Handbook of
POLITICAL MARKETING

ADVISORY BOARD MEMBERS

Handbook of
POLITICAL MARKETING

Bruce I. Newman Editor

Sage Publications, Inc.
International Educational and Professional Publisher
Thousand Oaks ▪ London ▪ New Delhi

For information:

SAGE Publications, Inc.
2455 Teller Road
Thousand Oaks, California 91320
E-mail: order@sagepub.com

SAGE Publications Ltd.
6 Bonhill Street
London EC2A 4PU
United Kingdom

SAGE Publications India Pvt. Ltd.
M-32 Market
Greater Kailash I
New Delhi 110 048 India

Printed in the United States of America

Library of Congress Cataloging-in-Publication Data

Main entry under title:

Handbook of political marketing / edited by Bruce I. Newman.
    p. cm.
  Includes bibliographical references and index.
  ISBN 0-7619-1109-X (alk. paper)
  1. Campaign management. 2. Electioneering. 3. Marketing. I.
Newman, Bruce I.
  JF2112.C3 H365 1999
  324.7—dc21   99-6226

This book is printed on acid-free paper.

00 01 02 03 04 05 7 6 5 4 3 2

Acquisition Editor:	Harry Briggs
Editorial Assistant:	MaryAnn Vail
Production Editor:	Astrid Virding
Editorial Assistant:	Karen Wiley
Copy Editor:	D. J. Peck
Typesetter/Designer:	Christina M. Hill
Indexer:	Cristina Haley

Contents

SECTION I: Conceptual and Historical Origins of Political Marketing

SECTION II: Management of Political Campaigns

SECTION III: Analysis of the Political Marketplace

POLITICAL RESEARCH METHODS

SECTION IV: Development of Political Strategy

SECTION V: Execution of Political Campaigns

ELECTION CAMPAIGNS

LOBBYIST, INTEREST GROUP, AND GOVERNMENTAL CAMPAIGNS

SECTION VI: Political Marketing and Democracy

*This book is dedicated
with all my love
to my two children,
Todd Paul Newman
and Erica Lynn Newman.*

Foreword

It has been nearly 40 years since John F. Kennedy campaigned for the presidency and introduced what was considered a revolutionary approach to campaigning that involved the latest, sophisticated marketing and communication strategies. Widely heralded as the first "modern" presidential campaign in U.S. history, Kennedy's quest was adroitly recounted in Theodore White's classic account of the campaign, *The Making of the President 1960* (White, 1961).

White's colorful narrative details the political skills and sophistication that Kennedy, along with his family, friends, and staff, brought to the presidential race, in effect reinventing the process of running a national political campaign in America. As pollster Lou Harris sent interviewers door-to-door to conduct personal surveys with voters and then mailed their results in for tabulation by hand, other Kennedy aides organized piles of three-by-five index cards, each representing a target voter to mobilize in the crucial West Virginia and Wisconsin primaries. The political ads of the era had all the charm and innocence of a wholesome Wonder bread commercial, and the first televised presidential debates captured the attention of the nation and set new records for the size of a television audience. On Election Night, the Kennedy clan gathered together and phoned local party bosses, big city mayors, and ward leaders in a frantic effort to gauge the election return process.

If Kennedy were alive today and approaching his 80th birthday, no doubt he would be amazed and intrigued to witness the way in which modern political campaigning has changed since he first redefined the process in 1960. Indeed, the advances and changes in political campaigning and marketing over the past 40 years parallel the explosive innovations that have been made in so many other fields with ties to technology such as communication, science, and medicine. Today, political campaigns at all levels, from national races to state and local contests, depend on increasingly sophisticated marketing techniques. Dial testing (in which panelists rate their reactions to political ads frame by frame on equipment that constantly monitors every change in their responses), instant tracking polls (in which public reaction to breaking news events is measured and analyzed in a matter of hours), and complex computer databases that produce highly specialized models of voter contact are now the norm in the political arena. Every comment of the modern campaign is quicker and more sophisticated than its 1960 counterpart. And although all of these modern marketing techniques might have produced more sophisticated campaigns, they have not necessarily yielded a better set of candidates or a more involved or informed electorate.

Although evidence of the profound effect of these innovations is visible everywhere and has become the subject of a great deal of analysis and commentary, a serious, systematic, and thorough treatment of this important topic has been lacking to date. This book is an important source that brings together a broad base of knowledge in a wide variety of disciplines related to political marketing and communication. Whether the reader is a trained political scholar or an average observer with no formal background in politics, this book provides valuable and important information for anyone interested in understanding American, British, and European political culture.

PETER D. HART
Founder and Chief Executive Officer
Peter D. Hart Research Associates

Reference

White, T. H. (1961). *The making of the president 1960.* New York: Atheneum Books.

Preface

This is a handbook about the practice and theory of marketing in political systems around the world, or what has come to be known as political marketing. Political marketing is the application of marketing principles and procedures in political campaigns by various individuals and organizations. The procedures involved include the analysis, development, execution, and management of strategic campaigns by candidates, political parties, governments, lobbyists and interest groups that seek to drive public opinion, advance their own ideologies, win elections, and pass legislation and referenda in response to the needs and wants of selected people and groups in a society. This handbook brings together, in a single volume, the cutting-edge thinking of academics and political professionals who are experts in their related fields that fall under the umbrella of political marketing. Both consultants and scholars from nine different countries have contributed chapters that give a "state of the art" review of the role of marketing in political campaigns. The handbook goes beyond the conventional subject matter in the field of political marketing in two significant ways.

First, it bridges the theory development of academics who study and carry out research on political marketing with the practice of these techniques by consultants working on campaigns. Several chapters include a combination of authors who are practicing and theorizing about political marketing. This is a critical step that needs to be taken to connect the advances made by both into a cohesive body of work.

Second, it integrates the thinking of experts from nine different countries. Although each of the countries examined operates in a different political system, the common thread among all of them is the similarity in their use of political marketing practices. Accounting for cross-cultural differences will be paramount to understanding and predicting future changes in both established and developing democracies. Furthermore, it will form the basis for the next critical juncture in the field of political marketing, which is the development of a cross-cultural theory of political marketing.

Democracies around the world are relying on the same market-driven procedures to run their political systems that corporations use to ensure success in the commercial marketplace. This reliance stems from a shift in emphasis on pragmatism over ideology as political leaders become more poll driven and responsive to the needs and wants of the people. In fact, it has become nearly impossible to win elections without the use of marketing. It also is becoming increasingly important for politicians in office to rely on marketing to successfully pass legislation. As we enter the new millennium, it is my hope that this handbook will offer all participants in the political process a better understanding of how we can strengthen democracies around the world by making government more responsive to the will of the people.

This volume is compelling reading for any professional who is interested in understanding and predicting the future of politics. Political practitioners who are interested in the latest strategic and technological advances being used to run successful political campaigns in countries around the world will want to have a copy of this handbook as a reference guide in their offices; these include candidates seeking office at all levels, political consultants, lobbyists, political action committee executives, fund-raisers, pollsters, government officials, political advertising specialists, journalists, public relations executives, direct mail consultants, telemarketers, marketing researchers, and political party managers and officers. Academics and students who study politics and how democracies are changing in the United States, United Kingdom, and Europe will find this handbook to be an excellent textbook for use in university classes across a wide spectrum of disciplines; these include political science, political communication, political marketing, advertising, sociology, journalism, political management, direct marketing, and other related fields. Finally, academic researchers who study voting behavior will find the handbook to be an invaluable source of the latest theoretical and methodological advances in the field.

BRUCE I. NEWMAN

Acknowledgments

The successful completion of this handbook would not have been possible without the help of several people. First, I thank Harry Briggs, my editor at Sage Publications, who originally approached me with the idea to edit a book on political marketing. Harry was a constant source of encouragement throughout the project and provided me with all the resources I needed to complete the job. It continues to be a pleasure to work with you, Harry. I also thank all the wonderful professionals at Sage who have been involved in the editing and production of my book, especially MaryAnn Vail, D. J. Peck, and Astrid Virding. Thank you for making Sage a company with which I continue to enjoy working.

I invited a select group of people early on in the project to work with me and serve as advisory board editors. Because this was an international project, the board included people from four different countries. Each advisory board editor worked with me to find the people (or, in some cases, the person) whom he thought would be able to contribute a chapter on a specific area of political marketing in which they were experts and then participated in the review and editing of each chapter. Without fail, each of the advisory board editors was successful in attracting leading experts in the academic and consulting worlds in their respective areas in the field.

I could not have completed this project without the help of each of the advisory board editors (listed alphabetically), whom I thank for the tremendous effort put into this project: George Bishop (professor of political science and fellow at the Institute for the Data Sciences, University of Cincinnati), Andrzej Falkowski (professor of experimental psychology, Catholic University of Lublin), Jon B. Gould (visiting scholar at the Institute of Governmental Studies, University of California, Berkeley), Phil Harris (co-director of the Centre for Corporate and Public Affairs, Faculty of Management and Business, Manchester Metropolitan University), Philip Kotler (S. C. Johnson and Son distinguished professor of international marketing in the Kellogg Graduate School of Management, Northwestern University), Michael L. Mezey (dean and professor of political science in the College of Liberal Arts & Sciences, DePaul University), Richard M. Perloff (professor of communication, Cleveland State University), Christian Scheucher (senior adviser to the leadership of the Austrian People's Party), and Günter Schweiger (professor and head of the Institute of Advertising and Market Research, Vienna University of Business and Economics).

I also thank each and every one of the authors who helped to make this handbook a reality. The success of this project rests with the flexibility of the authors, who willingly shaped and revised their chapters to ensure that each one fit into the master plan around which the handbook was built. Because so many of the authors are internationally recognized as leading authorities in their respective fields, suffice it to say that this handbook is blessed with an enormous pool of talent. I thank each author (in alphabetical order) for contributing the highest quality work that an editor could ever hope for: Michaela Adami, Nigel Allington, Paul R. Baines, Knut Bergmann, Patrick Butler, Neil Collins, Wojciech Cwalina, Rob Daves, Dietmar Ecker, Andrzej Falkowski, Hanne Gardner, Jon B. Gould, Phil Harris, Andreas Herrmann, Jürgen Hofrichter, Frank Huber, Dennis W. Johnson, Lynda Lee Kaid, Dennis F. Kinsey, Neil Kotler, Philip Kotler, Sidney Kraus, Gregory G. Lebel, Barbara Lindsay, Andrew Lock, Hans Lugmayr, Dorina Miron, Pama Mitchell, Philip Morgan, Dan Nimmo, Daniel Odescalchi, Nicholas O'Shaughnessy, Richard M. Perloff, Fritz Plasser, Eric W. Rademacher, Lilia Raycheva, Mike Rice, Jennie Roberts, Jolán Róka, Judith-Rae E. Ross, Christian Scheucher, Hans Schmid, Dan Schnur, Günter Schweiger, Christian Senft, Elaine Sherman, Jennifer A. Steen, Wayne P. Steger, Michael Strugl, Alfred J. Tuchfarber, Craig Varoga, Nadja Vetter, Klaus Weissmann, Wolfram Wickert, J. Harry Wray, and Dominic Wring.

Finally, I thank my family members for being so supportive of me as I took time away from them to work on this project. Judy, your constant encouragement and our many hours of discussion about politics helped me to survive the journey. Todd and Erica, believe it or not, even our discussions about politics proved to be of great value to me as I was forced to think about the future of our democracy every time I looked in your young eyes so full of hope and excitement. Dad, I cannot count the number of times I picked up the phone and asked you for your advice, which always was imbued with wisdom and deep concern for the welfare of our country. Thank you.

Introduction

The handbook is organized around 40 chapters broken down into six sections that provide an exhaustive review of political marketing:

Section I: Conceptual and Historical Origins of Political Marketing
Section II: Management of Political Campaigns
Section III: Analysis of the Political Marketplace
Section IV: Development of Political Strategy
Section V: Execution of Political Campaigns
Section VI: Political Marketing and Democracy

The first section, "Conceptual and Historical Origins of Political Marketing," begins with an introduction to the evolution of the field of political marketing from experts in the fields of marketing, political communication, and political science in the United States, United Kingdom, and Ireland. It centers on *theory development in the field*. In the first chapter, Philip Kotler and Neil Kotler bridge the conceptual underpinnings between the application of marketing in business and political markets with a framework that ties the two disciplines together. The authors conclude that marketing cannot guarantee victory but will ensure that a political campaign is systematic, efficient, and voter oriented and will promote greater responsiveness in the political process. In the second chapter, Richard Perloff takes a historical view of political marketing and makes the point that the seeds of contemporary politics were really planted as far back as the early 1800s in the United States. The chapter documents the use of political communication strategies in these early "popular" campaigns and brings us forward to the more recent use of "merchandised styles of campaigning." The author concludes that the electoral system in the United States needs changing and makes the observation that campaign reform should be seen in a historical light.

In the third chapter, Dominic Wring reviews advances in the field in Britain, the United States, and other countries in the final part of the 20th century. The author uses that cross-cultural perspective to point out the overlap in growth in political marketing among several different academic disciplines. The chapter identifies three converging factors that account for what Wring predicts will be continued growth in the field well into the 21st century. In the fourth chapter, Patrick Butler and Neil Collins put forward a conceptual framework of political marketing that bridges the disciplines of political science and marketing and takes into account advances in the field in different countries. In the process of bridging the two fields, the authors compare and contrast the central focus of each discipline—political science on institutional relationships, the legislative process, and public policy; marketing on campaign strategies and management. In the final chapter of this section, Dan Nimmo offers historical background on the development of the permanent campaign, which he identifies as the reduction of governance to a perpetual extension of campaign strategies and tactics. The author goes back to 18th-century England and the early 19th century in the United States to document the tie between marketing and governance.

The second section, "Management of Political Campaigns," is devoted to the *day-to-day running of political campaigns* and looks at the various roles that consultants play in political organizations. This section includes chapters by academics and consultants in the United States and Europe. The political consulting industry has grown significantly over the past decade and has become a fixture in politics in democracies all over the world. Consultants are used to carrying out many different managerial functions of a campaign. The first two chapters in this section report on the general role of consultants in political campaigns. In the first chapter, Fritz Plasser, Christian Scheucher, and Christian Senft discuss the results of a survey conducted with political operatives from several different countries in Europe. Interviewees included political consultants, party managers, media experts, pollsters, and advertising experts. The results of the survey are then used as a benchmark to compare the management of political campaigns in Europe to those in the United States, and the conclusion is drawn that the United States is the international "role model of campaigning." The authors then develop two competing models of the diffusion of modern campaigning from the United States.

In the second chapter, Dennis F. Kinsey presents a literature review of the roles and tasks that consultants play in campaign organizations. The review bridges the academic and practitioner-oriented viewpoints toward political consulting. The author calls for more communication between scholars and consultants to advance the knowledge in this area. The third chapter covers the management of volunteers. Gregory G. Lebel presents a comprehensive overview of how this process has changed with technology over the years. Throughout the chapter, the essentials of managing a volunteer staff are covered including campaign organization and staffing issues, categories of volunteers, planning, recruitment, management, and motivation. In the end, and even with all the technological changes that have occurred in politics, the author makes the point that volunteers, the ground troops of a campaign, involve the same critical components that existed a generation ago.

In the fourth chapter, Dan Schnur addresses the importance and difficulty of coordinating a candidate's message in the media. The author separates free media from paid media and discusses the different strategies that must be followed to effectively communicate a message in both types of outlets. The chapter concludes with a discussion of how to reinforce a message between the paid and free media and how consultants should deal with the news media. In the final chapter of this section, Jennifer A. Steen addresses the role of fund-raising in American political campaigns. The author makes the point that the tactics used to raise funds vary from one campaign to another and depend on the strategy used, the type of office sought, the size of the election district, and the relevant campaign finance laws. The chapter presents an overview of successful strategies and tactics that are commonly used.

The third section, "Analysis of the Political Marketplace," consists of two subsections, one on political research methods and one on modeling voter behavior. Both subsections address the *analysis of the needs and wants of voters*. The first subsection, "Political Research Methods," has contributions from both professional pollsters and academic researchers in the United States and Europe. Polling procedures and their relationship to message development are investigated in this subsection. In the first chapter, Pama Mitchell and Rob Daves speak to the growing importance of media polls, one of the tools that journalists use to report political news. The chapter explains how news organizations use political polling and how journalists use poll results in their coverage of politics. The authors then outline the differences between the uses of polling by candidates and their consultants and by news organizations. In the second chapter, Eric W. Rademacher and Alfred J. Tuchfarber review the use of preelection polls in political campaigns, focusing primarily on candidate-centered campaigns. The chapter reviews the role that polls have played in American electoral history and gives a description of the different types of information collected for campaigns. The authors conclude with an overview of some of the procedural and methodological issues researchers deal with when conducting polls in general and preelection polls in particular.

In the third chapter, Jürgen Hofrichter discusses exit polls and their implications for election campaigns. The author begins with an overview of the history of exit polls and then looks at the organization and methodology of exit polling with respect to sampling, questionnaire construction, fieldwork, data analysis, and the presentation of results. The chapter draws a distinction between exit polling in the United States and that in Germany, and it goes into depth on the use of exit polling in German election campaigns. In the final chapter of this subsection, Craig Varoga and Mike Rice discuss four different types of research: candidate (or "opposition") research, issues research, public opinion research, and targeting research. For each type of research, the authors identify what it is, the problems associated with conducting that type of research, using it in campaigns, testing it, and monitoring the progress of a campaign through the use of that type of research.

The second subsection, "Modeling Voter Behavior," looks specifically at understanding the voter, with chapters that document the use of various methodologies and models developed by American and European researchers. This section goes beyond polling and provides conceptual frameworks that can be used to explain and predict the behavior of voters. In the first chapter, Bruce I. Newman puts forward a predictive model of voter behavior. The model can be used to understand why voters choose one candidate over another by providing a psychological explanation behind the choice behavior of the people studied. The model was used by the author as the basis for an empirical study carried out for senior presidential aides in the Clinton White House to reposition the president in his successful reelection campaign in 1996. In the second chapter, Andrzej Falkowski and Wojciech Cwalina put forward a model of voter behavior that is used to carry out an empirical study on the 1995 Polish presidential election. The model uses a sequential process that connects the candidate's image to a voter's feelings, intentions, and decision to vote for a particular candidate. Based on the results of the study, the authors determine how candidates' images change in relation to voters' emotional attitudes toward them vis-à-vis their reactions to advertisements used during the campaign. The authors draw several conclusions with respect to the use of the model as the basis for political advertising construction and focus group testing of political advertisements.

In the third chapter, Frank Huber and Andreas Herrmann put forward the theoretical basis for developing what the authors refer to as a value-oriented model of candidate appraisal. The model relies on the use of means-end theory to connect voter values to various attributes of a politician. Measures of customer satisfaction are then used to determine the extent to which the politician corresponds to the voter's values. The authors draw comparisons between products and voters to extend the use of this modeling process to the political sphere. In the final chapter of this subsection, Dorina Miron investigates nonvoting behavior. The chapter provides a comprehensive review of the research findings and theoretical developments in the area of nonvoting. The author pays particular attention to the role of mass communication as an antecedent of nonvoting. Research findings on nonvoting from several different countries are summarized.

The fourth section, "Development of Political Strategy," is broken down into two subsections that detail how messages are developed and communicated in the political marketplace. Components of a strategy closely mirror the same tactical issues that are used for any product sold to consumers in the commercial marketplace, but with a greater emphasis placed on how the strategy is communicated. So, this section is broken down into tactical issues and political communication. In particular, the subsection on political communication is critical because it is the area in which the most amount of money is spent on political campaigns.

The first subsection, "Tactical Issues," has contributions from researchers and consultants from the United States, Europe, and the United Kingdom. In the first chapter, Günter Schweiger and Michaela Adami address the use of nonverbal imagery by politicians and political parties. According to the authors, the same rules that apply to companies apply to political parties. Examples from several different countries are used to back up their assertion. The authors suggest that image measurement in the political context is very rare and that, instead, political consultants rely on polling to measure images. After reviewing different operational approaches to the measurement of images, the authors present their own image measurement system called NVI (nonverbal image measurement). A methodology for using NVI for a political candidate or party is outlined and discussed, and examples are provided to support the use of this system. In the second chapter, Elaine Sherman discusses the role of direct marketing in political campaigns. The author presents a historical overview of the use of direct marketing in political campaigns, making reference to specific campaigns to identify selected milestones in its use as a strategic tool. Direct marketing is used for many different purposes in the course of a political campaign, each of which is reviewed by the author, who concludes with a case history of the use of direct marketing in the 1996 reelection campaign of Bill Clinton.

In the third chapter, Sidney Kraus addresses another important strategic tool used in many elections—televised debates. The author provides an overview of televised debates in American presidential campaigns. He then describes the participant observation methodology that he used to collect data on previous presidential debates and makes connections between debates and commercial arenas based on these data. The author concludes with a discussion of how marketing techniques have been used in televised presidential debates and the role that marketing plays in the process of electing a president. In the final chapter of this subsection, Paul R. Baines discusses two very commonly used strategic tools in marketing campaigns: market segmentation and product positioning. The use of these two strategic tools in political campaigns is reviewed in light of cross-cultural differences that exist in political systems around the world. The author also provides a review of the comprehensive models of political marketing.

The second subsection, "Political Communication," addresses the role of political communication in the development of a political strategy and includes chapters contributed by American and European academic researchers and consultants. In the first chapter, Lynda Lee Kaid presents a comprehensive overview of the use of advertising in political campaigns. The author identifies two defining characteristics of modern political advertising—control of the message and use of mass communication channels for the distribution of the message—and discusses each of these areas. Throughout the chapter, the author cites examples and literature from democracies around the world. In the second chapter, J. Harry Wray looks specifically at television advertising in the United States. The author gives a historical preface to the use of television in politics and then proceeds to review the significant features of American television. The author gives a detailed analysis of the effect of television on electoral politics, drawing on examples from recent elections at all levels of office. The chapter concludes with the author reflecting on the impact that television has had on democracy.

In the third chapter, Knut Bergmann and Wolfram Wickert discuss the use of selected communication strategies used in election campaigns in the Federal Republic of Germany. The authors begin with a comparative assessment of the use of political communication in Germany and the United States. They then use recent elections in Germany to elaborate on the use of various communication strategies employed. In the fourth chapter, Lilia Raycheva presents a case study of the role of television and other media in the democratization of Bulgaria. The author discusses the media system in Bulgaria in general and the impact that privatization of various media has had on the growth of social change and democratic transformation in Bulgaria. In the final chapter of this subsection,

Jolán Róka takes a reflective look at the impact of the media on public opinion. The author begins with a historical overview of public opinion, reviewing some of the classic theories devoted to this subject. The author then discusses the technological advances in the field of communication and how they influence public opinion formation. The chapter concludes with a discussion of recent elections in Hungary and the United States and the role that the media played in them.

The fifth section, "Execution of Political Campaigns," is devoted to discussion of *the implementation of strategy* and includes chapters written by American, British, and European academics, consultants, and politicians. This section is broken down into two subsections. The first subsection covers campaigns run by candidates and politicians who are seeking either election or reelection to office and looks at recent campaigns in the United States, the United Kingdom, and Western and Central Europe. The second subsection looks at political campaigns run by lobbyists, interest groups, and governments and includes chapters that present case studies and campaigns carried out in the United Kingdom and the United States.

The first subsection, "Election Campaigns," begins with a chapter by Judith-Rae E. Ross, who takes a close look at the role of the "political machine," its origins, and the impact it actually had on some recent local elections in the United States including one in which the author herself was a candidate. The author also gives a historical overview of the Chicago political machine and how the operation of the machine played out during the era of Richard J. Daley, former mayor of Chicago. The next chapter by Phil Harris, Andrew Lock, and Jennie Roberts reports on the 1997 general election campaign in the United Kingdom. The authors pay considerable attention to the press coverage of the campaign, and identify the prominent issues and personalities covered and how they varied from one newspaper to another. The chapter concludes with a note on the lack of attention that political marketers pay to understanding advertising effectivenesss in election campaigns.

The next two chapters in this section cover elections recently held in Austria. The chapter by Hans Schmid and Dietmar Ecker presents an overview of the 1995 national campaign in Austria, looking closely at the public relations strategies employed by the major parties. The authors also provide insights into the personal postures employed by each of the respective leaders, and the issues they advocated. The next chapter by Michael Strugl, Hans Lugmayr, and Klaus Weissmann present a case study of the elections in Upper Austria that took place in 1997. The authors begin with a description of the Upper Austria region and the unique political situation that existed at the time. They then go through a step-by-step analysis of the marketing campaign strategy employed, reporting on the development of the campaign concept, positioning studies, international campaign research, role of the consultants, and an in-depth explanation of why the People's Party won the election. In the final chapter of this subsection, Daniel Odescalchi presents an inside look at recent elections in Hungary and Bosnia-Herzegovina from the eyes of a political consultant who was involved in shaping campaign strategy for parties in both countries. The author describes how political parties in Eastern European countries set up their campaign organizations and the tactical steps that were followed in their effort to win. The author then discusses the campaign strategy developed and employed by Steve Forbes in 1996 in his bid for the U.S. presidency.

The second subsection, "Lobbyist, Interest Group, and Governmental Campaigns," starts with a chapter by Phil Harris, Hanne Gardner, and Nadja Vetter, who report on strategic lobbying campaigns and explain why the area has grown internationally. The authors present an analysis of the Sunday trading case that looks at the laws in the United Kingdom that enabled shops in England and Wales to trade on Sundays. The case study analyzes the campaign strategy that was used to direct the lobbying efforts of various pressure groups and how that resulted in the passage of laws to support the campaign. In the second chapter, Nigel Allington, Philip Morgan, and Nicholas O'Shaughnessy discuss the use of political marketing as a governing tool. The authors outline the campaign to sell the British people on the idea of privatization, pointing out the uniqueness of this campaign as one that centered on an idea that was sold in a commercial marketplace, as a product, to meet the multiple objectives of the politicians who launched it. The authors analyze the execution of four specific case studies that illustrate how the British government carried out its general campaign. In each case, the advertising and marketing strategy used to promote the government's program is analyzed in detail, with a conclusion that explains why the campaign was successful.

In the third chapter, Barbara Lindsay analyzes the influence of women voters in the United Kingdom and the United States. The author makes the point that public opinion no longer can be viewed as gender neutral and that women as an interest group must be given special consideration by political marketers. The author examines the nature of the gender gap in voting and looks at the issues that won over the women's votes in elections in the United States (in 1996) and in the United Kingdom (in 1997). The chapter concludes with a discussion of gender perspectives in U.K. political parties, women's lobbies, and the media. In the final chapter of the subsection, Wayne P. Steger analyzes the use of political marketing as a governing tool by legislators in the United States. The author makes the point that legislators carry out research on their constituencies, create and distribute programs tailored to their needs, and then promote themselves based on their accomplishments. The author concludes with a comment about the importance of money as the costs of carrying out campaigns continue to increase.

The sixth section, "Political Marketing and Democracy," deals with the impact that marketing is having on the evolution of democratic governance and what needs to be done to ensure that we, as a society, do not lose *control of the forces of political marketing*. Several critical issues that must be dealt with in the future include campaign finance reform, technology and the Internet, negative advertising, and money. The chapters in this section are written by American and British academics, some of whom have previous experience as consultants. Each of the chapters points to areas of the discipline that are shaping politics in significant ways and how each will influence democracy in the future.

In the first chapter, Jon B. Gould addresses the serious issue of campaign finance and why reforms have not worked. The author gives a historical overview of campaign reform and discusses the forces within the political system that have brought about the problem that exists today. Throughout his chapter, the author provides both a legal and a political perspective on the development and problematic attempts at campaign reform. Although the author is not convinced that the reforms he suggests as a potential solution will be enacted anytime soon, the chapter concludes with some realistic ideas on how to fix a political system that is in serious trouble. In the second chapter, Dennis W. Johnson predicts that the Internet will be an important political communications tool in the campaigns in the next decade. In his support for this assertion, he quotes Microsoft Chairman Bill Gates, who believes that the Internet will be the "primary conduit" for political discourse in future elections. The author covers several significant developments that will come with the creation of what he calls the "Net citizen" including better citizen access to campaign and policy information, easier voter registration, and on-line debates. The author gives considerable attention to how campaigns in the future will be conducted on the Internet and what the implications of this will be for voters. The chapter concludes with a realistic appraisal of the first "cyberspace election."

In the third chapter, Nicholas O'Shaughnessy raises some very serious concerns about the comparison of political marketing with political propaganda. The author takes note of, and cites the growing use of, negative advertising in American elections and makes the theoretical connection between the manipulation and bias one finds in these campaigns and the definition and use of propaganda in elections. The author then argues that marketing by itself does not capture the changes that have evolved in politics and makes the case that political communication is really a marketing-propaganda hybrid. The final chapter of this section, and of the book, addresses what is perhaps the most serious issues of concern to our democracy, that is, the role of money in politics. In this chapter, J. Harry Wray argues that to fully understand the problematic role of money, there must be a clear understanding of what he refers to as very common but ambiguously used terms in our political lexicon, that is, "politics" and "democracy." The author takes us through a carefully laid out explanation of what both terms mean to Americans and then defines them to take a close look at the role of money in political life. The author then puts forward and supports the argument that as a result of the confluence of three central facts—privately financed political campaigns, great economic inequality, and escalating campaign costs—the American system of campaign financing is problematic and, therefore, serves to subvert democracy. The author discusses the consequences for society and democracy. The author ends this chapter on a note that lies at the heart of the motivation for putting this handbook together and is worth quoting: "Democracy might be a comparatively new idea and an unfinished dream, but it is a dream worth pursuing."

SECTION I

Conceptual and Historical Origins of Political Marketing

Political Marketing

Generating Effective Candidates, Campaigns, and Causes

PHILIP KOTLER
NEIL KOTLER

Political marketing, the making of successful candidates and causes, is a major growth industry affecting virtually every citizen and institution. In the 1992 election, in excess of $550 million was spent on electing a president, a doubling in presidential campaign spending since 1980. That same year, all candidates for congressional seats, both House and Senate, spent nearly $630 million. In the 1996 presidential election, more than $894 million was spent.

While campaign spending is skyrocketing, more and more dollars are seeking after fewer and fewer voters. In the presidential election of 1996, voter turnout dipped to 49%, the lowest turnout as a proportion of eligible voters since 1924. Turnout in local and state elections often falls between one fifth and one third of eligible voters.

Campaigning for office always has had a marketing orientation. A survey of 200 political consultants, conducted by the Pew Research Center for the People and the Press in 1997–1998, indicates that quality of the campaign message was a top factor in winning an election along with money and the extent of partnership in a district.

Candidates, to be successful, have to understand their markets—the voters and their basic needs and aspirations and the constituencies they represent or seek to represent.

Marketing orientation means that candidates recognize the nature of the exchange process when they ask voters for their votes. And candidates have to view their campaigns from the point of view of the outcomes for voters, constituencies, and financial donors, the consumers in political campaigns. If a candidate can make promises that match the voters' needs and can deliver on some of these promises once in office, then the candidate ultimately will increase voter satisfaction, the sense of responsiveness of political institutions, and public satisfaction with the candidate.

Political Marketplace

Marketing strategy lies at the heart of electoral success because it compels a campaign to put together, in a relatively short period of time, a forceful organization that mobilizes support and generates a winning coalition of disparate and sometimes conflicting groups.

Years ago, candidates, especially at the local and state levels, were likely to face homogeneous and cohesive constituencies. Such constituencies allowed candidates to articulate broad and diffuse themes and to concentrate on projecting positive, charming, and reassuring personalities. In recent years, however, political arenas have become more heterogeneous, contentious, and fragmented. Voters are likely to be issue oriented as well as attuned to candidates' personal qualities. Agreements that once characterized small-scale politics have been supplanted by single-issue politics, widely divergent opinions and preferences, and tremendous diversity in lifestyles, motivations, and interests.

Organizing a political campaign historically involved building coalitions of voters, constituencies, and financial donors. Coalition building presupposed a spirit of compromise, adjustment, and acceptance of even marginal gains in the short run in the expectation that major gains would occur over the long haul. The rise of single-issue causes and constituencies and the growing force of special interest groups now require candidates to carefully map out the universe of opinion, emotion, and interest and to skillfully tailor appeals to different voter segments and target groups.

Electoral districts and, therefore, political campaigns differ widely among each other. A candidate in a small district dominated by single-issue politics, for example, faces the choice of either running as the champion of a single-issue group or running as a rebel or reformer who seeks to mobilize new voter segments that are less ideological or more middle of the road. The fact that only a minority of the electorate in any given electoral district bothers to cast ballots, in typical elections, raises the possibility for reformers to use new issues, causes, and appeals to mobilize new groups of voters. Research on voter turnout and citizen dissatisfaction with politics and government suggests that candidates could profitably learn from the attitudes of voters in their districts and the desire for empowerment that usually propels citizens, however disappointed with or even alienated from the electoral process they might be.

Besides the growing prominence of money in political campaigns, another notable development is the growing use of negative advertising against opponents. A result of raising large amounts of campaign funds, negative ads, whether paid for by a candidate's own organization or the party organization, can cripple

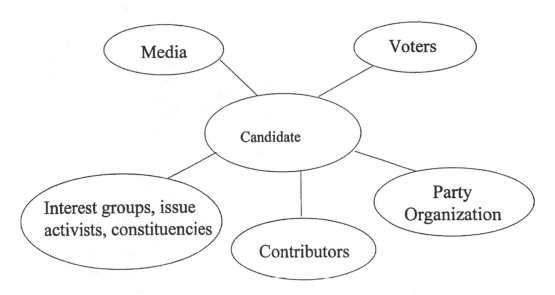

Figure 1.1. Five Markets in Political Campaigns

a candidate's opponent, regardless of the candidate's merit or appeal. The injection of negative personal attacks on candidates also means that candidates subject to such attacks have to spend as much time in answering the attacks as they do in articulating and advancing ideas and issues.

As a general rule, candidates face five different markets in organizing political campaigns (Figure 1.1): (a) voters who are in the habit of casting ballots in elections (not the same people as eligible or registered voters); (b) activists, interest groups, and organized constituencies who wield clout in votes and donations (e.g., labor and business, civil rights organizations, law-and-order advocates); (c) the media, which can make candidates visible, if not laudable, or can keep candidates in the shadows of campaigns; (d) party organization, which exists in most (but not all) districts; and (e) donors and financial contributors, who might or might not reside in the district in which a candidate is running.

A further word about the role of media in political campaigns is appropriate. The media market plays a unique role in campaigns. Print and electronic media are vehicles of both communication and sales in the political marketplace. As the perceptual screen through which candidates communicate to voters and through which voters view candidates, the media are critical intermediaries between candidates and the other campaign markets. Media can favor one candidate over another, exerting their influence covertly in the extent of a candidate's coverage or overtly in editorial endorsement and sponsorship of campaign events.

Media can either highlight, underplay, or diminish particular features of a candidate or a candidate's position on issues, casting these in a negative or positive light. These media-shaped images conveyed to voters are sticking points in the voters' minds. These images become powerful symbols that identify and/or define a candidate, sometimes quite early in a campaign.

Marketing Applied to Political Campaigns

Candidates always will market their candidacies in some way. The real question is how to do it effectively and efficiently. This chapter focuses on candidate rather than cause marketing, although the two often are intertwined. It aims to show candidates how they can develop effective goals and strategies, based on solid research, and how they can marshal campaign staff, volunteers, the organization itself, and other resources to build successful campaigns.

Political marketing shares much in common with marketing in the business world. In business marketing, sellers dispatch goods, services, and communications (e.g., advertising) to the market, and in return, money (consumer purchases), information (consumer research), and customer loyalty are received. In campaigns, candidates dispatch promises, favors, policy preferences, and personalities to a set of voters in exchange for their votes, voluntary efforts, or contributions. Candidates seek to develop personalities not unlike the images that manufacturers project for their products. Candidates in districts dominated by parties seek the approval of the party organization, which is not unlike the company image that businesses project. Candidates enter primary elections that are analogous to market tests for commercial products and services.

Despite the similarities, there are several areas of significant difference between candidates and political campaigns, on the one hand, and product development campaigns in the commercial world, on the other. The political arena usually is highly charged with beliefs and emotions, as well as conflict and partisanship, that rarely characterize the consumer's choice of commercial products. At the same time, although sharp beliefs and emotions stir political activists, activists generally constitute a small minority of the electorate. For most citizens, politics appears to be something to be avoided much of the time, and this avoidance can easily be misinterpreted as the low salience that politics appears to possess among the broad public. Because citizens typically invest little time in politics (and so lack detailed information about candidates, parties, and issues), politicians and first-time political candidates alike generally enjoy only limited visibility in the public mind.

A key challenge for a first-time candidate especially is to build an appealing image and message and then capture high-level visibility. Another challenge is to deal with the high-intensity politics of the activists and also, at the same time, transform the low salience or low-intensity politics of typical citizens into a more engaged politics that makes electoral participants out of more and more citizens.

Yet another challenge for most candidates, despite the inroads of single-issue politics, is to build coalitions of disparate voting segments and blocs—individuals, groups, and organizations. Building coalitions in the campaign world is not unlike the technical partnerships that computer companies form with other companies or that manufacturers form with suppliers and distributors; they are similar to the joint marketing alliances of for-profit firms such as Coca-Cola and Philip Morris with cultural organizations such as museums and performing arts organizations.

The Candidate Marketing Map

Figure 1.2 shows the candidate's marketing situation in further detail.

Stage 1: Environmental Research

The environment is the setting and context in which a candidate organizes a campaign. It defines the issues, opportunities, and the threats that a candidate faces. Environmental factors include the state of the economy (either in a local district or in the nation as a whole), the mood of the electorate, and critical issues and concerns. The environment also includes what some political analysts argue is the "personality" or profile of an electoral district—whether a district or constituency is activist or not (or whether it is liberal or conservative), whether it has favored incumbents or inclines toward candidate turnover, and whether the electorate actively votes or shows low voter turnout. The extent to which a single party organization dominates a district is another key environmental variable.

Also included in the environment are the critical factors of demographics and sociographics, namely, the age, income, education, status, lifestyle, and attitudinal characteristics of the voters and of different voter segments. Environmental factors also include the electoral rules (e.g., single-member districts vs. multimember districts, at-large offices vs. district-based offices), the type of government bodies and system, and the number and characteristics of a candidate's opponents in the campaign. In this phase of the marketing map, a candidate is well advised to invest in as much research as is possible.

Stage 2: Internal and External Assessment Analysis

In any marketing situation, including political marketing, the seller (candidate) has to undertake *assessment* of both the internal and external situations. A candidate has to assess his or her *strengths and weaknesses,* and the strengths and weaknesses of the campaign organization, at whatever stage of development. A candidate's situation is different, depending on whether he or she is an incumbent, a challenger who has run against the same incumbent in another contest, or a first-time candidate. External assessment involves identifying the strengths and weaknesses of one's opponent or the set of opponents in the campaign.

Assessment also involves identifying the *opportunities* a particular campaign offers (e.g., the retirement of an incumbent and a match between two newcomers; an opportunity to create a new issue, cause, or voting segment). Similarly, the assessment phase of a campaign also identifies *threats* or dangers that a candidate (or party organization) faces (e.g., a voter backlash against a party or candidate identified with a particular faction resulting from a political scandal). Whereas the first phase involves considerable research, the second phase in campaign marketing involves analyses.

1. Environmental Research ⇨ 2. Internal and External Assessment Analysis ⇨ 3. Strategic Marketing ⇨ 4. Goal Setting and Campaign Strategy ⇨ 5. Communication, Distribution, and Organization Plan ⇨ 6. Key Markets and Outcomes

1. Environmental Research

State of the Economy (jobs, inflation)

Mood of Electorate (voter satisfaction or dissatisfaction)

Critical issue & concerns of electorate

Demographics of electorate

Party organization dominant or independent oriented

Incumbency or reform minded district

High or low voter turnout district

2. Internal and External Assessment Analysis

Candidate is incumbent or challenger

Campaign issue opportunities

Candidate strengths & weaknesses

Campaign organization strengths & weaknesses

Competitor Strengths & weaknesses

3. Strategic Marketing

Segmentation
Voter segments in electoral district (age groups, income, education, single-issue activists, ethnic voters, ideological groups)

Targeting

Positioning
Candidate image versus opponents' images (e.g. build an image of an energetic candidate, provider of constituency services, moderate on issues, accessible and friendly)

4. Goal Setting and Campaign Strategy

Positioning, Personal Style, and Candidate Concept Personal attributes to be highlighted in image building

Positioning of background and Qualifications

Political Philosophy
• Core messages

Choosing Issues and Solutions

5. Communication, Distribution, and Organization Plan

Retail and Wholesale Campaign Mix
• Personal appearances
• Publicity
• Advertising (choice of media, message, format and design
• Endorsements

Organizational Resource Mix
• Fundraisers and development staff
• Issues & research staff
• Media and publicity staff
• Party and interest group staff
• Volunteers and party workers

6. Key Markets and Outcomes

Voter Party Constituency Segments

Contributor Segments

Media and Publicity Segments (TV, radio, newsprint, web sites, columnists)

Figure 1.2. Candidate Marketing Map

Stage 3: Strategic Marketing

A basic principle in marketing is that the consumer public is not of a single cloth, homogeneous and uniform, but rather consists of different segments, the behaviors of which have to be understood. In this phase of political campaign marketing, a candidate's organization has to focus on analyzing the electorate in a given district and campaign. Certain characteristics of a given electorate (in a city or state) will remain stable over a long period. On the other hand, electorates can change from one campaign to another. For example, an attractive and energetic reform-minded candidate, in particular circumstances, can mobilize new voter segments and reconfigure a set of issues and concerns.

A marketing-centered campaign organization will first identify the universe of voter segments that exist in a given district including segments of registered voters who might or might not vote in a given campaign. The organization then has to determine the mix of voter segments that a candidate can realistically target and coalesce into a majority bloc. For example, Candidate A, as an incumbent, might seek a coalition of older, affluent, and conservative-minded citizens. Candidate B, facing an incumbent who has grown stale among critical voter segments, might seek to shape a coalition of young and middle-aged voters who are reform- or liberal-minded, identify strongly with particular issues, and are available to work hard for a new political personality on the scene.

A third phase in strategic marketing applied to campaigns is to position a candidate effectively in relation to his or her opponents and then to build candidate image, campaign concept, and set of policy preferences and issues that will effectively communicate the candidate's strengths and appeals.

Stage 4: Goal Setting and Campaign Strategy

The fourth stage on the candidate and campaign marketing map involves developing objectives and goals (measurable benchmarks and magnitudes of desired change) that a candidate can use in determining how well the campaign is doing, what the weaknesses and lagging areas are, and what things can fill the gap. At this stage, a candidate, based on the prior research, has to develop an image, a concept as relates to issues and policy preferences, and a set of messages and communications that will carry forth the candidate's image and the campaign's selling proposition.

Stage 5: Communication, Distribution, and Organization Plan

The fifth stage in the marketing map involves tactical marketing and the use of marketing tools such as product and promotion that are widely used in commercial and nonprofit marketing. At this stage, a candidate has to figure out the most effective and efficient way in which to allocate a campaign organization's resources, for example, the mix of research, fund-raising, and media and publicity or the mix of using volunteers for personal appearances and "retail" campaign events (e.g., small-scale fund-raisers, "meet-the-candidate" nights, local endorsements) versus the use of funds to build a full-blown media campaign (i.e., "wholesale politics").

Stage 6: A Candidate's Key Markets—Voters, Donors, and Media

The sixth and final stage in the marketing map consists of reaching the candidate's markets (i.e., contributors' dollars, voters' votes, and other forms of support including word-of-mouth endorsements to other voters) and building media exposure and publicity, as measured by the number of times a candidate is mentioned in news stories and opinion pieces, the endorsements a candidate receives, and the extent of campaign coverage and advertising. In this final stage, the candidate and his or her campaign organization are focused on outcomes—the number of messages necessary to mobilize voter turnout, the number of votes needed in the various precincts of an electoral district, and so on. In districts where party organizations are dominant, candidates will have to work with their parties as critical players. In other districts, candidates might have to develop their own organizations insofar as traditional party organization is weak or non-existent.

Marketing and the Campaign Process

Decisions on campaign strategy, issues, advertising, appearances, and funding have to be made early in a campaign and involve getting started and getting nominated and elected.

Getting Started

There are three ways in which to become a candidate. One is to run as an independent by announcing candidacy and building an organization from scratch. A second is to wait for an existing party organization to select its nominee. The third is to join a party organization and to actively seek its nomination for a particular office. Any aspirant faces the following series of decisions from the start:

- Party decision
- Role decision
- Timing decision

Party Decision

The aspirant must decide, in most cases, which political party to join. Just as a product is not much without a company, a politician is not much without a party identification. The party, as well as the media, provides a communication and distribution system for reaching voters. The party's image makes credible a personal image. It defines a candidate's personal marketing concept more sharply.

A candidate may choose a party purely on the grounds of having strong political views that are more consistent with one party than another. But for the candidate without strong party preferences, the questions are different. Which party or family brand would add more strength to his or her political career? Which has more of a future in local or national politics? In which party is the leadership vacuum greater? In some cases, a candidate will choose to run against a party organization or to present himself or herself as an independent.

Role Decision

The political aspirant also must determine what role he or she wishes to play in an organization and how the media will communicate that role. The major roles in political organizations are loyal party worker, gadfly or rebel, and statesman or stateswoman.

The loyal party worker regularly attends organizational meetings, volunteers for assignments, carries them out efficiently and uncontentiously, and exhibits the traits of a dependable person whose interest in the welfare of the organization is paramount.

The gadfly plays a provocative part in the organization's meetings; challenges mainstream proposals; and urges innovation, critical discussion, and institutional soul searching. This role guarantees early attention and, under certain conditions, can lead to a leadership role in an organization. At the same time, it is a high-risk strategy because it is noisy and boat-rocking and might make early enemies for the candidate.

The statesman or stateswoman falls between the loyal party worker and the gadfly. This type of aspirant participates in group discussions, makes judicious and well-balanced suggestions, and avoids acting aggressively or exhibiting a personal ambition. He or she takes on a mediator role.

A candidate faces other types of role decisions. Incumbent candidates already have defined their political roles during the time they served in office, although they can continue to redefine roles and the perceptions citizens have of their roles. First-time candidates can shape their images in terms of one or more defined political roles of which the electorate is aware. One classic politician role is *constituency service or problem solver.* In this role, a politician devotes full-time to providing services such as access to social security offices and to Medicare and Medicaid information, offices, and appeal mechanisms. This role involves going after federal funds and jobs for the politician's districts. A first-time candidate can appeal to voters on such a platform, especially if the incumbent fails in this role.

Other roles a candidate can identify with and promise are those of *policy worker, fixer,* and *visionary leader* who can promise the electorate a new approach to policy problems, a new paradigm for thinking about issues, or a new electoral coalition.

A candidate also has to consider the political educational role that he or she projects in the campaign and, if successful, in public office as well. Candidates face the question of whether they have to mobilize new voters and an expanded voter base to succeed or whether they will benefit in having low voter turnout. In certain cities that have strong political machines, such as Chicago and St. Louis, candidates who enjoy strong party support often benefit from low voter turnout (i.e., mobilizing voters who are reliable from the party point of view and discouraging from voting others who are not predictable).

Research on political attitudes and voter behavior has demonstrated that citizen disaffection with and even alienation from campaigns, elections, and political institutions is, at the close of the 20th century, at an all-time high. For this reason, there are opportunities for some candidates, who are resourceful in ethical, inspirational, and educational ways, to raise the awareness and involvement level of the voters in their districts. The amount of resources a candidate wishes to devote to political education and the empowerment of voters depends on particular situations, candidate goals, and other factors. Although opportunities for candidates to organize campaigns that can empower citizens are vast, clearly any single candidate can make only a slight dent in a negative political culture, and such a candidate also can meet resistance from citizens who are skeptical or cynical about moral and educational appeals in campaigns.

Timing Decision

One should not join a party one day and announce his or her availability for that party's nomination the next day. Normally, an aspirant spends months or years learning the ropes, building friendships, getting to form connections, and doing fieldwork. He or she avoids announcing a political goal until the time is right. If ambition is revealed too early, then the aspirant invites blocking efforts from actual or potential rivals. It is not unlike commercial marketing, wherein rivals do not announce plans for new products until they are sure of distributor support, sufficient resources, and ultimate market success.

The aspirant should wait for an opportunity that will accelerate his or her career. For example, by working actively for a rising star within an organization, the aspirant can advance his or her career and avoid being identified with a loser. The opportunity also might take the form of an issue in which the aspirant is particularly qualified to do battle.

Once a candidate has announced his or her intention to run for office, everything changes. The candidate must now assume a leadership role, win popular trust, and make convincing the chances of success. Throughout, the aspirant has to study the party organization because it serves as the "market" at this stage of the electoral game. What type of candidate does the organization want? What is the recruitment and adoption process? How can one create maximum convergence between the party's recruitment process and the potential candidate's attributes?

Getting Nominated and Elected

Because most candidates have to enter primaries and run against others seeking a party nomination, this campaign arena can be viewed as a test market or trial run. The marketing activities required to win a primary campaign and a subsequent general election vary, just as the size of voter segments involved and the nature of voter interests vary in both election types. Primary campaigns usually are arenas in which ideology and partisan attitudes most prevail. Primaries, after all, are party affairs. Primary electorates are smaller and more homogeneous than general election electorates. Candidates who reach the general election face broader, more diverse, and fragmented voter segments. Aggregating and coalescing disparate segments is a key challenge. In many cases, candidates in general elections have to move to the middle of the road to reach diverse voters and, therefore, have to shed ideological appeals.

The activities common to both stages and arenas are as follows:

- Marketing research
- Product concept and strategy
- Communication and distribution strategy

Marketing Research

The first rule of effective campaigning is for the campaign to reflect the interests of the voters. Some candidates feel that they already know voters' opinions and that dollars invested in marketing research would mean fewer dollars available for advertising. But even if a candidate could guess the major issues in a campaign, he or she is not likely to know their relative importance to various groups or how the voters feel about the issues without research. Manufacturers do not develop and launch a product on a hunch. They carefully research the major market segments, analyzing consumers' needs, desires, product involvement, and loyalties. Some consumers never will buy a given product, some will be loyal to competitive brands, some will buy the new brand because of the company's reputation, and some are independent and will switch brands.

Campaigns are now conducting comparable types of sophisticated research such as "geodemographic" analysis involving "clusters" of voter types within a district, past voting patterns, and involvement levels of voters in each precinct.

Is there anything in modern marketing research not already being used in voter research? Very definitely yes. Much voter research takes the form of opinion polling that is reminiscent of the "nose-counting" phase of marketing research 30 years ago. When marketers began to recognize that buying motives went deeper than what the yes/no answers of opinion polling were showing, there was a wave of motivation research. Marketing researchers then began to experiment with in-depth interviewing methods such as free association, thematic appreciation tests, and open-ended questions. They also began to run group discussion panels to reveal a deeper dimension to consumers' attitudes toward products.

Later, marketers began to employ multivariate statistical techniques such as multiple regression analysis (to reveal relations between various marketing stimuli and consumer responses), discriminant analysis (to determine the variables that predicted the probable group affiliation of consumers), factor analysis, and cluster analysis (to determine optimal grouping of individuals). Today, marketing researchers are making great use of multidimensional scaling techniques to identify the major attributes defining a product's perceptual space, the position of competing products in that space, and the characteristics of ideal products.

The nagging question remains the same: How much marketing research spending is feasible for the candidate in view of the alternative payoff from direct promotion? Business firms know that nothing is gained by spending advertising money on the wrong message or on the right message when it reaches the wrong audience. The candidate also has to conduct enough marketing research to feel confident about formulating the best message and about identifying the best media for reaching the intended audience.

Product Concept and Strategy

Voters rarely get to know candidates. Most lack the time or interest to explore their political choices. They generally vote on the basis of the candidates' images as shaped by the media or previous identifications.

Although candidates attempt to transmit particular images of themselves to voters, the transmitted images are not always the perceived ones. Voters have different perceptions and needs, and as a result, they see candidates in a variety of ways that the candidates might not intend. In addition, voters are exposed to stimuli from other sources that modify the candidates' intended images.

The candidate who wishes to succeed cannot leave his or her image making to chance. Clothes, manner, statements, and actions shape the impressions made on people. The term used in marketing to orient image planning for a product is *product concept*. It is the major theme around which buyer interest is built, the "unique selling proposition" or "promised benefit" of the product.

The candidate must choose a product concept for marketing. Does the candidate want to come across as the hard-hitting reformer, the mature statesman, or the deep thinker? Part of this choice involves ascertaining what the image of the opponent is and determining an effective positioning strategy. The product concept is not just a slogan. It is the basis for planning and organizing the entire campaign. It shapes the coalitions that are formed, issue positions that are embraced, statements that are made, public appearances, the allocation of effort to voter segments, and many other decisions.

How does the candidate choose a product concept from the multitude of themes available? The major issues of an election, as seen and felt by the voters, have to be determined. Voters, after all, are seeking something from the candidates—a promise or an answer to the problems they face. The candidate must listen to the voters' message with a third ear to learn what type of symbolic reassurances the voters want. In this way, a candidate can choose a major theme or product concept.

Given several contending product concepts, the candidate should avoid choosing one that is unnatural or unbelievable, no matter how much it might match the voters' needs. The candidate will be placed in too many situations that test sincerity.

Because there will be many feasible concepts from which to choose, pre-campaign concept testing is necessary. A list of possible concepts can be shown to a sample of targeted voters who are asked to rank or rate them in terms of interest or preference. Voters then indicate how strongly they feel about candidates who are honest, experienced, or conservative. Usually, the majority of voters are in need of a certain type of political leader. By conducting a concept survey, a campaign can find out what type is most in demand. The final choice of a concept should be influenced by both market research and the opposition's expected product concepts.

The candidate should not automatically seek the most ideal concept but rather should choose the one that puts him or her in the best position to offset the product concepts adopted by the other candidates. This is called *product positioning*. If an opponent is a "law-and-order candidate," then would an opposing candidate be more effective as a "civil rights person" or as a "fiscal watchdog"? Because the voter market is composed of many segments, the candidate should devise concepts that will influence a certain market share of each segment over his or her opponents' concepts.

Two additional points can be made about the choice and use of a concept. The candidate must decide how much emphasis to place on the chosen concept. At one extreme, a particular concept can be projected in all talk and action. This is the policy of concept specificity. Or, a product concept can be used more loosely and discriminatingly. This is the policy of concept diffuseness. In commercial marketing, a product can be advertised strongly as offering one major benefit or weakly (and by implication) as offering a variety of benefits including one in particular.

By pursuing concept diffuseness, the candidate might fail to come across to the voters as having any specific identity. Such a strategy might be appropriate for a majority party candidate who believes that partisan voting will bring the victory. On the other hand, the candidate who practices specificity can raise visibility and win the strong support of certain groups while alienating others.

The candidate also can assume a secondary concept as well as a primary one. The candidate can wear two images so long as they are not boldly inconsistent and do not confuse the best use of scarce resources. For example, a candidate might decide on being primarily a law-and-order person and secondarily a fiscal conservative. The primary concept could be projected at mass meetings of, for example, business groups. It is important, however, to avoid trying to be all things to all people.

Given the increasingly single-issue focus of voters' behavior today, the candidate has to be careful about concept consistency. Yet, unlike firms that concentrate on winning the biggest share of a highly profitable but relatively small market segment, the candidate's ultimate task is to attract the broadest possible voter coalition. A computer manufacturer might be content to dominate one market segment while leaving the rest to competitors. The candidate, on the other hand, has to be a "market aggregator" rather than a "market concentrator." He or she must find the umbrella concepts that encompass different groups. This often involves having to deal with both a small number of intense, single-issue adherents who are already mobilized and a large number of unattached and disparate voters who are potentially mobilizable. The trade-offs that are made in the appeals are unavoidable. However, the candidate can control only certain stimuli. Voters also are influenced by their peers, the media, opponents, candidate surrogates, and fortuitous events.

Communication and Distribution Strategy

The candidate's concept should become the basis for planning communication and distribution programs. The concept must be packaged into statements and actions that are matched and distributed to targeted voters. Whether or not the candidate chooses to speak from prepared remarks versus speaking extemporaneously on television or radio, or before mass rallies versus intimate gatherings, is a factor in the tactical development of a campaign. Everything the candidate does communicates something to voters. Strategies should be formed for each of three communication distribution programs:

- A paid advertising program
- A personal appearance program
- A volunteer program

A paid advertising program. Political advertising has come a long way from the days of billboards and posters. Customized appeals through mailings to targeted groups are as important as mass appeals via print and electronic media. Copy no longer can be left to amateurs. The candidate might want to hire an advertising agency to develop the basic components—the method, substance, and frequency of message delivery; management of the candidate's appearances; the size of ads; allocation of the budget over the various media categories; and the percentage of the budget that will be spent each week up to Election Day.

But the candidate should not abandon all judgment and must be comfortable with the advertising messages. Advertising can turn people off as well as on.

A personal appearance program. If a candidate is attractive, then he or she would do well to increase exposure by appearing before as many voters as possible. Meeting a candidate personalizes and intensifies a voter's interest in the election and often ensures his or her vote. A heavy emphasis on personal appearances is not prudent, however, when the candidate bores, confuses, or disappoints voters. Such candidates would do better to minimize their appearances or to agree to them only under highly controlled, favorable circumstances.

The candidate who emphasizes voter exposure is, of course, rarely able to reach every voter. Personal channels consist of rallies, club meetings, coffees, and random appearances at places such as busy street corners. A rally gives the candidate a chance to present his or her positions on the basic issues to a varied audience. The club meeting is a vehicle for meeting special groups such as businesspersons or church members who might not attend a rally. Coffees give the candidate an opportunity to meet friendly and curious neighbors or acquaintances in intimate surroundings so that he or she can project a personal side. Although random meetings on street corners tend to be brief and superficial, they usually involve a broad cross section of potential voters and are relatively inexpensive interactions between candidates and potential voters.

The candidate's schedule usually is severely limited, but some time should be put aside to motivate party workers, volunteers, and committed voters. Time for appearances must be judged in terms of vote potential—the number of uncommitted voters who might be in attendance, the number of opinion leaders, and the chance that an appearance will be covered by the media. The scheduling of a candidate's appearances still is a developing art. It is not yet handled with the same analytical rigor with which the analogous "sales call problem" is in commercial marketing.

The candidate also must think of specific promotional ideas to attract attention. Not only is the candidate competing against an opponent, but on television and radio he or she is competing against candidates running in other races, commercial product advertisements, soap operas, and news reporting of thousands of other events happening in the world. The job is one of event management, that is, the effective staging of events designed to draw the most favorable attention to the candidate. Examples might include the announced plan to walk from one end of the city to the other, the calling of a news conference to make an important announcement, and an appearance at a major sports event.

A volunteer program. Although a candidate cannot be in two places at one time, he or she can use surrogate speakers and volunteer workers to reach voters. A speaker's bureau, consisting of various supporters who are articulate and individually effective with different types of groups, can be formed. But every attempt should be made to match the speaker to the audience—an older person for senior citizens, a woman for women's organizations, a college student for younger voters. Studies of personal selling effectiveness show that effectiveness is optimized when there is a match between the speaker and the audience.

The candidate also needs volunteers who can carry out a multitude of tasks including mailings, canvassing and registering voters, providing transportation, and policing polling places. Managing volunteers effectively has many similarities to managing a sales force. Volunteers must be kept enthusiastic, work quotas must be set, and accomplishments must be monitored.

What Marketing Can Do

With marketing research, positioning strategy, product concept development, and communication and distribution planning, the candidate will be prepared to wage a good fight for votes. These techniques do not guarantee victory. Conscious marketing only promises to maximize the candidate's potential. It cannot necessarily sell a bad candidate, and lack of careful planning will not always harm a good candidate. But applying standard marketing techniques to political campaigning will at least ensure that the campaign's planning is systematic, efficient, and voter oriented. Marketing can promote the most effective use of scarce resources, generate valuable information for both the candidate and the voters, and promote greater responsiveness in the political process.

2

Elite, Popular, and Merchandised Politics

Historical Origins of Presidential Campaign Marketing

RICHARD M. PERLOFF

Hardly a day passes during a presidential campaign without some critic commenting on the sorry state of the nation's quadrennial conversation about politics. Things are too merchandised, too impersonal, too mediated, and far too dominated by marketing considerations, critics say. Those who defend the status quo are quick to point to positive aspects of today's campaign, but there is little disagreement that today's campaign is an exercise in political marketing.

Consumed as we are by activities in the present, we often forget that presidential politics was not always a marketing game. A little more than a century ago, politics was a passionate pursuit, a spectacle that captivated millions of Americans from diverse economic classes. Two centuries ago, politics was an elite man's game, an activity too precious and important to be left to the masses. Campaigns have changed in a variety of ways over the past 200 years. This chapter reviews the major trends in the style of presidential campaign communication in an effort to provide some background and perspective to our contemporary discussions of political marketing. Too often, we forget that the characteristics of today's marketing campaign were influenced and shaped by factors in the past. By looking back at the campaigns of yore, we gain perspective on the present; we obtain a deeper appreciation of what is unique about the contemporary campaign, how

AUTHOR'S NOTE: I appreciate the comments of Robert Dinkin on an earlier version of this chapter.

we came to this historical moment, and why. A historical analysis helps us to understand that the roots of the contemporary campaign can be found not in the advertisements of Rosser Reeves during the 1950s or in Franklin D. Roosevelt's manipulation of radio during the 1930s. Instead, the seed was planted in the late 1800s, with the movement from popular politics to a merchandised presidential campaign (McGerr, 1986). In this chapter, I review the movement from the elite political campaigns of the late 18th century to grassroots campaigning in the Jacksonian period. I discuss the metamorphosis from the flamboyant and colorful politics of the mid-19th century to the merchandised politics of the late 1800s and early 1900s. I then take advantage of the vista that this historical review provides and offer some general statements about the changes and continuities in the quadrennial American presidential contest.

Elite Politics

Like most things, active campaigning for public office developed slowly. In postrevolutionary America, many political activists sneered at vote seeking by candidates. As one New Jersey critic noted, a candidate is "a detestable and dangerous wretch when his popularity has been 'sought after' by *day light* and by *candle light.*" A Connecticut congressman, reflecting on the open solicitation of votes, remarked, "Should any person have the effrontery or folly to make such an attempt, he may be assured of meeting with the general contempt and indignation of the people" (quoted in Dinkin, 1989, p. 14).

The negative attitude toward active campaigning had its roots in the Founding Fathers' republican philosophy of government. Republicanism emphasized public virtue and "disinterested public leadership"; it assumed that people would willingly give up their private interests to work for the common good (Wood, 1992, p. 229). Campaigns initially were thought to be unnecessary. In the republican view, "Candidates did not have to do anything to get elected; they simply had to allow those who knew them to recognize their virtue" (Troy, 1996, p. 8).

The Founding Fathers also feared that the few would manipulate the many. They worried that unscrupulous leaders would abuse their power and direct "demagogic appeals" at a public that was unaccustomed or unable to distinguish between charlatans and statesmen (Troy, 1996). Fearing that the public lacked the political acumen to make sound electoral choices, the founders hedged their bets, opting for a democratic election but instituting an electoral college to ultimately select the president. Thus, active and aggressive campaigning violated the founders' philosophical predilections. They believed that "for republics to prosper, men of character had to sacrifice personal interests for the public good. . . . Popular campaigning was not only dangerous, it was improper, illegitimate, and unnecessary" (p. 8).

Yet, for all the preaching, the practice of politics was different. The American frontier spawned values such as individual liberty and popular democracy. The reality was that candidates had to get elected, and to get elected they had to persuade their brethren to vote for them. So, candidates for Congress or state office were expected to deliver public speeches wherever people were gathered— typically horse races, cockfights, or barbecues. Not surprisingly, liquor flowed freely at these events. Thus, early in the nation's history, we glimpse the development of an ambivalence toward campaigning that remains to this day. This tension between republican and democratic values, between passive candidates and active ones, and between restrained oratory and unbridled appeals to the masses, began in postrevolutionary America and has stayed with us, as can be seen in the criticism that greets both reluctant candidates (e.g., Bob Dole) and energetic ones (e.g., Bill Clinton), whose apparent ease at the gift of gab in presidential debates has been bemoaned by those who find it insincere and unbecoming of a president.

In postrevolutionary America, there was limited acceptance of the notion that candidates should campaign for state and congressional office. This tolerance did not extend to the presidency. Troy (1996) notes,

> Originally, presidential candidates were supposed to "stand" for election, not "run." They did not make speeches. They did not shake hands. They did nothing to betray the slightest ambition for office. Candidates were supposed to stay on their farms in dignified silence, awaiting the people's call, as George Washington had done. (p. 7)

Washington, with his stately, dignified manner, embodied the republicans' dream—a nation in which character and ethos reigned, a society in which people sacrificed their private pursuits for the larger good and worked out problems peacefully and without rancor. But this 18th-century dream would soon give way to 19th-century realities, for a host of major economic and cultural developments would soon influence the dynamics of the American presidential campaign.

The 1800 Election

In the early 1800s, there was fierce debate among political activists, and it frequently was carried out in the partisan newspapers of the day. True to the republican doctrine, presidential candidates did not venture out into the public to offer their views or to seek votes. In 1800, John Adams and Thomas Jefferson spent the election campaign on their farms. But their minions were not so passive.

The Republicans made considerable use of posters, handbills, and pamphlets to promote the candidacy of Jefferson. One Republican leader bragged to Jefferson that he and his allies had "literally sprinkled Georgia and No[rth] Carolina *from the mountains to the sea*" with pamphlets (quoted in Fischer, 1965, p. 130, emphasis in original). Unquestionably, the major weapon in the campaign arsenal was the partisan press, whose editors made no bones about their staunch support for one of the candidates and who engaged in "no holds barred" attacks on the opposition.

The Republicans launched broad attacks on the Federalists, intimating that the latter's policies would push the government toward the sort of monarchical control that the colonists had successfully repelled in the revolution. In fact, as Ellis (1997) notes, the Federalists' plans "for a proactive federal government empowered to shape markets and set both the financial and political agendas" were "more a precocious precursor of [20]th-century New Deal values than an archaic attempt to resuscitate the arbitrary authority of medieval kings and courts" (p. 132). Yet, Federalist policies, particularly Adams's questionable imposition of the Sedition Act, enflamed the Republicans, and the Republican press hit the Federalists hard during the fall campaign. The Federalists, for their part, ignored the Republicans' charges and instead stressed that Adams, as president, had preserved peace and prosperity (Dinkin, 1989).

Not content to rely exclusively on ideology, partisans of both sides resorted to personal attacks. Republican editors smeared Adams, charging that he was a monarchist plotting to set up a "dynastic succession with his sons" (quoted in Troy, 1996, p. 13). Federalist supporters called Jefferson an atheist and a traitor and accused him of raping a slave. (Little did they know that the latter charge would appear in another form in 1802 when the Federalist press carried the sensational allegation that Jefferson had a sexual relationship with a slave, Sally Hemings. Charges and countercharges continue to fly today in the wake of evidence of a DNA match between Hemings and Jefferson descendants.)The press attacks of 1800 reflected the increasing tendency for the political to become personal as well as the striking differences in philosophy between the Federalists and the Jeffersonian Republicans. Without question, both parties recognized the need to use available newspapers to sway voters to their causes. "The engine is the press. Every man must lay his purse and his pen under contribution," Jefferson counseled Madison (quoted in McCormick, 1982, p. 65).

Ever since Mott (1962), journalism historians have referred to this early period in American history as the "dark age of American journalism." Although there is reason to be critical of the scurrilous attacks launched on political leaders (but see Rosenfeld, 1997), it also is important to recognize that such criticism fulfilled a larger function for the political system. It helped to make the press more popular, thereby establishing it as a major institution in American political life (Fischer, 1965). More important, the partisan attacks helped to pave the way for the full-scale development of political parties. Parties, during their heyday, helped to democratize American politics by putting people in touch with candidates for public office.

Applying the criteria of our own era, we would judge the discourse of the late 18th century to be coarse and uncivil. In fact, much of it was. As De Witt Clinton's biographer remarks, "Government in his [Clinton's] time . . . was an almost impenetrable maze of double-dealing in which an honest man found it hard not to lose his way" (Pessen, 1985, p. 159). Yet, there was a silver lining in this cloud of partisan warfare. Fischer (1965) notes, "Behind the smoke and flame of party strife, developments of deep significance were taking place" (p. 148). Parties were forming and people were using established outlets to express their Hobbesian political strivings. Indeed, historians have long believed that the most significant aspect of the 1800 election is that control of government passed peacefully from one political party to another, Aaron Burr's subsequent shooting down of Alexander Hamilton notwithstanding (Cunningham, 1971, p. 134).

Finally, it is important to emphasize that for all the partisan attacks and electioneering during the 1800 election, this was not a national campaign. No national political organizations had yet emerged, and there was no overall direction given to state party leaders, who, for the most part, acted independently (Dinkin, 1989). Furthermore, the campaign still engaged only the most educated and affluent members of the public. Political participation still was limited to White men who owned property. However, change was afoot, and by 1825, property (although not race and gender) restrictions had been removed, thereby extending the vote to most White men. At the same time, advances in transportation and communication put more Americans in touch with each other and reduced the time that it took for people to learn of major events. The stage was set for what historians have called the second party system and for what political communication scholars might call the first bona fide presidential election campaigns.

The Jacksonian Period

The 1828 Election

Presidential campaigns changed dramatically during the period between 1824 and 1852. During this era, loosely called the Jacksonian period because Andrew Jackson and his followers ushered in many "democraticizing" changes in popular politics, the nation witnessed the rise of a number of institutions that have remained as fundamental components of the electoral system. These include party platforms, nominating conventions, and national campaign committees. The reforms significantly increased democracy in that they gave the public a greater voice in the nomination process. However, they had their limits. Presidential politics would not be in the hands of the masses; indeed, the very notion would send the Founding Fathers into convulsions. Instead, politics would be run, to a considerable extent, "by small numbers of men organized into tightly knit groups best described as political machines" (Pessen, 1985, p. 156). Even so, the changes that occurred during the Jacksonian period did succeed in replacing a secret system of designating candidates with one that took place in public, made it mandatory for parties "to undertake to mobilize a mass electorate" (p. 156), and "helped to make democracy acceptable to Americans" (Wood, 1992, p. 305).

The changes grew out of the 1828 election that pitted John Quincy Adams, a distinguished but charismatically challenged political leader, against Jackson, a man who came to be known as "the hero of New Orleans" and "the urbane savage" (Bugg, 1962; Remini, 1971). The campaign witnessed the formation of the first truly national campaign organization, spearheaded by Jackson lieutenant Martin Van Buren, and more generally the emergence of a new class of political professionals dedicated to mastering the art of winning elections. Recognizing that the public was a new force in politics, the Jacksonian Democrats held barbecues, staged rallies, and promoted their candidate by planting hickory trees and erecting hickory poles in town squares. Although Jackson espoused a democratic philosophy, he was a man of republican temperament (at least when it came to presidential campaigns). Jackson delivered no speeches in 1828. However, he was determined to avenge his loss to Adams in 1824, so he worked behind the scenes, communicating frequently with aides and meeting with state party delegations.

Jackson's supporters devoted much of their persuasive energies to creating a vast network of party newspapers (Dinkin, 1989). Of the 600 newspapers in the country at that time, more than 300 actively supported Jackson and lavishly praised "Old Hickory" while denouncing Adams. Once again, the uncivil nature of the Jacksonians' attacks (and those of the pro-Adams newspapers as well) made mincemeat of today's partisan campaigning. Remini (1971) notes that the Jacksonian newspaper editors "stooped to invoking religious bigotry" and "trifled with minority groups by concocting lies about Adams," charging that the Adams administration had referred to the Dutch as "the stupid Dutch" or "the ignorant Dutch" (p. 420). Pro-Adams editors retaliated, charging that "General Jackson's mother was a common prostitute." A pro-Adams newspaper in Cincinnati charged that Andrew and Rachel Jackson had been adulterers and that Rachel was a bigamist and Andrew her seducer (Dinkin, 1989, p. 45). (In fact, Rachel had left her abusive husband, Lewis Robards, and married Jackson. She assumed that Robards had filed for divorce. Later, she learned that he never had filed divorce proceedings.)

Once again, although the campaign revealed the darker side of journalism and human nature, it also had a functional element: It energized people, bringing more ordinary people into politics and changing attitudes toward political parties, groups that the Founding Fathers feared but that, for all their problems, helped to put ordinary people in touch with elites. With more people becoming more politically aware, deferent attitudes that characterized the first political party system of the early 1800s were on the wane (Dinkin, 1989). As Troy (1996) observes, "Even old-fashioned democrats like Jefferson and Madison would appear too patrician; these gentlemen were never called 'Tom' or 'Jemmy.' The era of 'Old Hickory,' Andy Jackson, had begun" (p. 15).

Historians have long debated the meaning of Jacksonian democracy and the sources of its power (Bugg, 1962; Hammond, 1962; Pessen, 1985; Schlesinger, 1945). Was Jackson a democrat who ably represented ordinary men and women, or was he a demagogue who exploited the masses to increase his power? Did he reduce disparity of condition, or did he maintain an inegalitarian status quo? Whereas there are divergent opinions on these issues, there is consensus among historians that Jackson expanded the powers of the presidency and transformed presidential campaigns (Troy, 1996). After Jackson, a candidate had to be not only a person of "distinguished character" (republican virtue) but also a person of "ability and energy" (a democratic value) (p. 15). Although Jacksonian democracy was more complex and less egalitarian than popular myth suggests, there is little doubt that the Jacksonians expanded the parameters of presidential politics, stimulating millions of people to get involved in national campaigns, and laying the foundation for the mass campaigns that were just around the corner. These changes were not lost on Alexis de Tocqueville, who was touring America during 1831–1832 and was impressed by Americans' "inveterate habit of forming groups to obtain common social goals" (quoted in Ryan, 1997, p. 8). "No sooner do you set foot upon American ground than you are stunned by a kind of tumult," he wrote, adding that "almost the only pleasure which an American knows is to take a part in the government and to discuss its measures" (quoted in Chambers, 1971, p. 684). To be sure, some of de Tocqueville's ideas were exaggerated, a function of his own personal biases (Pessen, 1985). Nonetheless, the Frenchman was onto something, for there was much that was vital in the American public sphere in those days. The Jacksonian Democrats ably reflected and shaped Americans' burgeoning interest in the body politic. It would be no exaggeration to say that the evanescent—but immensely democratizing—force of public opinion took on many of its modern contours and assumed much of its significance during the raucous Jacksonian period.

The 1840 Election

The year 1840 turned out to be a highly significant one in American politics. In that year, Troy (1996) observes,

> Millions of Americans entered the political process not only as voters but [also] as partisans attending caucuses, conventions, committee meetings, and rallies. . . . As passionate as the religious revivals sweeping the country, as efficient as the new factories sprouting throughout the land, the rival Whig and Democratic parties inspired and organized the masses. . . . Popular politics became the new American religion, as two and a half million men streamed to the polls—[10] times the number enrolled in churches. (p. 20)

The 1840 race marked the first truly popular presidential election campaign. It was odd that all this happened in 1840, for although the candidates that year, Whig William Henry Harrison and Democrat Martin Van Buren, were capable politicians, they were neither the most compelling orators of the era nor the most distinguished statesmen that the country had to offer. But the times were ripe for change. There was a steady increase in the right to vote, a significant upsurge in voting in presidential elections, major developments in political party organization, and a strong feeling on the part of the public that politics was not just for the high and mighty but rather for every man (Chambers, 1971). "To involve the masses, no novelty was too inane," observes Troy (1996), citing as examples "song, slogans, floats, coonskin caps, popular newspapers with rough-hewn names like *The Log Cabin,* [and] revival-like 'camp' meetings more suitable to the Second Coming than the first Tuesday after the first Monday in November" (p. 20). As before, newspapers added fuel to the fire, intensifying interest in the race. In 1830, America boasted 906 newspapers, of which 100 were dailies. Just 10 years later, with the "penny press" attracting readers and making money, the number of newspapers rose significantly. In 1840, there were 1,577 newspapers, of which 209 were dailies (Chambers, 1971). The newspapers remained highly partisan, promoting Harrison or Van Buren avidly.

It was Harrison, not Van Buren, who would break with tradition and become the first presidential candidate to deliver a stump speech on the campaign trail. He was an unlikely candidate for the role of "people's candidate," as Boller (1996) notes. Unlike Jackson, who had experienced poverty as a child, Harrison was the son of a governor, had attended college, and was living on an affluent farm in North Bend, Ohio, when the Whigs first took an interest in his candidacy. Like Jackson, he had commanded troops in battle, both in the Battle of Tippecanoe in 1811 and during the War of 1812. However, he lacked Old Hickory's military pedigree. If the truth be told, Harrison was attractive to Whig Party leaders precisely because he never had held a major elective office and, therefore, was not likely to alienate key portions of the electorate (Dinkin, 1989).

Confident that voters would reject Van Buren because they blamed him for the economic panic of 1837, during which many businesses failed and unemployment skyrocketed, the Whigs steered clear of taking positions on the issues. Instead, Harrison and the Whigs waged an image campaign, promoting Harrison "as the log cabin–hard cider candidate who, unlike the high-falutin' Martin Van Buren, was plain, simple, down-to-earth, and very much of, by, and for the people" (Boller, 1996, p. 66).

It was quite a spectacle. "The log cabin–hard cider campaign had to be seen to be believed," Boller (1996, p. 66) notes. Thousands gathered at Whig rallies. Parades went on for miles, and they featured speeches, songs (e.g., *The Harrison Cause,* which might be sung to the tune of *The Star-Spangled Banner*), Tippecanoe badges (commemorating Harrison's now controversial battle against the Shawnee Indians at Tippecanoe, Indiana), Tippecanoe shaving cream, hard cider, and more log cabin paraphernalia than you could shake a Whig stick at.

Harrison's managers sought to persuade voters that their man embodied the rustic, hardy, down-to-earth life of frontiersmen and that he "would come to Washington and drive away the corrupt Van Buren regime" (Dinkin, 1989, p. 50). Today, their strategy of linking Harrison with popular values might be analyzed by invoking psychological concepts such as higher order conditioning or associative network representations. Or, the strategy might call to mind political ads that portrayed "Jimmy Carter in a work shirt and blue jeans addressing voters from his home in Plains[, Georgia,] or Ronald Reagan splitting firewood or riding horseback on his ranch" (Jamieson, 1984, p. 12). No doubt, as Jamieson (1984) observes, in the age of television, Harrison's attempt to pass himself off as a man of the frontier would have been exposed by a celebrated journalist who would have pointed out that, although Harrison did own a log cabin in North Bend, he had been born of patrician stock with a silver spoon in his mouth.

In 1840, however, there was no such thing as investigative reporting. Furthermore, the Van Buren newspapers that contained this information reached only Van Buren partisans, not the Harrison supporters or what few undecided voters there were in 1840. To be sure, the Van Buren camp tried to undercut Harrison's credibility, raising questions about his intellectual capacities and tagging him "General Mum" for his reluctance to take positions on the issues. In fact, they raised so many questions that Harrison finally felt that he had to answer their charges, thus becoming the first presidential candidate to take to the stump to defend himself. Yet, for the most part, "Old Tip" equivocated, preferring to tell stories about his military exploits than to outline his positions on the issues. But although his strategy was disappointing, from the standpoint of issue education, it was right on the money when viewed from the vantage point of campaign tactics. Harrison bested Van Buren, capturing 234 electoral votes to Van Buren's 60.

Although Harrison died shortly after taking office, his imprint was left on the American political campaign. Whether by design or by passively acquiescing to the advice of his managers, Harrison influenced the style of presidential campaigning. More generally, as Chambers (1971) notes, the 1840 election

> served to set the presidency and presidential elections as the focal point of American politics and popular attention. The year also brought the popularization of national politics to its zenith and established its character in American life; never again could the Washington community go its way heedless of a national public. (p. 684)

Yet, questions remained. Had Harrison persuaded voters or manipulated them? Had he convinced them that he was the better man for the job? Or, had his handlers instead duped the public through adroit candidate image making? Was the vaunted vox populi deserving of de Tocqueville's praises, or was it as susceptible to demagoguery as the Federalists had feared?

Taking stock of 1840, it is important to point out that good things did come of the log cabin–hard cider campaign. The campaign stimulated interest in politics, helping to make presidential politics America's civic religion during the mid-19th century. More people participated in an election that year than ever before. It can plausibly be argued that the electorate behaved responsibly by rebelling against the burdens of economic depression and launching a crusade against the party in power (Chambers, 1971; Gunderson, 1957). Yet, the campaign, like most campaigns before and after, was a creature of its time. It improved on the status quo by bringing forth new electoral strategies, but it failed to raise a variety of issues that desperately needed to be discussed such as slavery, inequality of conditions, and urban squalor.

The Age of Parties and Popular Politics

The 1840 election marked the official burial of the age of elite politics. "No longer would voters follow after leaders who looked down on the people and dealt with a limited clientele in the electorate," notes Chambers (1971, p. 684). Into the vacuum stepped party leaders and organizations. For half a century, political parties would mediate between government and the public. During the mid-1800s, parties would develop the structures that would last for nearly half a century—professional organizations, platforms, conventions, spectacular campaigns, and affiliation with a partisan press. Parties fulfilled numerous functions for the country and its citizens. Dinkin (1989) notes that as government began to play a larger role in the nation's political and economic life, individuals, social groups, and even sections of the country saw that they could gain a great deal from favorable government policies. This motivated them to work harder to elect their preferred candidates to office. Parties became the mechanism to accomplish this goal. The effects of parties were complex; they rewarded corruption, but they also provided a mechanism for ordinary people to get involved in politics. They also led to major social changes, as can be seen in the effects of the Republican campaign to halt the spread of slavery, a crusade that excited poet Henry Wadsworth Longfellow, and (to a lesser extent) in the Populist effort to reform American economic policies (Dinkin, 1989; Fite, 1971).

Until the last quarter of the 19th century, parties discouraged presidential candidates from speaking out. "Throughout the 1840s and 1850s," Troy (1996) notes, "both Democrats and Whigs craved available, pliable candidates. Parties emerged from conventions united behind one candidate, who, respecting republicanism and the platform, kept silent, content to be waved as an icon before partisan crowds" (p. 45). Thus, the continuing, if rocky, commitment to republicanism discouraged presidential candidates from speaking their minds on social issues. Slowly, however, candidates began to take to the stump. In 1860, Stephen Douglas, beset with inadequate campaign finances and an ineffective party organization, realized that his only hope of winning election was to hit the campaign trail. One Illinois newspaper, reflecting both republican values and a pro-Abraham Lincoln bias, ridiculed the "Little Giant":

> Douglas is going about peddling his opinions as a tin man peddles his ware. The only excuse for him is that he is a small man, [so] he has the right to be engaged in small business; and small business it is for a candidate for the presidency to be strolling around the country begging for votes like a town constable. (cited in Dinkin, 1989, p. 81)

Lincoln took the more republican posture. Although his views on slavery were known to many, he said little about the issue and avoided campaigning in public. His restraint was based on both personal style and political strategy (i.e., his belief that he could do his cause considerable harm if he offended large numbers of voters). Like Jackson, he worked behind the scenes to harness support for his candidacy while his advisers developed posters, articles, and even full-length biographies that touted Lincoln's virtues including the soon-to-be-mythical notion that he had split rails as a younger man. Lincoln was the better man for the job, and his moral and political agenda no doubt saved the country (Morison, 1971). But Douglas was ahead of Lincoln on the issue of strategy. Over the course of the 19th century, presidential candidates increasingly took a more active posture, a change that Troy (1996) says had its roots in a host of structural factors including "the spread of liberal democracy, the strengthening of the presidency, and the continuing transformations in technology and the press" (p. 80). Expectations for candidates changed in light of the growing recognition that corruption plagued urban political machines and that politics had become less populist than unseemly. Leading editors and activists urged candidates to reveal their opinions and take to the stump.

Candidates did so cautiously, well aware that republican values still were in force and that, as the *New York Times* proclaimed as late as 1892, the notion of a president campaigning "disgusts the people." Thus, during the last quarter of the 19th century, candidates experimented with a variety of ideas for reconciling the time-honored conflict between republican and democratic values. James Garfield and Benjamin Harrison delivered scores of speeches to the throngs who converged on their homes. In 1896, William McKinley launched a front porch campaign that attracted hundreds of thousands of people to Canton, Ohio. The silver-tongued orator, William Jennings Bryan, delivered 600 speeches in 27 states. According to Troy (1996).

> These innovations helped obliterate the ideological and actual distance between the candidate and the people that buttressed the republican taboo. No longer mere icons, candidates now appealed directly to the people, who learned much about each candidate—from his shoe size to his worldview. Public communication with large audiences became more important than informal letters to individual voters. The gentleman was no longer speaking to his neighbor privately; rather, the leader was exhorting his followers publicly. (pp. 106-107)

The Press

From the Jacksonian period through the end of what Mark Twain called the "Gilded Age," newspapers had close ties to political parties. Some editors, such as Thurlow Weed, also were party leaders. Reflecting on the mid-19th-century press, one journalist observed that the newspaper "was not a newspaper at all. It contained little news of a general character and almost no local intelligence. It was simply the organ of a party" (cited in McGerr, 1986, p. 18). The contemporary distinctions between facts and opinions and between news and editorials, murky as they might be, were lost on the mid-19th-century editor, who believed that news should serve the party's ideology.

In those days, news bias (if the term can even be said to have existed) was not a bad thing but rather a good one, an indication that a newspaper was standing up for what it believed. Editors distorted information so that it favored their party's side, sometimes falsifying election returns and frequently writing stories so that they portrayed their side as attracting huge, exuberant crowds while minimizing the number of partisans who showed up to see the opposing party candidate. Headlines such as "The Millions Have Spoken and Liberty Is Proclaimed Throughout the Land" frequently were used to celebrate the victory of the newspaper's candidate (McGerr, 1986, p. 21).

McGerr (1986) notes that newspapers and parties worked well together because they needed each other. Newspapers provided a forum for parties to reach voters, furnishing them with well-written partisan propaganda. Editors received financial capital from parties including advertising, contracts for printing campaign materials, and even subsidies paid by politicians during election years. Newspapers announced their partisan affiliation by listing the names of the party's candidates on their mastheads each day.

Although newspapers became increasingly independent of political parties during the 1880s and 1890s, they still colored news in partisan shades. Even during the 1896 election, some news stories were written to obviously favor the newspaper's candidate. It is fair to say that for much of the second half of the 19th century, newspapers depicted the world in partisan terms and encouraged readers to view it in absolutist ways. While acknowledging the costs of this portrayal of politics, some scholars have viewed it as more positive than negative. Dissatisfied with the dispassionate style of today's political reporting that may inhibit participation in political causes, McGerr (1986) argues that "by reducing politics to black-and-white absolutes, the [19th-century] press made partisanship enticing. . . . Through combative editorials and lavish victory displays, news-papermen declared that one's partisan attachment must be publicly asserted, defended, and celebrated" (p. 21).

Popular Politics

Perhaps the most distinctive aspects of 19th-century presidential campaigns were the spectacular displays of partisan politics, exuberant rallies, and "army-style" marches in the streets, the latter an outgrowth of the emphasis placed on discipline during the Civil War (Dinkin, 1989; Jensen, 1971).

Shortly after the parties nominated their candidates, hundreds of men formed political clubs. Party workers, immigrants, and tradesmen all formed clubs. Each club selected officers, established rules of operation, and coordinated members' participation in campaign events. Torchlight parades (featuring the lighting of fireworks and the burning of "red fire" that provided a colorful hue), pole-raisings, banner-raisings, barbecues, ox roasts, and rallies that mixed long candidate speeches with songs and picnicking were common during this era (Dinkin, 1989, pp. 65-66).

So, too, were military-style marches in the streets, organized by uniformed marching companies. In October 1876, at the height of military-style campaigning, four marching companies composed of immigrants and sons of immigrants—men who worked in hard labor jobs by day and proudly marched as members of campaign armies by night—gathered in New Haven, Connecticut, wearing military-style caps and holding kerosene torches. By early evening, the men proceeded through the city streets, their torches lit, a brass band leading the way. Later, an enormous flag with the name of the beloved Samuel Tilden, Democrat of New York, flew from a rooftop while the crowd, now estimated at 3,000 people, heard six speakers lambast the Republican Party and call on the men to vote a straight Democratic ticket (McGerr, 1986).

The Tilden march was typical of those that occurred during this time. It reflected the belief that people (in essence, White men) ought to actively partake in politics and should vote in presidential elections. During the last half of the 19th century, as many as 25% of voters actively participated in campaigns; from

1876 to 1900, a whopping 77% of the electorate voted in presidential elections (Dinkin, 1989; McGerr, 1986).

Issues were discussed passionately, often publicly and often with prejudice. On a local level, debates focused on topics ranging from immigrants' rights to prohibition of alcohol. Discussions of temperance got heated, as when a Democratic partisan charged that Republicans "hated the Germans because they would drink beer even on Sundays" (Dinkin, 1989, p. 61). Debates often could turn ugly, as when race or abolitionism was discussed. In some cases, the outcome was violence directed at newspaper editors, particularly those, such as African American journalists, who took positions outside the mainstream discourse (Nerone, 1994). Of course, not all discourse was violent. There was lively discussion of economic issues, such as tariffs and the gold standard, reflecting concerns about income disparities between the rich and the poor.

During the Gilded Age, politics was a major leisure time activity, an emotional, active pursuit that (unlike today) was perceived to be highly relevant to people's private lives. "Party affiliation ranked on the same level as religious or family affiliation," notes Dinkin (1989, p. 63). "Party membership was a part of men's identity; as such, their partisanship had to be paraded and asserted in public," observes McGerr (1986, p. 14). Participation in politics no doubt fulfilled a number of social and psychological functions for White men growing up in the mid-1800s. Men identified with their political parties in the same way as people today affiliate with city sports teams or participate vicariously in the lives of celebrities. Politics served both instrumental and symbolic functions. Men, particularly those who had just emigrated from Europe, depended on party bosses to bring jobs and (in some cases) money for their families. But more symbolically, politics offered people a way in which to transcend the gritty and often unjust here and now. It offered a ready-made identity—membership in a marching company or party club that embodied ideals and values they respected. It gave people a feeling that they were part of something larger than the self and were partaking in a cause that was right and just, even if participants did not always grasp the ways in which big-city machines were using spectacular events to build their largesse.

Merchandised Politics

The forerunner to today's marketing campaign developed slowly, but inexorably, over the course of the late 19th and early 20th centuries. The "merchandised style of campaigning," to use Dinkin's (1989) phrase (cf. Jensen, 1971), and "advertised politics," as McGerr (1986) calls it, evolved from frustrations with the popular politics of the Gilded Age. Jensen (1971) and Dinkin (1989) argue that popular, spectacular campaigns began petering out in 1892, and McGerr (1986) traces the beginning of their decline to 1876, when Tilden mounted the first "educational-style" campaign. An emphasis on education and dissemination of facts pervaded the politics of the 1880s and 1890s and then was supplanted by merchandising and marketing-oriented campaigns. The change from spectacular politics to educational and merchandised politics occurred slowly. It began in 1876, could be seen in 1884 when campaign leaders paid great attention to polls and issue-oriented materials (with one state headquarters organized like "the management of some business enterprise"), and was in full swing in 1896 (p. 76).

There were many forces pushing for change. A first nudge came from the liberal reformers who played an active part in politics during the 1870s and 1880s. The reformers were educated, affluent, and often highly elitist. (Some called for an educational requirement for suffrage.) Reformers railed against the ideology of partisanship, pointing to the enormous power parties wielded and to the corrupt party machines. Placing their faith in the nascent field of social science, the provision of facts (rather than opinions), and the exercise of cool and dispassionate political reflection, liberals expressed hope that campaigns would rely on education. They yearned for a "less emotional, more intellectual public life," notes McGerr (1986, p. 58).

The liberals pushed through major reforms. They replaced the corrupt practice, whereby parties circulated ballots listing only their nominees, with the secret ballot. They pushed successfully for civil service reform and presidential primaries. By the time that the first presidential primaries occurred in the early 1900s, the change from the popular politics to the new progressive politics was complete.

A second factor pushing campaigns toward change was the decline in enthusiasm for spectacular politics. "As memories of the Civil War faded," McGerr (1986) notes, "people lost the martial interest that was one facet of campaign spectacle" (p. 147). In 1916, an Indiana reporter came across a kerosene torch from the 1892 campaign and wondered why men enjoyed carrying things that spilled oil onto clothes. The public had grown tired of the noisy campaigning, perhaps feeling disillusioned with parties and also sensing that torchlight parades were out of sync with the ambience of a nation preparing to enter the 20th century. No doubt, liberal reformers' criticism of old-style campaigns and newspaper exposés of Boss Tweed (Leonard, 1986) also increased the sense of public ennui. Responding to (while simultaneously shaping) the new sentiments, party officials of the late 1800s opted to spend more of their funds on printed materials designed to educate voters rather than on torches, banners, and bands.

The first educational-style campaign occurred in 1876, when Tilden's campaign managers distributed millions of pieces of campaign literature describing the candidate's background, drafted editorials for Democratic newspapers, and sent out speakers to partisan meetings across the country.

Although Tilden lost the battle for the election, probably due in part to the corrupt actions of electoral college officials, he won the campaign war. Educational politics became more popular after 1876. The passage of a federal civil service law helped to diminish the power of political parties. It also served to promulgate the norm that campaigns should be fought less, as the *New York Tribune* put it, in "Chinese fashion . . . with loud noises and a dreadful beating of gongs" (cited in McGerr, 1986, p. 83). In 1888, there were noticeably fewer marching companies and torchlight processions than there had been in years past. "Everywhere, politicians emphasized polls, organization, and literature," notes

McGerr (1986, p. 98). The emphasis on education made sense during an era when fewer voters could be counted on to slavishly follow the marching orders of the party's commanding officers.

A third factor pushing campaigns away from spectacle was the increasing division of the economic classes. For many years, wealthy and working class men had worked together in campaigns, bonded by their allegiance to party. But walkouts and strikes, such as the Homestead Strike of 1882, pushed the classes apart. In addition, upper class men, who previously had encouraged people of all economic stripes to participate in partisan displays, lost faith in popular politics, preferring instead the reformist educational approach.

A fourth factor was the increasing application of the business model to politics. Frustrated with corrupt bosses, liberal reformers hoped that a business approach would shake up presidential politics. A quid pro quo quickly developed; political activists recognized that big corporations could help finance campaigns, and businessmen realized that they gained by helping elect candidates who owed them favors.

A fifth ingredient was the development of new leisure time pursuits. From the 1840s through the 1870s, politics was the main source of entertainment for White men of the working, middle, and upper classes. Toward the end of the 19th century, new forms of entertainment appeared—vaudeville, amusement parks, baseball, and the like. With the development of leisure as a value and the emergence of a host of new leisure time pursuits, there was less interest and time for political spectacle. Advertising, consumption, and new modes to symbolically experience life quickly gained a foothold, leading to the decline in political theater.

Finally, the press pushed campaigns away from noisy partisan displays. A growing number of newspapers took up the banner of independent journalism. Younger editors shared educational reformists' frustration with party politics and agreed that newspapers should not be the tools of political parties (McGerr, 1986; Rutenbeck, 1990). At the same time, as the newspaper field became more prosperous and business oriented (Baldasty, 1992), there was added incentive to pitch stories to a heterogeneous collection of readers, which militated against partisan journalism. Reporters also increasingly regarded journalism as a profession and began to see themselves as part of a vocation that was considerably different from politics. The result was front-page news that more clearly separated fact from opinion. These stories undoubtedly cultivated a more complex view of politics. Investigative stories, such as the *New York Times'* exposés of Boss Tweed, undermined faith in political parties, and sensational coverage à la William Randolph Hearst trivialized exuberant partisan displays (Leonard, 1986; McGerr, 1986).

The press changed popular politics not just by painting a less colorful, partisan landscape for readers but also by making political speeches quickly available to the masses. When readers knew that the gist of a candidate's speech would later be reprinted in the newspaper, they lost their enthusiasm for listening to hours-long flamboyant oratory. Politicians also delivered speeches less spontaneously, knowing that the text would be reprinted in the newspaper and would be available to thousands (Dinkin, 1989). Although oratory was not dead and would make a comeback with Bryan in 1896, some of the old-style dynamism was gone, a casualty of the new era.

Thus, for a variety of reasons, the popular politics of the mid-19th century was in decline by the 1880s, and visibly so by the early 1890s. In 1892, the *New York Herald* noted an "exceptional calmness" and an "unprecedented absence of noisy demonstrations, popular excitement, and that high-pressure enthusiasm which used to find vent in brass bands, drum and trumpet fanfaronade, boisterous parades by day and torchlight processions by night" (Dinkin, 1989, p. 97).

The 1896 Campaign

The spirited 1896 presidential campaign marked an official beginning of advertised politics—the unabashed introduction of marketing-type techniques into presidential politics. The change had been coming, as I have noted, and the use of business techniques could be seen in earlier campaigns. But it all came together in 1896.

What made 1896 unique was the fact that both candidates participated actively in the campaign and both discussed the issues (e.g., the gold standard vs. free silver, the latter a symbol of justice to Democrats and of irresponsibility to Republicans). There was, of course, a sharp contrast between Bryan's fiery campaign oratory, available to all who cared to listen during his 29-state, 500-speech tour (the most extensive tour yet conducted by a presidential candidate), and that of McKinley, who preferred a dignified, scripted campaign, directed by Republican Chairman Mark Hanna, campaign manager nonpareil.

Hanna systematically applied the principles of modern business to presidential campaigns. He employed more experienced workers at campaign headquarters, used up-to-date bookkeeping practices, expanded polling operations, relied on the telephone to keep track of campaign developments, and brought campaign finance into the modern age. Hanna raised between $3.5 million and $7 million for the Republican campaign, perhaps three times more than had been raised in any previous campaign (Dinkin, 1989). Standard Oil alone gave $250,000. Although he was portrayed as greedy and corrupt in the press, Hanna "took pains to avoid situations where favors were implied in return for contributions," Dinkin (1989) notes, and "probably was one of the more honest political figures of the day" (p. 106). Yet, Hanna helped to initiate the system in which businesses underwrite presidential candidates' campaigns.

As the campaign unfolded, Hanna became increasingly concerned about Bryan's ability to attract huge, enthusiastic crowds. He urged McKinley to stump. McKinley refused but agreed to wage a front porch campaign, speaking to hundreds of thousands of visitors to his Canton home. Although it is commonly believed that McKinley delivered off-the-cuff, spontaneous speeches to well-wishers, in fact many of the meetings had been carefully planned in advance, with details worked out by Hanna. In some cases, as Fite (1971) notes, "McKinley knew what questions would be raised, and he had time to give close attention to his replies" (p. 1817).

Known to his colleagues as a "phrase maker," Hanna reveled in clever slogans and symbols. In fact, Hanna was so proficient in reducing complex issues to simple phrases and in linking McKinley with positively held American values that Theodore Roosevelt felt moved to remark, "He has advertised McKinley as if he were a patent medicine." Hanna's emphasis on advertising strategies paralleled the emergence of modern advertising in the 1880s and 1890s. During this period, Kodak created the slogan "You press the button; we do the rest" (McGerr, 1986). Hanna, shrewd businessman and creative marketer that he was, quickly realized the implications that advertising had for politics, and he used it shrewdly in 1896. The technique caught on. Early in the new century, political leaders recognized that the same pithy slogans and colorful illustrations that agencies used to sell products could be employed to promote candidates. In 1908, both the Republicans and Democrats ran ads in newspapers. That same year, segments of Bryan's Labor Day speech were shown on film.

McGerr (1986) maintains that the 1896 campaign paved the way for the politics of the 20th century. He notes,

> The campaign of 1896 offered the essence of [20th]-century political style: emphasis on the personality of the candidate rather than on his party; concentration on the nominee and national headquarters rather than on events in communities; careful packaging of the candidate, whether on posters or on his front porch; and pictures and slogans—the tools of advertising—to sell him to the voters. (p. 145)

Now, to be sure, the 1896 campaign differed in important ways from 20th-century campaigns. Old-fashioned party campaigning still was in vogue, spectacular events and rallies still occurred, candidates interacted a great deal with voters in person, and (on the Democratic side at least) the use of mass mediated appeals played second fiddle to old-fashioned political oratory. It would take nearly an entire century, and a host of political, cultural, and technological developments, before the presidential election could be aptly described by a marketing model.

Yet, in other ways, the handwriting was on the wall in that 1896 race. Not only was the spectacular politics of the mid-19th century in sharply less abundance, but the Tilden-style educational politics that characterized elections of the previous decade worked for the first time in tandem with a business-oriented approach, spearheaded by Hanna. The mixture of education and merchandising soon would become the norm in presidential campaigns, with merchandising supplanting education inasmuch as it seemed more capable of reaching and influencing masses of American voters.

The changes were readily apparent in the first elections of the new century. Candidate speechmaking (foreshadowing candidate-centered politics), short speeches, tailoring appearances to the press, and a focus on personal appeals soon became de rigueur. To be sure, some of the hoopla continued in 1900 when Bryan's Democrats organized spectacular outdoor rallies. But by 1904, the *New York Times* proclaimed that "campaigning is only a political name for advertising." And 4 years later, a reporter could write that "campaign management has come to follow strictly the lines of publicity adopted in business" (cited in McGerr, 1986, p. 159). By 1916, a political writer observed that "the old-fashioned political spellbinder" had been replaced by the "skilled advertising expert," who boils down issues and presents them in a way that average people can understand (p. 168). During the 1920s, in the aftermath of elite and (to some extent) public consternation about the power of U.S. propaganda during World War I, writers began to decry the abilities of image makers to manipulate the mass public. On one level, the criticism of advertising experts was a new phenomenon. On another level, it was as old as the republic itself, for it dated back to the ambivalence the framers themselves harbored toward candidate advocacy and unbridled presidential campaigns.

Conclusions

Presidential campaigns are quintessentially American institutions. The notion that candidates ought to publicly court the favor of the electorate could only emerge in a nation whose founders rejected aristocratic culture, with its hierarchy and all-encompassing en loco parentis, and instead embraced a republican society that offered new, egalitarian conceptions of the individual, the family, and government (Wood, 1992). Although the revolutionary generation disdained the notion of campaigns, the generations that succeeded it gradually took up the banner of campaigns, realizing that they are fully consonant with the culture's long-held belief that persuasion is preferable to coercion.

This whirlwind tour of American campaign history has revealed the many continuities and changes in campaign communication. The continuities are striking. Throughout American history, campaigns have been vibrant and colorful but also strident and divisive. Partisan attacks and uncivil discourse have been the order of the day. The press always has played an important part in American campaigns. It served as the mechanism by which candidates could launch partisan attacks in the late 18th century. Throughout the 19th century, it provided parties with a mouthpiece for reaching voters, and it helped to shape and construct a world of exuberant partisan attachment. During the era of merchandised politics, it helped campaigns educate and persuade masses of voters. What is more, the incestuous relationship between politics and journalism dates back to Jefferson, who gave a printer a lucrative government printing contract, and also to Jackson, who had as many as 57 reporters on the federal government payroll (Perloff, 1998). Some 30 years later, Lincoln befriended *Chicago Tribune* editor Joseph Medill, and Medill returned the favor by helping to get Lincoln nominated in 1860. And long before journalist Patrick Buchanan tossed his hat into the ring, editor Horace Greeley declared his interest in the job and even managed to get nominated. The press has worked hand in hand with party elites, and yet it has provided a mechanism for ordinary people to participate, both materially and symbolically, in politics.

Today's criticisms of political marketing can be usefully viewed in the context of a century or more of such excoriations, including the observation of the *New York Evening Post* in 1872 that the methods by which voters elect leaders are "execrable" and a reporter's lamentation in 1916 that "the old-fashioned political spellbinder, who has made the hustings 'resound' in past campaigns, is being put out of business by the skilled advertising expert" (cited in McGerr, 1986, p. 168; Troy, 1996, p. 77). Criticism of campaigns is not new. It dates at least as far back as the late 1870s, when liberal reformers denounced the excesses of party spectacles.

Finally, presidential campaigns never have been totally democratic; they never have been controlled primarily by masses of ordinary Americans (nor would such a proposition have been endorsed by the Constitution's framers). For better or worse, campaigns always have been shaped to a considerable degree by elites—political elites in the late 18th century, party leaders in the 19th century, and marketing gurus in the late 20th century. And although campaigns have touched on pressing issues in some elections (e.g., 1896) more than others, they never have been primarily about issues, particularly those that fall outside the realm of mainstream discourse. Slavery, lynchings, and urban squalor are among the issues that received short shrift in presidential campaigns of the 18th and 19th centuries.

There have been numerous changes in presidential campaigns over the past two centuries. During the early years, republican virtue dominated as candidates steered clear of making public appearances. The elite stage of campaigns gave way to party-dominated popular politics, a style that began during the Jacksonian era and lasted through the Gilded Age. During this era, party leaders ran the show, often using heavy-handed, corrupt techniques to maintain power. At the same time, campaigns were enormously popular and captured the interest and imagination of large numbers of White voters. This stands in striking contrast to the cynicism and apathy that typify today's presidential contests.

Campaigns always have been about persuasion, but the nature of the persuasion has changed. At first, elites tried to convince other elites through newspaper articles and informal communications. Next, stump speeches, pole-raisings, and spectacular events became the hallmark of American campaign persuasion. Unlike today, when presidential communications typically target undecided voters, these ceremonies were geared toward the overwhelming majority of partisan voters. They were designed to access people's partisanship and to induce them to translate attitudes into political behavior. As educated politics and then advertised politics replaced exuberant partisanship as the major political style in America, persuasive efforts took on a more dispassionate and strategic orientation. As a result of cultural, political, and technological developments too numerous to discuss in this chapter, the hybrid campaigns of the late 19th century evolved and metamorphosized into today's marketing-style presidential elections, dominated as they are by public relations, polling, and candidate-centered political campaigns. Contemporary campaigns try to manage impressions and to highlight issues, as campaigns have done for more than 150 years, but the persuasive orientations are dictated by marketing considerations and by the technical and economic needs of the news media, particularly television.

TABLE 2.1 Display of Political Values in Public by Presidential Candidates and Ordinary Citizens

Century	Degree of Public Expression	
	Candidates	*Citizens*
18th	Low	Low
19th	Low	High
20th[a]	High	Low

a. Particularly the latter years.

Other changes revolve around the yin and yang of public and private values. The past 200 years have witnessed a transformation in the display of these values by candidates and voters. During the late 18th century, republican virtue reigned; candidates' privacy was protected and respected. During this era of elite politics, few members of the public actively participated in campaigns; it was largely an elite man's campaign. A half century later, in the age of popular, party-based politics, stumping was on the rise, but presidential candidates still were not expected to campaign actively; republican dignity remained intact. By contrast, many voters participated actively and publicly in campaigns, with participation reaching its peak during the years of exuberant army-style campaigning.

In our time, as a result of the evolution to merchandised politics and then to the marketing style (Newman, 1994), candidates are expected to campaign actively in public and, what is more, to reveal their innermost personal secrets. Candidates are public personalities; their private lives are grist for the mass media. Republican dignity, although not dead, plays second fiddle to seamless public performance. By contrast, the public keeps its own views private. People share opinions with others in the privacy of their living rooms, nestled before their omnipresent television sets. Few participate in public forums or rallies. Participation is mediated, indirect, and filtered through the press. Although the structural barriers to public participation that were erected during the 18th and 19th centuries have been lifted, social and psychological impediments remain (Table 2.1).

This discussion simplifies the matter to some extent. For ease of discussion, I have treated 20th-century campaigning as an entity, thereby minimizing differences between merchandising and marketing and between campaigns of the pre- and posttelevision age. But the important point is that the determination of what is deemed appropriate for the public and private spheres has changed dramatically over the past 200 years and will continue to change so long as people elect candidates and candidates campaign to get elected.

It is tempting, of course, to suggest that things were better in the "old days," particularly during the era of popular politics, when there was rowdy, passionate participation in presidential campaigns. Indeed, McGerr (1986) suggests that something vital was lost in the move from spectacular to advertised politics. Yet, one must stringently guard against the all-too-human tendency to assume that the past was more positive than it really was (Mitchell, Thompson, Peterson, & Cronk, 1997), for as critics like McGerr would be quick to acknowledge, not all

Americans could participate exuberantly in the army-style campaigns. Although Blacks and women occasionally participated in partisan displays, they were not exactly encouraged to do so, and it was effectively impossible for them to partake on a regular basis. The second half of the 19th century was, after all, an era of horrendous sexism and racism, the latter a particular blight on the American character, as historical scholarship continues to demonstrate (e.g., Williamson, 1997). Moreover, it is not immediately clear that there is anything ennobling about political participation that seemed to emerge almost reflexively as a function of religious and ethnic loyalties rather than as an outgrowth of a thoughtful and reasoned consideration of issues. What makes the type of knee-jerk partisan participation of the mid-19th century worthy of emulation, particularly if one suspects, to paraphrase Socrates, that the unexamined political life is not worth living?

But if romanticizing the past is less than useful, then discarding it is a recipe for disaster. History helps us to appreciate the differences between the campaigns of today and those of the past. It aids us in understanding how we have come to this place in space and time, and it gives us a rich lens for examining today's presidential communications. The marketing campaign did not develop out of thin air; instead, it evolved over time and as a response to the inequities and dysfunctional aspects of the popular party-based campaign, in much the same way as popular politics emerged when elite politics no longer could serve the complex needs of the burgeoning culture. By reviewing the past and the many takes on it provided by historians, we may become somewhat less critical of the raucous, coarse nature of American politics, realizing that politics always has been a rough-and-tumble profession. We may appreciate the strengths of today's campaign—its absence of structural impediments to political participation, the reduction of fraud, and the emphasis placed on democratic appeals to the electorate. At the same time, we are likely to be more aware of the deficits in the contemporary campaign—the replacement of republican faith in the willingness of citizens to work for the public good with a cynical distrust of candidates and organized political groups, the decline in popular participation in campaigns, and the corrosive influence that money (doled out by megalobbyists and multinational firms) exerts on presidential politics.

Unquestionably, the system needs changing. The theme of this chapter has been that attempts to both change and understand campaigns should take history into account, for history provides us with perspective on the present. It helps us to see the pleasant and not so pleasant aspects of contemporary campaigns in a more objective light, thereby helping us to make more informed judgments and providing those who wish to reform campaigns with visions of how to go about this seemingly impossible, but enormously important, task.

References

Baldasty, G. J. (1992). *The commercialization of news in the nineteenth century.* Madison: University of Wisconsin Press.

Boller, P. F., Jr. (1996). *Presidential campaigns* (rev. ed.). New York: Oxford University Press.

Bugg, J. L., Jr. (1962). Introduction. In J. L. Bugg, Jr. (Ed.), *Jacksonian democracy: Myth or reality?* (pp. 1-5). New York: Holt, Rinehart & Winston.

Chambers, W. N. (1971). Election of 1840. In A. M. Schlesinger, Jr., & F. L. Israel (Eds.), *History of American presidential elections 1789-1968* (Vol. 1, pp. 643-744). New York: Chelsea House.

Cunningham, N. E., Jr. (1971). Election of 1800. In A. M. Schlesinger, Jr., & F. L. Israel (Eds.), *History of American presidential elections 1789-1968* (Vol. 1, pp. 101-156). New York: Chelsea House.

Dinkin, R. J. (1989). *Campaigning in America: A history of election practices.* New York: Greenwood.

Ellis, J. J. (1997). *American sphinx: The character of Thomas Jefferson.* New York: Knopf.

Fischer, D. H. (1965). *The revolution of American conservatism: The Federalist Party in the era of Jeffersonian democracy.* New York: Harper & Row.

Fite, G. C. (1971). Election of 1896. In A. M. Schlesinger, Jr., & F. L. Israel (Eds.), *History of American presidential elections 1789-1968* (Vol. 2, pp. 1787-1874). New York: Chelsea House.

Gunderson, R. G. (1957). *The log cabin campaign.* Westport, CT: Greenwood.

Hammond, B. (1962). The Jacksonians. In J. L. Bugg, Jr. (Ed.), *Jacksonian democracy: Myth or reality?* (pp. 92-106). New York: Holt, Rinehart & Winston.

Jamieson, K. H. (1984). *Packaging the presidency: A history and criticism of presidential campaign advertising.* New York: Oxford University Press.

Jensen, R. (1971). *The winning of the Midwest: Social and political conflict, 1888-1896.* Chicago: University of Chicago Press.

Leonard, T. C. (1986). *The power of the press: The birth of American political reporting.* New York: Oxford University Press.

McCormick, R. P. (1982). *The presidential game: The origins of American presidential politics.* New York: Oxford University Press.

McGerr, M. E. (1986). *The decline of popular politics: The American North, 1865-1928.* New York: Oxford University Press.

Mitchell, T. R., Thompson, L., Peterson, E., & Cronk, R. (1997). Temporal adjustments in the evaluation of events: The "rosy view." *Journal of Experimental Social Psychology, 33,* 421-448.

Morison, E. (1971). Election of 1860. In A. M. Schlesinger, Jr., & F. L. Israel (Eds.), *History of American presidential elections 1789-1968* (Vol. 2, pp. 1097-1152). New York: Chelsea House.

Mott, F. L. (1962). *American journalism* (3rd ed.). New York: Macmillan.

Nerone, J. (1994). *Violence against the press: Policing the public sphere in U.S. history.* New York: Oxford University Press.

Newman, B. I. (1994). *The marketing of the president: Political marketing as campaign strategy.* Thousand Oaks, CA: Sage.

Perloff, R. M. (1998). *Political communication: Politics, press, and public in America.* Mahwah, NJ: Lawrence Erlbaum.

Pessen, E. (1985). *Jacksonian America: Society, personality, and politics* (rev. ed.). Urbana: University of Illinois Press.

Remini, R. V. (1971). Election of 1828. In A. M. Schlesinger, Jr., & F. L. Israel (Eds.), *History of American presidential elections 1789-1968* (Vol. 1, pp. 413-492). New York: Chelsea House.

Rosenfeld, R. N. (1997). *American Aurora.* New York: St. Martin's.

Rutenbeck, J. B. (1990). Editorial perception of newspaper independence and the presidential campaign of 1872. *Journalism History, 17,* 12-22.

Ryan, M. P. (1997). *Civic wars: Democracy and public life in the American city during the nineteenth century.* Berkeley: University of California Press.

Schlesinger, A. M., Jr. (1945). *The age of Jackson.* Boston: Little, Brown.

Troy, G. (1996). *See how they ran: The changing role of the presidential candidate* (rev. ed.). Cambridge, MA: Harvard University Press.

Williamson, J. (1997). Wounds not scars: Lynching, the national conscience, and the American historian. *Journal of American History, 83,* 1221-1253.

Wood, G. S. (1992). *The radicalism of the American revolution.* New York: Knopf.

3

The Marketing Colonization of Political Campaigning

DOMINIC WRING

In a survey of trends and debates in political science, Almond (1990, p. 121) identifies five analogies often used in the analysis of political competition. Despite parallels with the military, sporting, theatrical, and religious arenas, the conception of a political market has become perhaps the most enduring metaphor for interparty rivalries. Publication of Downs's (1957) seminal study *An Economic Theory of Democracy* served to considerably strengthen the comparison. Since then, the analogy has derived additional support from the fact that the marketing approach and its tools have invaded the electoral environment in which competitive political organizations must operate. Several influential authorities have sought to develop the concept of the "political market," most notably democratic theorist Joseph Schumpeter:

> Party and machine politicians are simply the response to the fact that the electoral mass is incapable of action other than a stampede, and they constitute an attempt to regulate political competition exactly similar to the corresponding practices of a trade association. (Schumpeter, 1943, p. 283)

In seeking to account for the growing popularity and relevance of the market as a metaphor and a tool of analysis for elections in Britain, not to mention elsewhere, it is necessary to understand the connection among three interrelated theoretical developments. The first involves the emergence of what psephologists have termed "volatility" and the perception that voters are increasingly exercising a greater degree of "consumer sovereignty," abandoning their previous supposedly stable partisan allegiances. Second, transformations in the wider social and economic environment during the course of the 1980s precipitated profound cultural change, with commercialism having colonized many areas of civic life with the philosophy and practices of the market. Politics has not been excluded from this process. Third, the study and practice of marketing have grown considerably over the past decade and now encompass new developments in the field of non-profit-making management. Consequently, a good deal of attention is beginning to be focused on understanding and, in selected cases, on influencing the practices of organizations such as charities, governmental agencies, and political parties.

Politics:
The Rise of the Volatility Debate

British general election results between 1945 and 1970 were characterized by the stability of the main competitors' shares of electoral support. In each of the eight campaigns that took place during this period, the two parties of government, Labour and Conservative, obtained approximately 85% of the popular vote between them. It was not until the elections of 1974 that this relatively static pattern of voting behavior began to change (Denver, 1994, p. 149). The catalyst of change was a growth in support for the Liberal and Scottish Nationalist parties. In their search to explain the development of what they termed "volatility," political analysts began to consider alternatives to a hitherto dominant theory of electoral behavior that had emphasized the stability rather than the weakness of partisan allegiances (Crewe & Denver, 1985).

During the 1960s, the party identification model of voting helped to popularize the notion of a partisan but stable British electorate (Butler & Stokes, 1969). Electoral alignments were primarily explained by structural factors. Demographic variables such as age, race, and (especially) class were judged to be the best predictors of voter intention. However, the advent of major social change, coupled with a serious decline in support for the two major parties during the 1970s, helped to initiate a debate aimed at understanding the changing pattern of electoral behavior. Two main alternatives to party identification, the radical and choice models, were offered as explanations for increasing volatility in the "electoral market" (see Harrop, 1986, for details). The sum of a sometimes intensive and rather complex debate helped to shift the analytical focus of psephology away from the study of factors explaining the steadfastness of voter allegiances and toward consideration of those that helped to account for the apparent increase in partisan instability.

The choice model of voting, originally popularized by Downs (1957), supported the idea of the voter as sovereign consumer in the electoral marketplace (see also Himmelweit, Humphreys, & Jaeger, 1985). Downs's work also gave consideration to the nature of political competition and helped to popularize a now familiar adage of modern politics: For a party to maximize voter support, the party must align itself closer to its principal opponents' position. By no means the only interpretation to be drawn from political market analysis, the "center-ground" thesis nevertheless is the most common one and continues to condition a great deal of contemporary electoral discourse.[1] Consequently, when faced with defeat, Labour and Conservative leaders often are advised to court the center, squeeze the Liberal vote, or appeal to middle England/class/income voters. Even critics of the market model of voter and party behavior concede that the analogy has had a significant impact on the popular understanding of electoral politics (Wellhofer, 1990).

Culture and Economics: The Entrepreneurial Decade

The second factor responsible for popularizing the importance of political marketing in Britain relates to changes in the social and economic climate that occurred during the 1980s. The election of the Conservative government in 1979 heralded the beginning of a steep decline in U.K. manufacturing output. By contrast, the decade also witnessed a major expansion in the tertiary sector, particularly in the marketing services industry. By the end of the 1980s, U.K. advertising as a share of gross national product was second only to that of the United States (Davidson, 1992, p. 63). The link between politics and advertising was symbolically sealed in the durable relationship that existed between the ruling Conservatives and their advisers, Saatchi and Saatchi. This highly publicized partnership helped to promote the cause of professional political communications as well as the fortunes of client and agency. The party went on to win a further three elections, whereas the firm briefly became owners of the world's largest group of advertising companies (Kleinman, 1987). As Davidson (1992) points out, "By the end of the eighties, it was just impossible to talk about politics without talking about communication, about consuming policies" (p. 78).

The political right in the guise of premier Margaret Thatcher and her Conservative supporters lauded marketing as an important aspect of modern economic activity. Their opponents were a good deal more skeptical. Historically, the left had been unsympathetic to a process seen to be irredeemably imbued with the very capitalist ethos that encourages "consumer fetishism" (Williams, 1981). During the 1980s, some socialists began to reconsider the role of marketing, treating it as a serious phenomenon that needed to be analyzed within the context of a debate over the politics of consumption. Thus, a few critics on the left began to argue that the hitherto dominant producer-centered understanding of economic relations obscured the mobilizing potential presented by an increasingly powerful consumer movement. Notably, in one contribution to the *New Times* manifesto, Mort (1990) argued that because Labour had constantly been associated with the austerity of the 1940s rather than with affluence that coincided with Conservative rule between 1951 and 1964, the party could hope to succeed only if it was able to radically remodel itself and overhaul its popular image in the process.

In the aftermath of the 1992 election defeat, an influential section of the Labour Party sought to redevelop the theme of consumption politics as a popular strategy (Blair, 1992). In so doing, these thinkers advocated the need to acknowledge the importance of social changes and the necessity of Labour to align itself with the customer against vested interests such as the large banking and finance corporations. Such moves reflected the desire of the so-called party "modernizers" to reorientate Labour away from its most obvious association with producer groups in the shape of its allies in the trade union movement (Webb, 1995).

Marketing:
The Development of Societal Concerns

The emergence of political marketing analysis has its roots in a debate initiated by a pair of leading management theorists more than 25 years ago. With the publication of their groundbreaking analysis of nonprofit organizations, Kotler and Levy (1969) found themselves in the vanguard of a group of marketing scholars committed to challenging their subject's traditionally narrow preoccupation with commercial activity (see also Lazer, 1969; Lazer & Kelley, 1973). In their seminal piece, Kotler and Levy (1969) argue that "the crux of marketing lies in a general idea of exchange rather than the narrower idea of market transactions."

Taking up this revised definition, Kotler and Zaltman (1971) identified a new and distinct field of "social marketing" in the belief that the work of nonprofit organizations could benefit from the adoption of an approach pioneered in business. Kotler and his colleagues were by no means the first to advocate the application of marketing in public sector work; as early as 1919, an American conference had been held on the theme of marketing in government (Graham, 1994). Nevertheless, they succeeded in that they provoked a major discussion of their thesis in a way that previous pioneering work on the same theme had not (Wiebe, 1951).

Despite initial criticisms of Kotler and Levy's (1969) "broadening" thesis (Carman, 1973; Luck, 1969), analysts began to accept the need to study and develop understanding of the noncommercial sector (Hunt, 1976; Nickels, 1974; O'Leary & Iredale, 1976). Consequently, analysis of social marketing has since entered into the subject mainstream (Elliott, Unsworth, Gavel, Saunders, & Mira, 1994; Kotler & Roberto, 1989). Recent research has focused on a diverse group of public bodies such as charitable, religious, and governmental agencies (Crompton & Lamb, 1986; Fine, 1992; Graham, 1994; Kotler & Andreasen, 1991; Tam, 1994). Parallel to these concerns, interest also has begun to turn to the question of party politics and, more specifically, how candidates campaign to win elections.

Under conditions of liberal democracy, election campaigning forms the means by which competing party elites persuade the public of their ability and fitness to govern. As such, it constitutes an important civic function revolving around voting, an activity that for many in the population forms their only engagement with politics. In Britain, mass electioneering developed during the course of the 19th century following three major extensions of the franchise in 1832, 1867, and 1884. Modern political campaigning dates from 1918 and the advent of near universal suffrage. By 1928, every adult over 21 years of age was assured of at least one vote, regardless of gender or property qualifications. Since then, the nature and media of political communication have changed. Terms such as "image makers" and "spin doctors" are now part of the popular electoral lexicon, and the phrase "political marketing" has become a recognized part of academic discourse. A cursory glance at material on the subject in Britain and abroad indicates a steady growth in publications since 1980 and a more marked increase during the 1990s. This is perhaps understandable given the major changes in media, marketing, and technology that have taken place during this time.

Studies in American Campaigning

The literature on election campaigns is dominated by material originating from the United States. Whereas American scholars monopolize debate in several areas of political science, their preeminence in the field of political communication is augmented by a unique set of local factors. In short, a thriving industry built around elections in the United States services candidates for everything from municipal dog catcher to national president. Such an environment has encouraged the professionalization of campaigning, perhaps unsurprising given the frequency with which contests for congressional seats alone take place.[2] Consequently, the scale and number of these elections have provided scholars with ample opportunity to study this particular type of mass political behavior.

One of the earliest and most important studies of professional election campaigning appeared in the mid-1950s. Kelley's (1956) *Professional Public Relations and Political Power* examines developments in political communications including the launch and evolution of the first full-service consultancy, Campaigns Inc., during the 1930s. Significantly, Kelley's study probably was the first to make use of the phrase "political marketing." In his other major contribution to the literature 4 years later, Kelley (1960) took a less case-specific but nonetheless interesting approach to the analysis of campaigning. The importance of the subject matter in this work was underlined by the presidential race that took place late in the year when the second book was published. The narrowness of the 1960 result, coupled with the respective professionalism of the campaign teams (particularly the one working for successful candidate John F. Kennedy), was adjudged by some commentators to have been crucial to the electoral outcome. Analysis of the Kennedy strategy formed the basis of White's (1962) respected and acclaimed study, *The Making of the President 1960.*

Toward the end of the 1960s, analysis of electioneering began to shift from generalities to focusing more on the impact that media and new technologies were having on strategies. By far the most famous of these studies was *The Selling of the President,* McGinniss's (1969) account of the publicity-conscious machine supporting Richard Nixon's successful 1968 bid for the White House. Perry's (1968) pioneering investigation into the changing nature of campaign technology, appropriately titled *The New Politics,* also made an impression not least in Britain, where one senior Labour Party official alerted colleagues to the potential lessons to be learned from the book by warning that candidates "will be promoted and marketed like the latest model automobile" (Pitt, 1968). Other important material followed, including *The Election Game* (Napolitan, 1972) and *Boys on the Bus,* Crouse's (1972) classic study of pack journalism on the presidential campaign trail. Academic material on the burgeoning campaigns industry also appeared, most notably in the form of Dan Nimmo's (1970) *The Political Persuaders* and Rosenbloom's (1973) critical study, *The Election Men.*

During the mid-1970s, a new school of campaign analysis began to come to the fore. Using quantitative methods pioneered by Lazarsfeld, Berelson, and Gaudet (1944) in the earliest academic studies of voting behavior, researchers attempted to measure and assess the impact and effect of political advertising on the electorate. A steady stream of publications attempted to evaluate changes in public reaction to a variety of campaign strategies and initiatives (Atkin & Heald, 1976; Kaid, 1976; Palda, 1973; Patterson & McClure, 1976). In sum, these studies suggested that whereas advertising played a minor role in the most important elections, it could have a significant impact on the outcome of less high-profile contests. In respect of the latter type of campaign, attention focused on the apparent ability of appeals to influence voters who watched an above average amount of television, possessed lower levels of educational attainment, and had little prior political commitment (Rothschild, 1978).

Aside from the development of quantitative-based studies, marketing scholars also began to take an interest in electioneering. Foremost among these were Kotler and Shama (Kotler, 1975; Shama, 1974, 1976). Comprehensive textbooks on how to devise strategy and best manage electoral organizations also appeared (Agranoff, 1976; Steinberg, 1976). These, together with the highly sophisticated strategies deployed on behalf of successful presidential candidates Jimmy Carter and Ronald Reagan, helped to reinvigorate interest in campaign analysis. Whereas some chose to concentrate on the important electoral function of television coverage (Patterson, 1980), other researchers decided to focus on what were perceived to be the increasingly central roles played by polling research and paid advertising within the political communications process (Diamond & Bates, 1984; Jamieson, 1996; Perry, 1984). More recently, another study has attempted to chart and analyze the impact of direct marketing in elections (Godwin, 1988).

The growing interest and recognition that professionalism and the mass media have assumed a dominant influence in terms of modern campaigning has gathered a negative reaction from some. In his classic study into *The Rise of Political Consultants,* Sabato (1981) challenges the notion that the growth of the elections industry is necessarily beneficial to American democracy. Similar sentiments underpin more recent work on the subject (Gold, 1987; Jamieson, 1992; Margolis & Mauser, 1989). In contrast to the approach of these studies, other accounts have sought to assess the effect of electoral professionals on more traditional forms of party organization and strategy (Luntz, 1988; Peele, 1982).[3]

The obvious overlap between politics and marketing apparent in much of the growing literature on American campaigning written during the 1980s has revived management specialists' interest in the subject. In his pioneering work, Mauser (1983) shows how it is possible to use new product development, a tool popular in conventional business, to devise successful electoral strategies. Other scholars, including Newman and O'Shaughnessy, have developed the literature on political marketing in the United States, offering general overviews of the subject (Newman & Sheth, 1985, 1987; Niffenegger, 1989; O'Shaughnessy, 1987; Schoenwald, 1987) as well as more detailed case-based material on the most recent presidential races (Newman, 1994; O'Shaughnessy, 1990).

Campaigning in an International Context

Aside from the growth in specialist literature on electioneering in the United States, several scholars in other countries have begun research into developments in and around their regions. Unlike the American research, which is increasingly subdivided and focused on specific cases or campaign activities such as polling or advertising, the international literature tends to group the study of techniques together under the generic term "political marketing." The fact that several independent scholars from different democracies have recognized the growth of this phenomenon over the past two decades tends to reinforce the belief that there is a major change taking place in the way modern elections are being conducted.

A large amount of the non-American material on political marketing has been produced by researchers in Europe. Several French writers have been to the fore in this development. These include Lindon (1976), who completed his study, *Marketing Politique et Social,* in the mid-1970s. In 1980, a group of mainly French scholars including Charlot, David, and Piotet convened at Liege University to consider the growing importance of the phenomenon in Western Europe (Piotet, 1980). Since then, other Gallic academics have been actively researching and writing about the subject (Bobin, 1988; Boy et al., 1985; Le Seac'h, 1981; Maarek, 1995), a trend reinforced by the decision of the *Revue de Marketing Francaise* to devote a special edition to politics (Marti, 1988). Significantly, the 1988 national elections in France and the United States formed the backdrop to a comparative study of presidential campaigning in the two countries (Kaid & Gerstle, 1992).

Wangen (1983) has pioneered the study of political marketing in Germany. More recently, his work has been joined by that of Wortmann (Farrell & Wortmann, 1987; Wortmann, 1989). Mazzoleni (1991) has investigated the growth of the phenomenon in Italy, whereas a pair of experts have charted developments in Spain (Roces & Rives, 1982). Despite being one of the smallest member states in the European Union, Ireland has been well served with analysis by Farrell, Butler, and Collins (Butler & Collins, 1993; Farrell, 1986; Farrell & Wortmann, 1987).

Other research completed on political marketing includes material from countries as far afield as Canada (Leiss, Kline, & Jhally, 1990), Australia (Tiffen, 1989), New Zealand (Denemark, 1991), and Colombia (Salazar Vargas, 1994).

In addition, there are several comparative analyses of campaigning. These include *Electioneering,* a study of practices in various countries edited by Butler and Ranney (1992). Developments in selected democracies also are featured in another comprehensive collection edited by Bowler and Farrell (1992). Two books edited by Kaid survey trends in political advertising throughout the world (Kaid & Holtz-Bacha, 1995; Kaid, Nimmo, & Sanders, 1986). This trend toward comparative analysis looks set to continue as the democratization process continues within Eastern and Central Europe, Latin America, and the Far East.[4]

Political Marketing in Britain

The impact and enduring importance of political marketing in Britain has been documented most comprehensively in the wealth of material that has appeared in the run-up to and after the 1992 general election.[5] These pieces include Harrop's (1990) critical review of the subject matter in *Parliamentary Affairs.* Whereas O'Shaughnessy (1990) uses a chapter to contrast British and America electioneering, Bruce (1992) devotes the bulk of his book to studying campaigning in the two countries. A former advertising executive and director of communications for the Conservative Party, Bruce draws on his professional experience to observe developments in a book punctuated by sometimes interesting, if highly opinionated, commentaries. Rees (1992), a television producer, covers similar ground to Bruce in parts of *Selling Politics,* a book based on the BBC "Timewatch" series of the same name.

The 1990s have witnessed the publication of several important academic commentaries on the development of political marketing in Britain. In *Packaging Politics,* Franklin (1994) offers a comprehensive and critical review of the role played by modern media and marketing techniques within the political process. Wide in scope, the book outlines the changing nature of broadcasting and press reporting, central and local government public relations and news management strategies, and the national and regional parties' campaign apparatus. In *Election Campaigning,* Kavanagh (1995) takes a different perspective, concentrating on the professionalization of electioneering in the postwar period. The bulk of his research considers the strategic evolution of the parties at the national level and the political importance of advertising, polling research, and mass media since the 1950s.

Based on her thesis (Scammell, 1991), Scammell's (1995) *Designer Politics* offers an in-depth insight into the way in which marketing reshaped politics during the 1980s. The book is particularly useful because it analyzes changes in both Conservative Party and governmental communication strategies. Separate sections consider the historical perspective and the Thatcher leadership. Other work on the evolution of Conservative campaigning has been completed by Cockett (1994). On the Labour Party, Wring (1996, 1997a) offers a historical overview comparing and contrasting the organization's approach to political communication. Webb (1991), Shaw (1994), and Sackman (1996) concentrate on the way in which marketing was used to reshape the party during the critical latter part of Neil Kinnock's leadership, which eventually gave rise to Tony Blair and his "New" Labour Party of the late 1990s. Significant assessments of contemporary political communication and marketing in Britain also can be found in Jones (1995), McNair (1995), Negrine (1996), O'Shaughnessy and Wring (1994), Rosenbaum (1997), and Sackman (1992).

Beyond the discipline of political science, a wider academic community has begun to take an interest in electoral behavior. For their part, key management journals such as the *European Journal of Marketing* (Butler & Collins, 1994; Lock & Harris, 1996; Reid, 1988) and *Journal of Marketing Management* (Smith & Saunders, 1990; Wring, 1997b) have featured major contributions to the literature on political marketing in the United Kingdom. Significantly, the first of these titles opted to publish a special issue in 1996, and a panel on the topic was featured as a major strand at the 1997 U.K. Academy of Marketing Conference, the leading national umbrella organization for the discipline.[6]

Of additional and symbolic importance is the increasing interest being paid by the marketing trade press to party political affairs. Given their specialization, some of this coverage in media such as *PR Week, Marketing Week, Campaign,* and *Marketing* has been less willing to reflect the consensus among political correspondents and party professionals when it comes to reporting strategic developments. During the 1992 election, this source of coverage offered a welcome rejoinder to some mainstream television and newspaper commentaries that tended to overgeneralize and promote the view that the main participants were either wholly competent or ineffective.

Conclusions

The late 20th-century phenomenon of political marketing arises from three converging factors. First, within the political sphere, there is growing recognition that there has been a marked rise in so-called voter volatility over the past three decades. In tandem with this, analysts have become increasingly interested in applying rational choice theory to the study of electoral behavior. Underpinning such an approach is the view that the competition for votes mirrors that of a business pursuing a share of a consumer market. This, in turn, derives support from and revitalizes the importance of the work of earlier democratic theorists, most notably Downs and Schumpeter.

Second, industrial change during the 1980s afforded the tertiary service sector an even greater role within the economies of major Western countries such as the United Kingdom. This, in turn, has consolidated and advanced the cultural importance and power of marketing, one of the sector's most important component parts. As a consequence, advertising and market research agencies are increasingly exerting considerable influence over society and, more specifically, over the political process. Marketing as an approach and set of techniques has become increasingly indispensable to those fighting modern election campaigns.

Third, there has been a significant growth in public sector marketing, reflected by an increasing academic appreciation of the importance of management in the non-profit-making sector. Politics is a key dimension of this trend. As has been shown in this chapter, a number of international scholars working independently of one another have begun to identify and analyze the concept and practice of political marketing. This trend looks set to continue well into the 21st century.

Notes

1. For example, midway through the 1992 election (March 25), BBC *Newsnight* featured analysis by Peter Kellner and John Kay clearly derived from Downs's work on the parallels between politics and business. Kellner argued that, in the same way as rival businesses sometimes are located in close geographical proximity to one another to compete for customers, politicians also might seek to position themselves ideologically closer to maximize their votes, hence the common refrain of political strategists about the need for parties to appeal to the electoral centerground or, in the British case, so-called "middle England."

2. A third of U.S. Senate seats and all House of Representatives seats are contested every 2 years, with the presidency contested every 4 years. The term *professional,* increasingly common in the literature, is used here to mean the extent to which specialist advisers and state-of-the-art technologies are integral to the organization of campaigning.

3. The definitive study into the effect of professionalism on party organization has been conducted by Panebianco (1988). Related material also has appeared in the journal *Political Communication* and in two collections of essays (Nimmo & Sanders, 1981; Swanson & Nimmo, 1990). It should be added that the launch of titles such as this, together with the burgeoning series of books on the subject published by Praeger (e.g., Denton, 1991), helps to underline the vibrant state of research in the field.

4. The interest of the mainly U.S.-based body of campaign consultants in foreign elections can be detected in the activities of organizations such as the American Association of Political Consultants, the International Association of Political Consultants, and the party-linked National Democratic and National Republican Institutes. Recently, non-American strategists such as Sir Tim Bell also have been active advising presidential candidates in countries such as Chile and South Africa.

5. Prior to the 1980s, commentary on the professionalization of election campaigning can be found in Rose's (1967) classic work, *Influencing Voters,* and the regular "Nuffield" studies of which McCallum and Readman (1947) was the first in the series. The 1959, 1964, 1992, and 1997 studies are especially good for analyzing the impact of the media and marketing on political communication (Butler & Kavanagh, 1992, 1997; Butler & King, 1965; Butler & Rose, 1960). See also the Cambridge University Press series on political communications that includes Crewe and Harrop (1989).

6. Similar panels appeared at the Political Studies Association meetings of 1995 and 1996, and a group of academics also have convened conferences in Cambridge, United Kingdom, in both of these years (Henneberg & O'Shaughnessy, 1996).

References

Agranoff, R. (1976). *The management of election campaigns.* New York: Holbrook.
Almond, G. (1990). *A discipline divided.* Newbury Park, CA: Sage.
Atkin, C., & Heald, G. (1976). Effects of political advertising. *Public Opinion Quarterly, 40,* 216-228.
Blair, T. (1992, May). Pride without prejudice. *Fabian Review,* p. 3.
Bobin, J. P. (1988). *Le marketing politique: Vendre l'homme et l'idee.* Editions Milan Media.
Bowler, S., & Farrell, D. (Eds.). (1992). *Electoral strategy and political marketing.* Hampshire, UK: Macmillan.
Boy, D., et al. (1985). Le marketing political. *Pouvoirs, 33,* 121-130.

Bruce, B. (1992). *Images of power: How image makers shape our leaders.* London: Kogan Page.

Butler, D., & Kavanagh, D. (1992). *The British general election of 1992.* Hampshire, UK: Macmillan.

Butler, D., & Kavanagh, D. (1997). *The British general election of 1997.* Hampshire, UK: Macmillan.

Butler, D., & King, A. (1965). *The British general election of 1964.* London: Macmillan.

Butler, D., & Ranney, A. (Eds.). (1992). *Electioneering: A comparative study of continuity and change.* Oxford, UK: Clarendon.

Butler, D., & Rose, R. (1960). *The British general election of 1959.* London: Macmillan.

Butler, D., & Stokes, D. (1969). *Electoral change in Britain.* London: Macmillan.

Butler, P., & Collins, N. (1993). Campaigns, candidates and marketing in Ireland. *Politics, 13,* 3-8.

Butler, P., & Collins, N. (1994). Political marketing: Structure and process. *European Journal of Marketing, 28,* 19-34.

Carman, J. (1973). On the universality of marketing. *Journal of Contemporary Business, 2,* 4.

Cockett, R. (1994). The party, publicity and the media. In A. Seldon & S. Ball (Eds.), *Conservative century* (pp. 547-577). Oxford, UK: Oxford University Press.

Crewe, I., & Denver, D. (Eds.). (1985). *Electoral change in Western democracies.* London: Croom Helm.

Crewe, I., & Harrop, M. (Eds.). (1989). *Political communications: The British general election campaign of 1987.* Cambridge, UK: Cambridge University Press.

Crompton, J., & Lamb, C. (1986). *Marketing government and social services.* New York: John Wiley.

Crouse, T. (1972). *Boys on the bus.* New York: Ballantine.

Davidson, M. P. (1992). *The consumerist manifesto.* London: Routledge.

Denemark, D. (1991). Electoral instability and the modern campaign: New Zealand Labour in 1987. *Australian Journal of Political Science, 26,* 260-276.

Denton, R. (Ed.). (1991). *Ethical dimensions of political communication.* New York: Praeger.

Denver, D. (1994). *Elections and voting behaviour in Britain* (2nd ed.). Hemel Hempstead, UK: Harvester Wheatsheaf.

Diamond, E., & Bates, S. (1984). *The spot: The use of political advertising on television.* Cambridge, MA: MIT Press.

Downs, A. (1957). *An economic theory of democracy.* New York: Harper & Row.

Elliott, G., Unsworth, D., Gavel, K., Saunders, J., & Mira, M. (1994). Social marketing: Conceptual and pragmatic observation from a current Australian campaign. *Journal of Marketing Management, 10,* 581-591.

Farrell, D. (1986). The strategy to market fine gael in 1981. *Irish Political Studies, 1,* 1-14.

Farrell, D., & Wortmann, M. (1987). Party strategies in the electoral market: Political marketing in West Germany, Britain, and Ireland. *European Journal of Political Research, 15,* 297-318.

Fine, S. (Ed.). (1992). *Marketing the public sector: Promoting the causes of public and non-profit agencies.* New Brunswick, NJ: Transaction Publishers.

Franklin, B. (1994). *Packaging politics: Political communications in Britain's media democracy.* London: Edward Arnold.

Godwin, R. (1988). *One billion dollars of influence: The direct marketing of politics.* Chatham, NJ: Chatham House.

Gold, P. (1987). *Advertising, politics, and American culture.* New York: Praegar.

Graham, P. (1994). Marketing in the public sector: Inappropriate or merely difficult? *Journal of Marketing Management, 10,* 361-375.

Harrop, M. (1986). Voting and the electorate. In H. Drucker, P. Dunleavy, A. Gamble, & G. Peele (Eds.), *Developments in British politics* (pp. 35-59). London: Macmillan.

Harrop, M. (1990). Political marketing. *Parliamentary Affairs, 43,* 277-291.

Henneberg, S., & O'Shaughnessy, N. (1996). *Proceedings of the Conference on Political Marketing.* Cambridge, UK: Judge Institute of Management Studies.

Himmelweit, H., Humphreys, P., & Jaeger, M. (1985). *How voters decide* (2nd ed.). Milton Keynes, UK: Open University Press.

Hunt, S. D. (1976). The nature and scope of marketing. *Journal of Marketing, 40,* 17-28.

Jamieson, K. H. (1992). *Dirty politics: Deception, distraction, and democracy.* New York: Oxford University Press.

Jamieson, K. H. (1996). *Packaging the presidency.* Oxford, UK: Oxford University Press.

Jones, N. (1995). *Soundbites and spin doctors.* London: Cassell.

Kaid, L. L. (1976). Measures of political advertising. *Journal of Advertising Research, 16*(5), 49-53.

Kaid, L. L., & Gerstle, J. (1992). *Mediated politics in two cultures.* New York: Praeger.

Kaid, L. L., & Holtz-Bacha, C. (Eds.). (1995). *Political advertising in Western democracies*. London: Sage.

Kaid, L. L., Nimmo, D., & Sanders, K. R. (Eds.). (1986). *New perspectives on political advertising*. Carbondale: Southern Illinois University Press.

Kavanagh, D. (1995). *Election campaigning: The new marketing of politics*. Oxford, UK: Blackwell.

Kelley, S. (1956). *Professional public relations and political power*. Baltimore, MD: Johns Hopkins University Press.

Kelley, S. (1960). *Political campaigning*. Washington, DC: Brookings Institution.

Kleinman, P. (1987, September). The research market: Did psychographics win the general election? *Admap*, pp. 16-18.

Kotler, P. (1975). Overview of political candidate marketing. *Advances in Consumer Research, 2*, 761-769.

Kotler, P., & Andreasen, A. (1991). *Strategic marketing for non-profit organisations* (4th ed.). Englewood Cliffs, NJ: Prentice Hall.

Kotler, P., & Levy, S. J. (1969). Broadening the concept of marketing. *Journal of Marketing, 33*(1), 10-15.

Kotler, P., & Roberto, E. (1989). *Social marketing: Strategies for changing public behaviour*. New York: Free Press.

Kotler, P., & Zaltman, G. (1971). Social marketing: An approach to planned social change. *Journal of Marketing, 35*, 3-12.

Lazarsfeld, P., Berelson, B., & Gaudet, H. (1944). *The people's choice*. New York: Columbia University Press.

Lazer, W. (1969). Marketing's changing social responsibilities. *Journal of Marketing, 33*(1), 3-9.

Lazer, W., & Kelley, E. (1973). *Social marketing: Perspectives and viewpoints*. Burr Ridge, IL: Irwin.

Le Seac'h, M. (1981). *L'etat marketing*. Paris: Editions Alain Moreau.

Leiss, W., Kline, S., & Jhally, S., with Shwetz, A., and Yonin, Y. (1990). Fantasia for the citizen: The nature and uses of political marketing. In W. Leiss, S. Kline, & S. Jhally (Eds.), *Social communication in advertising* (pp. 389-404). Scarborough, Ontario: Nelson Canada.

Lindon, D. (1976). *Marketing politique et social*. Paris: Dalloz.

Lock, A., & Harris, P. (1996). Political marketing: Vive la difference! and other contributions to special edition on political marketing. *European Journal of Marketing, 30*(10/11), 21-31.

Luck, D. (1969). Broadening the concept of marketing: Too far. *Journal of Marketing, 33*, 53-55.

Luntz, F. (1988). *Candidates, consultants, and campaigns: The style and substance of American electioneering*. Oxford, UK: Blackwell.

Maarek, P. (1995). *Political marketing and communication*. London: John Libbey.

Margolis, M., & Mauser, G. (1989). *Manipulating public opinion*. Pacific Grove, CA: Brooks/Cole.

Marti, C. (1988). Clausewitz et Campagnie. *Revue Francaise de Marketing, 16*(1), 7-11.

Mauser, G. (1983). *Political marketing: An approach to campaign strategy*. New York: Praeger.

Mazzoleni, G. (1991). Emergence of the candidate and political marketing: Television and election campaigns in Italy in the 1980s. *Political Communication and Persuasion, 8*, 201-212.

McCallum, R. B., & Readman, A. (1947). *The British general election of 1945*. Oxford, UK: Oxford University Press.

McGinniss, J. (1969). *The selling of the president*. New York: Trident.

McNair, B. (1995). *Introduction to political communication*. London: Routledge.

Mort, F. (1990) The politics of consumption. In S. Hall & M. Jacques (Eds.), *New times* (pp. 160-172). London: Lawrence & Wishart.

Napolitan, J. (1972). *The election game and how to win it*. New York: Doubleday.

Negrine, R. (1996). *The communication of politics*. London: Sage.

Newman, B. (1994). *The marketing of the president: Political marketing as campaign strategy*. London: Sage.

Newman, B., & Sheth, J. (Eds.). (1985). *Political marketing: Readings and annotated bibliography*. Chicago: American Marketing Association.

Newman, B., & Sheth, J. (1987). A review of political marketing. *Research in Marketing, 9*, 237-266.

Nickels, W. G. (1974). Conceptual conflicts in marketing. *Journal of Economics and Business, 27*, 140-143.

Niffenegger, P. (1989). Strategies for success from the political marketers. *Journal of Consumer Research, 6*(1), 45-51.

Nimmo, D. (1970). *The political persuaders*. Englewood Cliffs, NJ: Prentice Hall.

Nimmo, D., & Sanders, K. (Eds.). (1981). *Handbook of political communication*. Beverly Hills, CA: Sage.

O'Leary, R., & Iredale, I. (1976). The marketing concept: Quo vadis? *European Journal of Marketing, 10*(3), 146-157.

O'Shaughnessy, N. (1987). America's political market. *European Journal of Marketing, 21*(4), 60-67.

O'Shaughnessy, N. (1990). *The phenomenom of political marketing*. Hampshire, UK: Macmillan.

O'Shaughnessy, N., & Wring, D. (1994). Political marketing in Britain. In H. Tam (Ed.), *Marketing, competition, and the public sector* (pp. 246-270). Harlow, UK: Longman.

Palda, K. (1973). Does advertising influence votes? An analysis of the 1966 and 1970 Quebec elections. *Canadian Journal of Political Science, 6,* 636-655.

Panebianco, A. (1988). *Political parties: Organisation and power.* Cambridge, UK: Cambridge University Press.

Patterson, T. (1980). *The mass media election*. New York: Praeger.

Patterson, T., & McClure, R. (1976). *The myth of television power in national politics*. New York: Putnam.

Peele, G. (1982). Campaign consultants. *Electoral Studies, 1,* 355-362.

Perry, J. (1968). *The new politics: The expanding technology of political manipulation*. London: Weidenfeld & Nicolson.

Perry, R. (1984). *The programming of the president*. London: Aurum.

Piotet, J. P. (Ed.). (1980). *Le marketing politique*. Etudes et recherches No. 18, Department of Science Politique, Universite de Liege.

Pitt, T. (1968, December). More on American elections. *Labour Organiser,* No. 553.

Rees, L. (1992). *Selling politics*. London: BBC Books.

Reid, D. (1988). Marketing the political product. *European Journal of Marketing, 22*(9), 34-47.

Roces, C., & Rivas, J. (1982). *Marketing electoral.* Madrid, Spain: Iberico Europea de Ediciones.

Rose, R. (1967). *Influencing voters: A study of campaign rationality*. London: Faber & Faber.

Rosenbaum, M. (1997). *From soapbox to soundbite: Party political campaigning in Britain since 1945*. Hampshire, UK: Macmillan.

Rosenbloom, D. L. (1973). *The election men: Professional campaign managers and American democracy*. New York: Quadrangle.

Rothschild, M. (1978). Political advertising: A neglected policy issue in marketing. *Journal of Marketing Research, 15,* 57-71.

Sabato, L. (1981). *The rise of political consultants: New ways of winning elections*. New York: Basic Books.

Sackman, A. (1992). Bringing the party to market: A political marketing approach to election campaigning in Britain. In *Manchester papers in politics* (No. 12, Papers in Politics series). Manchester, UK: University of Manchester, Department of Government.

Sackman, A. (1996). The learning curve towards New Labour: Neil Kinnock's corporate party 1983-92. *European Journal of Marketing, 30*(10/11), 147-159.

Salazar Vargas, C. (1994). *Marketing politico*. Bogota, Colombia: Japro Editores.

Scammell, M. (1991). *The impact of marketing and public relations on modern British politics: The Conservative Party and government under Mrs. Thatcher.* Unpublished Ph.D. dissertation, London University.

Scammell, M. (1995). *Designer politics: How elections are won*. Hampshire, UK: Macmillan.

Schoenwald, M. (1987). Marketing a political candidate. *Journal of Consumer Research, 4*(2), 57-63.

Schumpeter, J. (1943). *Capitalism, socialism, and democracy*. London: Urwin.

Shama, A. (1974). Political marketing: A study of voter decision-making process and candidate marketing strategy. *Annual Proceedings of the American Marketing Association, 4,* 381-385.

Shama, A. (1976). The marketing of political candidates. *Journal of the Academy of Marketing Sciences, 4,* 764-777.

Shaw, E. (1994). *The Labour Party since 1979: Crisis and transformation*. London: Routledge.

Smith, G., & Saunders, J. (1990). The application of marketing to British politics. *Journal of Marketing Management, 5,* 295-306.

Steinberg, A. (1976). *The political handbook*. Lexington, MA: Lexington Books.

Swanson, D., & Nimmo, D. (Eds.). (1990). *New directions in political communications: A resource book*. Newbury Park, CA: Sage.

Tam, H. (Ed.). (1994). *Marketing, competition, and the public sector.* Essex, UK: Longman.

Tiffen, R. (1989). *News and power.* North Sydney, Australia: Allen & Unwin.

Wangen, E. (1983). *Polit-marketing: Das marketing-management der politschein partein*. Opladen, Germany: Westdeutscher Verlag.

Webb, P. (1991). Election campaigning, organisational transformation, and the professionalisation of the Labour Party. *European Journal of Political Research, 21,* 267-288.

Webb, P. (1995). Reforming the Labour Party-trade union relations: An assessment. In D. Broughton, D. Farrell, D. Denver, & C. Rallings (Eds.), *British elections and parties yearbook 1994* (pp. 1-14). London: Frank Cass.

Wellhofer, E. S. (1990). Contradictions in market models of politics: The case of party strategies and voter linkages. *European Journal of Political Research, 18,* 9-28.

White, T. (1962). *The making of the president 1960*. London: Cape.

Wiebe, G. D. (1951). Merchandising commodities and citizenship on television. *Public Opinion Quarterly, 15,* 679-691.

Williams, R. (1981). Advertising the magic system. In R. Williams (Ed.), *Problems in materialism and culture*. London: Verso.

Wortmann, M. (1989). *Political marketing: A modern party strategy*. Unpublished Ph.D. dissertation, European Institute, Florence, Italy.

Wring, D. (1996). From mass propaganda to political marketing: The transformation of Labour Party election campaigning. In C. Rallings, D. Farrell, D. Denver, & C. Broughton (Eds.), *British elections and parties yearbook 1995* (pp. 105-124). London: Frank Cass.

Wring, D. (1997a). *Political marketing and the Labour Party: The relationship between campaign strategy and intra-organisational power*. Unpublished Ph.D. dissertation, Cambridge University, UK.

Wring, D. (1997b). Reconciling marketing with political science: Theories of political marketing. *Journal of Marketing Management, 13,* 651-664.

4

A Conceptual Framework for Political Marketing

PATRICK BUTLER
NEIL COLLINS

To make progress in political marketing, scholars must draw from the disciplines of political science and marketing. Attempts to merge two diverse research areas are replete with problems of context, understanding, and approach. Whereas political scientists tend to focus on institutional relationships, the legislative process, and public policy, the concern of marketing researchers is with campaign strategies and management. Although these difficulties must be acknowledged, they cannot be allowed to limit progress in the integrative study required in the field.

Developing theory from the two fields demands a greater specificity at the conceptual level than might be the case for a discussion within a widely shared literature. A future research agenda requires an awareness that the democratic process is valuable and fragile. Indeed, it is under threat in many parts of the world. Marketers rarely will apply themselves to a more serious topic than the way in which the political elites and their electorates communicate.

Public choice theorists and earlier political writers such as Downs (1957) have used ideas drawn from economics to examine political behavior. The use of the term "market" in this analogy is, therefore, not a real innovation. In keeping with insightful approaches taken by Denton (1988), Reid (1988), O'Shaughnessy (1990), and Niffenegger (1989), this chapter continues to use the analogy of parties as companies and voters as purchasers. Recently, Olson (1998) suggested that if the market is an analogy for elections, then the election campaign would be market day, whereas the Parliament would be the bourse. Unlike the earlier economics-derived ideas, however, the marketing discipline would seek to incorporate an emphasis on long-term interactive relationship rather than on simple exchange. Thus, marketing would have a focus on what political scientists would refer to as party allegiance, electoral volatility, civic duty, and the like.

A notable overconcentration on situation-specific tactics is clear in much of the literature. Thus, particular television performances, new logos, or advertising campaigns are analyzed in isolation. As Mauser (1983) points out, the result is a failure to examine marketing at the level of strategy. This is a crucial omission, for it limits the horizon of political marketing research and understanding. A greater appreciation of strategic considerations would help place into perspective those tactical and operational issues that some political scientists use to dismiss marketing as irrelevant and unethical.

Because marketers have developed a body of knowledge and technical expertise directly related to the analysis and persuasion of large groups of people, their discipline can contribute to an understanding of politics. Marketing scholars' interest in consumer motivation and behavior denotes the importance of the long-term view. Political scientists generally have overlooked this field, with consequent failure to fully use the insights of the marketing discipline.

Political scientists have defined marketing too narrowly; the marketing discipline has not engaged the political arena with enough conviction. Despite well-recognized recent progress by marketers in the field (e.g., Harris, 1996), there is no established paradigm or agreed focus of study. No other area of marketing research would attempt to build theory on the study of duopolies. Most political markets have more than two significant players, and few are regulated by a "first past the post" system. Although the United States dominates the world's media, its presidential form of government contrasts sharply with the parliamentary systems of most Western democracies. For these reasons, the model here is deliberately pitched at the broad generic level.

The Conceptual Framework for Political Marketing Characteristics

The basis of the framework is that political marketing exhibits both "structural" characteristics, such as the nature of the product, the organization, and the market, and "process" characteristics that define, develop, and deliver value. By drawing out these characteristics and examining them for marketing implications, the campaigner is better equipped to conceptualize the environment and develop appropriate strategies.

When characterizing other marketing "industries," writers have focused on the most heuristically useful features for addressing management problems. For example, the emphasis on the product will be familiar to students of services marketing; Shostack (1977) and others conventionally stress intangibility, perishability, heterogeneity, and inseparability to differentiate service products. In the not-for-profit field, Blois (1987) suggests that the characteristics of the organization are the most insightful. In public sector marketing, the nature of the citizen as consumer and other peculiarities of the market are brought to the fore (Walsh,

TABLE 4.1 The Structural and Process Characteristics of Political Marketing

Structural Characteristics	
The product:	Person/party/ideology
	Loyalty
	Mutability
The organization:	Resource base
	Amateurism and volunteers
	Negative perception of marketing
The market:	Regulations and restrictions
	Social and ideological affirmation
	The counterconsumer
Process Characteristics	
Value defining:	Establishment of core values
	Value aggregation
	Leaders and candidates
Value developing:	Specification of choice
	Communication standards and style
	Media attention and political polls
Value delivering:	Office-policy dichotomy
	Periodic market
	Tactical voting

1995). However, it can be argued that the weakness in these approaches is their singular emphasis on one factor or another. In the framework here, all of these factors are drawn together as the structural characteristics.

In regard to the most appropriate way of understanding marketing processes, delineating the actual political or electoral process of a democracy is not necessarily the most advantageous. Here, we are attempting to capture the peculiar process aspects of politics that would be of concern to marketing observers and practitioners in "going to market." So, bringing some model from the marketing arena to bear on politics is more apt to offer the type of insights sought by campaign managers. Many process models are available. Marketers conventionally perceive their domain in terms of the market research process, buyer behavior processes, planning processes, new product development processes, and the like. Furthermore, Murray and O'Driscoll (1996), for example, have sought to explain marketing in organizations in terms of the four *core* processes. In this case, a set of three broad marketing processes are used to analyze the political context: value-defining processes, value-developing processes, and value-delivering processes (Webster, 1997). The concept of value underpins the process dimension of the model. In going to market, the value proposition—the reason to buy—must be defined, developed, and delivered. Indeed, the process dimension here resonates with the systems theory approach often found in political science (e.g., Easton, 1981). The outcome is the development of a generic and more robust model of the features that characterize political marketing. These characteristics are outlined in Table 4.1.

It is important to note in the development of the framework that the characteristics discussed do not necessarily need to be perceived as *unique* to political marketing. Rather, they are included on the basis that they are *distinctive* enough to this to warrant particular attention by marketers. That is, the characteristics or features of political marketing outlined in the framework are judged to be worthy of special consideration because of the implications they have for marketing decisions in the field. Furthermore, although the discussion of any one factor may be useful, it is the overall integration of the structural and process characteristics that makes the model applicable in the field.

The Structural Characteristics of Political Marketing

The Political Product

The marketing traits of the political product are considered in three parts: the multicomponent (person/party/ideology) nature of the offer, the significant degree of loyalty involved, and the fact that it is mutable (i.e., it can be changed or transformed in the postelection setting).

Person/Party/Ideology

In the context of political elections, the product or offer is made up of several distinct components that usually (although not necessarily) are indivisible. These are the candidate, the political party, and the ideology. Nominating candidates calls into question issues such as their competence and resources, their past records and promises for the future, and their degrees of autonomy given the need to adhere to the party line. Confusion and even contradiction among the components of the offer is a pronounced trait in this context. For example, a voter might support the only candidate of his or her preferred party despite not having any confidence in the candidate personally. Similarly, a voter might support a candidate's stance on an important local issue despite not wanting his or her political party to win power on a national basis.

One marketing implication of this multicomponent offer is that the components cannot be offered separately. This situation results in particularly complex trade-offs of costs and benefits. As Bean (1993) shows in his comparative analysis of electoral influences in Australia and New Zealand, practitioners need to be alert to the contrasting features of particular electorates. New Zealand voters, for example, give greater salience to the image of the party leader than do their counterparts in Australia.

Loyalty

Political parties and candidates command an extraordinary level of loyalty. A dominant feature of Western European politics is continuity of support, despite growing evidence of electoral volatility (Heath, Jowell, & Curtice, 1986; Lane, 1993). Voter loyalty is especially marked in first-order elections such as national parliamentary elections (Reif, 1985). In second-order elections such as those to local councils or to the European Parliament, a greater degree of volatility exists. Similarly, by-election and mid-term votes often are protests, rejecting some aspect of one party's record rather than stating loyalty to another.

For campaign managers, a high degree of loyalty allows parties or candidates a certain flexibility in shifting policy. However, it also can mitigate against party switching, thereby constituting a barrier to entry to new parties and groups. Some electoral arrangements (e.g., the primaries in the United States) and preferential voting systems (e.g., the majority of European Union member states) permit loyalty to be expressed both to the party and to particular candidates. In these contexts, campaign managers can accommodate a more diverse set of loyalties.

Mutability

A notable property of political marketing is that the "purchase" is alterable even in the postpurchase setting. Unlike the situations in the United States, it is quite common in many democracies for parties that compete vigorously during elections to enter coalitions. Although in many cases pacts are formed prior to elections, some voters would not have supported a particular party or candidate had they known the postelection outcome. Also, the coalition can signify a failure to win outright by one party but can be a successful outcome for another party whose objective had been to win only enough seats to influence power.

A number of implications for marketing arise; the credibility of the parties involved in coalescing is questioned, as might be the entire political process. The political party involved might be subject to charges of bad faith. Political parties must address the problem of being honest with their supporters before the election and of appeasing them after the election and coalition. Essentially, difficulties may arise from asserting distinct policies during a campaign and then compromising on them after the election. The potential for devaluation of the political process and for cynicism arising out of this type of situation is largely dependent on cultural and traditional factors.

Marketing Strategies Relating to Product Characteristics

One strategic implication for marketing arising from product characteristics is that appeals to the electorate based on the rational presentation of single issues are unlikely to succeed in the long term. Market segmentation and positioning must be cognizant of the congruence among the candidate, the party, and the message. People are judged by their policies, and policies are judged by the people who put them forward. Strategists should attempt to "brand" policies and ideas and to build barriers to entry so as to "own" important issues.

The significance of very loyal supporters underlines the importance of winning first-time voters because people's first electoral choices tend to be enduring. Furthermore, loyalty enables strategies that follow a "brand extension" approach such as coattailing in multimember constituencies.

In regard to the problem of postpurchase mutability, the appeasement of dissatisfied (former) supporters usually is addressed by a strategy of pointing to the achievement of greater objectives through compromising on lesser issues. Marketing communications should stress continuity of principle and past record rather than dramatic changes in direction.

The Political Organization

Political organizations here are considered to be those intending to win positions in public office through the election process. Distinctive marketing characteristics of political parties include their resource bases, the importance of amateurs and volunteers, and the perception of professional political marketing within the organizations.

Resource Base

Political parties, like other organizations, have very varied resource bases. In the political market, such resources may derive from a charismatic leader, easy access to public attention, skillful staff, and historic capital. But as Ware (1996) puts it, "At the risk of some oversimplification, it can be argued that there are two main 'generalised' resources that can be used in an election campaign—money and labor. To a surprisingly large extent, they are not interchangeable" (p. 296).

The relative reliance of parties on these two major resources varies from market to market because of regulation. In the United States, for example, the relatively liberal laws on campaign expenditure and the lower reliance on mass party membership compared to that in Europe have made money the key resource. In other candidate-centered markets (e.g., Ireland), money also is important. It is probable that, given the increased significance of computers, polling, and direct mailing, money is likely to increase in significance relative to labor.

Skilled staff at headquarters and in the field are an important resource for most parties, but the largest numbers by far are the volunteer workers (discussed later). One problem with this resource, however, is finding something engaging to do between election campaigns. Many commentators have seen the decline in mass party membership as a problem for democracy. On the other hand, public participation in single-issue pressure groups is increasing. Internet-based communications may enable new forms of instant information flows between political institutions and citizens. As an organizational characteristic, however, the change in the balance of party resources probably matches the substitution of labor-intensive marketing by capital-intensive political marketing. The implications for management consequently emphasize the need to keep abreast of changing business information technologies.

Amateurism and Volunteers

Most political marketing activity takes place at local levels. Party activism is developed over several years of committee meetings, constituency panels, canvassing during elections, and the like. In such circumstances, technical advice often is seen as supportive rather than as crucial to the process of decision making. Thus, at the core of political marketing, there is the propensity to value the nonexpert. The high status afforded the committed amateur in many societies traditionally has been reflected in political organizations.

In common with many other not-for-profit organizations, political parties and groups at all levels rely heavily on a volunteer workforce and often on a volunteer management team. Electoral marketing cannot be completely divorced from the ongoing political marketing undertaken by incumbents and opposition alike. The necessity, especially in the United States, to attract money continuously to pay for past and future campaigns has led to the retention of permanent marketing professionals by individuals and parties. Given these circumstances, volunteers are more likely to be reduced to carrying out low-level tasks at the instruction of the professionals than participating in local policy-level discussion and debate. It is likely, however, that this reliance will decline in the coming years. Certainly, in political circles in the United States, "the phenomenon of political marketing has . . . led to the demise of the volunteer" (O'Shaughnessy, 1990, p. 102) and to the rise of the political consultant. Marginalized volunteers might be easier to control in terms of their activities, but their enthusiasm might be more readily dissipated.

An implication of the dependence on volunteers is that efforts need to be made to retain their enthusiasm through a feeling of proximity to power or of a significant contribution to a worthwhile cause. Organizations neglect the social dimensions of work at their peril. For political parties, this function often is fulfilled through conferences, conventions, and other quasi-social events. Parties in power have a decided advantage in dispensing state largesse to their volunteers.

Negative Perception of Marketing

Given the nature of political party organizations, the reasons for membership, the historical traditions, and the amateur and volunteer status of participants, it is not altogether surprising that marketing is perceived in a negative manner at grassroots levels in many countries. However, the United States, because of its commercial history and strong commitment to market forces, might be relatively more open to overt marketing practices in politics. Broadly, a common attitude is of marketing as unethical and trivializing. According to Smith and Saunders (1990), the fear exists that politicians might increasingly focus on narrow short-term issues just because they are popular, with the result that matters of greater substance become hostage to fortune. However, many anxieties expressed about political marketing are felt by Harrop (1990) to be based on exaggerated assessments of their impacts.

The perceived devaluation of the integrity of the political process mitigates against the employment of marketing terminology, even though the well-supported political campaign might be founded on sound marketing principles and techniques. Members of nonprofit organizations such as charities hold similarly adverse views of marketing. This arises from a belief that they know what is best for their customers. A similar conviction might dissuade political party members from a marketing orientation.

Given this difficulty, the implication is that marketing concepts and practices must be addressed with special sensitivity. Drafting in external experts whose allegiance to the cause is not clear or might have only been purchased could imply an inability on the part of amateur and volunteer group members to campaign effectively. The consequences of such a message might be severe.

Marketing Strategies Relating to Organization Characteristics

After the acquisition of resources, the management and balancing of finances and people is the central administrative task of the political party. Resource deployment, as in any organization, demands clarity of purpose in the first instance. The organization must be clear in its strategic campaign directions and the activities necessary for the achievement of its objectives because these are the determinants of the relative importance and roles of the core resources.

Volunteers are likely to have a certain sense of loyalty, not just to a party in abstract terms but also to a particular candidate or senior figure. It is sensible to target these influential people first to aid diffusion of the market orientation and to garner support for campaign strategies. Their assistance will be crucial in generating a "trickle down" effect. Negative perceptions of marketing can be overcome only by showing—indeed proving—that the marketing orientation is not necessarily unethical or unworkable. The ethical dimension certainly is the more difficult issue, so there is some merit in showing the benefits of marketing techniques in the shorter term. For example, cases of electoral successes clearly facilitated by professional marketing research and communications will help to persuade activists of the value of a marketing approach.

The Political Market

The electorate constitutes a political market. Of significance to marketing are the following characteristics of the electoral marketplace: civil and legal regulations and restrictions abound, the vote is a forceful social and ideological affirmation, and there exists a "counterconsumer" in the electorate.

Regulations and Restrictions

To understand the political market in any country, the analyst must focus on the regulatory environment. The political context involves a particularly high level of regulations and restrictions. For obvious reasons, the governance of a democracy requires that a minimum extent of equity be applied and be transparent. Such views are manifested in advertising and campaign spending restrictions. For example, in spending, most democratic states have restrictions on candidates' budgets to prevent the outright "purchasing" of votes. The emphasis is not so much on the content of the communication as on the absolute amount of the expenditure. In most commercial market contexts, these would be independent.

So, whereas in the United States a candidate can buy any time on television, in most markets the amount of time on television is restricted. Indeed, in some places, such time is confined to publicly provided space for political broadcasts. Such are the reasons for politicians opening garden fetes, announcing plowing championship winners in rural communities, and modeling Easter bonnets; they are staged events masquerading as news so as to be presented on news programs.

The implications of such restrictions for campaign strategists are that innovative ways of promoting candidates are critical. Where exposure cannot be bought outright, it must be cleverly manufactured. The danger, of course, is the trivialization of the candidate and the party.

Social and Ideological Affirmation

In democratic communities, the election is seen as a cornerstone of civil society. For the vast majority of people in the likes of South Africa, the significance of the franchise far outweighs immediate considerations of particular policies and personalities. The importance of elections is reflected in the ways in which they are conducted. The legal requirements are strict; state institutions are involved and are affected both by the process and the outcome. In marketing terms, this feature suggests that campaigns must be carried on with dignity and that political institutions must be treated with respect. The paradox remains, however, that campaigns that should be dignified are characterized in part by hoopla and triviality. Given this, only a thorough understanding of the electorate—its culture, values, and expectations—will enable the marketer to avoid counterproductive gaffes.

More than most other consumption activity, the vote is an act of social affirmation. The major social cleavages in society are expressed in elections. In Belgium, for example, the vote reflects the identity and language issue before matters of unemployment, the economy, and the like. Most political communications tend to affirm existing commitments. The prior assumptions of the electorate restrict the marketing maneuverability of the parties.

Marketing implications include the problems associated with addressing new issues. This is especially the case if such issues are seen to challenge the long established axioms of party support. In addition, the importance of social affirmation adds weight to the objective of "getting the vote out," that is, ensuring that the traditional supporters do actually get to the polling stations.

The Counterconsumer

A phenomenon not experienced in other marketing contexts is the counterconsumer. Within the electorate might be a group that is not merely interested in its preferred candidate winning an election but possibly more (or only) interested in preventing another candidate from taking office. This objective is pursued through negative communications during the campaign and through the process of tactical voting. The counterconsumer's vote is motivated by a desire to prevent a particular outcome rather than to support the candidate in whose favor the vote is cast. The temporary realignment of the Italian party system in the 1992 election, it is suggested, was due to the fact that 80% of those supporting the successful minor parties did so to prevent the election of Christian Democrats and Socialists. In Northern Ireland, in the assembly election following the Belfast Peace Agreement of 1998, nationalists and unionists voted tactically in a proportional representation system, against their initial instincts, to maximize their political interests.

The consequence of this characteristic is the need for marketers to understand election and voting procedures so that a defensive stance can be planned. The competition in this scenario is not just from voters choosing opposing parties or candidates but also from those with a vested interest in a candidate losing.

Marketing Strategies Relating to Market Characteristics

The value of strategic qualitative information becomes evident when dealing with the electorate. Regulations, values, and perceptions must be understood in such an ideologically charged situation to ensure compatibility between the offer and the "core values" of supporters. The development of a credible position for the electorate requires an extraordinary empathy, which necessitates top-quality feedback through both formal and informal channels on a continuous basis. The counterconsumer is a particular problem for the political marketer, who might need to ensure that other aspects of the campaign are instrumental in limiting the political damage that this group can cause.

The Process Characteristics of Political Marketing

The process characteristics in a political marketing situation can be described as the market operations peculiar to this context. They amount to the "rules of the game" and are concerned with procedures and systems that condition marketing activities. The focus on "delivered value" is increasingly important in the management of marketing. In politics, parties and candidates traditionally have stressed core values as the basis of existence and the principal means of differentiation from opponents. Hence, the emphasis on values has real meaning for both marketers and political scientists. Here, we consider value-defining processes that enable the assessment of the organization and its electorate's concerns, value-developing processes that enable the creation of positions and policies to meet those concerns, and value-delivering processes that enable the transformation of policies into political action.

Value-Defining Processes

Value-defining processes enable the assessment of the organization and its electorate's concerns. They include the process of establishing or affirming core values and of aggregating competing claims to those values and delineating limited numbers of options.

Establishment of Core Values

The value-defining process seldom is started from scratch. New political parties often are formed by dissatisfied elements from within existing entities. For both new and old parties, however, it is important to establish, renew, and refine core values. Politics is essentially about reconciling claims for state action that are quintessentially competitive. Therefore, parties must appeal to the electorate by appearing to articulate the core values of significant sections of it. Often, such values are about class, religion, or ethnic identity. Some political markets are defined by reference to other fundamental social cleavages that owe their origin to major historic discontinuities such as war, new state formation, and cataclysmic economic events. The process of defining these core values might involve charismatic leadership, although as Weber's famous typology suggests, tradition or rational procedures might be the more enduring.

Core values do not need to be very specifically delineated. Indeed, the content of policy might appear to nonpartisan observers to contradict core values. It is important, however, that a party's supporters see continuity as well as change. The implication for successful management is the need to reconcile central identities with market realities. The correct market response will depend on the party's strategic analysis (Collins & Butler, 1996). The more narrow and specific the core values of a party, the more challenged it will be as circumstances change.

Value Aggregation

All political parties must attract sufficient supporters to remain viable. In some markets, the status of "political party" and the right to compete are dependent on achieving a threshold of support. If the core values of the party resonate with significant sections of the electorate, then there inevitably will be conflicts of interest within the organization as well as with other parties. For example, a party whose core values revolve around religion or language usually will need to reconcile the interests of farmers and consumers or of employers and employees. The larger the market share a party seeks, the more complex the processes of articulation. In most cases, values are articulated in a continuous cycle of informal discussion, position papers, conferences, and party meetings. As in other businesses, the process will display a range of openness, hierarchy, and trust. Political parties are, however, seldom able to achieve the level of discipline that business firms regard as normal. This process characteristic is to an extent governed by the organization feature highlighted earlier.

Such processes of aggregation have implications for procedures of inclusion. It will be critical for managers and administrators to follow the rules of the organization, encourage wide participation, and establish consensus.

Leaders and Candidates

The process of value definition is crucially influenced by the selection of candidates and leaders. In effect, like other businesses, parties are in large part a reflection of their full-time "employees." Most important is this corp of people on which the party will draw to fill state office if the occasion arises. Broadly speaking, in parliamentary systems, this is the membership of the legislature. Elsewhere, it is those in elected public offices.

Candidate selection is a part of the value-developing process. Thus, for example, the values of women, racial minorities, and various social classes have become more distinctively defined as parties have adjusted to recruitment-to-office procedures. Because this part of the value-defining process is so significant, party strategists have concentrated on adjusting it to reflect marketing imperatives. As mentioned earlier, this can cause friction in organizations with a structured dependence on amateurs and volunteers.

Value-Developing Processes

Value-developing processes enable the creation of positions and policies to meet the concerns articulated and aggregated in the definition stage. The particular process issues that distinguish politics include the specification of voter choice, the communication standards and style of electoral competition, and the extraordinary level of attention from the media and the public.

Specification of Choice

The characteristics identified in this analysis of political marketing are part of a continuous process. Nevertheless, it is useful to regard the specification of choice as a stage after value defining. In these terms, it involves the development or policy positions or, at least, clear parameters for discussion or compromise. Like other businesses, parties seek to attract customers through the claims they make about their offers. Most commercial organizations, notwithstanding worker councils and employee share ownership schemes, are not as inherently democratic as political parties. The open articulation of opinions at conferences and the full range of rational and charismatic approaches make for a rich experience that rarely is seen in other contexts. Parties are not simply responsive in this process. Their ability to manage market expectations or to set the policy agenda depends greatly on their market position in terms of size, the demography of their support, and skill.

Implications for parties are ironic. On the one hand, it is at this stage that most media attention is focused, so statements must be seen as newsworthy and innovative. On the other hand, policy needs to be couched in a rhetoric that maximizes its appeal to the party's supporters and the wider electorate.

Communication Standards and Style

Politics is largely concerned with the processing of ideas. Elections are one mechanism through which some people's ideas come to prevail over those of others. It is unusual, however, for substantive debates on policy to be the main focus of political marketing. Three decade ago in the United States, Nimmo (1970) noted that "election campaigns are fought not 'on the issues' but [rather] on the themes," the purpose of which is to "simplify complex public issues into brief, clear, recognisable statements to the advantage of the candidate" (p. 44). Ronald Reagan garnered much support in U.S. presidential elections by dwelling on themes—appealing to the masses with a broad focus, symbolism and emotiveness, rather than with the specific positions and programs that are followed only by the "political nation." Identifiable symbols, ceremony, and rhetoric would appear to be of more benefit in vote-catching terms than would the development and explanation of policies. Many political "debates" on television are merely shows in which rehearsed set pieces are proffered in fear of making a blunder. The same type of insubstantial statements appear in the print media, but only the editors of quality newspapers produce verbatim reports of political texts in their entirety as opposed to "sound bites." Newton (1990) reports that the ratings of news and current affairs programs fall during elections as people "react against the deluge of election coverage" (p. 12).

Advertising standards in political marketing differ significantly from those in other contexts. The practice of negative advertising is unique to politics, with the relatively tame comparative advertising being the nearest commercial equivalent (O'Shaughnessy, 1990). This facility to engage in disparaging communications even at deeply personal levels, and often by anonymous surrogates, is not uncommon in politics. The capacity to generate anxieties, doubts, and fears is augmented by the brevity of television spots and news coverage sound bites that do not allow time for qualification or defense.

The inherent conflict is that whereas more political information is delivered faster to more people than ever before through the instant mass media, the political content of such information and reporting tends to be sensationalized, personalized, and trivialized. Most countries attempt some control of political advertising and communications. In some instances, broadcast time is made available according to agreed formulas, and in others, budgetary limits are set. Such restrictions would be intolerable in commercial marketing. The marketing implication of this increasing emphasis on style is that presentation is critical; in fact, repetitive references to manifestos and policies are much less important (Reid, 1988).

Media Attention and Political Polls

The attention paid to political and electoral issues, especially during elections, is unrivaled in any other marketing setting. In particular, television coverage of politics and elections is influential. Even outside of the electoral context, the ongoing coverage of political events and processes—leading to the notion of the "permanent campaign"—provides opportunities unknown in other businesses.

Of particular interest to marketing professionals is the actual influence of such coverage on the electorate. Social scientists disagree on the nature and extent of the power of the mass media. It is difficult to disentangle the media's influence from that of education, religion, and the like. The same message can be received and interpreted by different people in different ways (Newton, 1990). At a minimum, however, there is broad acceptance of the agenda-influencing power of the mass media in political terms. Although the quantity of coverage is significant, the television medium, from which most people now get their political information, is one of semiconcentration by the audience (Denver, 1989). Thus, the danger lies in the simplistic reporting of short news items.

Unlike most market research reports, political polls are continuous and subject to wide and intense debate. Polls are now conducted and published within hours during elections. Their immediacy precludes great depth of information, but fundamental attitudes and preferences can be addressed. Polls cover current voting intentions, perceptions of party leaders, government performance, current issues, and much more. They also differ from other marketing research because they are available to the market as well as to the "manufacturer."

The publishing of polls and the subsequent debate influence several aspects of the political process (Crewe, 1990); party morale and policy formation may be acutely affected as well. Party activists and policymakers tend to be surrounded by people holding similar political views, so external polls provide a source of relatively reliable information.

The implication for marketing of media attention is the necessity to develop media expertise that focuses on photo opportunities, set-up walkabouts, and situations flattering to the candidate masquerading as "news." Also of major consequence for political marketing is the provision of information in late polls that enables voters to practice tactical voting.

Value-Delivering Processes

When the political offer has been defined and developed in terms of the value proposition, it ultimately must be delivered. The distinctive characteristics of politics that affect the delivery of political offers include the office-policy dichotomy, the periodic nature of elections, and the employment of tactical voting procedures in the market.

Office-Policy Dichotomy

By their success in elections, parties are able to fulfill the expectations that they represent in two ways: They may be able to advance their particular policy priorities or to enjoy the rewards of office. Clearly, both may be achieved, but the second usually is less openly pursued. In party systems (e.g., that in Britain), where two major parties compete for the monopoly of government power, head-to-head, office, and policy rewards are hard to distinguish. In most political systems, however, either power is dispersed among various institutions, such as the residency, courts, and legislature, or it generally is wielded by a coalition of parties. Delivering policy goals might be less straightforward than placing party supporters in government, administrative, or quasi-administrative positions. Legal, constitutional, and practical considerations might set limits on a "to the victor goes the spoils" approach. Many parties' core values, however, revolve around ensuring that more of their ethnic, linguistic, gender, or other groups are placed in positions of authority. Given that today's policy changes might not be shown to have been a success until long after the government has lost power, the immediate rewards of office might seem particularly attractive. Some small parties in a pivotal position in coalition formation might have much more ability to deliver office than does policy.

Periodic Market

A characteristic of the political marketing process that differentiates the context markedly is the periodic nature of elections. Whereas most markets operate on an ongoing basis, the importance of the election to the power, standing, and success of political market participants is critical. Notwithstanding the varying temporal nature of other markets (e.g., stock markets operate in minute time frames, major construction projects have cycles of many years), the importance of the win-lose dimension of a single election in many political markets has enormous consequences. Political careers and futures might be wholly dependent on single voting outcomes. Voting patterns do not just reflect current attitudes about parties and candidates. Because the vote is periodic, it becomes the prime opportunity for direct communication by the citizen to the party. In some instances, the electorate's strong sense of loyalty to a party or candidate might enable forgiveness for past broken promises. In other cases, elections are an opportunity for the public to punish past transgressions.

The implications of the periodic nature of political elections are that all competition ultimately is focused on the election, so regardless of whatever happened in the past, the party or candidate needs to be in good standing come decision time.

Tactical Voting

The process of tactical voting differentiates electoral marketing from other contexts. It is analogous to a negative purchase. Tactical voting occurs when voters vote for a candidate other than their favored one so as to defeat their least favored candidate. Measuring the extent or outcomes of tactical voting is difficult, but there is evidence that it has become more common in recent years (Denver, 1990). Encouraging tactical voting might form an important part of the local marketing plan. This market operation does not exist in other commercial markets. The marketer here must understand the complexities involved and analyze polling data for possible signals in this regard (Smith, 1989). The implication for the marketer is that this situation demands subtle and precise targeting of political effort. The difficulty is that planning might require support-ers behaving in a counterintuitive manner by acting on marketing criteria rather than on ideological criteria.

Marketing Strategies Relating to Process Characteristics

The tendency toward themes rather than issues reflects the attention paid to style rather than to substance. In elections, communications often steer toward similarities rather than differences. For example, Smith (1989) stresses the importance of speechwriters focusing on problems rather than on the more divisive solutions. Although not wishing to trivialize further much of what passes for political debate, the strategy lesson is that presentation must be given its due weight. Elections might not be decided by the pitch of a minister's voice or by the color of the backdrop at a party conference (Harrop, 1990), but it is important not to devalue completely the importance of subliminal and nonrational elements in voting behavior.

The different rules and standards relating to political advertising force market-ers to use news programs to convey their messages. In relation to television coverage, the smart *word* often is more likely to be edited in than is the smart *idea,* hence the calculated use of sound bites in speeches. A program of photo opportunities, briefings, speeches, and the like is necessary to make news of intrinsically promotional activities.

The marketing strategy of election campaigning must be cognizant of the lessons derived from polling data. If the product appears to be experiencing consumer resistance, then it might need to be repositioned in quick order.

Because the critical decision forum for most political markets is the election, the resources of the organization must be focused on success at that point. Whatever the effect on the ongoing running of a political office, this requires the ongoing analysis of the impact of nonelectoral decisions and activities on the ultimate decision point.

Conclusions

The marketing analysis offered in this chapter has eschewed references to some key concepts with which political science approaches political parties. It has not differentiated parties by their place on the left-right spectrum, the sophistication of their ideology, or the morality of their core values. Voters too have been treated as customers rather than as citizens of democratic states. The analysis here attempts to gain insights from the parallels among parties, commercial firms, not-for-profit organizations, and the other more usual focuses of marketing analysis. Nevertheless, it is important to note Ware's (1996) warning: "An analogy with consumers' behaviour in the market . . . cannot be pushed very far before it constitutes a misrepresentation of the political process" (p. 358).

Ultimately, politics is about state power and moral choices. On a day-to-day basis, however, political managers face many of the same dilemmas as do other businesses. It is at the level of strategy that they may gain from the analogy made here. We are attempting to develop a broader political model that places the insights marshaled here in a context that gives political marketing a fuller meaning. It seems safe to say that the effect of marketing strategies on voting usually is marginal. The recipients of the message, however well packaged and targeted they might be, are far from neutral or easily influenced. If conversion is the criterion, then most marketing efforts are wasted. Research on political campaigning effects is not straightforward.

In considering the theoretical implications, it is important to note that the model is a synthesis of material from two separate disciplines. Therefore, it will be evaluated for its significance in relation to different criteria by political scientists and marketers. The former will seek answers to questions concerning the impact of marketing on electoral outcome, political significance, and policy direction; the latter will concern themselves with issues of professional management practice in political organizations, enhancing the relevance of marketing and effective implementation. It is hoped that the debate will enrich research in both areas.

References

Bean, C. (1993). The electoral influence of party leader images in Australia and New Zealand. *Comparative Political Studies, 26,* 111-132.

Blois, K. (1987). Marketing for non-profit organisations. In M. J. Baker (Ed.), *The marketing book* (pp. 404-413). London: Heinemann.

Collins, N., & Butler, P. (1996). Positioning political parties: A market analysis. *Harvard International Journal of Press/Politics, 1*(2), 63-77.

Crewe, I. (1990). Matters of opinion. *Social Studies Review, 6*(2), 47-52.

Denton, R. E. (1988). *The primetime presidency of Ronald Reagan.* New York: Praeger.

Denver, D. (1989). *Elections and voting behaviour in Britain.* London: Philip Allan.

Downs, A. (1957). *An economic theory of democracy.* New York: Harper & Row.

Easton, D. (1981). *The political system* (3rd ed.). Chicago: University of Chicago Press.

Harris, P. (Ed.). (1996). Political marketing [special issue]. *European Journal of Marketing, 30*(10/11).

Harrop, M. (1990). Political marketing. *Parliamentary Affairs, 43,* 277-291.

Heath, A., Jowell, R., & Curtice, J. (1986). Understanding electoral change in Britain. *Parliamentary Affairs, 39,* 150-164.

Lane, J.-E. (1993). The twilight of the Scandinavian model. *Political Studies, 41,* 315-324.

Mauser, G. A. (1983). *Political marketing: An approach to campaign strategy.* New York: Praeger.

Murray, J. A., & O'Driscoll, A. (1996). *Strategy and process in marketing.* Hemel Hempstead, UK: Prentice Hall International.

Newton, K. (1990). Making news: The mass media in Britain. *Social Studies Review, 6*(1), 12-15.

Niffenegger, P. B. (1989). Strategies for success from the political marketers. *Journal of Consumer Marketing, 6*(1), 45-51.

Nimmo, D. (1970). *The political persuaders: The techniques of modern election campaigns.* Hemel Hempstead, UK: Prentice Hall International.

Olson, D. M. (1998). Party formation and party system consolidation in the new democracies of Central Europe. *Political Studies, 46,* 432-454.

O'Shaughnessy, N. J. (1990). *The phenomenon of political marketing.* Hampshire, UK: Macmillan.

Reid, D. M. (1988). Marketing the political product. *European Journal of Marketing, 22*(9), 34-47.

Reif, K. (1985). Ten second-order national elections. In K. Reif (Ed.), *Ten European elections* (pp. 1-36). Gower, UK: Aldershot.

Shostack, G. L. (1977). Breaking free from product marketing. *Journal of Marketing, 41*(2), 73-80.

Smith, C. R. (1989). Speechwriting: An acquired art. In L. J. Sabato (Ed.), *A reader in modern American politics* (pp. 104-112). Glenview, IL: Scott, Foresman.

Smith, G., & Saunders, J. (1990). The application of marketing to British politics. *Journal of Marketing Management, 5,* 295-306.

Walsh, K. (1995). *Public services and market mechanisms: Competition, contracting, and the new public management*. Basingstoke, UK: Macmillan.

Ware, A. (1996). *Political parties and party systems*. Oxford, UK: Oxford University Press.

Webster, F. E. (1997). The future role of marketing in the organisation. In D. R. Lehmann & K. E. Jochs (Eds.), *Reflections on the futures of marketing* (pp. 1-17). Cambridge, MA: Marketing Science Institute.

5

The Permanent Campaign

Marketing as a Governing Tool

DAN NIMMO

Compare two journalistic assessments of political campaigns and governing in the last half of the closing decade of the 20th century. In one, Goldman (1996) closes the special election issue of *Newsweek* coverage of the 1996 U.S. presidential election by noting that, in the campaign, "the great issues of the day never got addressed." Bill Clinton's victory depended on a "Clintonism" that was "nearer to the New Democratic platform he ran on [4] years ago than to the New Deal and Great Society traditions." It was, writes Goldman, "less an ideology than an assemblage of tactics forced on him by the necessities of dealing with a hostile Congress and of getting himself reelected." In short, to govern is to campaign via the "Small Deal" to speak to concerns of everyday life—"V-chips and school uniforms, breast cancer and tobacco, time off for family emergencies and longer stays in maternity wards." It was to run government on "tiny ideas" (p. 127).

Well into his final presidential term, Clinton's approach continued the "Small Deal," still "Putting People First," in the words of his 1996 campaign slogan. Clinton traveled the country, serving up daily items for the evening news with the regularity of Blue Plate Specials in a 1950s diner—volunteerism, national school testing for fourth graders in reading and for eighth graders in mathematics, "racial diversity" in communities, supervised child care, strict rules on mammograms, and "earned" over "social" promotion between grades in public schools, all "essentially local issues elevated to national prominence, not innovations at the federal level" (Kurtz, 1997, p. J10).

The second journalistic appraisal of political governance cum campaigning appeared June 6, 1997. The British prime minister, New Labourite Tony Blair, was but a month in office. The day following his election, he announced outside Downing Street, "We won as New Labour and will govern as New Labour." Now, in an address to a conference of representatives of European socialist parties, Blair warned that they must change with the times and avoid needless government intervention in private industries or else they will "die." In reporting Blair's remarks on the BBC World Service, the anchor of *Britain Today* called on George Jones, political editor of the *Daily Telegraph,* Jones observed, "In many respects, [Blair] is still campaigning." Blair's speeches since his election, said Jones, contained the same material and arguments of his campaign addresses. Jones argued that this accounted for Blair's prolonged "high popularity." In fact, he concluded, this was quite the opposite of John Major's government defeated in the May election. "Conservatives became too concerned with governing and lost touch with public opinion" (BBC World Service, 1997a). Then, 2 months later, assessing Blair's "First One Hundred Days," Jones observed on the BBC World Service that the Labour government still was "campaigning" as though it were the "party in opposition," a form of "supply-side politics" with a specific policy announcement each day—a tiny issue of narrow focus with a quotidian interest (BBC World Service, 1997b).

The two assessments are telling. Both suggest that to campaign is to touch public opinion and be governed *by* it. To govern for its own sake, on the other hand, is to lose touch with public opinion. Hence, *governors risk office by governing*. So, contemporary leaders campaign not to govern; they govern to campaign. Is this the "permanent campaign" prophesied two decades ago, the inevitable derivative of a world of political marketing (Blumenthal, 1980)? Or, is it a contemporary manifestation of a centuries-old fact of democratic political life? What consequences derive from the (re)emergence of the permanent campaign in either case?

The Standard Account of the Permanent Campaign

The origins of the phrase "the permanent campaign" are obscure, probably dating to the interminable military conflicts of earlier centuries. The label entered the journalistic and scholarly literature of electoral politics nearly two decades ago with publication of Blumenthal's (1980) volume on political consultants; it used the phrase in its title. Blumenthal's volume embellished a view that political scientists (e.g., S. Kelley, 1956, 1960; Nimmo, 1970), journalists (e.g., McGinnis, 1969), and political consultants (e.g., Baus & Ross, 1968; Napolitan, 1972) had advanced for years—that the arrival of a professional class of political consultants had altered the landscape of modern political campaigns. Blumenthal (1980) writes that political consultants "are permanent, the politicians ephemeral" (p. 1).

Put simply, elected politicians rise and fall, win and lose; political consultants survive countless elections. So that they too can extend their longevity, "embattled" politicians turn to a permanent cadre of technical operatives. Consultants respond with "the permanent campaign, the doctrine of the consultants," dogma that Blumenthal (1980) likens to Leon Trotsky's "permanent revolution" (i.e., "The revolution is built by making the revolution" and "goes on forever"). "Like

Trotsky's permanent revolution, the permanent campaign is a process of continuing transformation. It never stops, but [rather] continues once its practitioners take power" (p. 8). To apply the principle, Blumenthal argues, "governing is turned into a perpetual campaign" that "remakes government into an instrument designed to sustain an elected official's public popularity." Governing *to* and *through* endless campaigning (e.g., Clinton, Blair) secures politicians' legitimacy by stratagems that enhance the governor's credibility. "Credibility is verified by winning, staying in power. And legitimacy is confused with popularity" (p. 7).

Blumenthal traces the lineage of the permanent campaign beyond Trotsky's doctrine of permanent revolution; perpetual campaigning also derives from perpetual marketing in a consumer-oriented society. Prior to permanent campaigning, the rule was "a political campaign ends with an election; a soap campaign can last for years" (Blumenthal, 1980, p. 2). As politics grew more market oriented during the 1950s, the ruling imperative was that political campaigns, like sales campaigns, also must last for years. For politicians aspiring to public office, this involved prolonged campaigns beginning not just months but rather years before Election Day. For officeholders seeking to remain in power, it turned office itself into a full-time campaign platform.

Of the various political operatives whose careers and campaigns Blumenthal (1980) profiles, only one—Edward L. Bernays—was active prior to the last half of the 20th century. Blumenthal describes Bernays as a "forerunner" of the modern political consultant. The permanent campaign and the elite corps of political technicians who direct it constitute a "new process of American politics" (p. 10), a derivative of the post-World War II era with its conjunction of several trends: mass diffusion of television technology, decline of political parties, widespread popular participation via electoral and campaign reforms, and birth of political marketing. The "new process" evolved in stages. First was a precursor stage marked by "the advent of television and the decline of political machines" (p. 2). Second was the presidential election of 1952, when the campaign of Dwight Eisenhower was the first to hire an advertising firm in a national contest. Subsequently, "ad agencies sold candidates like soap" (p. 3). The stage ended with the selling of Richard Nixon as president in 1968. Third, in a stage running to 1980, consultants used aggressive strategic doctrine in perpetual campaigning for candidates' permanence in office.

Blumenthal is one of many observers who date a new process in American politics from the Eisenhower era. A recent volume on political marketing declares that "for the term 'political marketing' to have descriptive value, it must replicate most of the processes involved in consumer marketing. . . . This would make it an almost exclusively post-Second World War phenomenon" (O'Shaughnessy, 1990, p. 17), "largely a television activity" (p. 46). Similarly, a related analysis of political communication notes, "The genesis of modern political marketing is entirely rooted in the history of political communication in the United States" (Maarek, 1995, p. 7) in three stages: infancy (1952–1960), when "the 1952 presidential election marks the start of political marketing in the United States" (p. 11); adolescence (1964–1976), with increasing sophistication in television techniques; and adulthood (post-1980), with global exportation of U.S. political marketing. Another recent analysis argues that "increasing specialization and division of labor among campaign professionals" means that the political marketer conducts overlapping perpetual campaigns—"first, as initiator of policy proposals that get candidates elected; second, as public lobbyist organizing post-election policy campaigns on behalf of the official the consultant elected to office" (Nimmo, 1996, p. 37).

It appears that marketing concepts have drastically altered, in numerous ways and for better or worse, political campaigns since the Eisenhower era (Newman, 1994). In the "good old days," politicians campaigned sporadically, not continually; campaigns were of brief rather than unending duration; campaigns were preludes to governing, not products of governance; and campaign consultants were "on tap" but not yet "on top." Now U.S. President Clinton, British Prime Minister Blair, and all elected democratic leaders hold power through permanent campaigning, the logical extension of marketing to politics in a consultant-centered, nonparty world.

Is this received view of the origin, growth, and current state of the permanent campaign and its relationship to political marketing so? As Toulmin (1990) says in his critique of the received view of modernity, "Too often, what everyone *believes,* nobody *knows*" (p. 12, emphases in original). Conventional wisdom might be but a capsulized version of matters far short of complete. In their incompleteness, standard accounts appear as burlesques, polemics, or caricatures, thus *partisan* by way of being *partial* (Burke, 1959). Consider one such caricature: "In a large sense, the new technology of political campaigning portends a view of the electoral process quite different from that envisioned by practitioners of either old or new politics" (Nimmo, 1970, p. 197). Such judgments guide less than beguile understanding of contemporary campaigns to the degree that they are premature or misinformed. Hence, in assessing the state of marketing as a contemporary governing tool, it is well to begin by examining whether the standard account of the permanent campaign is adequate to assist our task.

Reconsidering Political Marketing and Permanent Campaigns

Perhaps because of the tendency to regard political marketing as of post-Eisenhower origins, students of political campaigning rarely probe the relationship of governance and marketing in earlier times. If they do, they speak of marketing not as a commercial activity but rather as a form of rhetoric, propaganda, or persuasion. Typical is O'Shaughnessy's (1990) tracing of the "ancestry" of political marketing to its "ancient antecedents" (e.g., propagandistic symbols and myths of religious cults and the Egyptian pharaohs, schools of rhetoric in Athenian Greece, propaganda techniques in Roman times). For example, "The schools of rhetoric in Athenian Greece were in a sense propaganda seminaries since they trained their acolytes in all the arts of persuasion," and the assemblies of Greece "offered the chance to employ such formally acquired skills" (p. 18). Setting aside the problems in confusing rhetoric with propaganda (Combs &

Nimmo, 1993), an identification of marketing *as* rhetoric ignores a key lesson in Greek political theory.

The *agora,* the marketplace of ancient Greece, joined commerce and politics, that is, marketing and governing. The agora was a hotbed of political conflict, discourse, and decision.

> For the Greeks have always met to talk. . . . [Yet] even in the hottest argument, persuasion is not the main object. For a Greek, argument is less the crossing of rapiers than the erection of parallel columns. Each party builds his own column. Argument is piled on argument as block on block. The two opposing columns rise side by side, each completely independent and oblivious [to] the other. He who has finished his column first and crowned it with a flowery capital is considered the winner. (Rodocanachi, 1948, p. 159)

And of what did they talk perpetually for the sake of winning, not persuading? If Plato is a guide, then they talked of the nature of the "well-ordered state." Thereby, they constructed an insightful association of the polity and the market.

In *The Republic,* Book II, Plato asks a question about a husbandman arriving at market. There is no one to exchange with him. "Does he leave his calling and sit idle in the marketplace?" Not at all. He "will find people there who, seeing the want, undertake the office of salesman." Who are these salesmen?

> In *well-ordered states,* they are commonly those who are the weakest in bodily strength and, therefore, of *little use for any other purpose;* their duty is to be in the market and to give money in exchange for goods to those who desire to sell and to take money from those who desire to buy . . . a class of retail traders. (Jowett, 1952, p. 317, emphases added)

If a political community is well ordered—organized in a viable way, stable, and benefiting from able rule—then marketing, although a necessary activity, is not controlling; tradesmen are on tap, not on top. But what of states not well ordered? What of those states in which organization is fragmented and selfish interests proliferate and compete and, without leadership, fail to coordinate the whole? *The Republic* speaks of those in Book IV:

> Are there not ill-ordered states in which the citizens are forbidden to alter the constitution; and yet *he who most sweetly courts those who live under this regime* and indulges them and fawns upon them is skillful in anticipating and gratifying their humors is held to be a great and good statesman . . .? (Jowett, 1952, p. 345, emphasis added)

Here, Plato succinctly describes, and foreshadows, Blumenthal's (1980) "permanent campaign, the doctrine of the consultants" (p. 8), the "doctrine" in all its particulars—marketers who in "well-ordered" states are of "little use for any other purpose" than bringing buyers and sellers together, who in "ill-ordered" states assume *political* roles (i.e., in campaign marketplaces, they buy and sell credibility, elect officials, strategically exploit officials' legitimacy via perpetual campaigning/

governance, enhance officials' credibility, and complete the cycle with a marketed reelection).

If this Platonic description be so, then permanent campaigning and the dominance of marketing in governance occurs principally in ill-ordered and not well-ordered states. Thus, is permanent campaigning a sign of a state so ill ordered that governance falls to political marketers in perpetuity, or is it a sign of a state in transition with marketers rebuilding a well-ordered regime? Ponder the following selected British and American possibilities.

Whigs, Wilkes, and the Publicans

W. T. Kelley (1956), Brink and Kelley (1963), and other students of the evolution of marketing, promotion, and advertising have documented that a negative image of the salesman prevailed in the Greco-Roman world, as evidenced in the views of Aristotle and Cicero; in medieval judgments such as those of Thomas Aquinas; and throughout the arrival of peddlers, traders, merchants, and guilds in the early Renaissance. The late Renaissance and the subsequent spawning of industrialism witnessed a shakeup of social orders. What once was well ordered was now threatened, for "the outpouring of products initiated by the industrial revolution necessitated the tapping of distant markets" and, thereby, "emphasized the importance of the marketing process," breaking "sanctions against free trade and, significantly, against advertising and selling goods" (Brink & Kelley, 1963, p. 24). Capitalism redefined the relationship between politics and marketing, and it introduced permanent campaigning as well.

The story of this redefinition is perceptively related by Brewer and his colleagues in a study of commercialization in the 18th century (McKendrick, Brewer & Plumb, 1982). Key to the origins and nature of permanent campaigns is Brewer's chapter titled "Commercialization and Politics." Brewer (1982) analyzes the transaction at the nub of political marketing and, thereby, the permanent campaign (i.e., commerce exploited on behalf of political interests *and* politics exploited on behalf of commercial interests).

Britain during the 18th century was a place and time of political, economic, and social upheaval. Behind a facade of well-ordered Hanoverian society was a fundamental tension between two clienteles, one aristocratic and the other entrepreneurial. In this ill-ordered reality, marketing as a governing tool emerged. Prior to the 18th century, British politics was a patrician activity, a prestigious obligation; plebeians had no role other than to obey. With capitalism, however, rose a bourgeoisie comprised of neither patricians nor laborers but rather tradesmen, shopkeepers, and professionals. Unlike plebeians, these entrepreneurs did not serve, nor were they the clients of, the aristocracy. To a middle class, "courtly politics," the politics of patrician privilege conducted in royal palaces and the benches of parliament, "seemed increasingly unattractive" in the 18th century; "a more broadly based market and a more equitably grounded politics" were "desirable and mutually reinforcing replacements for the old order" (Brewer, 1982, p. 198).

What particularly galled the emerging class of tradesmen, shopkeepers, small merchants, and professionals was a patronage system nurtured for decades by Whig oligarchs. That system awarded government contracts, loans, and sundry bonuses to patrician landowners, moneyed interests in London, and well-to-do business clients of courtly politics. In return, the beneficiaries supported Whig claims to political power and legitimacy. It was an embryonic form of the permanent campaign.

Moreover, members of the rising entrepreneurial class shut out of patronage were the very persons increasingly burdened with taxes, customs, and excise duties on corn, tea, sugar, tobacco, spirits, beer, salt, glass, and the like. To break Whig patronage and unshackle the tax yoke, the new entrepreneurs sought "opening up of politics and of enterprise in tandem; in the eyes of predominantly urban and bourgeois groups, the two were seen as an interconnected problem whose solution was mutually reinforcing" (Brewer, 1982, p. 200). Key to that solution was the role played by a host of voluntary associations, principally clubs and masonic and pseudo-masonic groups organized by entrepreneurs in trades such as ceramics, coinage, clothing, printing, and bookselling. Members of associations bonded to cope with indebtedness resulting from business risks and taxation, to offer barter and credit, and (*importantly*) to act as interest lobbyists outside courtly politics. Three groups were especially instrumental in wedding marketing to politics: brewers, innkeepers, and tavern proprietors. They formed the cadre of a radical movement that promoted economic and political reform.

> They saw the value (and profit) of using recently refined marketing and advertising techniques to publicize their cause, and [they] perceived how the interests of the politicians could be harmonized with certain commercial groups. . . . There was a hard core of radicals—centered in the clubs—who saw radical politics as a vehicle for creating a polity in which moveable property would play a new and more powerful role. (p. 261)

In 1763 began a ceaseless campaign that converted marketing into a tool of governance. The April 23 issue of *The North Briton,* a newspaper with a history of criticism of the king and his ministers, published a scathing attack accusing ministers of despotism, corruption, and sewing discord across the land; it called for an end to the regime. Under a warrant that did not identify the author, printer, or publisher of that issue (No. 45), the Crown searched homes, seized papers, and imprisoned 50 suspects. One was John Wilkes, a member of Parliament—"a rake," wrote Churchill (1957, p. 166). Wilkes protested the warrant as illegal. Nonetheless, he was charged with seditious libel and was outlawed. Undaunted Wilkes ran again for Parliament in 1768 and was elected, only to be expelled. In the by-election to fill the seat, Wilkes ran and won. Parliament declared the election void and then declared Wilkes's opponent the victor (having polled only 296 votes to Wilkes's 1,143). Wilkes again was jailed, this time for publishing an obscene parody of Alexander Pope's "Essay on Man" titled "Essay on Women." Released from jail in 1770, Wilkes won election to Parliament and as Lord Mayor.

The furor over the Wilkes affair involved matters dear to the new entrepreneurs. There was the constitutional issue regarding an independent press; entrepreneurs relied on the press for information to calculate business risks. Also key was the constitutional definition of legal warrants. And there was the matter of "the whole machinery of [18]th-century corruption exposed to the public eye" (Churchill, 1957, p. 166), a derivative of a patronage system that tradespeople and professionals had denounced as corrupt for years. Small wonder that business-oriented associations, clubs, and masonic groups campaigned for more than 7 years on behalf of Wilkes's cause. It was their cause as well—freedom from economic bondage to patricians and political independence from courtly patronage.

> In fighting for liberty—or independence—Wilkes was pursuing a higher value, one that promised to create a commercially freer, politically self-reliant body politic which, in turn, would produce national unanimity, harmony, and good feeling. Precisely because Wilkes promised to change the rules of politics in this way, he appealed to tradesmen, shopkeepers, and members of the middling sort. (Brewer, 1982, p. 233)

Wilkes was marketed in a perpetual saturation campaign—the envy of any contemporary politician. "Wilkites used the techniques and methods of organization derived from the world of business, so the tradesman and entrepreneur treated *politics as a commodity* whose purchase could bring him profit" (Brewer, 1982, p. 238, emphasis added). Thus, an "exclusively post-Second World War phenomenon" of political marketing that replicates "most of the processes involved in consumer marketing—research, advertising, personal selling, product management, and so on" (O'Shaughnessy, 1990, p. 17) was actually conceived much earlier. An interlocking network of voluntary associations of tradesmen, merchants, shopkeepers, and professionals who sold Wilkes were both political marketers and the purchasers of a wide variety of Wilkes's promotional commemoratives, artifacts, and commodities. "The centre, the hard core of the market for politics, and one which provided continuity between periodic expressions of jubilation which often proved enormously profitable to the potter, publican, and printer, were the clubs and societies" (Brewer, 1982, p. 238).

Wilkes had no spin doctors and no televised sound bites. But he had widely marketed equivalents; ceramic makers merchandised porcelain figures of Wilkes, teapots inscribed with "45" (*The North Briton* issue number) under the spout, pots with a portrait of "John Wilkes, Esq. The Patriot," snuff boxes with images of Wilkes and of Liberty, mugs, punch bowls, plates, and the like, adorned with political slogans—"Let not liberty be sold/For silver nor gold." Medals cast in gold, silver, and base metal sold similar images and sentiments. Wilkite coats had specially embroidered buttonholes for commemorative buttons, rings, and handkerchiefs. A Wilkes wig bore 45 curls. An endless variety of Wilkite jewelry, tobacco pipes, candles, candlesticks, flagons, cakes, confections, fruits, breads, and print matter captured buyers.

Publicans, "no strangers to the sort of organizing, entertaining, treating, and celebrating that were an essential part of politics" (Brewer, 1982, p. 241) were especially imaginative in selling Wilkes and his (and their) cause. Aside from providing cheap beer on Wilkes's birthday, inscribing pots with "Wilkes and Liberty," using special cups and tankards commemorating the cause, and displaying inn and pub signs with the Wilkes likeness—all conventional promotional schemes—publicans moved in novel directions. "Wilkes Head" hostelries, taverns, and inns opened in London and in various provincial and market towns. Brewers and publicans created regularly scheduled mock elections celebrating liberty, Wilkes, and brew. For example, "The Garret election was a manufactured political event, revived and revamped by members of the victualizing trades to create the sort of market that usually occurred only when a parliamentary election took place" (Brewer, 1982, p. 243). In addition to mock elections, publicans modified the calendar of the market and of politics by creating and adding as recurring fixtures on the Wilkite political market calendar (to go along with all conventional religious and royal holidays). Included were Wilkes's birthday, each date of the parliamentary elections that he had won but been denied office, and the date of Wilkes's release from the King's Bench. The plethora of dates honoring Wilkes made for a perpetual calendar of political campaigning.

The Marketing of Party Government

One might dismiss the Wilkes movement as but an interesting historical footnote, a precursor of political marketing and the permanent campaign, if it were not for two points. First, the political marketing of Wilkes led to subsequent tangible political reforms—a parliamentary redistribution of seats, an increase in the franchise, an end to political appointees to the House of Commons, the secret ballot, and the like. Even though the new class of entrepreneurs was locked out of political power—and its attendant legitimacy—at the time of Wilkes's arrest in 1763, their ceaseless permanent campaigning paid subsequent dividends in a union of marketing and governance that would grow ever more profitable in centuries to come.

Second, the permanent campaign surrounding Wilkes was a prototype of what would occur increasingly in the 19th and 20th centuries well before the arrival of television. That is, political interests, whether holding or aspiring to public office, adopted "the political ideology of our age," namely, "the political campaign" that "combines image making with strategic calculation" (Blumenthal, 1980, p. 7). Governors began governing to campaign and campaigning to govern. Indeed, in Britain only two decades after Wilkes's first arrest, William Pitt (the Younger) employed marketing technique. He consulted political operatives to plan upcoming parliamentary elections. A "small expert group of politicians began to take the parliamentary pulse"; a secret report calculated numerically the partisan composition of the likely postelection Parliament with the sitting body. The report "convinced Pitt that a majority in the Commons could be obtained"; the king dismissed his ministers, "and the ensuing elections created a majority which William Pitt preserved into the next century. The plan had been justified, and the nation at large accepted the result as the true verdict of the country" (Churchill, 1957, p. 245; see also Ehrman, 1969, pp. 123-127, for a detailed account of the strategic plan).

As parliamentary reforms in Britain were enacted in the Great Reform of 1832, the product of the earlier permanent campaign for Wilkes, party politics in America were shifting from a well-ordered to an ill-ordered republic. And just as the ill-ordered Hanoverian regime had sparked a full-fledged political marketing campaign, so too did elaborate political marketing emerge in the United States. With the exception of John Adams's election to the presidency in 1796, the young (but well-ordered by Platonic standards) American republic was guided by a succession of aristocratic plantation presidents for the first quarter of the 19th century. The Jeffersonian Democratic Party and the weakened Federalist Party both were directed by party elites. Leaders' policies and principles constituted the party platforms, and leaders subsidized and directed a party press. Through party caucuses, they circulated executive and legislative offices among themselves, and they controlled patronage. The situation had much in common with the ascendant patronage system of the 18th-century British Whigs. Agrarian and commercial interests that were not beneficiaries of elite patronage sought reform. As the Federalists vanished and the Jeffersonians fragmented, the "Era of Good Feeling" ebbed. A period of ill-ordered party strife extended until the conflict over slavery rended the nation.

Vital in the development of political marketing and permanent campaigning was the period between 1824 and 1840. It saw the end of congressional control of nominations to major office, fragmentation of party organization, and proliferation of trade, religious, political, and social voluntary associations. Conditions led de Tocqueville (1969) to observe,

> Great parties convulse society; small ones agitate it; the former rend it, and the latter corrupt it; the first sometimes save it by overthrowing it, but the second always create unprofitable trouble. America has had great parties; now they no longer exist. (p. 175)
> . . . Better use has been made of association, and this powerful instrument of action has been applied to more varied aims in America than anywhere else in the world. (p. 189)

After a half century, the Wilkes scenario was transplanted to American soil. In 1828, President John Quincy Adams sought reelection. Andrew Jackson, plurality electoral vote winner in 1824 but loser to Adams in what Jackson sympathizers trumpeted as the "corrupt bargain," ran for a second time. The 1828 campaign was a ceaseless campaign, waged throughout the whole of Adams's administration. With an eye on the election, Adams advocated a national program—a national bank, protective tariff, and federal improvement program including roads, turnpikes, and subsidies for science and education. Although the phrase did not enter the political lexicon until the 1860s, Jacksonians in Congress knew a "porkbarrel" when they saw it, and they appropriated large sums to the states, not to Adams's national proposals.

Jackson's electoral victories in 1828 and 1832 reinforced the ill-ordered polity. Perpetual campaigning persisted throughout Jackson's tenure and was magnified in 1834 when remnants of Adams's old National Republicans, anti-Jackson factions among Democrats, and anti-Masons loosely allied to form the Whig Party. They contested the 1836 election and finished second to the Jacksonians' Martin Van Buren. Whether by coincidence or by design, one cannot say, but the Whig marketing campaign for the U.S. presidency in 1840 was a rerun of the Wilkes campaign in 18th-century Britain. Whig marketers also foreshadowed, in the absence of television, the election conventional wisdom credits as the first marketing campaign for the presidency, namely, Eisenhower's in 1952. Whig marketing of candidate William Harrison has been described many times (e.g., Boller, 1996; Combs & Nimmo, 1993). Only the essentials require recapitulation.

With states removing property and taxpaying requirements for voting, the electorate in 1840 was substantially increased in size. To appeal to an expanded electoral market, Whigs created a marketable commodity. Harrison, a man of modest military achievement, became the "Hero of Tippecanoe." A man of social standing with a plantation background and living in comfortable means, Harrison was merchandised in the "log cabin–hard cider" campaign as homespun, barely more than dirt poor, "Ol' Tip." As with Wilkes, all manners of commemoratives advertised the populist fervor—popular slogans and songs such as "Tippecanoe and Tyler Too" and *The Log Cabin Song,* imagery such as "The Farmer's President" and "The Soldier of Tippecanoe," Old Cabin Whiskey sold in log cabin-shaped bottles and brewed by E. C. Booze Company ("booze" became a synonym for whiskey), coonskin caps, newspapers, books, pamphlets, 10-mile-long torchlight parades, giant-sized mudballs rolled from town to town (to "Keep the Ball Rolling"), lengthy rallies, barbecues, and a flood of free hard cider. True to a later era of marketing candidates, Harrison was urged to heed the advice of a campaign consultant: "Say not one word about his principles or creed"; indeed, "say nothing—promise nothing . . . [and] let no committee, no convention, no town meeting ever extract from him a single word about what he thinks now or will do hereafter. Let the use of pen and ink be wholly forbidden as if he were a mad poet in Bedlam" (Boller, 1996, p. 70).

Conclusion: Rethinking the Chronology of Political Marketing and Permanent Campaigning

Suffice to say that the Whig campaign's marketing features were repeated several times during the pre-Eisenhower era—marketing-informed 1912 Republican presidential primaries pitting William Howard Taft against Theodore Roosevelt, a 1933 mayoralty contest in New York City, and Upton Sinclair's 1934 campaign for California governor (Anderson, 1970). Marketing features adorned all of the presidential "advertising" campaigns between 1916 and 1980 in which "control of significant features of the race . . . passes from the party to commercial agencies or . . . specialized campaign management firms" (Jensen, 1980, p. 48).

Bearing in mind the close tie between governance and marketing since the ancients, between commercialization and politics since the 18th century, and the role of marketing in times of fragmented political order, a revision of the conventional historical development of the relationship of political marketing to permanent campaigning (Blumenthal, 1980; O'Shaughnessy, 1990; Maarek, 1995) is appropriate. It follows revisionist lines of marketing's development (Fullerton, 1988).

Era of Antecedents (before 1700s). This period is characterized by small, almost nonexistent political markets in controlled, well-ordered states where electoral clienteles were shrunk by restricted franchises, low voter turnouts, and non-accountable elites. Campaigns, not to say permanent campaigns, are largely unnecessary in prerepublican, precapitalist times.

Era of Origins (1760s-1840s). Dating from the mid-18th century in Great Britain and the early 19th century in America, this period is marked by proliferating voluntary associations, challenges to and decline of ruling parties, expanded political participation and demands for electoral reforms, and the emergence of marketing to augment and/or replace party-centered campaigns. Campaigns endure, and governance is aimed at securing or holding legitimate office.

Era of Party Markets (1950s-1970s). In Great Britain and America in the early 19th century, reforms expand electoral markets, campaigns for office, and party efforts to institutionalize marketing techniques in adjusting to the popularization of politics. In Britain, the central offices of the Conservative Party and the National Liberal Party make campaign efforts continuous and national in scope. In America, following Reconstruction, Democrats and Republicans undergo "critical realignment" in 1896 (Key, 1955) and then a succession of partisan-marketed, packaged appeals for party regimes—the Square Deal, New Freedom, Normalcy, New Deal, Fair Deal, Eisenhower Crusade, Great Society, and New Nixon.

Era of Total Campaigning (to date). Campaigns of Margaret Thatcher in 1979 and Ronald Reagan in 1980 erase vestiges of lines between campaigning and governance. Campaign marketing is continuous, unrelenting, specialized, refined, and media comprehensive. It occupies a *total environment* of politics, "reaching and encircling" the whole of every citizen, surrounding each "by all possible routes in the realm of feelings, as well as ideas," by "playing on" conscious and unconscious will and need, "providing a complete system for explaining the world, and . . . immediate incentives to action" (Ellul, 1965, p. 11).

If such a revision is worthy of discussion, then a few concluding points are suggested. First, the development of permanent campaigning in Anglo-American democracies has been of extended duration, involving subtle and dynamic relationships among political parties, voluntary interest associations, commercialization, changing campaign techniques, and inventions in media technology. The contemporary state of political marketing as a tool of governance arrived by a process far more protracted and complicated than that captured in the creationist theory that dates it from the advent of television; the gospels of Batten, Barton, Durstin, and Osborne; and the crusade of "The Man From Abilene." Whatever democratic dislocations, political ills, and social injustices we might trace to marketing as a tool of governance, they took a very long time to evolve. No baptism by congressional-mandated campaign reform will sweep them away in a single election cycle.

Second, the consolidation between marketers and politicians on behalf of mutual interests forged in the 18th and 19th centuries became a permanent merger. "A fundamental characteristic of politics in market-oriented systems" is to assign "many or most of the great organizing and coordinating tasks of society to business enterprises" (Lindblom, 1979, p. 520). During the 20th century, this includes, via political marketing, both campaigning and governance. Merchandisers, motivated by market inducements more than constitutional commands, acquire a vested interest in governing policies that reward marketing skills rather than punishing them. Hence, "many lines of policy that, however attractive they might look for, say, energy conservation or environmental protection," are forgone (p. 520). To the degree that they undercut inducements to perform that entrepreneurs take for granted, such policy lines have limited appeal in strategic doctrines of permanent campaigning. Hence, in marketed governance, these policy lines often are dismissed and even vetoed if they threaten campaign goals.

Finally, the relationship between party government and marketed government is subtle. Analysis leads us to suspect that each phenomenon is the cause and effect of the other. If so, then sophisticated measures of political marketing in government need not be assumed to be the death of political parties, as many lament. Indeed, it might be that political marketing can build and *restore* party government, not *replace* it. That claim professional marketers make, be they Frank Lutz, who drafted the Republican Party's "Contract With America," or British Labour Party consultant Peter Mendelson, who recrafted Old Labour into New Labour. So too do politicians such as former U.S. House Speaker Newt Gingrich and Labour Prime Minister Blair, who heeded marketing advice.

Only time, a longer time than between the close of the 18th century and the start of the 21st century, can speak to the full potential of marketing's restorative or destructive effects. As reformers ponder adjustments, they best recall Simmel's words in "The Stranger": The "trader as stranger" is a "person who comes today and stays tomorrow" (quoted in Wolff, 1950, p. 402). Political traders no longer are Plato's figures of "little use for any other purpose." They stay to govern today, tomorrow, and (perhaps) forever.

References

Anderson, W. (1970). *Campaigns*. Pacific Palisades, CA: Goodyear.

Baus, H. M., & Ross, W. B. (1968). *Politics battle plan*. New York: Macmillan.

BBC World Service. (1997a, June 6). Comments by George Jones. *Britain Today,* 1115 hours UCT.

BBC World Service. (1997b, August 8). Comments by George Jones. *Britain Today,* 1221 hours UCT.

Blumenthal, S. (1980). *The permanent campaign: Inside the world of elite political operatives.* Boston: Beacon.

Boller, P. (1996). *Presidential campaigns.* New York: Oxford University Press.

Brewer, J. (1982). Commercialization and politics. In N. McKendrick, J. Brewer, & J. H. Plumb (Eds.), *The birth of consumer society* (pp. 197-262). Bloomington: Indiana University Press.

Brink, E. L., & Kelley, W. T. (1963). *The management of promotion.* Englewood Cliffs, NJ: Prentice Hall.

Burke, K. (1959). *Attitudes toward history.* Berkeley: University of California Press.

Churchill, W. (1957). *The age of revolution.* New York: Dorset.

Combs, J. E., & Nimmo, D. (1993). *The new propaganda.* New York: Longman.

de Tocqueville, A. (1969). *Democracy in America.* New York: Anchor.

Ehrman, J. (1969). *The Younger Pitt: The years of acclaim.* New York: Dutton.

Ellul, J. (1965). *Propaganda.* New York: Vintage.

Fullerton, R. A. (1988). How modern is modern marketing? Marketing's evolution and the myth of the "production era." *Journal of Marketing, 52*(1), 108-125.

Goldman, P. (1996, November 19). The Small Deal. *Newsweek,* pp. 126-127.

Jensen, R. (1980). Armies, admen, and crusades: Struggles to win elections. *Public Opinion, 3*(5), 44-49, 52-53.

Jowett, B. (Trans.). (1952). *The Republic.* In W. Benton (Ed.), *Great books of the Western world* (Vol. 7, pp. 295-442). Chicago: Encyclopedia Britannica.

Kelley, S., Jr. (1956). *Professional public relations and political power.* Baltimore, MD: Johns Hopkins University Press.

Kelley, S., Jr. (1960). *Political campaigning.* Washington, DC: Brookings Institution.

Kelley, W. T. (1956). The development of early thought in marketing and promotion. *Journal of Marketing, 21*(7), 62-67.

Key, V. O., Jr. (1955). A theory of critical elections. *Journal of Politics, 17,* 3-18.

Kurtz, H. (1997, July 27). The city that can put you to sleep. *Dallas Morning News,* pp. J1, J10.

Lindblom, C. E. (1979). Still muddling, not yet through. *Public Administration Review, 6,* 517-526.

Maarek, P. J. (1995). *Political marketing and communication.* London: John Libby.

McGinnis, J. (1969). *The selling of the president 1968.* New York: Trident.

McKendrick, N., Brewer, J., & Plumb, J. H. (Eds.). (1982). *The birth of consumer society.* Bloomington: Indiana University Press.

Napolitan, J. (1972). *The election game.* Garden City, NY: Doubleday.

Newman, B. I. (1994). *The marketing of the president: Political marketing as campaign strategy.* Thousand Oaks, CA: Sage.

Nimmo, D. (1970). *The political persuaders.* Englewood Cliffs, NJ: Prentice Hall.

Nimmo, D. (1996). Politics, media, and modern democracy: The United States. In D. Swanson & P. Mancini (Eds.), *Politics, media, and modern democracy* (pp. 29-47). Westport, CT: Praeger.

O'Shaughnessy, N. J. (1990). *The phenomenon of political marketing.* London: Macmillan.

Rodocanachi, C. P. (1948). *Athens and the Greek miracle.* Boston: Beacon.

Toulmin, S. (1990). *Cosmopolis.* Chicago: University of Chicago Press.

Wolff, K. H. (Ed.). (1950). *The sociology of Georg Simmel.* Glencoe, IL: Free Press.

SECTION II

Management of Political Campaigns

6

Is There a European Style of Political Marketing?

A Survey of Political Managers and Consultants

FRITZ PLASSER
CHRISTIAN SCHEUCHER
CHRISTIAN SENFT

In the United States, the top figures of the political consulting business are political stars recognized nationwide, and popular political pundits often receive more mass media attention than do the candidates they consult and whom they are supposed to help toward electoral victory (Nimmo & Combs, 1992, pp. 97-117). Despite this fact, the empirical knowledge about the professional self-esteem of the members of this new power elite is limited even in the United States (Althaus, 1998, pp. 70-71; Bowler & Farrell, 1998; Thurber, 1998). To date, only a few studies have provided insight into the professional attitudes and the ethical codex of political consultants (Althaus, 1998; Faucheux, 1994; Kolodny & Logan, 1998; Luntz, 1988; Petracca & Wiercioch, 1988). It was as late as 1997 that the American University's Campaign Management Institute initiated a multiyear research project including an extensive investigation of the political consulting industry in the United States by conducting the first ever survey of the campaign profession (Pew Research Center, 1998).

The state of knowledge in Western Europe is far more deficient and unsatisfactory. It is true that several international comparative studies published during the past years provided information about the practice of political marketing and campaign strategies in selected Western European countries (Bowler & Farrell, 1992; Butler & Collins, 1994; Butler & Ranney, 1992; Collins & Butler, 1996; Harris, 1996; Kaid & Holtz-Bacha, 1995; LeDuc, Niemi, & Norris, 1996; Swanson

& Mancini, 1996). However, there has not yet been a study focusing on the professional self-definition of European political consultants and campaign managers.

A great number of studies have been done on the position and importance of political consultants in the process of democratic competition in the United States (Farrell, Kolodny, & Medvic, 1998; Friedenberg, 1997; Johnson-Cartee & Copeland, 1997a, 1997b; Medvic, 1998) and the strategies and practice of political marketing in the United States (Arterton, 1992; Mauser, 1989; Newman, 1994; Sabato, 1981; Scammell, 1997; Selnow, 1994; Shea, 1996; Thurber & Nelson, 1995). This contrasts with Western Europe, where the only comparably intensive study was for the United Kingdom (Franklin, 1994; Kavanagh, 1995, 1996; O'Shaughnessy, 1990; Scammell, 1995), where Tony Blair's New Labour campaign clearly was influenced by observation of the U.S. presidential campaigns (Butler & Kavanagh, 1997, pp. 56-57). With the exception of France (Bongrand, 1993; Kaid, Gerstlé, & Sanders, 1991; Maarek, 1992, 1995) and Italy, where the "marketing party" Forza Italia and the election success of television tycoon Berlusconi made "marketing politico" the subject of scientific research from 1994 onward (Mancini & Mazzoleni, 1995; Mazzoleni, 1996), Germany is the only country for which comparatively informative studies are available (Dombrowski, 1997; Grafe, 1994; Pfetsch & Schmitt-Beck, 1994; Radunski, 1996; Schönbach, 1996).

In recent years, the "Americanization" of the political process in Europe has triggered an intensive and controversial debate about the consequences of modernizing campaign practices in Western Europe (Åsard, 1997; Farrell, 1996; Irwin, 1997; Kavanagh, 1997; Negrine & Papathanasopoulos, 1996; Norris, 1997; Pfetsch, 1998; Semetko, Blumler, Gurevitch, & Weaver, 1991; Wring, 1997). On the one hand, the debate has focused on the influence of the American consultancy business on European campaign practices (Farrell, 1998). On the other hand, the hypotheses of the Americanization of European politics has been countered by the theory of modernization that explains the progressive professionalization and medialization of political competition in Europe (Swanson & Mancini, 1996). To date, the controversy has failed to fully answer the critical question of whether there is a European style of political marketing.

The European Context of Political Marketing

The institutional context of political marketing practice in Europe differs fundamentally from the situation in the United States (Farrell, 1996, 1998; Lane & Ersson, 1996; Swanson & Mancini, 1996). A comparison of the institutional background of political marketing in 16 European countries with the institutional context in which political marketers, consultants, and campaign managers operate in the United States reveals few similarities between the individual European countries and the competitive situation in the United States. Campaigns in the United States are candidate centered, money and media driven, professionalized, and highly individualized. In most European democracies, on the other hand, campaigns follow the traditional model; they are party centered and labor intensive, receive free television time, are publicly funded, and are managed by party staff. The relevance of the candidate-centered, capital-intensive versus party-centered, labor-intensive distinction for campaign consultants is that "in the former case there is much more scope for individual candidates to employ their own specialists to fight election campaigns; by contrast, in a party-centered system, such as most of Western Europe, it is more likely that the political parties will have their own campaign professionals as full-time employees" (Farrell, 1998, p. 174). However, candidate-centered versus party-centered styles of campaigning constitute only one important criterion of distinction. Other especially relevant context factors of political marketing practice are as follows:

1. The electoral system (e.g., majority vote system vs. proportional election system, density of the election cycle, candidate vs. party elections)
2. The system of party competition (e.g., number of party activists, number and strength of ties in society, ability of the organization to mobilize party followers, member vs. voter parties)
3. The legal regulations of election campaigns (e.g., public vs. private campaign financing, budget limits, access to television advertising, time limits for official campaigns, candidate nomination, primaries)
4. The media system (e.g., public vs. dual vs. private media systems, differentiation of the media system, level of modernization, professional roles of journalists, autonomy of mass media)
5. The national political culture (e.g., homogeneous vs. fragmented cultures, hierarchical vs. competitive political cultures, degree of trust in the political process, political involvement)
6. The degree of modernization in society (e.g., degree of societal differentiation, industrialized vs. information society, socioeconomic mobility)

In light of the criteria just mentioned, the situation of political competition in Europe differs substantially from that in the United States in terms of the institutional background. A "first past the post" electoral system, such as that in the United States, can be found only in the United Kingdom. The maximum time between elections for the lower house (House of Representatives) in the United States is only 2 years, whereas the average in European democracies is 4 years. Only the United States has an entirely privately organized television system, whereas in most European countries state-owned broadcasting networks operate in addition to private television channels. Only in the United States is it possible to buy unlimited television time for political broadcasts; in Europe, paid political television ads are either subject to numerous legal restrictions or forbidden by law (Kaid, 1997; Kaid & Holtz-Bacha, 1995). Thus, looking exclusively at the institutional background, there are strict limits on the Americanization of political competition in Europe.

Although there are significant differences in the institutional backgrounds of the political marketing processes in Europe and the United States, there are structural trends showing that the two processes are becoming more similar

(Wilson, 1998). For example, most European party systems are characterized by a continued dealignment process, weakening both traditional party loyalties and party identification among the European electorates (alton, 1996; Schmitt & Holmberg, 1995). At the same time, volatility is rising and the proportion of floating votes is increasing (Franklin, Mackie, & Valen, 1992), whereas voter turnout is on the decline (Blondel, Sinnott, & Svensson, 1997). Since the 1980s, traditionally strong party systems, such as those in Sweden, Germany, and Austria, have been facing the erosion of their party organizations, declining membership rates, and a decreasing ability to mobilize their voters (Katz & Mair, 1992, 1994).

Fierce competition between public and private television channels, progressive personalization, and "infotainment" also have brought about sweeping changes in the media systems and the political communication process, bringing them increasingly closer to the media-driven process in the United States (Iyengar & Reeves, 1997; Østergaard, 1997). Decreasing trust in political parties and the political elite in most Western European democracies (Dalton, 1997; Inglehart, 1997, pp. 293-323), increasing political dissatisfaction, the challenge posed by the formation of right-wing populist parties (Betz & Immerfall, 1998), and a rising proportion of negative voters have fundamentally changed the competitive situation in European party systems. One reaction to the erosion of voter loyalties and the decline of organizational strength is the ongoing professionalization of the political parties (Mair, Müller, & Plasser, in press), which also leads to changes in the practice and strategies of political marketing.

Research Design

Is there a European style of political marketing? This question can be answered only by the political consultants and party managers themselves. Thus, the core of our research design consisted of a personal survey of experts conducted in January and February 1998. Because the aim of the European Consultants Survey was to identify a European view of political marketing, 50 political marketing experts from all parts of Europe were asked about their opinions and attitudes. The interview partners were select party managers, political consultants, media experts, pollsters, and advertising experts (see Appendix). The interviewees were selected according to the practical relevance of their work in campaigns, advertising, communication management, and strategic political consulting.

Professional interview partners were chosen from the membership lists of the International Association of Political Consultants (IAPC), the World Association of Public Opinion Research (WAPOR), and the European Democratic Union (EDU) Campaign Conference; the lists of the parties represented in the European Parliament; and the participant lists of various international conferences that were available. These addresses were supplemented by recommendations of party managers and experts of individual countries. Although we tried to achieve a balanced selection of interview partners according to their countries of origin and activities, we must acknowledge that the investigation used a relatively higher proportion of experts from German-speaking countries. One reason for this was that the regional origin of the authors ensured easy access to German and Austrian experts. Another is that the market for political consulting services is larger in Central and Northern Europe than in Southern Europe. There is a demand for such services in Southern Europe, but it is largely filled by consultants from other European countries (mostly Germany, Great Britain, and France) and from the United States, and specific political consulting markets have developed only in certain places. Overall, the regional distribution of the interviewees reflects the density and professional level of the political consulting business in Western Europe. Nearly 50% of our sample consisted of external political consultants (strategic consultants, media and television consultants, pubic relations experts, and pollsters). The other half consisted of party managers and staff of political parties involved in campaign and communication planning.

The experts who were selected spent, on average, half an hour answering the questionnaire's 27 questions about opinions and professional attitudes. Whereas most were closed questions, 5 open questions were added to round out the picture. Supplementary background questions helped to place the answers in the professional context of the interviewees. The seven-page questionnaire was designed to focus on six thematic areas: general understanding of marketing, success factors for campaigning and candidates, importance of parties, cooperation between parties and political consultants, and the scientific-professional background of the interviewees.

These are the same focal points that formed the core of Luntz's (1988) qualitative survey of 36 top consultants in the United States. We took over some of his questions verbatim to make spot comparisons possible, but we also took into account the questionnaires of Faucheux (1994) and Althaus (1998). In the formulation and sequence of the questions, we emphasized clarity and a conversational interviewing style. This was an advantage in cases where time constraints made it necessary to interview the experts in written form. The great majority of interviews were conducted by phone, with a small proportion carried out face-to-face. Because the questions were closed ones, interviewees were asked to choose from a scale of answers consisting of three to five options. Thus, the measuring level was limited to nominal and ordinary scales. The answers were processed by means of SPSS. The focus of the analysis was on frequency counts and distribution. By combining different parameters by means of factor analysis, we also were able to investigate their influence on the diverging marketing attitudes and to determine whether there is a special style of political marketing in Europe.

European Perspectives of Political Marketing

If there really is a specific European style of political marketing, then it must be reflected in a pronounced European concept of marketing on the part of the consultants and party managers. In our survey, we first asked the experts which

TABLE 6.1 Professional Definition of the "Political Marketing" Concept ($N = 50$, percentages)

	Very Close	Fairly Close	Only Exceptional
Please tell me, for each of the following definitions of the concept of "political marketing," whether it is very close to your political marketing practice, fairly close, or applies only in exceptional cases. "Political marketing" means the following:			
a. Long-term communication to build up competence and trust among the electorate	58	35	7
b. Directions for strategic planning and development of campaigns	50	40	10
c. Management technique for political communication	38	40	22
d. Techniques for the definition of and communication with strategic target groups	33	48	19

SOURCE: European Consultants Survey, Question 7.
NOTE: Due to missing answers, N's may differ slightly for some questions in later tables.

definitions of political marketing came closest to their professional concepts of marketing (Table 6.1). The surprising result was that few European consultants identified definitions in which techniques and strategies were important. Although they conceded that political marketing offers a large set of tools ranging from target group definition to complex communication techniques, European consultants maintained that a marketing concept aimed exclusively at electoral victory is too restricted.

It is true that half of all European consultants and party managers associate political marketing with guidelines for the strategic planning of campaigns. Nearly 60% of them, however, emphasized that the essence of political marketing is its long-term impact, specifically the communication of competence and the creation of trust. They indicated that a campaign that aims at a "quick sell" confuses politics with consumer products, quickly becomes stale, and is not credible. Therefore, it is necessary to strengthen the competence of the political actors and build a basis of trust among their voters by using the communicative strategies of the marketing mix.

This opinion is especially prevalent among "unconnected experts," those consultants and managers who tend to distance themselves from American marketing practices. Fully 60% of those in this group said that they were oriented toward a long-term model of relationship marketing and drew their strategies and activities from this model. By contrast, members of the group with a stronger affinity toward the U.S. model and close contacts with the American consultancy business (U.S.-connected experts) emphasized a primarily campaign-oriented concept and the technical uses of political marketing.

The consultants and party managers interviewed saw the communication of central messages to the target group as the central task of political marketing

TABLE 6.2 Central Tasks of Political Marketing (*N* = 50, percentages)

Based on your experience, what would you consider to be the central task of political marketing?	
1. Target group-specific communication of the message or issues	37
2. Profiling the candidate's image	21
3. Dialogue with the voters	14
4. Strategy for building trust	12
5. Promotional communication with the voters	10

SOURCE: European Consultants Survey, Question 6.

(Table 6.2). Addressing strategically defined target groups and developing specific issue competence are the basis for creating a clearly defined image profile. The definition of the tasks of political marketing again emphasizes the long-term perspective of political marketing activities and stresses the strategic creation of trust and campaigns focusing on dialogue as the keys for the successful implementation of the concept of political marketing.

In past years, political marketing has undergone dramatic changes that have affected the basic understanding of marketing and its tasks as well as the context in which political managers operate. Asked what they see as the most influential change in political marketing practice, half of all European experts cited developments in the media system, and one out of three emphasized the importance of electronic media, especially television. The fact that the communication of politics and the image creation of parties and candidates take place predominantly via electronic mass media has increased both the importance of professional media management and the necessity of visualizing messages. One out of four respondents saw the increasing differentiation of the European media landscape as a new opportunity for political marketing, one that makes it possible to communicate central campaign messages better to specific target groups. In this respect, the special importance of private television channels is expected to increase in the coming years.

The importance of television has moved the candidate into the center of strategic marketing considerations. A third of the consultants and party managers interviewed saw the candidate as the most important factor of a political campaign. The trend toward personalization and individualization of the political process also influences the professional orientation and strategies of political and media consultants. However, the speed of the electronic mass media also places increased demands on the reaction time of the campaign management. European consultants clearly stressed the necessity to react immediately and to integrate just-in-time messages and situational interpretations into topical media reports. This makes the increased use of state-of-the-art communication technologies in political marketing an absolutely necessary precondition for a successful campaign. However, the respondents still stated that a clever and well-planned strategy is the decisive basis for planning and that tactical and marketing-technical considerations are of secondary importance. Without a consistent strategy, it is impossible to successfully conduct issue management and professional public relations.

The majority of European political consultants interviewed regarded political marketing practice in the United States as a role model. Developments in the United States and the progress in campaign management set high standards even for those who do not think that the techniques and strategies can be adapted to the European or regional context. (Only one out of six respondents believed that the U.S. model of political marketing could also be applied to Europe.) According to the experts, the U.S. style of political marketing, adapted to the institutional and cultural specialties of the European campaign situation, is by far the most professional technology of the democratic acquisition of power. They stated that if there is a European style of political marketing, then its core is a modification of the American role model.

In keeping with the importance of electronic mass media in the political process, one out of four respondents placed special importance on adopting techniques of media management. In the opinion of political consultants, using spin control and event management in the media to create a clear public image has become indispensable in Europe. One out of four European experts predicted an increase in the importance of techniques such as database marketing, direct mail, and telephone marketing. European managers obviously are fascinated by these techniques because they provide far more personalized access to the voter and, as dialogue marketing, surpass the distant and one-sided presentation of politics. The basis of these techniques, however, is better knowledge of the needs and wants of the voters, which would in turn allow the methods of market and opinion research to be used more professionally in Europe (e.g., focus groups, moment-to-moment research techniques).

European political consultants saw the differences in the electoral systems as the main factors that limit adopting U.S. campaign strategies and techniques. Because of the single-member districts in the United States, candidates are at the center of the contests. The experts interviewed maintained that the personalization of campaigns also can be observed in Europe, but not to the same extent as in the United States. In addition to institutional and procedural differences between the United States and Europe, one out of five respondents also stressed differences in the sociocultural mentality and political-cultural traditions that make the adoption of the U.S. marketing concept problematic.

This means that political marketing faces the same problems as does consumer or business marketing. In all of these cases, crossing cultural borders makes it necessary to reconsider the marketing tools used and to adapt them to regional and cultural specialties. Even transnational products such as Coca-Cola and McDonald's have encountered obstacles in their global marketing activities that sometimes required substantial modifications of their product concepts. Considering politics' more complex framework, no global political marketing strategy would have the slightest chance of success.

In addition to institutional and cultural barriers, the far-reaching adoption of U.S. political marketing know-how also faces budgetary restrictions. Many of the

TABLE 6.3 Factors Influencing the Chances of a Political Candidate's Success (means)

How important are the following factors for the success of a political candidate? The number 1 would mean "very important," and 5 would mean "quite unimportant." You can weight your evaluation in between.

1. Personality/image	1.22
2. Ability to communicate well through the media	1.26
3. Presence in the media (especially on television)	1.33
4. Central campaign message	1.67
5. Leadership qualities	1.72
6. Issue competence	1.95
7. Rhetorics/being a good speaker	2.10
8. Unified party support	2.14
9. Looks and personal habits	2.30
10. Professional media and television consultants	2.48
11. Political experience	2.59

SOURCE: European Consultants Survey, Question 17.

techniques that European experts believe have great future potential, such as database management, track polling, and telephone marketing, require extraordinary financial resources that are (at least at present) not available in the campaign budgets of Western European parties. This restriction also applies to Western European media systems, although they have developed rapidly and become increasingly differentiated since the 1980s. At the national level, the media system is far less complex than the 212 television markets, more than 1,000 television stations, and more than 1,500 daily newspapers that determine political communication planning in the United States.

Success Factors of a Campaign

"How can we win this campaign?" is the question political managers most frequently are asked by candidates and parties. Although the specific context, complexity, and differences of the various campaigns must be taken into account, it still is possible to identify the factors that, in the view of European experts, are central to the success of political marketing (Table 6.3).

For three quarters of the political consultants surveyed, the crucial point of a campaign is the candidate (Table 6.4). This evaluation clearly confirms the current trend of the personalization of politics. The aim of a campaign is to establish a clear profile for the product, which is the personality of the top candidate. Creating a clear candidate profile and conveying this image to the voters via mass media is a central task. From the point of view of political managers, a successful candidate seeks media exposure, is able to conduct successful impression management, and gets his or her central message across to the audience. Key factors in so doing are the presentation of the candidate's factual competence and leadership qualities. According to political managers, political experience is of secondary

TABLE 6.4 Success Factors of a Campaign (percentages)

	Very Important
How do you evaluate the importance of the following factors for the success of a campaign? Please tell me, for each factor, whether you believe it is very important, important, or not so important.	
1. Personality and image of the candidate	75
2. Control over topics of mass media reporting	71
3. Strategic positioning toward the competitors	66
4. Campaign budget	41
5. Issues/thematic positions	39
6. Information about expectations/motives of target groups	34
7. Strong and effective party organization	30
8. External advisers and campaign consultants	18

SOURCE: European Consultants Survey, Question 5.

importance, but this by no means implies that relevant issues are not important. Whereas half of the consultants interviewed said that candidate image is more important than issues, a third of those interviewed saw both factors as equally important. Issue competence is extremely relevant, but it is the combination of the candidate's image and the relevant, target-specific messages that forms the basis of a successful campaign.

In Europe as elsewhere, election campaigns are conducted predominantly in the mass media, and television assumes a central significance. For example, three quarters of European experts indicated that reports issued through well-planned news management are a decisive criterion for the success of an election. In the opinion of political consultants, professional spin control, issue building, and issue framing also are highly relevant factors in European campaigns. In addition, two thirds of the interviewees stated that it is important to create a clear strategic position in relation to the competitors in a campaign. Ideally, it must be possible for the voter to clearly identify the candidate, the party, and its image as well as to differentiate them from the competitors.

The significance of active news management through the political agents lies first and foremost in its goal of influencing the framing of mass media reporting. Parties and candidates, however, have little direct influence on news reports (free media). Therefore, it is all the more important to address the potential voter by means of advertisements that can be designed freely (paid media). The extraordinary importance of the electronic media for campaigning also was revealed in the evaluation of media in terms of their advertising value. Public television was regarded as the most important advertising medium. If the parties in individual countries are given free television time, then access to television is regulated for all political contestants. Purchasing air time for political television ads is banned by law in most European countries. In cases where it is possible to buy television time and to run ads, political consultants especially appreciate the flexible times for commercials on private television because it allows them to target specific voters and to address them quickly. Local private television stations are becoming more important because they allow for message differentiation according to strategic target groups.

Daily newspapers are a more attractive print medium than weekly publications or monthly magazines. However, a difference is made between national issues and regional sections. Some experts gave more attention to the latter because the messages can be more efficiently adapted to the target segments.

With regard to magazines, respondents frequently commented that this important advertising medium is not being used efficiently. Although the scope of most magazines is more limited than that of daily newspapers, readers often devote more time and interest to individual reports in magazines. Special interest magazines, in particular, offer a wealth of various possibilities that better media planning could use more efficiently.

Direct mail aims at addressing strategically defined voter target groups. Sending target-specific mail and getting information and messages across represents an advertising potential that still is being insufficiently exploited in Europe. For this reason, political consultants predicted an increase in the importance of direct mail for the political marketing mix. One quarter of those interviewed favored using the same database marketing techniques as are used in the United States. Such methods currently are restricted by law in Europe (data protection). Furthermore, the extremely high costs would have to be integrated into campaign budgets. Finally, successfully using the potential of this promotional tool would require extensive practical experience and special experts.

In view of the traditional importance of billboards and street posters in European campaigns, it is surprising that the interviewees assigned only average relevance to posters as communication tools. This is all the more surprising given the large share of a party's campaign budget that is earmarked for billboards and posters. With a few country-specific variations, however, the experts were unanimous in their opinion that posters generally have a mobilizing effect only on voters loyal to the party and that they stimulate short-term discussions at best. Posters and billboards are used to create a visual presence in the streets; they attract attention but are convincing only in exceptional cases.

Consultants and party managers also were less than enthusiastic about the current chances for political communication through the Internet. Most European parties now have specially designed Web sites on the Internet that Web surfers occasionally visit. Traditional party conventions also have adapted to the standards of cyberdemocracy, making them accessible to interested people via the Internet, and more and more chat dialogues are being offered. Experts stated that the people who take advantage of these possibilities are an important but still relatively small group that is likely to gain in importance as more people have easy access to the Internet. Four fifths of the interviewees assumed that a professional representation of candidates and their issues on the Internet will be indispensable in the future and that the Internet will open up new opportunities in political marketing such as for organizational networking, fund-raising, and voter mobilization (Corrado & Firestone, 1996).

Whereas the new methods of political communication offer the political parties new options, they also change the structure of campaign budgets. Advertising

TABLE 6.5 Importance of National Party Organizations for Parliamentary Elections ($N = 50$, percentages)

	Total	U.S. Connected	Unconnected
How important are the national party organizations in the election of their candidates?			
Very important	50	17	70
Somewhat important	46	78	26
Little or no importance	4	6	4
Has the importance of the national party organization for parliamentary campaigns become more important, become less important, or stayed the same in recent years?			
Become more important	34	12	48
Become less important	43	71	26
Stayed the same	23	17	26

SOURCE: European Consultants Survey, Questions 15 and 16.

and media costs already eat up a large portion of the financial means available. Half of the respondents predicted an increase in campaign costs in the coming years, based on increased use of new communication and advertising methods.

Because of this development, parties will be under increasing pressure to find new sources of financial support. Our results parallel those of Luntz's (1988, p. 239) investigation, as 88% of the U.S. consultants interviewed in 1986 predicted an increase in campaign costs. Even the 50% of European experts who assumed that expenses will remain the same foresaw changes in the structure of the expenditures. Because the proposed budgets will remain roughly the same, we can assume that an optimized use of resources will lead to the phasing out of classic campaign media such as the use of campaign posters. In future European campaigns, like those in the United States since the 1980s, television and especially direct mail will consume a large part of the available budgets.

What is the significance of national party organizations in a campaign? Political experts' answers to this question varied greatly (Table 6.5). For the candidates of the political parties, the organizational apparatus and the financial and technical support are indispensable factors in successful campaigning. One half of the interviewees assigned a very important role to the national party organization. Simultaneously, the trend toward increased personalization and the development toward media-driven campaigning, like that in the United States, will cause the party organizations to gradually lose importance, according to 43% of the respondents. This is especially true in cases where a candidate is able to build a strong basis of support outside of the traditional party organization. Those interviewees who are predominantly oriented toward the U.S. practice of political marketing (U.S.-connected experts) distanced themselves more from party organizations than did those respondents who are more closely linked to traditional European campaign practices (unconnected experts). Whereas roughly three quarters of the U.S.-connected experts had the impression that the relevance of party organizations for parliamentary elections has decreased in recent years, fully half of the unconnected experts believed that the importance of the party organizations is increasing.

According to three quarters of the European consultants, candidates have become a lot more experienced in employing campaign techniques. They no longer delegate the tasks of strategy formulation and campaign management exclusively to party managers and external consultants; instead, they take an active personal role in campaign planning.

Degree of Professionalization of European Political Consultants

The political consultancy business in the United States has already gone a long way toward establishing most of the criteria essential for an independent profession—a clearly defined market for special services, a clear definition of professional roles in the relationship with clients, a separate professional association, an academic career path, and a codex of professional and ethical guidelines (Althaus, 1998, pp. 300-309). By contrast, European consultants and political managers currently are at a much lower degree of professionalization. This becomes obvious if one looks at membership in professional groups such as the IAPC, the European Association of Political Consultants, and the WAPOR.

The IAPC, founded by Joseph Napolitan and Michel Bongrand in Paris in 1968, had 90 members in 1997. Of these members, 45 were from the United States and 20 were from Latin America, Australia, Turkey, and Russia. Only 25 IAPC members were from Western Europe, and of these, 10 were from Germany and 6 from Sweden. The IAPC organizes annual conferences that last for several days and publishes an internal newsletter. Its members come from different professions such as full-time employees of political parties, professional political consultants, heads of political polling firms, film producers, advertising experts, and specialists for public affairs and government relations. Thus, the IAPC is a highly professionalized expert forum but definitely is no representative professional association for Western Europe. The same is true of the WAPOR; most of its members are representatives of commercial polling firms, survey specialists, and university academics.

Only one third of the consultants and party managers interviewed belong to professional associations. In this respect, political consultants differ from party managers. Whereas half of all political consultants are members of professional associations, only one out of 10 party managers is a member of a professional group. However, membership in a professional association says relatively little about the real degree of professionalization. For party managers in Western Europe, platforms such as the campaign conference of the EDU (an organization of Christian democratic or conservative parties) and the regular meetings of the advertising and communication managers of the social democratic or socialist parties provide forums for transnational contacts. Every year, both platforms host several conferences and workshops at which leading party campaign experts exchange and analyze their professional experience and discuss current strategies.

The EDU Campaign Conference convenes roughly every 6 months in a European city. The participants typically are leading staff of Christian democratic or conservative parties from the United Kingdom, Sweden, Norway, Finland, and Germany. Less frequently, participants come from France, Spain, Austria, Greece, Cyprus, Malta, and Eastern European countries such as Hungary, Slovakia, and Poland; rarely do they come from the Czech Republic, Slovenia, and Lithuania. The meetings, which usually last for 2 days, provide for intensive informal contacts and the chance to discuss past and future campaigns in terms of strategy, media work, and (especially) implementation. Other strategic questions, such as the confrontation with New Labour or right-wing populist parties, are discussed at great length. The so-called new media, especially the Internet, play an increasingly important role in the discussions.

The advertising and communication managers of the European social democratic parties usually meet in Brussels, Belgium, every 4 to 6 weeks in intensive phases or otherwise quarterly. Key issues are networking and cooperation among the social democratic parties, strategy questions with strong focus on implementation, and sometimes on-site fact finding such as a visit to the New Labour headquarters. Top figures from the U.S. consultancy business are regularly invited to report on the newest trends and innovations in U.S. campaign practices. There also are organized field trips to observe campaigns, and an efficient transnational information and contact network provides for a mutual transfer of know-how.

In comparison with the situation in the United States, the communication channels of know-how transfer in Europe are significantly more fragmented, more informal, and more strongly aligned along the boundaries of ideological and programmatic party alliances. Similarly, the market for strategic consultancy services is more strongly segmented by party-political loyalties, personal relationships of trust, and the ideological background of external consultants. This also is true of professional qualifications. A national campaign training seminar, such as the one that *Campaigns & Elections* offers several times a year in Washington, D.C., for candidates, consultants, and party managers of both the Republican and Democratic parties, would be totally unthinkable in today's Western Europe. Practical political marketing know-how in Western Europe is developing within the relatively enclosed ideological camps of conservative or social democratic parties.

Western Europe also differs from the United States in that there are no specialized university courses of study for political marketing or political management. To date, university programs such as the Graduate School for Political Management at the George Washington University are missing from the European academic landscape. Very few university departments deal intensively with theories and models of the practice of political marketing, and where courses are offered, they are limited to special lectures or workshops. Despite the relatively deficient situation regarding education and qualification, most European consultants and party managers place very high demands on professional marketing or campaign experts. Topping the list of requirements is knowledge of the latest U.S.

TABLE 6.6 Demands Made on a Professional Political Marketer ($N = 50$, percentages)

	Yes	No
What is absolutely necessary in order to be a professional political marketer?		
1. Knowledge of the latest U.S. campaign literature	64	36
2. Regular observation of campaigns in the United States	63	37
3. Study of political or communication science	50	50
4. Personal contacts with U.S. campaign consultants	39	61
5. Study of business and marketing	28	72
6. Contact with specialized university institutes	27	73

SOURCE: European Consultants Survey, Question 25.

campaign literature and regular observations of campaigns in the United States. In the absence of a European political marketing identity or a European definition of the political marketing profession, the majority of the consultants and political managers interviewed look to the United States for a role model (Table 6.6).

Fully half of the consultants and political managers interviewed regarded the study of political science or communications as an indispensable prerequisite for a profession as a political marketer. Only one out of four named a degree in business administration or marketing as a necessary qualification. Similarly, because of the lack of programs, only a minority of the respondents considered contacts with relevant university departments absolutely necessary for the professional profile of a political marketer.

The professionalization of an occupational group also is defined by standardized information contacts through specialized journals or specialist literature. This context also confirms the function of the United States as the role model for European political marketing practices. Roughly 60% of the European consultants and political managers interviewed at least occasionally read *Campaign & Elections,* the most widely read monthly magazine for campaign experts. Roughly one fourth of the respondents reported that they at least occasionally read academic journals such as *Political Communication, Public Opinion Quarterly,* and *Electoral Studies.* Only one out of 10 respondents regularly reads the *European Journal of Marketing,* one of the leading publications in its field. In this respect, political consultants show a stronger interest in U.S. journals than do party managers. The same journals also are of greater interest to persons who are professionally more oriented toward U.S. campaign practices. Approximately three fourths of U.S.-connected experts said that they draw professional information and ideas from *Campaign & Elections* and frequently use academic journals such as *Public Opinion Quarterly, Party Politics,* and the *International Journal of Press and Politics.*

In summary, the degree of professionalization of European consultants and political managers is much lower than that of U.S. consultants and campaign managers. Professional associations play a much smaller role in the process of occupational qualification, and the platforms and training opportunities provided by transnational party associations are more important. The possibilities for training are ideologically segmented and oriented along party lines, and university training and continuing education are largely deficient. What is significant is the importance of political marketing know-how from the United States as a role model for European political marketing practice. Roughly 40% of the European consultants and political managers interviewed said that they orient their professional self-awareness along U.S. standards and make intensive use of transatlantic sources of information and experience.

The United States as a Transnational Role Model?

European experts regard political marketing practice in the United States as "the cutting edge of electioneering innovation" (Blumler, Kavanagh, & Nossiter, 1996, p. 59). During election campaigns for the U.S. presidency, hundreds of European campaign experts and party managers visit the candidates' campaign headquarters and try, through briefings with leading campaign specialists, to get information about technical and promotional innovations that they can use in planning their national election campaigns. Thus, it is no exaggeration to refer to the United States as the international "role model of campaigning" (Scammell, 1997, p. 4). The transnational diffusion of U.S. campaign and marketing techniques is enhanced by the internationalization of the campaign consulting business (Farrell, 1998). In recent years, top consultants from the United States have, in cooperation with Western European political and communication consultants, opened political consulting firms in London, Paris, and Stockholm. Especially in off years (i.e., years in which there are no congressional or presidential elections), U.S. consultants are particularly interested in finding customers in Western Europe, Latin America, and (increasingly) Eastern Europe. Even at the height of election cycles in the United States, some top consultants have not signed lucrative contracts with the candidates and still are available for consulting jobs outside the United States. In most Western European countries today, hiring U.S. consultants to help plan campaigns and strategies, even in a limited role, is the ultimate indication of professionalism.

The diffusion of the "modern model of campaigning" is accomplished in the form of an

> international network of connections through which knowledge about new campaign practices and their uses is disseminated constantly across national borders by independent consultants for economic reasons, by ideologically kindred political parties for political reasons, and by the mass media to aspiring political candidates and interested members of the public worldwide. (Swanson & Mancini, 1996, p. 250)

However, the diffusion of U.S. campaign and marketing techniques is not a linear process leading to a uniform standardization of Western European cam-

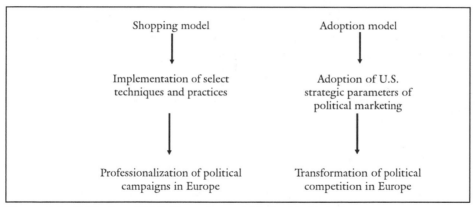

Figure 6.1. Diffusion of U.S. Campaign and Marketing Techniques

paign practices. The most widespread model of adopting select innovative practices and techniques from U.S. election campaigns seems to be the "shopping model." Certain techniques and organizational routines of professional campaign practices in the United States are imported, modified according to the national context of political competition, and implemented. For example, in its campaign for the 1998 Bundestag elections, the German SPD set up a campaign coordination center, similar to the one New Labour created for the British campaign for the House of Commons in 1997. Both were clearly inspired by the "war room" of the 1992 Clinton campaign. The shopping model primarily focuses on concrete and down-to-earth techniques that can easily be implemented in the national context while maintaining the specifically European campaign style and philosophy of political marketing. The idea is to optimize and professionalize national campaign know-how without adopting the cornerstones of strategic marketing logic as practiced by U.S. consultants and political managers.

The "adoption model," on the other hand, probably will have a greater impact on political competition in Western European democracies. In this case, the European observers show a tendency to adopt those strategic parameters of U.S. consultants and campaign experts that are deemed to define future developments better than the traditional European campaign and marketing philosophy. The adoption of the U.S. parameters of political marketing signifies a turning away from conventional organizational campaigning and programmatic-ideological continuity and a focus on candidate image, strategic product development, target marketing, news management, spin control, permanent campaigning, and negative advertising. If the shopping model means a transition from "amateur campaigning" or "labor-intensive campaigning" to "capital-intensive campaigning" (Farrell, 1996), then the adoption model means breaking the European tradition of party-centered campaigning and a clear transition from "party logic" to "media logic" (Figure 6.1) (Blumler, 1990).

The consequences of the adoption model are reinforced by the structural trends in media-centered democracies (Figure 6.2) in which political competition increasingly presents itself as a "competitive struggle to influence and control

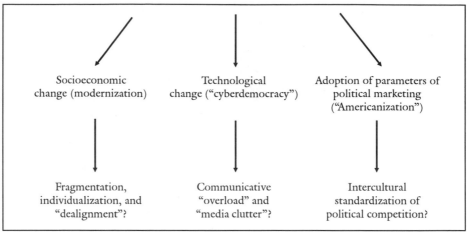

Figure 6.2. Structural Trends in "Media-Centered Democracies"

popular perceptions of key political events and issues through the major mass media" (Blumler, 1990, p. 103). Gurevitch and Blumler (1990) have created a transnational pattern to describe the current lines of tension in media-centered democracies:

> High prioritization of media strategies and tactics among would-be political influentials.
>
> "Source professionalization," or the extensive involvement in the promotion of such strategies and tactics of publicity advisers, public relations experts, and campaign consultants.
>
> Intensification of conflict between politicians and journalists, with the former seeing themselves as engaged in competitive struggle, not only with their political opponents but also with the press itself, over which version of political reality will reach the public.
>
> Increased uneasiness among journalists about their own role in political communication given their vulnerability to news management.
>
> Increased circulation of negative messages about political actors, events, and decisions. (p. 323)

The data from our European Consultants Survey allow us to make a cautious evaluation of the impact of the orientation toward the United States as the "role model of campaigning." For this purpose, the consultants and political managers interviewed were divided into two groups. We termed one group "U.S.-connected experts." The members of this group are characterized by their relatively greater proximity to and acquaintance with the practices of U.S. campaigning. They are persons who answered the question "What is absolutely necessary in order to be a professional marketer?" by stating that both regular observations of campaigns in the United States and knowledge of the latest U.S. campaign literature are absolutely necessary professional standards. Thus defined, the U.S.-connected experts constituted roughly 40% of our sample of European consultants and

TABLE 6.7 Differences in the Definition of the Concept of "Political Marketing" (percentages)

	Very Close to Respondent's Personal Political Practice		
	U.S. Connected *(n = 20)*	Unconnected *(n = 30)*	Percentage Point Difference
a. Long-term communication to build up competence and trust among the electorate	58	58	0
b. Direction for strategic planning and development of campaigns	53	48	5
c. Technique for the definition of and communication with strategic target groups	45	25	20
d. Management technique for political communication	40	40	0

SOURCE: European Consultants Survey, Question 7.

political managers. Respondents who considered neither criterion as essential for the standards of a professional political marketer were assigned to the group of the "unconnected experts," that is, consultants or party managers whose professional self-definitions are not based primarily on their knowledge of U.S. marketing practices.

The first interesting differences in the professional self-definition of the U.S.-connected experts and the unconnected experts were revealed in the respondents' understanding of the concept of political marketing (Table 6.7). Most of the unconnected experts saw political marketing as long-term communication to build up competence and trust in their professional practice. For the U.S.-connected experts, targeting marketing (a technique for the definition of and communication with strategic target groups) was nearly as important as relationship marketing (building up competence and trust).

In the evaluation of the success factors of a political campaign, there also were interesting differences between the U.S.-connected and unconnected interviewees (Table 6.8). European consultants who lean strongly toward U.S. standards in their professional self-definition considered strategic news management and spin control as more important success factors than did unconnected experts. Analogously, the personalities and images of the candidates, as well as their strategic positioning in relation to the competitors, were more important for the U.S.-connected respondents than for the unconnected interviewees. The U.S.-connected experts saw the available campaign budget as especially important, thus orienting themselves to the model of cost-intensive, high-tech/multimedia campaigning, whereas the unconnected experts considered the campaign budget a secondary factor in the success of a campaign.

As expected, the most striking difference between the two groups was in their assessment of the importance of traditional party organizations. Whereas roughly

TABLE 6.8 Success Factors of a Campaign According to U.S.-Connected and Unconnected Experts (percentages)

	Factor Is Very Important		
	U.S.-Connected *(n = 20)*	*Unconnected* *(n = 30)*	*Percentage Point* *Difference*
1. Control over topics of mass media reporting	87	64	+23
2. Personality and image of the candidate	83	71	+12
3. Strategic positioning toward the competition	70	58	+12
4. Campaign budget	57	33	+24
5. Issues/thematic positions	41	37	+ 4
6. Information about expectations/motives of target groups	42	25	+17
7. Strong and effective party organization	17	37	−20
8. External advisers and campaign consultants	25	10	+15

SOURCE: European Consultants Survey, Question 5.

half of the unconnected experts saw an increase in the importance of national party organizations for parliamentary elections, approximately two thirds of the U.S.-connected respondents believed that the importance of party organizations will decrease over time. The two groups' evaluation of the importance of national party organizations for the selection of top candidates was diametrically opposed. Only one out of five U.S.-connected respondents assessed the role of national party organizations as very important, whereas three quarters of the unconnected interviewees attributed a very important role to national party organizations. Orientation toward U.S. campaign practices, regular observations of campaigns in the United States, and knowledge of the newest U.S. campaign literature obviously influence the professional self-definition of European consultants and political managers.

The data from our European Consultants Survey allow us to tentatively conclude that the U.S.-connected experts have already made the transition from the shopping model to the adoption model and have assimilated not only the occasional technical and organizational innovation but also the central strategic parameters of campaign logic in the United States into their professional self-definition. Orientation toward the modern model of campaigning (Swanson & Mancini, 1996) and the imperatives of the "modern publicity process" (Blumler, 1990), both highly developed in the United States, a textbook case of media-centered democracy, also have led to a surge of modernization and professionalization in the European practice of political marketing. This development is already evident in some countries (e.g., Great Britain, Germany, France, Italy) where it has influenced political campaign logic more strongly than in Scandinavian and Southern European countries.

APPENDIX

Interview Partners

Mario Ballerini (Italy), Ludger Beerfeltz (Germany), Rune Bjerke (Norway), Peter Boenisch (Germany), Michel Bongrand (France), Marc Bousquet (France), Jacob Broberg (Sweden), Simon Buckby (Great Britain), Antonio Dalle Rive (Italy), Michael Dolley (Great Britain), Pascal Drouhaud (France), Christian Dürig (Germany), David Farrell (Great Britain), Peter Frei (Switzerland), Andreas Fritzenkötter (Germany), Wolfgang Gibowski (Germany), Klaus Golombek (Germany), Roberto Grandi (Italy), Sepp Hartinger (Austria), Per Heister (Sweden), Volker Hoff (Germany), Manfred Kienpointner (Germany), Peer Krause-Kjair (Denmark), Bo Krogvig (Sweden), Michael Kronacher (Germany), Heinz Lederer (Austria), Susanna Loi (Italy), Claude Longchamp (Switzerland), Matthias Machnilg (Germany), Coordt von Mannstein (Germany), Konrad Maric (Austria), Marco Marturano (Italy), Arve Mathisen (Norway), Rainer Nick (Austria), Phil Noble (United States), Velipekka Nummikoski (Finland), Peter Radunski (Germany), Volker Riegger (Germany), Lothar Rolke (Germany), Peter Rumpold (Austria), José Luis Sanchez-Armelles (Spain), Jesus Sepulveda-Recio (Spain), Michael Strugl (Austria), Alec Taylor (Austria), Peter Ulram (Austria), Christos Valtarados (Greece), Hans-Joachim Veen (Germany), Matthias Wambach (Germany), Peter Westenthaler (Austria), and Werner Wolf (Germany).

References

Althaus, M. (1998). *Wahlkampf als Beruf: Die Professionalisierung der Political Consultants in den USA.* Frankfurt, Germany: Peter Lang Verlag.

Arterton, C. (1992). The persuasive art in politics: The role of paid advertising in presidential campaigns. In M. P. McCubbins (Ed.), *Under the watchful eye: Managing presidential campaigns in the television era.* Washington, DC: Congressional Quarterly Press.

Åsard, E. (1997, October). *Not so "Americanized" after all? A comparison of political campaign ads in Sweden and the United States.* Paper presented at the international conference on "Images of Politics," Amsterdam.

Betz, H.-G., & Immerfall, S. (Eds.). (1998). *The new politics of the right.* New York: Macmillan.

Blondel, J., Sinnott, R., & Svensson, P. (1997). Representation and voter participation. *European Journal of Political Research, 32,* 243-272.

Blumler, J. G. (1990). Elections, the media and the modern publicity process. In M. Ferguson (Ed.), *Public communication: The new imperatives.* London: Sage.

Blumler, J. G., Kavanagh, D., & Nossiter, T. J. (1996). Modern communications versus traditional politics in Britain: Unstable marriage of convenience. In D. L. Swanson & P. Mancini (Eds.), *Politics, media, and modern democracy: An international study of innovations in electoral campaigning and their consequences.* Westport, CT: Praeger.

Bongrand, M. (1993). *Marketing politique* (2nd ed.). Paris: PUF.

Bowler, S., & Farrell, D. M. (Eds.). (1992). *Electoral strategies and political marketing.* New York: St. Martin's.

Bowler, S., & Farrell, D. M. (1998, June). *The internationalization of election campaign consulting.* Paper prepared for presentation at the conference on "Campaign Consultants in Election Campaigns," Washington, DC.

Butler, D., & Kavanagh, D. (1997). *The British general election of 1997.* London: Macmillan.

Butler, D., & Ranney, A. (Eds.). (1992). *Electioneering: A comparative study of continuity and change.* Oxford, UK: Clarendon.

Butler, P., & Collins, N. (1994). Political marketing: Structure and process. *European Journal of Marketing, 28,* 19-34.

Collins, N., & Butler, P. (1996). Positioning political parties: A market analysis. *Harvard International Journal of Press/Politics, 1,* 63-77.

Corrado, A., & Firestone, C. (Eds.). (1996). *Election in cyberspace: Toward a new era in American politics.* Washington, DC: Congressional Quarterly Press.

Dalton, R. J. (1996). *Citizen politics: Public opinion and political parties in advanced Western democracies.* Chatham, NJ: Chatham House.

Dalton, R. J. (1997). *Citizens and democracy: Political support in advanced industrial democracies.* Mimeo, University of California, Irvine.

Dombrowski, I. (1997). *Politisches marketing in den massenmedien.* Wiesbaden, Germany: Universitats-Verlag.

Farrell, D. M. (1996). Campaign strategies and tactics. In L. LeDuc, R. G. Niemi, & P. Norris (Eds.), *Comparing democracies: Elections and voting in global perspective.* Thousand Oaks, CA: Sage.

Farrell, D. M. (1998). Political consultancy overseas: The internationalisation of campaign consultancy. *Political Science & Politics, 31,* 171-178.

Farrell, D. M., Kolodny, R., & Medvic, S. K. (1998, September). *The political consultant/political party relationship: A health warning for representative democracy or a welcome advance.* Paper prepared for delivery at the annual meeting of the American Political Science Association, Boston.

Faucheux, R. (1994, February). The political pro poll: An exclusive C & E survey of America's political consultants and party leaders. *Campaigns & Elections,* pp. 58-59.

Franklin, B. (1994). *Packaging politics: Political communications in Britain's media democracy.* London: Edward Arnold.

Franklin, M., Mackie, T. T., & Valen, H. (Eds.). (1992). *Electoral change: Responses to evolving social and attitudinal structures in Western countries.* Cambridge, UK: Cambridge University Press.

Friedenberg, R. V. (1997). *Communication consultants in political campaigns: Ballot box warriors.* Westport, CT: Praeger.

Grafe, P. (1994). *Wahlkampf: Die Olympiade der demokratie.* Frankfurt, Germany: Eichborn Verlag.

Gurevitch, M., & Blumler, J. G. (1990). Comparative research: The extending frontier. In D. L. Swanson & D. Nimmo (Eds.), *New directions in political communication: A resource book.* Newbury Park, CA: Sage.

Harris, P. (Ed.). (1996). Political marketing [special issue]. *European Journal of Marketing, 30*(10/11).

Inglehart, R. (1997). *Modernization and postmodernization: Cultural, economic, and political change in 43 societies.* Princeton, NJ: Princeton University Press.

Irwin, G. A. (1997, October). *Americanisation: Infiltration or imitation?* Paper presented at the international conference on "Images of Politics," Amsterdam.

Iyengar, S., & Reeves, R. (Eds.). (1997). *Do the media govern? Politicians, voters, and reporters in America.* Thousand Oaks, CA: Sage.

Johnson-Cartee, K. S., & Copeland, G. A. (1997a). *Inside political campaigns: Theory and practice.* Westport, CT: Praeger.

Johnson-Cartee, K. S., & Copeland, G. A. (1997b). *Manipulation of the American voter: Political campaign commercials.* Boulder, CO: Westview.

Kaid, L. L. (1997, October). *Political television advertising: A comparative perspective on styles and effects.* Paper presented at the international conference on "Images of Politics," Amsterdam.

Kaid, L. L., Gerstlé, & Sanders, K. (Eds.). (1991). *Mediated politics in two cultures: Presidential campaigning in the United States and France.* New York: Praeger.

Kaid, L. L., & Holtz-Bacha, C. (Eds.). (1995). *Political advertising in Western democracies.* Thousand Oaks, CA: Sage.

Katz, R. S., & Mair, P. (Eds.). (1992). *Party organisations: A data handbook on party organisations in Western democracies, 1960-1990.* London; Sage.

Katz, R. S., & Mair, P. (Eds.). (1994). *How parties organize: Change and adaption in party organisations in Western democracies.* London: Sage.

Kavanagh, D. (1995). *Election campaigning: The new marketing of politics*. Oxford, UK: Oxford University Press.

Kavanagh, D. (1996). New campaign communications: Consequences for British political parties. *Harvard International Journal of Press/Politics, 1,* 60-76.

Kavanagh, D. (1997, October). *Media and elections: An unhappy marriage?* Keynote address delivered at the international conference on "Images of Politics," Amsterdam.

Kolodny, R., & Logan, A. (1998). Political consultants and the extension of party goals. *Political Science & Politics, 31,* 155-169.

Lane, J.-E., & Ersson, S. O. (1996). *European politics*. London: Sage.

LeDuc, L., Niemi, R. G., & Norris, P. (Eds.). (1996). *Comparing democracies: Elections and voting in a global perspective*. Thousand Oaks: Sage.

Luntz, F. L. (1988). *Candidates, consultants, and campaigns: The style and substance of American electioneering*. Oxford, UK: Basil Blackwell.

Maarek, P. J. (1992). *Communication et marketing de l'homme politique*. Paris: LITEC.

Maarek, P. J. (1995). *Political marketing and communication*. London: John Libbey.

Mair, P., Müller, W. C., & Plasser, F. (Eds.). (in press). *Party responses to the erosion of voter loyalties in Western Europe*. London: Routledge.

Mancini, P., & Mazzoleni, G. (Eds.). (1995). *I media scendono in campo: Le elezioni politiche 1994 in televisione*. Nuova ERI, Turin, Italy.

Mauser, G. A. (1989). Marketing and political campaigning: Strategies and limits. In M. Margolis & G. A. Mauser (Eds.), *Manipulating public opinion*. Pacific Grove, CA: Brooks/Cole.

Mazzoleni, G. (1996). Patterns and effects of recent changes in electoral campaigning in Italy. In D. L. Swanson & P. Mancini (Eds.), *Politics, media, and modern democracy: An international study of innovations in electoral campaigning and their consequences*. Westport, CT: Praeger.

Medvic, S. K. (1998). The effectiveness of the political consultant as a campaign resource. *Political Science & Politics, 31,* 150-154.

Negrine, R., & Papathanasopoulos, S. (1996). The "Americanisation" of political communication: A critique. *Harvard International Journal of Press/Politics, 1,* 45-62.

Newman, B. I. (1994). *The marketing of the president: Political marketing as campaign strategy*. Thousand Oaks, CA: Sage.

Nimmo, D., & Combs, J. E. (1992). *The political pundits*. Westport, CT: Praeger.

Norris, P. (1997). The rise of postmodern political communication. In P. Norris (Ed.), *Politics and the press: The news media and their influence*. Boulder, CO: Lynne Rienner.

O'Shaughnessy, N. I. (1990). *The phenomenon of political marketing*. London: Macmillan.

Østergaard, B. S. (Ed.). (1997). *The media in Western Europe: The Euromedia handbook*. London: Sage.

Petracca, M. P., & Wiercioch, C. (1988, April). *Consultant democracy: The activities and attitudes of American consultants*. Paper presented at the annual conference of the Midwest Political Science Association, Chicago.

Pew Research Center. (1998). *The views of political consultants* [survey]. Washington, DC: Author.

Pfetsch, B. (1998). Government news management. In D. A. Graber, D. McQuail, & P. Norris (Eds.), *The politics of news, the news of politics.,* Washington, DC: Congressional Quarterly Press.

Pfetsch, B., & Schmitt-Beck, R. (1994). Amerikanisierung von Wahlkämpfen? In M. Jäckel & P. Winterhoff-Spurk (Eds.), *Politik und Medien*. Berlin: Vistas Verlag.

Radunski, P. (1996). Politisches kommunikationsmanagement: Die Amerikanisierung der wahlkämpfe. In B. Stiftung (Ed.), *Politik überzeugend Vermitteln: Wahlkampfstrategien in Deutschland und den USA*. Gütersloh, Germany: Bertelsmann-Stiftung.

Sabato, L. J. (1981). *The rise of political consultants: New ways of winning elections*. New York: Basic Books.

Scammell, M. (1995). *Designer politics: How elections are won*. New York: St. Martin's.

Scammell, M. (1997). *The wisdom of the war room: U.S. campaigning and Americanisation*. Research Paper No. R-17, Joan Shorenstein Centre.

Schmitt, H., & Holmberg, S. (1995). Political parties in decline? In H.-D. Klingemann & D. Fuchs (Eds.), *Citizens and the state* (Beliefs in Government, Vol. 1). Oxford, UK: Oxford University Press.

Schönbach, K. (1996). The "Americanization" of German election campaigns: Any impact on the voters? In D. L. Swanson & P. Mancini (Eds.), *Politics, media, and modern democracy: An international study of innovations in electoral campaigning and their consequences*. Westport, CT: Praeger.

Selnow, G. W. (1994). *High-tech campaigns: Computer technology in political communication.* Westport, CT: Praeger.

Semetko, H. A., Blumler, J. G., Gurevitch, M., & Weaver, D. (1991). *The formation of campaign agendas: A comparative analysis of party and media roles in recent American and British elections.* Hillsdale, NJ: Lawrence Erlbaum.

Shea, D. M. (1996). *Campaign craft: The strategies, tactics, and art of political campaigns.* Westport, CT: Praeger.

Swanson, D. L., & Mancini, P. (Eds.). (1996). *Politics, media, and modern democracy: An international study of innovations in electoral campaigning and their consequences.* Westport, CT: Praeger.

Thurber, J. A. (1998). The study of campaign consultants: A subfield in search of theory. *Political Science & Politics, 31,* 145-149.

Thurber, J., & Nelson, C. (Eds.). (1995). *Campaigns and elections American style.* Boulder, CO: Westview.

Wilson, G. K. (1998). *Only in America: The politics of the United States in comparative perspective.* Chatham, NJ: Chatham House.

Wring, D. (1997, October). *Americanization: Journalistic rhetoric or political reality?* Paper presented at the international conference on "Images of Politics," Amsterdam.

7

Political Consulting

Bridging the Academic and Practical Perspectives

The "bad boys and girls" of politics, political consultants, have convinced politicians that running a successful campaign begins with hiring the right consultant. These days, it is rare for serious candidates to run for office without the advice of professionals. Having savvy consultants on board no longer is perceived as just a distinctive advantage; rather, it is perceived as a necessity. It is this growing trend that has seen the political consulting business become a $6 billion industry (Churchill, 1996).

Consultants have gradually taken on a large and central role in the practice of American democracy. Yet, their influence on the political campaigning process has not been the focus of much academic inquiry or theory development. Several scholars have lamented the lack of research on political consultants (Medvic & Lenart, 1997; Sabato, 1981). When contrasted with the impressive amount of academic research on the political process, political communication, and campaigning more generally, an obvious gap in our understanding of political consulting is exposed.

This chapter bridges the academic and practical perspectives toward political consulting. Those who do consulting for a living and those who study political marketing rarely communicate. However, there are interesting overlaps between the academic and practical perspectives. Consultants' view of their craft—their

AUTHOR'S NOTE: I thank the following for reading and commenting on earlier drafts: Steven H. Chaffee, Steven J. Collins, Christiane M. Pagé, and Richard M. Perloff.

theories and guiding values—is the focus of this chapter. More specifically, consultants' use of research and theories of political communication is compared to what academic research tells us about political campaigning.

Level of Campaign

The attention of the political marketing scholar's gaze usually is federal election campaigns, specifically the campaigns for president of the United States. The presidential election is the highest visibility election, arguably the most important and the one that generates the most interest from the media and the public. In addition, massive amounts of data often are available for secondary analysis, so the scholar need not spend precious grant money conducting original survey research.

The practitioner, on the other hand, works on elections at the local, state, and federal levels. These include city council races, mayoral campaigns, school board elections, judicial races, state legislative races, county office elections, gubernatorial races, and other statewide office elections as well as congressional and presidential campaigns.

Thinking About Campaigns

The political scholar is interested in developing theory and advancing science, exploring communication processes and effects, and identifying contingent conditions (i.e., trying to understand political communication effects by documenting who is affected, when, under what circumstances, for how long, etc.). The practitioner is interested in winning elections.

Scholars develop elaborate theories of political campaigns and voter choice. Newman and Sheth's (1987) comprehensive theory of political choice behavior postulates that voters' choice is driven by up to five values: issues, social imagery, candidate personality, situational effects, and epistemic value (i.e., curiosity factor). This theory includes rational decision making, stereotyping, emotion, and consumer behavior concepts.

Popkin (1991) views voters more as rational decision makers. His theory of "low-information rationality" or "gut reasoning" is derived from the Columbia University voting studies conducted during the 1940s, the economic theories of Anthony Downs, and cognitive psychology. Low-information rationality involves the use of information shortcuts and rules of thumb. Information that people need in their everyday lives also is the information that voters can and do apply to their political judgments and choices.

Scholars also develop models of successful campaigning. Newman's (1994) model of political marketing integrates four components—candidate focus, the marketing campaign, the political campaign, and environmental forces—to explain how presidential candidates can be marketed. Consultants, however, are quick to point out that candidates are not "sold" like bars of soap (Perloff & Kinsey, 1992). Newman (1994) agrees that candidates cannot be marketed like a product. Candidates are "service providers," and Newman's model of political marketing reflects the distinction.

In a similar expression of wisdom, Popkin (1991) distinguishes between a product choice and a vote choice. The voter is viewed as a "public investor," not as a private consumer. Public choices (the vote) differ from private choices. The incentives to gather information are different in each instance. This influences when information gathering will be searching and when it will be superficial, when voter beliefs will be accurate and when they will be misleading, and when those beliefs will be stable and when they will be transient.

Practitioners' most common complaint about scholars is that they lack insight and political instincts. Scholars understand the scientific method, and their studies are rigorous. However, they do not "know" politics. How could they? Those who study political marketing are not involved in nearly as many campaigns as are practitioners. This might be true, but many scholars have some practical political campaign experience. Their campaign work might be mostly pro bono, but nonetheless, scholars often are experienced in the real world of politics.

Sharing of Knowledge

The academic research on political marketing and political communication is widely available. Political scholars are members of the "community of scholars." It is their "job" to conduct research and to share their results with other scholars through journals and conferences.

Consultants' work, on the other hand, is proprietary. It is proprietary in the sense that consultants do not want to give away their "trade secrets" and their means of making a living to other consultants. In addition, their work is proprietary because political consultants need to know all about their candidates—the good, the bad, and the ugly—and their candidates could be hurt if others were privy to that information. Consultants use their intimate knowledge of candidates to strategize successful campaigns—to understand what to emphasize, what to protect or head off, and what is not necessary to respond to if used in an attack by the opposition. This proprietary information is not easily pried from the "hold them close to the vest" consultant.

What we do know about consultants typically comes from the popular press. We also glean insight from a handful of participant observation studies (Diamond & Bates, 1988; Kern, 1989; Luntz, 1988; Nesbit, 1988), an empirical assessment study of consultants' beliefs about voters and the impact of political advertising (Perloff & Kinsey, 1992), and *Campaigns & Elections* (the trade magazine for political consultants).

Types of Consultants

There are several types of consultants involved in political campaigns—media consultants, direct mail specialists, fund-raisers, general strategists, and pollsters.

Media consultants generally are responsible for the overall message development and the electronic campaign media. They write the scripts and produce the television and radio ads. The media consultants also are responsible for determining the ad "buys"—decisions on when, where, and how often to broadcast each ad. The decision on ad placement is an important strategy that has received little attention from scholars (West, Kern, Alger, & Goggin, 1995).

Direct mail specialists focus on the writing, producing, and dissemination of campaign literature. Examples of typical campaign literature include a simple letter from the candidate or supporter; a postcard highlighting an issue or two; a simple one-color, two-fold brochure; and a multicolor, multipage booklet outlining the candidate's experience, issue positions, and the like.

Fund-raisers are the consultants responsible for developing plans for, and raising the money necessary to run, a political campaign. These consultants use techniques ranging from neighborhood "coffee klatches" and simple mail appeals for campaign contributions to elaborate fund-raising dinners with celebrity hosts.

General strategists concentrate on the large picture, the integration of all phases of the campaign. The general strategist often is the campaign manager directing when and where volunteers will distribute literature and pulling the other consultants together for strategy sessions.

The pollster s the person responsible for conducting public opinion research to help gude the campaign strategy, planning, and ongoing evaluation. For this reason, the pollster is arguably the most important consultant on the team. All other activities stem from the interpretation of the research data. Benchmark polls often are the first manifestation of a campaign, conducted a year or more in advance of Election Day. These early polls test potential issues, gauge the strengths and weaknesses of the candidate and the candidate's opponent(s), determine target audiences and how best to reach them based on their communication behaviors, and reveal the themes that will strike a responsive chord and inspire attention to the campaign.

Whereas all consulting specialties are integral to the successful political campaign, it is the media consultant who tends to be featured in the popular press and in post-Election Day interviews. The media consultant waxes eloquent about the brilliant strategy, message construction, and voter targeting that led to the victory, yet he or she rarely mentions that all these things were driven and put on track by the research and pollster.

Even if media consultants do not publicly recognize the important role of the pollster in political campaigns, the campaign managers and candidates do. A recent study of congressional elections noted that polling experts were the most widely used consultants (Medvic & Lenart, 1997). This was true for incumbents, open seats, and challengers and was true for both Democrats and Republicans.

Media consultants were the second most frequently used consultants, followed by fund-raisers.

The Message

The message, "your rationale for running [and] the most compelling reasons why voters should vote for you and not for the opposition," must be communicated in all campaign activities (Faucheux, 1994, p. 46). Consultants overwhelmingly believe that it is the strength of the candidate's message that makes the difference between winning and losing. A recent survey of 200 political consultants (Pew Research Center, 1998) found that consultants view the quality of the candidate's message as more important than the amount of money available to the campaign, the partisan makeup of the district, and the candidate's abilities as a campaigner. By a margin of three to one, consultants "think that a weak message is a bigger barrier to electoral success than a weak campaigner" (p. 2).

Winning in most elections requires convincing more than half of those voting to vote for your candidate. This often requires persuasion, "an activity or process in which a communicator attempts to induce a change in the belief, attitude, or behavior of another person or group of persons through the transmission of a message" (Perloff, 1993, p. 14). Research is used for developing persuasive messages and understanding how to send them. Polling and focus group research is the bread and butter of campaign research methods.

However, a more sophisticated understanding of political marketing and persuasive messages requires consultants to gain "access to the voter's subjectivity" (Gopoian & Brown, 1988, p. 114). Having access to the voter's subjectivity means having a deep understanding of the voter's point of view and information that allows the creation of a powerful message to strike a responsive chord when communicating with voters. This requires a methodology for the scientific study of subjectivity—Q methodology (Brown, 1980, 1986; McKeown & Thomas, 1988; Stephenson, 1953). The insight gained from a scientific approach to political subjectivity is impressive. Scholarly illustrations with candidate imagery can be seen in the works of Nimmo and Savage (1976) and Thomas and Baas (1996). Subjectivity and campaign issues are addressed by Mansfield and Hale (1986) and Wattier (1986).

Practitioners have been slow to embrace the notion of gaining access to the voter's subjectivity. Practitioners' use of subjective measures still is somewhat limited. This might be because of the sophisticated statistical analysis required by Q methodology (i.e., Q factor analysis) or the hesitation to move away from the staple campaign research techniques of polls and focus groups. Some examples of practitioners' use of Q methodology include the selection of a campaign slogan (Kinsey, 1991) and the selection of campaign issues (Kinsey & Kelly, 1989).

Once a message is developed, it must be received by the voters. Many media consultants advocate an often followed theory of campaigning—redundancy works. "Keep the message local and simple, and say it to as many voters as possible and as many times as possible. When you think you've said it enough, say it again" (Wachob & Kennedy, 1997, p. 33). From this perspective, repetition is deemed to be the "secret to success" (Sweitzer & Heller, 1996). This view of redundancy—repetition is an unbounded good—represents a folk belief in the business. As some studies show (e.g., Becker & Doolittle, 1975), there is a repetition threshold in audiences; after so many repetitions, the intended effect washes out and might even boomerang, causing an adverse effect for a given audience member.

From an academic perspective, repetition and redundancy are achieved within and across channels of communication. Practitioners' view of these ideas is similar to the "convergence" view outlined by Chaffee (1982): "Convergence occurs when different channels provide the same or overlapping messages" (p. 60).

Consultants do not rely on one medium to get their messages out. Political consultants believe in a mixed communication approach to campaigning, that is, the use of multiple channels of communication.

Channels of Communication

Let us take a closer look at practitioners' views toward campaigns as manifested through various channels of communication. Practitioners generally believe in the power of media. Perloff and Kinsey (1992) note that consultants believe that ads manipulate people into feeling a certain way about a candidate. Anecdotal evidence of powerful media effects abound in the political trade magazines (Struble, 1997). But Murray Fishel, president of Grassroots Political Campaigns and founder and former director of the nation's first graduate program in political campaign management, notes that consultants do not scientifically test to see whether what they have done had the intended effect. "Consultants' views are colored by whether or not they've won the election. . . . If a consultant wins an election, then he or she thinks [that what he or she] did was effective" (Fishel, personal communication, October 14, 1998).

Television

Consultants believe that a candidate generally should spend most of his or her campaign funds on television advertising (Perloff & Kinsey, 1992). This, of course, assumes that the campaign is large enough to even consider the use of television. Some smaller, lower visibility elections do not have the budgets necessary to buy television ads. Instead, these lower level campaigns focus on door-to-door campaigning and targeted voter contacts (Fishel, 1983a, 1983b; Fishel & Kinsey, 1984).

Commercials are valuable weapons for candidates (West, 1993). West's review of research on televised political advertising found that commercials influence how voters learn about candidates, help them identify priorities, and influence their standards of assessment and attributions of blame. Perhaps nothing has inspired more political communication research than has television advertising.

Political advertising on television has an exalted place in the study of political communication. Perhaps this is so, in part, because it might be the "most feared form of political communication" (Kaid, 1981, p. 249). Political ads often are a source for campaign issue information (Patterson & McClure, 1976). Political advertising is hard to avoid (Chaffee & Choe, 1981) and is easily accessible (Atkin, Bowen, Nayman, & Sheinkopf, 1973).

Kern (1989) suggests that there is a consensus among consultants that the best ads evoke powerful feelings and trigger emotional associations. Perloff and Kinsey (1992) found that consultants believe that the best way in which to reach voters is to appeal to their emotions. It is not surprising, then, that when Kaid and Davidson (1986) interviewed producers of political ads in three statewide races, they concluded that "producers for both challengers and incumbents are preoccupied with reaching the voter/viewer emotionally." However, consultants also believe that advertising on television exerts a great deal of impact on cognitive learning (Perloff & Kinsey, 1992).

The academic literature tends to support consultants' beliefs in this area. Television is a good source of information about candidates' personal qualities or image (McLeod, Glynn, & McDonald, 1983; Sue, 1994). In addition, television is relied on heavily for news about politics (Roper, 1983), and people gain political knowledge about issues from watching television news (Chaffee & Yang, 1990; Drew & Reeves, 1980; Iyengar, Peters, & Kinder, 1982; Leshner & McKean, 1997).

There has been a substantial increase in practitioners' use of targeted video for direct voter contact. In a discussion of new channels of mass communication, Ron Faucheux, editor and publisher of *Campaigns & Elections* magazine, notes that there was an 82% increase of targeted video use during the 1996 election cycle over the prior cycle because, like television, "videos work" (Faucheux, 1997).

Newspapers

Consultants also see communication behavior differences in voters. These differences generally follow well-established academic research. For example, one Arkansas political consultant explains, "Newspaper advertising appeals to the rational voter" (Russell, 1996, p. 42). Newspapers are seen as reaching other important voter groups such as ticket splitters, swing voters, opinion leaders, elites, and the elderly (Wilson, 1994).

Newspapers often are compared to television in political communication studies (Chaffee and Schleuder, 1986), and more often than not, newspaper use is found to be more highly correlated with political knowledge (of various sorts) than is television use. After an extensive review of the academic literature on how citizens acquire knowledge for their political decisions, Chaffee and Kanihan (1997) conclude,

> The contribution of television news and the newspaper to political knowledge tends to be complementary. People seek information via print, but uniformed individuals

who are not especially seeking information learn more from television. . . . The newspaper covers political content in greater depth and is used more by those who are more involved in politics. (p. 427)

Direct Mail

Direct mail is a medium used extensively by political consultants yet infrequently studied by political communication scholars. Targeted direct mail, palm cards, brochures, and other voter contact devices are designed and written with an audience in mind. Audience segmentation is fundamental in literature distribution. For example, one consultant segments the voters into four types—noninterested voters, casual voters, interested voters, and policy "wonks" (i.e., the most informed voters in the electorate)—to maximize campaign effectiveness by designing literature that will appeal to each type (Hildebrand, 1996). Others use direct mail to "narrowcast" or send messages that are made particularly salient to voters based on the choice of targeting strategy—voter history, political party, geography, age, gender, renter or home owner, income, race/ethnicity, or sexual orientation (Terris & Jaye, 1995).

Radio

Radio is another medium widely used in political campaigns. Consultants see radio as "the most intimate of all media—its impact is significant because the images it conveys exist in the listeners' minds" (Sweitzer & Heller, 1996, p. 41). It also works best "when it is used to complement television, and . . . by putting the two together, your campaign will earn far more bang for your media dollar than if you relied solely on [television]" (p. 41).

Radio also is viewed as perhaps the best medium for negative ads. It is seen as less confrontational than the "in-your-face" television. Consultants feel that they can produce a harder hitting message on radio than on television because there is less chance for negative voter backlash (Goodman, 1995).

The academic research on radio reveals a slightly different picture. People rarely cite radio as a main source or as the most believable source when presented with conflicting news accounts (Gentry, 1987; Griffiths & Goodman, 1989), and radio listening rarely seems to predict political knowledge or behavior (Garramone & Atkin, 1986).

Interpersonal Communication

Interpersonal communication is another technique incorporated into most campaigns. One consultant reminds the candidate that every person he or she meets is an investment in the candidate's future. "Whether it's a factory tour, a trade show, or a county fair, meeting the public face-to-face is important not only to the person you're meeting but also to those watching your interaction" (Peck, 1996, p. 47).

The academic research on interpersonal communication reveals that political discussions often are viewed as a supplement to mass media (Chaffee, 1982), and studies have shown correlations between use of newspapers or television and frequency of political discussions (Shaw, 1977). Mass media facilitate political discussions (Schudson, 1978; Chaffee, 1972). In addition, when mass media information about campaigns is scarce, people will use interpersonal discussions to obtain political information (Trent & Friedenberg, 1983). However, interpersonal channels rarely are seen as a "primary news source" (Robinson & Levy, 1986, p. 161).

Downs (1957) suggests that political discussions are a necessary part of a democracy. He argues that people do not feel confident about what they have learned from the media until they have discussed it with others. Even when voters know about an issue, they might be unaware of the many relations between government and their lives; interpersonal discussion helps to make those connections. Katz and Lazarsfeld (1955) had high hopes for the role of interpersonal discussions in politics. They viewed interpersonal discussion as a way for people to "generate" and "maintain" common ideas fundamental for democratic society. They saw interpersonal discussion as providing "anchorage points" for individual opinions, attitudes, and values. The sharing of opinions and attitudes was viewed as the key to understanding the role of mass media in society. They saw the encouraging signs of political participation and not disabling evidence of media-driven atomistic society.

Interpersonal communication is a major component of Popkin's (1991) theory of the reasoning voter. Voters rely on the opinions of others as a shortcut in evaluating the information they receive from media. "The campaign and the media only send the initial messages; until these messages have been checked with others and validated, their full effects are not felt" (p. 46).

Political discussions tend to take one of two forms: heated discussions between people with divergent views or cooler discussions between those sharing similar views (MacKuen, 1990). Although much evidence suggests that people are more willing to talk about politics in compatible rather than contentious situations (Beck, 1991; Glynn & McLeod, 1984; Huckfeldt & Sprague, 1987; Noelle-Neumann, 1974, 1984), people also do engage in political discussions with disagreeing partners (Huckfeldt & Sprague, 1987; Straits, 1991).

Chaffee (1982) notes that the process of discussion includes "finding out, telling, asking, and being asked" (p. 67). People are important information sources (Robinson & Levy, 1986). Political discussions are characterized by persuasion attempts and opinion change more often than are nonpolitical discussions (Greenberg, 1975).

The earliest election campaign studies suggested that interpersonal discussion might be more influential than mass communication (Berelson, Lazarsfeld, & McPhee, 1954; Lazarsfeld, Berelson, & Gaudet, 1944). Kinsey and Chaffee (1996) noted a strong correlation between people talking about the campaign and a decrease in then President George Bush's job rating. Their survey of California voters during the 1992 primary election campaign, for example, found that talking to others about the campaign was the strongest predictor of a decrease in Bush's job rating in an analysis that included television news and advertising, newspapers, and radio. Pfau, Diedrich, Larson, and Van Winkle (1995) found similar powerful interpersonal communication effects. In a survey of Democratic primary voters in South Dakota, interpersonal communication was a particularly strong predictor of voters' attitudes toward candidates and the likelihood of voting for a particular candidate. However, a follow-up study by Pfau and his colleagues (1997) during a Republican primary 4 years later found no interpersonal communication effects.

World Wide Web

The Internet or World Wide Web is just starting to be used in political campaigns. Unlike the other forms of communication, it is not yet a very good voter contact tool. The Internet's real value might lie in simply providing more information to voters, particularly the information seekers. One political consultant, who specializes in the Internet, says that heavy Internet users today "are about 70[%] registered voters, mostly under 35 [years old], well educated, politically independent, and even a bit cynical, individualistic, tending toward libertarian" (Noble, 1996, pp. 27-28). A recent survey of 270 candidates found that campaigns use the Internet simply as another information source, providing information about the candidate (Faucheux, 1998).

Negative Campaigning

The recent focus of scholarly attention to political advertising has been on negative campaigning. Driven by normative views of the democratic process, several scholars have critiqued the so-called "dirty politics" prevalent in much of today's political advertising (Ansolabehere & Iyengar, 1995; Jamieson, 1992; Johnson-Cartee & Copeland, 1991).

Practitioners understand and believe much of the criticism of negative campaigning. For example, Perloff and Kinsey (1992) found that consultants believe that negative ads intensify voters' distrust of politicians. However, consultants do not believe that once a negative atmosphere is in place, positive media do not work. Negative campaigning does not poison the campaign water, from a consultant's perspective. This is one reason why practitioners feel that a candidate can attack the opposition even before he or she has made a positive impression on voters. In addition, and presumably for the same reasons, practitioners do not believe that it is necessary to avoid negative advertising during the early phases of a campaign (Perloff & Kinsey, 1992).

It is doubtful that consultants will stop using negative ads anytime soon. Consultants strongly believe that negative ads can exert a powerful impact on voters' attitudes toward a candidate and that people remember negative information better than they do positive information (Perloff & Kinsey, 1992), a view well established in attitude theory and research (Kanouse & Hanson, 1972). In addition, even if one did not want to "go negative," sometimes campa' drawn into that exact mode. Consultants strongly believe that a candidat afford to ignore attacks by an opponent (Perloff & Kinsey, 1992).

Some consultants have turned their understanding of voters' disgust of negative campaigning into a strategic advantage. One pollster tested the impact of a "clean campaign pledge" in a congressional benchmark poll. The clean campaign pledge gave the candidate an opportunity to draw a clear distinction between him and his opponent (an opponent who refused to sign the clean campaign pledge) without "going negative" (Wilson & St. Claire, 1997).

Consultants continue to use negative ads but have developed rules of thumb for their use; the statements of fact about one's opponent must be accurate, and a fair representation about the "public" record of one's opponent must be given (Doak, 1995; Goodman, 1995; Schlackman & Douglas, 1995). Because of "adwatch" journalism and the attention of academics, negative campaigning is now "cleaner and fairer. . . . Voters get more information, both good and bad, about political candidates" (Doak, 1995, p. 21). A recent study of adwatches suggests that we might see fewer of them in the future. Journalists might be assessing whether adwatches are worth the time, resources, and space devoted to them and whether producing adwatches is a "proper" role for the press to play in elections (Greer, 1998).

As Ansolabehere and Iyengar (1995), paying homage to V. O. Key's classic view of the electorate, correctly state, "Voters . . . are not fools, nor are they fooled by political advertising" (p. 63). Consultants know this, and they acknowledge that there are conditions under which ads are unlikely to work such as when voters have strong views about an issue or a candidate (Perloff & Kinsey, 1992). Still, they believe that people can acquire a lot of information from watching political ads (Perloff & Kinsey, 1992). Consultants' views also reflect some of the scholarly research on theory of attitude change, for example, that individuals are likely to take a person's physical appearance into account under low involvement (Perloff, 1984; Petty & Cacioppo, 1986).

Concluding Remarks

Practitioners do not generally read the academic literature on political marketing or talk about the "theory" of their craft. However, even though not articulated, all consultants are guided by theories. Many of these theories revolve around powerful media effects. Some are supported by the academic literature, and some are not.

This chapter has started the process of bridging the academic and practical perspectives toward political consulting. Those who do consulting for a living and those who study political marketing rarely communicate. This is a shame. As we have seen, there are interesting overlaps between the academic and practical perspectives. Yet, there still are gaps in our understanding. Given the important role that consultants play in the practice of American democracy, more communication between the academy and the field might be fruitful.

A closer working relationship between consultants and scholars could help the advancement of knowledge in this area and could lead to interesting research questions. For example, scholars could get involved in the early stages of a campaign and design research for the empirical assessment of the practice. Scholars could evaluate and test some of the campaign activities or theories that consultants never test. Scholars could focus more attention on the whole range of local and state campaigns in which consultants are involved.

Consultants have much experience in the practice of political campaigning. This experience and practice could help inform the political marketing scholars research and point to areas that perhaps the scholars would not see without the consultants' help.

References

Ansolabehere, S., & Iyengar, S. (1995). *Going negative: How attack ads shrink and polarize the electorate*. New York: Free Press.

Atkin, C. K., Bowen, L., Nayman, O. B., & Sheinkopf, K. (1973). Quality versus quantity in televised political ads. *Public Opinion Quarterly, 37,* 209-224.

Beck, P. A. (1991). Voters' intermediation environments in the 1988 presidential contest. *Public Opinion Quarterly, 55,* 371-394.

Becker, L. B., & Doolittle, J. C. (1975). How repetition affects evaluations of and information seeking about candidates. *Journalism Quarterly, 52,* 611-617.

Berelson, B., Lazarsfeld, P. E., & McPhee, W. N. (1954). *Voting*. Chicago: University of Chicago Press.

Brown, S. R. (1980). *Political subjectivity: Applications of Q methodology in political science*. New Haven, CT: Yale University Press.

Brown, S. R. (1986). Q technique and method: Principles and procedures. In W. D. Berry & M. S. Lewis-Beck (Eds.), *New tools for social scientists: Advances and applications in research methods* (pp. 56-76). Newbury Park, CA: Sage.

Chaffee, S. H. (1972). The interpersonal context of mass communication. In F. G. Kline & P. J. Tichenor (Eds.), *Current perspectives in mass communication research* (pp. 95-120). Beverly Hills, CA: Sage.

Chaffee, S. H. (1982). Mass media and interpersonal channels: Competitive, convergent, or complementary? In G. Gumpert & R. Cathcart (Eds.), *Inter/media: Interpersonal communication in a media world* (2nd ed.). New York: Oxford University Press.

Chaffee, S. H., & Choe, S. Y. (1981). Newspaper reading in longitudinal perspective: Beyond structural constraints. *Journalism Quarterly, 58,* 201-211.

Chaffee, S. H., & Kanihan, S. F. (1997). Learning about politics from the mass media. *Political Communication, 14,* 421-430.

Chaffee, S. H., & Schleuder, J. (1986). Measurement and effects of attention to media news. *Human Communication Research, 13,* 76-107.

Chaffee, S. H., & Yang, S. (1990). Communication and political socialization. In O. Ichilov (Ed.), *Political socialization, citizenship education, and democracy* (pp. 137-157). New York: Columbia University, Teachers College Press.

Churchill, A. (1996, February). Marketing political consultants: Follow your own advice. *Campaigns & Elections,* pp. 52-53.

Diamond, E., & Bates, S. (1988). *The spot: The rise of political advertising on television* (rev. ed.). Cambridge, MA: MIT Press.

Doak, D. (1995, July). Attack ads: Rethinking the rules. *Campaigns & Elections,* pp. 20-21.

Downs, A. (1957). *An economic theory of democracy*. New York: Harper & Row.

Drew, D., & Reeves, B. (1980). Learning from a television news story. *Communication Research, 7,* 95-120.

Faucheux, R. (1994, May). The message. *Campaigns & Elections,* pp. 46-49.

Faucheux, R. (1997, June). Creative video ideas: Inexpensive ways to produce campaign messages. *Campaigns & Elections,* pp. 31-32.

Faucheux, R. (1998, September). How campaigns are using the Internet: An exclusive nationwide survey. *Campaigns & Elections, 19,* 22-26.

Fishel, M. (1983a, Spring). Electoral targeting, part 1: For the do-it-yourself campaign. *Campaigns & Elections,* pp. 11-19.

Fishel, M. (1983b, Summer). Electoral targeting, part 2: For the do-it-yourself campaign. *Campaigns & Elections,* pp. 4-19.

Fishel, M., & Kinsey, D. (1984, Winter). Electoral targeting, part III: Computerizing the process. *Campaigns & Elections,* pp. 61-66.

Garramone, G. M., & Atkin, C. K. (1986). Mass communication and political socialization: Specifying the effects. *Public Opinion Quarterly, 50,* 76-86.

Gentry, F. (1987, April). Radio news in the television age. *Radio-Television News Directors Association Communicator,* pp. 18-19.

Glynn, C. J., & McLeod, J. M. (1984). Public opinion du jour: An examination of the spiral of silence. *Public Opinion Quarterly, 48,* 731-740.

Goodman, A. (1995, July). Producing TV: A survival guide. *Campaigns & Elections,* pp. 22-24.

Gopoian, J. D., & Brown, S. R. (1988). Public opinion and campaign strategy. In S. Long (Ed.), *Political behavior annual* (Vol. 2, pp. 103-124). Boulder, CO: Westview.

Greenberg, S. R. (1975). Conversations as units of analysis in the study of person influence. *Journalism Quarterly, 52,* 128-131.

Greer, J. (1998, August). *The birth of adwatches: Political advertising becomes front-page news.* Paper presented at the annual meeting of the Association for Education in Journalism and Mass Communication, Baltimore, MD.

Griffiths, T. A., & Goodman, R. I. (1989). Radio news directors' perception of involvement in advertising and sales. *Journalism Quarterly, 66,* 600-606.

Hildebrand, S. (1996, May). Writing and designing campaign literature: How to reach the four voter groups. *Campaigns & Elections,* pp. 38-39.

Huckfeldt, R., & Sprague, J. (1987). Networks in context: The social flow of political information. *American Political Science Review, 81,* 1197-1216.

Iyengar, S., Peters, M. D., & Kinder, D. R. (1982). Experimental demonstrations of the "not-so-minimal" consequences of television news programs. *American Political Science Review, 76,* 848-858.

Jamieson, K. H. (1992). *Dirty politics: Deception, distraction, and democracy.* New York: Oxford University Press.

Johnson-Cartee, K. S., & Copeland, G. A. (1991). *Negative political advertising: Coming of age.* Hillsdale, NJ: Lawrence Erlbaum.

Kaid, L. L. (1981). Political advertising. In D. D. Nimmo and K. R. Sanders (Eds.), *Handbook of political communication* (pp. 249-271). Beverly Hills, CA: Sage.

Kaid, L. L., & Davidson, D. K. (1986). Elements of videostyle: Candidate presentation through television advertising. In L. L. Kaid, D. D. Nimmo, & K. R. Sanders (Eds.), *New perspectives on political advertising* (pp. 184-209). Carbondale: Southern Illinois University Press.

Kanouse, D. E., & Hanson, L. R. (1972). *Negativity in evaluations.* Morristown, NJ: General Learning Press.

Katz, E., & Lazarsfeld, P. E. (1955). *Personal influence.* New York: Free Press.

Kern, M. (1989). *30-second politics: Political advertising in the eighties.* New York: Praeger.

Kinsey, D. (1991). Selecting a winning campaign slogan. *Operant Subjectivity, 15,* 1-10.

Kinsey, D., & Kelly, T. C. (1989). Mixing methodologies: An aid in developing Q samples. *Operant Subjectivity, 12,* 98-102.

Kinsey, D. F., & Chaffee, S. H. (1996). Communication behavior and presidential approval: The decline of George Bush. *Political Communication, 13,* 281-291.

Lazarsfeld, P. E., Berelson, B., & Gaudet, H. (1944). *The people's choice.* New York: Duell, Sloan, & Pearce.

Leshner, G., & McKean, M. L. (1997). Using TV news for political information during an off-year election: Effects on political knowledge and cynicism. *Journalism and Mass Communication Quarterly, 74,* 69-83.

Luntz, F. I. (1988). *Candidates, consultants, and campaigns: The style and substance of American electioneering.* London: Basil Blackwell.

MacKuen, M. (1990). Speaking of politics: Individual conversational choice, public opinion, and the prospects for deliberative democracy. In J. A. Ferejohn & J. H. Kuklinski (Eds.), *Information and democratic processes* (pp. 59-99). Urbana: University of Illinois Press.

Mansfield, M. W., & Hale, K. (1986). Uses and perceptions of political television: An application of Q technique. In L. L. Kaid, D. D. Nimmo, & K. R. Sanders (Eds.), *New perspectives on political advertising* (pp. 268-292). Carbondale: Southern Illinois University Press.

McKeown, B. F., & Thomas, D. (1988). *Q methodology* (Quantitative Applications in the Social Sciences series, No. 66). Newbury Park, CA: Sage.

McLeod, J. M., Glynn, C. J., & McDonald, D. G. (1983). Issues and images: The influence of media reliance in voting decisions. *Communication Research, 10,* 37-58.

Medvic, S. K., & Lenart, S. (1997). The influence of political consultants in the 1992 congressional elections. *Legislative Studies Quarterly, 22,* 61-77.

Nesbit, D. D. (1988). *Videostyle in Senate campaigns: The managers look at '84.* Dover, DE: Auburn House.

Newman, B. I. (1994). *The marketing of the president: Political marketing as campaign strategy.* Thousand Oaks, CA: Sage.

Newman, B. I., & Sheth, J. N. (1987). *A theory of political choice behavior.* New York: Praeger.

Nimmo, D. D., & Savage, R. L. (1976). *Candidates and their images: Concepts, methods, and findings.* Pacific Palisades, CA: Goodyear.

Noble, P. (1996, July). Net the vote. *Campaigns & Elections,* pp. 27-28.

Noelle-Neumann, E. (1974). The spiral of silence: A theory of public opinion. *Journal of Communication, 24*(2), 43-51.

Noelle-Neumann, E. (1984). The spiral of silence: A response. In K. R. Sanders, L. L. Kaid, & D. Nimmo (Eds.), *Political communication yearbook* (pp. 43-65). Carbondale: Southern Illinois University Press.

Patterson, T. E., & McClure, R. D. (1976). *The unseeing eye: The myth of television power in national elections.* New York: Putnam.

Peck, L. (1996, April). Face-to-face campaigning: How to work a room. *Campaigns & Elections,* pp. 47-48.

Perloff, R. M. (1984). Political involvement: A critique and a process-oriented reformulation. *Critical Studies in Mass Communication, 1,* 146-160.

Perloff, R. M. (1993). *The dynamics of persuasion.* Hillsdale, NJ: Lawrence Erlbaum.

Perloff, R. M., & Kinsey, D. (1992). Political advertising as seen by consultants and journalists. *Journal of Advertising Research, 32*(3), 53-60.

Petty, R. E., & Cacioppo, J. T. (1986). The elaboration likelihood model of persuasion. In L. Berkowitz (Ed.), *Advances in experimental social psychology* (Vol. 19, pp. 123-205). New York: Academic Press.

Pew Research Center. (1998). *The views of political consultants: Don't blame us.* Available on the Internet: http://www.people-press.org/con98rpt.htm.

Pfau, M., Diedrich, T., Larson, K. M., & Van Winkle, K. M. (1995). Influence of communication modalities on voters' perceptions of candidates during presidential primary campaigns. *Journal of Communication, 45*(1), 122-133.

Pfau, M., Kendall, K. E., Reichert, T., Hellweg, S. A., Lee, W., Tusing, K. J., & Prosise, T. O. (1997). Influence of communication during the distant phase of the 1996 Republican presidential primary campaign. *Journal of Communication, 47*(4), 6-26.

Popkin, S. L. (1991). *The reasoning voter: Communication and persuasion in presidential campaigns.* Chicago: University of Chicago Press.

Robinson, J. P., & Levy, M. R. (1986). Interpersonal communication and news comprehension. *Public Opinion Quarterly, 50,* 160-175.

Roper, B. W. (1983). *Trends in attitudes toward television and other media: A twenty-four year review.* New York: Roper Organization.

Russell, J. (1996, July). Homespun campaigning: How a tough race for a regional judgeship was won with newspaper ads and a well-timed media mix. *Campaigns & Elections,* pp. 42-43.

Sabato, L. J. (1981). *The rise of political consultants: New ways of winning elections.* New York: Basic Books.

Schlackman, R., & Douglas, J. B. (1995, July). Attack mail: The silent killer. *Campaigns & Elections,* pp. 25-26, 62, 67.

Schudson, M. (1978). The ideal of conversation in the study of mass media. *Communication Research, 5,* 320-329.

Shaw, E. F. (1977). The interpersonal agenda. In D. L. Shaw & M. E. McCombs (Eds.), *The emergence of American political issues: The agenda-setting function of the press* (pp. 69-88). St. Paul, MN: West.

Stephenson, W. (1953). *The study of behavior: Q-technique and its methodology.* Chicago: University of Chicago Press.

Straits, B. C. (1991). Bringing strong ties back in interpersonal gateways to political information and influence. *Public Opinion Quarterly, 55,* 432-448.

Struble, K. (1997, June). Creative video ideas: Inexpensive ways to produce campaign messages. *Campaigns & Elections,* pp. 24-27, 32.

Sue, V. (1994). *The role of television reliance in evaluating the personal qualities of political candidates.* Ph.D. dissertation, Department of Communication, Stanford University.

Sweitzer, D., & Heller, D. (1996, May). Radio tips: 10 ways to give your campaign ads more punch. *Campaigns & Elections,* pp. 40-41.

Terris, M., & Jaye, E. (1995, September). The art of the self-mailer: How to grab voter attention step-by-step. *Campaigns & Elections,* pp. 34-35.

Thomas, D. B., & Baas, L. R. (1996). The postelection campaign: Competing constructions of the Clinton victory in 1992. *Journal of Politics, 58,* 309-331.

Trent, J. S., & Friedenberg, R. V. (1983). *Political campaign communication: Principles and practices.* New York: Praeger.

Wachob, B., & Kennedy, A. (1997, February). Beating B-1 Bob: How underdog Democrat Loretta Sanchez ended Bob Dornan's congressional career. *Campaigns & Elections,* pp. 32-34.

Wattier, M. J. (1986). Discovering campaign themes: Reinforcement with Q method. *Election Politics, 3,* 20-23.

West, D. M. (1993). *Air wars: Television advertising in election campaigns, 1952-1992.* Washington, DC: Congressional Quarterly.

West, D. M., Kern, M., Alger, D., & Goggin, J. M. (1995). Ad buys in presidential campaigns: The strategies of electoral appeal. *Political Communication, 12,* 275-290.

Wilson, C., & St. Clair, G. (1997, April). The runner's last lap: How Jim Ryun refused to go negative, lost a big lead, then recovered in the final week to win a U.S. House seat. *Campaigns & Elections,* pp. 34-36.

Wilson, T. W. (1994, March). Newspaper advertising: The comeback medium. *Campaigns & Elections,* pp. 35-36.

8

Managing Volunteers

Times Have Changed—Or Have They?

GREGORY G. LEBEL

Once upon a time, campaigns were simple, home-grown affairs. Even presidential contenders with high-stakes candidacies refrained from big, expensive, manipulative productions as they assumed the role of candidate. A century ago, presidential candidates considered it undignified to appear to be actively seeking nomination and election. Rather, they awaited the people's decisions, always orchestrated by the network of precinct workers and bosses. But these affairs were relatively inexpensive and low profile.

Candidates for other national offices relegated the running of their campaigns to local political party operatives or members of their staffs. A congressman's chief of staff or other tested and trusted aide would shift every electoral cycle into the campaign manager role, assembling the usual cadre of local party pros to engage in what essentially amounted to a get-out-the-vote effort. Likewise, challengers sought the help of their local party leaders in bringing the party faithful to the polls on Election Day. Campaign budgets were low, and often general visibility was lower still. Campaigns were inside affairs run by close confidants of the candidate and fueled by party money, party staff, party prospects, and other inside resources. Virtually no one from the outside got into these affairs.

From bids for seats on local school boards and city councils to races for governorships and the U.S. Congress, campaigns were run relatively cheaply, often with low profiles, and they were developed and carried out by small bands of citizens whose skills included good political intuition and the ability to develop a message and organize a handful of party regulars and volunteers. The need for skills in polling and analysis, targeting, media production and placement, and targeted direct mail was unheard of until just recently.

With the dawning of the television age and the candidate-centered campaign, everything changed. Men and women seeking their party's nomination no longer pleaded their cases before the party regulars and elders. They increasingly went directly to the voters. As party identification and commitment weakened among voters, would-be officeholders at all levels sometimes even downplayed their partisan connections with an eye toward the vote-rich trove of those registered as independents and crossover voters.

Professionals Dominate

Since the 1950s, professional political consultants have increasingly replaced party figures and transplants from incumbents' staffs in running most (if not all) aspects of campaigns. This situation exists in presidential, U.S. Senate, U.S. House, gubernatorial, and big-city mayoral races. It also is the case in legislative races in larger states, and increasingly consultants have taken over some roles even in local races such as city council and school board contests.

As recently as Gerald Ford's presidential campaign in 1976, Ford would admit to only limited knowledge of his own direct mail consultants' activities and complained about the incursion of consultant-driven direct mail efforts for some time after leaving office. Candidates often feared that public awareness of the involvement of "Madison Avenue types" would negatively affect their public images. Now, the acquisition of top-rated, nationally known consultants is treated by the campaign as both a tactical goal and a major press event, cited as an early indicator that the candidate is indeed serious enough to attract the top echelon of the professional consultant pool. Names such as Pat Caddel, Bob Squier, Lance Tarrance, Peter Hart, Robert Goodman, Lee Atwater, and Roger Ailes have struck fear in the hearts of would-be candidates when they were added to their opponents' rosters of "hired guns." Incumbents likewise use news of consultant signings as a means to scare off potential challengers; the specter of sheer firepower being amassed against them in the person of media experts, pollsters, and direct mail wizards whose campaign win columns are as well documented as, and often touted more loudly than, their candidates' voting records can frighten even veteran politicians.

How does this change the makeup and needs of the campaign in its day-to-day activities? Whereas political professionals have a major impact on the mega-campaign, the day-to-day campaign continues to unfold as it always has. While consultants are hammering out overall campaign strategies and tinkering with tactical refinements, the daily grind of campaigns must and does go on. Someone must be there quite literally to unlock the doors each morning at the headquarters. Someone must ensure that the candidate's schedule is distributed to the candidate, staff, and media. Someone must precede the candidate to campaign events to ensure that the campaign maximizes the value of each moment of candidate time. Someone must be in contact with constituencies and potential voters to shore up supporters and persuade those who have not yet made up their minds. Someone

must be organizing and carrying out door-to-door and telephonic voter identification and "get out the vote" (GOTV)[1] activities in conjunction with direct mail
and media efforts. Someone must be updating the campaign Web site and writing
and distributing media releases. In short, if there is no one on the ground to make
the most of the strategic and tactical efforts of high-paid consultants and senior
campaign staff, then much of it is wasted effort.

There is a story in political circles about the presidential candidate whose
campaign consultants had developed an elaborate and impressive detailed daily
progression of activities based on the strategic plan developed at the top. Every
major decision maker in the campaign was given a copy many inches thick. For
each day, specific projects were listed. The computer program required that state
campaign officials respond to daily queries generated by the computer regarding
the status of various projects. Campaign officials in the early primary and caucus
phase would review and update the document with fierce regularity. In the final
days of the campaign in one early battleground state, a national staffer arrived at
the state headquarters from Washington, D.C., to assess the campaign's prospects
on the ground. But when the national operative arrived, there was no evidence
of GOTV activity. Upon investigation, he discovered that the state staff had been
simply telling the computer what it wanted to hear to avoid questions. In a closet
in the headquarters sat boxes containing thousands (and thousands of dollars
worth) of computer-generated indexed walking cards (used for voter identification in door-to-door canvassing efforts) intended for voter persuasion and
identification efforts. The boxes were unopened. Nothing had been done. No one
had been made responsible for seeing that this specific activity had actually taken
place. The national campaign's efforts were lost for lack of follow-through on the
ground. No one had been responsible and accountable for carrying out the
nationally developed strategy where it mattered.

In another past primary contest in the state of Maine, the importance of
volunteer-centered activity became painfully clear for one well-heeled, would-be
member of Congress. The candidate in question, running for the Republican
nomination in an open seat for the U.S. Senate, had it all—high name recognition
as a member of a long-standing and prominent Maine family and lots of money
thanks to a family fortune that was at the candidate's disposal. As primary day
drew near, the candidate far outflanked the hapless opponent in money spent,
broadcast ad time, and (of course) in the polls. The candidate was so far in the
lead as the campaign approached its final weeks that the campaign consultants
and staff made the decision to forgo any on-the-ground GOTV effort. There was,
in their minds, simply no need. No volunteers had been called in to list likely and
probable supporters, no door-to-door reminders of the approaching election were
envisioned, and no phone banks were put in place. Primary day dawned sunny
and unseasonably warm for the state of Maine in June. The day was so balmy, in
fact, that citizens headed for the outdoors as soon as they could. The combination
of the unseasonable weather and every assurance that their candidate could not
lose distracted too many of the candidate's supporters from voting. And with no
mechanism in place to remind them and exact their promise to get to the polls,
the campaign officials could only sit and watch their supporters—and their

chances—dissipate. The opponent, on the other hand, had scores of volunteers calling, reminding, driving, and re-calling identified supporters throughout the day. The result surely is not in question at this point. The unbeatable candidate lost in a record low-turnout election in which the opponent capitalized on a well-organized, volunteer-based GOTV effort.

This miscalculation on the part of the candidate's consultants was based on a misunderstanding of the volatility of voter turnout and a failure to take advantage of the availability of committed supporters who could have made the difference in the election.

Campaign Organizations and Staffing Issues

It has been said that campaign organization is a contradiction in terms, and most campaigns prove that maxim to be true. By their very nature, political campaigns defy traditional organizational rules. Unlike other structured organizations such as for-profit businesses and nonprofit groups, campaigns do not have the luxury of time in developing staffing patterns, building mutual confidence, and putting together the right mix of talents, experience, and personalities that most longer range organizations take for granted. Instead, campaign managers must cobble together a staff comprised of people with varying skill levels who might or might not have ever met, let alone worked together before. These people must form a cooperative and focused working unit, develop and implement complex projects, and analyze and react to a fast-changing environment—all under often intense media scrutiny—within a matter of a few short weeks. When all that is accomplished (to some degree), the entire organization functions for less than a year before it disbands after the election.

But these temporary organizations share something critical to their survival with more long-term entities. They must develop systems for maximizing two key factors: communication and accountability. As with any organization of individuals, all of whom are working toward the same goal, each individual must be able to communicate both vertically and horizontally. Managers and supervisors must be able to express to their subordinates expectations and time lines for task completion. Subordinates must have the tools to comprehend their instructions from above and the means to interact with their coworkers in completing those tasks. Equally critical, this communication system must afford managers the ability to hold each other and subordinates accountable for the efficient and effective completion of assigned tasks. This accountability, built on a solid communication system, is the basis for quick, effective decision making and the necessary assessment and fine-tuning of campaign projects and goals.

But campaigns differ from other organizations in another important way. They rarely are made up entirely of people who receive remuneration for their efforts. Indeed, most campaigns are comprised primarily of individuals who provide their services on a purely voluntary basis. This distinction requires that campaign managers have a thorough understanding of the dynamics of volunteer management. Paid staff, too, must recognize the peculiar dynamics that exist in volunteer-dominated organizations.

Categories of Volunteers

Volunteers come in many guises. Highly skilled, politically savvy party stalwarts are as likely to appear at the candidate's door as are first-time volunteers who might have a personal commitment to the candidate and other individuals with no previous campaign experience.

A particular type of volunteer is not the individual who signs up to work in the headquarters on Wednesday evenings between 6:30 and 9:30. The earliest volunteers often are those who are sought after by the campaign and who agree to sit on one of several campaign committees. These committees are the seed from which campaign structure will sprout in time. Their members have specific needs and interests that must be recognized and dealt with by senior campaign staff. The three most visible and crucial committees in any campaign are the finance committee, the steering committee, and the "kitchen cabinet."

The finance committee is composed of individuals who are committed to raising campaign funds for the candidate. These individuals usually have considerable personal worth of their own, some of which they are willing to contribute to the campaign. In addition, finance committee members bring to the table contacts with other financially well-off individuals. These contacts will, if all goes well in the course of the campaign, be parlayed into additional large contributions to the campaign coffers.

The steering committee is populated by individuals whose medium is not cash but rather political influence. Men and women whose opinions are respected in the community are targets of any steering committee. These individuals, in joining a candidate's steering committee, are willing to let their names, reputations, and contacts be used to bring on other influential opinion leaders. They are the stuff of "inside baseball" politics in that their pull is mainly among other influential individuals in the political and media communities.

Finally, the so-called kitchen cabinet is made up of the candidate's closest and most trusted advisers. These often are women and men who have been through past campaigns with the candidate and whose loyalty and political instincts have been tested by time. Members of the kitchen cabinet need unparalleled access to the candidate and often double as key advisers once the successful candidate moves into political office.

What members of these committees all share is their volunteer status. They are aboard for exactly the same reasons as are canvassers, phone bankers, letter writers, and envelope stuffers. They believe in what the candidate stands for, and they believe that the candidate can win. They are investing their money, contacts, time, and prestige in an individual's quest for political office. In return, they expect different things from paid staff, just as their counterparts do in the less rarefied levels of the campaign. They believe that they are acting in the public good, expect access to the candidate, and crave the excitement of a political campaign.

The second important set of volunteers the campaign must seek out and enlist are those who will fill key positions within the campaign staff. These volunteers most often are drawn from the ranks of party regulars and staffers from earlier campaigns. The campaign always should be on the lookout for new faces in this echelon of volunteers because they constantly require replenishment. Volunteers at this level are particularly difficult to line up when there is a large number of races on the ballot. Candidates and their campaigns often begin the campaign season competing with each other for people with experience to fill key campaign positions.

These positions vary somewhat, but they always require more than a casual connection with the campaign apparatus. County, precinct, and district organizers, as well as finance and legal staff, often are drawn from these ranks. These individuals, by virtue of their often lengthy involvement in electoral politics, bring with them not only their expertise but also their own networks of other players in the district or state. Because of this, pivotal individuals often are the object of intense competition during the early days of the campaign. The decision by a well-known and respected individual to contribute his or her efforts, expertise, and influence to a particular candidate sends a message to party regulars and to electorally oriented issue advocacy groups that this is a candidacy that must be taken seriously. These individuals have coattails as well. They bring with them, either overtly or de facto, other volunteers at high levels as well as below. Their worth in the early stages of the campaign is difficult to overstate.

The third level of volunteers consists of those people whose specific high-level political experience is minimal or nonexistent. If recruited properly, nurtured wisely, and treated well, these volunteers will be not only the load-bearing structure that holds much of the campaign together but also the raw stuff of future upper level volunteers. The prudent manager constantly is on the lookout for new blood—volunteers whose innate ability, interest, and skills render them prime candidates for promotion within the volunteer ranks. Campaign managers should be willing to try out volunteers in higher stakes positions if they are to build the organization with the depth and flexibility necessary to wage a successful campaign. The campaign's investment here is measured in time and attention. Campaign managers are well advised to set challenging, measurable, short-term goals and to track closely the progress of the volunteers in question. Successful completion of one task should lead to another and another until one has achieved a level of confidence in the volunteer's ability to take on a substantive and ongoing campaign role.

Rank-and-file volunteers bring to any campaign a level of enthusiasm that should not be underestimated. Most voters will have face time with only one of these volunteers. An enthusiastic, helpful, articulate encounter is second only to meeting the candidate or the candidate's family in its ability to persuade voters. But volunteer enthusiasm must be nurtured, or else it will wane and die and the volunteer will vanish. There are three important aspects of this nurturing that the campaign must be prepared to handle: planning, recruitment, and management.

Planning

Successful use of volunteers requires early and ongoing and rigorous planning. How one recruits volunteers, what motivates them, and what they do once they have been lured into the campaign have not changed that much in the past 20 years. It still is pretty low-tech stuff at heart. But new technology enhances recruiting and tracking efforts and has added new needs to the tasks the manager asks volunteers to undertake.

Before seeking out the first volunteer, the manager must spend time developing a volunteer plan. Volunteers are a scarce resource that must be used efficiently and wisely if the campaign is to maximize their benefit. The manager or volunteer coordinator must use the campaign plan to develop a slate of volunteer tasks with detailed goals, directions, time lines, and evaluation components. These tasks should be developed in conjunction with key campaign staff who are responsible for field, media, fund-raising, GOTV, visibility, phone banking, and other labor-intensive projects that will draw on the campaign's human capital. Once the tasks are detailed and placed on a calendar, each manager must make an assessment of the number of volunteers necessary to meet set goals in the time allotted. For example, a canvass of 10,000 households to be completed in 2 weeks will require considerably more volunteers than will a phone bank that will occur over a 6-week period. The volunteer coordinator must know what volunteers the campaign needs and when it needs them. Once projects have been developed and set into the campaign calendar, then—and only then—volunteer recruitment can begin in earnest.

Recruitment

But where to find these people? Volunteers come in all shapes, sizes, levels of skill, types of interests, and levels of motivation. There are some logical first steps in recruiting those who will provide a best fit with one's campaign needs. The manager should look first to friends of the candidate and friends of campaign staff. They are most likely to share both the campaign's vision and the belief in the candidate's viability. But these individuals, although high on commitment, might be rather low on needed skills. The manager should look next to party regulars and individuals who have worked in past campaigns. They will bring know-how but might require convincing that the candidate is the one steed to whom they should hitch their proverbial wagons. This combination often provides the core volunteer list from whom one will build outward. Networking from these individuals can offer a wealth of new prospects. Everyone who joins the campaign should, as their first project, identify and recruit their friends and colleagues. Nothing else will do.

Once this process is in place, the manager should turn to those whose interest in the campaign is driven by other demands and interests that are further from the manager's core interests. Students often are looking for volunteer opportunities either to fulfill course requirements or to beef up their resumés for future reference. Colleges should continually be included in recruiting efforts, keeping in mind that early in the semester is more lucrative than the end of the semester. Fortunately, most general election campaigns are coming together as fall sessions start and are over before they must compete with end-of-term papers and examinations. High school students can prove to be helpful volunteers as well.

Students in the 11th and 12th grades often are sufficiently mature and interested in the political process to be of help. They are tireless additions to door-to-door efforts and provide high levels of excitement at campaign events.

Volunteers should be recruited at every opportunity. Tapping into holiday card lists, fellow members of organizations, and even alums of the candidate's college must not be overlooked. The development of a solid base of volunteer support is one of the first good indicators of the campaign's likely success. Conversely, the manager's inability to build such a core should serve as a red flag.

Once the volunteer core is in place, the manager should begin to expand it and never stop. Volunteers are everywhere; they are simply waiting to be asked. At every campaign event or gathering, the manager should make sure that someone is assigned to recruiting new volunteers. Every request for financial support should include the opportunity to offer other types of support as a volunteer. The campaign's Web site must prominently feature a volunteer recruitment page that pitches volunteers on the campaign, gathers volunteer information, and prompts an immediate and specific reply from the campaign.

The campaign must develop a compelling message to entice volunteer support. This message is a version of the campaign's general message—in essence, its case for electing the candidate. The case is the campaign's guiding vision. It explicates who the candidate is and why voters should vote for him or her. The message to potential volunteers is a variation on this central component of the candidacy. Volunteers are like voters in that they are attracted to public figures who express similar views on issues and offer appealing solutions to the perceived challenges facing voters. Each volunteer recruited will come initially because he or she has been touched by some aspect of the message. The candidate's reason for being in the race must be clear and compelling for it to work as a recruiting tool. And it *must* work.

This message can and should be expanded on to maximize the recruiting appeal to specific segments of the population. Older people likely will be interested in one's stand on health care and social security, whereas young parents might be most swayed by one's thoughts on children's issues and education policy. The manager should make sure that the targeted supporters hear the strongest message that can be put forth so as to increase their interest, excitement, and sense of investment in the campaign. But volunteers also are like investors; they are being asked to invest a uniquely valuable commodity in the campaign—their time. Like potential financial contributors, potential volunteers must believe that their investment will pay off, that is, result in a winning campaign. So, volunteers will be attracted to candidates with whom they agree and whom they believe can be successful. The challenge to the campaign from the candidate on down is to attract, convince, and secure commitments from these individuals based on the twin pillars of the candidate's case and prospects of election.

Once the manager has aroused their interest, he or she should make it easy for them to commit. Volunteer sign-up cards should be ubiquitous. Campaign literature, tables at events, volunteers helping at those events, and the campaign Web site all should feature volunteer sign-up forms. These forms are really quite simple. Names, addresses, and telephone numbers should be accompanied by fax numbers and e-mail addresses (at both work and home). The cards should ask the volunteers whether they can work at the headquarters or prefer to work at home, days and hours of the day available, and types of work of greatest interest. The manager should list the things needed most—data entry, phone work, office management, letter writing, and the like. The cards should be easy and clear.

Once these data are collected, the volunteers should be contacted before 24 hours elapse. The manager's excitement at the volunteers' interest will double their commitment instantly. One should determine early whether phone or e-mail is most effective for ongoing communication with each volunteer. The more people one can communicate with by e-mail, the faster and more efficient the effort will be. This initial contact should include a hearty "thank you" and a request for some specific action. The volunteer should be invited to come to a volunteer night at the headquarters, where the campaign will be discussed and volunteers assignments made. The manager should ask the volunteers to begin writing letters to voters in their precincts. Whatever the task or event, the manager should engage each volunteer during this conversation or else probably will lose him or her. Each contact one has with every volunteer is an opportunity to increase the volunteer's investment in the campaign effort. Each contact in which one fails to exact some further commitment of help diminishes that investment. Of course, these early requests also allow the manager to determine whether this individual will follow through on his or her commitments. Weeding out the unreliable before push comes to shove is an essential part of the recruitment effort. Three failures to make good on a promise should relegate a particular supporter to the back of the pile, assuming that the manager has done enough to engage the volunteer.

The manager never should stop recruiting. In fact, each volunteer should have as a prime task providing at least two more volunteers from his or her own circle of friends and associates.

Management

Okay, the manager has got the list of volunteers, it is growing every day, and the volunteers are ready to work. Now what? Now, the manager needs to know what his or her requirements are and when they will come due. A thorough campaign plan that includes a weekly resource budget is essential if the manager is to work smoothly with volunteers. The campaign's resource budget should include events, projects, and other campaign activities listed on a calendar. Included in the information should be a listing of resources needed to complete each entry. Resources include not only money and candidate time but also volunteer needs. The need for drivers, literature table staffers, petition promoters, sign makers, headquarters staff, letter writers, and telephone workers should be thought out and included on the resource budget for each day of the campaign. The manager should treat volunteers and staff just like one treats money in this aspect of the campaign. In fact, the manager will learn that they often are interchangeable. Where the manager can load up on volunteers, he or she often can save the cost of expensive professional services. I have overseen the preparation of huge amounts of food by volunteers to feed the media, convention delegates, and other volunteers where catering would have cost thousands of dollars. One can feed people with little money and find a way in which to engage volunteers whose only (but extremely significant) contribution is to cook.

In addition to the resource calendar, the campaign staff should know how to request volunteer help. A volunteer request sheet provides that mechanism. Now, the volunteer coordinator can match the campaign's needs to the preferences and availability of the volunteers. One effective means of organizing volunteers is with a "day captain" system. This works in part because the manager establishes teams of volunteers who work together on certain days of the week. Team members establish a camaraderie, and the manager delegates some of the detail responsibility to others.

First, the manager must designate daily volunteer team captains—one for each day of the week. These must be very reliable volunteers on whom the manager can depend completely. Each of these captains builds his or her own network of volunteers who are available on the day or night of the week for which the captain is responsible. At the beginning of the week, the manager should review the campaign's needs for that week and contact each captain with the volunteer needs for each day in the week as well as the nature of the work required. It is then the responsibility of the daily captain to provide the volunteers necessary to complete the day's volunteer tasks. This approach does not remove all responsibility from the volunteer coordinator. Careful assessment of the progress of each captain is essential, and ultimate responsibility for seeing that the campaign's staff needs are met remains with the coordinator. Furthermore, the manager must maintain a backup list of volunteers with special talents or more flexibility to get through the rough and thin spots.

This approach helps manage some, but not all, of one's volunteers and volunteer needs. Especially big or ongoing projects will require different approaches. Weekend door-to-door canvasses will require tapping into student volunteers or political clubs and organizations. A database with times, interests, and contacts will serve the manager well as he or she continually seeks to match resources with needs. Maximizing the effectiveness of a volunteer operation requires accurate, consistent, and ongoing record keeping. A computer database should be built that includes all the basic information about individuals who volunteer to work on the campaign. Name, address, telephone, fax, e-mail, and pager numbers all must be entered along with scheduling information. A complete individual record of volunteers' activities will allow the campaign to make quicker, more accurate decisions about who from the volunteer pool is best suited to each project. A lack of accurate and current information will result in mismatches, angry supporters, and lots and lots of *former* volunteers—not a recipe for campaign success in anyone's book.

Any new job requires a period of training, and volunteer jobs are no different. Volunteer coordinators must be prepared to provide a basic introduction to the campaign, its goals, and its procedures to all new volunteers. These individuals want to feel a part of an important undertaking. Treating them as full members of the staff is essential in developing a high level of support and reliability. If volunteers sense that the manager regards them as unnecessary, inconsequential, or even bothersome, then they will act accordingly by not showing up on time (or at all) or by doing marginal work (or worse). Volunteers also must understand that some of what they will hear around the headquarters is privileged information. They must be made to understand that nothing heard in the office should leave the office. Again, the best way in which to ensure this loyalty is to treat volunteers as valued, trusted members of the team. Equally important is one's insistence on discretion among paid staff. Sensitive information said in private is not subject to repetition by others. Campaign staffers who exercise care in what they say and where they say it are the best insurance against leaks.

Direct voter contact, which is best provided by a well-trained and vigorous volunteer staff, is less efficient as measured by the total number of voters and potential voters actually contacted, but it is quite effective on the individual voter. The key issue here is in targeting. Putting persuadable likely voters in contact with campaign volunteers through canvass operations is an excellent use of resources because of the cognitive difference between reading campaign literature and meeting and interacting with a representative of the candidate. This two-way communication personalizes the candidate and humanizes the campaign in ways that printed materials and broadcast advertising cannot. In addition, visibility in the field strongly promotes a bandwagon effect among voters in the district.

Volunteers can help a campaign make up for a lack of financial resources. They can offset lagging polling numbers by providing the campaign with a story to tell and an alternative means of measuring campaign organization and candidate appeal. The appearance of large numbers of volunteers in a community in a narrow time period can be parlayed into free media coverage that helps discredit low numbers in public opinion surveys. These volunteers also can provide the visibility that could be bought in broadcast time if the resources were available. In short, volunteers not only are a source of reliable labor but also can be incorporated into the campaign plan to augment and enhance other components of the campaign process.

In a primary campaign I was involved in several years ago, we mounted a massive 6-week, door-to-door canvass that included limited canvassing by the candidate himself. Each weekend, we deployed hundreds of young volunteer canvassers into the streets of swing precincts. At the same time, we ran radio ads featuring the voice of the candidate indicating that he would be going door to door the following day and expressing his interest in talking with voters. At the end of the weekend, we ran similar ads with the candidate thanking the citizens of the city involved for their hospitality, followed by a pitch for their support. Sandwiched between these two ads were two days of heavy "warm" canvassing[2] by volunteers and some door-to-door voter contact by the candidate himself. At the end of each weekend, voters in that part of the state were abuzz about the fact that our candidate had been in their neighborhood (whether or not he actually had been on their respective streets), raising his name recognition exponentially.

This points to another important aspect of volunteer efforts such as these. It is crucial that volunteer activities—canvassing, literature drops, visibility efforts, rallies, and the like—reinforce and be reinforced by the campaign's mass media efforts and general message. If the campaign is focusing on education, then at least some volunteer activities should be focused on school-related activities. Likewise, a large volunteer effort can be enhanced by making it a part of the campaign's media message for that week (as we did in that primary campaign).

There are particular tasks that volunteers are best suited to handle. They include warm canvasses, cold canvasses and literature drops, voter registration drives, absentee ballot efforts, phone banks, hosting and facilitating house parties and coffees, staffing candidate appearances and factory gates and commuter gathering points, and all GOTV efforts. These efforts are relatively short term, are task specific, and require a minimum of prior campaign experience, although this is not to say that volunteers can carry out any of these tasks without careful training and supervision by more experienced staff.

Even with proper training, things can go awry. In one recent campaign, I sent a group of eager college students forth to "leaflet" a neighborhood, that is, to deliver campaign literature to the homes in the area. I instructed these fresh volunteers on what they should and should not do, being careful to remind them that it is illegal to place campaign literature in U.S. mailboxes. After some time, one student came back for more, saying that he had placed the flyers on cars parked along the street adjacent to the headquarters. My worst fears were realized when I saw that he had placed the flyers on windshields of mourners attending services at the funeral home next door. He removed them promptly, and I never forgot to add this caution to my literature drop training. Training and oversight are keys to successful volunteer management.

Motivation

Volunteers in the late 1990s look very much the same as they did 20 years ago. They still are people who are attracted to active involvement in the political process through the electoral system. They are people who feel that they have some time to invest, are willing to devote that time without financial compensation, and believe that their involvement will make a difference in some way. Although it would be comforting to assume that people volunteer on political campaigns solely or chiefly because they believe that their efforts will make the world or the country a better place, this is not necessarily the case. A commitment to principle naturally is high on the list of motivations, but other driving forces include meeting new and interesting people, being in the center of important activity, improving personal contacts through close association with political figures and their circles, improving employment prospects through contacts, and even simply taking advantage of an opportunity to get out of the house.

These various motivations do not diminish the value or commitment of individual volunteers, but campaign staff should understand and recognize the different motivations and their manifestations. Keeping things on track requires ensuring that people's individual agendas do not get in the way of campaign goals and objectives. The smooth running of the campaign requires that personal needs take a back seat to the success of the general effort. Volunteers who habitually gravitate toward the candidate and tend to show up in snapshots on a regular basis probably are not focusing on the tasks assigned to them (unless, of course, they are working as personal aides to the candidate). Balance is key in assessing whether a volunteer's personal agenda is becoming problematic. Staff must not hesitate to direct volunteers away from inappropriate activities or locales and back to assigned tasks.

Just as well-trained, motivated volunteers can be a campaign's greatest asset, so too can untrained, poorly supervised volunteers be detrimental to the rest of the campaign's efforts. In the event that a volunteer refuses or is unable to produce the results expected of him or her, dismissal is a viable option. Most campaign staffers balk at the prospect of sending away free help on the sole basis that it is free. This is dangerous thinking. Allowing inadequate or disruptive individuals to remain involved in the campaign suggests that staff are unwilling to carry out the necessary effort to maintain and renew volunteer staff. Furthermore, volunteers who are not carrying their weight create disillusionment, resentfulness, and even more disruption among other volunteers. Campaign staffers should apply the same rules of expectations and conduct to volunteers as are expected of paid staff.

Once they are recruited, volunteers stay because they feel needed and believe that their contributions are important. This does not happen by itself. By definition, volunteers often are at the low end of the campaign hierarchy, with the least access to the candidate and senior staff. Constant reinforcement is essential not only from the volunteer coordinator but also through regular visits by the campaign manager and other senior staff and, occasionally, by the candidate. Brief and periodic volunteer events in which the candidate spends 15 minutes with volunteers before a rally or other event reinvigorates volunteers and reminds them why they are taking time from their families, friends, or studies to be there.

In addition, campaign staff are well advised to be on constant lookout for volunteers whose skills exceed the tasks to which they are assigned. Promoting from within is essential in small campaigns. Learning to recognize underused talent is a paramount skill among senior campaign professionals. The manager should look for volunteers who always find better, more efficient ways in which to complete tasks or who seem to be the ones organizing groups of volunteers into more cohesive groups. The manager should listen for those who voice ideas or whose interest and knowledge are above average. Once these "movers and shakers" have been identified, they should be tested. The manager should give them small, short-term tasks that require more than rote effort. For example, they should be asked to organize a small phone banking operation or to recruit local volunteers in a particular neighborhood. The task should be clearly defined and short term to avoid wasting time and resources if the experiment fails. But testing out these individuals is the best way in which to find new talent in a situation where new talent is of prime importance.

This effort to find and develop volunteers' skills is part of the campaign's ongoing evaluative component. Like paid staff, volunteers require supervision, monitoring, and ongoing evaluation. Without this, the campaign loses control of an already slippery aspect of campaign management.

Summary

Campaigns still are about garnering more than 50% of the vote (in most elections). But the process for getting there has evolved dramatically during the past several years. Increased reliance on professional consultants, more sophisticated polling methods and analysis, the increasing centrality of television and other broadcast and narrowcast media, and the growth of computers in managing virtually every aspect of the campaign have changed what campaigns look like on a day-to-day basis. As recently as the early 1980s, computers were not staples in campaign headquarters. Today, the potential for success of a campaign of any size without computer capacity must be viewed with intense skepticism.

Nonetheless, the ground troops of a campaign—its volunteers—involve the same critical components that existed a generation ago. Identifying potential volunteers is key to a successful recruitment effort. Once brought in, volunteers must be trained, managed, and engaged in campaign projects in ways that maximize their benefit to the campaign's overall plan. Ongoing recruitment, careful scheduling and management, and regular assessment of volunteers ensure that these campaign investors will help move the campaign toward its short-term objectives and its long-term goal—success at the polls on Election Day.

Notes

1. GOTV includes activities such as organized telephone calling and door-to-door canvassing to encourage potential supporters to vote.

2. A canvass is "warm" when the canvasser knows the names and party identifications of household members. This information usually is available from voter registration data. A canvass is "cold" when the canvasser has no specific information about the household prior to the interaction.

9

Greater Than the Sum of Its Parts

Coordinating the Paid and Earned Media Message

DAN SCHNUR

The most difficult thing for most candidates and campaign workers to remember is how little interest most people have in what they are doing. Most people do not care very much about politics. They do not care about government unless it is bothering them about something, and they are even less interested in campaigns. So, engaging the attention of the electorate, and maintaining that attention long enough to teach voters something about the candidates, is an extraordinarily difficult and resource-consuming process.

The news media are acutely aware of their audience's lack of interest in politics. Because the owners of most commercial news outlets, both broadcast and print, are in business to realize a profit, they try to give their audience what market research tells them that audience desires. So, even when they provide news about current events, only a very small part of that news is related to politics or government.

Because there are only a certain number of minutes in a newscast, and only a certain number of column inches in a newspaper, there is a tremendous competition for what type of news is covered. A half-hour local television newscast, minus commercials, runs for 22 minutes. If the competition for that time includes local, state, national, and international news, as well as weather, sports, movie reviews, and other non-news feature stories, then the opportunity to cover issues related to politics and government is very small.

To the extent that a news organization does devote some time to the political process, the competition for coverage is just as intense. A candidate for, say, the

143

state legislature is competing not just with his or her opponent but also with every other candidate for every other office in every election in which a portion of the viewing or reading audience is eligible to participate. Every one of those candidates—whether running for the U.S. Congress, for the state legislature, for local or county office, for governor, or for president—is competing for a relatively thin slice of the available news coverage.

This process becomes even more complicated and challenging when one takes into account the explosion of entertainment and information options that technology has brought to the average voter. Although the rapid rise of cable television, talk radio, and the Internet provides communication opportunities for candidates that might not have existed previously, it has become easier than ever for the public to avoid political news. For every viewer watching CNN or C-Span, there are countless others watching all-sports, all-music, or all-movie channels who rarely (if ever) are reached by the candidates' messages.

The same dynamic exists when the means of communication shifts from news coverage to paid advertising. Because the average consumer is bombarded with so many different commercial messages throughout his or her daily life selling so many different products (and so many other candidates), the ability of a single paid advertisement to affect the targeted voters is extremely limited.

The practical result of this competition is that only a small fraction of campaign dialogue ever reaches the shrinking percentage of the audience that is actually going to vote. In increasing numbers, citizens are simply deciding not to vote at all, as voter registration and turnout statistics demonstrate. And those who do vote are making their decisions with only a very limited amount of the available information at their disposal.

For candidates and their campaign staffs, whose success or failure depends on their ability to reach, engage, and persuade as many of these potential voters as possible, the task in the face of this level of competition is formidable. To effectively communicate a persuasive message to the electorate, the campaign must develop a message that can take advantage of that small window of opportunity into the voters' consciousness when it is available. Candidates must develop a message that is short, simple, and direct enough to squeeze through that window, and they must repeat that message as often as possible through every means at their disposal.

Narrowing the Message

This chapter does not deal with the various necessities involved in developing a winning campaign message. That task alone could take up an entire treatise. But the ability to *communicate* that message consistently through all available forms of campaign media cannot be overstated. There is so much competition for the voters' attention that any significant differentiation in the substance or presentation of the campaign message will simply create yet another level of competition. Not only is the candidate combating the various campaign messages of other politicians, but the candidate also is competing with each of the other messages emanating from his or her own campaign.

For this reason, it is critical to limit the number of issues *proactively* addressed by the campaign. A candidate that attempts to reach the voters on more than a small number of issues runs the risk of developing a message too broad and too complex for that narrow window of opportunity. So, although a candidate must be able to respond to inquiries on any relevant topic, a campaign should restrict its paid and earned media efforts to no more than three issues over the course of the election cycle. The candidate should target specific audiences with specific issue concerns, of course, but a message directed to the general electorate almost always should reflect one of those three primary issues.

Similarly, an effective message should be able to be summarized in a relatively brief statement by the candidate. The use of a "sound bite," an 8- to 10-second phrase articulated by the candidate, can explain an issue quickly and succinctly. This increases the chances that the campaign message (or at least a simplified version of that message) will be included in the day's news coverage. Although the sound bite is particularly useful for television and radio coverage, a brief quote also is helpful for newspaper reporters and is a way in which to quickly encapsulate a more complex issue position in a small amount of space.

We have seen this dynamic often in politics. As president, Ronald Reagan traveled to Berlin to deliver a lengthy and substantive speech about the end of the cold war. But all that the audience back home heard him say was "Mr. Gorbachev, tear down this wall!" And that was all they needed to hear.

Similarly, in his 1991 campaign for the U.S. Senate, Pennsylvania Democrat Harris Wofford concentrated his campaign's message on the importance of health care reform, an issue almost impossible to address without lengthy, detailed policy proposals. Although Wofford offered specifics to interested reporters and voter groups, he framed his candidacy around a single sound bite. "If a criminal has a right to a lawyer," he said, "then you have the same right to a doctor." Wofford came back from 40 points behind in the polls to win that year, and it is safe to say that a lot more people heard the sound bite than read the proposal.

Lest the readers call this cynical, let me say upfront that a candidate must be prepared to answer questions in greater depth as well. A candidate who is unable or unwilling to discuss policy matters to a greater degree of specificity quickly loses credibility with the reporters covering the campaign. All the snappy sound bites in the world will not help a candidate recover from a reputation as a lightweight. So, although sound bites are a way of reinforcing the campaign's message, let us not forget that sound bites only represent the message; they do not become it.

Paid Versus Free Media

When campaign professionals talk of campaign communication, they differentiate between two types of coverage: paid and free media. For the sake of establishing a common definition, let us say that paid media encompass not only radio, television, and newspaper advertisements but also any other form of mass message dissemination that incurs a direct financial cost to the communicating entity. Therefore, our definition of paid media also includes direct mail and phone bank programs as well as door hangings, billboards, bumper stickers, videos, flyers, brochures, handouts, campaign souvenirs, and the like.

Free media (also known to campaign message specialists as "earned" media), therefore, are defined as any forms of mass communication that a campaign can use without offering direct financial compensation to the transmitting agent. So, this definition includes not only print and broadcast news coverage but also other communication mechanisms such as talk radio, public access television, mass e-mail and other Internet activity, and personal and surrogate public appearances.

Every one of these communication mechanisms, whether paid or free, is employed by a campaign because it provides the opportunity to reach some segment of the electorate with the candidate's message. Specifics such as the amount of detail provided, the style and tone of the message delivery, and the opportunity for other sources to interfere in that message's transmission might vary to some degree. But the greater the consistency in delivering that message from one form of communication to another, the more likely that message will penetrate the consciousness of some segment of the campaign's target audience.

Particularly in the context of free media, the ability of a candidate to continue to deliver a consistent version of his or her message can be extremely difficult. It is an understandable element of human nature to want to avoid saying the same thing over and over again, particularly when a portion of the audience (e.g., campaign staff, reporters) have heard the message repeated on numerous previous occasions. To a candidate concerned about the effect of repeating his or her message too frequently, I offer the following thought: When the candidate is sick to death of hearing the same exact words come out of his or her mouth time after time, when the candidate's own advisers wince when they hear those words yet another time, and when the reporters covering the candidate's campaign roll their eyes in mock agony because they have heard him or her deliver this message so many times without variation, then the candidate is just beginning to get that message into the head of the very first targeted voter.

Because voters receive their news from so many different sources, the consistency of the candidate's message each time is even more critical. A voter might read a story in the morning newspaper, catch the evening news on television, or listen to the local news radio station while driving to or from work. That voter is far more likely to retain the campaign's message if it is reinforced through each of these individual communication opportunities with as little variation as possible.

So, the candidate should suck it up and keep repeating the message. It is the only way that most people will ever hear it.

Controlling the Message Through Paid Media

The most significant advantage of paid media is that the candidate's message can be delivered precisely as was originally intended without any interference or distortion from outside sources. That level of control allows the campaign to shape the message so that it reflects on the candidate most positively. Not only are the words in the message presented as purely as possible, but depending on the form of paid media communication, the campaign also can control other elements of the message that can reinforce the information being delivered to the voters.

In a television advertisement, the campaign managers can strengthen the particulars of their candidate's message through the use of any number of audio or video techniques. The lighting can be made brighter or darker to create a certain mood. Different types of music or other background noise (e.g., sirens, children's laughter, car horns, gunfire) all can add to the strength of the ad. Setting, clothing, and even camera angles can dramatically affect the way in which the audience reacts to the message's presentation. In the 1988 presidential campaign, for example, George Bush's campaign ran an advertisement detailing Michael Dukakis's positions on a variety of defense-related issues. The specifics of the charges were soon forgotten, but the unflattering footage of Dukakis riding in a tank that played while the candidate's positions were being summarized left a visual impression that still persists years later.

Similar opportunities exist for free media as well. The location of a news conference, the backdrop in front of which the candidate is positioned, and the presence of other participants all can serve to strengthen the candidate's message and increase the possibility that it will be received by the audience. When is the last time you saw a candidate talk about crime without a line of police officers standing behind him or her?

The impact of visual imagery is so powerful that, in the case of television news coverage, many campaign strategists believe that the words uttered by the reporter or candidate in a news story are less important than the video footage the station uses to frame the piece. Predictably, as campaigns have gone to greater and greater lengths to place their candidates in visually pleasing settings, news reporters and producers have gone to similar effort to explain the campaigns' intent. Some have even attempted to avoid using the backdrops in their coverage altogether.

Paid media have the ability to reach an audience that might otherwise be successful in avoiding political information. A voter who does not regularly read the front page of a newspaper or watch television news is less likely to avoid political information that arrives unexpectedly during a commercial break in an entertainment program. This window increases the pressure to create an advertisement that is as enticing and arresting as possible; a viewer who is armed with a remote control device is unlikely to devote his or her attention to political information unless it is presented in a sufficiently dramatic or exciting manner.

Although broadcast advertising does not require that the audience take action to receive the campaign message, a different imperative holds with most other forms of paid media. A letter from the candidate, or another direct mail piece, is unlikely to be opened unless there is information on the envelope that suggests that it would be in the recipient's interest to open it. Once open, the letter or brochure is unlikely to be read unless the information is presented in some type of compelling fashion.

Direct mail specialists, therefore, tend to use photographs, large and colorful typefaces, and other visually stimulating images to encourage the voter's interest. The 1997 campaign in San Francisco to build a new football stadium sent out regular mail pieces with pictures of Jerry Rice, Steve Young, and other 49er stars on the cover, all designed to appeal to the resident with more interest in the Super Bowl than in the voting booth. By the time the unsuspecting readers had opened the mailers, they had already received the campaign's political message.

A communication mechanism such as direct mail can target a voter much more precisely than can broadcast advertising. But the importance of consistency of message still is critically important. Although a letter to specific groups (e.g., environmentalists) can address an issue outside the campaign's primary focus, the message communicated through direct mail must be articulated in such a way as to remind the recipient of other times when the candidate has communicated with him or her through other formats. Even appeals for campaign contributions sent to potential donors should reflect as small a variation on the central campaign message as possible.

Types of Messages

There are three different methods by which information can be presented through paid media: positive messages, negative messages, and comparative messages.

A classic example of positive message presentation is the "Morning in America" television ad produced for the Reagan-Bush reelection campaign in 1984. A deep-voiced narrator talked soothingly of economic and foreign policy progress achieved over the previous 4 years while the camera showed scenes of an idyllic, small-town America illustrated by new homes under construction and factory openings. A viewer without access to other forms of political information could have easily assumed not only that no Democratic candidate was running but also that no election was being held at all.

Since then, voters have become accustomed to seeing their candidates presented in similar settings—candidates with their families, candidates walking by the water, candidates talking (or listening) to "average," middle class men and women. A candidate introducing himself or herself to the voters, or reminding them of the candidate's past achievements, is most likely to deliver a positive message.

A candidate trailing in the polls, on the other hand, tends to go negative. An effective negative communication will lower support for the candidate's opponent. However, negative communications often cut support for the candidate leveling the attack as well as for the recipient of the attack. So, the calculated risk in any negative communication is that the target of the criticism might lose more support than will the communication's instigator. Obviously, a candidate running behind his or her opponent is more likely to take that risk than is a candidate with an advantage.

Because negative campaigning can cause an adverse reaction among voters, it is a technique employed much more regularly through paid media, usually in a context that does not involve the candidate himself or herself. Similarly, the most frequent presentation of negative messages in the free media is accomplished by a surrogate speaker on behalf of the candidate. In both cases, the candidate is insulated to minimize the potential loss of support.

There is an inherent contradiction in negative campaigning. Although voters claim to disapprove of negative campaigning, and reinforce their claim by opposing those candidates who engage in such activity, the same voters tend to retain a much higher percentage of information transmitted through negative campaigning than through other forms of message communication. Negative message presentation tends to contain a larger amount of factual information, whereas the information in a positive message usually is more subjective in nature. So, despite the potential downside to disseminating negative information about the opposing candidate, campaigns continue to do precisely that because they know that the information involved has a much greater chance of being retained by the voters.

The most effective method for message presentation, however, is a message that compares information about the campaign's candidate and the opposition. Voters generally are wary of claims made through paid media communications, so offering information about one candidate alongside that of a potential alternative provides a level of credibility that often is missing from a message that provides information about only one candidate.

We saw this technique in the 1996 presidential contest when the Clinton-Gore campaign ran ads on the issue of family leave. Bill Clinton's advisers knew that voters were unlikely to be persuaded by a message that simply told them about the president's efforts in that area. The campaign managers also understood that a commercial that only attacked Republican candidate Bob Dole on the same issue was not much more likely to have a significant impact. But by putting together an advertisement that contrasted Clinton's position with that of the Republican Congress, they established credibility both for the support of Clinton's position and for their attack on the Republicans—and, by extension, on Dole.

Like negative message communications, a comparative message provides factual information for the voter to review. But it also provides a positive contrast that encourages the voter to choose one candidate rather than simply discouraging participation altogether. Voters are less harsh in their judgment of a candidate who mitigates the dissemination of negative information by comparing relevant facts from his or her own record. They also are as likely to retain the negative information offered as if they had received it in a purely negative context.

The Challenge of Communicating Through Free Media

The largest downside of paid media, predictably, is that they cost money, a resource of which most campaigns have only a limited amount. So, although a paid media campaign would allow the candidate to maintain complete control over the campaign's message, it is a prohibitively expensive option for all but the wealthiest candidates. This means that nearly all campaigns must attempt to deliver their messages through free media as well.

Message consistency, although essentially important to campaigns, is much more difficult to achieve through the free media. At the same time that a candidate is attempting to repeat his or her message with as little variation as possible, the objective of the news media is to find something previously unreported to pass on to that same audience. So, the tension between the candidate's goal not to create news and the goal of the news media to find news on which to report is an ongoing one.

James Carville, the Democratic strategist, likes to describe the strategy for maintaining a constant message in culinary terms. He suggests that the most effective way in which to feed the news media a steady diet of the campaign's message is to slightly vary the way in which each meal is served, with a slightly different topping or side dish to give them something new to satisfy their journalistic imperative. But the basic message, the entrée, remains constant to provide the necessary reinforcement to the ultimate audience, the voters.

Suppose that a candidate wants to spend several days reinforcing his or her education plan to the voters. Instead of delivering precisely the same message each day, the candidate can talk about reducing class size on the first day, improving teacher training on the day after, expanding after-school programs on the day after that, and so on. The essential message of a candidate who cares about education is unchanged. But different elements of that message provide the news media with different information on each successive day for continued coverage, allowing the campaign to continue to communicate its message to the voters unabated.

Dealing With Reporters

Many candidates and campaign workers make the mistake of thinking that the news media are the audience that they must satisfy. Because reporters covering the campaign are the physical manifestation of the mass audience, it is extremely easy to forget that the news media are only the conduit through which the campaign's message passes, not the message's ultimate destination.

Candidates such as Reagan and Clinton, two of the most gifted communicators to appear on the political landscape in recent years, always have known that the voters are the audience to whom they are communicating their messages, not the reporters with whom they happen to be speaking. Conversely, less talented communicators running for office frequently allow their exchanges with the news media to degenerate into verbal jousting matches, forgetting that winning debatings point with reporters is much less important than delivering their messages to the electorate.

The most difficult challenge that a candidate faces in dealing with the news media is answering reporters' questions without wandering from the message he or she is attempting to deliver. A candidate who refuses to answer questions from the news media loses credibility for himself or herself and the campaign. But if the candidate allows the reporters covering the race to dictate his or her message agenda, then the candidate loses the ability to communicate that message to the voters. There are two important points that a candidate and his or her campaign must keep in mind in these situations. First, the candidate and campaign managers always should decide in advance what news they want to make whenever there is a scheduled meeting with representatives of the news media. Second, the candidate must be prepared for questions on any number of subjects and must be ready to turn those questions back to the subject at hand.

The nature of their job demands that reporters find news to report. Thus, it makes much more sense to provide new information to them that reinforces an element of the campaign's message. Although the campaign's control over its message in these situations is not absolute, it certainly is much greater than if the news media are left to their own devices to identify a news story worthy of their attention. By planning to release new tidbits prior to any interaction with the news media, the candidate has a much better chance of attracting helpful news coverage.

No matter how newsworthy the candidate's announcement might be, however, the reporters almost always will have questions relating to other subjects. A candidate should strive to find a way in which to answer the reporters' questions in a manner that allows him or her to include information relating to the campaign's central message or to the news being announced that day. For example, a candidate announcing a proposal on education reform who is asked about crime can talk about how education and job training can prevent young people from turning to crime. This type of give-and-take with the news media can be a precarious exercise. A candidate who appears evasive to reporters' questions will appear to be uncooperative or, even worse, uninformed. A good way in which to avoid this problem without veering too far away from the campaign's central message is for the candidate to answer these questions in as nonprovocative a manner as possible. In other words, the candidate should concentrate on making news only on the subject that he or she came to address.

The importance of preparation before any encounter with the news media cannot be overstated. Prior to interviews, press conferences, or even photo opportunities, the candidate's advisers should prepare a list of questions likely to be asked by the news media and rehearse those questions, and their answers, with the candidate. The candidate should be ready to answer questions not just on the subject matter at hand but also on any other current news story relevant to the campaign. A good rule for campaign staff is to *never let the candidate hear any question for the first time from a reporter.* If the question is initially posed in a preparation session, then the candidate and advisers can discuss possible answers to that question before they see it in quotes. By the time a candidate hears the same question from the news media, he or she will have had the opportunity to think through possible responses and to answer the question so as to help (or at least not hurt) the campaign's overall message.

Early in his 1988 presidential campaign, Bush agreed to a live interview with CBS anchorman Dan Rather. When Bush advisers Roger Ailes and Pete Teeley found out from network sources that Rather planned to spend the entire interview focusing on Bush's alleged role in the Iran-contra affair, they took time before the interview to thoroughly prepare their candidate. In the interview, Bush came out swinging, defending his own behavior and questioning Rather about having recently stormed off the news set when a tennis match ran late and delayed the beginning of his newscast. Although Bush probably still would have been able to answer Rather's questions, the additional preparation helped to change the complexion of the interview.

The strategy of message control by redirection also can be useful when responding to charges leveled by an opponent through either free or paid media. Here, a campaign has several options. On the one hand, it can respond to a charge that it believes to be damaging, even if it takes the campaign away from its agreed-on message. But that strategy runs the risk of confusing the electorate by introducing additional elements into the candidate's message. Another alternative is to ignore the attack and simply reinforce the campaign's primary message. The risk here, however, is that failing to respond to an opponent's criticism suggests that the criticism is valid.

The dilemma is obvious. One of the oldest rules of politics is to never leave an attack unanswered. But frequently, a decision to respond to such an attack takes away time, attention, and money from the issues the candidate needs to emphasize.

There is a third alternative. Much in the same way as a skilled candidate can take a question on an unrelated topic and turn it into a discussion of the campaign's message, a campaign's paid media can attempt to redirect the charge onto favorable issue turf. When California Governor Pete Wilson prepared for his reelection campaign in 1994, his advisers realized that Democratic candidate Kathleen Brown probably would attack his record on education. Rather than enter into an extended debate over an issue favorable to Democrats, Wilson's campaign decided to shift the debate back to their own turf. In responding to Brown's criticisms on education spending, Wilson pointed out that several billion dollars of taxpayer money was being used for the education of children of illegal immigrants rather than U.S. citizens and legal residents. Brown's attack was answered, but with Wilson's own issue, illegal immigration.

Why the News Media Are *Not* the Enemy

The second major lesson of campaign communication is that a candidate and his or her staff must nurture their relationship with the reporters covering the campaign. Politicians of both parties frequently fall into the trap of believing that the news media are the enemy and treating them accordingly. This almost always is a recipe for disaster.

There is no greater mistake a candidate or campaign can make than to develop an adversarial relationship with the news media. There is an old saying, "Never pick an ink fight with someone who buys it by the barrel." A reporter who is angry with a candidate can let the whole world know about it (or at least the portion of the world that watches the reporter's newscast or reads his or her newspaper). A candidate or campaign staffer, on the other hand, has limited resources to tell that audience the other side of the story. Besides, using a campaign's limited resources to do combat with a reporter instead of the other candidate is invariably a waste of those resources.

It is understandable why candidates often think that the news media are the enemy. In the course of the typical candidate's daily activities, nearly every person with whom he or she interacts offers some type of positive reinforcement for the campaign. A candidate whose day is filled with speeches to supporters, meetings with advisers, and phone calls with donors rarely encounters any negative feedback at all, save the occasional refusal to contribute. Even unfavorable poll numbers usually are presented to the candidate in some type of positive light to keep his or her spirits up.

But the overwhelming majority of reporters are not in the business of supporting candidates. They do not have to be friendly. Because a candidate does not have the opportunity to see his or her opponent interact with the news media, the candidate is unable to see that most reporters treat candidates in exactly the same manner. So, the candidate frequently comes to believe that the reporters' equivocal behavior is directed only at him or her.

By their nature, reporters are suspicious of official statements and explanations. If every public statement from an elected officeholder or candidate told the entire story, then there would be no need for reporters to serve as anything more than stenographers. So, the role of political reporters is to attempt to identify the information that is not formally (or willingly) made available to the public. These conflicting pressures are particularly great during campaigns, when candidates must continually repeat their messages to reach the voters and reporters must find something new to report to justify coverage.

Reporters also are influenced by market factors. Simply put, controversy and conflict attract larger audiences of the viewing and reading public. Although an increasing number of news organizations have begun to seek out positive news in the communities they cover, public interest in political news is, to a large extent, driven by information that is out of the ordinary. The same competitive pressures that keep news organizations from covering stories about all the planes that land safely in favor of the spectacular crashes drive political coverage as well.

Politicians, community leaders, and other interested parties regularly engage in group hand-wringing sessions about the news decisions of the media. But because candidates do not have control over those processes, it is much more useful to figure out how to use those tendencies to the advantage of the candidate or campaign. And just as a poor craftsman tends to blame his tools for his own failures, an unsuccessful campaign worker or candidate invariably blames the press.

Although there certainly are exceptions, most members of the news media go to great lengths to keep their own political preferences out of their reporting. If reporters show a bias, it usually is toward the candidate who is more interesting to cover because such a candidate tends to make their work more enjoyable and can help to place their stories up front in the newspaper or on the newscast. Generally speaking, this bias of sorts is applied on a roughly equal basis to candidates of both parties.

There is another reason to make the extra effort to treat reporters well: Campaigns need them. One should think of the news media in the same way as one would think of a coworker with whom he or she is not particularly friendly. Eventually, one might need that coworker's assistance on some work-related project, and that individual is much more likely to help if one has not been overtly hostile during the time the two have worked together. The same principle holds with the reporters covering one's campaign. They are much more likely to be cooperative with someone who has treated them decently over the time of their professional relationship. This does not necessarily mean that the coverage will be favorable if one's dealings with the media generally are cordial, but it is almost guaranteed that the coverage will be better than it would be if one were constantly at war with the media.

Candidates and their advisers frequently discuss the idea of refusing to communicate with a reporter or news organization they believe to be hostile. This almost always is a self-defeating strategy that should be avoided in all but the most extreme cases. The reporter and his or her news organization are going to report on the campaign whether or not the candidate is talking to them. All the candidate will accomplish by shutting them out is to withhold his or her explanations and message from the reporter's audience.

Reporters usually are working on several stories and projects simultaneously. They need to know why a particular story is important to them and to their audience before committing to cover that story. Just as candidates compete with each other for the voters' attention, it is equally critical to realize that the candidate is competing for the time of each individual reporter. So, the more attentive that a campaign can be to each reporter's deadlines, schedules, and other needs, the more likely it is that the news media will provide coverage for that campaign's announcements and other public events.

Finally, one should remember that reporters are human beings and like to be treated as such. If the candidate cannot convince himself or herself of this, then the candidate should learn to hide his or her feelings because the candidate needs the reporters more than they need the candidate.

Reinforcing the Message Between Paid and Free Media

In addition to the prohibitive financial cost, there is another downside of relying exclusively on paid media to deliver a campaign's message to the voting public. Voters generally tend to attach less credibility to a message they receive through paid media than through news coverage. Even though public trust in the news media has declined significantly in recent years, trust in politicians is even lower. Instinctively, voters know that a message they receive through paid media has been developed solely to serve the interests of the candidate.

Therefore, there is a necessary balancing act between free and paid media. Although paid media provide an opportunity to deliver the candidate's message repeatedly without outside interference, they face built-in interference from the recipients of that message. Conversely, the advantage of conveying that same message through news coverage is that voters tend to accept it with significantly less reservation, even if it is not always received by the voters in precisely the form that the candidate or campaign originally intended.

A successful campaign uses its paid and free media to mutually reinforce each other. The credibility of the message delivered through news coverage can transfer when the voters receive a similar message through paid media. Similarly, a message delivered repeatedly through advertising or mail can serve to jog the voter's thought process when a related message, even if somewhat diluted, is received through the free media. The advantage of coordinating the candidate's message between paid and free media carries another benefit as well. Over the course of a campaign, voters become increasingly unable to recall the original sources of information they have received. The information compiled in their memories mixes together as the campaign progresses, so a message that originally was delivered through one form of media often is identified with another.

When Wilson was preparing to run for reelection as California's governor in early 1994, his advisers showed draft campaign commercials to focus groups in the San Fernando Valley that contained news footage of illegal immigrants crossing the U.S.-Mexico border. Although the ads never had aired on television, several of the focus group participants recognized the news footage and concluded that they had seen the commercials before.

This dynamic presents a great advantage for a campaign that uses paid advertisements. Voters do not like to admit that they rely on paid media for political information, so they convince themselves that the information they often recognize about the candidates came to them through the free media instead. In the process, they attach greater credibility to the paid messages, convinced that they have been filtered by the news media and not just created by the campaigns themselves. The greater the similarity that exists between the messages delivered through paid and free media, the more likely the voters are to confuse the sources of those messages and the more likely they are to attach credibility to information that was presented to them through advertising or other forms of paid media.

Another common technique that highlights paid media is to appropriate information and/or opinions from the news media and to insert them into paid media. Using a newspaper headline, endorsement, or excerpts from other favorable coverage gives the ad greater credibility while maintaining complete control over that message.

A final thought to keep in mind when weighing a campaign's paid and free media communications is the relative impact of the two means in different campaign settings. The importance of paid media, although always significant, increases in races for offices with lower levels of voter interest. Presidential campaigns, for example, receive a disproportionately large amount of free media coverage, which lessens the relative importance of paid media communications. Statewide campaigns for governor and senator receive somewhat less coverage from the news media, so paid media becomes proportionally more important. The further down the ticket a campaign is located, the smaller the amount of news interest it receives and the greater the impact that paid media can have on the voters. So, a race for school board, city council, or another low-interest office can be decided almost exclusively on the basis of a paid media message in the absence of significant attention from the news media. Because television advertising usually is prohibitively expensive for a local campaign, lower cost paid media such as direct mail and door hangings usually become the dominant form of communication.

The other factor that affects the level of news coverage and public attention, of course, is the amount of competition that exists for that attention. In most circumstances, the size of the media market in which the campaign takes place, and the number of voters that the market reaches, is a reliable indicator of the level of that competition. A campaign for U.S. Congress in the Los Angeles media market, which reaches voters in two dozen separate congressional districts, will be virtually ignored by the news media. The same race in a more rural media market, on the other hand, will receive extensive coverage because of the relative lack of competition for the news media's attention. For better or worse, candidates for office in larger media markets will, therefore, tend to place a larger amount of importance on paid media communications.

Limits on Paid and Free Media Communication

Bruce Cain, a University of California professor, postulates a theory of adversarial democracy that argues a directly inverse relationship between the size of a constituency and the level of trust and interpersonal communication that takes place. Looking at this theory from the perspective of a candidate or campaign adviser, it is increasingly more difficult to effectively communicate with a larger constituency and increasingly more difficult to gain the trust and support of voters in that constituency.

The logistical challenges of communicating with thousands (if not millions) of voters presents obstacles unimaginable to our Founding Fathers. A candidate for statewide office in California determined to deliver his or her message in person to voters could not hope to reach even the smallest fraction of the electorate without relying heavily on mass communications of both paid and free media. In modern-day campaigning, a rally of supporters for a candidate is important only to the extent that the enthusiasm that they exhibit can somehow be conveyed either on the evening news or as part of the candidate's campaign advertisements. As cynical as this might sound, consider that a candidate for statewide office in California who begins the campaign year shaking hands in downtown San Diego would be lucky to reach Los Angeles before Election Day. Therefore, voters between Los Angeles and the Oregon border would have to be reached through other means or else go without the candidate's information.

Handling External Events and Information

This trend toward mass communication makes effective paid and free media essential for winning campaigns. However, it is important to remember that a message communicated to voters through the mass media is only part of the stored information that an individual calls on in making his or her decision on Election Day. Every voter is the product of his or her own life experiences and is shaped by memories that take place from the earliest times of childhood until the moment in which the individual actually steps into the voting booth. Voters also are influenced by their surrounding communities, families, friends, neighbors, and coworkers with whom they communicate without the need for mass media.

Not only do these life experiences and community influences play a significant part in political decision making, but they might be as important as (or more important than) the information provided through paid and free media. Interpersonal communication is the strongest defining factor in the formation and maintenance of a community, and information provided through these interpersonal (and intrapersonal) conduits carries a much higher level of trust and credibility than does a message delivered through mass communication mechanisms.

Similarly, there is information being delivered to voters every day through the news media that is not directly related to the campaign but that has the potential to greatly affect its outcome. Factors such as economic recovery or recession, a high-profile violent crime, an environmental accident, civic unrest, and political corruption all can dramatically alter an election campaign even after the race is already well underway.

The best candidates and campaigns react to these external factors much in the same way as they would respond to questions from the news media or to attacks from opposing candidates that have the potential to take the campaigns off-message. They find a way in which to incorporate outside events into their campaign messages and to use them as examples that can help to deliver those messages. It always is much easier, especially in a competitive media environment, to become part of an existing story that already captures the public's interest than to create a new story and convince the public to become interested in it. So, using a real-life incident to further the candidate's message is an excellent way in which to engage voters' attention in the campaign.

Conclusion

Although there always are outside influences beyond a candidate's or campaign's control, a campaign message carried to the voters through paid or free media almost always is consequential to the voters' decisions. So, in a race that is otherwise competitive, the strength of a message communicated and coordinated effectively through paid and free media can have a significant effect on the campaign's outcome.

But as important as paid and free media can be to a candidate's message, their importance increases dramatically when the message is reinforced through both forms of mass communication. Making sure that a common message is received by the voters through both forms of mass communication dramatically increases the potential impact of each. So, it seems that, as in so many other circumstances, the whole of political communication is greater than the sum of its parts.

10

Money Doesn't Grow on Trees

Fund-Raising in American Political Campaigns

JENNIFER A. STEEN

Running for office is drudge work. Political candidates endure a grueling schedule of meetings, travel, and appearances, campaigning morning, noon, and night every day of the week. The aspiring officeholder enjoys little time with his or her family and even less time resting and recuperating. The candidate forfeits all privacy, submitting to intense public scrutiny of his or her personal and professional lives. And the candidate must shed all inhibitions to ask friends and strangers alike to help in his or her quest. A handful of politicians find these aspects of public life invigorating, but for most, they are a distasteful but necessary means to an end.

Without question, the least enjoyable campaign activity also is the most inevitable—raising money. Money doesn't grow on trees, but most candidates wish it did because the necessity of funding a competitive campaign forces them to beg, cajole, and grovel for hundreds of hours. Only in the smallest, least competitive election district can a candidate avoid expenditures for some type of communication, whether bumper stickers, brochures, or a 30-second television ad. Recently, an increasing number of candidates have forgone fund-raising and self-financed their efforts with personal wealth, but the vast majority still turn to friends, family, and sympathetic communities for the individual contributions that sum up to a campaign treasury.

The size of the fund-raising burden varies from a few hundred dollars in town council contests to several million dollars in U.S. Senate elections. In 1996, the median amount raised by successful Senate candidates, net of candidates' loans and contributions to their own campaigns, was $2,930,000. The median amount raised by winning House candidates was $626,000 (Federal Election Commission, n.d.). In campaigns for the California state legislature, the median amount spent by winners was $676,000 for the senate[1] and $299,000 for the assembly (Citizens' Research Foundation, n.d.).

Popular metaphors characterize fund-raising as prostitution and extortion. Under the former, politicians are presumed to offer votes or other official favors in exchange for campaign contributions. Under the latter, powerful officeholders threaten to punish groups by thwarting their agendas if financial support is not provided during the campaign. A handful of politicians might fit these images. For example, Chicago Alderman Jesse Evans recently was convicted on several corruption charges, among them exchanging his approval of a rock crusher in his ward for a $10,000 campaign contribution (Gillis, 1997).[2] However, most candidates fall far short of such extremes.

Raising money is more accurately described as solicitation. People do not part with their money readily, and certainly not unless they are *asked*. Each fund-raising method—direct mail, telemarketing, events, candidate calling, and the like—is simply a different way of asking for a contribution. This reality underlies much of the squeamishness about the campaign finance system; to fund a competitive effort, candidates must actively solicit financial support, and many worry that the process renders candidates "beholden" to their contributors rather than their election district constituencies. The view of fund-raising as an inherently corrupt act is popular, and many public interest groups have documented a correlation between campaign contributions and issue positions. But the system's defenders argue that money follows—and does not dictate—votes and positions. Many of my former colleagues in political campaigns claim (and truly believe) that politicians take positions on principle, and contributions from like-minded groups are offered to enhance election prospects, not to change issue stances.

Political scientists have tried to nail down the relationship. Does money buy positions, or do positions attract money? Wright (1985) studied five federal political action committees (PACs), all perceived as among the most influential in Washington, D.C., and concluded that the dominant PAC strategy was to contribute to candidates who *already* were sympathetic to the group's interests. In Wright's study, PAC support had a negligible effect on U.S. representatives' positions, as expressed in roll call votes. Another researcher examined committee behavior in the U.S. House and found that organized interests influence only activity with "low public visibility" (Schroedel, 1986, p. 387). Others have determined that PAC influence is indirect; contributions buy access for lobbyists, and lobbying contact tends to affect positions, but without the lobbyists' activity, contributions had no effect (Langbein & Lotwis, 1990; Wright, 1990).

Although the process of soliciting contributions one by one might appear unseemly, it does strengthen the ties between the candidate and at least part of the constituency. To finance a campaign, a candidate must reach out to local groups[3] and individuals. In the course of soliciting contributions, the candidate forges relationships, mobilizes communities, learns about the issues the constituents favor, and unites segments of the community in a common effort. By making contributions, individuals and groups make a commitment that binds them to the candidate. Of course, building this type of relationship is the goal of all campaign activity, but the bond can be stronger when cemented by a financial investment than when borne of other political activity.

The structure of a fund-raising effort parallels the other aspects of the campaign. Each division—press, political, field, or media—follows a plan with two components: strategy and tactics. The *strategy* identifies target communities and determines the message that will elicit support, whereas *tactics* are the means of delivering the message to the targets. Press, political, field, and media operations all are in the business of voter contact; that is, they target electoral support or *votes*. The finance team targets financial support or *contributions*.

The basic formula for fund-raising strategy is invariant across campaigns. The candidate's fund-raising consultant or finance director must determine the characteristics of likely contributors and then identify specific individuals with those characteristics. In essence, *why* and *who* are the first two questions the fund-raisers must ask. The answers to the *why* and *who* questions are different for every campaign, but the need to answer these questions early is universal. Once the targets and their motivations have been identified, the campaign must decide *how* to solicit the contributions. The mix of tactics varies by campaign and depends in part on the fund-raising strategy. Tactics also are dictated by structural factors such as the type of office sought, the size of the election district, and the relevant campaign finance laws.

Fund-Raising Strategy: Who Gives and Why?

Fund-raising is asking for money, and a candidate cannot ask for money unless he or she is talking to someone. The candidate can "talk" through a mass-produced letter or a paid phone bank, but in either case, the candidate needs a name and an address or telephone number. Just as a campaign manager identifies likely voters who can be persuaded to support the candidate at the polling booth, the finance director or fund-raising consultant targets prospective givers who can be induced to support the candidate with their checkbooks. Before identifying the *who*, however, the campaign must address the *why*. People do not give unless they are asked, but even when asked, most do not give without a compelling reason. The first part of a fund-raising plan, then, enumerates the reasons why a person or group would contribute to the candidate.

Fund-raising strategy and campaign strategy overlap structurally and substantively. Both must answer the *why* and *who* questions, and the answers to *why* often are the same. But the answers to *who* usually are different; potential contributors are not a neat subset of potential voters. Some financial supporters live outside the election district and, therefore, are ineligible to participate at the polling booth. And, of course, some contributions come from organizations—PACs in federal elections as well as corporations, unions, and other associations in most state elections—that cannot vote as organizations and whose members might not even be electoral constituents.

Rational choice theory offers a useful explanation for the difference between voters and contributors. Both take action because the expected benefits exceed the cost of the act. The greater benefit an actor derives from the outcome (the candidate's victory), the more the actor is willing to do to ensure that outcome. Suppose that Jones and Smith both care about the environment but that Smith is more ardent than Jones. Jones cares just enough to expend the time and energy to go to the polls and vote for a conservationist candidate, but it is not worth it to him to take the extra step of contributing financially. To Smith, it is very important that the conservationist candidate take office, so Smith is willing to pay a little more, that is, to make a campaign contribution *and* vote. For some people, it might be less costly to write a check and send it to the candidate than to apply for and cast an absentee ballot, so they contribute but do not vote. Consider, for example, 1998 California gubernatorial candidate Al Checchi, who contributed $14,500 to Dianne Feinstein's 1990 campaign for governor but did not vote in her 1994 U.S. Senate reelection battle with Michael Huffington (Chance, 1997; Smith, 1997).

The *why* of campaign contributions generally falls into one of four categories: affection, agreement, access, or antipathy. *Affection* and *agreement* both are reasons to contribute to and vote *for* a candidate. By contrast, contributors seeking access might not even prefer the candidate over his or her rivals but are covering their bets in case the candidate wins. *Antipathy* contributors want to block the opponent more than help the candidate. High-profile, ideologically extreme candidates can inspire such behavior. For example, U.S. Representative Loretta Sanchez's campaign reported that former Representative Robert ("B-1 Bob") Dornan's decision to seek a rematch in 1998 boosted Sanchez's receipts overnight. These cases are atypical, so I focus on the first three contribution incentives.

Affection

The first group a candidate usually turns to is his or her family and friends. Regardless of political positions, a candidate's immediate family members usually are quite receptive to a fund-raising appeal. They care personally about the candidate and want to see him or her succeed. Most candidates have friends and associates who feel similarly, although perhaps not quite as intensely as do family members. Checchi explained his $1,000 contribution to 1996 Republican presidential candidate Steve Forbes, a family friend, by saying, "I don't happen to agree with Steve or most of his politics, but as a courtesy to him, I made a contribution" (Smith, 1997, p. A1).

Many fund-raising consultants, who think of fund-raising targets in terms of lists, refer to this group as the "Christmas card list." Although not all candidates celebrate Christmas, it is not surprising that most individuals with ambitions for elective office keep in touch with hundreds of acquaintances made throughout their lives with greetings in December. Whether the list is Hanukkah cards or just the personal address book, this is the first source of contributors with the affection incentive.

Sometimes, the affection incentive is cued in individuals who do not even know the candidate personally. A candidate often appeals to those who share some type of group identification, whether it is based on ethnicity, alma mater, or other apolitical affiliations. In my household, we recently received a letter from Jonathan Miller, a candidate in Kentucky's 6th congressional district. The letter targeted alumni of a Harvard College student group, and the Harvard alumnus in the house smiled as he announced that he would indeed send a token donation, although he had neither met nor heard of Miller previously. In such cases, warm feelings certainly are not as strong as among the candidate's family and friends, so the members of these target groups usually must have other reasons, whether ideological or issue oriented, that reinforce the group identification motivation to contribute.

Agreement

Most people who care about election outcomes are concerned with some issue or policy. If they feel strongly, then they might believe that a campaign contribution is a good investment. The intensity of their preferences can be estimated by their level of outwardly visible engagement with the issue. For some, the engagement is economic. For example, small business owners care deeply about the minimum wage, and farmers care deeply about agricultural subsidies. For others, there might be no objective source of their involvement. Clean air benefits everyone equally, but some people seem to care about it more than others. We do not know why they do, but often they express these feelings with political activism and, therefore, are as identifiable as those with economic stakes. Thus, membership groups are a rich source of campaign contributions based on policy or ideological agreement. Of course, a candidate can and should sit down with his or her finance committee and brainstorm the names of individuals who share the candidate's ideas, but the list produced probably would not be long enough to fund a competitive campaign. The campaign must cast a wider net by targeting organized groups. Members of professional associations (e.g., trial lawyers, doctors, realtors) will be motivated by their economic interests, and members of political groups (e.g., Sierra Club, National Organization for Women, National Rifle Association) have a proven record of putting up money in support of political causes.

The notorious "incumbency advantage" extends to targeting organized interests. During a campaign, both the incumbent and challenger will choose perhaps three issues on which to focus their messages. Each can turn to groups affected by the three issues, but the challenger might find it difficult to court groups outside this circle. A candidate who does not emphasize a group's pet issue cannot make a compelling prima facie case for financial support, and organizations are skeptical of campaign promises that are not widely broadcast. By contrast, an incumbent has an established voting record that offers groups a strong incentive to support the incumbent, even when the group's concerns are not the centerpiece of the candidate's campaign.

Access

Many organizations and some individuals are directly affected by legislation and regulation, and for most, the interaction continues over time. The livelihood of western ranchers is subject to continued grazing rights on federal lands, developers' projects hinge on local zoning ordinances and building codes, and union members work under conditions established by state law. You can bet that these entities want to enjoy friendly relations with their U.S. representatives, county supervisors, or state senators, depending on the nature of their interests. They regard a candidate as a current or future officeholder, and even if the candidate does not generally champion the entity's position, it is in the association's, company's, or union's interest to be able to maintain a dialogue. Thus, many contributions are motivated not by policy agreement but rather by the need for access.[4] Recall that political scientists indicate that this money is well spent, as PAC influence seems to operate through lobbying activity, and the lobbyists have a much easier time getting in the office door when their organizations have made campaign contributions (Langbein & Lotwis, 1990; Wright, 1990). In competitive elections where the outcome is unpredictable, many such groups will contribute to both sides, although perhaps more heavily to one because of issue/ideological agreement, so that no matter who wins, the group's government affairs representative can get his or her phone calls returned.

Many prospective contributors have multiple, sometimes cross-pressured, reasons to support or oppose a candidate. The strength of an agreement incentive might be less than the strength of an access incentive, and within the agreement category, there might be conflicting or reinforcing dimensions of different intensity. In one campaign on which I worked, many traditional givers told me that they appreciated my candidate's position on most issues, but they disagreed so strongly with his stance on abortion that they would not make financial contributions. The same candidate enjoyed support from organized interests that were not close to him ideologically but wanted "insurance." Anticipating his possible victory, those groups wanted to be able to work with him and, therefore, were motivated to contribute as a gesture of goodwill. In my dealings with the first group, the candidate and his fund-raisers (myself included) always emphasized the candidate's strong record on issues other than abortion. Although that group was ambivalent, it did have an incentive to contribute, and I tried to cue that incentive. For many of these group members, the balance of the weak pros and the strong con was such that they never responded favorably to our message. With the second group, we would remind prospects of the closeness of the race so that they would not forget that our candidate might be the guy to see at the capitol the following year.

Fund-Raising Tactics: Reeling in the Contributions

Once a campaign has identified its fund-raising targets, it must determine *how* to ask for the contributions. The task is to communicate to the prospects that the candidate's victory offers some benefit to them, that is, to give the prospects an incentive to contribute. There are five options: personal solicitation by the candidate, personal solicitation by a finance committee member or staff person, direct mail, telemarketing, and events. Different targets require different tactics, and the targeted contribution amount is the most important factor. For example, one does not invite a potentially lucrative donor (called a "max-out" in campaign lingo after the ability to contribute up to the applicable legal limit) to a $25 barbecue. The max-out prospect might like to go to the barbecue, and he or she might especially like to get off with only a $25 contribution. To secure a larger amount, a candidate must ask for it personally. Conversely, smaller ("grassroots") donations should be collected en masse at large events. A candidate simply does not have the time to solicit 100 $20 contributions one at a time.[5]

Personal Solicitation by the Candidate

Large contributors want to be personally asked for their support. In federal races, very few $1,000 checks arrive in the mail in response to an event invitation or even the most persuasive letter ever written. Large donors want to hear the candidate's voice and size up the investment. That is, after all, how many big donors view their contribution—as an investment. A candidate's friends and family might give because they like the candidate, but those who give because of agreement or access—those who want a certain policy promoted or who want to cultivate a relationship over time—give now to get something later. The giver expects to derive some benefit from the candidate's election, but the return is not necessarily a quid pro quo favor. A handful of contributors have such high expectations, and some officeholders are willing to oblige, but for most contributors, it is sufficient payoff to see the candidate take office and vote according to the positions he or she espoused during the campaign.

Of course, investors do not plunk down cash without doing some research, and because most candidates are not personally acquainted with most big donors (especially in the larger budget races and among nonincumbents), the prospects want to check them out. They want to talk to the candidates in person, ask them specific questions, and see how they handle themselves. A contributor/investor wants to assure himself or herself of three things: (a) that the candidate is viable and has a shot at winning; (b) that if the candidate wins, he or she will pursue the policy on which the candidate and the contributor agree; and (c) that the candidate really needs the money.

Research is not the only reason why prospects want to talk to candidates. If this were the case, then incumbents would not have to call prospects themselves. After all, incumbents have demonstrated that they can win, they have established records in different policy arenas, and they are personally known to their existing contributor list (although not necessarily to new prospects). This does not let them off the hook, however. In the culture of political fund-raising, norms have evolved, and donors *expect* to be asked personally for money. If they do not receive that courtesy, then they often withhold contributions. Fund-raising solicitations sometimes can boil down to flattery; the candidate calls, tells the prospect how crucial his or her support has been, expresses gratitude, and lets the prospect know that the candidate cannot win without his or her help. It is human nature to respond favorably to this type of attention.

A personal request from the candidate is by far the most effective solicitation. Usually, such requests are made by telephone, which is why campaign fund-raising is called "dialing for dollars." Depending on the size of the campaign budget, most candidates spend 2 to 4 hours per day raising money over the phone. Campaigns schedule "call time" along with public appearances, private meetings, and personal matters.[6] Fund-raising staff ferociously defend their allocation against encroachments from other schedule requests, especially because 4 hours of scheduled call time often translates into 2 hours of actual calling. Candidates are renowned among finance operatives for arriving late, taking frequent breaks, using fund-raising time to make personal calls, and cutting off call time early. It is easy to sympathize with this behavior, as 4 hours of begging for money would seem like a "degrading, disgusting, demeaning experience," as Hubert Humphrey described fund-raising. But fewer calls means fewer receipts and thus fewer resources available for contacting voters. Call time and fund-raising are easier for candidates who understand that they are not asking for charity. As mentioned earlier, only friends and family give out of the kindness of their hearts. Everyone else wants something. Thus, the relationship is a two-way street. The contributor and the candidate share some interest, and they both can advance this interest if the candidate runs for office and the contributor helps the candidate pay for it. Candidates can make fund-raising less painful if they conceptualize it as generously giving the prospect the opportunity to achieve his or her own goals. I have witnessed many candidates come around to this way of thinking in the final 2 weeks of a campaign, when the heat is on and they are tired of taking "no" for an answer.

Before call time, a fund-raiser will have prepared a stack of "call sheets" containing background information that the candidate needs to make an effective pitch. Basic information includes the prospect's name, telephone number(s), and giving history, and often the call sheet includes notes about the prospect's business or political interests and his or her family as well as details of the prospect's last contact with the candidate. Each call sheet also includes the exact amount the candidate should ask for, which has been carefully researched by the fund-raising staff. If a candidate makes a vague request, then he or she is very likely to receive less than the prospect could have given. Asking for too much usually is better than asking for too little, although staff do try to avoid embarrassing the prospect (and the candidate) by scripting a request for much more than the prospect can afford.

During call time, a staff member sits with the candidate and takes notes on each conversation. The most important content of each call is the amount of the pledge made. Many prospects decline to contribute or even to commit to later support, and others offer to raise money or host events. Some candidates are very engaged in fund-raising and every other aspect of their campaigns, so they themselves remember well who offered to do what. Others hate fund-raising so much that they are thinking too much about how to terminate the calls and do not retain the facts of the conversations as well. In either case, it ultimately is the staff's responsibility to follow up with each contact and collect the full amount of the pledge, so the staff person must gather as much information about the commitment as possible. Many candidates facilitate this by doing call time on a speakerphone and letting the fund-raiser listen to both sides of the conversation.

Some candidates maximize the number of contacts during call time by "pre-calling." As the candidate wraps up one call, a staff person uses a second line to get the next prospect on the phone. The candidate can then move seamlessly from one prospect to the next without wasting time dialing, holding, or leaving messages. Many candidates hate this because they welcome any break they can get from asking for money. They might net more from a more efficient operation, but for many of them, it is psychologically bruising to make request after request like a stream of rapid fire. Pre-calling is not always an effective strategy, especially for first-time candidates, because prospects generally do not appreciate hearing "Hello, please hold for Mr. Ambitious" when they pick up a call. Prospects seem much more tolerant of pre-calling by incumbents.

As noted previously, a personal request is persuasive. It also is effective because it is just plain hard to say "no" to someone personally. A prospect can easily hang up on a telemarketer or ignore a letter, but when a candidate is on the other end of the line, human decency kicks in. Prospects know that fund-raising is agonizing, and it often is as embarrassing for them as it is for the candidates. It is easier for many of them to say "Yeah, I'll send you a little something" than to hem and haw an excuse.

Personal Solicitation by a
Finance Committee Member or Staff Person

Candidates need help. Whether running for mayor or governor, a competitive candidate must collect hundreds of contributions. The candidate must solicit several times the number he or she collects because prospect response can vary widely but rarely exceeds 50%. Recruiting a finance committee lessens the burden and increases receipts dramatically. The finance committee members provide prospects and, as often as possible, convert those prospects to donors. Fund-raising can operate like a phone tree; the efficiency of contacts improves exponentially if the candidate calls on 10 friends, who each call on 10 friends to help, who each call on 10 more friends, and so on. The best fund-raising operations are *not* just a candidate and the paid staff; they entail an army of volunteers or members of the community who solicit contributions.

Once a finance committee person has enlisted in the fund-raising effort, he or she often is treated as a secondary candidate. One typical maneuver is for a fund-raiser to visit the finance committee member in the latter's office and brief him or her. The exercise parallels the first meetings with the candidate—combing through the Christmas card list, business rolodex, association rosters, and memory banks for names of people who might contribute to the campaign or, better yet, might come on board as lay fund-raisers themselves. Just like a candidate, the finance committee person considers the reasons to support a candidate and matches them to people he or she knows.

Finance committee members can dial for dollars, and many do. Asking for money personally generally is easier when one asks on behalf of another instead of for himself or herself. Others send personal letters to their lists of prospects. Some organize events (e.g., a breakfast with business colleagues, an in-home reception). The guests invited to these events usually must have committed to contribute, and the events are just an opportunity to collect the checks.

One trap that many campaigns fall into is using the finance committee as a planning committee. A finance committee's job is not to plan events, coordinate invitations, draft letters, or suggest ad scripts. This does not stop many of them from trying, especially with respect to the latter.[7] Each of these activities simply distracts the fund-raising volunteers from their primary task: soliciting contributions. In addition, finance committees frequently are underused. The members' names go on stationery or event invitations, but they do little to reel in commitments. This is a huge waste of human resources, the moral equivalent of printing brochures and not mailing them. Finance committee members can be of tremendous help to a fund-raising operation when they follow the script and concentrate on asking for money.

Direct Mail

Candidate calling targets individuals on the basis of individual interest or leadership status in a group that contributes organizationally such as a PAC or, in nonfederal races, a corporation, labor union, or other organization. A campaign also can target a group for individual contributions from its members, and this usually is done with direct mail or, increasingly, telemarketing.

A group most often is targeted because the candidate appeals to its members on the basis of the common characteristic that identifies them as a group. For example, members of Planned Parenthood presumably favor abortion rights and, therefore, would endorse a pro-choice candidate. Museum subscribers support arts funding, environmentalists like environmental protection, and accountants prefer Byzantine tax codes. Candidates who share these positions can send a form letter to each group member, discussing the shared interest and asking for financial help. Each of the preceding examples is a membership group with a membership list, so these groups make excellent targets for direct mail fund-raising. Some groups do not have formal members but still are readily identifiable. Campaigns (or their list vendors) can use surname dictionaries to target ethnic communities with appeals based on either substantive or descriptive representation. For example, Jewish donors often are targeted by federal candidates who offer a pro-Israel message. Hispanics and most Asian groups also can be targeted, and sometimes they are courted with an "elect one of our own" message. Such tactics might seem cynical, but they work well and, therefore, are unlikely to fade away.

The ripest target group members are those who already have contributed to the candidate, either earlier in the cycle or in previous campaigns. Members of this group already have calculated that it is worth it to them to support the candidate financially, and once committed to the campaign, it behooves them to protect their investments by contributing again. Money is the lifeblood of campaigns, and donor resolicitations are the red blood cells of campaign money. Campaigns tend to resolicit their donors about once every 6 weeks until the final 2 months of the campaign, when the mailing schedule often is stepped up to 3- or 4-week intervals. At least one consultant recommends that her clients mail to their in-house lists every week during the final stage of the campaign (Hart, 1992).

Increasingly, campaigns have been targeting groups whose shared characteristic has nothing to do with politics explicitly. Data vendors purchase catalog and magazine subscription lists and repackage them for political clients. With any new list, whether purchased from a data vendor or supplied by a supportive organization, the campaign conducts a test before sinking the costs of production and postage into mailing the entire list. The size of the test depends on the size of the list, but for the smallest universe, 200 pieces is the minimum that should be sent. The average profit per piece is estimated from the test sample, and statistically the expected variation is quite large, certainly large enough that the campaign might easily overestimate the projected yield with a sample smaller than 200.

Direct mail is most effective when it is immediately followed by phone calls. The second contact serves as a combination reminder/guilt trip that dramatically increases response rates in most cases.

Telemarketing

Telemarketing, like direct mail, has a much larger clientele now than it did 10 years ago. Technology has decreased costs of lists used in both media, and the advent of the automatic phone dialer has increased the efficiency of telephone operations, making it more affordable for lower budget campaigns. Telephone appeals still are much more effective for statewide candidates; creating a targeted calling list for a typical legislative or congressional candidate usually yields too few names to make the endeavor cost-effective, at least in the short run. Down-ballot candidates who can afford to invest in list development (i.e., to pay for several rounds of calls even though the early ones will cost more than they raise) might be able to use telemarketing profitably over the long run.

Exceptions include "celebrity" candidates who have appeal outside their geographic constituencies as well as their opponents. These candidates tend to be on an extreme end of the political spectrum and can motivate both opposition and support. Fund-raising consultant Chris Schwenkmeyer observes that "anti-campaigns" often are the most effective ones; they open up a national target

audience to the candidates who take on controversial figures (personal communication, February 24, 1998). A negative message, cueing the antipathy incentive
discussed earlier, seems to play especially well with small-dollar givers. Schwenkmeyer notes that during the brief duration of unified Democratic Party control
of the White House and Congress, telephone fund-raising for Democratic candidates slowed considerably. It took a new "bogeyman," House Speaker Newt
Gingrich, to get small donors back into action.

Telemarketing sometimes is coordinated with direct mail to a single universe,
but more typically it is a complementary tactic. Some fund-raising consultants
have found that traditional direct mail is not very effective with telephone donors,
who tend to be "impulse buyers." Just as direct mail pieces are followed up with
reminder calls, telephone commitments are followed up with mailed pledge cards
and response envelopes. Yields vary by list, but a typical success rate is 75% of
targets contacted, with 10% to 12% of contacts pledging and 50% of pledges
returned.

Events

Many first-time candidates and their enthusiastic but politically inexperienced
"kitchen cabinets" (i.e., their closest and most trusted advisers) think that the way
in which to raise money is to throw a party and charge admission. Even veteran
politicians often prefer event fund-raising, perhaps because it is less personally
excruciating to send a polite invitation than to issue a pleading letter. Making an
appearance at a nice reception also is a lot more fun than call time. Fund-raising
operatives, who can spend up to three quarters of their time arranging the logistics
and riding herd on follow-up, tend to feel exactly the opposite. Events incur huge
overhead costs and drain valuable staff and volunteer time. Their net profit per
hour of labor is incredibly small, making them the least efficient way in which to
raise money. However, in most races, events are a necessary evil. There is no other
way in which to collect checks from many small contributors and even some big
ones. Certain contributors require a "retail" approach; they feel as if they are
paying something for nothing if they just send checks in response to mail or
telephone appeals. These supporters need free hors d'oeuvres and a "grip-and-
grin" photo with the candidate.

Events are not completely worthless. Barbecues, house parties, and pancake
breakfasts are the "bread and butter" of local elections. Events also can offer an
effective way in which to harness star power when an especially prominent
political figure offers support to the candidate.[8] Such endorsers could do more
for the campaign by mailing an appeal to their own list of dedicated supporters
and enlisting their top-tier finance volunteers to help the candidate, but that just
does not happen very often. A politician's lists are one of his most valuable
resources; the lists are painstakingly developed over a long career, and most
politicians guard this resource very closely. The next best thing a political celebrity
can do is offer himself or herself as a lure to people who will pay to meet the
celebrity. I once coordinated a fund-raiser at Pamela Harriman's home in Sun
Valley, Idaho, and it was staggering to see the number of people who showed up

just to meet the legendary Democratic doyen. My colleagues and I had been courting some of the guests for months, but it took this retail opportunity to get them to contribute to our candidate's campaign.

Even with a big name as a draw, a campaign cannot just mail invitations and wait to see who shows up. The hook might enhance turnout and attract a few curiosity seekers, but without the usual legwork, the event certainly will not meet its potential for cash infusion and might even be a flop. Several years ago, I planned a garden party at which the governor of my candidate's state was the special guest. Trying to expand our donor network, we recruited a new group of volunteers to serve on the event host committee. All of these people were thrilled to have their names appear with the governor's on the invitation, but they were not too keen on asking all of their friends to ante up the ticket price. The event was a total disaster, and greeting the governor at the curb to give him fair warning ("Sir, there are 10 excited people waiting to meet you") was one of the low points of my professional career.

Small-dollar events also serve to build political support, which is essential to candidates at all levels. The retail aspect of events refers not to the financial transaction but rather to the enhancement of the guest's attachment to the candidate. It can make a small donor feel like part of the campaign team to attend an "exclusive" (at least more exclusive than a rally or a public appearance) event and stand in a room full of compatriots getting a pep talk (stump speech) from the team captain. Many campaigns harvest volunteers at grassroots fund-raising events.

Tailoring the Mix of Tactics

All of the tactics described in the preceding subsections can vary in their effectiveness. The level of the office sought and the governing campaign finance regulations are the two most important determinants of a campaign's tactical mix. Unique circumstances such as running against a high-profile, controversial opponent also guide the fund-raising approach.

Federal elections are subject to the Federal Election Campaign Act, which limits the total amount of contributions from one individual to $1,000 per election. Thus, contribution limits make wide-reaching appeals to small donors essential for candidates for the U.S. House or Senate. Such appeals are best made through direct mail and, for statewide candidates, telemarketing. Candidates for local office have a much smaller universe of potential donors and, therefore, are more reliant on fund-raising events in their communities.

Money Doesn't Grow on Trees . . . or Does It?

The key to campaign fund-raising is repetition, reinforcement, and relentlessness. A campaign plan can map out a brilliant strategy, but the candidate and the fund-raising team must ask, ask, and ask some more. Each of the tactics outlined in the preceding subsections requires repeated contacts—personal letters and staff contact to follow up candidate calls, reminder phone calls to direct mail and event invitees, mailed pledge cards to telemarketing donors, and so on.

The initial contact plants a seed by introducing the prospect to the candidate and showing the prospect that supporting the candidate promotes the prospect's own interest. That prospect might not give the first time he or she is asked, but with each new campaign interaction, the prospect's incentives are reinforced. The campaign nourishes the seed with each meeting, letter, and phone call. Finally, the prospect decides to contribute, perhaps to get the campaign to leave him or her alone, but more likely because he or she has judged the candidate to be a good investment.

A dedicated candidate with a skilled fund-raising team can cultivate an orchard of money trees, with contributions ripening every day. The campaign should not try to harvest contributions too soon, that is, before cueing the prospect's incentives. But tireless execution of a well-laid finance plan certainly will bear fruit, enabling the candidate to fund the other aspects of the campaign.

Notes

1. At first glance, it might seem odd that the California senate races are more expensive than U.S. House races, but California is the only state with more members of the House (52) than of the state's upper chamber (40), and state senate districts are significantly larger than House districts.

2. It is interesting that the vast majority of corruption cases do *not* involve campaign contributions. My search for colorful examples of the politician-prostitute and the politician-extortionist produced a long list of names, but in only a very few cases did the individual deposit tainted money into a campaign account. Most just took the money personally. Apparently, the currency of corruption—at least of proven corruption—is *not* the campaign contribution. Or, perhaps there are so few examples because it is much harder to prove that a campaign receipt involves an illegal exchange.

3. Most federal PACs contribute to candidates only at the request or with the approval of a local affiliate. The member unions of the AFL-CIO are the best example of this rule. Before a national union will contribute federal PAC funds to a congressional candidate, a local affiliate in the candidate's district must formally request the contribution.

4. This is why incumbents in noncompetitive districts often amass huge "war chests." Their donors do not contribute to enhance electoral prospects; rather, they contribute to keep a smooth working relationship.

5. The amounts that qualify as "large" or "grassroots" vary by election. In California state elections, contribution amounts currently are unlimited by state law, so candidates can (and do) collect funds in $100,000 increments. Their time obviously is spent more efficiently pursuing such large chunks rather than $1,000 or smaller contributions. A city council candidate, on the other hand, might have a total budget of $10,000 or less and, therefore, will need to spend part of each day chasing after individual $50 and $100 donations.

6. Federal officeholders are prohibited from making fund-raising calls from official phones. Members of Congress often schedule call time at the national party committee offices—both parties have telephone stations set up for their members—or at the offices of their fund-raising consultants.

7. Everyone associated with a campaign is an amateur media consultant. When I worked as a fund-raiser, I thought that it was just the finance committee. But when I joined a media consulting firm, I learned otherwise.

8. Many campaigns misjudge the drawing power of their local elected officials. "Especially prominent" means president, vice president, Senate majority leader, House speaker, and (sometimes) governors and U.S. senators.

References

Chance, A. (1997, February 25). As a voter, Checchi has imperfect record in '90s. *Sacramento Bee,* p. A3.

Citizens' Research Foundation. (n.d.). Amounts raised or spent in selected state legislative contests 1991-1996. Available on Internet: http://www.usc.edu/dept/crf/data/contests.html.

Federal Election Commission. (n.d.). Untitled database of candidate campaign finance information for 1995-1996 cycle. Available on Internet: http://www.fec.gov/fec/hstap1.zip.

Gillis, M. (1997, October 17). Evans sentenced to 41 months in bribery case. *Chicago Sun-Times,* p. 3 (Sports).

Hart, N. (1992, September). Buddy, can you spare a grand? *Campaigns & Elections,* pp. 47-50.

Langbein, L. I., & Lotwis, M. A. (1990). The political efficacy of lobbying and money: Gun control in the U.S. House, 1986. *Legislative Studies Quarterly, 15,* 413-440.

Schroedel, J. R. (1986). Campaign contributions and legislative outcomes. *Western Politics Quarterly, 39,* 371-389.

Smith, D. (1997, May 19). A political wheeler-dealer. *Sacramento Bee,* p. A1.

Wright, J. R. (1985). PACs, contributions and roll calls: An organizational perspective. *American Political Science Review, 79,* 400-414.

Wright, J. R. (1990). Contributions, lobbying, and committee voting in the U.S. House of Representatives. *American Political Science Review, 84,* 417-438.

SECTION  III

Analysis of the Political Marketplace

Political Research Methods

11

Media Polls, Candidates, and Campaigns

PAMA MITCHELL
ROB DAVES

In a bitterly fought 1996 campaign for the U.S. Senate in Minnesota, Republican Rudy Boschwitz was trying to take back his seat from Democrat Paul Wellstone. In an effort to blunt the sting of the latest poll by the Minneapolis *Star Tribune,* which showed Boschwitz slipping, the campaign's managers cranked up the fax machines to Republican "fat cat" contributors. Their fax claimed that the newspaper's poll was flawed because it asked the trial heat question after question about their candidate's negative advertising. It also suggested that the poll interviewed too many Democrats.

The poll had done neither. The *Star Tribune*'s polling director recognized that the party was only doing its job—protecting its candidate—but asked for a correction and an apology. Neither was forthcoming.

Welcome to the rough-and-tumble world of candidates and media polls. This chapter is devoted to one of the tools that journalists use to report political news—the media poll. Media polls have been around almost since the beginning of modern survey research during the 1930s and 1940s. Political marketers might be familiar with the 1936 *Literary Digest* polling fiasco, when the magazine used a sample from lists heavily skewed toward upscale Republican voters. That poll incorrectly forecast the presidential election, whereas others such as Gallup and Roper correctly predicted Franklin D. Roosevelt's election (Roshco & Crespi, 1996). Since then, refinements in sampling procedures, questionnaire methods, and statistical techniques as well as better ways of ascertaining likelihood to vote have made preelection polls remarkably accurate in their ability to allow journalists to tell their readers, listeners, and viewers what the public is thinking about and who is ahead in any given election campaign (see Rademacher & Tuchfarber's chapter in this book [Chapter 12]).

This chapter explains how news organizations use political polling, that is, how journalists think about polling as they go about their coverage of politics—both the politics of public policy and the politics of election campaigns. It outlines the differences between the uses of polling by candidates and their consultants, on the one hand, and by news organizations, on the other.

The chapter discusses seven main issues: (a) players in the political milieu who use polling, and how polls done for news organizations differ from other polls; (b) how journalists use polling information (both their own and that from other sources); (c) the effects of media polls on campaigns and on the electorate; (d) how candidates respond to media polls; (e) the exit poll and how journalists use exit poll findings; (f) the curse of pseudo-polls and the ethics of polling; and (g) a glimpse at what political marketers can expect from media polls in the future.

The Players: Who Does What and Why?

In the game of election politics, there are many players. Among them are reporters (who gather the news) and editors (who frame and order the news), candidates, political consultants (including hired pollsters), and (not least) the voters. Nearly all use polling for various purposes at different times, and all have a vested interest in the election outcomes and the effects that polls might have on those outcomes.

Political consultants work in many milieus. Special interests—lobbyists, trade organizations, and the like—use polling for various reasons such as making sure that public policymakers hear public opinion about their key areas of interest and drawing attention to a social need. Their goal often is to make sure that political power is used for the benefit of their group's interest—to elect specific candidates, ensure passage of favorable legislation, and/or create a positive public image of the groups or their members.

There are many other players in the national political arena who conduct polls. For example, there were at least nine nationwide polls conducted regularly during the 1996 election campaign (Mitofsky, 1998). Many of the national media polls consist of partnerships between a television network and a major newspaper. The first such partnership was between CBS News and the *New York Times,* begun during the 1970s (Moore, 1995). The *Atlanta Journal-Constitution* partners with WSB-TV in Atlanta for election polling only, and the *Star Tribune* regularly has KMSP-TV as a broadcast partner for its Minnesota Poll.

Many academic institutions become players in state election campaigns. Their polls, often located in survey laboratories such as the ones at Ohio State University, the Institute for Research in the Social Sciences at the University of North Carolina (UNC) at Chapel Hill, and Marist College, use their polls as laboratory exercises for students, and many team with media partners to offset costs. The *Journal-Constitution,* for example, regularly partners with Georgia State University in conducting statewide polls and with UNC-Chapel Hill for a biannual southern regional poll. Private organizations that have no stated political agendas also conduct polls involving public policy and election campaigns. At the national level, these include organizations such as the Pew Research Center for the People and the Press. There also are many local and state polls, most conducted by academic institutions and news organizations. The earliest continuously published polls were the Iowa and Minnesota polls, begun in 1943 and 1944, respectively, and the Field Poll in California, which began in the latter part of that decade.

Polls conducted locally by news organizations now reach into all media markets in the United States. A 1989 Roper Center survey of news organizations found that 82% of large-circulation newspapers (115,000 daily circulation or higher) and 56% of large television stations were substantially involved in news polling. These media outlets served as principal sponsors and/or agencies for conducting news polls, and nearly all of them reported the use of polling for election coverage (Ladd & Benson, 1992). Although no similar study of media polling has been done during the 1990s, we believe that at least as many media outlets now regularly sponsor election-related polls.

Political parties and candidates—or more specifically, campaign consultants hired for the job—also do political polling.

What Makes Media Polls Different?

Political campaigns do polling for reasons considerably different from those of news organizations. For campaign consultants, the poll is essentially market research. Consider the various places that campaign polling fits into marketing. Polling exists to help identify the need for a product or service (or candidate), to test market communications such as video and print ad copy, to identify desirable traits, and to segment the market (Newman, 1994; see also various chapters in this book). For news organizations, the use of political polling is a bit more straightforward. Most news organizations poll because they believe that it is news to know who is ahead and who is behind, and why, in an election campaign. Thus, it is their practice to do "horserace" polls that give a precise estimate of the outcome "if the election were held today." But if one substitutes "candidate" for "product," it is not hard to see how a campaign consultant uses polling. Diane Feldman, a pollster who specializes in election campaigns for Democrats and progressive special interest organizations, thinks about the difference between her role as one that shapes the election and the role of journalists as reporting on how an election looked *yesterday:*

> The media look at a [poll] prediction as if it's static. I have no interest in that for my clients. Instead, what I'm trying to do is to advise [a campaign] about how the candidate should allocate resources in the final days. You can foreshadow the election to a degree, but my job [as a campaign strategist] is to try to change what you've foreshadowed if you see a problem with my candidate's campaign. My job is to make you wrong if you're showing that my candidate is behind. (personal communication, October 10, 1997)

To understand why news organizations conduct polls—any polls, not just political polls—political marketers must understand the concept of *news judgment*. News is something that a journalist considers important, something that readers, viewers, or listeners ought to know about or that is interesting. For example, many journalists consider it important that people know which candidate is ahead or behind or whether the race is close. That information is useful to journalists when they decide which stories to cover on the campaign. But more than that, it is a service to readers or viewers. Many people, however, disagree that such information is news. Former U.S. Representative Tim Penny, a Democrat who represented the second district in Minnesota, is one of many critics of horserace journalism and believes that current journalism pays too much attention to the horserace aspect of an election and too little to what candidates are saying about their beliefs on the issues. He also does not think that knowing the "horserace numbers" constitutes news (personal communication, February 19, 1999).

But just as candidates use polling information to help to manage their campaigns, such as who the candidate sees and where the candidate goes, they also use polls to affect their campaign workers and supporters and to influence reporters. For example, when campaigns are close, an underdog candidate might release current polling numbers to show supporters that a little extra effort might put the candidate over the top. In the same situation, leaders often choose not to release their poll results for fear that workers will slack off and that supporters might not bother to vote. Thus, media pollsters believe that we have an even more important reason to conduct political polls—to ensure that there is a disinterested third party whom readers trust to report objectively where the race stands.

Types of News Polls

News organizations use polling as a reporting tool, covering public opinion, collective behavior, and voter intention just as they would cover any story that meets the news judgment threshold. They use polls to do many things, for example, to support investigative projects and survey the public about lifestyles. News organizations' polls can be categorized as either election or nonelection.

Election polls often fall into one of several general types—horse race/tracking polls, polls that measure issues, panel studies, deliberative polls, or exit polls. These categories are not distinct ones, however, because often one survey will do double duty by measuring attitudes about issues and measuring the trial heat in the same questionnaire. But it is useful for political marketers to understand the methods, uses, and implications of each.

Horse Race/Tracking Polls

These are the best known of all polls done by news organizations and are simply measures of the support for each major candidate. Early in the campaign, horse race polls are conducted among registered voters, or the voting age population, and might be limited to asking about name recognition and general image measures. Later in the campaign, pollsters try to limit the sample to those who are most likely to vote, or they weight their sample to reflect a "probable electorate" to gain more accuracy and make it easier for reporters to write with confidence about the results of the poll.

Determining who is likely to vote in a preelection poll is a significant challenge for both media pollsters and those working for candidates. Some use a screen at the beginning of the survey and exclude those deemed "unlikely voters," that is, those who are not registered, say they have not voted in the past, or say that there is a chance that they will not vote in the election in question. (For a more complete discussion about how pollsters identify likely voters, especially in the 1996 presidential election, see Daves, in press; see also Rademacher & Tuchfarber's chapter in this book [Chapter 12].)

Polls That Measure Issues

This is more of a type of question than a type of poll. These measures can be done anytime during the campaign. Early in the campaign, determining public opinion about selected issues helps journalists to understand what is on voters' minds and what key issues candidates will try to address. Later in the campaign, issue measures might help to understand why a candidate is weaker or stronger or is ahead or behind. Media pollsters often use questions that test awareness and salience, or importance, to voters.

Panel Studies

Panel studies are surveys in which respondents from one poll are reinterviewed at a later date. They are used most often to help understand the effects on candidate support of single events—usually debates—during a campaign. After a televised debate, interviewers call back the respondents from an earlier poll—the panel—and question their reactions to the debate. Although the panel study is an extremely dicey way in which to precisely measure levels of candidate support, it can be useful in testing the effect on the electorate of some specific event (Daves, 1999).

Deliberative Polls

The deliberative poll is a relatively new tool for journalists, involving both measuring and influencing public opinion. Deliberative polls survey a representative sample of some population and try to give respondents balanced, objective, and factual information about a topic or collection of topics. The concept of a deliberative poll was fleshed out most fully by University of Texas government professor Jim Fishkin, who wanted to overcome what he says is one of the basic dysfunctions of American democracy—the lack of real citizen deliberation in election campaigns (Fishkin, 1991). In deliberative polling, a sponsoring news organization invites poll respondents to meet with reporters and researchers and leads small group discussions about the topics from the poll. Finally, respondents are reinterviewed after these deliberations to determine any shifts or changes in their positions. Deliberative polls are expensive, time-consuming, complicated, and difficult for journalists to cover well. They can be useful for studying opinion formation and change and for involving citizens in the public political debate, but they are less pertinent in measuring candidate support.

Another important and widely used type of media poll, exit polls, is discussed in some detail later. (See also Hofrichter's chapter in this book [Chapter 13].)

How the Press Uses Election Polls

In *Warfare Without Bloodshed,* Clift and Brazaitis (1996) are not the first to liken a political campaign to a military campaign. One can extend the metaphor to journalists, who use polls as part of their artillery in covering political campaigns. It helps in understanding how journalists use election polls if we classify them into three general types: "our" polls, the polling that the reporter's own organization does; "their" polls, the polling that other media organizations do; and candidate/campaign polls and other polls. The collection of all these sources often is referred to as "the polls," for example, "The polls show that Dole is edging up" or "the polls say that Dole doesn't have a prayer."

"Our" Polls

This is the best poll, of course, often because the reporter has had a chance to influence, if not help write, the poll questions and to plan the timing of the interviewing. Nearly all news organizations give their own polls bigger play than they do the polls of other news organizations, and they certainly give their own polls bigger play than they do candidate or campaign polls. For "our" polls, newspapers often publish stories outlining the poll results. Such stories usually contain at least three elements: what the trial heat numbers are (or who is ahead and who is behind), why the news organization thinks that is so and what it might mean for the immediate future, and some quotes from the relevant campaigns reacting to the results and from poll respondents who discuss their positions. In addition to the main story, there often are several graphics that outline the poll results, perhaps demonstrating several key points in the news story.

Television reports rarely give more than 1 or 2 minutes to a poll story because time is a precious commodity in a 30-minute news broadcast. For "our" polls, television coverage usually is composed of a lead-in (i.e., the anchor's transition from the prior story to the poll story), the television reporter's stand-up and voice-over while the poll results are graphically displayed, and the tag out (i.e., when the anchor winds up the story and transitions to the next story).

"Their" Polls

The results of polls of competing news organizations often are printed or broadcast but usually are not played as prominently or given the same amount of space as a news organization might give its own poll. Often, polling organizations that have their own polling units ignore competing media polls. That does not mean that reporters do not file them away mentally for a paragraph in the day's campaign story about "the polls." But unless a competing poll shows something quite unexpected or otherwise proves newsworthy, it is given short shrift.

Candidate/Campaign Polls and Other Polls

Unless there is a dearth of polling information in a campaign, which might occur in local races, many journalists all but ignore (at least in print or on the air) candidate polls. Journalists might be suspicious of a campaign poll's findings, knowing that candidates and campaign managers rarely release polling information that shows the candidate behind or in an otherwise bad light. Consequently, when campaign-sponsored polls are released, reporters frequently ask campaign representatives questions such as "Why do the numbers show what they do?" and "Why did you choose to release them now?" Political marketers would do well to advise the campaign representatives who deal with reporters to be able to answer these questions.

Journalists use polls for many reasons. As mentioned earlier, they use polling information later in the campaign to track who is up, who is down, and why. More sophisticated political reporters also use poll data to keep tabs on shifts in party identification among various demographic subgroups in the electorate that help explain voter attitudes. Journalists also try to use polls to measure other influences on campaigns. For example, in 1996, the *Star Tribune* used its Minnesota Poll to explore the effect of Boschwitz's negative advertising against the incumbent, Wellstone, in the general election, concluding that Boschwitz's negative advertising was adversely affecting his chances for unseating Wellstone (Baden, 1996).

Timing of Media Polls

Preelection media polling usually falls into several distinct periods over an election cycle. Depending on how close it is to Election Day, who we want to survey and what we want to ask them about will vary. For those whose business is politics, almost as soon as the ballots have been counted on Election Day, the next campaign begins. But for the media pollster, an election cycle usually lasts no longer than about a year. The first round of media polls usually occurs a few months before the primaries, when journalists want to get a detailed overview of the upcoming races. The networks and their big-city newspaper partners focus this stage of polling on national samples and, in presidential election years, on early primary states such as New Hampshire. Smaller news organizations often concentrate on their own local and statewide contests. Polls taken months before primaries often are called "baseline" polls because they provide a starting place or point of comparison for subsequent polls.

The purposes of baseline polling include finding out what matters to the voters right now—learning which issues are uppermost in their minds—and measuring name recognition and favorability ratings of likely candidates for important races. At this point, pollsters often include all adults 18 years of age or over in the sample, or the voting age population, rather than only those who say they currently are registered to vote because there still is plenty of time for people to register to vote.

As an important primary approaches, media pollsters tighten those respondent screens so that in the final pre-primary poll in a statewide campaign, they usually interview adults who say that they are registered and also plan to vote in the primary. Now, the focus of the questioning also shifts emphasis from issues to candidates, and media pollsters especially want to know which candidates the interviewees plan to vote for in the primary.

After the primaries but before the fall campaign, screening methods sometimes revert to registered voters, tightening once again as the general election approaches. The horse race emphasis continues throughout the rest of the cycle because the question of who is ahead retains its legitimate news value in the judgment of most editors. Toward the end of the campaign, media polls also might try to measure the effects of advertising and other campaign tactics used by the candidates. Most important for their credibility and professional pride, it matters a lot to media pollsters that their final preelection horse race measure closely matches the outcome on Election Day.

Effect of Media Polls on Elections

Although most observers agree that media polls have had an effect on campaigns and elections, there is less agreement about what those effects have been (Asher, 1998). To sort out the effects of media polls on campaigns, first we consider the different dynamics of published polls at various times during a political campaign—the early days before and just after primary elections, during the general election campaign, and the days just prior to Election Day when campaign managers focus on turnout.

Early Days

One of the early goals of campaign managers is to get name recognition of their candidate high enough in media polls so that reporters will begin to pay attention to him or her. Higher name recognition among the public and among partisans is important for two reasons: money and volunteers. Wellstone's run at Boschwitz's U.S. Senate seat in Minnesota in 1990 is a good example. Early in the campaign, media polls had shown that Wellstone initially had low name recognition. The campaign addressed that problem with a series of clever, award-winning ads. But after the primary election, he still had trouble raising money because he was perceived as a flaky, liberal college professor running against a long-established, relatively popular moderate Republican senator. Just after the September primary, however, the *Star Tribune*'s Minnesota Poll showed Wellstone within 3 percentage points of Boschwitz. Just 3 days after the poll results were published, "Wellstone's mailbox overflowed with checks," causing his campaign manager to comment that it was "literally raining money" (McGrath & Smith, 1995, p. 217). Wellstone went on to defeat Boschwitz narrowly, in part because the media poll had demonstrated that he was indeed a viable candidate.

Reporters and editors traditionally have given third-party candidates less attention than they have major party candidates. Candidates who are not perceived as acting like "real" candidates—by holding press conferences, issuing position papers, trying to raise money, and so on—often get the cold shoulder from journalists despite having jumped through all the legal hoops such as paying the filing fees. Thus, a poor showing in media polls early on, especially for third-party candidates, can result in getting less press coverage, or "free media," than those candidates who do well in early polls.

It also is true that other, nonpartisan groups active in election campaigns ignore candidates who do not have good showings in media polls. The League of Women Voters is a large and, in some areas, influential political organization. Many league chapters that often sponsor candidate debates and other forums rely on "independent polls"—often meaning media polls—to set minimum levels for candidates to be included in their debates. In North Carolina at one time, the league had a 15% rule; that is, if a candidate did not have at least 15% name recognition, then he or she would not be invited to participate in debates. That is true of league chapters in other states as well, although the guidelines might differ by chapter.

General Election Campaign

Many political consultants readily concede that although media polls might have the greatest impact on fund-raising and worker morale during the primary and caucus season, media reports of poll results continue to influence the candidates' fates throughout the campaign. Even presidential campaigns cannot afford to poll continuously for months on end, so the media polls can give campaigns additional data and provide a kind of "reality check" to compare to their own polls (McBride, 1991). Polls conducted in particular states by local media also help campaigns decide how to target resources. For example, a September 1992 *Journal-Constitution* poll showing Democratic presidential candidate Bill Clinton within striking distance of George Bush in typically Republican Georgia might have prompted the Democrats to pump more money into the Atlanta television market during the campaign's final weeks. (Clinton narrowly won Georgia in 1992.)

In recent years, both of the major parties have seen presidential candidates declared virtually dead by media polls weeks before the vote. On the eve of the final debate between Bush and Michael Dukakis in October 1988, ABC led its evening news broadcast with the results of polls conducted in all 50 states showing Bush with a huge advantage in electoral votes, strongly suggesting that Dukakis would lose in an electoral landslide. This news occurred even as ABC's latest national poll had Bush ahead by only 5 percentage points in the popular vote. Critics of ABC's handling of the story objected to its timing prior to the debate because it contributed to unrealistically high pressure on Dukakis to "ace" the debate (Moore, 1995). Similarly, polls in the early fall of 1996 showing Bob Dole up to 20 percentage points behind Clinton might have colored press coverage of Dole's campaign and given him a "can't win" tag.

A somewhat special case of poll effects occurs when media polls either miss the story or get it wrong. As hard as it might be for them to admit, media pollsters occasionally make mistakes of omission or commission, some of which might adversely affect political campaigns. In the 1992 New Hampshire presidential primary, the joint network exit poll significantly overestimated the showing of Patrick Buchanan, giving Bush only a 6 percentage point win, when in fact Bush won by more than three times that margin. As a result, "The networks, and the newspapers with early deadlines, treated the GOP primary as a real horse race, energizing the Buchanan campaign and creating an aura of Bush vulnerability that was, as it turns out, vastly exaggerated" (Moore, 1995, p. 366). Similarly, some national polls had Clinton as much as 18 percentage points ahead of Dole on the final weekend of the 1996 campaign, whereas others measured the Clinton lead much closer to the 8 percentage points he eventually tallied on Election Day (Panagakis, 1997). This discrepency between some of the polls and the election outcome prompted political scientist Everett Carl Ladd to roundly criticize many of the national polls for their work in the 1996 election. Ladd, in a piece for the *Chronicle of Higher Education* that later was published in the *Wall Street Journal,* called for a blue ribbon commission to look into what he called the most inaccurate polling since the 1948 election (Ladd, 1996). At the 1997 conference of the American Association for Public Opinion Research, however, a panel of media pollsters defended their work as being no less accurate than in many previous elections and certainly more so than the 1948 preelection polling. Ladd said that although he remained critical of the way in which polls are used in the democratic process, he regretted "the polemical excess of the piece" (Daves, 1997).

Whit Ayres, a Republican political pollster based in metro Atlanta, believes that the "wrong" 1996 preelection polls might have oversampled Democrats, a flaw he also believes occurred that same year in a *Journal-Constitution* Georgia poll, to the detriment of one of his clients. That poll, published in early October, had Republican U.S. Senate candidate Guy Millner trailing Democrat Max Cleland by double digits at a time when Ayres's own polling showed Millner trailing by just a few percentage points. In the newspaper's sample, the proportion of Democrats had jumped from about one third of the state's electorate to more than 40%, suggesting that either the Democrats were gaining ground in Georgia or the particular sample was skewed. The newspaper chose the former interpretation over the protests of the Millner camp, and a later newspaper poll found the Democratic proportion back at 33% with Cleland's lead correspondingly narrowed. (He eventually squeaked by to narrowly win the seat.)

Ayres says that "a media poll can make or break a campaign in its last [3] weeks" and that a poll showing the candidate far behind "creates the impression that the campaign is destined to lose—so the money dries up and the campaign *is* destined to lose." On the other hand, polls showing one's candidate ahead can "open the floodgates" of campaign contributions. Because of that magnitude of impact, Ayres urges the media to report not only their own polls but also the results of partisan polls taken at approximately the same time (personal communication, February 11, 1998).

Other Polling Effects

Another more general criticism of the influence of media polls has to do with their emphasis on horse race results. Although surveys taken late in the campaign might ask numerous questions about why voters feel the ways in which they do—about positions on issues and assessment of the strengths and weaknesses of each candidate's character and background—the media often lead their poll stories by reporting the relative standings of the candidates. Some observers have charged that this horse race emphasis causes people to evaluate candidates not on their positions regarding issues or their personal character but rather on how electable they are (Traugott, 1992). But it is at least arguable that editors exercise sound news judgment by leading with the horse race because as the election nears, the most important part of the story really might be who is likely to win (Kagay, 1991). Furthermore, polls that show a close race might have a positive effect on the electorate in that they actually could increase voter participation by making members of the public feel that their votes can make a difference (Traugott, 1992).

Scholars and media professionals also have studied the effect, if any, of polls on election turnout. Researchers try to answer questions such as whether Dole's position in the polls contributed to a lower turnout in 1996 than in the more competitive 1992 general election and whether projections of a winner—at least partially determined from exit polls—in east and central time zones discourage voting in western states.

Two of the most widespread concepts related to the effect of polls on voting behavior have been dubbed the "bandwagon" and "underdog" effects. "Some argue that polls that show one candidate ahead of another increase the incentives for supporters of the trailing candidate to change their preference and climb on board the winning candidates' bandwagon," explains political scientist Herb Asher. "Others emphasize underdog effects. Sympathetic voters, they claim, rally around the candidate the polls show to be losing" (Asher, 1998, p. 129). Researchers so far have produced only limited evidence supporting either of these effects. Some have posited that Jimmy Carter's electoral momentum during the primaries in 1976 might have come in part from voters seeing his high poll standings in other states and then jumping on his bandwagon, but no studies have shown that polls were more influential than a number of other factors in Carter's rise (Hickman, 1991). Lavrakas, Holley, and Miller (1991) found both bandwagon and underdog effects in a preelection poll during the Bush-Dukakis race in 1988, although "even with an underdog effect three times as large as a bandwagon effect, Bush's lead over Dukakis still was sufficient to win the election" (p. 172). Not surprisingly, voters who made up their minds late in the race were most likely to exhibit either the bandwagon or underdog effect.

Also looking at the 1988 presidential election, McBride (1991) concludes that although a slight underdog effect might have accounted for a late surge by Dukakis, other explanations could well have accounted for the drop in Bush's support. McBride also posits that both the underdog and bandwagon effects seem more likely to occur in subpresidential races where voters are less well informed about the candidates. In some of those races, voters might "look for some means of cutting their information costs in order to make their ballot choice" (p. 192). In studying that 1988 presidential election, Lavrakas et al. (1991) might have identified a more disturbing effect of media polls. Their work, incorporating a panel design that repeatedly reinterviewed a sample of registered voters both before and after the November election, found that "approximately 20% of registered nonvoters may not have voted because their awareness of preelection polling news stories made them think a Bush victory was a forgone conclusion," suggesting that reporting of preelection media polls "influences persons within the electorate and affects their behavior" (p. 175).

If true, then such an influence has to concern and even dismay journalists involved in preelection polling. But the media are not likely to stop conducting preelection polls because they strongly believe that trying to find out how citizens are responding to the candidates competing for public office represents not only a legitimate tool but also a compelling news tool.

Candidate Reaction to Media Polls

Most journalists who have covered numerous elections agree that candidates have fairly predictable responses to media polls, depending on whether they are ahead or behind. One frequent response, no matter whether the candidate is out in front or behind, is that "the only poll that's important is the one on Election Day." Candidates who are ahead are most likely to play down the importance of a poll, hoping that volunteers will keep volunteering, donors will keep donating, and the campaign will not lose or run out of steam. News stories report their reactions, for example, "It's because our supporters are working hard and because voters agree with me on the issue." But candidates who show poorly have somewhat less predictable responses. One is to criticize the results, claiming that the polls are different in some way from what the candidates' own polling shows. Often, however, candidates who do not like the results of media polls go after the news organizations or their pollsters, attacking question wording, interpretation, and/or the methodology. (All of these have happened to the authors of this chapter.)

Following are some examples of "war stories":

- In the 1998 Ohio gubernatorial election, one major party accused a pollster of biasing the interpretation of his university's nonpartisan poll, which was cosponsored by a newspaper. The party claimed bias because the pollster had given money to the opposing party's candidate.

- In the 1996 U.S. Senate election in Minnesota, the head of the Republican Party faxed a media poll's results to key donors and other party faithful, misrepresenting the findings. The criticisms eventually found their way into a national magazine, which had to correct them.

- In New Jersey, Governor Christine Whitman took umbrage with the results of an Eagleton Poll, and a member of her cabinet attacked the poll in the state's general assembly.

- In Minnesota, Governor Arne Carlson did not like the results of a poll that showed how one of his pet issues was faring among the population. So, he attacked the poll and its director, calling it a "push poll" and challenging the ethics of the news organization. (It was not a push poll; see the later section for a discussion of that type of non-poll.)

In some of these instances, political operatives, usually campaign managers or candidates themselves, attacked media pollsters for findings that the campaigns did not like. Quite often, a candidate will have the campaign's pollster review the media poll's methods to find possible flaws. This tactic has become so common that it became the topic of a panel at the 1998 conference of the American Association for Public Opinion Research, the most prominent professional organization for media pollsters. At that panel, one of the present authors called on politicians to find a better way in which to resolve these disputes, perhaps by using nonpartisan, academic-based experts to critique media polls rather than politicians' own hired gun pollsters (Daves, 1998).

Exit Polls

Exit polls represent one of the most valuable, if often controversial, types of polls conducted by the news media (see Hofrichter's chapter in this book [Chapter 13]). Journalists who have access to exit poll data throughout an Election Day, including many primary elections in presidential races, use early information to guide their election night coverage. Preliminary results from exit polling not only help editors decide which campaigns will be hosting victory celebrations but also provide valuable data about the issues and concerns that have resonated with voters. Complete exit poll data, which goes through adjustment and weighting after official vote tallies are in, provide a wealth of information about what the voters said at the ballot boxes.

The first systematic exit polling was conducted for CBS News in 1967 in a Kentucky gubernatorial race and was expanded to 20 states for the 1968 presidential election (Moore, 1995). By the early 1970s, the other television networks had created exit polling operations of their own. Exit polls are complicated, expensive undertakings that for many subsequent years were conducted competitively by the television networks and their newspaper partners. Largely for economic reasons, in 1990 the networks combined exit polling into a single joint operation, Voter Research and Surveys (VRS), and further consolidated in 1993 when VRS merged with the News Election Service, the organization responsible for providing vote tallies for media use on election nights. The new entity became Voter News Services (VNS), which sells exit poll results to media clients throughout the United States (Barnes, 1993). VNS conducts national samples of voters as well as statewide exit polls in dozens of states.

"In presidential [election] years, we conduct exit polls in every state, and in the off-year, in all states holding a race for U.S. Senate or governor," says Lee C. Shapiro, director of media service for VNS. "This information is provided to our six member organizations as well as to over 200 local news outlets—print, radio, and television—on Election Day." For the general election in 1996, VNS conducted exit polls in approximately 1,500 precincts with a total of nearly 70,000 voters participating in the sample. "The data are collected and processed on Election Day with a very quick turnaround time," adds Shapiro. "However, prior to being released, the data [are] subject to an enormous amount of quality control; [they are] scrutinized by political and statistical analysts as well as put through numerous computer models" (personal communication, January 1998).

Journalists often find exit polls more useful than other types of election-related polling because these polls represent the opinions of actual voters, not just those who claim they plan to vote. Political reporter E. J. Dionne of the *New York Times* writes that exit polls "can strengthen the democratic process by allowing reporters to explain what voters are trying to say at the moment they are saying it" (Dionne, 1992, p. 159).

Table 11.1 shows an example of an exit poll table, which VNS sends electronically to subscribers on Election Day and updates throughout the day and evening. This final version from the 1996 presidential election reflects weighting to adjust the sample to account for actual vote totals so that the top row of numbers shows the final popular vote of 49% Clinton, 41% Dole, and 8% Ross Perot, with percentages rounded. The table then tells us which demographic groups voted for each candidate—information we would not have without an exit poll—and also shows in the final column the differences between these breakdowns and those in the 1992 presidential vote. For example, men (48% of the sample) split their vote at 43% Clinton, 44% Dole, and 10% Perot, which was 2 percentage points more Democratic than in 1992. Women (52% of the sample) voted 54% Clinton, 38% Dole, and 7% Perot, a 9 percentage point gain for the Democratic ticket over 1992. Additional tables address issues and candidate qualities as well as other demographic and behavioral variables, all broken down by presidential vote.

State exit polls analyze a state's presidential vote as well as top statewide races, providing extremely useful information for journalists and others examining election results. Television networks and newspapers that have access to exit polls use them both to identify likely winning candidates before official vote totals are tallied and to analyze voting patterns. And, as is true with other types of polls, television and newspapers use exit polls in ways characteristic of the various

TABLE 11.1 Voter News Service Exit Poll Table: 1996 Presidential Election (percentages, N = 16,359)

	All	Clinton	Dole	Perot	Democratic Change From 1992 Presidential Election
Selected respondents		49	41	8	
Sex					
Male	48	43	44	10	+2
Female	52	54	38	7	+9
White					
Men	48	38	49	11	
Women	52	48	43	8	
Race					
White	83	43	46	9	+4
Black	10	84	12	4	+1
Hispanic	5	72	21	6	+11
Asian	1	43	48	8	+12
Other	1	64	21	9	+7
Age					
18-29 years	17	53	34	10	+10
30-44 years	33	48	41	9	+7
45-59 years	26	48	41	9	+7
Over 60 years	24	48	44	7	−1

SOURCE: Voter News Service, Copyright 1996. Used with permission.

media. Whereas television's immediacy leads to an emphasis on using exit polls to help "call" races—to announce which candidates have won their campaigns—newspapers' longer lead time and relative depth allow for greater emphasis on deciphering the *why* and *how* questions of what the voters did that day (Asher, 1998).

The controversial nature of exit polls stems mostly from charges that the television networks rely on these data to project winners before all the polling places have closed. For example, in 1980 the networks declared a Ronald Reagan victory—and Carter conceded the election—before the polls had closed on the West Coast. The evidence is inconclusive about whether turnout in the western states was affected by the early call in 1980, but the networks have since agreed not to call election results in any state until its polls have closed (Asher, 1998; Traugott, 1992).

Criticism of television's reliance on using exit polls to project election winners centers on the suspicion that "these media projections violate [a voter's] individual right to make a private decision that will have an impact on the electoral process" (Traugott, 1991, p. 137). Citizens sometimes feel that broadcast of exit poll results has too great an influence on people who have not yet voted. Media sponsors of Election Day polling argue that any legal restriction placed on reporting of exit poll results would constitute a violation of the press's First Amendment rights. One proposal to eliminate the potential problem of voters in the West being influenced by reports of results in eastern time zones is to establish uniform voting hours throughout the United States. But the media are not likely to voluntarily curtail their use of exit polls, nor are they likely to rely too heavily on them to report the outcomes of tight races, if only because the media cannot afford to call them wrong.

Non-Polls/Pseudo-Polls

As newspaper pollsters, we repeatedly urge reporters and editors to guard against the publication of information based on bogus survey research or "pseudo-polls." These unreliable polls, which come in many guises, are simply nonscientific polls that purport, implicitly or explicitly, to represent public opinion but that in fact have methodological flaws that render the results nonrepresentative. Those flaws almost always can be traced to the fact that the results are not based on random probability samples. But media outlets often receive releases from publicists who claim to have surveyed public opinion when in fact no scientific sample was employed.

Types of pseudo-polls include 900 number phone call-ins conducted by television or radio stations, which are based on self-selected samples. Editors also learn to be wary of information publicized by officeholders or office seekers based on questionnaires returned from mass mailings in their districts because the findings might not employ proper sampling methods and might include biased questions. A type of pseudo-poll that has become notorious during the 1990s is the push poll, which has been called political telemarketing under the guise of survey research (Gawiser, 1995). The American Association for Public Opinion Research (1997) defines the push poll as a telemarketing technique that feeds voters "false or misleading 'information' about a candidate under the pretense of taking a poll to see how this 'information' affects voter preferences" (p. 11). But the true intent of this technique is not to measure but to manipulate public opinion, "to 'push' voters away from one candidate and toward the opposing candidate" (p. 11).

The Internet and Other Computer Applications

Computer technology has both streamlined the conducting of legitimate surveys and added to the array of pseudo-polls that threaten to undermine public confidence in the profession. On the positive side, researchers have used computer-assisted telephone interviewing (CATI) for a decade or more. Interviewers read questions off a screen instead of a paper questionnaire and enter responses, thus cutting out the need for a separate data entry step, and computer programs also efficiently handle telephone samples while a poll is being conducted. For the news media, CATI's chief benefit might be that the technology's faster turnaround time—the time between completion of interviewing and distribution of tabulated results to editors—allows for a much more timely reporting of those results (Frankovic, 1992).

Computers and touch-tone telephones also have made it possible to gather information without even using interviewers. This attractive cost-cutting method has been called "CATS" (for completely automated telephone surveying) and consists of recorded questionnaires in which respondents enter their own answers. The methodological problems affecting the quality of results obtained in this way are legion, encompassing everything from short field times, to lack of a way in which to select respondents within households, to insufficient callback procedures (Traugott, 1995). Although households may be selected at random, the other problems associated with CATS relegate the method to the realm of the pseudo-poll.

The Internet also has brought the home computer version of the radio or television call-in—the on-line poll. Prodigy and America Online, as well as on-line versions of many local newspapers, frequently ask users to participate in "polls" about all types of topics. Again, because the samples are self-selected, the survey research profession generally does not consider on-line polls valid. But research comparing Prodigy's measures of presidential approval ratings and a variety of trial heats in statewide elections with scientific poll results has shown a remarkable consistency, prompting some softening toward on-line polling within the profession (Maisel, Robinson, & Werner, 1995; Werner, 1997). We do caution that on-line polling will have only limited uses unless and until a method for probability sampling can be devised.

Media Polls in the Future

Looking into our crystal ball, we believe that political marketers can expect the media to continue to sponsor election polls in the quantity we have seen during the 1990s. The market for media polls seems saturated, as most of the news organizations that can afford to conduct surveys already are doing so. Unless a major economic downturn hits, these organizations are likely to persist in using quantitative public opinion as a tool for reporting the news. We also anticipate a further proliferation of pseudo-polls over the next few years. As more Americans become Internet users, on-line polls seem likely to increase. The software for Web surveys is easily available, giving virtually anyone with Web page design experience the ability to conduct surveys. Internet surveys can be a useful tool for allowing readers and viewers to interact with the news organization and with each other. The Internet also offers promise to political marketers trying to collect information about supporters and as a method for supporters to contact the campaign. But until the sampling hurdle is cleared, political marketers need to take Internet surveys with the appropriate grains of salt and be wary of these efforts to collect on-line opinions.

Another development that the authors hope to see is greater accountability for accuracy among media polls. There have been relatively few presidential elections in which media polls had serious problems. One of the first was in 1948, and certainly the 1980 election challenged the nation's pollsters. In 1996, some polls underestimated turnout and overestimated the size of the Clinton lead. Because of those and other problems, public opinion researchers are renewing their efforts to develop ways in which to judge the accuracy of preelection polls (Mitofsky, 1998).

During the past two decades, media polls have cemented their place in the political landscape, and the political marketer will do well not only to understand the reasons why journalists conduct polls but also to consider the potential effects of media polls.

References

American Association for Public Opinion Research. (1997). *Best practices for survey and public opinion research and survey practices AAPOR condemns.* Ann Arbor, MI: Author.

Asher, H. (1998). *Polling and the public: What every citizen should know* (4th ed.). Washington, DC: Congressional Quarterly.

Baden, P. L. (1996, October 15). Wellstone pulls ahead of Boschwitz: Results suggest Republicans' negative ads are backfiring. *Star Tribune* (Minneapolis), p. A1.

Barnes, J. (1993). The polling business: VRS and NES—the fusion ticket. *The Public Perspective, 5*(1), 17-18.

Clift, E., & Brazaitis, T. (1996). *War without bloodshed: The art of politics.* New York: Scribner.

Daves, R. (1997, Summer). Plenary hears about 1996 polling controversy. *AAPOR News,* p. 5. (Ann Arbor, MI: American Association for Public Opinion Research)

Daves, R. (1998, May). *Pummeling the pollsters: Case studies of how politicians attempt to tar the messengers—The case of the push poll accusation.* Paper presented at the annual conference of the American Association for Public Opinion Research, St. Louis, MO.

Daves, R. (1999). Deliberative polling: Fitting the tool to the job. In M. McCombs & A. Reynolds (Eds.), *The poll with the human face: The National Issues Convention experiment in political communication.* Mahwah, NJ: Lawrence Erlbaum.

Daves, R. P. (in press). Who will vote? Ascertaining likelihood to vote and modeling a probable electorate in 1996 preelection polls. In P. J. Lavrakas & M. W. Traugott (Eds.), *Election polls, the news media, and democracy.* Chatham, NJ: Chatham House/Seven Bridges Press.

Dionne, E. (1992). The illusion of technique: The impact of polls on reporters and democracy. In T. Mann & G. Orren (Eds.), *Media polls in American politics* (pp. 150-167). Washington, DC: Brookings Institution.

Fishkin, J. (1991). *Democracy and deliberation: New directions for democratic reform.* New Haven, CT: Yale University Press.

Frankovic, K. (1992). Technology and the changing landscape of media polls. In T. Mann & G. Orren (Eds.), *Media polls in American politics* (pp. 32-54). Washington, DC: Brookings Institution.

Gawiser, S. (1995, Fall). Push polls: Next wave of dangerous pseudo-polls. *AAPOR News,* pp. 1, 8. (Ann Arbor, MI: American Association for Public Opinion Research)

Hickman, H. (1991). Public polls and election participants. In P. Lavrakas & J. Holley (Eds.), *Polling and presidential election coverage* (pp. 100-133). Newbury Park, CA: Sage.

Kagay, M. (1991). The use of public opinion polls by the *New York Times:* Some examples from the 1988 presidential election. In P. Lavrakas & J. Holley (Eds.), *Polling and presidential election coverage* (pp. 19-56). Newbury Park, CA: Sage.

Ladd, E. (1996, November 19). The pollsters' Waterloo. *Wall Street Journal,* p. A22.

Ladd, E., & Benson, J. (1992). The growth of news polls in American politics. In T. Mann & G. Orren (Eds.), *Media polls in American politics* (pp. 19-31). Washington, DC: Brookings Institution.

Lavrakas, P. J., Holley, J. K., & Miller, P. (1991). Public reaction to polling news during the 1988 presidential election campaign. In P. J. Lavrakas & J. K. Holley (Eds.), *Polling and presidential election coverage* (pp. 151-183). Newbury Park, CA: Sage.

Maisel, R., Robinson, K., & Werner, J. (1995). Creating a benchmark using on-line polls. *The Public Perspective, 6*(2), 8-10.

McBride, F. (1991). Media use of preelection polls. In P. Lavrakas & J. Holley (Eds.), *Polling and presidential election coverage* (pp. 184-199). Newbury Park, CA: Sage.

McGrath, D., & Smith, D. (1995). *Professor Wellstone goes to Washington.* Minneapolis: University of Minnesota Press.

Mitofsky, W. (1998). Was 1996 a worse year for polls than 1948? *Public Opinion Quarterly, 62,* 230-249.

Moore, D. (1995). *The superpollsters: How they measure and manipulate public opinion.* New York: Four Walls and Eight Windows.

Newman, B. I. (1994). *The marketing of the president: Political marketing as campaign strategy.* Thousand Oaks, CA: Sage.

Panagakis, N. (1997). Incumbent races: A national perspective. *The Public Perspective, 8*(1), 21-23.

Roshco, B., & Crespi, I. (1996). From alchemy to home-brewed chemistry: Polling transformed. *The Public Perspective, 7*(3), 8-12.

Traugott, M. (1991). Public attitudes about news organizations, campaign coverage, and polls. In P. Lavrakas & J. Holley (Eds.), *Polling and presidential election coverage* (pp. 134-150). Newbury Park, CA: Sage.

Traugott, M. (1992). The impact of media polls on the public. In T. Mann & G. Orren (Eds.), *Media polls in American politics* (pp. 125-149). Washington, DC: Brookings Institution.

Traugott, M. (1995). "CATS" dissected. *The Public Perspective, 6*(5), 1-3.

Werner, J. (1997, May). *Self-selected on-line polls in selected 1994 state-wide races.* Paper presented at the annual meeting of the American Association for Public Opinion Research, Norfolk, VA.

12

Preelection Polling and Political Campaigns

ERIC W. RADEMACHER
ALFRED J. TUCHFARBER

Polls are political intelligence. However, as with all forms of intelligence, what is learned depends on the care with which the information is gathered and the sophistication with which it is interpreted.

—*Charles W. Roll, Jr., and Albert H. Cantril,* Polls: Their Use and Misuse in Politics
(1972, p. 17)

Since the early 1960s, American political campaigns have increasingly relied on information gathered using "preelection polls," that is, sample surveys of voters conducted by private organizations to assist in the development and execution of campaign strategy and tactics. As a result, in contemporary campaigns, there is great temptation to simply "do a poll." However, for campaigns that wish to *effectively* use preelection polling, there is no such thing as *simply* doing a poll. This is the case because of at least two important realities. First, although polls can be used to gather information on a myriad of topics, from voter perceptions of candidates and issues to "the relative merit of competing ideas, hypotheses, and theories" related to strategic and tactical development, such information is of little value if strategists have no design as to how the information will aid in their ability to chart and/or modify the campaign's course (Mellman, Lazarus, Rivlin, & Grove, 1991, p. 24).

The second reason why using polls in a campaign is not a simple procedure is that, in reality, the actual administration of a poll (what most people envision as

AUTHORS' NOTE: We thank Terri Byczkowski and William Mason for their comments on earlier drafts of this chapter.

an interviewer calling citizens on the telephone and asking them questions) is just one stage of a larger process. The strategy of a political campaign often is carried out in stages, and errors in execution at any of these stages can spell disaster on Election Day. The same thinking can be applied to the process involved in conducting polls. "Just as the strength of a chain depends on the strength of each of its links, the quality of a public opinion poll is only as good as the quality at each of its stages" (Cantril, 1991, p. 91). Although campaign organizations usually are not charged with troubleshooting errors that can occur at each of these stages (this responsibility is left to the research organizations), they are left to judge the quality of the research that has been conducted. Thus, it is important that those working actively for candidates, as well as those observing the role of polling in political campaigns, gain some awareness of the basic procedural and methodological issues that underlie this research process.

The goal of this chapter is to provide a guide that allows readers to better understand the use of preelection polls in political campaigns, with a primary focus on candidate-centered campaigns. We construct this guide in three stages. First, we briefly review the role that polls have played in American electoral history. Next, we provide a description of the different types of information that are collected for campaigns as well as the types of polls conducted over the course of a campaign. Finally, we provide an overview of some of the procedural and methodological issues that researchers face when conducting polls in general and preelection polls in particular.

Before we begin, however, two caveats are in order. First, this chapter cannot possibly provide a comprehensive primer on survey research methods. However, there are several well-regarded texts that address this subject (Babbie, 1990; Dillman, 1978; Fowler, 1993; Frey, 1989). Second, we cannot possibly cover each of the methodological issues confronting those who conduct polls in general, or preelection polls, in the detail they deserve. Fortunately, however, reports on methodological issues specifically affecting the conduct of preelection polls, and how various organizations have dealt with them, are available (Crespi, 1988; Perry, 1960, 1962, 1972, 1973, 1979; Traugott & Lavrakas, 1996; Tuchfarber, Rademacher, Downing, & Smith, 1998; Voss, Gelman, & King, 1995).

With these caveats aside, we begin with a brief description of the history of preelection polls and the extension of private polling into American political campaigns.

A Brief History of Preelection Polls in American Political Campaigns

The history of preelection polls dates *at least* as far back as 1824, when "proto-straw polls" of presidential voter preferences were taken by political operatives and others in various settings (Smith, 1990; see also Robinson, 1932). By the turn of the century, more elaborate media-sponsored "straw polls" were conducted, often by newspapers, in an effort to project winning candidates in elections for local, state, and national offices. Such polls measured voter preferences using ballots distributed in newspapers, by mail, and through the "personal canvass," where newspaper employees collected voting intentions "wherever people could be found" in places such as factories and theaters and on street corners (Robinson, 1932, p. 53).

Straw polling reached a height of popularity during the 1920s and early 1930s, thanks in part to the successful election projections of one nationally syndicated magazine, the *Literary Digest*. In presidential election years during the period, the *Digest* mailed millions of mock ballots to lists of people compiled from sources such as telephone directories and automobile registration lists, and it reported the results of the ballots that were returned ("The *Digest* Presidential Poll," 1936). The *Digest* became the best-known straw poll after successful presidential election projections between 1920 and 1928 culminated in its 1932 estimate of Democrat Franklin D. Roosevelt's victory within 1 percentage point ("Roosevelt Bags 41 States," 1932; see also Converse, 1987, p. 11; Katz & Cantril, 1937). Despite this accuracy, the *Digest* poll faced its share of critics. Several analysts argued that the demographic characteristics of those who returned ballots to the *Digest* did not resemble the composition of the larger electorate, especially in relation to economic and geographic characteristics. For this reason, the critics contended, the *Digest* poll was doomed to eventually fail (Gallup, 1936; Robinson, 1932; Roper, 1936).

Leading up to the 1936 election, the *Digest* touted its poll as the " 'Bible' of millions," and Goodyear found enough public interest in the poll to sponsor a segment reporting *Digest* poll results on NBC Radio while at the same time distributing a "Poll-O-Meter" scorecard at its dealerships ("The *Digest* Presidential Poll," 1936; Goodyear, 1936). However, the *Digest*'s streak of projecting presidential winners ended that year, when its final poll showed Republican Alf Landon ahead of Roosevelt by a wide margin ("Landon 1,293,669; Roosevelt 972,897," 1936). Postelection analyses of the *Digest*'s failed projections attributed the error to some combination of socioeconomic bias in the lists the *Digest* used to determine where to send ballots, the low percentage of people who returned ballots, and differences in the voting preferences of those who returned the ballots they received and those who did not (Bryson, 1976; Katz & Cantril, 1937; Robinson, 1937; Squire, 1988).

Although the *Digest* failed in 1936, several organizations, including the American Institute for Public Opinion Research led by George Gallup, were successful in projecting the Roosevelt victory (Gallup, 1936).[1] These organizations primarily conducted in-person interviews and sought to control one area where the *Digest* was weak: the demographic composition of the entire group of voters interviewed. This control was exercised through "quota sampling," which mandated that a certain number of voters from various demographic and geographic groups in the electorate be interviewed to ensure that each group was represented in proportion to what was expected to be their composition of the electorate.[2]

The success of the 1936 election projections resulted in what Bradburn and Sudman (1988) dubbed "the almost overnight acceptance of public opinion polls by politicians and the general public" (p. 22). This acceptance continued during the early 1940s, when successful election projections by Gallup's organization and others created an "aura of infallibility about the polls" (Frankovic, 1992a, p. 121; see also Field, 1990, p. 36). This success fostered the extension of survey research into many facets of American life and led to the proliferation of organizations conducting research in both the public and private sectors. It also was during this period that the potential for polling research as a participating partner in the conduct of political campaigns was first explored. In 1946, pollster Elmo Roper was retained by Jacob Javits to measure the similarities between Javits's stated positions on issues and the positions of voters in the New York U.S. House of Representatives district in which he was running (Javits, 1947).[3]

Before the use of private polls by political campaigns could fully take shape, however, the confidence in polling built since 1936 was shattered, at least temporarily, in November 1948. The three major national polling organizations, led by Gallup, Roper, and Archibald Crossley, each projected a victory for Republican Thomas Dewey over Democrat Harry Truman, underestimating Truman's vote share by between 5% and 13% (Albig, 1956). This failure to project the presidential winner led to widespread criticism of the polls and the pollsters themselves ("The Press," 1948; "The Real Losers," 1948; "Stumping the Experts," 1948). One observer suggested that preelection polls be banned and that "the American Association for Public Opinion Research make the ban a part of its ethical code" (Chase, 1948, p. 629). But the toughest assessment came from a committee set up to investigate the failure of the 1948 polls by the Social Science Research Council (1949), which concluded, "The pollsters overreached the capabilities of the public opinion poll as a predictive device in attempting to pick, without qualification, the winner of the 1948 election" (p. 600). The council identified several culprits in the 1948 polling failure including errors in the methods used to select individuals to be interviewed, problems with the identification of nonvoters and likely voters, the failure to detect late shifts in voting behavior, and the inability to accurately allocate undecided voters to the candidates (pp. 608-611).

The failure to project the presidential winner in the 1948 presidential election began a revolution that changed the methods employed in the conduct of all polls. Since 1948, polling in the United States has been marked by several trends including (a) the move away from personal interviewing toward interviews conducted by telephone; (b) the move away from quota methods for selecting respondents toward probability methods using random sampling, which seeks to ensure that all respondents in a defined population of interest (e.g., all registered voters in the United States) have a known chance of being selected for an interview; (c) the move toward the use of computers for data collection, management, and analysis including the use of computer-assisted telephone interviewing; and (d) the proliferation of organizations involved in survey research, with the emergence of many new academic and private organizations conducting survey research at the local, state, and national levels (Crespi, 1988; Gawiser & Witt, 1994).

Another change since 1948 has been the increasing participatory role of polls in election campaigns. Javits's hiring of Roper offered one example of how polls might be used by campaigns, as did Rosser Reeves's consultation of Gallup when developing themes for the first presidential campaign commercials in 1952 (Diamond & Baker, 1984). But the large-scale expansion of private polling into political campaigns began during the late 1950s and early 1960s. Harris (1963) estimates that in 1962, three fourths of all gubernatorial candidates, two thirds of all U.S. Senate candidates, and approximately one tenth of all U.S. House of Representatives candidates used private polls over the course of their campaigns. By 1968, *Congressional Quarterly* proclaimed "Political Pollsters Head for Record Activity" ("CQ Fact Sheet," 1968), and that activity has continued since as the influence of polls and pollsters on political campaigns at all levels has grown dramatically to the point where "polling dictates virtually every aspect of election campaigns, from fund-raising, to electoral strategy, to news coverage" (Moore, 1995, p. 359). Certainly, the relationship between private polling and political campaigns has evolved markedly from the role played in the 1946 Javits campaign to the level played 50 years later in the 1996 presidential campaign, where at least one piece devoted to chronicling ties between consultants charged with polling, strategy, and advertising concludes, "The election was won and lost on the message—the ability to divine the hopes, fears, and desires of voters, then craft the ideas, words, and images that would best reach them" (Stengel et al., 1996, p. 76).

Attempting to divine the hopes, fears, and desires of voters is one role that private polling plays in contemporary American political campaigns. It is a consideration of this role that we turn to next.

The Research Question: Why Conduct Preelection Polls?

In the formative stages of a campaign, strategists must determine what role, if any, polling is to play in the campaign. An analysis of congressional, state, and local campaigns by Conway (1984) portrays such a decision to use (or not to use) polls as resting largely on three factors: the nature of the constituency (e.g., size of district, diversity of constituency), campaign characteristics (e.g., financial resources, sophistication of candidate and campaign staff), and the electoral contest (e.g., competitiveness of the contest). Of the factors Conway discusses, the campaign characteristic of *cost* probably is the most important consideration in judging whether, and how, to use polling over the course of a campaign. If we consider the example of the costs of conducting private polls in a political jurisdiction, the size of a U.S. congressional district, one recent report estimates that (a) an early, thorough sounding of voters (approximately 400 interviews) can cost $12,000 to $16,000; (b) a later poll, conducted on more narrow topics with the same amount of voters, can cost $8,000 to $12,000; and (c) a "tracking poll," which monitors voter preferences in specific candidate races over a period of time (e.g., 20 days at 200 interviews per day), can cost $60,000 to $80,000 (Faucheux, 1995, p. 23). Given that most campaigns allocate between 5% and 10% of their budgets to polling, there are some campaigns where such costs will make the use of surveys prohibitive (Conway, 1984, p. 101; Mellman et al., 1991, p. 23).

Several other considerations can affect the decision to use polling in a campaign including the level of diversity in a constituency and the competitiveness of a race. In political jurisdictions with diverse constituencies, polls can be valuable in determining the layers of opinion, if any, that exist. Such a constituency might require a thorough polling program because candidate support might vary by population subgroup, issues might affect various groups differently, and candidate messages might resonate differently with various subgroups within the electorate. By contrast, as Conway (1984) observes, "The research necessary to plan an effective campaign, including the selection of issues, campaign media themes, and targeted voter groups, is simplified in a relatively homogeneous constituency" (p. 101). In less competitive races, the point is an obvious one: Although no polling always is risky, an extensive polling plan beyond an early poll and a late follow-up poll might not achieve much more than satisfying the curiosity of the most paranoid of campaign managers or strategists.

If it is determined that polling is to be an integral part of the campaign, then an early poll can tell a campaign a great deal about the viability of running a campaign in that election year. Once the decision to go ahead with the campaign has been made, the goal of polling research in the campaign's formative stages becomes (a) the determination of which voter groups need to be the focal points, or targets, of the campaign's attention and (b) what messages need to be delivered to these and other constituencies to achieve victory on Election Day. Later, when a campaign has implemented its strategy and begun tactics designed to appeal to targeted voters, the research goal becomes one of determining what messages and themes are working to effectively persuade or energize voters and what part of the campaign, if any, is not having the desired effect.

Before going into detail about various types and timing of preelection polls and the information they collect, it is important to discuss the relationship between campaign strategists and the political polling organization that is commissioned. Whereas there are several models of this relationship, a model in which both the strategists and the pollster construct the topics of exploration is closest to the ideal. Campaign strategists have a better feel for their candidate and the constituency involved. Pollsters bring to the table experience with the types of methods most appropriate in exploring constituent attitudes and preferences as well as dynamics characteristic of the type of race that is being run. Thus, it is critical that *both* the campaign strategists and the pollster contribute to the design of an election polling program. In the same way as the average campaign strategist should not be expected to be able to design and execute a public opinion poll, the pollster cannot be expected to define what a candidate believes, or what a campaign should set out to accomplish, by simply going out and asking voters what they would like to see and hear from a candidate. Such plans are doomed to fail. Mellman et al. (1991) sum up the campaign-pollster relationship by advising campaigns,

> A pollster cannot "find" a message for a candidate. A candidate must feel and believe his or her message. The candidate and campaign staff [have] to be able to articulate for the pollster what it is the client feels and believes. And the campaign must also be able to fill in this story with specifics. Biography, issue positions, values, accomplishments, vision, and character are all grist for the questionnaire mill. Failing to provide your pollster with these raw materials will result in your receiving an inferior product. (p. 24)

In the relationship that established between the campaign and the polling organization it commissions, the organization brings to the table experience with the various types of information preelection polls can provide for a campaign. These are best illustrated through a discussion of three types of polls that are conducted at different stages of a campaign: benchmark polls, follow-up polls, and tracking polls.[4]

Benchmark Polls

The earliest poll that is conducted, either just before or just after a candidacy is declared, is the benchmark poll. Benchmark polls often are intentionally lengthy in content and usually represent the candidate's most thorough sampling of opinions during the campaign (Mellman et al., 1991). This type of poll, as its name implies, also provides a standard or baseline of indicators by which the campaign can be evaluated as it progresses toward Election Day.

Benchmark polls are timed to assist campaigns in gathering information of importance to planning the campaign. The first critical piece of information they can provide is the level of name recognition of candidates who might compete in the race as well as the standing of potential candidates using a "trial heat" question, which pits candidates in head-to-head match-ups against one another. Such information can be critical, as Crespi (1989) notes, in helping strategists to plot campaign strategy and tactics:

> Perhaps the single most common use of private polls is to measure the voting strengths and weaknesses of competing candidates. . . . Knowing whether a candidate is ahead or behind, by how much, and how standings differ between demographic segments of the electorate contributes to realistic assessments of what has to be achieved if a campaign is to be won. This knowledge can be of great value to campaign organizers and strategists in determining intensity of campaigning, in allocating campaign resources, and in targeting campaign efforts to specific populations. (p. 22)

Identifying target groups in the electorate obviously is an essential component of campaign strategy. In the formative stages of campaigns, it is critical to have adequate information about subgroups within the electorate, allowing campaign strategists to gauge, for example, which groups clearly support a candidate, which groups clearly do not, and those "swing voters" who (a) do not consistently vote for candidates of one party or another, (b) might be persuadable toward a campaign that addresses their key concerns, and (c) often represent the difference between winning and losing.

Benchmark polls also can aid in the determination of voter reactions to the candidates, their messages, and their themes. Voters frequently are asked questions that assess voter disposition (favorable or unfavorable) toward candidates and, perhaps most important from a strategic standpoint, the strengths and weaknesses voters perceive in the candidate and his or her opponent(s) both personally (e.g., reputation, character, personality) and politically (e.g., occupational experience, performance in office).

Finally, benchmark polls also can identify "what is bugging the constituents"— the key issues that voters feel the candidates should be addressing—as well as the impact that positions on particular issues might have on the likelihood of voters to support a candidate on Election Day (Grieve, 1996, p. 197; see also Crespi, 1989, p. 24).

Follow-Up Polls

The benchmark poll often is followed up by a shorter poll or polls, referred to as "follow-up" or "vulnerability" polls earlier in the election period and as "brushfire" polls toward the latter stages of a campaign (Sabato, 1981, p. 76). These polls are relatively shorter in length and focus on a few specific issues in a more in-depth fashion. If strategists have developed themes and messages using information gathered in a benchmark poll, then follow-up polls can be used to test voter reactions to a series of potential messages or slogans under consideration for use by the campaign. For example, an analysis of the use of polls in Bill Clinton's 1996 presidential campaign describes how voter reactions to certain slogans—"Building a Bridge to a Second Term," "Building a Bridge to the Next Four Years," "Building a Bridge to the Year 2000," and "Building a Bridge to the 21st Century"—was one of the determining factors of the latter's choice as a central theme in the campaign (Stengel et al., 1996, p. 90). Toward the end of the campaign, preelection polls might be used to observe voter reactions to candidate messages and issue positions or to measure voter intensity on a particular issue that emerges late as important in the campaign. The goal of this research is to monitor the impact that a particular message or issue has on the candidate's standing among voters.

Tracking Polls

Tracking polls are conducted continuously or semiregularly throughout the latter stages of a campaign. These polls can be conducted as a series of very short brushfire polls or as a series of very short daily polls. Usually, tracking polls contain only a few questions, the centerpiece of which is the trial heat question pitting the candidates against each other, as well as basic demographic questions and perhaps a very limited number of questions that monitor the impact of issues on the campaign or of messages on target voter groups. In charting candidate progress, tracking polls are useful in evaluating how well a campaign strategy and its tactics are working on the electorate as a whole and among key groups the campaign has targeted. They also can be used to determine whether or not an opponent's campaign is having an impact on voters (Asher, 1995, p. 106; Blakeman, 1995, p. 24; Sabato, 1981, p. 76).

Now that we have explored some of the roles that preelection polls have played, and can play, in political campaigns, we move to a discussion of the various procedural and methodological issues that face researchers who conduct polls.

Links in a Chain:
Stages and Errors in Preelection Polls

The conduct of a preelection poll is part of a larger research process. Whereas there are many levels and stages of a political campaign, there also are many stages in the process of conducting a preelection poll. A simplified version of these stages includes (a) the development of a research design, which includes specifying whether to study registered or likely voters, selecting an interviewing method (e.g., telephone interviewing), and constructing the instrument that contains the questions asked of respondents (i.e., the questionnaire); (b) the actual administration of the poll, which includes measuring voter preferences, attitudes, and opinions; (c) data processing, which includes tabulating interview results; and (d) the analysis stage, which includes interpreting results and presenting them to clients.

In this section, we briefly cover several components of a wide range of procedural and methodological issues that are faced when conducting polling for political campaigns. In focusing on the research design and analysis stages, we identify some of the potential sources of error at these stages, with the intent of leaving the reader with information that aids in the evaluation of the polling results they are presented with as well as the quality of those results.

Research Design:
The Sample Survey and the Telephone Interview

A key part of the research design stage is determining who to interview and how interviews are to be conducted. We can simplify things from the outset by stating that much of the information gathered in preelection polls, including information gathered for political campaigns, is now collected using sample surveys administered over the telephone (Crespi, 1988; Traugott & Lavrakas, 1996).[5] Whereas the term "survey" might be familiar enough, the addition of the word "sample" in front of it might not. A sample survey is conducted based on the premise that if proper probability methods are employed, generalizations can be made about a larger population using information collected from a smaller subset, or *sample,* of that population (for more extensive discussions of sampling, see Henry, 1990; Kalton, 1983; Kish, 1965).

Whereas the researchers commissioned to conduct a poll usually will determine the methods necessary to draw an adequate sample of a population, the campaign probably will be consulted on the population that is to be studied. In preelection polls, two types of populations are of greatest interest: *registered voters* and *likely voters*. Because many registered voters do not show up at the polls on Election Day, and attitudes and opinions of registered voters might differ from those of likely voters on various questions in which the campaign is interested, organizations often choose to study likely voters (Perry, 1973).

How are voters then chosen for interview? Most organizations will use probability sampling methods to randomly select voters for inclusion in a sample or will purchase a sample list from another organization that specializes in constructing randomly generated samples. The goal in using probability methods is to ensure that all members of a given population have the opportunity to be included in a sample and that each population member's probability of being selected in the sample is able to be determined by the organization conducting the poll. Such methods then allow analysts to calculate the degree to which the information obtained from a sample reflects the results that would have been obtained had the entire population of interest been interviewed.

Typically, organizations compile, or purchase, lists of phone numbers generated at random using one of two sources: voter registration lists or lists generated through a technique known as random digit dialing (RDD). One common method is to construct a sample of registered voters from registered voter lists available through state or local boards of elections. Whereas a voter registration list might seem like the best place to begin when trying to construct a sample of voters, voter registration lists often are out of date, provide limited information about telephone numbers, include ineligible voters, and exclude newly registered voters (Marquette, 1996, p. 138).

An alternative method that has come into wider use, and has been found to deal effectively with some of these problems, is RDD. RDD sampling methods can be used if a researcher is able to identify all of the possible working telephone exchanges within the political jurisdiction in which an election takes place. Using this information about exchanges, a computer program can be used to generate a random sample of telephone numbers, allowing each household with a telephone number to be assigned a known probability of inclusion in the sample (Klecka & Tuchfarber, 1974, 1978; Tuchfarber & Klecka, 1976). Whereas a registered voter list will provide a specific voter name and telephone number to contact, an RDD list provides only a telephone number for a household. Thus, a second stage of respondent selection must be undertaken.

Once an RDD sample of households has been generated, each household in the sample must be contacted. Upon contacting a household, however, the person answering the telephone is not necessarily the person who is to be interviewed. At this point, a registered voter must be randomly selected from within the household using one of a variety of techniques. For example, one commonly used technique instructs the interviewer to identify the registered voter living in the household who had the most recent birthday, which results in the selection of a registered voter from within the household while avoiding bias introduced by interviewing a voter who happens to be home at the time or a person who commonly answers the telephone in a household of multiple eligible respondents (Oldendick, Bishop, Sorenson, & Tuchfarber, 1988; for a discussion of other selection techniques, see Kish, 1965; Trohldahl & Carter, 1964; Waksberg, 1978).

It should be pointed out that there are drawbacks to using RDD and instances in which it might be a less appropriate approach to selecting respondents. From a cost perspective, there might be a large cost incurred in drawing and contacting an appropriate RDD sample in political jurisdictions that lack neatly constructed boundaries given that phone exchanges overlap political boundaries (Mellman et al., 1991, p. 26).

Research Design and the Potential for Error

The research design stage is one point at which researchers attempt to plan and try to limit errors that are common in all polling research (Groves, 1989; Lessler & Kalsbeek, 1992). Perhaps the best launching point for this discussion is the understanding that, as Groves (1989) notes, "To many readers of survey results, sampling error is erroneously interpreted as a summary measure of all the errors in the estimates. . . . Sampling error represents only one component of *total error*" (p. 293, emphasis added).

The notion of total survey error includes a variety of potential sources of error, from those that occur because of a failure to reach all respondents selected to be interviewed, to various errors that can be attributed to the questionnaire that is constructed, to errors attributable to the individual conducting the interviews (for more on the concept of total survey error, see Anderson, Kaspar, Frankel, & Associates, 1979; Converse & Traugott, 1986). For the purposes of this chapter, we focus on two general aspects of survey error: sampling error and nonsampling error (Anderson, Kaspar, Frankel, & Associates, 1979; Henry, 1990; Lessler & Kalsbeek, 1992). Sampling error, which is commonly referred to in reports of poll results in the popular press, occurs because information is gathered from a sample rather than from an entire population. Nonsampling errors occur because of flaws that go undetected in various components of the research process such as an inadequate sample, questionnaire construction, survey administration, and tabulation and reporting of results. We turn to these two issues next.

Sampling Error

To illustrate the concept of sampling error, assume that a statewide poll of likely voters finds that candidate "Smith" has 75% name recognition among likely voters. The use of a probability sampling technique such as RDD allows us to determine the precision of our name recognition result, or the difference between the result obtained from our sample of statewide voters and the expected result had we interviewed the entire population of registered voters in the state. This difference between the sample result and the actual population result is called sampling error. Sampling error is comprised of a margin of error and a level of confidence. The margin of error is a range (above and below the sample percentage) within which the actual population result is likely to fall. The confidence level is an estimate of the likelihood that the actual population result will fall within the range established by the margin of error. Thus, if it is determined that candidate Smith has 75% name recognition with a margin of error of ±4% at the 95% confidence level (a commonly reported level of confidence), then what is essentially being said is that if we were to take 100 samples of the population, the name recognition of candidate Smith will fall between 71% and 79% (i.e., 75% ±4%) approximately 95 times.

In evaluating the results of any poll, the sampling error gives only one indicator of survey error. The researcher can reduce sampling error when creating the research design by increasing the size of the sample to be interviewed. It is important to be aware that "the size of the population from which a sample of a particular size is drawn has virtually no impact on how well that sample size is likely to describe the population" (Fowler, 1993, p. 33). The calculation of sampling error is based on the number of individuals interviewed in the *sample,* the desired confidence level, the desired margin of error, and the proportion of the sample that offers a particular response.

At this point, we digress for a moment to our previous discussion of survey cost. Any campaign that uses polls must balance cost and precision against one another. In the survey design planning stages, careful attention must be paid not only to the size of the overall sample but also to the size of subgroups within the sample. Here is where cost and precision necessarily conflict. As we described earlier, campaign planning often requires information not only about the population but also about subgroups within the population. To reduce the error that is associated with key subgroups, the overall size of the sample must be increased. However, as Faucheux (1995) notes, "Sample size . . . is like a box of chocolates; the more, the better, but the more you get, the more it costs" (p. 23).

Nonsampling Error

The truth about the multitude of nonsampling errors involved in survey research is that even the most watchful eyes sometimes fail to appropriately plan for or detect them. Many of the same general nonsampling errors plague nonelection and preelection polls. These errors include, but are not limited to, "nonresponse error" (i.e., error resulting from not interviewing the entire sample) and "measurement error" (i.e., error due to problems associated with the questionnaire such as poor question wording) (Groves, 1989, p. vi; Lessler & Kalsbeek, 1992).

One type of error that has the potential to plague all polls is nonresponse error, which occurs when the respondents selected in the sample are unable to be located or refuse to answer questions they are asked. Nonresponse error can plague poll results when members of the sample who *were* contacted hold views that differ from those in the sample who *were not* able to be contacted or who refused to answer questions. The degree to which an organization "works a sample" (including how many follow-up calls are made to reach respondents and the organization's efforts to convert initial refusers) can have special importance in election surveys. Traugott (1987) found that persistence in attempting to reach respondents resulted in both different sample compositions (e.g., more calls meant the sample became more balanced in terms of the numbers of self-identified Democrats and Republicans) and, just as important, "differences in observed levels of support for political parties and candidates" (p. 54). The good news is that more recent political polls conducted by polling firms continue to get accurate estimates even in the face of falling response rates.

The subject of measurement error necessitates a discussion of questionnaire design and construction. The questionnaire is the written form of the ideas that campaigns want to test and the information they need to collect. Although it is potentially a source that will greatly aid a campaign, it also can be the campaign's worst enemy—a source of error that can severely affect the quality and usefulness of the information that is gathered. This error is captured in the ways in which the results of a poll can vary widely as a result of, among other things, the format of questions, the way in which questions are worded, and the order in which questions are presented. More exhaustive explorations of these topics as they relate to survey research in general are readily available, but here we focus on some of the issues that are particularly important in the construction of preelection polls (for further discussion of errors associated with various aspects of the questionnaire, see Converse & Presser, 1986; Schuman & Presser, 1981; Schwarz & Sudman, 1992; Sudman & Bradburn, 1982; Tanur, 1992).

In any poll, the form of the question used—closed or open—makes a difference in the amount and type of information that is gathered (Schuman & Presser, 1981). A closed-form question limits respondents to a predefined set of answers, whereas an open-form question allows respondents the opportunity to answer at length without limitation. On critical questions that a campaign might ask, such as the most important problem in the minds of voters, likes and dislikes about candidates, and reasons for preferring one candidate over another, the open form of a question might be preferable to a closed form. In any closed question, there is necessary potential for measurement error in that the researcher might not cover all of the possible responses to a question. As Fowler (1993) notes, the use of the open-form question has the following commendable properties: "They permit the researcher to obtain answers that were unanticipated. They also may describe more closely the real views of the respondent. Third, and this is not a trivial point, respondents like the opportunity to answer some questions in their own words" (p. 82). However, there also are many instances in which the closed-form question is more appropriate than the open-form question. For example, a closed-form question is necessary in testing campaign slogans that have been prepared by strategists.

The art of wording questions used in polls has long been a topic of study. Although the 100 considerations that Payne (1951) suggested be made when *wording* questions for inclusion in polls might be difficult to live up to, in polls, as in everyday life, it is important to remember that the answers received usually are framed by the questions asked. With this in mind, the "KISS" (keep it short and simple) maxim often is appropriate in the wording of questions, especially in the telephone format, where it is difficult to present a series of complex considerations to the respondent (Frey, 1989). The words used to elicit information on topics of interest to the campaign must be weighed carefully, as Groves (1989, pp. 450-451) notes, because words can be unfamiliar or not understood by a respondent, take on different meanings to a single respondent, or take on different meanings among a number of respondents. For example, if a campaign wished to gather information about the topic of affirmative action, and the polling organization asked voters whether they "favored or opposed affirmative action" without specifics about the issue, then researchers would run the risk that individuals will attach varied and different meanings as to what constitutes affirmative action and what does not (Sigelman & Welch, 1991).

The complex dimensions characteristic of an issue such as affirmative action, as well as other issues such as abortion and the economy, are good examples of why no poll should probe attitudes on the topics of greatest interest to the campaign using a single question. For example, research has shown that most answers to questions that ask whether a respondent favors or opposes "abortion" in general miss the fact that respondents have different opinions on abortion, depending on whether or not the questions ask about the topic in general or about specific circumstances such as the case of a defect in the baby or when the woman's life is endangered by her pregnancy (Tuchfarber & Rademacher, 1998).

The wording used in the presentation of an issue question to a respondent also is important. For example, research has shown that providing two sides of an issue can result in markedly different results than if respondents are simply asked to agree or disagree with a particular issue stance (Bishop, Oldendick, & Tuchfarber, 1982a; Hedges, 1979).

It also is possible that the wording of a question will contain a phrase or word that has no meaning to respondents whatsoever. Assurances that respondents understand what is intended by the question are critical to gauging the value of the results of the question. Research has found that "nonattitudes" can exist in survey responses, as respondents will, on occasion, answer questions on topics "so remote from and irrelevant to citizens' concerns that they do not hold real opinions on [them]" (Asher, 1995, p. 24; see also Bishop, Oldendick, & Tuchfarber, 1980; Bishop, Tuchfarber, & Oldendick, 1986; Converse, 1964). Because respondents sometimes will answer questions on topics about which they have little or no information, it is helpful to consider the types of response alternatives provided to respondents by researchers when closed-form questions are used. There is a line of research that demonstrates that large differences in results can occur when one includes, or does not include, an "undecided" or "don't know" response alternative (Bishop, Oldendick, & Tuchfarber, 1980, 1983; Schuman & Presser, 1981). This effect also has been found in results using trial heat questions in preelection polls. Marquette (1991) found the inclusion of an "undecided" response alternative can produce a smaller gap between candidates tested than when an "undecided" response is not offered, but the end result also is a large increase in the percentage of voters who say that they are undecided (p. 28; see also Marquette, 1996, p. 126). This leads to problems with how to allocate those voters at the end of the campaign when final projections must be made.

Another problem in question presentation is the leading question, which, as its name implies, "guides" a respondent toward a particular response. Such questions provide the campaign little meaningful information and have the danger of creating delusions that the voting public holds a particular issue stance when in fact it does not. Sometimes, however, polling organizations will pitch the idea to engage in a practice of using leading questions, which contain positive information about their client and harshly negative information about their client's opponent—known as "push polling." However, this unethical practice should be staunchly resisted, if for no other reason than its use has become a burden to campaigns, which have been put in a position of having to defend against media, voter, and opponent criticism about the practice (Clymer, 1996; Edsall, 1996).[6]

There also has been a great deal of research on the impact that a previous question or questions has on subsequent questions in the survey (Bishop, Oldendick, & Tuchfarber, 1982b, 1984; Schuman & Presser, 1981; Schwarz & Sudman, 1992). The most important question order consideration in preelection polls relates to the purpose of the trial heat question to the campaign. A recognition of the strong possibility that an issue question or other type of question might bias one candidate over another has led many pollsters to take great care in asking the trial heat question first in preelection polls. In his review of preelection polling, Crespi (1988) notes that his discussion with survey directors found the following:

> A concern voiced in many of the personal interviews is that asking questions about issues and the candidates before asking for candidate preference can shape the "perceptual environment" and bias poll results. With a few exceptions, pollsters position the voting preference question early in the interview, before any substantive questions on issues or on attitudes toward the candidates. (p. 104)[7]

The issue of order as it pertains to voter preference questions is illustrated by Asher (1995), who reports the results of a poll conducted by the Harris organization during the 1980 presidential primaries. The poll first asked respondents about their presidential preference and then proceeded to ask a series of questions about, among other things, the U.S. economy and the hostages being held in Iran. Toward the end of the interview, respondents were asked again whom they would vote for in the primary. "Surprisingly, over the course of the interview, support for President Carter declined sharply. The only explanation for this drop was that as respondents thought about Carter's record, their views of him became more negative" (p. 52). There is other evidence of the effect that the order of questions surrounding the presidential preference question can have on its results. Frankovic (1992b) speculated that differences among several organizations in the support they were showing for presidential candidates in 1992 depended on the proximity of the candidate favorability and vote preferences question. For example, the *New York Times*/CBS News poll showed Ross Perot with lower levels of support than other candidates, but the poll asked respondents to rate candidates before the presidential preference question, which might have meant that "those who have said they don't know enough about Mr. Perot have probably been inhibited from saying they would vote for him" (p. 23). Crespi and Morris (1984) found evidence of a question order effect in a trial heat poll that included questions about two races in Connecticut: a gubernatorial race and a U.S. Senate race. The authors concluded, after finding differences in the results when the order of the two races were switched, that "when designing questionnaires to measure voter preferences in more than one race, particular attention should be paid to the effect that cross-pressures may be exerting on the electorate" (p. 589). Finally, sensitivity to the order in which candidate names are presented to respondents also is important. Morin (1988) reported the results of a 1988 Roper organization survey that found Democratic candidate Michael Dukakis to enjoy a 12 percentage point lead over Republican candidate George Bush if Dukakis's name was read first in the vote preference question but only a 4 percentage point lead when Bush's name was read first.

Last, but certainly not least, one additional source of measurement error that we have not discussed is the bias that interviewers can introduce into the results of a survey. Some of the most important questions to be asked of any polling organization are how researchers train, oversee, and monitor interviewers as part of their quality control measures to ensure that interviewers administer the questionnaires in a manner that produces standardized, consistent, identical administration of the questionnaire.

The Analysis Stage:
Compensating for Error Through Weighting

Whereas errors of the measurement variety are difficult to compensate for unless they are detected in advance, sample inadequacies can be remedied, to a large extent, through weighting. It is not uncommon for the results of a poll of the general population, as a result of nonresponse error, to overrepresent some groups within the population (e.g., interviewing a higher percentage of women than are represented in the population) while underrepresenting other groups (e.g., interviewing a lower percentage of African Americans than are represented in the population). Once data collection has been completed, researchers analyze demographic data to determine the degree to which the demographic characteristics of the sample mirror the expected demographics of the population, often using U.S. Bureau of the Census information as a guide.

In the case of a preelection poll, if the sample does not resemble what the researcher believes to be the registered voter or likely voter population, then data adjustment, or weighting, often is used to adjust sample demographic characteristics so that they more closely resemble expected population characteristics. In larger political jurisdictions, there often are census data or exit poll results that can help to guide thinking as to what percentages of what groups will make up the registered voter population or will make up the likely electorate.[8] Both the campaign and the organization conducting the poll should have a voice in the determination of the target demographic and geographic characteristics of the registered voter and likely voter populations prior to the conduct of the poll.

Crespi's (1988) review suggests that such weighting, at least in the case of preelection polls used for election projection, is a common practice. However, organizations use different variables, and different combinations of variables, when adjusting data to more adequately represent the expected electorate. These variables include sex, age, race, political party identification, education, geography, and size of household (p. 34; see also Voss et al., 1995). For example, the public polling organization with which we are associated, the University of Cincinnati's Institute for Policy Research, uses an election methodology that sets target percentages for variables such as sex, race, and region of the state in its final Ohio Poll statewide election surveys of Ohio voters. Such a methodology is based on lengthy research, which means that the weighting component of analysis, like other components, must be solidified long in advance of the actual administration of the survey.

The Analysis Stage:
Potential for Error in the Special Case of Election Projection

When preelection polls are conducted to track a candidate's progress in the final stages of a campaign, their results sometimes are used in an attempt to project the likelihood of the candidate winning the election. Prior to the conduct of late preelection polls, those private and public pollsters who engage in preelection projections of final election results face three additional problems that can introduce error into results: (a) identification of likely voters, (b) turnout estimation, and (c) the allocation of undecided voter preferences. These problems also must be considered and planned for as part of research design, long before the actual administration of the survey.[9]

Identification of Likely Voters

The first problem that researchers face in election projections is related to the identification of likely voters. Asher (1995) observes that in preelection projection, "probably the most difficult task that pollsters face is estimating which of their respondents will actually vote" (p. 126). The quality of the screening questions used to determine vote likelihood is very important given that research by Perry (1973) and others has found evidence that in some instances, likely voters and nonvoters can differ markedly in reporting who they will vote for.

Several approaches to the identification of likely voters have been attempted, from simply determining whether or not an individual is registered to vote, to determining registration and the likelihood a respondent places on his or her voting on Election Day, to asking several questions so as to determine vote likelihood (Crespi, 1988; Freedman & Goldstein, 1996, p. 575; Saad, 1997). Several examples of the types of screening questions that various organizations and researchers have used to identify likely voters are available. The University of Cincinnati's Institute for Policy Research typically determines vote likelihood in its Ohio Poll election surveys using questions that ascertain each respondent's registration status, past turnout history, and interest in the upcoming election as well as the likelihood the respondent places on voting (Tuchfarber et al., 1998). The Gallup organization has used up to nine indicators to determine likely voters in its presidential election surveys since 1952. These include questions asking respondents about their registration status, the certainty they would vote, whom they voted for in the previous presidential election, how often they vote, and how much thought they have given to the upcoming election (Perry, 1979; Saad, 1997).

Turnout Estimation

Once the screening questions are chosen to determine vote likelihood, there are several approaches that can be used to make final estimations that separate likely voters from nonvoters for the purpose of analysis. Some organizations interview only those individuals who answer in specific ways that identify them as likely voters (e.g., respondents tell pollsters that they are registered to vote and definitely will vote in the upcoming election). Others interview all registered voters and then use answers to vote likelihood questions to construct a scale of voting likelihood, which later is used to weight respondents based on their probability of voting. Still others analyze results gathered only from those who obtain a vote likelihood score above a certain threshold on the turnout scale. Finally, some organizations use some combination of these approaches (for reports on the ways in which these approaches vary by organization, see Crespi, 1988; Freedman & Goldstein, 1996; Voss et al., 1995; for experimental research in this area, see Freedman & Goldstein, 1996; Petrocik, 1991; Traugott & Tucker, 1984).

The key to any analysis of vote likelihood is the estimation of what turnout will be on Election Day. Typically, organizations can easily determine what percentage of the registered voters they interview say they will vote on Election Day or meet criteria that would classify them as more likely or less likely to vote. Estimation of actual turnout is not so easy. There are several indicators that might be used in a calculation of possible turnout, including turnout in a previous election of a nature similar to the one in question (e.g., turnout in the previous gubernatorial election), and in the case of statewide or countywide elections, some organizations are able to use turnout estimates made by state or local election officials as a guide to how high (or low) election turnout will be.

Once pollsters determine how expected turnout compares to the level of turnout reflected in their sample, they have several options for adjusting their data, as described previously. Turnout estimation is key to the way in which these options affect results because it often is the basis for determining the probabilities that might be used for each respondent or the score on a turnout scale that qualifies one as a likely voter. Thus, error in this estimation can cause results to differ markedly from what occurs on Election Day.

From the point of view of a campaign, it is most useful to have portraits of likely voters in high-, medium-, and low-turnout elections at their disposal. This allows one to assess the level of support a candidate has under several turnout scenarios and how a campaign might need to react accordingly.

Allocation of Undecided Voter Preferences

Finally, when using trial heat questions in an attempt to gauge voting preferences, voters frequently say that they do not know who they will vote for on Election Day. Although tracking the movement of undecided voters throughout the campaign is helpful in determining a candidate's ability to attract this voting group, undecided voters are difficult to contend with in preelection projection. Because there is no "don't know" option on the Election Day ballot, researchers engaging in election projection must use available clues in an attempt to make inferences about how these respondents will vote (Asher, 1995; Perry, 1979; Traugott & Lavrakas, 1996; Tuchfarber et al., 1998). In an effort to combat this problem, organizations try to lessen the number of undecided voters in trial heat questions through the use of two techniques. First, questions often are asked that stress who respondents would vote for *today* as opposed to in the future. Second, respondents who say they "don't know" who they will vote for often are asked whether they "lean" toward one of the candidates (Crespi, 1988; Mendelsohn & Crespi, 1970).

Organizations traditionally have made one of two choices with the undecided voters that remain; either they have allocated undecided voters to candidates based on some set of assumptions, or they have assumed that undecided respondents will not vote. Whereas the latter choice was more common during the 1930s and early 1940s, several different methods have been adopted or tested by analysts since then in an effort to allocate undecided voters. For example, the Institute for Policy Research uses a "swing voter" variable in its candidate election projections, which scales information respondents provide regarding partisanship, past voting behavior, and vote preferences in candidate races as well as allocating "independent" undecided voters to the challenger if there is an elected incumbent in the race (Tuchfarber et al., 1998). Another strategy suggests allocation of undecided voters in greater proportion to the challenger in races where an incumbent seeks reelection. This reasoning is based on the "Incumbent Rule" introduced by Panagakis (1989, 1997; see also Crespi, 1988, p. 144), which argues that in two-candidate races, undecided voters tend to favor the challenger in local and presidential elections, so large proportions of the undecided vote should be allocated to the challenger. Other allocation methods use side information, as Crespi (1988, p. 110) found allocation formulas including information ranging from party identification to opinions on issues and the ratings of candidates. Still others have used allocation models that distribute undecided voters to candidates in the same proportion as the decided voters (Daves & Warden, 1995; National Council on Public Polls, 1997). However, as Daves and Warden (1995) conclude, "It is still tricky to allocate undecideds among candidate choices. . . . If one allocates undecideds among the candidate choices, it would be advisable to use several methods . . ., particularly if issues salient to the specific election are included with demographics as predictor variables" (p. 115).

Conclusion

In this chapter, we set out to provide a guide that would help readers to better understand the reasons why preelection polls are conducted and the mechanics of their operation. At this point, we would be remiss if we did not offer some final advice about the use of the information that is contained here. The first point that needs to be made pertains to those campaign strategists and campaign workers who might see or have use for the information that polls provide for political campaigns. If properly conducted, polls can provide a great deal of useful information, or "intelligence" in Roll and Cantril's (1972) terms, that can aid many decisions that are faced in the conduct of a campaign. For example, strategists charged with crafting a campaign's key messages and themes can learn a great deal from polls that gather information about important issues in the election. Later, strategists charged with purchasing media time can use information about voter reactions to the themes and messages that are constructed to make media buys. In both of these examples, information generated by polls is research that aids decision making but is not the "be all and end all" of how decisions should be made. We make this point as part of a broader point: No campaign should simply subvert itself to its pollsters and expect automatic victory. Various members of campaign staff are hired because of their expertise in particular areas, and this expertise should not be locked in a drawer once polling information begins to penetrate the campaign. As we have stressed, the ideal relationship between campaign strategists and pollsters is one in which collaboration allows each to provide their respective expertise in the planning and execution of political polls. Once the information is collected, the organization charged with polling usually will report results and make recommendations as to the course the campaign should take. This information should be taken under consideration, along with other information and expertise that campaign staff bring to the table, in final decisions that are made. Although polling has become an important part of campaigns, it cannot alone drive a campaign toward success on Election Day. Information generated by polling research is a powerful tool, but it must be used in concert with other information that the experts charged with running various areas of the campaign bring to the table to have maximum effectiveness.

A second point to be made is that this chapter has provided several ideas for evaluating the quality of the polling information presented to a political campaign as well as the quality of the organization that is conducting the polling. We did not cover all of the standards by which the quality of polls and organizations should be judged. However, readers can use our discussion to begin to think about the array of considerations they might wish to employ in judging the quality of information that has been collected including information about things such as the population of study, the sample, question wording and order, and the degree to which the results are subject to problems due to sampling and nonsampling error. In terms of evaluating the organizations conducting polls, stronger research firms will present their approaches to remedying many of the problems we have discussed in their discussions of research design. Thus, the degree to which polling organizations express awareness of these issues certainly is an indicator of their quality and experience in the field.

Some final points relating to the selection of an organization also need to be made. One may look at a resource such as *Campaigns and Elections: Political Blue Pages 1997–1998,* which lists approximately 200 organizations that conduct research in the category of "Polling: Survey Research and Analysis," and wonder what other considerations one should make in selecting the best organization to hire to meet a campaign's needs. In addition to some of the suggestions contained in this chapter, Hamilton (1995, p. 30) outlines a number of helpful considerations in choosing a polling organization. First, the polling organization and the campaign must be able to develop a strong working rapport because the pollster and other key campaign staff will need to work together to achieve success. Second, the choice of any organization should take into account the experience an organization has in researching similar races and the "feel" the pollster has for the political jurisdiction in which the race is being run. Finally, an organization that is not overwhelmed with clients also is preferable because the campaign might need to have the pollster's ear in a pinch. Unfortunately, it often is the case that the more successful organizations also have large numbers of clients (for obvious reasons), so striking an agreement about "attention" in advance is good policy.

Notes

1. In addition to Gallup's American Institute for Public Opinion, these organizations included *King Features Syndicate* (polling directed by Archibald Crossley) and *Fortune* (Elmo Roper and Brad Cherington) (Cantril 1937, p. 100; Katz & Cantril, 1937, p. 164).

2. For example, Gallup's organization reportedly chose "representative" counties in each state and then interviewed respondents using both personal interviews and mail surveys while ensuring that respondent quotas were met based on party registration, urban and rural populations, income, age, and gender (Robinson, 1937, pp. 47-48).

3. This use of polling has been referred to by some sources as "the first *paid* privately conducted poll for a political candidate" (Sabato, 1981, p. 4, emphasis in original; see also Nimmo, 1970). Sabato (1981) and Roll and Cantril (1972) also report that prior to the 1932 election, George Gallup used polling to assist his mother-in-law's secretary of state candidacy. Roll and Cantril (1972) also note that a number of candidates commissioned Gerald Lambert to conduct polls for their campaigns during the 1940s (see also Lambert, 1956).

4. While we focus on some of the traditional survey-based forms of research, we would be remiss in not mentioning the important role that "focus group" research can play in a campaign as well as in the survey process itself. A focus group does not use surveys in the traditional fashion but rather "is a small collection of individuals (a dozen or less), selected nonrandomly to reflect age, sex, race, economic, or lifestyle characteristics, brought together under the leadership of a trained discussion leader to talk generally about the campaign and the candidates" (Sabato, 1981, p. 77). Focus groups can be insightful in terms of the way in which voters are thinking about and talking about candidates and issues, which in turn can aid pollsters in the formulation of questions and the construction of surveys. Focus groups also are commonly used to assess reactions to the various types of media used in a campaign.

5. Therefore, in this discussion, we always must keep in mind that organizations using telephone surveys are reaching only those registered voters *with* telephones. Although approximately 95% of American households have telephones, one organization recently estimated that 25% to 30% of

American households are not listed in published telephone directories (Cottreau, 1997). Failure to reach these individuals is an example of what Groves (1989) calls "coverage error," or where some members of the population being studied have no chance of being selected into the sample (p. 83). If those registered voters excluded from the sample differ substantially in important ways (e.g., less supportive of the particular candidate being studied) from those with phones, then the results will be subject to error due to their exclusion (for further discussion of this issue, see Keeter, 1995).

6. The American Association for Public Opinion Research (AAPOR) joined with the National Council on Public Polls in condemning such "polls" in early 1996, stating, "A 'push poll' is a telemarketing technique in which telephone calls are used to canvass potential voters, feeding them false or misleading 'information' about a candidate under the pretense of taking a poll to see how this 'information' affects voter preferences. In fact, the intent is not to measure public opinion but [rather] to manipulate it—to 'push' voters away from one candidate and toward the opposing candidate" (AAPOR, 1996).

7. The placement of the vote preference question also might be an intentional tactical decision that involves the inducement of an order effect. As Kagay (1992) observes, "By asking questions about certain issues or traits of the candidates before asking the respondent his or her choice, [pollsters] seek to simulate learning that they presume voters will undergo during the campaign. This technique can be particularly useful to a candidate's private pollster in market testing campaign themes" (p. 101).

8. Organizations using RDD sampling methods frequently also weight to adjust for unequal selection probabilities. For example, voters living in households with multiple telephone numbers have a higher probability of being selected than do voters from households with one telephone number. Also, voters from single-voter households have a higher probability of being selected than do voters from households with multiple voters.

9. For a consideration of how one organization has dealt with these issues over time, one would be well served to consult the works of Perry (1960, 1972, 1973, 1979).

References

Albig, W. (1956). *Modern public opinion*. New York: McGraw-Hill.

American Association for Public Opinion Research. (1996). Statement condemning push polls. Available on Internet: http://www.aapor.org/ethics/pushpoll.shtml.

Anderson, R., Kaspar, J., Frankel, M., & Associates. (1979). *Total survey error*. San Francisco: Jossey-Bass.

Asher, H. (1995). *Polling and the public: What every citizen should know*. Washington, DC: Congressional Quarterly.

Babbie, E. R. (1990). *Survey research methods* (2nd ed.). Belmont, CA: Wadsworth.

Bishop, G. F., Oldendick, R. W., & Tuchfarber, A. J. (1980). Experiments in filtering political opinions. *Political Behavior, 2,* 339-369.

Bishop, G. F., Oldendick, R. W., & Tuchfarber, A. J. (1982a). Effects of presenting one versus two sides of an issue in survey questions. *Public Opinion Quarterly, 46,* 69-95.

Bishop, G. F., Oldendick, R. W., & Tuchfarber, A. J. (1982b). Political information processing: Question order and context effects. *Political Behavior, 4,* 177-200.

Bishop, G. F., Oldendick, R. W., & Tuchfarber, A. J. (1983). Effects of filter questions in public opinion surveys. *Public Opinion Quarterly, 47,* 528-546.

Bishop, G. F., Oldendick, R. W., & Tuchfarber, A. J. (1984). Interest in political campaigns: The influence of question order and electoral context. *Political Behavior, 6,* 159-169.

Bishop, G. F., Tuchfarber, A. J., & Oldendick, R. W. (1986). Opinions on fictitious issues: The pressure to answer survey questions. *Public Opinion Quarterly, 50,* 240-250.

Blakeman, B. W. (1995, August). Tracking polls: How to do them. *Campaigns & Elections,* pp. 24-25.

Bradburn, N., & Sudman, S. (1988). *Polls and surveys: Understanding what they tell us*. San Francisco: Jossey-Bass.

Bryson, M. C. (1976). The *Literary Digest* poll: Making of a statistical myth. *American Statistician, 30,* 184-185.

Cantril, A. H. (1991). *The opinion connection: Polling, politics, and the press*. Washington, DC: Congressional Quarterly.

Cantril, H. (1937). How accurate were the polls? *Public Opinion Quarterly, 1,* 97-105.

Chase, S. (1948, December 4). Are the polls finished? *Nation,* pp. 626-629.

Clymer, A. (1996, June 27). Association of political handlers attacks ruse polls as unethical. *The New York Times,* p. A20.

Converse, J. (1987). *Survey research in the United States.* Berkeley: University of California Press.

Converse, J. M., & Presser, S. (1986). *Survey questions: Handcrafting the standardized questionnaire.* Beverly Hills, CA: Sage.

Converse, P. E. (1964). The nature of belief systems in mass publics. In D. Apter (Ed.), *Ideology and discontent* (pp. 206-261). New York: Free Press.

Converse, P. E., & Traugott, M. W. (1986). Assessing the accuracy of polls and surveys. *Science, 234,* 1094-1098.

Conway, M. M. (1984). The use of polls in congressional, state, and local elections. *Annals of the American Academy of Political and Social Science, 472,* 97-105.

Cottreau, A. (1997, June 30). A better way to poll? Listed-number samples vs. RDD in election surveys. *The Polling Report,* pp. 1, 6-7.

CQ fact sheet on political polling: Political pollsters head for record activity in 1968. (1968, May 3). *Congressional Quarterly Weekly Report,* pp. 992-1000.

Crespi, I. (1988). *Pre-election polling.* New York: Russell Sage.

Crespi, I. (1989). *Public opinion, polls, and democracy.* Boulder, CO: Westview.

Crespi, I., & Morris, D. (1984). Question order and the measurement of candidate preference in the 1982 Connecticut elections. *Public Opinion Quarterly, 48,* 578-591.

Daves, R. P., & Warden, S. (1995). Methods of allocating undecided respondents to candidate choices in pre-election polls. In P. Lavrakas, M. W. Traugott, & P. V. Miller (Eds.), *Presidential polls and the news media* (pp. 101-119). Boulder, CO: Westview.

Diamond, E., & Baker, S. (1984). *The spot: The rise of political advertising on television.* Cambridge, MA: MIT Press.

The *Digest* presidential poll is on! (1936, August 22). *Literary Digest,* p. 1.

Dillman, D. A. (1978). *Mail and telephone surveys: The total design method.* New York: John Wiley.

Edsall, T. B. (1996, February 12). Dole camp acknowledges "push poll"; Critical questions asked about GOP rival Forbes. *Washington Post,* p. A8.

Faucheux, R. (1995, August). Pricing polling: The going rate. *Campaigns & Elections,* p. 23.

Field, M. (1990). Opinion polling in the United States of America. In M. Young (Ed.), *The classics of polling* (pp. 34-45). Metuchen, NJ: Scarecrow Press.

Fowler, F. J. (1993). *Survey research methods* (2nd ed.). Newbury Park, CA: Sage.

Frankovic, K. (1992a). AAPOR and the polls. In W. Mitofsky & P. Sheatsley (Eds.), *A meeting place: The history of the American Association for Public Opinion Research* (pp. 117-154). Ann Arbor, MI: American Association for Public Opinion Research.

Frankovic, K. (1992b, July 27). Reading between the polls. *The New York Times,* p. A23.

Freedman, P., & Goldstein, K. (1996). Building a probable electorate from preelection polls: A two-stage approach. *Public Opinion Quarterly, 60,* 574-587.

Frey, J. H. (1989). *Survey research by telephone.* Newbury Park, CA: Sage.

Gallup, G. (1936, November 1). America speaks: Institute gives Roosevelt 315 electoral votes. *Cincinnati Enquirer,* sec. 4, pp. 1, 26.

Gawiser, S. R., & Witt, G. E. (1994). *A journalist's guide to public opinion polls.* Westport, CT: Praeger.

Goodyear. (1936, September 19). A quarter of a billion ballots [advertisement]. *Literary Digest,* p. 27.

Grieve, R. R. B. (1996). *The blood, sweat, and tears of political victory . . . and defeat.* Lanham, MD: University Press of America.

Groves, R. M. (1989). *Survey errors and survey costs.* New York: John Wiley.

Hamilton, B. (1995, August). Hiring a pollster: Four keys. *Campaigns & Elections,* p. 30.

Harris, L. (1963). Poll and politics in the United States. *Public Opinion Quarterly, 27,* 3-8.

Hedges, B. (1979). Question wording effects: Presenting one or both sides of a case. *American Statistician, 28,* 83-99.

Henry, G. T. (1990). *Practical sampling.* Newbury Park, CA: Sage.

Javits, J. (1947). How I used a poll in campaigning for Congress. *Public Opinion Quarterly, 11,* 222-226.

Kagay, M. R. (1992). Variability without fault: Why even well-designed polls can disagree. In T. E. Mann & G. R. Orren (Eds.), *Media polls in American politics* (pp. 95-124). Washington, DC: Brookings Institution.

Kalton, G. (1983). *Introduction to survey sampling.* Beverly Hills, CA: Sage.

Katz, D., & Cantril, H. (1937). Public opinion polls. *Sociometry, 1,* 155-179.

Keeter, S. (1995). Estimating telephone noncoverage bias with a telephone survey. *Public Opinion Quarterly, 59,* 196-217.

Kish, L. (1965). *Survey sampling.* New York: John Wiley.

Klecka, W. R., & Tuchfarber, A. J. (1974). Random digit dialing as an efficient method for political polling. *Georgia Political Science Association Journal, 2,* 123-142.

Klecka, W. R., & Tuchfarber, A. J. (1978). Random-digit dialing: A comparison of personal interviews. *Public Opinion Quarterly, 42,* 104-114.

Lambert, G. (1956). *All out of step.* Garden City, NY: Doubleday.

Landon 1,293,669; Roosevelt 972,897: Final returns in the *Digest's* poll of ten million voters. (1936, October 31). *Literary Digest,* p. 1.

Lessler, J. T., & Kalsbeek, W. D. (1992). *Nonsampling error in surveys.* New York: John Wiley.

Marquette, J. (1991). Response form effects in election polling. *The Public Perspective, 2,* 28.

Marquette, J. (1996). How to become a wise consumer of campaign polling. In D. M. Shea (Ed.), *Campaign craft: The strategies, tactics, and art of political campaign management* (pp. 121-145). Westport, CT: Praeger.

Mellman, M., Lazarus, E., Rivlin, A., & Grove, L. (1991, May). Benchmark basics and beyond: How to get the most out of your most important poll. *Campaigns & Elections,* pp. 22-32.

Mendelsohn, H., & Crespi, I. (1970). *Polls, television, and the new politics.* Scranton, PA: Chandler.

Moore, D. W. (1995). *The superpollsters: How they measure and manipulate public opinion in America.* New York: Four Walls Eight Windows.

Morin, R. (1988, October 16). Behind the numbers: Confessions of a pollster. *Washington Post,* pp. C1, C4.

National Council on Public Polls. (1997, February 13). *Polling council analysis concludes criticisms of 1996 presidential poll accuracy are unfounded* [press release]. Fairfield, CT: Author.

Nimmo, D. (1970). *The political persuaders: The techniques of modern election campaigns.* Englewood Cliffs, NJ: Prentice Hall.

Oldendick, R. W., Bishop, G. F., Sorenson, S. B., & Tuchfarber, A. J. (1988). A comparison of the Kish and Last birthday methods of respondent selection in telephone surveys. *Journal of Official Statistics, 4,* 307-318.

Panagakis, N. (1989). Incumbent races: Closer than they appear. *The Polling Report, 5,* 1-3.

Panagakis, N. (1997). Incumbent races: A nationwide perspective. *The Public Perspective, 8,* 24-26.

Payne, S. (1951). *The art of asking questions.* Princeton, NJ: Princeton University Press.

Perry, P. (1960). Election survey procedures of the Gallup Poll. *Public Opinion Quarterly, 24,* 531-542.

Perry, P. (1962). Gallup Poll election survey experience. *Public Opinion Quarterly, 26,* 272-279.

Perry, P. (1972). Election survey methods. In G. Gallup (Ed.), *The Gallup Poll: Public opinion 1935-1971* (pp. xxxi-xxxiii). New York: Random House.

Perry, P. (1973). A comparison of the voting preferences of likely and unlikely voters. *Public Opinion Quarterly, 37,* 99-101.

Perry, P. (1979). Certain problems in election survey methodology. *Public Opinion Quarterly, 43,* 312-325.

Petrocik, J. R. (1991). An algorithm for estimating turnout as a guide to predicting elections. *Public Opinion Quarterly, 55,* 643-647.

The press: The great fiasco. (1948, November 15). *Time,* pp. 63-66.

The real losers. (1948, November 8). *Newsweek,* pp. 13-14.

Robinson, C. (1932). *Straw votes: A study of political prediction.* New York: Columbia University Press.

Robinson, C. E. (1937). Recent developments in the straw-poll field. *Public Opinion Quarterly, 2,* 45-51.

Roll, C. W., & Cantril, A. H. (1972). *Polls: Their use and misuse in politics.* New York: Basic Books.

Roosevelt bags 41 states out of 48. (1932, November 5). *Literary Digest,* pp. 8-9.

Roper, E. B., Jr. (1936). Forecasting election returns. *Review of Reviews, 44,* 58-59.

Saad, L. K. (1997, May). *An historical analysis: Presidential candidate preferences according to likelihood to vote—The Gallup Poll, 1952-1996.* Paper presented at the annual meeting of the American Association for Public Opinion Research, Norfolk, VA.

Sabato, L. (1981). *The rise of political consultants.* New York: Basic Books.

Schuman, H., & Presser, S. (1981). *Questions and answers in attitude surveys: Experiments on question form, wording, and context.* New York: Academic Press.

Schwarz, N., & Sudman, S. (Eds.). (1992). *Context effects in social and psychological research.* New York: Springer-Verlag.

Sigelman, L., & Welch, S. (1991). *Black Americans' views of racial inequality: The dream deferred*. New York: Cambridge University Press.

Smith, T. W. (1990). The first straw? A study of the origins of election polls. *Public Opinion Quarterly, 54,* 21-36.

Social Science Research Council. (1949). Report on the pre-election polls and forecasts. *Public Opinion Quarterly, 12,* 599-622.

Squire, P. (1988). Why the 1936 *Literary Digest* poll failed. *Public Opinion Quarterly, 52,* 125-133.

Stengel, R., Pooley, E., August, M., Birnbaum, J. H., Duffy, M., McAllister, J. F. O., Novak, V., & Edwards, T. M. (1996, November 18). Masters of the message; Inside the high-tech machine that set Clinton and Dole polls apart. *Time,* pp. 76-96.

Stumping the experts. (1948, November 4). *The New York Times,* p. 28.

Sudman, S., & Bradburn, N. (1982). *Asking questions: A practical guide to questionnaire design.* San Francisco: Jossey-Bass.

Tanur, J. (Ed.). (1992). *Questions about questions: Inquiries into the cognitive bases of surveys.* New York: Russell Sage.

Traugott, M. W. (1987). The importance of persistence in respondent selection for pre-election surveys. *Public Opinion Quarterly, 51,* 48-57.

Traugott, M. W., & Lavrakas, P. J. (1996). *The voter's guide to election polls.* Chatham, NJ: Chatham House.

Traugott, M. W., & Tucker, C. (1984). Strategies for predicting whether a citizen will vote and estimation of electoral outcomes. *Public Opinion Quarterly, 48,* 330-343.

Troldahl, V., & Carter, R. (1964). Random selection of respondents with households in phone surveys. *Journal of Marketing Research, 1,* 71-76.

Tuchfarber, A. J., & Klecka, W. R. (1976). *Random digit dialing: Lowering the cost of victimization surveys.* Cincinnati, OH: University of Cincinnati, Police Foundation.

Tuchfarber, A. J., & Rademacher, E. W. (1998, March 8). *Ohioans divided on abortion, but most favor new laws restricting access* [Ohio Poll press release]. Cincinnati, OH: University of Cincinnati.

Tuchfarber, A. J., Rademacher, E. W., Downing, K., & Smith, A. E. (1998, May). *Accuracy in pre-election polling and projections: Lessons from the telephone vs. mail battle in Ohio.* Paper presented at the annual meeting of the American Association for Public Opinion Research, St. Louis, MO.

Voss, D. S., Gelman, A., & King, G. (1995). Review: Preelection survey methodology. *Public Opinion Quarterly, 59,* 98-132.

Waksberg, J. (1978). Sampling methods for random digit dialing. *Journal of the American Statistical Association, 73,* 40-46.

13

Exit Polls and Election Campaigns

JÜRGEN HOFRICHTER

This chapter is about exit polls and their implications for election campaigns. Because the public is confronted with results of both preelection surveys and exit polls on Election Day, the two first should be distinguished. Preelection polls, based on representative sample surveys before Election Day, are now mostly conducted as telephone interviews and measure vote intention, issue attitudes, and other political preferences of respondents who might or might not participate in an election (see Rademacher & Tuchfarber's chapter in this book [Chapter 12]). By contrast, exit polls are representative Election Day polls that measure voting behavior of actual voters immediately after the individual act of voting. Within selected precincts, interviewers ask voters who have just cast their ballots to fill out a self-administered questionnaire immediately after leaving the polling station. Exit polls are an invention of the electronic news media and are used to predict election outcomes before all votes are counted. In addition to answering the question of who won, they provide analytical information to answer the questions of who voted for the winner and why he or she won.

This chapter first provides a brief overview of the history of exit polls. Next, the organization and methodology of exit polling are described with respect to sampling, questionnaire construction, fieldwork, data analysis, and presentation of the results during Election Night. The chapter concludes with a discussion of the role of exit polls in political marketing. With respect to the methods, a comparative perspective between the United States and Germany is applied. With respect to the history of exit polls, Great Britain during the 1990s is included as

AUTHOR'S NOTE: I thank George Bishop, Wolfgang Hartenstein, Richard Hilmer, Max Kaase, and Michael Kunert for their helpful comments on earlier versions of the chapter.

well because of the significant problems of the British polling industry in predicting the outcome of the 1992 general election and the resulting effect on exit polls in Great Britain.

Brief History of Exit Polls

Reporting on Election Night includes the prediction of election results as early as it is reliably possible and the provision of analytical information explaining the election outcome. The available data sources are preelection surveys, precinct returns, and exit polls. Exit polls were developed during the late 1960s to cope with specific problems of other data sources. The results of preelection surveys might vary too much from the actual election results to be the major source of analytical information on Election Night because voters can change their preferences and their intentions to participate in the election during the final days of the campaign.[1] In addition, the number of voters in preelection surveys usually is not big enough (1,000-1,500 nationwide) to allow for a detailed analysis of voting behavior in particular subgroups (e.g., newly registered first-time voters). With respect to precincts, researchers also attempted to include aggregate information about precincts classifying them into analytical categories such as urban or rural, Black or White, and so on. Thus, so-called "tag" or "analytical" precincts with disproportionate concentrations of certain types of voters often were selected. The precinct returns were grouped, and the vote in each analytical group was analyzed. These aggregate categorizations on the precinct level might, however, be misleading for representing personal characteristics of voters; for example, Blacks in "ghettoized" precincts might vote differently compared to the vote of all Blacks, so that a prediction of the total Black vote based on selected Black precincts could be inaccurate (Levy, 1983, p. 55; Mitofsky, 1991, pp. 85-86). The exit poll method provides more reliable information than do preelection surveys, on the one hand, and it provides good estimates of the election outcome earlier than do precinct returns, on the other.

Before presenting a brief history of exit polling, some remarks about differences between the media systems and the electoral systems in the United States and Germany are noted. In the United States, preelection polls have been used by the media since the 1930s. The dominance of television networks over newspapers in the coverage of Election Nights began in 1956 with the second Dwight Eisenhower versus Adlai Stevenson election. The pluralistic and highly competitive media system has long been playing a key role in the coverage of elections. In 1964, the CBS anchorman announced that Lyndon Johnson was going to be the next president shortly after 9 p.m. in the eastern time zone. Since then, there has been a debate about devaluing the western vote by announcing results on television before all polls are closed. In Germany, there are no problems due to different time zones, and polls uniformly close at 6 p.m. Television coverage started much later, and the German television system has been a closed and regulated system, with two public channels dominating the market until the late

1980s, resulting in a different context of political communication from that in the United States. The German electoral system is a system of proportional representation. A party's share of the vote is transferred into roughly the same amount of seats, and the focus is on predicting party share. The electoral system in the United States is a majority system in which the winner takes all, and the focus is on predicting the winning candidate.

United States

The first exit poll was carried out in 1967 in a Kentucky gubernatorial contest by the CBS News Election and Survey Unit along with several other methodological experiments. Exit polls were first used for analytical purposes only. NBC News have used exit polls for projections since the mid-1970s, and CBS News and ABC News both started to do this in 1982. However, the 1980s also was the time of an "exit poll controversy" (Mitofsky, 1991, p. 89). It was sparked by NBC News projecting Ronald Reagan's victory over Jimmy Carter at 8:15 p.m. in the eastern time zone (i.e., 2 hours and 45 minutes before the polls in the western time zone closed). As a consequence, exit polls and projections came under heavy attack. It was argued that particular candidates had lost their seats due to reduced turnout because of the publication of the result of the presidential election. Although no hard evidence was found in various studies, anti-exit poll laws were passed in several states.[2] However, the news media announced their results as they always had and challenged the anti-exit poll laws in court. The first lawsuit against the state of Washington was decided for the plaintiffs, and the media went to court successfully against the laws in other states as well. During the controversy, there were two major points in election reporting by the media that were heavily criticized: (a) announcing a winner before a state closed its polls and (b) publishing analyses that clearly indicate who the winner would be before poll closing. The media agreed to refrain from these activities to end the controversy. Since the 1960s, it has been argued that polls should be closed at a uniform time across the nation rather than interfering with the networks' First Amendment rights to broadcast news. A uniform poll closing legislation has, however, not yet been enacted (for details on the history of exit polls and the controversy in the United States, see Levy, 1983, and especially Mitofsky, 1991).

Since 1990, exit polling in the United States has been organized centrally. Voter Research and Surveys (VRS) was formed by ABC, CBS, NBC, and CNN as a central institution designing and conducting exit polls to reduce the costs involved in collecting exit poll data and making projections. In 1993, these networks formed Voter News Service (VNS), adding the Associated Press and combining the VRS activities with the News Election Service. VNS is now responsible for exit polls for the major television networks and a variety of additional users (Edelmann & Merkle, 1995, p. 2). Exit polls are now widely used for the coverage and analysis of most presidential primaries and for general elections such as contests for president, senator, and governor as well as for seats in the House of Representatives and even for local elections in cities such as Cincinnati and New York.

Germany

In Germany, the systematic coverage of national elections for public television started in 1965 with reporting on the national election of September 19; the first public television channel, the ARD, published the first projection, and the second public television channel, the ZDF, published provisional results. The *Institut für angewandte Sozialwissenschaft* (INFAS) provided the know-how for the ARD. In close cooperation with researchers from the United States, INFAS had implemented the methods developed in the United States, using then newly available computer resources. INFAS was responsible for the election coverage of the ARD up to 1996. Since 1997, *Infratest dimap* is the partner of the ARD for electoral research and reporting. Between 1964 and 1974, the ZDF cooperated with a group of political scientists at the University of Mannheim, which developed the methods and techniques for the channel's election coverage and was influenced by the development in the United States. Out of this original group of electoral researchers at the University of Mannheim, the *Forschungsgruppe Wahlen* (FGW) emerged, and it has been contracted by the ZDF since 1974 to support the channel's coverage of German Election Nights. Exit polls during national or state elections in Germany have almost exclusively been carried out by these institutes working for the two major public television channels.

The first exit polls in Germany were conducted by INFAS on June 4, 1978, for elections in the two federal states, Niedersachsen and Hamburg.[3] The results of these exit polls were published at 6 p.m., immediately after the closing of the polls. The 1978 "prognoses" were very close to the actual results at such an early time on Election Night. The early availability of the election outcome led to a German exit poll controversy, with debates about issues such as protecting the "secret ballot" and the dignity of the voter and the act of voting as well as the older issue of restricting publication of survey results before Election Day. Exit polls came under heavy attack (Schultze, 1980), and a law against exit polls was discussed. As a result of the debate, the two public television channels opted for a strategy of voluntary self-restraint, especially with respect to surveys on Election Day, and refrained from exit polls for more than a decade.

The exit poll methodology was reintroduced into German electoral reporting in 1990. The Berlin Wall had fallen in October 1989, and on October 3, 1990, the German Democratic Republic (GDR) joined the Federal Republic. In March 1990, the first free parliamentary election of the *Volkskammer* (people's chamber) in decades took place in the GDR. State elections in the five new East German federal states took place on October 10, 1990, and the first general election in unified Germany was held on December 2, 1990, together with the first election in reunified Berlin. With respect to the analysis of elections in East Germany, no previous election results were available, so that the method of "tied samples" and "tied projections" using past voting results, which was applied to predict West German election outcomes, was not available (see Methodology section). In view of the quality of the exit polls during the 1970s, it could be expected that the method would provide reliable data early on Election Night. In fact, the exit poll for the Volkskammer election led to a very accurate prognosis, which was an enormous success because the election outcome was unexpected, as the Conservative Alliance scored a clear victory over the Social Democratic Party that had been in the lead in the preelection surveys. Exit polls were carried out for all elections in 1990, and since then, the exit poll instrument has become an unquestioned and integral part of German election reporting for the two public television channels. Election Days in Germany are on Sundays, and on Election Nights, the first highlight is broadcast at 6 p.m. sharp. Both major public television channels individually publish their so-called prognoses based on their respective exit polls. Following the prognoses, German Election Nights in the electronic media are characterized by the competition between the two major public channels regarding the coverage of elections.[4]

Exit Polls in Great Britain During the 1990s.

In their final preelection polls during the 5 days before the 1992 general election, the five major British polling institutes—Gallup, Harris, ICM, MORI, and NOP—averaged a 1.1 percentage point Labour lead and predicted a hung Parliament. The final result was a 7.6 percentage point lead for the Conservatives, giving them a 21-seat victory. This margin of error was far beyond sampling error, and the 1992 general election is widely known as the British election in which "the pollsters got it wrong." The mean error gap between the leading and second party was 8.7 percentage points in 1992, as compared to an average error of 3.3 percentage points in the final preelection polls from 1945 to 1987. As a consequence, the Market Research Society set up a research committee comprised of pollsters, academics, and experienced market researchers not involved in opinion polling, which reported the results of its investigation in July 1994 (Market Research Society, 1994). Three major reasons were believed to account for the projection error. The first was *late swing,* which was substantially influenced by the Conservative Party's campaign strategy during the final days. Labour was believed to be in the lead by 4 to 7 percentage points on Sheffield Wednesday (i.e., 8 days before the election). The Conservatives, however, spent nearly all of their advertising money during the final 3 days challenging voters intending to vote for the Liberal Democrats that they would open the door for a Labour government (slogan: "Letting Labour in"). Thus, the Conservatives were able to attract the ballots of many "floating voters." The second reason was *differential refusal.* Conservative voters were less likely to reveal their vote intentions than were supporters of the Labour Party ("shy Tories"). The third reason was *inadequate sampling.* The quotas set for the interviewers and the weights applied after interviewing did not reflect with sufficient accuracy the social profile of the electorate at the time of the election (Worcester, 1997a, 1997b, 1998).

The 1992 election had a substantial impact on polling and, in particular, on exit polls in the United Kingdom. In 1992, two national exit polls were carried out—one for the BBC by NOP and one for ITN by MORI. The error in the exit polls was much smaller than that in the preelection polls; the exit polls showed 4 and 5 percentage point leads for the Conservative Party. ITN did broadcast the vote share once, whereas the BBC results never were broadcast. The channels instead concentrated on the seat forecasts in marginal districts, translating the vote share into seats. The models used for projections of seats were, however, more faulty than the exit poll data on which they were based (Worcester, 1997a, pp. 32-34; 1998). As a result, the BBC was embarrassed over its 1992 exit poll and over polling in general. This resulted in the development of strict guidelines for opinion polls (BBC, 1996) and a restrictive policy with respect to commissioning and reporting polls. In particular, no national exit poll was commissioned for the European elections in 1994. MORI, however, conducted an experimental exit poll in London on behalf of the Electoral Reform Society that produced highly accurate results. MORI also came under pressure from the BBC to publish the exit poll results, although the exit poll was carried out mainly to test the method in view of the next general election in 1997. The London exit poll showed a high degree of accuracy, with a maximum difference in party share of one percentage point per party compared to the official London results (Braunholtz & Atkinson, 1995, Worcester, 1997a, p. 33). With respect to the 1997 general election, two exit polls were carried out—one for the BBC by NOP and one for ITN by MORI—which produced very satisfactory predictions, but the British ambivalence about polls and exit polling is likely to continue.[5]

The Methodology of Exit Polling

Exit polls share many important characteristics with normal surveys, where interviewers collect empirical information from representative samples that is processed and analyzed. However, exit polls have particular logistical and economic constraints and a rather unique time frame; a vast amount of data are collected across a wide geographic area, the data are returned for central processing, the data are continuously analyzed, and conclusions are presented. All this is done simultaneously on Election Day, and the quality of the work is assessed almost immediately (i.e., within hours) in comparison to the outcome of the election.

Selecting the Voters

The best possible probability sample of voters for an exit poll is, of course, the basis for an accurate prediction of the election outcome. Probability sampling of individual voters using voting registration data, however, is not available. Votes are cast in voting precincts, and a two-stage sample design is applied, selecting precincts first and then the voters within the precincts. A representative sample of precincts has two purposes. First, it should produce a representative sample of voters filling out the exit poll questionnaire on Election Day. Second, after poll closing and counting of ballots, complete precinct returns are reported immediately to a central computing installation by telephone for projections. The returns provide the input for models of computer projections that attempt to predict the outcome before the total vote has been counted. The exit poll can be carried out in all sample precincts, or it can be carried out in a random subsample of the total precinct sample.

Before the sample is drawn, the precincts are grouped into different strata, taking into account factors such as the regional dimension and past voting behavior (e.g., administrative and geographical units, major parties' share of the vote).[6] It has then to be decided which precincts to include in the sampling frame. Special precincts, such as those in hospitals and asylums, have particular characteristics and, therefore, could be excluded. Small precincts with few voters could be excluded for cost-benefit reasons. The absentee vote, of course, also cannot be included in a sample of voters at the ballot box.[7] Samples can then be drawn by systematic random choice from a stratified list of precincts independent of precinct size. This method leads to a self-weighting sample. A number of samples can be drawn, and after the quality is assessed, the best sample would be chosen. The most important quality factor is the representation of the result of the past election in the "tied sampling procedure."[8] Major problems are that precincts are subject to change between elections due to mobility and generational change. Most practical problems result from changes in the number of voters between elections and from changes in the boundaries of precincts. Local communities are responsible for the design of precincts, and usually no central registration and/or data are available. If precinct boundaries have changed, then the discrepancy between old and new boundaries has to be resolved.

On Election Days in the United States, many different elections take place. The president, senators, governors, members of the House of Representatives, and various local officials are elected. This leads to complex sample designs for exit polls covering the different contests, whereby poll closing time and type of voting equipment also are relevant dimensions in the United States. Up to the 1990s, the different networks and newspapers used different approaches (for an overview of different sample designs used in the exit polls in the 1980 elections, see Levy, 1983, pp. 56-58). After the founding of VRS and then VNS, exit polls were organized centrally. Precincts for VRS exit polls in 1992 were selected in a "stratified sample proportionate to the number of votes cast in the 1988 presidential election" (Mitofsky & Edelmann, 1993, p. 2). In VNS exit polls, a probability sample of voting precincts within each state that represents the different geographic areas across the state and the vote by party is selected. Precincts are selected with a probability proportionate to the number of voters in each precinct, with the exception of precincts with large minority populations, which are sampled at a higher rate than other precincts. The national sample is a subsample of the state samples of precincts.

With respect to the second stage of sampling, the voters to be interviewed within the precincts also are selected on a systematic random basis. Thus, all voters casting their ballots in person have the same chance to be selected. The interviewers are provided with a skip interval and are told to select every kth voter. Intervals usually are tied to expected voter turnout and the total number of interviews desired. In the United States, the interval can range from every voter in precincts with a small number of voters up to every 70th voter or more in the largest precincts (Levy, 1983, p. 59). In Germany, maximum precinct size is fixed by law at about 2,500 persons entitled to vote, so the variation in the skip interval is much smaller.

The size of the exit poll samples depends on the complexity of the voting area and the states or constituencies for which projections are requested. The exit poll operation of VRS for the 1992 general election in the United States comprised 1,310 precincts. Exit polls were carried out in all states, and including state polls, about 177,000 voters were interviewed (Mitofsky & Edelmann, 1993, p. 2). In German state elections, sample size varies between 150 and 200 precincts,[9] and samples for general elections include a minimum of about 400 precincts. The sample for general elections can be designed to allow separate predictions for East and West Germany because there still are systematic differences in voting behavior. If projections for specific regional units (e.g., constituency, city) are required, then sample size can be increased accordingly, whereby a minimum size of about 30 precincts is recommended for projections. There are, however, some specific aspects of the German electoral system that also might influence sampling. A party needs either 5% of the valid vote or three directly won constituency seats to be represented in Parliament.[10] In 1994, the East German-based Socialist Party (PDS) won four constituency seats in former East Berlin and was represented in Parliament, although it had only 4.4% of the valid vote. If the PDS would again be represented in Parliament, then the coalition options for national government probably would be affected. Relevant constituencies, therefore, have to be included in the sampling frame for the general election in September 1994 to be able to give a reliable estimate with respect to the PDS early on Election Night.

Questionnaire Design

In the United States, respondents usually are asked to answer between 20 and 50 questions; in Germany, exit poll questionnaires typically include between 10 and 20 questions. Questionnaires are printed on two sides of a letter-sized page. The questions include self-report of the votes just cast; recall questions on past votes; time of the vote decision; and measures of demographic variables such as sex, age group, education, occupation, religion, and trade union membership in Germany. In the United States, measures of income, party identification, and political ideology as well as major factors influencing the vote decision, attitudes toward candidates, and issue preferences are included in addition. This type of information usually is collected in preelection surveys in Germany. Questions are closed-ended, and contingent questions are avoided. Scales are collapsed into moderately broad ranges. In Germany, the scaling of age groups usually is, for reasons of comparison, adapted to the categories that are applied by the census office publishing the electoral statistics.

During the VRS exit poll operation in 1992, a national exit poll and polls in all states were carried out, during which multiple questionnaires and split-ballot forms were used. The questionnaires were identified by color and bound into pads. Each pad had the different questionnaires interspersed so that neither interviewer nor respondent could influence which type of questionnaire was handed to a particular voter. Because the names of candidates running for senator and governor in the individual states were listed, questionnaires varied between states. There were three different national questionnaires. Split-ballot experiments on the order of answering categories for two questions were carried out, and in total, 204 different versions of the questionnaires had to be printed. The different versions of the national questionnaire also included network-specific questions. These preparations, of course, also involved creating the respective computer programs and files for reporting the results. To list the names of the candidates running for seats in the House of Representatives would be preferable; however, this would have increased the number of questionnaire versions to about 1,200. Therefore, only the candidates' parties were listed, and the interviewers had the names on their clipboards. Many voters do not know to which parties popular incumbents and candidates belong, and this led to a bias with larger errors in those races where popular candidates won their seats by wide margins, drawing votes from supporters of both parties. When congressional names are listed, the bias disappears (Mitofsky & Edelmann, 1993, pp. 3-5).

Exit poll questionnaires today normally are self-administered secret ballot questionnaires. The respondent folds the completed questionnaire, puts it in an envelope, and deposits it in a ballot box provided by the interviewer. Secret ballot questionnaires reduce refusals and other evasive responses in comparison to face-to-face interviews (Bishop & Fisher, 1995) and also respect the privacy of the vote.

Collecting the Data

The task of Election Day interviewers usually is twofold. First, they collect information from a sample of voters in their designated precincts throughout the day. Second, they report precinct results to election headquarters after the counting of all votes. VRS Election Day interviewers were recruited and trained by professional survey research organizations in 1992 or were recruited and trained by VNS in 1994. In the first case, mostly professional interviewers were hired. In the second case, college students and other interested personnel also were recruited. Infratest dimap uses primarily the regular Infratest field staff of about 3,000 interviewers in Germany. For state elections, especially in city-states, additional recruiting is necessary. Interviewers get a comprehensive instruction manual and all the necessary field material. Additional instructions are given from field headquarters via telephone, and local supervisors also are included in organization and training. Central training sessions can be organized when the costs are acceptable (e.g., in cities). A few days before the election, interviewers identify the locations of their precincts, check the telephone facilities, and transfer test data from their precinct locations to central headquarters.

Interviewers are told to arrive at their designated precincts before opening time of the polls on Election Day. In locations with several precincts in the same building (e.g., schools), they have to identify their precincts and check the number of exits from the building. They identify themselves to election officials and collect information about their precincts.[11] In cooperation with the officials, they determine their interviewing positions and put up their ballot boxes as close as possible to the voting site exits. Depending on precinct size and skip interval, there can be one or two interviewers per precinct, or interviewers can be supported by "counters" who identify the voters who the interviewers should approach. The voters to be interviewed are selected by applying a skip interval. After leaving the polling place, every *k*th voter is approached and asked to complete the questionnaire. Either the skip interval can be set to generate adequate numbers of interviews or quotas can be set to determine the number of interviews in each interview period. Skip intervals may be fixed in all precincts or can be tied to the number of voters and expected turnout. It might be necessary, however, to modify the interval due to field conditions in certain precincts. If more than one exit is available for voters of the target precinct or more than one precinct is located in a polling station, then the interval has to be adapted as necessary. Different strategies can be used following refusals and misses. Either the skip count starts again to select the next voter or the interviewer is expected to convince the very next person after the one who refused to participate or was missed.

If the voter participates in the exit poll, then he or she puts the completed questionnaire in an envelope and into the ballot box. If a voter refuses to fill out the questionnaire, then the interviewer marks the voter's sex, estimated age group, and race (in the United States) on a sheet. In the United States, this demographic information also is marked for those voters who the interviewers miss during peak periods. The information about refusals and misses is transferred to headquarters together with the information from the individual questionnaires. Field time usually covers the entire Election Day; it is split up among interview time, time of data transfer to headquarters, and breaks. In the VRS 1992 exit poll operation, interviewers worked 50 minutes of each hour. During their breaks, they did hand tallies of the number of respondents who said that they voted for each candidate. Three times during the day, they telephoned the results of their hand tallies and the individual responses to each question to a central site using the respective code numbers for the individual answers. Before the reading of the individual responses, the questionnaires were subsampled by the operator receiving the call. Subsampling produced 62,000 questionnaires, of which 15,300 were national questionnaires (Mitofsky & Edelmann, 1993, p. 3). Infratest dimap interviewers register with headquarters early in the morning, transferring precinct data regarding the number of voters. Interview periods and data transmission times are prescheduled and are roughly equally distributed throughout Election Day.

Response rates vary. For the VRS and VNS exit poll operations in 1992 and 1994, the figures were 61% and 54%, respectively (Edelmann & Merkle, 1995). For the three recent German state elections, response rates in the Infratest dimap exit polls were between 70% and 72%. It is reported that up to 10% do not fill out the back side of U.S. exit poll questionnaires, which are longer than the ones used in Germany (where about 2% do not fill out the back side of the questionnaires).

After poll closing time, interviewers attend the public count of ballots. They are provided with sheets similar to official sheets for reporting the results to census offices. Interviewers are instructed to copy the results of their precincts as soon as they are available and to telephone them immediately to election headquarters. Precinct returns are checked and processed. Either they can be processed in election headquarters (VNS) before being distributed at prescheduled time points to the participating media (United States), or they can be processed in the central television studio after having been checked by election headquarters (Germany).

Weighting Exit Poll Data

Exit poll samples can be designed to be self-weighting or can be designed by using unequal probabilities of precinct selection. In exit polls, refusals and misses may lead to a bias and have to be controlled and eventually corrected by weighting. In addition, the absentee vote has to be taken into consideration. Weighting requires reliable estimates for the universe, that is, the voters of the current election. Weights can be computed by taking into account sample design, information available from official sources (e.g., electoral statistics), and information collected in the exit poll (e.g., recall of last vote, information about refusals and misses). Two weights directly refer to sample design if the sample is not self-weighting. A precinct weight takes into account unequal probabilities of precinct selection. In the VNS 1996 national exit poll sample, precincts with large minority populations, which were selected at a higher rate, received smaller weights than did other precincts of the same size. A within-precinct weight takes into account the probability of respondent selection. In the 1992 VRS exit polls and the 1996 VNS exit polls, noninterview adjustments were made for voters who were missed by the interviewers or who refused to be interviewed. This was based on their observed age, race, and sex.

In contrast to the situation in the United States, information from an official electoral statistic usually is available, allowing the sociodemographic adjustment of an exit poll sample, in Germany. National and state census offices register voting behavior in five age groups[12] for men and women separately by providing ballot sheets in different colors to the different groups in a representative sample of precincts. This information about voting behavior according to age and sex is published some months after an election. Based on these data about past voting behavior and turnout in different groups and past turnout in the sample precincts, the distribution of voters according to region, age, and sex can be used as an estimate for the sociodemographic adjustment of an exit poll sample. Unfortunately, this electoral statistic was suspended for the general elections in 1994 and 1998.

Another option for weighting exit poll data is weighting by recall. The exit poll questionnaire may include recall questions providing information about past voting behavior for the current electorate. However, recall questions have specific problems. Some voters do not remember their last voting decisions or "remember" them incorrectly, for example, because they want to belong to the winners (bandwagon effect). Some voters in the last election have died, and new voters are now part of the electorate. Turnout varies between elections. However, despite various known effects on answers to recall questions, experience has shown that the distribution of the recall question often reflects past vote results in a mean-ingful way. The adjustment of the distribution of the recall question according to the actual past electoral results, therefore, provides useful information on Election Night, and recall weights for different past elections may be computed.

In summary, weighting in exit poll attempts to correct for effects that also are known from other surveys, for example, higher refusal rates of elderly women and respondents refusing to report their votes for radical parties. Different weighting schemes can be applied such as weighting according to the estimated sociodemographic structure of the voters, weighting according to recall data, and weighting according to other factors (e.g., absentee vote). Different weights provide different results in different elections. As experience is accumulated, further research is needed on the utility of these alternative techniques.

Analyzing and Presenting the Results on Election Night

In Germany, the research institutes are responsible for the analysis and graphi-cal on-air presentation of all information regarding the election on Election Night. The task consists of the delivery of the "prognosis" of the election outcome to be broadcast at 6 p.m.; continuous computer projections of the share of the vote and the distribution of seats based on incoming precinct returns; the presentation of ready-to-broadcast graphics analyzing the results based on preelection survey data, exit poll data, and precinct data; and, finally, the presen-tation of regional results and the final results.[13] To fulfill these tasks, Infratest dimap has developed an integrated computer program combining electoral databases, data processing and analysis, prediction models, and the production of television graphics.[14]

On Election Day, exit poll results are transferred into the studio and analyzed periodically. They allow the observation of voting patterns known from previous elections.[15] Information about turnout might be available from the statistical officials at certain time points on Election Day. All available information is accumulated and evaluated constantly to feel the pulse of the election. The German electoral law forbids the publication of exit poll results before poll closing time, and preliminary data on Election Day usually are kept confidential by the institutes.

At poll closing time (i.e., 6 p.m. sharp), both major public channels (ARD and ZDF) simultaneously publish their prognoses of the election outcome based exclusively on data from their respective exit polls. Although the quality of the prognoses differs from election to election, they usually are accurate estimates of the election results. The prediction of the results for smaller parties may be decisive and can be rather difficult if the party share is close to 5% or if the party has a chance to win three direct constituency seats.[16] National and state govern-ments are mostly coalition governments of a big party and a smaller party. The political result of an election with respect to government formation often depends on the availability of a small party as a coalition partner for a bigger party. In some cases, only the final result shows whether a party is above or below the 5%

threshold. In these cases, Election Day remains rather exciting until late into the night.[17]

After 6 p.m., precinct returns start coming in and are filed into the computer models for the predictions and estimations of seat distribution. Later in the night when constituency results are available, they also are used in projection models. Precinct returns arrive at differential rates, with smaller precincts being earlier than precincts with more voters. On Election Night, different estimation models can be applied for computer projections—ratio estimates, difference estimates, and regression estimates (Hoschka & Schunk, 1977). The projections are "tied projections" based on the "tied sample" of precincts. The FGW reported its experience that difference estimates were more reliable with respect to the larger parties, whereas ratio estimates provided better results for the smaller parties at the beginning of Election Night when only part of the returns from the precinct sample were available (Gibowski, 1985, p. 343). The application of regression models can be recommended only when the number of actual precinct returns amounts to about 30. The different projection methods also can be applied by using a stratified approach, that is, by computing results for specific groups of precincts. Stratification and poststratification, quality control, and other refinements taking into account important factors that may vary between elections (e.g., rate of absentee vote, difference between the vote at the ballot box and the absentee vote) and between types of elections are applied to provide the best estimates. This is a process of continuous learning from election to election.

The integrated computer program also provides a variety of analytical ready-to-broadcast television graphics that have been prepared using the different information sources (e.g., voting behavior in different social groups from exit poll data; attitudes toward parties, candidates, and issues from preelection survey data). In addition to these individual-level data, a service for analyzing the election on the aggregate level is provided. The sample precincts are categorized according to regional, economic, social, and political factors (e.g., region, city, rates of unemployment, strength of parties). Prestructured tables periodically provide the party results for each aggregate category and the wins or losses in comparison to the results of the selected previous election. In addition to the precinct level, this type of aggregate analysis is available at the level of constituencies later at night.[18] Information on the context and the environment of the voters, therefore, is combined with individual-level information.

The situation on Election Day is much different in the United States due to the different time zones and a different division of labor between the media and the polling institutes (Mitofsky & Edelmann, 1993, pp. 5-8). VRS provides data via formatted cross-tabs on computer screens showing vote by demographics, by issue preferences, and by other questions asked in the exit poll. Each participating network and news organization gets the results of its questions and is responsible for its own analysis. In contrast to the German situation, preliminary data based on the respective shares of the exit poll interviews that have been collected and processed up to particular time points are available throughout Election Day. They are, however, for internal information only. There are guidelines regarding the use of the information, some of which were not observed in 1992. It was agreed that VRS would call the winners of the different state contests before the winners were announced by the networks. The media got the information regarding in which state the poll indicated that a candidate had won and which candidate it was, and they agreed not to publish results prior to poll closing time in the individual states. The percentages for the candidates in state contests were not available for on-air use immediately after closing of the polls. They were provided when the estimates could be based on actual precinct returns. Although this agreement was widely kept, a problem of confidentiality emerged; It was impossible to keep election results confidential before they were broadcast. The basic idea was to provide preliminary data throughout the day that could be used to develop story ideas. The preliminary exit poll results were, however, communicated to other media people, the business community, and the political elites. Preliminary results were even published, although they were marked as "not for air." The freedom to communicate and to interpret complex statistical information available from noon until late at night, therefore, proved to be too tempting. Mitofsky and Edelman (1993) view this loss of control and the distribution of preliminary data as "not a healthy development" (p. 7).

Not to publish results before the polls are closed is rather uncontroversial with respect to state contests in the United States. Regarding the national exit poll results, however, things are different. The winner of the presidential contest is known after the candidate has received the necessary number of 270 electoral college votes, which often is the case before all polls in the western states are closed. At 9 p.m. in the eastern time zone, the polls are closed in 41 states. If the presidential contest is decided, then the winner can be announced by the networks. This inevitably leads critics to believe that the vote in the western states is devalued ("Critics Believe TV Devalues," 1996). It would, however, be very difficult for journalists to pretend not to know who is going to be the next president when giving a political analysis or comment. In 1992, participants had reached an agreement to "use their best judgment when to report their analyses of the national election" (Mitofsky & Edelmann, 1993, p. 7). In 1996, it was agreed not to publish a result before a candidate had won the necessary votes in the electoral college. So long as uniform poll closing legislation is not enacted, this problem, which has been a controversial issue for decades, will remain unsolved.

On Election Night in 1992, VRS made projections on 133 statewide contests for president, senator, governor, referenda, and the like, where exit polls had been carried out with respect to 114 of the 133 contests. The results of 67 contests were predicted using exit poll data; the method used was "poststratified ratio estimates that involve quality control and other refinements" (Mitofsky & Edelmann, 1993, p. 8). The projections regarding the other 66 contests used actual vote returns and cumulative vote counts in counties.

National estimates for the 1992 presidential election were provided from 7 p.m. until midnight at each hour and were computed as follows. The weighting of the national exit poll data by the reciprocal of the probabilities of selection produced an unbiased estimator. This estimator was improved by using all data available for a state at a given time. VRS computed poststratified ratio estimates in each state by "taking advantage of the correlations with past election results" (Mitofsky & Edelmann, 1993, p. 9). All data available at a particular time were used. At first, only exit poll data were available, and these were replaced by actual votes from sample precincts after poll closing. Later, vote returns by county were available as well. The best estimates from each state were then combined to make subregional estimates (i.e., East, Midwest, South, West). The national exit poll results (based on a subsample of precincts) within each subregion were then adjusted (forced) to those estimates. Without this procedure, Democrat Bill Clinton's margin over Republican George Bush would have been overstated by 5 percentage points (p. 9).

Evaluating Exit Poll Projections

A few hours after publication, prognoses and predictions based on exit polls are directly validated by comparison with the election result. In 1992, VRS correctly predicted all winning candidates in its projections including those 67 based on exit poll data only. The median presidential contest predicted at poll closing time had an 11.5 percentage point margin between the winner and his nearest opponent. The median after poll closing time was 4.4 percentage points. For the contests with smaller margins of victory, the projection models used either actual vote returns or cumulative vote counts in counties. The national estimates in 1992 improved from hour to hour with the gradual completion of the sample. The margin of Clinton's victory over Bush decreased from an estimated 10 percentage points at 8 and 9 p.m. in the eastern time zone to 9 and 8 percentage points at 10 and 11 p.m. When the polls were closed and the sample was complete at midnight, the margin was 7.5 percentage points. This was an overstatement of Clinton's lead by 1.6 points, as compared to the final result. The phenomenon of overstating the Democratic candidate has occurred in presidential elections as well as in state elections, and in general, a small but persistent bias in favor of the Democrats has been found (Mitofsky, 1991, p. 96; Mitofsky & Edelmann, 1993, pp. 9-10). It seems to be comparable to the problem of the shy Tories in Great Britain.

In Germany, the prognoses at 6 p.m. sharp are the first published estimates of the election outcome. In the prognoses, party shares of the vote for up to seven parties are estimated. The analysis of 34 prognoses published by the two channels on 17 Election Nights since the general election in 1994 shows that the cumulated difference between the prognoses and the final results has varied between a minimum of 0.9 percentage point and a maximum of 11.2 percentage points. The least accurate prognosis of both institutes (11.2 percentage points) was the one for the election in the eastern state of Saxony in 1994. The maximum cumulative differences for the other 16 elections were 7.8 percentage points (INFAS and ARD) and 7.2 percentage points (FGW and ZDF). The average cumulated difference for the 17 elections was 5.1 points for both institutes. With respect to predicting individual party share, bigger parties are estimated less accurately than smaller parties. The average cumulated differences between estimates and final results were 1.4 percentage points for the Social Democratic Party and 0.4 percentage point for the Liberal Party.

Projections based on precinct returns are calculated continuously on Election Night and published periodically according to the needs of the respective channels. The projections improve with increasing numbers of precinct returns. Within the first hour after poll closing, Infratest dimap and FGW projections for the three recent state elections based on the then available returns had cumulated deviations of about 2 to 4 percentage points from the final results. In projections based on all returns from the sample precincts, the cumulated differences compared to the final results in the three elections varied between 0.4 and about 2 percentage points. Some elections are "easier" than others; there are variations between elections regarding the speed and the amount of precinct returns at particular time points, and there are variations between the institutes. But the margins of error are relatively small, although the task of predicting and analyzing voting behavior in Germany has become more difficult in unified Germany due to increasing volatility.

The Role of Exit Polls in Political Marketing

Exit polls have been developed to reduce certain problems of preelection surveys, and they provide a unique database. They are based exclusively on interviews with voters and usually comprise a substantial number of interviews. Thus, very reliable information about the individual vote decision and the sociodemographic structure of different groups of voters is available. U.S. exit polls also include many important variables such as issue attitudes and party and candidate preferences. The analysis of previous exit polls from VNS and archived exit polls could provide useful information before campaigns, on the one hand, and the measurement of campaign effects in an exit poll on Election Day could provide vital feedback and a validity check for the political marketing of candidates, on the other.

The U.S. presidential election in 1992 demonstrated convincingly that political marketing has become a key factor in getting elected and reelected. In his analysis of Clinton's victory, Newman (1994, p. 12) presents a framework of political marketing and describes the role of survey research and polling in the process. Candidates are characterized as service providers offering political leadership in exchange for votes, and during the campaign, they have to market themselves and their campaign platforms. In political marketing, survey research and polling are crucial to fulfill the various tasks such as voter segmentation; candidate positioning; and the development, implementation, and control of the campaign strategy. For identifying the needs of voters, the profile of voters, and the segments most likely to support a candidate's positions, different empirical research instruments are available—focus groups, benchmark surveys, "trial heat" surveys, tracking polls, cross-sectional and panel surveys, and exit polls (pp. 115-119; see also

Mitchell & Daves's chapter in this book [Chapter 11] and Rademacher & Tuchfarber's chapter in this book [Chapter 12]).

Before or in early stages of campaigns, and before the extensive application of other empirical research instruments, secondary analyses of exit poll data could be used to test and further develop multivariate models of voting behavior and to identify multivariate predictors of party and candidate preferences. Based on such secondary analyses, improved questionnaires could be constructed for voter segmentation and candidate positioning.

Whereas the course of the campaign is observed with the help of preelection surveys, the success of the campaign is judged on Election Day. With the help of an exit poll on Election Day, political marketers can acquire data to figure out why their candidate won or lost. An exit poll is the only survey method in which the questions are answered by actual voters, as compared to registered or likely voters in other surveys, so it provides the most reliable information on candidate images and issue preferences in the various voter segments. Pre- and postelection surveys are influenced by various effects, such as social desirability and the bandwagon effect, that hardly influence exit polls to such an extent. Thus, exit polls could be carried out as a reality check for the political marketing of candidates. Exit polls should be carried out according to professional rules as described in this chapter, and users should be aware of the implications and guidelines when interpreting exit poll data.

Because the question of projections before poll closing time is a controversial issue in the United States, exit poll data also could be analyzed to determine whether projections of the results for U.S. eastern states have any influence on the turnout of certain types of voters in the U.S. western states.

Notes

1. With the availability of telephone interviews, however, fieldwork nowadays can be carried out until Election Day.

2. The states were Florida, Georgia, Hawaii, Kentucky, Minnesota, Montana, Ohio, South Carolina, South Dakota, Washington, and Wyoming. The laws declared it illegal to conduct an exit poll within 300 feet of the polling place, which made it impossible to carry out a valid exit poll. Other states, especially California, Illinois, and Texas, tried to "impose the strictures of electioneering statutes on exit polls" (Mitofsky, 1991, p. 91).

3. See INFAS (1990, p. 26). The German term for exit poll nowadays is *Wahltagsbefragung* (Election Day survey).

4. The term *Prognose* (prognosis) is used in Germany for the 6 p.m. prediction based on the exit poll data only, and it is used in this chapter only when referring to this particular operation in Germany. Projections provided later on Election Night (*Hochrechnungen*) are based on precinct returns.

5. Following the 1992 predictions, there still is a conflict between the media, namely the BBC and the British polling industry. Polling institutes have accused the BBC of censoring political poll findings and of "ghettoizing" poll reports (Worcester, 1997a, pp. 29-34). The critique of the 1992 poll performance led to methodological efforts and improvements by the polling institutes. Poll performance and especially the use of quota polls are, however, subject to a controversial ongoing debate in Great Britain (Curtice, 1997).

6. Voting differs between regions, due mostly to different religious affiliations and differences in the occupational structure. Past voting behavior is highly correlated with current voting behavior.

7. In Germany, the absentee or postal vote is organized in postal precincts (*Briefwahlbezirke*) that are counted separately on Election Night. In general elections during the 1990s, the postal vote has amounted to more than 10%. In state elections in city-states such as Hamburg, it has amounted to about 20%.

8. "Tied sample" means that the basis for the prediction of the current election is a sample of the precincts of the preceding election, representing the result of the preceding election as closely as possible. In Germany, the preceding election can be a general election, a state election, or a European election.

9. The figures for the recent Infratest dimap exit polls were as follows: Hamburg, 200 precincts and about 9,300 interviews (September 21, 1997); Niedersachsen, 150 precincts and about 7,400 interviews (March 1, 1998); Sachsen-Anhalt, 150 precincts and about 8,500 interviews (April 26, 1998).

10. In the general election and in most state elections in Germany, voters have to cast two votes—the first for a direct candidate running in a constituency and the second for a party list valid for the state as a whole. Direct seats are won by receiving a majority of the first vote, and the total number of seats allocated to a party is determined by the share of the second vote. In most elections, half of the number of total seats are allocated to candidates running for direct seats. However, these candidates often also have secure places on the party lists.

11. In Germany, this refers to the number of voters entitled to vote and the amount of the absentee vote. In the United States, this can refer to the number of actual votes cast up to the prescheduled reporting times (Levy, 1983, p. 62).

12. The age groups are 18 to 24, 25 to 34, 35 to 44, 45 to 59, and 60 years or over.

13. A preliminary final result is published after the count is finished later at night by the census office responsible for the electoral statistic for the respective election.

14. The first German television channel, ARD, is a cooperation between different regional broadcasting companies in the federal states. As a consequence, there might be a central television election studio, additional regional studios in different locations, and radio studios that have to be supported simultaneously.

15. Older German Catholic voters are, for example, more inclined to vote for the Christian Democrats and to cast their ballots after their Sunday church attendance before noon.

16. See note 11.

17. In two recent state elections (Hamburg, September 21, 1997, and Niedersachsen, March 1, 1998), a right-wing party and the Liberal Party missed parliamentary representation by only a small margin, getting 4.97% and 4.86% of the vote, respectively. In the case of Niedersachsen, this resulted in an absolute majority of seats for the Social Democratic Party. After his victory, the prime minister of the state, Gerhard Schröder, was nominated as the party's candidate for the chancellorship in the September 1998 general election. Schröder then defeated the 16-year incumbent, Helmut Kohl, in the general election and became chancellor of a new coalition government of the Social Democratic Party and the Green Party.

18. The aggregate analysis on the constituency level is available later on Election Night, after the constituency votes have been counted, and is used for further analyses after the election. Part of the aggregate information about the constituencies and the previous results in the constituency is available from the statistical offices, and part is computed by the institute.

References

BBC (1996). *Producers Guidelines 1996*, Chapter 20: *Opinion Polls.* Available on Internet: http://www.bbc.co.uk/info/editorial/prodgl/20.htm.

Bishop, G. F., & Fisher, B. S. (1995). "Secret ballots" and self-reports in an exit poll experiment. *Public Opinion Quarterly, 59,* 568-588.

Braunholtz, S., & Atkinson, S. (1995). What can we learn from June 9? Voters in the 1994 European Parliament election. In *British elections and parties yearbook 1995* (pp. 1-13). London: Cress.

Critics believe TV devalues western votes. (1996, November 5). *USA Today,* p. A1.

Curtice, J. (1997). So how well did they do? The polls in the 1997 election. *Journal of the Market Research Society, 39,* 449-461.

Edelmann, M., & Merkle, M. (1995, May). *The impact of interviewer characteristics and Election Day factors on exit poll data quality.* Paper presented at the annual conference of the American Association for Public Opinion Research, Fort Lauderdale, FL.

Gibowski. W. (1985). Hochrechnung. In D. Nohlen & R. O. Schultze (Eds.), *Pipers Wörterbuch zur Politik 1: Politikwissenschaft, Theorien, Methoden, Begriffe* (pp. 342-343). Munich: Piper.

Hoschka, P., & Schunk, H. (1977). *Comparison of regression-, difference-, and ratio-estimates in sample theory.* GMD-Mitteilungen Nr. 42, Birlinghoven castle, Sankt Augustin.

Institut für angewandte Sozialwissenschaft. (1990). *25 Jahre Wahlberichterstattung für die ARD.* Bonn, Germany: Author.

Levy, M. R. (1983). The methodology and performance of Election Day polls. *Public Opinion Quarterly, 47,* 54-67.

Market Research Society. (1994). *The opinion polls and the 1992 general election.* London: Author.

Mitofsky, W. (1991). A short history of exit polls. In P. J. Lavrakas & J. K. Holley (Eds.), *Polling and presidential elections coverage* (pp. 83-99). Newbury Park, CA: Sage.

Mitofsky, W., & Edelmann, M. (1993, May). *A review of the 1992 VRS exit polls.* Paper prepared for presentation at the annual meeting of the American Association for Public Opinion Research, St. Charles, IL.

Newman, B. I. (1994). *The marketing of the president: Political marketing as campaign strategy.* Thousand Oaks, CA: Sage.

Schultze, R.-O. (1980). Wahltagsbefragung: Chance und Gefahr. *Zeitschrift für Parlamentsfragen, 11,* 73-92.

Worcester, R. M. (1997a, July). *How do polls influence public attitudes and voting intentions?* Paper prepared for presentation at the Wilton Park Conference. (Available from MORI)

Worcester, R. M. (1997b). *The media and the polls: Pundits, polls, and prognostications in British general elections.* MORI research paper.

Worcester, R. M. (1998). *Letter to our readers from March British public opinion.* Adapted from an article published in *Press Gazette* (United Kingdom) on March 7, 1997. Available on Internet: http://www.mori.com/pubinfo/polls.htm.

14

Only the Facts

Professional Research and Message Development

CRAIG VAROGA
MIKE RICE

Facts can be stubborn things.

In 1934, Hollywood executives funded a relentless campaign against Upton Sinclair, the Democratic nominee for California governor that year. Sinclair, an avowed Socialist, was battered by attacks based on his own writings, "words he had written years or even decades ago. . . . There was nothing he could do about that." Sinclair responded ineptly—and lost the election (Mitchell, 1992).

In 1991, David Duke, "former" Nazi sympathizer and Ku Klux Klan (KKK) wizard, won a runoff berth in Louisiana's gubernatorial election. One week into the runoff, a statewide poll showed Duke trailing by only 4 percentage points. For the remainder of the runoff, Duke was battered by attacks based on his documented Nazi and KKK activities. Duke responded ferociously—but lost the election (Bridges, 1994).

The defeats of Sinclair and Duke were attributable to many causes, not the least of which were documented, fact-based research programs that reminded voters of the candidates' pasts.

Research

"Practical politics consists in ignoring facts," writes Adams (1961), a man of letters and a presidential descendant. But in a rejoinder, it also is observed that "ignoring facts means one thing and being ignorant of facts means another. Longevity in office rewards the politician who does his [or her] homework" (Baus & Ross, 1968).

Facts. Homework. By any other name, that is research.

There are four types of research that form the intellectual foundation of modern campaigns:

- Candidate research
- Issues research
- Public opinion research
- Targeting research

Without these four types of research, campaigns lose. With them, campaigns increase their chances of winning.

Candidate research, often called "opposition" research, is a comprehensive analysis of public records relating to both the candidate and his or her opponent. It is the campaign's intellectual foundation and begins the process of transforming plain information into "intelligence" or actionable information. Candidate research is the political equivalent of what is called "competitive intelligence" in the business world. Both have the same goal—to "anticipate your competitors' moves, learn from their successes and failures, and identify new opportunities" (Parker, 1994).

At the beginning of the 1996 election cycle, candidate research was reported to be the component that "really fuels the campaign machine—providing raw information that can be used strategically" (Keller, 1996). In 1990, *Campaigns & Elections,* the trade publication of campaign professionals, first began listing candidate research as a separate category in its annual "Political Pages" of campaign vendors. Approximately 25 firms or individuals were listed. In its 1998 edition, the equivalent number had grown to 42 (Persinos, 1994).

Issues research provides the information that informs a candidate's proposals or accomplishments on policy matters (e.g., taxes, crime, education, national security). Issues research, often in the form of position papers or policy announcements, enables the candidate to tell voters why he or she is running.

Public opinion research, addressed later in this chapter as a "development" tool, is the identification and measurement of public opinion using polls, focus groups, mall tests, and other methods. The best public opinion research goes below the surface (e.g., who is winning or losing) to answer fundamental questions. What are voters thinking? What issues will motivate them to reject a front-runner in favor of a dark horse? Which voting blocs are most receptive to persuasion?

Targeting research is the half-art, half-science of identifying voters by geographic area (e.g., precinct, media market, urban/rural) and demographic group (e.g., race, gender, education, age, party registration, income level) to determine "base" and "swing" voters. Base voters almost always will vote for your candidate, whereas swing voters will require persuasion to vote for your candidate. Targeting research will help your campaign determine how to present its message through paid media (television, radio, and direct mail advertising) and earned media (newspaper and broadcast coverage of the campaign).

What Research Is Not

Candidate research often has gotten bad press; for example, it was dismissed in 1994 as a "cottage industry of life-ruiners" dedicated to publicizing "more and more on the personal pecadilloes [sic] of candidates" (Shalit, 1994). In explaining this bad press, the *New York Times* opined, "Opposition research has become stigmatized since the Republicans used it so aggressively against [Democratic presidential nominee Michael] Dukakis in 1988. . . . The fallout from that campaign left negative research in such disrepute that campaign aides are reluctant to discuss them" (Nagourney, 1996). Critics of candidate research often cite the perils of questionably obtained information. The critics are right to attack these tactics but are incorrect to call them research.

To understand candidate research, it is necessary to establish what candidate research is not.

Dumpster Divers

Dumpster divers are the midnight marauders who take their opponent's trash and go through it after it has been thrown away. Their activity falls into the category of "legal but stupid"—legal because trash becomes public property once placed curbside for garbage pickup, stupid because voters hate campaigns that get down (literally) in the gutter. Dumpster divers brag about sifting through pizza remains and old coffee cups. Their Holy Grail is finding a discarded memo or candidate schedule or some elusive campaign secret that will turn the entire election to their candidate. More likely, they get caught and become the focus of an embarrassing news story about how a campaign "has reached a new low" or how "the election has gotten dirty." As Talleyrand said of Napoleon, "It was worse than a crime; it was a blunder" (quoted in Kimball, 1995).

Cookie Cutters

Cookie cutters sell "one size fits all" research regardless of region, opponent, or personal background. They include the following:

- *Ideologues* who claim to have figured out the entire election before doing a speck of research: They often have a partisan ax to grind or cause to push that has nothing to do with voters in your state or district.
- *Chop shops* that peddle on-line sources as "original" research: Some so-called "professional" firms will take an electronic search, change the typeface, slap on a new headline, put it in a pretty binder, and then submit a big fat invoice for their "work."
- *Fly-by-nighters* who promise the sky but, after they get paid, will not return phone calls.

Spies and Private Investigators

Many campaigns boast about "moles" inside their opponents' operations. This psychological warfare usually is a bluff. Most so-called spies usually are loyal supporters with big mouths who say the wrong things to the wrong people. Or, they are lukewarm supporters playing both sides until the election outcome becomes clear. In the heat of battle, some campaigns hire private investigators to plug leaks, uncover moles, and/or document the scurrilous rumors that inevitably (and often falsely) engulf opponents. None of this is research. Or necessary.

In writing about the U.S. need for "central intelligence," diplomat George F. Kennan has good advice for politicians and campaign professionals: "I would say that something upward of 95[%] of what we need to know could be very well obtained by the careful and competent study of perfectly legitimate sources of information open and available to us in the rich library and archival holdings of this country" (Kennan, 1997). The road to electoral defeat is paved with cloak-and-dagger gumshoes hired to hide in shadows, only to be exposed in front-page, above-the-fold newspaper stories. When that happens, you have lost the moral high ground for the remainder of the campaign.

What Research Is

Candidate research is the retrieval and strategic analysis of documents obtained from libraries, databases, government agencies, and other public sources. A "well-managed" campaign will use "fair and accountable data which can be publicly verified" (Democratic National Committee, 1996). The results of a candidate research project are presented in written form with fact-based summaries and analyses of significant points.

Identifying Public Documents

As Kennan has noted, public archives are a rich trove of information. Sometimes, they can provide too much. In the mid-1970s, a 21-year-old Princeton University physics student, "using information obtained from unclassified sources," prepared a 34-page report said to contain plans for a "crude plutonium device weighing 125 pounds and allegedly carrying a charge one third as powerful as the one detonated over Hiroshima in World War II" ("Student Designs," 1976).

Candidate research begins with a retrieval of standard public documents including the following:

- Elected officials' records (e.g., floor and committee votes, minutes, travel documents, phone bills, staff reimbursements)
- Campaign contribution records
- Records of voter participation
- Court files including possible criminal activity and litigation history
- Property records and property tax payment histories

- Corporate and "DBA" (doing business as) records
- Newspaper, magazine, and journal articles
- Military service records
- Documents available on electronic databases and the Internet

These documents can be retrieved in-person or through written request from sources such as courthouses, county or city clerks, tax assessors, registrars of voters, newspaper morgues, public libraries, chambers of commerce, and the Federal Election Commission.

Problems Conducting Candidate Research

Official Resistance

Employees at government agencies often have a vested interest in an election's outcome. For example, the county clerk might be allied with your opponent, and in a partisan move, could instruct his or her employees to prevent anyone from obtaining copies of a lawsuit alleging financial misconduct against your opponent. Legislative clerks, in particular, have been known to give researchers the run-around about the availability of travel reimbursements, phone records, and office expenses when the requests concern the legislators who helped in hiring them.

These custodians of public records sometimes assert nonexistent rules to prevent the release of government documents. Official resistance might include a request for information not yet obtained (e.g., the subject's birthdate, social security number, or address) or unnecessary (e.g., a written release from the subject). The official excuses sometimes are ludicrous. For example, in a 1996 case, a clerk refused to conduct a manual search "through thousands of pages of government records" because that allegedly would violate state ethics laws, which "prohibit the use of public funds or property to influence the outcome of an election."[1] Other times, the excuses appear reasonable, with clerks explaining that they "don't have time today to look for them, but if you come back next week we'll see what we can do." The return visit, not surprisingly, meets with a similar excuse.

Records prepared with taxpayer dollars, generally speaking, are open for public inspection. These include expense reports, travel vouchers, phone bills, official correspondence, appointment calendars, voting records (minutes and journals of proceedings), executive orders, and other documents relating to official conduct. Exceptions to the general rule might include records that are restricted to protect an individual's right to privacy, public safety, or national security. For example, a person's income tax records are private and not subject to release. Likewise, most law enforcement records are not open to inspection because they contain information regarding criminal informants, investigations, and ongoing prosecutions. Most other public documents, however, can be obtained.

Faulty Analysis, Incorrect Sources

Reporters, it has been written, "are generalists who use no documents in preparing nearly three quarters of their stories. When documents are used, they are most often newspaper stories" (Jamieson, 1992). So, if it is in print, such as this book or a newspaper story, then it must be true. Right? Not necessarily.

In 1996, the *Fort Lauderdale Sun-Sentinel* ran a front-page story about ethnic street gangs flocking to the Internet. The reporter warned that gangs were using cyberspace to go on a global crime spree. But shortly thereafter, the newspaper recanted. The gang and the Web page cited in the news article were hoaxes created by a White 16-year-old living in a Michigan suburb (see also Weeks, O'Harrow, Pishvanov, & Light, 1996). Also in 1996, a New York University physicist tricked an academic journal into publishing a parody in which he mused that the physical laws of the universe (e.g., gravity) were culturally relative. When the physicist gloated publicly about his hoax, the journal's editors recanted, albeit reluctantly.

Hoaxes and uncorrected mistakes, especially those in print, can profoundly embarrass a campaign—or even destroy it. Just ask any candidate who has made charges against an opponent, only to see the charges blow up in his or her face when those allegations (e.g., drunk driving conviction, failure to pay child support, arrest record) are proven dead wrong. During the early 1990s, a member of Congress running for reelection issued a news release accusing his opponent of simultaneously holding two jobs as a congressional staffer, one of them a "no show" sinecure. As it happened, the opponent was not a "double-dipper" but rather had the same name as another staffer. The member of Congress was forced to apologize, an embarrassment that needlessly jeopardized what eventually was a successful reelection effort.

In a research-driven campaign, you will not make claims—especially attacks—without the ability to prove them.

Development

Analyzing the Information

With the advent of the Internet and other on-line resources, everyone has access to information at lightning speed. Increasingly, candidates ask, "Why do we have to hire a research agency when we can log on ourselves and get the information at a fraction of the cost?" The question is valid but has two faulty presumptions: (a) that information is self-evident (it is not) and (b) that analysis is either easy or unnecessary (wrong again). The goal of research is not quantity ("We got every property record going back 25 years") but rather quality ("The opponent sold one property at twice its assessed value to a campaign contributor who also received a no-bid contract from the county"). Consider the following examples:

- If the opponent failed to vote in a municipal election, is it enough to label him or her a nonvoter? Or, is it worth noting that the election the opponent missed was for the school board, undercutting his or her campaign pledge to be the "education mayor"?

- If court records indicate that the opponent was sued for not paying child support, is that information off limits? What if the opponent's campaign literature cites legislation he or she sponsored to crack down on "deadbeat" parents?

- If the opponent says that his or her business background gives him or her an advantage, is it valid to ask why two of the opponent's companies failed to pay franchise taxes?

By analyzing information, you can juxtapose a candidate's statements with his or her record. A candidate who pledges campaign finance reform but runs afoul of state election laws is fair game, as is a candidate who pledges to prosecute drunk drivers but who has an arrest record himself or herself for driving under the influence. The same holds true for office seekers who march to a pro-defense drumbeat but who evaded the draft by obtaining student deferments during the Vietnam War era. Analyzing. Cross-referencing. Placing things in context. Using them effectively during the campaign. These are the challenges and goals of a research-driven campaign.

Sharing the Information

If the campaign does not review the candidate research, then that is as bad as not doing the research in the first place. When the research is completed, campaigns should share it with the strategy team including candidate, manager, pollster, media consultant, communications director, and others "in the loop" or "at the table." Information unshared, unread, untested, and unvetted is an opportunity missed or a disaster waiting to happen.

Examples of unshared information and poor communication include a legislative campaign that documented the outlandish political ideology of the opponent but failed to forward the documents to the media consultant, a statewide candidate who falsified educational credentials and refused to come clean when confronted by the campaign's political advisers, and a press secretary who delayed returning a reporter's calls about a seemingly scandalous lawsuit and failed to alert the research team to the accusations (which were false but unrefuted in the first round of news coverage).

Vetting the Information

Outlandish, undocumented claims will blow up in anyone's face. In 1917, two English girls produced photographs purporting to show wood fairies at play "in the woods of Cottingley in the far-off region of Yorkshire." The photos created an international sensation. Skeptics who examined the pictures called them fakes. But Sir Arthur Conan Doyle, the creator of Sherlock Holmes (the greatest investigative mind in literature), "believed so strongly in their authenticity that he wrote a whole book, *The Coming of the Fairies* . . ., about them—and nearly lost his credibility forever" (Goldberg, 1998).

Few candidates believe in the tooth fairy, but many have selective recall and are unreliable narrators. They "often can't (and may not want to) remember what, or who, they did, said, smoked, slept with, or profited from during their lives" (Duffy, 1995). In 1994, U.S. Senate candidate Jim Miller challenged Oliver North to release his psychiatric records, but Miller then reluctantly admitted that he himself had undergone psychiatric treatment. The challenge backfired and contributed to Miller's loss to North in Virginia's Republican primary.

To vet information and prevent needless embarrassment, convene a conference of the strategy team. Summarize the findings. Determine whether you share any vulnerabilities with the opponent. Maybe you will not finalize the campaign's message, but you can at least kill the sort of foolishness that Miller attempted against North. As novelist F. Scott Fitzgerald observed, "No grand idea was ever born in a conference, but a lot of foolish ideas have died there" (Fitzgerald, 1956). Kill hypocrisy before it starts. When you set yourself up as sparkling clean, dust looks like mud.

Testing the Research

Once the candidate research is completed, it will be tested using focus groups and benchmark polls. The findings of this public opinion research will hone the campaign's message.

Focus groups are a collection of about a dozen individuals, all chosen demographically because of gender, occupation, income, or party registration, led in discussion by a trained moderator. The groups are used to simulate how issues and attitudes form over the course of a campaign. Focus groups are like test marketing. They often preview television advertisements or screen campaign messages. In 1988, the George Bush presidential campaign tested both the Willie Horton and flag issues in focus groups held in the spring. Later in the campaign, both issues (pretty or not) hammered the Dukakis campaign.[2]

Ideally, open discussion in focus groups will reveal insights into voter attitudes about candidate strengths and issues. In turn, these insights will enable the campaign to do additional candidate or issues research. For example, a heightened awareness of crime might require greater explanation of a candidate's legislative record on criminal justice issues; the same campaign might want to add detail to its own anticrime plan.

Focus groups are just one development tool to revise tactics and hone strategy. No prudent campaign will base its entire strategy on the outcome of one focus group because a verbose member in one group can dominate and skew the discussion. In 1989, NBC used focus groups to test a half-hour show starring an unknown comedian. The research report dismissed the pilot as "weak," the characters as "weird," and the overall audience reaction as "lukewarm." According to *TV Guide,* "No segment of the [focus group] audience was eager to watch the show again" (Robins, 1996). After nearly a decade of critical acclaim, high ratings, and numerous Emmys, *Seinfeld* left prime time as one of the most successful comedies in television history.

Benchmark polls are used to scientifically measure the findings of focus groups including campaign themes, issues, and candidate research. A benchmark poll is approximately 20 minutes long and poses various questions to voters including negative arguments against your candidate and the opponent. It includes enough respondents (600-800 for a city or congressional race, 800 or more for a statewide election depending on the size of the state) to get information within geographic and demographic groups.

A benchmark poll is a tool to build a strategic consensus within the campaign. It also is useful in silencing kibitzers who have the candidate's ear and articulate bullies who make "bad advice sound good while driving into silence less aggressive or more cautious advisers," in the words of Theodore Sorensen, President John F. Kennedy's lawyer and speech writer (Sorensen, 1963).

When hiring pollsters to do your benchmark survey, it is important to know whether they have other clients in your state and whether these present a potential conflict of interest. Ask whether the pollster uses lists of registered voters in selecting the sample so that you get a higher concentration of likely voters. If, instead, the pollster selects the sample by phone numbers, make sure that he or she draws the numbers randomly (rather than from a phone book) to avoid undercounting mobile, swing, and younger voters. You will want to know what type of "screen" they use in the questioning to eliminate unlikely voters as well as their call-back procedures to ensure a representative demographic sample.[3] Finally, you will want to make sure that the phoners are sufficiently trained and supervised and that the callers' accents are appropriate to your area.[4]

Once the poll is completed, make sure that your pollster gives you a blunt, objective view of the political situation. Require verbal and written recommendations. In a statewide race, get a geographic breakdown of results to customize your campaign strategy by the various media markets. Share research with other consultants and key staff. Use this research to sharpen your message and targets.

Protect your benchmark poll from budget slashers who would either cut it completely or delay it until it was useless. And you should not try to save money by doing an in-house poll, even when the person running your volunteer phone bank says he or she once worked at a polling firm or when your phone bank vendor says it does all the calls for the college professor who polls for your local television station. Even if luck strikes and you get it 90% right, that still is 10% wrong—enough to hurt you in a tight race.

Monitoring Your Progress

Tracking polls are used at the end of a campaign to monitor the ballot contest—who is ahead and who is behind. This research enables the campaign to make last-minute adjustments in strategy. If you are ahead, then your message of lowering taxes and improving schools might be working despite the opponent's negative ads. But if you are falling behind, then you might need to respond to charges that you did not pay taxes owed to the school district.

There are two types of tracking polls: (a) weekly, with a sample size of at least several hundred, and (b) nightly, with 100 to 200 respondents, in which pollsters "roll" the survey over several nights and average results to reduce fluctuation due to a smaller sample size. Costs vary depending on the district and sample sizes. Statewide surveys cost more than congressional polls.

Tracking polls are vastly different from benchmarks, which are longer, costlier, and designed to identify long-term voter attitudes and overall election strategy. Tracking polls are used to spot last-minute trends and to adjust tactics including changes in the final television buy, candidate schedule, debate plans, "get out the vote" targets, and spending needs. Most campaigns prefer nightly surveys because they provide decision makers with continuous information including a vivid sense of the opponent's options.

A skittish campaign will overanalyze and become paralyzed when confronted by too much data. But that is not a research problem; it is a management crisis. Used effectively, tracking polls can help fix a losing campaign. In 1982, U.S. Senator John Danforth seemed poised to lose to his Democratic challenger, Harriet Woods. But Danforth's campaign used numerous tracking polls to adjust its end game, ultimately winning in a nail-biter finish.

Message Discipline

"Message discipline" is a recent term but hardly a new concept. In 1935, after Louisiana Senator Huey Long was shot and still was conscious but close to death in a Baton Rouge hospital bed, he barked out one final order to his entourage: "I don't want anybody to issue any statements or do any talking until I get out of here. I'll issue all the statements" (quoted in Zinman, 1993).

In modern campaigns, message discipline is research driven—keeping it simple, telling the truth, remaining focused, and responding rapidly.

Keeping It Simple

The simplest message—"It's the economy, stupid"—often is the most profound and memorable. That is because it has been vetted (confirmed by economic data) and tested (reflecting voters' anxiety about job security).

The U.S. Army's 1962 field manual summarizes the power of putting it simply: "Simplicity contributes to successful operations. Direct, simple plans and clear, concise orders minimize misunderstanding and confusion. If other factors are equal, the simplest plan is preferred" (Summers, 1984). Sounds easy, but as management guru Peter F. Drucker observes about business executives, "The most time-consuming step in the process is not making the decision but [rather] putting it into effect" (Drucker, 1966).

Telling the Truth

It is 3 p.m. on a Friday afternoon. The opponent has just had a news conference and has begun airing a new radio ad accusing your candidate of directing millions of dollars in state contracts to a campaign contributor who owns a construction company. What do you do?

If you neglected to do research on your candidate, then you are about to swerve off your campaign's central message and possibly lose the election. You can deny the accusation, but you do not have the facts to disprove it. Your only choice is to hit back with a counteraccusation, but that will not dispel the odor of malfeasance about to envelop your campaign.

On the other hand, if you have done research on your candidate, then you should have the facts to handle the accusation. If you have nothing to hide, then your best strategy is telling the truth. Immediately, gather all relevant documents, organize them into a packet, and distribute copies to the news media. Prove in indisputable terms that the opponent is peddling falsehoods and misleading information. If there is some truth in the opponent's accusations but it is out of context, then again tell the truth. Put it back into context, explain the facts, and get back to the message that scores points for your campaign. Most reporters and voters eventually will recognize who is telling the truth. You just need to speed that recognition. As Shakespeare wrote, "There is no terror in your threats, for I am armed so strong in honesty" (quoted in Cross & Brooke, 1993).

Remaining Focused

One of the biggest challenges in a campaign is remaining focused when everyone around you—or so it seems—wants to go off-message. In these instances, message discipline means returning to the research. What were each candidate's strengths and weaknesses? What were the findings of the benchmark poll? Are the tracking polls encouraging, or do they indicate that nothing has worked—and so it is okay to go off-message?

Some advisers will forcefully argue that it is necessary to use every weapon from the candidate research. But having what campaign veterans call "nuclear capability" (e.g., a divorce proceeding with messy personal details) does not mean that you should strike first. Although personal attacks can damage the other side, they are messy and can backfire just as often.

Candidates and managers would do well to remember a story that former House Speaker Tip O'Neill told about President Harry Truman. In 1953, after Dwight Eisenhower moved into the White House, Truman told several Democratic freshmen that he had no use for Eisenhower. But Truman added, "Leave his family alone. . . . If I ever hear that one of you attacked the wife or a family member of the president of the United States, I'll personally go into your district and campaign against you" (O'Neill, 1994).

Other distractions include reporters. Answer their questions directly; do not evade. But if you have an additional point to make (even if unrelated), then make it. You might not get another chance. Stay focused when a reporter says, "Oh, and just one more question." As Richard Nixon, episodic paranoia and constitutional disgrace aside, explained, "Forget the other [10 questions] he [or she] asked; this is what he [or she] really came for" (Nixon, 1990).

Responding Rapidly

Psychologists have noted that "voters retain negative messages four or six times as readily as positive ones" (Birnbaum, 1995). Therefore, the risk in not responding rapidly to a negative message is significant because voters will forget the good and remember only the bad stuff about you. Candidate research will enable you to strike at your opponent's heart when you are under fire:

- If they attack you for a specific campaign contribution, did they also accept money from the same source?
- If they attack you on an unpopular issue, is their current position consistent with their past statements?
- If an "independent" third party attacks you, can you quickly prove that the third party has political or financial links to your opponent, thus impugning its motives?

Similarly, public opinion research will enable you to gauge the effectiveness of the attack and your response:

- Are you ahead or behind in the polls?
- Do you have a large lead, or is it within the margin of error?
- Did you include this possible attack in your benchmark poll? If it hurt your candidate, was it a deep or shallow cut?
- If the charges are libelous, then consider suing. Litigation will prolong the story, but it also might add credibility to your denial.

The benchmark for a successful rapid response is how the 1992 presidential campaign of Bill Clinton defused Gennifer Flowers' claims of a long-term extramarital affair with the then governor of Arkansas. Just 2 days before the story broke in the network news, Clinton was leading former Massachusetts Senator Paul Tsongas by only 5 percentage points among New Hampshire primary voters (Royer, 1994). As the feeding frenzy hit, the campaign did not hide but instead chose to confront the story directly by booking the governor and his wife, Hillary Clinton, on the CBS news show *60 Minutes.* According to Clinton adviser James Carville, "We wanted as big an audience as we could get. It was Super Bowl Sunday, and they said they would give us the time right after the Super Bowl." Campaign pollster Stan Greenberg affirmed the "big audience" strategy "so that no one could ever say through the rest of this campaign that we did not confront the issue" (quoted in Royer, 1994).

The stakes were the presidency itself. According to Bill Shore, a consultant that year to Bob Kerrey's presidential campaign, "If Clinton survived the story, he was going to be very tough. It was a story that [either was] going to kill him or was going to make him very strong, which is what happened" (quoted in Royer, 1994).

After the Clintons appeared on *60 Minutes,* a Tsongas poll found Clinton's lead actually increasing, from 5 to 15 percentage points (Royer, 1994). Clinton had survived, and he would go on to survive additional crises in New Hampshire before gaining 25% of the vote, a respectable second to Tsongas—good enough to be "The Comeback Kid" and eventual winner of the biggest prize anywhere in politics.

Conclusion

During the second half of the 20th century, a professional class of advisers and staff (media consultants, pollsters, managers, and "spin doctors") has formed to service political campaigns in the American do-or-die electoral system. Candidate research specialists are the most recent to stake their claims as campaign professionals.

Despite its recent professionalization, research (by many other names) has been part of public and political life for thousands of years. During the Roman Republic, Cicero advised his brother, a candidate for consul, to make his opponents "know that they are observed and watched by you" (quoted in Yonge, 1853). And Sun Tzu remarked in *The Art of War* more than 2,000 years ago, "He who exercises no forethought but makes light of his opponents is sure to be captured by them" (quoted in Clavell, 1983).

Like any weapon, political research can be used for noble purposes or can be abused for less honorable ends. Louisiana and the United States undoubtedly are better places because Duke, the "former" Nazi sympathizer and KKK wizard, was not elected governor of that state in 1991, at least in part due to attacks documenting his demagogic and racist activities. Conversely, the fallout and disrepute that stigmatized the Republican presidential campaign in 1988 no doubt have cast an occasional pall over "negative" research. But arguably, a more research-driven campaign might have enabled Dukakis to respond more rapidly and, hypothetically at least, minimized the fallout from the Republican attacks.

The bottom line is that campaigns that use research win. Those that do not use it lose.

Notes

1. Of course, there is nothing unethical about producing public records.

2. The Bush campaign and its allies claimed in both paid and earned media that Dukakis had released a convicted murderer on furlough, during which this criminal had raped and terrorized a Maryland family. The Bush campaign also insinuated that Dukakis was less patriotic because the Massachusetts governor had vetoed legislation mandating the recital of the Pledge of Allegiance in Massachusetts schools.

3. If, for example, the polling firm samples only those voters who are at home on a Friday evening, then it might undercount young and single individuals.

4. A voter is more likely to participate in a poll if the caller has a similarly sounding accent.

References

Adams, H. (1961). *The education of Henry Adams*. Boston: Houghton Mifflin.

Baus, H. M., & Ross, W. B. (1968). *Politics battle plan*. New York: Macmillan.

Birnbaum, J. H. (1995, November 6). The pat solution. *Time*.

Bridges, T. (1994). *The rise of David Duke*. Jackson: University of Mississippi Press.

Clavell, J. (Ed.). (1983). *The art of war, Sun Tzu*. New York: Dell.

Cross, W. L., & Brooke, T. (1993). *The Yale Shakespeare*. New York: Barnes & Noble Books.

Democratic National Committee. (1996). *Campaign training manual: Research*. Washington, DC: Author.

Drucker, P. F. (1966). *The effective executive*. New York: HarperCollins.

Duffy, M. (1995, May 15). In search of skeletons. *Time*.

Fitzgerald, F. S. (1956). *The Crack Up*. New York: New Directions.

Goldberg, V. (1998, February 1). Of faeries, free spirits and outright frauds. *The New York Times*.

Jamieson, K. H. (1992). *Dirty politics: Deception, distraction, and democracy*. New York: Oxford University Press.

Keller, A. (1996, January 29). Inside the secret profession that digs up the dirt that makes the negative ads. *Roll Call*.

Kennan, G. F. (1997, May 18). Spy and counterspy. *The New York Times*.

Kimball, R. (1995, May). [Book review]. *American Spectator*.

Mitchell, G. (1992). *The campaign of the century: Upton Sinclair's race for governor of California*. New York: Random House.

Nagourney, A. (1996, April 3). Research the enemy: An old political tool resurfaces in a new election. *The New York Times*.

Nixon, R. M. (1990). *In the arena: A memoir of victory, defeat, and renewal*. New York: Simon & Schuster.

O'Neill, T., with Hymel, G. (1994). *All politics is local and other rules of the game*. Holbrooke, MA: Bob Adams.

Parker, E. (1994, April). Learn from the masters of competitive intelligence. *Success*.

Persinos, J. (1994, August). Gotcha! *Campaigns & Elections*.

Robins, J. M. (1996, September 21). Seinfeld aces ultimate test: Time. *TV Guide*.

Royer, C. T. (Ed.). (1994). *Campaign for president: The managers look at '92*. Hollis, NH: Hollis Publishing.

Shalit, R. (1994, January 3). The Oppo boom. *New Republic*.

Sorensen, T. C. (1963). *Decision making in the White House: The olive branch or the arrows*. New York: Columbia University Press.

Student designs $2,000 atom bomb. (1976, October 8). *The New York Times*.

Summers, H. G., Jr. (1984). *On strategy: A critical analysis of the Vietnam War*. New York: Dell.

Weeks, L., O'Harrow, R., Jr., Pishvanov, N., & Light, C. (1996, December 5). The homey home page newspaper taken in by gang site hoax. *Washington Post*, p. B7.

Yonge, C. D. (Ed.). (1853). *Treatises of M. T. Cicero on the nature of the gods; on divination; on fate; on the republic; on the laws; and on standing for the consulship*. London: Henry Bohn.

Zinman, D. (1993). *The day Huey Long was shot*. Jackson: University Press of Mississippi.

Modeling Voter Behavior

15

A Predictive Model of Voter Behavior

The Repositioning of Bill Clinton

BRUCE I. NEWMAN

The successful reelection campaign of President Bill Clinton in 1996 can be attributed to the market orientation of his campaign strategy. Through the use of sophisticated information technology, the president's marketing consultants were able to identify a theme that resonated with the hearts and minds of a majority of voters. The president repositioned his programs as opening up new opportunities for the American voters and their children, branded by the president and his campaign organization as the "age of opportunity." Winning reelection in 1996 hinged on the ability of the president to convince Americans that there still was hope for them and their children to achieve the "American Dream."[1]

Using a model of voter behavior, this study identifies exactly what the American Dream meant to four broad segments of voters, all of whom cross the boundaries of party affiliation and candidate preference; that is, each of the four segments of voters is found in the Democratic and Republican parties, and each of the three political leaders studied (Bill Clinton, Bob Dole, and Colin Powell) was potentially attractive to all four segments, but for different reasons. Although Powell had dropped out of the race, he was included in the analysis because at the time this study was undertaken he represented the "ideal" American Dream candidate to many voters in the United States. Powell still was considering a run for the White House at the time the data were collected for this study.

The four segments of voters studied were differentiated on the basis of the "value" they sought in a president. In other words, just as companies in the commercial marketplace have to create value to attract customers, so too does a candidate in the "political marketplace" who is seeking to carve out a niche for himself or herself that separates the candidate from the competition. To win reelection, the president had to position himself at the center of the political spectrum by appealing to a majority of voters on a nonpartisan basis and attracting as many voters as possible from three voter blocs: his supporters, Powell's supporters, and Dole's supporters. This could have been accomplished only by identifying the "value" that each voter bloc sought in a leader.

An important part of any political campaign is the candidates' spending of money and time to promote their ideas (Newman, 1994; Newman & Sheth, 1985b) and manufacture their images (Newman, 1999). Thus, it has become important to understand why voters behave the way they do in addition to conducting polls that indicate who is going to vote for whom and by what margin one candidate will win or lose an election. By understanding why voters value one candidate over another, their behavior can be better understood, which will enable campaign organizations to spend their time and money most wisely.

A Model of Voter Behavior

A model of voter behavior developed by Newman (1981) and tested on several elections (Newman & Sheth, 1985a, 1987) proposes a number of cognitive beliefs that may come from a wide range of sources including the voter, word-of-mouth communication, and the mass media. In addition, the model incorporates the influence of an individual's affiliation with groups of people in his or her social environment (Lazarsfeld, Berelson, & Gaudet, 1944) and the influence of party affiliation and past voting behavior (Campbell, Converse, Miller, & Stokes, 1960). This model was used as the basis for the conduct of this study (Figure 15.1).

The fundamental axiom of the model is that voters are consumers of a service offered by a politician, and similar to consumers in the commercial marketplace, voters choose candidates based on the perceived value they offer them. The model proposes that there are five distinct and separate cognitive domains that drive voters' behavior. A key proposition of the model is that voter behavior can be driven by a combination of one or more of the domains in a given election. The model consists of the following components.

Political Issues

The Political Issues component represents the policies a candidate advocates and promises to enact if elected to office. For example, voters concerned about their children's education will be more inclined to vote for a candidate who promises to enact laws that make education more affordable. Or, elderly voters worried about getting health care as they age will be receptive to a candidate who has ideas on how to deal with financial issues in the health care system (Campbell et al., 1960; Converse, 1964; Downs 1957; Flanigan & Zingale, 1983; Key, 1966; Nie & Anderson, 1974; Nie, Verba, & Petrocik, 1976; Popkin, Gorman, Phillips, & Smith, 1976; RePass 1971).

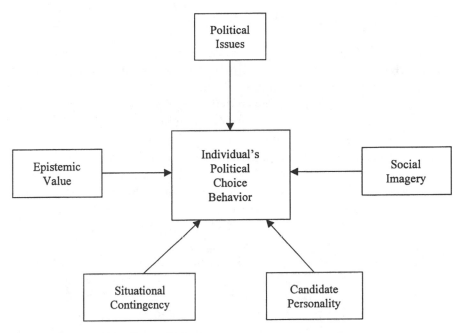

Figure 15.1. Model of Voter Behavior

This dimension is captured on the commercial side by companies that appeal to consumers with products that promise high quality, lower prices, and other benefits that have a rational appeal. For example, Miller Lite was promoted for many years as a beer that both tastes great and is less filling, two benefits that would appeal to consumers who choose a brand of beer for rational reasons.

Social Imagery

The Social Imagery component represents the stereotyping of the candidate to appeal to voters by making associations between the candidate and selected segments in society (e.g., the support Dole received in the 1996 election from business leaders and the National Rifle Association, the support Clinton received from unions and environmentalists). The use of imagery can be very powerful here as the candidate manufactures an image in the minds of voters on the basis of his or her associations, with the possibility of that image being either positive or negative in the minds of voters, depending on which group the candidate is trying to associate himself or herself with (Asher, 1980; Berelson, Lazarsfeld, & McPhee, 1954; Campbell & Cooper, 1954; Key, 1966; Natchez, 1970; Newman, 1999; Nie et al., 1976).

In the commercial marketplace, this is similar to Michael Jordan endorsing a product such as Gatorade (a sports drink) in the hope that consumers will buy it simply because it is linked with a sports superhero. Candidates, like products, get stereotyped in people's minds as a result of their association with selected individuals and groups of people.

Candidate Personality

The Candidate Personality component also represents the use of imagery in a slightly different way. Here, the candidate is emphasizing his or her personality traits to help reinforce and manufacture an image in the voters' minds (e.g., Dole's emphasizing his experience in the Senate in the 1996 election as a way of making voters feel more secure about him, Clinton's claiming to have new ideas to help bring the country into the next millennium in an effort to create an excitement about his candidacy). This is no different from Ronald Reagan's consistently being seen in front of flag-waving Americans in both of his presidential campaigns to create an image of the man as a true patriot (Bowen, Broh, & Prysby, 1976; Campbell, 1983; Campbell & Cooper, 1954; Downing, 1965; Gant & Davis, 1984; Kessel, 1984; Mendelsohn & O'Keefe, 1976; Natchez & Bupp, 1968; Newman, 1999; Nimmo & Savage, 1976).

When we compare this to consumers in the marketplace, marketers do play on emotions by using the right setting, appeals, and background to create a mood that affects consumers' decisions to purchase a particular brand. For example, Volvo advertises the fact that its automobiles have advanced safety features to create a sense of security in those consumers looking for a car that will provide protection for their children.

Situational Contingency

The Situational Contingency component represents that dimension of voters' thinking that could be swayed by "hypothetical events" described during the course of the campaign that voters are led to believe could happen. A candidate's opponents often use this as a means of creating the illusion that one candidate is better to deal with certain situations than the other candidate in an effort to get voters to switch their allegiance. For example, some voters might have been prepared to switch to Powell if he ran for president if they thought that he would be better able to lead the country as an outsider when the other candidates all were perceived to be insiders who would rely on the same deal-making tactics if elected (Campbell et al., 1960; Howard & Sheth, 1969; Triandis, 1971; Vincent & Zikmund, 1975).

Marketers also rely on this dimension as the basis for appealing to consumers and getting them to switch from one brand or company to another. For example, McDonald's and Burger King constantly are engaged in attempts to lure one another's customers by opening up new stores in conveneint locations. Similarly, long-distance telephone companies are becoming more creative in their attempts to get customers to switch providers by offering better deals and more complete telecommunication packages.

Epistemic Value

The Epistemic Value component represents that dimension which appeals to voters' sense of curiosity or novelty in choosing a candidate such as was the case in 1992 when Ross Perot ran against Clinton and George Bush on the basis of his outsider appeal. To many voters, Perot represented a candidate who was an outsider to the mainstream politician and was seen as someone who offered a much different and unique brand of politics. It is interesting to note that 4 years later, the novelty wore off for many voters, and Perot lost his appeal. In 1996, this same dimension also captured the desire on the part of some voters who voted for Dole either because they simply were sick and tired of Clinton's administration or they wanted to see a new face in the White House (Berlyne, 1963; Faison, 1977; McAlister, 1982; McAlister & Pessemier, 1982; Rogers, 1979).

Marketers rely on this tactic when appealing to consumers' desire to acquire the latest and newest products in the marketplace. Examples of products sold on the basis of the Epistemic Value dimension include hi-tech gadgets, computers with innovative features, and new and improved versions of products that represent a change of pace to consumers.

Overview of the Study

The study was designed to serve as the basis for segmenting the voters vis-à-vis their perceptions of what the American Dream meant to them and the specific beliefs related to it. The study sought to determine meanings attached to the American Dream; the extent to which voter choice is based on the ability of a candidate to make it easier to achieve the American Dream; the extent to which each leader is perceived to make the American Dream either easier or harder for people to achieve; and the ability of Clinton, Dole, and Powell to appeal to the following four main voter segments:[2]

1. "Rational" voters (driven by their American Dream expectations): This segment is defined by identifying issues and policies that voters associated with their American Dream and was operationalized by using the Political Issues component of the model.

2. "Emotional" voters (driven by the feelings aroused by their desire to achieve the American Dream): This segment is defined by linking voter feelings to the attainment of their American Dream and is operationalized by using the Candidate Personality component of the model.

3. "Social" voters (driven by the association of different groups of people and their ability to achieve the American Dream): This segment is defined by connecting the American Dream to different sterotypes in society and is operationalized by the Social Imagery component of the model.

4. "Situational" voters (driven by situations that might influence their decision to switch to another candidate): This segment is defined by situations and events that would either make their American Dream easier or make it more difficult to achieve and is operationalized by the Situational Contingency component of the model.

Testing the Model

Instrument

The instrument was broken down into three major parts. The first part covered the political background of the respondents. These questions centered on general perceptions of the American Dream, the role it played in the respondents' lives, and whether the respondents thought it was getting easier or harder to achieve. This section also included questions about whom the respondents would vote for if the election were held on the day they filled out the questionnaire. Finally, there were a series of questions that measured the extent to which each of the candidates would make it either easier or harder for the respondents to achieve their American Dream.

The second part of the questionnaire covered the four voter types just identified.[3] Several sources were used to generate the statements for each component. First, major news magazines and major and local newspapers were analyzed. Next, on the basis of the respondents' intentions to vote for a candidate, 10 to 20 respondents were identified for each of the three candidates and were asked in-person to identify their salient beliefs for each component in the model. The final list of statements was generated by rewording and screening out the salient beliefs identified by the literature survey and the in-person interviews. Following is a sample of the statements for each of the four components:

1. *Rational voters* (10 statements): These included a series of statements covering the American Dream measured on a binary scale (*agree/disagree*). *Example:* I believe the American Dream can
   a. cause me to lose focus on my family.
   b. offer me financial stability.
   c. cause me to burn out and acquire unhealthy stress on the job.
   d. offer me more freedom to take risks in my life and work.
2. *Social voters* (10 statements): These listed groups—college educated, White men, foreign men, motivated people, and the like—that were likely to acquire the American Dream. A binary scale (*most likely/least likely*) was used to measure whether respondents thought that a group was likely to acquire the American Dream.
3. *Emotional voters* (12 statements): These listed a series of feelings toward the respondents' attempts to achieve the American Dream—happiness, disappointment, excitement, fear, and the like—that were measured on a binary scale (*yes/no*).
4. *Situational voters* (13 statements): Measured on a binary scale (*easier/harder*), these were statements of hypothetical situations that might influence the respondents to switch their allegaince to another candidate. *Example:* If you knew that a candidate could make education more accessible, would you switch your vote to him?

   To the extent that each of the issues and policies listed was connected to the respondents' American Dream, it could have caused them to switch their allegiance to another candidate.

The third and final part of the questionnaire covered standard demographics about the voters.

Sampling and Data Collection

The questionnaire was pretested to detect either conceptual or operational flaws. The data were collected over a 3-week period. A total of 400 respondents were surveyed in-person in several malls in the greater metropolitan Chicago area. Only those respondents who indicated that they planned to vote in the 1996 presidential election were invited to fill out the questionnaire. A variety of malls located in different sections of the city were chosen in an attempt to get as broad a cross section of respondents as possible.[4] From the 400 respondents surveyed, 327 questionnaires were used in the analysis. A profile of the sample is listed in Table 15.1.

Data Analysis

The principal statistical technique used to carry out the data analysis was discriminant analysis.[5] Pairwise discriminant analyses were carried out between respondents who indicated that each candidate would make it either easier or harder to achieve their American Dream. In these analyses, the criterion variable was Question 1 in Table 15.2, and the predictor variables were the items listed in Tables 15.3 to 15.6. The procedural details and the mathematical theory underlying discriminant analysis are found in several books.[6]

The data also were analyzed by carrying out a series of pairwise *t* tests between segments of voters who indicated an intention to vote for either Clinton, Dole, or Powell (i.e., Clinton-Dole, Clinton-Powell, Dole-Powell).[7] This analysis offered an insight into voter beliefs by comparing segments of voters who intended to vote for their preferred candidate without reference to whether he would make their American Dream either easier or harder to achieve.[8] In addition, four separate factor analyses (with a varimax rotation) were carried out on the items identified in each of the four components operationalized in the model.[9] In other words, one factor analysis was carried out on the 10 statements used to measure the Political Issues component, another on the 10 statements used to measure the Social Imagery component, another on the 12 statements used to measure the Candidate Personality component, and another on the 13 statements used to measure the Situational Contingency component.

Results

The majority of the respondents (77%) indicated that the American Dream is not out-of-date. When asked to rank order a list of meanings that they attached to the American Dream, respondents rated "financial security" at the top of their list, followed by "freedom of choice" and "raising a family" (Table 15.2). When

TABLE 15.1 Sociodemographic Profile of the Sample

	Percentage
1. Home ownership	
a. Rent	66
b. Own	33
2. Sex	
a. Male	55
b. Female	45
3. Employment	
a. Full-time	74
b. Part-time	10
c. Not employed at present	16
4. Social class	
a. Lower class	1
b. Lower middle class	8
c. Middle class	49
d. Upper middle class	36
e. Upper class	6
5. Income (annual)	
a. Under $20,000	7
b. $20,000-$49,999	31
c. $50,000-$74,999	25
d. $75,000-$124,999	21
e. $125,000-$200,000	9
f. Over $200,000	7
6. Age (years)	
a. 18-24	13
b. 25-34	36
c. 35-44	22
d. 45-54	13
e. 55-64	9
f. Over 64	7
7. Education	
a. Grade school	2
b. High school/trade school	8
c. Some college	19
d. College degree	48
e. Master's/doctorate	23
8. Race/ethnicity	
a. White	85
b. African American	8
c. Hispanic	2
d. Asian	3
e. Other	2
9. Family life cycle	
a. Young, single	24
b. Single parent with children	5
c. Young couple, living together	3
d. Young couple, living together with children	3
e. Young married, no children	12
f. Young, single, living with parents	1
g. Family with small children	15
h. Older, unmarried	5
i. Family with teenage children	10
j. Family with grown-up children	12
k. Senior citizens	10

TABLE 15.2 Specific Issues Related to the American Dream

1. "The American Dream" is a concept that has been talked about for many years in this country. Do you think it is out-of-date? (If you check *yes,* please suggest a better term.)

   a. No, 77%
   b. Yes, 23% (American opportunity, personal goals, social equity, financial security, equal rights, personal freedom, next generation)

2. Which of the following meanings do you attach to *your* American Dream? (Check off the top five, numbering them 1, 2, 3, 4, and 5.)

Frequency of Responses	*Ranked No. 1 (N = 327)*
a. Financial security	99
b. Freedom of choice	62
c. Raising a family	47*D
d. Personal fulfillment	19
e. Children's welfare	17*C
f. Stronger religious commitment	16*D,**P
g. Job happiness	14
h. Job security	13
i. Home ownership	11
j. Children's education	8
k. Progressing in career	5

*Statistically significant difference in response between Clinton and Dole supporters (superscript C indicates that Clinton supporters rated it more important; superscript D indicates that Dole supporters rated it more important), **Statistically significant difference in response between Clinton and Powell supporters (superscript P indicates that Powell supporters rated it more important).

3. If the 1996 election were held today, who would you vote for? (Check off only one name.)

	Frequency (N = 327)
a. Bill Clinton	128
b. Bob Dole	64
c. Newt Gingrich	21
d. Ross Perot	10
e. Colin Powell	81

To what extent is your choice based on the ability of your preferred candidate to make it easier for you to achieve *your* American Dream?

To a very large extent	14%	17%	22%	23%	7%	5%	9%	To a very small extent

NOTE: These percentages were similar across the three leading candidates.

4. To what extent do you think each of the following political leaders would make it either easier or harder for you to achieve *your* American Dream? (percentages)

	Clinton		*Dole*		*Powell*	
	Easier	*Harder*	*Easier*	*Harder*	*Easier*	*Harder*
a. Bill Clinton	94	5	9	91	53	47
b. Bob Dole	14	83	91	9	35	65
c. Newt Gingrich	10	88	61	39	29	70
d. Colin Powell	56	43	70	30	93	5
e. Ross Perot	31	67	49	51	57	43

(continued)

TABLE 15.2 (Continued)

5. Do you think that the American Dream of equal opportunity, personal freedom, and social mobility has become easier or harder to achieve during the past 10 years? (percentages)

	Clinton	Dole	Powell
a. Easier	33	30	24
b. Harder	67	70	76

6. Do you think that the American Dream of equal opportunity, personal freedom, and social mobility will be easier or harder to achieve in the next 10 years? (percentages)

	Clinton	Dole	Powell
a. Easier	17	22	21
b. Harder	83	78	79

7. Do you believe that it is getting easier or harder for the younger generations to achieve the same level of prosperity as did their parents? (percentages)

	Clinton	Dole	Powell
a. Easier	13	11	12
b. Harder	87	89	88

8. Do you believe that the news media are credible or noncredible in their reporting on presidential candidates? (percentages)

	Clinton	Dole	Powell
a. Credible	46	40	51
b. Noncredible	54	60	49

9. Please indicate which of the following media outlets you use to stay informed about politics. (percentages)

	Clinton		Dole		Powell	
	Yes	No	Yes	No	Yes	No
a. Television	91	9	92	8	93	7
b. Radio	75	25	65	35	85	15
c. Newspapers	87	13	88	12	81	19
d. Magazines	65	35	56	44	72	28

respondents were asked to rank the meaning of "stronger religious commitment," a significant difference was found between both Powell and Dole voters and Clinton voters. In other words, both Dole and Powell voters saw the American Dream as having a religious connotation, whereas Clinton voters did not.

More than 75% of the respondents (from a moderate to greater degree) said that their choice for the presidency was based on the fact that their candidate would make it easier for them to achieve their American Dream. When asked to rate each of the three candidates on his ability to make the American Dream easier or harder to achieve, each of the respective segments of voters thought that their preferred candidate would do a better job at making their American Dream easier to achieve. However, only Powell's supporters indicated any level of confidence that the other two candidates also would make it easier, although not with the same level of support as they gave to their own candidate. In a similar vote of confidence, both Dole and Clinton supporters thought that Powell would make it easier to achieve their American Dream, again with less support than they gave their own preferred candidates. However, both Clinton and Dole supporters had no confidence in the other candidate's ability to make their American Dream any easier to achieve (Table 15.2, Question 4).

When the respondents were asked to rate each candidate with respect to a series of questions on whether they thought the American Dream would be easier or harder to achieve in the past, in the future, and for their children, the results across the three candidates' supporters were strikingly similar. Most respondents agreed that the American Dream had become more difficult to achieve in the past 10 years. Even more respondents agreed that the American Dream would become more difficult to achieve in the next 10 years. Finally, most respondents agreed that the American Dream would be even more difficult for their children to achieve. In other words, there was strong general agreement with the idea that changes needed to be made to make it possible for people to achieve their American Dream (Table 15.2, Questions 5-9).

Based on the components in the model, the voter segments were then profiled vis-à-vis the four voter types: rational, emotional, social, and situational (Tables 15.3-15.6).

Rational Voters

A review of Table 15.3 suggests that the voters who intended to vote for Clinton, Dole, or Powell had very similar perceptions with respect to the benefits and problems associated with their American Dream. The only significant differences that did exist were found when respondents were asked whether their American Dream would offer them financial security. Significant differences were found between Powell and Clinton supporters and between Powell and Dole supporters. In both cases, a greater percentage of Powell voters thought that their American Dream would offer them financial stability.

One problem that all three segments identified was the difficulty of achieving their American Dream due to the increasing cost of living, with more than one half of the respondents agreeing with this statement. However, on the positive side, fewer than one quarter of each segment indicated that they would have difficulty achieving their American Dream because of a lack of control. In other words, people realized that their American Dream was getting more difficult to achieve but believed that it still was possible to achieve. A review of the factor

TABLE 15.3 Profile of "Rational" Voters: Based on Pairwise *t* Tests and Factor Analysis

A. Pairwise *t* tests:

"Rational" voters will vote for the candidate whom they believe will make it easier for them to achieve their American Dream. The following "benefits" and "problems" are connected to the American Dream and were measured with the following questions:

Please indicate whether you agree or disagree that the following benefits and problems are associated with *your* American Dream (percentages of those who agree).

My American Dream can _____	Clinton	Dole	Powell
1. Cause me to lose focus on my family	21	31	19
2. Offer me financial stability*,**	85	83	92
3. Cause me to burn out and acquire unhealthy stress on the job	48	41	46
4. Lead to my disappointment	46	46	48
5. Offer me more freedom to take risks in my life and work	75	70	79
6. Lead to my self-fulfillment	86	80	89
7. Be difficult to realize because I have no control over achieving it	23	16	21
8. Lead to more personal time for myself	64	56	59
9. Be difficult to achieve due to the increasing cost of living	66	60	71
10. Offer me job security	60	65	57

NOTE: The percentages listed under each political leader reflect the thinking of those respondents who indicated that they would vote for him if the election were held on the day the study was conducted.
*Statistically significant difference between Dole and Powell, **Statistically significant difference between Clinton and Powell.

B. Factor analysis with varimax rotation[a] (there are two underlying dimensions):
    Dimension 1:   Questions 2, 5, 6, and 8 (optimistic/achievable)
    Dimension 2:   Questions 1, 3, 4, 7, 9, and 10 (pessimistic/defeatist)

a. The dimensions identified for each factor were determined by carrying out a varimax rotation and identifying factor loadings with an absolute value greater than or equal to .45. Due to space limitations, the rotated factor structure is not included in the table.

analysis suggests that there were two major underlying dimensions behind this cognitive domain: an optimistic/achievable domain and a pessimistic/defeatist domain.

Emotional Voters

A review of Table 15.4 indicates that again, the voters who intended to vote for Clinton, Dole, or Powell had very similar perceptions, this time with respect to the feelings they associated with their American Dream. The only significant differences that did exist were found on the feelings of loneliness and disappointment they experienced when attempting to achieve their American Dream. Clinton supporters felt more loneliness and disappointment than did both Dole and Powell voters. The factor analysis revealed three underlying dimensions—two negative (alienation/mad and fear/stress) and one positive (optimism). Although there was not a significant difference on the next two dimensions, Clinton supporters also indicated slightly stronger feelings of guilt and worry in their attempts to achieve their American Dream.

TABLE 15.4 Profile of "Emotional" Voters: Based on Pairwise *t* Tests and Factor Analysis

A. Pairwise *t* tests:

"Emotional" voters will vote for the candidate who gives them a certain level of comfort and emotional security. The following "feelings" were connected to the attempt that people make in their efforts to achieve their American Dream and was measured with the following questions:

Please indicate whether you have personally experienced any of the following feelings associated with your attempt to achieve *your* American Dream (percentages of those who said yes).

I feel _____ as I attempt to achieve my American Dream	*Clinton*	*Dole*	*Powell*
1. Happiness	81	83	76
2. Appreciation/thankfulness	77	82	74
3. Guilty	17	15	16
4. Fearful of failing	42	43	48
5. Excited	78	72	76
6. Angry	34	26	28
7. Increased confidence	74	78	74
8. Lonely**,***	31	16	20
9. Disappointed**,***	36	25	27
10. Proud/good about myself	85	87	93
11. Worried	58	52	57
12. Concerned that we are in a "crisis" in this country	66	66	71

NOTE: The percentages listed under each leader reflect the thinking of those respondents who indicated that they would vote for him if the election were held on the day the study was conducted.
**Statistically significant difference between Clinton and Powell, ***Statistically significant difference between Clinton and Dole.

B. Factor analysis with variamx rotation[a] (there are three underlying dimensions):

Dimension 1:	Questions 6, 8, and 9 (alienation/mad)
Dimension 2:	Questions 2, 5, 7, and 10 (optimistic)
Dimension 3:	Questions 3, 4, and 11 (fear/stress)

a. The dimensions identified for each factor were determined by carrying out a varimax rotation and identifying factor loadings with an absolute value greater than or equal to .45. Due to space limitations, the rotated factor structure is not included in the table.

Social Voters

The profile of social voters (Table 15.5) is, to a great degree, consistent with what one would intuitively think when looking at the voters who are aligned with each of the three candidates. For example, there was a significant difference between Powell supporters and both Clinton and Dole supporters with respect to African American people being more likely to achieve the respondents' American Dream. Powell supporters thought that African American people were more likely to achieve their American Dream.

Similarly, there was a significant difference between Dole and Powell supporters with respect to upper class voters being more likely to achieve their American Dream. Dole supporters were more likely to think that upper class people would achieve their American Dream. However, somewhat counterintuitive was the fact that Dole supporters indicated a higher likelihood than Clinton voters that high school-educated people were more likely to achieve their American Dream. The

TABLE 15.5 Profile of "Social" Voters: Based on Pairwise *t* Tests and Factor Analysis

A. Pairwise *t* tests:

"Social" voters will vote for the candidate who is associated with specific sociopolitical groups in society. The following groups were connected to the achievement of the American Dream and were measured with the following questions:

Not everybody achieves the American Dream. Which of the following groups of people do you believe are most and least likely to achieve *your* American Dream? (percentages of those who indicated most likely)

	Clinton	Dole	Powell
1. Lower class	7	11	13
2. College educated	98	98	96
3. White men	92	94	92
4. Foreign born	44	50	50
5. African American people*,**	26	24	38
6. Upper class*	91	95	87
7. Lucky people	71	75	74
8. High school-educated only**,***	13	24	25
9. Risk takers	76	83	85
10. Motivated people	96	95	98

NOTE: The percentages listed under each leader reflect the thinking of those respondents who indicated that they would vote for him if the election were held on the day the study was conducted.
*Statistically significant difference between Dole and Powell, **Statistically significant difference between Clinton and Powell, ***Statistically significant difference between Clinton and Dole.

B. Factor analysis with varimax rotation[a] (there are four underlying dimensions):

Dimension 1:	Questions 1, 4, 5, and 8 (least likely: lower classes)
Dimension 2:	Questions 2, 3, and 6 (most likely: higher classes)
Dimension 3:	Question 7 (most likely: lucky people)
Dimension 4:	Questions 9 and 10 (most likely: hard-working)

a. The dimensions identified for each factor were determined by carrying out a varimax rotation and identifying factor loadings with an absolute value greater than or equal to .45. Due to space limitations, the rotated factor structure is not included in the table.

factor analysis revealed very interesting results by isolating three dimensions of people who were more likely to achieve their American Dream (higher class people, lucky people, and hard-working people) and one dimension of people who were less likely to achieve their American Dream (lower class people).

Situational Voters

The last voter type is situational voters. Several significant differences were found here, indicating that the likelihood of a voter switching allegiances, at least at the point in time when this survey was carried out, were very fluid. From a strategic point of view, this is a very important segment of voters to understand because it provides an insight into "swing" voters. The first observation one could draw when looking at Table 15.6 is that the percentages across all three voter segments are fairly high. With the exception of one question (indicating that the

TABLE 15.6 Profile of "Situational" Voters: Based on Pairwise *t* Tests and Factor Analysis

A. Pairwise *t* tests:

"Situational" voters are driven by change and will *switch* their votes to another candidate if certain conditions exist. The following list represents a broad range of issues and policies that were important to voters' ability to achieve their American Dream:

Certain conditions motivate people to behave differently from their regular behaviors or habits. If you knew that one of the candidates for the 1996 presidential election *(other than the one you now prefer)* could accomplish any one of the following items, would you switch your vote to him? (percentages of those who said yes)

	Clinton	Dole	Powell
1. Make education more accessible	75	66	70
2. Lower housing costs**	64	55	51
3. Create more equal opportunity	73	62	65
4. Reduce the need for two incomes*	70	78	63
5. Increase financial aid for education***	35	23	28
6. Increase job security**	76	74	62
7. Reduce crime rates	83	88	85
8. Decrease unemployment	76	66	75
9. Increase economic growth	81	83	82
10. Make home ownership easier to attain	70	66	63
11. Bring about a greater social consciousness***	74	60	69
12. Increase levels of self-employment	54	57	57
13. Reduce racial tensions	82	74	78

NOTE: The percentages listed under each leader reflect the thinking of those respondents who indicated that they would vote for him if the election were held on the day the study was conducted.
*Statistically significant difference between Dole and Powell, **Statistically significant difference between Clinton and Powell, ***Statistically significant difference between Clinton and Dole.

B. Factor analysis with varimax rotation[a] (there are two underlying dimensions):

Dimension 1: Questions 1, 2, 3, 8, 10, 11, 12, and 13 (enhancing societal welfare)
Dimension 2: Questions 4, 5, 6, 7, and 9 (improving economic and crime conditions)

a. The dimensions identified for each factor were determined by carrying out a varimax rotation and identifying factor loadings with an absolute value greater than or equal to .45. Due to space limitations, the rotated factor structure is not included in the table.

respondents would switch to another candidate if he increased financial aid for education), more than one half of the respondents indicated that they would switch candidates on each of the other 12 questions.

Significant differences between Clinton and Powell were found in two areas: lower housing costs and increasing job security, for which Clinton supporters said they were willing to switch to another candidate. Significant differences between Clinton and Dole were found in two areas: bringing about a greater social consciousness and increasing financial aid for education, for which Clinton supporters again indicated a willingness to switch to another candidate. The factor analysis summed up this section very neatly by isolating two underlying dimensions for which respondents indicated a willingness to switch to another

TABLE 15.7 Discriminant Analysis Results for Clinton Supporters: Three Most Important Variables Listed for Each Segment

A. Segment 1: President Clinton will make American Dream easier
1. I would switch to another candidate who would create more equal opportunity (discriminant coefficient = .68)
2. I feel happy in my attempt to reach my dream (discriminant coefficient = .52)
3. My American Dream will lead to more personal time for myself (discriminant coefficient = .38)

B. Segment 2: President Clinton will make American Dream harder
1. I would switch to another candidate who would reduce crime rates (discriminant coefficient = −.52)
2. I would switch to another candidate who would make education more accessible (discriminant coefficient = −.39)
3. My American Dream can offer me financial stability (discriminant coefficient = −.39)

Group means
    Easier = 0.49
    Harder = −0.70
    Eigenvalue = .35
    Wilks's lambda = .73
    Chi-square = 41.02
    Degrees of freedom = 45
    Significance = .64

Classification analysis

| | Predicted | | |
Actual	Easier	Harder	Number of Participants
Easier	75	19	94
Harder	18	48	66

NOTE: Correctly classified: 76.8%.

candidate: the enhancement of societal welfare and the improvement of economic and crime conditions.

Easier Versus Harder Segments

A review of the discriminant analysis results in Tables 15.7 through 15.9 pinpoints some of the specific reasons behind why respondents thought each of the three candidates would make it either easier or harder for them to achieve their American Dream. For example, respondents who believed Clinton would make it easier for them to achieve their American Dream indicated that they would switch to another candidate who would create more equal opportunity. They also indicated that they felt happy as they attempted to achieve their American Dream and that they believed the dream would lead to more personal time for themselves (Table 15.7).

Respondents who believed Clinton would make it harder for them to achieve their American Dream again indicated that they would switch to another candi-

TABLE 15.8 Discriminant Analysis Results for Dole Supporters: Three Most Important Variables Listed for Each Segment

A. Segment 1: Bob Dole will make American Dream easier

1. I feel fearful of failing in my attempt to reach my American Dream
   (discriminant coefficient = −.52)
2. I feel increased confidence in my attempt to reach my American Dream
   (discriminant coefficient = −.41)
3. I would switch to another candidate who would reduce crime rates
   (discriminant coefficient = −.37)

B. Segment 2: Bob Dole will make American Dream harder

1. My American Dream can offer me more freedom to take risk in my life and work
   (discriminant coefficient = .51)
2. I feel proud/good about myself in my attempt to reach my dream
   (discriminant coefficient = .49)
3. Foreign-born people are least likely to achieve my American Dream
   (discriminant coefficient = .39)

Group means
  Easier = −1.07
  Harder = 0.82
  Eigenvalue = .89
  Wilks's lambda = .52
  Chi-square = 80.92
  Degrees of freedom = 46
  Significance = .001

Classification analysis

| | Predicted | | |
Actual	Easier	Harder	Number of Participants
Easier	54	12	66
Harder	8	78	86

NOTE: Correctly classified: 86.8%.

date who would reduce crime rates and make education more accessible. This segment of voters also said that they thought their American Dream would offer them financial stability. What is perhaps most interesting in this analysis is that the two strongest predictor variables for both the easier and harder segments were their willingness to switch. It suggests that Clinton supporters might have been looking for a reason to switch but never found Dole to be the candidate to whom they could turn.[10]

The discriminant analysis results in Table 15.8 suggest that respondents perceived Dole's ability to make their American Dream either easier or harder to achieve vis-à-vis their emotional connections to the dream. Respondents who believed Dole would make it easier for them to achieve their American Dream felt fearful of failing and, at the same time, felt increased confidence as they attempted to achieve the dream. They also said that they were willing to switch

TABLE 15.9 Discriminant Analysis Results for Powell Supporters: Three Most Important Variables Listed for Each Segment

A. Segment 1: Colin Powell will make American Dream easier

1. I would switch to another candidate who would increase levels of self-employment (discriminant coefficient = –.48)
2. High school-educated people are most likely to achieve my American Dream (discriminant coefficient = –.42)
3. My American Dream can be difficult to achieve due to the increasing cost of living (discriminant coefficient = –.32)

B. Segment 2: Colin Powell will make American Dream harder

1. My American Dream can be difficult to realize because I have no control over achieving it (discriminant coefficient = .58)
2. I would switch to another candidate who would increase job security (discriminant coefficient = .40)
3. Foreign-born people are most likely to achieve their American Dream (discriminant coefficient = .38)

Group means
Easier = –0.47
Harder = 1.47
Eigenvalue = .70
Wilks's lambda = .58
Chi-square = 63.80
Degrees of freedom = 46
Significance = .04

Classification analysis

	Predicted		
Actual	Easier	Harder	Number of Participants
Easier	92	17	109
Harder	8	27	35

NOTE: Correctly classified: 82.6%.

to a candidate who would reduce the crime rate. Respondents who believed that Dole would make it harder for them to achieve their American Dream believed that the dream would offer them more freedom to take risks in life and work and, at the same time, to feel proud or good about themselves as they attempted to achieve the dream.[11]

The discriminant analysis carried out for Powell (Table 15.9) revealed a broader based set of reasons behind why respondents thought he would make their American Dream both easier and harder. One could conclude from this that, as a candidate, Powell appealed to voters on more levels. Respondents who believed Powell would make it easier for them to achieve their American Dream indicated that they believed he would make the dream possible for high school-educated people and that it would be difficult to realize the dream because of the increased cost of living. They said that they would be willing to switch to another candidate if he would increase levels of self-employment. Respondents who believed Powell would make it harder for them to achieve their American Dream thought that it would be difficult to realize the dream because they have no control over achieving it and that Powell would make the dream possible for foreign-born people. These respondents indicated a willingness to switch to another candidate who would increase their job security.[12]

Positioning Strategy

The "age of opportunity" was successfully connected to the American Dream by President Clinton repositioning himself as the leader who would make the changes necessary for the dream of the younger generation to become reality. The president was able to convince voters that their struggles of today would lead to opportunity for their children tomorrow, and by so doing, he energized the electorate.

To his own supporters, the president was able to identify with their struggle toward achieving their American Dream. This was communicated by presenting himself as the "caring" candidate and pointing to the several programs he had initiated that bolstered that image. Clinton responded to his constituents by advocating programs that were geared to the welfare of voters' children and reinforcing the idea that achievement of the American Dream will lead to more personal time for people to spend with their families.

To Dole supporters, the challange to Clinton was more difficult. More than 90% of these voters did not think Clinton would make the American Dream easier for them to achieve. The results of this study suggested that the president needed to target voters in this segment with a message that centered on family and religion. This segment was more concerned than either the Clinton or Powell supporters about losing focus on their families in their attempts to achieve the American Dream.

To Powell supporters, achievement of the American Dream would have been a very effective device to move these voters over to Clinton because of the importance they placed on this issue. Messages that centered on religious commitment and financial stability were very effective areas to target to this group of people. The president benefited from the fact that these voters perceived him as being better able than Dole to make it easier for them to achieve their American Dream. These voters also felt a loss of control over their ability to achieve their American Dream. So, efforts to reinforce their ability to make their American Dream come true would have been another effective strategy to appeal to this segment of voters.

To both Powell and Dole supporters, issues that were of importance to them included reducing crime rates, reducing racial tensions, and increasing economic growth, all three areas that were emphasized by the president during his tenure in office. The study revealed that there were two central themes related to the American Dream that were of critical importance to all voters: that the dream would offer them financial stability and that the it would lead to their self-fulfillment.

One of the most important initiatives of the 1996 presidential campaign that enabled Clinton to get reelected was his ability to convince voters that the American Dream was getting easier to achieve, that he was the person who would give them a sense of control over their own destinies, and that the "age of opportunity" would make that happen for them. A leader ultimately is in the business of selling hope to his people, and as this study revealed, the American Dream was at the heart of all voters' hopes and concerns. By positioning himself as the leader who could make the American Dream a possibility for voters' children, the president was able to win reelection.

Conclusion

At the presidential level, a campaign must be anchored with an emotional message that cuts across party and sociodemographic lines. When marketing a president, there must be a broad-based appeal that is easy for voters to comprehend. Although the American Dream has different meanings to voters, it is an important construct in their evaluation of candidates. Even though the American Dream for many people is fizzling out, they still have a need to know that it will be made possible for their children. It was through this emotional connection that voters have with their children that the president was able to connect with voters of all persuasions. His vision centering on the "age of opportunity" was very much tied into and based on the perception that he would be able to make voters' American Dream a possibility if he were reelected. In fact, the president's State of the Union message in January 1996 incorporated the theme of restoring the American Dream for all Americans. Most people would argue that for an incumbent president, that message is the kickoff for his presidential campaign.

Similar to the American Dream of home ownership, or even of owning a pair of Michael Jordan athletic shoes, marketing has at its roots the ability to convince consumers or voters that a product or a presidential candidate will help to make their American Dream come true. The marketing of cosmetics, cigarettes, stereos, clothing, and most other goods is sold on the basis of imagery and emotional appeals. The situation is no different in politics, where people put their faith and hope in a single human being to make the world a better place in which to live. The restoration of the American Dream was a strategy that was born out of such logic.

When the president spoke about building a bridge to the future, he was implicitly talking about making it possible for people's American Dream to come true. From a marketing perspective, the challenge to the president was to define what the American Dream meant to different segments of voters and determine how best to incorporate those appeals in a promotional campaign. The study reported here presented the operationalization of a model of voter behavior that was used as the basis for defining four different types of voters. Each type of voter thinks about the American Dream in slightly different terms and presented to the president the opportunity to build a promotional campaign in creative ways that offered a diversity of advertising approaches. By incorporating a market-orientation into his campaign, the president was able to reach out to voters regardless of party affiliation.

The winner of a presidential election is the candidate who can successfully position himself or herself to the center of the political spectrum. The vision presented in this chapter afforded the president an alternative route for getting to that magical center of the political spectrum. It also gave him the opportunity to connect voters to the many issue initiatives he spoke about during the campaign. A dream can easily be conceptualized on an emotional plane, but it must be implemented with very rational proposals that convince voters that it is possible for them to obtain what they are reaching for. As with any marketing campaign, the fundamental core must come from research that identifies what consumers value in the product. The results reported in this chapter outlined some of the values that voters were looking for in a candidate in the 1996 presidential election and provided the basis for the successful strategy employed by Clinton and his team of advisers.

APPENDIX

A Vision for America:
The Restoration of the American Dream

The challenge facing the president is to move public opinion in the direction that he thinks is best for the country. The president has not been successful in his attempts to achieve this challenge for two reasons: (a) the lack of a cohesive message that connects to the concerns of most Americans, that is, *future economic security for them and their children and no hope of achieving their American Dream*, and (b) the use of improper channels of communication to convey his accomplishments to the American people. Citizens are looking to the president to present them with a vision for America, one that connects with their hearts and minds. *The restoration of the American Dream* is a vision that can make the president successful in this regard.

- It is a vision that applies to everyone.
- It has both an emotional and a rational appeal.
- It will serve as an "informational anchor" to which Americans can connect the legislation the president initiates.
- It can be used to break down the American electorate on the basis of *benefits* that government offers to *all* people.

The vision is best communicated by using three channels of communication, with appeals determined by a nationwide segmentation analysis of the electorate.

The results of the analysis will identify what the American Dream means to various political and sociodemographic groups in society.

1. *A prime-time news conference* should be held to announce the president's new vision to the American people. This venue should be repeated as often as possible to update the American people on the successful implementation of the vision.

2. *Regional "American Dream Summits"* should be held around the country to generate an excitement and interest in the president's new vision by interest groups and the media, the two key groups of opinion leaders who will help communicate the message to the public.

3. *Empower "well-respected" opinion leaders* (e.g., community and religious leaders, educators, local government officials) who will rely on word of mouth to build up a grassroots channel in addition to using talk radio and other more traditional media.

This strategy will work because it allows the president to talk about himself in a personal and positive way to which average Americans can relate. The president can define himself as someone who has lived the American Dream, working his way up from the bottom to the top, and who is now the *leader of the free world* (instead of letting the competition define him as a *Democrat*).

Notes

1. On March 20, 1995, I was invited to the White House to meet with senior aides to the president. At that meeting, I proposed a vision for the president that centered on the theme "The Restoration of the American Dream" as a way for him to win reelection in 1996 (the vision statement can be found in the Appendix). The research results that are reported in this chapter are based on a study I carried out in October 1995 and presented to George Stephanapolous in a meeting at the White House on February 8, 1996. The study investigated how the president should reposition himself to the American people vis-à-vis their perceptions of his ability to restore the American Dream.

2. It should be pointed out that the operationalization of the model was adapted to fit the purpose of the study, which was not only to predict and explain voter behavior toward a candidate but also to adapt some of the components in the model to explain voter perceptions of the American Dream. In other words, the model was used to explain how each of the voter types (as defined by the different components in the model) viewed various dimensions of the American Dream.

3. The Epistemic Value component was not operationalized in this study because of the difficulty of applying this cognitive domain to the study of the American Dream. The decision not to use it in the survey resulted from the responses that were generated in the focus group prior to setting up the questionnaire. It should be noted that this domain has been operationalized in several other studies of voting behavior, and it contributed to the explanation of variance in the data in a very significant way.

4. It should be noted that this sample did not precisely mirror a cross section of the American electorate and was skewed toward a white, younger, more highly educated, higher income cross section of the population. Hence, the conclusions reported in this study more closely reflect the aspirations of middle class and upper middle class voters.

5. Discriminant analysis is ideally suited to the model's operationalization because discriminant analysis begins with known groups such as voters. In applying the model, the objective is to classify these known groups on the basis of values driving choice, namely the independent variables listed for each voter type. Discriminant analysis accomplishes this by maximizing between-group variance and minimizing within-group variance to create mutually exclusive and collectively exhaustive groups. Once the groups have been distinguished, discriminant analysis allows the researcher to

determine which variables account for the greatest discrimination. Those values that discriminate significantly are associated with large coefficients, resulting in implications to strategy development. The predictive power associated with a discriminant model can be evaluated by comparing the predicted versus the actual group memberships, as identified in the questionnaire. Thus, classification analysis provides an indication of the theory's predictive validity. The results from the classification analysis can be used to develop a marketing strategy.

6. See, for example, Haire (1950), Jackson (1983), and Klecka (1980).

7. Other candidates' names also were listed (e.g., Ross Perot, Newt Gingrich) but were not checked off very often.

8. For all pairwise *t* tests carried out in this study, a *t* value was considered to be statistically significant at the .05 level.

9. Factor analysis is a data reduction technique that identifies the underlying dimensions (or ways in which respondents group questions together in their minds) of a set of questions. This technique was used to identify the underlying dimensions of the questions used to profile each of the four voter segments.

10. The classification analysis revealed a relatively low prediction rate of 76.8%, suggesting that these results were not that strong. However, it still can be used to glean some insight into the psychological makeup of those who responded to the survey.

11. The prediction rate in the classification analysis for this discriminant function was 86.8%, suggesting that a greater reliance could be put on the results reported.

12. The prediction rate in the classification analysis for this discriminant function was 82.6%.

References

Asher, H. (1980). *Presidential elections and American politics*. Homewood, IL: Dorsey.

Berelson, B., Lazarsfeld, P. F., & McPhee, W. N. (1954). *Voting: A study of opinion formation in a presidential campaign*. Chicago: University of Chicago Press.

Berlyne, D. E. (1963). Motivational problems raised by exploratory and epistemic behavior. In S. Koch (Ed.), *Psychology: A study of science* (Vol. 5, pp. 284-364). New York: McGraw-Hill.

Bowen, B. D., Broh, C. A., & Prysby, C. L. (1976). *Voting behavior: The 1976 election*. Washington, DC: American Political Science Association.

Campbell, A., Converse, P. E., Miller, W. E., & Stokes, D. E. (1960). *The American voter*. New York: John Wiley.

Campbell, A., & Cooper, H. C. (1954). *Group differences in attitudes and votes: A study of the 1954 congressional election*. Ann Arbor, MI: Survey Research Center.

Campbell, J. E. (1983). Candidate image evaluations. *American Politics Quarterly, 11*, 293-314.

Converse, P. (1964). The nature of belief systems in mass publics. In D. Apter (Ed.), *Ideology and discontent*. New York: Free Press.

Downing, J. (1965). What is a brand image? *Advertising Quarterly, 1*, 13-19.

Downs, A. (1957). *An economic theory of democracy*. New York: Harper & Row.

Faison, E. W. J. (1977). The neglected variety drive: A useful concept for consumer behavior. *Journal of Consumer Research, 9*, 172-175.

Flanigan, W. H., & Zingale, N. H. (1983). *Political behavior of the American electorate*. Boston: Allyn & Bacon.

Gant, M. M., & Davis, D. F. (1984). Mental economy and voter rationality: The informed citizen problem in voting research. *Journal of Politics, 46*, 132-153.

Haire, M. (1950). Projective techniques in marketing research. *Journal of Marketing, 14*, 649-656.

Howard, J. A., & Sheth, J. (1969). *The theory of buyer behavior*. New York: John Wiley.

Jackson, B. B. (1983). *Multivariate data analysis: An introduction*. Homewood, IL: Irwin.

Kessel, J. H. (1984). *Presidential parties*. Homewood, IL: Dorsey.

Key, V. O. (1966). *The responsible electorate*. New York: Vintage.

Klecka, W. R. (1980). *Discriminant analysis*. Beverly Hills, CA: Sage.

Lazarsfeld, P., Berelson, B., & Gaudet, H. (1944). *The people's choice: How the voter makes up his mind in a presidential campaign*. New York: Columbia University Press.

McAlister, L. (1982). A dynamic attribute satiation model of variety-seeking behavior. *Journal of Consumer Research, 9*, 141-150.

McAlister, L., & Pessemier, E. (1982). Variety-seeking behavior: An interdisciplinary review. *Journal of Consumer Research, 9,* 311-322.

Mendelsohn, H., & O'Keefe, G. J. (1976). *The people choose a president: Influences on voter decision making.* New York: Praeger.

Natchez, P. B. (1970). Images of voting. *Public Policy, 18,* 553-588.

Natchez, P. B., & Bupp, I. C. (1968). Candidates, issues, and voters. *Public Policy, 17,* 409-437.

Newman, B. I. (1981). *The explanation and prediction of voting intentions and actual voting behavior in a presidential primary race.* Unpublished doctoral dissertation, University of Illinois at Urbana-Champaign.

Newman, B. I. (1994). *The marketing of the president: Political marketing as campaign strategy.* Thousand Oaks, CA: Sage.

Newman, B. I. (1999). *The mass marketing of politics: Democracy in an age of manufactured images.* Thousand Oaks, CA: Sage.

Newman, B. I., & Sheth, J. N. (1985a). A model of primary voter behavior. *Journal of Consumer Research, 12,* 178-187.

Newman, B. I., & Sheth, J. N. (1985b). *Political marketing: Readings and annotated bibliography.* Chicago: American Marketing Association.

Newman, B. I., & Sheth, J. N. (1987). *A theory of political choice behavior.* New York: Praeger.

Nie, N., & Anderson, K. (1974). Mass belief systems revisited: Political change and attitude structure. *Journal of Politics, 36,* 540-587.

Nie, N. H., Verba, S., & Petrocik, J. R. (1976). *The changing American voter.* Cambridge, MA: Harvard University Press.

Nimmo, D., & Savage, R. L. (1976). *Candidates and their images: Concepts, methods, and findings.* Pacific Palisades, CA: Goodyear.

Popkin, S., Gorman, J. W., Phillips, C., & Smith, J. (1976). Comment: What have you done for me lately? Toward an investment theory of voting. *American Political Science Review, 70,* 779-805.

RePass, D. (1971). Issue salience and party choice. *American Political Science Review, 65,* 389-400.

Rogers, R. D. (1979). The neglected variety drive [commentary]. *Journal of Consumer Research, 6,* 88-91.

Triandis, H. C. (1971). *Interpersonal behavior.* Pacific Grove, CA: Brooks/Cole.

Vincent, M., & Zikmund, W. G. (1975). An experimental investigation of situational effects on risk perception. In B. B. Anderson (Ed.), *Advances in consumer research* (pp. 125-129). Provo, UT: Association for Consumer Research.

16

Methodology of Constructing Effective Political Advertising

An Empirical Study of the Polish Presidential Election in 1995

ANDRZEJ FALKOWSKI
WOJCIECH CWALINA

For many years in studies of electoral behavior, the approach that stresses the role of demographic variables as the main determinants of that behavior has dominated (Heath, Jowell, & Curtice, 1985; Lazarsfeld, Berelson, & Gaudet, 1944; Lipset, 1980). However, even among such oriented researchers, there always have been numerous differences about which features among the wide repertoire of demographic characteristics are the most important ones in predicting electoral behavior of the citizens. Attention was drawn to special significance of class identification (Centers, 1949), sex (McAllister & Studlar, 1992), age (Jankowski & Strate, 1995; Powell & Thorson, 1990), socioeconomic status (Canady & Thyer, 1990), race/ethnicity (Landa, Copeland, & Grofman, 1995; Tam, 1995), social context and influence of the neighborhood (Canache, Mondak, & Conroy, 1994), and occupational involvement (Sobel, 1993).

Another important trend in analyses that has gained support from many researchers is recognition of party affiliation or identification as well as recognition of partisanship (Butler & Stokes, 1974; Campbell, Converse, Miller, & Stokes, 1960; Converse, 1964) as the main determinants of electoral behavior.

However, these two, often complementary approaches, are subjected to strong criticism that stresses the ever decreasing power of electoral behavior predic-

AUTHORS' NOTE: We thank Bohdan Roznowski for performing some of the statistical analyses.

tions formulated on the basis of demographic variables and points to considerable differences in their influence in various countries (Antoszewski, 1995; Banaszkiewicz, 1995; Page, 1977; Riley, 1988).

The search for factors influencing voters' electoral decisions also is directed to groups of variables other than demographic ones. Studies are conducted on determinants of electoral behavior such as political culture (Morgan & Anderson, 1991; Morgan & Watson, 1991), a sense of political alienation (Korzeniowski, 1994; Seeman, 1975), system of values guiding voters (Braithwaite, 1997; Heaven, Stones, Nel, Huysamen, & Louw, 1994; Rokeach, 1973), both politicians' and voters' attitudes toward various political and social issues (Kessel, 1972; Nie, Verba, & Petrocik, 1976), image of the candidate or of the political party (Hacker, 1995; Osgood, Suci, & Tannenbaum, 1957; Sullivan, Aldrich, Borgida, & Rahn, 1990).

Constructing more complex and universal models of voting behavior is a significant trend in these studies. Attempts at systematizing and taking into account a greater number of connected determinants were undertaken by researchers such as Johnston, Pattie, and Allsopp (1988); Newman and Sheth (1985); and Singh, Leong, Tan, and Wang (1995). Among these studies, especially Newman and Sheth's (1985), this model is fairly popular with researchers. It already has been verified in the countries of Western Europe and now also is being tested in Poland (Cwalina, Falkowski, & Roznowski, 1997b).

Along with the evolution of research approaches concerning analysis of voting behavior, the conviction that this behavior has rational foundations became gradually weaker. However, although the rationality of human actions has been questioned, especially as a result of psychological research (Kahneman, Slovic, & Tversky, 1982; Tversky & Kahnemann, 1974; Zajonc & Markus, 1982), it still has many adherents, especially among politologists and economists (Becker, 1976; Lupia & McCubbins, 1997; Popkin, 1991). On the other hand, it has been shown that emotions are a significant factor influencing all—and not just political—human behavior (Goleman, 1995; Isen, 1993; Zajonc, 1980). In many studies, it was found that the emotional attitude toward candidates or political parties is a very good predictor of voters' decisions (Abelson, Kinder, Peters, & Fiske, 1982; Granberg & Brown, 1989). Aronson, Wilson, and Akert (1994) even metaphorically suggest that people vote with their hearts rather than with their minds. Wattenberg (1987) found that about one third of all voters know practically nothing about particular politicians and still have strong feelings about them. Lott, Lott, and Saris (1993) found that in the 1988 presidential election in the United States, the preference for the candidates was significantly correlated with the feelings toward them, with the levels being $r = .68$ for George Bush and $r = .60$ for Michael Dukakis. Bush won the election. Singh at al. (1995) analyzed voters' attitudes immediately before the 1988 general election in Singapore, and on the basis of multiple regression equations, they obtained predictions of voting intention on the basis of feelings toward the party and its candidates on the level of $R^2 = .36$ $(p < .0001)$.

Appreciation of the motivating role of emotions also is connected with the changes that occur in planning the electoral strategies for particular candidates or political parties. Special importance is ascribed here to television political advertising. Availability and popularity of this medium have made experts in political marketing treat television as the basic communication channel through which voters are supplied with information about the candidates and through which also their political preferences are influenced.

The Effect of Television Political Broadcasts on Voters

The pioneering studies on the effect of television on voters' behavior carried out during the 1940s and early 1950s proved that its influence is minor or even nonexistent (Berelson, Lazarsfeld, & McPhee, 1954; Lazarsfeld et al., 1944). However, a rapid expansion of television, and the resulting greater availability of television, led to total rejection of the earlier views.

In this way, at the end of the 1950s, the myth was created about an extra-ordinary power of this medium (Diamond & Bates, 1992; Faber, 1992; Negrine, 1994). Because of this, Trenaman and McQuail (1961) began to research the actual strength of television as a means of forming voters' attitudes through advertising spots of various political parties and, in fact, did not discover anything that would indicate changes in voters' attitudes and behavior under the influence of advertising. This hypothesis about minor or specific influence of political advertisements on voters' decisions also has been confirmed by current research conducted in many different countries (Caspi, 1984; Cohen & Wolfsfeld, 1995; O'Keefe & Sheinkopf, 1974). It has resulted in creation of a doctrine concerning the effects of information according to which, as Harrison (1965) presents, television can, at best, only strengthen viewers' beliefs but, in fact, cannot change currently held opinions.

Blumler and McQuail (1968), who carried out more detailed research on this phenomenon during the 1964 British parliamentary elections, reiterated the opinion that so-called deep-seated attitudes remain impervious and cannot be changed by the influence of television. However, those authors predict that it is possible to shape the image of a given reality among those persons whose undecided relationship to a given situation has been ascertained, that is, those who hold an unclear position. Blumler and McQuail maintain that undecided voters depend more on the television campaigns of political parties than on other sources of information about them. This was demonstrated by the significant increase in popularity of the Liberal Party among voters unsure of their decisions. Thus, it could be said that the general intuition of those authors concerning the effects of television advertising suggests an ease in controlling the behavior of undecided voters and a difficulty in this type of controlling among voters already convinced of their choices.

These intuitions also have been confirmed by later research on the influence of television advertising on voting decisions (Atkin, Bowen, Nayman, & Sheinkopf, 1973; Chaffee & Choe, 1980; Faber & Storey, 1985; Wolfsfeld, 1992).

An important element of this research is the fact that it allows undecided voters to be identified as being that segment of the population whose beliefs can be shaped under the influence of television broadcast. If the number of these undecided voters is large, then the possible victory of a given party in, for example, parliamentary elections will, to a large extent, depend on the effective strategy of its advertising campaign.

Television Political Advertising: Emotional Appeals and the Candidate's Image

Since the moment the first political broadcast was shown in 1952 by Dwight Eisenhower running for the office of U.S. president, this way of electoral communication has become the dominating element of all political promotion strategies (Diamond & Bates, 1992). Until the 1960s, hard-sell advertising played the main role; it was based on repeating the persuasion broadcast several times to "cram" it into potential voters' minds. However, after that period, an important change occurred in the way of appealing to the viewers. The transition to soft-sell advertising, or advertising whose main aim is to affect viewers through an emotional broadcast, is closely connected with media specialist Tony Schwartz (Perloff & Kinsey, 1992). Arguing that people already had strong attitudes about political issues, Schwartz (1973) contended that the job of advertising is to surface the feelings voters already have and give them a direction by associating them with values and meaningful images. The influence of such an approach still is present in political advertising, with consultants now, as Kern (1989) observes, especially keen on creating negative broadcasts attacking their political opponents.

Influencing voters' emotional relation to a candidate or political party is connected with creating images of particular participants in the electoral competition (Feofanov, 1995; Kaid & Holtz-Bacha, 1995; Sullivan et al., 1990). Image is a picture of a special type created for a particular aim that, by evoking certain associations, gives the object additional values (e.g., social-psychological, ethical, relating to personality) and, in this way, contributes to an emotional perception of him or her. Values with which the image enriches the object might not be justified at all by his or her real characteristics; it is sufficient that they have a definite meaning for the recipient. The task of the image is to secure a more emotional reception of the advertised object without disfiguring its essence (Feofanov, 1995; Garramone, 1983; Ogden & Peterson, 1964). Studies conducted so far in many countries confirm the hypothesis that political advertising effects a change in voters' picture of the candidate and leads to a reconfiguration of the arrangement of features of which that picture is composed (Cwalina, Falkowski, & Roznowski, 1997a; Holtz-Bacha & Kaid, 1995; Kaid & Chanslor, 1995; Kaid, McKinnon, & Gagnere, 1996; Mazzoleni & Roper, 1995).

Model of Effect of
Political Advertising on Political Decisions

A decided majority of analyses conducted so far have been focused exclusively on the changes in the candidate's image resulting from the advertisements (Kaid & Chanslor, 1995; Kaid & Holtz-Bacha, 1995). However, they do not try to reveal the relations among the created image, one's emotional attitude toward the candidate, and the voting intention. These aspects of political advertising's effect, however, provide little understanding for voters' overall behavior if they are analyzed separately. One can only say that viewing the spots leads to a decrease or an enhancement of the candidate's evaluation without a possibility of analyzing the consequences of this evaluation for the electoral decision. Thus, to find out whether the spots in fact change voters' image of the candidate in such a way that voters are more or less sure whether to vote for a particular candidate or even are going to switch candidates (i.e., change their decisions), it is necessary to find a link among the following four components:

1. Cognitive-affective elements (candidate image)
2. General feelings toward the candidate
3. Intention for whom to vote
4. Decision for whom to vote

These components are in a causal relationship to one another, which can be presented in the model of the influence of spots on voters' behavior (Figure 16.1). The significant aspect of the model is that each of the components is linked to another one and, therefore, should not be analyzed separately; rather, it should be analyzed in the context of the rest of the components.

Using this model, an empirical study was conducted in 1995 during the Polish presidential elections. The results of this study were supposed to provide the answers to two questions:

1. How do the candidates' images change in relation to one's emotional attitude toward those candidates under the influence of advertisements?
2. How can efficient political advertising be constructed?

The answer to the first question is directly connected with a verification of the proposed model of the effect of political advertisements on voters. Directions about construction of efficient advertising require acceptance of a definite theoretical perspective, and they are discussed in a later section of the chapter.

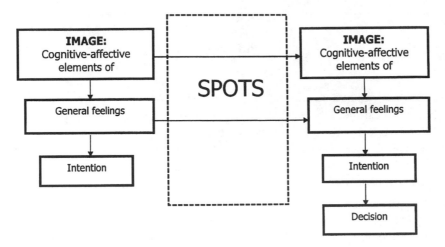

Figure 16.1. Sequential Model of the Influence of Spots on Voters' Behavior

Methodology of Research

The empirical studies were carried out between November 10 and November 18, 1995, during the period between the first and second ballots of the Polish presidential election. Of the 13 candidates running for the presidential office, 2 passed to the second ballot: incumbent Lech Walesa and the leader of the postcommunist Democratic Left Alliance, Aleksander Kwasniewski (for more details, see Cwalina, Falkowski, & Roznowski, in press).

Sample

The participants were students of political science and sociology from three Polish universities—the Lodz University, the Maria Curie-Sklodowska University of Lublin, and the Catholic University of Lublin—and students of postgraduate studies of the School of Social Communication affiliated with the Catholic University of Lublin. A total of 203 participants ages 18 to 52 years (average age = 20.95) were tested. The sample was composed of 124 women (61.4% of the total test group) and 78 men (38.6%).

Support for each candidate was distributed as follows. Of those tested, 53.9% expressed their desire to vote for Kwasniewski (he obtained 51.7% of the votes in the election), whereas 46.1% were prepared to vote for Walesa (he obtained 48.3% of the votes in the election). These results confirm the representative quality of the research sample and also indicate the division of the voters into two electorates: supporters of Kwasniewski and supporters of Walesa.

The participants were divided into 10 experiment groups. Each group consisted of 20 persons on average. A single experiment lasted for 45 minutes on average.

Procedure and Method

The participants were not informed about the true aim of the experiment, that is, the effect of political advertising. They were told that the experiment had the role of a preelection opinion poll among young people. Next, they were asked to complete the study questionnaire and to watch the advertisements prepared for them.

The experiments consisted of two stages. In the first stage, each experimental group anonymously completed a pretest questionnaire. Next, the groups watched 4 political advertisements, which were chosen at random from a group of 22 advertisements used by each of the two candidates for their television election campaigns. Participants were shown two advertisements of Walesa and Kwasniewski alternately. After the viewing of the advertisements, the experimenter handed out a postquestionnaire.

In the introduction to the pretest questionnaire that was completed before watching the ads, demographic data of each participant were included—age, sex, and place of residence—along with political preference, degree of interest in politics, and responses to open-ended questions about the characteristics of an ideal president.

The first of the two main research methods was the "feelings thermometer" scale. This scale denotes the voters' emotional attitudes toward a given candidate. This measurement was done for each of the candidates by marking points on the section describing the feelings temperature in relation to the candidate being advertised on a scale of 0 to 100 degrees.

The other main research method consisted of the 14 seven-degree semantic differential scales describing the candidates according to dimensions defined by pairs of adjectives of opposite meanings. The semantic differential is an accepted and commonly used method of analyzing political candidates' images (Kaid, 1995; Osgood et al., 1957).

The posttest consisted of the same feelings thermometer and semantic differential scales, open-ended questions concerning the content of the political advertisements and their evaluation, and a declaration as to which candidate the participant would vote for in the second round of elections.

Results

To empirically define the relations among the components of the model regarding the effect of advertising on voters' behavior, the statistical methods of discriminant analysis and multiple regression analysis were used.

On the basis of their voting intention, the participants were divided into two electorates: one for Walesa and one for Kwasniewski. Such a division, consistent with the model, takes into consideration the fact that members of each of the electorates see the candidates differently, that is, have different images of them. This is similar to *switch gestalt* demonstrations, where if two people look at the

TABLE 16.1 Numbers and Percentages of Participants Classified Into Particular
Electorates on the Basis of Their General Emotional Attitudes Toward
the Candidates: Results of Discriminant Analysis

| Observed Intention From General Feelings Thermometer to Vote on | Predicted Intention From General Feelings Thermometer to Vote on | | | | | |
| | Kwasniewski | | Walesa | | Overall | |
	n	Percentage	n	Percentage	N	Percentage
Kwasniewski	91	94.8	5	5.2	96	100
Walesa	5	6.1	77	93.9	82	100
No declaration	6	24.0	19	76.0	25	100

same picture, they can see two different things (e.g., an old woman or a young woman, a duck or a rabbit, to cite two well-known examples of switch gestalt in psychology).

Emotions Toward the Candidate and Voting Intention

The position was taken that effective advertising either consolidates (i.e., reinforces) or weakens the support for a candidate in a particular electorate. In other words, effective spots cause inflow or outflow of voters in the electorate. It also was assumed that the feelings thermometer is a good predictor of which candidates voters intend to vote for. Thus, the hypothesis is that voters choose the warmer candidates.

The discriminant analysis was used to check whether the general feelings toward the candidate is a good predictor of voting intention. Table 16.1 includes the numbers and percentages of participants correctly classified into Walesa's and Kwasniewski's electorates on the basis of the feelings thermometer toward both candidates. The prediction for both electorates was fairly accurate, as 94.4% of all the participants were classified correctly (94.8% for Kwasniewski's electorate and 93.9% for Walesa's electorate).

Because voting intention is based on the feelings thermometer scale, the relationship between the candidate's image and the thermometer can be defined for the voters of a given electorate.

Influence of Spots on the Candidate's Image

This relationship can be defined with the use of multiple regression analysis in which the feelings thermometer as a dependent variable is accounted for by semantic differential adjectives. The results of regression analysis are shown in Table 16.2.

An analysis of the data from Table 16.2 allows us to ascertain that in Walesa's electorate, the semantic differential accounts for the thermometer variance in a

TABLE 16.2 Adjectives Accounting for the Feelings Thermometer Variance Based on Multiple Correlation Analysis With a Division Into Electorates

			Variance Accounted for	
Candidate	Experimental Conditions	R^2	Characteristics (adjectives)	(percentage)
Walesa's electorate				
Kwasniewski	Pretest	.46	Honest**	13.19
			Friendly*	9.06
			Aggressive*	7.02
			Attractive*	5.86
			Believable	4.53
	Posttest	.44	Aggressive**	26.33
			Believable**	25.45
			Qualified*	5.94
Walesa	Pretest	.39	Friendly**	15.19
			Honest*	11.19
			Believable*	7.05
			Strong*	4.98
			Unsophisticated	4.72
	Posttest	.43	Honest**	23.28
			Aggressive*	8.92
			Believing Christian*	6.98
			Unsophisticated*	5.25
			Friendly	4.45
Kwasniewski's electorate				
Kwasniewski	Pretest	.51	Honest**	27.87
			Attractive*	10.06
			Friendly*	5.14
			Unsophisticated*	4.39
			Calm	3.85
	Posttest	.55	Respectable**	10.87
			Friendly*	9.72
			Believable*	6.70
Walesa	Pretest	.15	Strong*	6.92
			Open for world	3.61
			Unsophisticated	2.94
	Posttest	.17	Open for world*	7.29
			Honest*	4.23

*Level of significance = .05, **Level of significance = .001.

similar percentage for both candidates. The average sizes of R^2 from the pretest to the posttest for Kwasniewski and Walesa were .45 and .41, respectively. The different situation was evident in Kwasniewski's electorate. Here, the semantic differential accounts for the thermometer variance in a different percentage for both candidates. The average sizes of R^2 from the pretest to the posttest for Kwasniewski and Walesa were .53 and .16, respectively.

Therefore, we state that in Walesa's electorate, the thermometer for both candidates is basically identically sensitive in relation to the image of the given candidate, defined by significant adjectives of the semantic differential. The size of multiple correlation indicates a possibility of "regulating" this thermometer by manipulating the image that is broadcast for the voters of both candidates, which is achieved by concentrating on adjectives carefully selected in the process of regression analysis. In other words, voters from Walesa's electorate are susceptible to the influence of information in relation to both candidates. Their beliefs, therefore, are not polarized.

A totally different situation presents itself in Kwasniewski's electorate. In this case, the thermometer is sensitive only to voters' own candidate and is not sensitive to the opposing candidate, in whose case the small multiple correlation indicates a lack of possibility of regulating the thermometer by controlling his image. The voters from this electorate, however, react to their candidate within the range of adjectives that are selected in the process of regression analysis but are equally "cold" in relation to the other candidate, irrespective of the image he presents. Thus, this electorate has strongly polarized beliefs.

But we are interested in the influence of watching the spots used in the experiment on voters' overall cognitive behavior, not on only part of it (i.e., on the image of the candidate). In other words, it is not sufficient just to look at the difference in adjectives before and after watching the spots. The differences in R^2 must be analyzed (i.e., the difference in variances of adjectives accounting for the thermometer variance) before and after viewing the spots.

Thus, we could see, in fact, a minor effect of spots on cognitive behavior of both Walesa's and Kwasniewski's voters. One can say that spots did not influence the relationship between the image and the feelings (it is on the same level of intensity, i.e., about the same R^2 values for the pretest and posttest). However, they change some elements in the candidate's image. After viewing the spots, a reconfiguration of items in the voters' minds occurred that is shown by a different set of adjectives accounting for variances of the thermometer after viewing the ads from the one before watching them (Table 16.2).

It seems clear that after watching the spots, the pictures or images of the candidates have been changed within the overall cognitive behavior, which links all the components of the model—image, feelings, intention, and decision. In other words, after watching the spots, voters are sensitive to different adjectives. We can "warm up" or "cool down" the feelings toward the candidates by manipulating the selected and previously mentioned characteristics of the candidates' images in a promotional advertising strategy.

These characteristics of the image are operationalized by adjectives of the semantic differential. As has already been shown, these feelings are in a significant and direct relationship to voters' intention. This is what we understand by the influence of political spots. All the components of the model—image, feelings, intention, and decision—are linked.

The Influence of Spots on Feelings Toward the Candidate

The regression methodology that has been presented so far is used to evaluate the influence of spots on candidates' images, and it shows the change of the voters' images in a way that links these images with the feelings. However, this methodology does not say whether these feelings, in fact, have been changed under the influence of political advertisements.

An analysis of feelings change can be carried out within the framework of decision processes in perception. Precise premises for decision processes in perception were implicit in the base of the so-called "New Look" described in detail by Bruner (1973) as a theory of perception oriented toward personality and one in which the concept of spheres of uncertainty played a key role (see also Falkowski, 1995; Green & Swets, 1966; McNicol, 1972). That is, a lot of research in the field of perception and personality was carried out with the use of ambiguous stimuli such as weakly lit words or images, pictures with a wide variety of meanings, and short expositions of signals. In these quite poor conditions, the reactions of the receivers being tested for recognition of stimuli are defined by factors connected to motivation to a larger extent than by the action of the stimuli themselves. The authors developing this research trend generated various expectations among the participants in a given experimental situation, and the changes in reaction that they observed were connected to changes in motivation. Therefore, they concentrated on the so-called behavioral context in the process of perception. The important factor in this case is the assumption that the greater the degree of uncertainty, the greater the chance of activating behavioral factors in perception and the greater the possibility of controlling participants.

In the presented analysis, the discriminability or sensitivity of the d' index, which shows the voters' level of differentiation between candidates, is important. To calculate d', data on the feelings thermometer must be presented as a regular statistical distribution. It is possible to reconstruct two distributions of the feelings thermometer corresponding to X and his rival, Y, for experimental results of a presidential election. The size of d' is equal to the difference between the mean statistical distributions of X and Y expressed in units of standard deviation, corresponding to the difficulty in differentiating between X and Y. Large values of d' indicate an easy way of differentiating (i.e., a great difference between the mean statistical distributions, M_X and M_Y), whereas small values of d' indicate great difficulty (i.e., a small difference between the means of these distributions). Thus, we can infer that difficulty in decision making is proportional to the degree to which these distributions overlap.

An analysis of the voting situation in a given electorate should, therefore, be carried out from the point of view of the overlapping distributions. Thus, the larger the overlap between them (a large sphere of uncertainty), the more the voters of this electorate, despite their preference for a particular candidate, represent a similar emotional attitude toward X and Y and, therefore, might be more susceptible to the influence of information. A minor polarization of beliefs appearing among them qualifies them as being the sector of undecided voters. On the other hand, in the case where the distributions overlap to a small extent (a minor degree of uncertainty), we are dealing with a great degree of polarization of beliefs, that is, with very decided voters. Therefore, the degree of the sphere of uncertainty is a parametrical coefficient differentiation of X and Y, that is, the size of d'.

TABLE 16.3 Discriminability of d' Indexes in the Pretest and Posttest and Their Changes

	Pretest	Posttest	Change
Kwasniewski's electorate	2.00	1.75	↓
Walesa's electorate	1.30	1.15	↓

The mathematical formula to calculate d' is presented by the following equation:

$$d' = \frac{M_X - M_Y}{\sigma_{X-Y}},$$

where σ_{X-Y} is the standard deviation of the difference between distributions X and Y of the temperature of the feelings toward the candidates, and M_X and M_Y are the arithmetical means of distributions X and Y.

Hence, if d' is not changed after viewing the spots (i.e., it is the same before and after watching them), then it means that the spots have not influenced the voters' feelings or their voting intention. However, in a special case, with the same d', the arguments that the voters use to account for their decision to vote for a particular candidate might change. Such an operation may be defined as occurrence of some features of the image (adjectives of the differential) accounting for the thermometer variance before viewing the spots and of other ones after seeing the spots. This is similar to switch gestalt, which we observe for all candidates.

The discriminability of d' indexes in the pretest and posttest is presented in Table 16.3. As can be seen from the table, spots made voters in both electorates more uncertain (we notice a decrease in d' for both cases).

On the basis of these results, it can be said that the spots promoting the candidates running for the office of the president of Poland influenced voters. Voters' perceptions of the candidates' images and their emotional attitudes toward them changed.

Construction of Effective Political Advertising

The obtained results show that there are statistically significant relations among the candidate's image, the emotional attitude toward him, and the intention to support him in the elections. It also is known that political advertisements may lead to a reconfiguration of features of which the candidate's image consists and also may influence the voters' general feelings toward him. (In the present study, advertisements contributed to an increase in voters' uncertainty.) From the considerations presented in the introduction, it follows that the effect of ads is significant when they are directed to voters who are not yet sure for whom they will vote. Can this information be used for constructing an effective political advertisement? How should a candidate be presented in it?

Answers to these questions can be provided within the methodology taken from the decision theory of perception that already has been presented.

Decision Processes in Perception
Applied to an Analysis of Political Preferences

In analyzing political preferences in the light of the decision theory of perception, one must start from the data of the feelings thermometer because, as noted earlier, an analysis of these data allows the degree of polarization in voters' beliefs to be defined. We can state that the effectiveness of the influence of information (e.g., a political advertisement on changing voters' opinion) is conversely proportional to index d'.

Now, the basic problem arises: How is it possible to prove or account for the probable effectiveness of the influence of information within the undecided voting segment and the lack of its effectiveness within the decided segment? The solution to this problem would lead to specific directions about construction of an effective political advertisement.

Consequently, it is important to recollect the semantic differentials characterizing both political sides from the point of view of the electorate, as was presented earlier in the methods of studying political preferences. In the research conducted until now that has employed the methods of the feelings thermometer and semantic differential, the results obtained in each of these methods were dealt with separately (Kaid & Holtz-Bacha, 1995). However, as was shown earlier, the relation between these two different methods may be defined with the use of multiple regression analysis.

Taking into account the analysis of the distributions of the data on the feelings thermometer, it may be supposed that the best prediction of these data (large multiple correlation) occurs when the figures greatly overlap. This indicates that fluctuations on the feelings thermometer are very sensitive to significant adjectives on the semantic differential. On the other hand, failure to obtain such a prediction of feelings with the help of adjectives on the semantic differential (small multiple correlation) occurs when the amount of overlapping of the distributions is very small. More precisely, the lack of such a prediction (i.e., of a relationship of the feelings thermometer to the differential adjectives) should appear for the rival side or candidate in a given electorate. Thus, it may be anticipated that an increase in the overlapping of data in the thermometer distributions occurs concurrently with an increase and evening out of the size of the multiple correlation and, hence, the effectiveness of predicting these data through adjectives on the semantic differential. It should be stressed here that the proposed analysis is a detail operationalization of Blumler and McQuail's (1968) intuition that political advertising is only able to influence undecided voters' beliefs.

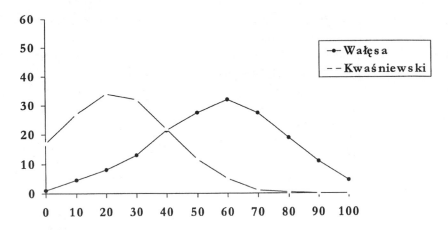

Figure 16.2a. Feelings Temperature Distribution for Walesa and Kwasniewski in Walesa's Electorate Before the Advertising Spot

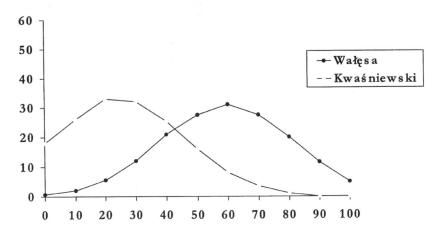

Figure 16.2b. Feelings Temperature Distribution for Walesa and Kwasniewski in Walesa's Electorate After the Advertising Spot

It is now easy to see that the confirmation of this hypothesis would lead to practical suggestions for a method of constructing political advertisements. Hence, in the context of the presented operationalization, the segment of undecided voters should be identified first on the basis of the data of the feelings thermometer and then by selection of significant adjectives on the semantic differential on the basis of multiple regression. Advertisements would be created on the basis of these adjectives.

An Analysis of Distributions

Distributions of the feelings thermometer data were carried out separately for the pretest and posttest with a division into electorates, and they were approximated to normal distributions. Figures 16.2a, 16.2b, 16.3a, and 16.3b present

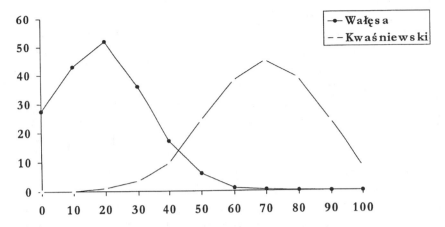

Figure 16.3a. Feelings Temperature Distribution for Walesa and Kwasniewski in Kwasniewski's Electorate Before the Advertising Spot

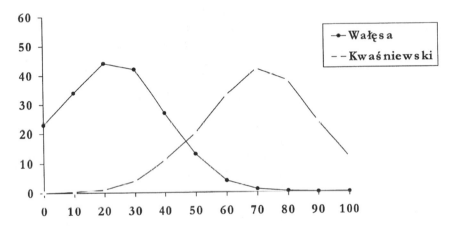

Figure 16.3b. Feelings Temperature Distribution for Walesa and Kwasniewski in Kwasniewski's Electorate After the Advertising Spot

the temperature distribution for each of the candidates among a defined group of voters before and after viewing the advertising spot.

An analysis of these figures allows us to state that Walesa's voters were less decided in their choice than were Kwasniewski's voters. The feelings temperature distributions in the case of the former electorate clearly overlap more considerably than in the latter one. Thus, we can assume that Walesa's electorate was comprised of the segment of undecided voters having a similar emotional attitude toward both candidates, whereas among Kwasniewski's electorate the difference in feelings temperature toward each candidate was much greater.

To precisely express the differences in the degree of certainty in the two electorates, the emotional distributions were presented on a voter operating characteristic (VOC) curve, thus allowing for a precise definition of the degree of sensitivity in differentiating between the two candidates. The curve is analogous to the receiver operating characteristic (ROC) curve used within the framework of decision processes in perception. (The formulas transforming the distributions into the VOC curve are presented in the Appendix.)

In Figure 16.4, the difference in the degree of sensitivity of emotional differentiation between the two candidates can be clearly observed in the case of both the first and second electorates. In Walesa's electorate, the sizes of d' before and after viewing the advertising spots were 1.30 and 1.15, whereas in the case of Kwasniewski's electorate, the sizes were 2.00 and 1.75, respectively. It is interesting to note that in both electorates, the sensitivity indicator diminishes in size.

The data of the thermometer that have been presented give grounds for testing the following hypothesis: The most satisfactory accounting for these data while using the adjectives of the semantic differential occurs when particular distributions greatly overlap. In the present situation, it should be predicted that Walesa's electorate is the one in which this accounting is better compared to Kwasniewski's electorate.

If we take into account that Walesa's electorate is the undecided segment (small d') in comparison to the decided electorate of Kwasniewski (large d'), then the hypothesis of a greater sensitivity to information among the undecided can be confirmed. In a logical fashion, this statement may be presented in the following way:

$$d_{I}' > d_{II}' \geq |R^2_{IX} - R^2_{IY}| > |R^2_{IIX} - R^2_{IIY}|,$$

where d_{I}' and d_{II}' are indicators of emotional sensitivity in differentiating between two political states in the first (I) and second (II) electorates, respectively; R^2_{IX} and R^2_{IY} are the variance sizes accounting for the thermometer on the basis of the semantic differential in the first electorate (I) for political sides X and Y, respectively; and R^2_{IIX} and R^2_{IIY} are the variance sizes accounting for the thermometer on the basis of the second electorate (II) for political sides X and Y, respectively.

It will now suffice to put proper values from Tables 16.2 and 16.3 into the preceding formula to be able to check the described relationship. If X denotes Kwasniewski, Y denotes Walesa, I denotes Kwasniewski's electorate, and II denotes Walesa's electorate, then we obtain the following logical formulas:

Pretest: $2.00 > 1.30 \Rightarrow |0.51 - 0.15| > |0.46 - 0.39| \Rightarrow 0.36 > 0.07$

Posttest: $1.75 > 1.15 \Rightarrow |0.55 - 0.17| > |0.44 - 0.43| \Rightarrow 0.38 > 0.01$

The results of the preceding analyses confirm the hypothesis that was put forward.

In Walesa's electorate, it would be possible to effectively control the behavior of voters by presenting either of the candidates in television political advertisement spots in a warm or icy fashion and, therefore, change voters' beliefs and electoral decisions. Kwasniewski's electorate, on the other hand, would basically be insensitive to efforts made to evoke such changes. This is in accordance with

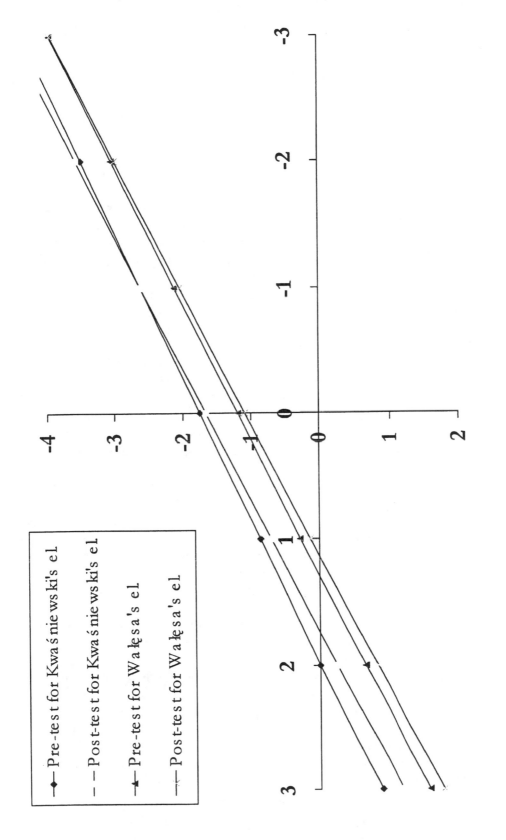

Figure 16.4. Voter Operating Characteristic Curves for Feelings Temperature in Relation to the Candidates in the Case of Electoral Division

the theory of Blumler and McQuail (1968) that established figures cannot be changed by political advertisements.

Final Remarks

The concept of empirical methodology in the field of political advertising research that has been presented in this chapter adapts the cognitive theory of human functioning in a very precise way to contemporary research in the practice of mass media influencing voters' behavior. In this study, the basically general intuition of Blumler and McQuail (1968) in relation to the influence of political advertising made it possible to compose a very exact method of measuring the degree of indecisiveness among voters and to make a precise analysis of the possibilities of shaping the image of a given political reality. We may now consider the practical application of this concept. That is, preselected adjectives in an analysis of multiple regression constitute the dimensions in which a given political option is pictured in the minds of voters; therefore, they identify the structure of voters' beliefs. Thus, construction of an effective advertisement should include the image of a given political side defined by these adjectives. Undoubtedly, effectiveness of these advertisements is dependent on the degree of indecisiveness among voters, which in this study has been operationalized by sensitivity index (d') of the emotional differentiation between two political sides. An important consequence of this is the necessity of segmenting voters and identifying their undecided segments within which the effectiveness of political advertising should be the greatest.

According to this concept, the effects of such an advertisement should cause a polarization of voters' beliefs. This may be seen in the increase in differences in "temperature" on the feelings thermometer, that is, in the increase of the sensitivity index d' (growing distance between distributions of feelings thermometer in the segment of undecided voters). An effective advertisement causes an exodus of the voter beyond the sphere of uncertainty.

Selecting the features of the image that influence voters is a starting point for work on such a presentation of the candidate that is consistent with the conception accepted by the political consultants. Information obtained in this way allows one to ascertain the stage of their work with the candidate and what should be improved.

Moreover, the presented strategy of research and of analyzing the effect of political advertisements might prove to be useful for evaluating advertisements (e.g., in focus groups) before they are presented to the viewers.

It is important to note that the proposed concept may be used in a much wider sense than merely within the context of researching political advertising. It also can be very easily adapted to the area of marketing that deals with creating promotional advertising strategies for various products and services corresponding to a demographic and psychographic segmentation of the market.

APPENDIX

Formula for Voter Operating Characteristic Curve

From the point of view of the parameters of the distributions, X and Y, the equalization of the VOC curve in a standarized coordinate may be expressed (with the assumption that the variances of both distributions are equal, i.e., $\sigma_X = \sigma_Y$) by the following equation:

$$Z_X = \frac{1}{\sigma_X} Z_Y - \frac{1}{\sigma_X} d', \text{ where } d' = \frac{M_X - M_Y}{\sigma_X},$$

where σ_X is the standard deviation of the distribution X, d' is the sensitivity coefficient, M_X and M_Y are the means of distributions of the two entities, Z_X is the ordinate of the VOC curve, and Z_Y is the abscissa VOC curve (Green & Swets, 1966; McNicol, 1972).

To accommodate the preceding equation to an analysis of the VOC curve, it is necessary to reshape it. This is because in the research on voting preferences, the variances of X and Y are not equal to each other. Thus, in keeping with Swets's (1973) suggestion, it is necessary to substitute the parameter $\frac{1}{\sigma_X}$ with the quotient of standard deviation of the two entities $\frac{\sigma_Y}{\sigma_X}$. Therefore, the final equation of the VOC curve takes the following shape:

$$Z_X = \frac{\sigma_Y}{\sigma_X} Z_Y - \frac{\sigma_Y}{\sigma_X} d',$$

which, after simplification, is as follows:

$$Z_X = \frac{\sigma_Y}{\sigma_X} (Z_Y - d'),$$

whereas, taking into account different variations of distributions:

$$d' = \frac{M_X - M_Y}{\sigma_{X-Y}},$$

where σ_{X-Y} is the standard deviation of differentials between two different distributions. Inserting this parameter is the result of the concept of Thurstone's law of comparative judgment (Coombs, Dawes, & Tversky, 1970).

References

Abelson, R. P., Kinder, D. R., Peters, M. D., & Fiske, S. T. (1982). Affective and semantic components in political person perception. *Journal of Personality and Social Psychology, 42,* 619-630.

Antoszewski, A. (1995). O zwiêkszenie skutecznosci prognoz wyborczych. In W. Sitek (Ed.), *Czy mozna przewidzies? Socjologiczno-metodologiczne doswiadczenia polskich badań przedwyborczych* (pp. 67-86). Wroclaw, Poland: Ossolineum.

Aronson, E., Wilson, T. D., & Akert, R. M. (1994). *Social psychology: The heart and the mind.* New York: HarperCollins.

Atkin, C., Bowen, L., Nayman, O. B., & Sheinkopf, K. G. (1973). Quality versus quantity in televised political ads. *Public Opinion Quarterly, 37,* 209-224.

Banaszkiewicz, A. (1995). Wybory 1991, 1993: Zmiany sympatii politycznych. In S. Gebethner (Ed.), *Wybory parlamentarne 1991 i 1993 a polska scena polityczna* (pp. 273-286). Warsaw, Poland: Wydawnictwo Sejmowe.

Becker, G. (1976). *The economic approach to human behavior.* Chicago: University of Chicago Press.

Berelson, B., Lazarsfeld, P., & McPhee, W. (1954). *Voting: A study of opinion formation in a presidential campaign.* Chicago: University of Chicago Press.

Blumler, J. G., & McQuail, D. (1968). *Television in politics.* London: Faber and Faber.

Braithwaite, V. (1997). Harmony and security value orientations in political evaluation. *Personality and Social Psychology Bulletin, 23,* 401-414.

Bruner, J. S. (1973). *Beyond the information given: Studies in the psychology of knowing.* New York: Norton.

Butler, D., & Stokes, D. (1974). *Political change in Britain: The evolution of electoral choice.* London: Macmillan.

Campbell, A., Converse, P. E., Miller, W. E., & Stokes, D. E. (1960). *The American voter.* New York: John Wiley.

Canache, D., Mondak, J. J., & Conroy, A. (1994). Politics in multiparty context: Multiplicative specifications, social influence, and electoral choice. *Public Opinion Quarterly, 58,* 509-538.

Canady, W. K., & Thyer, B. A. (1990). Promoting voting behavior among low income Black voters using reminder letters: An experimental investigation. *Journal of Sociology and Social Welfare, 17*(4), 109-116.

Caspi, D. (1984). Following the race: Propaganda and electoral decision. In D. Caspi, A. Diskin, & E. Gutmann (Eds.), *The roots of Begin's success* (pp. 245-272). Kent, UK: Croom Helm.

Centers, R. (1949). *The psychology of social classes.* Princeton, NJ: Princeton University Press.

Chaffee, S. H., & Choe, S. Y. (1980). Time of decision and media use during the Ford-Carter campaign. *Public Opinion Quarterly, 44,* 53-69.

Cohen, A. A., & Wolfsfeld, G. (1995). Overcoming advertising and diversity: The utility of television political advertising in Israel. In L. L. Kaid & C. Holtz-Bacha (Eds.), *Political advertising in Western democracies* (pp. 109-123). Thousand Oaks, CA: Sage.

Converse, P. E. (1964). The nature of belief systems in mass public. In D. E. Apter (Ed.), *Ideology and discontent* (pp. 206-261). New York: Free Press.

Coombs, C. H., Dawes, R. M., & Tversky, A. (1970). *Mathematical psychology: An elementary introduction.* Englewood Cliffs, NJ: Prentice Hall.

Cwalina, W., Falkowski, A., & Roznowski, B. (1997a, November). *Image and general feelings toward the candidate as the determinants of voter behavior: A comparative analysis of Poland, France, and Germany.* Paper presented at the Second Research Planning Group Meeting, "Television and Politics in Evolving European Democracies," Paris.

Cwalina, W., Falkowski, A., & Roznowski, B. (1997b). *Raport z badań wyborczych dla AWS Region Dolny Slask.* Lublin, Poland.

Cwalina, W., Falkowski, A., & Roznowski, B. (in press). Television spots in Polish presidential election. Chapter prepared for L. L. Kaid (Ed.), *Television and politics in evolving European democracies.* New York: Nova/Science.

Diamond, E., & Bates, S. (1992). *The spot: The rise of political advertising on television* (3rd ed.). Cambridge, MA: MIT Press.

Faber, R. J. (1992). Advances in political advertising research: A progression from if to when. *Journal of Current Issues and Research in Advertising, 14*(2), 1-18.

Faber, R. J., & Storey, M. C. (1985). Advertising and candidate choice: A profile of voters influenced by political commercials. In N. Stephens (Ed.), *Proceedings of the 1985 American Academy of Advertising* (pp. 123-127). Tempe, AZ: American Academy of Advertising.

Falkowski, A. (1995). *A similarity relation in cognitive processes: An ecological and information processing approach.* Delft, Netherlands: Eburon.

Feofanov, O. A. (1995). Wspólczesna reklama polityczna. *Aida Media, 10*(17), 5-6.

Garramone, G. (1983). Issue versus image orientation and effects of political advertising. *Communication Research, 10*(1), 59-76.

Goleman, D. (1995). *Emotional intelligence.* New York: Bantam Books.

Granberg, D., & Brown, T. (1989). On affect and cognition in politics. *Social Psychology Quarterly, 52,* 171-182.

Green, D. J., & Swets, J. A. (1966). *Signal detection theory and psychophysics.* New York: John Wiley.

Hacker, K. L. (Ed.). (1995). *Candidate images in presidential election.* Westport, CT: Praeger.

Harrison, M. (1965). Television and radio. In D. Butler & A. King (Eds.), *The British general election of 1964* (pp. 156-184). London: Macmillan.

Heath, A., Jowell, R., & Curtice, J. (1985). *How Britain votes.* Oxford, UK: Pergamon.

Heaven, P., Stones, C., Nel, E., Huysamen, G., & Louw, J. (1994). Human values and voting intention in South Africa. *British Journal of Social Psychology, 33,* 223-231.

Holtz-Bacha, C., & Kaid, L. L. (1995). Television spots in German national elections: Content and effects. In L. L. Kaid & C. Holtz-Bacha (Eds.), *Political advertising in Western democracies: Parties and candidates on television* (pp. 61-88). Thousand Oaks, CA: Sage.

Isen, A. M. (1993). Positive affect and decision making. In M. Lewis & J. M. Haviland (Eds.), *Handbook of emotion* (pp. 261-277). New York: Guilford.

Jankowski, T. B., & Strate, J. M. (1995). Modes of participation over the adult life span. *Political Behavior, 17*(1), 89-106.

Johnston, R. J., Pattie, C. J., & Allsopp, J. G. (1988). *A nation dividing? The electoral map of Great Britain 1979-1987.* London: Longman.

Kahneman, D., Slovic, P., & Tversky, A. (Eds.). (1982). *Judgment under uncertainty: Heuristics and biases.* Cambridge, MA: Cambridge University Press.

Kaid, L. L. (1995). Measuring candidate images with semantic differentials. In K. L. Hacker (Ed.), *Candidate images in presidential election* (pp. 131-134). Westport, CT: Praeger.

Kaid, L. L., & Chanslor, M. (1995). Changing candidate images: The effects of political advertising. In K. L. Hacker (Ed.), *Candidate images in presidential election* (pp. 83-97). Westport, CT: Praeger.

Kaid, L. L., & Holtz-Bacha, C. (Eds.). (1995). *Political advertising in Western democracies: Parties and candidates on television.* Thousand Oaks, CA: Sage.

Kaid, L. L., McKinnon, L. M., & Gagnere, N. (1996, May). *Male and female reactions to political broadcasts in the 1995 French presidential election.* Paper presented at the International Communication Association Convention, Chicago.

Kern, M. (1989). *30-second politics: Political advertising in the eighties.* New York: Praeger.

Kessel, J. (1972). Comment: The issues in issue voting. *American Political Science Review, 66,* 459-465.

Korzeniowski, K. (1994). Political alienation in Poland in days of systemic transformation. *Polish Psychological Bulletin, 25*(3), 187-200.

Landa, J., Copeland, M., & Grofman, B. (1995). Ethnic voting patterns: A case study of metropolitan Toronto. *Political Geography, 14,* 435-449.

Lazarsfeld, P., Berelson, B., & Gaudet, H. (1944). *The people's choice: How the voter makes up his mind in a presidential campaign.* New York: Columbia University Press.

Lipset, S. M. (1980). *Political man: The social bases of politics.* Baltimore, MD: Johns Hopkins University Press.

Lott, B., Lott, A., & Saris, R. (1993). Voter preference and behavior in the presidential election of 1988. *Journal of Psychology, 127,* 87-97.

Lupia, A. W., & McCubbins, M. D. (1997). *The democratic dilemma: Can citizens learn what they need to know?* New York: Cambridge University Press.

Mazzoleni, G., & Roper, C. S. (1995). The presentation of Italian candidates and parties in television advertising. In L. L. Kaid & C. Holtz-Bacha (Eds.), *Political advertising in Western democracies: Parties and candidates on television* (pp. 89-108). Thousand Oaks, CA: Sage.

McAllister, I., & Studlar, D. T. (1992). Gender and representation among legislative candidates in Australia. *Comparative Political Studies, 25,* 388-411.

McNicol, D. (1972). *A primer of signal detection theory.* London: George Allen & Unwin.

Morgan, D. R., & Anderson, S. K. (1991). Assessing the effects of political culture: Religious affiliation and county political behavior. *Social Science Journal, 28,* 163-174.

Morgan, D. R., & Watson, S. S. (1991). Political culture, political system characteristics, and public policies among the American states. *Publius: The Journal of Federalism, 21*(1), 31-48.

Negrine, R. (1994). *Politics and the mass media in Britain* (2nd ed.). London: Routlege.

Newman, B. I., & Sheth, J. N. (1985). A model of primary voter behavior. *Journal of Consumer Research, 12,* 178-187.

Nie, N., Verba, S., & Petrocik, J. (1976). *The changing American voter.* Cambridge, MA: Harvard University Press.

Ogden, D. M., & Peterson, A. L. (1964). *Electing the president: 1964.* San Francisco: Chandler.

O'Keefe, M. T., & Sheinkopf, K. G. (1974). The voter decides: Candidate image or campaign issue? *Journal of Broadcasting, 18,* 403-412.

Osgood, C. E., Suci, G. J., & Tannenbaum, P. H. (1957). *The measurement of meaning.* Urbana: University of Illinois Press.

Page, B. I. (1977). Election and social choice: The state of evidence. *American Journal of Political Science, 21,* 639-668.

Perloff, R. M., & Kinsey, D. (1992). Political advertising as seen by consultants and journalists. *Journal of Advertising Research, 32*(3), 53-60.

Popkin, S. (1991). *The reasoning voter: Communication and persuasion in presidential campaigns.* Chicago: University of Chicago Press.

Powell, F. C., & Thorson, J. A. (1990). Political behavior: Voting participation of inner-city elderly Blacks compared to other populations in a medium-sized city. *Psychological Reports, 67*(1), 64-66.

Riley, M. (1988). *Power, politics, and voting behavior: An introduction to the sociology of politics.* London: Harvester-Wheatsheaf.

Rokeach, M. (1973). *The nature of human values.* New York: Free Press.

Schwartz, T. (1973). *The responsive chord.* Garden City, NY: Anchor.

Seeman, M. (1975). Alienation studies. *Annual Review of Sociology, 1,* 91-123.

Singh, K., Leong, S. M., Tan, C. T., & Wang, K. C. (1995). A theory of reasoned action perspective of voting behavior: Model and empirical test. *Psychology and Marketing, 12*(1), 37-51.

Sobel, R. (1993). From occupational involvement to political participation: An exploratory analysis. *Political Behavior, 15,* 339-353.

Sullivan, J. L., Aldrich, J. H., Borgida, E., & Rahn, W. (1990). Candidate appraisal and human nature: Man and Superman in the 1984 election. *Political Psychology, 11,* 459-484.

Swets, J. A. (1973). The relative operating characteristic in psychology. *Science, 182,* 980-1000.

Tam, W. K. (1995). Asians: A monolithic voting bloc? *Political Behavior, 17,* 223-249.

Trenaman, J., & McQuail, D. (1961). *Television and political image.* London: Methuen.

Tversky, A., & Kahnemann, D. (1974). Judgment under uncertainty: Heuristics and biases. *Science, 185,* 1124-1131.

Wattenberg, M. P. (1987). The hollow realignment: Partisan change in a candidate-centered era. *Public Opinion Quarterly, 51,* 58-74.

Wolfsfeld, G. (1992). Voters as consumers: Audience perspectives on the election broadcast. In A. Arian & M. Shamir (Eds.), *The elections in Israel 1992* (pp. 235-253). Albany: State University of New York Press.

Zajonc, R. B. (1980). Feeling and thinking: Preferences need not inferences. *American Psychologist, 35,* 151-175.

Zajonc, R. B., & Markus, H. (1982). Affective and cognitive factors in preferences. *Journal of Consumer Research, 9,* 123-131.

17

A Value-Oriented Model of
Candidate Appraisal

FRANK HUBER
ANDREAS HERRMANN

How individuals perceive and think about candidates, issues, and political events has been the focus of considerable research and theoretical development in political cognition. Researchers in political cognition, drawing on theoretical models from cognitive psychology (Hamill, Lodge, & Blake, 1985; Hastie, 1986; Lau, 1986; Lodge & Hamill, 1986), behavioral decision theory (Iyengar, 1990), and social cognition (Conover & Feldman, 1984; Iyengar, Kinder, Peters, & Krosnick, 1984), have conceptualized the domain of political behavior as a particularly rich, naturalistic context in which to examine theoretical issues that are central to an understanding of human cognition. At the same time, these investigations have begun to contribute new insights to, and perspectives on, long-standing concerns in political science such as the nature of public perceptions and evaluations of political candidates.

Until recently, political scientists, while recognizing the importance of candidate images, have *not* provided theoretical or rigorous empirical analyses of the role of candidates and their images in electoral choice (Campbell, Converse, Miller, & Stokes, 1960). In reaction to this view, scholars during the late 1960s began to analyze the impact of short-term forces on the vote, looking especially at the role of issues. The central argument was that issues, instead of being short-term disruptions of otherwise stable partisan choices, could be seen as systematic determinants of voters' decisions (Kessel, 1972). One theoretical approach to explain issues voting is the spatial model of electoral competition (Downs, 1957). One important contribution of the spatial approach was the emphasis on choice as based on a comparison between the two alternative candidates, seen in that case as a collection of policy alternatives.

Other models of voter choice posited less demanding calculations than the spatial model, in which summary candidate assessments played a critical role (Brody & Page, 1973). Indeed, the decision rule in these models is that individuals vote for the candidate receiving the highest net evaluations. More methodologically complicated models have been developed to examine the causal determinants of these summary assessments (Markus, 1982; Markus & Converse, 1979), but they have lacked a systematic theoretical account of the processes that underlie voters' impressions of political candidates. Given these results, scholars of political behavior have recognized for some time that the focus should shift from predicting vote choice per se, as reflected in the component models of voter choice (Stokes, 1966), to understanding the nature of the candidate appraisal process. To explain that process, it might be useful to take an interdisciplinary point of view and integrate insights from the marketing theory.

One confirmed marketing theory suggests that consumers do not purchase a package of attributes but rather purchase a complex set of utility components, and another school of thought asserts that stimulating forces (e.g., attitudes, values, ends) possess greater relevance as motives for individual actions. The "means-end" theory, to which considerable attention has been devoted by researchers in recent years, enables the attributes relevant to the performance quality to be associated with the determinants of behavior (sets of values). Only by accentuating the characteristics of a politician or a political campaign along these lines can such values be accomplished and can this accomplishment subsequently be reflected in the customers' satisfaction with a performance of a candidate or campaign.

This chapter explains an approach we developed that sheds more light on the appraisal of candidates with respect to two new aspects. First, we use the model (described later) to take account not only of the voter decision-relevant characteristics of a politician but also of the behavior-forming utility dimensions and values of the voters. Second, we attempt to analyze the success of the measures initiated by the campaign strategist on the basis of the voters' satisfaction ratings. The measurement of voters' satisfaction in this context represents a controlling tool. Before commencing a detailed discussion of our integrative approach, however, we provide a short literature review and a summary of the essential aspects of the means-end and satisfaction concepts. Finally, we document the advantages of our approach with the aid of a pilot study supported by the management of one of the more popular parties in November 1997.

Candidate Appraisal

Research on political cognition has stimulated renewed interest in the study of candidate images as preeminent factors in the voters' world. The crucial factor behind the intensification of research activities in this area is the "personalization" of electoral campaigns. This term describes the growing concentration of campaigns on the top candidate of each party. During the past few decades, the candidates for the office of U.S. president have, to a large extent, shed their dependence on party organizations. Instead, they have engaged themselves in an offensive strategy to win voters' favors with the aid of electoral campaign organizations that have been set up specifically for this purpose, are self-financed through donation appeals, and are tailored entirely to the candidates' own persons. In Europe, electoral campaign planning and organization still are the domain of the party headquarters. However, candidates for top political office are increasingly becoming the key strategic elements of their own electoral campaigns. Among the German parties, the Christian Democratic Union in particular has for years openly and consistently pursued a policy of personalized electoral campaigning (Radunski, 1986). In the meantime, the Social Democratic Party has likewise become more receptive to this strategic electoral approach. In the 1994 federal election, the role played by "presidential styles" of electioneering achieved such significance that this election is considered by many observers to be the turning point on the road toward large-scale personalization of electoral campaigns.

As a result, the research activities of political scientists are now focusing to an ever greater extent on the candidates' own persons. Lau (1986) and Miller, Wattenberg, and Malanchuk (1986), for example, rely on an understanding of information processing based on schema theory (e.g., Taylor & Crocker, 1981) and use responses to the open-ended, like-dislike questions from the University of Michigan Center for Political Studies (CPS) national elections surveys to identify "information processing proclivities" among the mass public. Similarly, Miller and his colleagues (1986) categorize citizen responses to the open-ended, like-dislike questions into those dealing with candidates, issues, and groups. They find that candidate-directed comments cluster into five generic dimensions that are stable at the individual level across elections, suggesting that individuals do not respond to candidates as idiosyncratic figures.

Works by Kinder and others have examined the candidate appraisal process. These works have made extensive use of the new CPS candidates appraisal batteries to develop a theoretical framework for understanding the perception and evaluation of presidential candidates. In particular, Kinder's (1986) analysis of these measures reveals that individuals think about the candidates in stable, structured ways. Thus, in contrast to the early perspectives on vote choice, recent research suggests that the candidate appraisal process does not represent an idiosyncratic response to the vagaries and particular characteristics of a given election contest. Rather, these findings support the notion that, when thinking about political candidates, people tend to rely on the same information processing capabilities that guide their thinking and actions in other, nonpolitical domains (Feldman & Conover, 1983; Kinder & Fiske, 1986).

In nonpolitical domains, we find different research streams that try to explain human information processing. One of them says that a wide variety of political cues and other types of concrete information are abundantly available to the voters, and potentially all of this information can be used when evaluating candidates. In addition, it seems reasonable to state that voters decide not for an agglomeration of attributes but rather for a complex of utility components

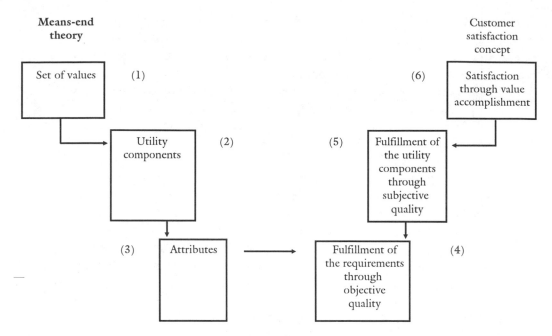

Figure 17.1. Value-Orientated Approach to Achieving Customer Satisfaction

(Lancaster, 1966; Myers & Tauber, 1977). This idea appears plausible, as voters are only rarely aware of all the beneficial attributes of a candidate. In many cases, it also is true to say that different attributes provide a concrete benefit and that one attribute can affect different utility areas.

There is, however, cause to doubt that the utility expectations of the buyer do, in fact, constitute the "ultimate explanation" of decision behavior. On the contrary, the motives for individual actions can be better accounted for by stimulating forces such as a set of values and the formation of an intention. Nevertheless, very little attention is paid to these hypothetical constructs when specifying a candidate's performance. There are two reasons for this. First, numerous studies have documented the unsatisfactory association between these variables and decision behavior. It is an undisputed fact that specific behavioral patterns cannot be predicted, for example, on the basis of specific motives (Nieschlag, Dichtl, & Hörschgen, 1994). Second, there is no theory in existence at the present time that describes the interaction between the hypothetical constructs and the relevant utility components and commodity attributes. Consequently, no evidence is available to support the notion that marketing activities are conceived according to the stimulating forces of voting behavior. The various problems that are raised in this connection can be solved by a value-oriented approach from the point of view of marketing theory (Figure 17.1).

The means-end theory is used to integrate the set of values of a voter (Element 1) with the utility components (Element 2) or the attributes (Element 3) of a politician. An analysis of customer satisfaction provides information regarding the extent to which the politician (Element 4) corresponds to the voter's conception of utility (Element 5) and to his or her set of values (Element 6).

Essential Aspects of the Means-End Theory

In consumer research, the means-end theory posits that linkages among attributes of the product, the consequences of consumption, and the personal values of consumers underlie consumers' decision-making processes (Herrmann, 1996). Because this approach has advantages to explain the appraisal of political candidates as well, we clarify this concept as follows. *Means* are products or services, whereas *ends* are personal values important to consumers. In an application to consumer research, the means-end theory seeks to explain how a person's choice of a product or service enables him or her to achieve the desired end states. This type of framework consists of elements representing the major consumer processes that link personal values to behavior.

Two assumptions underlying the model are that (a) all consumer actions have consequences and that (b) all consumers learn to associate particular consequences with particular actions they may take. Consumers derive consequences from the consumption of products or services. Consequences may be desirable (benefits) or undesirable; they may stem directly from consuming or from the act of consumption or may occur indirectly either at a later point in time or from others' reactions to the consumers' consumption behavior. The central aspect of the theory is that consumers choose actions that produce desirable consequences and minimize undesirable consequences.

The means-end idea was founded during the 1970s and 1980s, when Tolman's work served as a basis for Howard, Cohen, Myers, Shocker, and others to elaborate the first means-end models (Cohen, 1979; Howard, 1977; Myers & Shocker, 1980). Their approaches all share the same objective of amalgamating a selected stimulating force (e.g., set of values, goals in life) with the physical-chemical-technical commodity attributes relevant to the conception of marketing activities. The means-end model developed during the 1980s by Gutman and Reynolds can be considered a combination of all previously known approaches (Gutman, 1982; Reynolds & Gutman, 1988). As Figure 17.1 shows, the fundamental structure of this model consists of three elements: *attribute, utility component,* and *set of values.*

It is initially useful to break down the attributes according to their level of abstraction (Johnson, 1984; Peter & Olson, 1990; Tversky & Hemenway, 1984). An attribute is considered to be concrete if its various levels describe the physical-chemical-technical constitution (e.g., "with heel supports") of a product (e.g., Nike sports shoes). It can generally be observed directly or measured objectively, and it often exhibits a finite number of discrete states. Whereas this type of attribute normally is able to reflect only one facet of a phenomenon, an abstract attribute permits a comprehensive description of a commodity (e.g., "good fit"). The level of this type of attribute in a particular product depends on the subjective opinion of the individual rather than on objective facts.

According to Vershofen's utility theory, the functional utility of a product is derived from its physical-chemical-technical attributes (Bauer, 1989; Vershofen, 1959). This utility specifies the usefulness of the commodity and embraces the consequences of the product's actual use (e.g., "can run faster"). The socio-psychological utility, on the other hand, includes all extras that are not vital to the actual function of the product, for example, product attributes that enhance the aesthetic appearance of the commodity or the social acceptability of the buyer (e.g., "feel relaxed after running").

Graumann and Willig (1983) suggest that sets of values represent series of individual standards that remain constant over a period of time, serving to formulate goals in life and to put them into practice in everyday behavior. Thus, a set of values constitutes an explicit or implicit conception of ideals, characteristic of the individual concerned, that controls the choice of a particular mode, instrument (means), and goal (end) of conduct. This view also is held by Rokeach (1973), who defines a set of values as "an enduring belief that a specific mode of conduct or end-state of existence is personally or socially preferable to an opposite or converse mode of conduct or end-state of existence" (p. 5). By "an enduring belief in preferable modes of conduct and end-states of existence," Rokeach does not simply mean a cognitive representation or conception of what must be done and achieved. Instead, he attributes affective and conative components to the set of values (or the goals in life) over and above the cognitive component. This idea stems from Rokeach's definition of the term "value" as an "intervening variable that leads to action when activated" (p. 7).

It follows from this definition that a distinction needs to be drawn between terminal (end-states of existence) and instrumental (modes of conduct) values. The terminal values, which embody desirable goals in life, can be further subdivided into personal values and social values. The group of personal values includes inner harmony, serenity, and maturity in love, whereas the class of social values includes global peace, national security, and a world full of beauty. The instrumental goals in life, which represent desirable forms of behavior, consist of moral and achievement-oriented values. Examples of moral values include tolerance, a willingness to help, and a sense of responsibility, whereas the set of achievement-oriented values include attributes such as logical, intellectual, and imaginative. In our example, "physical fitness" can be classed as an instrumental value and "self-esteem" as a terminal value.

Using the specified means-end elements of the example, we can construct a chain that represents a small part of the knowledge structure of an individual. A consumer's intention to purchase a product (e.g., Nike sports shoes) initially causes the concrete (e.g., "with heel supports") and abstract (e.g., "good fit") attributes associated with it to be activated. This impulse is then propagated via the functional (e.g., "can run faster") and sociopsychological (e.g., "feel relaxed after running") utility components, before finally reaching the instrumental (e.g., "physical fitness") and terminal (e.g., "self-esteem") values.

Most important for understanding the idea is that personal values are beliefs people have about important aspects of themselves and the goals toward which they are striving. Personal values are the penultimate consequences of behavior for people, be they feelings of self-esteem, belonging, or other value orientations (Rokeach, 1973). In this sense, personal values are part of the central core of a person. Thus, personal values as core aspects of self are held to provide consequences (the term "consequences" here refers to the outcomes accruing to the person from behavior such as consuming a product or voting for a candidate) with positive or negative valences. Personal values, in other words, determine which consequences are desired by a person and which are undesirable (Sheth, Newman, & Gross, 1991).

Because it is attributes that produce consequences, we must consider the attributes that products, services, or (in our special case) political candidates possess. Therefore, we also must make ourselves aware of attribute-consequence relations. Overall, the attribute-consequence-value interrelations are the focus of the theory. Values provide the overall direction, consequences determine the choice of specific behavior in specific situations, and attributes are the contents of the actual products, services, or politicians that produce the consequences.

The Satisfaction Concept

According to this theory, a party or candidate is faced with the constant challenge of achieving maximum possible voter satisfaction. The significance of the satisfaction rating for assessing the quality of a party or candidate derives from its function as an indicator of actual voting behavior (Huber & Herrmann, 1997). The (dis)satisfaction is the outcome of a complex information processing process that essentially consists of a desired-actual comparison of a certain experience, with the vote for a party or candidate (actual) and the expectations regarding the fitness of the performance for its intended purpose (desired) (Anderson, 1994). The congruence or divergence yielded by this comparison between the perceived quality and the anticipated quality is expressed as the voter's (dis)confirmation.

Whether or not an individual considers his or her expectations to be confirmed by a decision for a candidate or party, so that the individual is satisfied with the performance, is primarily dependent on the perceived quality. Quality perception is directly linked to the experience and can be defined as a global judgment in relation to the fitness of a performance for its intended purpose (Zeithaml, 1988). The individual concerned assesses each attribute that is of relevance to him or her regarding its suitability (Element 4) and then integrates the partial ratings in accordance with a decision-making rule to obtain a quality judgment (Element 5). The voter's expectations represent a specific level of quality that he or she hopes to find in the commodity. They serve as a yardstick for appraisal by the voter. The level of expectation is determined, first, by previous experience (Fornell, 1992). Second (and this applies in particular to situations in which a voter gave his or her vote to a candidate who, or a party that, will be in power for the first time), the voter obtains, in addition to other preliminary information, an idea of the quality of the contemplated candidate or party, above all from the available alternatives. If the candidate in question matches the voter's conceptions in every respect, then the voter will be satisfied with the quality (Element 8). The relevance of a satisfaction rating to the success of a candidate or party is evident.

As numerous studies have demonstrated, satisfied voters exhibit considerable loyalty.

Another factor having a positive effect on the success of a candidate or party is the more marked inclination of satisfied voters to relate the advantages of a candidate (and perhaps also the disadvantages of the rival candidate) to other voters. This word-of-mouth advertising is distinguished by a high level of credibility; consequently, the task of canvassing new voters is simplified.

The extent to which a candidate is in line with voters' wishes is expressed by the satisfaction ratings. It is they who provide the necessary information about the success and, therefore, play a central role within the controlling system framework. By gathering judgments, it is possible to extrapolate means for improving the quality of a campaign or for assimilating it more closely with the conceptions of potential and actual voters.

On the Value-Oriented Appraisal of a Candidate: A Case Study

The Hierarchical Representation of the Means-End Chain

The object of our study was to get a deeper understanding of how voters evaluate candidates and, based on that information, to give advice on how to design a campaign. Various interviewing instruments of qualitative market research can be used to reconstruct, and subsequently visualize, the previously mentioned elements of the means-end chain and the relationships that exist among these components. The most relevant methods are the repertory grid approach, the laddering interview, the content analysis, and the laddering method. It is the interaction of these analysis techniques that enables the determinants of individual behavior to be identified.

The repertory grid method attempts to determine the attributes that are significant for an individual's choice of a politician (Bannister & Fransella, 1981). For this purpose, the voters are presented, in a series of interview rounds, with different triplets of candidates and then prompted to name those attributes that create a similarity between two of the three candidates while simultaneously establishing a dissimilarity from the third. This process continues until the voters are unable to specify any new attributes and a comprehensive attribute list, including details of the number of mentions, has been produced. Next, the voters are asked to name the two levels of each relevant attribute that exhibit the greatest contrast (dichotomy) and represent the positive and negative attribute poles. Finally, the respondents are requested to state whether the level of the various attributes corresponds more closely to the positive pole or the negative pole. The various attributes can then be analyzed regarding their similarity. The evaluation criterion is the value referred to by Kelly (1955) as the "matching score." This is calculated as the sum of the concurrent level values in two rows. A high matching score indicates a positive association. Possible redundancies in the list of attributes that may result from discrepancies in the linguistic and semantic use of the respondents can, therefore, be identified and eliminated.

The laddering interview represents a useful tool for determining the utility components of candidates and the sets of values. The objective of this nonstandardized interview is to investigate the behavior-forming forces that determine an individual's choice of commodity. From the methodical point of view, it consists of a series of consecutive *why* questions designed to cause the respondents to reveal certain facets of their imaginations, from abstract product attributes to terminal values.

On this basis, the laddering interview can be described as an investigation technique comprising a series of interview rounds. The first round is concerned with establishing why the concrete attributes identified by means of the repertory grid method carry such weight for the voters' choice of a particular candidate. The abstract attributes that are reconstructed from the answers form the basis for examining the functional utility components of the politicians in question in the second round. The aim of the third round is to develop a conception of the psychological utility components associated with the relevant marques while taking account of the respondents' previous mentions. The interview continues until the individuals have disclosed the desired information about their instrumental and terminal values (Herrmann, 1996).

Once the data have been collected, the contents of the interview must be analyzed. The purpose of this content analysis is to reconstruct the social reality of the respondents. The central propositions of any document can be revealed using words, sentences, and paragraphs. The researcher's decision to employ a particular linguistic unit (configurations) depends on where the pointers to the determinants of individual behavior are concealed. In this case, the persons charged with analyzing the raw data defined a total of 35 categories. Table 17.1 shows the system of categories developed with the aid of the content analysis.

The individual components can be subjected to a paired comparison; subsequently, the means-end chains can be represented in a frequency table. This so-called implication matrix contains the frequencies of all the direct relationships that are mentioned by the respondents between two immediately consecutive elements of the cognitive chains. Thus, this phase of the analysis involves not only aggregating the qualitative statements but also transforming them into quantitative data. The relationships documented with the aid of the implication matrix are then converted into a graphical form, referred to as the hierarchical value map, to enable them to be illustrated more clearly. It does not make sense, however, to visualize all these relationships when transforming the data. Rather, it is more useful to define a cutoff level. Therefore, the aggregated hierarchical value map can be restricted so that it contains only relevant relationships, that is, relationships that are located above a specified frequency level (Figure 17.2). The process of determining all the linkages that exceed this threshold value one row at a time forms the methodical core of the laddering method.

Chains that represent small parts of the knowledge structure of an individual can be constructed using the specified means-end elements. A voter's intention to choose a certain politician, for example, initially causes the concrete attributes

TABLE 17.1 Categories of the Fictitious Means-End Analysis

KP 1	=	Sex	PSN 3	=	Honesty
KP 2	=	Age	PSN 4	=	Ability to communicate
KP 3	=	Highest previous political office	PSN 5	=	Sincerity
KP 4	=	School diploma	PSN 6	=	Pleasantness of manner
KP 5	=	Family background	PSN 7	=	Credibility
KP 6	=	Size of staff to date	PSN 8	=	Trustworthiness
AP 1	=	Looks (physiognomy)	PSN 9	=	Receptiveness
AP 2	=	Charisma	IW 1	=	Impressing others
AP 3	=	Outward appearance (clothes)	IW 2	=	Success
FN 1	=	Technical competence	IW 3	=	Accepting responsibility for others
FN 2	=	Ability to lead	IW 4	=	Mastery of difficult situations
FN 3	=	Intelligence	IW 5	=	Satisfaction/well-being
FN 4	=	Ideological background	IW 6	=	Aesthetics
FN 5	=	Capability	TW 1	=	Social acceptability
FN 6	=	Authority	TW 2	=	Safety
FN 7	=	Ability to deal with conflicts	TW 3	=	Self-realization
PSN 1	=	Social competence	TW 4	=	Tolerance
PSN 2	=	Sympathy			

NOTE: KP = concrete attribute; AP = abstract attribute; FN = functional benefit; PSN = psychosocial benefit; IW = instrumental value; TW = terminal value.

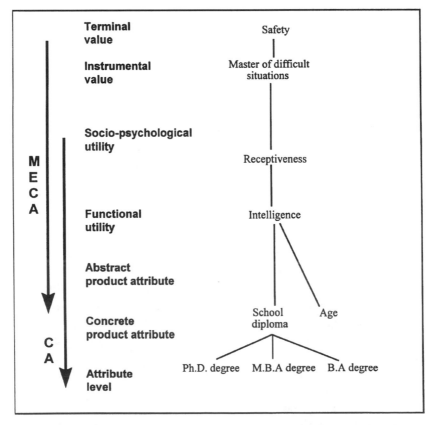

Figure 17.2. One Branch of the Hierarchical Value Map Representing the Knowledge Structure of a Fictitious Voter

NOTE: MECA = means-end chain analysis; CA = conjoint analysis.

(e.g., school diploma) associated with it to be activated. These attributes enable the buyer to realize functional (intelligence) and psychosocial (receptiveness) utility components. The utility dimensions are, in turn, a reflection of the voter's instrumental (mastery of difficult situations) and terminal (safety) values (Figure 17.2). Thus, the school diploma represents a means of safety in our fictitious example. However, it does not symbolize the "aesthetic" value.

The need to take account of sets of values when presenting a candidate or conceptualizing a campaign also can be demonstrated with an example from the automotive industry. If it is assumed that the length of the front section of the vehicle is an important criterion for a potential car buyer, then the knowledge that this attribute helps to raise the customer's self-esteem will inspire the product designer to devise a different body shape than if the value associated with the attribute were safety. Thus, this knowledge of the *why* should exert a decisive influence on the development of new seats or on modifications to existing ones.

Although the information yielded by the means-end analysis helps the researcher to identify the value and utility structures according to which certain attributes are considered by a particular voter segment to be relevant to the voting decision, it cannot provide an answer as to the concrete levels these attributes should have. If a crucial role is played by the "age" attribute, for example, then the researcher will be unable to make a definite statement at the end of the means-end analysis concerning the actual age a candidate should be so that the voter is willing to vote for that person.

The Conjoint Study

For a party strategist to obtain additional clues, the focus of the next step must be to determine the preferences for specific attributes or attribute levels (Elements 3 and 4). The preferability of a particular attribute is dependent on the position of the value in the individual's personal value hierarchy. The more central the value's position, the more avidly the individual will attempt to fulfill this end by means of an appropriate course of action and the more importance he or she will attach to the presence of an attribute that promises to live up to this value. These preferability differences can be measured using the conjoint analysis.

Conjoint analysis consists of a series of psychometric methods, the purpose of which is to determine the partial contributions of individual attributes (e.g., the appearance of the seats or the ease with which they can be adjusted) toward the formation of the global judgment (e.g., the preference for a particular marque of car) from empirically obtained global judgments concerning multiattributive alternatives (e.g., the fact that a certain type of seat is fitted inside the vehicle) (Bauer, Herrmann, & Mengen, 1996). The presented alternatives are the result of a systematic combination of the levels of several different attributes that have been identified as significant within the framework of an experimental design. Thus, we do not combine the individual, attribute-specific judgments to form a global judgment (compositional approach); rather, we follow precisely the oppo-

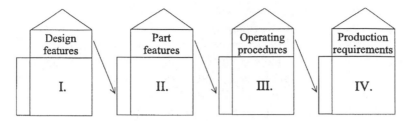

Figure 17.3. The "House of Quality" as a Starting Point for Planning a Product

site procedure in extracting the partial contributions of the individual attributes and their levels from the global judgments (decompositional approach).

The "full-concept" or "full-profile" method asks voters participating in the conjoint analysis to rank, order, or score a set of political cards according to preference. On each of these cards, a full profile of a given candidate or party is represented and a different combination of features appears. Consider, for example, a candidate's card that describes a politician who has a political position in a federal institution, is 56 years old, has an M.B.A. degree, and already has had the responsibility for more than 300 people in his last managerial position. The respondent has to evaluate this profile against the profile of another candidate's card that describes a politician who has a political position in a federal institution, is 66 years old, has a B.A. degree, and already has had the responsibility for more than 1,000 people in his last managerial position. The list of features can be easily expanded to include various ideological factors and issue-related views (e.g., abortion, environmental protection). The only limitation is the statistical degree of freedom, which forces the researcher to add candidates (observations) parallel to the addition of factors. Too many candidates and features might put a burden on respondents in trying to rank or score in a meaningful way. Similar to the marketing world, some candidates (like products or services) may be real, flesh-and-blood candidates, and some may be imaginary. Similar to the marketing world, a good conjoint analysis might force the party or political adviser to look out for a candidate who is unknown in name yet known in features and characters if victory is given the highest priority.

Furthermore, in the multilayer model proposed here, this method bridges the gap, in marketing theory, between the means-end approach and the "House of Quality" (HoQ) approach. The HoQ, which represents the first phase of the quality function deployment (QFD) methodology, is concerned with translating the purchase decision-relevant attributes of a product that have been established, for example, within the framework of a conjoint study into design features (Figure 17.3). It is important to point out that these design requirements are not design solutions that do not appear until the second house (part deployment). These design features subsequently are transformed into part features during the parts development phase. The aim of the work preparation phase is then to define crucial operating procedures on the basis of the specified part features. The crucial operating procedures, in turn, serve to determine the production requirements in greater detail.

The HoQ approach itself is part of the QFD, which can be described as a concept to product quality design, which attempts to translate the "voice of the customer" into the "language of the engineer." The customer's wants often are called the *whats* or what QFD ultimately is supposed to improve. Furthermore, it is necessary to determine the *hows* or the design requirements that will determine how the *whats* are to be fulfilled. The design requirements should be expressed in measurable terms (e.g., the amount of pressure required to close a door system from the outside). The core principle of this concept is a systematic transformation of customer requirements and expectations into measurable product and process parameters. From the methodical point of view, it would appear useful to subdivide a quality planning process derived from customers' expressed wishes into four separate phases (Hauser & Clausing, 1988).

Because the HoQ is a very successful tool in the business of products, it also is worth being used in the business of elections. Instead of imposing characteristics of the candidates on the voters and asking the voters to rank candidates accordingly, it begins with the means-end analysis identified most important requirements or utility dimensions for political candidates in a given election. By means of the systematic diagram method (Mizuno, 1988), the strategic planner develops a hierarchical system of goals and means, which at its most concrete level contains a comprehensive set of quality attributes of the political candidate. In the next step, these attributes are coupled by means of the so-called "Q matrix" to the operational and human resource factors that affect them. To indicate the strength of the relationship between voter requirements and campaigning activities, one can use the "mean gap scores," that is, the calculated discrepancies between voters' perceptions and their expectations. Specific areas for improvement are those with particular negative total gap values. With the HoQ approach, the campaign strategist identifies a variety of functional characteristics that correlate highly with voter requirements and subjective satisfaction scores. Thus, it has more degrees of freedom in its ability to detect determinants of political popularity than does the conjoint analysis. To gain full knowledge about the cognitive structure of the votes, it makes sense to combine all of these instruments.

Whereas the results of the means-end analysis merely provide the persons responsible for a candidate with an overview of the value and utility structures as well as the attributes that are relevant to the voting decision, the voters reveal in the conjoint interview their order of preference for these variables and the relevance attached to individual attribute levels. These attribute levels, in turn, represent one element of the HoQ. Subfactors such as the "social competence" of a candidate are derived in the HoQ from attribute bundles, which are generated on the basis of the functional elements important to the voters. In our case, this could be the extraversion of the candidate. In the voters' view, for example, the candidate should be "talkative," "assertive," "outspoken," and "outgoing" (Cohen, 1995; Griffin & Hauser, 1992; Hauser & Clausing, 1988; Mizuno & Akao, 1994).

Because in the case we have constructed here the social competence exerts a considerable influence on the decisions of voters, the task of the campaign development department is now to establish which of the technical features affect the attributes important to the voters and to what extent.

Finally, the voters must be interviewed again to establish the fitness of the modified attribute for its intended purpose. This time, they are asked to impart their satisfaction ratings to the interviewer. The appraisal is founded on direct interviews with voters and on the experience acquired by these voters over a period of time. If the political campaign corresponds to the voters' wishes, then the staff of the candidate can assume that the satisfaction values are high. This should inspire the candidate to perform even better in the future.

Summary

It can be stated that when the means-end chains and the HoQ are constructed, the starting point must be the wishes of the voters. Unlike the HoQ method, however, the means-end interview does not attempt to determine the relevant quality expectations of voters or the various characteristics of the candidate (attributes important to the customer). As mentioned earlier, it is the attributes important to the voter (so-called *whats*) and the design features (so-called *hows*) that make up the foundations of the HoQ. The results of the means-end studies serve as additional reinforcement for these foundations. Subsequently, the central objective is to discover the motives that guide an individual's actions. The action-guiding attributes that are generated (the *whys*) represent the "ultimate explanation" of a voting decision. The resulting improved understanding of the relationship between the voters' stimulating forces and the benefits derived from the candidates subsequently enables both campaign strategists and party experts to identify new bases for explaining present voter values and for designing future ones.

References

Anderson, E. W. (1994). Cross-category variation in customer satisfaction and retention. *Marketing Letters, 5,* 19-30.

Bannister, D., & Fransella, F. (1981). *Der Mensch als Forscher: Die Psychologie der Persönlichen Konstrukte.* Münster, Germany: Lange Verlag.

Bauer, H. H. (1989). *Marktabgrenzung: Konzeption und Problematik von Ansätzen und Methoden zur Abgrenzung und Strukturierung von Märkten unter besonderer Berücksichtigung von marketingtheoretischen Verfahren.* Berlin: Duncker & Humblot.

Bauer, H. H., Herrmann, A., & Mengen, A. (1996). A method of achieving maximum-profit product design on the basis of conjoint measurement. *Pricing Strategy & Practice, 4,* 28-33.

Brody, R. A., & Page, B. I. (1973). Indifference, alienation, and rational decisions: The effects of candidate evaluations on turnout and the vote. *Public Choice, 15,* 1-17.

Campbell, A., Converse, P. E., Miller, W. E., & Stokes, D. E. (1960). *The American voter.* New York: John Wiley.

Cohen, J. B. (1979). The structure of product attributes. In A. D. Shoker (Ed.), *Analytic approaches to product and marketing planning* (pp. 54-86). Reading, MA: Addison-Wesley.

Cohen, L. (1995). *Quality function deployment: How to make QFD work for you.* New York: Free Press.

Conover, P. J., & Feldman, S. (1984). How people organize the political world: A schematic model. *American Journal of Political Science, 28,* 95-126.

Downs, A. (1957). *An economic theory of democracy.* New York: Harper & Row.

Feldman, S., & Conover, P. J. (1983). Candidates, issues, and voters: The role of inference in political perception. *Journal of Politics, 45,* 810-839.

Fornell, C. (1992). A national customer satisfaction barometer: The Swedish experience. *Journal of Marketing, 56,* 6-21.

Graumann, C. F., & Willig, R. (1983). Wert, Wertung, Werthaltung. In H. Thomae (Ed.), *Enzyklopedie der Psychologie,* Vol. 1: *Theorien und Formen der Motivation* (pp. 313-396). Göttingen, Germany.

Griffin, A., & Hauser, J. (1992). Patterns of communication among marketing, engineering, and manufacturing. *Management Science, 38,* 360-373.

Gutman, J. (1982). A means-end chain model based on consumer categorization processes. *Journal of Marketing, 46,* 60-72.

Hamill, R., Lodge, M., & Blake, F. (1985). The breadth, depth, and utility of class, partisan, and ideological schemas. *American Journal of Political Science, 29,* 850-870.

Hastie, R. (1986). A primer of information-processing theory for the political scientist. In R. R. Lau & D. O. Sears (Eds.), *Political cognition.* Hillsdale, NJ: Lawrence Erlbaum.

Hauser, J., & Clausing, D. (1988). The House of Quality. *Harvard Business Review, 16,* 63-73.

Herrmann, A. (1996). *Nachfragerorientierte Produktgestaltung: Ein Ansatz auf der Basis der Means-End-Theorie.* Wiesbaden, Germany: Gabler.

Howard, J. A. (1977). *Consumer behavior: Application and theory.* New York: McGraw-Hill.

Huber, F., & Herrmann, A. (1997). The satisfaction of voters: Empirical testing of a dynamic model to measure different vote satisfaction profiles. In P. Harris & E. Schuster (Eds.), *Academy of Marketing conference proceedings: Marketing without borders* (pp. 1353-1357). Manchester, UK: Manchester Metropolitan University.

Iyengar, S. (1990). Shortcuts to political knowledge: The role of selective attention and accessibility. In J. A. Ferejohn & J. H. Kuklinski (Eds.), *Information and democratic processes* (pp. 160-185). Chicago: University of Chicago Press.

Iyengar, S., Kinder, D. R., Peters, M. D., & Krosnick, J. A. (1984). The evening news and presidential evaluations. *Journal of Personality and Social Psychology, 46,* 778-787.

Johnson, M. D. (1984). Consumer choice strategies for comparing noncomparable alternatives. *Journal of Consumer Research, 11,* 741-753.

Kelly, G. A. (1955). *The psychology of personal constructs.* New York.

Kessel, J. (1972). Comment: The issues in issue voting. *American Political Science Review, 66,* 459-465.

Kinder, D. R. (1986). Presidential character revisited. In R. R. Lau & D. O. Sears (Eds.), *Political cognition* (pp. 233-255). Hillsdale, NJ: Lawrence Erlbaum.

Kinder, D. R., & Fiske, S. T. (1986). Presidents in the public mind. In M. G. Hermann (Ed.), *Political psychology.* San Francisco: Jossey-Bass.

Lancaster, K. J. (1966). A new approach to consumer theory. *Journal of Political Economy, 32,* 132-157.

Lau, R. R. (1986). Political schemata, candidate evaluations, and voting behaviour. In R. R. Lau & D. O. Sears (Eds.), *Political cognition* (pp. 95-126). Hillsdale, NJ: Lawrence Erlbaum.

Lodge, M., & Hamill, R. (1986). A partisan schema for political information processing. *American Political Science Review, 80,* 505-519.

Markus, G. B. (1982). Political attitudes during an election year: A report on the 1980 NES Panel Study. *American Political Science Review, 76,* 538-560.

Markus, G. B., & Converse, P. E. (1979). A dynamic simultaneous equation model of electoral choice. *American Political Science Review, 73,* 1055-1070.

Miller, A. H., Wattenberg, M. P., & Malanchuk, O. (1986). Schematic assessments of presidential candidates. *American Political Science Review, 80,* 521-540.

Mizuno, S. (1988). *Management for quality improvement: The seven new QC tools.* Cambridge, UK: Cambridge University Press.

Mizuno, S., & Akao, Y. (1994). *QFD: The customer-driven approach to quality planning and development.* Tokyo: Asian Productivity Center.

Myers, J. H., & Shocker, A. D. (1980). *The nature of product related attributes.* Working paper, University of Chicago: University of Chicago Press.

Myers, J. H., & Tauber, E. (1977). *Market structure analysis.* Chicago: University of Chicago Press.

Nieschlag, R., Dichtl, E., & Hörschgen, H. (1994). *Marketing* (17th ed.). Berlin: Duncker & Humblot.

Peter, J. P., & Olson, J. C. (1990). *Consumer behaviour* (2nd ed.). Homewood, IL: Irwin.

Radunski, P. (1986). Wahlkampf in den 80er Jahren. *Aus Politik und Zeitgeschichte, 11,* 34-45.

Reynolds, T. J., & Gutman, J. (1988). Laddering theory, methods, analysis, and interpretation. *Journal of Advertising Research, 28,* 11-31.

Rokeach, M. (1973). *The nature of human values.* New York: Free Press.

Sheth, J. N., Newman, B. I., & Gross, B. L. (1991). Why we buy what we buy: A theory of consumption values. *Journal of Business Research, 22,* 159-170.

Stokes, D. (1966). Some dynamic elements of contests for the presidency. *American Political Science Review, 60,* 19-28.

Taylor, S. E., & Crocker, J. (1981). Schematic bases of social information processing. In T. E. Higgins, P. C. Herman, & M. P. Zanna (Eds.), *Social cognition: The Ontario Symposium* (Vol. 1). Hillsdale, NJ: Lawrence Erlbaum.

Tversky, A., & Hemenway, K. (1984). Objects, parts, and categories. *Journal of Experimental Psychology, 13,* 169-193.

Vershofen, W. (1959). *Die Marktentnahme als Kernstück der Wirtschaftsforschung.* Berlin: Duncker & Humblot.

Zeithaml, V. A. (1988). Consumer perceptions of price, quality, and value: A means-end model and synthesis of evidence. *Journal of Marketing, 52,* 2-22.

18

Grabbing the Nonvoter

DORINA MIRON

As early as 1954, Rosenberg looked at individual-related causes of political apathy and observed, "Theoretically, there is no limit to the factors which can fail to stimulate an individual to political activity" (Rosenberg, 1954, p. 361). To further complicate the problem, the majority of nonvoting factors are context bound—linked to local structures, traditions, and events. Consequently, the turnout problems faced by political marketers around the globe are extremely complex and diverse, and the knowledge gained from each experience and each study is rather hard to generalize. But awareness of this problem should not discourage students of nonvoting and political marketers. The present analysis is intended to provide them with a comprehensive picture of research findings and theoretical developments that may be used as a starting point in the examination of specific situations, irrespective of geographic location, and as a framework for solving nonvoting-related problems. Special emphasis is placed on the role of mass communication as an antecedent of nonvoting.

Because most information about nonvoting that currently is available in academic journals reflects American politics, some aspects of voter turnout in Europe, particularly in Romania, are discussed to illustrate the differences between turnout problems and ways in which to deal with them in Western democracies and in the emerging Central and Eastern European democracies.

Major Approaches to Nonvoting

The nonvoting literature explores the topic from three angles. The *critical* perspective focuses on the impact of nonvoting on society as a system and on social groups as system components. It is concerned with the democratic principles of representativeness and legitimacy. The *pragmatic* approach deals with the effectiveness and efficiency of activating potential supporters of the campaigning party or candidate and of "passivizing" opposing candidates' supporters. As the critical and the pragmatic schools matured, they adopted a scientific approach and opened their doors to theory building. Their new shared interest in relationships, processes, and group functions bridged their essentially adversarial positions due to values, that is, criticists' primacy of society and pragmatists' primacy of individuals. The *theoretical* approach started from descriptions and evolved in the direction of explanation and prediction.

From a critical perspective, voting is a major form of political participation in a democracy. Therefore, low voter turnout casts doubts on the representativeness and legitimacy of the elected leaders. This has become a serious problem in the United States, which is a low-turnout society by both international and historical standards (Teixeira, 1992, pp. 5-11). Only about one in three American citizens of voting age voted in post-Watergate elections (Boylan, 1991, p. 33), and turnout figures in the United States continue to decrease slowly but steadily, threatening to turn one of the world's leading democracies into a "miniocracy" (Zaccheo, 1976, p. 16).

Immediately after the demise of communism in Central and Eastern Europe, people were thrilled with the potential virtues of pluralistic democracy and were very eager to exert their newly acquired rights and to test in elections the political power gained through legislation. Although uncertainty and confusion were high, political fluidity was perceived by citizens as a challenge and a stimulus for self-assertion. The downfall of communism triggered an explosion of political parties, private newspapers, and political programming on radio and television. The fierce struggle for power among political parties and its intense dramatization by a self-serving media industry interested in changing its image after 50 years of Communist propaganda, attracting audiences, and gaining power over its political clientele resulted in incredibly high levels of media consumption, political interest, partisanship, and participation in the elections. But a regression to the mean is occurring in Eastern Europe. The people who were disgusted with the Communist leaders during the 1980s are now disappointed with the performance of the new elites, and they again tend to withdraw from the political process.

In addition to decreasing voting rates, major critical concerns have been expressed in connection with the uneven rate of turnout decline across social groups, with the decline being sharper with those groups least likely to vote in the first place (i.e., the poor and less educated, minorities, the young) (Teixeira, 1992, p. 80). Critical researchers also looked at consequences of nonvoting in terms of social dysfunctionality. Underprivileged and minority groups were found to be the culprits (i.e., the nonvoters), and at the same time, they were the losers. Such scary "naturally occurring" antidemocratic phenomena directed researchers' attention to the causes of nonvoting and stimulated theoretical efforts toward factor identification, their ranking, and ultimately their articulation in causal models.

Factor inventories developed from the critical perspective include (a) socio-psychological variables of voters and nonvoters and (b) external (i.e., system) variables describing the political machine, the economic environment, the legal framework, the cultural climate with traditions and fads, and the mass media as links between politicians and the public. Although most variables are the same as those considered in pragmatic research, their systematizations from the critical perspective tend to structure turnout variables in such a way as to point to the forces involved in the political game for the purpose of holding them responsible for nonvoting as a threat to democracy. One domain of interest in critical studies on nonvoting is that of political actors' interest in the participation or abstention of certain categories of the population that might account for their actions (i.e., "manipulations") to selectively enhance or reduce voter turnout. Such studies look at the values as well as the hidden and overt agendas of candidates, parties, media, and lobby groups, and they deal with agenda setting (McCombs & Shaw, 1972) as agenda manipulation. An equally important category of aspects from the critical perspective is that of consequences of nonvoting for the sociopolitical system as a whole (in terms of conflicts of interest among social groups and dysfunctionality of specific system substructures). This area of investigation produces "cultural" studies in the field of communication, but mostly political science literature.

The critical approach, which accompanied and fueled race and gender reformist movements in the United States, does not appear to be the dominant paradigm in nonvoter research if we judge by the proportion of critical/pragmatic studies published in academic journals. Increasingly competitive election races convinced parties and individual candidates to invest heavily in expert marketing research capable of addressing the possibility of enlarging candidates' electoral bases by tapping the nonvoter pool as well as the possibility of reducing opposing candidates' electoral bases by at least confusing and disactivating their voters if conversion was unlikely.

One category of turnout factors that pragmatic researchers look at includes the "givens," that is, the *independent variables* of turnout. The inventory of givens usually discussed in turnout studies has developed through converging efforts from both critical and pragmatic quarters. They include (a) eligible voter demographics such as age, gender, ethnicity, marital status, education, occupation, income, social class, and place of residence; measures of social connectedness (i.e., personal relationships and religious, union, political, and other affiliations); and current patterns of media consumption (in terms of source preferences as well as exposure schedule and duration); and (b) system descriptors such as economic indicators that determine both the perception of effectiveness of the economic system and the objective and perceived well-being of various voter groups; the current legislative framework; the political system in place at the time of the campaign (i.e., the system's structure of parties, each with its internal structure in organizational, ideological, and power terms); cultural soft points and idiosyncrasies (e.g., a population's sensitivity to social distance or personal attacks); and the expertise and infrastructure available for the campaign (both in-house resources developed by each party or candidate and external commercial sources including the mass media system, with its own infrastructure, values, routines, current hierarchy of penetration and credibility, and each medium's audience profile).

At any point in time, the givens may be regarded as "constants" that determine predispositions for certain groups to abstain from voting and relative to which campaign strategists estimate the possibility of manipulating the mediating variables of the campaign to influence voter turnout, which is the goal and the ultimate dependent variable.

The *mediating variables* of turnout include (a) targets for intervention such as potential voters' motivation to participate in the political process, both by investing resources of time, effort, and money and by voting (which depends on potential voters' values and interests including interest in politics and election campaigns) related to the sociopolitical system in general (at local, state, and federal levels) and to political actors in particular; potential voters' opinions, beliefs, attitudes, and affects (in terms of valence and intensity) related to the political system and all major political agents engaged in the electoral process (including the candidates and the voters themselves as decision makers); potential voters' degree of leaning toward (or against) one or several candidates; potential voters' opinions, beliefs, and attitudes about a large variety of issues, especially those that have been politicized (i.e., given prominence in the political and media discourse), both traditionally and in the recent past; potential voters' attitudes toward various media and their patterns of media consumption; the patterns of information acquisition, storage, and retrieval as well as of decision making predominant in the major social categories of the voting population (e.g., campaign intervention may be aimed at increasing attention, helping information storage by providing connective cues, switching processing from a peripheral mode to a central/systematic mode, manipulating retrieval through priming, or stimulating group decisions likely to be more risk taking and more stable due to the groupthink phenomenon); the media's current interests and attitudes toward the political process and the political actors engaged in the electoral competition; and (b) means of intervention such as situation maps, roles, and scripts (i.e., means of structuring the electoral process in the desired way = the strategic level); campaign messages (i.e., instruments or conveyors of structure = the production level, including all types of communication, verbal and nonverbal, organized as a flow of information, a sequence of events, or a dissemination of symbolic materials).

Mediating variables have a natural mobility due to their multiple relationships, whose relative importance tend to change spontaneously and fast over time. The efforts of campaign teams are directed toward gaining control over the mediating variables, that is, being able to shape through campaign output those electorate and situation features that account for voting behaviors. This makes the knowledge of potential causes of nonvoting as valuable and useful as the knowledge of means to influence voting behavior.

The "independent"/"mediating" distinction among turnout variables is not clear-cut and absolute. The level of education, for example, can be raised through campaign information to the extent that the targeted group is susceptible to educational messages (which depends on selective exposure and retention) that are related to prior knowledge and attitudes and that are dependent on other variables. The patterns of media consumption also are borderline between given and mediating. They are rather stable but can be altered, at least temporarily, by feeding a certain medium with sensational news or determining a radical change of position of a certain medium, that is, capturing or antagonizing it. As the audience is naturally alert to changes, a radical change seldom fails to be noticed and to cause increased exposure to the medium in question.

Last but not least, *campaign products* (e.g., information, events, tangible gifts) may be regarded as intervening between the givens and the mediating variables of turnout; that is, they are dependent on givens and are antecedents of the mediating variables.

As we can see, the picture of turnout variables is complex and fuzzy, and the variable system is open. Therefore, studies on concrete situations cannot produce recipes for full control and guaranteed success. Researchers can only refine the knowledge of possible variables and relationships relevant to turnout, and they can test and evaluate cause-and-effect models in terms of their descriptive generality (i.e., domain of applicability) and predictive power.

Context Sensitivity and Differential Effects of Nonvoting Factors

Space limitations for this chapter preclude a complete, systematic presentation of nonvoting factors. Some findings about certain variables have been selected for comparison purposes to highlight differences associated with geographic location.

Differential effects of *gender* on voter turnout currently are diminishing in Western democracies, as birth control allowed women to enter the labor market and to assume increasingly equal family and social responsibilities. The right to vote was on the top of feminist movements' agendas. Parties willing to tap the new voter pool simply endorsed feminist agendas, thus co-opting the group. But gender role stereotypes vary tremendously around the world, interacting with economic factors and various aspects of culture, especially religion and education. To the degree a social structure keeps women in inferior positions and politics is a macho game, women tend to be politically alienated. Any major democratization movement will involve bringing women front stage simply because the group includes half of the population. In Romania, for example, women used to distrust and boycott male Communist politics. Among the very first laws abolished after the 1989 revolution was the antiabortion law of 1966 that had forced women under 45 years of age to bear a minimum of four children.

In connection with *age,* life-cycle effects were documented. Older groups tend to have higher turnout rates (Teixeira, 1992, p. 76). This creates an age gap. In the United States, for example, the difference in turnout rates between the 21- to 24-year and the 65- to 74-year age groups was 20 percentage points in 1964. By 1988, turnout had declined by 6 percentage points for people in the 55- to 64-year age group and by 13 percentage points for those in the 21- to 24-year age group, indicating that the gap is widening over time (Teixeira, 1992, p. 76). The 1972 enfranchisement of the 18- to 20-year age group in the United States caused a 5.7% drop in turnout relative to 1968 (Matsusaka, 1995, pp. 105-106),

and every successive 18- to 20-year age group that entered the American electorate since 1972 has voted at a lower rate than the group preceding it (Teixeira,
1992, p. 76). Polltaker Peter Hart voiced a general fear that the United States
might end up with a "lost generation" of voters (quoted in Zaccheo, 1976, p. 16).

In addition to the age gap, a cohort phenomenon was identified in the United
States, with the New Deal generation being consistently more active in elections
than the preceding and subsequent generations (Teixeira, 1992, pp. 75-81).
Culturally distinct cohorts might be explained through education, dominant
philosophy, shared dramatic experiences, and/or large birthrate fluctuations with
economic and cultural consequences. In Romania, for example, the baby boom
caused by the 1966 antiabortion law burdened the poverty-stricken population
with a generation of undesired, ill-fed, unhealthy, improperly educated, nervous,
frustrated, and socially aggressive youth. That generation was the main force of
the 1989 revolution and the mass for political maneuvers in the subsequent
struggle for power. When communism collapsed, those young people were in
their 20s, desperately competing for jobs with their better educated elders.
Political fluidity keeps stimulating their self-assertive and opportunistic intervention in the political process. Reformist political parties in Romania have specialized in targeting the young, whereas leftists were left with the victimized old
generation, threatened with extermination through inadequate pensions and
medicare. This example indicates that age effects on voting are highly contextu-
alized, and this factor does not automatically mean youth abstention, so it requires
a nonstereotypical approach.

Miller (1992) also warns about the difficulty of identifying age group characteristics relevant to voting behavior. He studied the turnout of the American New
Deal generation over time in comparison with that of preceding and subsequent
generations. His conclusion was that only a minor part of generational differences
can be attributed to differences in party identification and social connectedness.
The larger portion of generational turnout differences cannot be accounted for
by a declining sense of political efficacy or citizen duty or by lessened interest in
campaigns and election outcomes (p. 1).

Education is relevant to turnout because it produces cognitive mobilization
(Flickinger & Studlar, 1992, p. 11); that is, it provides information processing
and social skills, enhances citizens' ability to handle bureaucratic obstacles,
increases access to information, and develops people's understanding of complex
social mechanisms (Teixeira, 1992, p. 33). The less educated cannot deal with the
overflow of political information (Campbell, Converse, Miller, & Stokes, 1960,
p. 476); they feel confused and ineffective, and they tend to withdraw from the
political process. According to Palfrey and Poole (1987), individuals with high
levels of political information are more likely to vote, but they tend to be more
extreme than those with low levels of information (p. 511).

Research during the 1990s refined the picture of the relationship between
education and nonvoting. Bennett (1990) argues that a linear relationship no
longer holds. He finds that "nonfinishers" of programs at all levels tend to show
a weaker participation and that age-related issues such as social security and
medicare have stimulated older and less educated people to become more politi-

cally active (p. 56). Flickinger and Studlar (1992) remark that higher education makes people relatively impervious to the influence of short-term factors on their propensity to vote (p. 11).

Education traditionally was found closely related with *income* and perceived class membership, which also are related to occupation. In Romania, under communism, high school education was mandatory, illiteracy was practically nonexistent during the 1980s, and the levels of income were not significantly different between people with and without university degrees. Higher income used to be an attribute of the ruling class of Communist Party leaders and the military on which they relied. After the 1989 revolution, intellectuals (who had felt unappreciated and underpaid under communism) lost ground to entrepreneurs because economic gain was increasingly associated with market mobility, personal adaptability, and "gut feeling" speculations rather than with competitive production based on science and technology. Consequently, Romanian intellectuals threatened with marginalization and poverty, and reluctant to get involved in "dirty" politics, formed a Civic Alliance and then a Civic Alliance Party led by a prominent literary critic. They hoped to attract student support, but the opposition alliance, the Democratic Convention, elected a university professor as a presidential candidate and stole away the electorate of the intellectuals' party. "True" intellectuals in Romania now abstain because of perceived meaninglessness of political participation. They tend to be older and to distance themselves from the "opportunistic," "narrow-minded," and "unprincipled" youth.

Research on economic voting in the United States (e.g., Brody & Sniderman, 1977; Caldeira, Patterson, & Markko, 1985; Wolfinger & Rosenstone, 1980) found that persons experiencing financial difficulties are less likely to vote because the preoccupation with personal economic problems diminishes their attention to political community matters. According to Brody and Sniderman (1977), the ethic of self-reliance in American culture encourages people to regard personal economic problems as their own responsibility and not to expect government to deal with their difficulties (p. 353). Kinder and Kiewiet (1979) hypothesize that economic discontent and political judgments inhabit separate mental domains (p. 523). Rosenstone (1982) proposed a mobilization model that contradicted the cultural approach and predicted that economic difficulty would enhance voting. Southwell (1988) tried to explain the divergent views, emphasized the notion of conditional effects in the theory of economic voting, and hypothesized that personal problems may activate turnout when they are "socially located" (p. 275), that is, when people look outward and make connections between self and society. She found that race and class, but not national unemployment rates, had a significant impact on the changes in voter turnout in the United States from 1974 to 1982 but that personal unemployment still depressed turnout (p. 283). Southwell concluded, "We cannot rely on the conventional wisdom that unemployment and turnout are inversely related. . . . While partisan intensity, age, education, and region retain their strong relationship to turnout, the effects of race, class, and unemployment display more volatility from year to year" (p. 285).

The cultures of Central and Eastern European countries developed under communism in the opposite direction. Whole generations grew up under Communist control and were educated to accept government control and to believe in its legitimacy. After the downfall of communism, when the economies of those countries adopted the free market model, citizens felt betrayed by their governments. Poor economic performance at the national level still is attributed by the population to the incompetence and weakness of elected leaders, not to the capitalist noninterventionist approach. In this context, extremists (both left and right), nationalists, and fundamentalists with dictatorial personalities and inflammatory discourse enjoy large audiences and considerable voter support, especially from underprivileged groups, and often manage to gain parliamentary immunity.

The general wisdom is that low education, low income, and youth depress voting. Teixeira (1992) calls this a "demographic skew in turnout rates" (p. 59). From a psychological perspective, people with internal locus of control, who are self-assertive and have a high sense of self-efficacy (which is generally the case with the rich, the more educated, and the older), tend to attach more meanings and derive more benefits from voting. But Piven and Cloward (1988) noticed that turnout effects of education, income, and age in Western Europe are weaker than in the United States, which means that the high correlation might be specific to the contemporary American electoral system (pp. 115-116).

Occupation and income are believed to mediate personal relevance of social processes, and of the political process in particular, as well as the perception of personal stake and social duty. But Teixeira (1992) argues that involvement in public affairs is both psychologically determined and media based (p. 39), that is, spontaneous and induced. This brings into discussion the impact of the *mass media* on voter turnout.

Reagan (1981) constructed a cumulative index of voting in three U.S. elections between 1976 and 1980 and found it negatively correlated with the use of electronic media (insignificant $r = -.051$ for television, significant $r = -.183$ for radio) and positively correlated with the use of print media (r's between .232 for daily newspapers and .150 for weekly newspapers). A significant negative impact of television viewing also was found by Morgan and Shanahan (1992), but it disappeared under multiple simultaneous controls in 11 out of 14 national samples surveyed by the National Opinion Research Center between 1975 and 1989 in connection with five U.S. presidential elections held between 1972 and 1988. Blumler (1983) conducted a comparative study in six Western European countries and found that exposure on television to the 1976 campaign for the European Parliament elections was a significant predictor of voter turnout in five countries. Wald (1985) tested two path models of effects on voter participation, one based on the closeness hypothesis and the other assuming a selected information flow. In both models, media exposure correlated with turnout at low but significant levels ($r = .13, p < .01$). These and more quantitative data indicate that exposure to the media and to campaigns carried by the media do influence turnout, even if the impact is generally low compared to that of other factors. Research findings corroborate the general impression that because the mass media provide most of the contact people have with candidates for major offices (Boylan, 1991, p. 33), the press is an important player in the electoral process and cannot be omitted from the picture of nonvoting factors.

Habitual exposure to the media is believed to increase political cynicism and ultimately to depress turnout. The most frequent explanation is the newspeople's "gotcha mentality" (Key Porter, quoted in Gordon, 1995), which is a distortion of the watchdog function of the press into an adversarial disposition toward politicians, combining negativism, sensationalism, and scapegoating. This mentality propagates the professional cynicism of most journalists into the public (p. 9). Rieder (1996) observes, "Accentuating the positive is almost a violation of the macho code. It's a sign of terminal naïveté" (p. 6), a rationale and tactic that might serve the journalists well but whose side effect might be the transfer of a negative perceptual frame to the electorate, prejudicing the population against politicians and disengaging citizens from the political process.

The attitudes that filter and frame the information appear to have a stronger impact on turnout than information pure and simple because information never is pure and simple. While endorsing the alienation explanation of decreasing turnout, Wolfinger, Glass, and Squire (1990) emphasize its emotional aspects— "disaffection," "malaise," and "distrust" coming from a perception of failure of the political system, a feeling that it "is rotten or at least unresponsive" (p. 554). In addition, Weaver (1994) observes that voters also are sensitive to and resent the joint efforts of politicians and the media to impose their own agendas on the electorate, so instead of involvement, the outcome of such efforts is more likely to be voter alienation (p. 351).

Worries about the influence of media content on voting through gatekeeping, framing, agenda setting, editorializing, persuasion, priming, and the like are supplemented by concerns with the differentiated effects of the various media. The conventional wisdom is that print has a positive effect on turnout, whereas broadcast media (especially television) have a negative impact. Gans (1990) casts a heavy but overgeneralizing blame on television, claiming (with no empirical support),

> It has served to atomize our society; weaken our institutions; reduce participation by making people spectators and consumers rather than involved participants; decrease reading, comprehension, and conversation; and increase public confusion. It gives information in undifferentiated blips and by highlights of the most visually exciting. It has, in addition, established unreal expectations for our political system by creating heroes and as quickly destroying them and by offering in its advertising panaceas that give the society a belief it can have equally rapid panaceas. (p. 536)

In the case of television, the negative aspects of coverage for which journalists may be held responsible are aggravated by medium-specific problems—the priority of the visual, the potential of contrasts and emotionality to arrest and hold attention, the speedy pacing and kaleidoscopic structure of content, and the "please all for advertisers' sake" orientation. Gans (1990) lists among the consequences of television's both technical and economic constraints the medium's inability to focus on more than two candidates at a time, its disinterest in substance and issues and its preference for drama, its arrogance in predicting outcomes of political processes by polling and controlling campaigns, its low sensitivity to both politicians and the public, and its destruction of the sense of history and the political process (p. 536). To these, Hart (1996) adds the fragmentary, juxtaposed, kaleidoscopic presentation resulting in "cameo politics" (p. 109). Gitlin (1996) describes television coverage as "an extended 'horizontal' cacophony," where "significance bleeds from one story into another" (pp. 83-84). Politicians are willing to put up with all this because television has the advantage of instant and massive penetration, and they have chosen to adapt the political process to fit the medium. The question is, "To what gains or costs to the public?" Here, we address the effects only in terms of voter turnout.

As early as 1962, Campbell raised the question of whether television reshaped politics. He looked at some statistics for an answer and observed that radio produced a revolution before the advent of television. Radio broadcasts of campaign events were put on the air in the United States in 1924 but did not achieve full coverage of the electorate until after the 1932 election. Between the elections of 1932 and 1940, the turnout records jumped more than 8 percentage points, and the off-year congressional vote increased even more markedly, from 33.7% in 1930 to 44.1% in 1938. Campbell's (1962) explanations were that, on the one hand, radio reached the less educated and the less involved sections of the population and that, on the other, this was a time of depression and political urgency. When television was introduced during the late 1940s, it was expected to stimulate political interest and participation. Indeed, according to Campbell,

> In the presidential elections of 1952, 1956, and 1960, the turnouts were considerably higher than in the elections of 1944 and 1948, but if we drop back to the period just before the war, we find that turnouts in 1936 and 1940 were almost as high as they have been in the most recent elections. There has been a small proportionate increase in the presidential vote during the television era, although it has fluctuated and, at its lowest point in 1956 (60.6%) [relative to 1962, the year when the article was written], exceeded by only a percentage point the high of the pretelevision period. (p. 11)

The small and inconsistent impact of the new medium on turnout prompted Campbell to ask three key questions (which may be rephrased and asked again whenever a new medium enters the market): "Was there a virgin area of the population not being reached by the mass media when television came on the scene? Was television as effectively different from existing media as radio had been a generation earlier? Was there an unsatisfied demand for political communication in the electorate when television appeared?" (p. 13). Campbell's answer to the first question was no. The answer to the other two questions seems to be yes, television is different (its specificity was briefly presented earlier), and television very likely meets higher and/or different needs from a uses-and-gratifications perspective. First and foremost, television has the spectacular capacity to accommodate politicians as actors and the electorate as a willing-to-be-entertained audience, which results in the showiness of today's politics, meaning staging on the politicians' side and passivity and vicarious experience on the electorate's side. Hart (1996) argues that television produces an overwhelming passivity in viewers even when making them feel politically involved (p. 109). Television has the potential to project the electorate into a virtual reality while the real political game may be played off-stage, in an invisible and inaccessible reality. According to Hart, "By making politics easy, television has made citizenship easy, and that is a dangerous thing" because "people are at their most arrogant when they are being ocular: 'I've seen it, so it must be true'" (p. 110). This view is not new; we can trace it back to the 1940s, when Lazarsfeld and Merton (1948) launched the concept of the narcotizing dysfunction of the media. People "drift lazily across the [televised] political landscape" and "pay less and less attention" (Hart, 1996, p. 118). Watching becomes more and more habitual and functions as a surrogate of direct political participation (p. 114).

Contemporary viewers' laziness and superficiality in Western democracies is (paradoxically) aggravated by higher education that brings about a growing reliance of the electorate on the power, neutrality, and infallibility of statistics. During the early 1990s in United States, the chance that a projection could be wrong dropped below 1 in 200 (St. Thomas, 1993, p. 2). What can we reasonably expect a voter to do when confronted not only with early election night projections but also with preelection estimations that tell people who will win before anybody has a chance to cast a vote? Potential voters who are satisfied with the projections very likely will say "Why bother if my candidate is going to win anyway," whereas those who are discontent probably will shrug their shoulders and choose not to fight a lost battle. Both categories are susceptible to developing a belief that voting is a mere ritual and that an individual vote cannot change anything anymore. Added to the already mentioned general dissatisfaction with politicians, this feeling of technical powerlessness and individual insignificance can only aggravate alienation and decrease turnout.

Moreover, most election-related polling conducted or sponsored by the media is not issue centered but rather outcome focused, and it promotes a "horse race" style of coverage and campaigning (Barber, 1992; Dinkin, 1989; Patterson & McClure, 1976). According to Patterson and McClure (1976),

> A presidential election is surely a super contest with all the elements that are associated with spectacular sports events: huge crowds, rabid followers, dramatic do-or-die battles, winners and losers. It is this part of the election that the networks emphasize. . . . In its own way, a presidential election has all the pageantry, color, glamour, and decisiveness of the Kentucky Derby. . . . The opinion polls are cited frequently, indicating the candidates' positions on the track. The strengths and weaknesses of all the participants are constantly probed, providing an explanation for their position and creating drama about how the race might change as they head down the home stretch. The feverish activity that accompanies the campaign provides the back-barn setting that lends color and "inside dope" to the coverage. . . . Crowds are . . . testimony to the drawing power of the candidates and certain proof of what is at stake as they near the finish line. (pp. 40-42)

The image of the electoral process created by television coverage is not one of dignity but rather one of gambling. Some voters might not like horse race/gambling politics and might not wish to be involved in it.

During the 1990s, American media started to educate the public about the polling techniques used to create statistical pictures that match candidates' campaign goals. Such materials conveyed to the electorate an additional discouraging message that "in practice, American politics has come to be run by full-time insiders" (Boylan, 1991, p. 35). Hitchens (1992) provides a list of "classical" types of polling manipulations, going from "piss them off," rush them, confound them tactics to sampling, interview timing, suggestive or confusing question phrasing, and answer option design. To these, we can add choice of statistical procedures, choice and use of control variables, and other technicalities. But the essence is the same as that highlighted by Hitchens: "A good pollster is like a good attorney, and [he or she] fights for the result that the commissioning party expects or needs" (p. 51). A poll is successful to the extent that it shapes "fluidity," that is, the "chaos and ignorance" that pollsters (and the politicians behind them) seek to control, to shape into a pattern, and to build up as "momentum." Hitchens bitterly but humorously argues that "money and press coverage follows the polls as doggedly as trade follows the flag; speed is of the first importance" (p. 52).

This new reality of poll campaigning, on the one hand, dazzles voters with a huge array of hard data (most of which are irrelevant to them) and, on the other, elicits bandwagon (Lazarsfeld, 1944) or spiral-of-silence (Noelle-Neumann, 1984) effects, depending on whether estimations and projections match voters' preferences. Information overload shifts a voter's attention from analyzing the meanings of the data toward checking his or her own position relative to the general trend. If the voter "fits," then he or she might be stimulated to go along or bandwagon; if the voter does not fit, then he or she will either abstain from voting or "adjust" to avoid social marginalization (Noelle-Neumann, 1984).

One more issue that has just started to kindle researchers' interest is the development of new media technologies, and their potential for interactive political communication, that is generally expected to stimulate and increase participation in political decision making. Gitlin (1996), nevertheless, is skeptical about new media's potential for strengthening democracy. He argues that Internet and other linkages based on affinity and selectivity are conducive to "public sphericules" rather than a large forum for public debate (p. 81), and at the same time, they will deepen the "gulf" between the information saturated and the information deprived, aggravating the class division between politocracy and the rest (p. 82). Although the new forms of political participation made possible by new technologies (e.g., computer-based political communication, teleconferencing, televoting) might revolutionize politics and totally replace (in the future) the current system of voting, thus substantially reducing abstention, such forms of political communication have not yet reached the mass level, and their use so far has been merely experimental.

The general demobilizing effect of the mass media undermines both traditional and emerging democracies. It should be noted, nevertheless, that at the incipient stages of democratization, while the new political agents are struggling to build up constituencies and while the balance of power is uncertain and changing, the mass media are in a favorable position to assume a stronger role in directing the political show and game, and they tend to play politicians against one another to produce dramatic clashes that increase media consumption and reliance. Ball-Rokeach and DeFleur's (1976) dependency model explains the phenomenon through people's acute anxiety and need for information under conditions of fast change and high uncertainty.

In spite of such temporary upsurges in political concerns and media reliance, the key words in popular analyses of mass reactions to national political crises remain cynicism, alienation, rejection, and apathy (Miller, 1992, p. 5). Looking at historical trends, Teixeira (1992) found that partial or total distrust of government in the United States increased from 22% in 1964 to 74% in 1980 (p. 31). Flickinger and Studlar (1992) refer to a similar situation in Western Europe, where interest in politics reportedly is rising and citizens are becoming interested in a growing range of issues, but at the same time, there is a growing dissatisfaction with democracy as people see politicians' activity as less satisfactory and their own political action (including voting) as less relevant (pp. 8-9). Consequently, turnout in Western Europe is either fluctuating within a previously established range or declining (pp. 1, 3).

The situation in Central and Eastern Europe is different. The balance of power among political forces still is unsettled, and most politicians do their utmost to pull down the existing political structures and to push for early elections, hoping to improve their positions at a faster pace. This creates dramatic tension that is eagerly amplified by self-serving media. The electorate in the former Communist countries of Europe is more frequently exposed to political crises than are Western voters, and the former is maintained in a state of quasi-permanent decision-making alert. People's eagerness to vote and change politicians in positions of power has become "chronic." It seems that the population has been conditioned to enjoy effecting changes that politicians keep proposing. A continual splitting up and merging of parties creates an illusion of novelty and resourcefulness of politics despite the almost closed pool of politicians, and it retards the development of voter cynicism toward the system and estrangement from the political process.

A seminal qualitative study by Rosenberg (1954), based on 70 unstructured interviews with American nonvoters, established an essential link between individual and institutional factors of voter turnout. Rosenberg found that political participation tended to be inhibited by (a) social restraint (caused by perceived threats to interpersonal harmony, occupational success, or self-image); (b) feelings of futility of political activity (associated with perceived personal inadequacy, insignificance, or weakness); unmanageability of the political machine and of political forces; unresponsiveness of elected representatives; remoteness of the decision-making process and anonymity of the centers of power; the gap between ideal and reality, that is, between the factual and normative orders of society; no real differences among parties and candidates; and (c) the absence of spurs to action, more precisely, the psychologically noncompelling nature of politics, the lack of immediate satisfactions and of noninstrumental gratifications, the media focus on politicians and systemic problems rather than on voters' personal needs, and the fact that the outcomes of political activity do not satisfy individual urgent and direct needs (p. 349). Rosenberg's conclusion was that "many people are not politically apathetic" (p. 366), and he called for research on what can be done to get them involved.

The importance of contextual factors cannot be overemphasized. According to Piven and Cloward (1988), the political context determines whether the demographic or sociopolitical factors will have a significant effect on participation and just what those effects will be (p. 117). The same thing can be said about the legislative, economic, and even cultural factors. Yet, why do we tend to consider voter-related factors first? Leighley and Nagler (1992) compared individual influences on voter turnout (age, race, gender, education, family income, marital status, union membership, and occupation) and systemic influences (closing, party competition, state education, per capita income, state union strength, and presidential margin). Based on data from the 1984 presidential elections in the United States, those authors concluded that individual correlates of voting are unaffected by the inclusion of systemic variables and that individual demographic factors are the predominant predictors of turnout, whereas the systemic factors are at best marginal in importance for predicting political participation (p. 735).

Other researchers credit *institutional factors* of nonvoting with stronger but, to some extent, mutually canceling effects. Based on aggregate data, Kleppner and Baker (1980) showed that turnout in the United States was advantaged about 5% by political attitudes but disadvantaged 13% by the party system and institutional factors and up to 14% by the registration laws. Moreover, attempts by Kim, Petrocik and Enokson (1975) to disentangle the effects of rules, party competition, and socioeconomic characteristics showed that besides main effects, interactions occurred between contextual variables and individual characteristics.

One of the most powerful contextual factors that affects voter turnout is *electoral legislation.* Variables found particularly relevant to nonvoting are unicameral or bicameral legislative bodies, simple direct vote or national election proportional representation, frequency of elections, election levels and simultaneity, registration requirements and procedures, workday or weekend elections, and the like. Rosenberg (1954) pointed out that electoral periodicity is not resonant with human reactions, and citizens resent discontinuity of control (pp. 358-359). This psychological factor makes new media technologies very attractive for developing a direct and permanent involvement of constituencies in decisional processes. Communication technologies may revolutionize not only the voting but also the whole political structure by reducing the role of periodical elections and power delegation.

According to Piven and Cloward (1988), various features of the electoral system affect different groups differently. Legal and administrative barriers to voting impinge less on the well-off and well educated than they do on the poor and uneducated (p. 119).

Another crucial category of turnout variables is that of features of the *political structure* at the national and party levels. Multipartyism and the complexity of governing coalitions are conducive to voter confusion and abstention. On the other hand, intensifying competition and convergence toward the market ideal results in candidate indistinctiveness and increases the importance of special candidate features likely to strike a sensitive chord with a large group of voters. In another development, consistently low turnout has enhanced the power of cohesive, active support groups that often are decisive for the election outcome. Parties that control such groups might find general abstention advantageous and might turn it into a campaign goal. Piven and Cloward (1988) appreciate that the institutional arrangements are crafted precisely to demobilize the groups whose politics are threatening and disruptive. They argue that the political system determines whether participation is predicated on class-related resources and attitudes (pp. 119-120).

A controversial aspect of the electoral climate believed to affect turnout is competitiveness, that is, race *closeness*. It enhances the dramatic quality of a race, generates excitement, and is intuitively expected to stimulate participation. But Wald (1985) compared two models of turnout decision, under the selective information flow hypothesis and under the closeness-turnout hypothesis, and found perceived closeness insignificantly related to turnout under both hypotheses. Knack (1997) also challenged the idea of closeness effects, arguing that no closeness-related differences can be discerned in the general downward trend of turnout in the United States from 1960 to 1988 (p. 25). Moreover, closeness did not play a significant role in the 6% increase in turnout from 1988 to 1992.

Researchers are unanimous in emphasizing penetration of party organizations, *strength of alignment* between parties and social groups, *political mobilization,* and the quality of contacts between party and citizens (Teixeira, 1992, p. 53) as means of stimulating potential supporters to vote. Teixeira (1992) complains that in the United States, party organization is very weak (especially at the local level), and the links between parties and social groups are relatively blurry (p. 17). But the issue is not whether or not parties make such efforts or whether or not the efforts are successful. The major question is whether, under intense competition and budget limitations, the contacts between a party and social groups have superior efficiency compared to other campaign activities (e.g., spots, sponsorship of sports events). Such strategic questions can only be answered within a systemic approach.

Theories and Models
That Cast Light on Nonvoting

Several communication theories have been used as a framework for more or less critical approaches to voter abstention. For example, the effects of education, class/income, and age on turnout may be explained in the light of Tichenor, Donohue, and Olien's (1970) knowledge gap theory. Those authors posited that highly correlated demographics such as social class, education, occupation, and income, usually expressed synthetically through a socioeconomic status index, interact with the mass mediated flow of information and produce a knowledge gap, that is, a differential growth in knowledge. On the other hand, advertising-driven television tends to target upscale audiences. Consequently, lower classes find most of the information carried on television irrelevant to them, and they gradually cease to pay attention to it. Brantgarde (1983) found that higher socioeconomic status groups in Sweden tend to assume the role of generating and disseminating information, which indicates that the knowledge gap practically results in an influence gap. Brantgarde's conclusion echoes Sallach's (1974) media hegemony theory that describes the mass media as controlled by the dominant class and pictures them as instruments used by that class to exert control over the rest of society. Such views are complemented by Ball-Rokeach and DeFleur's (1976) media dependency theory that predicts higher reliance on mass-mediated information about aspects of social (and political) life to which citizens have no direct access. Media dependency is expected to increase in times of change, conflict, uncertainty, and insecurity, which have become the "normal" conditions of contemporary life in many parts of the world. These theories push mass media front stage as key players in the social process in general and the political process in particular. Actually, the communication theorists of the 1970s revamped Lippmann's (1922) idea that people do not react to social realities but rather react to pictures in their heads, derived from the symbolic world produced by the press. This line of thought suggests that when certain categories of population get estranged from the political process and do not exercise their right to vote, the mass media need to be examined as a possible flawed link between politicians and the electorate.

The demobilizing effect of the media might be one answer to the "puzzle of participation" in America (Brody, 1978), where both legislation improvements facilitating registration and the steady rise in the level of education failed to reverse the decline in turnout rates.

Olsen (1972) championed the idea of increasing voting turnout by getting people involved in any organized social activity (p. 318). The mobilization version of the social participation theory predicts that involvement in voluntary, special interest, nonpolitical associations increases members' information, social interaction, and leadership skills; makes salient the public affairs political issues; and provides resources. The mediation version of the theory posits that associations give political elites a channel for contacting constituencies. In Olsen's research, the Social Participation Combined Index correlated significantly with voting turnout (mean eta = .40), and the correlation remained significant after controlling for age, education, media and direct party contacts, and political orientation (p. 330). Olsen argued that political orientations are intervening variables and concluded that once they are partialed out as an independent factor, the dimension of social participation becomes the most important predictor of voting (p. 331).

A warning is in order here. Diffusion-of-innovation studies (1940s-1960s) also emphasized the importance of social connectedness and networking, but political and organizational studies on groupthink (e.g., Janis & Mann, 1987) revealed the potential of group membership to modify individual decisions and actions toward internal conformism and external risk taking. When potential voters are targeted in organized groups, the dynamics of effects should be expected to differ from effects on unstructured pools of independent voters.

On the pragmatic side of turnout research, the massive efforts made during the late 1970s and early 1980s, mostly by the National Coalition for Black Voter participation and by the Republican Party to "get out the vote," managed to raise registration by only 2.5% between 1980 and 1984 and to increase turnout by only 0.7% (Piven & Cloward, 1988, p. 181). Other examples are the "motor voter" registration programs at the state level between 1988 and 1992 that accounted for less than 1% of the 6% turnout increase in 1992 (Knack, 1997, p. 30). These facts indicate that the American electorate is resistant to organizational pressures; therefore, internal processes, especially personal motivation, should become the focus of researchers' and strategists' attention. On the other hand, research on campaigns that addressed nonvoter variables individually points to the generally low effectiveness of such approaches, which invites the alternative of a system approach.

The preferred method for investigating turnout factors during the 1980s was the multivariate analysis (Cassel & Hill, 1981; Cassel & Luskin, 1988; Shaffer, 1981). The purpose of such studies was to simplify the picture of possible causes of nonvoting and to identify the most powerful predictors. Abramson and Aldrich (1982) found the best predictors of turnout to be the decline in partisanship and political efficacy. Shaffer (1981) and Kleppner (1982) added age to the other two. But Cassel and Luskin (1988) warned that models with few variables gain in generality at the expense of explanatory power because they do not account for most of the turnout decline (p. 1321). The situation seems to be worse when researchers address turnout increase. Knack (1997), for example, could account for only 2 percentage points of the 6% increase in U.S. presidential election turnouts between 1988 and 1992. On the other hand, the explanatory power shrinks as we add variables that have acted to increase turnout, and the burden of explanation drifts away from partisanship and political efficacy as we add other variables (Cassel & Luskin, 1988, p. 1327). A compounding problem in recent times might be the change in the relative weight of nonvoting factors that accompanies the political dealignment tendency in the United States. These observations explain why research on nonvoting factors needs to be an ongoing process, and there is no fixed and universally applicable formula for anticipating the rate of abstention. Yet, Flickinger and Studlar (1992) express doubts about the usefulness of such efforts:

> Is there a distinctive explanation for observed turnout decline? . . . No single factor emerges with a strong claim. Turnout patterns appear to be the product of a complex interplay of forces—some exercising a boosting effect and others a depressing effect. . . . It is difficult to generate a common multivariate model to provide an adequate explanation across all countries and across both individual and aggregate levels. (p. 14)

Turnout prediction algorithms are based on regressions on a wide range of factors susceptible to depressing turnout. What one finds in this type of analysis depends on the input variables. Petrocik's (1991) algorithm, for example, focused on voter variables. His research showed that the single best correlate of voting is stated intention to vote (p. 644). He improved Traugott and Tucker's (1984) technical approach by introducing a correction for respondents' inflated professed intentions to vote. That correction enhanced by 50% the predictive power of the method. According to Petrocik's (1991) findings, the American citizens least likely to vote, stated intentions notwithstanding, are those least typical for the modal middle class American—recent residents of communities who are less educated, lower income, younger, less religiously observant, Black, not in stable family situations, and living in the South (p. 644).

Merrifield's (1993) purpose was different. He was not interested in turnout prediction but rather was interested in identifying ways in which to increase turnout. Consequently, his input variables were very different. He used political and institutional independent variables known to have an impact on turnout (e.g., line item veto, debt limits, balanced budget requirements, elasticity of income and sales tax revenue, number of legislators, bi- or unicameral state legislature, nonpartisan elections). Merrifield developed an econometric model to assess the effectiveness of these variables in reducing nonvoting. His model included economic, demographic, and even physical (e.g., weather) control variables. Merrifield's empirical findings supported the hypothesis that nonvoting can be reduced by eliminating constraints on voters' and/or elected decision makers' powers (p. 659).

The most popular approach in designing pragmatic turnout models is economic. It posits that although voting is a low-cost activity, it involves some investment of time and effort in registration, collecting and processing information, and ultimately casting the ballots. As to the benefits of voting, they are available to everyone, voters and nonvoters alike. Because the probability of a lone individual's vote affecting an election outcome is minuscule, the concept of making a difference in terms of election results is not enough to account for the force that drives citizens to vote. As observed by Teixeira (1992), most of the expected value is expressive or symbolic (p. 12). The act of voting becomes worthwhile to the extent it has meanings that are associated with the values cherished by individuals, which explains the huge intervention potential of campaigns to guide voters' understanding of the political situation and of their role in it. Moon (1992, p. 124) also recognized the importance of noninstrumental factors and extended the early outcome-contingent models of turnout (Downs, 1957; Riker & Ordeshook, 1968) to include consumptive benefits derived from the act of participating (e.g., sense of self-efficacy, partisanship, and solidarity; satisfaction of exercising one's prerogatives and fulfilling one's duty).

Within the value-based marketing framework, Teixeira (1992) proposed a historical explanation of turnout decline in the United States, arguing that various factors influenced turnout simultaneously in opposite directions and that their intensity varied over time, resulting in fluctuating turnout rates. Legislative reforms facilitated voter registration, which helped to improve participation. On the other hand, major-minor party fusionism reduced party competition and deflated turnout rates. But the key negative factors, according to Teixeira, were the decay of party mobilization (i.e., the weakening of links between parties and voters) and the weakening of alignment between parties and social groups. These organizational aspects of political life are believed to be the main cause of the weakening feeling of civic duty and of the diminishing perceived benefits of voting (p. 22). According to the same author, the turnout decline in Western democracies is aggravated by a social trend that we can do little to counteract—the decay of social connectedness in general (i.e., weakening family, religious, and local community ties due to increased population mobility and changing societal and personal values).

When Carter (1984) examined the effects of early projections on voter turnout in the 1980 U.S. presidential elections, using as a framework Downs's (1957) expected utility model and Ferejohn and Fiorina's (1974) minimax regret model, he anticipated that postannouncement turnout would be depressed by the publicized estimations because of perceived irrelevance of personal vote (i.e., instrumental utility) and loss of uncertainty-related excitement (i.e., consumption/ entertainment utility). Carter's hypothesis was not supported, so he further hypothesized that voting is driven primarily by civic duty, that is, fulfilling an ethical obligation and/or avoiding social opprobrium (p. 200).

One of the most valuable attempts to synthesize and articulate existing knowledge into a comprehensive model of voting turnout that includes the media, among other factors, belongs to Dennis (1991), who classified explanations of turnout into three groups: atheoretical theories (based mostly on electorate demographics), alienationist theories (including the media as a cause of political cynicism and abstention), and rationalist or economic theories (which assume voters' evaluation of the costs and returns of voting). Dennis tested the alienationist and rationalist models for predictive power and noticed that they were significantly correlated (phi = .486), which suggested a substantive overlap in the two theories. Together with the atheoretical demographics, the alienationist and rationalist variables in Dennis's study accounted for as much as 54% of total turnout variance, which indicates that a three-pronged approach is highly effective. But the more complex the system of turnout variables, the lower the significance of each variable. In Dennis's three-pronged model, for example, the media factor ("information motivation") was an insignificant predictor of voting, although it predicted political alienation at beta = .14, (p = .02), and the alienation block of variables entered first in the regression equation accounted for 35% of total turnout variance (N = 275).

Recent developments in voter turnout theory were geared toward synthesizing the market and information approaches. Matsusaka (1995) embedded the information theory in the standard rational voter theory (p. 112) and proposed a rational voter model based on utility maximization under limited information conditions. Looking at the costs of information acquisition, he found that married people enjoy economies of scale, education and age improve information processing, and longtime residence in a community ensures better contextual knowledge (pp. 93-94). Matsusaka's assumption was that the consumption payoff to an informed vote should exceed the payoff to an uninformed vote (p. 97). He posited that the decision to vote depends on a person's confidence, which depends on his or her general knowledge and raw information; the contribution of new information to the decision depends on the clarity of received signals (p. 98). Matsusaka's model can account for the low turnout of youth, for the widening participation gap due to a widening knowledge gap, for the effects of generation-related disillusionment (e.g., the depreciation of the American model of society due to the Vietnam war, the Watergate scandal, and other scandals, aggravated periodically by economic difficulties), for the effects of the decline in party affiliation, and for the effects of increasing political "turbulence" (pp. 108-110). Matsusaka highlighted a fundamental difference between the cynicism explanation and the information theory explanation of declining turnout. According to his information model, citizens abstain not because of social and political alienation but rather because they do not feel capable of making prudent decisions (p. 110), and the act of voting under high uncertainty becomes meaningless. Matsusaka's information model of turnout appears to be more consistent with evidence that citizen duty in the United States remained high and constant over the period of turnout decline (Brody, 1978).

The latest wave of economic-informational models explains phenomena unaccounted for by cynicism models—the facts that democratic and attitudinal predispositions can be offset by campaign stimuli (Piven & Cloward, 1988, p. 116) and that Western citizens are not irrecoverably apathetic and do respond to "good" campaigns. The pragmatic value of such models resides in their explication and operationalization of "goodness" as information clarity and consistency and in their emphasis on the need for a new message to fit the knowledge previously acquired by the audience and to be logically connected with the information simultaneously delivered by other sources.

Dealing With Nonvoting in the Future

Politicians around the world constantly watch American politics for guidance and inspiration. To a large extent, what is being done and what works in the United States tends to become the rule, or at least a desideratum, for younger democracies. The underlying assumption is that the campaign models produced by the biggest financial resources and the best technology must be the fastest and surest ways to win.

Essentially, the new American campaign approach is money based. Money buys expertise and access to mass media, and success is a matter of efficient investment, that is, minimizing costs and maximizing benefits. Consequently, electoral battles ceased to be waged on a wide front; they tend to concentrate around candidates' vulnerable features, critical issues, and audience susceptibilities. Voters no longer are politically involved in the traditional sense; party affiliation and activity have become almost irrelevant. Voters are consumers who buy political services offered by competing specialized providers, who rely heavily on marketing expertise.

Foreigners who look at the American standard of living as the ultimate outcome and effectiveness measure of the American political system come to admire, envy, and imitate the American market model including its political sector. Imitators tend to ignore not only their own disproportionately and dysfunctionally smaller resources but also the invisible part of the system—intangibles such as traditions and culture. The result is that imitators cannot match the research that underlies the success of American politicians, and they transplant ready-made scenarios that often prove discordant with local culture and boomerang against the most "Westernized" candidates. This appears to have been the case of President Iliescu of Romania, who sought reelection in 1996. His campaign manager hired American consultants (Dobrescu, 1997), who recommended an aggressive approach, with negative spots about both the second- and third-ranking presidential candidates and threatening citizens with possible consequences of electing any of the incumbent's challengers (pp. 178, 180). But Romanians historically were fed up with threats from Communist leaders, and after the first ballot, most supporters of opposition candidates—who had been estranged by Iliescu's negative campaign—chose to vote for the opposition leader.

As the American campaign model evolves toward tactical strikes, which might target the increasingly numerous nonvoter groups on the condition of superior efficiency relative to other targets, the emerging democracies gradually are learning that American recipes might be more costly and less effective than home-researched and developed campaigns. Although the general global practice seems to develop in the tactical direction set by the American campaign experts, the choices for targets and means are likely to follow locally generated and culturally idiosyncratic algorithms. This trend will escalate the costs of consulting. The visual media appear to retain their preferred status with campaign strategists, which will further enhance the role of emotionality and nonverbal communication, will increase the costs of sleek production, and will cause the market value of advertising talent to skyrocket.

References

Abramson, P. R., & Aldrich, J. H. (1982). The decline of electoral participation in America. *American Political Science Review, 76,* 502-521.

Ball-Rokeach, S. J., & DeFleur, M. L. (1976). A dependency model of mass media effects. *Communication Research, 3*(1), 3-21.

Barber, J. D. (1992). *The pulse of politics: Electing presidents in the media age.* New Brunswick, NJ: Transaction Publishers.

Bennett, S. E. (1990). The education-turnout "puzzle" in recent U.S. national elections. *Electoral Studies, 9*(1), 51-58.

Blumler, J. G. (1983). Communication and turnout. In G. Blumler (Ed.), *Communicating to voters* (pp. 181-209). Beverly Hills, CA: Sage.

Boylan, J. (1991). Where have all the people gone? Reflections on voter alienation and the challenge it poses to the press. *Columbia Journalism Review, 30,* 33-35.

Brantgarde, L. (1983). The information gap and municipal politics in Sweden. *Communication Research, 10,* 367-373.

Brody, R. A. (1978). The puzzle of political participation in America. In A. King (Ed.), *The new American political system* (pp. 278-324). Washington, DC: American Enterprise Institute for Public Policy Research.

Brody, R. A., & Sniderman, P. M. (1977). From life space to polling place: The relevance of personal concerns for voting behavior. *British Journal of Political Science, 7,* 337-360.

Caldeira, G. A., Patterson, S. C., & Markko, G. A. (1985). The mobilization of voters in congressional elections. *Journal of Politics, 47,* 490-509.

Campbell, A. (1962). Has television reshaped politics? *Columbia Journalism Review, 1,* 10-13.

Campbell, A., Converse, P. E., Miller, W., & Stokes, D. (1960). *The American voter.* New York: John Wiley.

Carter, J. R. (1984). Early projections and voter turnout in the 1980 presidential election. *Public Choice, 43,* 195-202.

Cassel, C. A., & Hill, D. B. (1981). Explanations of turnout decline. *American Politics Quarterly, 9,* 181-194.

Cassel, C. A., & Luskin, R. C. (1988). Simple explanations of turnout decline. *American Political Science Review, 82,* 1321-1330.

Dennis, J. (1991). Theories of turnout: An empirical comparison of alienationist and rationalist perspectives. In W. Crotty (Ed.), *Political participation and American democracy* (pp. 23-65). Westport, CT: Greenwood.

Dinkin, R. J. (1989). *Campaigning in America: A history of election practices.* Westport, CT: Greenwood.

Dobrescu, P. (1997). *Iliescu contra Iliescu.* Bucuresti, Romania: Diogene.

Downs, A. (1957). *An economic theory of democracy.* New York: Harper & Row.

Ferejohn, J., & Fiorina, M. (1974). The paradox of not voting: A decision theoretic analysis. *American Political Science Review, 68,* 525-536.

Flickinger, R. S., & Studlar, D. T. (1992). The disappearing voters? Exploring declining turnout in Western European elections. *West European Politics, 15*(2), 1-16.

Gans, C. (1990). Remobilizing the American voter. *Policy Studies Review, 9,* 527-538.

Gitlin, T. (1996). Television's anti-politics: Surveying the wasteland. *Dissent, 43*(1), 78-85.

Gordon, C. (1995, June 19). The real threat to Canada's future. *Maclean's,* p. 9.

Hart, R. P. (1996). Easy citizenship: Television's curious legacy. *Annals of the American Academy of Political and Social Science, 546,* 109-119.

Hitchens, C. (1992, April). Voting in the passive voice: What polling has done to American democracy. *Harper's Magazine,* pp. 45-52.

Janis, I. L., & Mann, L. (1987). Admiral Kimmel at Pearl Harbor: A victim of groupthink? In D. L. Yarwood (Ed.), *Public administration, politics, and the people* (pp. 251-261). New York: Longman.

Kim, J.-O., Petrocik, J. R., & Enokson, S. N. (1975). Voter turnout among the American states: Systemic and individual components. *American Political Science Review, 69,* 107-131.

Kinder, D., & Kiewiet, D. R. (1979). Economic discontent and political behavior. *American Journal of Political Science, 23,* 495-527.

Kleppner, P. (1982). *Who voted? The dynamics of electoral turnout, 1870-1980.* New York: Praeger.

Kleppner, P., & Baker, S. C. (1980). The impact of voter registration requirements on electoral turnout, 1900-1916. *Journal of Political and Military Sociology, 8*(2), 17-19.

Knack, S. (1997). The reappearing American voter: Why did turnout rise in '92? *Electoral Studies, 16*(1), 17-32.

Lazarsfeld, P. F. (1944). *The people's choice: How the voter makes up his mind in a presidential campaign.* New York: Duell, Sloan, and Pearce.

Lazarsfeld, P., & Merton, R. (1948). Mass communication, popular taste, and organized social action. In W. Schramm (Ed.), *Mass communications* (pp. 429-503). Urbana: University of Illinois Press.

Leighley, J. E., & Nagler, J. (1992). Individual and systemic influences on turnout: Who votes? 1984. *Journal of Politics, 54,* 718-740.

Lippmann, W. (1922). *Public opinion.* New York: Macmillan.

Matsusaka, J. G. (1995). Explaining voter turnout patterns: An information theory. *Public Choice, 84,* 91-117.

McCombs, M. E., & Shaw, D. L. (1972). The agenda-setting function of mass media. *Public Opinion Quarterly, 36,* 176-187.

McLeod, J. M., & McDonald, D. G. (1985). Beyond simple exposure: Media orientations and their impact on political processes. *Communication Research, 12*(1), 3-33.

Merrifield, J. (1993). The institutional and political factors that influence voter turnout. *Public Choice, 77,* 657-667.

Miller, W. E. (1992). The puzzle transformed: Explaining declining turnout. *Political Behavior, 14,* 1-44.

Moon, D. (1992). The determinants of turnout in presidential elections: An integrative model accounting for information. *Political Behavior, 14,* 123-140.

Morgan, M., & Shanahan, J. (1992). Television and voting 1972-1989. *Electoral Studies, 11*(1), 3-20.

Noelle-Neumann, E. (1984). *The spiral of silence: Public opinion, our social skin.* Chicago: University of Chicago Press.

Olsen, M. E. (1972). Social participation and voting turnout: A multivariate analysis. *American Sociological Review, 37,* 317-333.

Palfrey, T. R., & Poole, K. T. (1987). The relationship between information, ideology, and voting behavior. *American Journal of Political Science, 31,* 511-530.

Patterson, T. E., & McClure, R. D. (1976). *The unseeing eye: The myth of television power in national politics.* New York: Putnam.

Petrocik, J. R. (1991). An algorithm for estimating turnout as a guide to predicting elections. *Public Opinion Quarterly, 55,* 643-647.

Piven, F. F., & Cloward, R. A. (1988). *Why Americans don't vote.* New York: Pantheon Books.

Reagan, J. (1981). *Media exposure and community integration as predictors of political activity.* Ph.D. dissertation, Michigan State University.

Rieder, R. (1996). A skeptical view of the cynicism epidemic. *American Journalism Review, 18*(5), 6.

Riker, W. H., & Ordeshook, P. C. (1968). A theory of the calculus of voting. *American Political Science Review, 62,* 25-42.

Rosenberg, M. (1954). Some determinants of political apathy. *Public Opinion Quarterly, 18,* 349-366.

Rosenstone, S. J. (1982). Economic adversity and voter turnout. *American Journal of Political Science, 26,* 25-46.

Sallach, D. L. (1974). Class domination and ideological hegemony. *Sociological Quarterly, 15,* 38-50.

Shaffer, S. D. (1981). A multivariate explanation of decreasing turnout in presidential elections, 1960-1976. *American Journal of Political Science, 25,* 68-95.

Southwell, P. L. (1988). The mobilization hypothesis and voter turnout in congressional elections, 1974-1982. *Western Political Quarterly, 41,* 273-287.

St. Thomas, L. (1993). The media and exit polls and predictions. *St. Louis Journalism Review, 22*(153), 2-3.

Teixeira, R. A. (1992). *The disappearing American voter.* Washington, DC: Brookings Institution.

Tichenor, P., Donohue, G., & Olien, C. (1970). Mass media flow and differential growth in knowledge. *Public Opinion Quarterly, 34,* 159-170.

Traugott, M. W., & Tucker, C. (1984). Strategies for predicting whether a citizen will vote and estimation of electoral outcomes. *Public Opinion Quarterly, 48,* 330-343.

Wald, K. D. (1985). The closeness-turnout hypothesis: A reconsideration. *American Politics Quarterly, 13,* 273-296.

Weaver, D. (1994). Media agenda setting and elections: Voter involvement or alienation? *Political Communication, 11,* 347-356.

Wolfinger, R. E., Glass, D. P., & Squire, P. (1990). Predictors of electoral turnout: An international comparison. *Policy Studies Review, 9,* 551-574.

Wolfinger, R. E., & Rosenstone, S. J. (1980). *Who votes?* New Haven, CT: Yale University Press.

Zaccheo, M. (1976, September 13). The turned-off voter. *Newsweek,* p. 16.

Development of Political Strategy

Tactical Issues

19

The Nonverbal Image of Politicians and Political Parties

GÜNTER SCHWEIGER
MICHAELA ADAMI

Politics is much too serious to leave it to politicians!

—*Charles de Gaulle (former president of France)*

Focusing on the distribution side of a market, marketing includes all strategic and tactical aims to sell a product to a target group. The quality of these decisions depends, to a great extent, on the information made available to the decision maker.

In the case of political decisions, a candidate or party is sold to the public. The goal is to maximize votes, however broad the target might be defined. Yet, the implications of marketing knowledge to political strategies cannot be realized without a very critical focus.

Comparing company requirements to political markets, the difference seems to be narrow but nice (Table 19.1). The same rules for marketing targets of a company apply to a political party: It tries to sell its product. The product can be defined as a program that, or a candidate who, has to be sold to a special regional, demographic, or psychographic segment or a group of voters with a special behavior pattern.

The marketing mix has to be much more sophisticated because contents of marketing statements are loaded with emotions, desires, needs, and wants. However, the decision is not only up to the consumer but also predicted by a given date up to which the decision has to be made, without any regard to the stage of decision the consumer is in. In addition, the voter has no physical prices he or she can compare. Yet, each party and each candidate has its very special value that

TABLE 19.1 Marketing Goals

Company Competition	Political Competition
Enforcement of market access	Overcoming access obstacles
Global and regional distribution goals	Increasing the share of voters
Selling to new market segments	Reaching new target groups
Increasing degree of public knowledge	Increasing degree of public knowledge
Increasing preference for a product	Increasing preference for a party, program, or candidate
Increasing intention to buy	Increasing intention to vote

SOURCE: Ehrenberger (1995).

affects the preferences of a voter. A statistical survey of voter behavior and voting trends can be an indicator for further marketing decisions.

These values are much more sophisticated and less programmatic than simple-party contents because contents become interchangeable. Values in the past have been defined by strong personalities, and they still are.

Success in political markets can be measured as the result of a party at the very point of an election. So, let us consider the German elections of 1998. The candidate of the Christian Democratic Party was Helmut Kohl, who had led the country as a strong chancellor for four decades. His innovative, far-sighted political means helped to prepare a new century in Germany and even Europe. He managed to settle a triple strike: He deepened the European Union (EU) by preparing the currency union and the treaty of Maastricht, and he enlarged the EU by adding Sweden, Finland, and Austria to the community. Furthermore, he reduced the fear of France to create a dominant German position in the EU and the fear of Poland to create a unified Germany. Kohl helped to deepen and enlarge the EU, to unify Germany, and to convince the rest of Europe to approve all that. But he lost the election. Why?

He lost because his picture in the media was that of an old man, a political charger, and a bad-tempered man concerning the media. He was no slim, smiling, handsome political follower and did not fit in the political picture of a smooth 21st century. And his opponents?

The Social Democrats clearly won these elections, although their candidate, Gerhard Schröder, was strictly against the German unification and was a political waverer without any brave political decisions in the past. But now he is the chancellor of Germany. Why?

It is because he was the handsome politician, showing his white teeth while embracing the audience and the media. He knew how to communicate perfectly, and he was the potential politician with sex appeal and a slim, smooth character for the next century.

Marketing for Political Brands

The idea of a classical brand has been put to a far broader approach recently, which affects not only a widening but also a deepening of the definition. Culture, society, and social ideas have taken up marketing instruments that create the values of brand capital.

However, strong oppositions to treating a political candidate as a brand or even as a product have been stated in expert literature. "To convey the impression that the marketing of candidates is similar to the marketing of a bar of soap is to oversimplify and minimize the uniqueness of the marketing application to politics" (Newman, 1994, p. 9). This might be true so far as low-involvement products are concerned.

Soap is, for most of us, a low-involvement product. We do not spend too much time on making our decision because soap does not cost too much money, and our social status is not closely connected to our decision. Just imagine going into a shop and buying a bottle of mineral water. You rarely compare prices, colors, smells, and ingredients in making your decision; instead, you rely much more on the brand you use. You only change when you have not been satisfied the last time.

But what is the difference between the decision process for buying a car and that for electing a president? Let us assume that a person is very interested in cars; in fact, his car is more important to him than his wife. He glances over the fence to see his neighbor's car, and he decides to buy a new one. The decision is very important to him. He will collect a lot of information, comparing prices, shapes, and colors. He will think about horsepower, acceleration, and technical features. He is a highly involved buyer.

So, the consumer is forced into a process of complex decision making when the product has the following features:

- Is important to the consumer
- Is continuously of interest to the consumer
- Entails significant risks
- Has emotional appeal
- Is identified with the norms of a group

In the case of an election, it might be true in many cases that voters (i.e., buyers) inform themselves well (very long before the election takes place), read the newspaper, watch the news on television, read the political programs, and compare the candidates. Let us assume that a voter does. According to science, the human being is an "eye animal." Now, what does the voter see on television? He or she sees politicians who spent hours and hours with their image consultants, training their body languages and choosing their words rather than their programs. What does the voter see in ads in newspapers? He or she sees health, strength, beauty, and sex appeal. Is the voter aware of these facts? How does he or she decide for whom to vote, according to contents or to looks? Now, let us assume that a voter is not interested in politics; he or she knows the parties only superficially. Is this individual a sovereign voter? Is not the story of the sovereign buyer a fake? Are the candidates or parties a type of brand in the eyes of a voter?

So far as voter behavior is concerned, these points become important in the election process. But according to Assael (1992), the same situation exists as when a consumer wants to buy a new car. In such complex situations, the consumer tries to inform himself or herself as well as possible. In complex decision making, the consumer evaluates brands in a detailed and comprehensive manner. More information is sought, and more brands are evaluated, than in other types of decision-making situations (p. 39).

Voter behavior has been studied in much the same manner as has consumer behavior—as a decision-making process to engage in a certain action, including the processes preceding and following that action. Both the voter and the consumer are viewed as individuals receiving information—possibly seeking it out, then processing it to reach predispositions to respond, and finally responding toward the goal object (Newman & Sheth, 1987, p. 21).

To orientate himself or herself on the complicated market of different candidates and parties, the voter uses much the same patterns as when comparing brands. To be recognized as a brand so far as the consumer is concerned, it is necessary to give a product pithiness, independence, remaining and liable quality, goodwill, and availability.

The product of political marketing strategies is a candidate who has to be promoted with those messages. The candidate has to be accepted as a branded product of a company called a political party. The candidate's slogans and contents have to fit; they have to be credible, authentic, and relevant for the target group.

If one would have to make a job description for a political candidate, what skills would one request? Probably an interchangeable style, charisma, and trustworthiness.

Pithiness can be stated by means of brand names and brand symbols. Therefore, the name of the party has to inform the voter and give the voter basic information about targets as well as values and appreciation of a party. The candidate has to represent these values and add his or her name and personality to build a symbol of orientation.

Continuously constant quality and uniqueness are necessary contents of all public communications. Because there is no measurable price of a political brand, goodwill and brand capital are direct values for the voter. The availability of a candidate can be comprised in confidence of the voter that the candidate will be able to fulfill his or her future duties physically, psychically, and mentally.

Political targets justify brand marketing in a political environment without any doubt. "The input side of a brand is uncontestedly communication" (Trommsdorf, 1997, pp. 4-5). Political communications such as advertising, public relations, and personal presentations of the candidate have a very special marketing message. The target of all these is to present the brand as unique and credible.

Marketing has been using pictures for years to create and communicate an image. Because the synergy effects of branding and politics are not new so far as visual communication is concerned, political strategies have been treated like brand marketing decisions in the past.

The Internet, for example, is a new channel of communication and a new chance to place political parties as brands. The Social Democratic Party, for example, tries to underline a new brand identity that states a new solidarity with people. The new brand of the party is Viktor Klima, the federal chancellor in charge of Austria. His face can be seen on each page, which creates a new brand identity. His name is a symbol, and his unique selling proposition is sold as social conscience combined with political knowledge (*Die Presse* [Vienna, Austria], September 12, 1997). His present image is to create a style of technical politics. Mass media tend to call him a mechanician of politics. His problem is that he was not the federal chancellor when his party was elected by the Austrian nation. He followed his predecessor, Franz Vranitzky, after the retirement of the latter. His political instrument is his political power, control, and might that protects his political influence at the moment. But he tries to avoid problems rather than trying to solve them. The new image he tries to create is the image of a Machiavellian mastermind. But it is in question whether these features are strong enough to create a new brand as is currently being tried by the Social Democrats.

By comparison, the Austrian Freedomite Party tries to reestablish itself as very spectacular and aggressive. It tries to accomplish this the other way around. Jörg Haider, chairman of the party, is a personified brand who rises above his political opponents with means of clear and plain party discipline, party politicians who are dependent on him, and very strong native roots. So, the political party as a brand depends absolutely on the image of Haider. His personal pithiness and independence are real brand assets. His strategy is comparative advertising and is even more aggressive than that of Pepsi and Coca Cola. It is doubtful whether Haider could defend his image if he had to change from opposition to governmental power.

Haider also tries to establish his international image in comparison to well-known politicians and parties with strong branding activities. "Like [Bill] Clinton, I am not against foreigners but [rather] in favor of native habitants. We can learn a lot from the immigration laws of Bill Clinton. The only difference between me and Tony Blair is his name" (quoted in *Die Presse*, March 25, 1998).

The election campaign for the federal president of Austria, who was elected on April 19, 1998, showed that image and brand pithiness are more important than promises of other candidates and parties. The Austrians trusted in the experience and reliability of the president in charge, Thomas Klestil, who originally was nominated by the Austrian People's Party. He managed to be voted in again, despite his opponents, health problems in the past, and no shining example so far as his family situation was concerned. Opinion researchers found that the image of Klestil as a qualified candidate was much too strong for his opponents. The other candidates tried to create noninterchangeable images to set off against the brand of Klestil.

But branding, as stated earlier, needs continuously constant quality and availability of the product. Besides Heide Schmidt, all other candidates were new and had to be presented to the public with their very own selling propositions. The strategy failed because a lot of the stated advantages and promises have been interchangeable for the voters, and Klestil remained the only established reliable brand. The opponents' slogans included the following: "Democracy Means Strengthening Backbones," "Knowledge and Conscience," "View and Circumspection," "Successful Under One's Own Stem," "Don't Give Up Neutrality," and "Democracy Needs Security." "Political programs became totally unimportant. Image and brand marketing strategies won this election" (*Die Presse,* April 21, 1998).

In Germany, for example, the campaign for the elections for Parliament in 1998 was very exhausting for the candidates but not for the voters. Nobody wanted to "bore" the voters with programs, contents, and conceptions. "The program am I," stated Kohl, the chancellor in charge. He was noninterchangeable and pithy, with remaining quality and a strong personality. He was a personified brand. His strategy was branding. The campaign was based on a competition between lifestyles and emotions. Even his opponent, Schröder, tried to imitate his style and be a better brand of "Kohl" to beat him with his own weapons. Schröder tried to be a slimmer, younger Kohl with more sex appeal. He won. Yet, the problem is that some of the opposite parties' contents do not fit into this image. But contents did not win this election.

A very similar situation has taken place in the United Kingdom. Just a short time ago, forecasts were gloomy. The old left wing would leave its hiding place immediately after it had won the election. Like a wolf in sheep's clothing, the Old Labour Party would hide behind Tony Blair's New Labour Party, the Tories predicted a year ago and played with the fear of change.

According to the opinion researchers MORI, the Labour Party could manage to achieve 54% of the vote, which is at least 10% more than a year ago. But what has happened? The clue is the new brand—Blair. He walks a very straight line, is clever and cool, has got style without classifying, is uncomplicated, and is available. He is like an outstanding product in a mass of supermarket politicians (Peter Mandelson, quoted in *Die Presse,* April 30, 1998). He has a crew whose members try to make and strengthen his image—the "spin doctors." At this time, they add a serious touch to his charm.

So far as image and strong politicians are concerned, Blair moves in good company with one of his predecessors, Margaret Thatcher. Her style has become legend. Her image created her brand—Thatcherism. Saatchi and Saatchi tried to give her the touch of the toughest man in the government.

Scandals sometimes help to strengthen a brand. In the case of Perrier, for example, the fact that benzyl had been found in some bottles forced the bottled water company to take all bottles from the market immediately. Perrier could profit by the scandal; it now has an even healthier image in the United States than it did before.

But what about politicians? Can a scandal help a candidate to take an even stronger position? It can if the responsible persons know how to manage a crisis:

- *Prophylaxis:* Possible negative situations have to been prepared for with training. Public relations has to build a goodwill buffer around the brand.
- *Transparency:* If a crisis arises, the situation has to be made transparent to the public immediately. To disclose the truth bit by bit gives the impression of a surprised sinner. In the case of Clinton, the nation is divided. Everyone believes, nobody knows.
- *Measuring the impacts of the scandal and reacting appropriately:* In the case of the former president of Austria, Kurt Waldheim, it was attempted to establish the man

from New York in Austria who had no strong national roots. The Jewish World Congress made him pay for his past. Yet, the scandal helped Waldheim to become a candidate with strong Austrian roots in the eyes of the Austrian voters. The Austrian nation thought that the scandal was a top theme in the U.S. mass media, but apart from a few east coast newspapers, nobody was interested in Waldheim (*Die Presse,* April 21, 1998).

- *Arguments that match the target group*

The trend to create strong brands in the political market will go on because the decision-making process is very similar to the consumption process where high-involvement goods are concerned. Slogans and signs will become even more important. The reason to vote for a candidate no longer will be a party's contents but rather will be the world of experience that is built around a person or party. Market researchers no longer will have to compare political programs but rather will compare images of candidates and parties.

Image as Subject of Social Statement

Political Choice Behavior

A voter is a buyer. Experts observe several differences between buyer and voter behavior. For example, Rossi points out that voting decisions are less rational than buying decisions (cited in Newman & Sheth, 1987).

Yet, in the world of interchangeable products, and often similar prices and conditions, the consumer no longer is able to make his or her decision according to rational facts. The consumer also has to base his or her decision on models using latent constructs such as image. Unlike Rossi, I do not believe that the consumer always is able to predict the consequences of his or her decision.

The consumer builds a pool of brand alternatives. If the consumer has to decide on a product, then he or she recalls the processed information and decides. But how can the consumer consider alternatives rationally when he or she is in contact with hundreds of brands a day. Because of the consumer's limited brain storage capacity, he or she can recall only an evoked set of brands (Mayerhofer, 1995). So, the basis of the consumer's decision is the image of a brand.

An individual votes for his or her party not only automatically and traditionally but also impulsively if the phenotype of the brand "party" appeals to him or her as a whole. The voter wants to be confirmed in his or her wishes, needs, and motives, using the aims of a party (Ehrenberger, 1995).

According to Kapfer (1990), the followings points are important for the voter in making his or her decision:

- Image of a candidate
- Principles of a candidate
- Capability of a candidate

- Quality of a candidate
- Availability of a candidate
- Representation of a society
- Optical phenotype

Election campaigns are the time when political parties try to convince voters of their qualities. In a time of low party loyalty, the image of the top candidate is the most important thing for voters to decide (Schönbach, 1993).

To bridge the gap between what political scientists know about electoral behavior and the notion that voters are consumers, professional campaigners and journalists, as well as political scientists and economists, use the concept of image (Nimmo, 1974, p. 771).

The problem of the latent variable image in this context is its definition. In the German literature, a very intensive discussion has taken place to define the image construct and to differentiate it from the concept of the attitude model.

Mazanec, for example, states that both models have to be separated very strictly; image focuses on the emotional-affective, and attitude focuses on the cognitive profile of a decision process. On the other hand, Krober-Riel defines image as a multidimensional attitude construct and tends to replace image by a more explicit attitude definition. Herzig concludes that the building of attitude and image is not a separated process but rather proceeds hand in hand (cited in Herzig, 1990).

In a large part of the American literature, image and attitude are used like synonyms, and both affective and cognitive elements are put together. There seems to be a general consensus among attitude researchers that attitudes consist of one or more of these three elements: affect (like-dislike emotive tendency toward an object or concept), beliefs (cognitive profile related to the object or concept), and behavioral intention (response tendency of approaching or avoiding the object or concept) (Raju & Sheth, 1974, p. 80).

In American literature, on the other hand, the cognitive element of a world of experience is combined with image models, just the other way around compared to that in German literature. "Image, in short, has many different denotative meanings that make it a poor concept for a scientific analysis of public relations" (Gruning, 1993, p. 264).

Furthermore, image in American social science is used as model of an imagery process. Therefore, the artistic concept of image sees "image" as something that a communicator creates, that is, constructs and projects to other people, who often are called "receivers." In psychology, by contrast, receivers construct meanings (i.e., images) from their personal observations of reality or from the symbols given to them by other people (Gruning, 1993, p. 270).

In this chapter, we refer to the image model as the whole picture that a voter stores of a candidate or program. The decision-making process is not necessarily based on specific knowledge of a party's program and impartial, verifiable information to build an evoked set of political brand; rather, it may be based on impressions and nonrational evaluation criteria.

According to Mayerhofer (1995), "Images are pictures and imaginative con-structs which have a comprehensive effect and have to be considered globally, which show a high degree of complexity, [and] which remain stable and inflexible but can be influenced" (p. 56).

Presently, there are many examples where the imagery process and the image theory already have been used in election campaigns. The management of Haider, candidate of the Austrian Freedomite Party, has produced and published a series of pictures showing Haider in the Austrian mountains with an uncovered chest and a smile. The message is that of a young, healthy, handsome politician for Austria who has strong roots in the country and loves nature (and women).

But image is not an invention of the present. For example, Adolf Hitler stated that each form of propaganda has to be close to people and meet their emotional state. The less scientific the information in a statement is, and the more that emotions and feelings become weapons, the more success the statement will have.

Image signs and symbols always have accompanied political parties, for example, the swastika of Hitler or the red elephant of Republicans. Or, consider the image campaigns of Schröder, the chancellor of Germany; Klima, the chan-cellor of Austria, and Blair, the prime minister of Great Britain; the new socialists present themselves as testimonials for toothpaste. Did they win their elections because of political strategies, or did they win because of better salesmanship?

So, how can a political party manage to form an image and sell it to the voters?

Means of Political Communication

From the perspective of social science, one of the best-developed theoretical approaches to the production of images is that of "impression management," where an image can be seen as the impression that a person or an organization makes on another individual.

Impression management means focusing the target group and defining the communication strategies. Image management means designing the political message in the form of slogans, signs, and strategies. A political campaign has to be planned in detail like a marketing campaign. A sophisticated media plan has to be established.

A political party or candidate has three means of communicating a message:

- *Public relations:* The voter regards the message published as true because he or she trusts in newspapers and mass media. The possibilities to underline an image massage are small only because media tend to exaggerate and act as if only bad news were good news.
- *Personal contact:* The candidate can try to control his or her phenotype and be available for the public. The candidate can send a very harmonized message to different target groups and catch them in their state of decision making.
- *Advertisements:* Images can be created and strengthened. Any content can be put into a marketing message without alteration by the media using sophisticated psycho-logical marketing knowledge.

A candidate not only represents a political point of view but represents an ideology as well. The personalization of political contents is important not only for journalists but also for parties. But the fact that parties and candidates are brands gives mass media enormous power.

According to the state of a political campaign, it is important in what type of state mass media come into sight—during an election campaign, after an election campaign, or in times when image has to be processed without a distinct election target.

The deciding points of communication between politicians and voters are made with means of media. Therefore, a communication success is an election success. The contents of political messages have to be encoded by marketing specialists and decoded by voters. So, the message has to be simple, global, distinct, clear, and within anybody's grasp. It has to match the wishes, desires, and needs of the target group.

To transmit an image message, political marketing specialists not only use words in the form of slogans and explanations but also base their campaigns on pictures. We stated earlier that image is a complex model that uses pictures and imaginative constructs. It is assumed that image is stored in the human brain as a picture and a verbal code (dual code theory).

So, information can be processed verbally and as a picture. As stated earlier, humans are primarily visually oriented. Pictures send all-embracing messages and tell the most important things both credibly and quickly. Pictures used to transmit information should be precise, rich in contrast, and free of unnecessary details. Pictures tend to have a better effect than words for the following reasons:

- Pictures have an information value that very easily can be overlooked. Accordingly, pictures in an advertisement are fixed and stored prior to words. This also is important because elements that are fixed earlier can be better stored and remembered.

- The activating potential of pictures can be created by means of its contents or design elements and can be controlled and dosed relatively well, as compared to text elements. The activation of pictures stimulates the processing of information.

- A person has a nearly unlimited capacity for the reception of imagery information. The extent of imaginative material that can be received and stored by far exceeds the capacity for the reception and storage of cognitive information.

- The more concrete and pictorial information is designed, the better it can be remembered. According to the theory of dual coding, pictures can more or less (according to the theme) replace verbal information (Schweiger & Schrattenecker, 1995).

Let us try to make the preceding sentences more obvious with a very easy example. Both of the following examples express almost the same thing:

A black triangle
with a white
circle in it.

The pictorial information is more precise than the verbal information. Now, which one is easier for you? Which one did you fix on first? If we asked you to write down the easy sentence, would you remember it in a few minutes? What about the symbol?

So, pictures have a lot of advantages in the very first step of making information easier when creating an image. Remember the following (Schweiger, 1985):

- Pictures are usually fixed and stored prior to words.
- Pictures tend to have a higher activating potential than texts.
- Imagery research has proved that pictures can be remembered better than words.
- Pictures are at the very least as suitable as verbal stimuli to create a positive product image and to convince the consumer to buy.
- Attitudes and images can be changed without slogans.

Image Measurement in Political Contexts

Marketing research and image measurement in a political context is very rare. Instead of structured methods, polling is used. Polling presents a descriptive overview of various segments of the electorate at different points in time. By the use of sophisticated statistical analysis, marketing research is used to isolate and explain dimensions of the candidate's strategy that cannot be determined by polling alone. Polls most often are used to give an overall description as opposed to a deep analysis of why voters think the way in which they do. The reason for this is that polls usually are used for media consumption and, therefore, must be concise and easy to interpret (Newman, 1994, p. 117).

Nevertheless, important decisions are based on the results of such research. The quality of these decisions depends, to a great extent, on the information made available to the decision maker. When political decision making and marketing efforts merged in recent years, and successful parties and candidates became brands, the demand for qualified methods became stronger. The election process is a consuming process, and image is the most important factor in the decision process. Therefore, image measurement in political contexts is the basis for a qualified decision.

Marketing researchers generally use verbal methods to measure the image of a political candidate. Different scales and methods are used to determine the motives and wishes of a voter who is a consumer. Verbal methods means that a person is asked to express his or her meaning by means of words. For example, questions are asked, or emotions are translated into words, and a person has to choose these words and/or express his or her meanings through other words. It is not important whether these interviews are conducted personally or by means of a telephone or computer.

There are five general operational approaches to the measurement of images and attitudes (Tull & Hawkins, 1984):

1. Inferences based on self-reports of feelings, beliefs, and behaviors

   - *Rating scales:* These require the rater to place a (verbal) attribute of the object being rated at some point along a numerically valued continuum or in one of a numerically ordered series of categories.

   - Attitude scales
     - *Semantic differential scale:* This requires the respondent to rate the attitude object on a number of itemized, 7-point scales bounded at each end by one of two bipolar adjectives.
     - *Staple scale:* This is a simplified version of the semantic differential scale. It is unipolar, with values ranging from +5 to –5.
     - *Likert scale:* This requires a respondent to indicate a degree of agreement or disagreement with each of a series of statements related to the attitude object.
     - *Multidimensional scaling:* This is applied to a variety of techniques for representing objects—brands, stores, products—as points in a multidimensional space where the dimensions are the attributes that the respondents use to differentiate the objects.
     - Conjoint measurement

2. Inferences drawn from observation of overt behavior
3. Inferences drawn from responses to partially structured stimuli
4. Inferences drawn from performance of objective tasks
5. Inferences drawn from the physiological reactions to the attitudinal object

The methods of the first point frequently are used in marketing research, even with political background. Yet, the person is forced to translate his or her image conceptions into words without regard for the fact that an image is stored as pictures and imaginative constructs.

At the Vienna University of Business and Economics, a new method of image measurement has been developed—the method of nonverbal image measurement (NVI). Pictorial stimuli are used in addition to verbal stimuli to reflect the different dimensions of images.

Let us take a simple example. Assume that we want to measure the image of a car brand. In the process of research, the image dimensions have to be developed—sportsmanship, luxury, pollution, status symbol, sex appeal, quality, safety, modernity, and so on.

The researcher has to decide which dimensions can be translated into verbal stimuli. Some dimensions are not suitable to be operationalized verbally. For example, owners of prestigious German cars usually do not attribute the term "prestige" to a Mercedes. In this case, a nonverbal, pictorial stimulus that communicates the term prestige outside the world of car brands is used in the research process. Denotative aspects of the image, on the other hand, usually are better operationalized with verbal stimuli, for example, the handling of the car in our car example. The researcher has to find the best operationalization of the different dimensions. The goal has to be a survey that achieves the best possible quality relating to validity, reliability, and objectivity.

Let us take the example of our car brand. The pollution dimension can be expressed through a verbal statement, "The throwing out of Brand X pollutes the environment." The respondent can answer on a scale from 1 to 6, where 1 = *agree* and 6 = *disagree*.

The same game can be played with a nonverbal stimulus. A picture of a forest suffering from pollution can be presented to the respondent, who has to relate the picture to Brand X on a scale from 1 to 6.

If pictures are used, they have to be very clear so far as the measured dimensions are concerned so as to give all respondents the same prerequisites. Therefore, pictures have to be measured; all dimensions included in the picture have to be shown and made known to the researcher. This can be done by exploration by the researcher or by a survey. If a picture is very vague and indistinct to the respondents, then it is not suitable for research.

In the case of NVI, the respondent is asked to view the pictures and to relate them to the attitude object using either scales or a nominal base.

The advantages of NVI are as follows:

- The methods better fit into the imaginative construct of image that is stored and processed in pictures and even constructed with means of pictures.

- There is no need for a double translation. To measure an image of a subject (e.g., brand, company), a researcher using verbal methods translates complex attitudes into single-dimensional verbal attributes to design a questionnaire and make respondents relate an attribute to the subject. To use the results for advertising, these attributes have to be translated into pictures again. These problems can be avoided entirely by using nonverbal methods.

- International studies and multinational target groups become more important. Verbal methods have to translate the questionnaire into different languages. Plain pictures can be used without translation. This fact underscores the call of many marketing researchers for a standardized international or even transnational method to consider brand personalities.

- Respondents tend to have a certain aversion to answering unpleasant questions or to giving negative or socially undesired answers. Picture scales help these persons to give necessary answers and are not so easy to peer through.

- Pictures also help to make available sensations and perceptions that are difficult to verbalize or are not even consciously available for the marketing researcher.

- The implementation of NVI helps to create a richer bouquet of image facets and helps to distinguish the different objects of attitude.

- Pictures make it easier to realize the emotional-connotative component of images.

- Pictures make an interview more interesting and diversified to the respondent.

Because NVI is a rather new method, it is not totally clear yet under which circumstances and for which products it is suitable. Certainly, the processing of pictures needs more time and money than do pure verbal sets. But if the results are better so far as quality measures (e.g., validity, reliability, objectivity) are concerned, then this is the right way to go.

Furthermore, the results of verbal and nonverbal methods cannot be compared regarding the different levels of abstraction. Pictures used in NVI have to be clear and distinct. The Institute of Marketing Research and Advertising at the Vienna University of Business and Economics tries to standardize NVI methods with regard to validity, reliability, and objectivity as well.

Nonverbal Image Measurement as an Instrument of Political Marketing Measurement

Because image models are based on complex dimensions, political marketing researchers try to use a huge variety of verbal dimensions put onto a scale to draw a picture of the mind of a voter.

We collected a few of the attributes and statements that are used to convert image dimensions of a candidate into verbal statements in the present political marketing research literature (Table 19.2). If these dimensions have to be put into a questionnaire as verbal stimuli, then the respondent will have problems, for example, in relating the embezzlement attribute to a candidate. But the honesty dimension can be measured very simply by means of the pictures.

So far, the NVI method has not been applied to measure the image of political parties or candidates. Based on the experience, the Institute of Advertising and Marketing Research suggests the following procedure to measure the image of political parties or candidates.

1. The dimensions that describe the political parties and candidates are selected. Examples include contents of political programs, leadership, credibility, and attractiveness (as shown earlier in the verbal dimensions).

2. Stimuli are selected. The first step would be to select stimuli that are able to describe the party or candidate so as to distinguish the party or candidate.

   - *Verbal stimuli:* future oriented, conservative

   - *Nonverbal stimuli:*

     – *Pictorial stimuli* such as Picture 66, "family playing football" (Figure 19.1), to cover the family orientation dimension, teamwork, fun

   - *Acoustical stimuli* such as marching music to measure the traditional orientation

3. Finally, the set of stimuli is presented to the respondents. They will, for example, be asked the following questions:

   - Example of a nominal scale: "To which of the following parties does the picture apply?" The respondent might mention just one or more parties.

   - Example of an ordinal scale: "How well does the following [statement, picture, tune . . ., for example, picture of "family playing football"] fit into Party X?"

TABLE 19.2 Image Attributes of a Political Candidate

Dimension	Positive Attribute	Negative Attribute
Honesty	Honest Credible A man of his word Transparent Reliable Honest reputation	Entangled in scandals Embezzlement Breach of contract
Quality	Knowledge Educational background Capable Mastermind Experienced	Does not know how to manage a government No business knowledge No international experience Not qualified
National roots	Available Represents our country Knows the needs of our nation Traditional Interested in our culture Loves our country	Foreigner Does not know the history of our country
Strength	Strong Winner Carries his point Energetic Tough Successful	Weak Loser Without backbone
Passion	Loves his job Cares for our nation Helping hands Modern ideas Sporty Family orientated Young Knows our problems	Stubborn Emotionless

4. The result of such a study would be the relative frequencies; for example, how many respondents attributed a picture to the parties of interest. Further statistical analysis could be done by correspondence analysis. The final result of such a study would show the common image space of the political parties.

We would see the positions of the parties and candidates as well as the stimuli used in the research in a correspondence map. The dimensions would give us further information such as in which dimensions the parties differ and in which they are seen to be similar.

Now, let us look at a brief example of how such a study could take place. Party X wants to know what type of image it has among its potential voters. There is a special candidate for Party X called Candidate A. Party X has two strong opponents, Party Y with Candidate B and Party Z with Candidate C.

Figure 19.1. Picture 66: "Family Playing Football"—Passion Dimension; One Attribute: Family Orientation

Two image dimensions that Party X wants to test are honesty and family orientation. The party decides to make a survey and ask about 100 respondents. The party decides to use nonverbal stimuli for each dimension.

The honesty dimension is translated into the pictorial stimuli in Picture 836, "handshake" (Figure 19.2). To measure the dimensions of Picture 836, the party asked an additional 100 persons what they associate with this picture. Let us assume that 95% of the respondents included the honesty dimension in a wider sense. Because the respondents were forced to translate their constructs of attitudes, feelings, and emotions toward this picture into words, the verbal measurement of pictures is subject to discussion, and other methods are going to be developed.

The family orientation dimension is translated into Picture 66, "family playing football." The party might use an ordinal scale and ask respondents the following question: "How well does picture "handshake" [showing the picture] fit into Party X? Please use a scale from 1 to 6, where 1 = *picture fits well* and 6 = *picture doesn't fit at all*." The question is repeated with all stimuli, all parties, and all candidates.

After the survey, the results are tested for any significant results and put into a correspondence analysis to create an image map and make the result more obvious. Figure 19.3 gives an example of how the result might look.

Now, Party X knows its position very well; it is seen as an honest party, but it is not seen as family oriented. Its candidate has a very similar position. Party Y is

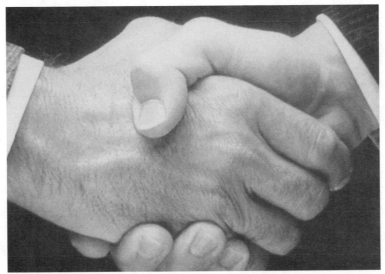

Figure 19.2. Picture 836: "Handshake"—Honest Dimension; One Attribute: Reliable

seen as honest (less so than Party X) and family oriented, and its candidate is seen as similar but less honest and placed more into the direction of embezzlement. Party Z is seen as attractive but connected with embezzlement; however, its candidate has got a good chance, as he is seen as sexually attractive and honest.

As a result, Party X could very well use Picture 836 as part of its election campaign if it wants to take advantage of its honest image.

By means of pictures, it is easier to characterize the image of a candidate. The different dimensions do not have to be translated but can be measured by means of complex constructs such as pictures. It is even possible to take pictures that have to be used in an electoral campaign and see whether the dimensions are really combined with the candidate of a party. It also is possible to draw distinct pictures of the opponents or to test whether the images of all candidates have the same intensity and strength. A unique selling proposition can be realized and used for further campaigns.

It is even possible to use in the next campaign some of the pictures that were used as image measurement instruments and were strongly connected with a party or candidate.

Conclusion

The method of nonverbal marketing research opens a dimension in the wide field of research that has not been accessible so far. It is an instrument that gives the possibility of coming much closer to the complex construct of image, not just so far as political image is concerned. Pictures help to draw a map of the feelings, emotions, and attitudes of a consumer or voter. It catches the respondent where he or she is.

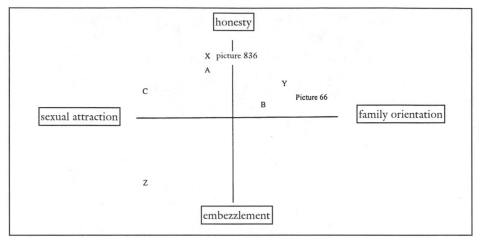

Figure 19.3. Image Space of Parties

Combined with verbal methods, NVI helps to draw a status quo of an image space that is much wider and full of variety. The quality of research will achieve an enormous gain because constructs that could not be measured with words alone can now be made approachable.

So, believe it: One picture does express more than a thousand words.

References

Assael, H. (1992). *Consumer behavior and marketing action.* Boston: South-Western.

Ehrenberger, J. (1995). *Political communication.* Unpublished master's thesis, Vienna University of Business and Economics.

Gruning, E. J. (1993). On the effects of marketing, media relations, and public relations: Images, agendas, and relationships. In W. Armbrecht, H. Avenarius, & U. Zabel (Eds.), *Image und PR* (pp. 264-295). Opladen, Germany: Westdeutscher Verlag.

Herzig, O. (1990). *Verbale und nonverbale Imagemessung: Ein Methodenvergleich.* Master's thesis, Vienna University of Business and Economics.

Kapfer, L. (1990). *Wir verbessern das Erscheinungsbild der Volkspartei.* Vienna, Austria: Politische Akademie.

Mayerhofer, W. (1995). *Imagetransfer: Die Nutzung von Erlebniswelten für die Positionierung von Ländern, Produktgruppen, und Marken.* Vienna, Austria: Service Fachverlag.

Newman, B. I. (1994). *The marketing of the president: Political marketing as campaign strategy.* Thousand Oaks, CA: Sage.

Newman, B. I., & Sheth, J. N. (1987). *A theory of political choice behavior.* New York: Praeger.

Nimmo, D. (1974). *Images and voters' decision-making process.* Knoxville: University of Tennessee Press.

Raju, P. S., & Sheth, J. N. (1974). *Nonlinear, noncompensatory relationship in attitude research in combined proceedings.* Montreal.

Schönbach, K. (1993). Images der Kanzlerkandidaten im Wahlkampf 1990: Einflüsse von PR und politischer Werbung im Vergleich. In W. Armbrecht, H. Avenarius, & U. Zabel (Eds.), *Image und PR* (pp. 215-226). Opladen, Germany: Westdeutscher Verlag.

Schweiger, G. (1985). Nonverbale Imagemessung. *Werbeforschung und Praxis, 4,* 126-134.

Schweiger, G., & Schrattenecker, G. (1995). *Werbung.* Stuttgart, Germany: Gustav Fischer Verlag.

Tull, S. D., & Hawkins, I. D. (1984). *Market research.* New York: Macmillan.

Trommsdorf, V. (1997). *Markenmanagement und Kommunikation.* Vienna, Austria: Werbeforschung und Praxis.

20

Direct Marketing

How Does It Work for Political Campaigns?

ELAINE SHERMAN

Direct marketing has become an integral part of modern political campaigns. With rapidly changing software and hardware technologies, direct marketing will play an ever increasingly important role in the future of politics. Although direct mail and telemarketing have been used for years, they have increased in frequency and changed in terms of how they are used and who the specific target audiences are. Technological innovations, including the growth of the Internet, are providing opportunities to secure better information through the availability of more sophisticated databases. These developments have led to greater opportunities to target smaller groups with more customized messages and to build better relationships with potential supporters.

Today, marketing techniques used in the commercial world are being embraced by politicians. This includes focusing more on the issues that are important to voters rather than just selling a candidate as a "commodity" (Newman, 1994). In the current political environment, there are a variety of important strategic functions in which direct marketing efforts can play a pivotal role. At the core is the task of communicating a candidate's message, often through a variety of media including direct mail, infomercials, videos, telephone, cable television, and the Internet. Given the more informed and diverse electorate, modern pollsters constantly are modeling databases, tracking the perceptions of their audiences, gauging the influences of their messages, and noting shifts in attitudes and behavior.

AUTHOR'S NOTE: I thank Hal Malchow of Malchow, Adams & Hussey for his important insights concerning various campaigns and his generous contributions of materials included in this chapter.

With costs of campaigns escalating, there has been increased pressure to find potential donors. However, voters still have little incentive to make contributions, particularly given that they often view the candidates with some degree of cynicism (Corrado, Mann, Potter, Octiz, & Soraufet, 1997, p. 106). Despite these obstacles, one key direct marketing-related objective of all political fund-raisers (regardless of party) is to build a large database of potential supporters and convert them into donors. Among existing donors, a primary function is to get them to give more money.

Direct marketing plays other important roles in politics by helping to "get out the vote" for a particular candidate or issue. In the 1996 presidential campaign, more sophisticated direct marketing techniques allowed political candidates to more accurately target prospects to raise funds and to do a better job of building databases. Despite these advances, the value of direct marketing sometimes is underrated. Even in the 1996 presidential campaign in which direct marketing proved to be a valuable tool, its worth had to be vigorously promoted by its advocates. The example in the following paragraph is an example of how direct marketing's usefulness can convert those who are skeptics.

After the 1992 presidential campaign, Bill Clinton's popularity took a sharp tailspin. In an effort to get increased support, the firm of Malchow, Adams & Hussey was selected to handle the Democrat's direct marketing fund-raising effort. In the spring of 1995, one of its first nationwide mail pieces, a closed-face envelope with a picture of the White House, was sent to 600,000 individuals on Democratic National Committee (DNC) lists. The message stressed that President Clinton said that the recipient was a friend and that he or she was wanted as part of the steering committee (Appendix A). It was a soft call for money, with no explicit plea for money until the "P.S." at the end of the letter. The White House was concerned that the letter was not a direct enough call for money. To support his belief in the power of this soft sell approach, a member of the marketing team placed a wager with Hillary Clinton that it could pull in $2 million. To back up his conviction, he wagered his house. The good news is that it pulled in $3.5 million and, therefore, he still owns his house. Not all direct marketers are that enthusiastic about the power of direct mail pieces (Hal Malchow, personal interview, June 18, 1998).

Selected Milestones in the Use of Direct Marketing in Political Campaigns

The volatility of presidential primaries and campaigns has fostered creative ways for candidates to capture the attention of prospective voters and donors. One of the early efforts to use direct mail in political campaigns was undertaken by Morris Dees, who used his knowledge of direct mail in commercial enterprises to make it more productive as a political fund-raising tool.

Dees, a successful direct mailer, became involved in Senator George Mc-Govern's bid for the 1972 presidential nomination. When asked to send out a letter announcing McGovern's candidacy to newspapers and targeted supporters, Dees realized that this could be an opportunity to combine the news with an appeal for campaign donations. Just sending a newsletter without an order form was something that a good commercial direct marketer definitely would not do. In addition, instead of the standard one-page letter in a business envelope used by political campaigners at that time, he created a seven-page letter mailed in a personal-size envelope. McGovern's disapproving staffers rejected the long letter and condensed it to one page (although leaving in the fund-raising appeal). Dees's direct mail intuition suggested that a longer letter would be more effective, so he sent out his seven-page letter (ignoring the McGovern staffers). This mailing of 200,000 (more than the number requested) was paid for with his own money. The mailing drew a 15% response. As McGovern's finance director, Dees continued to raise more than $24 million from 600,000 small donors. The financing of a major portion of a presidential campaign through small gifts by mail set a precedent for future elections ("Not Politics as Usual," 1993). For example, Ronald Reagan's 1976 and 1980 campaigns continued to use direct mail following this general formula.

Another stimulus to increased use of direct marketing techniques was Roger Craver. He founded a company that successfully used telemarketing to increase the overall fund-raising success for advocacy issues and political campaigns. The company provided information services for fund-raising and pioneered the use of the computer in political fund-raising (Daly, 1993). Furthermore, during the early 1990s, the increased pressure for funding to support the increasing cost of television advertising spurred other new fund-raising directions (Cross & Smith, 1993). With finance reforms limiting some contributions, and a new attitude among some voters from self-interest to public spirit, political strategists during the 1990s realized that a broader base of supporters was the appropriate strategy for fund-raising and getting out the vote (Morris, 1997, p. 86). New interactive communication technologies, and new ways of using traditional media, were used to generate new interest. For example, in the 1992 presidential campaign, Jerry Brown used a toll-free telephone number to secure $4.5 million in campaign funds. Ross Perot's infomercials and his use of toll-free numbers provided a large database of support. Clinton used video messages as a new direct mail approach. In this environment, a critical factor for success became database fund-raising (Rapp, 1993).

The database contains not only potential and actual supporters' names, addresses, phone numbers, and records of contributions but also histories of individuals' activities on behalf of the campaign or cause including voter registration information. Encouraging responders to become full-fledged supporters (not just donors) helped to build a powerful political organization for candidates. Maximizing the size of a candidate's database and creating strong bonds with potential supporters, including grassroots support, were aided by a variety of media including mail, phone, and fax.

Building long-term relationships with donors became a new focus rather than just short-term techniques to obtain quick donations. In this political climate, the database becomes the critical information core for communication and involvement. The focus also shifts from a select list of best contributors to a more broad-based group of supporters. In the old climate, repeat contributors became the focus of a more intense appeal, whereas noncontributors were dropped to inactive status and largely ignored. This approach resembled a donor pyramid in which a small number of larger dollar donors were pressured to give more with more frequency, creating an atmosphere of excessive pressure of intensive solicitation. Moreover, this approach was not as feasible in the new political environment of small donors. Formerly ignored nonresponders or small contributors were increasingly being recognized as useful potential voters or volunteers.

Better knowledge of potential supporters encouraged a shift from simply bombarding prospects with messages to building relationships with them. Perot's campaign illustrates this approach with the use of massive telephone conferences and computer bulletin boards to recruit volunteers. Both image makers and fundraisers were increasingly using databases to build relationships with supporters.

Finally, more sophisticated modeling technology helped strategists to find where they could put their direct marketing techniques to best use. Finding where the voters' turnout is heaviest became critical information for planners. This new use of information was important in the Clinton campaigns. Computer-generated maps indicated information such as the locations of potential converts to Clinton, which messages worked in specific neighborhoods, and which states were "must-win" ones. Other maps tracked competitors and their advertising. Although geodemographics and tracking were not new to the business community or political campaigns, Clinton's staff mapped crucial information daily. These developments can be attributed to the late Paul Tully, who developed a sophisticated analysis of how and where swing voters could be found and won over by Democratic candidates in the closing days of the 1992 campaign (Barnes, 1992). Tully was one of the pioneers of the Geographic Information Systems. Tully worked with the National Committee for an Effective Congress Services (NCECS) to produce maps indicating how a Democratic candidate could win the White House. His maps linked key issues to past voting patterns in key states. Thus, maps were used by political strategists to make key analytical decisions. Maps aided in pinpointing markets where specific messages were most likely to persuade voters. Maps also helped to identify the most effective ways in which to raise and spend campaign funds. Although Bush also used computer maps in 1992, they were more simplistic in nature (Montage, 1993).

This focus on "persuadable voters" continued into the next election. Direct marketing played a pivotal role. It became commonplace to drop mail in towns where there were high percentages of persuadable voters. For example, if there were high-performing Democratic districts with a great deal of "stay-at-homes," then their numbers could be calculated from NCECS data in terms of past performance. After these people were identified, overlays of their profiles, such as demographic data and issues that were important to them, could be established. Encouraging them to get out and vote was a key component of a successful strategy.

But political direct marketing still differs from commercial direct marketing in that individual campaigns often are shorter in duration, are more intense, and have only limited funds when contrasted with the multimillion-dollar direct mail campaigns commonly carried out by leading commercial marketing firms. Often, the emphasis is more on the present than on the future. If the candidate does not win, then there will be no future relationship. Often, the information sought from databases still is much simpler and revolves around two key questions: *"Where* are our potential donors and voters?" and *"How* can we persuade those undecided to come out and vote for our candidate?" These strategies often are not so much dependent on demographics and psychographic details as they are a function of simple numbers and issues (Ben Sawyer, personal interview, July 30, 1998).

The Basics of Direct Marketing

According to Stone (1997), "The basic purpose of any direct marketing program is to get a measurable response that will produce an immediate or ultimate profit" (p. 6). The Direct Marketing Association, a professional trade association, has another widely accepted definition. It defines direct marketing as "an interactive system of marketing which uses one or more advertising media to effect a measurable response and/or transaction at any location" (cited in Stone, 1997, p. 4). This definition implies a two-way dialogue with the target market, giving the consumer or voter a chance to respond. The response can be by any vehicle including phone, mail, print, broadcast, kiosk, fax, or personal computer. The notion of a measurable response is a key to the growing popularity of direct marketing. It implies that direct marketers can trace the "history" of the response, store it in a database, and gauge how effective the communication has been, that is, measure the type of response that it generates.

In the case of political fund-raising, the fund-raisers can evaluate which mailing pulled in the best response in terms of factors such as recency, frequency, and monetary value of the donations. Characteristics of donors, such as their demographics and geographic locations of the best responders, can be analyzed for each campaign. This information can be used to plan future campaign strategies. Direct marketing differs from general marketing in that it seeks an immediate response from the prospect such as giving a contribution or requesting information. General marketing often focuses on changing attitudes or building loyalty. However, the longer range objectives of many direct marketers are to establish long-term relationships. The successes of direct marketing programs, particularly in the commercial arena, often are dependent on three factors: the *list* (which today often is an enhanced database), the *offer,* and the *creative execution* (Stone, 1997, p. 6). Here, the discussion is concentrated on lists and database management.

List Selection and Politics

As the costs of list rentals and postage continue to climb, there is increased pressure to find new ways in which to identify political donors. More accurate targeting of known and potential donors is very important for more effective political campaigns. Screening lists with the assistance of new technologies and using various statistical techniques are helpful. There are many alternative political lists available, ranging from individual candidate supporters to issue-oriented supporters. Lists that contain supporters of "more extreme causes," and lists labeled either "liberal" or "conservative," tend to generate higher response rates. For the 1996 presidential campaign, a variety of alternative list sources were sought to develop new prospective donors and voters.

To raise money for Bob Dole's presidential campaign, the Republican National Committee (RNC) sought to rent lists from upscale catalog companies. At that time, fund-raisers such as the RNC usually paid $50 to $65 per 1,000 names from list firms such as Mokrynski & Associates, Millard Group, and AZ Marketing. The average response rate generated was less than 1.5% (Kiley, 1996, p. 29).

Other political figures running for office also are using more creative alternatives to get lists of donors. In 1996, two candidates from Massachusetts, Attorney General Scott Harshbarger and U.S. Senator John Kerry, raised political funds by using lists of donors who contributed to the Massachusetts Special Olympics (Hayward, 1996).

Clearly, mailing lists for electoral campaigns are developed from many sources. Because the information used to create these lists is acquired from a variety of external sources, the lists may, at times, come into conflict with individuals' rights to privacy. New techniques have been developed to assess privacy implications from different sources of personal information.

Database Marketing and Its Relationship to Political Campaigns

New data targeting techniques have had an important effect on political campaigns. The ability to target potential persuadable voters to get out and vote for a particular candidate has already been discussed. Databases also have had an important influence on fund-raising. New uses of database techniques have helped the Democratic Party, particularly in the 1996 presidential election.

> One of Clinton's strengths in the 1996 election was that he scared off potential rivals for the party nomination by his prodigious fund-raising. Early in 1995, several of his advisers developed a preemptive plan called "Peace Through Strength." The purpose was to deter any challengers by raising an enormous amount of money. By the end of 1995, Clinton had raised a record amount of cash in record time, $27 million. (Sabato, 1997, p. 83)

This effort has resulted in better use of lists and database marketing. Database marketing today is widely recognized as a key to successful direct marketing. Information from a database can facilitate more meaningful communications because the message can be targeted to the specific interests of the voters. Therefore, precisely targeted groups can be identified, and more relevant messages can be created. This is very different from responding to a general list containing only names and addresses. Today, both responders and nonresponders are profiled. Mailings can be converted into databases with greater ease. Exploring databases gives us clues as to how responders react, including where and when they take action. Some underlying tenets of these databases include the importance of some groups of responders compared to other responders and nonresponders. Various responders are likely to share some characteristics (which can be used to segment the entire group), and past behavior often is a good predictor of future behavior. From a long-term perspective, one can calculate the lifetime value of customers (or donors), not just the revenue from a single transaction (Roberts, 1997).

Database marketing also implies specific statistical models that can be produced by in-depth quantitative analysis. A firm that has a computerized mailing list and simply mails or telephones an entire list at regular intervals is not practicing database marketing. Data are collected and maintained at a more individual level. Furthermore, the data allow for tracking the effectiveness of messages in effecting attitudinal or behavioral change. Finally, they provide an important method for building relationships with respondents. Databases have facilitated the implementation of sophisticated market segmentation. A particular strength of database marketing is the ability to split mass markets into smaller or even niche segments and to measure responses and test the effectiveness of more precisely targeted messages. To illustrate, in 1996, the National Republican Senatorial Committee decreased mailing costs and increased donor acquisition through the use of computer modeling. Different selection techniques worked for different mailers, so testing and evaluations are important. In addition, Malchow, Adams & Hussey acquired 7 million prospects for the DNC using chi-square automatic interaction detector (CHAID) analysis. Following is that story.

A Case History

In early 1994, the firm of Malchow, Adams & Hussey took over the DNC account. At that time, both Democrats and Republicans had been experiencing declining donor returns. An examination of the Democratic database revealed a static donor file with core lists of 1.5 million prospect names (those who might be expected to give money considering that they previously had donated to candidates or political causes). In addition, there were high acquisition costs to obtain new donors (approaching $20 per donor). Initial strategies to increase the donor base included a move to larger envelopes, more personalization, and a more interactive format with handwritten laser fonts. However, lack of adequate funding limited the ability to substantially increase the size and scale of the program to reach new donors.

A productive step came with the search for strategies to make catalog customers, charitable donors, and other nonpolitical lists work. The objective was to identify a method to eliminate Republican names from the mailings. Initially, a list of registered Republican voters in the state of California was obtained. The list was run against all of the California prospect names that the DNC had mailed in the first four mailings of 1995. This resulted in a 35% "hit rate" using these names from catalog users. This file also eliminated 15% of those names from Liberal lists. After accounting for all costs, a net savings of 22 cents for every name eliminated was achieved (i.e., every name that matched one on a Republican list). After duplicating this effort for other states, the Republican eliminator file (which contained a file of registered Republicans and primary voters) saved the DNC an estimated more than $1 million in prospect losses. It increased net performance of all mailings by about 13%. In addition, the effect was an increase in marginal and nonpolitical lists, so the range of lists available to the DNC expanded dramatically. It is important to understand that "targeting is just as much about what names you don't mail as which names you mail" (Malchow, 1995). Furthermore, a new lifestyle selector technique enabled the profiling of those individuals having characteristics that indicated they would be poor prospects. The eliminator files can model such individuals and increase the ability to eliminate wasteful potential mailings to poor prospects (Malchow, 1995).

A second strategy (developed by Hal Malchow) to increase the efficiency of mailings consisted of creating new software programs such as *Zap*. This system provides information about the returns of mailings. A great deal of information can be generated including demographics of favorable and unfavorable zip codes. Those who are the most likely prospects can be sorted, and new strategies can be implemented. For example, it was found that if a prospect has the same nine-digit zip code as a DNC donor, then returns increase by 40%. In the same vein, it appears that those individuals on catalog buyer lists who are in lower income zip codes are more likely to respond positively to DNC mailings. These new prospects can be matched to profiles of those in similar zip codes.

A third component of the improved use of lists was a result of using better statistical analysis such as the regression analysis and statistical technique (known as CHAID) to isolate productive voter files. The result of these new techniques was that by 1996, the total number of Democratic Party donors had increased significantly and reached the million-donor mark (Malchow, personal interview, June 18, 1998; see also Malchow, 1995).

In total, more than 50 million pieces of mail were sent at an overall cost per donor of less than $2. This valuable Democrats list of more than 1 million donors could then continue to be used as a house file, being segmented for various specific campaigns to build names before the election. Thus, database marketing had a significant impact on the presidential election by identifying a large base of potential supporters. Even among the undecided voters, these targeting techniques allow planners to consider a wide variety of variables (geodemographic, demographic, and lifestyle) that can help to define clusters of potential and undecided voters. These new targeting techniques have revolutionized direct mail. The Democrats were able to generate a significant base among small donors because of these targeting techniques (Malchow, 1995).

In elections since 1996, computer-managed databases are increasingly being used to target specific groups with unprecedented precision. One key strategy is to ignore the majority of apathetic party members who are less involved with upcoming elections and to focus on smaller groups who are more concerned and involved with the issues (e.g., union members, anti-conservatives, environ-mentalists, gun owners, abortion rights defenders, religious right).

Direct Mail Offers and Political Campaigns

Direct mail often is chosen by political marketers because of its ability to be personalized and flexible. Each recipient can be targeted, not only by name and address but also by the messages to which he or she is most likely to respond. This creates the sense of a personal contact. In addition, messages on the envelope, such as "A Special Note From the President," can help to grab attention and ensure that the envelope will be opened immediately and the message possibly read. Another advantage of direct mail is its selectivity. The value of mapping and sending mail to specific target voters already has been discussed.

In addition, particular groups, such as high donors, can be selected, and messages can be targeted with extra precision. Another benefit of direct mail is its flexibility. The limitations of time and space that affect other media, such as television ads, are not limitations when using direct mail. Messages can be customized with greater creativity. They can be tested and compared to other mailings. This idea of testing against a control provides an opportunity to gauge how effective the new direct mailing is in increasing response rates. This ability to test is one of the major attractions of direct mail marketing. Today, there are many variations in direct mail packages. Graphic and visual communication is becoming more important as the desire to have more rapid and powerful communication with prospects increases. Still, over the years, there has been a standard mailing package that often is used, although with more modifications than ever before. This standard package includes the following: outer envelope, letter, brochure, order form, and reply card or envelope (Geller, 1996). The outer envelope sets the tone of the mailing. For example, a picture of the White House on the envelope would not use "way out" colors. Once the envelope is opened, the key piece in a direct mail package is the letter. It is the *direct* communication with the prospect. It positions the candidate or issue and explains why support should be given. It usually is more personalized. For fund-raisers, the postscript is very important. Often, the appeal is reinstated or something relevant, such as an initial plea for a donation, is highlighted. The brochure also can help to set the mood. Asking for funds for a political cause can be in the form of a detailed brochure illustrating how some groups can be helped or how some causes can be positively affected. An additional way in which to encourage response is to include response cards or envelopes. They lift the response rate by making certain that a request for funds will not be ignored because the respondent has to look for a stamp.

Political fund-raisers in the 1996 presidential campaign tried a variety of methods to seek donors, often soft-pedaling their pleas for money. An early success was direct mailings in 1995, asking prospects in Virginia and Maryland to join the Primary Committee for the Clinton/Gore Campaign. The envelope was oversized and white, with simple black lettering and a picture of the White House in the left-hand corner. The outside envelope stated that a certificate was enclosed. The inside letter invited the recipient to become a member of the "Honorary Steering Committee" for the president's reelection campaign. A red, white, and blue large certificate of committee membership was enclosed with the respondent's name already on it. A response form to let the committee know the certificate was received and the respondent's name was spelled correctly also was included. Only in the "P.S." was there a soft plea for donations (Appendix B). The notion of becoming involved with this effort was the focus, not the plea for funds. This campaign was very successful (Malchow, personal interview, June 18, 1998). Other successful Democratic direct mail campaigns included giving a response poster and a bumper sticker with campaign kits; this campaign drew a 6% response. It was followed up with another appeal to those who gave on the first mailing; this follow-up drew a 13% response.

The Republicans also used a variety of direct mail campaigns to obtain support. In one campaign, Dole used direct mail pieces to ask prospects to become participants in the RNC. The mailings emphasized a sense of belonging and making the recipients believe they could be important to the success of the campaign.

According to Malchow, who devised many of the successful direct marketing campaigns discussed in this chapter, an important contribution to the success in political marketing is the political environment. For example, in 1995, Clinton had no Democratic opponents, whereas the Republicans were fighting among themselves. Clinton was raising money for nonexistent primary opponents. At that time, $7.0 million to $7.5 million was raised in the mail for the Clinton/Gore Committee at a cost of $1.6 million, a substantial net gain. More money was raised in the first part of 1996, another $1.1 million raised at a cost of $200,000. Thus, the Clinton/Gore Committee, which was a separate entity from the DNC, raised $9 million, mostly from direct mail efforts early in the political process. The cost was only $2 million (Malchow, personal interview, June 18, 1998). This treasure chest was able to pay for early television ads and helped Clinton to state his stand on issues and to define his image in the campaign early on.

Another interesting direct mail package was created by Malchow, Adams & Hussey for the DNC. The purpose of this direct mail effort was to obtain special contributions for the Clinton/Gore 1996 campaign. The campaign's strategy was to compile the results from a previously mailed survey and to return these to the president's adviser, James Carville, for tabulation and interpretation. Therefore, this package was signed by Carville. The package looked very official on campaign stationery and using an "official business" teaser. A memo format personalized the donor's name and emphasized it with a yellow highlighted look. A lift letter, signed by Carville, thanked the donor for participating in the survey and asked for a contribution. A delivery verification form was included to confirm that the confidential memo had been received. The response rate was nearly 12% and netted more than $50,000 for the president's campaign.

One other successful creative use of direct mail involved the celebration of Clinton's 50th birthday. A birthday letter from Hillary Clinton, including a very large card, was sent to 165,000 people. Of these, 28,000 responded with birthday greetings. In addition, 20,000 people gave money. Eventually, this appeal rolled out to a wider base and eventually secured about $500,000. A follow-up for Clinton's next birthday continued to be a big success. Everyone who sent something got a signed picture of the president. Of those recipients, 15% sent donations.

Another change has been in the "vote-by-mail" campaigns for other political offices. In the past few years, there have emerged technologies allowing for more proficient vote-by-mail campaigns. During these election periods rather than on Election Day, databases help to target respondents with personalized messages. In the future, profiles of these voters will be used to carry on effective interactive dialogues with supporters. These profiles will consist of all the information about the individuals that has been accumulated over time to improve the impact of direct marketing messages (Grigsby, 1996).

Other Media Used in Political Direct Marketing: Television, Radio, and Print

Reflecting on the 1996 presidential campaign, some political analysts perceived that many voters appeared disinterested in the actual campaign (Herrnson & Wilcox, 1997, p. 122). This viewpoint was supported by the smaller than usual televison audiences for the presidential and vice presidential debates. It appeared that "by the end of the Republican convention, most voters had made up their minds, and no amount of advertising, issue posturing, or debating points could change that" (p. 122).

This was partially a result of Clinton's campaigning early with a media blitz. The need for large campaign budgets, fueled by the high costs of televison advertising, caused both parties to find innovative ways in which to acquire contributions. Fund-raising was a key approach in this presidential race. Many campaign commercials posed as "issue ads." These ads were supposed to merely discuss the issues of the day and not technically ask for contributions for the federal campaigns. The ads were, in reality, practically indistinguishable from regular commercials that the candidates planned for themselves. A sizable portion was spent before the nominations.

The DNC spent $42 million on issue ads before Clinton was nominated (Jackson, 1997, p. 238). These issue ads were not counted as part of the spending limits. In addition, a sizable portion of the funds went to pay for expensive direct mail programs aimed at smaller donors, especially telemarketing programs. For example, the RNC spent $61 million in 1996 on fund-raising expenses. Some $18.7 million went to its "Victory '96" program in an attempt to get out the vote (p. 245).

Furthermore, $30.5 million was spent on issue ads. These large expenditures put pressure on fund-raisers to find new donors to finance these efforts. Because the pool of traditional donors had shrunk since the 1980s and early 1990s, list brokers employed alternatively nontraditional ways in which to find prospective donors. Some creative methods to supply active names included advertising on MTV and using infomercials and the World Wide Web to find prospects for political mailers. Republicans even generated responses from second-tier lists such as cigar smokers (Ryan, 1996). Both the DNC and RNC set up Internet sites to help attract younger voters.

Integrating a campaign is another important task. The media increasingly are used not only for development of lists but also for candidates to communicate directly with voters. For this task, the broadcast media appear particularly effective. Candidates can use television and radio to develop important issues and to show different sides of their personalities that are in touch with voter interests. Clinton used these techniques effectively 16 months before the election to recast potential voters' perceptions. Although these televison ads were not a direct appeal for money, they did call for a direct response such as asking for information. The tracking of these results provided information to help craft future direct mailing to prospective voters. Reflecting on the 1996 election, integrated marketing strategies and early television advertising were keys to Clinton's success.

Polling and Direct Marketing

Polls are valuable instruments in modern American political campaigns. In past presidential campaigns, a variety of polls were conducted including candidate polls, media polls, tracking polls, and exit polls. There has been a tremendous surge in polling since previous presidential campaigns. One estimate suggests that "from September 1, 1996, to Election Day, there were about 300 national polls checking presidential preferences. There were about half as many in 1992 and only 10 such polls in 1968" (Bode, 1997, p. 269).

A poll has been defined as "a systematic, scientific, and impartial way of collecting information from a subset, or sample, of people that is used to generalize to a greater group, or population, from which the sample is drawn" (Lake & Harper, 1987, p. 5). A poll is a measurement at one point in time; therefore, it resembles a snapshot of public opinion. It can change at any future time, based on a variety of events. Polling differs from market research, which can use either a variety of complex statistical tools or psychologically based qualitative methodologies to secure deeper insights on which to formulate a candidate's strategic options. The media often use poll results to create political profiles of various demographic groups. In a political contest, polling often is used as a predictor of where the various candidates are in relation to each other (Newman, 1994, p. 117).

Polling for the 1996 presidential campaign was steeped in controversy because most well-known pollsters predicted a larger victory for Clinton over Dole than actually occurred. For example, the CBS/*New York Times* poll predicted an 18 percentage point spread, compared to the actual 6 percentage point spread (Bode, 1997, p. 269).

From a direct marketing perspective, call-in polls (with 900 and 800 phone numbers) often are used after political debates and presentations. It is well established that they can be very misleading. Those calling in almost never are a random sample (Newman, 1994, p. 118).

In addition, the wording of the questions is very important and can change the outcomes. Many anomalies occur with simultaneous tracking by different pollsters on the same issue that can produce conflicting numbers. These unexplained variations might partially be the result of the fast-paced lifestyles of many voters, especially those who often are not home, making it more difficult to obtain their input. Time frames for polling, the day of the week, and the time of day often reflect changing lifestyle patterns and cause discrepancies. For example, as a political pollster, I have noticed that with the great increase in commercial telemarketing, there has been an increase in the resistance to respond to telephone polls. Better planning and evaluation of polling techniques is needed to make polls more useful.

One of the major reasons attributed to Clinton's successful 1996 campaign was his ability to pick a few key issues and keep focused on them. Polls helped him to isolate which issues were most important. The ease and decreasing costs of obtaining computer-generated political campaign information has made polling popular, not only for national campaigns but also for local elections. One problem is that the effectiveness of interpreting the results rests with the competency of the political consultants. Telephone contact programs and direct mail development need the guidance of skilled market researchers and pollsters as well as intuitive political strategists.

Telemarketing

Politicians still use telephones to isolate relevant concepts and to discuss them with important targets. The phones still are a quick way in which to ask for help, donations, and votes. Phones usually are not the medium best developed for probing issues. Time is a factor. Today, targets are difficult to keep on the telephone because people are more time pressured and bombarded with more calls. People need to believe that they can make a difference. Some of Clinton's successful appeals dealt with this strategy. Being asked to join a group early in the campaign was important. Often the "softer" approach, where funds were asked for only as a secondary step or an "afterthought" motive, worked well. More recently, with the growing antagonism of many people to receiving unsolicited calls, a major potential problem facing the industry is the privacy issue. Answering machines, time-pressured voters, and fear that personal information will be used for inappropriate purposes are making people more wary of telephone pollsters and fund-raisers.

Direct Marketing and New Technologies

Despite all the limelight, the Internet drew mixed reviews from many campaign consultants. By some accounts, it was not very successful as a voter contact tool in the 1996 presidential election. "More campaigns wasted more money on home pages than they should have" (C. Allen, quoted in "Lessons Learned," 1997, p. 17). Web pages were used more often by professional team members for communicating with each other than for fund-raising or for influencing undecided voters. Agreeing with these sentiments, Malchow feels that the Internet did not have a substantial impact on political funding during the presidential campaign (personal interview, June 18, 1998). The disappointing results might be partially attributed to the nature of the Internet, which is customer driven. Whereas direct mail marketers have the advantage to seek out and direct messages to their prospects, on the Internet the potential donors have the control to search out what they want. Because most people do not seek out opportunities to give money, the Internet has limited success as a fund-raising tool. Malchow believes that although a number of clubs and some political organizations have general Web sites (e.g., on America Online), the volume of hits (people visiting the sites) is high relative to the amount of money raised (which is low by comparison).

Another problem with the Internet for reaching potential voters is that, unlike television, it is not universally available, and on-line information reaches only highly interested voters. People have to want to go to a political site and get information, in contrast to television viewing, where they watch a program and inadvertently view the political ad (Raney, 1998).

Whereas some political consultants view the Internet as not mature enough to be an effective medium to convey political messages, others who are more enthusiastic hail candidates' Web sites as one of the most visible innovations of recent campaigns. Through the Web, voters and the press have wider access to campaign materials. A variety of "fun" devices, such as virtual voting booths and creative graphic presentations of issue information, are available. In the future, some optimistically see the Internet as more fully integrated into the message-generating apparatuses of many political campaigns. It also might eventually become an important persuasion tool. Web sites in the future certainly are going to become very valuable sources of information for potential voters. Some envision campaign and issue-sponsored Web sites as more and more government agencies and nonprofit organizations bring their issues and causes to voters via the Internet.

Voters can access massive amounts of information on complex ballot issues. In California, Taxpayers Against Frivolous Lawsuits, the coalition that opposed Proposition 211 (dealing with securities lawsuits), developed a highly trafficked Web site. The site was updated frequently, and visitors were able to download information and view a complete list of opponents. More than 6% (500,000) of Californians who voted in November 1996 used the Web to obtain election information (Allen, cited in "Lessons Learned," 1997).

More recently, e-mail slate cards have emerged as a more direct high-tech campaigning tool. E-mail electioneering was created in California in the spring of 1998, where candidates were running for office electronically. This new way of reaching large numbers of voters might change the face of campaigns in future elections. Robert Barnes, a political consultant, bought more than 750,000 e-mail addresses from various advocacy and subscriber associations. Computer campaigning, using e-mail links to candidates' Web sites, offers voters a chance to ask questions, request information, and read more about candidates (Elias, 1998).

The Future of Political Direct Marketing

The following are some thoughts about direct marketing and the future of political marketing:

1. There will be new uses of databases to create more enriched profiles to select which voter groups can be targeted more frequently and effectively.
2. There will be more emphasis on building relationships with voters through personalized and interactive communications.
3. There will be more sophisticated Web sites and specialized kiosks that will be updated constantly to give new information, spot trends, and hold interactive dialogues with supporters.
4. Messages will be sent through a variety of targeted media including more focused direct mail and newsletters that can personalize messages to supporter groups.
5. There will be more frequent interactive dialogues with politicians, giving people the opportunity to voice their views in chat boxes, electronic newsletters, and Web sites.
6. There will be more innovative polling, with on-line polls adding another dimension for profiling potential supporters.
7. New technologies will be used more frequently to expand the overall size of the voting population whose members are exposed to political marketing messages that are targeted to them. Computer campaigning, using e-mailed slate cards linked directly to candidates' Web sites, will offer voters a chance to "speak to candidates" and establish dialogues.
8. Eventually, there will be more vote-by-mail using the Internet as it becomes more secure with "smart card" technology.

The 1996 presidential election demonstrated the unpredictable nature of American politics. In 1994, Clinton suffered the Republicans' takeover of Congress and a reduction in public support. Yet, by the end of his first term, he emerged a winner. It is expected that by the millennium, new voter targeting, using a variety of predictive models, will go beyond usual list analysis. They will be much more sophisticated, enabling communication with broader markets.

It seems clear that the world of corporate direct marketing is increasingly being employed successfully in the marketing of political candidates and cause-related marketing.

Chevy Chase, MD 20815-7219

BILL CLINTON AND AL GORE, JR.

hereby recognize

▬▬▬▬▬▬▬▬

as a member of the National Steering Committee

of the Clinton/Gore '96 campaign.

President of the United States

Vice President of the United States

CLINTON GORE

APPENDIX C

Clinton/Gore '96

Memorandum

To: Steering Committee Members

From: ▇▇▇▇▇▇▇ Director of Operations

Subject: Campaign Start-Up

Date: November 1, 1995

CC: ▇▇▇▇▇▇▇▇▇ National Finance Chairman

The President has asked me to brief you on the start-up of the campaign and our important first tasks.

Filing Announcement

On April 14, 1995, White House Press Secretary Mike McCurry announced that President Clinton had authorized the formation of the Clinton/Gore '96 Primary Committee, Inc. - formalizing his intent to seek reelection. In his statement, McCurry emphasized many of the themes that President Clinton will repeat in the campaign ahead -- growing the middle class, protecting children, expanding educational opportunities, continuing the war on crime and building on the economic recovery that has already created over 6 million new jobs.

He also emphasized the real choice before Americans and the difference between his vision for our nation and that embodied in the Republican "Contract With America." As the real agenda of this new Congress has become clear, polls show Americans are placing greater trust in President Clinton and his ideas for our nation's future. There is no question that we face a tough reelection campaign. But the polls show that the President's standing has improved over the past few months. And the "Contract With America" is becoming a problem for Republicans in the 1996 campaign.

Early Goals

The presidential primaries do not officially begin until early next year, but the reelection committee faces several immediate goals.

CLINTON GORE

November 1, 1995

████████
████████
Chevy Chase, MD 20815█████

Dear █████████:

On behalf of President Clinton, I want to thank you for agreeing to serve as a member of the honorary Steering Committee for the President's reelection campaign.

I have enclosed your certificate recognizing your membership on the Committee. To save money, we have sent this certificate third class. For this reason, I would appreciate your returning the enclosed confirmation form to let us know that you have, in fact, received your certificate and that your name is correctly spelled.

Your help in the months ahead will be critical to winning an election victory that is so important to our future in America. The President sends you his warmest thanks for your friendship and support at the outset of this campaign.

Sincerely,

Joan C. Pollitt
Treasurer

P.S.   The first and most important task facing this campaign is raising funds for the campaign ahead. I have enclosed a short briefing memo prepared by █████, Director of Operations for Clinton/Gore '96. Any gift you could make would be greatly appreciated.

CONFIRMATION OF RECEIPT

To: Joan Pollitt, Treasurer
      Clinton/Gore '96
      PO Box 57277
      Washington, DC 20037

From: ████████
      ████████
      Chevy Chase, MD 20815█████

☐ I acknowledge that I have received my certificate recognizing my membership on the honorary National Steering Committee of President Clinton's reelection campaign.
☐ My name on my certificate is:
   ☐ Correctly spelled   ☐ Incorrectly spelled (please indicate correct spelling below:)

_____

☐ Along with my confirmation of receipt, I would like to make a contribution in the amount of:
      ☐ $25   ☐ $50   ☐ $100   ☐ Other: $_____

Please be sure to fill out the required information on the other side.

21052002   00271497

383

A3F AAAB94

BILL CLINTON

Madison, SD 57042

Dear John,

Over the next few weeks, I will begin my reelection campaign in the state of South Dakota.

And before beginning my campaign in your state, I want to invite you to become a member of the South Dakota Citizens for Clinton/Gore Committee.

Membership on this important committee is an honorary position. It is my way of saying thanks for your loyal support as a Democrat. And it is also my way of asking you to join me in this historic campaign. By joining, you will be making a statement of support that will mean a lot to me personally.

All members of the committee will receive updates on the progress of the campaign. You will have an opportunity to provide my campaign team with written input about the political situation in your area. You will also receive a certificate recognizing your membership. But no meetings or formal duties are required.

I have enclosed a reply card for you to indicate whether or not you accept this invitation. Whatever your answer, please respond soon so that I will know your decision, and we can finalize the committee's membership roster.

Time is short. Election day will be here sooner than we think.

And as you consider your decision, I hope you will consider the importance of this historic election. We are involved in a political struggle that will determine the future course of our nation as we enter a new century, and a new millennium.

P.O. Box 19827, Washington, DC 20036
Paid for by Clinton/Gore '96 GELAC

Will we continue my efforts to restore the American Dream, to grow the middle class and shrink the underclass? Or will America pursue a different vision which reduces government to an entity without room for helping children, community responsibility or sensible regulation to protect ordinary Americans?

You understand the importance of the task ahead. My message to you is that I need your partnership to succeed in the most challenging campaign I have ever faced.

The outcome will be decided not by political strategists or newscasters or powerful special interests. This election will be decided by individual citizens who become involved and give of themselves for the candidate of their choice.

Please let me know that I will have your support in the campaign ahead. With the commitment of dedicated Democrats such as you, I know we can win an important victory for the values we share.

Thank you in advance for your help and support.

Sincerely,

Bill Clinton

P.S. One of our important challenges is raising funds for the campaign ahead. Membership on the Citizens for Clinton/Gore Committee does not require a contribution of any kind. However, if you can afford to send a gift, I will be greatly appreciative of any help you can provide. Please respond today!

Reply to The President

TO: Bill Clinton

FROM:

Madison, SD 57042-

Please verify that your name and address are spelled correctly, and indicate any changes above.

b07b1010

Thank you for your invitation to serve as a member of the South Dakota Citizens for Clinton/Gore Committee, an honorary position reserved for dedicated South Dakota Democrats.

☐   **YES! I accept your invitation to become a member of the South Dakota Citizens for Clinton/Gore Committee.**

☐   NO. I appreciate your invitation but respectfully decline.

☐   I want to do my part to help launch the reelection committee operations by making a personal contribution of:

$_____

Please make your check payable to the Clinton/Gore '96 GELAC Fund, and return it in the enclosed envelope to **Clinton/Gore '96 GELAC, P.O. Box 19827, Washington, DC 20036.**

Thank you for your support.

Please be sure to complete the required information on reverse.

Your contribution to Clinton/Gore '96 GELAC will be used solely to pay for the campaign's legal and accounting services to comply with federal law. Federal law prohibits the use of private contributions to pay a publicly-funded general election candidate's campaign expenses. The campaign cannot accept corporate, union or PAC contributions.

Federal law requires that you sign below and return this stub with your contribution.

My contribution is designated for the Clinton/Gore '96 GELAC Fund.

Signature:_____

Date:_____

Federal election law requires political committees to report the name, mailing address, occupation, and name of employer for each individual whose contributions aggregate in excess of $200 in a calendar year.

Occupation: _____
Name of employer:_____
☐ Check if self-employed.

Your contribution to the Clinton/Gore '96 GELAC Fund will help us cover necessary legal and accounting expenses for the campaign. Your cooperation will help us make the most efficient possible use of your contribution. Even if you have made a contribution to Clinton/Gore '96 Primary Campaign, you may contribute up to $1,000 in personal funds to Clinton/Gore '96 GELAC.

Your contribution will be used in connection with federal elections and is subject to the limits and prohibitions of the Federal Election Campaign Act. Your contribution is not tax-deductible as a charitable contribution for federal income tax purposes.

Paid for by Clinton/Gore '96 GELAC.

 RECYCLED PAPER

References

Barnes, J. A. (1992, October 3). A Democrat who never said never. *National Journal,* p. 2281.

Bode, K. (1997). Final thoughts. In L. Sabato (Ed.), *Toward the millennium: The elections of 1996* (pp. 261-290). Boston: Allyn & Bacon.

Corrado, A., Mann, T. E., Potter, T., Octiz, D. R., & Soraufet, F. J. (1997). *Campaign finance reform.* Washington, DC: Brookings Institution.

Cross, R. H., & Smith, J. A. (1993, January). The coming turnaround in political fund raising. *Direct Marketing,* pp. 16-19, 70.

Daly, V. (1993, September). Craver's uncommon causes. *Direct Marketing,* pp. 41-42.

Elias, T. (1998, June 3). Computer campaigning. *Newsday,* p. C3.

Geller, L. (1996). *Response: The complete guide to profitable direct marketing.* New York: Free Press.

Grigsby, J. (1996). Vote-by-mail: A catalyst for change in political marketing. *Public Relations Quarterly, 41*(3), 30-33.

Hayward, E. (1996, May 28). Fund-raiser preys on charity donors, Part 1. *Boston Herald,* pp. 1, 6, 14.

Herrnson, P. S., & Wilcox, C. (1997). The 1996 presidential election: A tale of a campaign that didn't seem to matter. In L. Sabato (Ed.), *Toward the millennium: The elections of 1996* (pp. 121-142). Boston: Allyn & Bacon.

Jackson, B. (1997). Financing the 1996 campaign: The law of the jungle. In L. Sabato (Ed.), *Toward the millennium: The elections of 1996* (pp. 225-260). Boston: Allyn & Bacon.

Kiley, K. (1996, September 1). The GOP comes calling. *Catalog Age,* p. 29.

Lake, C. C., & Harper, P. C. (1987). *Public opinion polling: A handbook for public interest and citizen advocacy groups.* Washington, DC: Island Press.

Lessons learned. (1997, February). *Campaigns & Elections,* p. 17.

Malchow, H. (1995, March). Luncheon address presented at the spring conference and exhibition of the Direct Marketing Association.

Montage, C. (1993, February). Clinton follows computer maps to White House. *American Demographics,* pp. 13-15.

Morris, D. (1997). *Behind the Oval Office.* New York: Random House.

Newman, B. I. (1994). *The marketing of the president: Political marketing as campaign strategy.* Thousand Oaks, CA: Sage.

Not politics as usual. (1993, November). *Target Marketing,* pp. 20-25.

Raney, R. F. (1998, July 30). Politicians woo voters on the Web. *The New York Times,* pp. G8-G12.

Rapp, S. (1993, June 1). The direct road to the White House. *Direct,* p. 90.

Roberts, M. L. (1997, Fall). Expanding the role of direct marketing databases. *Journal of Direct Marketing, 1*(4), 26-35.

Ryan, M. (1996, June 3). In '96, 2nd tier lists for 1st class business. *DM News,* pp. 26, 43.

Sabato, L. (1997). Presidential nominations: The front-loaded frenzy of '96. In L. Sabato (Ed.), *Toward the millennium: The elections of 1996* (pp. 37-92). Boston: Allyn & Bacon.

Stone, B. (1997). *Successful direct marketing methods.* Chicago: NTC/Contemporary Publishing.

21

Televised Debates

Marketing Presidential Candidates

SIDNEY KRAUS

A controversy in the study of political communication is whether it is ethical to apply commercial persuasion techniques to political campaigning, particularly when electing a president. The charge is made that the contexts of the two arenas, commerce (markets) and government (politics), require different protocols. The commercial arena has products and services that are offered for sale in the marketplace, and mass communication channels (e.g., television) are used for commercial advertising to gain the attention and allegiance of the consumer. The political arena is seen by many as a place for discussing issues affecting citizens and the country, identifying and selecting leaders, and maintaining democracy. One is concerned with the "bottom line," the other with the welfare of the polity. Critics who decry applying commercial marketing techniques to political campaigns argue that we should not "sell candidates like bars of soap." Sabato (1981) insists that "a live candidate is simply not as flexible a product as a bar of soap." He quotes Robert Goodman, George Bush's 1980 consultant: "You can try to inspire certain attributes [in candidates]. But you don't have the complete freedom that you do when you're dealing with a bar of soap" (p. 144). These critics insist that using commercial techniques to convince voters to elect a candidate for president demeans both the political process and democracy.

For some time now, the voter has been likened to the consumer, the candidate to the product, and advertising in a political campaign to advertising in a commercial campaign. The comparisons yield negative and positive assessments. Consider the cynical views of Kent (1928), a reporter for the *Baltimore Sun*. In 1928, he insisted that voters do not pay attention to political ads. Those ads, Kent said,

utterly lack the pulling power of the ordinary advertisement. What is overlooked by the political managers who pay for these advertisements and by the professional men

TABLE 21.1 Marketing/Commerical Term Equivalents in Election Campaigns

Marketing/Commercial	*Election Campaigns*
Companies/corporations	Political parties/organized blocs
Product/service	Candidate/issue
Competition (other products/services)	Competition (opponents)
Advertising	Advertising
Market share (sales)	Percentage of votes
Consumers	Citizens (voters, electorate)
Profit	Election
Consumer analysis	Voter analysis
Market identification	Constituency unit
Market research	Election research
Modeling, forecasting	Modeling, vote intention
Focus groups, survey research	Focus groups, survey research
Point-of-purchase	Exit polls
Shelf life	Terms
Image building	Image building
Persuasion techniques	Persuasion techniques
Communication channels	Communication channels
Campaign advisers	Campaign advisers
Product demand	Voter turnout
Business firms	Political parties

who prepare them is that "selling" a candidate to the voters is not like selling ordinary merchandise to the consumers. . . . The fundamental mistake, of course, is in thinking that the voters, like the consumers, make merit the real test. . . . Merit is not the thing that sways the voter, prejudice is. (pp. 349-356)

In 1969, the paperback cover of McGinniss's *The Selling of the President 1968* displayed Richard Nixon's face on a package of cigarettes. McGinniss (1969) argued,

Advertising in many ways is a con game. . . . Human beings do not need new automobiles every third year. . . .

It is not surprising, then, that politicians and advertising men should have discovered one another. And once they recognized that the citizen did not so much vote for a candidate as make a psychological purchase of him, [it is] not surprising that they began to work together. (p. 20)

Jamieson (1984) notes further that ads are part of the mix that voters pay attention to and "provide an optic through which presidential campaigns can be productively viewed" (pp. 446-447).

When considering the election and commercial campaigns in marketing terms (Table 21.1), the candidate is essentially the equivalent of the product, political ads are like commercial ads, persuasion strategies are identical, and the use of media for coverage obtains in each domain.

Mauser (1983) considers the comparison and suggests,

The claim that marketing concepts and techniques are applicable to political campaigning depends upon the extent to which commercial marketing resembles electoral campaigning. If we adopt a managerial perspective, we find that the problem situation confronting the political campaigner is strikingly similar to that facing the marketing manager.

He notes three overall similarities: competition, decision makers, and communication channels and persuasion.

A more direct and striking comparison can be found in the characteristics, training, and job descriptions of key personnel in political and commercial appointments. For example, media advisers, sometimes referred to as image makers, often come from the business sector and assume *temporary* roles in a political campaign—temporary because campaigns generally have a beginning point and an abrupt ending. In that regard, it should come as no surprise to see public relations professionals, journalists, television talent, polling experts, and others moving in and out of commerce and politics. That movement, of course, brings *skills and values* from one domain to another. The interchange seldom is sharp and divided. Rather, it is blurred, making it difficult to isolate skills and values to one or the other territory. Nevertheless, business values (especially in terms of persuasion) somehow have been placed beneath that with which leaders in a democracy should be identified. Given the political scandals in the last half of the 20th century, perhaps that relationship should be reversed.

Although the contexts and *some* protocols are different, there is a symbiotic relationship between commercial and political campaigns, and *nowhere is that relationship more pronounced than in campaigns for the office of president of the United States.*

I examine this relationship by reviewing prototypical events and occurrences in and associated with *televised presidential debates*. First, I briefly provide an overview of televised debates in presidential campaigns. Second, I describe the participant observation methodology that allowed me to gather data firsthand at most of the sites from which the debates were televised (Kraus, 1962, 1979, 1988, 1999). It is from these data that I make the connection between the debates and commercial arenas. Third, I discuss how marketing techniques were used in televised presidential debates and associated events. Finally, I consider the influence of commercial marketing techniques on the process to elect a president.

Televising Presidential Debates

Given that voters get most of their information about candidates and issues from television (Blumler & McQuail, 1969; Buchanan, 1991; Kraus & Davis, 1976; Patterson, 1980; Patterson & McClure, 1976) and that voters often make their assessments about presidential candidates from watching debates (Buchanan, 1991; Kraus, 1988, 1999), it is fortunate that televised presidential debates have been institutionalized. With the rising costs of political advertising and the problems associated with candidate fund-raising, television networks have been

TABLE 21.2 Televised Presidential Debates

Year	Number	Candidates
1960	4	John F. Kennedy vs. Richard M. Nixon
1976	2	Jimmy Carter vs. Gerald R. Ford
	1 (vice president)	Walter F. Mondale vs. Robert Dole
1980	1	John B. Anderson vs. Ronald Reagan
	1	Jimmy Carter vs. Ronald Reagan
1984	2	Walter F. Mondale vs. Ronald Reagan
	1 (vice president)	George Bush vs. Geraldine Ferraro
1988	2	George Bush vs. Michael Dukakis
	1 (vice president)	Dan Quayle vs. Lloyd Bentsen
1992	3	Bill Clinton vs. George Bush vs. Ross Perot
	1 (vice president)	Al Gore vs. Dan Quayle vs. James B. Stockdale
1996	2	Bill Clinton vs. Bob Dole
	1 (vice president)	Al Gore vs. Jack Kemp

urged to provide free air time to presidential candidates. In addition, some political observers see the need to mandate candidate participation in presidential debates (Buchanan, 1991; Kraus, 1988, 1999).

There have been seven presidential campaigns in which candidates have debated on television in the general election (Table 21.2). The three major networks at the time (ABC, CBS, and NBC) sponsored the debates in 1960 after Congress suspended the requirement that all candidates for the office receive equal time on television (Section 315 of the Communications Act of 1934). Debates did not occur in election years between 1960 and 1976; one or another candidate refused to debate in each election, mostly because of a substantial lead in the polls and reluctance to give an opponent television exposure. In 1975 and 1976, Congress and the Federal Communications Commission set conditions that allowed the broadcasters to televise debates without providing equal time as they did in 1960. The League of Women Voters sponsored debates in 1976, 1980, and 1984, and the Commission on Presidential Debates has sponsored debates since 1988.

Participant Observation and Retrospective Interviewing

Much of this section is extracted from Kraus (1999) and is a condensation of the methodology employed to gather the information. Many of the observations in presidential election years—1976 through 1996, with the exception of 1992—came about because of the opportunity to occupy a given role (e.g., on-site television reporter) or because the media, debate sponsor, or candidate staff contacted me (e.g., as a general resource, for specific information). In each case, permission to observe was obtained prior to the debate or media/political event. In some instances, permission was given as the event developed. These roles, and the individuals arranging permissions to assume them, have been noted in my previous debate publications. I never hid my professional identity or purpose for occupying a role; sometimes, because of the sheer quantity of people, disclosure to all attendees was not feasible (e.g., at a political rally, in the debate hall). Table 21.3 shows the principal roles (and/or credentials) occupied in events and with organizations in each presidential election year. Observations varied depending on the role, time, place, structure, and content of the event. Briefings about upcoming events, meetings, and the like were not always available. Itineraries, locations of site-specific activities, and significant actors relating to aspects of the debates usually were obtained and/or contacted through cohorts (e.g., media personnel, debate staff, candidate staff politicians, local academicians).

As the observations increased over the years, and as the results of the observations were distributed to academic and professional outlets, it became easier to anticipate events associated with the debates. But even with exposure over time—my being identified as a researcher of the debates—it remained difficult to gain access to certain events. Most often *closed* to observers were the candidates' debate negotiations, briefings, and private rehearsals. Obtaining permission to observe television pool and network meetings and pool rehearsals was difficult. Meetings of the debate sponsor boards and staffs, as well as their interactions with candidates, were not open to the public and often were not available for research observations or for the press. Interviews with key personnel in institutions connected to the presidential debate process also were difficult to come by and to conduct *on the spot*. Hence, employing the technique of retrospective interviewing (Merton, Fiske, & Kendall, 1990)—recalling shared events and activities to obtain reactions to them—was necessary and invaluable.

Marketing Techniques in Televised Debates

For this chapter, my notes on the observations were reviewed to provide the basis for identifying marketing techniques used in the commercial setting and adopted or employed in televised presidential debates. To supplement this investigation, I looked at videotapes of the debates and advertising clips used in the political campaigns. For present purposes, the items reviewed may be grouped under the guiding principle of *establishing an overall image of the candidate that voter-viewers perceive as desirable for a president*.

The debate preparations of candidates and their campaigns were part of the strategies to establish, build, and maintain a *positive image* in the voters' minds. From the point of view of the campaign advisers, a voter with a favorable image of the candidate is a voter who would vote for the candidate. This observation might need to be restructured considering the recent reaction of the electorate to President Bill Clinton's job performance (positive) and character (negative) ratings.

TABLE 21.3 Participant Observation Roles Occupied and Credentials Issued During Presidential Campaigns, 1976–1996

1976
  News, Carter-Mondale Campaign
  Audience, guest of the LWV (all debates)
  Press, LWV (all debates)
1980
  Campaign press, U.S. government
  Press, presidential forums, LWV
  Television crew, presidential forums, LWV
  Iowa debates pool, LWV
  Staff, presidential candidate forums, DMRT
  Press, presidential candidate forums, DMRT
  Audience, presidential candidate forums, DMRT
  ABC-TV News, Democratic and Republican National Conventions
  CBS-TV News, Democratic and Republican National Conventions
  NBC-TV News, Democratic and Republican National Conventions
  Outside (NBC-TV) pool, Democratic and Republican National Conventions
  Pool, Republican National Convention
  News, Democratic National Convention
  Audience, guest LWV (all debates)
  Press, LWV (all debates)
  Television crew, LWV (all debates)
  Staff, Williamsburg presidential debate, LWV
  ABC News, Baltimore debate
1984
  Campaign press, U.S. government
  Press, LWV (all debates)
  Press, trip of the president to Dallas
  Preconvention, Democratic National Convention
  Press, Democratic National Convention
  Visitor, ABC News, Democratic National Convention
  CBS News, Democratic National Convention
  NBC News, Democratic National Convention
  Media workspace, Republican National Convention
  CBS News, Republican National Convention
  Press, LWV (all debates)
  Press, debate hall, LWV (all debates)
1988
  WUAB-TV Cleveland (CNN-TV), political analyst
  Preconvention, Democratic National Convention
  Press, Democratic National Convention
  CNN-TV, Democratic National Convention
  Radio-television booth, Republican National Convention
  Media, Winston-Salem presidential debate, CPD
  Media, Omaha vice presidential debate, CPD
  Media, Los Angeles presidential debate, CPD
  ABC-TV, broadcast pool, Los Angeles presidential debate
  Pool, Los Angeles presidential debate, CPD
1996
  CNN-TV pool, Hartford presidential debate
  ABC-TV pool, St. Petersburg vice presidential debate
  CBS-TV pool, San Diego presidential debate
  General media, San Diego presidential debate, CPD
  Debate hall, San Diego presidential debate, CPD
  Moderator (rehearsal), San Diego presidential debate

NOTE: LWV = League of Women Voters; DMRT = *Des Moines Register and Tribune;* CPD = Commission on Presidential Debates.

Although it is difficult to parse the various strategic stages in marketing televised debates, for present purposes, these strategies are grouped into three categories: polling and survey research, debate practice and performance, and tracking studies and tracking polls. These are not mutually exclusive categories, but each has a core that can be observed as unifying the activities within it. While discussing the categories, I explain strategies behind them and make comparisons to commercial marketing.

Polling and Survey Research

Much like commercial market managers measuring consumer acceptability and purchasing of products and services, candidates gauge their standing with the electorate and do so almost on a daily basis. The similarity is especially note-worthy when comparing product/opponent competition. Competitive strategies in both domains require using two essential ingredients: persuasive messages and mass communication channels. These messages and to whom and how they will be diffused *initially* are decided on, in large part, by audience (electorate and market) research, systematically tracked *during* the delivery process, and evaluated as to their effect. Although the comparison might be obvious, it often is dismissed because of attitudinal barriers.

The symbiotic relationship between polling and debating can be seen in candidates' representation of issues and their efforts to establish favorable images. Polls help to identify those issues that the electorate cares about and that candidates discuss in debates. Candidate images are formed in the minds of televised presidential debate viewers.

Essentially, voters merge their perceptions of candidates' positions on issues with their images of the candidates. This merger has been confirmed in studies during the 1960s and 1970s. For example, in a study of the 1960 presidential debates, voter-viewers' images of Nixon and John F. Kennedy were correlated with the voters' identification of key campaign issue positions of the candidates. Similarly, in a study of the 1970 California gubernatorial election, campaign themes were determined by identifying key issue positions that were correlated with Democratic voters' perceptions of Jesse Unruh and Ronald Reagan (Kraus & Smith, 1962; Mauser, 1983, pp. 143-165).

Personality (attractiveness) of the candidate, projection of an image, and issue development are endemic to televised presidential debates. Restated in business terms, attractiveness (appealingness) of a product, projection of a positive image, and issues associated with the product are endemic to commercial presentations of a product. These variables—attractiveness, image, and issues—serve as impor-tant aspects of monitoring the *content* of a campaign. Ultimately, the debates become a "political and media yardstick for measuring political candidates" (Schmuhl, 1994, p. 103).

Voters' reactions to the debates come in the form of answers to questions about personality, image, and issues. These questions and answers are part of the business of polling. Polls and surveys play an important part in assessing winners and losers in debates.

TABLE 21.4 Numbers of Debate Poll Questions, by Topic and Year

Year	Number of Questions Asked	Personal Characteristics of Candidates	Debate Interest	Influence Vote	Who Won	Issues Separating Candidates
1960	14	1	7	2	4	0
1968	4	0	2	1	1	0
1972	3	1	2	0	0	0
1976	58	6	25	9	17	1
1980	111	34	34	31	8	4
1984	188	39	48	41	31/11[a]	18
1988	235	85	34	26	42/36[a]	12
1992	130	17	30	49	25/6[a]	3
Total	743	183	182	159	128/53[a] (181)	38

SOURCE: Adapted from Kraus and Ross (1996). Used with the permission from *The Public Perspective*.
NOTE: In contrast to the presidential election years listed in the table, other years reveal little polling activity on the debates (e.g., 1974, 1 question; 1979, 3 questions; 1986, 1 question; 1990, 2 questions).
a. Second number indicates questions about media influence as to who won.

Perhaps the most important feedback that a political (commercial) campaign receives is the polling (survey research) data devised to help in the development of strategies and tactics. These data give a running account of how the electorate (market) is reacting to campaign events, how voters (consumers) feel about candidate (product) issue positions, and how the voters would vote "if the election were held today." Sponsors of presidential debates have paid attention to polls that show the amount of public interest in debates. In the general presidential campaign, voters are asked several questions related to televised debates (Table 21.4).

Survey research is an important part of determining voters' views and attitudes toward candidates. This research influences how presidential candidates prepare for and perform in televised debates.

Debate Practice and Performance

Since 1976, candidate advisers (much like product and marketing managers' campaign planning) have prepared candidates for debates in election campaigns. Televised debates allow the candidates to present their credentials to be president to the electorate. Advisers use this venue to motivate candidates to adhere to a specific plan—a marketing plan, if you will.

Although not as methodologically sophisticated, the candidates' marketing plan for a series of televised debates resembles parts of Steffler's (1971) phases of new product development (see also Mauser, 1983, pp. 66-81) in which *marketing goals* are established, *product concepts* are evaluated and tested, and *packaging designs* matching the concepts are created.

Similarly, there are essentially two phases in the candidates' televised presidential debates marketing plan. The first phase is to devise those strategies and preparations that will project the candidates as *presidential* in both appearance and behavior, knowledgeable about the issues, and capable of governing the nation. The second phase is to get voters to feel positively toward the candidates. Defining what the electorate identifies as presidential usually is accomplished with focus groups or survey research.

Steffler's (1971) first phase primarily includes locating, assessing, and developing new products according to management specifications. His first phase proceeds from defining the market, to determining product concepts comparing consumer judgments through a series of (interview) samples, to converting the perceptions into models, to analyzing preference data with multidimensional scaling techniques. The second phase seeks to match the packaging (advertising) of the new product with the concepts originally developed.

Making a comparison to Steffler's topology with the preparation for televised presidential debates, the tasks run from identifying the issues that the electorate cares about to identifying the characteristics it seeks in a president, combining both for presentation on television.

Much like the marketing team sets out to package and promote a product in a competitive market, the candidate's staff prepare a briefing book that provides a review of the issues and a characterization of the opposition—the opponent's position on issues and his or her attributes and negatives. The candidate studies the briefing book, and the staff responsible for conducting debate rehearsals usually set up a mock debating practice site that includes furniture and an atmosphere similar to that which will be used in the debate telecast.

In these practice or rehearsal sessions, various presentational aspects of debates are tested (product testing). The candidate is confronted by a stand-in panel or moderator and by a stand-in opponent(s). At times, these rehearsals are videotaped for criticism and playback to the candidate. Focus groups may be used after a debate, and their reactions can be incorporated into briefing sessions prior to the subsequent debate. There is, of course, no substitute for being "issue literate"; recall the 1992 vice presidential debate between Senator Al Gore, Jr., and Admiral James Stockdale, the latter of whom was totally unprepared for the debate (Carlin & McKinney, 1994, p. 180).

Essentially, the purpose of rehearsals is to pretest a plan for the acceptance (selling) of the candidate to the electorate using persuasive rhetorical devices (e.g., repetition, memorable phrases, sound bites) that will be replayed in subsequent media outlets (e.g., television news and talk shows, various print media) and influence the electorate's view of the candidate as evidenced in public opinion polls about who won the debate.

Marketing activities require constant measurement of progress toward relative goals (sales and election). Tracking occurs in the development of commercial and political ads as well as in debates by assessing winners and losers.

Tracking Studies and Tracking Polls

A common practice in the commercial marketplace is to use tracking studies to help measure marketing effectiveness. Basic measures include brand awareness, awareness of advertising for individual brands in a product category, and association of brands with specific attributes. For example, companies may obtain weekly, monthly, or quarterly estimates of the percentage of people who recall having seen ads for particular brands. The data are based on sampling either the general population, a target consumer segment, or both. The awareness measures can then be aligned with advertising or other marketing communications during the same time frame to assess whether consumers were affected by these programs. Specific methods for doing this type of analysis vary, but in some cases, econometric modeling techniques are applied to develop a quantitative estimate of change in awareness per dollar of spending, ad rating points, or other standard measures of communication activity.

Many consumer packaged goods marketers also buy weekly data for their categories that include sales, prices, in-store promotions, coupon distribution, and the like from companies such as A. C. Nielsen and Information Resources Inc. Collected via UPC checkout scanners and in-store audits from a nationally representative sample of supermarkets, these data can be used to build econometric models that estimate the short-term impact of different marketing activities on consumer purchase volume. These models can be applied to forecast consumer demand or, in a "what if" mode, to compare sales results for a range of different marketing scenarios.

Analogous to the awareness index is the attempt by media and campaign pollsters to continuously monitor candidate name and issue recognition as well as vote intention. The change in percentage of voters intending to vote for a candidate or an issue after an ad is aired is the "equivalent" of a marketing effectiveness evaluation.

Perhaps the most obvious marketing political comparison is the measurement of the reactions of audiences (e.g., consumers, voters, segmented groups) to commercial and political ads designed for different media channels—television, radio, print, and the like. One technique used in commercial and political persuasion campaigns instantaneously measures the consumers' or voters' on-going reactions to a television spot. The respondents hold keypads and press buttons to indicate favorable or unfavorable reactions to the ad as they view it. Second-by-second or minute-by-minute calibrations form an overall index, essentially predicting the acceptance or rejection of the spot among members of the electorate or consumers. Also, the moment-by-moment view of commercial (spot) reactions can be used diagnostically to identify what specific elements of a message of execution are received positively (or negatively) by the respondents.

This technique has been used by partisan groups to assess how well their candidates perform in presidential debates. In recent elections, some television stations have presented the data in graphs as the measurement is being made in "live" performances. But the most ubiquitous device for obtaining information about presidential debates is the public opinion poll.

A recent examination of polls about presidential debates from 1960 through 1992 separated the questions asked into six categories: personal characteristics of candidates, debate interest, influence on vote, who won, media influence as to who won, and issues separating candidates (Table 21.4). Of 743 questions asked, 181 were about who won the debates. When a candidate wins a debate, the inference is that it will help win the election. Since 1984, a total of 53 questions were asked to measure media influence as to who won. This finding is interesting given the history of the media's involvement in predicting election winners. In the 19th century, newspapers had reporters canvass voters to gauge public sentiment about issues and candidates. These assessments were conducted with *straw polls* of local groups, often not representative of the electorate to whom the reporters referred in their stories.

As I have noted elsewhere,

> Straw polls dramatically fell victim to the inadequacies of the market research techniques and sampling methods of the times when, in 1936, the *Literary Digest* predicted that the Republican nominee, Alfred M. Landon, would win the presidency over Democrat Franklin Roosevelt. The *Digest*'s poll was conducted by mailing millions of ballot cards . . . [and] brought about a sampling error that overpredicted the support for the Republican presidential candidate. . . .
>
> In 1933, with the knowledge that errors associated with sampling could be reduced by using probability techniques to measure public opinion, George Gallup founded the American Institute of Public Opinion . . ., [and with the cooperation and financial support of the media,] a market for *opinion* had been established. The Gallup Poll had arrived. (Kraus, 1988, pp. 105-106, emphasis in original)

Over the years, market research techniques also have been honed by experts in both business and political sectors.

Again, it is important to note the interchange of personnel between business and political staffs and the polling institutions that serve the media, business, and politics. Many in these interchanges belong to a culture unique in Western society. They are *image merchants* (Heibert, Jones, Lorenz, & Lolito, 1971) but prefer to be called marketing or political consultants. Whatever they are called, they bring the same box of tools to help construct images of products as they do to promote persuasive images of presidential candidates.

Shortly after World War II and the advent of television, political consultants emerged, largely from the business sector (Agronoff, 1976; Kelley, 1956; Nimmo, 1970). As the field grew, they formed the American Association of Political Consultants, and political consultant firms, distinct from advertising agencies, rose to prominence, especially in presidential campaigns. This rise was seen by some as damaging to the political party system and to democracy itself (Sabato, 1981).

But the fact remains that television allowed candidates to go directly to the voters, bypassing the political parties. It was inevitable, then, that there would be a demand for political specialists who *also* were experts in the use of television, image making, marketing, and knowledge about survey research and the use of polling in campaigns.

Their *goal was not to educate the voter but rather to win the election*. In the eyes of those who are repulsed by the use of commercial marketing techniques in elections, using education as a driving force in a political campaign would be more acceptable.

These television and media experts know that when winning in a given time period (Election Day) drives a campaign, the resources (marketing and persuasion) used are those that have been proven successful in previous political and commercial campaigns. Under this paradigm, money is a major factor because most campaign plans rely on heavy use of television to bring the images of the candidates and the issues they stand for to the voters.

Presidential debates are seen as affecting the outcome of the election (turnout at the polls and the vote) and as an advantage for the nonincumbent and/or the underdog because televised debates represent free national time, legitimize the campaign, and are covered by the media. (The number of media personnel covering the debates on-site range from 2,300 to 3,500.)

Eventually, debate performances (winners and losers) are part of the input for projecting election outcomes. But initially, data are collected to help prepare candidates for the televised encounters. Like industries that assess their products in a variety of ways, presidential campaigns track winners and losers in and out of debates.

A Concluding Note

In this brief discussion, similarities between commercial and political campaigns, between research applications in the marketplace and in the polity, and between marketing and political debates have been identified as integral parts of campaigns. We may categorize these campaigns, grouping them by commercial, political, or other designations. Although not necessarily mutually exclusive, we may arrange campaigns in terms of *strategic brands* communication campaigns (Schultz & Barnes, 1999), *persuasive* campaigns (commercial, political, and social) (Plau & Parrott, 1993), *public* communication campaigns (Rice & Atkin, 1989), and *information* campaigns (Solmon, 1989). Regardless of the differences in the classifications, the persuasive and marketing techniques are strikingly comparable in both fields.

This conclusion might not be welcomed by those who oppose "selling candidates like bars of soap," but although the rhetoric (selling and soap) might appear debasing, the methods employed are applied artfully and scientifically. Consumers and voters are accustomed to receiving messages in both fields in much the same way.

One significant difference, however, is that the consumer buys the product over and over again. The voter elects the candidate on Election Day, and that is all.

References

Agronoff, R. (Ed.). (1976). *The new style in elections campaigns* (2nd ed.). Boston: Holbrook.
Blumler, J. G., & McQuail, D. (1969). *Television in politics: Its uses and influence*. Chicago: University of Chicago Press.

Buchanan, B. (1991). *Electing a president: The Markle Commission research on campaign '88.* Austin: University of Texas Press.

Carlin, D. B., & McKinney, M. S. (1994). *The 1992 presidential debates in focus.* Westport, CT: Praeger.

Heibert,, R., Jones, R., Lorenz, J., & Lolito, E. (Eds.). (1971). *The political image merchants.* Washington, DC: Acropolis.

Jamieson, K. H. (1984). *Packaging the presidency: A history and criticism of presidential campaign advertising.* New York: Oxford University Press.

Kelley, S. (1956). *Professional public relations and political power.* Baltimore, MD: Johns Hopkins University Press.

Kent, F. (1928). *Political behavior.* New York: William Morrow.

Kraus, S. (Ed.). (1962). *The great debates: Background, perspective, effects.* Bloomington: Indiana University Press.

Kraus, S. (Ed.). (1979). *The great debates: Carter vs. Ford, 1976.* Bloomington: Indiana University Press.

Kraus, S. (1988). *Televised presidential debates and public policy.* Hillsdale, NJ: Lawrence Erlbaum.

Kraus, S. (1999). *Televised presidential debates and public policy* (2nd ed.). Mahwah, NJ: Lawrence Erlbaum.

Kraus, S., & Davis, D. (1976). *The effects of mass communication on political behavior.* University Park: Pennsylvania State University Press.

Kraus, S., & Ross, M. (1996, August/September). Polling on presidential debates, 1960-1992. *The Public Perspective,* pp. 57-59.

Kraus, S., & Smith, R. (1962). Issues and images. In S. Kraus (Ed.), *The great debates: Background, perspective, effects* (pp. 289-312). Bloomington: Indiana University Press.

Mauser, G. A. (1983). *Political marketing: An approach to campaign strategy.* New York: Praeger.

McGinniss, J. (1969). *The selling of the president 1968.* New York: Pocket Books.

Merton, R. K., Fiske, M., & Kendall, P. L. (1990). *The focused interview: A manual of problems and procedures* (2nd ed.). New York: Free Press.

Nimmo, D. (1970). *The political persuaders.* Englewood Cliffs, NJ: Prentice Hall.

Patterson, T. (1980). *The media election.* New York: Praeger.

Patterson, T., & McClure, R. D. (1976). *The unseeing eye: The myth of television power in national elections.* New York: Putnam.

Plau, M., & Parrott, R. (1993). *Persuasion communication campaigns.* Needham Heights, MA: Allyn & Bacon.

Rice, R. E., & Atkin, C. K. (1989). *Public communication campaigns.* Newbury Park, CA: Sage.

Sabato, L. J. (1981). *The rise of political consultants: New ways of winning elections.* New York: Basic Books.

Schmuhl, R. (1994). *Demanding democracy.* Notre Dame, IN: University of Notre Dame Press.

Schultz, D. E., & Barnes, B. E. (1999). *Strategic brand communication campaigns.* Lincolnwood, IL: NTC/Contemporary Publishing Group.

Solmon, C. T. (1989). *Information campaigns: Balancing social values and social change.* Newbury Park, CA: Sage.

Steffler, V. J. (1971). *New products and new enterprises: A report of an experiment in applied social science.* Irvine: University of California, Irvine.

22

Voter Segmentation and Candidate Positioning

PAUL R. BAINES

The political systems in operation around the world are different. For example, whereas a preferential party-centered system operates in Australia, a "first past the post," candidate-centered system operates in the United States. As a result, it is likely that certain marketing techniques will be more appropriate than others for use in political campaigns in different countries. The literature comparing electoral systems, their political effects, and the marketing implications is relatively sparse. The differences that exist between electoral systems and their consequences for voting behavior have considerable implications for the type of approach that party strategists take when devising their campaigns (Farrell, 1996; Granberg & Holmberg, 1995).

Scammell (1997) suggests that the factors dictating whether campaign techniques used in one country can be used in another are the electoral system and structure of party competition, whether the campaigning is candidate centered or party centered, the structure of regulation, restrictions on media and paid advertising, the structure of the media, and the strengths and distinctiveness of the national cultures. Although this chapter is written from a general perspective, readers should understand that adjustments should be made for cultural, infrastructural, electoral, and political peculiarities when devising voter segmentation bases and candidate and party strategies. Whereas there are a variety of publics with which the candidate or political party has to be concerned (see Kotler & Kotler, 1981; Sweeney, 1995), this chapter focuses on perhaps the most important group of all—the voters.

The importance of the voters in an election campaign is paramount because ultimately it is the voters who cast their choices with their ballots. Usually, certain groups of voters are disproportionately more important than others in the campaign. For example, for the U.K. political parties to gain a seat, they must change a seat's allegiance (i.e. the overall partisanship of a particular constituency);[1] they should communicate with those voters that are most likely to change their votes. Thus, in a Liberal Democratic Party seat where the Labour Party is the main opposition, strategists would be keen to encourage Labour supporters to vote for the Liberal Democrats while also attempting to gain tactical votes[2] from the Conservative Party supporters by encouraging them to vote Liberal Democrat because they would not want the Labour Party to gain the seat. Such tactical voting does not tend to occur in a dominant two-party system because there is no alternative for whom to vote. But although this has tended to be the case in the United States in the past (because it has had a two-party system), there are now opportunities for tactical voting with the increase in the standing of third-party candidates (e.g., Ross Perot).

One of the most important types of voter in elections, constantly referred to in both academic and newspaper articles, is the floating voter. The floating voter can be regarded as a voter who is unsure for which candidate or party to vote. Generally, this voter is either an independent, someone who has not previously voted (for age or other reasons), a voter considering changing his or her choice, or a voter who does not know for which candidate or party to vote. In the United States, split-ticket voters[3] would be an ideal category of voters to target (because they also demonstrate less party loyalty), but this category of voters is very difficult to target, and it has been argued that these voters have no specific demographic profile (Kitchens & Powell, 1994).

Hayes and McAllister (1996) state, "From a marketing perspective, floating voters could be considered individuals with no brand loyalty" (p. 139). They suggest that floating voters tend to be less politically aware and, therefore, more difficult to communicate with, and they argue that those voters in the middle of the ideological spectrum (e.g., where far left is communist and far right is fascist) are more knowledgeable voters who might be a better segment to target. Converse (1962) demonstrates that less politically aware voters are just as hard to convert as those voters who are knowledgeable and committed.

Thus, segmentation of voters becomes an important process in political marketing because the voter market is not homogeneous and different voter groups contribute more or less to different campaign outcomes. The importance of positioning a candidate or party correctly can be illustrated, from a British perspective, by Heath, Jowell, and Curtice (1985), who suggest,

> For the floating voter, there is a less close fit between [his or her] own values and . . . perceptions of where the parties stand. The floating Conservative voter was more likely to report that [he or she] lay to the left of [his or her] party, while the floating Labour voter tended to lie to the right of the Labour position. (p. 95)

This argument is supported by Himmelweit, Jaegar, Stockdale, and Stockdale (1978), who state that converts have a stronger stance on their new party's ideological position and that, as a result, political parties should attempt to convert such floaters with political messages designed to maximize this phenomenon.

Thus, in many political campaigns, because there is a need to target specific voters who are more likely to affect the outcome, political strategists should divide the electorate into a number of homogeneous segments of voters. Political strategists should determine which segments are most likely to contribute to a candidate's or party's success in the election and should position the candidate or party with these segments of voters. The basis of this chapter is to suggest how the voter market should be segmented and how parties and candidates should position themselves.

Segmentation and Positioning in Political Campaigning

The acceptance of marketing as a discipline capable of being applied in the political campaigning process has only recently taken effect in Western Europe. The use of marketing techniques has been much more prominent in U.S. presidential campaigns. For example, Dwight Eisenhower is renowned for the 1952 presidential campaign in which he sent out a number of different fund-raising letters to different groups of the population—with each letter containing different issues—and then based his subsequent voter persuasion campaign on the letter containing the issues that received the best response (in terms of donations).

The underlying process in political campaigning is the exchange of promises for votes, and this process occurs through the communication of programs, policies, and ideas in return for information (relating to these policies, ideas, and programs) from the electorate about how parties and candidates can position themselves and segment the market better. Although the exchange relationship does not fit neatly into marketing theory (Lock & Harris, 1996; O'Cass, 1996; O'Leary & Iredale, 1976; Wring, 1997), marketing techniques can be applied if they are modified accordingly.

The segmentation and positioning processes involved in political campaigning differ considerably when compared to segmentation and positioning in the commercial marketing process. The difference between the two arises from the following factors:

1. There is less information from voters than from consumers because the social stigma attached to voting is far stronger than that compared to buying a commercial product or service.

2. The amount of funding available to political parties generally is very limited; therefore, research has tended to be accorded less significance than its counterpart in commercial research. As a result, in most countries, political marketing research is limited to opinion research through questionnaires and focus groups. Some attempts are made by U.S. political consultants to segment voter populations using statistical procedures such as chi-square automatic interaction detector (CHAID), but these tend to be by the more experienced research agencies working with large campaign teams (e.g., those for presidential nominees or gubernatorial candidates).

3. Positioning a product and positioning a candidate or political party are two very different processes. Whereas successful products are positioned such that their images are clear, consistent, credible, and competitive (Jobber, 1995, p. 225), political positioning is more difficult because politicians deal with a higher level of uncertainty, as plans for government policy have a subsequent impact on the corporate environment; companies may attempt to block aspects of the policy from becoming law through commercial lobbying efforts.

4. The intangible nature of the political marketing process, and the fact that the voters' choice in the political process is more emotional, restricts the capacity for image re-creation, although when re-creation does occur, it tends to take much longer and to require more incremental changes (as with Bill Clinton between 1992 and 1996).

There is a need for parties and candidates to formulate policies based on identifying key individuals' interests and enthusiasms (O'Shaughnessy, 1987; Reid, 1988). Smith and Saunders (1990) state that the following four methods have been used for political market segmentation in the past.

Geographic. This method was used by the British Liberal Democrats in southwestern England during the 1997 British general election. Shelley and Archer (1994) point out that Clinton's strategy in the 1992 U.S. presidential election campaign was to concentrate on gaining the 270 electoral college seats necessary to become president by further concentrating on the far western states (especially California), Clinton's home state of Arkansas, and Vice President Al Gore's home state of Tennessee as well as on neighboring Georgia, Alabama, Kentucky, Mississippi, Louisiana, Oklahoma, and Texas. Other examples of geographic targeting include the use of age, gender, street location, and other census data. Yorke and Meehan (1986) have advocated the use of ACORN[4] as a segmentation base.

Behavioristic. Smith and Saunders (1990) cite Downs (1957), who argued that most voters would not expend a large amount of effort in learning about parties' and candidates' policies and instead would select parties only on the basis of their general propositions; this relates significantly to the fact that U.S. political strategists constantly mention the need to repeat and reinforce one single theme. Perhaps a more common behavioristic segmentation base is loyalty to a party, which can be used to target voters (when they are asked for whom they are going to vote at the next election) with canvassing techniques that can then be used to locate key voters.

Psychographic. Ahmed and Jackson (1979) suggest using this method for segmenting the electorate for the Canadian provincial elections. In their study, they used respondents' attitudes toward welfare to produce different market segments.

Demographic. Robbin (1980) states that traditional methods in political market segmentation use data such as registration statistics, regional electoral history, and census data and that these are much more useful in segmenting voters than are other methods. Hughes (1984) disagrees, arguing that geopartisan data are much better than geodemographic data. This is likely to be the case because geopartisan data allow the strategist to make the distinctions among voters for particular political parties, which is of more direct interest.

The interactions among segmentation, positioning, and targeting are neatly described in the literature by Baer (1995), who suggests, "Candidates should form a strategy that has an overall theme (broadcast message) and maintains momentum but also effectively targets specialized groups (narrowcast message)" (p. 61). There is a need for political strategists not only to target the small groups of floating voters that can change the pattern of an election result but also to communicate with the wider audience in general. It is of little use to garner the votes of the floating voters if one cannot keep the larger body of voters that voted for the candidate previously.

To successfully market the candidate or party, political marketers should fully understand the reasons why voters have previously selected their candidate and alter the packaging of agendas and the substance of the agendas themselves so as to reflect the changing needs of the electorate. Newman and Sheth (1985) suggest that the following factors effect voter choice in U.S. elections: the issues and policies of the candidate, social imagery and the particular segments of society that support the candidate, the emotional feelings aroused by the candidate (e.g., nationalism, anger, hope), the candidate's image in terms of personality traits, current events in the domestic and international situations, personal events in the voters' lives, and epistemic issues such as the offering of something new.

Strategists should be concerned with those issues that the electorate considers to be important and how to encompass such issues within a coherent theme. To fully design a coherent competitive message, it is necessary to determine the competition within each individual voting district so that an appropriate policy platform can be designed to counteract the opposing candidates or parties. To attempt to convert supporters of other parties, political strategists need to use policies, issues, and reasoned arguments to attempt to win the battle for the minds of the voters. Often, voters support candidates or parties with whom they might not actually agree. This is illustrated graphically in Table 22.1 (Newman & Sheth (1987, p. 135). From the table, it can be clearly seen that candidates have a number of ways in which they need to communicate with their voters. These options led Newman and Sheth (1987) to suggest the following strategies when positioning a candidate.

Reinforcement strategy. This strategy is used for those voters who have voted for the right candidate for the right reasons. The intention of the strategy is to reinforce the voters' choice by communicating to them the message that they have made the right choice, and this would envisage a positive campaign such as targeting 1992 Clinton voters in the 1996 U.S. general election.

Rationalization strategy. This strategy should be used when the right candidate has been chosen for the wrong reasons. Thus, strategists need to communicate carefully with this segment of the electorate to modify these voters' attitudes

TABLE 22.1 Candidate Strategy Options

Candidate	Values	
	Right	*Wrong*
Right	Right candidate Right reasons	Right candidate Wrong reasons
Wrong	Wrong candidate Right reasons	Wrong candidate Wrong reasons

SOURCE: Newman and Sheth (1987, p. 135).

accordingly or, alternatively, to "connect" with them using other more convergent attitudes. In the United Kingdom, this strategy should have been used to counter the Labour Party charges against the Conservative Party that taxes had been increased 22 times despite the fact that the party previously had campaigned on a tax reduction platform; in the United States, it should have been used when Lyndon Johnson was elected president in 1964 on an anti-Vietnam War platform and subsequently escalated U.S. involvement in that area.

Inducement strategy. This strategy applies to those voters who pick the wrong candidate for the right reasons. Thus, this strategy attempts to explain to voters that their values are consistent with the candidate's or party's values. This strategy was successfully used by Tony Blair and the Labour Party by reengaging the support of the working classes (which had been taken away, to some extent, by the Conservative Party throughout the Thatcher period) in the 1997 British general election and by Clinton in the 1992 U.S. general election when he regained the support of what had been termed the "Reagan Democrats."

Confrontation strategy. This is where the wrong candidate is selected for the wrong reasons. Essentially, the voters are either picking the candidate or party because the candidate or party is the "best of a bad bunch" or are voting *against* the other parties or candidates (a combination of antivoting and tactical voting).[5] This type of strategy is best suited for a negative or comparative campaign such as that used by Perot in the 1992 U.S. presidential election or the campaign run by the Liberal Democrats in the 1997 British general election.

Once the agenda for the constituency has been developed and the political strategists have determined who needs to be contacted (having identified who the floating voters are and how they can be reached), the constituency organization must deliver its message through the various media. Locally, this is achieved using door-to-door and telephone canvassing, political literature, and local meetings. At the national level, different methods are used in the various countries around the world because there are different electoral and political laws, systems, and cultures operating.

The Political Marketing Process and Strategy Formulation

There is a strong relationship between political marketing strategy and the political product. The political marketing strategy process involves the promotion of the candidate or political party, and their associated issue and policy stances, to the electorate. Research affects this process in a number of ways. For example, Kavanagh (1995) states that polling organizations can provide political campaigns with the following relevant marketing information:

- *Election timing:* When the government has the power to determine when to hold an election,[6] polls can be used to determine when the mood is most favorable for commencement of the general election.
- *Image building:* Polls provide parties with a "snapshot" of how the voters perceive them. In the United States, pollsters conduct benchmark surveys to determine the candidate's name recognition level, the candidate's electoral strength vis-à-vis the opponents, and citizens' assessments of an incumbent officeholder's performance (Asher, 1995, p. 104).
- *Policy:* Blair has suggested setting up a "people's panel" to test the viability of future government policy. This panel would involve approximately 5,000 specialist members of the electorate who scrutinize draft government policy (Etienne, 1998). Clinton also has used polls to help in the development of government policy.
- *Tracking:* Parties and candidates can use polls to pinpoint their potential strengths and weaknesses over time. Bob Teeter was the first to set up daily interviewing of voters in 1972 (Moore, 1995, p. 198). Blakeman (1995) argues that a good tracking program allows for the evaluation of the effectiveness of a candidate's own—as well as opponents'—strategies and tactics.
- *Targeting voters:* In addition to asking voters questions on issues, pollsters usually include questions to determine the demography of voters for particular parties and candidates. In the 1997 British general election, it was thought that "Worcester women"[7] represented an important target group for the Conservative Party because they were underrepresented in the previous general election and were thought to be Conservative floating voters. To some extent, in the United States, this is analogous to "soccer moms" who were identified as a target through polling.

Candidates and parties also conduct qualitative research into individuals' thoughts and values using focus groups (general discussion groups of between 8 and 12 people) and dial groups (used to measure respondents' attitudes toward candidates' television campaign advertisements in the United States). Such techniques allow strategists to build up a more detailed picture of voters' needs, desires, and wants that enhances positioning and enables the candidate or party to make more educated decisions regarding the positioning strategy.

Maarek (1995) illustrates his version of the political marketing process in Figure 22.1. Maarek states that political strategists first need to determine the "main line of the campaign" or theme. Then, it is necessary to determine what the public's opinion is, what the opposition's "standpoint" (or theme) is, and what resources are available to the campaign.

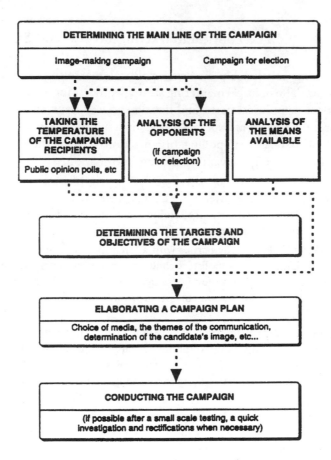

Figure 22.1. Determining the Main Line of the Campaign
SOURCE: Maarek (1995).

Strategists consequently identify the target segments and which media need to be used to reach them before finally conducting the campaign. In this model, it is assumed that segmentation and positioning, on the national level, *are* the political marketing process.

The model shown in Figure 22.2 relates to the coordination of local campaigning activity by the national party to project a systematic and unified message by political parties. Thus, this process attempts to minimize the dichotomy that occurs in British general elections (and, to a lesser extent, in U.S. elections for national office), where the electorate tends to vote on party labels within a localized context.

In the model in Figure 22.2, it is suggested that political strategists collect data on individual voting districts regarding voter registration; collect census data; and conduct constituency market research into voters' attitudes, opinions, hopes, and desires to determine which individual voting districts are most liable to changing their allegiance from one candidate or party to another.

The next stage requires determination of the competition and identification of the profiles of the different segments within each of the marginal voting districts,

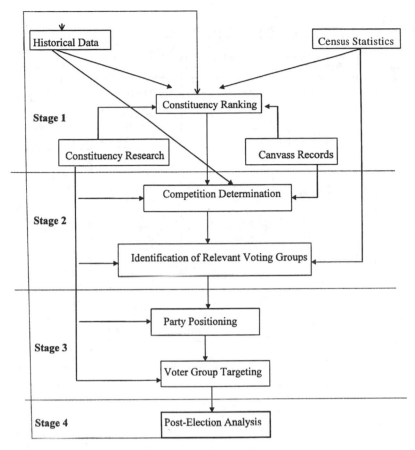

Figure 22.2. Political Planning Model for Local Campaigning
SOURCE: Baines, Yorke, and Lewis (1998).

that is, those that are most likely to influence the overall result of the election campaign. This, then, allows the candidate or party to establish position and target the relevant supporter groups in each constituency to win the overall campaign.

Finally, the campaign planning team should conduct a postmortem examination of how and where the campaign succeeded and failed. In this model of political marketing planning, political market segmentation and positioning are influenced by competition determination, census data, constituency research, and identification of the relevant voting groups. Again, political market segmentation and positioning are crucial to the whole process.

Newman (1994, p. 12) illustrates a different notion of political marketing (Figure 22.3) by taking into account the fact that there are different candidate foci. For example, whereas one party might focus simply on its policies (product concept), another party might focus on what it feels the electorate wants (marketing concept). Yet another party might focus on getting its image across (selling concept) or simply appealing to the voters' partisan nature (party concept).

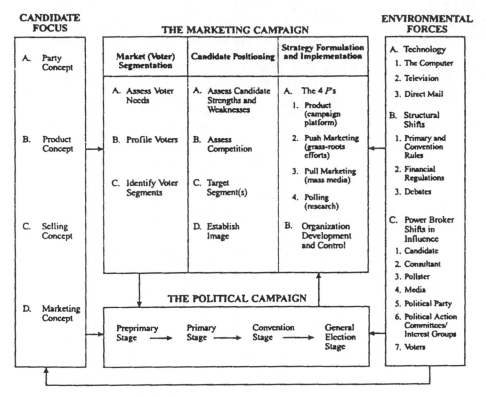

Figure 22.3. Newman's Political Marketing Process Model
SOURCE: Newman (1994).

Newman (1994) also takes into account the effects of the stages in the election campaign that are relevant to the process. For example, he argues that the market segmentation and positioning strategies for a primary campaign would be very different from those for a general election campaign. In addition, he argues that environmental forces such as technology, structural shifts in the political process, and shifts in the influence of power between political agents all affect the political marketing process. Clearly, technology has had a significant effect on segmentation and positioning because sophisticated computer applications can now be used to profile voters (e.g., using neural networks) and the issues they consider important.

The environment has a significant impact on how voters are segmented, targeted, and positioned because different rules and regulations are in force around the world. For example, in the United Kingdom, it is illegal to advertise a political party using broadcast media such as television and radio. Similarly, in France, polling is not allowed to be reported in the final week of the election. Financial regulations also may be imposed in different countries. For example, in the United Kingdom, constituencies have stringent expenditure ceilings (carrying the penalty of an election being declared null and void). As a result, some constituency work is carried out in the party's name and, therefore, comes under national party expenses (for which there are no ceilings).

The models describe different facets of positioning within the political marketing process. Nevertheless, all the models indicate that focused research should be conducted into the determination of the competition and voters' opinions and attitudes, that the electorate should be segmented, and that careful media planning needs to take place if the candidate or party is to be positioned effectively.

It is important to realize that these models are guidelines as to the basic aspects of the political campaigning process. There are aspects of marketing that are pertinent to campaigning in most countries, yet there also are cultural nuances that often must be taken into account. Baines, Newman, and Harris (1998) state that political consultants and marketers need to take account of the differences in political systems when positioning candidates and parties because there often are different factors prevailing on the conduct of political campaigns. Examples of such factors include the electoral system, the campaign organization structure (external consultant or internal party campaign executive), the funding methods available to parties (private, public, or mixed system of funding), and the extent to which candidates' and parties' messages are allowed to be disseminated.

Thus, specific aspects of media planning are different in the various countries. For example, scheduling in the United States is different from that in the United Kingdom because U.S. campaigns run over a longer time period. Similarly, the types of media (e.g., television, radio, press, billboard) available to political consultants and campaign executives in the various countries are different, but the process of positioning (outlined in the previous paragraphs) generally is the same.

Determining Positioning Strategy

The political positioning process is a determination of how best to portray a candidate or party to the relevant segments of the electorate so as to persuade the voters to vote for the candidate or party again or to switch from supporting another candidate or party.

It is important for a candidate or political party to understand its own strengths and weaknesses because this allows the strategists to determine what the candidate or party can and cannot do. Clearly, a small regional party cannot lay claim to governing the whole country because this would not be credible. It could, however, lay claim to managing the local council or other local offices. In the United States, opposition researchers are hired, not just to look at the strengths and weaknesses of the opposition (in terms of voting records, stances on issues, inconsistency of stance, and any relevant personal details that might affect the holding of office) but also to conduct the same type of research on their own candidate. The results of this are fed into the positioning process.

Baines (1996) suggests that U.K. candidates and political parties should determine who their main competition is within each constituency because it is unlikely to mirror the national scene due to differences in partisan allegiance in different areas of the country.

TABLE 22.2 Political Market Positions, Strategies, and Examples

Position	Characteristics	Strategic Directions	Examples
Leader	Highest share Acknowledged orientation point Continuous attack	Expand total market Expand share Defend share	National Congress (India) PRI (Mexico)

Challenger	Chosen to depose
	   leader
	May be several chal-
	   lengers
		Attack leader
		Attack similar com-
		   petitors
		Attack smaller com-
		   petitors
			Partido Popular (Spain)
			Labour party (United
			   Kingdom)

Follower	Purposeful concentration
	   on target market
	Imitative rather than
	   innovative
	Local/regional strengths
	Broad line
		Clone
		Imitate
		Adapt
			Center party (Norway)
			Progressive Democrats
			   (Ireland)

Nicher	Leader in narrowly de- fined market or niche Specialist appeal	Create niche Expand niche Defend niche	Les Verts (France) Yisreal Ba-Aliya (Israel)

SOURCE: Butler and Collins (1996).

Butler and Collins (1996) suggest that political parties should think pragmatically about their electoral prospects and the strategies that are adopted. For example, a "nicher" cannot hope to become leader in a short space of time. A niche party should instead expand the niche before moving into more mainstream politics such as when the Green Party won 14% of the European election vote in 1989. This vote share subsequently dropped dramatically as the major European parties imitated its policies. In this case, the Green Party failed to defend its niche. The range of strategies open to political parties after determining their competitive positions is illustrated in Table 22.2.

Once a candidate or political party has determined who its competitors are, what its own and its competitors' strengths and weaknesses are, and which competitive strategy it will adopt, it is necessary to target the appropriate segments with the appropriate message and policies.

The positioning evaluation tool in Table 22.3 illustrates how candidates and political parties can determine whether their policies should hold a position of strength within the portfolio and the extent to which those policies should be communicated on the basis of the strength of importance that voters attach to those policies and how central they are to the candidate's or party's ethos or mission.

Baines, Lewis, and Ingham (1998) argue that candidates and political parties should determine which issues are of most importance to the electorate. However, this is not to say that political parties and candidates should follow a purely populist agenda (this may be more or less possible depending on the political traditions in the voting district concerned) or that the extent to which policy

TABLE 22.3 Positioning Evaluation Tool

	High	
Environment *	Electorate's viewpoint of importance of issue	Law and order *
	Housing	Centrality to party ethos
Low	Medium	High
* Drugs	Low	* Europe

SOURCE: Adapted from Baines, Lewis, and Ingham (1998).

platforms should be modified (in terms of how much of the future government budget they have allocated to them, how much space they occupy in the manifesto, the extent to which they are being actively investigated by working parties, etc.) and the extent to which the policy platforms should be communicated (how many advertising spots or party political broadcasts and other media should be devoted to the dissemination of a specific issue) depend on the extent to which an issue is part of a candidate's or party's ethos and how important the electorate feels the issue is.

In the case of an issue that the electorate feels is important but is of low centrality to party ethos (e.g., the environment in Table 22.3), the party needs to build up the issue's agenda and hold communications constant until its agenda sufficiently represents the targeted section of the electorate's perspective. Communications can be increased at a later date, depending on the changing state of the electorate's feelings (as determined by tracking polls). With an issue such as Europe, where the electorate views the issue as relatively unimportant,[8] but where the issue was considered as highly central to the party's ethos, there is a need to reduce the policy agenda in this area while building communications until the public comes to recognize the importance of the issue from a political perspective.

The candidate's and party's aim is to move issues from the bottom left-hand sector of Table 22.3 to the top left-hand sector of the table by increasing communications surrounding the issue and increasing the issue's impact on the candidate's or party's agenda, in line with voters' expectations and needs. In Table 22.3, the axes are concerned with centrality to party ethos and the electorate's viewpoint of importance of issue because certain issues were found to differentiate the parties (Baines, 1996). However, in systems where issues are less able to differentiate candidates or parties, positioning should occur using other axes (determined through polling and research) that allow maximum differentiation on those factors that determine voters' choice.

Candidates and political parties need to determine whether there are any issues that currently are not being covered by any political candidate's campaign. Attempting to uncover new issues that tie in with a campaign's overall theme and allow connection with the voters is the art of political campaign management and tends to be generated through focus group discussions with voters and "brainstorming" sessions.

The central tenet of the political positioning problem is the creation of a consistent image that is centered around a single theme with strongly tied-in underlying issues while the competition is attempting to undermine consistency and credibility. Thus, candidates' and political parties' campaign teams constantly attempt to perform this action through "spin-doctoring" and the use of "rapid rebuttal," where political parties send out press releases either to deny allegations made by competing parties (e.g., the party has presided over the largest decline in spending on the National Health Service for the last x number of years) or to plant stories that shed a negative light on the opposing parties. This process requires considerable computerization because voting records, press releases, manifestos, speeches, and party literature for all candidates and parties over a lengthy period all must be readily accessible.

In the United States, rebuttal tends to occur through the placement of bought advertising spots. In some cases, media consultants may anticipate that an opponent will make a certain claim and have an advertising spot already paid for and designed to deal with such a claim. This "game" between political consultants often constitutes who wins and loses in a close election.

Voter Targeting

The most traditional method of communicating with the voters is the use of political literature. "Direct mail succeeds because, unlike any other media, it can deliver a specialized message to distinctive groups, made personal through the agency of new technology and therefore engendering unique loyalties" (O'Shaughnessy & Peele, 1985, p. 56).

Owen (1992) writes that in the 1992 British general election campaign, "Labour . . . used canvass returns to target categories of voters with computer-printed letters" (p. 7). Owen does mention that this process can cause problems when people are targeted incorrectly. For example, a former Democrat voter might be targeted as a Democrat when he or she has become an Independent. In the United Kingdom, recent research suggests that only around 47% of the people receiving official government pamphlets find them very or quite useful (Marsh, 1996).

O'Shaughnessy (1987) argues that in America, "the low-involvement, high-viewing recipient is most susceptible to attitude change" (p. 61). Rust, Bajaj, and Haley (1984) state that "television viewership appears to be negatively related to voting participation, with the anomalous exception of the lowest television viewership quintile" (p. 185). Thus, it would not seem to make sense to target high-viewing members of the electorate if they do not vote. Political parties and candidates should be careful to ensure that their communicational messages are targeted to the appropriate audiences. In the United States, it is much easier to target voters because broadcasting companies have detailed demographic details of their audiences gathered through research conducted by audience research boards that help to price television advertising slots for both commercial and political advertising. U.S. consultants also advertise their candidates on cable channels, which tend to have even smaller and more highly specified populations (because they operate in smaller areas). Thus, targeting is much less of a problem in the United States than in the United Kingdom, where it tends to occur more through the use of newspaper and billboard advertising (with increasing use of direct mail).

Where candidates and parties cannot afford advertising, or where it is not allowed, they have to attempt to maximize favorable reporting about themselves on the major news network channels through earned media. In addition, they have to adopt significant grassroots efforts to ensure that their messages are disseminated by more traditional means (e.g., door-to-door canvassing, direct mail, town meetings). Most campaigns try to tie the two together so that they are mutually reinforcing. Thus, reporters are invited to join campaigns while in action.

Conclusion

Ideally, voter segmentation and candidate positioning combined represent the process in which political strategists determine who their most influential supporters are, determine how they can be reached, and devise a plan to determine how best to project the image of that candidate or party in such a manner that it is consistent with the voters' ideals, wants, and needs (where these are known by the voters themselves) and the image is consistent with the candidate's or party's ideology and previous policy statements and actions. This process is aided by marketing research techniques that enable the construction of a picture of voters' attitudes and opinions. Where the voters do not know their own ideals, wants, and needs or are incapable of communicating them (as in many burgeoning democracies), the process relies on the anticipation of these factors by political strategists and the determination of a "connection," mainly by intuition.

The electorate is communicated with through broadcast messages (generally policy propositions mainly for name recognition and voter education purposes) and through narrowcast messages (mainly for voter persuasion purposes). It is important that strategists communicate through both media with one consistent theme. This theme helps to unite the candidate's or party's campaign team and project a consistent message that voters will remember and understand. However, different political systems have peculiar cultures, electoral systems, media structures, and electoral laws, and all of these factors may affect the voter segmentation and candidate or party positioning strategies. Despite this, the general process of positioning candidates and political parties in different countries remains the same. Strategists should pay particular attention to the environment in which they are working, and systematic research is advised so as to take the particular political market's cultural characteristics into account.

Notes

1. A constituency in the United Kingdom generally consists of approximately 70,000 voters. There currently are 659 such constituencies (seats) in the British Parliament.

2. Tactical voting is referred to as "strategic" voting in the U.S. political science literature and occurs when a voter votes for his or her second choice for a candidate to defeat the first-place candidate because this candidate has a better chance of defeating the first-place candidate than does the preferred (third-place) candidate.

3. Split-ticket voters are members of the electorate who vote for one party for one race and another party for another race because voters may be asked to make a number of choices between different public offices on the same ballot. An example of this behavior might be voting Democrat for U.S. Senate and Republican for the House of Representatives.

4. ACORN (a classification of residential neighborhoods) is a system designed by CACI Ltd. in London to classify individuals by the types of houses in which they live (using "postcode" data, similar to zip codes in United States) in terms of their lifestyles and consumer purchasing patterns.

5. The difference between antivoting and tactical voting is that the voter who is antivoting does not necessarily attempt to maximize his or her choice by supporting the party or candidate with the best chance of winning.

6. For example, in the United Kingdom, the government sets the election date.

7. The Worcester woman was a mid-1930s housewife with a couple of young children and a husband in the "C2" category of the social grading scale.

8. The data used to formulate Table 22.3 were generated from a survey conducted in April 1996. For further details, see Baines, Lewis, and Ingham (1998).

References

Ahmed, S. A., & Jackson, D. N. (1979). Psychographics for social policy decisions: Welfare assistance. *Journal of Consumer Research, 5,* 229-239

Asher, H. (1995). *Polling and the public: What every citizen should know* (3rd ed.). Washington, DC: Congressional Quarterly Press.

Baer, D. (1995). Contemporary strategy and agenda setting. In J. A. Thurber & C. Nelson (Eds.), *Campaigns and elections American style* (p. 61). Boulder, CO: Westview.

Baines, P. R. (1996). *The relevance of strategic marketing planning for political parties.* Unpublished master's thesis, Manchester School of Management.

Baines, P. R., Lewis, B. R., & Ingham, B. (1998, July). *Political campaign and government marketing: An exploration of the positioning process.* Paper presented at the 5th International Public Relations Symposium on Public Affairs and Government Relations, Lake Bled, Slovenia.

Baines, P. R., Newman, B. I., & Harris, P. (1998, May). *New realpolitik: Political campaigning and the application of political marketing across cultures.* Paper prepared for presentation at the European Marketing Academic Conference, Berlin.

Baines, P. R., Yorke, D. A., & Lewis, B. R. (1998). *Marketing planning for U.K. political parties: Coordinated local campaigning.* Unpublished manuscript, Middlesex University Business School.

Blakeman, B. W. (1995, August). Tracking polls: How to do them. *Campaigns & Elections,* pp. 24-25.

Butler, P., & Collins, N. (1996). Strategic analysis in political markets. *European Journal of Marketing, 30*(10/11), 32-44.

Converse, P. (1962). Information flow and the stability of political partisan attitudes. *Public Opinion Quarterly, 26,* 578-599.

Downs, A. (1957). *An economic theory of democracy.* New York: Harper & Row.

Etienne, S. (1998, March). Does the people's panel lead a Blair revolution? *Research: The Magazine of the Market Research Society,* p. 16.

Farrell, D. M. (1996). Campaign strategies and tactics. In L. LeDuc, R. G. Niemi, & P. Norris (Eds.), *Comparing democracies and voting in global perspective* (p. 162). London: Sage.

Granberg, D., & Holmberg, S. (1995). *The political system matters: Social psychology and voting behaviour in Sweden and the U.S.* Cambridge, UK: Cambridge University Press.

Hayes, B. C., & McAllister, I. (1996). Marketing politics to voters: Late deciders in the 1992 British election. *European Journal of Marketing, 30*(10/11), 135-146.

Heath, A., Jowell, R., & Curtice, J. (1985). *How Britain votes.* New York: Pergamon.

Himmelweit, H., Jaegar, M., Stockdale, B., & Stockdale, J. (1978). Memory for past vote. *British Journal of Political Science, 8,* 365-384.

Hughes, R. N. (1984, Summer). Geopartisan vs. geodemographic data. *Campaigns & Elections,* pp. 27-35.

Jobber, D. (1995). *Principles and practice of marketing.* New York: McGraw-Hill.

Kavanagh, D. A. (1995). *Election campaigning: The new marketing of politics.* Oxford, UK: Blackwell.

Kitchens, J. T., & Powell, L. (1994, June). Ticket splitting: Dead or alive? *Campaigns & Elections,* pp. 34-35.

Kotler, P., & Kotler, N. (1981, Summer). Business marketing for political candidates. *Campaigns & Elections,* pp. 24-33.

Lock, A., & Harris, P. (1996). Political marketing: Vive la difference! *European Journal of Marketing, 30*(10/11), 21-31.

Maarek, P. J. (1995). *Political marketing and communication.* London: John Libbey.

Marsh, H. (1996, January 8). Are Britain's doors open for business? *Marketing,* p. 8.

Moore, D. W. (1995). *The superpollsters: How they measure and manipulate public opinion in America* (2nd ed.). New York: Four Walls Eight Windows.

Newman, B. I. (1994). *The marketing of the president: Political marketing as campaign strategy.* Thousand Oaks, CA: Sage.

Newman, B. I., & Sheth, J. N. (1985). A model of primary voter behavior. *Journal of Consumer Research, 12,* 178-187.

Newman, B. I., & Sheth, J. N. (1987). *A theory of political choice behavior.* New York: Praeger.

O'Cass, A. (1996). Political marketing and the marketing concept. *European Journal of Marketing, 30*(10/11), 45-61.

O'Leary, R., & Iredale, I. (1976). The marketing concept: Quo vadis? *European Journal of Marketing, 10*(3), 146-157.

O'Shaughnessy, N. (1987). America's political market. *European Journal of Marketing, 21*(4), 60-66.

O'Shaughnessy, N., & Peele, G. (1985). Money, mail and markets: Reflections on direct mail in American politics. *Electoral Studies, 8,* 55-64.

Owen, D. (1992, April 8). Election 1992: Message unclear amid the graffiti. *Financial Times,* p. 7.

Reid, D. M. (1988). Marketing the political product. *European Journal of Marketing, 22*(9), 34-47.

Robbin, J. (1980, Spring). Geodemographics: The new magic. *Campaigns & Elections,* pp. 25-33.

Rust, R. T., Bajaj, M., & Haley, G. T. (1984). Efficient and inefficient media for political campaign advertising. *Journal of Advertising, 13*(3), 45-49.

Scammell, M. (1997). *The wisdom of the war room: U.S. campaigning and Americanization.* Research Paper R-17, Joan Shorenstein Centre on the Press, Politics, and Public Policy, John F. Kennedy School of Government, Harvard University.

Shelley, F. M., & Archer, J. C. (1994). Some geographical aspects of the American presidential election of 1992. *Political Geography, 13*(2), 137-159.

Smith, G., & Saunders, J. (1990). The application of marketing to British politics. *Journal of Marketing Management, 5,* 295-306.

Sweeney, W. R. (1995). The principles of planning. In J. A. Thurber & C. Nelson (Eds.), *Campaigns and elections American style* (pp. 20-21). Boulder, CO: Westview.

Wring, D. (1997). Reconciling marketing with political science: Theories of political marketing. In *Proceedings of the 1997 Academy of Marketing Conference*. Manchester, UK: Manchester Metropolitan University.

Yorke, D. A., & Meehan, S. A. (1986). ACORN in the political marketplace. *European Journal of Marketing, 20*(8), 73-86.

Political Communication

23

Political Advertising

A Summary of Research Findings

LYNDA LEE KAID

Political advertising is a major tool in political marketing. In fact, political advertising has become the dominant form of communication between politicians and the publics they seek to lead. Most often, political advertising is used by political candidates seeking to influence electoral decisions, but it also frequently is used by political parties and by interest groups or individuals who want to influence voting decisions or public opinion on issues of national concern.

In the political campaign marketing process where candidates exchange political leadership for votes (Newman, 1994), political advertising is the pragmatic tool that allows the candidate to communicate to voters the superiority of his or her attributes over those of opponents. In devising advertising messages, candidates rely on traditional marketing research techniques to assess their strengths and weaknesses as well as those of their opponents (Newman, 1994; O'Shaughnessy, 1990), to position themselves accordingly, and then to target or segment the voters/market with appropriate messages.

The defining characteristics of modern political advertising are (a) control of the message and (b) use of mass communication channels for message distribution. As a marketing tool in politics, political advertising's greatest advantage is its ability to completely control the message conveyed to the public. With political advertising, those seeking to influence voting decisions or public opinion can control every aspect of the message content and every aspect of the presentation or format of the message. Most other forms of political communication are subject to filtering or intervention by news media or other players in the political process. Those seeking to use political advertising to influence voting and public opinion also benefit from political advertising's distribution through mass media channels, allowing a tremendous reach and penetration of the controlled message.

Earlier definitions of political advertising also suggested that it was characterized by its paid nature (Kaid, 1981). However, with the growth of new communication technologies, it is no longer true that all political advertising is "purchased" in the traditional sense. Political advertising spread through the Internet, for example, would not fit this traditional definition. In addition, in many countries (particularly European democracies), controlled political messages are distributed through mass channels where the time is given or provided to candidates and parties as well as sometimes sold (Kaid & Holtz-Bacha, 1995).

In U.S. elections, television advertising's dominance is evidenced by the massive expenditures that campaigns devote to it. In the 1988 presidential campaign, candidates George Bush and Michael Dukakis together spent more than $80 million on electronic advertising (Devlin, 1989). With three candidates in the race, 1992 spending was more than $120 million combined for Bush, Bill Clinton, and Ross Perot (Devlin, 1993), and the 1996 presidential campaign topped even the 1992 expenditures with Clinton, Perot, Bob Dole, and their respective parties spending nearly $200 million on advertising time (Devlin, 1997). Millions more are spent on state- and local-level races and by political parties and independent entities.

Money alone is not the test, of course, but it is an important indication of how candidates and their managers see the election. "Adwatches" testify to the media's judgment of advertising significance (Kaid, Gobetz, Garner, Leland, & Scott, 1993), and televised political spots affect agenda setting for television and newspaper coverage as well (Roberts & McCombs, 1994).

Whereas in the United States buying in the media for television spots is virtually unlimited and results in campaigns producing many different ads, most other Western democracies provide free time for candidates on television or operate with a dual system of public and private time, whereby some small amount of time is given and other time may be purchased. This approach is described for several of these systems as operated in France, Germany, Britain, Italy, Israel, and others in *Political Advertising in Western Democracies* (Kaid & Holtz-Bacha, 1995).

Because political advertising has increased steadily as a marketing tool in democracies throughout the world over the past five decades, this chapter examines the characteristics of modern political advertising and reviews the research findings on its effectiveness. Although political advertising certainly has flourished in all mass media channels from television to newspapers, from radio to direct mail, from the Internet to display advertising, this review concentrates on the most prevalent form of political advertising—televised political spots.

As social scientists during the 1970s began to break away from the pessimistic media effects prescriptions of the "limited effects" model (Klapper, 1960), many discovered that the principles accepted by minimal effects researchers did not apply as readily to political television advertising as to other mass media phenomena. Even by 1981, when the first comprehensive review of the literature on political advertising was published in the *Handbook of Political Communication* (Kaid, 1981), it was possible to say that researchers had discovered that political advertising had identifiable cognitive, affective, and behavioral effects. In a summary of research on advertising effects, Perloff (1998) also concluded, "Clearly, political spots can affect voters' evaluations of candidates and their interpretations of political events" (p. 374). The current body of literature on political television advertising falls into two basic areas: research on the *content* or characteristics of the advertising and research on the various *effects* of the advertising.

Characteristics of Televised Political Advertising

Political scholars and researchers have taken many approaches to describing the content of political advertising. Some have taken an approach that is primarily historical, critical, and interpretive, relying on subjective analysis (Devlin, 1989, 1993, 1997; Diamond & Bates, 1984, 1988, 1992; Jamieson, 1984, 1992, 1996). Other scholars have applied more systematic methods (Joslyn, 1980; Kaid & Johnston, 1991). Several key concerns have dominated studies of the content of televised political advertising—issue versus image content, negative versus positive content, and various other content considerations.

Issues Versus Images

No topic has been more dominant across the five decades of research on political advertising than the discussion of whether or not campaign commercials are dominated by image information or issue information. This concern, of course, is rooted in the classic democratic voting model that insists that rational voting decisions should be made on the basis of policy issues (Berelson, 1966), not on the basis of a candidate's image. One of the perennial criticisms of television advertising in politics is that it trivializes political discourse by concentrating more on candidate personalities and images than on issues. This has proven to be an unfounded concern; research has shown that most ads, usually between 60% and 80%, concentrate more often on issues than on candidate images (Joslyn, 1980). Patterson and McClure's (1976) classic study of the 1972 presidential campaign found not only that issue information overshadowed image content but also that the issue content of political spots outweighed the issue content of television network news during the campaign. Other work confirms this finding in regard to the 1972 presidential race (Hofstetter & Zukin, 1979), and Kern (1989) reinforced these findings in her studies of spots during the 1980s. Findings on the last three presidential campaigns also have substantiated that issues are stressed in spots more frequently than are images (Kaid, 1991a, 1994, 1998). In analyses of the 1996 primaries, researchers also have discovered that candidate messages (advertising and speeches) were giving substantial attention to issues and definitely were more issue substantive—by a margin of three to one—than was television news (Center for Media and Public Affairs, 1996; Lichter & Noyes, 1996).

Other studies at varying levels of races have found that issue content is predominant over image content in political television spots (Elebash & Rosene,

1982; Latimer, 1984), although some researchers have found that candidates for lower level races rely on a substantial amount of personal appeals in their spots. Typical of these findings are those by Latimer (1989a, 1989b), who found that Alabama state legislative candidates focused on image traits in their spots.

Although this research debunks the notion that political television spots are dominated by image information, it is important to note that the concentration on issues does not always mean that candidates are providing substantial arguments or explaining complex policy issues. Even Joslyn's (1980) early analysis of spots indicated that the percentage of spots with specific policy issue information was much lower than the overall number of issue spots. In a later analysis of 500 spots from 1960 to 1984, Joslyn (1986) found that ads focusing on prospective policy choices were the least frequently occurring type. Payne, Marlier, and Baukus (1989) reinforced this notion in their analysis of 1988 presidential primary spots when they concluded that issues are treated more in the form of vague policy preferences and that spots are replete with emotional and cultural images and symbols. West (1993) analyzed sets of typical and prominent spots across a number of years and was equally critical of the lack of substantive, specific policy positioning by candidates, although he noted that spots have become more policy oriented, not less so, in recent presidential elections.

One of the most well-developed studies of issue and image content in political spots was conducted on the 1980 presidential primary spots by Shyles (1983, 1984a, 1984b, 1988). Shyles found a strong emphasis on defense and foreign policy in the 1984 primary ads. He also found that candidates in the presidential primary used the spots to convey their image characteristics and that the choice of issue or image content also related to the presentational style of the spots (Shyles, 1984b). For example, spots that focused on the candidates' images tended to be head-on candidate presentations with candidates in formal attire.

Researchers also have noted the increasing difficulty in distinguishing between issues and images in campaign messages. Traditionally, issues have been viewed as statements of candidate positions on policy issues or preferences on issues or problems of public concern, whereas images have been viewed as the concentration on candidate qualities or characteristics (Kaid & Johnston, 1991; Kaid & Sanders, 1978). Many researchers have acknowledged that this dichotomy is, in fact, a false one. As Rudd (1986) pointed out in his observation of spots from the 1982 Idaho gubernatorial campaign, issue spots often are used to bolster aspects of a candidate's image.

Negative Versus Positive Ads

In the past two decades, the controversy over negative and positive spots has raged. Although this might seem like a relatively new concern to some, analyses of spots over time indicate that negative spots have been a factor in all presidential campaigns (Kaid & Johnston, 1991, in press). Johnson-Cartee and Copeland (1991, 1997) also have done a great deal to enhance our understanding of negative spots in their books, which categorize and analyze the strategies used in a wide variety of negative ads.

However, it is unquestionably true that there has been a real increase in the number of negative spots used in presidential campaigns in the past two election cycles. Although the percentage of negative ads in presidential campaigns from 1952 through 1996 is only about 38%, in the 1992 and 1996 campaigns, negative ads made up more than half of the advertising content of both major party candidates. In both 1992 and 1996, Clinton reached all-time highs in the proportion of negative ads in a presidential campaign, with 69% of his ads being negative in 1992 and 68% being negative in 1996 (Kaid, 1994, 1998; Kaid & Johnston, in press).

One of the clear findings about negative ads is that they tend to be more issue oriented than positive ads. Kaid and Johnston (1991) reached this conclusion from a study of more than 800 presidential ads aired between 1960 and 1988. West (1993) reached similar conclusions in his content analysis of typical and prominent ads: "It is somewhat surprising to discover that the most substantive appeals actually came in negative ads" (p. 51).

Other Content Considerations

The conceptualization of "videostyle," first laid out by Kaid and Davidson (1986), also focuses on the content of political spots and suggests that it is possible to understand a candidate's mode of self-presentation in spots by analyzing the verbal, nonverbal, and production characteristics of the candidate's political advertising. Videostyle has been used to describe characteristics of presidential spots (Kaid & Johnston, 1991, in press), to analyze spot styles of incumbents and challengers (Kaid & Davidson, 1986), and to determine differences in male and female candidate styles (Bystrom, 1995). Some researchers have examined the types of claims and arguments used in political spots. In an analysis of logical claims in 1972 Richard Nixon and George McGovern ads, Buss and Hofstetter (1976) found that the use of logical fallacies was not a dominant strategy; instead, ads used cognitive maneuvers to identify issue stands or information about the candidate. On the other hand, Baukus, Payne, and Reisler (1985) suggested that the arguments contained in spots often are so abbreviated that they are misleading and difficult to prove. The misleading or ethical content of political spots is a difficult area for assessment (Kaid, 1991b). The only systematic analysis of ethical content focused on the technological distortions in the ads (Kaid, 1996) and found a growing use of technologically based ethical concerns in ads from 1980 through the present (Kaid, 1998; Kaid & Noggle, 1998). As O'Shaughnessy (1990) lamented, "Political marketing and its technological articulation can conceal real intentions, fine-tuning the lie" (p. 156).

Effects of Spots on Voters

There would be very little reason for analyzing spot content or for assessing patterns in videostyle if there were no evidence that political spots have identifiable effects on voters. Such evidence is not difficult to find, confirming that candidates who spend millions on advertising campaigns are not completely off the mark. Most of the effects studies rely on survey research or experimental designs to measure the effects of spots. The most well researched of these effects fall into three categories: (a) effects on voter knowledge levels, (b) effects on voter perceptions of candidates, and (c) effects on voting preferences.

Effects on Knowledge Levels

American voters are not considered to be particularly well informed. Studies abound verifying that many cannot name their current congresspersons, let alone the candidates for upcoming offices or the issues at stake in various electoral contests. Certainly, the minimal effects tradition, with its emphasis on the significance of selective processes in thwarting media effects, had lowered expectations about the possibility that political advertising would be successful in communicating information to voters.

Nonetheless, one of the earliest surprises in political advertising research was the finding that political television commercials do a good job of communicating information, especially issue information, to voters regardless of partisan selectivity. One of the earliest research findings about political advertising was its ability to overcome selective exposure (Atkin, Bowen, Nayman, & Sheinkopf, 1973; Surlin & Gordon, 1976). This was a very important finding because it confirmed that spot advertising was successful in getting the candidate's message to all voters, not just those who already supported the candidate or party.

One cognitive effect of great interest to political marketers is candidate name identification, the equivalent of brand name recognition in product marketing. Research has provided evidence that exposure to political spots enhances candidate name recognition (Kaid, 1982). In fact, in a study of the 1992 California U.S. Senate races, West (1994) found paid advertising exposure to be a better predictor of candidate recognition than either television news or newspapers.

A great deal of evidence now supports the claim that exposure to political ads also can influence voter recall about specific campaign issues and candidate issue positions (Atkin & Heald, 1976; Martinelli & Chaffee, 1995). Although Faber and Storey (1984) reported that voters' recall of political spots in the 1982 Texas gubernatorial race was only 34%, the split between information they did recall was evenly distributed between issues and image information. Certainly, others have found that there are differences in the types and levels of information recalled from spots and that the type of information recalled can be structured somewhat by what viewers are cognitively attuned to or "seeking" from the ads (Garramone, 1983, 1986). The type of ad also can affect voter recall levels, with some research showing that image ads can produce greater recall of information (Kaid & Sanders, 1978), particularly when a candidate is less well known (Schleuder, 1990). However, negative ads generally produce higher levels of recall than do positive ones (Basil, Schooler, & Reeves, 1991; Johnson-Cartee & Copeland, 1989; Lang, 1991; Newhagen & Reeves, 1991).

In fact, voters learn more about issues from television ads than from television news (Kern & Just, 1995; McClure & Patterson, 1974; Patterson & McClure, 1976) and even more than from televised debates (Just, Crigler, & Wallach, 1990), although more recent multivariate analyses suggest that television news sometimes is a better predictor of overall information acquisition in political campaigns (Zhao & Chaffee, 1995).

Receiver characteristics also can affect ad recall. Early research posited the notion that voters with low levels of campaign involvement are most likely to be affected by political spots (Rothschild & Ray, 1974), as are undecided voters and late deciders (Bowen, 1994).

Agenda-setting theory also has played a role in understanding the cognitive effects of political advertising. The issue content of ads has been shown to affect judgments of ad salience for voters (Bowers, 1977; Ghorpade, 1986; West, 1993; Williams, Shapiro, & Cutbirth, 1983) and to affect the news agendas of media outlets (Roberts & McCombs, 1994; Schleuder, McCombs, & Wanta, 1991).

The structure and design of a political spot also might explain the greater effectiveness of some ads compared to others. For example, researchers have demonstrated that the structure and design of ads can affect recall (Lang, 1991; Lang & Lanfear, 1990). Emotional aspects of a political ad can affect viewer recall (Lang, 1991). The presence of music in an ad can enhance visual recall (Thorson, Christ, & Caywood, 1991a), and an ad's visual structure can affect content recall and candidate evaluation (Geiger & Reeves, 1991).

Effects on Candidate Evaluations

The finding that exposure to political spots can affect candidate image evaluation has been confirmed in both experimental and survey research settings (Atkin & Heald, 1976; Becker & Doolittle, 1975; Cundy, 1986, 1990; Hofstetter, Zukin, & Buss, 1978; Kaid, 1991a, 1994, 1997a, 1998; Kaid & Chanslor, 1995; Kaid, Leland, & Whitney, 1992; West, 1993). Some of the most convincing evidence for the effects of spot viewing on candidate perceptions comes from multivariate analysis. West (1993) analyzed survey and voting data from 1972 through 1992. Controlling for demographic variables such as political party, education, and gender, West found that seeing a candidate's ads had a significant impact on judgments of candidate likeability and information on candidate issues and traits.

As with the recall of spots, the type of spot may be related to the effect on candidate image evaluation. For example, issue ads seem to be particularly effective in raising a candidate's image ratings (Kaid, Chanslor, & Hovind, 1992; Kaid & Sanders, 1978; Thorson, Christ, & Caywood, 1991a, 1991b). Viewer predispositions also can affect evaluations of candidates as a result of spot exposure (Donohue, 1973; Meyer & Donohue, 1973).

Usually, the effects of spots on candidate images have been in a positive direction, but sometimes the results have shown that the effects also can be negative, particularly as a result of spots attacking the opponent (Kaid & Boydston, 1987; West, 1994). Although a few studies have not found strong effects of spots on candidate evaluations (Meadow & Sigelman, 1982), others have found that the effects often are mixed. For example, in a study of the 1992 California U.S. Senate races, West (1994) found that exposure to spots did not have a uniform effect on the candidates; sometimes the candidate's favorability rating was not affected at all, sometimes the effect was positive from exposure to the candidate's own ads, and sometimes the effect was negative as a result of exposure to the opponent's attack ads.

In fact, there is now a substantial body of research that specifically addresses the effects on candidate images and voting behavior from exposure to negative or attack ads or comparing negative ad exposure to positive ad exposure. Early research suggested that those with low information-seeking habits were more likely to accept and be influenced by negative ads (Surlin & Gordon, 1977). Findings from experimental studies have suggested that positive ads are more effective than negative or comparative ads at affecting attitudes toward candidates (Hill, 1989; Kahn & Geer, 1994).

It should be noted that this does not mean that negative ads have proven ineffective; it only means that some experimental studies have shown them to be less effective than positive spots. One of the reasons why negative ads have not proven to be as effective in some studies is that negative ads can produce a backlash effect on the image of the candidate sponsoring the ad (Garramone, 1984; Merritt, 1984), but third-party or independent sponsorship can offset this problem (Garramone, 1984, 1985; Garramone & Smith, 1984). Attacks that focus on the opposing candidate's issue positions are more effective than those attacking the opponent's character or image (Kahn & Geer, 1994; Pfau & Burgoon, 1989; Roddy & Garramone, 1988). For a candidate who is the target of negative attack spots, rebuttals have proven to be helpful in blunting the effects of an attack (Garramone, 1985; Roddy & Garramone, 1988), and inoculation also can provide some advance protection against the effectiveness of opponent smears (Pfau & Kenski, 1990).

Effects on Voter Preferences and Behavior

There also is strong evidence that political television spots have behavioral effects. The most obvious of these are effects on voting decisions. Such effects often have been found in experimental and survey studies (Cundy, 1986; Kaid & Sanders, 1978; Mulder, 1979), and the effects seem to be especially strong for late deciders (Bowen, 1994). Hofstetter and Buss (1980) found that exposure to last-minute paid advertising was associated with late changes in vote decisions and ticket splitting. In his study of the 1992 California U.S. Senate races, West (1994) identified some effects of exposure to ads on vote preference for Barbara Boxer, but not all other candidates were similarly affected.

As with recall and image formation, receiver variables seem to play a role in advertising effects on voting behavior. Early studies suggested that the voting decisions of low-involvement voters were more easily affected by political ads (Rothschild & Ray, 1974). However, in the 1988 Minnesota U.S. Senate race,

Faber, Tims, and Schmitt (1993) found that higher levels of enduring and situational involvement, as well as attention to television news, resulted in greater effects for negative ads on vote preference. In fact, many of the studies that have measured negative ad effects on recall and candidate image also have identified effects on voting behavior, leading to a clear conclusion that negative ads do affect voting preferences (Ansolabehere & Iyengar, 1995; Basil et al., 1991; Roddy & Garramone, 1988).

The context in which ads are shown also can affect vote likelihood. For example, negative ads are particularly likely to affect vote decisions when shown in a news environment (Kaid, Chanslor, & Hovind, 1992).

There also has been concern that political television spots might affect voter behavior in another way besides actual voting decisions. Some have suggested that the voter negativity toward attack ads might turn voters off to voting at all, thus lowering turnout. The most publicized findings in this regard are those of Ansolabehere and Iyengar (1995), who suggested that exposure to negative ads reduces voter turnout by 5% (see also Ansolabehere, Iyengar, Simon, & Valentino, 1994). However, other studies have found little relationship between exposure to negative ads and intention to vote or lower levels of trust in government (Garramone, Atkin, Pinkleton, & Cole, 1990; Martinez & Delegal, 1990).

Political Advertising in International Perspective

The need of political leaders to market issues and personal qualifications to voters is not a uniquely American problem. Political candidates and parties in most democratic systems face the fundamental problem of how to communicate with and persuade voters to accept their leadership. Televised political ads, or party political broadcasts, have become important to many democratic systems because they provide a solution to this problem that also has the advantage of being under the direct control of the candidate or party. Despite this fundamental advantage to political advertising, the roles of such messages, their content and styles, and their effects vary across democratic systems. In *Political Advertising in Western Democracies,* Kaid and Holtz-Bacha (1995) discussed the various media, cultural, and political system differences that affect the role that such messages play in a number of democratic systems. These differences often prompt researchers to throw up their hands in despair, lamenting that the differences are so great that no meaningful comparison is possible. However, some comparisons of political spot broadcast content and effects across Western democracies are possible.

Perhaps the most distinguishing aspect of the American system is its commercial nature. Because television stations are primarily private entities selling advertising time, American candidates at every level of elective office are free to buy nearly unlimited amounts of advertising time on television. Also distinctive to the American system is the almost unregulated nature of the message content;

candidates and parties can say or do almost anything in political spots because the value placed on free speech rights in the United States insists that political speech be unfettered (Kaid, 1991b). Although other democracies often have been accused of "Americanization" of their political television offerings, some limitations on the adoption of American practices have been imposed by media, political, and cultural system differences. Probably the most noticeable difference is in the quantity of spot advertising allowed because most other countries allow only limited purchases of time—or none at all—instead providing free time on public channels to candidates and parties (Kaid & Holtz-Bacha, 1995). Whereas in many countries this free-time system might commonly alot 3, 5, or 10 spots per candidate or party in an election campaign, the major U.S. presidential candidates in 1996 purchased time in the general election campaign for more than 100 spots, costing nearly $200 million (Devlin, 1997).

A few comparisons of content of political spots across countries (including Germany, Britain, France, Italy, Poland, Romania, and Israel) have revealed that political ads in most democracies concentrate more on issues than on candidate images (Holtz-Bacha, Kaid, & Johnston, 1994; Kaid, 1997b; Kaid & Holtz-Bacha, 1995; Kaid & Tedesco, 1993). Although most countries are not immune to the attack mode of political communication, the United States is the only country in which negative ads have become the dominant format for political spots in national elections (Kaid, 1997b). The use of emotion also is a common feature in spots across cultures, although Great Britain and France are more successful at emphasizing logical proof in their broadcasts.

Other democracies have not often measured precisely the effects of political spots on voters. As with other aspects of political television and the possible Americanization of their systems, most countries have preferred to assume that party broadcasts were not very important to voters. However, research on early party election broadcasts in Britain suggested that they did affect voter knowledge levels (Blumler & McQuail, 1968; Scammell & Semetko, 1995) and might have had some effects on undecided or low-interest voters. Research on the first unified national election in Germany in 1990 showed that spots had effects on chancellor candidate images and on voter recall and emotional responses (Kaid & Holtz-Bacha, 1993).

Subsequent research findings on the effects of political broadcasts in other countries also show remarkably similar trends. Experiments conducted with the same basic procedures (pretest/posttest designs with intervening exposure to sets of political ads) and measuring instruments (semantic differential scales to measure candidate image) have shown that exposure to political television messages can have definite effects on a candidate's image, regardless of the country or political culture (Kaid, 1997b). Sometimes the effects are positive, as they were for Bush in 1988 and 1992, for Clinton in 1996, for Romania's Emil Constantinescu in 1996, for Poland's Lech Walesa in 1995, and for Britain's Tony Blair in 1997. Sometimes, however, exposure can mean a negative reaction, as it did for Dole in 1996 and for Jacques-René Chirac in France in 1988 and for Mino Martinazolli in Italy in 1992.

Research on effects of spots across countries also shows some interesting gender differences. Women reacted much differently from men when viewing spots, somewhat in line with voting behavior findings on the "gender gap" in voting. For example, women voters rated Clinton (1996 U.S. election) and Blair (1997 British election) much higher than they did the candidates' opponents, Dole and John Major. Overall, the gender comparisons across several countries suggest that "female voters are more likely to be affected by exposure to political spots, and when they are, the spots are more likely to result in higher positive evaluations for the candidates than is true for male voters" (Kaid, 1997b, pp. 20-21).

Political Advertising in the Context of Voter Decisions

Overall, there is no question that political television spots have proven to be an effective marketing tool for candidates at all levels and across countries. Although this review has not attempted to break out all of the individual effects of spots, it also is clear that different types of spots might have different types of effects. Some spots are more effective at eliciting recall of information and providing voters with some idea of the salience of candidate issue positions. Other types of spots can build and sustain candidate images and communicate to voters about a candidate's strengths and weaknesses of character. Both of these outcomes, effects on issue learning and on formation of candidate images, have some effect on voting decisions. Some spots also seem to have direct effects on vote likelihood.

For much of the 20th century, scholars and politicians alike attributed most of the variance in voting behavior to partisan affiliations. The definitive work in the field of voting behavior attributed voting to a fourfold model—political party, issues, candidates, and groups—and declared political party to be the dominant component (Campbell, Converse, Miller, & Stokes, 1960). Even when issues or candidates were thought to rise in importance, the model believed that attitudes toward them were filtered through a partisan lens. Perhaps it is ironic that it was a real lens—the actual lens of television—that changed all that. Media consultant Tony Schwartz, who produced the famous "Daisy Girl" spot for Lyndon Johnson in 1964, observed long before others seemed to understand what it meant that in the past, "political parties were the means of communication from the candidate to [the] public. The political parties today are ABC, NBC, and CBS" (Schwartz, 1984, p. 82).

Although this comment might seem out-of-date in a media world that now offers not just ABC, NBC, and CBS but also CNN and scores of other independent and cable choices, the spirit of the comment still is important. Candidates in the United States need not rely on parties. They rely on mass media to carry their messages. Because television spots are the most direct way of doing that, providing them with proven effectiveness, it is easy to understand why candidates would choose television as their primary means of communicating with voters.

References

Ansolabehere, S., & Iyengar, S. (1995). *Going negative: How political advertisements shrink and polarize the electorate*. New York: Free Press.

Ansolabehere, S., Iyengar, S., Simon, A., & Valentino, N. (1994). Does attack advertising demobilize the electorate? *American Political Science Review, 88,* 829-838.

Atkin, C., Bowen, L., Nayman, O. B., & Sheinkopf, K. G. (1973). Quality versus quantity in televised political ads. *Public Opinion Quarterly, 37,* 209-224.

Atkin, C., & Heald, G. (1976). Effects of political advertising. *Public Opinion Quarterly, 40,* 216-228.

Basil, M., Schooler, C., & Reeves, B. (1991). Positive and negative political advertising: Effectiveness of ads and perceptions of candidates. In F. Biocca (Ed.), *Television and political advertising* (Vol. 1, pp. 245-262). Hillsdale, NJ: Lawrence Erlbaum.

Baukus, R. A., Payne, J. G., & Reisler, M. C. (1985). Negative polispots. In J. R. Cox, M. O. Sillars, & G. B. Walker (Eds.), *Argumentation and social practice* (pp. 236-252). Annandale, VA: Speech Communication Association.

Becker, L. B., & Doolittle, J. C. (1975). How repetition affects evaluations of and information seeking about candidates. *Journalism Quarterly, 52,* 611-617.

Berelson, B. (1966). Democratic theory and public opinion. In B. Berelson & M. Janowitz (Eds.), *Reader in public opinion and communication* (pp. 489-504). New York: Free Press.

Blumler, J. G., & McQuail, D. (1968). *Television in politics*. London: Faber and Faber.

Bowen, L. (1994). Time of voting decision and use of political advertising: The Slade Gorton-Brock Adams senatorial campaign. *Journalism Quarterly, 71,* 665-675.

Bowers, T. A. (1977). Candidate advertising: The agenda is the message. In D. L. Shaw & M. E. McCombs (Eds.), *The emergence of American political issues* (pp. 53-67). St. Paul, MN: West.

Buss, T., & Hofstetter, C. R. (1976). An analysis of the logic of televised campaign advertisements: The 1972 presidential campaign. *Communication Research, 3,* 367-392.

Bystrom, D. (1995). *Candidate gender and the presentation of self: The videostyles of men and women in U.S. Senate campaigns*. Doctoral dissertation, University of Oklahoma.

Campbell, A., Converse, P., Miller, W., & Stokes, D. (1960). *The American voter*. New York: John Wiley.

Center for Media and Public Affairs. (1996, May/June). Whose campaign did you see? *Media Monitor,* pp. 1-4.

Cundy, D. T. (1986). Political commercials and candidate image: The effects can be substantial. In L. L. Kaid, D. Nimmo, & K. R. Sanders (Eds.), *New perspectives on political advertising* (pp. 210-234). Carbondale: Southern Illinois University Press.

Cundy, D. T. (1990). Image formation, the low involvement voter, and televised political advertising. *Political Communication and Persuasion, 7,* 41-59.

Devlin, L. P. (1989). Contrasts in presidential campaign commercials of 1988. *American Behavioral Scientist, 32,* 389-414.

Devlin, L. P. (1993). Contrasts in presidential campaign commercials of 1992. *American Behavioral Scientist, 37,* 272-290.

Devlin, L. P. (1997). Contrasts in presidential campaign commercials of 1996. *American Behavioral Scientist, 40,* 1058-1084.

Diamond, E., & Bates, S. (1984). *The spot: The rise of political advertising on television*. Cambridge, MA: MIT Press.

Diamond, E., & Bates, S. (1988). *The spot: The rise of political advertising on television* (2nd ed.). Cambridge, MA: MIT Press.

Diamond, E., & Bates, S. (1992). *The spot: The rise of political advertising on television* (3rd ed.). Cambridge, MA: MIT Press.

Donohue, T. R. (1973). Impact of viewer predispositions on political TV commercials. *Journal of Broadcasting, 18,* 3-15.

Elebash, C., & Rosene, J. (1982). Issues in political advertising in a Deep South gubernatorial race. *Journalism Quarterly, 59,* 420-423.

Faber, R. J., & Storey, M. C. (1984). Recall of information from political advertising. *Journal of Advertising, 13*(3), 39-44.

Faber, R. J., Tims, A. R., & Schmitt, K. G. (1993). Negative political advertising and voting intent: The role of involvement and alternative information sources. *Journal of Advertising, 22*(4), 67-76.

Garramone, G. M. (1983). Image versus issue orientation and effects of political advertising. *Communication Research, 10,* 59-76.

Garramone, G. M. (1984). Voter responses to negative political ads. *Journalism Quarterly, 61,* 250-259.

Garramone, G. M. (1985). Effects of negative political advertising: The roles of sponsor and rebuttal. *Journal of Broadcasting and Electronic Media, 29,* 147-159.

Garramone, G. (1986). Candidate image formation: The role of information processing. In L. L. Kaid, D. Nimmo, & K. R. Sanders (Eds.), *New perspectives on political advertising* (pp. 235-247). Carbondale: Southern Illinois University Press.

Garramone, G. M., Atkin, C. K., Pinkleton, B. E., & Cole, R. T. (1990). Effects of negative political advertising on the political process. *Journal of Broadcasting and Electronic Media, 34,* 299-311.

Garramone, G. M., & Smith, S. J. (1984). Reactions to political advertising: Clarifying sponsor effects. *Journalism Quarterly, 61,* 771-775.

Geiger, S. F., & Reeves, B. (1991). The effects of visual structure and content emphasis on the evaluation and memory for political candidates. In F. Biocca (Ed.), *Television and political advertising* (Vol. 1, pp. 125-144). Hillsdale, NJ: Lawrence Erlbaum.

Ghorpade, S. (1986). Agenda setting: A test of advertising's neglected function. *Journal of Advertising Research, 26*(4), 23-27.

Hill, R. P. (1989). An exploration of voter responses to political advertisements. *Journal of Advertising, 18,* 14-22.

Hofstetter, C. R., & Buss, T. F. (1980). Politics and last-minute political television. *Western Political Quarterly, 33,* 24-37.

Hofstetter, C. R., & Zukin, C. (1979). TV network news and advertising in the Nixon and McGovern campaigns. *Journalism Quarterly, 56,* 106-115, 152.

Hofstetter, C. R., Zukin, C., & Buss, T. F. (1978). Political imagery and information in an age of television. *Journalism Quarterly, 55,* 562-569.

Holtz-Bacha, C., Kaid, L. L., & Johnston, A. (1994). Political television advertising in Western democracies: A comparison of campaign broadcasts in the U.S., Germany, and France. *Political Communication, 11,* 67-80.

Jamieson, K. H. (1984). *Packaging the presidency.* New York: Oxford University Press.

Jamieson, K. H. (1992). *Packaging the presidency* (2nd ed.). New York: Oxford University Press.

Jamieson, K. H. (1996). *Packaging the presidency* (3rd ed.). New York: Oxford University Press.

Johnson-Cartee, K. S., & Copeland, G. (1989). Southern voters' reaction to negative political ads in 1986 election. *Journalism Quarterly, 66,* 888-893, 986.

Johnson-Cartee, K. S., & Copeland, G. A. (1991). *Negative political advertising: Coming of age.* Hillsdale, NJ: Lawrence Erlbaum.

Johnson-Cartee, K. S., & Copeland, G. A. (1997). *Manipulation of the American voter.* Westport, CT: Praeger.

Joslyn, R. A. (1980). The content of political spot ads. *Journalism Quarterly, 57,* 92-98.

Joslyn, R. A. (1986). Political advertising and meaning of elections. In L. L. Kaid, D. Nimmo, & K. R. Sanders (Eds.), *New perspectives on political advertising* (pp. 139-184). Carbondale: Southern Illinois Press.

Just, M., Crigler, A., & Wallach, L. (1990). Thirty seconds or thirty minutes: What viewers learn from spot advertisements and candidate debates. *Journal of Communication, 40,* 120-133.

Kahn, K. F., & Geer, J. G. (1994). Creating impressions: An experimental investigation of political advertising on television. *Political Behavior, 16,* 93-116.

Kaid, L. L. (1981). Political advertising. In D. D. Nimmo & K. R. Sanders (Eds.), *Handbook of political communication* (pp. 249-271). Beverly Hills, CA: Sage.

Kaid, L. L. (1982, Spring). Paid television advertising and candidate name identification. *Campaigns & Elections,* pp. 34-36.

Kaid, L. L. (1991a). The effects of television broadcasts on perceptions of political candidates in the United States and France. In L. L. Kaid, J. Gerstlé, & K. Sanders (Eds.), *Mediated politics in two cultures: Presidential campaigning in the United States and France* (pp. 247-260). New York: Praeger.

Kaid, L. L. (1991b). Ethical dimensions of political advertising. In R. Denton (Ed.), *Ethical dimensions of political communication* (pp. 145-169). New York: Praeger.

Kaid, L. L. (1994). Political advertising in the 1992 campaign. In R. E. Denton, Jr. (Ed.), *The 1992 presidential campaign* (pp. 111-127). Westport, CT: Praeger.

Kaid, L. L. (1996). Technology and political advertising: The application of ethical standards to the 1992 spots. *Communication Research Reports, 13,* 129-137.

Kaid, L. L. (1997a). Effects of the television spots on images of Dole and Clinton. *American Behavioral Scientist, 40,* 1085-1094.

Kaid, L. L. (1997b, October). *Political television advertising: A comparative perspective on styles and effects.* Paper presented at the International Conference on Images of Politics, Amsterdam.

Kaid, L. L. (1998). Videostyle and the effects of the 1996 presidential campaign advertising. In R. E. Denton (Ed.), *The 1996 presidential campaign: A communication perspective* (pp. 143-159). Westport, CT: Praeger.

Kaid, L. L., & Boydston, J. (1987). An experimental study of the effectiveness of negative political advertisements. *Communication Quarterly, 35,* 193-201.

Kaid, L. L., & Chanslor, M. (1995). Changing candidate images: The effects of television advertising. In K. Hacker (Ed.), *Candidate images in presidential election campaigns* (pp. 83-97). New York: Praeger.

Kaid, L. L., Chanslor, M., & Hovind, M. (1992). The influence of program and commercial type on political advertising effectiveness. *Journal of Broadcasting and Electronic Media, 36,* 303-320.

Kaid, L. L., & Davidson, J. (1986). Elements of videostyle: Candidate presentation through television advertising. In L. L. Kaid, D. Nimmo, & K. R. Sanders (Eds.), *New perspectives on political advertising* (pp. 184-209). Carbondale: Southern Illinois University Press.

Kaid, L. L., Gobetz, R. H., Garner, J., Leland, C. M., & Scott, D. K. (1993). Television news and presidential campaigns: The legitimization of television political advertising. *Social Science Quarterly, 74,* 274-285.

Kaid, L. L., & Holtz-Bacha, C. (1993). Audience reactions to televised political programs: An experimental study of the 1990 German national election. *European Journal of Communication, 8,* 77-99.

Kaid, L. L., & Holtz-Bacha, C. (Eds.). (1995). *Political advertising in Western democracies.* Thousand Oaks, CA: Sage.

Kaid, L. L., & Johnston, A. (1991). Negative versus positive television advertising in presidential campaigns, 1960-1988. *Journal of Communication, 41,* 53-64.

Kaid, L. L., & Johnston, A. (in press). *Videostyle in presidential campaigns.* New York: Praeger.

Kaid, L. L., Leland, C., & Whitney, S. (1992). The impact of televised political ads: Evoking viewer responses in the 1988 presidential campaign. *Southern Communication Journal, 57,* 285-295.

Kaid, L. L., & Noggle, G. (1998). Televised political advertising in the 1992 and 1996 elections: Using technology to manipulate voters. *Southeastern Political Review, 26,* 889-906.

Kaid, L. L., & Sanders, K. R. (1978). Political television commercials: An experimental study of the type and length. *Communication Research, 5,* 57-70.

Kaid, L. L., & Tedesco, J. (1993). A comparison of political television advertising from the 1992 British and American campaigns. *Informatologia, 25,* 1-12.

Kern, M. (1989). *30-second politics: Political advertising in the eighties.* New York: Praeger.

Kern, M., & Just, M. (1995). The focus group method, political advertising, campaign news, and the construction of candidate images. *Political Communication, 12,* 127-145.

Klapper, J. (1960). *The effects of mass communication.* New York: Free Press.

Lang, A. (1991). Emotion, formal features, and memory for televised political advertisements. In F. Biocca (Ed.), *Television and political advertising* (Vol. 1, pp. 221-243). Hillsdale, NJ: Lawrence Erlbaum.

Lang, A., & Lanfear, P. (1990). The information processing of televised political advertising: Using theory to maximize recall. *Advances in Consumer Research, 17,* 149-158.

Latimer, M. K. (1984). Policy issues and personal images in political advertising in a state election. *Journalism Quarterly, 61,* 776-784, 852.

Latimer, M. K. (1989a). Legislators' advertising messages in seven state campaigns in 1986. *Journalism Quarterly, 66,* 338-346, 527.

Latimer, M. K. (1989b). Political advertising for federal and state elections: Issues or substance? *Journalism Quarterly, 66,* 861-868.

Lichter, S. R., & Noyes, R. (1996). *Campaign '96: The media and the candidates* (first report to the Markle Foundation). Washington, DC: Center for Media and Public Affairs.

Martinelli, K. A., & Chaffee, S. H. (1995). Measuring new-voter learning via three channels of political information. *Journalism and Mass Communication Quarterly, 72,* 18-32.

Martinez, M. D., & Delegal, T. (1990). The irrelevance of negative campaigns to political trust: Experimental and survey results. *Political Communication and Persuasion, 7*(1), 25-40.

McClure, R. D., & Patterson, T. E. (1974). Television news and political advertising: The impact of exposure on voter beliefs. *Communication Research, 1,* 3-31.

Meadow, R. G., & Sigelman, L. (1982). Some effects and noneffects of campaign commercials: An experimental study. *Political Behavior, 4,* 163-175.

Merritt, S. (1984). Negative political advertising. *Journal of Advertising, 13,* 27-38.

Meyer, T. P., & Donohue, T. R. (1973). Perceptions and misperceptions of political advertising. *Journal of Business Communication, 10*(3), 29-40.

Mulder, R. (1979). The effects of televised political ads in the 1975 Chicago mayoral election. *Journalism Quarterly, 56,* 336-340.

Newhagen, J. E., & Reeves, B. (1991). Emotion and memory responses for negative political advertising: A study of television commercials used in the 1988 presidential election. In F. Biocca (Ed.), *Television and political advertising* (Vol. 1, pp. 197-220). Hillsdale, NJ: Lawrence Erlbaum.

Newman, B. I. (1994). *The marketing of the president: Political marketing as campaign strategy.* Thousand Oaks, CA: Sage.

O'Shaughnessy, N. J. (1990). *The phenomenon of political marketing.* New York: St. Martin's.

Patterson, T. E., & McClure, R. D. (1976). *The unseeing eye: Myth of television power in politics.* New York: Putnam.

Payne, J. G., Marlier, J., & Baukus, R. A. (1989). Polispots in the 1988 presidential primaries. *American Behavioral Scientist, 32,* 365-381.

Perloff, R. A. (1998). *Political communication: Politics, press, and public in America.* Mahwah, NJ: Lawrence Erlbaum.

Pfau, M., & Burgoon, M. (1989). The efficacy of issue and character attack message strategies in political campaign communication. *Communication Research Reports, 2,* 52-61.

Roberts, M., & McCombs, M. (1994). Agenda-setting and political advertising: Origins of the news agenda. *Political Communication, 11,* 249-262.

Roddy, B. L., & Garramone, G. M. (1988). Appeals and strategies of negative political advertising. *Journal of Broadcasting and Electronic Media, 32,* 415-427.

Rothschild, M. L., & Ray, M. L. (1974). Involvement and political advertising effect: An exploratory experiment. *Communication Research, 1,* 264-285.

Rudd, R. (1986). Issue as image in political campaign commercials. *Western Journal of Speech Communication, 50,* 102-118.

Scammell, M., & Semetko, H. A. (1995). Political advertising on television: The British experience. In L. L. Kaid & C. Holtz-Bacha (Eds.), *Political advertising in Western democracies* (pp. 19-43). Thousand Oaks, CA: Sage.

Schleuder, J. (1990). Effects of commercial complexity, party affiliation, and issue vs. image strategies in political ads. *Advances in Consumer Research, 17,* 159-168.

Schleuder, J., McCombs, M., & Wanta, W. (1991). Inside the agenda-setting process: How political advertising and TV news prime viewers to think about issues and candidates. In F. Biocca (Ed.), *Television and political advertising* (Vol. 1, pp. 263-310). Hillsdale, NJ: Lawrence Erlbaum.

Schwartz, T. (1984). *Media: The second God.* New York: Anchor.

Shyles, L. (1983). Defining the issues of a presidential election from televised political spot advertisements. *Journal of Broadcasting, 27,* 333-343.

Shyles, L. (1984a). Defining "images" of presidential candidates from televised political spot advertisements. *Political Behavior, 62,* 171-181.

Shyles, L. (1984b). The relationship of images, issues, and presentational methods in televised spot advertisements for 1980's American presidential primaries. *Journal of Broadcasting, 28,* 405-421.

Shyles, L. (1988). Profiling candidate images in televised political spot advertisements for 1984: Roles and realities of presidential jousters at the height of the Reagan era. *Political Communication and Persuasion, 5,* 15-31.

Surlin, S. H., & Gordon, T. F. (1976). Selective exposure and retention of political advertising. *Journal of Advertising, 5,* 32-44.

Surlin, S. H., & Gordon, T. F. (1977). How values affect attitudes toward direct reference political advertising. *Journalism Quarterly, 54,* 89-98.

Thorson, E., Christ, W. G., & Caywood, C. (1991a). Effects of issue-image strategies, attack and support appeals, music, and visual content in political commercials. *Journal of Broadcasting and Electronic Media, 35,* 465-486.

Thorson, E., Christ, W. G., & Caywood, C. (1991b). Selling candidates like tubes of toothpaste: Is the comparison apt? In F. Biocca (Ed.), *Television and political advertising* (Vol. 1, pp. 145-172). Hillsdale, NJ: Lawrence Erlbaum.

West, D. (1993). *Air wars: Television advertising in election campaigns, 1952-1992.* Washington, DC: Congressional Quarterly Press.

West, D. (1994). Political advertising and news coverage in the 1992 California U.S. Senate campaigns. *Journal of Politics, 56,* 1053-1075.

Williams, W., Shapiro, M., & Cutbirth, C. (1983). The impact of campaign agendas on perception of issues in 1980 campaign. *Journalism Quarterly, 60,* 226-231.

Zhao, X., & Chaffee, S. M. (1995). Campaign advertisements versus television news as sources of political issue information. *Public Opinion Quarterly, 59,* 41-65.

24

Through a Glass Darkly

Television and American Electoral Politics

J. HARRY WRAY

On April 30, 1939, the Radio Corporation of America opened the nation's first regular television service from the World's Fair in New York City. The telecast featured addresses from two presidents: Franklin D. Roosevelt, president of the United States, and David Sarnoff, president of RCA. Of the two, Sarnoff's address was the more memorable. He called the new technology "an art which shines like a torch of hope in a troubled world" and proclaimed that it was one that "we must learn to utilize for the benefit of all mankind" (quoted in Kisseloff, 1995, p. 43).

Sarnoff's exuberance was not broadly shared at the time. The next day's *New York Times* gave extensive coverage to the fair but did not report on RCA's exhibit. News coverage was dominated by the hugely popular livestock exhibits; the General Electric and General Motors exhibits; and the fair's crown jewel, Perisphere, whose central feature was Democraticity, a visionary and fanciful representation of the American city of the future. No doubt, RCA's Sarnoff was thought to be engaged in a measure of corporate hucksterism. Although one may quarrel with the underlying sentiment of Sarnoff's address, his assessment of the significance of television was sound. Television technology has transformed society, fundamentally altering lifestyles and social relationships as well as restructuring political institutions and processes.

Television emerged as a central artifact of American culture during the post-World War II years, and its emergence was dramatic. During the 12 years between 1948 and 1960, the proportion of television-owning households in the United States zoomed from 1% to 90%. The significance of television can be partly understood by recognizing the larger cultural meaning of this era. The nation emerged from the trials of the Great Depression and the war to a position of unrivaled economic and military ascendance. Many economists had feared that the end of the war would return the nation to recession or worse. This was avoided. On the contrary, pent-up demand stimulated continued economic growth. The "American Dream" seemed at last to be within reach of everyone. Families flocked to suburbia. In the 1940s, 9 million people lived in the metropolitan areas surrounding central cities; in the subsequent decade, that number more than doubled (Judd & Swanstrom, 1998, p. 163). These trends were accelerated when Republican President Dwight Eisenhower initiated the largest public works project in U.S. history—the National Highway Act.

Between 1949 and 1959, the number of persons living in poverty was cut nearly in half (Danzinger & Gottschalk, 1995, p. 57). The economic problems of America had been solved, so the economic conventional wisdom ran, by John Maynard Keynes. What remained was the not-so-daunting task of managing the country's affluence (Galbraith, 1958). The economic conventional wisdom was complemented in political science by those who saw an end to politics. Politically, America had become that shining city on the hill of which the Puritan Jonathan Edwards once dreamed, the model toward which other right-thinking nations would naturally aspire. As with economics, it was felt that the major political problems had been solved. All that remained was to tinker with an efficiently administered state (Bell, 1965).

Television was partly cause and partly consequence of this optimism. It stood as a dazzling technology, a manifestation of American brilliance and know-how. But television was a technology of a very particular sort; it presented pictures and images of the society to itself. Not only did people see themselves on the news, but through programs such as *I Love Lucy, Father Knows Best, Amos and Andy,* and *Ozzie and Harriet,* television recreated and promoted America's cultural self-image. The American Dream, being one of the self rising to comfortable affluence and autonomy, always has been a private dream. The family sitcoms of the 1950s reflected this sensibility. Life was easy and good, and problems were small and resolvable.

The flight to suburbia, the enormous investment in a national highway system, and the extension of television into people's everyday lives are similarly ironic. Each is presented as community enhancing, yet each is destructive of community as well. People go to the suburbs in part to find community with people like themselves. Jackson (1985) shows, however, that even the architecture of suburbia, with freestanding homes, the elimination of front porches, and the rise of enclosed backyards, worked against personal contact with neighbors. The national highway system was justified in part by promising easy contact with distant communities (Lewis, 1997), yet its effect also was to obliterate, circumvent, or obscure communities and to replace them with the unending sameness of easy-access strip malls. And television, which promised to be a window to the world, also retired people to endless hours on isolated sofas.

The election of 1960, closing the postwar decade, stands as a watershed in American political life. It is interesting for many reasons. Two of the most extraordinary characters of 20th-century American politics, John F. Kennedy and Richard Nixon, were pitted against each other. In terms of popular vote, it stands as the closest election in U.S. history. Most analysts give Kennedy a razor-thin victory in the popular vote, but a complex ballot in Alabama makes even this claim questionable. The excitement of the election was increased by Kennedy's Catholicism and by the fact that a perilous cold war made leadership choices seem more significant. A higher proportion of the electorate participated in that election than in any election since women had been granted suffrage in 1924, and no election since has witnessed that level of popular participation.

All of these things make the 1960 election interesting. What makes it a watershed is that for the first time, television played a major role in politics. The election serves as a crucial transition in the way in which candidates are presented to voters and the way in which voters think about choices. Nixon and Kennedy agreed to hold three nationally televised debates, and for the first time in history, the nation would witness two presidential candidates going toe-to-toe on the same stage. The first debate drew a huge television audience. From a contemporary perspective, that debate seems tepid. Both candidates were polite, formal, and articulate. The questioning newsmen were deferential. To viewers at the time, however, it was enthralling.

There was a curious and largely unanticipated development in the public discussion following the debate. Some attention was given to the issue positions of the candidates, but the most interesting and electric discussion was about candidate image. Commentators noted that Kennedy seemed rested and self-assured and that his blue suit contrasted nicely with the gray background of the set. Nixon was well spoken, but it was noted that, with his gray suit, he tended to blend into the background. Nixon's "5 o'clock shadow" also became a matter of public discussion.

By a narrow margin, according to polls, the public thought that Kennedy had won the first debate. Most analysts concluded that the reason for the Kennedy victory had little to do with the substantive arguments of the candidates. Rather, Kennedy was seen as winning because he projected a more compelling image. Given the ultimate closeness of the election, Kennedy's "victory" in that first historic debate was considered quite significant.

In office, Kennedy systematically cultivated television. Against the advice of his staff who considered it too risky, he became the first president to regularly schedule televised news conferences. These news conferences, during which he frequently displayed his charm and humor, turned out to be political pluses for Kennedy. His wife, Jacqueline, led television journalists (and the nation) on a dramatic "White House tour." Moreover, the style of the Kennedy administration seemed particularly suited to television. The talk about "getting the nation moving," the emphasis on vigor and action, and the Camelot glamour were hungrily gobbled up by a medium particularly adept at conveying motion and drama.

To recap this historical preface, television comes to the people precisely at the time when huge numbers of people seek the more private, isolated, and limited environs of suburbia. Isolation is exacerbated as people increasingly move over a system of highways consciously designed to separate them from their environment. This narrowing of experience increases the importance of television as a source of information about the culture. Isolation is overcome by the pictorial representations on the small screen, but the legacy here is ambiguous, for television watching also increases isolation. It is not surprising that sociologists and social psychologists of this period were writing about the emergence of a faceless mass society. No doubt, Riesman's (1952) *The Lonely Crowd* and Whyte's (1956) *The Organization Man* were attracted to television in part out of a sense of lost intimacy.

Since 1960, television has become increasingly central to Americans' culture. Estimates about how much time Americans spend watching television are difficult for a number of reasons, but a consensus figure is 30 hours per week. It clearly is their major leisure time activity. It has become the major way in which Americans learn about themselves. Television also has become increasingly central to political life. Today, about two out of three Americans report that television is their major source for information about politics. To understand what this means politically, it is first important to consider the distinctive properties of the medium of U.S. television.

Properties of U.S. Television

One of the most distinctive features of American television is the extent to which it is a vehicle for commercial advertisers. American television stations are engaged in the business of selling audiences to advertisers. With small exaggeration, it has been called the umbilical cord of consumer society. In exchange for licenses to use the public airwaves, the government does establish broad and vague parameters regarding tastefulness, and it requires a minimal commitment to some public interest programming. So long as they remain within these boundaries, stations are free to do whatever is deemed necessary to maximize profits.

No other television system in the world is as single-mindedly devoted to commercial interests. In some systems, advertising is banned; in the rest, it is more constricted. Nearly all other systems have a clearer sense of public responsibility than does the American system, with one consequence being better funded and more vigorous public broadcasting. In the United States, public broadcasting faces the constant pressure of financial cutbacks, and in recent years, public stations have been forced to accept advertising to sustain themselves.

Most Americans who have not traveled abroad are surprised to learn that the television systems of other nations differ from the American system. Americans are so conditioned by their own experience that it is hard to imagine television being any other way. The constant commercial interruptions of programming, altering the rules of athletic events to allow more time for commercials, the seamless transitions in which Olympic champions glide from award ceremonies into McDonald's for an order of fries—all these appear not as Fellini outtakes but rather as part of a natural television world.

This was not always the case. In his definitive history of American broadcasting, Barnouw (1966) notes that in the early days of radio, most stations were owned by colleges and universities. The development of private stations increased a concern for profits, but turning the airwaves over to commercial interests was extremely controversial. Many thought that advertising on radio was a desecration, and legislation was introduced in Congress to ban it. As secretary of commerce during the 1920s, Herbert Hoover expressed serious reservations about the propriety of advertising on radio. Despite this concern, there never was a serious national debate over the proper administration of the airwaves as there was, for example, in Canada. Instead, private interests won a war of attrition. In the beginning, advertisers were careful to offend public sensibilities as little as possible. The earliest advertisers, such as Browning-King, simply attached names to programs. When specific ads emerged initially, they appeared only between programs.

Television's pervasiveness is such that its form seems ineluctable. Both the experience of other countries and the American history suggest that the current U.S. system is the result of political and social decisions the country has made. The point is neither to decry nor to exalt these decisions but rather to recognize their significance, as the resulting system reverberates through American culture. At this point, I call attention to one of these consequences.

Once television is organized around the principle of selling audiences to commercial interests, it is inevitable that audience size becomes central in determining what is seen on television. Like any medium, television has strengths and weaknesses in communication, and audiences are attracted by the things it does well. As a visual medium, television is at its most compelling in conveying drama, spectacle, and action. It helps the viewer to get "up close and personal" to see the person behind the story. Television is less good at discourse—at the rational consideration of competing ideas. In this area, print is far superior to the electronic media.

Consider the advantages that print enjoys. Discourse requires attention and thought, qualities that are congenial to reading. The reader may move at a self-determined pace, pause, reflect, reread, and so forth. All of these are vital to discourse. Regardless of the level of attention, television washes over the viewer. It cannot wait for reflection; it must move on. Because the viewer cannot become part of television's discourse, discourse on television is dreary. People tend to switch channels when confronted with "talking heads." As television news producers have gained a firmer grasp of their medium, news stories have shortened. Graphics are now vital, and they busily occupy the background even when the anchorperson is on screen.

Television does carry news programming featuring talking heads, but these usually are found at those times when viewership is low. Although these programs help stations to meet their public interest obligations, network executives have long known that they are not money makers. Even for these programs, the pulls of good television are substantial. The reason that the McLaughlin Group has evolved into a tightly scripted pie-throwing contest is because such antics help to attract audiences.

There is an additional characteristic of television that separates it from other media: The inherent properties of television are such that its essence is obscured. The deceptiveness of television is that it imparts a sense of "being there," of observing events firsthand instead of having them mediated. The industry actively promotes this illusion through aphorisms such as "you are there," "and that's the way it is," and "the camera's eye never blinks." The viewer can be lulled into thinking he or she is seeing reality unfiltered. There is a vast difference between a citizen asking "Did you see the article about the riots in South Los Angeles?" and "Did you see the riots in South Los Angeles?" The difference is in the conscious recognition of mediation.

Although viewers of television might have the sense of "being there," they are there in a special capacity—as voyeurs. They are silent and unobtrusive observers of television's "reality." This leads to a final property of television relevant to our considerations: Watching television is inherently passive. The familiar slang terms for television viewing—"vegging out" and "couch potato"—are apt. Philosophers have noted that humans are action-oriented creatures in the sense that they seek to dominate and control their environment. Conjuring images such as the preceding ones from the more docile plant kingdom seems appropriate to the world of television watching. Television washes over one in incessant waves. Levels of attention are a matter of indifference to the form of the medium; the programming continues regardless. There are exceptions, of course—moments of enthralling drama that deeply engage the viewer. But watching people watching television over time, seeing the slack-jawed, glassy-eyed viewer occasionally moved to a chuckle or a grunt, will quickly convince the observer that passivity is the norm for television viewing.

In sum, several properties of television are relevant to an understanding of the medium's effects on electoral politics. It is a commercial medium that sells audiences to corporate interests. To maximize profits, it is fundamentally concerned with building audience size. The properties of television are such that it can most effectively do this through depicting drama, personality, and intimacy. These are conveyed to a largely passive audience that is unlikely to be aware that it is experiencing a medium as opposed to reality itself. It is the blend of these factors, combined with the fact that most Americans get their information about politics from television, that has transformed the country's electoral politics.

Television's Effects on Electoral Politics

A few years ago, Norman Vincent Peale, one of the most popular moralists of 20th-century America, wrote an extraordinary paean to television. He wrote that television personalities have become "cherished friends" to millions of people. Although he admitted not knowing Tom Brokaw personally, he stated, "I like him; he's got a good face and a calm, friendly style" (Peale, 1984, p. 4). This remarkable statement, coming from an intelligent person, suggests television's extraordinary capacity to convey a sense of intimacy and personality. No doubt, this capacity is augmented by the fact that watching usually occurs in intimate settings, characteristically the home—perhaps even in bed.

When voters make decisions about candidates, representative democratic theory holds that issues must be of primary concern. People must evaluate candidate positions on matters they care about and use these assessments in their voting decisions. It also is recognized that the personal character of candidates is important and that voters may rationally opt for a candidate with good leadership qualities even while finding more common ground with another candidate on issues. The rational voter is one who considers both character and issues in voting decisions.

Television has reconfigured the way in which Americans think about politics by dramatically elevating the personal in political life. It directs public attention to the personalities of politicians. Students of American politics have widely documented extraordinary levels of political ignorance in this society. Some seem to take a perverse delight in revealing how little Americans know of even elementary political facts. What is missed in this assessment is that in some senses, Americans know more about politicians than ever before. Or, at least they think they do. Americans know intimate details about politicians' private lives, things that were unimaginable prior to the era of television politics. Americans know these in part because newscasters, aware of their medium's strengths, seek them out and in part because politicians, recognizing a new political era, willingly reveal them. Politicians reveal personal data because they realize that they must build compelling images of their personae. What Wills (1983) calls "the requirement of charisma" is a necessity of the television age.

A sense of political character is, of course, a legitimate part of any voting decision. But there are two things about television's elevation of the personal that are worrisome. The first is that, because of television's sense of being there, citizens are likely to miss the fact that the sense of the personal being conveyed is false—a political contrivance. The parade of politicians' families before television cameras may mask the reality of family dysfunction. Al Gore dancing to the music of Fleetwood Mac tells us nothing about what he actually thinks of that group or of dancing. He is image mongering, politicking in the television age.

The second thing that is problematic about the elevation of the personal is that it crowds out other types of information vital for a healthy democracy. As Henny Youngman might say, "Take Bill Clinton. Please." Long before we learned of the particular types and locations of his alleged sexual encounters with Monica Lewinsky and various other women, long before we were encouraged to think about telltale characteristics of his genitalia, we already knew of his preference for boxer shorts over jockeys, of his apparent distaste for pot, of his simultaneous penchant for jogging and Big Macs, of his passing ability on the saxophone, of his half-brother's struggle for stardom, of the hard times he and his wife Hillary had experienced in their relationship, and of the poignancy of seeing their daughter Chelsea off to Stanford University. These are the types of things that pass for political knowledge in the new era. The problem is not so much this knowledge per se but that we are so awash in the sea of the personal that we know little else.

The emphasis on the personal in political life encourages a peculiar view of campaigns—peculiar for a society that values democracy. For any large, complex, representative democracy, elections are important because they provide a rare opportunity for a broad, direct expression of public sentiment with respect to the outstanding issues of the day. Television's emphasis on personalism reduces this opportunity. It encourages an alternative view—the sense that political campaigns are personal odysseys. Elections devolve into dramatic candidate "horse races," with polls dominating the news of the campaign season. Issues are overwhelmed by coverage of strategy and tactics. When they do appear in newscasts, almost invariably, issues are shaped by the imperatives of personalism. In television's instinctive search for intimacy, issues are simply devices used by candidates seeking political advantage. Thus, Bob Dole opposes abortion *because* of the strength of the Christian right in the Republican Party, and Clinton supports abortion rights *because* he is trying to curry favor with the National Organization for Women.[1]

Television also has made significant contributions to the erosion of political parties as mass-based organizations. In a society that never has been particularly enthusiastic about politics, political parties have not been broadly esteemed historically. Their importance to representative democracy commonly goes unrecognized. No mention is made of parties in the Constitution; indeed, the founders were wary of the "mischiefs of faction." In the earliest days of the republic, however, the main author of the Constitution, James Madison, became a leader in establishing the world's first political party. To enact policies, the nation's first politicians soon came to realize that alliances were necessary, especially in the American system that dispersed power. The next generation of politicians, spearheaded by President Martin Van Buren, came to recognize that parties also provided vital linkage between the citizens and government (Remini, 1959).

These "linkage" contributions were widely recognized by academics, if not by the general public. The term of art used by political scientists during the 1950s to describe American parties was "agents of interest aggregation." Parties contributed to democracy by building coalitions of interests. Successful coalitions were durable and established broad "governing ideas" that brought coherence to government. Certainly, leadership and management of opinion were evident, but the conventional wisdom had it that ideas, at least to some extent, flowed upward through mass-based parties to the corridors of power. As opposed to business hierarchies, party structures were seen as "stratarchies" in which deference relations were reciprocal. Top party leaders needed those below as badly as those below needed them. The metaphor for this association is Kennedy striking a deal with Mayor Richard Daley of Chicago to carry Illinois in the 1960 election.

In the pretelevision era, such deal making was commonplace. It was far from idyllic. It could be distorted, even perverted. Yet, one also could see that democracy often was at least crudely served. In striking bargains, politicians develop obligations. It is hard to imagine how else representative democracy can function.

With the dawning of the television era of politics, the integrative functions of parties began to erode. Structures linking masses to elites became irrelevant as television began to place politicians directly into citizens' homes. In the 1960 elections, only 13 states held primaries. This meant that politicians had to strike many bargains with the types of interests that were represented at state nominating conventions. Such interests typically had a keen sense of what they wanted out of politics, and what they wanted went beyond candidate image. Characteristically, they asserted policy claims. National conventions were exciting, and not simply because one could observe the wanton pursuit of power. They were exciting because issues were at stake. In 1960, Nixon selected Henry Cabot Lodge as his running mate to appeal to the Republican moderates of the eastern establishment. In reaction to this, Republican conservatives, who already had grown restless with Eisenhower moderateness, started a grassroots movement that led to the nomination of Barry Goldwater four years later. These two conventions witnessed the Republican Party struggling with fundamental questions of identity.

As television became more important to politics, politics began to conform to the requirements of that medium. Primaries are much more telegenic than the type of closed-door, back-room politicking that typified the pretelevision era. Candidates on the campaign trail were telegenic and made good footage for the evening news. Because primaries made good television, their coverage dominated evening news shows. The television industry brought significant publicity and revenue to the states that held primaries as they followed candidates "along the campaign trail." For this reason, and for others as well, states started switching to primary systems for presidential nominations. By 1976, approximately two thirds of the states had adopted primary systems. The effects of this on bargaining and building durable governing coalitions also were clear. In his acceptance speech at the Democratic Party convention of that year, Jimmy Carter proclaimed—proudly and without irony—that he had gained the nomination without making a single deal with any politician. The flip side of this is that no politicians had made deals with Carter either, so he brought no structure of power to the task of governance. Campaigning on personal integrity and decency, popular during the post-Watergate years, and bolstered by the new personality-centered media system, his actual political ideas were unmoored.

It is possible to conclude that the expansion of primaries encouraged by television has enhanced democracy. After all, primaries were seen by progressive reformers early in this century as doing exactly this. Progressive reformers imagined, however, that primaries would allow people at least indirectly to express their sentiments on important issues. Perhaps in an earlier age this would have been true, but the television era makes this possibility moot. As we have seen, television does not encourage decision making on the basis of issues; rather, it elevates personality at the *expense* of issue deliberation.

Political party adaptation to television also can be seen in the changing character of political conventions. Once highly dramatic because they were so full of conflict, conventions originally made great television. The struggle between conservatives and moderates at the 1964 Republican Convention, the struggle at the Democratic Convention over civil rights in that same year, and the turmoil over the war in Vietnam at the 1968 Democratic Convention all made wonderful television. These made for wonderful politics as well because they involved struggles over central questions of governance. Hard as it is to believe in today's political milieu, party platform sessions were the stuff of high drama.

Televising these extraordinary and chaotic events was not so good for the parties, however. It was too much airing of dirty linen in public. In pretelevision days, various party factions could fight like hell in comparative privacy. Now, voters seemed to punish parties that they believed were too divisive. So, both parties, through a series of rule changes, sought to reduce conflict at the convention and, therefore, to "appear" better on television. The logic was obvious and has led to what we have today—3-day infomercials masquerading as political conventions. Conventions no longer aggregate interest, nor do they air and mediate conflict. Poignant films of presidential and vice presidential nominees are shown in prime time; scripts with minute-by-minute timing are widely disseminated and meticulously followed. Everyone knows where to stand on stage and how long to applaud. Convention hall interiors, color schemes, and the like are matters of high policy. The entire point is to get the maximum "bounce" in the polls for party nominees. In making themselves presentable for television, however, conventions have become far less telegenic. The result is that fewer people now watch them, and gavel-to-gavel network coverage is a thing of the past.

American political parties always have been loosely organized and comparatively easy to co-opt. Now, however, they are more porous than ever. Partisan identification is shrinking, dramatically so among younger voters. As parties become more technologically sophisticated and professionalized, the need for citizen volunteerism that historically has energized the parties is diminishing (Verba, Schlozman, & Brady, 1995). Although millions of Americans still identify with one of the two major political parties, the intensity of that commitment is less. It probably no longer is realistic to think of parties as mass organizations. They are, more accurately, structures that candidates, in the pursuit of office, penetrate, co-opt, and bend to their short-term purposes.

The diminution of bargaining in electoral politics creates a void. How are politicians to convince voters that they are worthy of support? The answer is personal marketing. Even as television helps to erode political parties as mass organizations, it provides its own solution—the personal marketing of candidates. Here, advertising becomes essential, and television is a marketer's dream. There are three reasons why this is so.

First, television has achieved a level of social penetration that is unrivaled historically and unapproached by other media. Its audience is vast, including literati and illiterates alike. This provides the marketer with extraordinary choices. A vast market can be reached at a single moment by advertising on a popular time slot. But the vastness of the audience also allows for highly focused ads targeting selected regional and demographic groups.

A second reason television is such an effective advertising instrument is that, unlike the major print alternatives, it plays to a captive audience. Magazine advertising, for example, may be readily ignored by the reader. Reading an ad requires an affirmative decision on the part of the reader. Whole sections of newspaper advertising may be readily ignored by the reader who is not interested in shopping. By contrast, television advertising is seductive. The television viewer is lured into commercials in part by inertia, in part because ads always are paced more rapidly that other types of television content, and in part because programming is calibrated around commercials. Dramatic shows are paced to maximize commercial efficiency, and the rules of sport are altered to be more accommodating as well. Even the most ardent channel surfer cannot avoid all television advertising; it is too ubiquitous, often occurring seamlessly on the program itself, and its timing is too well coordinated by networks.

Perhaps the most important reason why television is the sine qua non of modern advertising has to do with interesting developments in capitalism itself. The moral underpinning of capitalism always has revolved around the dignity and worth of the individual. The assumption of individual rationality emanates from this conviction. The virtue of capitalism, as its theorists see it, is that individuals have the ability to make well-reasoned decisions about what is best for them and ought to be allowed to do so. As capitalism has developed, however, events have conspired to make its moral foundation tenuous. Advertising, which begins as an ally of reason in that it provides information necessary for consumers to make rational choices, has become increasingly concerned with subverting reason. This development flows out of the internal logic of capitalism. Profit maximization and competition have driven corporations to make increasingly emotional claims about products and to attach products to sentiments (e.g., sexual desire) having nothing to do with the products themselves and, therefore, to subvert rationality. The rational individual, the foundation of capitalism, becomes the problem—the entity that must be undone.

It is the move toward sentiment in the advertising industry that elevates the significance of television as an advertising medium, for television is the unparalleled medium of sentiment. Novels, of course, can be extraordinarily sentimental, but the authors must labor to build the sentiment. No medium approaches the ability of television to create sentiment in the little packets required by advertising. No one remembers magazine ads. Everyone can recall dozens of memorable television ads. People buy theater tickets to see a compendium of the best television ads of the previous year. People regularly integrate television commercials into their everyday lives by humming jingles, borrowing quips, and so on. For many, the "Bud Bowl" carries as much interest as the Super Bowl itself.

In politics, it is reasonable to assume that politicians concerned with marketing themselves are lured by that marketing dynamo, the television screen. Thus, television fills the void it has helped to create. As politicians have been increasingly concerned with marketing, some critics have complained that they are selling themselves as if they were "bars of soap" and that this subverts the dignity of the political process. Perhaps so, but this criticism obscures an important distinction between political and economic markets: The goals of the "sellers" differ fundamentally in the two markets. In the economic market, the goal is to maximize transactions and, therefore, maximize profits; in the political market, the goal is to complete more transactions than opponents. The competition between Doritos and Tostitos, for example, is not necessarily zero-sum competition. It is important that they outsell each other only if this ensures a maximization of their own sales. If their marketing activities together produce a greater predisposition to consume chips in general, then they are mutually reinforcing. On the other hand, if Doritos seeks to dominate the market by discrediting Tostitos, then

Tostitos might well retaliate. One company may sell more than the other, but if the results of these marketing strategies are such that the consuming public becomes suspicious of chips in general and, therefore, switches to popcorn, then both companies lose.

In the political market, the goal is not to maximize transactions (votes) but rather to have more of them than the competition. Unlike the economic market, there is a payoff to attacking the competition, even with the expectation of retaliation, because the point is to win, not to maximize votes. This is why, despite pledges to the contrary at the outset of campaigns, nastiness usually is returned in spades. With unmoored and skittish voters making impulsive decisions among television-generated images, candidates recognize that they have little choice. This difference in the political and economic markets reveals a significant democratic dilemma. Democracy needs widespread participation; in their desire to win elections, politicians adopt strategies that increase cynicism and turn people away from politics.[2]

There always has been an element of hucksterism in American politics. Political gimmicks that help candidates to sell themselves are as old as the republic itself. What has changed in the television era is the increasing centrality of marketing strategies in political campaigns. Through the 1960s, political professionals around candidates would make the strategic campaign decisions including decisions about television ads and tactics. Nixon was the first candidate to bring marketing professionals into his inner circle in his successful 1968 campaign. Since that time, they have become increasingly dominant. Richard Morris, Clinton's campaign manager in 1996 until Morris's fondness for prostitutes made him a political liability, serves as the archetype. He is a consummate professional—a hired gun. He will work—and has worked—for Democrat Clinton or Republican Trent Lott. His loyalties extend only to his immediate client, with the point being to get that client elected. Living by the aphorism that in the long run we are all dead, he is indifferent to durable policy coalitions.

Today, the entire campaign is orchestrated around marketing considerations. Getting the best visuals possible is a daily concern. Campaign events are staged simply because they will make good visuals. Put George Bush in front of a flag factory. Show Clinton in his "buscapade" through small hamlets in search of America. Groups that might provide undesirable visuals are kept blocks away from candidates and are replaced by well-screened crowds. Polls and focus groups are used constantly, with an eye to what works and what "hot button" issues may be effectively exploited by the candidate. Never mind that the issues might have nothing to do with actual government policy. Only the short run matters. Speeches are laced with a few zingy phrases that television news programs find irresistible. They also may be used later in campaign ads. Focus groups are used to determine opponent vulnerabilities, and these are played on in candidate speeches and negative campaign ads. The candidate needs only to stay "on message." Spin doctors, a position unheard of just 20 years ago, now frequent campaigns. Their job is to make sure that the media get the message the campaign intends.

Perhaps the greatest indication of the emergence of televised marketing as the central aspect of political campaigns can be seen in the increasing irrelevance of the print media. Campaigns are so staged that there is little to report beyond the constantly churning polls. As the only game in town, newspapers have begun carrying news stories about the televised ads themselves. Television's story is *the* political story.

In lieu of the discourse required for effective democratic political campaigns, some analysts have noted the emergence of "sound bite democracy." It has taken time for television to bend politics to its own purposes. The earliest televised conventions, for example, featured cameras focusing on the convention rostrum for hours on end. Television executives soon discovered that more interesting programming was to be found in behind-the-scenes dramatic conflict, so reporters went scurrying about the convention hall trying to uncover it. (Some politicians came to believe that reporters were encouraging conflict for their own self-interests.)

Television's evolving coverage of politics extends to the campaign trail. Adatto (1990) has carefully studied the evolution of sound bites—uninterrupted statements made by candidates—carried on network newscasts. In the 1968 presidential campaign, the average sound bite was 42 seconds, and nearly a quarter of all sound bites exceeded 1 minute in length. Just 20 years later, the average sound bite had been sliced to 9 seconds, with only 4% running as long as 20 seconds. News producers recognize that the more abbreviated statements make for better television.

This has led to political adaptation. Politicians need to make the news, and they need to make it effectively. They recognize that, on television at least, they will be allotted only 10 seconds of fame. So, the search for punchy sound bites is of surpassing importance. Thus, the public is treated daily to quips that have momentary appeal but that are disconnected from the tasks of governance. Perhaps the most famous sound bite in recent years—and one that was exactly 9 seconds in length—came from Bush during his 1988 acceptance speech at the Republican Convention—"Read my lips. No new taxes." From the perspective of a sound bite, it was brilliant. It referenced a popular idea, and its style worked against a "wimp" image that troubled Bush. The Bush campaign used the phrase in televised ads, and it probably contributed to his victory in that election. But as policy, given the huge deficit of the time, the pledge was not such a good idea, and Bush was forced to impose new taxes during his administration. In the ensuing election, the pledge came back to haunt him. He appeared to be a wimp after all. The sound bite that had helped to elect him in 1988 contributed to his defeat four years later.

Further evidence of the emergence of sound bite democracy can be seen in the evolution of presidential debates. There was enormous excitement prior to the first Kennedy-Nixon debate in 1960. A new technology, television, would be used to serve and extend democracy. For the first time, candidates for the nation's highest office would share the same stage to discuss the outstanding issues of the day before a nationwide audience. To the credit of both candidates and questioners, they did exactly that. The assessment of the debate, however, focused almost exclusively on image and style.

Since that time, candidates have become increasingly aware that presentation dominates substance. The assessment of issues takes a back seat to personal appearance and "zingers." Candidates must seem self-assured, and they must get off a few zingers in the debate if they are to "win." Consider the things that stand in our collective memory of presidential debates—Gerald Ford's misstatement about East Europeans "living in freedom," Ronald Reagan's self-deprecating joke about his age, Lloyd Bentsen's "You're no John Kennedy" retort to Dan Quayle, Michael Dukakis's inability to offer a pithy response about whether he would change his mind regarding capital punishment if his wife were raped and murdered, Clinton's indignant defense of his patriotism, Bush furtively checking his watch. It is at such moments that television debates are won or lost.

Let us briefly recapitulate the argument to this point. Although it might not be true, as Marshall McLuhan put it, that the medium is the message, media vary significantly in their capacities to convey information. Because television has become the dominant vehicle of communication in politics, it is important to identify its inherent properties. In the United States, television is organized around the principle of selling audiences to advertisers, which leads it to a concern for audience size. Television draws larger audiences, and therefore makes more money, doing the things it does well. What it does best is convey drama, intimacy, and personalism. As a consequence, it emphasizes these aspects of politics when it considers that sphere of human activity. It is important to note that television producers are not acting maliciously; they are just doing their job, creating good television.

By emphasizing those aspects of politics that television effectively communicates, it also has reconfigured the political world. The relationship is reciprocal. Television wants to do what it does well; politicians, needing television, increasingly orchestrate their activities around the types of things most likely to get on television. What is unfortunate is that the things making for good television and the things making for good democratic politics are not the same. The television era has drawn us toward political personality and away from issue deliberation, it has contributed to the demise of political parties as mass (and therefore representative) organizations, it has brought marketing (and, one is tempted to suggest, impulse buying) to the center of American political life, and it has ushered in the era of sound bite democracy.

Television has done more as well. Not only has television, through its manner of presentation, reconfigured the process of politics, it also has reshaped the popular response to that process. To understand this, it is crucial to recognize both the ubiquity of the viewing experience and the phenomenological context in which that experience is received. Lives grow more isolated. Increasingly, we travel in hermetically sealed capsules over superhighways that neutralize the environment. People live in homes, perhaps located in the rapidly proliferating gated communities, that further separate them from each other. From there, we may venture out to the "controlled environment" of the shopping mall. Social psychologists have noted that stress is on the rise in American society. Perhaps this is one reason why television watching is so extensive; it allows people to "veg out." Whatever the reason, television viewing now dominates people's leisure time. Even when people venture out into the world looking for a good time, television exerts its influence. It is ironic that one of the most popular sitcoms in recent times was *Cheers,* a running story about a group of improbable characters finding solace and comfort through fellowship in a cozy bar. Go into a bar today and what you will find is people watching television—perhaps reruns of *Cheers.*

What this means is that television is increasingly Americans' window to the world—a surrogate reality. People's sense of urban areas, for example, is bound to the images they see on *Chicago Hope, NYPD Blue,* the evening news, and so forth. So it is with politics, and for democratic politics, this is a disaster. Television generates both passivity and cynicism, which are equally destructive of a vibrant democratic polity. It promotes passivity because, as Postman (1985) shows, television viewing is inherently passive, and whatever is shown on television is contorted into a form of spectacle and entertainment. On television, politics no longer is the arena of public discourse in which citizens have important stakes; it is the competing sagas of individual politicians. As the world turns, people's job is to watch.

Passivity also is encouraged by the cynicism that television engenders.[3] Cynicism is promoted in a number of ways. The relentless pursuit of the personal story in politics has driven newscasters to plumb the imagined thought processes of politicians. When issues are presented to the public, they almost invariably are represented as strategic decisions. Politicians rarely are seen as doing anything out of conviction and belief; they are nothing more than creatures of calculation. The proliferation of negative ads contributes to a sense that politicians, in general, are reprehensible. Finally, the highly marketed and spin doctor-promoted images that are shown stretch, and occasionally exceed, the boundaries of credibility. The created images are false, and occasionally this falseness breaks through.

Television's corruption of a vibrant democratic politics is not the product of a demonic mastermind. If that were so, then change might be more easily accomplished. It is rather the result of a logical concatenation—of small and immediately rational decisions leading to epic irrationality. There is some evidence that the natives are restless. People today do understand that politics is not working, and they vaguely sense that the media (which for them mean television) have something to do with this.

As this was being written, Clinton's continuing sex saga was dominating the news. The greater his infidelity, the higher the level of support for him. Perhaps his spin doctors should imply that he has an unusual fondness for small animals. His approval ratings might then set records. What is going on? Careful polling shows that the public does not approve of Clinton's alleged sexual escapades; his personal character ratings have dropped. But the public is even more disapproving of the media that push this story with such intensity. To complicate this conflict, media executives recognize that stories about Clinton's sex life draw big audiences. Out of this confusion, there is a glimmering recognition, not yet seen clearly but rather through a glass darkly. It is the recognition that although television might give viewing citizens what they want, it does not give them what they need.

Notes

1. For an excellent exegesis of the manner in which news media reference the putative political motives of candidates regarding their positions and choices, see Fallows (1997).

2. Bennett (1996) provides empirical evidence to suggest that these are the actual effects of campaign advertising.

3. For interesting assessments of the contributions that television makes to political cynicism, see Hart (1994), Fallows (1997), and Starobin (1995).

References

Adatto, K. (1990, May 28). The incredible shrinking sound bite. *The New Republic,* pp. 20-23.

Barnouw, E. (1966). *A history of broadcasting in the United States* (Vol. 1). New York: Oxford University Press.

Bell, D. (1965). *The end of ideology.* New York: Free Press.

Bennett, L. (1996). *The governing crisis.* New York: St. Martin's.

Danzinger, S., & Gottschalk, P. (1995). *America unequal.* New York: Russell Sage.

Fallows, J. (1997). *Breaking the news.* New York: Vintage.

Galbraith, J. K. (1958). *The affluent society.* Boston: Houghton Mifflin.

Hart, R. P. (1994). *Seducing America.* New York: Oxford University Press.

Jackson, K. (1985). *The crabgrass frontier.* New York: Oxford University Press.

Judd, D. R., & Swanstrom, T. (1998). *City politics.* New York: Longman.

Kisseloff, J. (1995). *The box.* New York: Viking.

Lewis, T. (1997). *Divided highways.* New York: Viking.

Peale, N. V. (1984, December 22). Television is a force for good in the world. *TV Guide,* pp. 4-6.

Postman, N. (1985). *Amusing ourselves to death.* New York: Viking Penguin.

Remini, R. V. (1959). *Martin Van Buren and the making of the Democratic Party.* New York: Columbia University Press.

Riesman, D. (1952). *The lonely crowd.* New Haven, CT: Yale University Press.

Starobin, P. (1995, March/April). A generation of vipers. *Columbia Journalism Review, 33*(6), 25-32.

Verba, S., Schlozman, K. L., & Brady, H. E. (1995). *Voice and equality: Civic volunteerism and American political life.* Cambridge, MA: Harvard University Press.

Whyte, W. H. (1956). *The organization man.* New York: Simon & Schuster.

Wills, G. (1983). *The Kennedy imprisonment.* New York: Pocket Books.

25

Selected Aspects of Communication in German Election Campaigns

KNUT BERGMANN
WOLFRAM WICKERT

This chapter describes a few aspects of the communication strategies used in election campaigns in the Federal Republic of Germany. It seeks to illustrate the validity of theoretical statements regarding the conduct of election campaigns on the basis of examples taken from the general election held in Germany in 1994, with particular emphasis on examples provided by the Christian Democratic Union (CDU) and its leading candidate and party chairman, Helmut Kohl. The chapter also includes references to the campaign that led up to the general election held on September 27, 1998. This is particularly interesting in view of the trend toward "Americanizing" the way in which German election campaigns are conducted. A comparison of the two campaigns also is interesting because of the apparent similarity of situations. Hardly anyone in Germany believed that the coalition consisting of the CDU, the Christian Social Union (CSU, its sister party in Bavaria), and the Free Democratic Party (FDP) would be in a position to form a government again after the 1998 election. The polls were similarly bad for the governing coalition in 1994, but in the latter case the trend started to reverse in favor of the incumbent parties about 4 months before the election.

The General Conditions for Political Communication in Germany

The general conditions for political communication in America are comparable with those in Germany to only a limited degree. Differences in election laws play a considerable role. In most cases, Germany's personalized system of proportional representation prevents a given party from obtaining an absolute majority and, as such, from being able to govern without a coalition partner. For this reason, Germany could be referred to as a *coalition-based democracy*. The need to form coalitions makes it appropriate, in many cases, to show a certain amount of consideration for one's potential coalition partners. In past general elections, the CDU has been very kind to its liberal partner, the FDP, and has given it the space it needs to project its own identity. Because its presence in the Bundestag recurrently has been in doubt due to the need to get at least 5% of the vote to get in, the FDP has regularly conducted its campaigns with a view to getting "second votes" (crucial under the German electoral system for the distribution of seats in Parliament) from people who normally would be inclined to cast both of their votes for the CDU and CSU.

The state elections held between general elections continue to be important barometers of the public mood. Given that the legislative terms in the states are 4 years, just as at the federal level, there is a parallel between 1994 and 1998. A series of 18 elections was held in Germany at the various levels (local, state, national, and European) in 1994, concluding with the general election on October 16. The election of Roman Herzog to the position of federal president also was important, but it was not a direct election. In that election, the Social Democratic Party (SPD) made serious miscalculations in its strategy and, in so doing, presented itself to the public as not being capable of united action. Of course, not all the elections held prior to the general election were significant for the outcome of the latter, but some election results did have considerable effects. In 1994, the state election in Saxony-Anhalt was of particular importance. In 1998, it was the election in Lower Saxony that made that state's premier, Gerhard Schröder, the leading candidate for the SPD in the general election. Once again, the election in Saxony-Anhalt was important for the general election (this state election and the one in 1994 are dealt with in a later section), as was the Bavarian state election, held on September 27, 1998, just 2 weeks before the general election.

Party Platforms

There also are significant differences in political communication with regard to the ways in which issues are addressed. In the United States, candidates do not need to give very much consideration to their party organizations, which are comparatively weak, something that results in their being much less tied down to specific party platforms than could ever be the case in Germany. The lack of personnel structure in the American parties forces presidential candidates to hire external advisers for their campaign teams, and these people then bring their own ideas into play. In Germany, candidates are much more strongly tied to specific party platforms, and they can—and indeed must—refer back to career staff members in the party organizations. As such, Germany does not (yet) have a category of professionals who hire themselves out as *political consultants*. The advertising agencies responsible for designing and producing campaign ads, the importance of which often is overestimated for communication in election campaigns, are non-decision-making consultants who are required to follow rules laid down for them by the parties (Radunski, 1980, p. 37 ff; Wolf, 1987, p. 298).

A further difference is that in Germany, narrow limits are imposed on the use of the electronic media for political campaigning as a result of the comparatively small budgets available for campaign financing. It is not possible to address target groups in as differentiated a fashion in Germany as it is in the United States. In Germany, there are only 30 television channels available throughout the country (i.e., on cable) and very few local stations. The diversity of different stations found in America is not comparable with the situation in Germany.[1] Given the structure of the German media landscape, it is very difficult for political parties to engage in populistic campaigning directed at specific target groups in any way comparable with what is possible in the United States.

Campaign Financing

Major differences also exist with regard to campaign financing. German election campaigns are financed in part on the basis of donations, but to a much smaller extent than is the case in America. The laws on the financing of political parties impose strict limits on the amount of money available for campaigning. By law, parties that get more than 0.5% of the vote are granted public funds to help defray campaign costs in general, state, and European elections up to a limit of DM 230 million (DM 1.30 each for the first 5 million votes, and DM 1.00 per vote after that). Compared to corporate advertising budgets, the campaign financing budgets political parties have available to them are extremely modest. In Germany, a trend is emerging toward reducing the amount of money spent on election campaigns. With the sole exception of the SPD, the parties had less money available for campaigning purposes in 1998 than in the previous general election. No doubt, the reasons for this are to be found in declining memberships and a concomitant drop in party revenues, the general economic situation, the smaller volume of donations as a result of this, and the insight that expensive campaign efforts no longer are looked on favorably by a public that has become sensitive to the campaign financing issue.

The budget for the 1994 European and general elections was around DM 60 million for the CDU and DM 20 million for the CSU; a budget of between DM 75 million and DM 100 million was indicated for the SPD. In 1994, the CDU received an election campaign cost subsidy of DM 74 million, the CSU about DM 18 million, and the SPD nearly DM 90 million. No doubt, the party budgets for the 1998 campaigns will turn out to have been lower than in 1994. Only the SPD probably will have invested about the same amount as in 1994, despite the fact that this time there was not a European election creating a second nationwide polling date. The members of the FDP had approximately DM 10 million available to them, and Alliance 90/the Greens had a modest DM 5 million.

Personalization

German election campaigns are now similar to those in the United States in their use of campaign strategies that focus on the leading candidates. Personalization strategies could be summed up in the phrase "The leading candidate is the platform" (Grafe, 1994, p. 155). Of fundamental importance in this context is the assumption that the supposition of competence in favor of a party is based, first and foremost, on persons and not on platforms. In the eyes of campaign strategists, there is a need to simplify election issues anyway, and this is a good way in which to do it. This process of simplification is inevitable given that many political issues are based on matters removed from the experience and interests of individual voters and that a process of social change involving a breakdown of traditional social milieus and ties is making orientation in the political landscape more difficult. In difficult times, a charismatic leader helps to give a sense of direction both at the objective and emotional levels. Major importance attaches to the leading candidate's ability qua personality to be a mobilizing and decisive factor in attracting the support of potential nonvoters as well as undecided voters (Sarcinelli, 1991, pp. 483-486). As such, he is "not only a field marshal but also his side's best weapon" (Radunski, 1980, p. 9) and works both as "a director and a leading actor" (p. 11). The dominant role played by television also requires a large measure of personalization in campaign communication strategies.

Recent studies have shown that *perceived* expertise plays hardly any role at all in attracting voter support. Much more important are perceptions regarding the character of the candidate because voters make their decisions on the basis of criteria they are able to assess themselves and can observe in their own surroundings, things that in the final analysis are "general human qualities" (Kepplinger & Rettich, 1996, p. 82).

With regard to the role played by personalization in German general elections, it should be noted that the popularity of a chancellor is more a product of voter preferences for his or her party and less the case that the chancellor's party will benefit from his or her popularity as a person. However, there is a closer connection between the popularity of a CDU office holder and his or her party than is the case for the SPD; so far, public support for the Social Democrats has been largely independent of the popularity of their chancellors.[2] This finding would seem to indicate that personalization strategies might be of particular importance in CDU election campaigns. In actuality, the CDU recurrently has conducted strongly personalized campaigns. We need only think back to the Adenauer campaign in 1957 ("No experiments"), the Kiesinger campaign in 1969 ("The chancellor is what matters"), and the 1976 campaign ("Helmut Kohl—chancellor for Germany" and "Helmut Kohl—a man you can trust"). The CDU once again focused strongly on its leading candidate in the campaign for the 1994 general election. In 1998, this was done most prominently by the SPD. The party had in Schröder a candidate who came across very well in the media.

What personalization strategies produce for a given party in the way of results on Election Day is difficult to say. Kaase (1994), in a study of the 1990 general election, found that personalization does not have a *growing* influence on voter decision making, something that could have been assumed from what has been said heretofore (p. 226). The special situation created by the reunification of Germany in 1990 could have played a role here because a direct connection existed between the all-encompassing issue of reunification and the persons who were actively involved in the process, first and foremost Chancellor Kohl. In this case, personalization did not have to be made part of a campaign strategy. It was more or less taken care of automatically by media coverage.[3]

Above and beyond campaign strategy considerations, the personalization of political competition is a characteristic of the German political system. "The 'chancellor democracy' [is characterized] by a strong personalization of political competition which reaches its peak in general election campaigns" (Niclauss, 1988, p. 68). The antagonistic relationship between government and coalition is characteristic of the competitive democracy that exists in the federal republic. Niclauss notes in this regard,

> Strict separatism . . . and reduction to standpoints pro and contra were clearly already being used in the Adenauer era as instruments of power in the "chancellor democracy." Under the effect of this polarization, voters are faced with a decision to confirm the incumbent chancellor and his coalition or to vote for the opposition and their candidate. (p. 69; see also Niclauss, 1987, pp. 226-245)

The Americanization of German Election Campaigns

Despite the differences that exist in conditions for political communication in Germany and the United States, there has been talk for some time now of an Americanization of German election campaigns. A series of articles on this subject was published early in election year 1998.

Since the beginning of the 1980s, the term "Americanization" as used in this context has been equated with "professionalization." The professional conduct of an election campaign includes the following elements in particular: personalization, the use of outside consultants, the use of polls, and the "electronification" of campaigns and elections through the use of computers and the electronic media. With this in mind, we concur with Radunski (1996), who formulated this definition, when he notes with a view to 1994 that "the Americanization of politics . . . has long since become reality in Germany" (p. 39) given that the CDU, if not others, conducted a professional election campaign.

The meaning of the term "Americanization" needs to be expanded by a further component. Surprisingly, the term "New Politics," formerly used in the United States to describe the conduct of election campaigns with a marketing approach and clearly having an implication of its own, has not been used in the growing debate on the conduct of election campaigns in Germany. The meaning that has emerged over the past few years consists of two elements: (a) on the one hand, a certain amount of ideological flexibility, a turning away from the ideological foundations of one's own party, and possibly a certain amount of emptiness in the party program; and (b) on the other, the growing trend toward the tailoring political actions, above and beyond the normal theatrics, to the requirements of the media public and with their electioneering usefulness in mind. Thunert (1996) refers to this style of politics with regard to the United States as "the public presidency: governing in campaign style" (p. 16). In Tony Blair's time as prime minister of Great Britain, we also have seen government in the style of a permanent campaign. Germany still is a long way from phenomena of this type. For the year 1997, which deserves to be described as a year of standstill and reform blockage, it might be said that just the opposite was true. The government failed to gain approval for its tax reform, as neither of the two major parties was willing to enter into a genuine compromise so as not to maneuver itself into what might have been a less advantageous position for the general election.

Even though the term "New Politics" might have gone out of fashion, it provides a semantic parallel to an Americanized form of social democracy in Europe: New Politics–New Labour–New SPD.

The nature of German media coverage has reflected a further aspect of this process of Americanization. As in the United States, in Germany there is a tendency to report more on campaign strategies and less on campaign issues.

The Preeminent Importance of Television

As in all media-dominated Western democracies, tremendous importance attaches to television as a communication medium in election campaigns. There are three reasons for this:

1. Television is a powerful medium because of its ubiquitousness (Pfetsch & Schmitt-Beck, 1994, p. 234).
2. Television lends itself well to the pursuit of personalization strategies.
3. Television is a fast medium in which images can be broadcast live (Radunski, 1986, pp. 37-45).

Television also makes it possible to transport emotions. This ability to combine images with emotions lends great importance to the use of political symbols. In most cases, symbolic messages can be projected without a great deal of effort and expense. Recent studies on the use of the media in Germany have shown that over the past 30 years, the amount of time spent watching television has increased steadily along with the distances over which television programs are broadcast. In the case of the print media and radio, on the other hand, the amount of time spent reading newspapers and listening to the radio has stagnated or declined, indicating a loss of importance (Kiefer, 1996, pp. 235-248).

As a result of the enormous influence exerted by television, there is a need for the "visualization" (Bergsdorf, 1995, p. 48) of political happenings, and this is accompanied by processes of ritualization and personalization. It is nearly impossible to convey the multidimensionality and increasing complexity of political issues and decisions through the television medium. The visual information it provides determines the perceptions that people have of the character of a politician. Views regarding issues such as the political goals and the competence of a candidate are influenced more by written information (Kepplinger et al., 1994, p. 16 ff).

With regard to the agenda-setting function (i.e., the selection of events that are reported in the media), greater influence is ascribed to the print media than to television. Newspapers have a greater information capacity; as a rule, television will report a story only if it is important enough to have been reported previously in the print media (Schönbach, 1983, p. 463). But television also has its own selective filter. In a study of the 1990 general election in Germany, it was determined, on the one hand, that television coverage reported the events in question factually but, on the other, that it attributed more importance to some happenings than they deserved (Kepplinger et al., 1994, p. 148).

The Relationship Between Politics and the Media: Interdependence

The relationship between politics and the media is important for the choice of issues on the media's agenda of political reporting. This relationship is characterized by mutual give-and-take. Politicians provide (political) journalists events they can cover; the journalists see to it that their coverage of these events is shown to the public. Neither side can exist without the other; the relationship can be described as a "general political trade-off" (von Beyme, 1994, p. 324). The two are interdependent. For politicians, there is an opportunity to be seen due to the fact that journalists are dependent on events. It is obvious that at times when there is not much news, certain stories might be given coverage that otherwise would not have been given consideration. Election campaigns are faced with the need to bridge slow news phases such as this. Vacation times, particularly the summer vacation period (aptly called the "silly season"), require detailed timing on the part of the parties and the political players. In the relationship that exists between politics and the media, it is of enormous importance for a party and its candidates, particularly during election campaigns, to have the support of affiliated media.

Symbolism as a Means of Conveying a Political Message

An excellent way in which to attract media attention is to employ what is referred to as "political symbolism." The players in question use political symbols as a means of conveying political messages. According to Sarcinelli (1989), this includes "optical, acoustic, or linguistic stimuli" (p. 295) with which a message is expressed. Political symbolism means "the concrete use of political symbols, i.e., process-related actions and the possible political and strategic contexts in which they are used in the communication process" (p. 295). These symbols do not represent a policy, its contents, or individual politicians but rather are a vehicle for their perception; they become a "problem solution surrogate" (Sarcinelli, 1987, p. 242). By means of symbolism, the need to reduce complex issues to simple alternatives is given its due. The presentation of specific political issues can hardly do without symbolism. Applied stagecraft is part and parcel of political life. According to Offe (1976), this results in a "parallelism of theatrics and reality" (p. ix). Personalization strategies and what Grafe (1994) calls the "ceremonies of power" (p. 144) (i.e., status of office and insignias of power) are the most important elements of this symbolic form of conveying political messages.

As might be expected, exploiting the ceremonies associated with power produces a type of bonus obtained merely by virtue of holding the office in question given that, as a rule, they are available only to the person who holds that office. Even when an incumbent state premier takes over the role of chancellor candidate for the opposition, he or she has very little possibility of embodying national symbolism. In this context, it becomes clear what Radunski (1983) means when he says, "The bonus of office . . . is basically nothing other than a television bonus" (p. 132). The incumbent politician has a much easier time being seen on television than does his or her challenger due to the numerous symbolic events and the media coverage of them that the office brings with it. Schönbach and Semetko (1995) speak in this context of a "visibility bonus" (p. 55).

In the use of political symbolism, it is, first and foremost, visual stimuli that are consciously perceived. In many cases, the importance of language stimuli for the conveying of political messages is underestimated. The use of symbolic concepts for one's own ends, the control of terminology, and the symbolic content of language in general are excellent prerequisites for the symbolization of actions that take place as processes, and as such, they play an important role in the acquisition and preservation of political power (Bergsdorf, 1983, p. 33).

The Use of Political Symbolism in 1994

The strategy used by the CDU in the 1994 general election attributed major importance to the electronic media. Due to the high costs of campaigning in the *paid media,* the CDU's media campaign focused "primarily on providing news about politicians and on their public appearances, and less on television advertisements" (CDU-Bundesgeschäftsstelle, 1993, p. 73). This made campaigning, as well as the use of political symbolism, particularly important in the *free media.*

Symbolic events used in 1994 to highlight the chancellor's power and importance included the 50th anniversary of D-Day, when Allied troops landed in Normandy; the ASEAN conference; the world economic summit in Naples, Italy; the European Union (EU) summit in Corfu, Greece; the chancellor's speech commemorating the July 20 resistance movement against Hitler; the ceremonies marking the departure of the Western Allies and of Russian troops from the Federal Republic of Germany in the presence of their respective presidents and with live television coverage of parts of these events; and Germany's EU presidency in the second half of the year.

Particular importance was attributed in strategy planning to the EU presidency; it was seen as "a chance to decide the issues presented in the campaign leading up to the European Parliament election in favor of the CDU/CSU" (CDU-Bundesgeschäftsstelle, 1993, p. 48) by announcing specific European policy projects. This appears not to have been successful, however. Media analyses showed that the program of issues dealt with during the 6 months of the German presidency failed to elicit any significant interest in the media (*Medien Monitor*, August 1, 1994, p. 1). By contrast, two other events of those mentioned previously received strong media attention. The economic summit in Naples and U.S. President Bill Clinton's trip to Europe were among the 10 topics mentioned most often. There also was a great deal of interest in the visit paid to Germany by Chinese leader Li Ping. In this case, however, it would have to be assumed that this was not an advantage for the CDU in terms of political symbolism. Given the human rights situation in China and behavior that was an affront to his hosts, this guest of state generated headlines that were mostly negative. Other events of great symbolic power in 1994 were the participation of German troops in the framework of the Eurocorps in a military parade along the Champs-Élysées in Paris on the French national holiday, July 14, an event that stirred up considerable controversy in France, and their participation again in a parade held in Brussels, Belgium, a short time later marking the 50th anniversary of the liberation of Belgium in World War II.

Kohl not only received state visitors in Bonn but did so very visibly for the media in other locations as well. There was a meeting with President François Mitterand in the Alsace Region of eastern France, followed by a short trip across the border to Heidelberg, Germany, where Kohl had spent his university years. In addition, there was a visit to Schwerin, Germany, and the Island of Rügen with Spanish Prime Minister Filipe Gonzales. Most cabinet ministers met during the summer break with foreign counterparts—in some cases, in their home constituencies—and in this way took advantage of the German EU presidency. By contrast, the SPD candidate for chancellor, Rudolf Scharping (who had no foreign policy profile at all) was forced to go on a tour of foreign countries. As a result, he failed to attract much media attention. Jarren and Bode (1996) aptly sum up the difference between Kohl's and Scharping's activities with regard to their foreign policy presence and contacts with prominent foreign politicians: "The chancellor held court. The challenger had to travel" (p. 94).

Political Symbolism in the 1998 Election Campaign

The situation in the 1998 election campaign is somewhat different. In his capacity as premier of the state of Lower Saxony, SPD chancellor candidate Schröder also was president of the Bundesrat (based on a rotational system) for 1998, giving him a variety of possibilities to appear in public on occasions of symbolic significance.

A difference compared to 1994 is clear in connection with the CDU's prime issue—Europe. The EU summit held in Brussels early in May, at which the introduction of the single European currency (the euro) was decided, was a disaster for the Germans. In the debate surrounding the appointment of the president of the European Central Bank (ECB), the French obstinately insisted against the will of all the other member countries that Wim Duisenberg, the first ECB president, step down in favor of a French successor halfway through his term in office. As the protagonist of the Duisenberg support group, Kohl was criticized in Germany for not having prevented this. With this blemish on Kohl's record, the theme of a "united Europe" with the German chancellor as its architect, the drawing power of which CDU strategists were counting on, no longer could be used in the campaign, and it faded into the background. The situation was aggravated further by the fact that a majority of Germans reject the euro and would rather have kept the mark, a currency with which older people, in particular, have an almost emotional relationship. As a result of a majority of the population being against the euro, the European theme acquired a negative component for the CDU. There seemed to be emerging a parallel to the 1992 presidential election in the United States given that foreign policy successes lost their drawing power in view of domestic problems, foremost among them a high level of unemployment. The 1998 general election would be won or lost on the basis of domestic issues. The SPD did not make any attempt to claim a large amount of foreign policy competence for itself.

In contrast to the poor media management at the EU summit, after which Kohl fired his press spokesman, Clinton's visit in May in connection with the 50th anniversary of the Berlin airlift attracted strong media attention and resulted in positive television coverage. Of importance in this context was the fact that this was Clinton's first visit to an eastern German state. The CDU has been struggling with disastrously poor poll results in eastern Germany. As a result of the two mishaps in their media and event management, the SPD decided to leave the month of May entirely to the CDU and to come back into the focus of public interest after that. The SPD candidate's campaign team was presented at the end of May somewhat like a shadow cabinet. The media response to the presentation was not particularly positive, however, because the team did not contain any of the party-independent experts about whom there had been speculation beforehand, and on the whole the event could only be described as "mediocre."

The lineup for the prospective Schröder cabinet later was to take on a bit more color. Jost Stollmann, an entrepreneur in his early 40s who built up a very successful computer business and is without party affilations, was presented as a candidate for the office of economics minister who would be acceptable to voters at the center of the political spectrum. A political novice, Stollmann created an uproar in the ranks of the SPD with a number of statements made shortly after his nomination, some of which strongly contradicted the SPD platform. However, the excitement this evoked also created the impression among politically disinterested voters that the SPD was willing to recruit independent experts in an effort to address the problems the country faces. Stollmann ended up withdrawing his candidacy after the election. The same type of function was served by Michael Naumann, a publisher who has lived and worked in the United States for some time now whose role was as a candidate for office in the cultural sector to remobilize left-wing intellectuals in the ranks of the SPD.

The Role Played by the Electronic Media

The CDU and SPD strategies in 1994 clearly were directed toward running media-based campaigns (and this was the case even more so in 1998). Television ads were widely used.

The advantages of running campaign ads are obvious. They can be placed in effective time slots and guarantee a high level of public exposure; only posters attract a similarly high level of attention (Schulz, 1994, p. 321). In addition, they offer a forum for the presentation of political standpoints "unfiltered and un-influenced by journalistic selection" (Szyszka, 1996, p. 185). Radio and television ads have a high exposure rate and can prove to be an important source of information, particularly for politically disinterested members of the viewing and listening audiences (Holtz-Bacha, 1994, p. 346). In the 1990 general election campaign, two thirds of the population saw campaign ads on television and learned something about the election from them. In this information-providing function, they were more effective than television news programs; only posters scored better.[4]

What concrete effect they have on voting behavior cannot be determined. Above and beyond the normal difficulties encountered in extracting an individual factor from a bundle of factors that exert influence on voting decisions, this is a result of the fact that almost nothing can be said about who sees the ads; the structure of viewing audiences is strongly dependent on the given program environment. The situation is similar for campaign ads broadcast on the public television channels ARD and ZDF. It cannot be predicted to which viewing audiences they will be shown because it is not known in advance which party will be given the time slot in question.[5]

Air time on the two nationwide public channels is allotted to the parties in accordance with their importance; the CDU and SPD are each given eight 2½-minute time slots of free advertising time. In 1994, the two major parties also bought a great deal of advertising time on the private channels. The latter channels lowered the price they charged for campaign ads to 45% of the regular price. In 1990, the parties still had to pay the full price. In the run-up to the European Parliament election in 1994, the CDU ran 30-second ads on private television channels more than 150 times, and they ran them another 100 times in the run-up to the general election. The SPD ran ads 335 times on private television channels. No election campaign in the history of the Federal Republic of Germany had seen this much campaigning on privately owned television before. This rising trend continued in 1998.

The Internet and Intranet

A further component of electronic media-based election campaigning, an internal communications network through which ideas, speeches, and other texts can be accessed rapidly, was created at the CDU national headquarters. The system, KomSys, linked all the party's district offices with a central computer on which information and official party positions were available to users in real time.

The extent to which this communications medium was used is difficult to say. In the 1998 general election campaign, a new version of this system, Kandinet, was employed. For the first time, the SPD also made use of this possibility for their candidates and campaign staff to transfer data and information back and forth rapidly.

The Internet is used by the parties as an information medium for the general public on their home pages (e.g., http://www.cdu.de, http://www.spd.de). In addition, there are a number of Bundestag deputies who have personal home pages on the Internet.[6] In Germany, the Internet is used much less for political communication than it is in the United States. Internet postings in Germany are aimed primarily at young voters. Two Hamburg students created an independent Web site to serve as an information platform during the 1998 election campaign. It featured a media database, the possibility to engage in chats with politicians, and the opportunity to take part in on-line polls (http://www.wahlkampf98.de).

The Role Played by Television in the 1994 Campaign

In 1994, not only was Kohl active at campaign rallies, where he made constant appearances, he also was by far the politician seen most often on television (although, in contrast to his challenger, he did not appear on talk shows). In the course of the entire election year, Kohl was on television for more than 33 hours either in discussions (nearly 28 hours) or in freeze frames (5½ hours). By comparison, Scharping was on for a total of not quite 23 hours and did not come across as well as Kohl in discussions.[7] Kohl came off signficantly better in television statements lasting longer than 1 minute in the period from June 1 to October 14—the heated phase of the campaign. With a total of more than 10½ hours, Kohl was well ahead of the SPD candidate, who had 6 hours 50 minutes.[8]

When comparing these figures, the conclusion can be drawn that the media were a great deal less interested in presenting Scharping's campaign message to the viewing audiences. Certainly, the "incumbency bonus" played a role, but it also is possible that Scharping was a victim of the standards that apply to politicians who use the television medium. Kohl is definitely not the prototype of a telegenic politician, but over the years, he has acquired singular self-confidence and poise on camera with which he has been able to overcome his one-time image as "nerd of the nation."

Media Management

CDU media managers made skillful use of events in 1994 and tested new forms of campaigning in the media. Among other things, at the beginning of June, shortly before the World Cup started in the United States, Kohl appeared on the

SAT.1 soccer show and then, a short time later, flew to the United States at the expense of this private television channel to watch the opening game of the World Cup together with Clinton. There, he also met with coach Berti Vogts and the German team. The mutual admiration that existed between Kohl and Vogts became a subject of interest in the media. At the time, Vogts had not yet become a controversial figure in his role as coach of the national soccer team. The SPD candidate, on the other hand, committed what in this connection could be described as a nearly disastrous blunder. Scharping said that there were "better coaches than Vogts" and allegedly referred to him as being "on the verge of retirement." The import of this remark should not be underestimated. Soccer is the German national sport, comparable in popularity with baseball or basketball in the United States.

Due to his enormous presence in the media, Kohl could afford to avoid any media appearances that entailed risks such as television debates and talk shows. He avoided any public contact at all with Scharping so as not to enhance the latter's image. This probably was why, after a proposal to this effect was put forward several times by the SPD, the CDU stated that it did not want a debate between Kohl and his challenger, giving as the official reason that it would not be fair to its coalition partner, the FDP. But this was nothing new. Televised discussions with the candidates for the chancellorship, known in Germany as "elephant rounds," were held on only five occasions between 1972 and 1987. In recent years, chancellor candidates have limited themselves to giving interviews (Holtz-Bacha, 1996, p. 23).

Jarren and Bode (1996), who closely studied media management of the parties in "super election year" 1994, gave the CDU very good marks, in contrast to the SPD, which had to deal with a number of structural problems such as its candidate's lack of charisma (pp. 108-114). In her analysis, Friedrichsen (1996) comes to the conclusion that of all the parties, the CDU chalked up the largest amount of media presence across the board. The Christian Democrats also were the party that appeared most frequently as a player in the news, both in the print media and on television, although their success was greater in the latter medium. The governing parties were the initiators of nearly 60% of the news items reported (pp. 56-79, Tables 1 and 2). Schönbach and Semetko (1996) note a clear predominance of the coalition parties in the media, as was the case in 1990; in contrast to Oskar Lafontaine, the present party chairman (who ran as chancellor candidate for the SPD in 1990), Scharping was able to close the gap a bit between himself and Kohl (p. 157).

A significant problem that the SPD faced in 1994 was the fact that the media traditionally close to the party not only failed to support it in the manner expected but also echoed the criticism coming from the opposing side. The main reason for this was that the media close to the SPD clearly would have preferred a chancellor candidate other than Scharping, that is, the candidate who succeeded him 4 years later, Schröder. "A clear incumbency bonus" (Friedrichsen, 1996, p. 56) was evident in the media coverage in 1994. The CDU/CSU and the FDP used their better prerequisites for agenda setting to motivate coverage (Institut für angewandte Sozialwissenschaft [INFAS], 1994, p. 10). The SPD, on the other hand, failed to attract media attention with its attempts at staging "pseudo-events" and similar tactics. The Social Democrats were unable to get their political issues onto the media agenda, in contrast to the internal problems that plagued their party that year, which the media eagerly snapped up, evoking considerable public response (Friedrichsen, 1996, p. 59).

The Role Played by the Candidates

Both candidates had a major influence on the outcome of the election—Scharping through his weakness within the party, his errors, and his ineptness; Kohl as a dominant figure both on the political stage and in the media during that election year. In a direct comparison to his challenger, Kohl came out ahead in nearly every respect. Not only were the 1994 campaigns of the two major parties planned and carried out as personalized campaigns, but their intentions also were to get the media to focus on them in this way. As was the case in 1990, the candidates in 1994 were the "central element of media coverage" (Kepplinger & Rettich, 1996, p. 85), with the incumbent chancellor being the subject of media coverage more frequently than the SPD candidate. The media assessed Kohl's importance for his party's campaign as being much greater than Scharping's importance for his party (*Medien Monitor*, September 15, 1994, p. 4).[9] A qualitative analysis of media reports shows that depictions of Kohl tended to be more positive than negative, whereas depictions of Scharping in the media tended to be ambivalent.[10]

With regard to "experience" and "prestige abroad," public perceptions of Kohl came close to the level of an "ideal chancellor" (Jung, 1995, p. 126). The lack of experience and profile shown in many areas by the political newcomer, Scharping, was a major shortcoming for the Social Democrats. In the media coverage that took place in the course of the campaign, his unsharp contours became "increasingly vague" (Rudolph, 1996, p. 151). The similarities the challenger was said to have with the incumbent were more in Kohl's favor. Why should people vote for a copy when they could have the original?

In a large number of analyses and editorials, major importance was attributed to the role that Kohl played personally in winning the election for the coalition. Recurrent reference was made to Kohl's campaign experience, enabling him to cast his government's policies in a favorable light. In summary, it can be said that both candidates played very significant parts in determining the outcome of the election—Kohl in a positive sense for the CDU/CSU and Scharping in a negative sense for the SPD. The turning points in the election year were closely linked to Scharping, and the lack of media support for the SPD was primarily a result of who the candidate was. The candidates in an election campaign play a key role within their respective parties. The unity shown by the CDU/CSU was, first and foremost, a result of who its candidate was, a person who had no difficulty in gaining acceptance for his ways of thinking; the party stood united behind its candidate. The problems of the SPD were closely related to its party chairman's and chancellor candidate's isolation within the party and his lack of ability to gain acceptance and support for his views.

The Role Played by Campaign Posters

Posters are the second most important form of paid political advertising after radio and television ads. There is a long tradition of using posters as a political medium in Germany as well as in other European countries. In the past, they were one of very few means of public communication. The advent of the new electronic media has diminished their importance as a medium of (political) communication.

Even though they no longer are the "flagship of election campaign advertising" (Radunski, 1986, p. 37), as they still were being referred to in 1986, or "for the public, the number one election campaign medium" (Radunski, 1980, p. 111), as they still were viewed in 1980, posters continue to be "the most visible signs of an election campaign" (Grafe, 1994, p. 206), and their importance should not be underestimated. In the final phase of election campaigns, political posters exert effects that extend far into the realm of consumer goods advertising. By way of example, the tobacco industry, which is the largest renter of approximately 300,000 available advertising surfaces for large posters (accounting for about one fifth of the total), traditionally allows political parties to use these surfaces for their posters free of charge for a period of 10 days prior to a general election. Smaller formats, for which it is not necessary to rent large and expensive surfaces, are in some cases printed in numbers of 100,000 or more.

What effect posters have on voters has not yet been made the specific focus of a study. They are used to indicate moods, to give signals, to add, or to underline something in a campaign. But it is not possible to win voter support for a specific policy with posters (Radunski, 1980, p. 111). According to available estimates, 20% of election campaign budgets are used for posters (Langguth, 1995, p. 17); this figure shows the level of importance the parties continue to attribute to posters as a political advertising medium. The fact that posters are up prepares the minds of the public for further advertising measures.

Above and beyond the effects they have on streets and city squares, posters recurrently have been the subject of media coverage themselves. The dissemination of a campaign poster almost exclusively through the media has been referred to as "newsroom campaigning." A very successful example of this type of campaign in 1994 was the poster with the inscription "Government Without a Beard" and the "red socks poster." Very few of them were put up. For the most part, they were disseminated by the media.

The "Government Without a Beard" motif was the first important poster in the 1994 CDU campaign and has become a classic among German election campaign posters. It shows a portrait of Kohl with his head resting on one hand, thinking, a wry smile on his face, without the glasses he wears for image reasons but has not needed for a long time. Only two copies of this poster were hung up in public. This represented a major success in terms of newsroom campaigning because the poster attracted a large amount of media attention. The slogan "Government Without a Beard" was well chosen for its ambiguity. On the one hand, the word "beard" in German is associated with "having a long beard," that is, being old and inflexible. In other words, a government without a beard would be a new, modern, reform-minded government. On the other hand, the poster alluded to the fact that the SPD candidate wore a beard. Scharping's beard and his appearance in general became a theme that was to accompany him throughout the election year.

The "Red Socks Campaign" in 1994

The other poster that was successfully disseminated by means of the newsrooms was the CDU's aggressive "red socks poster." It was created in response to the situation after the state election in Saxony-Anhalt, held 3½ months before the general election. The result of the election was that the only way in which to form a majority government without involving the Party of Democratic Socialism (PDS) would have been to form a grand coalition between the CDU and the SPD, which had received nearly equal percentages of the vote. A coalition with the PDS, the successor to the SED that had been formed in 1946 in a forced merger of the SPD with the KPD in the Soviet occupation zone and that had imposed dictatorial rule in the German Democratic Republic, was unthinkable.[11]

After negotiations on a coalition between the CDU and the SPD failed, the SPD formed a minority coalition with the Greens, tolerated by the PDS, a situation that has come to be called the "Magdeburg model" (Magdeburg is the capital of the state of Saxony-Anhalt). The CDU took advantage of the formation of this government in the eastern German state to attack the SPD, accusing it of collaborating with left-wing extremists and, as such, of breaking a political taboo.

The CDU's anti-leftist campaign was symbolically expressed by the "red socks poster," which showed a red sock (representing the PDS) hanging on a clothesline and held in place by a green clothespin (representing Alliance 90/the Greens, the SPD's coalition partner) and flanked by the slogan "Let's move forward . . . but not with red socks on." Since then, "red socks" has become a common expression in German. This probably is the most widely known political poster in the country. The "red socks campaign" upset quite a few voters in eastern Germany, and some of the CDU state organizations there were anything but happy about it. In the final analysis, however, the mobilization of voter support for the CDU in western Germany, the ultimate aim of the campaign, surely more than made up for these negative effects. The underlying idea was that general elections are won or lost in western Germany. The five eastern German states together have about as many voters as does North Rhine-Westphalia, the most populous state in western Germany.

The importance of the "red socks campaign" for the outcome of the 1994 general election often has been overestimated. This campaign alone could not have accounted for the narrow lead that the governing coalition had nationwide.

The state election in Saxony-Anhalt and its consequences was not the only event in election year 1994 that determined how people would vote.

Turning Points in Election Year 1994

The crucial effects of the campaign were that it polarized views on issues, mobilized voters, and created a lack of unity in the ranks of the SPD. Feist (1996) sums it up quite nicely: "Contrary to popular opinion, Magdeburg was not the SPD's Waterloo; it was a hot-button issue that shuffled the deck again for everyone involved" (p. 66). "SPD Waterloo" is appropriate only with reference to the election of the German president at the end of May, in connection with which the SPD acted very ineptly in tactical terms. A CDU defeat in this election, which the SPD could have achieved with the support of FDP candidate Hildegard Hamm-Brücher, and the symbolic effect this would have had with regard to the coalition might well have been able to modify somewhat the change of public mood that was taking place as a result of an upswing in the economy. The European election in mid-June, the outcome of which showed a trend against the SPD, constituted a further turning point in 1994, as did the CDU party conference in Hamburg at the end of February where Kohl made a rousing speech. With a view to these events, Rudolph (1996) is right when he says, "The suspected major turning point [in the form of a change of government] broke down into a number of smaller turning points which, on top of everything else, conflicted with one another" (p. 147).[12]

Voter preference for the CDU/CSU increased steadily in the course of the year, whereas voter preference for the SPD, which had been higher than that for the conservatives at the beginning of 1994, remained constant but in the end was overtaken by the chancellor's party (Friedrichsen, 1996, p. 61). A U-shaped trend curve with regard to election results and polls taken between two general elections was seen again in 1994, albeit "no longer with the same ideal adherence to the rule as in the past" (Feist, 1996, p. 76).

The "Red Hands Campaign" in 1998

In 1998, the "red socks campaign" was revived in the form of a poster that showed the historical handshake of the chairmen of the KPD and the SPD when they merged to form the SED in 1946. The poster took up the SPD slogan for election year 1998, "We are ready," and included beneath it, "Germany be careful! CDU." What this was supposed to suggest was that the SPD was ready to have its candidate elected chancellor with the help of votes from the PDS. The SPD provided the "ammunition" for this revival of the anti-leftist campaign when it decided after the 1998 election in Saxony-Anhalt, which produced a similar result in terms of coalitions as it did 4 years earlier, to let the PDS continue to tolerate its coalition in the state assembly. Coalition talks between the SPD and CDU had failed prior to that. Viewed from a strategy standpoint, it can be assumed that under pressure from the national party executive, the CDU in Saxony-Anhalt had set the bar for a grand coalition so high that the talks were doomed to fail from the outset. In an evaluation of the results of this state election, which was seen as an important test of the mood of the electorate prior to the general election, the CDU, which received only slightly more than 20% of the vote and lost more than 10% in its role as an opposition party, was lucky in that (a) in 1994 it was given an opportunity to polarize public debate as a result of the continuation of the SPD minority government and in that (b) its devastatingly poor results due to the gains made by the right-wing extremist German People's Union (DVU), which got into the state assembly with 13% of the vote, had faded into the background.

The revival of the anti-leftist campaign ran into stiffer resistance than it did in 1994 from the eastern German CDU, which was afraid of long-term consequences in the form of a hardening of the split between eastern and western Germany.

The outcome of all this was that the CDU suffered its greatest losses in the 1998 general election in eastern Germany, dropping from 38.5% of the vote in the 1994 general election to 27.3%, whereas in the western part of the country, the party lost "only" 5.1%.

For many eastern Germans, the stigmatization of the PDS as an undemocratic and radical party is something they simply do not understand. In western Germany, former President Richard von Weizsäcker has become a leading critic of this way of dealing with the PDS and, in so doing, has evoked a strong response in the media.

The attempt on the part of the CDU to give the 1998 general election the appearance of a decision on policy direction between a stable center-right government consisting of the CDU/CSU and the FDP, on the one hand, and an unpredictable, leftist-oriented, red-green, and possibly dark red alliance (SPD, Alliance 90/the Greens, and the PDS), on the other, has made a more detailed debate on issues and ideas largely impossible. It is precisely a debate of this type that a number of CDU politicians called for as an adequate instrument for doing battle with the SPD—first and foremost, the very influential CDU/CSU parliamentary group chairman, Wolfgang Schäuble, who fully supported the "red socks campaign" in 1994 but tended to be against its revival.

Schäuble's desire for a debate on issues in the election campaign reflected a growing distance between himself and his mentor, Kohl, who in October 1997 had declared him the preferred candidate to succeed him. Schäuble was said to be working in the direction of a grand coalition with the SPD under his leadership after the 1998 election because, on the one hand, a coalition of this type would be the only way for the CDU to continue in government and because, on the other, it would be a chance for him to become chancellor. Schäuble, who has been confined to a wheelchair since being shot in an assassination attempt in 1990, staked initial claims to Kohl's successorship in an interview given early in 1997 in which he raised the question as to whether a disabled person like himself could become chancellor.

Positioning the CDU as the Lesser of Two Evils

The "red socks campaign" and its revival in 1998 were part of a CDU/CSU strategy to position themselves as a party that constitutes the lesser of two evils. This strategy clearly was evident in a number of places in the scenario written for the 1994 campaign. This was the case, for example, in the section on the SPD, where attention is focused on counteracting the strategy employed by the Social Democrats. Sowing seeds of doubt with regard to the ability of another party to govern does not necessarily mean constructive political leadership; what it means is that the members of the party in question feel that they are just a little better than the others. This strategy was appropriate to the extent that the assessment of the basic mood of the electorate was correct with regard to its desire not to take further risks. The same applied with regard to the campaign for the chancellorship insofar as the strong element of personalization that this involves. Also with regard to the issue of viability for the future, there is an evident effort on the part of the CDU to present itself as a party that is better than the others but without providing proof that this is actually the case. It is noted in the party strategy for 1994,

> For this reason, the CDU . . . will focus its political strategy on public debate of its concept for the future. This means that debate with the political opponents will have to be conducted, for the most part, on the lack of viability for the future shown by their policies and the lack of competence evident in their platform. (CDU-Bundes-geschäftsstelle, 1993, p. 39)

From this, the conclusion could be drawn that it is not its own competence in competition with other parties that makes the CDU/CSU better but rather the incompetence of the others.

On the other hand, it must be noted, in all fairness, that a party that has been in government over a longer period of time (in the case of the CDU, it had been 12 years in 1994) has a hard time letting go of things that are tried-and-true and moving ahead into entirely new areas. For a party such as the CDU, with a perception of itself as a people's party forced to strike a balance among a large number of different interest groups having different vested interests, this is particularly difficult to achieve. This applied to an even greater extent in 1998 than it did 4 years earlier.

The SPD pursued a successful strategy of portraying the Kohl government as being ineffective by refusing to compromise on a number of key issues, foremost among them tax reform. A "Kohl must go" mood spread in the electorate; Kohl was perceived as the personification of stagnation. As was the case in the United States in 1992, a general feeling developed that it was "time for a change."

In any event, the presentation of the CDU as a party that constituted the lesser of two evils was successful in 1994. The party's success at the polls was personified by the chancellor, who stood for continuity like no one else. The desire of the people for the status quo—for what had stood the test of time—and their fear of the new helped the CDU to win the election. Germans very likely did not vote for the CDU/CSU out of a conviction that things would actually get better but rather out of a hope that things would not get any worse. It was not the will of the people that anything should really change. In the INFAS (1994) analysis of the general election, we read that "the need for continuity . . . won out" (p. 10). The SPD failed to make it clear what would have been better with it in government, leaving the question open as to why Kohl should be replaced.

The fact that up until Election Day 1994, half of the German electorate felt that it was time for a change but in the end did not vote that way, speaks for the correctness of the thesis that the CDU was elected as a party seen as constituting the lesser of two evils. At the beginning of the year, 61% of the electorate felt that there was a need for change (INFAS, 1994, p. 6). Apparently, the voters failed to see an acceptable offer for a change of government. The positioning of the CDU/CSU was right on the money: "If the time was ripe for a change, in the eyes of the electorate, the SPD was not" (p. 10). By adding up the mistakes the SPD made in 1994 and the fundamental positioning of the CDU as a party that constituted the lesser of two evils, it can be said that the outcome of the 1994 election was not so much a result of the CDU winning the election but more a result of the SPD losing it.

The Role of the Bavarian Sister Party, the CSU

The Bavarian sister party is of great importance for the strategic positioning of the CDU. On issues important to conservative voters such as domestic security and foreigners, the CSU can make use of its positions, which tend to be to the right of those held by the CDU, to address these voters for the entire party. In this way, it is able to polarize public debate on such issues with standpoints that would not be acceptable in this form in the CDU alone. This makes it possible for the party as a whole to attract right-wing voters without giving the CDU/CSU a right-wing image. The overall impression created could be described, in conservative circles at least, as that of a center-right party. Seen from a campaign strategy standpoint, these positions need to be well coordinated. This is enormously important to ensure that the CDU and CSU are presented to the electorate as a coherent and united party. In 1994, they succeeded at this very well by presenting a joint election platform.

In 1998, this type of coordination with the CSU became a major problem for the CDU. As was the case in 1994, a state election was held in Bavaria shortly before the general election. For the CSU, the preservation of its absolute majority in Bavaria is more important than a good result for the CDU/CSU at the national level. The problem that arises from this became apparent in 1998 when the CSU attempted to set itself apart from the federal government with a view to improving its ratings at the state level. This led to a conflict between the CDU and the CSU over a common election platform. In the course of the controversy, Schäuble, the strong man in the CDU/CSU behind Kohl and a man with an excellent reputation among voters as a very competent, aggressive, and fair politician with an enormous ability to get things done, took a number of hits. Up to then, he was the most popular CDU politician and the only one able to compete with the SPD candidate in terms of approval ratings. After this dispute, Schäuble no longer was able to gain support for conducting an election campaign based on issues. A side effect of this lack of unity—and something that was desired by the CSU in Bavaria—was that the CSU was able to consolidate its position at the state level after a successful state election but was relegated to an opposition role at the federal level. Bavaria's ambitious premier, Edmund Stoiber, took advantage of a strengthened position to take over from former federal finance minister Theo Waigel as chairman of the CSU. This shows some of the importance that state elections can have for politics at the federal level.

Waigel resigned as party chairman right after the election. The result of the Bavaria state election came as a surprise, bringing slight gains for the CSU and losses for the SPD, but this did not have any effect on the overall trend at the national level. The possibility of any such effect coming about was destroyed by a careless comment made 2 days before the election by Family Minister Claudia Nolte revealing that the CDU had been secretly planning to raise taxes after the election.

The 1998 Election Campaign

Looking back on the first half of election year 1998, it is clear that the SPD was not willing to repeat the mistakes it had made in the previous general election. After the experience of 1994, the Social Democrats did the right thing by moving their campaign headquarters away from the party headquarters (the "war room" concept), based on the American example, because in this way the decision-making center for the campaign would remain largely unaffected by any party infighting.

The perfect staging of Schröder's nomination as SPD candidate the evening of the state assembly election in Lower Saxony, where the SPD was able to expand its absolute majority with Schröder as premier, bespeaks an enormous gain in professionalism on the part of the Social Democrats and the correctness of their strategy. The SPD succeeded very well in making this state election look something like an American primary (formal differences aside). The decision to field Schröder as the SPD candidate obviously had been made in advance. This is shown by the fact that after the Lower Saxony election, the SPD was able to conduct a creative, perfectly staged, and (with regard to campaign posters) original campaign at a high rate of speed. The strategy and artwork for the campaign could not have been completed overnight. It would seem as if the SPD had successfully misled the CDU, leading it to believe that Oskar Lafontaine was going to be the chancellor candidate and intentionally presenting itself up to that point in a plain and unconvincing manner. After Schröder became the candidate for chancellor, the SPD made very skillful use of every opportunity to create public exposure for him.

Obviously, the CDU had reckoned that the party chairman, Lafontaine, would become the SPD candidate, which would have been an ideal situation given that he had lost against Kohl in 1990 and is strongly leftist in his views. The CDU was totally unprepared for Schröder's nomination. After that, the CDU was unable to keep up with the pace of the SPD campaign and displayed unprecedented weaknesses. By way of example, the CDU's secretary general, Peter Hintze, and his counterparts from the CSU and FDP walked out of a live television broadcast, *Bonner Runde,* a traditional Election Night discussion with the secretaries general of the parties, on the evening of the Lower Saxony election because the program had been interrupted to show an interview with Schröder. This left people with the impression that they were poor losers. Since then, this behavior recurrently has been a subject of discussion in the media. A further indication of nervousness on the part of the CDU is the fact that at the end of May, just 4 months before the election, Kohl fired his press spokesman, Peter Hausmann, with whom he had not gotten along well for some time. Hausmann's successor, Otto Hauser, forfeited any sympathies the press corps might have had for him by acting arrogantly in his first press conference and then made a number of careless remarks that left a devastating impression on the public. For this, he became a target of strong criticism, not just from the media but also from the ranks of his own party.

At the same time, the CDU hired Hans-Hermann Tiedje as a consultant for its party headquarters. Like Peter Boenisch, who served as campaign adviser to Kohl in 1994, Tiedje is a former editor-in-chief of *Bild,* Germany's largest circulation tabloid. According to press reports, Tiedje received approximately DM 200,000 for his 4-month assignment as Kohl's personal campaign adviser. His being hired also evoked a considerable response in the foreign media. Tiedje has a dubious reputation, with a number of previous media projects he attempted having failed. Fellow journalists refer to him as "Rambo" because of the way in which he deals with people and the methods he uses. He allegedly offered his services to SPD candidate Schröder at the beginning of election year 1998.

In preparing for its election campaign, the SPD drew on outside expertise in numerous places. In the fall of 1997, the SPD party executive was advised by U.S. specialists Henry Sheinkopf and Doug Schoen. Dick Morris is said to have met with Schröder and his media adviser, Bodo Hombach. The SPD also received advice from Blair's media adviser, Peter Mandelson, who might be considered the prototype of a European "spin doctor." Borrowings from the 1997 "New Labour" campaign were very evident in the way in which the auditorium was arranged and decorated at the party conference that the Social Democrats held in Leipzig in April, where Schröder officially was appointed as the SPD chancellor candidate. The stagecraft involved was similar to that of party conventions in the United States. The campaign colors used by the SPD, red and blue, were borrowed from the Clinton campaign. The presentation of a red rose to Schröder after his appointment was something that was used by Blair in 1997 and that Mitterand discovered for European social democracy.

The SPD party conference in Leipzig was a perfect production—almost too perfect. Television viewers found the grandeur overwhelming. But for the photos that appeared in the print media—and they were the ones that counted—the composition was just right. Television images are short-lived, whereas printed photos are much less so.

A further analogy to the sister parties in other countries can be found in the SPD's campaign slogan, "The New Center." A slogan used at the Leipzig party conference, "The Strength of the New," was dropped immediately because it had been used by Siemens a few years earlier.

A further element of the professionally managed SPD election campaign was the installation of a new premier in North Rhine-Westphalia, Germany's most important state. After serving as state premier for nearly 20 years, Johannes Rau, who was the SPD candidate for the office of federal president in 1994 and was thinking of running again in 1999, ceded his office as premier to Wolfgang Clement, one of the most popular SPD politicians and a man with a good reputation in the business community. Clement, who was referred to as the "Prince Charles of German politics" for having had to wait so long before he could take office, is a close friend of Schröder and a figurehead symbolizing a modern SPD. The importance of Rau's replacement by Clement for the SPD's national campaign should not be underestimated. The point in time at which this would take place had been a subject of speculation for 2 years. It illustrates the interactive relationship that exists between state governments and election campaigns at the national level, and it shows how professional the SPD's campaign management was in 1998 as opposed to 1994. In choosing its candidate for president, the SPD gave consideration to the fact that it had long been Rau's personal dream to hold this office, even though his chances of being elected were not good in 1994. This turned out to be a disastrous move for the Social Democrats and their chancellor candidate in 1994, Scharping.

Most of the elements in the SPD campaign fall into the category of "professional." The process of Americanization is evident here. On the one hand, the SPD had in Schröder a candidate who responded excellently to the requirements of the modern media; on the other, he showed a certain amount of flexibility with regard to party platform and ideology. If they were to be stated in a nutshell, the fundamental strategy rules for the SPD campaign would be "not too heavy on the issues" and "the man is the message." The "New Center" was a *successful* attempt to attract more middle-of-the-road voters than ever before. In this connection, the party extended itself across an area that included the chancellor candidate, Schröder, who looked to the right, toward the center of the political spectrum, and the more left-leaning party chairman, Lafontaine, whose job it was to keep the party on course and see to it that the party presented an image of unity to the public.

Schröder is preeminent among those in the SPD who have close ties with the business community. He has excellent contacts in industry. By referring to him as a "CEO's kind of socialist," the SPD tried to dispel voter fears that an SPD government would induce a downturn in the economy.

As a result of the way in which Schröder positioned himself, the CDU/CSU was unable to conduct a classical campaign based on crass policy distinctions such as "economic stability" versus "Red-Green chaos." In addition to this, the general public assessed that the possibility that the SPD would be able to form a coalition with Alliance 90/the Greens was very slim. The assumption was that the most likely outcome of the election would be a grand coalition consisting of the SPD and the CDU/CSU—indeed, that this would be the only realistic possibility of forming a government. This impression made it possible for the SPD to move strongly toward the center. As it turned out, the SPD was right on course with its "New Center" strategy.

It was very interesting to observe the campaign conducted in 1998 by Alliance 90/the Greens. Although the Greens, under the leadership of their parliamentary party chairman, Joseph Fischer (who, because of his rhetorical ability, often was viewed by the general public as the real opposition leader in the Bundestag), seemed to have developed in the course of the past legislative term into a serious party capable of being part of a government coalition, they made a number of serious mistakes in the course of the election year.

Prominent among them were the decision taken at the Magdeburg party conference to triple the price of a liter of gasoline to DM 5 over a period of 10 years and against a compromise with regard to the German armed forces blue helmet mission in Bosnia. Ironically, these decisions were approved by a one-vote majority. The relief that was supposed to be provided to people as compensation for the gasoline price increase was not given any notice at all. The decision against the involvement of the German armed forces in international missions nurtured new doubts as to the reliability of the Greens in foreign policy matters, and this was widely exploited by the other political parties including the SPD, the Greens' potential coalition partner.

The CDU responded to the gasoline price decision with a "no to 5 marks per liter for gasoline campaign" so poorly done that it was almost painful to watch. Even though the campaign resulted in a great deal of media criticism and ridicule of the CDU, it drove a wedge into the Green Party and greatly upset its parliamentary representatives. The CDU strategy was aimed at pushing the Greens below the 5% barrier and eliminating them as a potential coalition partner for the SPD.

But the real disaster for the Greens was a statement made by their tourism expert, Halo Saibold, to the effect that Germans would have to limit themselves to one plane trip abroad every 5 years because of the atmospheric pollution caused by air travel. This was tantamount to patronage of the people—ecological fundamentalists trying to impose restrictions on their personal freedom. After that, the Greens' polls plummeted to close to the 5% mark for the first time in several years. In an attempt to correct this ominous trend, the Greens conducted a decidedly personalized election campaign for the first time ever, with a strong focus on their parliamentary group chairman. Fischer set up his own American-style campaign team, drawing on the support of volunteers and attempting to obtain donations from industry for his private campaign fund. In this sense, the Greens conducted two campaigns in 1998: their official campaign involving the party as a whole and a private campaign run by their parliamentary party chairman (although the two cannot really be seen as separate from one another). With a view to paving the way for their reelection to the Bundestag, the Greens held an extraordinary party conference at which their major objectives were listed in an abbreviated platform and an attempt was made to relativize the decisions in favor of raising the price of gasoline and against out-of-country missions for the German armed forces. The party conference was held at the municipal hall of the area of Bonn known as "Bad Godesberg." Ironically, it was here in 1959 that the SPD approved its "Bad Godesberg Program" with which it laid the foundation for its acceptability as a party in government, in particular by reformulating its foreign policy positions.

The Results of the 1998 Election

The election produced gains for the Social Democrats greater than what most of the public opinion research organizations had predicted. They received 4.5% more than in the previous election, giving them nearly 41% of the total and making them the strongest group in the German Bundestag for the second time in the history of the federal republic. For the first time, they have a clear lead over the CDU/CSU, which lost more than 6% and received just under 35% of the vote. The small parties were able to hold their own, the Greens and FDP lost slightly, and the PDS made slight gains.

This result can be seen as a type of plebescite against the incumbent chancellor, Kohl. The promise made by the Social Democrats to offer continuity along with (necessary) change had drawing power with the electorate. Germans did not want radical change; they wanted change tempered by moderation. Schröder's comment that he did not "want to do everything differently, but many things better" accurately reflected the public mood.

The parties in the defeated government coalition did not present the same united campaign front in 1998 that they did 4 years earlier. In addition, they committed a series of blunders. Kohl's attempt to project an image of himself as a statesman with major foreign policy achievements who, after the unification of Germany, now wanted to crown his career with the unification of Europe no longer matched the mood of the electorate the way it did in 1994.

There were manifest weaknesses in the way in which the CDU/CSU organized its campaign. A lack of unity among its leaders cast a shadow across the party's activities throughout the run-up to the election. In the end, there was a type of trilateral effort involving Kohl's immediate circle of advisers in the chancellery; the party executive led by the general secretary, Hintze, in a situation in which his power base was gradually eroding out from under him; and the CDU/CSU parliamentary party group led by Schäuble. It proved impossible to coordinate the efforts carried out by these three groups both in terms of communication and coordination with one another and in terms of their views on specific issues. On the whole, the CDU/CSU's campaign management earned low grades. It failed to offer the electorate a convincing platform, and it failed to make use of a good marketing strategy.

Unexpectedly for the CDU as well as for numerous political observers, the SPD learned from the mistakes it made in the past and borrowed successfully from the campaigns of Clinton and Blair. SPD chancellor candidate Schröder sought the support of undecided voters with his "New Center" domestic policy platform, and the SPD's party chairman, Lafontaine, motivated the powerful party organization to give Schröder its support.

With its "New Center" strategy, the SPD followed in the footsteps of Clinton and Blair on the "third way." After the "New Democrats" in the United States and "New Labour" in the United Kingdom, now there is the "New Center" in Germany. However, the SPD was able to do more with this than just win over middle-of-the-road voters; it also succeeded in mobilizing its own party membership, something that the CDU failed to do altogether.

The CDU/CSU lost a total of about 2.5 million of its voters, the vast majority (1.6 million) of whom went over to the SPD, whereas nearly 600,000 decided not to vote at all. It is clear that the Christian Democrats failed to mobilize their voter base. The Social Democrats, on the other hand, were able to gain the support of more than a half million people who previously had been nonvoters. It is noteworthy that never before had there been such a high percentage of voters who remained undecided up until just before an Election Day. About a fourth of the members of the electorate made their decisions during the final few days before the election. From now on, any election campaign strategy that wants to be successful will necessarily have to focus strongly on this group of voters.

The smaller parties lost some of their attractiveness for the electorate. As a consequence of the current high levels of unemployment (the issue with by far the greatest importance in deciding the outcome of the election) and the structural reforms that were urgently needed in conjunction with economic and monetary union, the voters tended to see the major parties as being more capable of resolving the problems Germany faces in the process of European integration.

Notes

1. The United States has around 1,000 television stations and 10,000 radio stations (national and local).

2. See Anderson (1996, pp. 358, 363). The 1972 general election was no exception. The SPD became the strongest party for the first and only time in the history of the federal republic in the so-called "Willy election," but support for Willy Brandt was much stronger than for the SPD (p. 350 ff). See also Norpoth (1977, pp. 564-572).

3. This is shown in the results obtained by Schönbach and Semetko (1994), who found strong "chancellor" and "government" bonuses in the media coverage (p. 330). See also Kepplinger, Brosius, and Dahlem (1994, p. 149).

4. See Holtz-Bacha and Kaid (1993, p. 47). They give a brief survey of what is so far almost exclusively American research on campaign ads on television and the techniques used in them.

5. See Holtz-Bacha (1994, p. 346). The number of viewers who saw the ads was between 800,000 (worst case) and more than 6 million (best case). Market share was as high as 25% (Holtz-Bacha & Kaid, 1996, p. 180).

6. Not surprisingly, the youngest member of Parliament, Matthias Berninger (who came into the Bundestag in 1994 for Alliance 90/The Greens at 23 years of age), has the best home page of the deputies who are on the Web (http://www.berninger.de).

7. See Jarren and Bode (1996, p. 88). These times were calculated on the basis of the 1994 volume of tables by Media Control.

8. These times were calculated on the basis of the data given by Jarren and Bode (1996, p. 103-114).

9. Kohl was named in more than half of the media reports on the CDU election campaign. Scharping was mentioned in only a little more than a fourth of the reports on the SPD.

10. See Kepplinger and Rettich (1996, p. 96). For a description of the candidates and their characteristics, see in particular p. 84 ff. See also *Medien Monitor* (October 18, 1994, p. 3).

11. A large proportion of today's PDS members are former members of the SED. The PDS took over the SED's assets.

12. See Rudolph (1996, p. 147). After the election of the federal president and the European Parliament election, the Germans no longer believed that a change of government would be possible, even though a majority of them would have welcomed it (Feist, 1996, p. 65). According to Noelle-Neumann's spiral-of-silence theory, the crucial question is not personal wishes but rather the expected outcome. From this point on, the SPD could have been in a spiral of silence.

References

Anderson, C. (1996). Wirtschaftslage und Politischer Kontext: Kanzlerpopularität und Kanzler-parteienpräferenz, 1950-1990. In O. W. Gabriel & J. W. Falter (Eds.), *Wahlen und politische Einstellungen in westlichen Demokratien* (pp. 343-369). Frankfurt, Germany: Lang.

Bergsdorf, W. (1983). *Herrschaft und Spruche: Studie zur politischen Terminologie der Bundesrepublik Deutschland.* Pfullingen, Germany: Neske.

Bergsdorf, W. (1995). Die öffentliche Meinung und das Fernsehen. *Trend Zeitschrift für Soziale Marktwirtschaft, 63,* 44-53.

CDU-Bundesgeschäftsstelle. (1993, October 8). *Wir sichern Deutschlands Zukunft: Scenario for the campaigns of 1994.* First version of internal strategy paper.

Feist, U. (1996). Wählerstimmungen und Wahlentscheidung 1994: Zeit für einen Wechsel? In H. Oberreuter (Ed.), *Parteiensystem am Wendepunkt? Wahlen in der Fernsehdemokratie* (pp. 59-76). Munich: Olzog.

Friedrichsen, M. (1996). Im Zweifel für die Angeklagten: Zur Wahrnehmung und Akzeptanz von Parteien im Superwahljahr 1994. In C. Holtz-Bacha & L. L. Kaid (Eds.), *Wahlen und Wahlkampf in den Medien: Untersuchungen aus dem Wahljahr 1994* (pp. 45-79). Opladen, Germany: Westdeutscher Verlag.

Grafe, P. (1994). *Wahlkampf: Die Olympiade der Demokratie.* Frankfurt, Germany: Eichborn.

Holtz-Bacha, C. (1994). Politikvermittlung im Wahlkampf: Befunde und Probleme in der Wirkungserforschung von Wahlspots. *Rundfunk und Fernsehen, 42,* 340-350.

Holtz-Bacha, C. (1996). Massenmedien und Wahlen: Zum Stand der deutschen Forschung—Befunde und Desiderata. In C. Holtz-Bacha & L. L. Kaid (Eds.), *Wahlen und Wahlkampf in den Medien: Untersuchungen aus dem Wahljahr 1994* (pp. 9-44). Opladen, Germany: Westdeutscher Verlag.

Holtz-Bacha, C., & Kaid, L. L. (1993). Wahlspots im Fernsehen: Eine Analyse der Parteienwerbung zur Bundestagswahl 1990. In C. Holtz-Bacha & L. L. Kaid (Eds.), *Die Massenmedien im Wahlkampf: Untersuchungen aus dem Wahljahr 1990* (pp. 46-71). Opladen, Germany: Westdeutscher Verlag.

Holtz-Bacha, C., & Kaid, L. L. (1996). "Simply the best": Parteienspots im Bundestagswahlkampf 1994—Inhalte und Rezeption. In C. Holtz-Bacha & L. L. Kaid (Eds.), *Wahlen und Wahlkampf in den Medien: Untersuchungen aus dem Wahljahr 1994* (pp. 177-207). Opladen, Germany: Westdeutscher Verlag.

Institut für angewandte Sozialwissenschaft. (1994, December). *Politogramm Report Wahlen: Bundestagswahl 1994.* (Wahl zum 13. Deutschen Bundestag am 16. Oktober 1994, Analysen und Dokumente). Author.

Jarren, O., & Bode, M. (1996). Ereignis und Medienmanagement politischer Parteien: Kommunikationsstrategien im "Superwahljahr 1994." In Bertelsmann Stiftung, *Politik überzeugend vermitteln: Wahlkampfstrategien in Deutschland und den USA* (pp. 65-114). Gütersloh, Germany: Verlag Bertelsmann Stiftung.

Jung, H. (1995). Zwischen Lust und Frust: Eine Analyse der Bundestagswahl vom 16. Oktober 1994. In G. Hirscher (Ed.), *Parteiendemokratie zwischen Kontinuität und Wandel: Die deutschen Parteien nach den Wahlen 1994* (pp. 99-168). Munich: Hanns-Seidel-Stiftung.

Kaase, M. (1994). Is there personalization in politics? Candidates and voting behavior in Germany. *International Political Science Review, 15,* 211-230.

Kepplinger, H. M., Brosius, H.-B., & Dahlem, S. (1994). *Wie das Fernsehen Wahlen beeinflußt: Theoretische Modelle und empirische Analysen.* Munich: R. Fischer.

Kepplinger, H. M., & Rettich, M. (1996). Publizistische Schlagseiten: Kohl und Scharping in Presse und Fernsehen. In C. Holtz-Bacha & L. L. Kaid (Eds.), *Wahlen und Wahlkampf in den Medien: Untersuchungen aus dem Wahljahr 1994* (pp. 80-100). Opladen, Germany: Westdeutscher Verlag.

Kiefer, M.-L. (1996). Massenkommunikation 1995. *Media Perspektiven, 5,* 234-248.

Langguth, G. (Ed.). (1995). *Politik und Plakat: 50 Jahre Plakatgeschichte am Beispiel der CDU.* Bonn, Germany: Bouvier.

Niclauss, K. (1987). Repräsentative und plebiszitäre Elemente der Kanzlerdemokratie. *Vierteljahreshefte für Zeitgeschichte, 35,* 217-245.

Niclauss, K. (1988). *Kanzlerdemokratie: Bonner Regierungspraxis von Konrad Adenauer bis Helmut Kohl.* Stuttgart, Germany: Kohlhammer.

Norpoth, H. (1977). Kanzlerkandidaten: Wie sie vom Wähler bewertet werden und seine Wahlentscheidung beeinflussen. *Politische Vierteljahresschrift, 18,* 551-572.

Offe, K. (1976). Editorial. In M. Edelman (Ed.), *Politik als Ritual: Die symbolische Funktion staatlicher Institutionen und politischen Handelns* (pp. vii-x). Frankfurt, Germany: Campus.

Pfetsch, B., & Schmitt-Beck, R. (1994). Amerikanisierung von Wahlkämpfen? Kommunikationsstrategien und Massenmedien im politischen Mobilisierungsprozeß. In M. Jäckel & P. Winterhoff-Spurk (Eds.), *Politik und Medien: Analysen zur Entwicklung der politischen Kommunikation* (pp. 231-252). Berlin: Vistas.

Radunski, P. (1980). *Wahlkämpfe: Moderne Wahlkampfführung als politische Kommunikation.* Munich: Olzog.

Radunski, P. (1983). Strategische überlegungen zum Fernsehwahlkampf. In W. Schulz & K. Schönbach (Eds.), *Massenmedien und Wahlen* (pp. 131-145). Munich: Olzog.

Radunski, P. (1986). Wahlkampf in den achtziger Jahren: Repolitisierung der Wahlkampfführung und neue Techniken in den Wahlkämpfen der westlichen Demokratien. *Aus Politik und Zeitgeschichte, 11,* 34-45.

Radunski, P. (1996). Politisches Kommunikationsmanagement: Die Amerikanisierung der Wahlkämpfe. In Bertelsmann Stiftung, *Politik überzeugend vermitteln: Wahlkampfstrategien in Deutschland und den USA* (pp. 33-52). Gütersloh, Germany: Verlag Bertelsmann Stiftung.

Rudolph, H. (1996). Ereignismodellierung: Der Wahlkampf in den Printmedien. In H. Oberreuter (Ed.), *Parteiensystem am Wendepunkt? Wahlen in der Fernsehdemokratie* (pp. 145-152). Munich: Olzog.

Sarcinelli, U. (1987). *Symbolische Politik: Zur Bedeutung symbolischen Handelns in der Wahlkampfkommunikation der Bundesrepublik Deutschland.* Opladen, Germany: Westdeutscher Verlag.

Sarcinelli, U. (1989). Symbolische Politik und politische Kultur: Das Kommunikationsritual als politische Wirklichkeit. *Politische Vierteljahresschrift, 30,* 292-309.

Sarcinelli, U. (1991). Massenmedien und Politikvermittlung: Eine Problem und Forschungsskizze. *Rundfunk und Fernsehen, 39,* 469-486.

Schönbach, K. (1983). Werden Wahlen im Fernsehen entschieden? Einige überlegungen zur politischen Wirksamkeit von Presse und Fernsehen. *Media Perspektiven, 7,* 462-468.

Schönbach, K., & Semetko, H. A. (1994). Medienberichterstattung und Parteienwerbung im Bundestagswahlkampf 1990. *Media Perspektiven, 7,* 328-340.

Schönbach, K., & Semetko, H. A. (1995). Journalistische "Professionalität" vs. Chancengleichheit der Regierung und Opposition: Ein Dilemma der aktuellen Berichterstattung im Wahlkampf. In K. Armingeon & R. Blum (Eds.), *Das öffentliche Theater: Politik und Medien in der Demokratie* (pp. 49-64). Bern, Germany: Verlag Peter Haupt.

Schönbach, K., & Semetko, H. A. (1996). Wahlkommunikation, Journalisten und Wähler: Fünf Thesen zum Bundestagswahlkampf 1990—Mit einem internationalen Vergleich und einem ersten Blick auf 1994. In H. Oberreuter (Ed.), *Parteiensystem am Wendepunkt? Wahlen in der Fernsehdemokratie* (pp. 153-164). Munich: Olzog.

Schulz, W. (1994). Wird die Wahl im Fernsehen entschieden? *Media Perspektiven, 7,* 318-327.

Szyszka, P. (1996). Medien politischer Selbstdarstellung oder politischer Kommunikation? Wahlwerbespots im Bundestagswahlkampf 1994. In O. Jarren, H. Schatz, & H. Weßler (Eds.), *Medien und politischer Prozeß: Politische Öffentlichkeit und massenmediale Politikvermittlung im Wandel* (pp. 185-197). Opladen, Germany: Westdeutscher Verlag.

Thunert, M. (1996). Regieren als permanente Kampagne: Stil, Strategien und Inhalte der amerikanischen Innenpolitik unter Präsident Clinton. *Aus Politik und Zeitgeschichte, 43,* 14-24.

von Beyme, K. (1994). Die Massenmedien und die politische Agenda des parlamentarischen Systems. *Kölner Zeitschrift für Soziologie und Sozialpsychologie Sonderheft, 34,* 320-336.

Wolf, W. (1987). Wahlkampf: Normalfall oder Ausnahmesituation der Politikvermittlung? In U. Sarcinelli (Ed.), *Politikvermittlung: Beiträge zur politischen Kommunikationskultur* (pp. 290-300). Opladen, Germany: Westdeutscher Verlag.

26

The Impact of Television on the Democratization Processes

LILIA RAYCHEVA

To understand the profound changes in the television system and its development trends in the new situation in Bulgaria, one should go back to the roots of political upheaval after the falling of the Berlin Wall.

The collapse of the totalitarian regime in Bulgaria brought about significant changes throughout its whole social system. For more than four decades, the Communist Party dominated the functions of the state, curtailing the rights and liberties of the people. An atmosphere encouraging social obedience in line with the propaganda requirements reigned in the country. The freedom of expression was limited. Normal political life was practically nonexistent in Bulgaria. Only two parties—the Bulgarian Communist Party and its satellite, the Bulgarian Agrarian People's Union (BAPU)—were legal in the country. Paradoxically enough, membership of the Agrarians in their own organization had to be approved by the Communist apparatus. There were no electioneering campaigns because there were no opposition parties, nor were any worthy sociological surveys carried out in the normal sense of the word. Monitoring of the public moods, if any, catered to a tight circle of the ruling party autocrats and never made their way into the media. The recurring results of 99% participation in the elections and support for the political status quo naturally aroused doubts in all thinking people, but any reliable information as to whether these data coincided with the real vote was lacking. The public swam in an informational fog.

The ideas of glasnost and perestroika launched after 1985 opened the doors for political discussions in Bulgaria. The first dissident associations, however small, found significant response among members of the public.

Several party leaders, feeling the threat of social unrest and trying to preserve the monopoly on power by reforming the Party according to the Soviet perestroika, staged a coup on November 10, 1989, removing Todor Zhivkov from his post as a general secretary of the Party and chairman of the state council. The political activity of the population surged up dramatically, and its legality no longer was questioned. Political rallies and demonstrations became the event of the day. Encouraged by the landslide of totalitarian collapse throughout Central and Eastern Europe, the opposition set up the Union of Democratic Forces (UDF) on December 7, 1989. This was a coalition of 16 pro-democratic parties and organizations that became the driving force of the real opposition against the ruling Communist Party. Although fragile, inexperienced, and of an obscure political profile, the opposition of that period immediately filled the yet vacant place of a public corrective immanent for the functioning of democracy.

One of the major political achievements, provoked by the new forces in society during that hot winter, was the abolishment of Article I in the Constitution, which guaranteed a leading role to the Communist Party in societal and state affairs.

In the meantime, dramatic changes took place in the mass media system as well. In a very short time, without gatekeeping or ideological control, the style and content of the broadcasts and the press departed very much from the former patterns. Political pluralism brought about the creation of different party organs. That is how early in 1990, political marketing boomed in Bulgaria. The same year marked the beginning of the political advertising telecasts in the country. However, although political advertising and campaigning in newspapers was free and uncontrollable, the Parliamentary Commission for Radio and Television set definite guidelines for the electronic media.

On June 10 and 17, 1990, elections were held for the Grand National Assembly, and the Bulgarian Socialist Party (BSP, successor of the former Communist Party) won the majority. The Grand National Assembly adopted a new Constitution on July 12, 1991. It was the first constitution of a Western type in the former Eastern Bloc countries. Although it had many imperfections, it proclaimed that Bulgaria is governed by the rule of law and set up the fundamental principles of a civil society in Bulgaria. Zhelyu Zhelev, the leader of the UDF and a longtime dissident, was elected president by the Grand National Assembly on August 1, 1991. Thus, he became Bulgaria's first non-Communist head of state since 1944.

The political advertisement telecasts and the strong press and radio involvement in defining the final choice of the voters started to play a significant role during the preelection campaigns from the very beginning of democratization of political life. Thus, the mass media brought about high politicization of the people in Bulgaria. Journalism operated as a mirror, frequently distorting the political processes in the country and yet still exerting considerable influence over the public opinion.

On October 1, 1991, new parliamentary elections were held, and the majority of votes went to the UDF. After inseparable domination of more than 45 years, the former Communist Party no longer was in power. In January 1992, Zhelev was elected president by the people. These elections were considered historic, being the first presidential elections since Bulgaria's liberation from Ottoman bondage in 1878.[1]

During a span of 8 years, two presidential elections (in 1992 and 1996), four parliamentary elections (in 1990, 1991, 1994, and 1997), and two local elections (in 1991 and 1995) were held; eight governments were appointed, and as a result of fierce political fights, all the legislative and economic processes were crawling at a low speed. This entailed new social and economic problems, the solutions to which were nowhere in sight. Thus, the country lost its momentum generated by the quick start of the democratic reforms, missed the chance to get integrated with the Central European countries into the important European structures, and could very well enter the 21st century under the already launched Currency Board.

This was how the multiparty political system was set in Bulgaria, which was a great democratic achievement. All these elections played an important part in laying down a basis for political marketing in the country, especially in the electronic media.

The Mass Media System

The democratization processes in society strongly influenced mass media development in Bulgaria (Petev & Raycheva, 1999). The liberalization and deregulation of the whole mass media system led to its decentralization and to the emergence of a pluralistic press and alternative electronic media. The establishment of a mass media market stimulated the development of new formats and styles of expression, thus fostering the higher selectivity standards of the audiences.

For a good 40 years, the mass media in Bulgaria were monotonous, instructive, and politically controlled. The censoring institution prompted the development of self-censorship in journalism, the lack of information entailed misinformation, and the absence of alternative press and broadcasting resulted in newspapers, magazines, and radio and television programs of a marginalized profile. There were some meek attempts to diversify the journalistic landscape, but as a rule, the mass media during that time period were carefully monitored by the Party headquarters. It was indicative that the perestroika processes, which started in the Soviet Union in 1985, dramatically increased the demand for Soviet press while the authorities restricted and controlled the access to it.

Several main trends in the mass media development accompanied the democratization processes in Bulgaria:

- *in political terms:* decentralization of the mass media system, accompanied by emergence of a pluralistic press, radio, and television
- *in legal terms:* liberalization and partial deregulation of the mass media system, which still is not supported by legislative basis
- *in economic terms:* emergence of a mass media market with an emphasis on privatization, especially of local radio and television networks and of periodicals

- *in social terms:* demassing and fragmentation of the audiences, accompanied by higher selectivity standards and better options for social feedback
- *in professional terms:* departure from the former standards and experimenting with new forms and styles of expression in the process of transition from totalitarian to libertarian and socially responsible journalistic contributions.

Print Media

During the early 1990s, a tremendous shift in the press industry originally heralded the age of deregulation of the printed media. In a short period of time, the tight Communist Party control mechanisms over the mass media were switched over to economically based principles. Some factors, such as the soaring prices of newsprint paper and print house services as well as higher distribution network expenses, sped up this transition.

According to the information of the National Statistical Institute (1995), 1,053 newspapers totaling 454,200,000 in circulation were issued in 1996, compared to the 381 newspapers with a total circulation of 879,663,000 in 1988. In the same year, there were 635 magazines and bulletins with a total circulation of 12,200,000, whereas the year 1988 saw the highest circulation—69,599,000 of 873 magazines and bulletins—a tendency indicative of the concentration processes unfolding in that period. However, the newspaper death rate also was remarkable. For example, in 1994, 303 newspapers ceased to be issued (National Statistical Institute, 1995).

The process of restructuring the printed media brought to life several types of periodicals. The politically affiliated press seemed to outnumber the others in titles but not in circulation. The fragmentation of audiences was particularly strong in the area of political disputes. Deeply biased, the partisan press did not offer safe grounds for political judgment. The piling contradictory political views, beliefs, and convictions greatly damaged the press credibility. A need for a social dialogue was painfully felt. The partisan periodicals, however, did not provide their readers with balanced news coverage presenting both sides of the story. This tendency reflected the "double mirror" information effects in a politically deeply frustrated society (Petev, 1995). Not surprisingly, the circulation of the partisan press tended to diminish. Thus, in 1989, the annual circulation of *Douma* was 198.5 million, whereas by 1995, it had dropped to 25.0 million. The respective figures for *Demokratzia* were 76.0 million and 15.5 million (St. Cyril and Methodius National Library, 1995).

The emergence of independent press was a thoroughly new phenomenon in the national media landscape. The greater part of the new periodicals declared themselves independent, although they never have reported their financial sources. Big press corporations emerged under the auspices of privatization and commercialization. Instead of indulging in political rhetoric, the main popular independent newspapers attracted broader audiences because of their pragmatic, "closer to everyday life" approach to current issues. While the political press was preoccupied with ongoing power clashes, the independent periodicals focused their attention on economic interests. It was these periodicals that coined up the new popular patterns of the graphic layout, the news presentation, and the new language styles. This clearly indicated the discarded tutelage of the Party and bureaucratic apparatus with their lexical clichés.

However, the rush of the alternative press, which declared itself politically independent, into the press market left little chance for the quality periodicals presenting unvarnished hard news, that is, a press that did not blur together the news and the interpretation. Nevertheless, one of the basic reasons for the establishment of the serious broadsheets was the general low credibility of the politically biased or independent tabloids.

In terms of content, all newspapers featured various themes—graft and corruption of civil servants, links of executive authorities with shady economic groupings, the looming Mafia structures, white-collar trespassing of the law in the new banks, sexual quirks of public figures, piquant stories of life at the top—things that, until recently, were journalistic taboos and subjects of gossip among the people. The public space was flooded by an avalanche of uncensored news carrying as their main message the shattered confidence in the state institutions.

The formation and development of a comparatively independent, diversified, and pluralistic press during this period can be regarded as a sign for the emergence of a "fourth estate" in the power structure, namely that of the mass media.

The development of the press in Bulgaria shows the following tendencies and basic dichotomies:

- Decentralization of the press system, accompanied by the concentration of information power in several press groups
- Overpoliticization of the partisan periodicals in contrast with establishment of politically nonaffiliated, commercialized press
- Diversification of the press market with significant changes in the social structure of the press readers
- Experimenting of new styles and formats and setting up new standards for the popular and quality newspapers

Electronic Media

Radio and television in Bulgaria for a very long time followed the state policy very closely because they remained funded mainly from the state budget. Another factor for their slow transformation was the related restrictive legislature. When the former structures of the Party-state control were disregarded, the leadership of radio and television in Bulgaria gained some professional freedoms in decision making, program setting, and economic policies. Certain developments could be traced in the liberalization of the presentation of content.

Currently, the Bulgarian National Radio (BNR) and the Bulgarian National Television (BNT) are the only two broadcasting institutions whose programs cover the entire territory of the country. By a decision of the Grand National Assembly on March 6, 1991, they also are proclaimed to be independent institutions, financed mostly out of the state budget. Since the early 1990s, BNR and

BNT have been allowed to earn extra financial income from advertising and co-production contracts. This marks an attempt to transform these state-controlled institutions into public ones.

The liberalized rules for licensing of local radio and television stations marked the outset of a rapid development of the private radio ("Ordinance No. 1," 1992). The advent of private television was nearly 2 years late.

After the political changes in 1989, the Parliament, the Parliamentary Commission for Radio and Television, and the Provisional Council for Radio and Television became the control bodies in charge of the work of the electronic media. The final part of the new Constitution of the Republic of Bulgaria contained a text according to which the parliamentary commission should exercise control over the national mass media (radio, television, and the telegraph agency) until the adoption of any new legislative regulation. Thus, the chairmen of these basic institutions did not have mandatory leadership, and they were to be nominated by this commission and approved by the Grand National Assembly. In consequence, the respective boards of directors were open to direct political pressures and influence, causing overall instability and lack of continuity in program policies. Throughout the 1990s, numerous replacements were made in the executive boards of both BNT and BNR. Problems pertaining to the freedom of expression, commentaries on hot political issues, journalistic investigations, and the like gave rise to interinstitutional tensions and even dismissals.

After years of extensive debate, on July 18, 1996, the National Assembly adopted a Radio and Television Act that proved to be incomplete, inconsistent, and practically nonworking. The president of the republic vetoed the act and returned it for further discussion. In spite of public discontent, the act was adopted on September 5, 1996, by the National Assembly without a single amendment. According to this act, a National Council on Electronic Media was constituted. However, its power was limited to the appointment of the top executives of the national electronic media. The new parliamentary majority in 1997 put on its agenda the voting of a new electronic mass media act.

The major iniquity of the legislative initiative aimed at regulating the activities and management of the electronic media in the country lies in its inability to attune the former stereotypes of thinking to the demands of the new reality. The perpetual generation of novel versions actually means that legislative initiative simply refuses to create practically applicable norms independent of situation-bound interests or more remote political priorities.

So, at this point, radio and television in Bulgaria operate basically on two levels: national (state) and local (private).

Radio broadcasting in Bulgaria stayed under a state monopoly until 1991. Until then, there was only one Sofia-located central broadcasting station with four channels and five regional stations. The launching of the private radio broadcasting and the further development of the public radio broadcasting caused some significant changes in the organization of BNR. The four nationwide channels shrunk to two 24-hour ones including regular intermissions from regional radio stations. Consequently, the share of the regional radio stations production increased, and the structure of their programs was considerably diversified. At the same time, BNR also had to change its program content and formats.

The first licenses for nongovernment radio stations were issued to several foreign radio broadcasting companies—the Voice of America, BBC-World Service, Free Europe, France International, and Deutsche Welle. This act was regarded as a tribute to these radio stations for their sensitivity to the democratization processes in Bulgaria. The first domestic private radio station, FM+, went on the air in October 1992. According to the data of the Committee for Postal Services and Telecommunications (1995), by the end of 1995, licenses were issued to 54 local FM radio stations and to 60 cable radio operators.

The new radio stations developed different formats and styles, targeting the niches in the listening audience. They quickly gained popularity. Whereas the national radio channels stuck to information modules and hard news coverage, the private radio stations diversified the program supply, providing the audiences with a broader range of personal views and commentaries. In addition, they felt themselves free to experiment with more flexible and attractive formats and styles. The necessary premises (financial, technological, and personnel) for private broadcasting on a national scale were at hand.

The availability of highly qualified radio professionals, the affordable prices of FM radio equipment, and the urgent need of the local communities to have their "own" radio channels focused on local events and issues—all these factors contributed to an unprecedented boom of private radio. The audiences gained the privilege to have alternative Bulgarian sources of information. Private radio developed under rather specific conditions. On the one hand, it had to compete with the national channels and, on the other, it had to compete with the foreign radio stations. This struggle for capturing the radio audiences resulted in bringing the radio broadcasts as close as possible to the problems and interests of the people during the difficult period of transition.

Irrespective of their diversity of styles and formats, the new radio stations developed a clear-cut identity thanks to their conspicuous support for democratization of public life. Growing credibility of their emissions considerably expanded their audience reach. In the crisis of January 10-12, 1997, Darrik Radio snatched its star chance with its extensive on-the-spot coverage of the dramatic clash between protesters and police around the Parliament building. It was even officially accused of encouraging and coordinating the social process by its live reports.

The private radio stations clearly strove to sustain the emerging civil society; they helped people to weather the moments of crisis by encouraging them to overcome their natural inclination for alienation. If one has to decide which medium has "the most human face," private radio with its active listeners' feedback undoubtedly will be the winner. It is by no means accidental that most of the taxicabs and public transport vehicles are tuned to private radio stations that expand the social space of otherwise isolated people.

The data of the National Statistical Institute (1995) show some important trends of the radio program dynamics during this period of transition. For example, in the comparatively uneventful year 1988, some 46,810 hours of programming were aired; the year 1989 witnessed 48,498 hours of radio broadcasts; and the year 1996 witnessed 276,276 hours. The structure and formats of the programs also were marked by change; within 1 year, only the time allocated to news programs drastically climbed up—from 19,090 hours in 1988 to 26,154 hours in 1989. A significant increase was achieved in the field of commercials. A major shift in radio programming reflected the introduction of the new radio formats.

To sum up, the changing radio landscape in Bulgaria is characterized by the following features:

- Lack of legal regulations
- General restructuring of the state radio system
- Emergence of commercial broadcasting stations
- Further development of public radio stations
- Setting up of first commercial networks, which will open the real competition on air
- Disturbing transborder radio flows
- Diversification of the radio audiences
- High degree of audience credibility
- Innovative elaboration of new journalistic styles and radio formats

The liberalization of *television broadcasting* in Bulgaria did not start until 1994. Along with the only one Sofia-located central television station, a network of four local television stations was created during the 1970s. In every county, a correspondent was providing films and videotapes, with local news to be aired on the national programs. The television news service was backed by its foreign correspondents working in Berlin, Warsaw, Prague, Paris, the Middle East, and Japan. Bulgaria was a member of Intervision (the international television organization of the socialist countries) and Eurovision (which supplied most of the foreign programs). Since 1993, the capacity of the four regional television centers has been used for airing local programs on Channel 1 during the hours free of national telecasting. The tendency is to expand this activity in the future. Russian television, Ostankino, is aired on a separate channel. France International shares another channel with CNN.

Whereas radio broadcasting already has reached the full-blown scale of market dimensions, television still is operating on a very modest footing. The nearly uncontrolled invasion of satellite and cable programs exerts additional pressure on the domestic audiovisual channels. Infiltration of foreign audiovisual products has an equally strong impact on the national broadcasting policies.

Compared to the other media, the changes in television were the slowest to come around because of the still existing state monopoly over the national telecasting, political pressures resulting in frequent replacements of television executives (in 8 years, nine general directors in quick succession headed BNT), lack of general research and development concepts, inefficient management and economic structure, outdated equipment, and so on.

Nevertheless, the development of state television throughout this period of transition underwent some significant shifts and transformations. Similarly to BNR, it was renamed Bulgarian National Television (from Bulgarian Television). This reflected the nascent notion of transforming it from a state institution into a public institution.

Currently, BNT has a mixed economic structure. Although state owned, it is not totally funded from the state budget; the principle of coproductions allows an inflow of private funds and an increase of advertising profits. This dual economic structure shapes up the current mixed status of both national channels. In 1992, they were separated structurally into two competing units—Channel 1 and Ephir 2—each with its own financial, structural, and program policies. The increase of foreign electronic mass media flows and the alternative domestic local productions fostered the innovative elaboration of new styles and formats. Many of the previous sections were closed or modified, and new ones were established. Hundreds of qualified workers lost their jobs, some of them owing to political reasons. The painful reforms, based on economic and political reasons, are still going on. The catch phrase of one of the former television bosses, "Television follows the winner," apparently had squeezed the most powerful means of communication in the country into the corset of self-restriction.

Alternative broadcasting is rapidly developing. There are now 18 licensed local television stations. More than 95 cable television operators are gaining popularity among their subscribers (Committee for Postal Services and Telecommunications, 1995). Because of the lack of strict regulations, no reliable statistics could be supplied on the community cable operators or on the quantity of satellite aerials. Bulgaria was among the first countries in Central and Eastern Europe to permit the receiving of satellite signals via individual aerials. The country also holds a licence for a satellite transponder with five channels that will cover its entire territory. However, some regulatory, financial, and technological adjustments remain to be accomplished to use this facility (Petrova, 1995).

Nova Televizia (New Television) is the first private television station, launched in 1994. Its basic program content mainly consists of imported and domestic dramas and movies. The opening of the 7 Dni (7 Days) television station in 1995 marked the beginning of competition in private telecasting in Sofia.

As an alternative source of information and entertainment, the private television channels attract audience shares, but it is too early to speak of strong audience drifts in their favor. Private television tends to develop an extensive time coverage of the potential audiences, starting with its programs early in the morning and finishing at midnight. Such a model, of course, does not encourage a high-quality supply of programs. Most of the programs are cheap imported productions, mainly from North and South America and Australia. They stand quite well with the television audiences because of the general similarity of personal, community, and institutional conflicts. The saturation of the private television air with such cheap audiovisual products often dims the original creative achievements of independent journalists. Nevertheless, the presence of private television diversifies the landscape of program supply. This encourages higher audience selectivity in program consumption.

The private air and cable channels made good use of deregulation to claim their market shares in a relatively short time. They launched new styles and formats, which at first might have seemed amateurish but quickly acquired professional dimensions. The lack of gatekeepers and self-censorship enabled the new television channels to react even faster and in a more adequate manner to topical political events in the country. The mere existence of alternative television, however, posed a challenge for the program diversification of the national television channels.

According to the National Statistical Institute annual data, the growth of the television programs is impressive; despite all the difficulties, the telecasts have increased dramatically (31,274 hours aired in 1996 vs. 5,886 hours aired in 1988). Another important trend is that the news programs air time on both national channels has doubled (1,168 hours in 1994 vs. 869 hours in 1988) (National Statistical Institute, 1995).

Since 1990, political advertising, marketing, and preelection campaigns have become quite common sights on the television screen (Raycheva, 1995). January 10, 1992, will remain in the history of Bulgarian political life, with the first presidential debate televised *live*.

In brief, there are several important trends that could be distinguished in the television system:

- Lack of legal regulations, which destabilizes the television system and leaves it vulnerable to outside interference
- General restructuring of the television system along economic, managerial, and program lines
- Emergence of local commercial broadcasting stations, which have entered into an acute competition with state television
- Setting up of private cable television that is strongly entertaining in character
- Increase of the international television program flows (beamed by the television channels in Bulgaria, transborder flows, and via satellite), which diversifies the audiovisual supply
- Increasing fragmentation of the television audiences
- Higher degree of audience credibility in comparison to other mass media
- Elaboration of new journalistic styles and formats (mainly in the commercial television stations)

So far, BNR and BNT have maintained the highest rates of audience credibility. According to different sociological surveys, their ratings were much higher compared to the deeply polarized press sources and the main state institutions of the presidency, National Assembly, government, and police (Gallup International, 1995).

In their interaction with the three main powers—the legislative, the judiciary, and the executive—the mass media were striving to win a position of their own that generally amounts to the functions of a "watchdog." Any attempts to gain the status of the fourth estate in the public structure, however, seemed yet premature; along financial and political lines, and in terms of commitment to their audiences, the media of the posttotalitarian period could hardly acquire the fourth estate status. Their impact in the sociopolitical space rather amounted to lobbying for various interest groups. In such a situation, the mass media could hardly manage to speak for themselves by ignoring the positions of the various pressure groups, some of which could even sanction them economically if they chose to do so.

It is quite obvious that to become the fourth estate, the mass media should have their own legitimate foothold in line with the European and international standards. Whether deliberately or not, the setting of such a foothold has been delayed for more than 8 years, a stretch of time long enough to be taken advantage of by the political, economic, and other elites in the country. Regrettably, the principles of liberalism proved dominant in the case of the nascent socially accountable journalism.

The social visibility of mass media weight in political life was manifested in at least six critical instances in recent years:

- The attack against President Petar Mladenov in 1990 that compelled him to resign
- The resignation of the next government, headed by Andrey Loukanov, also in 1990
- The mass media war launched by the government of Filip Dimitrov (UDF), which led to its toppling in 1992
- The ignominious exit of the government of Lyuben Berov under the Movement for Rights and Freedoms mandate in 1994
- The withdrawal of the Socialist government of Zhan Videnov in 1996
- The mass protests around the building of the National Assembly in the situation of a government crisis in 1997

Television and the Transition to Democracy

It was the mass media, of all institutions, that reacted to the processes of democratization in the fastest and most flexible way. While in Sofia, as a focal point of all centers involved in the changes, a feeling of these changes floated in the air and sufficed at the meetings and rallies. On the periphery, the changes were savored chiefly with the help of the mass media and especially of television. The organizers of the protest rallies in support of change, both in the beginning and at the end of the period under review, included the television institution as a point of influence and importance in their routes. The media kept fulfilling the dual function of transmitters (carriers) and stimulators of political changes despite the old patterns of self-censorship that have not died out yet in the journalist circles and the fact that the mechanisms of rigid censure started working in the peak moments of tension.

Similarly to the politicians, the journalists were not yet ready to adequately undertake their new roles. The principles and style of emerging journalism were created ad hoc; the turbulent events forced the journalists to learn and master their new mission by groping blindly around and at the price of professional risks. It was generally a quest for a free and socially significant expression, public control over the state institutions of authority, and an open statement of shouldering the responsibilities of the fourth estate in the transforming society.

It could be said that the consensus achieved by political forces in the roundtable discussions in 1990 for convocation of a Grand National Assembly marked the start of legalization of the democratic processes in Bulgaria. The major task of that assembly was to develop and adopt a new Constitution. Actually, the work on a legislative basis began with the preparations for convocation of the Grand National Assembly, outlining the main parameters of the future political activity in the country. Parallel with this, efforts had been made to establish rules for the organization and financing of the preelection campaigns. The appending tension was further enhanced not only by the pressing terms but also by the new and turbulent political situation created in the country. The long years of one-party dominance were replaced by an ever-cropping host of new political parties, unions, and organizations that constantly split, regrouped, and entered into coalitions, especially on the eves of forthcoming elections. Although the grave economic and social problems of the period of transition notably quelled the political activity of the population, they did not abate in the least the craving for power of certain persons and circles. By snatching the opportunity for telecasting the canvassing campaigns, television catalyzed this political reshuffling race.

Legislation created a number of normative documents that juridically regulated various aspects of the activities of the political parties in the preelection periods. Financing of the political parties and electioneering campaigns were some of the most sensitive and difficult for monitoring spheres. One certainly should allow here for the fact that the public opinion and expectations since the outset of democratization have had difficulties in accepting the private financial initiative in politics; that is why the governmental institutions were entrusted with the procedure and control of this type of activity. This was particularly valid for the political canvassing on the national electronic media, where firm rules were instituted and strictly observed. After 1992, with the emergence of the private radio and television stations, at first timidly and then more confidently in the recent 1997 elections, purchase of broadcasting time became possible under respective regulations.

The right of access to the national electronic mass media was a central issue in the preparation and unfolding of the election campaigns. The principle on which the normative documents rest had been synchronized with the contemporary practices in other countries. Thus, broadcasting time was divided between the participating parties and coalitions according to their parliamentary representation in the previous Parliament.

The elections for a Grand National Assembly in 1990 were the first to be held in a posttotalitarian situation. They were organized in an atmosphere of extremely brisk political activity. Numerous rallies and meetings were held nearly every day. These public efforts were accompanied by dramatic changes occurring mainly in the printed media.

The political advertising campaign in electronic media started approximately 50 days prior to the first round of the elections. According to a preliminary agreement, the political advertising campaign on television was organized in two forms: propaganda video ads and a political debates studio named *The Open Studio*. Both were aired in prime time, for nearly an hour, every working day under the heading of *Preelection Studio*. The campaign totaled more than 32 hours of political advertising, organized in 37 program blocks.

Although the political rivals were following their own advertising strategies and their crews worked separately, all of them had to use the facilities of BNT. There were several occasions on which the main powers, the BSP and UDF, engaged in some televised exchanges of blows. The most significant clash occurred during the week between the two rounds. Obviously, it was then when everyone became aware that this political game could have a serious and dramatic ending. Until that moment, the BSP programs were basically tolerant and moderate, but then the BSP aired an aggressive piece—a crosscutting of one of the young UDF leaders with footage from Bob Fosse's film, *Cabaret,* which showed the rise of Hitler Jugend in Germany. The allusion was transparent, and the hint was more than clear. In its next scheduled program, the UDF fired back. It showed an accidentally videotaped remark uttered by the then Bulgarian president, Mladenov (who served many years as minister of foreign affairs under Zhivkov), to the minister of defense at a December 1989 anti-Communist rally: "Maybe it's better to call the tanks." The unfortunate controversial remark later ignited a students' strike that provoked Mladenov's resignation. For the first time, television manifested its power to catalyze fundamental shifts in political life. It also plainly showed how easily the electronic media could become a political instrument in times of turmoil.

According to a survey of 200 journalists conducted by the School of Journalism and Mass Communications at the St. Kliment Ohridsky Sofia University (1990) in Sofia, the television advertisements played a significant role in determining the final choice of hesitating voters. Fully 25% confirmed that the programs of the preelection television studio definitely had influenced the political vote, whereas 16% thought that the voters' decisions were not influenced by the television political ads. More than half (55%) shared the opinion that these programs influenced the political vote to a certain extent, and 4% did not respond to this question.

The sociological agency, Sigma, conducted a survey of how the viewers evaluated the televised political campaigning. It asked the question "Which political power did best on the television screen?" 10 days prior to the first round and 10 days after the second round of the elections. The responses were as follows: 39.0% and 33.5% for the BSP before and after the elections, respectively; 19.6% and 24.7% for the UDF; and 13.9% and 15.8% for the BAPU. Sigma went even further in an attempt to poll the credibility of the media in the eyes of the audience. BNT topped the standings before and after the elections. The respective figures were 59.6% and 38.5% for BNT, followed by the BSP press with 44.7% and 36.3%, BNR with 31.0% and 33.8%, and the UDF press with 24.5% and 27.2% (Raykov, 1990). The high credibility of television after the elections slid by about 20%. This dramatic drop mainly reflected the rejection of the over-politicized programs by the audience.

The summer of 1990 witnessed a significant and distressing event. One evening, the television program was interrupted with news that a protester against BSP intended to commit a public suicide by setting himself on fire. Many people rushed to the square in front of the BSP headquarters, the tension escalated, and the building was set on fire. Thus, Bulgarian television generated informational obscurity and social insecurity, which took many viewers out into the streets and allowed for the manipulation of some of them into getting involved in the emotionally uncontainable situation in the square.

In the next election campaigns, the electronic media managed more balanced coverage of the political disputes. Furthermore, the radio and television programs encouraged a style of negotiation and positive thinking, thereby "taming" the politicians. The fierce crossfire was left to the press, which continued to lose credibility in the eyes of its readers.

Since the dissolving of the Grand National Assembly, the country has voted for Parliament three times. On account of the strongly politicized and econom-ically problem-rife situation, the 36th and 37th National Assemblies failed to complete their legally fixed mandate. Parliamentary crises entailed preterm elec-tions. In spite of some already established traditions such as the proportional voting system, the existing legislation was refined parallel to the preparation for the elections.

The normative documents regulating the access to the national mass media during the canvassing campaigns also underwent a notable development. For example, the Election of Members of the National Assembly, Municipal Council-lors, and Mayors Act of 1991 had only one article providing a right to access to the national mass media of all candidates for members of Parliament, parties, and coalitions ("An Act for Members of Parliament," 1991). The manner of this access was regulated by a decision of the Grand National Assembly. The Local Elections Act of 1995 introduced 13 new articles regulating the appearance of the political forces in the national media during the canvassing campaigns ("A Local Elections Act," 1995). The specific problems in each preelection situation were to be settled by the Central Electoral Commission (CEC) and the Council of Ministers. The dynamism of that decision making deserves mention.

The regulations for the television preelection appearances of 1991 generally followed the logic of the preparation rules for the Grand National Assembly. Strictly fixed in duration and form, political advertising was allowed to be aired only by the central national media and was fully financed by the state budget. In the 1994 elections, it became possible for the regional radio and television centers to join in as well by observing fixed regulations in the canvassing of candidates, who had registered lists in the respective constituencies. Funding again came from the state budget. The order of appearances on the national screen was determined by drawing of lots. The Central Election Committee introduced another impor-tant point in its decision for the 1997 elections: The television and radio stations and cable television stations owned by physical persons and legal entities could assign air time for canvassing of the parties, coalitions, and independent candidates under the same preliminary set conditions and prices. For the first time, it became possible to buy air time for political television advertising, although at the local television centers. Naturally, the political situation prior to the elections also was different.

The preelection campaign of 1991 was shorter than that in 1990. It lasted less than a month and was launched in three major forms: video ads, debates, and addresses. Strict regulations were in force again regarding the proper use of television time.

A sociological survey carried out by the Centre for Investigation of Democracy on the eve of the 1991 parliamentary elections showed indications of credibility decay. The statement, "The television, radio, and newspapers strengthen the tension in this country," got the following responses: *agree,* 36.9%; *disagree,* 39.0%; *uncertain,* 24.1%.[2]

Prior to dissolving the 36th National Assembly in 1994, the Parliamentary Commission for Radio and Television failed to suggest any rules for the state-owned electronic mass media during the preelection campaign. The rules voted by the Grand National Assembly had to be applied, no matter how outdated they were. Thus, the BNT undertook to get itself in good technical shape well in advance of the upcoming political fights on the air. A special commission was supposed to accept the submitted video ads 48 hours prior to their broadcast.

The preelection campaign lasted 1 month and was developed in two major forms: video ads and debates. The video ads were organized in blocks and aired three times weekly—on Mondays, Wednesdays, and Fridays. Tuesdays and Thursdays were left to debates. The weekends were free from television campaigning.

The 37th National Assembly, dissolved in 1997, already had adopted the Radio and Television Act. Its Article 31 provided for the radio and television programs in preelection times to be subjected to not only that act but also the respective election laws ("A Radio and Television Act," 1996). The rules for television canvassing were set with a CEC decision.

An indicative case of silencing the national television channels was the running of animated cartoons during the turbulent events in the wake of the critical parliamentary sittings on January 10, 1997. The cameras covered the discussions in the conference hall but never turned their eyes on the seething and hardly contained sea of people outside the building. At midnight, while members of Parliament and journalists still were besieged in the Parliament, BNT wished its viewers good night instead of showing the earlier promised report from the spot of action. Fragmented scenes of the clash shown on Ephir 2 only contributed to the informational dimness about the clash in front of the Parliament.

Along with this, the private television channels beamed contradictory reports with an emphasis on the sensational or unexpected angles. Some of these materials were rather questionable in terms of professional ethics because there were journalists who insisted in their reports that nothing extraordinary happened whatsoever. The effect of this inconsistent coverage of the event by the private television channels was similar to the informational blackout resorted to by BNT, and the people took to the streets simply to see what had happened. Once outside, they were easily caught in the tide of the general process. In other words, both

BNT and the private television channels indirectly and unintentionally had contributed to the escalation of tension and to participation in the social process.

So far, Bulgaria has managed twice to conduct successful presidential elections—in 1992 and 1996.

By a decision of the Grand National Assembly, the first presidential elections in the country were scheduled to be held early in 1992. The preelection campaign opened up in a tense atmosphere of restructuring of the political arena. No doubt owing to the continuing strong politicization of the country, 22 nomination pairs for president and vice president were filed. A two-round electoral system was adopted, allowing the two running nominees with the highest numbers of votes to run for the second round.

In the meantime, the newspapers were privatized fast, although radio and television still were under state monopoly. Once again, certain regulations were introduced for the television preelection campaign. Every nominated pair was entitled to two short (up to 5 minutes each) public addresses. The two finalists were expected to have a 1-hour televised debate.

A significant point of this advertising campaign was that most candidates were politically, psychologically, and professionally unprepared for such an undertaking. Confusion and misunderstanding ran high with regard to the rights and responsibilities of the president as stipulated by the Constitution. Some were lacking a mature approach to important administrative issues, whereas others had behavioral problems in front of the television camera.

There was a lot of naïveté and nonprofessionalism in this campaign, which helps to explain why only four nominated pairs managed to collect more than 2% of the votes in the first round.

January 10, 1992, will remain in the history of Bulgarian political life as a date marking the first presidential debate televised *live*. The opponents were Zhelev, the UDF candidate, and Velko Vulkanov, an independent candidate backed by the BSP. The debate was anchored by longtime journalist Dimitry Ivanov. Both candidates were supposed to have equal time limits within their shared time. The result, however, was 44 minutes for Vulkanov against 17 minutes for Zhelev (Pesheva, 1992). This imbalance was the fault of the anchorman, who was supposed to watch for the time limits. On the whole, the performance of Vulkanov was far more aggressive, whereas the behavior of Zhelev was much more restrained. According to some sociological surveys, the offensive behavior of Vulkanov probably earned him an extra 16.61% of the votes in the second round (Zhelev collected 8.19% more votes). However, in the long run, Zhelev won the election on January 12 with 52.85% of the votes against 47.15% for Vulkanov, thus becoming the first democratically elected president in Bulgaria.[3]

The 1996 presidential elections were preceded by escalation of social tension in the country as a result of the failures of the Socialist government. On the eve of the start of the election campaign, a member of Parliament, former prime minister, and imprint figure in the sociopolitical life of the country, Andrey Loukanov, was assassinated in front of his home. Contrary to the expectations of certain people, his tragic death postponed the start of the campaign but not the elections. Five new articles regulating the canvassing campaign of the candidates on the national electronic media were voted in the addenda to the Presidential Elections Act. A decision of the CEC regulated the rules for running the campaign on radio and on television in the following form:

- An introductory and closing address of the candidates for president and vice president registered in the lists at the CEC
- Debates
- Coverage of the demonstrations and meetings, concerts, and other events organized by the parties, coalitions, and independent candidates

The regional radio and television centers, as well as the local and municipal radio stations, could assign up to 2 hours a week to presidential canvassing including the time for debates. Moreover, the television and radio stations and cable television stations owned by physical and legal entities could sell canvassing time to all candidates at the same preliminary fixed prices. Thus, it became possible to purchase radio and television air time for political promotion, although on the local level.

A total of 13 nomination pairs for president and vice president were filed. A two-round electoral system was used again, allowing the two running nominees with the highest numbers of votes to run for the second round. The candidate of the Joint Democratic Forces was the definite favorite in these elections, owing to the public mood in the country. The first candidate of the Socialists, Georgi Pirinski, was disqualified 40 days prior to the elections on the grounds of not being a Bulgarian citizen by birth. The strong presentation of George Ganchev, with his well-schooled behavior in front of the television cameras, marked the first attempt at breaking up the bipolar model in the country. Hristo Boichev and Ivan Koulekov were a tandem of writers of comic works who ran in the presidential elections as a challenge to the high political passions in the country. Their television addresses voiced the mocking corrective of the Bulgarian people with their characteristically healthy common sense to the political spectacle that was performed. Although the pair did not actually crave power, they collected 57,668 votes.

According to the adopted rules, all presidential pairs of candidates were entitled to free introductory (7 minutes long) and concluding addresses in the first tour. On the final day of the election campaign, they were allotted 10 minutes for the balloting. The order was determined by drawing of lots organized by the CEC.

The debates were to be televised once a week, in 120 minutes of air time altogether, and participation in them was prepaid according to tariffs set by the Council of Ministers. For the regional centers, the sum was 80% of that paid to BNT.

Expectations (real or anticipated) of the then leading political party's political bureau encouraged self-censorship in journalists who strove to keep their privileged jobs at the national medium. For example, on the night of 1996 presidential elections, BNT cut out the press conferences of the major political participants after the announcement of the election victory of the opposition.

Runoff polls between the two top-scoring candidate lists were held on November 3. Petar Stoyanov won with a majority of 59.73% of the votes. His carefully built media image during the electioneering campaign certainly had contributed to his success.

A representative sociological survey, carried out by the National Center for Public Opinion Studies in May 1996, shows high credibility in BNT (55.6%) as a source of reliable information. BNR holds a much lower rate of credibility (37.9%) of the national audience 18 years of age or over (23.1% do not give credit to the mass media at all, and 11.1% do not follow the mass media) (NOEMA Company Ltd., 1994).

Conclusion

During the period of transition to a democratic society and a market economy, political life in Bulgaria faces manifold social and economic difficulties. The encouraging thing is that the political processes and changes in the country are carried out peacefully and that in spite of significant differences among the political forces, their reasonable behavior has so far not allowed any display of violence.

Practically all the existing mass media institutions undergo changes in their management, structure, and professional programs. On the other hand, disturbing is the fact that the legislative regulation of the mass media in Bulgaria is very limited. Problems pertaining to the intellectual property rights over the artistic and cultural media products, as well as to copyright and distribution rights, have not been settled yet. Mass media also brought about a high-level politicization of the people in Bulgaria.

In such a situation, BNT maintains a peculiar position. Although the printed media no longer are under state monopoly, the national electronic media still depend almost entirely on the state budget. In line with the regulations, they successfully carried eight preelection campaigns. Thus, in the process of political fighting for democracy, the foundations of televised political advertisement were laid down in Bulgaria. This reserved for television the great responsibility of molding the public opinion, especially in view of the fact claimed by the different sociological surveys that Bulgarians maintain the greatest confidence in television as compared to the other mass media.

The analysis of the political marketing in preelection campaigns on Bulgarian television during the period of transition prompts the following inferences:

1. Political pluralism was established in the country after four decades of one-party rule.
2. The print media market is fully established. Liberalization of radio and television already is underway.
3. Political marketing and advertising have made their advent.
4. Television became the most important medium for political campaigning.

5. New television genres, such as political video ads, political addresses, and political debates, were introduced. A significant success in terms of creativity was achieved.

6. For the first time in Bulgarian history, a public debate between the two candidates for president was held and aired on live television.

The mass media in Bulgaria were the first to perceive that conditions were ripe for a profound social change and have used them for their democratic transformation as a system. This, in turn, broadened the public space and the access to the media, sustaining the right to communication and creating the socio-psychological premises for irreversible social change. In this sense, the turbulent social processes in Bulgaria were catalyzed by the new mass media landscape.

Bulgaria still is subject to difficulties of the transitional period. The political status quo remains uneasy and unstable. The economic situation is critical and lacks perspective. The mass media system often operates as a fourth estate, strongly influencing the social attitudes, political opinions, and decision making on national priorities. The press, radio, and television are that power which sensitizes the nascent civil society to the challenges of sustainable democratic development.

Notes

1. Until the referendum in 1946, Bulgaria was a kingdom.
2. The representative sociological survey was carried out in 1991 by the Centre for Investigation of Democracy.
3. Out of 6,857,500 voters, 5,205,833 cast their ballots.

References

A local elections act. (1995). *State Gazette* (Sofia, Bulgaria), No. 68.

A radio and television act. (1996). *State Gazette* (Sofia, Bulgaria), No. 77.

An act for members of parliament, municipality councillors, and mayors elections. (1991). *State Gazette* (Sofia, Bulgaria), No. 69.

Committee for Postal Services and Telecommunications. (1995). *Report of the Committee for Postal Services and Telecommunications.* Sofia, Bulgaria: Parliamentary Commission for Radio and Television.

Gallup International. (1995). *Political and economic index* (Report 2595). Sofia, Bulgaria: Gallup International, Balkan British Social Surveys.

National Statistical Institute. (1995). *National Statistical Institute reports.* Sofia, Bulgaria: Author.

NOEMA Company Ltd. (1994). *Media credibility and journalistic ethics.* Sofia, Bulgaria: NOEMA Company Ltd., Social Studies and Marketing.

Ordinance No. 1 of the Committee for Postal Services and Telecommunications. (1992, June 18). *State Gazette* (Sofia, Bulgaria), p. 43.

Pesheva, M. (1992). *Television: The political machine.* Sofia, Bulgaria: Hercules Publishing House.

Petev, T. (1995). *Transitive democratisation of the Bulgarian press: Postponed victories.* In N. Genov (Ed.), *Sociology in a society in transition.* Sofia: Bulgarian Academy of Sciences.

Petev, T., & Raycheva, L. (1999). Mass media's changing landscape in Bulgaria (1989-1995). In *Journalism: Today and tomorrow.* Sofia: St. Kliment Ohridsky Sofia University, School of Journalism and Mass Communication.

Petrova, T. (1995). Radio and television legislature: Questioning trivial patterns. In *Journalism in totalitarian and post-totalitarian society*. Sofia, Bulgaria: St. Kliment Ohridsky Sofia University, School of Journalism and Mass Communication.

Raycheva, L. (1995). The impact of new information technologies on the Bulgarian mass media system. In *Drustvo I Tehnologija '95*. Rijeka, Bulgaria: Gradevinski Fakultet Sveucilista u Rijeci.

Raykov, Z. (1990). Elections and mass communications. *Bulgarski Journalist Magazine* (Sofia, Bulgaria), No. 11.

St. Cyril and Methodius National Library. (1995). *Bulgarian book catalogue*. Sofia, Bulgaria: Author.

St. Kliment Ohridsky Sofia University. (1990). *Mass media behaviour in "Elections '90"* [survey]. Sofia, Bulgaria: St. Kliment Ohridsky Sofia University, School of Journalism and Mass Communication.

27

Do the Media
Reflect or Shape
Public Opinion?

JOLÁN RÓKA

Public space, which allows at least two different types of interpretation, is one of the main categories of interpersonal communication. On the one hand, it means the social scene of the development and the realization of communication; on the other, it means the sociocultural process of public opinion formation. According to the science of engineering, public space is considered as a basic notion of city planning, indicating those territories of the urban environment that are legally accessible for everybody and should be distinguished from the legally restricted private space. Metaphorically, it functions as a stage where the performance of public life is taking place (Lofland, 1973).

Public space is interpreted by the social sciences as the structure of communication that is characterized by the linear sequence of media–conversation–public opinion–social action. Habermas (1996) explains public space or public sphere as a network for communicating information or points of view. In that network, the different tendencies of communication are synthesized into thematically arrangeable public opinions. Public space is reproduced by the communicative activity, and the natural language provides its general comprehension in the everyday practice of communication.

AUTHOR'S NOTE: This work was sponsored by RSS Grant 1013/94 and OTKA T O20275.

Public Opinion:
A Historical Overview

Public Opinion as Interpreted by Social Scientists

The scientific research of public opinion formation historically originates in social psychology. Of course, before its development but especially from the 18th century, a growing theoretical interest toward the nature and structure of public opinion could be observed. In the works of Plato, Aristotle, Locke, Rousseau, and others, the still existing notion of public opinion has been outlined, stating that public opinion is the social phenomenon that greatly influences people's social behavior and prospects.

> Older discussions of our subject do not differ much from modern writings in estimating the influence popular opinions exert upon the action of men; they differ in assessing the influence popular opinions have or should have upon the actions of statesmen and philosophers. It was common knowledge among older writers that opinions hold sway over the success, conduct, and morals of men. (Speier, 1949–1950, p. 377)

In the 18th century, the French rococo salons and the London coffeehouses contributed to a new wave of scientific involvement in the research of public opinion.

In the 19th century, the print media became the main source of social information. In the history of social sciences, Tarde (1922) was the first to reveal the agenda-setting function of news media, the linear sequence of press–conversation–opinion–action and the close inherence of the four components. Tarde's paradigm is based on the assumption that while the newspapers determine the majority of the daily topics of conversation, they activate, direct, and nourish first individual opinion and then public opinion; thus, they shape the social connections and actions. The central category in Tarde's paradigm is conversation, which is the most influential social power from the point of view of politics. Tarde believes that the print media have a direct impact on opinion only through conversation.

Katz considers Tarde's paradigm theoretically acceptable for public opinion and mass media research. Tarde was the first social scientist to say "(1) the press fuels conversation, (2) conversation shapes opinion, and (3) opinion triggers action" (quoted in Katz, 1991). In his sociological theory of mass media, Katz (very much like Tarde and, later, Lazarsfeld) attaches outstanding importance to communication (conversation), which possesses normative power. Communication can either stimulate further communication or cause silence to spread.

The importance of Tarde's essay was recognized first by Lazarsfeld for the developing social sciences. Lazarsfeld states that the scientific research of public opinion started unfolding in the works of historians, political science scholars, and sociologists at the beginning of the 18th century. This classical tradition was further elaborated by the empirists of the 20th century founding their statements on the modern social systems. According to Lazarsfeld, the formation of public opinion, in the sense we interpret the term nowadays, can be brought into connection with the appearance of the middle class, the institutions of democracy, the general education, and the mass media.

Some theorists define public opinion as the reified "voice of the people" that is the central category in most of the models of democracy, and its expression is determined by the technical possibilities of the historical era (Herbst, 1988). Others agree that public opinion is "a collection of individual opinions on an issue of public interest, and . . . these opinions can exercise influence over individual behavior, group behavior, and government policy" (Davison, n.d., p. 188).

Back (1988) believes that public opinion is the result of the social structure in which it is stated. Public opinion is perceptible, but the perception depends on the situation, the person, and (first of all) the society. "Yet, because the place of public opinion is different in different kinds of societies, its perception will be different as well" (p. 278). Back also emphasizes that the confusion of two extreme views can be traced in a number of public opinion theories; some of them are based on individual attitudes, others on the social whole. He thinks that the analysis of metaphors that reveals the relationship of the individual attitudes and the public opinion may contribute to the theory and practice of public opinion research. Similar ideas are reflected in Speier's (1949–1950) sociological theory. He distinguishes individual and public opinion. This distinction can be explained by the different modes of communication. Public opinion is the communication from the citizens to the government with the intention to determine and influence the government's structure and actions. This type of public opinion can emerge only in democratic society, not in autocratic society (which suppresses public opinion). Public opinion may include a secondary communication process, which means the interaction between citizens (Speier, 1949–1950).

Noelle-Neumann (1984) considers public opinion as a sociopsychological phenomenon that is characterized by the interaction of the dynamics of media creation and the dynamics of opinion creation. Iyenger (1987) also thinks that there is a close interrelationship between media presentation and opinion formation; although people are capable of explaining and discussing the topics and actions of general interest, and these explanations probably are politically consistent, they are "critically dependent upon particular reference points furnished in media presentations" (p. 828).

One of the main aspects of public opinion research refers to the hierarchical structure and the logical succession of mass media and opinion formation. The preceding mentioned and quoted statements belong to a wide spectrum of disciplines, but all possess in common the approval of the linear sequence of media–conversation (individual opinion)–opinion (public opinion)–action (both individual and social).

Tarde's Sociopsychological Theory of Opinion Formation

Tarde, one of the most outstanding sociologists of 19th-century France, was the first to declare as a scientific fact the consequential succession of social phenomena in the formation of public opinion in his essay, *L'Opinion et la Foule* (Tarde, 1922). The importance of his empirically oriented sociopsychological theory was reevaluated for public opinion and communication research by Katz (1991). Katz calls Tarde's essay a timely paradigmatic document, claiming that the media have an impact on public opinion only if they provide the topics of conversation among people. In Tarde's explanation, opinion is one of the hierarchical elements of the social mind, and he identifies it as "opinion proper, a totality of judgments," in contrast to "general wish, a totality of desires." "Opinion proper" is closely related to two other parts of the social mind: tradition and reason. They mutually nourish and restrict each other but differ in their reason, efficiency, and nature. From among the three branches of public mind, opinion is the last to develop but is the most capable of further growth. In the course of historical evolution, opinion has been overwhelming tradition and reason and has become omnipotent in social expansion.

In Tarde's (1969) definition, "Opinion is a momentary, more or less logical cluster of judgments which, responding to current problems, is reproduced many times over in people of the same country, at the same time, in the same society" (p. 54). This definition stipulates that the ideation of the similarity of ideas should arise among the citizens. In other words, the individual opinion should transform into public opinion.

Tarde believes that the major, most universal and steady factor of opinion formation is conversation, whose principal source used to be public discourse in classical times and in the Middle Ages, whereas it is the press in our times. He gives special attention to the social influence of conversation, analyzing it according to the categories of social relationships. First, from the linguistic point of view, conversation preserves and enriches the national language. Second, from the standpoints of religions, it is the most influential means of missionary work. Third, from the political point of view, it serves as a constant brake for the governmental policy. Fourth, from the economic standpoint, conversation forms and clarifies the value system. Fifth, from the ethics standpoint, it is a successful means of the struggle against egoism and extreme individualism. Sixth, from the aesthetic standpoint, conversation is the creator of social politeness and aesthetic code.

Tarde considers the press as a type of conversation that is uniform and international and might as well be called public letters or public conversation.

Evaluation of Tarde's Paradigm: Other Concepts of the Structure and Dynamics of Public Opinion

Tarde's (1922) essay is an essentially important document in the history of social sciences, stating the fundamental influence of conversation on political actions. This statement's validity is proved, according to Katz (1991), by analysis of the voters' activity and passivity.

> Conversation is a key to the difference between active and passive. The press does not exert directive influence; rather, it animates the agenda for conversation. "A pen sets off a thousand tongues," says Tarde. He is clearly on the active side of the debate; he invented it, claiming it was the defining characteristic of participatory democracy. Media–conversation–opinion–action are the constituents of Tarde's model, and it works, he implies, only in linear order. Political conversation is nourished by the newspaper; opinion is the result of conversation; economic, political, and cultural action depends on opinions. (p. 3)

At the macro level, Tarde believes that the press is the most important social phenomenon in the development of the European nation-states, which created the national integrity and provides the national agenda.

Tarde considers the press as independent and critical and as being able to supervise the actions of the government. At the micro level, the newspapers create the agenda of conversation in the salons and coffeehouses, providing topics of social character for discussion.

Tarde emphasizes that conversation and the press call into being the basic conditions of politics and discussing politics. It also is true that the press and conversation are closely interrelated; conversation without the press would remain on the level of rumor, and newspapers without conversation would be unable to exercise considerable influence. Consequently, in Tarde's two-step model of communication (as stated by Katz, 1991), the basic category is the effect and not the information, the unit of analysis is the group and not the individual, and the mutuality and equality of conversation is in the center of attention. In Tarde's model, opinion is created through conversation. He defines opinion as the totality of ideas on current topics that occupies the given community; as such, it is public opinion. Public opinion produces social activity, which is the expression of daily possibilities of choice. It also means that for Tarde, opinion equals evaluation.

Habermas (1996), much like Tarde, regards public space or public sphere as the basic communication network of public opinion formation. The difference, however, is that whereas Tarde studies the process of message transmission and public opinion formation in an all-social aspect, Habermas focuses his attention on the political public sphere. Even in that socially limited sphere, public discourse plays a significant role in creating public opinion, which calls forth political action embodied in political power both for the politicians and for the citizens with the right to vote. Habermas links up the communication channels of public sphere with the private sphere (e.g., family, neighbors, colleagues, friends, acquaintances), but he admits that the public sphere originates in social problems interpreted by the private sphere, and the connection of public and private spheres historically have been forming through mass media.

Aspects of Media System Structures and Public Opinion Formation

Media Presentation of Political Campaigns

Media, according to common understanding, have become a political institution in their own right by the end of the 20th century, possessing a derivative role in political processes as a means of social power. Their significance is clearly represented in the political (and especially election) campaigns. Media (and especially visual media), due to their agenda-setting effects, are able to assign importance to certain issues. In other words, what the media shine a spotlight on or ignore has its own consequences.

Among the media institutions, television has become the most powerful means for political influence. Television is primarily a visual means of communication; consequently, it is more of an event-oriented medium than an idea-oriented medium. Through visual images in appropriate combination with verbal expressions, it can manipulate symbols and meanings to influence the audience's political orientation.

It is a worldwide phenomenon that in election campaigns, television possesses the widest range of visual and verbal possibilities of persuasion. In Western democracies (especially the United States), television not only broadcasts the elections but also is the most important "performer" of the campaigns. This means that the voters believe mainly in the ideas and propositions that have a media voice. But it also is true that any medium can maintain its manipulative, influencing role if it is verbally and visually authentic and politically neutral. The increased role of television in political campaigns can result in misleading consequences, namely that the political debates will be dominated more by symbols, slogans, and personalities than by logical arguments. That is why television is not really adequate for changing or modifying the ideological views of the different social groups, for shaping the parties' identities, or for profoundly explaining their political programs. On the other hand, television is efficient for constructing the visual images of political leaders, for increasing their popularity rapidly, or for ruining their popularity immediately.

Consequently, the development of the communication technologies has radically reshaped the public space by the turn of the 21st century. Television has taken over the interactional role of conversation and has become the main source of public opinion formation, although the Internet, as a sphere of information transmission and indirect interpersonal communication, is growing increasingly effective in this regard.

The growing importance of communication technologies, including television in the political process, can be represented by election campaigns taking place in different political and media systems and in different time segments. The present chapter summarizes the main conclusions of the analysis carried out on the 1990 and 1994 Hungarian campaigns and the 1992 and 1996 American campaigns, thus demonstrating the impact of the fully fledged American traditions of political campaigning on developing democracies and their election systems. The necessity of that type of analysis was motivated by the evident fact that the American media system and its role in election campaigns, to a great extent, serve as a model for the evolving European democracies. What concerns the Hungarian election system is a crucial question to answer if the American traditions of political campaigning could be used. The answer is complex and vague, but in one respect it is clear: The tendencies, methods, and culture of political debating applied in the American election system, and the scientific apparatus behind the campaign, represent an obvious example to be followed and applied, of course, being put right to the Hungarian reality.

1990 and 1994 Parliamentary Elections in Hungary

In any election campaigns, there are at least four different channels for influencing the citizens' political beliefs and party preferences: television, radio, print media, and street posters. In Hungary, manipulation through these channels started to operate almost simultaneously both in 1990 and in 1994. The main form of discourse of the parties' media appearances became political advertisements. In political ads, the skirmishes and inner disputes between the parties, which rarely had reached public manifestation in the past, now became external and started to function as the basis of the public evaluation of the parties.

The Hungarian political parties realized the extraordinary importance of the media in the political campaigns as early as the first democratic Hungarian election in 1990, which subsequently led to the media war in 1993, that is, the never-ending disputes about the inconsistency of media independence and neutrality, on the one hand, and the controlling power of the governing parties, on the other. In 1993, the situation became quite dramatic, as television had become the target of the parties' political struggles. In Hungary, there was no media law officially accepted by the Parliament to regulate the functioning of Hungarian television until 1996. Hungarian society was facing its second democratic multiplier system elections among these confusing circumstances. The situation was further complicated by the fact that there were too many parties coming forward without clearly outlined political programs or with evident overlaps in their platforms. Even more disturbing was the parties' violent, often rude and negative campaigns against each other, which surely could render the formation of a coalition government more difficult after the elections. (It is a well-known fact that the more parties there are, the more divided the political agenda is, and it also means that it is more difficult to win the elections because the votes are distributed among several parties. The 1994 elections seemed to be a turning point, as none of the parties had a real chance for victory, so they were forced to form coalitions.)

It also means that the political culture has undergone a fundamental change since 1990, the time of the first multiparty elections. In 1990, nearly all of the various parties formed an ideological unity against the former Communist ideology. In 1994, there was no real threatening power after the collapse of communism, but there were a lot of different parties competing for the voters' support. This, of course, led to the increase in negative campaigning and to the bigger role for political extremists. The politicians' images received greater attention than the parties' images. On the whole, the political culture became more corrupt. That was the reason why the number of voters with uncertain preference increased to approximately 2 million (or 40%).

According to the public opinion polls, the majority of the citizens were certain only in their opposition to the government of that time because of the high unemployment rate, the drastic economic situation, the worsening public safety, and the like. The results of public opinion polls also showed that the media campaign of the elections had a great impact on the voters' voting decisions but did not bring about any restructuring. Three quarters of the interviewed persons admitted that the election campaign had some type of influence on their beliefs. The media impact might have affected 90% of those people entitled to vote. It also turned out, however, that the media campaign did not facilitate making a decision but rather rendered it more difficult to make a decision. But it largely contributed to stabilizing the existing political attitudes, especially for those potential voters who were lacking clearly outlined party preferences. It also is true, however, that the huge mass of the campaign information diverted the so-called politically passive voters from their intentions to vote.

In 1994, the broadcast campaign started on April 11 and ended on May 6, a day before the first round of party elections. All of the 15 parties that had managed to set up national lists got equal media voices—two time segments, with the first 5 minutes and the second 10 minutes. In 1990, the parties had been provided two 5-minutes segments for demonstrating their own political programs. The parties also had the opportunity to buy some space time (60 seconds) for the purposes of paid political advertising. In addition, twice a week, live telecasts of the party leaders' debates were transmitted. Consequently, the parties could make use of three audiovisual genres: political declaration commercials, political debates, and political advertisements. The first two genres provided mainly the verbal possibility for clarifying their standpoints, for ideological demarcation, for outlining the future perspectives, and for offering solutions to the most urgent social and economic problems in Hungary. The applied declaration style entailed an overemphasized verbality to the detriment of visuality. Even the 5- and 10-minute declaration commercials were mainly composed as a series of stills with scanty dynamism in the vital clips. This monotonous official manner could hardly catch the viewers' attention, which is why it was not able to fulfill its intended purpose—to manipulate and to win the votes of the uncertain 40%. Angelusz and Tardos (1994) emphasize that it was a significant drawback compared to the number of uncertain voters in 1990, which was just 18% to 20% right before the elections. The cause might have been the general distrust of a great number of voters in the political parties and their abstract, often alien style and rhetoric to the citizens.

Consequently, in 1994, three time segments (1, 5, and 10 minutes) were available for the political parties for the purposes of popularizing the party programs and candidates and of formulating appealing party images in the form of commercials. The free time of 5- and 10-minute commercials was provided by the network, whereas the paid commercials were sponsored by the political parties themselves. Most of the 5- and 10-minute commercials were of mixed formats, combining the features of testimonials, issue statements, and dramatizations, although some of the parties also applied the format of documentaries. The paid commercials were composed as video clips with symbolic meanings.

As a result of the parliamentary elections in 1994, the total seats in the Parliament were distributed among six political parties. In the concrete analysis of the verbal and visual symbols used in the commercials, attention is focused mainly on these parties and their agenda-setting strategies in the 5- and 10-minute advertisements.

The style and rhetoric of the commercials can be categorized into several groups and subgroups. Some of the parties tried to introduce a "new" style and rhetoric that might be characterized as being high-flown, pathetic, and borrowing the ideals from the politicians of the Reform Age in the 19th century. Some other parties used conversational style sometimes combined with irony. The rhetoric of the Hungarian Socialist Party (the winning party in 1994) was considered to be skillful, objective, and emphatic and including high-flown, literary elements if necessary. The didactic and vulgar style also was represented but was not generally characteristic. The most successful parties chose their style and rhetoric with high consciousness.

I already have mentioned that the explicit verbality remained almost ineffective, but the implicit verbality may have a long-term influence on the spectators' party preferences. The implicit verbality includes the implied message in the slogans and logos. The hidden meaning provides the variety in their connotation (e.g., Alliance of Free Democrats: "With Heart, Wit, Honesty," "We'll be successful together!"; Hungarian Democratic Forum: "Thanks for the Calmness. For the Power of Patience"; Hungarian Socialist Party: "Maybe Different! Maybe Better! The Reliable Solution"; Alliance of Young Democrats: "The Orange Ripens," "Solidarity").

The symbolism of the slogans is strengthened by the logo (or emblem) symbols (e.g., orange for the Young Democrats, flying dove for the Free Democrats, red-pink for the Socialists, cross for the Christian Democrats). These slogans and logos formulated the parties' symbolically demonstrated and visually communicated images together with plenty of other signs and codes. The codes contained implicit and explicit values referring to the characteristics of subcultures, cognitive structures, and ideology. In addition to the individual symbols, global symbols often contributed to the understanding of the messages. Among the global symbols, there were cars, roads, computers (high technology), undamaged countryside, different social groups, children, family, the building of Parliament, the mesh of modernism and tradition, and sport.

The most important values mentioned in the political programs were Hungarians, citizenship, enterpreneurism, safety, stability, Christianity, the homeland, expertise, privatization, and unemployment. Consequently, the most important attributes for the voters became human values, leftism or rightism, external or internal political attitude, social transformation, and radicalism.

The political parties also are characterized by the manners of persuasion they have chosen. In persuasion, the communicator (i.e., the political party) is supposed to aim at the cognitive abilities of the viewers. It is a psychological fact that if the message contains too much information, then the persuasion can turn "sideways," diverting the coder's attention from the main stream of the issues. Sideways persuasion contains a rich paradigm of guiding techniques with hidden motivations, key words, symbols, emblems, the evocation of tension or desire, and different psychological effects. In the broadcast campaign of 1994, a broad variety of persuasion techniques and elements was used—music, attack, setting, objects, performers, issues and images, general impression, and verbality.

In the spring of 1994, 15 political parties were competing for governing position. They had been trying to compose marketable party images for nearly 2 months. Whose image proved to be the most appealing was easily predictable after the first round of the campaign. The Hungarian Socialist Party and the Alliance of Free Democrats were the most successful in identifying themselves with the value order of the citizens and in developing the most acceptable agenda-building strategies.

The Hungarian Socialist Party built its campaign on the myth of the greater expertise of the last Communist government and on the feeling of nostalgia toward past values. Its symbol was the party leader and the smiling child face. Its program could be characterized as pragmatic and aimed at all the social layers of the society.

The broadcast campaign of the Alliance of Free Democrats also was based on the personality and individual values of the party's first man, whose image had been carefully constructed. He was imbrued with symbolic values, being the man of the future. He possessed all the necessary physical and mental requirements for becoming the prime minister—a thoughtful, hardworking politician who also was a good-looking man, husband, and one of them—so (as one of the ads declared) the people would desire to have a prime minister like him. The pronounced slogan closely corresponded to the visual image—"I trust him!"

1992 and 1996 Presidential Elections in the United States

The quest for the presidency in 1992 began as a kind of Kabuki drama played to an audience grown weary of its stylized makeup and its ritualized forms. Politics had become a game for professionals, men and women for whom America was not so much a country or an idea as an assemblage of movable "coalitions," "constituencies," and "target groups." They had grown technically expert at their work in the century and a half since winning elections had first emerged as a business rather than a civic duty. . . .

A presidential election has [come] to resemble a pilgrimage of the lame and halt to a holy place in the range of hopes, all, and [George] Bush—unlike a Roosevelt, say, or a Reagan—did not have the art to pretend that he could. Hope, which dies hard in America, would seek other vessels. Bill Clinton, the man who would emerge as the leading Democratic challenger, was a bright and talented politician, but his most compelling claim was that he was new. (Goldman, DeFrank, Miller, Murr, & Mathews. 1994, pp. 17-19)

One of the most obvious manifestations of the American democracy is the presidential election. Its events are inspired by the candidates, citizens, campaign managers, and strategists, but it is the manipulative function of the mass media that has got the biggest effect on its outcome. In the 1992 campaign, which took place in the midst of a more and more perfect technical background and sophisticated election strategies, at least three phenomena caught the attention. First, a new type of political personality came into sight—Ross Perot, the multi-millionaire Texan and independent from parties candidate who made use of media as a technical possibility for increasing his popularity. Second, following the technical revolution of television, the campaigns also underwent a considerable change. The campaign managers realized that one of the ways of successful campaigning is to organize minim campaigns, which are aimed at different social layers, and to mix the possibilities provided by the traditional and interactive media. Clinton's victory, as well as his party's victory, is due partly to introducing a new type of campaign management and partly to the personality and physical endowments of the presidential candidate, who was apt and talented at using nontraditional campaign strategies. Third, the campaign reports and messages became faster. It was strictly determined how much of a time segment (sound bite) could be used for the media presentation of the politicians. The tempo was dictated by the advertisements, and their production and broadcast were rather costly.

The everlasting dilemma of the campaign managers is how to manage to communicate most effectively with the voters. It is a well-known fact that the political campaigns are, first of all, communicative training in the course of which the most appropriate means should be used for creating and presenting the politician's and party's image to the voters. Being aware of that, the communication mix of the campaigns makes use of the advertisements and public relations as an integral part of their political strategies. One of the elements of that mix is the press release, which potentionally includes the strengthening of the priority issues of the campaign and the images. The political public relations experts believe that the media presentation of the press release renders it advantageous for the candidate and the campaign issues, and it directs the citizens' attention to them. The legitimacy is ensured by the media, as is the supposed objectivity of the release. The attention is brought about by the press presentation of the issue or, in other words, its appearance in the media agenda. The media agenda, in turn, creates the public agenda that forms the public opinion and stimulates for action. One of the main efforts of the 1992 American election campaign was to forward some issue-oriented press messages to the media and to call the public's attention to these issues. The agenda-setting analyses have proved that the audience and public preference for the key issues plays a much bigger role in the final outcome of the elections than used to be presumed.

Based on their understanding of the process, the Bush reelection camp had hoped to set an issue agenda for registered voters based on taxes, character flaws, economy, jobs, and foreign affairs as its top five issues. Their attack campaign was wedded to these issues, even though, as the Spearman's rank order correlations have shown, the registered voters' agenda differed remarkably from [that of] the Bush camp. . . .

As outsiders, the Clinton camp campaigned as agents of change who were in touch with the people and who would radicalize the government. Their agenda identified more closely with that of the registered voters. . . .

What emerges is the inability of Bush-Quayle to use press releases to redefine the issue agenda order for the registered voting public. Conversely, the Clinton-Gore staff enjoyed success by employing their releases to match [their] issue agenda order to that of registered voters. (Walters, Walters, & Gray, 1996, pp. 16-18)

On November 5, 1996, Clinton gained an easy but slight victory against Bob Dole (the Republican nominee) and Perot, but he did not manage to get the majority of the popular vote. (According to public opinion polls, 54% of citizens who voted for Clinton did not trust him. However, it is an indisputable fact that out of the 42 presidents in U.S. history, only 15 were reelected and only 11 managed to serve two full terms. Clinton is the second reelected Democratic president.) His success was promoted by his politician's and orator's image created by the mass media. The turning points of his victory were the presidential debates held on October 6 and 16. Clinton summarized the main results of the first 4-year term of his governing and expounded the most important issues of his program that corresponded with the pocket issues of the citizens in a quiet, thoughtful, objective, easy-to-understand style.

His newly introduced metaphor, "Bridge to the 21st century," is proof of the exceptional vision of an exceptional politician. The tone, the hidden allusions, and the symbolism of his speeches served an evocative function. His speeches were constructed strictly according to the rules of rhetorics and logics. His delivery was dynamic, and his speeches were expounded and suitable for the target audience. He is said to be the first president of the media era who is consistently able to control the tone and style of his speeches and to create the professional correspondence of the verbal and nonverbal levels of communication. Clinton's rhetorics (i.e., his way of thinking, symbolism, and language use) is, to a great extent, influenced by the rhetorical traditions (and especially the speeches) of John and Robert Kennedy and Martin Luther King.

The televised debates strengthened the direct implication of the slogan, "Bridge to the 21st century," both verbally and visually. Clinton created the impression of a politician who is for the prosperity and even better future of the nation, who understands the voice of the future, and who possesses much empathy; consequently, he is the embodiment of the postmodern president.

Clinton's reelection was very much due not only to the stability of the domestic and international politics but also to the positive and progressive image shaped by the media. In their creation, the carefully designed rhetorics and iconographics played an emphatic role. Clinton's presidency enforced the coherent, objective rhetorics that reshaped the political language and enriched it with the deep symbolism and specific world of ideas.

Summary

One of the greatest technical achievements of the 20th century is the invention of mass media, which form a multilateral connection with the institutions of democracy, especially with respect to public space. Tarde was the first to compose the linear sequence of public opinion formation in his sociopsychological paradigm, which is based on the logical succession of media–conversation–opinion–action.

The tendencies of public opinion formation have undergone a radical change during the 20th century. The audiovisual media, embodied with the functions of information and persuasion, came into being along with the rapidly developing means of telecommunications and helped to revolutionize the process of message transmission. As a result of that development, Tarde's four-component structure simplifies into three components (although the linearity of his paradigm remains unchanged): media–opinion–action. Television took over the traditional social role of conversation, which is a symptomatic phenomenon of the industrial and postindustrial societies. The individual in the modern society enters into a one-sided communication with television or into indirect interpersonal communication through the Internet. These happenings, of course, have their own consequences in how they affect the public space. In other words, for the man of today, the source of authentic information is the media (and especially audiovisual media).

The election campaigns of the 1990s proved that mass media play a global role in shaping and modifying the social reality. They develop a multilateral relationship with the institutions of democracy, especially with respect to the formation of public space. Most of our information about the presidential candidates and parties comes from the media, which are able to influence our ideological, political, and aesthetical views, concepts, and values by their visual and verbal means of manipulation and their agenda-setting possibilities. The opinion-forming function of the media can be followed up most clearly in the political campaigns; the tactics and strategies of the political campaigns that are aimed at the ideological persuasion of the citizens surely would be ineffective without their media presentation. But in democratic societies, the influencing role of the media and the persuasive function of the political campaigns differ strategically. Mass media become an influential social power due to their agenda-setting function, whereas in political campaigns the clue to success lies in the agenda building—in the ability of assimilation with public opinion.

References

Angelusz, R., & Tardos, R. (1994). Bizonytalan választók vagy rejtozködo nem választók. In L. Gábor, A. Levendel, & I. Stumpf (Eds.), *Parlamenti választások 1994*. Osiris-Századvég.

Back, K. W. (1988). Metaphors for public opinion in literature. *Public Opinion Quarterly, 52,* 278-288.

Davison, W. P. (n.d.). Public opinion. In *International Encyclopedia of Social Sciences*.

Goldman, P., DeFrank, T. M., Miller, M., Murr, A., & Mathews, T. (1994). *Quest for the presidency 1992*. Texas A&M University Press.

Habermas, J. (1996). *Contributions to a discourse theory of law and democracy*. Cambridge, MA: MIT Press.

Herbst, S. (1988). *Effects of public opinion technologies on political expression: Putting polls in historical context*. Paper submitted to AAPOR Student Paper Competition.

Iyenger, S. (1987). Television news and citizen explanations of national affairs. *American Political Science Review, 81,* 814-831.

Katz, E. (1991). *On parenting a paradigm: Gabriel Tarde's agenda for opinion and communication research*. Unpublished manuscript, Hebrew University of Jerusalem and University of Pennsylvania, Annenberg School of Communication.

Lofland, L. H. (1973). *A world of strangers: Order and action in urban public space*. New York: Waveland.

Noelle-Neumann, E. (1984). *The spiral of silence*. Chicago: University of Chicago Press.

Speier, H. (1949-1950). Historical development of public opinion. *American Journal of Sociology, 55,* 376-388.

Tarde, G. (1922). *L'Opinion et la Foule*. Paris: Alcan.

Tarde, G. (1969). Opinion and conversation. In T. N. Clark (Ed.), *On communication and social influence: Selected papers*. Chicago: University of Chicago Press.

Walters, T. N., Walters, L. M., & Gray, R. (1996). Agenda building in the 1992 presidential campaign. *Public Relations Review, 22.*

Execution of
Political Campaigns

Election Campaigns

28

The Machine Was Alive and Well and Living in Skokie

JUDITH-RAE E. ROSS

Say "political machine," and visions of smoke-filled rooms, Runyonesque precinct captains, and former Chicago Mayor Richard J. Daley come to mind. Phrases such as "The fix is in" and "You can't fight city hall," and terms such as "pull" and "clout," have become part of America's—and even the world's—vocabulary.

The machine's image is not flattering. It evokes visions of corrupt politicians and judges, unqualified candidates and ward healers, and unsavory business connections. For Chicagoans, images of the Richard J. Daley machine are intertwined with the 1968 Democratic Convention and Daley's overreaction against the demonstrators.

But like it or not, until fairly recently, many American cities were governed by elected officials slated by political machines, and some cities (including Chicago) continue to be so governed. Chicago's current mayor, Richard M. Daley (Richard J. Daley's son), looks and sounds a lot like his father.

Much has been written about the workings of the political machine and its less-than-perfect form,[1] but the machine actually promoted the functionality of a government that served, and continues to serve, its constituents. What follows is a look at the machine's origins, how its image affected it, and how it worked until recently in one suburban area—Niles Township, Illinois.

The political machine is unique, an institution never dreamt of by Franklin, Madison, Jefferson, or the other framers of the Declaration of Independence or the Constitution. The Founding Fathers assumed an electorate for which vigilance was the price of liberty. Their greatest fear was an out-of-control executive.[2] They expected the electorate would actively participate in their government and, to that end, created a governmental structure consisting of the legislative, executive, and judicial branches with a system of checks and balances to ensure equilibrium among them.

The Constitution's framers created a legislative-based federal government in which franchised White males would take turns serving in the House of Representatives. The Constitution defines the lawmaking branch, the legislative branch, in greatest detail. The legislative branch also levies taxes, defines the tenor of the judiciary through its confirmation of judges (or refusal thereof), and has the power to impeach and remove the president from office.[3]

No one who signed the Constitution in the late 18th century could foresee overcrowded industrial cities teeming with new immigrants who neither spoke English nor understood the intricacies of representative government. No one envisioned "dumbbell"-shaped tenements, all-night work shifts, or child industrial labor. The Jeffersonian idea that "The government that governs best governs least" worked well in the late 18th and early 19th centuries but could not cope with the needs of immigrant urbanites.

All political systems, even totalitarian ones, serve the needs of their constituents to some degree (Rakove, 1975, pp. 14-15). The political machine arose largely out of the need to deal with industrialization and the waves of immigration to America from Southern and Eastern Europe that formed industry's labor force at the end of the 19th century and the beginning of the 20th century (O'Connor, 1975, p. 9). It is the political counterpart to the factory, which runs the city and seeks to perpetuate itself by running the city effectively.

Most immigrants came to the United States because they were hungry. The "huddled masses" were preoccupied with survival—putting food on the table and personal safety. They had little or no interest in making laws (Crosby, 1993, pp. 298-299; Rakove, 1975, p. 14).

Many truly expected to find streets paved with gold. Those arriving from Russia or the Habsburg Empire also sought refuge from the Cossacks and the pogroms.[4]

Freedom did not mean the same thing in the late 19th century as it did a century earlier (or today). Then, freedom meant going to a synagogue or hearing mass without fearing for one's life. Freedom meant being able to live peacefully in one's community and to practice one's cultural mores and religious beliefs. It did not necessarily mean the right to dissent or make individual decisions.[5]

The Cook County Democratic machine, like all political machines of the time, concerned itself with the issues that concerned the new immigrants and their children—food, employment, and the right of religious and cultural survival. This executive-based governmental system, the antithesis of the legislative-based government envisioned by the Constitution's signers, gave the new immigrants and their children what they craved as they sailed by the Statue of Liberty into New York Harbor. The Cook County machine developed institutions to keep the immigrants (and later their children) safe, fed, and free to worship and live as they wished. It also gave them a chance for entrée into the system and hope for a better future (Rakove, 1975, pp. 7-8, 18; Royko, 1971, pp. 24-26, 62).

The new American understood the machine. It was patriarchal, like the Russian or Austrian-Hungarian Empire, and it was under the control of a boss. This boss made most executive decisions and had the final word on the slating of candidates. He guided the city's course, despite the fact that Chicago's ordinances mandate a weak mayor/strong council system.[6]

Indeed, why fight city hall? The mayor was much better than Czar Nicholas or Emperor Franz Josef. Besides, most immigrants came from and replicated cultures that also were based on hierarchies. Ward bosses did not upset them.

The Chicago machine had representatives in the neighborhood in roles such as aldermen, committeemen, and precinct ward committeemen (precinct captain for short). Often, these precinct captains were neighbors. The political machine is the urban counterpart to feudalism. Political appointments are latter day fiefs, and precinct captains are the equivalent of knights, even down to winning their precincts (Rakove, 1975, pp. 106, 112, 115; Royko, 1971, p. 60).

Like any successful machine, the Cook County machine succeeded in bridging the gap between city hall and the neighborhood. As a sort of equal opportunity precursor, the machine made it possible for the many ethnic groups to live and thrive by developing representation of the ethnic groups that lived within the city. Richard J. Daley made certain that the Irish, Italians, Greeks, Poles, Jews, and Blacks all had voices in the hall.

The Chicago machine gave the individual a personal contact, giving each voter access to government services or to receive favors. The precinct captain, the foundation of the machine's success, represented the machine to the voter. The captain put a human face on the system, linking the constituent to the mayor and to the government services that mattered most. Accessing the system was as simple as meeting with the precinct captain or perhaps going to the alderman or committeeman's office. The precinct captain made sure that a sick child got medical treatment and that a poor family received food or welfare services, just as he or she made sure pesky trees were trimmed and curbs were repaired (Rakove, 1975, pp. 29-31; Royko, 1971, p. 62).

All that was asked in return was a vote, but if that was not returned, then there was retribution. But for the former residents of the Russian and Austrian Hungarian empires and their children, this was not difficult to understand (Royko, 1971, pp. 17, 20).

Still, the reformers and muckrakers railed at its less-than-perfect election procedures, the peddling of influence, and the hiring of the unqualified (O'Connor, 1975; Rakove, 1975, pp. 22-24).

The officials of the Chicago machine reflected the values of most of their constituents. Richard J. Daley was a family man who lived in Bridgeport, a working class neighborhood. He worked his way through DePaul University Law School and worked his way up the party ranks through increasingly important offices, all the way to the mayor's office. His clothing was expensive and tasteful, and he was equally at home with presidents, royalty, business leaders, and neighbors. Daley never forgot his roots, and he started every morning by hearing mass. He has been likened to a chieftain by Eugene Kennedy and called "boss" by Mike Royko. How did Daley achieve that stature?[7]

The "boss's" strength came only in part from elective mandate. Chicago's mayors who served between Richard J. and Richard M. Daley—Michael Bilandic, Jane Byrne, Harold Washington, and Eugene Sawyer—certainly had that mandate, yet each of them failed to control the machine. With the exception of Washington, they all lost bids for reelection.[8]

The secret of Richard J. Daley's success as "boss" for most of his tenure as Chicago's mayor (1955–1976) was that he consolidated political and elective power, thereby finely honing the machine. The Daley machine resembled a pyramid that included elected officials, judges, industrialists, labor, and urban workers, with Daley at its apex and the neighborhood precinct workers at the base. Everyone reported to a higher patron, and the line of authority extended upward to the mayor (O'Connor, 1975, p. 13; Rakove, 1975, pp. 107-111, 113; Royko, 1971, pp. 63-68).

Entrance into the pyramid depended on a quid pro quo—a reward in the form of jobs, contracts, or office in return for loyalty to the machine. Loyalty to the machine meant obeying orders from superiors. There might have been some time for discussion, but once the order was given and the candidate slated, the machine's operative demonstrated loyalty by turning in a winning precinct, at least for local candidates, no matter who the candidate was.[9] Nothing was set in stone. Jobs and offices hinged on continued loyalty and winning precinct totals. "What have you done for me lately?" was asked by many an anxious committeeman as Election Day neared. At one time or another, every member of Chicago's machine worked a precinct, ringing doorbells (Kennedy, 1978, p. 50; Rakove, 1975, p. 115; Royko, 1971, p. 64). The system worked so long because most of Chicago's population believed that the machine represented their interests, and communal identities superseded individual ambitions.

But the machine was no match for the resurgence of individualism after World War II, the emphasis on individual rights, and the shift in population patterns. In some ways, the machine was the victim of its own success. The immigrants' children shared many of their parents' dreams. They, too, craved economic security, close families, and a better world for their children.[10] But this generation also was tempered by world events.

Growing up during the Depression, it knew hunger and sacrifice. Many worshipped Franklin D. Roosevelt while, like their parents, expecting government to provide economic help to those in need. They voted religiously, usually supporting liberal causes.

But many in this generation believed that loyalty meant not making waves, not questioning authority. In some ways, living under the Chicago machine had taught these lessons. Paradoxically, the machine, as Milton Rakove noted, was apolitical. To avoid alienating any constituencies, it did not take strong stands. "Don't make no waves" became an anthem of the 1950s—nationwide. Furthermore, as young adults, this generation had fought, or had held up the homefront, during World War II. This further strengthened their sense of loyalty to the government; after all, the United States was fighting for its life against tyranny. Few question authority under these circumstances.[11]

After the war, cheap houses began to lure this generation to suburbia, and the movement became a migration during the 1960s. Having acquired a picture window, barbecue, and swing set, young parents became more interested in the Parent-Teacher Association than in the precinct. Rakove noted that most of the suburbs were well governed, with their governments well entrenched. There was little incentive to be interested in politics.[12]

There also was a less honorable force propelling the suburban migration. African Americans migrated to Chicago in increasing numbers from the South during the 1950s and 1960s and began competing for jobs and settling in neighborhoods previously occupied by White ethnic groups. Many Whites fled what they perceived to be a threat to their neighborhoods. Rakove even hypothesized that the African Americans ultimately would take over the Chicago machine (Rakove, 1975, pp. 234, 282-283; see also O'Connor, 1975, p. 180).

Then there was the image problem. The struggle for civil rights and the war in Vietnam further blurred the definition of freedom. For the generation coming to age during the 1960s, freedom meant the right to dissent and to make personal choices. This individualism flies in the face of any political machine, especially one so finely developed as Chicago's (Kennedy, 1978, p. 225; O'Connor, 1975, pp. 203-204).

After the "police riot"[13] that occurred outside the 1968 Democratic Convention, the Daley machine looked autocratic, bigoted, corrupt, and out of touch with youth. The image was sharpened by the convictions of some of Daley's closest subordinates. Len O'Connor went so far as to chronicle Daley's fall.[14]

The decline of the Chicago machine during the 1960s and 1970s contributed to the rise of the political machine in many suburbs including Skokie, Illinois. Many of the Jews who had lived on the West Side and in Hyde Park in Chicago moved to Chicago's northern suburbs during the late 1950s and 1960s, and many of these people were regular Democrats (Rakove, 1975, pp. 233-256).

Skokie, together with the southern border of Niles Township, is part of Chicago's northern border. The township is comprised of the villages of Skokie, Lincolnwood, and Golf as well as parts of Niles, Morton Grove, and Glenview. These communities offered affordable housing, good schools, good parks, and good public transportation, all near Chicago. Skokie, especially, was receptive to this largely Jewish migration because the village sported three synagogues, and by 1960, it had a Jewish mayor, Myron (Mike) Greisdorf. There were some tensions between the descendants of Skokie's entrenched population and the village's newer residents. A high school race in the mid-1960s sparked some anti-Jewish literature.[15] By the 1970s, these tensions had cooled.

Some of Skokie's newer residents moved into the township's Democratic Party. An organization had been in place since World War II under Scotty Krier. By the 1960s, it was headed by State Representative Aaron Jaffe, who opened the organization to Skokie's newer residents.

In 1973, Calvin R. Sutker became the committeeman of Niles Township, and he forged the organization into a more traditional political machine, in many ways paralleling Chicago's. A gregarious man who had been a village trustee,

Sutker had a personality that attracted many of Skokie's newer residents. He was assisted by a smart administrator, Patricia Morowitz, who helped Sutker organize and strengthen the precinct operation.

The Niles Township regular organization did differ in some measure from the Chicago model. It took liberal positions and allowed some latitude for personal dissent. A good precinct captain still was expected to support the whole ticket, but it was accepted that certain candidates would fare better than others. For the most part, the organization's members knew and liked each other, so there was a familial feel.[16]

The organization prospered. It received national attention when presidential candidate Jimmy Carter visited the Niles Township Jewish Congregation in 1976 and again when he returned in 1978. Starting in 1977, the organization won the township board elections. It made an alliance with Skokie's local political party, the Caucus Party, and began winning more offices on school boards, park boards, and library boards, despite the fact that these were supposed to be nonpartisan boards.

Sutker was appointed head of the state Democratic Party during the mid-1980s, but not everything went his way. On Sutker's watch, the LaRouche candidates, a radical right splinter group, won Democratic candidates' slots for two offices, one of which was the governor's, during the primary in 1986.[17] Jaffe resigned his office as state representative in 1986 to accept appointment as a judge. Sutker had the power as Democratic Committeeman to appoint Jaffe's successor, an office coveted by some of the organization's brightest and best younger members. Sutker and the nominating committee decided to award the plum to *himself!* It looked as if Sutker placed his own ambition ahead of the organization's welfare. Sutker's image suffered. And image, as Richard J. Daley discovered during the 1970s, can make or break any politician.[18]

Sutker's image problems affected political power. He began having trouble finding jobs for the party faithful. To that end, he sought and won election as a Cook County commissioner. But this office did not produce the anticipated power to control a large number of patronage jobs. The Niles Township Democratic organization looked more vulnerable after 1994 than it had in many years. By 1997, Republican Committeeman Sheldon Marcus, who had almost successfully challenged Sutker's seat in the legislature, fielded a slate against the Niles Township board. It began to look as though he might succeed.

This turned out to be my first contested election. I had served as a trustee on the Niles Township board since June 1980. During that time, I was reelected four times. Elections had become old hat, but none of them had been contested. Our slate had been challenged in 1981, but the challengers failed to get enough valid signatures on their petitions, so they were thrown off the ballot. A court fight ensued, and our team won. No one filed against us in 1985, 1989, or 1993, although there had been rumblings in 1993. I spent most of my time during those elections circulating nominating petitions and working for contested candidates in other elections.

Why were there no challenges? For one thing, the township tended to vote for Democrats, and the Republican organization had been in disarray. A second obstacle was the legal requirement to field a slate with a candidate for every office on the board.

Most of the offices pose no problem. All that is necessary to be slated for township supervisor, clerk, or one of the four trustee slots is a willingness to come to meetings, some record of civic-minded activity, and no skeletons in the closet. The seventh office, township collector, lacks a defined function and collects no salary. But the eighth office, township assessor, is a different story. The assessor must take and pass courses and be certified by the state. Simply being a civic-minded candidate with a knack for numbers will not qualify one for the office. The opposition could find no one with the necessary credentials, so it could not legally field a slate.

Since 1977, our ticket's candidate for assessor had been Robert Hanrahan, a retired high school biology teacher with all the punches on his ticket. But all was not well between Hanrahan and Sutker. The municipal election of 1993 turned out to be the breaking point. Hanrahan publicly supported candidates opposed to those supported by Sutker in the Morton Grove municipal election, and a contentious contest ensued. The Morton Grove Action Party, the party Sutker supported, won.

Hanrahan still believed that Sutker would slate him again in 1997. Who else was there? Slating time came, and Sutker's organization slated Scott Bagnall, a lawyer with the requisite credentials but no experience, for township assessor. Hanrahan learned that one does not openly defy a committeeman and then expect that committeeman to send flowers.

Dumping Hanrahan ensured a contested election. The opposition now had a qualified candidate for assessor, thus completing its slate. The Township Coalition Party, headed by Republican Committeeman Marcus, was born.

Marcus's slate looked impressive. In addition to Hanrahan, Marcus had tapped interesting candidates who represented diverse interests in the township. Portraying his slate as a coalition bent on breaking the power of the Sutker machine, his was a slate of community activists claiming that they wanted to bring government back to the people.[19]

Marcus, a Morton Grove resident, led the slate. He hoped to draw Skokie's significant Jewish vote away from Tom McElligott, the township's supervisor.

Herbert Root, the Coalition Party's candidate for township clerk, had ties to Jewish organizations. Like Clerk Charles Levy, Root lived in Lincolnwood and had a political base there.

Let us not forget the collector's office. The Coalition Party's nominee, Gordon Kornblith, was an active member of Skokie's local political party, the Caucus Party, which was a coalition of Republicans and Democrats. The party had been allied with Sutker since 1977, but Kornblith had the potential to lure independent and Republican caucus voters to the Coalition Party.

Marcus had tapped four interesting candidates for trustees, each with a political base. Reno Masini is an architect. Like McElligott, Masini is a longtime member of St. Peter's Catholic Church, the largest and most diverse Catholic church in Skokie. The parish could have split between two favorite sons.

James Hammerschmidt worked in his brother's popular bowling alley and had been a fixture in Skokie for many years. He promoted his candidacy by networking with customers.

Robert Malooly had held a political appointment in state government and was experienced in working with pensions. The man understood local government and exuded efficiency.

Last, but not least, there was Lourdes Mon. Mon had run and lost against Sutker for county commissioner in 1994, but in the process, she had developed a reputation for being competent. Not only was she familiar with structuring budgets, she also belonged to an impressive array of civic organizations. Her credentials and background made her a very attractive, electable candidate. Mon and I seemed to be vying for the same constituency. Sutker asserted that Mon was specifically running against me.

The Republican revolution of 1994 also worked against the Sutker machine. After the Republican sweep of the legislature and state offices, a perception grew among many voters that entrenched incumbents, liberal ideas from the 1960s, and organization or machine candidates ought to go the way of the dinosaur. This was particularly evident in liberal Democrat Dawn Clark Netsch's lopsided defeat for governor.

After the 1996 general election, the Democrats regained the majority in the state legislature, but the outgoing Republican-dominated state legislature had struck a powerful blow against machine politics by passing a law outlawing straight party voting. Punching a straight ticket gave the lower slots on the ballot "coattails." What this meant for the township was that it no longer was possible to simply "punch 10" to register a vote for every Democratic township candidate.

In the contest for township trustee, the four candidates with the most votes would be elected. It was feared that if voters crossed to vote for one of the Coalition Party candidates, they might vote for other Coalition Party candidates.

Our slate was known to be Sutker's and the regular Democratic organization's, even though the slate had taken the name "Township Caucus Party."[20] We could be seen as poster children for tired, incumbent machine candidates. McElligott, candidate for supervisor, had served for 20 years, and I had served for 17. Youth was not on our side. Our youngest candidate, Bagnall, was 45 years old, and our oldest, Lester Brownstein, was 75. Photographing the Township Caucus Party en mass and making us look appealing was an artistic challenge.

Four of the eight candidates on our slate were lawyers. Prior to 1994, that would have been a plus, as law and politics seem to go hand in hand. But the image of Perry Mason has been replaced with images out of John Grisham. For some voters, musicians in houses of ill repute are ethically superior to lawyers or politicians.

Then there was the "tax" question and the township's progressive programming. The township board had started a legal program for senior citizens, creating a licensed child care center based on the ability to pay, and subsidized close to 50 community organizations in the amount of $700,000 annually. Welfare reform worried us because we could see that innocent children would go hungry. Niles Township raised taxes when there was good reason, but raising taxes and creating programs were seen as passé and wasteful after 1994. We were portrayed as political hacks.

Perhaps the reader might wonder why being on the Niles Township board was so important to me. After all, being a township official has little salary and few perks. But our work was making a difference. It was making life better for the citizens of the township. Being a township trustee gave me the opportunity to do something worthwhile for the community.

Okay, there was something else. I am cantankerous, and it bugged me that someone was trying to take my place and diminish, or possibly dismantle, the programs that the board worked so hard to build. I just was not going to let that happen without a whale of a fight.

Although the Niles Township Caucus Party was the creation of Sutker, it did represent different parts of the political and geographical spectrum in Niles Township. Not all of us were even Democrats.

Supervisor McElligott headed the ticket. He had been active in Skokie politics since the 1950s. McElligott had served as a trustee on the Skokie village board before coming onto the township board.

McElligott staunchly advocated affordable, quality child care. Under his direction, the board created the Niles Township Community Day Care Center. Creating affordable, quality child care during the 1980s, with that decade's emphasis on family values, was no easy task. But McElligott stood his ground, and the center flourished.

The clerk, Levy, is a detail-minded man. A Lincolnwood resident, Levy kept the township's offices running smoothly while making certain our meetings ran to the letter of the law.

The newly slated assessor candidate, Bagnall, is a lawyer with experience in real estate and had all the requisite credentials needed for the assessor's office. Bagnall was the youngest candidate on the ticket but had some name recognition. His father-in-law, Robert Fritzchall, was a trustee in Skokie.

Perhaps the slated candidate for collector was the most charismatic of all of us. Brownstein is a conservative Republican who deeply wanted to be the township collector. He worked diligently to make the collector's office a viable one. Brownstein is a hard worker and a wonderful person, and I was delighted he was on our ticket.

As for the trustees, Suzanne Schwartz, an independent, is the wife of now retired Judge Harvey Schwartz, former legal counsel to the Village of Skokie and a moving force of the Caucus Party. Harvey Schwartz had fought the planned Neo-Nazi March in Skokie in 1977, gaining semi-legendary status for doing so. Suzanne Schwartz shared in his glory. She also volunteered for a myriad of causes.

Levon (Lee) Tamraz was active in Morton Grove politics and was our board's fiscal conscience. He often sat during meetings with a calculator, making certain that we were not going into the red. Of all of us on the board, Tamraz was the most traditional.

Marshall Belgrad came from the Devonshire section of Skokie. A precinct captain since 1983–1984, Belgrad had run, and lost, in a bid for state senator in 1984. He did have name recognition.

As for me, I was the board's liberal. I had worked closely with McElligott on child care, acting as the board's liaison to the center since its creation. I also sat as the township representative to the Cook County Economic Development Association board in Evanston, "CEDA—Neighbors at Work." I felt like a sitting duck.

That is the thing about being a candidate; you are exposed. For all the talk about issues, people vote for—or vote against—you. Your ideas, your actions, and your personality combine to form a public image of you, and that image is exposed for public judgment. Your opponents very quickly seize on your weaknesses and strive to redefine your image to their advantage. Our image already had problems. I felt vulnerable—good and vulnerable.

We had our first candidate's meeting on February 20, 1997. During that meeting, Sutker and his aides told us their strategy. The party and the candidates would send out campaign literature and "friend-to-friend" cards, postcards sent to friends that touted the ticket. It was a classic machine strategy, relying on loyalties, networking friends and family.

Sutker and his son, Alan, largely funded the campaign, although each candidate was assessed $750. As we sketched out biographies for the campaign literature, we were exhorted to work very hard and were warned that the campaign would "get dirty." I knew that there were instances in my life that could be used against me. I have diabetes, and it has been a medically "interesting" case. Would the opposition start a whispering campaign? Would the fact that I had been antiwar during the 1960s come back to haunt me? Would my loyalty be questioned?

Our family had had some business reversals. Would we be forced to relive these painful episodes? My mother, Dorothy Elias-Lipstadt, and my stepfather, Elmer Lipstadt, live a mile away from us. Would they have to see all this in print? How would my stepbrother, Skokie resident Bruce Lipstadt, feel?

The Coalition Party stood a good chance of winning some of the offices in Niles Township in January or February 1997. Morton Grove was up for grabs. Hanrahan campaigned heavily in Morton Grove and Niles. Even Skokie's Caucus Party was not unanimous. One of the village trustees, Don Perille, was a Republican with friends on both tickets, and he refused to sign an endorsement letter.[21] There also was the fear that the Republican Party in Cook County might send in mercenary precinct workers in a move to bring Sutker down by defeating us.[22]

Yet, the dirty campaign never came to pass. Dan Obermaier, managing editor of the *Skokie Review,* and Kathy Routliffe, the township beat reporter for that newspaper, both asserted that Marcus could not employ the strategies that could have brought him victory. Marcus, Routliffe noted, was too decent to point out the chinks in our armor. "He did the wrong things for the right reasons," she told me. Obermaier added, "He didn't take the campaign seriously. You [us] put on your war paint." The Coalition Party realized that it faced an uphill fight. Believing that it was an impossible dream, it campaigned accordingly. We ran scared, a fear shared by the local Democratic Party. On March 26, during our final candidates meeting, Sutker threatened that if any one of us lost, he or she would "never run for public office again."[23]

Fear of losing had a plus side. It forced us to soul search, to look closely at ourselves, and to discover what we stood for. Once that was accomplished, we succeeded in shedding the tired machine image; we turned being machine incumbents into a plus. By mid-February, we began looking like seasoned public servants campaigning for approval of our mandates.

Our ticket worked as a team, yet each member developed a distinct public image. Schwartz got things started. About once a month, we would eat breakfast or lunch together and have nice long woman-to-woman talks. During one of these talks in late January, Schwartz told me that she was planning to do a private mailing to all the people she knew from her work in the school systems. The letter would showcase Trustee Schwartz's volunteer work and also would tout the entire ticket. Schwartz added that she followed her husband's advice. Harvey Schwartz had played a significant role in past Skokie Caucus Party's victories. Rather than answer allegations, Schwartz would stress the positives of her job on the board. That resonated with me. From then on, I spoke and wrote only of our positive agenda. Having a positive stance made a difference in my image—and in all of our images. We campaigned as if the opponents did not exist.

Perhaps the turning point came during our first board meeting on February 10, 1997. Previous to that meeting, the township had mailed to each home in the township its annual newsletter about our activities. All of the trustees were pictured, and our accomplishments were highlighted. I wrote about child care. The lead article in this newsletter concerned the township's plan to offer data processing classes for those who suffered from computer anxiety and who would not be comfortable in a community college setting. Our classes would begin literally with learning how to turn on the computer. A query about whether or not there would be any interest brought more than 800 replies.

In an attempt to save taxpayers' money, the township sought corporate help. Township Coordinator Ada Sutker Rabinowitz approached computer-oriented businesses in the area, asking whether they would cosponsor these classes. One company, U.S. Robotics,[24] consented on the condition that its participation would remain a secret for the time being.

Hanrahan attacked the computer classes, calling them an unnecessary program. Hanrahan also challenged recent changes in the township employees' work schedules. Full-time township employees had worked only 4 days a week because it was thought that there was not enough work for a 5-day week, and Marcus charged that the employees were living off the fat of the taxpayers.

After analyzing each employee's workload, it became clear that most of the staff were actually working a 5-day week already. The supervisor has the power to set work hours. The personnel policy was changed to reflect reality, and McElligott wrote a memo placing all full-time employees, including Hanrahan's, officially on a Monday-to-Friday work schedule. Hanrahan was furious.

All this came to a head during a regular township meeting on February 10, 1997, when McElligott was out of town. I am next in line of seniority, so when McElligott is out of town, I act as supervisor. I walked into that meeting and saw that Hanrahan and all of the Coalition Party ticket except Mon were present. I also noted that Routliffe, the *Skokie Review* reporter, was sitting in the back with her pad in hand. I prayed.

Hanrahan seemed almost menacing when he spoke up during reports from elected officials. I believe that he wanted to cow me and show the Coalition Party how effective he was. He rambled about his health[25] and then tried to make his resumé part of the record. He mentioned that U.S. Robotics was involved in the computer classes, which could have jeopardized the agreement with that company, and he questioned the necessity of the classes. It was a full-scale harangue. Afterward, I thanked him, and Belgrad, Tamraz, and I said that there had been a large response to the computer classes and that there was no duplication of these classes in the township. We went on, feathers unruffled, as if not much had happened. Hanrahan sputtered.

The question about personnel policy came up during new business. Hanrahan complained bitterly about McElligott's decision. I answered this one. Noting that most of the employees were working 5-day schedules anyway, I said that McElligott was only bringing all the employment schedules into "alignment." Hanrahan sputtered again, and I thought I saw Routliffe smile as she noted my response.

It was a long meeting. At 9 p.m., Hammerschmidt walked out. During citizens' comments, Marcus charged that our newsletter, which was printed at taxpayers' expense, was being used as campaign literature in Morton Grove. We denied this charge. Why bother to pass out the newsletter? It had already been mailed to every house in Niles Township anyway. None of the other Coalition Party candidates spoke.

Politically, the rest was a mop-up operation. No story ran in the *Skokie Review* that week on the township meeting, and U.S. Robotics' role remained undisclosed to the public until the company chose to go public. The *Review* later printed Marcus's charge but also printed the township's denial. Sometimes, you win battles and do not realize it. After that meeting, the Coalition Party never went toe-to-toe with us again.

Afterward, Marcus's coalition unraveled. Hanrahan started campaigning on his own, inveighing against the computer classes. But the classes flourished, which ended the issue. Mon also campaigned on her own and created separate campaign literature. But she passed it out in church lots on Easter Sunday, a provocative move.

Marcus's strategy finally boiled down to trying to paint us as hack tax-and-spend candidates. He promised a 33% tax cut and called us "downtown lawyers." But Niles Township residents understood that a 33% tax cut meant a 33% cut in services, and the idea lost its appeal.[26]

The press further helped to enhance our images. The *Skokie Review* sent out endorsement statements. These concentrated on our performance relating to taxation, our answers to welfare reform, and how our party intersected local government.[27]

I was concerned that my answers would put me solidly to the left of the Pioneer Press. Nonetheless, I stuck to my positions on the need for prudent taxation, affordable child care, good social services, and the township's role as a safety net.

I also stated that I did not believe in employing party cronies just because we marched in the same army.

When the *Skokie Review* came to my house on March 20, I would not open it. Only after Sutker's brother, Irwin, told me that I had been endorsed did I open the newspaper. There it was. Although the *Review* split its endorsements, noting that I was a professor at DePaul, the *Review* said I was a "thoughtful" candidate ("Our Endorsements," 1997). I was thrilled. Somebody had noticed.

As Election Day got closer, our ticket shed most of the negative images that Marcus had tried to foist on us. The *Skokie Review*'s preelection profile pointed out that all of us had roots in the community (Routliffe, 1997b). The second community newspaper in the township, the *Skokie Life*, put to rest the notion that we were tired incumbents. Its article ran with the headline "Experience Counts" and then listed our accomplishments (Almer, 1997).

Our campaign literature helped. My letter to my neighborhood might have defused the tax issue by pointing out that the township's annual tax assessment per family cost no more than a meal at The Bagel, a local restaurant. Tamraz and Levy used similar text in letters to their precincts.[28]

Family and friends proved invaluable. Our family had moved to Skokie in 1949, and my mother continues to be active in civic affairs. She announced to the Ezra Habonim/Niles Township Sisterhood that I was "her daughter, the candidate." My mother's endorsement worked magic. Erica Brief, wife of Rabbi Neil Brief, made phone calls on my behalf. When Irwin Duhl, the father of my teenage friend Harriet, heard about my candidacy, he went door to door at several condominiums in Morton Grove. Duhl was an officer in his condo association, and his word carried weight.

Voter turnout was light on Election Day, which was April 1, 1997. My son, Sol, and I were precinct captains in two adjacent precincts. The polling places for those precincts, as well as a third, were in the same crowded room in Agudath Jacob Skokie Valley Traditional Synagogue. The day dragged. My husband, Allan; Sol; his friend, Charlie; my student assistant, Julie Johnson; and her husband, Bob, all stood with me during the afternoon, greeting voters outside the synagogue and giving me much-needed moral support.

At long last, 7 p.m. finally came, and the polls closed. It took 20 minutes to prepare for the tally. The tape that chugged out the results revealed that I led in all three precincts, and in two of the three precincts, the Coalition Party had at most six votes for any of the offices.

Allan and I delivered our tallies to the party office and learned that our tallies were typical. We proceeded to the postelection celebration at Leona's in Skokie. Other members of our slate came, and they were smiling. Levy sat next to me and said, "Congratulations." I asked, "Is it official?" "It's not official until I say it's official," Levy answered with a smile. He added, "It's official."

The entire ticket had won by a margin of more than two to one. Of the eight candidates, I came in fourth, which was three positions above my ballot location. Winning an election is a feeling like no other. My ideas had been validated, I was liked, and it felt wonderful. The *Skokie Review* reported that Sutker's machine had triumphed (Routliffe, 1997a).

We were sworn in 6 days later. All seemed well. Then, things started to unravel for the township and Sutker's machine. Three families complained about the director of the day care center, demanding that the township fire her. For 3 months, there was very public bickering about the day care center that was well covered in the local press. After an investigation by the Department of Children and Family Services licensing authority, the day care center was exonerated, but the township board split over the center's future.[29]

The township had outgrown its quarters, and a remodeling was approved in principle. It appeared that three members of the board were in favor of expanding the day care center, and plans for a separate building were presented.[30]

The center's director had a routine meeting with the architect to give her input on the new center's plans. When the results of that meeting were placed before the trustees, one of the trustees became convinced that he been excluded from the planning process, so he changed his vote, swinging the majority against an expanded center and in favor of creating a second meeting room. One consequence of the failure to proceed with the expansion was that the center lost a $75,000 Community Development Block Grant. All of this received press coverage, and the board, and by extension the machine, had egg on its face.[31]

The primary election for congressional, state, and local offices occurred at roughly the same time as the day care debacle and also proved devastating to the Sutker machine. Long-term U.S. Representative Sidney R. Yates announced his retirement from office, and a bitterly contested, three-way primary fight for his seat followed. Each of the candidates was Jewish with fairly liberal stances. State Representative Jan Schakowsky, an Evanston resident, resonated well with women, minorities, and younger voters. State Senator Howard Carroll, a seasoned politician from Chicago, counted on Chicago's machine and longtime voters. J. B. Pritzker, a millionaire from a philanthropic family with little grassroots political experience, mounted an elaborate campaign targeted to the Orthodox Jewish vote.

Sutker backed Carroll, as did most entrenched politicians. Carroll called himself "the endorsed candidate." It was a hard-fought, bitter, and sometimes dirty campaign. When the dust settled, Schakowsky, the "dark horse," won, defeating Carroll and Pritzker—and Sutker.

Sutker also misjudged the state representative's race. Julie Hamos, a lawyer who wrote Illinois' domestic violence law, ran for the state representative seat vacated by Schakowsky. Despite the fact that Hamos was married to Sutker's close friend, Appellate Judge Alan J. Greiman, and possessed excellent qualifications in her own right, Sutker refused to endorse her, although on several occasions he spoke well of Hamos. He did not want to offend Hamos's opponent, Meribeth Mermall,[32] who was passing out Sutker's literature on the lakefront and claiming that she was the "true Skokie candidate." Hamos won by a landslide without Sutker's endorsement.[33]

Worst of all, Sutker challenged the Cook County board president, John Stroger, for his post. In so doing, Sutker challenged an endorsed incumbent. Stroger had Chicago Mayor Richard M. Daley's support, the support of the regular Democratic leadership, and the support of the African American community. Few issues separated them. Sutker, like Marcus, tried to make taxes an issue and played the race card in his commercials, hoping to gain support from the suburbs. None of these issues resonated with the voters.

A canny politician, Stroger challenged Sutker's nominating petitions, keeping Sutker's campaign in limbo until February. The results were clear on the night of the primary election. Sutker won less than 30% of the vote and had endeared himself to no one.[34]

Because of the combination of his disastrous campaign against Stroger, coupled with the fact that candidates for both state and U.S. representative had succeeded without his endorsement, Sutker lost clout. It was painfully clear; there were no jobs for ambitious precinct captains or entrées into industry. The Schakowsky and Hamos campaigns brought out voters who previously had stayed home and who took a dim view of the Sutker machine.[35]

None of this went unnoticed by the *Skokie Review*. The editorial of May 28, 1998, tore into Sutker for his lack of support for the expansion of the township's day care center and blamed him for the Village of Skokie's approval to expand businesses on Old Orchard Road. It also noted that Sutker's unsuccessful and ill-advised race against Stroger made Sutker incapable of even getting a traffic light for a dangerous intersection in Skokie.

Political machines can be effective only when they serve their constituents' needs, the *Review*'s editorial continued. Recent events had shown that the machine could neither serve its constituents nor deliver for its candidates, even when its leader was on the ticket.

The *Review*'s editorial concluded by lamenting, "The Democratic Party here once was quite effective at using its power to serve the people. The question now is: Will voters demand repairs to their aging machine? Or, will they wait until it breaks down entirely and junk it?"[36]

Notes

1. Writings on the Cook County political machine center largely on the power of the leader. For example, Royko (1971) describes Daley's rise and his ability to survive but also notes his ties to Bridgeport. Kennedy (1978) views Daley as a chieftain but describes that chieftain as vulnerable and capable of making errors (p. 240). O'Connor wrote two books about Daley. *Clout: Mayor Daley and His City* (O'Connor, 1975) concentrates on how Daley kept his power and operated. O'Connor notes that Daley never wanted to host the 1968 Democratic Convention. But in a later work, O'Connor (1977) describes the decline of Daley's machine and the machine's hold on Chicago. A most salient example of this decline occurred during a party meeting just before the election of 1976. The party regulars were "getting numb" from Daley's rhetoric. A woman actually walked out. "Daley followed her with his eyes, as if wanting to know where in hell she was going" (p. 176). Although Daley died close to 22 years ago, books and studies on him continue. Sullivan (1989) discusses Daley, the man and mayor. The machine continues to be discussed in terms of its mayors (Holli & Green, 1989). Rakove concentrates on the workings of and the workers within the machine. In his book, *Don't Make No Waves . . . Don't Back No Losers,* Rakove (1975) analyzes both the structure of the machine and its weaknesses and future. His more recent book, *Don't Want Nobody Nobody Sent* (Rakove, 1979), is an oral history of the precinct workers. Two things emerge from this study: the loyalty bonds necessary to enter the organization and the sense that even the most hard-bitten worker started out wanting to improve society. See also Gove and Masotti (1982) and Granger and Granger (1987).

2. The Declaration of Independence lists the errors of the executive, George III, as the reason for the break with the colonies. Fully 40% of the document is devoted to George's tyranny. He is termed an "absolute monarch." America did not have an executive until after 1787.

3. Article I of the Constitution of the United States is approximately three times as long as Article II describing the executive branch. Travelers to the United States, such as Captain Basil Hall during the 1820s and Frances Trollope during the 1830s, decried the American practice of serving only 2 years and then stepping aside for a neighbor.

4. After the assassination of Alexander II in 1881, anti-Jewish demonstrations rose to a fever pitch. Pogroms erupted throughout Russia and Eastern Europe in 1905. The Habsburg Empire suffered from repeated assassinations and national unrest. The many national groups that made up the empire wished to be independent. This unrest wreaked havoc with the economies of these two empires.

5. See Crosby (1993, p. 300) and Rakove (1975, p. 5). Rakove's first law of politics applies here: "The individual is influenced by principle in direct proportion to his distance from the political situation."

6. See Royko (1971). In Chapter 4, Royko describes the workings of the machine that Daley controlled. The aldermen, with few exceptions, were part of the political structure. See also O'Connor (1975, pp. 12-13).

7. See Note 1. See also Kennedy (1978, pp. xiii, 33-34) and Royko (1971, pp. 7, 19).

8. Washington, the first African American mayor to be elected in Chicago, died in office 7 months after being elected for a second term in May 1987. His effectiveness was hampered during his first term by a rebellion in the city council. A total of 29 aldermen, led by 10th Ward Alderman Edward Vrolydak, refused to follow Washington's program. The feud was dubbed "Council Wars" by Aaron Freeman.

9. Daley worked for Michael Howlett, despite the fact that he believed the election was lost. See Kennedy (1978, pp. 237-238), O'Connor (1977, pp. 172, 177), and Royko (1971, p. 17).

10. A look at the 1950s sitcoms and reading material confirms the endurance of the immigrant dream for the future. As late as 1955, Patty Bauler said, "Chicago ain't ready for reform." It was business and politics as usual in Chicago.

11. See Rakove (1975, pp. 5, 11). The onset of the cold war and the McCarthyism of the 1950s also intensified the wish to be loyal Americans by supporting the established political structure. Dwight Eisenhower used the slogan "You don't change horses in the middle of the stream" during his 1956 campaign.

12. Duis (1989) notes that industry had begun to move toward the outskirts of Chicago as early as 1925 (see also Plotkin, 1995). The first subdivision, Leavittown, Pennsylvania, was built shortly after World War II (Rakove, 1975, pp. 235-236).

13. The Walker Report used this term when it discussed the Chicago Police Department actions toward the antiwar demonstrators.

14. Alderman Thomas E. Keane, County Clerk Edward Barrett, former Governor Otto Kerner, Circuit Court Clerk Matthew Danaher, Alderman Paul Wigoda, and Public Relations Director Earl Bush all were convicted on various charges of corruption (Kennedy, 1978, pp. 256-263). O'Connor (1975, pp. 197-261) discusses Daley's decline (see especially p. 208). Daley's decline is the subject of O'Connor's (1977) *Requiem*.

15. The *Evanston Review* ran an ad showing the slated Jewish candidates with the caption "These are the Jew candidates"; the challengers were called "the American candidates." A few weeks after the slate had been elected, Anne Rasmussen, one of the challengers' strongest supporters, was found dead in her garage, an apparent suicide.

16. During a precinct captains' meeting with Sutker a week before the presidential primary in 1980, Sutker stressed that each captain work for the candidates about whom he or she felt the strongest. Sutker believed that by concentrating on individual strengths, each captain would shore up the other captains' weaknesses. For many years, the Democratic organization sponsored a golf outing that became a family affair.

17. Sutker lost his position as state central committeeman to Jeffrey Paul Smith, thereby also losing the chairmanship of the state Democratic Party.

18. See O'Connor (1977, pp. 182-183). Sutker was roundly criticized for appointing himself and had a tight race against Sheldon Marcus in 1986.

19. Marcus wrote a letter in January 1998 to the organizations funded by Niles Township, assuring the organizations that their needs would be considered and that his slate was composed of "community people who attended church and synagogue."

20. The local regular Democrats had taken a nonpartisan name for township elections since 1980. The decision to use "Township Caucus Party" made the Democrats look like part of the Caucus Party, the local political party comprised of both Republicans and Democrats.

21. The Skokie Caucus Party's elected officials who were uncontested in the 1997 race were asked to sign an endorsement letter for the candidates of the Township Caucus Party. Perille's refusal to sign could have signified a split in Caucus Party support, especially because Kornblith was active in the Caucus Party.

22. Sutker maintains that the county Republican organization sent in precinct workers to campaign for Marcus. He made this claim publicly at the Democratic organization meeting held on September 27, 1998.

23. I thank Obermaier and Routliffe of the *Skokie Review* for sharing their thoughts on the Niles Township election on May 20, 1997. The opinions they expressed were strictly their own and do not necessarily reflect the opinions of the *Review*'s publisher, Pioneer Press. Members of the Niles Township slate had gathered to sign election credentials when Sutker made that announcement. It gave me pause.

24. U.S. Robotics was bought by 3Com, which absorbed U.S. Robotics and moved out of Niles Township. U.S. Robotics no longer exists.

25. Hanrahan had been hospitalized for a heart-related condition.

26. These points were featured prominently in Marcus's campaign literature.

27. I wrote my answers to these questions and faxed them to the *Skokie Review* on March 11, 1997.

28. The campaign letter was written circa February 15, 1997. I changed the names of restaurants and highlighted different accomplishments for Tamraz's and Levy's letters.

29. The families first complained and presented a written case on May 19, 1997. The issue culminated in a packed meeting on July 28, 1997. The parents complained publicly, called the press, and accused me of being in the director's "pocket" and of "stacking the board." Neither was true. As the controversy continued, the township administrator, Morowitz, noted that these parents succeeded where Marcus had failed; they split the board.

30. The motion to hire Michael Williams & Associates to present plans for remodeling was approved on December 8, 1997. McElligott and I were in favor of expanding the day care center. As late as March 8, 1998, Tamraz also approved of the idea.

31. The meeting took place in mid-February 1998. Sandra Hoffman, the former director of the day care center, wished to meet with the architect, as did all the township staff. The Community Development Block Grant was approved February 12, 1998. After the township board voted not to expand the day care center (May 18, 1998), the grant was rescinded in early June.

32. Mermall was backed by State Senator Jeremiah Joyce, a foe of Mayor Richard M. Daley. One of Sutker's advisers, Barbara Panozzo, admired Joyce. Sutker apparently was attempting to keep good relations with all camps. However, Sutker did speak warmly of Hamos on several occasions.

33. Hamos received 62.7% of the vote.

34. The Niles Township regular Democratic organization held no regular meetings between January 1998 and September 27, 1998. Sutker held group meetings with his precinct captains during mid-February 1998. After his primary, he maintained a low profile.

35. I wrote a guest editorial for the *Skokie Review* on March 26, 1998, pointing out that Hamos and Schakowsky approached voters often overlooked by the organization and concluding that Skokie residents do not like to be told for whom to vote. During this primary, I served as Hamos's Skokie coordinator and briefed the Schakowsky campaign on issues and personalities in Niles Township.

36. See the editorial, "Shut Down for Repairs" (1998). Schakowsky (U.S. representative) and Hamos (state representative) won their respective elections in November 1998. Schakowsky is one of the two freshman whips. Sutker remains the Democratic committeeman of Niles Township but has not called many party meetings.

References

Almer, E. (1997, March 27). Experience counts. *Skokie Life,* p. 3.

Crosby, A. W. (1993). Ecological imperialism. In D. Worster & A. Crosby (Eds.), *The biological expansion of Europe, 900-1900* (Studies in Environment and History, Canto ed., pp. 294-308). Cambridge, UK: Cambridge University Press.

Duis, P. (1989). Symbolic unity and the neighborhood: Chicago during World War II. *Journal of Urban History, 1.*

Gove, S., & Masotti, L. H. (1982). *After Daley: Chicago politics in transition.* Champaign: University of Illinois Press.

Granger, B., & Granger, L. (1987). *Lords of the last machine: The story of politics in Chicago.* New York: Random House.

Holli, M., & Green, P. (1989). *Bashing Chicago's tradition: Harold Washington's last campaign.* Champaign: University of Illinois Press.

Kennedy, E. (1978). *Himself! The life and times of Mayor Daley.* New York: Viking.

O'Connor, L. (1975). *Clout: Mayor Daley and his city.* New York: Henry Regnery.

O'Connor, L. (1977). *Requiem: The decline and demise of Mayor Daley and his era.* Chicago: Contemporary Books.

Our endorsements in the township race [editorial]. (1997, March 20). *Skokie Review,* p. 13.

Plotkin, W. (1995, January). Abstract of Duis (1989) article on World War II and Chicago in *Journal of Urban History.* Available on Internet: http://unimeld.edu.au/infoserv/urban/hma/hurban/1995q3/0012.html.

Rakove, M. (1975). *Don't make no waves . . . Don't back no losers.* Bloomington: Indiana University Press.

Rakove, M. (1979). *Don't want nobody nobody sent.* Bloomington: Indiana University Press.

Routliffe, K. (1997a, April 3). Caucus wins town office. *Skokie Review,* p. 3.

Routliffe, K. (1997b, March 27). Voters' guide. *Skokie Review* (special section).

Royko, M. (1971). *Boss: Richard J. Daley of Chicago.* New York: E. P. Dutton.

Shut down for repairs [editorial]. (1998, May 28). *Skokie Review,* p. 18.

Sullivan, F. (1989). *Legend: The only inside story about Mayor Richard J. Daley.* Chicago: Bonus Books.

29

Limitations of Political Marketing?

A Content Analysis of Press Coverage of Political Issues During the 1997 U.K. General Election Campaign

PHIL HARRIS
ANDREW LOCK
JENNIE ROBERTS

Politicians and political parties devote a great deal of time and effort to constructing political messages during election campaigns (Gould, 1998). These are intended to influence voters directly and also to shape the pattern of media coverage. The activity is one aspect of what has come to be known as political marketing. However, despite the recent attention given in Britain to "spin doctors," it has not been established how easy it is for parties and politicians to manipulate voters' perceptions and press coverage. The research reported in this chapter attempts to give an objective picture of press coverage of political issues in the 1997 U.K. general election campaign, identifying the relative coverage of different themes and relating this to its impact on the fortunes of the major parties. We chose to focus on newspapers because these are a significant source of voter information and are not subject to the same requirements of balance of coverage as is television. In the United Kingdom, political parties, candidates, and interest groups are not permitted to advertise politically on television and radio; they cannot buy air time to be used for political purposes. We use content analysis for the study of the press because we believe that it is the method best suited to the nature of the problem concerned.

The data are derived from a complete study of five U.K. national newspapers from the announcement of the general election date to Election Day itself. The relative incidence of issues is identified, and the amounts of coverage of different newspapers are compared. We endeavor to relate this to the impact of specific issues on the major parties and to the political stances of the newspapers concerned. We also relate this to voters' priorities, as identified by opinion polls. On the basis of the analysis, we endeavor to draw some tentative conclusions about the impact of the political marketing and communication approaches adopted by the parties.

The Choice of Approach

A study of an election campaign and the press could have taken one of many different directions, and each would have required use of a different research framework. If the study had intended to discover the reasons behind the political stances taken by the various newspapers, then qualitative research such as observation and in-depth interviews would have provided the best method of finding relevant data. On the other hand, if the study had aimed to discover whether the views put forward by the newspapers had an impact on the readers of the newspapers, then surveys and quantitative analysis would have been preferable. However, previous studies suggest that neither of these two areas of study would have presented the researcher with satisfactory results. Blumer and Gurevitch (1981) argue that evidence drawn from research into effects on political behavior is complex, difficult to interpret, and often inconclusive. An approach based on interviews with journalists and editors would be an alternative, although considerable caution has to be applied to the resultant information and its interpretation.

Therefore, the study is based entirely on the data extracted from the newspapers during the election campaign. It was felt that the best way in which to judge the stance of a newspaper and the way in which it portrayed a political party was to see what the newspaper actually wrote. Of course, this also is what the readers of the newspaper are exposed to.

Content Analysis

Krippendorff (1980) describes content analysis as "a research technique for making replicable and valid inferences from data to their context" (p. 21). The term "content analysis" is approximately 50 years old, although there are examples of it dating back more than 100 years. McQuail (1977) cites Berelson's definition of content analysis: "the objective, systematic, and quantitative description of the manifest content of communication."

The first known quantitative newspaper analysis took place in 1893. It was a basic form of analysis with simply column inches counted (Krippendorff, 1980). Content analysis does not fit neatly into the positivist approach of research, nor is it completely in line with the interpretative approach. It is a combination of nomothetic methodology and ideographic methodology, being as it is, quantitative data drawn from subjective views of the content of the study. Therefore, it is a compromise between several different research methodologies and the one that could best meet the requirements of the study. The balance in the compromise depends on the research questions and the nature of the source material. It can be most likened to observation because it is analysis of the words of something or someone, in this case, newspapers. However, because of the large volume of material involved, the resultant analysis is of quantitative data rather than qualitative data, although the process of deriving the data from the material usually involves the exercise of judgment.

Content analysis has several characteristics that distinguish it from other methodologies. First, it is completely unobtrusive in that it is an analysis of something that already exists, in this case in written form. Second, it consists of unstructured material that must be analyzed and organized by those carrying out the study. Leading on from this, content analysis usually involves large volumes of data that could be used for many different purposes.

Content analysis can take a number of forms depending on the depth of study of the particular items of source material. As will be seen, in this case we were concerned with identifying the key themes of each article rather than going in-depth into the particular slant of each article.

Data Selection and Collection

Our definition of the election campaign period was March 18 to May 1, 1997. John Major called the election on March 18, and the unofficial campaign began at that time, although the official campaign did not start until later. The national daily U.K. London-based press was chosen for analysis. Although there are many important regional publications in the country, such as *The Scotsman* and the *London Evening Standard,* it was decided that problems of availability and time prevented the scope of the study from being widened to cover the regional press. Five newspapers were studied for their political coverage each day during the course of the election campaign. The five newspapers chosen—*The Guardian, The Times, The Sun,* the *Daily Mail,* and the *Daily Mirror (The Mirror)*—represented a cross section of political reporting and press political allegiances.

Because it could not be guaranteed that the newspapers were going to support a certain party in the election, the ways in which they recommended voting in the 1992 general election were considered when choosing the newspapers to analyze. Based on their particular political stances in the 1992 general election, three of the chosen newspapers supported the Conservatives and two suggested voting for the Labour Party. Two of the newspapers are broadsheet, "quality" publications; one, the *Daily Mail,* is a "quality tabloid," and the other two are "popular" tabloids (Table 29.1). Although it would be unclear until the election campaign was underway whether the newspapers would maintain the same

TABLE 29.1 Political Affiliations of Chosen Newspapers at the 1992 General Election

Newspaper	Type	Political Stance
The Times	Broadsheet	Conservative
The Guardian	Broadsheet	Labour
Daily Mail	Tabloid	Conservative
The Sun	Tabloid	Conservative
The Mirror	Tabloid	Labour

SOURCE: Times Books (1992), based on MORI analysis.

allegiances as in 1992, they were seen to illustrate the differences that exist between national newspapers in Britain today in terms of both reporting style and editorial stance.

Although the British national Sunday press also is an important source of information during an election campaign, these publications were not covered by the study because they usually are independent of weekly newspapers and, therefore, could not be directly compared. Because Sunday newspapers appear weekly, it was believed that it would not be possible to derive sufficient data from only six editions. By comparison, there were 45 editions of each of the selected dailies from March 18 to May 1.

The newspapers were collected daily during the course of the campaign, and the coverage was analyzed. To ensure comparability, only coverage featured in the main pages of the newspapers was used; features in supplements and magazines were discarded. Therefore, the coverage fell into one of two general categories: editorial comment or straight news reporting. It also was noted, in each instance, whether the story appeared on the front page of the newspaper or on the inside pages. It was a prime assumption that each newspaper puts the stories that it considers to be of most interest or importance on the front page. It also was noted, in each instance, whether the election campaign was featured as the main front page story or as a secondary story. In addition, it was recorded whether a newspaper chose not to run any election coverage on the front page.

Each story concerning the election campaign was categorized and coded according to the main issue being discussed. Where the story involved more than one principal issue, it was included in all relevant categories (in practice, this never exceeded two categories). An item was not included if it just mentioned the issue in passing; for example, the two main party leaders were mentioned in many articles, but it was only those articles that were specifically about them that were counted in the category for the purpose of the study. Many categories were identified at the outset, whereas several emerged in the course of the campaign (e.g., the stunts category, which included "Fitz the Bulldog," the great symbol of British resolution, and the giant "Rubber Chicken," employed by the Conservatives to follow and challenge Labour politicians to not be scared to tell the public what they would really do once in government).

In summary, the coverage was classified according to the subject of the article, the newspaper in which it appeared, the date of the article, whether the story was on the front page, and whether the article was news reporting or editorial comment.

Coding in content analysis requires judgment, even with this relatively simple scheme. Often, it is obvious whether an article is positive or negative about a party because of causal factors such as the headline and whether it is supportive of a policy statement. It is difficult to prove whether an article is biased toward one party or another, however, and even if a piece is judged to be positive or negative, that still is a subjective judgment to make, and another person might see it in a different light. As McQuail (1977) suggests, "We cannot make inferences about the effects of the press or the way it may be read from a description of content, nor can measurement of space in [itself] offer evidence on the quality of the press without some other value judgment being made" (p. 2).

One way of trying to overcome this problem is to analyze the issues that are generally seen as "safe territory" for the parties. For example, the issue of taxation usually is seen as a strong Conservative issue, and health and social policy often are considered to be Labour territory. It is by analyzing issues in this way, and the frequency with which they occur in the different newspapers, that a picture can be built of the ways in which the parties are being treated by the press. If this is used along with a judgment about the political slant of the articles, then reasonably safe conclusions about the sympathies of the newspapers may be drawn. Every effort, however, was made independently to judge fairly whether an article was positive, negative, or neutral (Table 29.2).

The Prominent Issues

Table 29.3 shows the division of the total election coverage taken from the five newspapers into the categories listed in Table 29.2. A later figure will show the ways in which the issues were divided among each of the newspapers. Table 29.3 shows that 13% was the largest percentage of coverage devoted to a single issue ("sleaze"). The two issues with the most articles written about them were sleaze and the European Union (EU). (Although the use of the term "sleaze" in the press had an obvious pejorative slant, we have retained it as the best descriptor of the content and slant of that category of coverage.) Together, these issues accounted for about one fifth of the election output in the five chosen newspapers. Therefore, it can be seen that although the percentage of coverage these issues received was not especially high, they were the subjects that the newspaper editors apparently viewed as most important during the campaign. One also may note that seven issues or topics account for nearly 50% of the total coverage in terms of numbers of articles.

A relatively high percentage of the total coverage (6%) was devoted to discussing the possible election result and the consequences of it. The election itself had become a talking point as well as the issues within it. The coverage given to the leaders of the two main parties also came near the top end of the scale, with Tony Blair being the subject of 7.8% and John Major the subject of

TABLE 29.2 Data Coding Frame and Description of Categories

Subject	Description of Articles/Examples
"Sleaze"	"Cash for questions"/Neil Hamilton/sex scandals
European Union	Debate over single currency/sovereignty
Tony Blair	Leader of the Labour party
Result and consequences	Suggested result/consequences of a Labour or Conservative victory
John Major	Leader of the Conservative party
Media	The role of the media in the campaign/change of allegiance by *The Sun*
Social issues	Welfare/benefits/homelessness
Economy	Economic issue/taxation
Education	Schools/universities/teachers
Unions	Trade unions/potential resurgence of their power
Scotland/Northern Ireland/Wales	Events in Scotland, Ireland, and Wales/devolution/terrorism
Polls	Results of opinion polls
Liberal Democrats	Liberal Democrat policies and personalities
Labour strategy/spin	Election strategy and role of spin doctors
National Health Service	Health/state of the National Health Service
Marginal seats, floating voters	Views on target seats/undecided voters
Celebrity endorsements	Which celebrities are voting for which parties
Labour members of Parliament	Labour candidates other than leader and deputy leader
Conservative members of Parliament	Conservative candidates other than leader and deputy leader
The Campaign	Length of campaign boredom factor
Attacks and accusations	One party attacking another party
Editorial	Editorial comment/not on specific issue but on election in general
Law and order	Crime/drugs/prisons
Manifestos	Each party's policy document
Chicken/bulldog	Stunts/the Tory chicken/Labour's Fitz the Bulldog
Margaret Thatcher	Involvement of John Major's predecessor
Cherie Blair	Wife of the Labour leader
Privatization	Labour policy on selling off of state assets
Televised debate	Proposed televised debate between party leaders
Michael Heseltine	Deputy Conservative leader
Youth/schools	Opinions of students and schoolchildren
John Prescott	Deputy Labour leader
Women	Women candidates in the election
Referendum party	Party against links with Europe
Conservative leadership	Who succeeds John Major if Labour wins
Conservative strategy	Election strategy
Norma Major	Wife of the Conservative leader
Business	Views of business leaders and the city
Other issues	Miscellaneous/do not fit any other category

another 5.3% of the coverage (13.1% combined). This suggests that during an election campaign, the leaders of the parties become more important than usual, with coverage often focusing on the leaders as well as on the policies of the concerned parties. Lock and Harris (1996) observe that the leader becomes a visible symbol of the political brand, sometimes even the brand itself.

TABLE 29.3 Content of Newspaper Election Coverage: March 18 to May 1, 1997

Subject of Article	Number of Articles	Percentage
"Sleaze"	222	12.5
European Union	169	9.5
Tony Blair	139	7.8
Result and consequences	107	6.0
John Major	94	5.3
Media	77	4.3
Social issues	75	4.2
Economy	61	3.4
Education	52	2.9
Unions	50	2.8
Scotland/Northern Ireland/Wales	49	2.8
Polls	49	2.8
Liberal Democrats	44	2.5
Labour strategy/spin	38	2.1
National Health Service	38	2.1
Marginal seats, floating voters	35	2.0
Celebrity endorsements	34	1.9
Labour members of Parliament	33	1.9
Conservative members of Parliament	32	1.8
The Campaign	30	1.7
Attacks and accusations	28	1.6
Editorial	24	1.4
Law and order	22	1.2
Manifestos	22	1.2
Chicken/bulldog	22	1.2
Margaret Thatcher	21	1.2
Cherie Blair	19	1.1
Privatization	18	1.0
Televised debate	17	1.0
Michael Heseltine	17	1.0
Youth/schools	15	0.8
John Prescott	14	0.8
Women	13	0.7
Referendum party	13	0.7
Conservative leadership	12	0.7
Conservative strategy	12	0.7
Norma Major	11	0.6
Business	9	0.5
Other issues	39	2.2
Total	1,745	100.0

Figure 29.1 also relates to the total coverage but shows only the top 10 subjects of coverage as a percentage of the total. It is these subjects that are worth looking at in more detail because they were those that made up the majority of election coverage. The top 10 issues or subjects accounted for 58% of the total articles written. This shows that certain issues are viewed with more importance than others by the press during an election campaign and that these issues are given more priority so far as coverage is concerned.

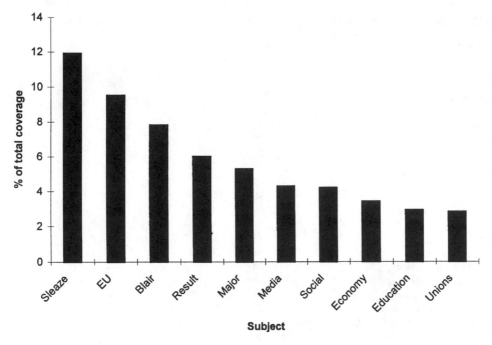

Figure 29.1. The 10 Leading Election Issues, by Total Coverage in Press
NOTE: EU = European Union.

The remaining 42% of the articles covered a wide range of subjects, issues, and personalities and can be seen to show the varied interests of the different newspapers. This also demonstrates the fact that there might be more stories than available column space in a day, so it comes down to editorial judgment as to which stories are featured and which are not.

As discussed earlier, the most popular issues were sleaze, the EU, the election result, and the two main party leaders. The media were the subject of a relatively high level of coverage, with articles discussing the role of the media in the campaign or the ways in which the media were reporting campaign events. This shows an increasing awareness of the role of the media in election campaigns and suggests that the parties' attempts at media management and the ways in which the parties are portrayed by the media are becoming the subject of increased scrutiny by the media themselves.

The rest of the top 10 were political issues and the policies of the Labour Party and Conservative Party relating to them. These four subjects were social issues (e.g., the National Health Service [NHS], benefits, welfare), education (which also is a social issue but was classified on its own because of the amount of coverage it received), the economy (including the perennial issue of taxation), and the Labour Party's relationship with the trade unions. These are standard issues in all postwar U.K. general election campaigns. As such, issues such as these normally would have been expected to receive more coverage than they did. This might reflect the fact that the policy differences between the parties on most of them appeared slight.

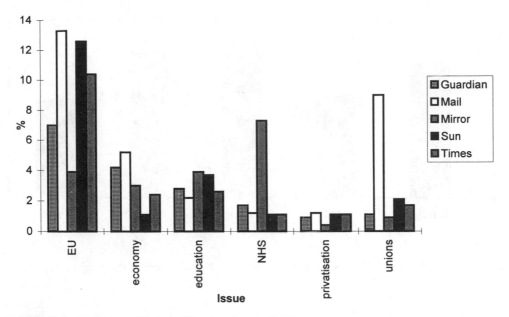

Figure 29.2. Coverage Given to Election Issues, by Newspapers
NOTE: EU = European Union; NHS = National Health Service.

Variations in Coverage Among Newspapers

Although the data relating to the total coverage received can show which issues generally were considered to be of importance during the election campaign, it is only when the amounts of coverage are split according to the newspapers in which they appeared that any real evidence can be discovered as to the ways in which the newspapers set their agendas during the campaign. Figure 29.2 divides the election coverage so that it can be seen which newspapers covered which issues and how frequently.

As can be seen in Figure 29.2, the agendas and loyalties of the individual newspapers begin to become apparent once the coverage is shown split by newspaper. The figure also shows the percentage of coverage in each newspaper devoted to each of the issues. The EU, and the debate over Britain's level of involvement in it, received a significant level of coverage in all the newspapers, but *The Mirror,* and to some extent *The Guardian,* devoted considerably less coverage to the issue than did the other newspapers. *The Times,* the *Daily Mail,* and *The Sun* all gave the issue a great deal of coverage. One should note that it had been chosen by the Conservatives as a key area for their political messages. As will be seen later, it does not appear (from opinion research) to have been a priority issue for most voters.

Other issues also saw clear variations in the amounts of coverage among the various newspapers. *The Mirror* wrote frequently about the NHS, whereas the *Daily Mail* saw the issue of unions as more newsworthy than did all the other

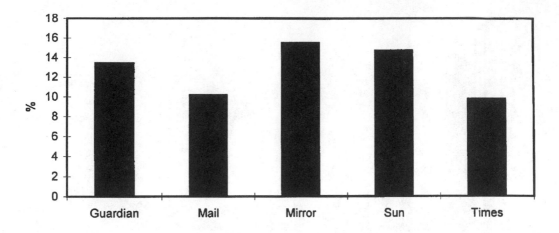

Figure 29.3. Percentage of Total Coverage Given by Each Newspaper to the Subject of "Sleaze"

newspapers. The NHS is a subject generally agreed to be a positive one for the Labour Party, whereas trade unions (or their perceived power) is a favorable subject for the Conservatives. The coverage given to these issues by *The Mirror* and the *Daily Mail* might indicate where their political sympathies lie.

All of the other issues shown in Figure 29.2 received similar amounts of coverage by each of the newspapers. The economy received the most attention from *The Guardian* and the *Daily Mail,* and the subject of education was covered more by *The Mirror* and *The Sun* than by the other three newspapers. The differences in the amounts of coverage received, however, were rather small and suggest that the issues were of similar importance to all of the newspapers.

The sleaze issue warrants a special mention. Figure 29.3 shows the percentage of coverage in each newspaper given to the subject. It was the biggest issue of the election campaign so far as amounts of coverage are concerned. It also is notable that all of the newspapers devoted the greatest number of articles to the sleaze issue, even when their amounts of coverage of other issues varied quite widely. Despite this, the sleaze issue did not exceed 16% of the coverage of any of the newspapers covered. *The Times* and the *Daily Mail* had slightly less coverage of the issue than did the others, but still more than on any other single subject. Their slightly lower amounts of coverage might suggest a certain level of sympathy for the Conservative Party by giving the issue less attention. By the same logic, the greater numbers of articles about sleaze in *The Guardian, The Mirror,* and *The Sun* might demonstrate that the sympathies of these newspapers did not lie with the Conservative Party.

A subject that received very little coverage was the Liberal Democrat Party, despite being widely accepted as a strong third party presence in British politics. The party did not even receive enough coverage to be a part of the top 10 subjects in the newspapers analyzed. The broadsheet newspapers, *The Guardian* and *The Times,* gave the third party more coverage than did the tabloids, but none devoted

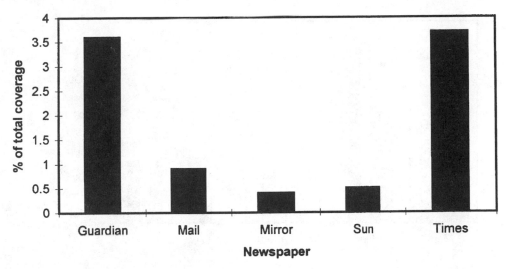

Figure 29.4. Percentage of Total Coverage Given by Each Newspaper to the Liberal Democrat Party

more than 4% of total coverage to the Liberal Democrats (Figure 29.4). This shows that the election campaign is dominated by the two main political parties and that smaller parties find it hard to gain any coverage at all, particularly in media that are not obliged to give "balanced" coverage. We believe that this squeeze on third-party coverage is characteristic of "first past the post" electoral systems, and we are actively involved in research to see whether similar effects are to be found in electoral systems based on proportional representation.

Coverage of Political Personalities

In any election campaign, personalities are very important. Figure 29.5 shows the percentages of coverage given by the newspapers to the different personalities within the campaign. The leaders of the two main parties come under the spotlight more than does anyone else. The leaders were the subject of 13% of coverage overall. Blair received more coverage than Major in all of the newspapers, although the *Daily Mail* gave the leaders the most equal amounts of exposure. This suggests that the Labour leader was of a higher profile than the prime minister during the campaign. *The Sun* seemed to almost ignore Major, whereas Blair was the subject of more than 8% of its coverage. This could imply that *The Sun* believed that ignoring the Conservative leader would do him harm. *The Mirror* devoted the highest percentage of its stories to the Labour leader— more than 10%—but still wrote a fair amount about Major as well. The percentage of articles written about the leaders is not necessarily telling until it is established whether the coverage is favorable or not. The focus of the newspapers on the two leaders shows that they became an easily recognizable focal point for

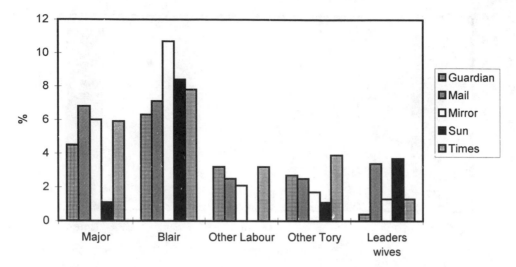

Figure 29.5. Coverage Given to Political Personalities, by Newspapers

attention during the election campaign. The relative perceived strengths of the two leaders appear to be reflected in the amounts of coverage, even before judgments are made about whether articles are favorable or unfavorable. Given that the leader is a significant component of the political brand, this would raise considerable questions about political marketing strategies for a party with a lower rated leader (Lock & Harris, 1996).

Other personalities from the two parties also were noticed by the press despite the leaders being the focus of the most attention. The articles were ones that featured political figures from either main party other than the two leaders and their wives. The broadsheets looked beyond the leaders into the parties more than did the tabloids, featuring similar percentages of stories about Conservative and Labour politicians. On the other hand, the mass popular circulation tabloid newspapers whose readers are interested in gossip, such as *The Sun* and *The Mirror*, took a greater interest in the wives of the two leaders than did the other newspapers, as did the *Daily Mail*.

Front Page Coverage

It was important to analyze the front page election coverage. The news seen as most important on any given day usually is given priority by being placed on the front page of the newspaper. The amount of coverage given to a issue on the front page of a newspaper helps to show whether an issue was seen as important on a particular day when compared to all the other stories on that day. It should be noted that stories are selected for the front page to sell newspapers, not necessarily because they influence party choice.

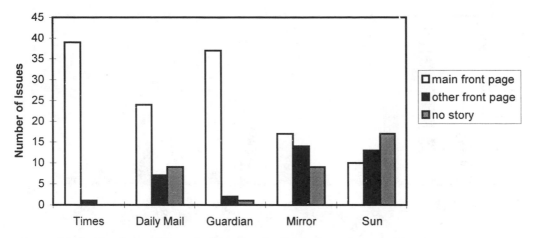

Figure 29.6. Numbers of Days the Election Was Front Page News, by Newspapers

It was interesting to see which newspapers gave the front page to election news during the campaign and which saw other stories as more newsworthy (Figure 29.6). The two broadsheet newspapers used election news on their front pages every day of the campaign, usually as the main story. This is in keeping with the idea that the quality newspapers see political events as important and cover them in some depth. The election clearly was the priority for the editors of *The Guardian* and *The Times* during the campaign. There were several days when the *Daily Mail* had other stories on the front page, but for more than half of the days of the campaign, the election was the main front page story. The election clearly was an important subject for the newspaper during the campaign, but other stories were seen as more important from time to time. The tabloids found other stories more interesting than the election on many occasions. The election made the main front page story in *The Sun* on only 10 days out of 40, whereas other stories made the main front page story on 17 days. *The Mirror* felt that other stories were more worthy of front page coverage than the election on about a quarter of the days of the campaign. *The Mirror* and *The Sun* obviously both saw the election as an interesting story, but only when there was a major issue to report and when other stories were not more likely to whet the readers' appetites. One ought to observe that there is space for fewer stories (often only one story) on a tabloid front page, and a general election is not the only story that sells newspapers.

Figure 29.7 shows the percentages of total front page coverage devoted to different issues. Sleaze was by some distance the subject of most front page coverage during the election campaign. Fully 23% of the total number of front page election stories concerned the sleaze issue. This shows that the issue that gained the most coverage overall also was seen as being one of the most important issues on many days of the campaign. The sleaze issue gained proportionally more front page coverage than coverage in general, which showed that it was the issue that received the most attention in the campaign.

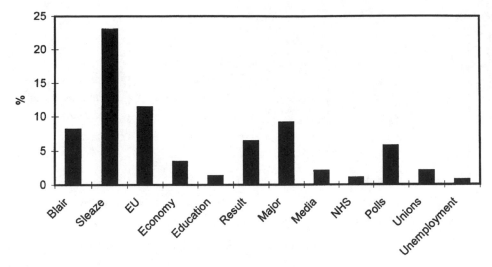

Figure 29.7. Subjects as Percentages of Front Page Coverage
NOTE: EU = European Union; NHS = National Health Service.

The next most popular subject in terms of total campaign coverage also was the second most popular front page story but lagged well behind the sleaze issue with about 12% of the coverage. The EU received a higher proportion of front page coverage than coverage in general, which shows that, like the subject of sleaze, the EU was a high-priority issue from day to day as well as overall. Again, the two main party leaders were the subjects of much front page coverage, although Major received more front page coverage than did Blair. This might not have been positive for the Conservative leader if the stories were featured on the front page and were not positive. The results of opinion polls were a popular front page subject. Nearly 6% of the stories were concerned with them. Polls seem to have been a subject that made the front page more frequently than the inside pages. This is because polls are very topical and are of major importance on the day in which the results are announced. The possible result of the election also was a common story, representing 6.4% of total front page stories.

Use of the Press by the Political Parties During a General Election

The major political parties in the U.K. general election of 1997 had very sophisticated media communications operations in place throughout the campaign. Parties have moved to a more regular war footing to fight campaigns, and the core national press, with its early-morning and subsequent stories, is used as agenda setters for the rest of the daily campaign. The press is monitored from the moment it is published, and journalistic contacts and stories even earlier, by the respective media watchers and managers of each party. Stories are developed and/or spun to support and counter what emerges from this monitoring process on an ongoing basis. The early-morning press stories become very much the agenda items in the party press conferences held at breakfast time later that day. These, in turn, stimulate the broadcast media and their reportage of the event.

The Millbank Tower media operation of the Labour Party supposedly was modeled after the "war room" in the Clinton campaign. The Millbank organization had a tight inner core including Peter Mandelson, Gordon Brown, press secretary Alastair Campbell, pollster Philip Gould, personal assistant Anji Hunter, Lord Irvine of Lairg, and chief of staff Jonathan Powell. A number of senior American advisers were known to be assisting operations but were kept away from the media for fear of scare stories. The group was surrounded by about 200 staff connected via fax machines, modems, and pagers to key shadow spokespersons and candidates in the target marginal constituencies and to ensure that the party remained "on message." Briefings to all these were sent overnight and more frequently as the campaign intensified. "The Labour Party designed its communications strategy down to the smallest detail, with a rebuttal unit under the direction of Adrian Menamin, ready for a rapid response to anticipated attacks" (Norris, 1998, p. 127). The Conservatives as the governing party, with Lords Saatchi and Gummer and Sir Tim Bell behind the scenes, had similar but less focused operations. The Liberal Democrats, with fewer resources, mounted similar-style operations but were more dependent on volunteers.

Summary and Discussion of Content Analysis

The evidence analyzed in the previous sections leaves no doubt about two main issues of the campaign: sleaze and the EU. This is the case whether it is front page coverage, inside page coverage, or editorial comment that is analyzed.

Sleaze was the most prominent issue of the campaign and was a strongly negative one for the Conservative Party. All of the newspapers covered wrote large proportions of unfavorable articles on the subject. Sleaze is an example of an issue that came to light and haunted a party throughout its election campaign, even though the party would have preferred for it to have been forgotten. It was placed so firmly on the news agenda that even the traditional ally of the Conservative Party, the *Daily Mail,* was unable to create a positive angle for the party out of the issue. It is not surprising that newspapers that were not sympathetic to the Conservative Party, such as *The Mirror, The Sun,* and *The Guardian,* were able to make the most of the story and keep it running for much of the length of the campaign.

It may be argued that the subject of sleaze is an example of agenda setting by the media. As Swanson and Mancini (1996) suggest, when an issue is given attention and prominence in the news media, it can become what voters believe to be important (p. 51). Sleaze was not an issue that voters initially felt was very important to them, but the large amount of coverage devoted to it made it an issue almost impossible to ignore (Burns, 1997). Lord Nolan, who had chaired the committee responsible for two reports on standards in public life, observed on BBC Television on November 5, 1997, that "the public perception of sleaze runs far ahead of the reality. . . . The press . . . has played its full part in the growth of cynicism." However, although the relative amount of coverage is linked to the party preference of the newspaper concerned, in journalistic terms, these were good stories to provide headlines. One should be careful not to overestimate the extent of deliberate agenda setting in this case.

The EU was the second most prominent issue in the press during the election campaign. The subject was unique in the campaign because it failed to follow traditional party lines. The issue divided politicians who usually saw eye to eye, and this made the debate particularly newsworthy. Although the subject of the EU is one over which Labour politicians are not completely united, coverage emphasized the divisions within the Conservative Party rather than the issues on which those divisions were based. *The Times* and the *Daily Mail,* both traditionally Conservative-supporting newspapers, made these divisions more prominent than did the other newspapers studied by focusing their attention on the Eurosceptic candidates from the Conservative Party. These also were the newspapers that gave the subject the most coverage. As a result, the large amount of coverage devoted to the EU had more major implications for the Conservative Party than for the Labour Party. Worst of all for the Conservative Party, and by extension best of all for the Labour Party, was the fact that both *The Times* and the *Daily Mail* chose not to endorse the Conservative Party wholeheartedly as they had done in previous elections; rather, they advised their readers to vote for whichever candidates in their constituencies were anti-European. In some cases, those candidates were not from the Conservative Party.

The two leading issues, in terms of coverage, both were damaging to the Conservative Party. The timing of the two issues meant that just as sleaze began to fade away, the EU issue came to the forefront of the campaign, meaning that there was a continual flow of negative news about the Conservative Party throughout the campaign. As a result, the Conservatives were permanently on the defensive and rarely in a position to positively attack Labour.

Voter Priorities

How far did the relative coverage of issues by newspapers reflect their salience for voters? A MORI poll on April 8, 1997, asked voters which issues were most important in helping them to decide which political party to vote for. The top eight issues, in order of importance, were as follows:

1. Health (68%)
2. Education (61%)
3. Law and order (51%)
4. Jobs (49%)

5. Social security (39%)

6. Tax (33%)

7. Economy (30%)

8. Europe (22%)

As can be seen, Europe was given much more prominence in the press than voters gave to it, and sleaze did not figure in the top eight issues at all.

The two issues that voters felt were the most important also occurred in the top five issues according to coverage. Health, or the NHS, was the most important issue to voters but made up only 2% of total coverage in the newspapers. This percentage is relatively low but still was quite high on the list of most frequently covered issues. Only *The Mirror* and *The Guardian* felt that the issue was important enough to be on the front page. Most of the coverage of the subject of health or the NHS was either positive toward the Labour Party or negative toward the Conservative Party. Even the *Daily Mail* was unable to be very complimentary about the Conservative record on health. Health generally has been seen as a strong Labour issue and continued to be so in 1997 (Scammell, 1995). Although the amount of coverage was relatively low, the fact that voters viewed the issue as important means that they were more likely to take notice of it and to note the negative public reaction to Conservative Party health policy (Donsbach, 1991). Newspapers that showed signs of being sympathetic toward the Labour Party devoted more coverage to the issue than did the others. Therefore, the health issue can be seen as important, both in terms of the concerns of voters and as a source of negative coverage for the Conservative Party.

Education was the second most important issue for voters in the election campaign. This issue was the subject of 2.9% of the total election coverage and shows again that the issues under debate in the press are not always those that are seen as important by voters and readers. Education was strongly promoted by Labour and was portrayed as such by the press. *The Guardian* and *The Mirror* covered the issue in a positive way for the Labour Party and featured the subject as front page coverage. *The Sun* and *The Mirror* wrote about the subject most frequently, and only the *Daily Mail* was negative about Labour Party education policy. The *Daily Mail* showed itself to be the most critical of the Labour Party, with *The Sun, The Mirror,* and *The Guardian* being most positive.

Future Research and Limitations of Political Marketing

It is apparent from 1997 U.K. general election voter questioning (King et al., 1998) and prior opinion polling (Heald, 1998) that past Conservative government supporters had switched allegiance to the Labour, Liberal,and Referendum parties more than 1 year before the election. Consequently, the generally agreed high-quality campaign of the Labour Party during the 4 weeks of the election campaign did not improve their standing; in fact, there is some limited evidence to suggest that support for Major actually improved over the period (Heald, 1998). In addition, Labour's marketing-focused Millbank operation resourced special campaigns and targeted 91 parliamentary seats that achieved a swing to Labour of 11.8% against the average swing of 9.9%. Interestingly, in the 54 nontarget seats won by Labour with no assistance from the Millbank marketing operation, the swing to Labour was 14.3%. This underlines some of the limitations and questions that marketing needs to address in this complex area.

If we look at the impact of newspaper coverage and stories on voting behavior, there is relatively little research in this area. We do not know whether there is a causal link among press coverage, editorial bias of a particular newspaper, and the way in which a voter behaves. We know that the press can influence and play a background role in reinforcing voter behavior (Scammell, 1995), but there is very little analysis of by how much, when, and why it is done (Gould, 1998). Again, there is plenty of room for future research and development of political marketing practice and theory.

One of the largest nonaddressed limitations of political marketing is the measurement of advertising effectiveness. In the 1997 general election campaign, the Conservative Party launched its "New Labour, New Danger" advertising campaign, which was devised by Saatchi and Saatchi to demonize the Labour Party and, consequently, to draw away its support. The Conservative Party spent the largest proportion of its advertising budget (£14.1 million) on this campaign to win the election. The evidence that has emerged (Heald, 1998; Powell, 1998) is that the "New Labour, New Danger" advertising campaign actually strengthened Labour support. Interestingly, Labour had been using focus groups and polling to test out policy and voter perceptions of the party for 3 years before the general election; thus, its advertising campaigns and messages were targeted very effectively (Gould, 1998). It is widely known that the Conservatives did not start regular polling and using focus groups of voters until 6 months before the election. Much of the management of the Conservative campaign rested with professional politicians who had limited political marketing experience, whereas Labour and Liberal Democrats had a dedicated group of politicians and managers who were aware of modern marketing methods. The latter won; the Conservatives lost.

Conclusions

The contrasts among relative press coverage of subjects, apparent voter priorities, and the messages stressed by the parties raise some interesting questions. Clearly, some of the coverage of the leading issues and the journalistic research on which it was based was intended to damage the fortunes of the Conservative Party. However, it would be dangerous to generalize this into an argument about agenda setting by the press. The similarity, which has been widely discussed, between the parties' policies on many of the topics regarded as priorities by voters made it difficult to construct newsworthy stories about them, particularly for the tabloids. As a result of the similarities, these issues were reduced to a general issue of relative competence. The Conservative Party started the election campaign well behind in the opinion polls, with apparent voter doubts about the party's competence. From a journalistic point of view, the attraction of the sleaze and "Tory divisions over EU" issues was that, whatever one's political opinion, they were strong stories, with considerable person interest aspects that would appeal to readers.

There are considerable questions for political marketers about communications and tactics in an election campaign. The 1997 U.K. general election might have been unusual in terms of the relative coverage of political issues. However, it seems that the parties had less influence on press coverage than might have been thought at the time. Labour was judged to have run a good campaign, selecting issues that were important with voters and developing an effective rebuttal system. The Conservative choice of issues seems to have misjudged voter concerns, but the party's campaign was swamped by the big stories and, as a consequence, was on the defensive throughout. One possible conclusion is that the important role of political marketing is longer term and that positioning and messages ought to be well established prior to campaigns. Although we agree with this, we believe that tactical promotion and communication are important but are subject to a version of what Keynes referred to as a principle of selection. He used the example of the opera, where if one person stands, he or she gets a better view; once everyone stands, there is no advantage for anyone. In the long run, tactical activities by parties will tend to cancel themselves out. This raises the standards of political marketing, but there is no observable effect unless one party falls down in one area or the other manages to innovate. Eventually, effective innovations will be copied and neutralized.

References

Blumer, J., & Gurevitch, M. (1981). Politicians and the press. In D. Nimmo & K. Sanders (Eds.), *Handbook of political communication* (pp. 467-493). Beverley Hills, CA: Sage.

Burns, T. (1997, September). *The impact of the national press on voters in 1997*. Paper presented at the Political Studies Association EPOP Conference, Essex, UK.

Donsbach, W. (1991). Exposure to political content in newspapers: The impact of dissonance on readers' selectivity. *European Journal of Communication, 6,* 155-186.

Gould, P. (1998). *The unfinished revolution: How the modernisers saved the Labour Party.* Boston: Little, Brown.

Heald, G. (1998, September). *Why Tory policy and political marketing failed in the 1997 general election campaign.* Paper presented at the Political Marketing Conference, Cork, UK.

King, A., Denver, D., McLean, I., Norris, P., Norton, P., Sanders, D., & Seyd, P. (Eds.). (1998). *New Labour Triumphs: Britain at the polls.* Chatham, NJ: Chatham House.

Krippendorff, K. (1980). *Content analysis: An introduction to its methodology.* London: Sage.

Lock, A. R., & Harris, P. (1996). Political marketing: Vive la difference! *European Journal of Marketing, 30*(10/11), 21-31.

McQuail, D. (1977). *Analysis of newspaper content.* London: Her Majesty's Stationery Office.

Norris, P. (1998). The battle for the campaign agenda. In A. King, D. Denver, I. McLean, P. Norris, P. Norton, D. Sanders, & P. Seyd (Eds.), *New Labour triumphs: Britain at the polls* (pp. 113-144). Chatham, NJ: Chatham House.

Powell, C. (1998, September). *Political campaigns: How they work*. Paper presented to the Advertising Association and Fabian Society the Labour Party Conference, Blackpool, UK.

Scammell, M. (1995). *Designer politics*. Basingstoke, UK: Macmillan,

Swanson, D. L., & Mancini, P. (1996). *Politics, media, and modern democracy*. Westport, CT: Praeger.

Times Books. (1992). *Sunday Times guide to the House of Commons, 1992*. London: Author.

30

Against the Fundamental Rules

HANS SCHMID
DIETMAR ECKER

Austria has had a Social Democratic federal chancellor ever since 1970. The Social Democrat Party (SPO) ruled Austria with a majority government until 1983, when the Social Democrats entered into a coalition with the Austrian Freedomite Party (FPO). This subsequently was dissolved by the then SPO Federal Chancellor Franz Vranitzky after Jörg Haider's seizure of power in the FPO in 1986. The so-called "grand coalition" between the Social Democrats and the conservative Austrian People's Party (OVP) has now been in power since 1986. It is not a particularly popular form of government, and over the past few years, there has been repeated discussion of a possible alternative constellation.

The year 1995 was dominated by a prolonged and controversial discussion about the consolidation of the national budget. The two parties in government, the SPO and the OVP, had to digest an election result that was not particularly luxurious in the national elections at the end of 1994 and, furthermore, were confronted with a considerable anti-Europe mood throughout the country. The largest opposition party in Austria, the FPO (under the leadership of Haider), seemed to have embarked on an inexorable path to the top.

At the same time, the former federal chancellor, Vranitzky (SPO), was sailing just as inexorably into the greatest popularity crisis of his 10-year period of office. Practically every major daily newspaper in Austria was speculating about the end of the Vranitzky era. Parallel to this, the need arose in the conservative OVP to finally grasp the right moment in time for a change of power in the country. The OVP had not been able to provide the federal chancellor since 1970, yet in the course of 1995 as a result of opinion polls, the party had come to see that there was an optimal situation for making a step in the direction of the chancellery. The leader of the OVP, Vice Chancellor Wolfgang Schüssel, had at the last moment succeeded in consolidating his party and bridging the gap to the Social Democrats in terms of popularity with the electorate.

In the autumn of 1995, both of the coalition parties were running neck-and-neck in all the opinion polls, each with about 31%. In contrast to the election of 1994, this situation signified a loss for the SPO of about 4% and a gain for the OVP of about 3%. In September, opinion polls showed that, for the first time in 27 years, the Social Democrats had become only the second strongest party.

In this situation, which was quite dramatic for the SPO, the new and very young Social Democratic minister of finance made a rather inept public statement about the deficit of the national budget that was corrected a few days later by the federal chancellor. Therefore, in September 1995, the SPO's minister of finance became the target of criticism by the OVP. Naturally enough, the negotiations about the national budget subsequently entered an extremely difficult phase.

In public, the impression arose that the SPO was incapable of reform, was inwardly shocked by the opinion polls, and was dominated by a conservative wing that was hostile to reform, and that the party leader and federal chancellor, Vranitzky, no longer had the party under control.

Another unwelcome fact for the largest party in government was the new and intensive courting of the OVP by Haider with the intention of making its leader the federal chancellor. This offer sparked off a discussion in the OVP, from which it emerged that, after 27 years, the time for a change of chancellor never had been more favorable than it was at the end of 1995.

SPO Overtaken in Opinion Polls for First Time

At the beginning of October 1995, the leadership of the OVP decided to end the coalition with the Social Democrats and, therefore, to provoke new elections. The SPO was shocked because it had not really believed that its coalition partner was capable of doing such a thing. During these days of early October 1995, the SPO was subjected to a barrage of attacks by the media and was stigmatized as the election loser even at this early stage.

Yet, it was precisely in those days that something happened to the OVP that could not be immediately recognized as a mistake. The party was making such incredible headway that clear reflection about the events at this point in time was really not possible; therefore, the mistake could not be corrected. The party leadership publicly announced that the actual reason for the end of the coalition was the fact that the coalition partner had become inflexible about cuts for early pensioners and that, therefore, one very important step for the consolidation of the national budget had proved impossible.

This mistake could not be recognized as such at the start of the election campaign in October. According to the opinion polls, the OVP had, in the eyes of the general public, become responsible for the financial rehabilitation of the budget (SPO, 22%; OVP, 28% [Institut für empirische Sozialforschung (IFES), 1995]). The OVP's euphoria was then reinforced by further survey data showing that only 23% believed that the SPO had the ability to create jobs, whereas 30% believed that the OVP had that ability (IFES, 1995). This poll increased the sense of impending doom among the Social Democrats. At this point in time, they had every justification.

A situation had arisen in Austria where a great many previously protected economic sectors were now gradually being exposed to international competition. For many people, especially older employees, the step of taking early retirement represented the chance of making a more or less satisfactory transition to the final parts of their lives. Furthermore, it is part of the Austrian mentality to believe that the pension is a well-earned right that cannot be tampered with by anyone.

It was, therefore, a question of mentality, and it should have activated all the energy for a strategy with a debate about pensions. Admittedly, at the start of the election campaign, the subject of economizing was extremely popular, and even the Social Democrats' election team was unsure about the analysis of the situation.

Budget Debate Will Lose Its Dramatic Impetus

Thus, it seemed to be clear what the OVP's election campaign should be based on to bring victory—the consolidation of the budget. All opinion polls supported this strategy. Even the sensitive pensioners agreed with this course during these weeks.

The Budget Does Not Interest the Public for Months

In a first fundamental analysis of the initial situation for the election, it was clear that the two competitors, the OVP and FPO, would make the budget economy measures the center of their campaigns because in this way they could pick up points from the Social Democrats.

However, it was clear to us that nobody can hope to maintain the dramatic element necessary for an election campaign by running such a public debate for 10 weeks. The annual budget discussion could hold the attention of the general public for at best 4 to 6 weeks, but after that, the public would lose interest. What is more, members of the public were, from this point onward at the latest, only interested in the definite effects of the budget on their own wallets. This experience was decisive for the coming strategy.

Confronted with this analysis, and also with the catastrophic image situation of the SPO with regard to its social capability, another separate theme had to be created that was independent of the budget debate being conducted in the media and in politics and that would have the greatest possible appeal for a broad section of the electorate. Once again, it did not matter at all how heavily the media criticized the Social Democrats, for our calculation was that in a few weeks, a situation would arise in the country that would be emotionally quite different.

Old Versus Young

Right at the start of the election campaign, we made a wrong estimate that later proved to be extremely useful because the knowledge we gained from it gave us a precise orientation for placing the emphasis of the Social Democratic election themes.

A few days after the end of the grand coalition, at the beginning of October 1995, the SPO placed an advertising spot in national television that showed a single mother with two small children. It depicted the terrible consequences that the OVP's budget economy measures would have for this family.

New Strategy Won From Mistakes

However, the result of this commercial was different from what had been expected. Hundreds of angry pensioners rang the hotline that had been set up in the Social Democrats' federal office. All were of the opinion that they themselves had not received any financial support from the state when they were young and had, nevertheless, managed to cope with everything. Now, it was a matter of economizing, and everybody should do their bit. Therefore, by and large, the pensioners also supported the abstract idea of economizing.

One other thing also became clear in these first few weeks, especially in the analysis made after this commercial: The concrete effects of the abstract idea of economizing had to be depicted for the target group that was relevant for the SPO.

The strategy, therefore, was born from the necessity of the hour. The defensive situation of the SPO, the catastrophic survey results for the Social Democratic federal chancellor and top candidates, and the terrible survey results regarding social capability meant that only one strategy was feasible: to run a campaign based on content (without the top candidates) for the first few weeks, suggesting that social democracy should take over the protective function for those segments of the population that could be severely affected by conservative economy measures (e.g., pensioners, workers, women).

Miraculous Stabilization

Until October 1995, the popularity of the SPO and its top candidates had been continuously plummeting; indeed, for many, it seemed to be heading toward a crash. By means of embarking on a new strategy (i.e., placing social capability and the protective function in the foreground), it was possible to pull out of this nosedive within a very short period of time. The Social Democrats stabilized their position in the opinion polls at about 31%, which (internally) could already be regarded as a success.

At the same time, the poll ratings for the sociopolitical image of the SPO soared. Whereas in October, only 33% were of the opinion that the SPO had the better proposals for creating more social justice, by the first half of November, that percentage already had risen to 40%. Over the same period, the conservative OVP lost 3% (IFES, 1995).

As for the question of its ability to create new jobs, the SPO ratings also soared. From October to mid-November, they rose from 23% to 30%. Over the same period, the OVP lost 7% and dropped to 23%.

After some 4 weeks of electoral campaigning, the pattern began to emerge that previously had been reckoned with. In the emotions of the population, the budget and economy measures gradually became replaced by worries about the development of social benefits. Economizing came to have fewer and fewer positive connotations, and the subject (which was well occupied by the OVP) became increasingly associated with drastic and largely negative changes in people's lives.

Where Is the Leading Candidate?

Thus, the goal for the first phase had been achieved, that is, stabilization after plummeting and preparation for the second half of the campaign, both emotionally and with regard to content.

One problem with this situation, at the beginning of November and about 6 weeks before Election Day, was the continued low image of the federal chancellor and leading candidate. From this problem was born the strategy for handling the television media that would later prove to be so successful.

Nevertheless, despite these initial successes, there was a great deal of uncertainty on the election team. How could we go on the offensive when the leading candidate was not popular with the voters? Yet, as it turned out in this matter as well, favorable circumstances, together with strategic mistakes made by the opponents, brought about a change in the situation.

ORF, the Austrian national television company, planned numerous discussions involving pairs of politicians, in the course of which each of the leading candidates from the five parliamentary parties would have the opportunity for discussions with all the others. In addition, two big rounds were planned in which all five candidates would engage in a discussion together.

The OVP's leading candidate, Schüssel, decided to take part personally in all of the pair discussions and, of course, in the big rounds. Schüssel ran a very aggressive campaign, so his strategy was to take advantage of every possible appearance.

Anyone who has ever done public relations work for politicians will know that the necessary aura to arouse emotional publicity often can only be achieved by reference to other personalities in public life. In the present case, this meant that the OVP and its top candidate actually "needed" the federal chancellor. From their point of view, he was the very incarnation of the state of standstill with regard to reform in Austria and bore the main responsibility for it.

In the first half of the election campaign, Vranitzky hardly appeared at all. He did not make any television appearances and otherwise kept in the background. In this way, the OVP was robbed of an essential element for the success of its attack—images on television of a weakened top candidate of the SPO. Intuitively, the conservative top candidate must have increased his criticism of the SPO and its party chairman to be able to emotionalize the dimensions of his attack, despite the lack of the actual incarnation of the target of his attack.

Two Different Emotional Worlds

Thus, the first half of the campaign saw a development that could not have been planned in the form it actually took. There was an aggressive opposition leader, Haider, and now there also was an aggressive vice chancellor, Schüssel. At the same time, there was a party that placed importance on social justice. At that point in time, it could not be seen whether this emotional constellation, which would later prove to be immensely favorable for the SPO, was decisive for the election. This phenomenon also is not described in existing literature about classical election campaigns.

The social circumstances and general mood a few weeks before Christmas favor themes that are not directed toward aggression and attack. Not until the November weeks, heading toward the second half of the election, did we become especially aware of this connection through an important event. It was not only because the question of social justice was increasingly replacing the economy measures as the dominant election subject, but also because we were receiving more and more well-meaning calls on the election hotline inquiring about the state of the leading candidate.

In letters to the party's central office as well, the spitefulness abated and swayed in the direction of inquiries about what the party chairman and federal chancellor actually had to say about the OVP's budget proposals.

In the meantime, through the many television appearances of Schüssel, it had become clear to Austrians what the conservative challenger wanted. He had, in part, been forced to repeat himself, and in so doing the novelty of his interviews had sunk asymptotically toward zero.

In parallel with this, the interest in the Social Democratic federal chancellor increased, and not only among callers and letter writers to the SPO central office. In their commentaries, many journalists also increased the pressure for clear positions from Vranitzky, calling for statements on his party's move to the left, indicated by the fact that it had pushed the social protective function into the foreground.

This constellation could not have been better for the SPO. Just 4 weeks before the election, both parties were level. The opposition challenger, Haider, increased his attacks on Vranitzky and, at the same time, courted the OVP in the direction of a joint government.

The two smaller opposition parties, the Liberal Forum and the Greens, had hardly any chance of public attention in this group of three because the question of what would happen within the group was too exciting. The SPO also was favored in the weeks before Election Day by this lack of publicity for the smaller parties because there was considerable overlapping with the two other parties in the segment of social liberal voters.

Thirst for Vranitzky

Eventually, over a few weeks, an unbelievable situation for an election occurred: A leading candidate, who at the start of the election campaign had reached a definite low in popularity among the voters, suddenly became increasingly desired emotionally, both by the public and by the media, even though in the first half of the campaign he had not actually appeared at all.

Something like that cannot really be planned. As mentioned earlier, this development was brought about by the aggressive strategy of both the conservative challenger and the Freedomite opposition leader, employed at a time when the emotional mood of the population was swinging toward the inner peace preceding Christmas. And the main election themes of the SPO corresponded to precisely this mood.

Against this background, it would be highly interesting to analyze by scientific methods the chances of aggressive candidates in election campaigns before Christmas.

Of course, it was helped by a strategic constellation in which Vranitzky possessed a high degree of credibility. He stood for the political isolation of Haider and, therefore, was ad persona the guarantor that the FPO would be kept out of the government.

In November (4 to 5 weeks before Election Day), this question developed into the second major election theme after the social question. The leading candidate of the OVP did not want to exclude the possibility of a coalition with the FPO, which gave Vranitzky the chance to play his best card at this point in time—the anti-Haider bonus.

Haider Must Be Kept Out of the Government

There were phases in the election campaign, above all in the first part, when the anger at the Social Democrats was so great that the question of Haider's participation in the government was not at the center of people's emotions. With the already described development, this situation changed dramatically. In October 1995, only 38% of the population thought that it was necessary to vote SPO to prevent Haider from getting into government. By the start of December, the percentage had increased by 11%. At the same time, the OVP lost 9% on this question. Only 10% believed that the OVP was a guarantor for keeping Haider out (IFES, 1995).

That showed vicariously the increasing importance of this subject in the course of the election. Today, one can admit that the great fear of those essentially responsible for the Social Democrats' election campaign was that the OVP would slam the door shut on Haider and lay claim to leadership of the country while at the same time inviting the SPO to join the government as a junior partner, as a social corrective as it were, offering the Social Democrats the Ministry of Social Affairs.

It would have been difficult for Vranitzky to come to terms with this variation because he would have been unable to fully play either his greatest strength of being the country's leading statesman or the anti-Haider bonus.

Vranitzky Filled the Vacuum

Yet, things happened differently, and an increasing need for social warmth arose in the country that could be translated into all political and emotional dimensions, whether in the form of protection for low earners, support for pensioners and single mothers, or (above all) the reassuring manner and calm, considerate appearance of Vranitzky. These were two characteristics for which he had been pilloried 8 weeks earlier and that had brought him terrible commentaries and a fall in popularity among voters. Yet, he filled the vacuum during this period.

A few weeks before Election Day, strong signs emerged that made it unlikely that the Social Democrats would suffer a defeat. Even if a neck-and-neck race was indicated by the opinion polls, the SPO's victory was already decided 3 weeks before the election.

The Last Evidence for a Change of Mood

During this phase, on December 5, there was the main television confrontation between Vranitzky and his challenger, the leading conservative candidate, Schüssel. At the same time, it was the federal chancellor's first big television appearance—just a short time before Election Day.

This final phase of the election was introduced by a series of posters in which Vranitzky was shown as representing the values of humanity and justice. As if it were being applied to him personally, something then happened in that decisive television discussion that, at first and shortly afterward, caused a feeling of depression within the SPO.

In the middle of the discussion, Vranitzky began to perspire heavily, a fact that was clearly visible to all television viewers. In this situation, Schüssel increased his attacks on the SPO and, therefore, also on Vranitzky. It seemed as if Schüssel had decided the duel in his favor. However, something completely different evidently transpired during this phase of the discussion. Vranitzky conveyed the impression that he was suffering from a cold, and this was in fact the case. This circumstance was at the center of the subsequent press reports.

Even during the program, the dispirited SPO election team received hundreds of angry calls on the hotline, primarily from elderly female voters who were angered by Schüssel's style of attacking an unhealthy federal chancellor in such a way. At this point, it became clear that the pensioners, who were the most decisive group for the outcome of election, would turn in the direction of the SPO.

A few days before the election, all Austrian pensioners received a letter from Vranitzky in which he explained the Social Democrats' position in guaranteeing pensions and promised not to allow any pension cuts, an economy measure that had been hinted at here and there by political opponents. This letter provoked a huge and very emotional discussion, and Vranitzky was subjected to fierce criticism. Time and again, it has been claimed that this letter decided the election in favor of the SPO. In actual fact, it simply fitted in well with the developments during the final weeks of the campaign and gave expression to a general mood.

The election result brought the SPO an increase of 4% of the votes, whereas the OVP and the FPO ended up with practically the same results as in 1994. Yet, in this election, many things happened that could not be explained by means of traditional international election campaign literature.

Conclusion

Today, we can regard as a fact that the Social Democrats consolidated their position as Austria's leading party on account of this election result. After his electoral victory, Vranitzky stayed in office for nearly a year before he handed over the federal chancellery to Viktor Klima, then minister of finance, who has been in that position since. The position of vice chancellor is held by Schüssel. Haider, head of the biggest opposition party, FPO, still plays his part.

So, on the whole, role allocation has not changed much. Since the 1995 elections, however, all parties have lost considerable interest in early elections, and positions and poll results have proved relatively stable.

What has increased dramatically, however, is the immediate use of political actions by the central figures who carry the messages. One press conference follows quickly after another, and interventions to get more appearances on prime time news programs, if only for seconds, have become more frequent.

In fact, this is a remarkable development given that the 1995 election campaign proved that political success is not necessarily connected with a constant presence in the media. This development in Austria, however, is not exceptional. As for successful social democrats such as Gerhard Schröder in Germany and Tony Blair (Labour Party) in Great Britain, exercising restraint was not exactly their top motto.

This might be a possibility of compensating for the loss of influence on the voters' everyday lives due to the priority of the economy, which is ever more accepted by politics. Politicians try to compensate for this deficit by struggling hard for presence in the media to keep the attention of their voters alive.

Politics, now facing different circumstances and acting in different fields as compared to only two or three decades ago, should increasingly internalize the laws of the entertainment business. In this regard, Austrian normalization after the extraordinary event of 1995 is no exception.

Reference

Institut für empirische Sozialforschung. (1995, October). [poll]. Vienna, Austria: Author.

31

The Impact of Dr. Joe's Strategic Positioning

A Case Study of a Successful Marketing-Based Election Campaign in Upper Austria

MICHAEL STRUGL
HANS LUGMAYR
KLAUS WEISSMANN

The election campaign of the Upper Austrian People's Party for the state Parliament in 1997 has mainly illustrated that positive campaigning based on a proactive issue and message strategy has led to success. Although the confidence in the establishment has been declining and the representative democracy is facing a crisis in legitimacy, new radical party extremist political movements with their populist leaders are rapidly rising. Those mentioned try to gain votes by simplistic and polarizing matters of explanations and argumentation. In this sociopolitical environment, the Upper Austrian People's Party succeeded in mobilizing the voters by positive messages and by changing the passively observing political consumers to active citizens. The People's Party achieved 42.7% of the votes and, therefore, was able to defend its leading position with its candidate governor, Dr. Josef Phüringer. The distance between him and the second strongest vote-getter not only was maintained but actually increased.

Upper Austria: A Dynamic Region in Central Europe

Upper Austria, the third largest state of Austria with 1.4 million inhabitants, has developed within the past decades from an agricultural to a highly industrialized region in Central Europe. From an economic point of view, Upper Austria underwent a deep crisis caused by the nationalized industry, which consequently included large losses of jobs and which had to be compensated in other economic branches.

Today, Upper Austria is a modern and prospering economic area, although the structure of society has changed dramatically. A mainly rural population has changed into one that has extended greatly into the urban areas. Nowadays, more than 40% of all inhabitants are living in cities and their suburbs.

Dramatic Changes in Voting Behavior

As a consequence, the voting behavior has changed seriously. Until the 1980s, the traditional party voters formed the majority. Nowadays, most of the voters are mobile and not directly linked with a specific party. The political order in Upper Austria is characterized by a multiparty system that is dominated by the People's Party. Since 1945, it has always recruited the governor. Similar to the second strongest party, the Social Democratic Party, the People's Party has suffered from losses. In the last election, the People's Party lost its absolute majority. Reasons for this can be found in the changed voting behavior and in the restructuring of Austria's political landscape during the 1990s. New political movements and parties have appeared on the political stage such as the Greens and the Liberals. In addition, the spectacular rise of the right-wing populist Freedom Party has had a dominant impact on the two traditional parties.

The Political System and the Significance of the 1997 Election for the People's Party

Upper Austria's Constitution provides that each political party that gains one mandate in one electoral district or gets more than 4% of the state vote is represented in the state Parliament (proportional representation). Based on a certain amount of the vote, each party is part of the government. The governor, who is the chairman of the government, is elected by the majority of the Parliament. Because of the conditions of the political system, the People's Party was facing its most important and difficult elections in its history. In the last elections, the People's Party had lost its absolute majority and now was competing with a new candidate. This time, the party was operating in a political framework with strong competition from 10 other parties running for representation (Figure 31.1).

The Starting Situation: An Unexpected Political Change in Upper Austria

Approximately 2½ years before Election Day, a decisive political earthquake surprised Upper Austria's political landscape. The longtime governor of Upper Austria and head of the government for 18 years, Josef Ratzenböck, resigned and passed his responsibility over to the next generation. More or less overnight, the

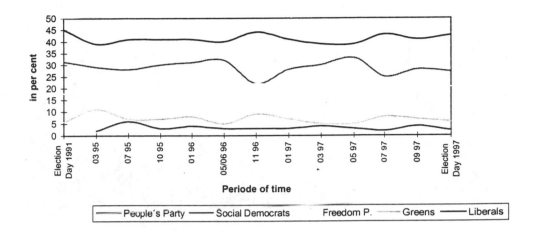

Figure 31.1. Parties' Preferences in Upper Austria

public was presented with a new face; a new governor appeared in the political spotlight. Neither the media nor the political insiders got directly involved in this process of position changing.

Simultaneous with the new governor taking over, an extensive reshuffling of the government took place. All conservative members of the government were exchanged, and those in the leading positions of the party's management were replaced as well.

Dr. Josef (Joe) Pühringer became governor and leader of the People's Party within 3 weeks. The well-organized management of the personnel policy and the fact that the public was excluded until the final act were signs of the well-structured internal party leadership. Apart from that, the party's image among the public was not to its manager's satisfaction. During this early stage of Püringer's governorship, the polls showed a 6% dropoff from the previous election result in which the People's Party had received 45.2% of the votes. The distance between the People's Party and the second leading vote-getter, the Social Democratic Party, was rapidly decreasing. It turned out that the People's Party had too few new and innovative answers to current affairs and problems of the country. The party suffered from a lack of political content, and former Governor Ratzenböck, while still popular, sometimes had not shown enough courage in his decision making.

The Political Atmosphere at the Point of the Change in Governor

For the public, the most important issues at the stage of the governor change were saving jobs (71%), battling crime (56%), fighting youth unemployment

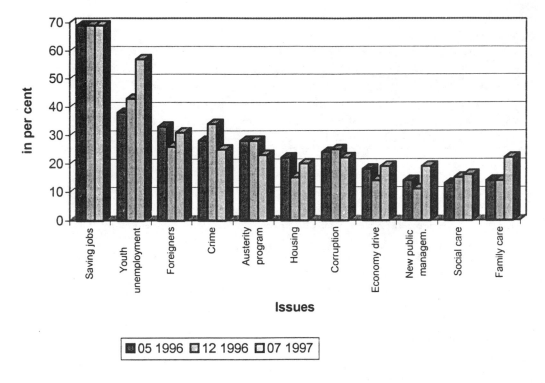

Figure 31.2. Dominant Campaign Issues

(51%), finding high-value housing (48%), fighting corruption (48%), and integrating foreigners (46%). Help for people who live in poverty also was demanded (43%). These issues needed the first priority for the new governor. As a consequence, the people's consciousness was deepened so far as the neccessity of finding a solution for unemployment was concerned (Figure 31.2).

Furthermore, the People's Party had lost its key credibility at this time, as well as its credibility in creating new jobs, because the standings in social and family questions were dominated by the Social Democrats. A decline in the People's Party's credibility in economic affairs also was obvious. One could recognize neither the party's profile nor its clear positioning. Moreover, this was underlined by a weakness of the People's Party on the national level, as the party had suffered losses in the national election of 1994. The Austrian nationwide atmosphere toward the People's Party in general had a rather negative effect on the Upper Austrian People's Party organization.

The new governor was criticized by his opponents from the very beginning. The Social Democrats and the Freedom Party immediately realized their chances of strengthening their positions in the political competition at the expense of the People's Party after the unexpected resignation of the popular former governor, Ratzenböck (Figure 31.3).

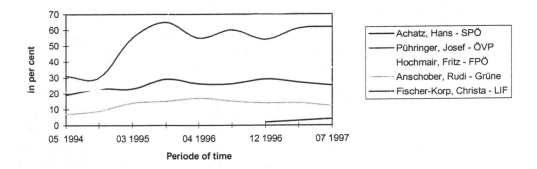

SPO   = Social Democrats
OVP   = People's Party
FPO   = Freedom Party
Grune = The Greens
LIF   = The Liberals

Figure 31.3. Sympathy Rates Toward the Candidates

The Introduction Campaign:
Action Rather Than Debate

The kickoff for the work of the team surrounding the new governor, Pühringer, was an exraordinary challenge because of the rapid change within the government that did not leave enough time to plan the beginning of the campaign. The start of the campaign was simultaneous with the development introducing the candidate himself. Although some of the organizational pre-work and a media-covered kickoff event were prepared, a general marketing concept for the candidate was missing.

The New Governor

Pühringer's predecessor, Ratzenböck, represented the classical type of a "father of the people." Most of the political observers had their doubts as to whether the new governor would succeed in obtaining political success and popularity. He had to avoid being viewed as a copy of his predecessor. The challenge was to stage Pühringer with his own personality and qualities. For this to be successful, the public had to be conditioned in its view of the new governor.

The campaign management succeeded in organizing the candidate's introduction campaign within a short period of time. In this very first step, the campaign focused on the extraordinary political qualifications of Pühringer that distinguished him from his predecessor. The positioning strategy was based on Pühringer's capacity for decision making that is characterized by his ability to address serious questions and offer solutions.

How an Emotional Issue Was Used to
Polarize the Country and to Position the New Governor

The construction of the hydroelectric power station in Lambach, a small town on the Danube River, had already been a long-term project of the Upper Austrian energy suppliers. Suddenly, the Lambach issue became a synonym for the quality of Pühringer's decision making. In the run-up to the 1997 election, the whole Lambach project was rejected not only by the other parties but also by the media and the environmental organization Global 2000. For the People's Party, however, Lambach became its political fate when Pühringer announced his affirmative vote for this project. In a first step, Lambach polarized the population's attitudes. In a second step, Pühringer established his clear supporting position, in contradiction to his opponents, which helped to reveal the voters' orientations. This clear position ended in massive support not only for the issue itself but also for the new governor.

An Excellent Start for the New Candidate

The party management agreed that the party's success was dependent on a highly profound acceptance of the candidate. Because of the ongoing party dealignment and the swing voters' orientation toward personalities rather than toward ideologies, it was necessary to match the person and the message. The interaction between Pühringer and the media became a decisive factor for the party's communications. The strong free media concentration on the candidate when he entered office directly affected his degree of fame, which increased from 79% to 85% during his first 8 months in office. At the end of the 9-month introduction campaign, 94% of all voters were familiar with Pühringer's name and positions.

Pühringer's degree of fame also correlated with his sympathy among the population. After becoming governor, his sympathy rate reached 55%, and at the end of the introduction campaign, that rate had increased by a further 10%.

The introduction campaign was based on advertising such as media ads, billboards, media impression management, and a motivation program for the party staff and volunteers. The decision for the hydroelectric power station in Lambach helped to establish Pühringer a strong issue profile. Just 6 months after assuming office, he had already reached the level of his predecessor.

The good functioning of the political marketing and the introduction campaign was due not only to the party's management but also to the candidate himself, who seemingly felt comfortable in his new position. Besides this upturn at the early beginning, it was necessary to strategically position the candidate with a lasting effect and to give the party a new content-oriented profile. With the support of an external consultant, an extensive study on political positioning was worked out based on detailed research in neighboring countries. The results were then tested on qualitative focus groups. Those focus groups also fulfilled the second function of a permanent link to the basis. They showed the rise, the fall, and the relevance of certain issues on the public agenda.

The Concept of Positioning

The introduction campaign and the clear positioning toward Lambach helped to establish the image of a person who polarized by showing a clear standing. This political strategy of depicting in black and white would not have led to a clear majority on Election Day because the electorate made other demands on the governor:

- As an ideal, the governor should be a person of integrity who has the ability to reconcile the different political ideologies and interest groups and, in so doing, to provide for social peace and prosperity. The stereotype of Pühringer, however, was diametrically opposed to this.
- The electorate wanted a governor whom it could show off, a strong person with a diplomatic character, a father figure who is accepted and appreciated by a great majority.

The concept of clear positioning could be justified so long as the introduction campaign was going on, but now his profile needed to include integrative and social components because these also correlated with Pühringer's temperament. Thus, he was willing to allow this additional positioning.

The Governor for Ordinary People

This additional repositioning of the governor also worked because the media supported this by showing him from his human side. The media strategy was based on personal talks and meetings with journalists during which the media could see the "real Pühringer," a person of integrity and social attitudes who sticks to a modest way of living, in other words, a governor for "ordinary" people (Figure 31.4).

The selection of media events was taken under consideration in the new positioning strategy. Instead of showing governmental presentations, pictures of Pühringer caring for the needs of fellow citizens were depicted.

Another Dimension:
The Situational Positioning Strategy

Apart from the personal positioning of the candidate, a second dimension that often is neglected in political advertising is as important as the first—the situational positioning. The personal positioning creates the candidate's image, which is evaluated in a positive sense correlating to the political position by the

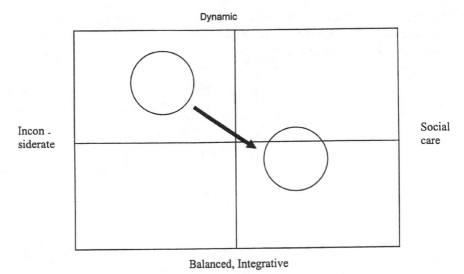

Figure 31.4. Change of Pühringer's Positioning

voters. Through this, the canidate's profile can be shaped, but this does not necessarily lead to the voters' support. Nevertheless, the voting behavior of swing voters mainly covers an apolitical dimension and follows a simple behavioral scheme: The crucial motivation for supporting a candidate correlates with the personal situation of the voters and how the voter experiences and evaluates his or her own reality.

If the mood of the majority regarding the situation of the country in general is positive, then the incumbent's chances of getting reelected are good as a guarantee for continuing in the present direction. If the voters feel uncomfortable with their situation and fear the future, and the political leaders are seen as being less effective, then the chances of the challenger increases under the condition of a strong profile and a clearly defined alternative.

Therefore, the incumbent has to undertake great efforts to present a positive picture of Upper Austria. That is why the public relations work was based on independent experts describing Upper Ausrtia as an example worth being imitated—as a country with the lowest unemployment rate and with a well-balanced budget (Figure 31.5).

Focus Groups: An Important Instrument for Navigating and Controlling

The traditional use of focus groups was supplemeted by presenting visuals. Pictures of different types of personalities were presented such as young and unconventional people, successful entrepreneurs, happy families, lonely elderly people, power women, and the like. The focus groups were then asked for their picture of an ideal governor. The task was to select a picture that correlated with

Positive prevailing situation, support for incumbent	Negative prevailing situation, support for incumbent
Me too: Political losing situation	Fundamentally based positions, ideologically located

Figure 31.5. Situational Positioning

Pühringer's desirable image. Applying this method supported a better understanding of the voters' impressions.

Conclusion of the Positioning Study

The positioning study concluded with the result that the People's Party could pattern itself after the Bavarian Christian Social Union (CSU). The CSU based its position strategy on a mixture between "high-tech and brass band," that is, a mixture among tradition, national sentiment, and pacemaker for a modern state policy. Therefore, the governor ideally should represent a combination of a traditionally anchored Upper Austrian person and a modern manager with special skills in moderation, mediation, and suggestion and with social competence (heart and understanding).

The Importance of Research and the Early Campaign Planning

In the spring of 1996, the management started to define and develop the campaign's concept for the 1997 autumn election. The campaign planning was based on the positioning strategy and a fundamental profound analysis of the political atmosphere in the country. In the spring of 1996, the public mood was strongly dominated by a fear of the future and pessimism in general. The reason lay in the austerity program of the national government, which had a deep impact on the economic situations of a large number of people. On the national level, the evaluation of the political representatives resulted in a negative atmosphere long before this negative public mood was spread among Upper Austria. It was mainly young voters (under 30 years of age), protest voters, and nonpartisan voters who were motivated in such a negative way.

International Campaign Research

The campaign management relied on international research that was based on the 1996 U.S. presidential election. Debates and discussions with consultants, fund-raisers, and political strategists from both sides of the political spectrum were included in the preparations for the forthcoming elections at home. The main findings that were later implemented in the Upper Austrian campaign were precisely documented:

- Media strategies, in particular intensified involvement in the use of regional and local media in the area of paid media activities
- Techniques for impression and event management and agenda setting for the statewide free media
- Professional productions of local events
- Effective use of telephone marketing
- Strategic planning of resources

Further information was gained by analyzing the election campaign of the Christian Democratic Union (CDU) in Germany's state elections of 1994; that campaign was addressed to the basic demands of the voters and successfully appealed to the national sentiment, the sense of community, the feeling of security, and the personal confidence in the candidate. Issue management and the correlation of the party's key credibility with the public agenda were the most important findings of this research. The basic elements of the CDU campaign, such as an introduction campaign, a separate campaign focusing on future opportunities, a campaign presenting the political achievements of the past, and an aggressive campaign strategy, were taken into consideration in establishing the Upper Austria campaign concept.

In both the United States and Germany, it turned out to be obvious that early planning of the campaign is a fundamental condition and that the constituency has to be well prepared for the election campaign. Although the final weeks of a campaign are the most important ones, during this late period only the strengthening of facts and special issues is possible. It is true that most of the voters come to their final decisions during the final 2 weeks before Election Day. It also is true that predispositions are formed long before that.

The Formative Influence of Professional Consultants

Because of the increasing importance of the media and professionalization in the world of political communication, it was necessary to use external consultants and their know-how. An extraordinary challenge was to combine and coordinate the experience of those consultants and to create an atmosphere of confidence and personal trust. The party's management was supported by an executive advisory board of pollsters, media consultants and journalists, advertising experts, and direct mail and telephone marketing agencies.

A carefully selected group of external consultants and the party's manager consequently met on a regular basis during the campaign in a type of "war room" where the main decisions were made during the campaign itself. The campaign manager, as head of the war room, was responsible for implementing and controlling the daily activities. Furthermore, it was his duty to make sure that the campaign was permanently focused on strategy and that the operative measures were strictly applied. A pollster fulfilled the special task of providing its database and in interpreting so as to control the communication's impact. One journalist played an important role by analyzing the party's media performance and the special events of the candidate.

One special feature was the careful selection of the campaign advertising agencies. Whereas the pollsters, the media, and the strategy consultants held a rather monopolistic position within the campaign team, a stong competition was found among the ad agencies. For the very first time, the party management decided to use several agencies. The leading agency was responsible for implementing the candidate's and party's performance and the campaign advertising strategy. A second agency was delegated to organize the grassroots campaign in the local units, the "get out the vote" activities, and the campaign addressing young voters. A third agency was entrusted with the free media planning and the public relations work. In addition, an agency was hired to lay out the advertisment in the newspapers, and a smaller one dealt with new media and the Internet.

This type of cooperation succeeded because of the high quality and high specialization of the consultants and the people involved; because of a wider potential of creative inputs, more flexibility, and broader resources; and because of a decisive knowledge transfer among all participants. Potential disadvantages included a higher amount of expenses, a higher effort in coordination, difficulties in the information transfer, and the risk of a split corporate performance. Retrospectively, one main conclusion can be drawn that only one agency would not have managed to launch this extensive election campaign.

The Campaign Strategy

The aims of the campaign strategy were based on three concepts:

- A fundamentally positive atmosphere in Upper Austria
- Positioning based on appropriate and credible issues
- Personalization focused on the new governor and his vision of the future

The People's Party combined its own strong issues with the main interests and concerns of the voters and mobilized its traditional voters to the same extent as its target groups and swing voters. The People's Party succeeded in dominating and driving their own issues and in distancing itself from matters beyond its competence and credibility with a strong focus on the state political affairs.

The whole campaign communication was focused on the governor's performance, whereas the other members of the state government played a special role in presenting their own competence and in communicating with their specially defined target groups.

The success of the People's Party can be explained with four essential factors, discussed in the following sections.

Presenting the Best Personnel Choice

The People's Party's candidate had the highest acceptance rate among the various candidates. Pühringer could maintain his leading position in the polls from the beginning on and was able to increase his popularity from 30% in September 1994 to 55% in March 1995, basically due to his position as governor. Subsequently, the introduction campaign was implemented and positioned the new governor as the leading person in the state. Pühringer raised his sympathy rate to 65% in October 1995.

The sympathy of the governor became the key motive for supporting the governor and his party on Election Day. Throughout the whole election campaign, Pühringer always had the capacity to keep his competitors from the Social Democrats and Freedom Party at a distance so far as the sympathy rate was concerned.

This success was based on the fact that Pühringer greatly enjoyed campaigning and had close contact with his constituency. Because the key factor in making a decision on Election Day was based on the personality of the candidates, the People's Party had the best chance to make the most of this constellation.

Polls showed that, apart from the candidate himself, the People's Party could offer the most attractive team for the government. The party had the most attractive mayors and local activists. Furthermore, the success of the People's Party also can be explained by the fact that it seemingly presented the best choices of personalities on all levels of political decision making in Upper Austria.

A Clear Issue Profile

The second decisive factor for the success on Election Day was the clear issue profile of the party. The party managed to harmonize its key credibility with the demands of the voters on the level of issue campaigning in the run-up.

Whereas the People's Party mainly showed competence in economic affairs and with a cutback in family issues, the strongest expectations of the constituency lay in the issue of maintaining and creating jobs. The People's Party had the ability to combine the issue of job growth with its competence in economic matters. The party presented the job issue, with all its various facets such as apprenticeship and education, as the most important aspect in defining Upper Austria's strong position as a value place for economy and investment. The key credibility of the party, therefore, correlated with the number one campaign issue.

The Social Democrats' access to this topic was different. They traditionally represent the working class as being able to rely on an expected credibility regarding the question of employment. Also in Upper Austria, they could hold this leading position. In October 1996, polls indicated that the Social Democrats had a leading position on this issue (40%) compared to the People's Party (34%). In the course of the campaign, the People's Party was able to gradually make up the difference, and in September 1997 the Social Democrats were for the first time overtaken by the People's Party on this issue. A similar situation could be observed so far as family issues were concerned. Raising the question of family issues, the Social Democrats had a weak leading position. From spring to summer, the People's Party was able to cause a turnaround in these proportions: The People's Party showed a competence rate of 35% compared to 32% for the Social Democratic Party. On this issue, however, the People's Party was faced with difficulties.

Although family matters could be counted in the People's Party key credibility and it was holding the minister for family affairs in Upper Austria, the party's strength was not crucial for the voters. Consequently, if the party wished to make up the difference in the family issue, then it would be necessary to create an atmosphere of consciousness and concern for accentuated policy in family questions among the voters.

A special campaign, first of all, communicated difficulties for families and the claim for more suppport for families. The campaign caused a stronger demand for intensified help for families. Therefore, a presentation of a statewide "family package" by the People's Party followed that was then strongly identified with the People's Party. The logic of decision making correlated with the logic of marketing tools. The family issue was not reduced to communicating with traditional voters or special targeted voters by the People's Party, but it represented the crucial factor for the whole area of social affairs. The Social Democrats, with their traditional social policies, were able to take the direct access to this issue, whereas the People's Party had to choose an indirect access starting with the family issue. Finally, the People's Party succeeded by doing so; it was not able to overtake the Social Democratic Party on the question of social affairs, but the distance could be narrowed. As mentioned previously, the People's Party could increase its competence in economic questions while the others, namely the Social Democrats and the Freedom Party, stagnated.

The different issue campaigns were an important element of the People's Party's election campaign, which aimed to sharpen the party's profile and to get differentiated in this political competition. One of the main goals was to ensure not to lose the broad spectrum of political contents; therefore, soft issues such as cultural and educational issues were not neglected. Finally, the People's Party was successful in getting rid of its image of being the party of retrenchment.

The Positive Prevailing Mood

The third winning factor for the People's Party was the fundamental change from a negatively dominated atmosphere to a mainly positive one as Election Day got closer. As the ruling party, the People's Party had to take strong efforts to create a positively dominated political atmosphere that favored the party's reelection. This turned out to be a great challenge because the starting situation was determined by the austerity budget savings of the Austrian government. In addition, the evaluation of the government strongly varied in Upper Austria. Whereas the nationwide government traditionally was judged in a critical sense, the state government got better ratings.

In early January 1997, the People's Party started the Upper Austrian campaign, meaning the part of the whole campaign presenting Upper Austria's outstanding position. The campaign was titled "Keeping Faith in Our Country—Creating Our Common Future" and was aimed at influencing the general mood of the constituency. By March 1997, the judging of Upper Austria government already was balanced (34% positive, 35% negative), whereas on the national level, pessimism in general still could be observed (27% positive, 47% negative). In July 1997, a turnaround in the public opinion in Upper Austria took place, as 38% of those polled said they thought government was going in the right direction in Upper Austria and 35% said it was going in the wrong direction. Shortly before Election Day in September, 58% of the electorate finally were convinced that Upper Austria had an efficient policymaking process. No doubt, this turnaround in the public polls concerning the basic public mood was the key reason for the success on Election Day in October.

The success of the Upper Austria campaign was mainly based on covering concete examples explaining the contrast between the Upper Austrian situation and the nationwide situation. Here, the balanced budget in Upper Austria can be mentioned. Thus, conveying politics by symbols was the decisive factor of the People's Party's performance in this election campaign.

The Implementation of the Campaign

The fourth winning factor for the People's Party was a professionally managed campaign that combined the traditional way of campaigning with modern elements. A powerful organization optimized the implementation of the campaign. The campaign consisted of a network of campaign concepts that resulted in synergy effects. The constituency should learn from the campaign that Upper Austria's situation—its standing and position—was outstanding compared to those of other regions in Europe. Furthermore, the constituency should learn that the People's Party, with its governor, would need all the confidence to continue the engagement for Upper Austria in the future as well.

The Upper Austria Campaign

The already mentioned Upper Austria campaign declared its goal to reduce the negative public mood in the state and to demonstrate the outstanding and powerful performance of Upper Austria. The basic economic figures such as unemployment rate, indebtedness, and economic growth, as well as other issues such as cultural benefits, pollution control, environmental policies, and medical care, were some selected parameters to demonstrate the outstanding position of Upper Austria. The constant repetition of this good news on all channels helped to distribute and communicate the main message. This campaign was presented not only by ads but also by strong free media activities and, therefore, was an extensive link to the general representation of the People's Party in this campaign.

Important Issues

The actual election campaign focused on four main issues: creation of jobs and a strong economy, family and social policies, education and the common future, and security. Every issue was implemented with a special campaign by using a balanced mixture of communication strategies in which all the key messages were constantly repeated. The campaign concepts were based on equal schemes.

In a first step, the campaign message, structure, and organization were presented to the party members and activists. Afterward, an effort was made to cover and drive the issue by the media. The media implementation was highly oriented to the different media formats, and the issues underwent an editorial prestructuring. In so doing, the party was able to dominate the political and media agendas. The ongoing public discussion was then supplemented by a special ad campaign that reinforced the campaign's message. Finally, the message was communicated and authentically interpreted on the grassroots level by mobilizing the party's staff and volunteers.

The Media Strategies

The People's Party followed two main directions with its media strategy. For the first time, a separate amount of the campaign budget was invested in regional small media activities. The consideration was a pragmatic one; the benefit was to communicate with a specially targeted audience on a regional basis by using a small part of the budget. Local free newspapers and cable television had high acceptance rates among the constituency; therefore, it was possible to optimize the media resources.

Apart from the media strategy for regional and local paid media communication channels, the party's management also tried to influence the editorial reporting through effective event management.

Furthermore, a separate series on the issue of "a common future" was organized with notable and considerable guest speakers from home and abroad. By involving these experts, the party was able to undergo an image transfer and to present credibility regarding the future. An important contribution was made by the "Forum for the Future," which developed a model for Upper Austria supported by interested people and experts and was then presented to the public. This model also was used for establishing a specific program for this election.

Proceeding from the perception that politics needed not only a convincing achievemet test but also a powerful vision of political shaping, the Forum for the Future strongly contributed to the development in Upper Austria with its prework, and this also favored the People's Party.

The Mobilization of the Campaign Basis and Grassroots

In January 1997, the campaign concept was presented to the campaign team and to local activists by the campaign manager in small motivation conferences. Both contents and form of this multimedia presentation conveyed high professionalism. This fact caused an early internal motivation effect among the campaign activists and volunteers, and it increased the party's capacity to launch the campaign. A further important part of communication was established through a campaign focused on debating and arguing, which helped to distribute the People's Party's messages in personal talks. This specially defined campaign titled "Politics From Person to Person" seized nearly all levels of the campaign organization. The governor and the members of the government emphasized personal contacts in their "afternoon meetings," just as the other delegates did in their deputy meetings.

A key goal of the campaign was to generate as many personal contacts as possible because the representatives and activists of the People's Party were superior to the competitors in directly contacting voters. A special network for all local activists that got continuous information via the Internet and "argument cards" (for campaign workers) had a strong effect throughout the state. The "Debate and Arguing Campaign" was one essential part of the communication strategies. This campaign also helped to prepare for continuous and rapid reaction to the competitors' actions.

Strategic Planning and Targeting of the Campaign Resources

In preparation for the strategic and operative planning of the campaign, a detailed statistical analysis of the previous election results was made. The election results of the 1995 national election and the 1991 state election revealed the potential of mobile voters, and this had to be strongly addressed by the People's Party. As a consequence, those local communities that would require the greatest effort were selected. Particularly in those areas, the main focus of the campaign was directed so far as issue campaigning and organizational grassroots work were concerned.

The Grassroots Strategy for Local Communities

The Debate and Arguing Campaign seamlessly developed into a mobilizing campaign in the final days of the campaign. An important dovetailing can be seen in combining the state campaign with the local community campaigns that were held on the same Election Day. The management of the People's Party made strong efforts to support the local campaigns and to involve the local activities in its own campaign. This organizational support of the state party had the effect of establishing a lead in the local competitions with other political parties. In so doing, the state party's and the governor's main messages were transferred to the regional and local campaigns.

A Special Teaser: Dr. Joe

The whole campaign was based on attracting no specially segmented target group except one—the youth segment. A separate campaign for young voters titled "Dr. Joe and the Future" had the goal of identifying and mobilizing young supporters and of "refreshing" the whole campaign. This campaign on the persona of Pühringer was based on the concept of a "teaser campaign" aimed at giving the party a younger image. The governor was depicted in a modern style by the use of young voters as a specially defined segment of the campaign. Retrospectively the concept succeeded in establishing "Dr. Joe" as a proper brand that still is used to describe Pühringer even today. In so doing, this new form of political communication was introduced and standardized in Upper Austria. Furthermore, specially targeted groups were contacted on the basis of a separate direct marketing plan with direct mailings and telephone activities.

Conclusions

Considering the findings of this marketing-oriented political campaign in Upper Austria, the following lessons were learned:

1. The incumbent will find himself or herself on the way to success only if he or she is aided by a positive prevailing mood among the public.

2. One cannot ignore the candidate's acceptance rate, meaning that the candidate must fulfill the public's projected standards for a candidate and must be accessible for his or her consultants.

3. The political issues that come up during a campaign must correspond to the demands of the constituency. The messages must be simple but not simplistic and must be presented in a highly credible way. Only then can confidence in the political representatives be generated.

4. One of the crucial winning factors can be defined by professional standards and by using proper and adequate measures for communicating with voters.

32

Democracy and Elections in the New East Central Europe

DANIEL ODESCALCHI

A drive through the countryside of either Hungary, Romania, Slovakia, or Bosnia-Herzegovina forces one to come to terms with the fact that in these countries during the 1990s, it still is common to witness a 40-year-old farmer walking across a field pulling an old plow with a steer. It is almost as if in many parts of these countries, the industrial revolution has not yet taken place. In many respects, society in these areas has changed very little during the past 50 years. When I arrived in Hungary to work for Prime Minister Jozsef Antall in 1992, most people still did not have telephones, and in rural areas, running water was being introduced to homes for the first time. By stark contrast, the dramatic end of communism has opened these countries up to the most modern campaign techniques available. The contrast between the old world and the new world was almost chilling. It was noticeable not only in the infrastructure of the country but also in the psyche of its people.

As a political consultant about to immerse myself in the emerging democracies of the region, there were lots of hurdles I was going to have to jump to make use of the techniques we take for granted in more modern democracies. The communications system, for example, was not conducive to modern campaigning. In many areas, telephones, faxes, and computers were missing from the standard arsenal that most political organizations naturally assume they have available when waging a campaign. Poor roads slowed down candidates running from one campaign appearance to another. I once was stuck behind a horse-drawn cart carrying hay for 45 minutes before the road widened enough for me to pass. For reasons such as these, unless one's political party had a strong organization in rural areas, one was severely limited in the ability to communicate with voters living outside of urban areas. The press often had its limitations as well, often carrying editorials as if they were hard news.

One of the greatest challenges facing a Western political consultant when entering the political fray of an emerging democracy is overcoming the psyche of the nation after 45 years of Communist rule. This psyche impregnated every aspect of society, from the intellectuals surrounding the prime minister to the blue-collar crowd surrounding the bus stops in working class neighborhoods. In each corner of society, the word "democracy" had many different definitions. I mention this because with the collapse of communism and the introduction of democracy, how people defined this new order affected their expectations of it. In Hungary, for example, the first democratically held election in 1990 was won by the party that best personified democracy and freedom. It was the Antall's party, the Hungarian Democracy Forum (MDF). The 1990 election was a clear rebuke of communism, with the breakaway "reform" Communists (now "Social-ists") receiving only 10% of the vote and the MDF-led government receiving 43%. The country was about to embark on a new life. An interesting observation at the time was the nation's fascination with its number one-rated television show, *Dallas,* about an opulently wealthy oil family from Texas. Those viewers who thought that this show represented democracy were bound to be disappointed, as many had become by 1992 as the MDF's popularity plummeted.

The voters' perception of what democratic life would be like obviously was important, but equally important was the perception of the newly elected demo-cratic politicians. This element is not as great a consideration in more mature democracies where politicians have a democratic tradition and history from which to draw. However, in the emerging democracies of Eastern Europe, this tradition did not exist, and the lack of this tradition resulted in a generation of political leaders with slightly skewed perceptions. These skewed preceptions had repercus-sions. All this had to be taken into account when assessing and learning the environment in which we were about to contest a series of elections.

In newly emerging democracies, there are certain distinct areas that need to be examined to clearly understand the environment in which elections were, and will be, contested. One obvious aspect to examine is the reality in which the voters perceive themselves. This is true in any democracy. In simple terms, a consultant needs to understand how the voters perceive their environment, the candidate, and the candidate's policies. Once this is understood, strategies must be developed that best communicate the specific benefits a candidate or party has to offer. These benefits should relate to the various problems that exist in the environment as the voters perceive them. The next area, which is unique to emerging democracies, is understanding the reality in which the newly elected politicians perceive themselves. The way in which they perceive democracy will effect the way in which they operate in a democracy. Then, of course, there are the deficiencies in the infrastructure to take into account. These areas are explored in more detail, as are the steps, or programs, that we developed to compensate for certain unique circumstances.

In the minds of the Hungarian voters, the MDF had successfully connected itself to the principles of democracy and freedom. As a matter of fact, people still associated the MDF with these principles 3 years later when the MDF became the most unpopular party among the six major parties. By September and October

1993, in a government-commissioned Gallup poll, respondents were asked whether they felt democracy was more representative of the new MDF-led government or of the former Communist-led government. Despite the party's low approval rating, 67% felt that the MDF-led government was more representative of democracy, compared to only 12% who felt that the former government was.[1] The same response was received when the word "democracy" was replaced with the word "freedom." But if people wanted democracy so much in 1990, then why was the MDF's popularity suffering so much in 1993? Was people's definition of democracy not living up to expectations? Other events taking place in the region also gave reason for concern. Just that year in Poland, Lithuania, and Estonia, the ruling parties comparable to the MDF could not even muster the 5% threshold to secure seats in Parliament. Like these parties, the MDF was about to contest its reelection campaign for a second term in office. As in these countries, polling data showed a strong shift in priorities away from values like democracy and more toward issues like unemployment.

This was understandable, and even in mature democracies, people's priorities shift during times of economic hardship. What was startling was the reaction that voters had to one of the pillars of democracy, the multiparty system. Hungary, prior to 1990, had a fairly orderly Parliament, or at least the citizenry was unaware of any bloodthirsty debates among its members of Parliament (MPs). This was mainly because there were no opposition MPs in Parliament. By 1992, parliamentary debates, an outgrowth of the multiparty system, were broadcast on national television and to focus groups. The response to these debates was a sense of disdain. Having never seen this before, people reacted by saying things such as "It's chaos," "The country is falling apart," and "The government has lost control." In the earlier mentioned Gallup poll, when respondents were asked which government was more representative of "order" and "discipline," 66% said that the former Communist government was more representative, compared to 11% who said the MDF-led government was. By this point, the trend showed that voters associated democracy with the lack of stability that engulfed their lives.

Many pundits blame economic conditions for the resurgence of the reform Communists (or Socialists). Although this no doubt was a major contributing factor, I think that it would be careless to leave it at that. The transformation from communism to democracy created an instability in the political, economic, and personal lives of people that they did not understand and for which they were not prepared. This led the Hungarian public to the conclusion that the present government was more or less to blame for the new "chaos." Interestingly enough, the prime minister of the former Communist government seemed to get exonerated from the blame (Gallup Hungary, 1993c). Under his leadership, the people had a sense of stability. For reasons to be discussed later, the MDF was unable to convince the electorate that it knew how to lead the nation out of the present crisis. In another poll 7 months before the May elections of 1994, when asked which party (out of the six major parties) had a program to lead the country out of this crisis, respondents placed the MDF last. By then, 87% of the respondents felt that the MDF-led government had no program to lead the nation. During this period, as the MDF was sinking in the polls, the Socialists were slowly gaining. Eventually, the Socialists would win by stating what conventional wisdom already implied. The Socialists' campaign slogan was simply "Expertise." It strengthened the negative impression that people had about the MDF and built on the perception that life was more reliable when the Socialists were in control of the previous Communist government.

Confidence in the present democratic structure in Hungary also was fading. Democracy encouraged debates in Parliament, and many voters felt that this was to the detriment of solving the country's problems. Many MPs found it difficult to explain the importance of democracy to those voters who found themselves disappointed with the results. One of the most vocal groups of voters were the pensioners, who also were the single largest voting bloc in the country. Opposition politicians had it easy because they could just criticize the government and leave the governing politicians to try to explain their policies. From this situation grew a natural distrust of both the governing MPs and the democratic process.

History undoubtedly had dealt the MDF-led government a difficult hand. Antall himself told members of his cabinet during the early days of the transition that they were part of a "kamikaze government." He knew well that the necessary steps toward democratizing the nation and liberalizing the economy were going to lead to hardships that the nation would find difficult to endure. However, the MDF-led government had problems other than its historic duty to change the direction of the country. The government also had different expectations of democracy that affected the way in which it approached governing. This was true not only in Hungary but in all the emerging democracies in which I worked. These politicians usually came out of the dissident movements that existed in their countries during the decades of communism. As dissidents, they had fought a secret war against communism that promoted democracy and freedom. But none of them had ever lived in a democracy or fully understood its intricacies. Their knowledge of democracy came primarily from books or the hearsay of those who traveled to the West. They understood that governments are voted in by popular vote. Once candidates won their elections, they went to Parliament and began drafting and voting on laws. In their minds, and justifiably so, they thought that if they did a good job, then they naturally would win reelection. It was in working with these dissident candidates that I would discover my greatest challenge.

Shortly after I arrived, I began interviewing various incumbent candidates. One of the first candidates I met was the parliamentary faction leader for the MDF. I asked him when he last visited his district. He scoffed as though I should have known the answer and said, "I was last there 2½ years ago during the elections." As it turned out, he never stayed in touch with his voters. I suddenly realized that, if this was indicative of the other candidates, the spiraling polling number should come as no surprise. When I explained the importance of communicating regularly with the voters to justify the necessity of certain initiatives and engaging them in regular dialogue, he became pale white. To my amazement, he asked, "I have to stoop to that level?" As I discovered, this attitude permeated every level of government, all the way up to the prime minister's office.

These politicians born from the dissident movements understood that they were voted into office by the public, but representing the public's interests was not as well understood. Their belief was that once they were in office, they were to make decisions on the public's behalf, so why go back to the district? This was not done maliciously. Antall truly believed that if he closed the doors to his office and made the right decisions, people would reelect him. Unfortunately, if politicians close their doors and the public does not see what they are doing, then the public assumes that they are doing nothing. The result was evident in a June 1993 Gallup poll revealing that only 15% felt that Antall was an effective prime minister and that 72% no longer trusted the government. Most politicians found it almost offensive when I encouraged them to meet and greet the public. Antall's handlers were totally against me subjecting him to this type of campaigning. In their eyes, it was below his stature to be seen with average people, and the public picked up on this.

This seemingly bizarre behavior of a candidate not greeting the electorate can, however, be explained. The only example these politicians had of how a politician should behave was that of the Communist politician. Under communism, it was not the court of public opinion that helped govern a nation; rather, it was fear of the police. The Communist MPs never were out "pressing the flesh" with their constituency; it was not necessary. In an effort to show that communism was for the working person, the only person to publicly do anything of the sort was the Communist prime minister. Every time we tried to encourage Antall to do anything that had to do with greeting the public, his handlers claimed that people would recall their former Communist leaders from the past. At times, it seemed as though I could not win. I often heard that the Western campaign techniques that I advocated were not meant for the region. One of the MDF vice presidents put it to me very succinctly: "These techniques may work on the ignorant American public, but Hungarians are too sophisticated to be massaged for support."

In short, I was faced with a number of disturbing elements. The electorate was losing faith in the transition to democracy and the leaders associated with it. The policies that would help articulate a solution to the transitional problems were not in the national dialogue. The political leaders did not understand the need to campaign using various techniques and messages. To top off this list, there was the lack of infrastructure that I was used to. This last point, however, was the least of my problems. My greatest problem was encouraging the politicians themselves to take action.

Although this behavior was not symptomatic of all the politicians, it did apply to most, especially the party leaders who were older and more ingrained in their past. One tactic I used to try to motivate them into action was to scare them with polling results. Of all the six major parties, the MDF ranked last when respondents were asked which party was concentrating on raising the standard of living for the average person. The MDF also ranked last when respondents were asked which party had a plan to lead the country out of its crisis situation. The majority of the respondents could not name one success that they felt the government could attribute to itself (Gallup Hungary, 1993d). The closer the Election Day came, the more support grew for the Socialist Party. It was the Socialists who attracted the most disgruntled voters, and among the Socialist sympathizers were the largest number of people who felt that the transition was not even necessary. But despite the results, the MDF leadership remained unpersuaded. As it turned out, polling was a science they did not believe to be accurate. Worse, they felt that all of the polling companies were manipulated by the opposition liberal parties. The chairman of the party once explained to me that the polls were manipulated to misguide me in the advice I was giving. I was faced with a party whose members refused to believe what the polling results showed. Thus, the way in which they perceived their environment was much different from the way in which the electorate perceived it. This led to some grave errors in the party's judgment and strategy.

One such dilemma surrounded a newspaper advertisement the party chairman had created. It was an advertisement thanking foreign companies for having confidence in the MDF and for moving their businesses to Hungary. In the ad, the party listed numerous foreign corporations. In a vain attempt, I explained to the MDF chairman that the electorate had a real problem with privatization; the electorate felt that foreigners were coming in and buying up—and, in some cases, "stealing"—the industrial resources of the country. Many felt that Hungary was an economic pawn to the West. What this ad did was strengthen the MDF's perceived negatives as well as the charges that the opposition was claiming. I even reminded the party chairman that the Liberal Democratic Congress in Poland, which was in charge of privatization, was one of the parties that never reached the 5% threshold to get back into Parliament. I was told that I did not understand the soul of the average Hungarian. The ad ran. The MDF had wounded itself.

There were, however, many candidates in the MDF who wanted to try running "modern" campaigns. Because the party had no real campaign headquarters to assist these candidates, I was able to convince the leadership to open an office called the Constituency Relations office. The sole purpose was to train staff and candidates on how to reach out to the electorate, whom they should reach out to, and how to develop messages that will help them to connect with the voters. Because the MDF as a party was so unpopular and the leadership seemed too gridlocked to make any strategic decisions, we decided to concentrate extra resources on the campaigns of the individual candidates.

Most candidates never imagined running campaigns for themselves. I often heard the argument that people did not vote for candidates, they voted for parties instead. There was some legitimacy to this argument because the way in which voting was structured, voters voted for a national party list. But they also voted for individual candidates in their respective districts, where, if we could do well, we could garner support and win seats. This also gave us a chance to dodge the national media, to do a guerilla warfare-style campaign and try to soften the image of the party. Most candidates, and voters for that matter, never had seen a candidate campaign in the district before. It was a very foreign concept to them, with a foreigner advocating it. Also, because none of the candidates believed the polling results, no one believed how unpopular they were or that the voters in their districts did not even know their MPs' names. Most never had dealt with the press, they avoided contact with the voters, and they had no idea what to say to either. The responsibility of the Constituency Relations office would be to overcome these hurdles with as much speed as possible.

First of all, there needed to be a mechanism by which I could get the candidates' perceptions of the environment more in line with those of the voters. We needed to make sure that we were contesting this election on the same plain. Two factors made it difficult for me to use Gallup or another polling organization for research to help the candidates in their districts. The first was that most candidates did not trust the polls, and the second was that the party could not afford to do polling in each district. The only solution was to begin polling with the help of party members, knowing in advance that its accuracy could be questionable. Through the Constituency Relations office, we organized and trained a volunteer army that could, each month, ask a minimum of 300 voters in each of the 176 districts five simple questions. The questionnaire served a number of purposes. The first question asked that the respondents name their districts' MPs. In most districts, of course, people could not do this, which immediately humbled most candidates. The danger here lay in the fact that if voters are unfamiliar with a candidate, then they will vote strictly according to party. If a candidate's party is unpopular, then by association, so is the candidate. The second question asked the respondents whether they knew anything that the candidates had done. Often, the response was "He didn't do anything." This gave me a chance to explain to the candidates the importance of always briefing the press and speaking to groups in their districts. The third question asked the respondents to list the concerns to which they felt the candidates should turn their attention. This helped the candidates to create the dialogue necessary to allow them to develop a connection with the voters. The final two questions of the questionnaire dealt with local issues.

Due to the poor infrastructure and lack of telephones in many areas, volunteers would approach voters in the marketplace or at busy bus and train terminals. Because we had less than a year until the elections, it was necessary that everything we did was designed to be as effective as possible. In an effort to build the trust that every candidate wanted to enjoy with the voters, the volunteers would hand out pre-signed "thank you" letters to all those who responded to the questionnaire. This letter read,

> I want to thank you for answering these questions. In the last year, I've spoken to many citizens, but to speak with everyone is simply impossible. This is why I've chosen the method of using questionnaires. I am asking these questions because I need to know your opinion in order to do my job well. If I understand your problems and expectations, then I can represent you better, and after all, this is my job. So that I may represent you to the best of my abilities, please write me with any additional thoughts you may have.
>
> I gladly await your letters. Write so that I can help!

The response to this surprised even me. It seemed as though people were starved for this type of attention and dialogue. Remember, this was new not only to the candidates but to the voters as well. We first started asking people to respond to the questionnaire and handing out the thank you letters in a district on the outskirts of Budapest for an MP by the name of Laszlo Dobos. Practically half of those who received the thank you letter that first weekend responded by writing him a letter. Some wrote comments such as "I've been disappointed by your party, but since I received this letter from you with your kind words, I will turn to you after all." Unfortunately, not everywhere was the response this good, but it was an opportunity to begin breaking through the perception barrier.

Once candidates who started working with the Constituency Relations office saw the results of their district polls, they quickly began looking for ways in which to promote themselves. They were shocked by how few of the people in their districts were familiar with them and that most people had no idea of their accomplishments. Because candidates had no idea where to start, we next needed to create mechanisms through which the candidates could promote themselves. We created a three-step outreach program.

First, candidates would be able to turn to the Constituency Relations office, where one of our staffers would help them design newsletters. Usually, the topics discussed in the newsletters were the same topics that voters offered in the district polls when asked on which concerns they would encourage the candidates to focus. Each candidate could do a monthly newsletter that would be distributed to most households in the district.

Second, we developed a press relations operation to assist the candidates with writing press releases, organizing press conferences, and developing themes. Traditionally, MPs never had to deal with the press, and many were dismayed that the press naturally did not cover their accomplishments. When we began this process, I visited an MP in his district located about 3 hours southwest of Budapest. He detailed how he had done many wonderful things to help the community and the country, yet the local newspapers never covered them. As if he were purposefully trying to contradict himself, he began waving full-page articles in front of me. The articles were written about him and even contained huge pictures of his smiling face. When I called his attention to the contradictory nature of his actions, he paused in dismay and said, "Dan, you don't understand. I had to go down to the publisher's office and tell him what I was doing." The Constituency Relations office made it so easy that a candidate simply had to call our office, and we would help the candidate brainstorm ideas. Then our staff would actually write the press release. We would create charts and graphs for press conferences and help research facts. We also would write sample press releases about national policy issues that each candidate could modify and distribute to the local and regional press. This helped to elevate the candidates' status in their districts and also helped to promote the MDF's national agenda throughout the country.

The third step consisted of developing personal outreach tools for the candidates so that they could meet with constituents and speak articulately about their concerns. Our office developed packages targeting various groups within each district. For example, we created packages aimed at pensioners, farmers, entrepreneurs, environmentalists, and teacher groups. Each package contained brief but vital demographic and policy information including charts, graphs, and interesting facts supporting the government's position. Most packages included a specialized questionnaire that the candidates could hand out at the beginning of the meetings and collect at the end. For attending the meetings, the voters also received personalized thank you letters from the candidates in the mail. Sample thank you letters also were included in the candidates' packages. By using this package, an MP who was a specialist in defense policy and knew nothing about the government's position on pensioners could sound articulate and concerned when meeting a group of pensioners. Each step of the way, we encouraged candidates to begin building a database of names.

From a tactical and logistical aspect, the Constituency Relations office became very important. We became a center on which local operations relied. There were many offices around the country without telephones, fax machines, or computers. For these outposts, we acted as a surrogate office, typing and faxing as well as consulting. We filled an important void that would help to catapult these offices into the 21st century. We also acted as mentors to candidates, party volunteers, and workers who were looking for guidance and assurance.

The Constituency Relations office also helped candidates and their workers to develop themes for their campaigns. Most candidates relied 100% on party money to pay for their campaigns, so it was a mistake to think or expect that all of the candidates would have their own consultants. The Constituency Relations office acted as 176 individual consultants.

Through this office, we developed ways in which candidates and their workers could begin developing good relationships with their constituents. Although this part of the campaign did not result in victory, it did show the fruits of our labor. The most unpopular member in the MDF was the privatization minister, Tamas Szabo. Most people thought that he was corrupt and untrustworthy because he sold Hungary's industries to foreigners. Yet, in his own district, he faired well and received more votes than the MDF did as a party. Aside from promoting the candidate, each element of the Constituency Relations office served a second purpose. Each element attempted to build the credibility of the democratic process and that of a representative government. The thank you letters people received during our district polling helped to explain why polling was important in a democracy. They also helped to strengthen the notion that politicians were there to help the voters. The fact that people could contact their representatives helped to strengthen the concept that they could influence their government. In essence, through the candidates, we tried to create a guerilla warfare-style campaign for the principles of democracy. On the national level, this became much harder to do for a variety of reasons, the main one being the lack of cooperation from MDF party leaders.

Nationally, we continued using Gallup, and I continued attempting to frighten the party leadership into action. In all the emerging democracies where I worked with politicians that blossomed out of the dissident movements, one element was constant. The issues they promoted usually were inconsistent with those with which the electorate was concerned. For example, the MDF leadership felt very strongly about the Hungarian minorities in neighboring countries. They saw the leaders of these minority organizations as fellow dissidents fighting for a greater cause. The MDF also expended incredible energy promoting Hungarian patriotism. The party leaders thought like dissidents and saw the world through dissident eyes. The way in which they perceived reality was very different from the way in which the average voter saw reality. To the dissident, issues of patriotism and Hungarian minorities living in neighboring countries were of major importance. Yet, to the average voter, issues of survival, unemployment, and inflation were most important. A September 1993 poll showed that employment and inflation were among the top three pressing problems for 77% of the population, whereas the Hungarian minority issue was among the top three for only 1% (Gallup Hungary, 1993b). The less mature the democratic system, the less the candidates seemed to focus on policy initiatives such as taxes, defense, and education.

In Bosnia, things were not much different. I had worked there with a coalition trying to promote multiethnicity as it campaigned against the strong nationalist parties. It was the first election since the end of the war. The electorate showed signs of war fatigue but continued to vote for the nationalist parties. Each ethnic group hoped that, in this way, it was ensured jobs for at least its people. The multiethnic parties did little to promote the idea of prosperity at the time and instead focused on multiethnicity. Unfortunately, Bosnian citizens of all ethnic backgrounds were more concerned with unemployment than with multiethnicity. For example, in January 1997, 59% of Bosnian Serbs felt that unemployment was the most urgent problem facing the country, whereas only 2% felt that political/ democratic reform was the most urgent.[2] After we shared polling results with the candidates, they were so torn between the concrete message that I advised about creating jobs and the plain message of multiethnicity that they missed their deadline to produce television commercials and nothing aired.

I met with the president of the Bosnian Republican Party as he prepared for the upcoming election. Earlier in his career, he had been the president of the leading Nationalist Croatian party. After the Bosnian war, the people was consumed with unemployment and rebuilding their lives, yet he continually spoke of democracy and freedom. Despite the recent poll, he claimed that he knew best what was right for the people. In an attempt to make a point, I asked him whether he was sure he understood the problems better then the single mother who comes home to three starving children each night. His response was "Of course, the only people left in Sarajevo are illiterates." It is difficult to engage a candidate with this mentality in developing a message necessary for a modern campaign that must show compassion and sensitivity.

Issues, as we know, are not the only aspect of a campaign. It is no secret that a good leading candidate can turn around the image of an entire party. One must look no further than Britain to see what Tony Blair has done for the Labour Party or to America to see what Bill Clinton has done for the Democratic Party. Upon arriving in Hungary, I was greeted by a prime minister who was severely ill with cancer. Instead of campaigning, he was receiving radiation therapy or was in Germany undergoing high-risk bone marrow transplants. This posed a bit of a problem. We had a campaign with no real full-time candidate, and even when we had a part-time candidate, his handlers blocked his participation. Regrettably, however, Antall passed away 3 months prior to the election. He was replaced by Peter Boross, the former minister of the interior, whose first words to me were

"You do your campaign, but leave me out of it." I still was left without a candidate for the nation's most important office.

One universal attitude in these countries was the electorate's desire for a strong-handed leader. The people wanted someone to take charge, to take control. Listening to phrases such as "It's chaos," "The country's falling apart," and the "Government has lost control" as the public's reactions toward certain democratic norms, it should come as no surprise that most Hungarians wanted an assertive, self-assured, and "hardened leader" (Gallup Hungary, 1993a). It was a natural reaction to expect given that prior to this chaos, they had years of iron-fisted rule. In Romania, while I was there to work with members of the Democratic Coalition, 88% of respondents believed that they needed specifically "authoritative" political leadership (FBIS-EEU, 1994). The new democratic leaders, however, spoke only of the necessity of democratic values. Although this was admirable, they came across as weak and out of touch. It seemed that the more democratic and polite a leader was, the more useless the public thought him to be. When Hungary's new prime minister, Boross, forbade the NATO planes to do bombing runs over Bosnia from Hungarian airspace, the international community was aghast, but his popularity jumped among the Hungarian public. To these people, he showed resolve and leadership qualities.

There also was a laissez-faire attitude among the politicians in the region. The old saying that a good plan today is worth more than a great plan tomorrow was not well received. The intensity of modern campaigning has yet to find its way into the blood of the region's candidates. I have sat through many meetings in which decisions never were made. In Hungary, the MDF never agreed on a campaign strategy; the campaign came to an end before a strategy was decided on. In Bosnia, television ads never got produced because no one could make a decision in time; the deadline passed, and nothing aired.

At the time that Boross's popularity rose because of his NATO decision, I was able to convince the leadership to use him actively in the campaign. It was already only 2 or 3 months before the elections, but Boross's popularity was double that of the MDF and only within 1 or 2 percentage points of the Socialist candidate for prime minister. We were pitching a campaign around the slogan "Sure steps—Secure future" in which we could insert different steps that the MDF or Boross would take and the expected results. We planned to highlight jobs, an increased standard of living, and lower inflation. Due to disagreements within the leadership, the plan never progressed, and the outcome was disastrous. We were left with huge billboards around the country with "Sure steps—Secure future" written across the top and a picture of Boross to the left. To the right was a picture of a boy writing graffiti that said, "We've grown a lot in 4 years." It was meant to imply that the country had grown a lot in 4 years, but the public took it to mean that the MDF had grown a lot. Gallup's data showed that voters' perception of the MDF was that the leaders were not well prepared and did not really know what they were doing. Our billboards actually strengthened this perception.

Making matters even worse was that citizens took to painting their own graffiti on our billboards. Next to the line "We've grown a lot in 4 years," citizens would write "Yes, taxes and unemployment!" It just so happened that 5 months before the election, in an open-ended Gallup poll, when respondents were asked what they believed the MDF-led government had accomplished, there was a strong undercurrent of sarcasm among the responses. Many people claimed that the MDF was successful at both raising taxes and increasing unemployment.

The billboards actually did more harm than good. It strengthened our negatives and created the perception that the MDF was admitting that it was unprepared to govern and was playfully saying that it had come a long way in the past 4 years. Meanwhile, the Socialists also had a billboard that strengthened our negatives and at the same time strengthened their positives. It had a picture of Gyula Horn, their prime ministerial candidate, and said only one word: "Expertise."

Because the MDF leadership's only experience came from its 1990 election when poetic slogans for democracy and an end to communism sent a powerful message, the party leaders were constantly trying to recreate that campaign. It was a knee-jerk reaction. One of the posters in 1990 was a picture of many of communism's memorabilia stuffed into a garbage can with "It's time for spring cleaning" written across the top. In 1990, issues were not important, but by 1994, people wanted to know what the MDF was going to do to improve their lives. As an attempt at a poetic gesture in 1994, the MDF leadership sent out 1 million packets of flower seeds as a random direct mail piece. The piece created no reason for people to consider voting for the MDF. It had only a picture of the MDF emblem and "a flowering future" written across the top. It would have been a nice gesture to give them to volunteers, but it was a big waste of money to randomly mail them out to the opposition's supporters.

The 1990 election was a euphoric period in history when the Communist structure that had governed the country had collapsed. The opposite of communism was democracy, and the MDF, with a loosely run campaign embracing democracy and freedom as well as rejecting communism, scored a magnificent win. To the MDF, this was a recipe for a successful campaign. The only problem was that times had changed, people's needs had changed, and the MDF's recipe for success no longer was appealing. The polls showed this, but one would have to believe the polls to learn from them. This was not specific to Hungary alone; in Bosnia and Romania, I encountered the same predicament.

The freedom of the press was one element of democracy that the dissident politicians knew was important if freedom and democracy were to remain. Despite their firm commitment to this principle, however, the novelty quickly wore off when the press launched attacks on them. As in all democracies, political parties have their favorite and least favorite press organizations. This was true in Hungary as well, but a fundamental difference was that in emerging democracies, both the press and the politicians were a bit uncertain of how to handle these newly found freedoms. One of the first official press conferences I attended for the prime minister's office was held by his chief of staff. Among the reporters present was a gentleman from a newspaper that recently had written an unflattering piece about the prime minister. When this reporter asked a question, the prime minister's chief of staff reprimanded him in front of everyone and told him that so long as his newspaper published articles like the recent one he had written, the newspaper should never expect an interview with the prime minister. In effect, he was punishing the newspaper.

The press also seemed to have a rough start once it became free. When I first arrived in the region, it was not uncommon to read a journalist's opinion written as a news story. Journalism centers quickly sprang up to educate journalists, and we began a series of workshops to educate politicians. As we entered the 1998 election cycle, this whole issue was normalizing.

The psyche of the electorate and the candidates always will prove to be the biggest impediment to modern electoral campaigns in emerging democracies. In Hungary, I would like to believe, the psyche of the electorate could have been overcome, but only if we, as consultants, would have had the full cooperation of the candidates. So long as candidates do not believe in polls and avoid the electorate, cooperation will be impossible. Older candidates in Slovakia, Bosnia, and Romania also resisted much of the campaigning style that we in the West have come to take for granted. Younger candidates are far more prone to embrace them. Younger candidates also are more open to discussing the uncomfortable issues of the transition process. During the early period of an emerging democracy, the job of a consultant is to become an election professor and hope that the pupils have an accelerated learning curve because, as we know, elections do not wait until everyone is ready.

In just about every country in which I worked, the party leadership was in a bit of disarray. In retrospect, this is not surprising. History thrust these politicians into an unexpected situation in which they had to focus on governing, message developing, party building, and (the most distracting of all political elements) fighting the daily partisan battles. This was one of the reasons why we placed such a great emphasis on creating a structure in which the individual candidate campaigns would support the party campaign instead of vice versa. As I stated earlier, due to the severe unpopularity of the MDF and the leadership's inability to adapt, we saw the individual candidate campaigns as a way in which to break down the wall that voters erected between themselves and the party. Also, because these campaigns were more sovereign, and hence more controllable, we were able to campaign in ways in which the party refused to campaign.

There were two problems with this plan. The first was that the state and maturity of Hungary's democratic evolution was not entirely up to the level of Western democracies. Although at the time the approach of the candidate campaigns supporting the party campaign did result in limited success, in a decade or so, it will have the same effect it would have in a Western democracy. Many voters, after emerging from 40 years of Communist rule, still thought more in terms of parties than in terms of candidates. In mature democracies, we are seeing a trend away from party loyalty and of more voters classifying themselves as being independent. The second problem stemmed from the unfortunate late start of the Constituency Relations office and the fact that only a fraction of the candidates took part in the program. Still, because of the effort of these candidates and the image they helped to create in various regions around the country, the MDF was successful in avoiding the same fate as their cousins in Lithuania, Estonia, and

Poland. After all the dust settled, the MDF was left standing. It did not win reelection, but it remained in Parliament as the largest opposition party.

All the elements that make up a successful campaign were at different levels of maturity in Eastern Europe. Strategies, mechanics, and logistics must work in concert with one another if a campaign is to be successful. Just like a symphony, each section relies on the other to complete a masterpiece. The mere fact that strategies from the MDF central campaign headquarters could not be approved put our campaign at a severe disadvantage. But even when strategies were implemented at the regional level, certain logistical realities, such as the lack of telephones and computers, created obstacles. In these new democracies, voter lists were not available, which made direct mail and phone banking operations suffer.

In stark contrast to the Eastern European phenomenon, for example, I returned to the United States afterward to join a group of consultants to help Steve Forbes, the billionaire entrepreneur, contest the Republican presidential primaries in 1996. In this campaign, there was no room for error because Forbes, who was a political novice, was virtually unknown to the voting public when we began. This meant that we had only 5 months to create a campaign in which he could compete against candidates who had prepared for this opportunity for decades. When I joined the campaign in September, Forbes was at 5% in the Gallup polls. By February 11, he was in a dead heat with the front-runner, Senator Bob Dole, at 25% (Gallup, 1996, pp. 18-22). Although Dole eventually would win the primary and go on to contest Clinton in the general election, it was a great feat for a political novice to become such a formidable challenger to a senator who had spent his entire adult life in public service. This feat was accomplished only through the careful coordination of strategy, logistics, and mechanics.

Strategy is the most basic element in political consulting because it lays the groundwork to how the other elements of a campaign will be employed. Strategy itself has two components: the message and the implementation. The strategy behind Forbes's message was to keep it simple because, within the short period of time allotted, we could not inundate the voters with many issues. One of Forbes's issues was a flat tax, and for the next few months, we built our campaign solely on that one issue. This might seem simplistic to some, but it was a sure way in which to guarantee that in the time the campaign had to establish itself, we could give Forbes an identity and positive name recognition. The fact that no one likes to pay taxes and that the flat tax appeared to be simpler and fairer made it attractive to the public. So attractive did it become through a series of television ads that by January 7, 51% of the voters felt that the flat tax would be better for the country than the existing tax code (Gallup, 1996, pp. 15-16).

Having the strategy of message decided on, the next step was to devise a strategy for implementation. We wanted to take our opponents by surprise, like a blitzkrieg—hit hard and hit quick. In the beginning, our main weapon was the 30-second television commercial. Millions of dollars were spent in states that played a key role in the primary process. Soon, the concept of a flat tax and its advocate, Forbes, were being talked about on all the national political talk shows. By the final week of January 1996, both *Time* and *Newsweek* had Forbes on the cover, and he was running neck and neck with Dole. As we flew into Iowa for the caucuses, I remember thinking that Forbes really stood a good chance of winning.

We would go on to lose both Iowa and New Hampshire because we were not fully prepared. The television medium alone was not going to be enough; it never is. But we won both Delaware and Arizona when we took full advantage of our polling and phone bank operations. In the United States, there is no such thing as "campaign silence" on Election Day. The extent of our silence is that within the vicinity of the buildings where people vote, one cannot campaign. This allowed us to continue our "get out the vote" operations right through to the last moment that people could vote. In Arizona and Delaware, we kept polling and phoning supporters to remind them to vote on Election Day. Through our last-minute polling, we were able to create a profile of those who were most likely to be Forbes supporters. Then, we ran the profile against our database of voters in both states and directed the phone banking operation to call only those who met the profile. As we continued this throughout the day, we saw our vote increase by nearly 1 full percentage point each hour. By the time the polls closed, Forbes had inched his way to victory in both states.

In Eastern Europe, this type of operation still was impossible during most of the campaigns in which I took part. Although Gallup's polling results proved to be quite reliable in Hungary, we still had the problem of communicating with the voters. The only way in which to strategically communicate with the voters was through the media. Target marketing to certain demographic groups through the use of direct mail, one of the most successful tools in the United States, was not feasible in Eastern Europe due to the lack of developed lists. Where in the United States the parties have in-house lists that they also make available to individual candidates, in this region these lists did not exist or were not made available. This, thankfully, is slowly changing.

Is there a future for political consultants in the region? Absolutely. However, there are some pitfalls. Western consultants often will be faced with defending their advice against the wicked complaint that, as foreigners, they cannot fully understand the voters of a particular country. This can be especially frustrating when the polls clearly indicate attitudes that the client flatly refuses to believe. There are certain universal problems in consulting that are magnified in this region. As mentioned previously, candidates in emerging democracies lack the historical tradition from where to draw their experiences. This will lead to temporary misunderstandings among the candidates, the electorate, and the consultants that will last until their democratic traditions develop. As emerging democracies mature, many of these problems will disappear.

Cost is another factor. Unless the candidate is leading the party ticket, relatively few candidates can afford to pay the cost of a Western consultant. MPs in Eastern Europe will have only a fraction of the capital available to congresspeople in the United States, much less senators. Their fund-raising opportunities are much more limited, and the sizes of their constituencies are smaller as well. They rely mostly on state funds to campaign. Fund-raising, the way it is done in the United States, still is a long way off. Once again, in their tradition and experience, candidates never asked for money. The concept is very foreign to them. We had some fund-raising successes where it was tried, but few candidates were willing to participate. As I helped certain candidates 4 years later, this process was slowly beginning to evolve as well.

Following the 1994 elections in Hungary, with the help of certain international pro-democracy foundations, I started a program called "Survival in a Democracy." This project was aimed at assisting the younger politicians in the new opposition parties to gain access to polling data and helping them to develop effective campaign strategies. Gallup was commissioned to periodically provide polling data, which was distributed and analyzed at conferences held for the members of these opposition parties. Foreign campaign experts and pollsters who worked with parties of similar ideology also were invited to speak.

Due to this and other efforts, great changes began taking place in the political landscape during the years following the 1994 election. Voter apathy still remained high, and most politicians continued their intellectual ramblings. However, by April 1998, the party of 35-year-old Viktor Orban found itself neck and neck with the Socialists (Batthyany Foundation, 1998). His party, the Federation of Young Democrats (FIDESZ), had taken a very active role in the Survival in a Democracy program. His party also was the only one to clearly promote concrete issues such as tax relief, faster economic growth to cut the jobless rate, a return to free university tuition, and crime reduction as its campaign message.

Despite the gains that FIDESZ made among decided voters, Gallup still showed that 45% of the electorate was undecided. That posed a danger because if only the party loyalists turned out for the elections on May 11, 1998, then it would help parties such as the Socialists and various fringe fanatical groups. On the day of the first round of elections (Hungary has a two-round election process), exit polls began painting a picture of what was to come. Among the five parties to exceed the 5% parliamentary threshold and move on to contest one another in the second round, the Socialists were in the lead with FIDESZ only a few percentage points behind. But voter turnout was the lowest since the end of communism, which also allowed a right-wing radical party, the Hungarian Truth and Life Party, to reach the 5% threshold for the first time. The apathy in the eastern part of the country, which did not enjoy the prosperity that the western part had experienced, caused voter turnout to be so low that the election results were pronounced null and void and would have to be recontested during the second round.

During the campaign, FIDESZ provided an optimistic and positive image of the future. By contrast, the governing parties used slogans such as "Keep the right direction" that gave apathetic voters no reason to get interested in the election. Another slogan the governing parties used was "Pay for one, get three," which played on the fear that if FIDESZ were to win, it would form a coalition with the right-wing extremist parties. During the 2 weeks between the two rounds of the election, the two prime ministerial candidates, FIDESZ's Orban and the Socialists' Horn, held a televised debate. Going into the debate, Horn's favorable rating was at 43% and his unfavorable rating was at 33%, compared to Orban's favorable rating of 46% and unfavorable rating of 34%. After the debate, Horn's favorable rating fell to 39%, and his unfavorable rating jumped to 47%. Orban was the clear winner, with everything to gain by the debate; his favorable rating jumped to 66%, and his unfavorable rating fell to only 18% ("A nézok szerint Orbán jobb volt Hornnál," 1998). It proved to be a bad judgment call on the part of the Socialists to debate the young, optimistic, and witty Orban. It was the turning point of the campaign.

As I wrote this in the summer of 1998, Hungary's newly elected prime minister was preparing to take office. He is Orban, who clearly won in the second round of the elections, which saw the highest voter turnout in the second round since the political change. This shows that democracy is well on its way.

All said and done, for the adventurous political consultant, emerging democracies are becoming a place to consider. If those willing to enter the political stage in the region are patient and creative in overcoming some of the present deficits, they will reap some big rewards sooner or later.

Notes

1. Data are from Gallup Hungary (1993c), based on 1,500 responses from a national sample. This was from a questionnaire titled "C".

2. See U.S. Information Agency (1997). Data from the poll are based on a total of 2,967 face-to-face interviews.

References

A nézok szerint Orbán jobb volt Hornnál [According to viewers, Orban was better than Horn]. (1998, May 21). *Világgazdaság* (Budapest, Hungary), p. 1.

Batthyany Foundation. (1998, April). *Report on the political situation* (Report 36, based on Gallup polls). Budapest, Hungary: Author.

FBIS-EEU. (1994, November). *Poll reveals attitudes toward privatization* (Document 94-211). Author.

Gallup. (1996). *Public opinion 1996*. Wilmington, DE: Scholarly Resources.

Gallup Hungary. (1993a, July). *What makes a good prime minister? Expectations and observations* [poll completed for the Hungarian government]. Budapest, Hungary: Author.

Gallup Hungary. (1993b, September). [Poll completed for the Hungarian government]. Budapest, Hungary: Author.

Gallup Hungary. (1993c, September/October). [Poll completed for the Hungarian government]. Budapest, Hungary: Author.

Gallup Hungary. (1993d, November). [Poll completed for the Hungarian government]. Budapest, Hungary: Author.

U.S. Information Agency. (1997, February). *Public opinion in Bosnia Hercegovina,* Vol. 4: *One year of peace* [poll commissioned by USIA and conducted by PULS in Hercegovina and central Bosnia and by Medium in Serbia]. Washington, DC: Author.

Lobbyist, Interest Group, and Governmental Campaigns

33

"Goods Over God"

Lobbying and Political Marketing: A Case Study of the Campaign by the Shopping Hours Reform Council to Change Sunday Trading Laws in the United Kingdom

PHIL HARRIS
HANNE GARDNER
NADJA VETTER

> To found a great empire for the sole purpose of raising up a people of customers
> may at first sight appear a project fit only for a nation of shopkeepers. It is,
> however, a project altogether unfit for a nation of shopkeepers, but extremely fit for
> a nation whose government is influenced by shopkeepers.
>
> —*Adam Smith,* The Wealth of Nations *(1776/1986, p. 4),*

The links among commercial interests, politicians, and political parties have attracted growing interest in the United Kingdom during the past 10 years. Until comparatively recently, there was only a very small number of articles covering this subject. However, interest has been growing especially in political marketing, pressure group, and public relations research areas (Jordan, 1991; Moloney, 1996; O'Shaughnessy, 1990; Richardson, 1993) and most recently in the United States (Mack, 1997). This case study outlines the growth in strategic lobbying in the United Kingdom and how it was used to change shopping hours regulation for competitive advantage to some of the major multiple retailers (or chains).

An indication of the scale of activity in this area, and one manifestation of the level of public concern at levels of undue influence on officials and elected representatives exerted by interest groups and lobbyists, has been the establishment of the Committee on Standards in Public Life, which has been assessing probity and recommending appropriate legislation and best practice. It is the first report (Nolan, 1995a, 1995b) that recommended standards for all public office-holders and elected representatives and that supported a voluntary code of practice for corporate lobbyists. This committee, following the retirement of Nolan, is now chaired by Lord Neill and has just reported, after extensive investigations, on the funding of political parties in the United Kingdom (Neill, 1998). The report makes very interesting reading as it highlights the political parties' needs to raise nearly £60 million from private business interests to fund their election campaigns. This clearly exerts strong pressure on political parties in the United Kingdom to have a strong financial link with business interests. It is surprising to note that in the marketing literature, there is very little published in this crucial strategic area, yet its importance is increasingly recognized (Harris & Lock, 1996).

Clearly, if we are to look at the strategic activities associated with lobbying, then we need a management definition of the practice. To arrive at a workable definition for corporate lobbying, we prefer Van Schendelen's (1993) view that it covers a multitude of practices and uses: "the informal exchange of information with public authorities as a minimal description, on the one hand, and as trying informally to influence authorities, on the other hand" (p. 3). This definition allows for both informal and formal contact.

To understand commercial political campaigning, which is rapidly becoming a very effective form of direct lobbying, we use the working definition that we have used previously: "mobilizing opinion to exert pressure on public authorities for commercial gain or commercial advantage" (Harris & Lock, 1996, p. 315).

Miller (1996) defines lobbying as meaning two things: (a) "representations based on careful research, usually followed by negotiation with several elements of central or local government—in short, working the system" and (b) "mobilization of public and media opinion where you seek to make government act against its will or where an issue needs to be given a higher place in the political agenda—in short, pressure" (cited in Andrews, 1996).

The use of lobbying within the British political process, particularly lobbying by pressure groups (Alderman, 1984; Jordan & Richardson, 1987; Moloney, 1996) or interest groups (Ball & Millard, 1986) is well documented. Corporate political lobbying, with the exception of major multinational campaigns that attract media attention, is less well known. One example was the U.K. brewers' lobbying to amend the Monopolies and Mergers Commission proposals on tied houses (Gallagher & Scott, 1994). In industrial markets, lobbying to obtain military contracts always has been of significance, although often conducted in secret. The recent highly visible lobbying by British Aerospace of the Ministry of Defence to put pressure on the German federal government to continue to finance the development of the European Fighter Aircraft is a prime example (Harris & Sherwood, 1994). Corporate lobbying in the United Kingdom has grown dramatically during the past 10 years (Attack, 1990; Hollingsworth, 1991; and, of course, Nolan, 1995a, 1995b, 1996a, 1996b, which include particularly useful, in-depth transcript evidence). The principal reasons for this growth appear to be the following:

1. Increased internationalization and competition in business markets that increases the importance of government, creating a competitive home business environment

2. Importation and influence of a more structured corporate lobbying system from the United States whose objective is to influence legislation affecting business markets

3. Increased corporate acquisition, merger, strategic alliance, and joint venture activity

4. A move away from consensual politics during the 1980s and early 1990s (those affected by proposals had to seek to ensure that their views were communicated as competently as possible or lose influence)

5. The growth of international and transnational government, which is generating substantial legislation affecting businesses, for example, on the environment. (McCormick, 1991)

This has brought lobbying at the national and European levels to ensure that the voice of business is heard when proposals are being formulated.

This list of reasons can equally be applied to the wider European scene. The modern business literature barely recognizes lobbying in the United Kingdom and European Union (EU), yet its impact over the past 10 years has been significant. There is a clear need within modern marketing, management, and public relations literature for a reevaluation of the importance and quantification of the extent of political lobbying as well as for a theoretical understanding of its strategic role. It is essential that more research is carried out in the fields of marketing, corporate strategy, and (in particular) the study of business relationships (Hakansson & Snehota, 1992) in industrial markets in which government plays a significant role as purchaser, regulator, or initiator of legislation.

> In reality, lobbying has increased, is increasing, and is not going to be diminished. Even our vaunted Constitution is really a framework of lobbying, for the Constitution is, essentially, whatever governments can get away with. Lobbying, persuasion, and opinion manipulation are the tugs at the sleeve of power. Government itself is a lobby. (Austin Mitchell, quoted in Jordan, 1991, p. 3)

The application of political marketing by commercial and not-for-profit organizations to influence governments and associated legislation to gain commercial or societal advantage is increasingly the case (Andrews, 1996; Harris & Lock, 1996), although gaining access to information and the evaluation of campaigns is causing researchers severe epistemological difficulties. There still is only a limited number of published articles on effective lobbying and campaigning to bring about strategic ends. This is a pity given that the growth of this area has been phenomenal in recent years, with more than 10,000 lobbyists being employed in Brussels, Belgium, which is now reputed to be the largest lobbying center in the world. The strategic lobbying campaign by the Shopping Hours Reform Council (SHRC) to change the English and Welsh Sunday trading laws is an attempt to fill part of that gap and to show how a lobby to benefit retailers was organized over 10 years.

Retailing and Introduction to the Sunday Trading Laws Case

Retailing in the United Kingdom has become one of the few growth industries, fueled from both consumer demand and multiple retailers' hunger for additional profits. Traditionally, women stayed at home and looked after their houses, cooked, and shopped. However, with the increase in the number of working women, there was a demand for longer opening hours, and to meet that demand, there was a need for additional employment. This societal change played into the hands of retailers able to offer part-time jobs to a predominantly female workforce. Extended trading hours allowed customers to shop when it suited them, and Sunday was seen by retailers as a day on which the whole family could spend leisure hours shopping.

Today, it appears that shopping has become a favorite leisure activity, with an estimated average of 2.5 hours per week spent on "essential" shopping and an additional 2.5 hours spent on "nonessential" shopping (Henley Centre for Forecasting, cited in Lansley, 1994).

Conspicuous consumption has been seen as a feature of the 1980s, but the Office for National Statistics estimates that 1997 produced the biggest growth rate since then, up 7% over 1996 consumption.

> Shop til you drop. Like exercise, it often seems to present itself as a form of therapy, designed to restore a sense of wholeness and well-being after long hours of unrewarding work. I feel like hell and go out for a run, and before I know it, everything is OK. Shopping serves the same purpose. It hardly matters what I buy. I just get a kick out of buying. (Lasch, 1991, cited in Gabriel & Lang, 1995)

The combination of "addicted" shoppers and retailers hungry for additional profit has become a dominant force in transforming the way in which we live and shop today. The retailers, in particular the multiple retailers, have sought to expand and capitalize on such behavior by expanding and developing out-of-town and edge-of-town centers providing thousands of square feet of extra selling space. Such facilities have allowed the one-stop shopping much loved by some British customers.

According to Nielsen (1996), 2% of shops now account for nearly 50% of turnover. Multiple retailers wanted their billions of pounds invested in such shopping centers to get better returns on their capital, and they saw Sunday trading as a means of achieving this. An additional 6 hours every Sunday was worth fighting for. This was most notably the case for "do-it-yourself" chains.

This was not so much the case for food retailers until 1992. B & Q (the do-it-yourself chain) estimated that 23% of turnover was gained on a Sunday. Because the chain costed itself over 6 days, 23% of turnover represented all of its profits.

The concentration and influence of the multiple retailers demonstrated just how well connected some were when it came to mustering their forces and mounting a campaign seeking the change that would allow Sunday trading.

The Sunday Trading Case

In July 1994, the new Sunday Trading Act received royal assent and came into force. It replaced the Shops Act of 1950 and enabled all shops in England and Wales to trade on Sundays. Although the hours of opening were limited by the size of the store, no restrictions were placed on the type of goods that could be sold. Over the previous 40 years, there had been numerous attempts to reform Sunday trading laws, all of which had met with vigorous opposition from people and groups wanting to preserve the traditional day of rest.

When reviewing a lobbying campaign, it often is difficult to access relevant information because of secrecy that routinely surrounds such activities. Therefore, it is useful to note that most of the research about the inner workings of the campaign are based on published materials provided by people directly involved or by interviews carried out by the authors with members of the respective campaigns.

A Nation of "Groupies": The Growth of Pressure Groups

May 1 was the date of the 1997 general election, and for most people, voting is the only opportunity to participate in the democratic process. Only a small and declining minority are actually members of political parties (Ware, 1996). More citizens are involved in pressure group activity than in political parties, as many feel that they can exert more influence on the issues that are of direct concern to them in this way. Therefore, pressure group activity represents an important part of the political process. Those involved are engaged in a wide range of activities designed to influence the course of government policy (Grant, 1995; Smith, 1989; Wilson, 1984).

During the 20th century, the scope of government has grown immensely and impinges on the lives of many different groups in society. The existence of hundreds of pressure groups suggests that nearly every aspect of society is represented—from pedestrians to civil liberties—and all are competing for the attention of the public, politicians, and civil servants. Many researchers argue that it is difficult to define pressure groups, but perhaps one of the most viable definitions of activities in this area is the following:

> A pressure group is an organization which seeks as one of its functions to influence the formulation and implementation of public policy, said public policy representing a set of authoritative decisions taken by the executive, the legislature, and the judiciary and by local government and the [EU]. (Grant, 1995, p. 9)

This definition is very general, as pressure group activities can range from informal to formal contacts. In the past, there have been various attempts to create typologies to categorize the groups. One of the most important distinctions is drawn between "sectional" or "interest" groups and "cause" groups. The former represent certain sections of society that are motivated by the common, often economic interests of their members. The cause groups are based on beliefs or ideologies, and their aim is to act in the interests of those beliefs. In general, the membership for cause groups is open to everybody, whereas the membership for sectional groups is limited to those who are part of the specific interest groups (Jones & Kavanagh, 1994). Grant (1995) argues that sectional groups are more likely to have highly specific issues and objectives that do not interest society as a whole but that can have a considerable impact on the profitability or even the future of an industry. He goes further to state that sectional groups are more likely to establish long-term organizations with invariably multiple objectives, in contrast to cause groups that may dissolve as soon as they have achieved their (often relatively simple) objectives. Although the SHRC campaign seems to fit the sectional classification, it was dissolved after attaining its objective. Furthermore, in this case, the interests of the group, an alliance of large retailers, corresponded to the interests of a considerable part of society—the consumers.

This illustrates the difficulties of categorizing pressure groups of different natures and widely varying interests. Various authors have tried to go further and develop other distinctions. One of these classifications is the "insider-outsider" distinction. This classification is based on alternative group strategies and on the susceptibility of government to those strategies. "Insider" groups are recognized by government and are consulted on a regular basis, whereas "outsider" groups either do not want to become insiders or are unable to gain acceptance. The distinction is based on the assumption that status is achieved by the pursuit of a certain strategy, a view that has been challenged by Jordan, Maloney, and McLaughlin (1992), who argue, "Even if pursuing an insider strategy is a precondition to attaining the status, there can be cases where the strategy is not enough" (cited in Grant, 1995, p. 16). They go on to state, "The key variable is that of resources, which can cover knowledge, technical advice or expertise, membership compliance or consent, credibility, information, [and/or] implementation guarantees" (p. 16). This is confirmed when considering the reasons for success of the SHRC campaign.

It is relatively rare for only one group to be active on a particular issue. Various groups will approach an issue in different ways, using a variety of strategies and techniques in their relations with government. Their key points of influence depend not only on the groups' strategies but also on their relationships with government. There is no single definitive route through which pressure groups exert influence. This chapter focuses on one approach that was taken during the Sunday trading campaign.

According to Harris and Lock (1996), the use of lobbying by pressure or interest groups is relatively well documented, whereas corporate political lobbying is less well known. However, corporate lobbying has increased considerably in the United Kingdom during the past decade. In the case of the SHRC campaign, pressure group campaigning was linked to corporate lobbying as it saw Britain's major retailers joined in a long-term campaign to reform the Sunday trading laws. Since the 1970s, there has been a proliferation of direct political pressure by companies, operating through their own government relations divisions or through paid lobbyists acting on their behalf, particularly in their dealings with Parliament.

Government-Business Relations

The 1980s were characterized by the retreat of state ownership in Britain, where privatization and deregulation were the order of the day. These changes had a major impact on government business relations. Grant (1993) identifies five roles that government occupies in relation to business: It can act as an owner, sponsor, regulator, customer, and policymaker. As a policymaker, government can significantly influence the context in which a company operates and makes decisions. However, Grant argues that it would be misleading to present the relationship between business and government only in terms of "a political struggle between lobbiers and lobbied" (p. 47). There is a mutual relationship from which government gains three types of benefits: information for policies, cooperation for their implementation, and consent for their implementation. Therefore government also depends on business. According to Jordan and Richardson (1982), "This exchange relationship is part of a long established tradition in Britain reinforced by civil service rules of consulting with affected interests" (cited in Grant, 1993, p. 49). Thus, industry is an active and officially recognized participant in the policy process.

According to Judge (1990), there seems to be increased attention by companies to Parliament. He argues that one explanation might be that the Thatcher government's aversion to vested interests meant that links with the civil service became more fragmented and that the voice of business no longer held the same weight in Whitehall (cited in Grant, 1993, p. 100). Therefore, business developed supplementary channels through which their voices could be heard. There currently is a tendency to approach more and more specific government departments and the EU because, as within the context of further integration, EU questions are a more central concern to government relations divisions. Miller (1991) argues that this misdirection of effort has been prompted by an exaggerated media interest in Parliament (which is easy to report) compared to what is invariably the real policymaking center of Whitehall, which is far less accessible (pp. 55-56).

However, there is not only one way of influencing; each case has its own characteristics. The case of the Sunday trading campaign shows that lobbying activity directed at Parliament might be one platform for influencing government. Trying to affect the climate of political opinion and, therefore, the parliamentary agenda is an important activity for pressure groups, but some issues inevitably will be accorded a higher priority than others. One wonders whether Michael Foster's Wild Mammals Bill (hunting with dogs) will fall foul of this policy priorities rule.

Historical Background

Modern-day legislation on Sunday trading dates back to shortly after World War II, when earlier legislation was consolidated in the Shops Act of 1950, which governed Sunday trading up until July 1994. The Shops Act allowed only the sale of a small variety of goods. Historically, the aim of the legislation had been to protect the interests of shop workers and small traders and to preserve the traditional character of Sunday. The restrictions on Sunday trading applied to England and Wales only because, in 1950, society's sentiment against the commercial infringement of Sundays in Scotland was considered to be strong enough to regulate itself.

Since 1950, the Shops Act became increasingly inadequate given societal changes that, coupled with changes in retailing, made Sunday trading more attractive for traders. The duty of enforcing the act lay with local authorities, but fines imposed on retailers for breaching the Sunday trading legislation had not kept pace with time and were more than covered by the profits of the day's trading. As a result, the act was widely ignored by retailers and only partially enforced by some authorities.

Consequently, there was general discontent with the provisions of the act, and between 1956 and 1983, there were no fewer than 19 attempts to change the law, ranging from proposals to enforce the existing restrictions to proposals significantly liberalizing the law. However, all these attempts failed (Warnaby, 1994). According to Kirkup and Wilkinson (1994), most attempts were lost because they were private members' bills and did not have the support of the government at the time. It was generally perceived to be impossible to change the law by this means because controversial subjects rarely are suitable for private members' bills without government support.

Past Attempts at Reform

During the early 1980s, the Conservative government under Margaret Thatcher, with its agenda of deregulation and privatization, took action. The Auld Committee (Command 9876, 1984) was established to consider changes to the Shops

Act. (It recommended the total abolition of any regulation of Sunday trading because none of the considered alternatives would "provide a fair or readily enforceable system" (Command 2300, 1993).

The government responded to the Auld Committee recommendations by introducing a bill proposing total abolition. In the meantime, its opponents grouped together, and the Keep Sunday Special Coalition (KSSC) was born. The KSSC enjoyed support from a broad coalition of interest groups including church groups and the Union of Shop, Distributive, and Allied Workers (USDAW). The KSSC mounted a very effective lobbying campaign, pressuring members of Parliament (MPs) to vote the bill down. Against this, the retailers backing deregulation delivered too little too late, and they were badly advised by a government too sure of its position. Burton (1993) argues that it was the partnership between the USDAW and the cooperative movement that opposed longer trading hours for shops that had most effect because this concentrated lobbying power had significant impact against a divided opposition of retail interests.

The bill failed in April 1986, at its second reading, by 12 votes. "Sunday trading earned a reputation as a political 'hot potato,' an issue that split all political parties and on which there appeared [to be] no consensus" (Kirkup & Wilkinson, 1994, p. 7). As a result, in its 1987 election manifesto, the Conservative Party committed itself to bringing sense to the law on Sunday trading. This manifesto was the beginning of a period of intense political lobbying that was to continue right through to 1993. The government would have preferred total deregulation because it would have been much clearer legally. But the parliamentary realities meant that total deregulation would not pass through Parliament. Therefore, compromise and partial deregulation was the only way in which to move forward. Numerous campaign groups, advocating very different solutions for reform, were involved in lobbying over this time period, but only four groups were considered seriously, among which the KSSC and SHRC were the major players.

Shopping Hours Reform Council

The SHRC was created in 1988 out of the frustration of the defeat of the Shops Bill in 1986 to promote the views of retailers and consumer organizations in favor of deregulation. Its core supporters are listed in Table 33.1.

The SHRC's sole objective was to liberalize shop hours, but after the 1986 defeat, it seemed unlikely that the government would reconsider total deregulation. Consultations among the SHRC, retail organizations, and the Home Office led to the adoption by the SHRC of a compromise package for reform, often referred to as "partial deregulation" (Kirkup & Wilkinson, 1994). These proposals would allow small shops to open at any time on Sunday and would allow larger shops to open for up to 6 hours selling the full range of merchandise.

TABLE 33.1 Core Supporters of Shopping Hours Reform Council

ASDA	Allied Maples, ASDA, Dales
Argyll	Lo-Cost
Boots	Boots the Chemists, Boots the Opticians, Children's World, Do It All, Fads, Halfords
Courts	Courts Furnishings
Dixons	Currys, Dixons, PC World
Kingfisher	B & Q, Charlie Browns, Comet, Woolworths, Superdrug
Ch. Robertson	Trago Mill
Sainsbury's	Sainsbury's, Savacentre, Homebase
Tesco	Tesco
WH Smith	Do It All, Our Price Music, Waterstones, WH Smith

SOURCE: Kirkup and Wilkinson (1994).

Keep Sunday Special Coalition

The KSSC was and still is funded by the Cambridge-based charity, the Jubilee Centre, a Christian research and campaigning organization with a wide network of church groups throughout the United Kingdom (Table 33.2).

After the government pledge in May 1987, the KSSC published the "REST Proposals," outlining its alternative to the existing law for Parliament to discuss. These proposals would prohibit all Sunday trading except for categories covering recreation, emergencies, social gatherings, and travel (REST), aiming to protect the special and distinctive character of Sunday (Askham, 1994). Critics argued that the KSSC's proposals would leave the existing situation partly unchanged and would continue to spread uncertainty. Furthermore, the burdens on the enforcement authorities would be considerable.

Retailers for Shop Act Reform

In October 1992, the Retailers for Shop Act Reform (RSAR) emerged as another campaign group. This group was supported by Marks and Spencer, the most profitable retailer in the United Kingdom, and by organizations such as the Association of Metropolitan Authorities. The RSAR's proposals were similar to those of the KSSC but were not quite as restrictive. Under this proposal, all shops would be allowed to open on the four Sundays before Christmas, but during other times of the year, only "convenience outlets" of no more than 3,000 square feet would be allowed to trade (Warnaby, 1994).

During the summer of 1993, talks took place between the KSSC and RSAR because it was felt that two options advocating strict limits for the regulation of Sunday trade might split the vote among supporters in Parliament. Before the vote in the House of Commons in December 1993, these proposals were incorporated with those of the KSSC.

TABLE 33.2 Associates and Supporters of Keep Sunday Special Coalition: 1988

Campaign associates

Association of Independent Retailers	Multiple Shoe Retailers Association
British Footwear Manufacturers Federation	National Chamber of Trade
British Hardware Federation	National Federation of Meat Traders
Conservative Family Campaign	National Federation of Sub-Postmasters
Cooperative Union	National Hairdressers Federation
Drapers Chambers of Trade	National Pharmaceutical Association
Federation of Sports Goods Distributors	Retail Fruit Trade Federation
Independent Footwear Retailers Association	Radio, Electrical, and TV Retailers Association
Independent Footwear Suppliers Association	Union of Shop, Distributive, and Allied Workers

Campaign supporters

Baptist Union
British Council of Churches
CARE Campaigns
Catholic Bishops Conference for England and Wales, General Secretariat
Church of England, Board for Social Responsibility
Church of Scotland, Church and Nations Committee
Free Church Federal Council
Methodist Church, Division of Social Responsibility
Mothers Union
National Board of Catholic Women
Pro-Sunday Coalition and the Shaftesbury Project
United Reformed Church, Church and Society Department

SOURCE: Keep Sunday Special Campaign (1988).

Total Deregulation

Those arguing for total deregulation, Sort Out Sunday (SOS), continued to campaign actively in the Sunday trading debate, despite the defeat of their model in 1986. They pledged for freedom of choice so that opening would be determined by commercial judgment and consumer demand (Gillespie, 1994).

The Legal Battleground: 1988–1992

The period 1988 to 1992 was characterized not only by intensive political lobbying on the Sunday trading reform but also by confusion among the courts and local authorities over the legality of the 1950 act itself and of the actions to enforce it. Retailers who continued to trade illegally on Sundays came into increasing conflict with those local authorities that chose to uphold the law. Between 1988 and 1992, there was considerable contention on the issue of whether or not the restrictions on Sunday trading conformed with the Treaty of Rome. During this period, a great number of courts in England, Wales, and

Northern Ireland, including the High Court, referred the issue to the European Court of Justice (ECJ) (Askham, 1994).

The issue began in 1988 with a test case between B & Q and the Torfaen Borough Council. It was for the court to decide whether the effect of the 1950 act on trade was "proportionate," in other words, no more than necessary to achieve the objective of worker protection. The ECJ decided that the Shops Act fell within the Treaty of Rome but that it was for the national court to decide whether the effect of the act was "justified" and "proportionate" (Askham, 1994; Warnaby, 1994).

The ECJ's response created a great deal of ambiguity in the application of the Shops Act, and U.K. courts were unable to hear Sunday trading cases until the ECJ's ruling in 1992. As a result, the country enjoyed a period of effective deregulation, and both the SHRC and KSSC criticized the government for its immobility and failure to resolve the confusion.

Further litigation followed the ambivalent judgment of the ECJ until the matter was again referred to the ECJ, this time by the House of Lords on a case again involving B & Q. The court in that case finally decided that the 1950 act was both justified and proportionate. Consequently, the Shops Act was judged to be compatible with European law and, therefore, enforceable (Askham, 1994; Kirkup & Wilkinson, 1994).

The Bill

Early in 1991, the Home Office became involved in extensive deliberations with representatives from each of the campaign groups in a vain attempt to come to a consensus decision that could be put before Parliament. The government seemed reluctant to declare an alliance with either side of the debate and wanted to act, but it needed a broader coalition to ensure that the bill would go through Parliament.

In January 1993, the KSSC secured the opportunity to present its proposal of reform to Parliament through a private member's bill. Initially, this caused considerable concern at the SHRC, but effective lobbying and a lack of parliamentary time led to its demise after the second reading and committee stages. The number of amendments tabled by the SHRC-friendly MPs ensured that the bill was talked out at the report stage in the House of Commons.

Finally, in July 1993, the government published proposals for a new Sunday trading law. The issue split all the political parties in Parliament. The government, fearing a repeat of 1986, indicated at an early stage that it would not commit itself to any one model for reform but instead offered a draft bill proposing four options (already detailed earlier) on which MPs would be permitted a free vote. In November 1993, the Sunday Trading Bill was published. The procedure used by the government to take the bill through Parliament was unusual. The bill was given a second reading on the general principle of the requirement to reform the law, achieving a majority with ease. Parliament was then left to choose among three options: total deregulation, the restrictive KSSC-RSAR proposal, and the SHRC proposal. Total deregulation was included to make the SHRC look like a concession. The debate on these three options took place on December 8, 1993.

The SHRC's proposals were adopted by a majority of 75. Thereafter, the bill still faced 6 months at Westminster before becoming law. Few changes were made, and the new act remained very similar to the original SHRC proposal. Its purpose was to liberalize shop opening on Sundays, to simplify enforcement, and to give effective employment protection (Askham, 1994).

Campaign Strategy

Who to lobby? How to lobby? There are no formal rules to follow, as each case has its own characteristics. The SHRC realized from the 1986 defeat that lobbying at Westminster alone would not secure the success of the campaign. It believed that the "reform must reflect the views of the consumers if it is to be workable, enforceable, and acceptable" (Kirkup & Wilkinson, 1994, p. 23). It opted for a mixture of campaigning and considered that, parallel to an effective campaign at Westminster, it would be vital to exert pressure in key MPs' own "backyards" (i.e., their constituencies) to counter the KSSC support network of churches across the country. Therefore, part of the SHRC's strategy was to develop, or to at least stimulate the perception of there being, a "grassroots campaign" (Kirkup & Wilkinson, 1994).

Grassroots Campaign

During the early stages of the campaign, when the bill was a distant prospect, campaigning centered on the constituencies of known opponents and in areas where councils actively enforced the Shops Act. The main tactic was to persuade MPs of local public support for more freedom to shop on Sunday. There were hundreds of constituencies in England and Wales to target. Furthermore, each constituency required its own mini-campaign that was tailored to the local physical, social, and political conditions, as well as the Sunday shopping patterns, in the area. Consequently, a full-time regional organizer was recruited, primarily for good political contacts in a major political party and an understanding of the political process in general. The regional organizer was supported by a regional public relations company to handle the media in the region. Their job was to publicize the activities of the regional organizer and to help tailor the national media strategy to the region. Snap surveys as well as interviews with the local press, radio stations, and (occasionally) television stations were commonly used techniques. Most journalists seemed to be supportive of liberalization. The Sunday shopping debate received wide coverage in the news columns and almost continuous discussion in the letter pages, particularly in the local press.

In addition, local supporters were recruited to monitor the campaign at the constituency level and, coordinated by bulletins, were urged to write letters to their MPs at crucial stages of the process at Westminster.

The Sunday Shopping Campaign

According to Kirkup and Wilkinson (1994), after the supermarkets began a widespread Sunday opening at the end of 1991 following the court of appeals decision, they increased their involvement with the SHRC, and the Sunday Shopping Campaign (SCC) was born. The SSC was essentially a public face for the SHRC's campaign. Significantly, however, the SSC gained the full support of the Consumers Association by focusing on the benefits of liberalization to shoppers.

The SSC's basic contention was that if shoppers wanted to shop on Sundays and workers were willing to work on Sundays, then they should be allowed to do so legally. The SSC gave voice to both of these groups, using the network of the SHRC's retail supporters' shops around England and Wales. Customers and staff were persuaded to lobby their local MPs in support of liberalization in general and the SHRC's proposal in particular. This gave an enormous boost to the SHRC's campaign in terms of visibility and the numbers of constituents declaring support for liberalization to their MPs. The SHRC then concentrated on publicizing the SSC's achievements and on lobbying directly with its political message (Kirkup & Wilkinson, 1994).

The Sunday Trading Campaign Managers

The Sunday Trading Campaign Managers (STCM) group was formed by the SHRC to oversee involvement with the SCC and SHRC campaign activities at the store level. STCMs were primarily experienced executives from each company, often from public relations or operations departments, who met on a regular basis. Individual store managers were charged with supervising local programs including inviting their MPs into the stores and encouraging customers and staff to write letters in support of liberalization. The general strategy was to keep the campaign sections separate so as to increase the MPs' perceptions that wide cross sections of their constituencies favored liberalization. However, the different sections needed to work hand in hand to achieve the desired success. Therefore, information and reports were constantly passed on to other areas of the campaign.

The STCM-SHRC network was first put to the test when the SHRC ran a 4-month bus campaign during the winter of 1992. A double-decker bus toured SHRC retail sites 5 days a week, including Sundays, raising the profile of the campaign locally and encouraging shoppers to write to their MPs. The success of this exercise paved the way for the highlight of the grassroots campaign, which acted as a springboard for the final push at Westminster. The Sunday of September 19, 1993, was designated National Sunday Shopping Day. In total, 1.7 million shoppers signed up in favor of liberalization, and a considerable volume of promotional material was distributed. Good coverage in press, radio, and television media was achieved. The main impact of the day was to demonstrate to MPs the huge popularity of Sunday shopping.

Marketing Reform at Westminster

The SHRC's Westminster lobbying machine was formalized and strengthened over the summer of 1993 in preparation for the introduction to Parliament of the government's Sunday Trading Bill. The SHRC's lobby committee consisted of its executive vice chairman and head of research, with a representative from each supporter company. This was either a senior executive, if the company undertook its own lobbying program, or an experienced professional lobbyist from an agency, such as Ian Greer Associates or GJW Government Relations, who had been recruited to the job. The committee reviewed target lists of MPs and peers and assessed new information that had been forwarded by the grassroots campaign and other sources. Each member of the committee was then allocated a number of key MPs to lobby, and briefings and face-to-face meetings were organized. When lobbying MPs, many lobbyists would argue that the first thing to do is to identify "key" MPs. However, in this case, it seemed a rather difficult task. The definition of a key MP changed as the campaign advanced, that is, as the MPs changed their positions on the issue when reacting to developments in their constituencies and/or at Westminster. Supportive MPs also were requested to lobby their colleagues.

Considering the division on the issue in the Conservative Party, a great deal depended on the opposition MPs. Two key developments influenced substantial numbers of MPs to consider partial deregulation. First, shop worker protection became a crucial issue at Westminster during the intensive lobbying that preceded and accompanied the introduction of the Sunday Trading Bill. The SHRC led the way in encouraging the government to arrive at a package of employee protection measures that helped satisfy skeptical MPs. Second, just before the bill's introduction, the USDAW's leadership dramatically reversed its traditional policy of opposition to Sunday trading after securing assurances from the SHRC's retailers that premium payments for Sunday work would be maintained voluntarily. The USDAW publicly backed the SHRC option, and when the bill was introduced, was joined by the Shadow Home Office team led by Tony Blair and Joan Ruddock.

Reasons for Success

According to Currie (1994), former Kingfisher executive Tim Clement Jones (personal interview at Labour Party Conference, October 2, 1996), and other informants, one of the main reasons for the success of the SHRC's campaign was the effective lobbying campaign. Yet, what makes a lobbying campaign effective or successful? Michael Shea compares lobbying to "growing asparagus" as "one should have started [3] years ago" (cited in Harris & Ziegler, 1996, p. 318). The following elements contributed significantly to the success of the SHRC's campaign, but they should be seen as a managed marketing campaign rather than as specific features.

Lobbying

The founding of the SHRC was not without controversy. According to Currie (1994), the KSSC accused the government of complicity given the association of key SHRC figures with the Tory Party. Suspicions grew about a rumored private arrangement in which the SHRC would press for reform and the government would concede. However, it can be argued that the 1986 defeat showed that the government's wishes were not always obeyed by the SHRC's network of significant contacts and supporters, who certainly were one of the major elements in the campaign.

It is useful to note that the 1986 defeat was the only piece of legislation lost at the second reading stage in Parliament by Thatcher's government. So, it did not happen very often. This gives some indication of the strength of opposition.

Contrary to criticism from the KSSC, the SHRC had very close links not only to the Conservatives but also to the Labour Party. Baroness Margaret Jay, for example, made a life peer shortly after joining the SHRC; was close to the Labour leadership; and was a very skilled SHRC chairman, communicator, and opposition politician in the House of Lords. Thus, the SHRC's contacts were spread across the parties at a high level.

Furthermore, active support and substantial know-how was provided by key people such as Des Wilson, an internationally known pressure group campaigner who is now BAA's director of public affairs (with responsibility specifically for obtaining assent for the development of Terminal 5 at Heathrow), and experienced consultants such as Ian Greer, GJW Government Relations, and other external advisers. This is a crucial factor to be considered in addition to the existing high-profile organizational structure composed of senior representatives of the retail members such as David Ramsden of Kingfisher, who held the post of executive vice chairman. Therefore, to have the right people in the SHRC at the right time and at the right place was a crucial element. The SHRC had its headquarters around the corner from Westminster.

Finally, since 1988, the SHRC was present at nearly all autumn party political conferences, holding receptions and having a stand in the exhibition area to support reform.

Resources

The financial power of the retailers allowed the SHRC to lead a high-profile campaign, whereas opposing groups had limited resources and, consequently, low-profile activities. This fact became clear in the stimulation of the grassroots campaign. Furthermore, it allowed the SHRC to use commissioned research to back its claims of public support for liberalization in general and its proposals in particular. Regular research and opinion surveys on a national and constituency level were carried out by organizations such as Gallup and MORI. The SHRC made good use of such survey responses in its campaign communications with the aim of reinforcing the general feeling of popular support for Sunday shopping.

Developing Grassroots Campaign Support

"Reform must reflect the views of the consumer if it is to be workable, enforceable, and acceptable" (Kirkup & Wilkinson, 1994, p. 23). This was the fundamental argument in the SHRC's grassroots campaign, which, according to Wilson, was crucial to the success of the overall strategy. Public support was vital in lobbying MPs in their constituencies. Wilson argues that it was most important to get consumers to write to their MPs and to get store managers to persuade MPs to come and see for themselves (quoted in Kellaway, 1993, p. 20). The store network of SHRC members represented an outstanding potential. The media also played an important role during the campaign, being used to amplify local campaigning activity.

Opposing Campaign Groups

Smith (1989) argues that pressure groups rarely achieve their objectives by virtue of their actions alone. According to Currie (1994), tactical errors were made by the opposing campaign groups such as policy changes by the KSSC that might have created confusion. The KSSC and RSAR campaigns seem rather limited in comparison to that of the SHRC. The KSSC's network rested on church groups whose individuals, although motivated, did not have the same resources at their disposal. The RSAR never invested in a grassroots campaign, although Marks and Spencer could have easily funded this type of activity.

Epitath

The campaign of the SHRC achieved its desired result. Its proposal passed through the parliamentary process virtually untouched.

The Sunday trading campaign, which represents one of the most protracted parliamentary battles, is a good example of the role and power of pressure groups in British politics today. After more than 40 years of confusion (particularly during 1991–1993) and failed attempts to reform the Sunday trading law, the 1994 act was the result of intensive lobbying and campaigning by various pressure groups and represents a case study of the power of a particular interest group to bring about policy change for commercial advantage.

However, there is no blanket definition for "pressure group," and fundamental problems of equality and weight of access persist. It is much more difficult for nonbusiness groups to succeed just on a low-profile basis. The large retail groups involved in this campaign had the necessary financial resources to throw behind the cause and were able to reinforce their economic power through pressure group activity. Their formidable lobbying power formed one of the most striking aspects of the campaign, as is illustrated in the following statement by Wilson: "I have an exceptional range of contacts. The reporters I knew when I started at Shelter in 1966 are now editors. The backbenchers are now ministers. The people I knew in [television] are now director generals. I know them all" (quoted in Kellaway, 1993, p. 20). Those lobbying in other regulated markets might be more discreet than this implies but would go along with the potential power of this type of activity (Andrews, 1996).

Sunday shopping is now established and is the second busiest shopping day in the week for retailers.

Conclusion

Strategic political lobbying by large corporations and coalitions of corporate interests is increasing dramatically as they seek to gain competitive advantage in global markets. Meanwhile, government at the national and supranational levels is increasingly attempting to regulate the environment, markets, and even lobbying. Thus, influencing government decision- and policymaking for strategic advantage has become an increasingly developed and organized business. To be able to operate in this complex and growing arena, one needs an appreciation of law, policy, politics, quality management skills, good connections in the process, and well-written research. As a consequence, a number of individuals, as well as groups, have now established themselves as well versed in political marketing and dominate this area. Political marketing skills were used to mount the campaign that amended Sunday shopping hours in the United Kingdom. The case is an example of how political marketing is being used in campaigning and lobbying by vested interests to gain commercial and/or strategic advantage.

The need for future research is essential, and some quality work has been done in the interest group and nongovernmental organization areas (e.g., by Greenwood, Jordan, and Pedlar), but very few case studies of campaigns have been written (Andrews, 1996). A typology of campaign styles; lobbying techniques; and the impact of "think tanks," pressure groups, and interest groups on the policy process needs to be developed. There is one glaring direct linkage between political marketing and strategic business and interest lobbying—the need for political parties to fund their activities to ensure survival. Interestingly, the need for political parties to fund longer and larger scale election campaigns using increased opinion polling and associated managerial staffing levels is placing a severe strain on the political parties' finances and has seen an unsurprising dramatic rise in earnestness in their development of closer links with business. To a large extent, this area has not been researched. We need to address these issues.

References

Alderman, G. (1984). *Pressure groups and government in Great Britain*. London: Longman.

Andrews, L. (1996). The relationship of political marketing to political lobbying: An examination of the Devonport campaign for the Trident refitting contract. *European Journal of Marketing, 30*(10/11), 76-99.

Askham, T. (1994). *A guide to the Sunday Trading Act 1994*. London: Butterworth.

Attack, S. (1990). *The directory of public affairs and government relations*. London: Berkeley International Recruitment Consultants.

Ball, A. R., & Millard, F. (1986). *Pressure politics in industrial societies*. London: Macmillan.

Burton, J. (1993). *Whither Sunday trading? The case for deregulation*. London: Institute for Economic Affairs.

Command 9876. (1984, November). *The Shops Act: Late night and Sunday opening*. London: Her Majesty's Stationery Office.

Command 2300. (1993, July). *Reforming the law on Sunday trading: A guide to the options for reform*. London: Her Majesty's Stationery Office.

Currie, A. (1994). Success of the Sunday shopping lobby. *Public Affairs Newsletter, 1*(2), 5.

Gabriel, Y., & Lang, T. (1995). *The unmanageable consumer*. London: Sage.

Gallagher, J. C., & Scott, R. (1994). Scottish & Newcastle Breweries. In P. Harris & F. McDonald (Eds.), *European business and marketing: Strategic issues*. London: Paul Chapman.

Gillespie, A. (1994, April). The Sunday shopping debate. *Business Studies*.

Grant, W. (1993). *Business and politics in Britain*. Basingstoke, UK: Macmillan.

Grant, W. (1995). *Pressure groups, politics, and democracy in Britain* (2nd ed.). Hemel Hempstead, UK: Harvester Wheatsheaf.

Hakansson, H., & Snehota, I. (1992). *Developing relationships in business networks*. London: Routledge.

Harris, P., & Lock, A. (1996). Machiavellian marketing: The development of corporate lobbying in the U.K. *Journal of Marketing Management, 12*, 313-328.

Harris, P., & Sherwood, R. (1994). British Aerospace. In P. Harris & F. McDonald (Eds.), *European business and marketing: Strategic issues*. London: Paul Chapman.

Harris, P., & Ziegler, S. (1996, July). Smoke gets in your eyes: The missing link, lobbying. In *Proceedings of the Marketing Education Group Conference*. Strathclyde, UK: University of Strathclyde.

Hollingsworth, M. (1991). *MP's for hire: The secret world of political lobbying*. London: Bloomsbury.

Jones, B., & Kavanagh, D. (1994). Pressure groups. In B. Jones (Ed.), *U.K. politics* (2nd ed.). Hemel Hempstead, UK: Harvester Wheatsheaf.

Jordan, G. (Ed.). (1991). *The commercial lobbyists*. Aberdeen, UK: Aberdeen University Press.

Jordan, G., Maloney, W., & McLaughlin, A. (1992). *Insiders, outsiders, and political access*. British Interest Group Project, Working Paper No. 3, University of Aberdeen.

Jordan, G., & Richardson, J. (1982). The British policy style or the logic of negotiation. In J. Richardson & G. Jordan (Eds.), *Policy styles in Western Europe* (pp. 4-5). Oxford, UK: Clarendon.

Jordan, G., & Richardson, J. (1987). *Government and pressure groups in Britain*. Oxford, UK: Clarendon.

Judge, D. (1990). *Parliament and industry*. Aldershot, UK: Dartmouth.

Keep Sunday Special Coalition. (1988). *The Rest Proposals: How to bring sense and consistency to the law on Sunday trading*. Cambridge, UK: Jubilee Centre.

Kellaway, L. (1993, December 16). Management: Campaign king cashes in his contacts book. *The Financial Times*.

Kirkup, M., & Wilkinson, S. (1994). *Campaigning for the reform of Sunday trading in England and Wales: A case study examining the approach taken by the Shopping Hours Reform Council*. Loughborough, UK: Loughborough University Business School.

Lansley, S. (1994). *After the Gold Rush*. London: Century.

Lasch, C. (1991). *The true and only heaven: Progress and its cities*. New York: Norton.

Mack, C. S. (1997). *Business, politics, and the practice of government relations*. Westport, CT: Quorum Books.

McCormick, J. (1991). *British politics and the environment*. London: Earthscan.

Miller, C. (1991). Lobbying: The development of the consultation culture. In G. Jordan (Ed.), *The commercial lobbyist*. Aberdeen, UK: Aberdeen University Press.

Miller, C. (1996, March). *The role of professional political consultants: The provider perspective*. Paper presented at the AIC Conference, "Lobbying: The Way Forward," London.

Moloney, K. (1996). *Lobbyists for hire*. Aldershot, UK: Dartmouth.

Neill, L[ord]. (1998). *Committee of Standards in Public Life, political party funding* (Vols. 1-2). London: The Stationery Office.

Nielsen. (1996). *Marketing pocket book*. Guilford, UK: Biddles.

Nolan, L[ord]. (1995a). *First report of the Committee on Standards in Public Life, Vol. 1: Report* (CM 2850-I). London: Her Majesty's Stationery Office.

Nolan, L[ord]. (1995b). *First report of the Committee on Standards in Public Life, Vol. 2: Transcripts of oral evidence* (CM 2850-II). London: Her Majesty's Stationery Office.

Nolan, L[ord]. (1996a). *Second report of the Committee on Standards in Public Life: Local public spending bodies, Vol. 1: Report* (CM 3270-1). London: Her Majesty's Stationery Office.

Nolan, L[ord]. (1996b). *Second report of the Committee on Standards in Public Life: Local public spending bodies, Vol. 2: Transcripts of oral evidence* (CM 3270-II). London: Her Majesty's Stationery Office.

O'Shaughnessy, N. J. (1990). *The phenomenon of political marketing*. Basingstoke, UK: Macmillan.

Richardson, J. J. (Ed.). (1993). *Pressure groups*. Oxford, UK: Oxford University Press.

Smith, A. (1986). *The wealth of nations*. London: Penguin. (Originally published in 1776)

Smith, N. C. (1989). Pressure groups: A management introduction. *Management Decision, 27*(5), 22-27.

Van Schendelen, M.P.C.M. (Ed.). (1993). *National, public, and private EC lobbying*. London: Dartmouth.

Ware, A. (1996). *Political parties and party systems*. Oxford, UK: Oxford University Press.

Warnaby, G. (1994). *Sunday trading: A case study of the sources of law*. Manchester, UK: Manchester Metropolitan University, Department of Retail and Marketing.

Wilson, D. (1984). *Pressure: The A to Z of campaigning in Britain*. London: Heinemann.

34

How Marketing Changed the World

The Political Marketing of an Idea: A Case Study of Privatization

NIGEL ALLINGTON
PHILIP MORGAN
NICHOLAS O'SHAUGHNESSY

This chapter discusses the political applications of marketing in a novel way, where marketing was enlisted not to win an election or to promote a manifesto or politician but rather to sell a radical political idea that was not even part of the party's electoral platform. The radical political idea that palpably changed the world was "privatization." The idea, moreover, had to be sold in a commercial marketplace, as a product, to fulfill the multiple and changing objectives of the British politicians who launched it. These objectives were to cut state expenditure and costs, to make money, to create more British Tories, to espouse popular capitalism, and to realize the old Conservative dream of a property-owning democracy (Marsh, 1991). The significance of privatization is twofold. First, it changed the course of history not only in Britain but also throughout the world because the changes were both revolutionary and replicated almost universally. Insofar as marketing is responsible for this, its political and historic status deserves reappraisal. Second, it is a case study in the evangelistic marketing of a "big idea." As such, it illuminates the possibility of taking marketing theory beyond its usual consumerist terrain in an attempt to answer some of the deeper philosophical questions associated with it.

This article describes how the astute use of marketing, a series of ad hoc campaigns rather than a grand general vision (because no such political foresight existed), helped to make this radical shift from state ownership to private control possible. Our thesis is that one of the most salient socioeconomic phenomena of our time was, in part, created and sustained by intelligent sociopolitical marketing strategies. This claim has some credibility if we accept that there was, in fact, no historical inevitability about the triumph of an economic ideology now sustained from Azerbaijan to Argentina. To accept these claims is to recognize a role for marketing beyond its traditional image as the purveyor of soap powder to that of an instrument sufficient to help reshape the global order, although important qualifications should be made. Privatization was an idea whose time had come and whose political attractiveness was underpinned by a straight appeal to acquisitive instincts.

The case of privatization certainly does suggest how critical marketing can be sometimes in what cultural theorists have termed the social construction of reality (Berger & Luckman, 1966; Hall, 1989; Searle, 1995). That is, the prevailing social order is not objective or indeed natural; rather, it is a synthetic and even arbitrary fabrication. In this process, communications phenomena are particularly important because they shape perceptions and make certain practices (which are, in fact, social constructs) seem simply the rational thing to do. The privatization campaign and the role of marketing within it are illustrations of this given that the idea of privatization would have seemed absurd to all political persuasions only a few years ago.

Privatization in the United Kingdom

Margaret Thatcher was not elected in 1979 on a mandate to introduce the privatization of Britain's extensive state-run industries. The Conservative Manifesto of 1979 did not even mention privatization, and it began to happen almost imperceptibly on a small scale as an opportunistic attempt to raise revenue for the Conservative government (something the Labour government had done before). The policy was generated by no higher ideal than this; there was no grand vision of a shrunken state and popular capitalism except in the private backrooms of the Conservative Party. The government simply began to sell shares held in a mixed bag of companies including ICL (a computer company), half of British Aerospace, Cable & Wireless, several British Transport hotels (including Gleneagles), and National Freight Corporation. It was not until Amersham, an atomic energy company, found a medical use for radioactive isotopes that a major privatization sell-off took place. More than a quarter of a million applications for shares were received through the post, and an instant profit of 35% was enjoyed by early buyers. Thus, privatization made buying shares an attractive proposition for the general public, and eventually 10 million people bought them, although many sold their shares for a a quick profit. The concept of a mass base in share ownership was almost a post hoc justification but later became a salient political-ideological motivation of the program.

In Britain, privatization radically transformed the economic and political landscape (Haskel & Szymanski, 1991). In the process, it put more than £80 billion into the Treasury's coffers, transferred more than 47 businesses employing 1,950,000 people into the private sector, and created more than 10 million new shareholders. In 1995, privatized companies contributed more than £2 billion a year, or£60 million a week, to the exchequer in corporation tax (Her Majesty's Stationery Office, 1995). The privatization policy achieved a fundamental shift in politics, the very framework within which all political debate was conducted. Hence, privatization was "naturalized" as an unquestioned assumption underpinning all political arguments.

The Global Impact of Privatization

Privatization is now a global phenomenon, and the significance of the Conservative privatization program is that it turned Britain into an experimental laboratory that was scrutinized by much of the world (Ramanadham, 1988, 1993). The success of Britain's privatization program emboldened governments everywhere, seeking to increase both their finances and the effectiveness of indigenous industry by imitating the British strategy. Insofar as marketing was critical to the success of Britain's privatization program, one may even ask the question "Did marketing change the world?" It significantly helped to establish a domestic model that became the basis for a reorientation of the global economic order—an industrial revolution—and some might actually argue that this was as significant as the original Bolshevik revolution (which it ultimately represents reaction against).

A few examples will suffice to illustrate the extent of privatization in the world today. Currently, the main water supplier of Lesotho is being commercialized. In Nepal, government-owned tea estates have been privatized, and future privatizations include hydroelectric systems and the national airline (Ramanadham, 1989). In Bangladesh, there is a new privatization law. In Romania, the power sector is being reformed. And in Azerbaijan, large-scale enterprises are about to be privatized. Even Vietnam is developing a privatization policy with the assistance of the right-wing London "think tank," the Adam Smith Institute, which provided the theoretical and conceptual case for privatization under Thatcher. Courses in the liberalization of railways have been run by the Adam Smith Institute for Bulgaria, Pakistan, Egypt, Ghana, Jamaica, Argentina, Chile, and Brazil (Ramanadham, 1989). The institute also has run advisory courses on privatization for Bosnia, Hungary, India, Iceland, Nepal, Indonesia, Thailand, Sri Lanka, South Africa, and Zimbabwe. To put the question in reverse order, "If the British government had never experimented with privatization, could we speak of such a shift in the global order today?" And, "If the British government had not purchased substantial help from London's sophisticated advertising industry, or if that industry had not developed such persuasive strategies to sell the initial privatization ventures with such success, would privatization (and the disruption it entails) have seemed a much less attractive proposition to the host of international watchers of Britain's laboratory?" Another point, of course, is that mass privatizations were occurring in Britain at the moment when international communism was fading away. Newly liberated governments and peoples were seeking a new model, and during this period in history, Britain seemed to represent the most fashionable one.

Social and Political Marketing and Marketing Theory

However, before proceeding further, the important question to be answered is "Does the selling of a political idea like privatization really constitute 'marketing'?" In 1960, the American Marketing Association (AMA) defined marketing as "the performance of business activities that direct the flow of goods and services from producer to consumer or user" (cited in Hunt, 1976). The subsequent history of the discipline was one of expanding this definition, a history that is important to us because we need to establish the legitimacy of the political marketing concept. Marketing as an academic study originated during the early years of this century, a derivative of applied economics that emphasized the analysis of distribution channels. Later, it focused on the increase of sales and then, under the guise of a behavioral science, on buyer or seller systems. Thus, by the stage at which the AMA sought a clear definition for it, the subject matter seemed clearly established. Pricing, market research, sales management, distribution, retailing, advertising, international marketing, purchasing, and so on all rested comfortably in the shade of its disciplinary umbrella.

But other academics were more skeptical. They noted that although other areas of human activity seemed to share analogous processes, these were excluded from their subject's conceptual embrace. For Kotler (1972), "The traditional conception of marketing would relegate this discipline to an increasingly narrow and pedestrian role." In 1965, a group at the University of Ohio described marketing as not just a business discipline but also a social process, and Lazer (cited in Hunt, 1976) pronounced that marketing should not remain a mere technology of the firm. Dawson (cited in Hunt, 1976) drew attention to the "social ramifications of marketing activity," and Kotler and Levy (1969) stressed that the concept should be expanded to embrace noncommercial entities such as the police and religious organizations. These moves opened up a potentially rich field of study, but they initially were resisted by those who felt that they would create conceptual vagueness and dilute the business focus. By becoming more academic, this subject would become less relevant and practical. Carman (cited in Hunt, 1976), for example, saw the "exchange of value" as the core marketing definition, so that processes such as politics, which did not involve this, should be rejected; however, 95% of marketing academics believed that their subject should include nonbusiness areas.

So, now there could be "social marketing" or "political marketing" or the organization's relations with nonclient groups ("consciousness three"). New definitions of the subject concentrated on the idea of the transaction. "Marketing is specifically concerned with how transactions are created, stimulated, facilitated, and valued" (Kotler, 1972). It is concerned with the "general idea of exchange rather than the narrower thesis of market transactions" (Hunt, 1976) and with "action undertaken by persons to bring about a response in other persons concerning some specific social object" (Hunt, 1976).

Although it is possible to identify definitions so abstract as to be meaningless, there could be no doubt now that the application of marketing to nonbusiness areas was a legitimate field of investigation, at least so far as marketing academics were concerned. "The political strategist, to the extent that he [or she] is effective, is a professional marketer" (Kotler, 1972; cf. Scammell, 1995). Marketing might legitimately interact with other subjects, such as psychology, that also studied transactions, although it was distinguished from them because "only in marketing is the transaction the focal point" (Hunt, 1976).

Relationship With Political Marketing

It could be argued that the selling of privatization was atypical of any category of marketing because it constituted a series of once-only sales for a mass consumer franchise. Unlike political marketing, there was a tangible product, the essence of which was the promise of an instant material gain, accompanied by a risk of immediate loss, although the perception of risk diminished after the first British Telecommunications (British Telecom) sale. At this level, there is a resemblance to the marketing of consumer services.

However, we would argue that the closest equivalent is with political marketing because the sales took place in the service of political ideology for political ends, and although a candidate was not being sold, a party political program certainly was. So, the context was a political and ideological one in which the sales occurred in an intense theater of public argument and controversy. Moreover, as with other political programs, privatization was at least initially based on selling a promise that might not be realized. The product itself, newly privatized shares, was a political symbol; to purchase them was to adhere to the political policy that produced them. Buying shares, like voting in an election, was part of the public construction and articulation of personality, as people would tell friends and neighbors what they had done. This identified the purchaser with a major social movement and what it symbolized.

Case Studies in Privatization

The following case studies illustrate some of the key points discussed heretofore and demonstrate how marketing can be used as a political tool (Newman, 1996) by the Conservative government to promote its political ends through the traditional avenues of marketing. Two of the early major privatizations, British Telecom and British Gas, are discussed, followed by two later privatizations of water and energy. In each case, the advertising and "marketing mix" used to promote the government's privatization program is analyzed in some detail. This is followed by a review of why the marketing of privatization was so successful. We conclude with a discussion of the lessons to be learned for marketing similar programs in the future.

Case 1: British Telecom

British Telecom (BT) was the share offer that, above all others, established the credibility of the privatization program. BT was the first public utility to be privatized, partly to raise capital for its much-needed modernization. It also was the first to use mass communication techniques (Rothschild, 1978). Before privatization, BT was a classic public sector industry, exhibiting all the negative characteristics of most nationalized industries at that time. As Sir George Jefferson, BT's chairman, noted, "BT didn't know the costs of its services. There were no qualified accountants. They didn't know what they owned." In the beginning, there was considerable resistance to privatizing BT from various sectors, not least from the general public. The Labour Party was against it in principle, the Post Office Engineering Union and the press were against it, and even the City of London was skeptical. As the maverick member of Parliament (MP), Norman Tebbitt, remarked, "The issue became one of how to persuade people in the city to raise £4 billion in a single flotation—something that had never been done before." Even Martin Jacombe, the head of Kleinwort Benson (the bankers chosen to lead the flotation), recognized that because BT was the biggest equity issue ever attempted in the world at the time, its success was in doubt.

The marketing strategists quickly realized that communication was key to a successful sell-off of BT, but the strategic objective was to appeal beyond the usual share buyers to the general public at large who, although they might consider an occasional gamble, had never thought of actually owning shares before. To do this required an attractive offer amplified via a massive advertising campaign to raise public awareness about the forthcoming flotation (British Telecom, 1984–1996).

The Function of the Advertising

The advertising function in the case of the BT privatization was to surface what people already knew from the press and other media and to further this existing momentum. Dorlands was the advertising agency chosen to create the campaign leading up to flotation. Hitherto, this company's main claim to fame had been a series of commercials it had developed that transformed Castrol from a mediocre company into a market leader. It aimed to do the same for BT. However, its demanding brief was to sell a product that initially had no price, no sale date, a 1-day sale, and a target audience that knew nothing about the product (Feldwick, 1990).

The campaign quickly ran into trouble with the Independent Television Commission (ITC), the public body responsible for licensing and regulating commercially funded television services. The ITC ruled that shares could not be advertised on television. However, Dorlands found a way around the ban by the simple device of developing a television commercial that featured a solemn voice reading out the content of the privatization act itself "by royal proclamation," as images of the nation—the countryside, shops, motorways, commuters, London, the White Cliffs of Dover—fled past. The television commercial said nothing about buying shares; rather, it simply urged people to "register for the BT prospectus" (British Telecom, 1984).

A fixed price share offer was chosen as the vehicle for selling the shares, which meant that public interest would be maximized. Also, advertising aimed to heighten institutional interest. This would be inevitable because once it was privatized, BT would be guaranteed a place in the Financial Times Index of 100 shares (FT 100) and, hence, would become part of any well-structured institutional portfolio. This advertising provided a benchmark for every subsequent sale. Numerous other communication devices also were used including "touring road shows" and a telephone "hotline" (which had been used before but never on this scale). However, even the hotline was overwhelmed, even though it was open 24 hours a day, 7 days a week, with 250 operators answering the often basic questions.

The results of this intense marketing campaign were highly successful. The issue closed nine times oversubscribed (11 million shares were applied for), so that scaling of applications for more than 400 shares became necessary. Shares went on sale on December 3, 1984, for £1.30, and within hours the price had risen by 87%. The initial underpricing of shares, a deliberate political act to alleviate buyer uncertainty, later led to criticisms that BT was sold off too cheaply. There was another dividend for the government. Many employees had demonstrated their support for privatization by applying for free shares in the company, so that it later became difficult for trade union representatives to claim that they were against privatization as a general policy. Privatization, therefore, offered Prime Minister Thatcher the opportunity of achieving two objectives simultaneously: winning voters' "hearts and minds" and effectively neutralizing some of the power of the unions. Hence, the BT flotation came to be perceived as a great success for the Conservatives. It demonstrated what could be achieved by a smart campaign. The Central Office of Information declared that the campaign had a positive impact on 16% of purchasers, a negative impact on 6%, and (somewhat surprisingly) no impact on the vast majority (78%). However, indifference to buying shares in privatized companies evaporated as the public gradually began to realize the personal advantages that could be derived from share ownership (Feldwick, 1990; National Audit Office [NAO], Department of Trade and Industry [DTI], 1984–1985; NAO, 1992–1993, 1993–1994).

Case 2: British Gas

Two years after the British Telecom flotation, British Gas was turned from a public sector monopoly to a private sector monopoly. Pre-flotation advertising stimulated public interest in the offer and, according to the Institute of Practitioners in Advertising, achieved an additional £200 million in revenue for the government (Feldwick, 1990).

Research at the time of the announcement of the sale indicated that, like British Telecom, British Gas suffered from the "dinosaur image" associated with most nationalized industries. To counter this, a corporate image-building advertising campaign was essential. The most interested groups were found to be men in the 35- to 54-year age group, ABC(1) socioeconomic groups, and other existing shareholders. The strategy articulated the concept of the "people's share offer" and attempted to create a feeling of not wanting to be left out of an exciting and financially rewarding opportunity. Television, radio, press, and poster campaigns were used, embracing people from every walk of life as participants. The marketing campaign formed a number of distinct phases; it aimed first to build awareness about the company, then indicated the terms of the offer, and later signaled the final phase between the publication of the prospectus and the final date for applications (NAO, Department of Energy, 1987–1988).

British Gas Advertising

Advertising used a flame motif as a symbol for spreading the word about the forthcoming British Gas flotation. Word-of-mouth advertising was particularly important to persuade people to urge each other on. A slogan was invented—"Tell Sid"—that endorsed and encouraged this process. (Indeed, so successful was the Tell Sid campaign that the slogan was adopted for the entire privatization program thereafter.) The idea behind it was that privatization represented good news for ordinary people because they could now get a piece of the action. Explicitly, it told them to spread the message, as persuasion from friends always is more influential. The agency, Young and Rubicam, wanted to personalize the campaign, to inspire, in their language, a process of "Chinese whispers." The "Sid" metaphor occurred in the information phase of the campaign as a conduit for building up, almost like a mini-soap opera, awareness of the terms of the offer. Information had to be passed on to Sid whenever the particular character saw him. People from all walks of life were shown whispering the phrase to each other—cleaner to dentist, dentist to patient, and so on. Sid himself, of course, never actually appeared, although one newspaper advertisement featured 40 men called Sid, for Sid is every man. In addition, various incentives were offered to British Gas customers, employees, and the public at large. In the largest direct mail campaign ever launched in Britain, more than 16 million letters were sent out to British Gas customers by its chairman, Dennis Rooke. The effectiveness of the advertising campaign was constantly monitored against preset criteria, and Survey Research Associates reported that it actually met or exceeded these requirements. A total of 4.5 million applications for shares were received, and just under half of these came from new share buyers. Once again, advertising as a medium of persuasion had proved its value (British Gas, 1984–1996; Feldwick, 1990).

Similarly, the sale of the aero-engine business, Rolls Royce, turned out to be a very cost-effective advertising campaign and one that, despite the volatility of its business, again proved to be attractive to ordinary people as well as professional investors. By this time, the Conservative government had been able to hone its marketing techniques so that the effect of advertising and the marketing mix combined to provide a very powerful and persuasive campaign. Press advertising predominated (in the so called "quality papers" and financial publications), and television was used for the final offer phase. Advertising purloined emotive symbols—the Rolls Royce company logo itself, coupled with World War II fighter planes (Spitfires and Hurricanes)—and conveyed essential information about the company with a particular emphasis on engineering excellence. An independent MORI poll conducted at the time reported that awareness of the company increased dramatically—from 22% to 64%—among experienced shareholders, and the level of interest generated surpassed that for other secondary privatizations such as British Aerospace, Cable & Wireless, and Britoil. And this was achieved on a much more limited budget. The offer closed oversubscribed by a factor of 10, and shares were clawed back from the institutions in favor of the small investors. Undoubtedly, the quality and potency of the advertising again were critical factors in the success of the sale (NAO, DTI, 1987–1988).

Privatization and the Marketing Mix

But the achievement of all these early privatizations was not simply a matter of creative advertising; it also was due to the successful integration of the other elements of the marketing mix. Better distribution channels were invented for this new mass consumer product, and the price was right. However, it was too attractive, according to critics who saw privatization as a give-away of state assets or, in the language of former British Prime Minister Harold Macmillan, "selling the family silver" (Chapman, 1990).

In the first British Telecom sales, costs to the consumer were minimized in a number of ways. Telephone vouchers were offered to buyers, as were bonus shares after a qualifying period. Payment in three installments lessened the initial outlay of individual buyers. British Telecom estimated the cost of these incentives at £171 million. Another twist was that advertising aimed at institutional investors sought to create the impression of a share shortage among them to increase revenue generation through higher share prices. A total of 10% of shares were reserved for employees and pensioners of the company (NAO, DTI, 1984–1985).

Nearly a decade later, in December 1991 and July 1993, the government offered for sale the second and third tranches of British Telecom. Again, these offers used the whole panoply of incentives and selling techniques that had been used individually, or in limited combinations, before. These incentives included bonus shares, discounts on the second and third installments, and vouchers for the sale and purchase of shares through share shops.

In general, the great British privatizations took care to involve private citizen applicants, and shares were clawed back from institutional investors in deference to these small investors. Generally, "loyalty bonuses" offered a powerful attraction. Graduated payments toward the share price were institutionalized, and proportionately high dividend benefits were available from the beginning through part-payment and bonuses, for example, in the sale of British Gas (Ramanadhan, 1988). Third, an array of pricing and sales channels were provided to attract a variety of customers. These included priority in the allocation of shares; installment plan payments (which raised the return on the initial investment); and incentives to buy and retain shares in the form of bonus shares, customer vouchers, and installment discounts (Ramanadhan, 1988).

The promoters of privatization also realized the great importance of innovative distribution channels in fields that previously had lacked them. By becoming mass retailers of shares, the vendors managed to create a perceptual association with consumer products and, indeed, to turn shares into consumer products. Thus, with the second British Telecom sale in 1991, share shops were established to demystify private sector share-dealing services. Share shops were to be used for the first time to make the issues as widely available as possible, and all applicants who made use of these outlets were to receive preferential treatment. Fully 75% of the 1991 offer and 59% of the 1993 offer were sold through the share shops. By the third sale in 1993, the 8 financial service providers with high street outlets in 1991 had metamorphisized into some 150 share shops accounting for 60% of the successful applications for shares (British Telecom, 1993–1994).

In the case of British privatization, one also has to add a fifth p to that conventional marketing mix litany of product, price, promotion, and place—namely, public relations. The sale of this product depends, perhaps critically, on a certain social atmosphere—its pressure and momentum. And this atmosphere had to be artificially produced because privatization was an untested theory, an untried gamble, and the site of political tension. It had to be engineered by the mass media. This is an example of the naturalization, or social manufacture of reality, so often discussed by critical theorists. Thus, the role of the media and their political support, together with their speculation and advice, was essential to these various campaigns. Free media interacted with purchased media to create that positive "climate" that Ellul (1973) sees as being so important to the success of propaganda. Thus, the press coverage hyped up the campaigns, stressed the "rich pickings" to be had, and (critically) explained the mechanics of how to purchase shares (although advertising played an informative role here as well). Another press role lay in stimulating and maintaining public confidence in the privatization process. The financial pages of the press, in particular, lent the product high credibility, which was important because the Conservative government was really selling a promise, something that was both intangible and uncertain (as the stock market crash of 1987 demonstrated so brutally). The leadership role and persuasiveness of politicians, particularly Thatcher, also were significant in what was portrayed as an exercise in popular mass democracy.

Case 3: Water

But as the privatization program expanded, public disquiet began to surface. This was especially true of the water and power industries. Water was seen to come, in former Cabinet Minister Michael Howard's words, "free from the sky."

Water, unlike steel, was perceived to be "natural"—a part of people's birthright and also "ours." People felt that they, the citizens, owned it. It was seen as plentiful, and the purification and distribution costs associated with it were more invisible, so in the public mind, there was an expectation of cheapness. Moreover, water was a natural monopoly, which made it difficult to introduce consumer choice or for consumers to switch to a competitor. Marketing, in this instance, met a highly charged problem of political resistance that it simply did not face in the other privatizations. The voices of interest groups of different political hues were raised in opposition. Fully 83% of the public, according to a MORI poll, were opposed to the sale. Indeed, a former leading minister on Thatcher's team, Tebbitt, has since claimed that the semantics of the water sales were entirely wrong. It should have been described to the public not as the water industry, with connotations of freeness and purity, but rather as the sewerage industry, which would have elicited an entirely different response and created some concept of cost.

In addition to this voluble constituency of public discontent, marketing recognized that investors might be more difficult to persuade. In the words of one commentator, "boring old water" did not seem a great growth prospect. For one thing, it was the victim of decades of underinvestment. The once hardy Victorian infrastructures were in need of repair, and the European Union demanded dramatic improvements in water quality. Politicians did not want to meet the costs. Indeed, for them, part of the beauty of privatization was that the subsequent odium, the political cost of price increases, would attach to the private organizations instead of government.

But the Conservative government sought to overcome any reluctance by investors with the device of the aptly named "green dowery," a generous public donation to cover debts and the many anticipated repairs that the new companies would receive as a free gift. Thus, the offer was oversubscribed 10-fold, with the usual criticism that the organization had been sold too cheaply—true, of course, but beside the point. Advertising was, and had become, the norm in these privatizations, witty and highly inventive—water cascading through pipes, splendid fountains gushed against a background of Handel's "water music." Elsewhere, little plastic ducks floated by and returned smoking cigars, a straight appeal to acquisitiveness. Slogans played well on the formula "H_2O," which became the leitmotiv of this campaign (NAO, Department of the Environment, 1991–1992).

Case 4: Energy

Energy represented the most awkward of all the privatizations because it contained costs that, as the organization of the sale progressed, were found to be unquantifiable. These costs include the open-ended ones of decommissioning the aging Magnox nuclear reactors, described as "1950s rust buckets," and a cost precept added to coal, gas, and oil electricity generation to align these with the higher costs of nuclear generation. The Conservatives had hoped to dispose of that entire industry, including its nuclear Achilles' heel, but was forced into a compromise, so that the decommissioning costs would now have to be sustained by a permanent tariff on electricity consumers. Marketing also faced a souring of the social atmosphere. The government itself was a victim of the hubristic belief that it could sell anything. But the regulators brought in to control natural monopolies such as gas and water had begun to bite, making privatization less attractive as an investment. Water customers, meanwhile, were furious at droughts, soaring bills, and the inflated salaries paid to water company directors, reviving an old insult to describe those enjoying the consequences of protected markets and inflated incomes as "fat cats." Again, the pricing of the offer was a political decision, and once again, the citizen investors got a bargain. But this time, the task given the marketers was as harsh in its way as with the first privatization, that of BT.

Privatization no longer was the flavor of the month. Recognizing that the best weapon to defuse hostility is humor, that is what the marketing strategy duly sought to use. Promoters created a character, "Frank N. Stein," a happy, electrically powered monster living a life of cheerful domesticity with his wife and family. The series unfolded vignettes of the family's life, assisted by plenty of sparking electricity and massive electric contraptions—Frank at the gym, Frank as a rock star, and so on. A pseudo-Vincent Price voice extolled the virtues of the offer—and persuaded 5% of the British public to buy. What the subtext of this advertising here is in effect doing is humanizing a horror figure. The whole sequence constitutes an interesting case study in marketing under conditions of adversity.

Why Was the Marketing of Privatization So Successful?

In the selling of privatization, marketing and particularly advertising were influential in the construction of the public mood—a rhetorical and imagistic strategy that contributed to the evolution of a distinct social climate. The special strength of marketing was that it offered an uncluttered image or even Utopian vision to a mass audience without the critical mediation of other agencies. But there also were particular strategies adopted in these campaigns that made them more successful than they otherwise would have been. As such, therefore, they offer lessons to future marketers of ideas, causes, and ideologies.

First, the advertising connected well and interpreted the zeitgeist of the age. It felt contemporary, reflecting the prevailing public mood or social climate of the 1980s. Symbols such as the bowler hat were borrowed from the spectacularly successful culture of the City of London, the wealth of whose workforce was deeply envied by other British citizens. The advertising success fully created the feeling of joining a vast celebratory national movement, and the people were really being asked to make a "death-defying leap onto a moving bandwagon."

Second, the campaign excelled at wit and humor. In Britain, humorous advertising is particularly valued because advertising to British homes traditionally had the character of an uninvited guest whose presence is made acceptable by humor; that is, it rewards the viewer. Humor might be low on credibility, but it is high as an attention-getting device or to deflect criticism when a product, a concept, or an individual is unpopular.

Third, the campaign drew its inspiration and symbolism from popular culture, as effective marketing so often must do. The entire campaign was, in fact, constructed around symbols to a degree unusual even in consumer marketing. But symbols are recognized by social anthropologists as critical in the construction of reality for most people. The anthropologist, May Douglas, states that the very highly educated have little concept of how potent symbols are to others. She gives the example of the dismay of Irish workers in London when the Catholic Church abolished the requirement for eating fish on Friday because to them it was a highly symbolic connection between a fondly remembered home in Ireland and the glory of Rome, and this campaign was image rich. The shares in themselves were symbolic—of wealth, of partnership in capitalism. In addition, the advertising used another potent symbol, nationalist imagery, as if buying shares in the ex-public estate was somehow engaging in a patriotic act. And as the major privatizations were occurring in the wake of the Falklands war victory, nationalist symbolism had ceased to seem anachronistic.

Fourth, much of the advertising was composed in a self-consciously "classic" vein with references to high culture to make share buying seem like a noble calling and then humanizing the process through wit, for example, featuring ballerinas dancing with bowler hats.

Fifth was the mobilization of cultural myths. The idea of empowering the "little guy" and seeing him avenged against institutional bullies and "the system" is prevalent across many cultures. That, for example, might explain the popularity of films by British comedian Norman Wisdom in Albania. Certainly, it has been a particularly powerful theme in the history of Hollywood. The Tell Sid campaign, the most famous and influential of all the privatization campaigns, consolidated this cultural resource with its idea of ordinary people benefiting from the democratization of corporate resources. The new myth was that they now had a share in the culture of the rich and could grow in stature.

Lessons for Marketing

Clearly, it is important to ask whether the experience of selling privatization in Britain offers any general lessons for marketing and the development of marketing theory. The core message in all cases cited was articulated via both paid and unpaid multiple media to the degree that it appeared to saturate the cognitive environment. Of course, it could be argued that such a phenomenon really represents a conceptual hybrid between marketing and propaganda, but the term "marketing" alone is overly narrow and fails to distinguish the subtleties of political situations. In World War I, British propaganda during the first few years was the private initiative of the London advertising industry, illustrating the point that there is direct transliteration between marketing and propaganda.

This case shows that marketing, when employed in conjunction with other communication methods, has the power to change things and even to change the world order. First, the campaigns enlisted the persuasive power of well-chosen symbols, around which the entire campaigns were constructed. Second, the campaigns played with popular culture, drawing their motifs and inspiration from culture, as much effective advertising usually does. Moreover, the campaigns identified and exploited the particular social climate of the 1980s. They were part of their times in the sense that the product is an expression of a prevailing public mood. This explains the success of much product advertising, especially when, as here, the core message is articulated via many media, both paid and unpaid. The sense was "Everybody is talking about it." The connection between marketing and the prevailing social value systems is an intimate one. These case studies affirm the persuasive impact of bandwagon effects and the enduring power of greed.

Conclusions

These privatizations represented not just the marketing of shares but also an economic ideology. The Conservatives were not elected in 1979 with any type of preordained plan to privatize or any popular mandate to do so. Nor was the initial objective particularly dictated by ideology. They aimed to avoid the redevelopment costs of a major part of the public estate being placed on the Treasury and also to raise the money necessary to sustain vote-winning tax cuts. Other consequences, which included reducing union power, increasing managerial efficiency, and ending the cash drain of the nationalized industries, were unsolicited benefits of privatization whose value was quickly recognized by the Conservatives. Privatization rapidly became the fulcrum of Conservative policy. In many ways, it was the Conservatives' *only* policy, and it structured the activity of the government. This all-fulfilling agenda made no intellectual or politically creative demands; anyone could follow the argument, and it filled an ideas vacuum. Deeper and more rooted problems, demanding analysis and not amenable to simple universal solutions (e.g., the continued underperformance in education, the "coarsening" of Britain's civic culture), were avoided because a single big idea could fill the political horizon.

There was a broader significance for British culture in this shift to the values of private individualism and away from the public virtues. In this process, privatization was a symbol, a reflection, and a cause, although it must be viewed in concert with other types of politically orchestrated movements such as the sale of public housing. Certainly, the case confirms the enduring power of bandwagon effects and (perhaps) greed. People began to view themselves in a different way, as proto-capitalists and as property owners rather than as workers. Many felt perhaps an authentic "city sense," the illusion of command over resources and unity with the men in red braces (i.e., professional city investors). The iconography of the marketing strategy helped to manufacture this fantasy. The Conservatives viewed privatization fundamentally as a way of creating more party members, the idea of the self-sustaining citizen or the "Essex man," as the newspapers called this brash new individual. Ownership of shares and council houses allegedly would create Tory voters. The emasculation of trade union power in Britain was another unsolicited but warmly greeted (by some) benefit. The privatizations also werc helpful to the Tories in a more instrumental way because the new property owners could be made fearful of socialist confiscation. For example, the Conservative Central Office bombarded shareholders with propaganda claiming that Labour would nationalize their assets, using mailing lists generated by various privatizations such as the British Telecom and British Gas share lists.

Others were more critical. We were, they claimed, in danger of breeding a "culture of contempt" (the phrase was the Archibishop of York's), a belief that the private system was the sole repository of virtue and that its antithesis, public service, was innately parasitic. This view was later strengthened by the tragedy of the private pensions scandal in which the government had persuaded many with occupational pensions to migrate to inferior private schemes. This began to surface a decade after the major privatizations. A buoyant private sector, and a demoralized public estate certainly wcre among the unanticipated dangers of privatization. Despite this, and even with the demise of the Conservative government, the public's belief in the benefits of privatizations remains virtually undiminished. This further confirms the importance of the power of marketing ideas in the political arena.

References

Berger, P. L., & Luckman, T. (1966). *The social construction of reality*. New York: Doubleday.

British Gas. (1984-1996). *Annual reports* (various years). London: Author.

British Telecom. (1984). *Prospectus*. Author.

British Telecom. (1984-1996). *Annual reports* (various years). London: Author.

British Telecom. (1993-1994). *Annual report*. Author.

Chapman, C. (1990). *Selling the family silver: Has privatisation worked?* London: Business Books.

Ellul, J. (1973). *Propaganda: The formation of men's attitudes*. New York: Knopf.

Feldwick, P. (1990). British Gas advertising. In P. Feldwick (Ed.), *Advertising works* (Paper No. 5, IPA Advertising Effectiveness Awards). London: Cassell.

Hall, E. T. (1989). *Beyond culture*. New York: Anchor/Doubleday.

Haskel, J., & Szymanski, S. (1991, December). Privatisation, jobs, and wages. *Employment Institute Economic Report*, pp. 1-6.

Her Majesty's Stationery Office. (1995). *Privatisation: Sharing the U.K. experience*. London: Author.

Hunt, S. D. (1976). The nature and scope of marketing. *Journal of Marketing, 40,* 17-28.

Kotler, P. (1972). A generic concept of marketing. *Journal of Marketing, 36,* 46-54.

Kotler, P., & Levy, S. J. (1996). Broadening the concept of marketing. *Journal of Marketing, 33,* 10-15.

Marsh, D. (1991). Privatisation under Thatcher: A review of the literature. *Public Administration, 69,* 459-480.

National Audit Office. (1992-1993). *The sale of the second tranche of shares in British Telecommunications* (HC568). London: Author.

National Audit Office. (1993-1994). *The third sale of shares in British Telecommunications* (HC663). London: Author.

National Audit Office, Department of Energy. (1987-1988). *Sale of government shareholding in British Gas* (HC22). London: Author.

National Audit Office, Department of the Environment. (1991-1992). *Sale of the Water Authority in England and Wales* (HC256). London: Author.

National Audit Office, Department of Trade and Industry. (1984-1985). *Sale of government shareholding in British Telecommunications plc* (HC495). London: Author.

National Audit Office, Department of Trade and Industry. (1987-1988). *Sale of government share-holding in Rolls Royce* (HC243). London: Author.

Newman, B. I. (1996, April). *Political marketing as a governing tool.* Paper presented at the Political Marketing Conference, Cambridge, UK.

Ramanadham, V. V. (Ed.). (1988). *Privatisation in the U.K.* London: Routledge.

Ramanadham, V. V. (1989). *Privatisation in the developing countries.* London: Routledge.

Ramanadham, V. V. (1993). *Privatisation: A global perspective.* London: Routledge.

Rothschild, M. L. (1978). Political advertising: A neglected policy issue in marketing. *Journal of Marketing Research, 15,* 58-71.

Scammell, M. (1995). *Designer politics: How elections are won.* London: Macmillan.

Searle, J. R. (1995). *The construction of social reality.* London: Penguin.

35

Interest Groups and the Political Process

Gender Issues

BARBARA LINDSAY

The results of the 1996 U.S. presidential election and the 1997 U.K. general election both demonstrated the power and importance of the women's vote. In the United States, the 1996 election marked the first time that the gender gap had exceeded a president's margin of victory (Williams, 1998). Bill Clinton's campaign undertook gender-based research and then specifically addressed women voters in terms of their different life experiences, priorities, and attitudes. In the United Kingdom, the majority of "floating" or "swing" voters were women (Fawcett Society, 1996). Women's votes, which had been responsible for keeping the Conservatives in power for decades during the 20th century, swung a massive 11% to Labour, compared to a 9% swing among men's votes (Stephenson, 1998, p. 108). The United Kingdom's Liberal Democrats nearly doubled their number of members of Parliament (MPs) from 26 to 46 after a general election campaign that aimed, for the first time, to be strongly "women friendly" in their target winnable seats and in their national media management.

Clearly, public opinion no longer should be considered as gender neutral, and the "interest group" that is women (52% of the population) merits special consideration by political marketers. The focus in this chapter concerns the implications of research into women's perspectives in the political process—the political parties, the polls, and the media. The aim is to examine the nature of the gender gap in voting behavior; issues of the representation of women with their different life experiences within the legislature; the record of campaigns (or lack thereof) in the winning of women's votes in the U.S. (1996) and U.K. (1997) elections; and gender perspectives of the U.K. political parties, women's lobbies, and media.

The Importance of the Gender Gap in Voting Behavior

Since 1945, opinion polls have recorded a difference in voting behavior between men and women, and this has become known as "the gender gap." It is particularly significant because it cuts across class, race, and regional differences that traditionally feature in left/right or geographical analyses of voting behavior.

Many of the factors relevant for discussion on the subject of the gender gap are common to both the United States and United Kingdom. The Clinton 1996 campaign identified the "soccer mom" as a typical floating or swing voter to be wooed—a working mother busy with her family and commitments to her local community who made up her mind during the few days before the election. In the United Kingdom, some talk in 1997 was of the parties' need to appeal to the "Worcester woman" rather than to the "Essex man" of the 1992 general election.

Looking at the U.S. statistics, it is reasonably claimed that it was women's votes in 1996 that allowed Clinton to remain in the White House for a second term. In 1992, 15% more women voted for him than for George Bush; in 1996, the gap widened to 18% (Granshaw, 1997). The gender gap difference in the proportion of women and men supporting Clinton widened from 4 percentage points in 1992 to 11 percentage points in 1996 (Norris & Carroll, 1997). If women had voted in the same proportions as did men, then Bush would have won. Women generally have been more likely than men to support Democratic presidential candidates. This gender gap persists across all age, income, and education groups. Discussing "statewide races" for governor and U.S. senator, Norris and Carroll (1997) state, "In every election since 1982, it has been possible to identify several specific statewide races where not only was there a gender gap, but also women's votes provided the margin of victory" (p. 3).

In the summer of 1996, the race for Congress showed similar wide disparities between men's and women's support for the Democrats and Republicans, so women's preference for the Democrats clearly was about parties more than about personalities (Page, 1996).

A gender gap of only a few percentage points can have a dramatic impact on election results. In Britain, the Fawcett Society, the leading women's organization campaigning for equality between the sexes, used Gallup's 1992 election survey and other up-to-date opinion poll data, including MORI polls, to persuade the U.K. parties of the importance of women's votes. In *Winning Women's Votes,* published for the party conferences in the autumn of 1996, the Fawcett Society (1996) established that the political parties were going into the 1997 general election campaign with knowledge of the following:

- In 1992, 82% of women had voted (and they are 52% of the population), compared to 79% of men, a difference of more than 1 million votes.
- Among those who voted Conservative in 1992, twice as many women as men were undecided for 1997 (12% women, 6% men).
- The majority of floating voters were women, with 23% being undecided as to how they would vote, compared to 16% of men.

- More than half (52%) of the women did not know which party to trust the most, compared to 35% of the men.
- More than a quarter (28%) of the women did not trust any of the political leaders, compared to 18% of the men.
- Across all class and regional differences, women were more likely to vote Conservative and less likely to vote Labour than were men. (Fawcett Society, 1996)

In the 1997 U.K. general election, Labour achieved a 179-seat majority in the House of Commons with 44% of the vote, compared to the Conservatives' 31% and the Liberal Democrats' 17%. MORI's research in May 1997 found the following:

- Approximately 44% of women's votes went to Labour, compared to 45% of men's.
- Approximately 32% of women's votes went to the Conservatives, compared to 31% of men's.
- Approximately 18% of women's votes went to the Liberal Democrats, compared to 17% of men's.

The gender gap on Labour's lead over the Conservatives, therefore, showed women's support to be 2 percentage points lower than men's, a very significant number of votes nationally for most elections.

As stated previously, U.K. opinion polls suggest that women still are more likely to vote Conservative than are men across all classes and regions. The only exception to this, according to the May 1997 MORI poll, is one age group, as women ages 18 to 34 years are more likely to vote Labour than are men of the same age group. Because 18- to 34-year-old women make up only 16% of the electorate, while women over 35 years of age make up 33%, on average women across the ages are more likely than men to favor the Conservatives.

Of strong significance when analyzing the gender gap is the fact that several U.K. studies showed women to be deeply alienated from party politics. One example is focus group research carried out by the Fawcett Society among women floating voters. The Fawcett Society (1997b) report, *It's Not Like Picking a Football Team,* found that many women in all age groups described politicians as untrustworthy, unlikely to keep their promises, and out of touch with the concerns of ordinary people. These women were not strongly attached to one party because they did not feel that any of the parties reflected their perspectives.

Women's Representation in Government

Throughout the American and British legislatures, it still is the case that only a small proportion of political representatives are women. Those few women who have broken through to power cannot reasonably be expected to represent all women. The political parties and women's organizations report problems in getting women selected for winnable seats, and there clearly is a shortage of women in the legislature who have perceptions and motivations relevant to the representation of the general population of women's particular experiences and "differences."

The women's movement, or women's liberation campaigns, started with a range of points based on needs and injustices that were focused strongly on calls for "equality," seen as equal rights and equal treatment with men. The women's movement then progressed, for many of its members, to calls for understanding that women are "equal but different" and a request for respect for those differences. This includes a request for respect for the responsibilities, vulnerabilities, and needs that are inherent in the differences between the sexes, primarily because women have the major domestic responsibilities, bear and usually rear the children, and act as carers to the sick and old. These responsibilities are expensive to fulfill in terms of both money and time. These unpaid responsibilities lead to financial deprivation including lack of (or lower) pensions for women, for example, and to the widescale "feminization of poverty" affecting millions of women and their children, which is a major problem in Western democracies, as it is elsewhere in the world.

Progress is needed in moving from respect for differences to a society based on "mutuality." This means a wish for recognition that the sexes are interdependent and that both women and men want the pleasures of family life and work with their respective responsibilities and vulnerabilities, fulfillments, and rewards. Current research on women's political views shows a wish for policy development that addresses the problems of the "long hours working culture" traditionally suffered by men and changes to a more family-friendly working culture suitable for either parent (Adcock, 1997).

The principles of the early battles for equal rights have largely been won, and women are free to vote, stand for election, compete in the workplace, and so on. However, the political importance of understanding the ways in which women's lives usually are different is not yet generally realized. Lovenduski and Randall (1993) express it as follows: "A problem with the early, simple demand for equality was that it assumed that differences between men and women were unimportant. Strategies based on such assumptions would inevitably actually disadvantage women, who would have to become like men if they were to benefit" (p. 59).

Winning Women's Votes: United States

The U.S. 1996 Democrat presidential campaign leaders recognized that women were not properly represented in politics, and they recognized the importance of women's votes. Clinton's team ensured that their candidate appealed to women. Presentation and style were carefully considered and organized, and women were visibly in the top-level team. Policies were explained in women's terms, a vision of "a better America for our children" was portrayed, and media relations were treated seriously. Page (1996) described the U.S. presidential election campaign in "Election '96: The Gender Gap" in *USA Today*. Commenting on a poll by the nonpartisan Pew Research Center that showed the Democrats to have a 27 percentage point lead in women's support over the Republicans whereas men's support was evenly divided, Page quoted Democratic pollster Celinda Lake: "This year's gender gap is of historic proportions, and it's rooted in what are emerging as very fundamental differences in attitudes between men and women, particularly around the role of government."

The Democrats' key campaign issues were selected on the understanding that Clinton had to be disproportionately popular with women to win. Although many issues are important to both men and women—the economy, education, health, crime, and so on—differences of views by gender were identified, and policy development was structured accordingly to give voters, especially women voters, what they had asked for. Page (1996) described how the Democrats recognized that certain issues had different responses from men and women, for example, on whether to cut back or strengthen government itself.

The Democrats held "At the Table" sessions throughout the states, where invited groups of women discussed their priorities and needs. A Democrat pollster described a trend of women making observations such as "I can imagine myself needing the safety net at some time for my family" and of men making statements such as "Just leave me alone." Women found tax breaks to be less important than ensuring that the safety net was intact (Page, 1996).

American women put a high priority on the following:

- Education, where they were not particularly interested in the Republican voucher schemes but rather in standards, discipline, and tax relief for student loans
- Health, where many older women were persuaded by the Democrats that the limited health care currently available to the old and sick—many of whom are women—was under threat
- Crime, where men wanted harsher sentences and women wanted protection, for example, gun control (Page, 1996)

The Democrat campaign had the following features:

- It included "get out the vote" programs that were targeting women in all 50 states.
- It arranged briefings for women leaders on the economy, the environment, education, and crime.
- It had a government paid staff of seven at the White House Office for Women's Initiatives and Outreach.
- It had more than 500 At the Table focus groups nationally that were chaired by Al Gore, Hillary Clinton, and Tipper Gore, among others.
- It had "What I Want the President to Know" forms for completion by focus group members, with each being acknowledged by the White House.
- It had Clinton saying that he wanted women to know that they have a voice in the White House. (Page, 1996)

By contrast, Republican Bob Dole said he intended to "engage women on the issues" and then suggested that his wife, Elisabeth, debate with Hillary Clinton. Republican New Jersey Governor Christine Todd Whitman said, "I think the gender gap comes from a perception that the Republican Party doesn't care about people." Senator Kay Bailey Hutchinson, a Texas Republican, said, "Republicans need to do a better job of . . . understanding women's concerns and speaking to them." Republican pollster Kellyanne Fitzpatrick, adviser to the Republican National Committee, complained that Dole failed to project a visual image of inclusiveness to women by being surrounded too often only by men (quoted in Page, 1996).

Winning Women's Votes:
United Kingdom

None of the U.K. parties in 1997 ran a gender-conscious campaign to compare with that of the U.S. Democrats. As the dissolution of Parliament and the start of the official general election campaign period became imminent, the parties appeared to recognize their need to win women's votes, but most politicians seemed to be unsure about the best way in which to gain women's support.

Members of U.K. women's research or lobby organizations believe that they have identified many of the reasons for this uncertainty. The Women's Communication Centre undertook a survey in which women answered Freud's question "What do women want?" on a postcard. A total of 10,000 replies with political responses were analyzed in terms of what the three main parties were offering. The main conclusion of the authors of the report is that "women's issues," and measures designed to address them, might figure prominently in the parties' strategy documents on women but do not feature strongly in the mainstream policy agendas. They claim that measures that would particularly benefit women are sidelined such as measures on child care, domestic violence, part-time workers' rights, low pay and equal pay, and support for carers. Also, they conclude that within mainstream government policy areas, women's priorities and concerns are different from those issues highlighted by the parties. "Unemployment is presented by all three parties as a key issue in the work debate. Yet for women, the critical issues revolve not so much around being in or out of work [as] around equal pay and access to pensions, child care, a minimum wage, genuinely flexible hours, parental leave, part-time workers' rights, and equal opportunities" (Adcock, 1997, p. vii).

The report's main conclusion echoes the Democrats' experience in America in finding that it is not that women do not understand the topics dominating national politics but rather that women think that important issues are missing from the debates being conducted by politicians. The authors conclude that existing political agendas are failing to address matters of significant importance to women and that women in the broad population should be consulted much more often and to a greater extent (Adcock, 1997, p. vii).

Women and U.K. Politics

At the 1997 general election, the number of women MPs doubled to 120, increasing to 18% from 9% of the total. The Labour government has 101 women MPs, the Conservatives 13, the Liberal Democrats 3, and others 3.

Labour's success in achieving this breakthrough in increased numbers of women MPs owes much to advance planning. The "Emily's List" campaign ("Early money is like yeast") raised funds for women candidates. Also, Labour initiated a policy of "positive action" to maximize the probability of an increased proportion of women MPs being elected for the party. It identified the "target seats" the Labour Party would need to win for the party to win the election, requesting constituencies to ensure that election candidates from half of these target seats were selected from all-women short lists. Some constituencies—but not enough—participated voluntarily, so Labour's headquarters imposed all-women short lists for selection on a sufficient number of constituencies to bring this important proportion of women to men candidates to 50% each. This did achieve the selection of women in many "strong" seats before the process was halted by two Labour men who won their case when they took the issue to an Industrial Tribunal under the Sex Discrimination Act. There is now a debate in the United Kingdom as to whether this tribunal decision could be overturned on appeal in view of European rulings concerning equal treatment in a political context (Diplock, 1998).

All the U.K. parties are now attempting to increase their numbers and proportions of women MPs, but they have different ideologies and methods and are in their respective processes of consultation, debate, and decision making.

The New Labour Government

The Labour government, in its first few days, appointed a secretary of state for social security, Harriet Harman, who also is minister for women. Working for her is Joan Ruddock, a junior minister for women, the only minister not to receive additional salary for her post. There is a strong focus on women's lives, but in the Fawcett Society's view, it is too orientated toward "welfare to work" policies and not sufficiently orientated toward valuing the role of the full-time mother who might have no choice as to whether or not she can work (Fawcett Society, 1997–1998). One of the early legislative acts of the new government was to make a cut in lone parent benefits, aimed at encouraging lone mothers into work. However, many mothers and carers have constraints placed on their own choices by their children's health or other family circumstances such as lack of good, affordable child care.

Some members of the United Kingdom's "women's lobby" are expressing concern that Labour's style is too "macho," that too many of its advisers are young and childless, and that there is greater concern for the success of "presentation" of policies rather than considered concern for their wide-scale social consequences and effects on the daily lives of women and children, many of whom live in poverty. There also is concern that solutions to problems are not being found in redistribution of wealth to mothers but rather in getting mothers into paid work when jobs are scarce and many are very low paid.

The Conservative Party:
Opposition to "Positive Action"

The Conservative Party remains opposed to positive discrimination measures. Under the leadership of William Hague, it is seeking to introduce "more professional" selection of candidates and training programs. One idea is "gender-blind" application forms. The party also is setting up a Conservative Women's Network, which will be in addition to the existing women's organizations that mainly meet during the day. The new network for working women will discuss ideas for reform and inform policy development (Conservative Central Office, 1997, p. 16).

Liberal Democrats:
The Gender Gap and "Positive Action"

The Liberal Democrats appeared to have a slow buildup to realization that the gender gap was important to them. A party-specific Fawcett Society presentation (which was done for all parties at the preelection autumn conferences) showed that in the Liberal Democrats' target marginal seats, they were ahead with the women's vote. The Fawcett Society's research-based advice that if they "looked after women, they would win" was heeded, and the party openly presented itself as the "party for women," achieving an increase in the number of women MPs from 26 to 46. During the 1997 general election campaign, the Liberal Democrats frequently used strong spokeswomen and were the only party to devote two entire press conferences to women's issues and perspectives.

The Liberal Democrats were, however, slow to realize the significance of their lack of women candidates in winnable seats and have only three women MPs. The party is now in the process of debate and submissions of conference resolutions to find improved gender balance methods of candidate selection for the next general election. "Zipping" will take place within the party for the next elections to the European Parliament, which means that men's and women's names will alternate on party list ballot papers. Five of the regional lists will lead with the name of a male candidate, four with the name of a female. The top names are, of course, the ones who win the seats if the party achieves sufficient votes.

Women's Lobbies

In the United States, women's organizations such as the National Organization for Women and the National Women's Political Caucus are very active lobbyists and have achieved a great deal. However, in this short chapter, the main focus is on the similar women's campaigns in the United Kingdom. There were a number of women's organizations working politically in the run-up to the May 1, 1997, general election.

Helen Wilkinson, then project director of Demos, the independent "think tank" on long-term political problems, coauthored with Shelagh Diplock, director of the Fawcett Society, *Soft Sell or Hard Policies* (Wilkinson & Diplock, 1996). They concluded,

> One symptom of the parties' failure to address the substance of women's needs is their disconnection from and distrust of party politics. . . . Women are certainly inclined to think of politics as a boys' club, out of touch with day-to-day reality. . . . Poll evidence consistently shows that women are less trustful of politicians and political parties than [are] men.

Their research found widely held opinions that "political meetings are boring, that politics is dominated by men, and that people only go into politics for themselves" (pp. 10-11).

The authors concluded,

> All these women are looking for a party which will deliver on its promises and make a real difference to the quality of their lives. . . . Women are well aware that national resources are scarce, but they want to be at the front of the queue when money becomes available or when spending is reallocated. (Wilkinson & Diplock, 1996, pp. 10-11)

These findings were echoed throughout the various sectors of the women's movement's research projects in the run-up to the 1997 general election.

Fawcett Society

Whereas valuable research and campaign work for women was done by Demos, the Women's Communication Centre, and other organizations, the United Kingdom's leading cross-party women's political lobbying organization is the Fawcett Society. The society is named after Dame Millicent Garrett Fawcett, who campaigned for women's suffrage and other rights throughout her long life, dying at 82 years of age shortly after seeing women get the vote on the same terms as men in 1928. Her memorial in Westminster Abbey reads, "A wise, constant, and courageous Englishwoman, she won citizenship for women."

Fawcett Society's "Listen to My Vote" Campaign: Public Opinion and the Political Process

In the United Kingdom during the 9 months or so before the May 1, 1997, general election, the Fawcett Society ran a "Listen to My Vote" campaign that aimed, first, to discover and articulate women's political opinions across Britain and, second, to use this information to influence the political process (e.g., the polls, parties, media), to recognize the importance of women's votes and women's political perspectives, and to give them a strong focus and high priority.

In many ways, the campaign was very successful, the women's movement and women's lobby in the United Kingdom were greatly strengthened, powerful progress was made within some sectors of the media on understanding some of the principles and issues, and the Fawcett Society became recognized as an authority on women's perspectives of political issues and practices.

The Listen to My Vote campaign aimed to reach beyond the national media to women across the country. A series of research reports was published and publicized, and "local action packs" were sent to more than 2,000 individual members and supporters of the Fawcett Society's objectives. Several thousand more were distributed in bulk to trade unions, the National Union of Students, women's community organizations, and many of the 8,000 local branches of the National Federation of Women's Institutes, the largest rural national charity in the United Kingdom with approximately 250,000 members whose involvement includes campaigning on high-profile issues such as human rights, the environment, and women's health. The packs contained a series of "how to" guides that assisted with local campaigning, letters to local press, and suggestions for publicity events. Accessible briefings were provided on key campaign areas—poverty, domestic and home life, employment and the gender gap—that gave women facts and figures to use in their campaigning. Many street stalls, public meetings, stunts, and events were held throughout the country, successfully publicizing the Fawcett Society campaign issues.

The Fawcett Society believes that women would achieve better representation of their interests with a proportional representation system of voting and is campaigning for it. A reform of the U.K. voting system was under review at the time of this writing. The Fawcett Society believes that poor representation of women is one of many failings of the current "first past the post" electoral system in single-member constituencies, which makes it possible for candidates in nearly all but marginal seats to ignore special interest group campaigns such as the women's lobby, which represents 52% of the population (Fawcett Society, 1997–1998).

The Listen to My Vote campaign officially was launched in September 1996, in time for the party conferences, with a report on the gender gap in voting patterns and political priorities titled *Winning Women's Votes* (Fawcett Society, 1996). The pollsters Gallup and MORI were extremely helpful to the Fawcett Society in providing full breakdowns of poll results so that gender analysis could take place across class, age, and region as well as gender. As reported earlier, these facts include that 23% of women were undecided voters, compared to only 16% of men, and that many more women did not trust any of the political leaders. Gender gap facts caught the attention of all the parties and the media.

A gender balance analysis was made of the three main party leaders' conference speeches as an indication of their understanding of their need to be women-friendly. Gender-specific words were counted (e.g., father, hero, serviceman, businessman, mother, widow, he, she), and the references to named men and women were counted.

Paddy Ashdown, leader of the Liberal Democrats, came out best with 32 "female" words compared to 30 "male" words as well as 11 references to named women compared to 5 to named men. However, he was criticized for failing to mention in his speech the policy document, *A Fair Deal for Women,* launched at the same conference. The Conservative prime minister, John Major, used 52 words referring to men and 22 to women, naming 14 men and 3 women. The Labour leader of the opposition, Tony Blair, used 74 words specifically referring to men and only 8 to women, naming 22 men and only 3 women. Blair's anecdotes were very "male" in character, and he ended his speech with a football metaphor.

Press interest in the Fawcett Society analysis of the speeches led to coverage of the fact that women were less likely than men to vote for Blair. A number of articles then focused on Blair's image, particularly his hairstyle and whether this was a significant factor in his lack of popularity with women. This infuriating assumption that women trivialize serious matters did have the compensation of affording the Fawcett Society media opportunities to promote information about the gender gap.

A series of Fawcett Society reports and briefings followed, aimed at reinforcing the message that women's priorities should be central to the general election. The focus of each report, which had a different subject or "angle," was how the political parties could appeal to women voters and win women's votes. The reports included the following.

The Best Man for the Job? This report examined the considerable barriers faced by women in getting selected as parliamentary candidates, particularly for winnable seats (Fawcett Society, 1997a). Postelection, the parties are now analyzing the reasons for fewer women being selected for winnable seats and are finding that women's problems can be described mainly with four *c*'s: cash, culture, confidence, and child care.

It's Not Like Picking a Football Team: Women Floating Voters at the 1997 Election. This research report combined polling data with the findings of a focus group carried out among floating voters in a marginal constituency. The women members of the focus group had diverse characteristics as to their social backgrounds, age, class, ethnicity, mother or childless status, and employment status. On the whole, the women started by saying that they "were not political," but when given questions describing possible political development with alternatives to discuss, they turned out to be highly political with strong views on policy for pensions (where the choice was between increased help with either state or private provision), choices between tax cuts or increased child benefits, a minimum wage or increased family credit, and child care issues (Fawcett Society, 1997b).

When asked about their lack of trust in politicians, a typical reply was "Their promises don't mean anything, do they?" (Fawcett Society, 1997b, p. 9).

The one complaint made by every single member of this group was about the confrontational, argumentative style of Parliament and media (Fawcett Society, 1997b, p. 11). When asked why women are more likely to be floating voters, a typical response was "We are more in touch with the effects of what has happened, whereas a man can be more distant" (p. 12). One woman stated, "It is almost like being a football supporter for some men, isn't it? You pick your team . . . [and] whatever that team does, you still support them" (p. 13).

Clearly, these responses from women floating voters in a marginal seat show that it is not, as claimed by many, women's lower intelligence that prevents them from understanding political issues and parties and from making choices. Rather, their uncertainty derives from their greater concern with the relevance to their own and their families' lives of the choices offered, coupled with their frustration in trying, and failing, to learn from the media what the various parties and candidates do have to offer. Women often are undecided until polling day itself. One survey found that a third of women were undecided a month before the election (Fawcett Society, 1997d).

Feminist Theory of Relevance to Political Campaigners

There are a number of feminist theorists whose work is likely to be of assistance to those, including political marketers, who seek increased understanding of how women traditionally have been perceived in relation to men and to wider society. Theories of a few of the most influential are described in brief here.

Simone de Beauvoir, in *The Second Sex,* argued that the inheritance of patriarchal cultures had created a general acceptance in society that the masculine is set up as the "norm" (and men still do run the major institutions, politics, religion, law, science, education, state structures, media, arts, sport, etc.), and the feminine is set up as "the other" and "lesser" (de Beauvoir, 1953). As discussed earlier, there still is a widespread view that to treat women as equal, one must treat them as men. This theory offers an explanation for the fear many politicians have that in treating women as different, they will be perceived to be treating them as other or lesser and thereby denigrating, patronizing, or otherwise insulting them (de Beauvoir, 1953).

Sherry Ortner, an American anthropologist, published in 1974 an essay, "Is Female to Male as Nature Is to Culture?," which added significantly to the existing nature/culture debate (Ortner, 1974). Ortner argues that women had been associated by men, through virtually all cultures and all time, with "nature" due to their childbearing and nurturing roles. Because conceiving a baby is not "clever"—it is nature's achievement—and cooking, cleaning, and attending to the family's domestic needs are not deemed to be clever either, this led to women's devaluation in the community. On the other hand, the masculine area—the area of "culture," the control and organization of the community—was deemed to be clever and, therefore, superior. The culture covers politics, religion, relations with other countries or groups, war/defense, education, science, the media and arts, and so on—the areas of power, authority, control, influence, and the making of money (Ortner, 1974).

Women have had the vote on equal terms with men in the United States and United Kingdom since the 1920s and have enjoyed many other forms of emancipation in the 20th century. It is clear from the research described earlier that a considerable number of women are now more confident of the value of their various roles in society, including the domestic, and are increasingly looking for political representatives who see merit and worth in their family lives and are willing to argue for some redistribution of wealth toward them, whether directly or through child care schemes, care for the aged, or other social benefits.

Nancy Chodorow, an American sociologist, argued in *The Reproduction of Mothering* that gender personality is shaped within the psychodynamics of the family (Chodorow, 1978). She believes that because "each child's initial relationship is to the mother, boys achieve male identity only in contradistinction from the mother" (Humm, 1995, p. 36). A growing boy, who usually is very affectionate and close to his mother in infancy, is unlikely to know much about what his father does in his job unless the father is a sportsman, soldier, spaceman, pilot, policeman, train driver, or fireman—the roles of boys' play. (It is no coincidence that all of these occupations involve uniforms or costumes denoting authority or status.) All boys know what their mothers primarily do—care for the family. A young boy knows from the entire culture around him that he must become "masculine" but has little knowledge of quite what that is. However, he knows that it means not being "feminine," that he must grow to be different from his mother, and that he must "cross a bridge" from the female world of the nursery to manhood to become his own man, a respected individual. Therefore, he sees masculinity, which he must achieve, as superior to femininity, which he must reject. On the other hand, in Chodorow's view, a girl, because of her continuing connection to the mother, as she learns how to mother and care for others, does not need, as a boy does, to repress her infantile experience or relational capacities. Chodorow concludes that girls and women are more likely to define themselves in relation to others (Chodorow, 1978).

The relevance of Chodorow's theories to political marketers is to recognize another important aspect of character in which women are equal but different. Research now shows that many girls grow into voting women who are more likely to want emphasis on social and community concerns than are men because they are accustomed from infancy to define themselves not so much as individuals but as members of a family and a community. Hillary Rodham Clinton showed that she was in harmony with this ethos in her book, *It Takes a Village:*

> Children are cradled in the family, which is primarily responsible for their passage from infancy to adulthood. But around the family are the larger settings of neighborhood, school, church, workplace, community, culture, economy, society, nation, and world, which affect children directly or through the well-being of their families. Each of us participates in several of these interlocking layers of the village. Each of us, therefore, has the opportunity and responsibility to protect and nurture children. . . . Just as it takes a village to raise a child, it takes children to raise up a village to become all it should be. (Rodham Clinton, 1996, p. 317)

The fact that the book's theme and title, of universal wisdom, is taken from an ancient African proverb is another strength in a multicultural society and illustrates one of the reasons for the Clinton administration's achievement of political popularity with women. However, the Democrats' WorkFair programs, getting mothers into paid work while others care for their children, run counter to this ethos. Similarly in Britain, the Labour government's Welfare to Work program, which included a cut in lone parent benefits early in its administration, is seen by many to fail to value motherhood.

Carol Gilligan (1982), an American psychologist and philosopher, argued in *In a Different Voice* that moral reasoning takes different forms in men and in women. Because women are concerned with the activity of care and children's moral development, they define morality as the understanding of responsibility and relationships, whereas men in general are more likely to claim that morality is defined by fairness that leads them to think of rights and rules. Here again, we see ways in which women are equal but different and a convincing rationale for their wide-scale different political priorities.

Carole Pateman (1988) argued in *The Sexual Contract* that in Western democracies "citizenship has been made in the male image" and that the belated inclusion of women to citizenship rights (only the 20th century) operates very differently from the original inclusion of men. Her main thesis is as follows.

First, the "social contract" is male and a "story of freedom." The typical male experience of life is of the free negotiation of a number of contracts, employment, pension, house and car purchases, and the like in their terms, duration, and cancellation possibilities. As the main family "breadwinner," the husband has the right to organize the family budget, to make long-term financial plans, and to live in a locality and in property that suits his needs.

Second, the "sexual contract" is female and a "story of subjection." The biggest contract in a woman's life is marriage, where the prevailing "normal" understandings and arrangements, based on a religious sacrament or its minimalist civil counterpart, must be accepted. There are no clauses to be negotiated in the marriage contract itself. In our still patriarchal society, even though she may earn herself, the wife's career will be broken by childbirth, and women on average earn considerably less than men whether working full-time or part-time. In the main, the wife and mother has to depend on her husband's consideration, generosity, good management, and foresight for her fundamental welfare and security.

Pateman (1994) observes, "Most democratic theorists see no special problem about women and citizenship and tacitly assume that motherhood stands outside politics. The contradictions and ambiguities in women's political position thus remain unrecognized" (p. 247). Here, we see reinforced the findings, from the United States and United Kingdom, that women's political priorities and issues are, in general, different from those of men. Women seek political protection from their vulnerabilities as society's carers; seek enabling legislation to assist them in combining working and family lives; seek a "safety net" in times of hardship; seek safety from crime; and seek a stable and healthy environment, increased incomes, and more control over their own financial affairs and futures.

The Media

In April 1997, the Fawcett Society published *Watching Women: Election '97,* a commissioned survey based on intensive monitoring of television news coverage during the crucial U.K. campaigning week of April 4-10, 1997 (Fawcett Society, 1997d). The research found that news coverage had been dominated by male politicians, reporters, presenters, experts, academics, and other professionals. "The television news teams are not fulfilling their public service obligation to inform by consistently not including women in their coverage" (p. 13). At this time, about a third of women voters were found to be undecided as to how they would vote. Monitoring did take place in the broadcast media to ensure party parity as required but failed to register the marginalization of women's roles and contributions, even when they did appear (Fawcett Society, 1997d).

Seeking explanations for the missing women and women's issues in the media, the Autumn 1997 issue of the Fawcett Society's (1997c) quarterly newsletter, *Towards Equality,* quotes broadcaster Bob Worcester of MORI:

> Opinion formers know they must follow the detail of the news, read the leader pages and editorial comment in the heavyweight newspapers as well as the news stories, watch other opinion formers, and debate and discuss current affairs in order that when their time comes, they will appear informed themselves and thereby enhance their own status as informed, educated, and influential. (p. 5)

The Fawcett Society's text below this quotation reads, "The evidence from a number of recent studies, including Fawcett's own analysis of the 1997 election media coverage, is that these political opinion formers are almost exclusively male" (p. 5).

One would have thought that during an election, when women's votes were to be wooed, the political parties would insist on fair representation of women politicians and issues. This is not generally the case. The influence of the parties' "spin doctors" often is strong in wanting communicators who will follow the agreed party line, and for the majority of parties most of the time, this is primarily a male agenda. In the week monitored by the Fawcett Society, excluding the three male party leaders, there were 127 appearances by men politicians and only 8 by women, none of whom appeared on any of the main BBC or ITV news broadcasts; instead, they appeared on more peripheral programs.

Speaking of the U.K. press's lack of women editors, Mary Ann Sieghart, lead writer for *The Times,* says that some editors give less weight to women's views and might think that women are more muddled thinkers (quoted in Fawcett Society, 1997c).

Linda Christmas (1997), author of *Chaps of Both Sexes,* quotes a recent survey by National Opinion Polls stating that "88% of women thought that national newspapers were biased against women, and 75% said that they could not name a national newspaper that was on their side at all" (p. 35).

However, it was not only the masculine culture of most of the media in policy discussion that thwarted women voters in their search for information on the policies being offered by the main parties. The widespread practice, particularly in the U.K. broadcast media, was to regard "news" as being the "horse race" or "gladiatorial contest" between the parties and between the leaders. Norris and Carroll (1997) confirm the same practice as occurring in the United States: "Campaign news commonly emphasizes the poll-driven horse race frame (who's ahead, who's behind)" (p. 1).

Equally unhelpful to those seeking information on which to base their votes was the number of interviewers who believed that their role was to engage in the contest themselves, clashing intellects with their political interviewees. Sancho-Aldridge (1997), in the Independent Television Commission's research publication *Election '97: Viewers' Responses to the Television Coverage,* carries a number of viewers' quotes on these themes including "Issues should be debated in more depth, more openly" (female, 45-54 years, p. 49), "I want clear, concise explanations of policies and views, not a 20-second sound bite and a lot of posturing" (female, 16-24 years, p. 49), and "I felt that the interviewers always had the intention [or goal] of trying to trip up the politicians. It was more like watching an argument than actually presenting information" (female, 16-24 years, p. 39).

Also relevant to this debate on the role of the media in politics is the question "What is news?" Sieghart says, "Papers are so obsessed with events rather than process, and I think that might be a male thing." She explains, "I would give prominence to social trend type stories: the way we live now and the sort of people we are. And I'd like to do more success stories because I am interested in how to solve problems" (quoted in Christmas, 1997, p. 24).

The Fawcett Society consider it a real achievement that its election media analysis report has had an enabling effect on women journalists who want to write serious women's perspectives but were prevented from doing so by their editors. They now have proof of past and existing inadequacies in political coverage. Mary Ann Stephenson of the Fawcett Society says that during the early stages of the society's research and its criticism of the lack of women's perspectives in the media, the standard response was to tell her that she was wrong, that her agenda was "feminist," and that the media covered issues of interest to "ordinary" women (personal communication, February 1998).

Conclusions

The debate about gender issues in the political process, or "winning women's votes," raises complex issues. Gender-specific knowledge of some aspects of public opinion is obtained by pollsters who traditionally have recorded whether a view was obtained from a man or a woman but frequently have failed to analyze their data in terms of the gender gap. Also, the questions asked frequently fail to address men's and women's different perspectives on a subject. There is now an established practice for some political parties or special interest lobby groups to request detailed gender breakdowns of poll data. The Democrats in the United States have had these practices at the heart of their campaigns, but the Fawcett Society is finding in the United Kingdom that, post general election, most key politicians have taken a view that the gender gap has closed and have reverted to treating women as being "inclusive with men" rather than equal but different.

Although there is an increasing number of women winning through to the legislatures, the numbers still reflect only a small proportion of the total, leaving the female population with inadequate representation in government. It is not reasonable to assume that such minority representation, split across parties into oppositional camps (and with media that rarely understand grassroots women's perspectives), can achieve real power to change the gender bias inherent in political institutions. Norris (1994) describes the "minimum threshold" argument as follows:

> When women are in a substantial minority within a legislature, they have to conform to the dominant procedures, practices, and norms of the institution. Hence, women who succeed in the current U.S. House of Representatives, the British House of Commons, or the French Assembly are more likely to resemble men in legislatures than women as a whole. (p. 49)

Norris points out that when women achieve significant numbers within the legislatures, past the minimum threshold (as in Scandinavia), they have confidence in their collective strength and "find their own voices" (p. 49).

The evidence is that "the women's vote" can be crucial to political success and that women's life experiences tend to be very different from men's. Research shows that it is the focus groups and women's organization research projects that are most effective at discovering the range of views within this area of public opinion and at articulating women's political priorities. Some politicians and journalists have described the belief that women's political opinions differ from men's as "patronizing." Stephenson (1998), the Fawcett Society's campaign manager, says in *The Glass Trapdoor* that "the implication seemed to be that the concerns of men were 'proper politics' and that suggesting women might think differently was to imply that they were not interested in serious political issues. Nothing could be further from the truth" (p. 139). Elections are won by building and keeping loyalty and by winning the support of floating voters. Women form a very much higher proportion of these undecided voters throughout political campaigns in the United States and United Kingdom, and the evidence is that many women still are looking for political agendas and priorities that address their own and their families' needs and aspirations.

References

Adcock, C. (1997). *What Women Want on Politics* (S. Tibballs, Ed.). London: Women's Communication Centre.

Chodorow, N. (1978). *The reproduction of mothering: Psychoanalysis and the sociology of gender.* Berkeley: University of California Press.

Christmas, L. (1997). *Chaps of both sexes: Women decision-makers in newspapers—Do they make a difference?* London: Women in Journalism.

Conservative Central Office. (1997). *Our party blueprint for change.* London: Author.

de Beauvoir, S. (1953). *The second sex.* Harmondsworth, UK: Penguin.

Diplock, S. (1998, January 13). [Letter to the editor]. *The Independent* (London).

Fawcett Society. (1996). *Winning women's votes: The gender gap in voting patterns and priorities.* London: Author.

Fawcett Society. (1997a). *The best man for the job? The selection of women parliamentary candidates.* London: Author.

Fawcett Society. (1997b). *It's not like picking a football team: Women floating voters at the 1997 election.* London: Author.

Fawcett Society. (1997c, Autumn). *Towards equality* (London).

Fawcett Society. (1997d). *Watching women: Election '97.* London: Author.

Fawcett Society. (1997-1998, Winter). *Towards equality* (London).

Gilligan, C. (1982). *In a different voice.* Cambridge, MA: Harvard University Press.

Granshaw, L. (1997, March). Lessons from America. *Women Liberal Democrat News* (London), p. 1.

Humm, M. (1995). *The dictionary of feminist theory.* Englewood Cliffs, NJ: Prentice Hall.

Lovenduski, J., & Randall, V. (1993). *Contemporary feminist politics.* Oxford, UK: Oxford University Press.

Norris, P. (1994). Elections and political attitudes. In M. Githens, P. Norris, & J. Lovenduski (Eds.), *Different roles, different voices* (pp. 47-50). New York: HarperCollins.

Norris, P., & Carroll, S. J. (1997, November). *The dynamics of the news framing process: From Reagan's gender gap to Clinton's soccer moms.* Paper presented at the annual meeting of the Southern Political Science Association, Norfolk, VA.

Ortner, S. (1974). Is female to male as nature is to culture? In M. Rosaldo & L. Lamphere (Eds.), *Women, culture, and society.* Stanford, CA: Stanford University Press.

Page, S. (1996, June 10). Vote '96: The gender gap. *USA Today.*

Pateman, C. (1988). *The sexual contract.* Cambridge, UK: Polity.

Pateman, C. (1994). Does sex matter to democracy? A comment. In M. Githens, P. Norris, & J. Lovenduski (Eds.), *Different roles, different voices* (pp. 245-249). New York: HarperCollins.

Rodham Clinton, H. (1996). *It takes a village and other lessons children teach us.* New York: Simon & Schuster.

Sancho-Aldridge, J. (1997). *Election '97: Viewers' responses to the television coverage.* London: Independent Television Commission.

Stephenson, M. A. (1998). *The glass trapdoor: Women, politics, and the media during the 1997 general election.* London: Fawcett Society.

Wilkinson, H., & Diplock, S. (1996). *Soft sell or hard policies: How can the parties best appeal to women?* London: Demos.

Williams, M. (1998, April 4). How Bill Clinton neutered the feminist movement. *The Independent* (London), p. 19.

36

The Permanent Campaign

Marketing From the Hill

WAYNE P. STEGER

Like firms, legislators market themselves and their services. They research their constituencies, they create and distribute programs and services tailored to the demands of their constituents, and they advertise themselves to their various constituencies. Whereas this chapter interprets legislators' governing and campaign activities in terms of a marketing framework, legislators and their campaign staffs increasingly do think about governing and campaigning in terms of marketing. One reason is that professionals with marketing backgrounds play a central role in many congressional campaigns. Developments in computer, travel, and communications technologies further advance political marketing by giving politicians market research and advertising options outside the traditional party framework. The ability to extract large sums of money contributes to marketing by giving members the independence from traditional party groups to engage in their own campaigns.

Political marketing fits within a broader economic approach that views democratic representation as an exchange process between constituents and elected officials. Elected officials secure programmatic benefits and provide services for constituents in exchange for political support (e.g., votes, money). Of course, exchanges in electoral systems differ from those in a market system (Newman, 1994, p. 10). In an electoral system, each voter has but one vote to offer, and it is the collective vote that determines which candidate's bundle of goods and services will be produced and distributed.[1] Moreover, only one candidate with the most votes in a given geographic area assumes office—a steep barrier to successful market entry. The production and distribution of goods and services also differs from that of private sector firms. Legislative policies are made through collective decisions by independently elected individuals serving in separate institutions sharing power (Neustadt, 1960, p. 33). Such a collective, yet fragmented, decision-making process also makes it difficult to reliably and validly attribute credit and blame for outcomes, which complicates the issue of pricing in political exchanges at the congressional level.

The Motives of Members of Congress

Understanding how and why legislators behave the way in which they do requires first assessing their motives. Most legislators today are career politicians who seek to remain in office or attain higher office over the course of their professional life spans. Doing so requires winning reelection to office repeatedly, especially in the U.S. House of Representatives, where members serve 2-year terms. Thus, reelection is a central concern of incumbents seeking to maintain careers in politics (Mayhew, 1974). Reelection frames legislators' views of their responsibilities, decisions in office, and relations with their constituents.

Although other goals matter to legislators, reelection is an instrumental and proximate goal for most incumbents. Aside from reelection, members of Congress variably value making good public policy (i.e., satisfying philosophical goals), representing constituents, and/or gaining power in Congress (Fenno, 1973). Attaining these goals usually requires reelection as an intermediary step. Changing legislative policy often requires years of effort to collect information, mobilize support, and build winning coalitions in Congress. Members usually need to get reelected several times to see their policy goals through to fruition. Even members of the relatively ideological Republican "Class of 1994" compromised principle for electoral expediency once it became clear that they would not accomplish their goals during the 104th Congress.[2] Effective representation and the accumulation of power in Congress require attainment of a certain amount of expertise or political know-how. Learning how the system works and establishing the connections needed to operate effectively within the system require time. Legislators need to be reelected repeatedly to satisfy these goals. Thus, reelection becomes instrumental and proximate to the attainment of most members' goals, even if they are not single-minded careerists.[3]

When members seek reelection, they are uncertain about their reelection prospects. Members of Congress fear electoral defeat, even though most do not appear vulnerable by common indicators. Incumbents enjoy high reelection rates, averaging above 90% in the House and above 80% in the Senate over the past three decades, and they typically win reelection with margins exceeding 60% of the vote. Such statistics, however, belie the difficulty of maintaining a political career in Congress. Even with reelection rates of 90% every 2 years, the odds of maintaining a political career in the House for 12 years are less than 60% for the typical representative. Large electoral margins in a previous election do not imply safety in a volatile electorate loosely anchored by partisan loyalties (Jacobson, 1992). Even apparently safe legislators can and do get defeated. As Mann (1978) notes, incumbents are "unsafe at any margin." Finally, electoral statistics fail to capture the uncertainty that members feel about their renomination and reelection

(Fenno, 1978, p. 36). Every incumbent knows some presumably secure colleague who was defeated in a primary or general election. These personal experiences bring home the point that incumbents themselves cannot take reelection for granted. The desire for reelection, combined with uncertainty about their reelection chances, motivates members of Congress to campaign incessantly. This is why political observers frequently talk about the permanent campaign in Congress. Members of Congress run scared; they act as if their chances of defeat are greater than might be the case in some objective sense, and they work hard to avoid that outcome (King, 1997).

Candidate-Centered Campaigns in a Self-Help System

Legislators today bear primary responsibility for their own campaigns. The candidate is both product and primary salesperson. Politicians use candidate-centered campaigns rather than party-centered campaigns. The focus of the campaign is the candidate and the services he or she will provide if elected rather than the political party with which he or she is affiliated. The image conveyed is "Smith, Republican for Congress" or simply "Smith for Congress" rather than "Republican Smith for Congress." The campaign message and themes are tailored to the political and philosophical preferences of their electoral constituencies. Candidates assemble their own campaign organizations, typically staffed with a mixture of campaign professionals and volunteers recruited from local party organizations and interest groups. Most congressional campaigns employ a campaign manager to handle strategy and coordinate the campaign effort; a professional fund-raiser skilled in direct mail and other forms of financial solicitation; a pollster to develop, conduct, and interpret surveys; and a media consultant and/or a press secretary to develop a "paid media" campaign and handle relations with the news media. Congressional campaigns use computer technologies to communicate with targeted groups of voters via direct and electronic mail. As more money becomes accessible, congressional candidates increasingly use broadcast media to reach voters whom their organizations and mailing lists do not reach.

Legislators use candidate-centered campaigns as a matter of choice and necessity. Candidates take responsibility for their campaigns in part because they cannot rely on the local political parties to deliver the vote and because running their own campaigns gives candidates more control over their fate than does the alternative. The decline of party loyalty and the rise of independent voters, coupled with increased split-ticket voting, makes the electorate volatile. Weak partisans and independent voters can and do vote for candidates of both parties. Candidates cannot be sure that voters who identify with their party will provide a margin of victory in most districts and states. The decline of local party organizations in many parts of the country means that candidates cannot rely on their party as a mechanism for communicating with and mobilizing voters through grassroots canvassing efforts. Candidates need to communicate with both partisan and nonpartisan voters, and they increasingly must do so with means outside the traditional party framework. Legislators use their offices and their own campaign organizations to communicate with voters.

Candidate-centered campaigns allow legislators to deviate from the party line when doing so is electorally advantageous. The decentralized character of American political parties and the autonomy of individual legislators in Congress allow them to tailor their issue positions to local constituencies. For example, a Democratic candidate in Oklahoma might adopt a pro-life position on the issue of abortion to be more electorally viable. Nationally focused congressional elections are uncommon. Such an instance did occur during the 1994 elections when Newt Gingrich sought to nationalize the focus of the congressional elections by getting all of the House Republican candidates to sign a "Contract With America." The contract, however, excluded many of the more controversial issues on which the Republican Party is divided, so even the exceptional 1994 elections allowed Republican candidates to adopt positions on social issues for local electoral considerations. Congressional elections typically follow Former House Speaker Tip O'Neill's counsel that "all politics is local."

Candidate-centered campaigns also help to insulate incumbents from national trends adversely affecting their party by giving them independence from their political party. By separating themselves from their party label or distancing themselves from an unpopular president of their party, members of Congress avoid collateral damage when scandals emerge or when the party gets blamed for failing to deal with the nation's problems. Such insulation against national trends matters because individual members have little control over the economy or the popularity of their party's presidential candidate. Deviating from the party line further benefits incumbents by undermining the informational value of the political party labels to voters. By lessening the informational value of party labels, voters look to other cues to make their decisions. Frequently, it is an incumbent's name recognition and image, not that of the party or of the party's presidential candidate, that voters think of when they decide who to vote for in congressional elections (Herrnson, 1997; Jacobson, 1992).[4] Incumbents gain because they can use their offices to build their name recognition and develop favorable images.

Thus, candidate-centered campaigns increase the importance of holding office and give legislators more control over their careers. Local constituencies gain because reelection-oriented legislators are responsive to local interests and concerns and have the flexibility and opportunities to satisfy many of these demands. Exchanges between constituents and their representatives, however, are not distributed equitably. Groups and individuals who pay attention to legislators' activities and who participate by communicating with their legislators, contributing money or time, and voting derive more value from political exchanges (although they also offer more to politicians). Legislators pay more attention to attentive, involved publics and tend to be more responsive to them when it comes to providing services and programmatic benefits. Legislators' differential responsiveness to various groups in society raises several normative concerns that I address later in the conclusion to this chapter.

Marketing From the Hill

Members of Congress campaign continuously because they want to maintain their careers yet cannot be sure of reelection. They must rely on their own efforts because they cannot rely on party identifiers to provide the margin of victory or on party organizations to communicate with and mobilize voters on Election Day. Legislators' concern with their next reelection and potential primary and general election opponents affects nearly everything they do in office. It shortens their time horizons for evaluating the value of policy options. It affects how they allocate their time among legislating, campaigning, raising money, meeting with lobbyists, visiting their districts or states, and so on. Reelection concerns affect the style of governing; rhetoric, symbols, and images matter to politicians performing for electoral audiences. Reelection concerns also affect the substance of governing as legislators work for or against numerous small amendments in committees and subcommittees and on the floor. Finally, legislators' reelection concerns affect what does not happen; legislators often are unwilling to make decisions that could cost them support in the next election cycle.

The following subsections focus on how legislators use their offices to market themselves. I begin with constituency research, followed by the production and distribution of programmatic benefits and services and then legislators' advertising activities.

Researching Constituency Interests and Preferences

Acquiring information about constituents is essential to legislators' legislative and campaign activities. Legislators use such information for deciding how to vote on issues and what services to provide to constituents. Their campaign staff use constituency information in forming campaign strategy, allocating resources, developing campaign messages and images, and identifying and targeting audiences for stylized communications. Such information also is used in soliciting campaign contributions. Groups considering an endorsement or a contribution (financial or manpower) often want information about a candidate's support, issue positions, and chances of winning before they make a public commitment.

Whereas legislators need information, they operate in conditions of variable uncertainty and risk; uncertainty varies across issues and over time, and acting contrary to constituent sentiment could cost them electoral support. Legislators need to continuously assess the concerns and opinions of their constituencies, and they increasingly must do so with methods other than traditional party organizational channels. Declining party identification and loyalty means that geographic constituencies are less predictable and more volatile. Redistricting and changing demographics create further uncertainty for legislators. The less partisan and the more heterogeneous their districts or states, the greater legislators' uncertainty about their reelection chances and the more they need to engage in constituency research. Declining local and state party organizations means that legislators cannot easily ascertain, through traditional party channels, the opinions and preferences of an increasing share of the electorate.

Legislators market themselves and their services to multiple audiences with differing concerns, interests, and preferences. Each district or state is composed of numerous constituency groups that pay attention to particular issues and that are more likely to be informed about and sensitive to a legislator's record on an issue or a set of issues. People who pay attention to politics and initiate communications with elected officials tend to be better educated, have higher incomes, hold higher status occupations, and belong to organized groups (Conway, 1991). These people matter for any legislator's reelection efforts because they are more likely to contribute money, volunteer during a campaign, and vote. Reelection-oriented legislators, therefore, need to be differentially attentive and responsive to different constituency groups on different issues. Legislators have to identify which individuals and groups are concerned with what issues, what their preferences are, and what they need to do to gain or maintain their electoral support. At the aggregate level, legislators need to be concerned with their positions on a wide range of issues, even though most individuals in their districts or states will be unaware of what their representatives are doing on any given issue.

Legislators especially need to identify the concerns and preferences of groups more central to their reelection efforts. Legislators establish different patterns of relations with their geographic constituencies, their electoral constituencies (the people whose support is needed to win the general election), their primary constituencies (the legislators' most ardent defenders back home), and their personal constituencies (their friends and political allies with whom they have the greatest and closest interactions) (Fenno, 1978). Legislators also pay attention to a number of nongeographically defined constituencies. Legislators need to be attentive to the people who comprise their campaign organizations—the professional staff and volunteers recruited from the ranks of party and interest group activists; party notables at the national, state, and local levels; and potential campaign contributors whose support must be solicited. Finally, legislators need to be attentive to local media—newspaper, radio, and television reporters and commentators who communicate with large numbers of voters.

Members of Congress use a variety of methods to gauge public opinion and monitor social, economic, and demographic changes in their districts or states. Most members, for example, keep tabs on their districts or states through traditional methods such as reviewing registration lists, evaluating the voting histories of individual precincts, and assessing various sources of demographic information. Legislators also gain feedback from their networks of friends and political allies who form their personal constituencies (Fenno, 1978). For example, Representative Bill Lipinsky, an Illinois Democrat, occasionally meets with Chicago aldermen and precinct chairs to identify supporters and set priorities for the delivery of services to areas in the district.[5]

Another common way in which legislators gather information is by traveling to their districts or states and meeting with constituents individually or in groups. Congress as an institution accommodates members' desire to visit their constituencies by providing them with ample travel budgets and by scheduling most legislative business between Tuesday and Thursday. Visiting one's district or state serves multiple purposes. Legislators solicit requests for assistance; listen to complaints; get constituent input on policy; shore up support among loyalists; consult with their friends and allies; advertise and claim credit for programs for the district or state; cultivate an image of competence, empathy, and identification as being "one of us"; and explain or justify their activities in Washington, D.C. (Fenno, 1978; King, 1997). Legislators are able to engage in direct interactive communication with their constituents to gain firsthand information about their concerns, complaints, and preferences. The particular topics and types of information gained through personal interactions with constituent groups vary, depending on the preferences of an individual legislator and the political culture of a given district or state (Fenno, 1978). Issues and policies tend to not be major topics in legislators' personal interactions with constituents (p. 153). Rather, legislators emphasize their accessibility and solicit requests for assistance from constituent groups and individuals (King, 1995).

Members of Congress have given themselves considerable resources to gather and process information about their constituencies. Legislators' personal staffs in their Washington offices and in the various district or state offices keep tallies of letters and phone calls by constituents. Although only a fraction of the voters communicate with their legislators (Conway, 1991), letters and phone calls are an important source of information. Monitoring letters and phone calls allows the staff to gain information about groups of people who matter for their legislator's reelection chances. People who call or write their legislator tend to be more knowledgeable about politics, are more likely to vote in elections, and are sufficiently motivated to act on their concerns and preferences. Such people often are willing to spend their time and money in campaigns and to vote, so pleasing them is important for legislators seeking reelection (Arnold, 1990, pp. 64-68). Moreover, writing letters and making phone calls are active expressions of one's preferences and opinions. Polls, by contrast, reflect passive expressions of opinion that indicate breadth of opinion but not intensity of opinion.[6]

Many legislators use the congressional frank—official mail sent free of charge— to generate constituency responses that staff members record and process for use in future communications. Brief questionnaires are attractive to legislators because they are inexpensive; they can be sent out at taxpayers' expense and can be worded to frame the legislators' positions in a positive light. The downside of such questionnaires is that the information generated might not be reliable because of biased wording and response rates (Rieselbach, 1995, p. 394). Still, they can be useful as a probe to identify groups within a geographic area for targeted communications. For example, Representative Steny Hoyer, a Maryland Democrat, uses the frank to mail a postcard questionnaire to every household in his district to give constituents an opportunity to request further information on various topics. Hoyer's staff keep records of the people making particular requests and then use the information to create a database for more targeted mailings to specific groups within the district (King, 1997, p. 23).

As legislators raise larger sums of money, an increasing number of them are using polls to keep track of constituency sentiment. Surveys are used to identify constituency concerns, demographics, interests, and preferences as well as to gauge an incumbent's strengths and weaknesses. Such information is then used for setting campaign strategy, allocating campaign resources, developing messages and presenting an image, and targeting specific groups within the district or state (Hamilton, 1996). Polls often are supplemented with focus groups to develop a more in-depth picture of constituent sentiment or mood. Focus groups are particularly important for assessing voter priorities among a number of different competing arguments and messages (p. 172). Pollsters and consultants use focus groups both to research constituency opinions and to assess voters' emotional and psychological reactions to messages, symbols, and candidate personalities to maximize the effectiveness of advertising messages.

Finally, lobbying deserves mention as part of legislators' efforts to gain information about constituent preferences. Legislators are the target of numerous attempts to contact and persuade them on matters of policy. Providing information to legislators about client concerns, interests, and preferences is a key part of the lobbying effort (Cigler & Loomis, 1995). Such political information is desired by politicians, yet it tends to be in short supply (Kingdon, 1989; Mathews & Stimson, 1975). In this sense, lobbyists act as an extension of a legislator's staff, helping to fill the "information vacuum" (Davidson & Oleszek, 1996, p. 346). Lobbyists are a legitimate part of the legislative process, even though political and representational asymmetries (inequities) result.[7] Constituency groups are differentially attentive to and affected by events in the political realm. These "special interests" also vary in their political participation and, hence, in their impact on legislators' reelection chances. Legislators' attentiveness to lobbyists and interest groups is especially keen if clientele groups have a presence in their geographic constituencies and/or contribute to their "war chests." Legislators concerned with reelection need to be differentially attentive and responsive to such groups, both as a matter of representation and for maximizing their reelection chances.

Production and Delivery of Services

The decentralized structure and operation of Congress gives legislators ample opportunity to claim credit for providing programs and services to their constituencies. The pervasive careerism among legislators has influenced the evolution of Congress's organizational and procedural structures in ways that facilitate their reelection efforts (Cooper & Brady, 1981; Polsby, 1968).[8] Legislators have established organizational structures and operational procedures to suit the needs of individual members as well as those of Congress as a whole.[9] First, legislators have created institutional structures, procedures, and norms that allow them to obtain programmatic benefits, often referred to as pork-barrel legislation, for their constituencies through mutually beneficial logrolls (Fenno, 1973; Shepsle & Weingast, 1981).[10] Second, the legislative process has structural biases that allow legislators the opportunity to block policy changes adverse to their constituency interests. Third, the collective nature of congressional decision making gives legislators opportunities to avoid blame for policies adversely affecting their constituencies. Finally, legislators have provided themselves with resources for providing constituents with assistance with their requests for service (Fiorina, 1989; Johannes, 1984). I focus on each point in turn.

Securing Programmatic Benefits for Constituencies

Legislators have several methods of directing federal money toward their constituencies. Most directly and overtly, members can earmark programs or projects for a specific constituency (i.e., a state, district, group, or company) during the authorization process, or they can set aside some of the funds for a program during the appropriations process. Less visibly, legislators can fix distribution formulas for grants or programs so that a given constituency has a better chance of qualifying for the program or project. By manipulating program criteria or qualifications, legislators can direct funds to a constituency even though the program is, prima facie, open to applications from anyone. Members also can pressure bureaucrats, who typically have some discretion for deciding who qualifies for a program or a grant, through their oversight activities or by direct intervention (i.e., making inquiries or recommendations).

Legislators also seek benefits for constituents by securing targeted tax breaks in the House Ways and Means Committee or in the Senate Finance Committee. Such tax breaks have become increasingly attractive as a result of the growing priority on balancing the budget and "pay as you go" agreements.[11] Robert Shapiro of the Progressive Policy Institute estimates that tax expenditures accounted for $47.7 billion in 1997 (cited in Dowd, 1997, p. 128). Tax policies also can be manipulated to give particular corporations or industries an advantage relative to competitors. For example, the 1997 tax act included a gradual reduction in the airline ticket tax from 10.0% to 7.5%, which was offset by a new levy on passengers on each leg of a flight between takeoff and final landing. Big carriers such as United stand to gain from the shift in taxes, whereas regional and discount carriers will see their taxes increase (Dowd, 1997).

Although most research on political marketing focuses on distributive programs, legislators can secure benefits for their constituencies through regulatory policy. Governments can create regulations that help or harm an industry or trade sector. Businesses may seek government regulations to gain an advantage relative to competitors (Stigler, 1971). For example, Congress could create a regulation (e.g., an import quota) that restricts competition and results in higher profits for a particular producer at the expense of other producers and even consumers. According to Gary Hufbauer of the Council on Foreign Relations, import quotas for sugar, textiles, and other goods are estimated to raise consumer prices about $110 billion annually (cited in Dowd, 1997, p. 128). Corporations, industries, and trade associations are quite willing to offer politicians financial support in return for potentially beneficial regulatory policies. It is not an accident that corporate, trade association, and labor union political action committees (PACs) consistently rank among the largest contributors to congressional campaigns.

Politics plays a key role in congressional decisions to spend money. Often, it is who wants what and who is in a position to demand it, rather than some other criteria such as merit or need, that determines spending priorities. Committee assignments, leadership positions, and seniority increase a legislator's ability to specify the allocation and distribution of federal funds to particular districts or states. The primary positions for steering money toward a district or state are memberships on committees and subcommittees—the policy committees that authorize programs, the appropriations subcommittees that allocate funds for programs, or the tax committees as noted earlier. The assignment process allows legislators to gain seats on committees or subcommittees with jurisdiction over policy affecting their states or districts (Fenno, 1973; Smith & Deering, 1990). Because most legislative work occurs in committees and subcommittees, panel members have the most direct and extensive opportunity and ability to steer money, for specific programs falling within the jurisdiction of the committees or subcommittees, to their states or districts. Non-committee members have less direct access to decisions distributing such projects. The asymmetries in influence over the substance of bills can be seen in the disparities in funds earmarked for committee and non-committee member districts. In the 1998 transportation bill, for example, members of the House Transportation and Infrastructure Committee received about $40 million apiece for road projects in their districts, with senior members on the panel getting even more and with Committee Chair Bud Shuster's district receiving about $110 million (Ota, 1998c, p. 1595). Shuster's district in Pennsylvania will receive about eight times the amount received by most representatives' districts (p. 1595).[12]

Committee members ultimately need the support of non-committee members to enact their bills into law. Norms of deference, reciprocity, and universalism operate to allow most members to benefit from committee power to distribute benefits (Fenno, 1973; Ferejohn, 1974). Committees often distribute programmatic benefits widely enough to attract the support of a winning coalition on the floor.[13] For example, the House Transportation and Infrastructure Committee's 1998 transportation bill included nearly $9 billion in earmarked funds for 1,506 highway projects and another $9 billion for 167 mass transit and 149 busing projects (Ota, 1998b, p. 1036). If all members reciprocate, mutually deferring to each other in their respective areas of jurisdiction, then legislators collectively create a system in which virtually every member has opportunities to steer money to his or her district or state. The system works best when the costs of projects are diffused while the benefits are concentrated and when different issues and policies are salient to different constituencies (Lowi, 1972). Legislators can make mutually beneficial exchanges of support without alienating substantial segments of their own constituencies.[14] Members agree to support other legislators' pet projects, which their own constituents are either indifferent to or only mildly disadvantaged by, in return for other legislators' support of their own pet projects that concentrate benefits in their own districts or states.

Both individually and in groups, legislators bargain and compromise to secure benefits for their constituents. The decentralized character of congressional decision making and the lack of strong political parties allow individual legislators to secure benefits for their districts and states. Senators are particularly potent bargainers because of rules that accentuate the power of individual legislators. Senators, for example, can threaten to filibuster a bill unless the managers of the bill accommodate them. Ending a filibuster formally requires a vote of 60 senators, which is a high hurdle in an institution comprised of independently elected individuals representing heterogeneous and often conflicting interests. Most often, filibusters are avoided or overcome through bargaining and compromising prior to formal debate and voting on a bill. The more restrictive rules of the House limit individual representatives' ability to hold out for projects benefiting their constituencies. Building winning coalitions in the House tends to be about mobilizing blocs of representatives (Oleszek, 1989, pp. 23-24). House members have developed informal alliances, called "caucuses," in which legislators with similar constituency interests band together to increase their bargaining leverage.[15]

Although it often is observed that the norms of deference and comity are declining (Uslander, 1994), the bargaining process might be changing form rather than declining. Legislators increasingly seek to earmark projects or funds in the pending bill in return for their immediate support of the committee bill on the floor rather than wait for repayment in kind on another bill at some future time.[16] The practice of earmarking projects or funds for specific districts or states has increased dramatically since the 1980s as federal funds have become more scarce and as legislators have put a greater priority on deficit reduction.[17] Moreover, the decline of reciprocity should not be overstated. As former Representative Tim Penny asserted, that is "how the system works. You help me; I help you. I don't blow the whistle on your pork; you don't blow the whistle on mine" (quoted in Pound & Pasternak, 1994, p. 36).

Bills passed in Congress typically incorporate numerous compromises and deals; few bills move through the House and Senate without additions and subtractions. The process of building winning legislative coalitions is messy, which helps to explain why people who pay more attention to legislative politics are more likely to be mistrustful of politicians and disdainful of Congress (Hibbings & Theiss-Morse, 1995). Although the process is unsavory, the end products are marketable to a wide range of interests. The compromises and deals needed to build winning coalitions throughout the legislative process effectively give large numbers of legislators in both chambers something that they can sell to their constituents. Citizens reap the benefits, be they a grain subsidy, park, post office, university building, weapons contract, or other program. Legislators reap the benefits of votes, money, and other forms of political support.[18]

Blocking Policy Actions Adverse to Constituency Interests

Legislators also seek to block proposals that would adversely affect their constituencies. Blocking actions typically takes one of two forms. First, legislators can block or dilute new proposals adverse to the interests of their constituencies. For example, senators from tobacco-producing states joined with senators philosophically opposed to government regulation of the economy to defeat the

McCain Bill, which would have dramatically increased federal taxes on cigarettes and imposed other regulations on the production and sale of tobacco products. Second, legislators can block or scale back proposals to cut existing programs currently enjoyed by constituents. Legislators on the defense committees, for example, have been quite successful at limiting post-cold war cuts in weapons systems built in their districts or states (Isaacs, 1994; Wright, 1996). When it comes to cutting current programs, most legislators, including many self-described budget hawks, take the "not in my district" approach.

The legislative process has several structural biases that advantage those defending the status quo. The sequential nature of the legislative process, coupled with decentralized decision making, creates numerous opportunities to stop a bill. To enact a bill, proponents need to assemble winning coalitions throughout the legislative process—in committees and subcommittees in both chambers, in the rules committee in the House, on the floors of both chambers, in conference committee, and again on the floors of both chambers, and finally, the president must approve or at least acquiesce to the bill. Opponents of a bill, by contrast, need a winning coalition against the bill in only one of these forums to defeat it. Also, committees' ability to block legislative policy is greater than their ability to enact changes in legislative policy (Shepsle & Weingast, 1987; Smith & Deering, 1990). Committees often have to accommodate the interests of numerous non-committee members to enact a bill. To prevent policy changes, they simply do nothing.[19] Finally, individual legislators, especially senators, can use their bargaining leverage to block policy changes that would adversely affect their constituencies.

The capacity to block policy changes creates opportunities for legislators to gain from political exchanges with constituency groups, especially in the corporate world. Legislators can engage in rent seeking by threatening to enact policy changes to extract political support from groups opposed to a change in such policies. For example, the threat of government regulation of tobacco products and advertising has motivated tobacco interests to contribute large sums of money to legislators who might be willing to oppose such regulatory legislation. According to the Center for Responsive Politics (CRP), Philip Morris was the largest single contributor to congressional races during the 1995–1996 election cycle, with $4.2 million in donations. Collectively, the tobacco industry combined contributed about $10.3 million for the 1996 elections.[20] Similarly, proposed changes in product liability laws have led the Association of Trial Lawyers of America to invest heavily in lobbying and contributions to legislators (Gettinger, 1997). According to the CRP, lawyers and lobbyists more generally contributed $51.7 million in the 1996 election cycle. The list goes on and on. In the past several years, we have seen agricultural, banking, communications, defense, electronics, financial, health care, insurance, labor, pharmaceutical, real estate, and transportation corporations, industries, trade associations, and unions contribute enormous sums of money to legislators and to the Democratic and Republican congressional campaign committees. Whether enacting or blocking policy changes, legislators secure immense sums of money from the private sector.

Blame Avoidance and Displacement of Costs

Legislators also seek to avoid blame for congressional decisions that could undermine their chances of reelection. Incumbent legislators have already established winning electoral coalitions in a previous election. Much of their reelection task involves maintaining their primary and general election coalitions. As such, legislators often avoid activities or issue positions that could alienate segments of their electoral and primary constituencies. Legislators also seek to avoid blame to deny potential opponents issues with which they can be criticized.

The collective action problems inherent in a system of separated institutions sharing power allow legislators to avoid blame for policies adversely affecting their constituencies.[21] Legislators can avoid blame for the collective performance of Congress by disassociating themselves from the institution. Many legislators, for example, run for Congress by campaigning against Congress. Congress's collective decision-making processes, coupled with its weak political parties, allow individual members to take positions tailored to their local constituencies. Legislators can take positions that distance themselves from a president, party leader, or policy that is unpopular with their primary and electoral constituencies. Legislators also avoid personal accountability by sidestepping substantive policy decisions. Congressional leaders often use procedural devices that allow legislators, in certain circumstances, to make decisions without directly or overtly appearing to do so. Motions to table (kill) an amendment, for example, allow legislators to avoid direct responsibility for controversial decisions. Legislators also may avoid blame by delegating authority to someone else for making the "tough decisions." The line item veto can be viewed as an example of such a blame avoidance mechanism. By giving President Bill Clinton the authority to eliminate funds for specific lines in appropriations bills, legislators increased Clinton's responsibility for budget discipline. This freed legislators to pursue credit via pork-barrel projects while blaming the president for killing such projects or for ballooning deficits if he did not.

If hard decisions must be made, then legislators opt for alternatives that displace the costs of their decisions on groups less central to their reelection efforts.[22] The political parties' strategies for balancing the budget are enlightening in this respect. Raising taxes and cutting existing programs are the primary proactive alternatives for cutting large deficits.[23] Since the 1980s, both political parties have proposed raising taxes and cutting expenditures. These proposals have distinct political biases. Republican tax increases and spending cuts have tended to adversely affect lower socioeconomic groups that are less likely to vote Republican. For example, the pain of the 1981 social security tax increase pushed by Bob Dole, fell disproportionately on lower and middle income wage earners because the FICA tax is both regressive and capped at $65,000 in taxable wages. The income tax increases in Clinton's 1993 deficit reduction package, by contrast, fell disproportionately on upper income Americans because the bill increased the top rate from 31% to 36%, with an additional 10% surtax for individuals making more than $250,000 in taxable income. The previously mentioned 1998 transportation bill illustrates how legislators displace the costs of spending cuts. The $216 billion transportation bill was about $20 billion over budget allowances, according to Congressional Budget Office projections (Ota, 1998a, p. 1385). Because of Congress's "pay as you go" rules, this spending overrun had to be offset with cuts in other programs or tax increases. Rather than give up some of the pork in the bill or raise taxes, the Republican-controlled Congress cut programs benefiting constituency groups that either tend to vote Democratic or have lower voter turnout—approximately $15.4 billion from veterans' medical benefits for smoking-related illnesses, $2.3 billion in social service block grants, $2 billion in public housing programs, $2 billion in state costs for administering Medicaid, and lesser amounts from programs such as food stamps (Ota, 1998a).

Constituent Services

The development of a large federal government has meant increased constituent demand for available government programs and services and increased demand for help dealing with agency officials responsible for delivering these programs (Fiorina, 1989).[24] Members have provided themselves with ample staff support, both in their Washington offices and in their district or state offices, to provide services to constituents. Legislators and their staffs act in an ombudsman-type role, intervening on constituents' behalf with federal agencies to facilitate the provision of government goods and services (Johannes, 1984). Typically, staff contact an agency (many federal agencies have congressional liaison offices to handle such requests) to request information, make recommendations for a constituent, expedite processing of constituent paperwork, and help in other ways to cut red tape. The services conducted by legislators' staff are extensive. Requests for help in finding government jobs are the most common type of constituent service request, followed closely by requests for help in dealing with problems relating to social security, veterans benefits, unemployment compensation, taxation, immigration, and miscellaneous legal problems (Davidson & Oleszek, 1996, p. 146; Johannes, 1984). Staff also frequently respond to constituent requests for government documents such as copies of bills, legislative reports, executive branch regulations, and tourist information (Davidson & Oleszek, 1996, pp. 146-147). Assisting constituents in applying for government grants or contracts is another type of service where legislators get involved in bureaucratic decisions, even when the relevant agency is at the state or local level (Rich, 1989, pp. 197-198). In general, legislators or their staff get involved whenever and wherever constituents interact with federal agencies.

The relations between legislators and federal agencies are conducive to ombudsman activities. Bureaucrats often feel compelled to respond to the inquiries or interventions of legislators. Congress controls several things that agencies want—budgets, personnel, organizational structure, and procedural operations. Bureaucrats face the potential imposition of sanctions—smaller budgets, fewer personnel, and less operation discretion—if they fail to accommodate legislators' requests (Johannes, 1984; Wildavsky, 1988, chap. 3). If legislators are not accommodated, then they can restrict bureaucratic discretion by writing into law specific guidelines dictating how bureaucrats will implement policies. These practices are known variously as micromanagement or procedural oversight (McCubbins, Noll, & Weingast, 1987). The threats of sanction—implicit or explicit, real or perceived—are especially credible if a legislator sits on an authorizing or appropriations subcommittee with jurisdiction over an agency.

Empirically, studies have shown that constituent service has significant electoral benefit for legislators, even though the number of people serviced varies considerably across districts and states (Fiorina, 1989; Johannes, 1984; Serra & Moon, 1994). Casework or constituency service is mostly profit for legislators; they make many more friends than enemies when their staffs provide services for their constituents (Fiorina, 1989, p. 180). Members gain goodwill among constituents, for example, when their staff help a senior citizen receive a missing or delayed social security check or Medicare benefit or when they help some constituency group apply for a federal grant for some program. Legislators act as if the electoral effects, even if marginal, matter simply because securing benefits for their constituents and providing them with services are factors affecting their reelection that they can control.

Advertising: Letting the Constituencies Know What Members Have Done for Them Lately

Legislators invest heavily in advertising and constituent communications because they need to promote themselves continuously. They advertise in a culture heavily influenced by Madison Avenue. They compete for voters' attention with advertisements from corporate America as well as from other politicians. They need to counteract and separate themselves from the continuous stream of cynical media stories of corruption, impropriety, and dubious deals obtained by various special interests. Legislators' advertising is aimed at establishing a high level of name recognition among their constituents, developing favorable images or impressions in the minds of their constituents, cultivating a sense of trust among their constituents for both proactive and defensive reasons, and deterring or weakening potential challengers.

Legislators seek to define the terms on which their constituents think of them. Most of the people back home are poorly informed about their legislators' activities (Cain, Ferejohn, & Fiorina, 1987; Stokes & Miller, 1962). Many policy matters do not directly affect constituents, and most people pay little attention to politics, especially political events not readily visible on television. Because much of what legislators do is below their constituents' radar screens, constituents' opinions and evaluations of their representatives tend to be poorly informed. Although constituents are not well informed about their actions, legislators fear that they will become so around election time and in ways that work against them. All legislators face potential opponents who will seek to undermine incumbents' images with negative advertising. The opinions of a poorly informed electorate are susceptible to influence by whatever information it does receive, so negative advertising can potentially be quite harmful to an incumbent's reelection chances (Ansolabehere & Iyengar, 1997, chap. 4). Legislators seek to define the terms on which constituents evaluate them before their next opponents have the opportunity.

Legislators market themselves and their services to multiple audiences with differing concerns, interests, and preferences. The decline of party membership among voters has made legislators' marketing task more difficult in this respect. As party membership declines, legislators' primary constituencies shrink relative to their electoral constituencies. The issue positions, messages, and symbols that play well with primary constituencies might not be as attractive to independent voters whose support is needed to win general elections. Legislators have responded by developing a multilevel approach using multiple media to appeal to voters generally and to narrower groups with messages tailored to their specific interests and concerns. First, they use ambiguous and vacuous slogans to appeal to voters more generally. Such slogans allow constituents to read what they want into them. Such slogans also deny opponents a specific target to attack. Who can argue with a candidate who promises to "bring [insert state name here] values to Washington" or "promote a strong America" or to "improve education" or "reduce crime"? By positioning themselves on the right side of "valence" issues, they appeal to the majority of voters and deny opponents a popular issue. Legislators then target specific audiences with stylized appeals communicated through focused media such as direct and electronic mail or radio and cable television programs with specific demographic audiences.

Members of Congress have given themselves ample resources to advertise themselves and their activities to their constituents. Legislators use the congressional frank to send newsletters to all households in their districts. According to a congressional research service report, legislators sent out approximately 363 million letters at a cost of $53 million during fiscal year 1994, the most recent year from which information is available (Pontius, 1997, p. 2, as cited in Davidson & Oleszek, 1998, p. 147). Members also have provided themselves with ample budgets for communicating with their constituents by phone, e-mail, and the Internet. E-mail and Web sites are useful because the people who use them tend to be better educated, wealthier, more politically aware, and hence more likely to participate in elections. Since the 1970s, members have televised sessions in which members make speeches to the viewing audience; the chamber is nearly always empty during these speeches, save for a few pages, staff, tourists, and watchdog members. Members also use the radio and television production studios provided by the political parties' congressional campaign committees to create news clips for local broadcast media and for their campaign commercials.

Members also use extensive travel budgets to visit their districts or states. Traveling to their districts serves the dual purposes of market research and promotion. Members spend time in their districts meeting with various constituency groups—local business leaders as well as representatives of civic groups, interest groups, and the like. During this time, members gain firsthand knowledge of constituents' concerns, interests, preferences, and requests for assistance. Members also use these trips to present themselves to their constituents, gain the trust of their constituents, and explain their activities in Washington, essentially providing constituents with rationales for their actions (Fenno, 1978). Legislators cultivate personal relations with their constituents that emphasize competence, identification with constituents, empathy, and trust (Cain et al., 1987; Fenno, 1978). Establishing personal relations with constituents, characterized by trust and empathy, facilitates legislators' reelection efforts by disposing constituents to accept the legislators' self-portrayals and explanations of their actions in Washington.

In addition to taxpayer-subsidized communications, legislators have advantages in generating free publicity on television and radio and in the print media. One reason why legislators are successful in generating "free media" coverage is that they are in a position to make news. Another reason is that legislators make themselves available to the media and hire staff to facilitate the media's coverage of themselves. All senators and virtually all representatives employ full-time press secretaries who manage relations with the media and who try to control the flow of information to constituents. Press secretaries routinely distribute news releases to local news broadcast and print media. Some press secretaries use satellite feeds to get their legislators on local television and radio news programs.

Gaining access to the media is less problematic than is controlling the image conveyed in the news media. Controlling the image conveyed in free media is important because advertising messages and images need to be consistent to be effective. Legislators can ill afford to say one thing while the media say something else. Image control has become more difficult because the news media have become more cynical about politics and politicians (Patterson, 1994). Legislators can affect their coverage, although it falls short of control. First, media coverage of politics is predictable. It is well known that the media seek stories that will attract readers and viewers. The media pay more attention to political competition, strategy, conflict, and scandals than to substantive policy issues or candidate qualifications (Robinson & Sheehan, 1983). Second, most coverage relates to what legislators say and do. Journalists rarely report on what goes unspoken or undone—or at least done but not visibly so. Legislators can manage their media coverage by scripting their actions and speeches for media coverage and then staying on script; by setting the location and timing of their speeches, meetings, and other events for maximum media coverage; and by cultivating the media by providing services for reporters and producers. Finally, legislators need to adopt a preventive approach to their public images, avoiding the appearance of impropriety by knowing where, when, how, and with whom they can make which deals and bargains.

Beyond their taxpayer-subsidized communications and free media, legislators engage in extensive paid advertising through multiple media. The most common method of paid advertising used by legislators is direct mail, which can be sent to targeted groups with messages tailored to group preferences and interests. As legislators raise more money, they are increasingly turning to television because more people obtain their political information from television than from any other medium and because television is a great medium for conveying images and emotional content. Herrnson (1997), for example, found that about 90% of senators and more than 70% of representatives used television advertising during their campaigns (p. 182). The main reasons why legislators opt not to use television are its high cost and its inefficiency when the media market and a district are dissimilar—mainly in urban districts where television markets encompass multiple districts. More often, legislators advertise on the radio, where they can target specific demographic audiences on particular radio programs. Nearly all senators and more than 90% of representatives use radio advertising, largely because of its lower cost compared to television advertising (p. 187). Newspapers are used less frequently by legislators—approximately 70% of House races and 80% of Senate races—because such advertising is less effective for communicating imagery and personalized messages (p. 188).

By nearly every indication, legislators' adverting efforts are successful. More than 90% of all voters recognize the names of their representatives, and more than 95% of voters recognize the names of their senators (Jacobson, 1992, pp. 116-121). By contrast, legislators' challengers have much lower rates of name recognition, especially in House races, where most challengers lack much political experience and have great difficulty in raising the money needed to afford the advertising necessary to build name recognition. Given a low level of political awareness by most voters, being a known commodity is extremely important to getting reelected. Indeed, name recognition has become an increasingly important factor in voting decisions as the political parties have declined (Herrnson, 1997, pp. 159-160). Not only do constituents recognize their representatives or senators' names, but about two thirds of them have favorable perceptions of their legislators (Jacobson, 1992, pp. 121-123). That two thirds of voters view their representatives favorably is remarkable given the media's highly cynical view of politicians and generally high levels of voter disapproval of Congress (Hibbings & Theiss-Morse, 1995). That legislators receive more favorable than unfavorable evaluations from their constituents matters because the more positive voters' perceptions of legislators are, the more likely voters are to vote for them (Jacobson, 1992, pp. 136-141).

A Final Note on Money:
The Mother's Milk of a Marketing Campaign

Conducting a continuous campaign is expensive. Campaign costs have been increasing as campaigns become more professionally managed, technologically sophisticated, and reliant on mass media. Legislators need large sums of money to hire pollsters and campaign and media consultants as well as to pay for the various forms of advertising not picked up on the taxpayers' tab. Computers, polls, mailing lists, direct mail, and media campaigns all require considerable outlays of money. These things are increasingly considered necessary in congressional campaigns because candidates are less and less able to rely on state and local party organizations to communicate with and mobilize large numbers of voters on Election Day.

Incumbents have a number of inherent advantages in absorbing the costs of continuous congressional campaigns. First, a large part of their marketing effort is subsidized by taxpayers. Legislators have given themselves ample travel and communications budgets. They have access to television and radio studios in the

House and Senate press galleries. They have press secretaries and other personal staffs to research their constituencies' preferences, provide services to constituents, and help advertise their own services and accomplishments. Legislators have many of the things money can buy by virtue of holding office in an institution structured by and for the benefit of its membership. Incumbents need less money to compete because they already have much of what money can buy, which is why incumbents face diminishing returns to their campaign spending. They start off with high name recognition and often have established favorable images among their constituents. Additional increments of paid advertising cannot dramatically increase their name recognition and improve their images (unless they need to repair their images with the help of professional handlers). Money matters far more for challengers, who typically begin their campaigns with low levels of name recognition.[25] Challengers have to raise money to establish campaign organizations and to buy the advertising needed to build name recognition, establish favorable images, and undermine the images of the incumbents. Their problem is that they often cannot raise the requisite funds and, therefore, must climb an incredibly steep hill to defeat incumbents.

The second advantage that incumbents enjoy when it comes to raising campaign funds is that they have greater access to and receptivity from the primary financial contributors—the congressional party campaign committees, PACs, and wealthy individuals. PACs in particular want access to make their cases for or against particular pieces of legislation. Incumbents are in a position to grant or deny access, and because most incumbents win reelection, they are likely to be in such a position after the next election. Incumbents raise substantially more funds than do their opponents. The disparity matters because the winners of congressional elections nearly always outspend the losers. According to a study by the Center for Responsive Politics, the average winner in the 1996 House elections spent more than two and a half times the average amount spent by the loser, whereas the average winner in 1996 Senate elections spent more than one and two thirds times the amount spent by the average loser.[26]

Money is perhaps most valuable to legislators for its deterrent effect on potential challengers. Challengers typically face an uphill battle in running against incumbent members of Congress. Challengers need to dramatically expand their name recognition, cultivate favorable images, give voters a reason to support them, and give voters a reason to reject the incumbents. Unless challengers are already well known and beloved to voters in their states or districts, or unless challengers have existing offices from which to develop these things, they need to obtain these things during the campaigns. Doing so is expensive. The problem for challengers is that they generally cannot raise the large sums of money to buy the advertising needed to increase name recognition, build favorable images, and attack the incumbents. The "catch-22" is that most challengers cannot raise enough funds unless and until Washington insiders estimate that they have a good chance of beating the incumbents. So, most of the time, the strongest potential challengers opt not to challenge incumbent members of Congress, preferring to wait until legislators die or retire before running for office (Jacobson, 1989; Squire, 1992).

Conclusions

Legislators are highly successful political marketers. They develop high levels of name recognition, cultivate favorable evaluations among their constituencies, raise large sums of money, and usually deter strong challengers. The vast majority of legislators go on to win reelection and do so by large margins. The very success of incumbent legislators raises several questions about the health of representative democracy in congressional elections. Are congressional elections fair, or do the biases favoring incumbents make them noncompetitive affairs? Do we have democratic governance for all the people or just those who pay attention, participate, and contribute large sums of money? How much choice do we, as voters, really have when our electoral decision often is between a well-known, well-promoted commodity and an unknown, inexperienced commodity?

One downside of members of Congress increasingly concerned with marketing themselves and their services is that representation of the American public becomes more utilitarian, a byproduct of legislators' efforts to maintain their careers. In an economic approach, politicians—like everyone else—are assumed to be motivated mainly by their desire to advance their personal interests. In this view, politicians seek programs and provide services for those who have something to offer toward their reelection. The resulting picture of democratic governance is one in which politicians are differentially responsive to various segments of the society, depending on their relative contributions (literally and figuratively) to the politicians' reelection aspirations. Representation of the "public interest" more generally occurs as a side effect of, or an externality to, the exchanges between politicians and their constituencies. In a sense, representation of the public interest is literally a public good (or a public bad, depending on one's own philosophical tastes).

It seems problematic, from the standpoint of normative democratic theory with its ideals of political egalitarianism, that legislators are disproportionately attentive and responsive to those subsets of society that contribute most heavily to their reelection. Organized groups with professional staff and lobbyists and moneyed interests gain representation to the detriment of those who do not participate or otherwise contribute to politicians' reelection. A downside of the increasing costs of congressional campaigns is that most incumbents spend considerable time and energy soliciting funds and, of course, granting the expected access to contributors. Legislators concerned with marketing themselves might be spending less time and energy becoming informed about issues and making "rational" policy choices. Perhaps even more worrisome than the time and energy devoted to campaign contributors are the policy consequences of such a system of exchange. The potential for moneyed interests to distort the representative functions of Congress is considerable. Is the U.S. Congress for sale?

There is, however, no consensus that the constitutional founders intended to have an egalitarian political system. It can be argued that the founders recognized social and political inequalities and created a political system that operates in the context of that reality. Ours might well be a pluralistic political system in which groups compete, albeit with unequal capacities, for political power and for favorable disposition of political issues. I shall defer to another time further thoughts on the juxtaposition of normative ideals and the positivist world in which we live.

Notes

1. Citizens and groups also may register their differential valuation of candidates by contributing time and money to candidates' campaigns.

2. Republican leaders became more willing to compromise with President Bill Clinton when polls showed increasing public dissatisfaction with the government shutdowns during the winter of 1995–1996, which were increasingly blamed on congressional Republicans.

3. Political marketing does not require the assumption that legislators be single-minded seekers of reelection. The assumption merely simplifies the logic. Legislators, for example, could seek the trust of their constituents to gain discretion in office, which could then be used to satisfy ideological goals shared with their constituents. The minimal assumption being made is that legislators provide programmatic benefits and services to constituents in return for political supports of some kind.

4. The disjuncture between the issue positions of candidates of the same party has consequences for governance. Political parties become less stable as bases for coalition building in Congress.

5. This information came from an interview with a participant in such a meeting in June 1998.

6. Politicians sometimes discount polls for this reason. Relying solely on polls can be hazardous given an uninformed public, divided opinion on issues, and the like. The American publics are notoriously ill informed about politics, yet they will offer responses to surveys. For example, in 1995, a *Washington Post* survey included a question asking people whether they thought that the Public Affairs Act of 1975 should be repealed. Fully 24% of the respondents answered yes and 19% answered no, even though no such act exists (Squire, Lindsay, Covington, & Smith, 1997, pp. 171-172).

7. Lobbyists and organized interest groups generally represent the better educated and wealthier segments of society (Cigler & Loomis, 1995).

8. The organization of Congress at a given point in time is a function of the current mixture of members' goals and the residual structures from previous Congresses. Changes in the mixture of goals and preferences lead to changes in organizational structures and procedures (Swift, 1989).

9. There are two theoretical frameworks for understanding the institutional structure and operation of Congress. Political marketing fits with the distributive theory of congressional organization, which holds that Congress is organized and structured to facilitate collective logrolls (Shepsle & Weingast, 1981). The alternative, informational theory of congressional organization, holds that Congress is structured to promote the collection and dissemination of information rather than the production and distribution of goods and services to particular geographic constituencies (Krehbiel, 1991). These theories are not necessarily incompatible. Congress could organize to generate information, but information could be used for self-interested ends by committees, parties, caucuses, or individuals that gather information.

10. Normative judgments about the value of such projects or programs depend on the eye of the beholder. We tend to view programs that benefit select groups with which we do not associate as pork, whereas we view more favorably those programs that benefit ourselves or groups with which we associate.

11. The 1990 budget deal included an agreement that new programs could not be created without coming up with funding for those programs. Given the difficulty of finding funding sources—either money allocated to existing programs (which have defenders) or raising taxes—it has become increasingly attractive for members to seek targeted tax breaks for their constituencies.

12. Ironically, the bill was renamed the "Transportation Equity Act for the 21st Century."

13. Committees' high level of success in enacting their bills also is attributed to (a) committee members' procedural prerogatives and privileges that advantage them in defending their bills against modifications by non-committee members (Shepsle & Weingast, 1987), (b) information asymmetries between committee members and non-committee members that advantage committee members' efforts to defend their handiwork on the floor (Krehbiel, 1991), and (c) committee members'

anticipation of potential sources of opposition and incorporate accommodations into their bills to minimize opposition (Evans, 1989).

14. Legislators of both parties have electoral incentives to engage in pork-barrel politics. Most Republicans are as eager as Democrats to earmark federally funded projects for their states and districts (Niedowski, 1997; Tumulty, 1995). Although most Republicans are avid pork-barrelers when it comes to their districts or states, there is a minority contingent of Republicans who vocally oppose such pork-barreling (Cohn, 1998). But even many of these self-proclaimed fiscal conservatives, including Newt Gingrich, Phil Gramm, and Trent Lott, conveniently ignore principle when it comes to projects for their own districts and states.

15. Congressional caucuses basically operate as cartels on specific issues, aggregating individuals' voting power to increase their bargaining leverage with those pushing the bills.

16. It is worth noting that the trend toward more explicit bargaining is less efficient than a system of tacit exchanges of support across policy areas because of the higher transaction costs inherent in extensive coalition-building negotiations. Legislators might be willing to absorb additional transaction costs in the present to reduce uncertainty about their own payoffs.

17. See "Slicing the Pork" (1994).

18. Note that new programs and money matter more than does continuation of previous projects or awards (Alvarez & Saving, 1997; Stein & Bickers, 1994). Legislators need to continuously seek benefits for their constituents to reap electoral rewards.

19. Although non-committee members can circumvent obstructionist committees, these options are costly to use (Davidson & Oleszek, 1998, chaps. 7-8; Oleszek, 1989).

20. See Center for Responsive Politics (n.d.).

21. Of course, legislators' efforts cannot be too transparent if they seek to credibly claim that they could not prevent adverse policies from occurring.

22. Legislators' understanding of their various constituencies becomes important in this respect because they need to know who they can and cannot afford to offend if push comes to shove.

23. The other strategies that governments have used to get rid of red ink are inflation and economic growth such that revenues exceed expenditures. Neither strategy is feasible for politicians at this time. Investors do not approve of inflationary strategies, and Federal Reserve Chairman Alan Greenspan would likely counteract political efforts to produce it. Economic growth or contraction is largely beyond the government's control, as George Bush learned to his chagrin and Clinton to his good fortune.

24. Fiorina (1989) also argues that the relationship is reciprocal; members' desire for bureaucratic assistance in the delivery of services to constituents has contributed to the growth of government over the past several decades. Legislators gain opportunities to claim credit both when they create programs and when they cut red tape as agencies implement programs.

25. This point is more relevant in House elections. Challengers in Senate elections are more likely to have held prior office, have better name recognition than the typical House challenger, and to be more capable of raising large sums of money.

26. The average winner in House elections spent $673,739, whereas the average winner in Senate elections spent $4,692,110. Note that these numbers do no account for whether the winner was an incumbent, a challenger, or an open-seat candidate.

References

Alvarez, R. M., & Saving, J. L. (1997). Deficits, Democrats, and distributive benefits: Congressional elections and the pork barrel in the 1980s. *Political Research Quarterly, 50,* 809-831.

Ansolabehere, S., & Iyengar, S. (1997). *Going negative: How political advertisements shrink and polarize the electorate.* New York: Free Press.

Arnold, R. D. (1990). *The logic of congressional action.* New Haven, CT: Yale University Press.

Cain, B., Ferejohn, J., & Fiorina, M. (1987). *The personal vote: Constituency service and electoral independence.* Cambridge, MA: Harvard University Press.

Center for Responsive Politics. (n.d.). *Tobacco legislation going up in smoke.* Available on Internet: http://www.crp.org.

Cigler, A. J., & Loomis, B. A. (Eds.). (1995). *Interest group politics* (4th ed.). Washington, DC: Congressional Quarterly Press.

Cohn, J. S. (1998, April 20). Roll out the barrel. *New Republic,* pp. 19-23.

Conway, M. M. (1991). *Political participation in the United States* (2nd ed.). Washington, DC: Congressional Quarterly Press.

Cooper, J., & Brady, D. W. (1981). Toward a diachronic analysis of Congress. *American Political Science Review, 75,* 988-1006.

Davidson, R. H., & Oleszek, W. J. (1996). *Congress and its members* (5th ed.). Washington, DC: Congressional Quarterly Press.

Davidson, R. H., & Oleszek, W. J. (1998). *Congress and its members* (6th ed.). Washington, DC: Congressional Quarterly Press.

Dowd, A. R. (1997, December). Look who's cashing in on Congress. *Money,* pp. 128-138.

Evans, C. L. (1989). Influence in congressional committees. In C. J. Deering (Ed.), *Congressional politics* (pp. 155-175). Homewood, IL: Dorsey.

Gettinger, S. (1997, November 29). Congress shaking its money maker. *CQ Weekly Report,* p. 2958.

Fenno, R. F., Jr. (1973). *Congressmen in committee.* Boston: Little, Brown.

Fenno, R. F., Jr. (1978). *Home style: House members in their districts.* Boston: Little, Brown.

Ferejohn, J. A. (1974). *Pork barrel politics: Rivers and harbors legislation: 1947-1968.* Stanford, CA: Stanford University Press.

Fiorina, M. P. (1989). *Congress: Keystone of the Washington establishment* (2nd ed.). New Haven, CT: Yale University Press.

Hamilton, W. R. (1996). Political polling: From beginning to the center. In J. A. Thurber & C. J. Nelson (Eds.), *Campaigns and elections: American style* (pp. 161-180). Boulder, CO: Westview.

Herrnson, P. (1997). *Congressional elections: Campaigning at home and in Washington* (2nd ed.). Washington, DC: Congressional Quarterly Press.

Hibbings, J. R., & Theiss-Morse, E. (1995). *Congress as public enemy: Public attitudes toward American political institutions.* New York: Cambridge University Press.

Isaacs, J. D. (1994, September/October). Not in my district. *Bulletin of the Atomic Scientists,* pp. 13-15.

Jacobson, G. C. (1989). Strategic politicians and the dynamics of House elections, 1946-1986. *American Political Science Review, 83,* 773-793.

Jacobson, G. C. (1992). *The politics of congressional elections* (3rd ed.). New York: HarperCollins.

Johannes, J. R. (1984). *To serve the people: Congress and constituency service.* Lincoln: University of Nebraska Press.

King, A. (1997). *Running scared: Why American politicians campaign too much and govern too little.* New York: Free Press.

Kingdon, J. W. (1989). *Congressmen's voting decisions* (3rd ed.). Ann Arbor: University of Michigan Press.

Krehbiel, K. (1991). *Information and legislative organization.* Ann Arbor: University of Michigan Press.

Lowi, T. J. (1972). Four systems of policy, politics, and choice. *Public Administration Review, 32,* 298-310.

Mann, T. (1978). *Unsafe at any margin: Interpreting congressional elections.* Washington, DC: American Enterprise Institute.

Mathews, D. R., & and Stimson, J. A. (1975). *Yeas and nays: Normal decision-making in the U.S. House of Representatives.* New York: John Wiley.

Mayhew, D. R. (1974). *Congress: The electoral connection.* New Haven, CT: Yale University Press.

McCubbins, M. D., Noll, R. G., & Weingast, B. R. (1987). Administrative procedures as instruments of political control. *Journal of Law, Economics, and Organization, 3,* 243-277.

Neustadt, R. E. (1960). *Presidential power and the modern presidents.* New York: Free Press.

Newman, B. I. (1994). *The marketing of the president: Political marketing as campaign strategy.* Thousand Oaks, CA: Sage.

Niedowski, E. (1997, July/August). Republican hypocrites. *Washington Monthly,* pp. 24-26.

Oleszek, W. J. (1989). *Congressional procedures and the policy process* (3rd ed.). Washington, DC: Congressional Quarterly Press.

Ota, A. K. (1998a, May 23). Congress clears huge transportation bill, restoring cut-off funding to states. *CQ Weekly Report,* pp. 1385-1387.

Ota, A. K. (1998b, April 25). Don't look for many pet projects to turn into road kill. *CQ Weekly Report,* p. 1036.

Ota, A. K. (1998c, June 13). Highway law benefits those who hold purse strings. *CQ Weekly Report,* pp. 1595-1596.

Patterson, T. E. (1994). *Out of order.* New York: Vintage Books.

Polsby, N. W. (1968). The institutionalization of the U.S. House of Representatives. *American Political Science Review, 62,* 144-168.

Pontius, J. S. (1997). *Congressional mail: History of the franking privilege and options for change* (Report No. 96-101). Washington, DC: Congressional Research Service.

Pound, E. T., & Pasternak, D. (1994, February 21). The pork barrel barons. *U.S. News & World Report,* pp. 32-36.

Rich, M. J. (1989). Distributive politics and the allocation of federal grants. *American Political Science Review, 83,* 193-213.

Rieselbach, L. N. (1995). *Congressional politics: The evolving legislative system* (2nd ed.). Boulder, CO: Westview.

Robinson, M., & Sheehan, M. (1983). *Over the wire and on TV.* New York: Russell Sage.

Serra, G., & Moon, D. (1994). Case work, issue positions, and voting in congressional elections: A district analysis. *Journal of Politics, 56,* 200-213.

Shepsle, K., & Weingast, B. (1981). Political preferences for the pork barrel: A generalization. *American Journal of Political Science, 25,* 96-111.

Shepsle, K., & Weingast, B. (1987). The institutional foundations of committee power. *American Political Science Review, 81,* 86-108.

Slicing the pork isn't easy. (1994, January). *Governing,* pp. 62-63.

Smith, S. S., & Deering, C. J. (1990). *Committees in Congress* (2nd ed.). Washington, DC: Brookings Institution.

Squire, P. (1992). Challenger quality and voting behavior in Senate elections. *Legislative Studies Quarterly, 17,* 247-263.

Squire, P., Lindsay, J. M., Covington, C. R., & Smith, E. R. A. N. (1997). *Dynamics of democracy* (2nd ed.). Dubuque, IA: Brown and Benchmark.

Stein, R. M., & Bickers, K. N. (1994). Congressional elections and the pork barrel. *Journal of Politics, 56,* 377-399.

Stigler, G. J. (1971). A theory of economic regulation. *Bell Journal of Economics and Management Science, 12,* 2-15.

Stokes, D. E., & Miller, W. E. (1962). Party government and the saliency of Congress. *Public Opinion Quarterly, 26,* 531-546.

Swift, E. K. (1989). Reconstitutive change in the U.S. Congress: The early Senate, 1789-1841. *Legislative Studies Quarterly, 25,* 175-203.

Tumulty, K. (1995, November 20). The freshmen go native. *Time,* pp. 70-71.

Uslander, E. M. (1994). *The decline of comity in Congress.* Ann Arbor: University of Michigan Press.

Wildavsky, A. B. (1988). *The new politics of the budgetary process.* Glenview, IL: Scott, Foresman.

Wright, M. (1996, October 14). Are aircraft carriers obsolete? *Fortune,* p. 44.

*Political Marketing
and Democracy*

37

You Can't Teach a Dead Dog New Tricks

The Problem of Campaign Finance and Why Reform Has Not Worked

JON B. GOULD

In the aftermath of the 1996 presidential campaign, sordid tales of fund-raising abuse have abounded. Most observers are now aware that President Bill Clinton offered overnight visits in the Lincoln Bedroom to top Democratic contributors, and no fewer than six congressional committees have investigated the Democrats' possibly illegal solicitation of foreign contributions. The Democratic National Committee alone has already returned more than $3 million in what it considers to be questionable donations, and one of the key figures, Democratic fund-raiser Johnny Chung, has agreed to plead guilty to illegal contributions (Sandalow, 1997).

Although much of the attention has been on the Democrats and on Clinton's "zeal for using the majesty of his office for partisan fund-raising purposes" (Sandalow, 1997, p. A3), the Republicans were themselves caught in illegal activities. Late in the presidential contest, Bob Dole's campaign vice chairman was fined more than $1 million and sentenced to 6 months under house arrest for making $120,000 in illegal political contributions (Shaw, 1996).

These stories only serve to confirm that the current system of campaign regulation is badly flawed. In response, several members of the press and public interest communities have called for fundamental campaign reform. So too have political leaders on occasion, with Clinton and Senate leader Trent Lott both trotting out their own competing proposals. To be sure, we might question their sincerity given that each man has done extremely well under the current system of campaign finance. But the question still remains: Although there can be little doubt that much is wrong with campaign regulation, how are we to reach consensus on the particular problems and respond with a better approach? With campaign reform controlled by those subject to it, such an approach has eluded Congress and the president.

History of Campaign Reform

This chapter addresses federal campaign finance reform, that is, reform of the system of funding presidential and congressional campaigns. I could just as well have added state and municipal races because "campaign finance at the state level share[s] many of the characteristics and problems commonly associated with the funding of federal campaigns" (Corrado & Ortiz, 1997, p. 338). But it is on the federal level that campaigns are most costly and where the stakes of improper influence are highest.

Federal campaigns are regulated by the Federal Election Campaign Act of 1972 (FECA), amended both in 1974 and 1979. In the aftermath of Watergate and the 1972 presidential campaign, Congress enacted the FECA to impose aggregate spending limitations on all federal campaigns as well as to restrict the amounts that individuals and organizations could give to candidates. After the U.S. Supreme Court struck down the spending caps in the case of *Buckley v. Valeo,* Congress reformulated the FECA to apply primarily to contributions. Under the law, individuals may give $1,000 to a federal candidate for his or her primary, general, or special election campaign. Corporations and labor unions are forbidden from using their treasury funds on behalf of candidates, although they or any other collection of individuals may form a political committee—better known to most as a political action committee (PAC)—to raise and spend election monies. PACs may only receive individual contributions of less than $1,000, but most may disperse up to $5,000 per candidate per election. Individuals may give up to $20,000 per year to political parties for use on federal campaigns and are limited to an annual total of $25,000 for all of their contributions on behalf of federal election activity.

Under the current law, candidates may spend as much as they can raise, with wealthy candidates allowed to finance their own campaigns. Public financing is not available for congressional races, although there is limited public funding for presidential candidates. During the primary campaign, presidential candidates are offered "matching funds" once they raise a certain threshold of contributions on their own. In the general election campaign, the two major party candidates may elect to receive full funding from the federal treasury provided that they agree not to raise any additional contributions for their own campaigns. Such funding also is available to independent presidential candidates, although the criteria to qualify are much more difficult. Both John Anderson in 1980 and Ross Perot in 1996 received public funding.

As part of its goal of "disinfecting" campaign fund-raising, the FECA requires federal candidates to disclose their contributions and expenditures by filing regular reports that are publicly available. These reports are filed with the Federal Election Commission (FEC), the governmental agency established by the FECA to monitor campaign practices and to enforce the terms of the federal election laws. The FEC is governed by six commissioners, divided equally between Democrats and Republicans, and maintains a staff of auditors, investigators, and attorneys to carry out its functions. A violation of the FECA is eligible for criminal prosecution by the Justice Department.

Defining the Problems

The biggest challenge in campaign reform is being able to define the exact problems. Because campaign finance laws, by definition, govern political activities, it is understandable that partisans might squabble over their own political fortunes. Public interest groups also weigh in, suggesting that politics is overrun with money and that corruption abides throughout the entire system. It is easy to get caught up in these debates with the inevitable result of losing track of the real problems. Nonetheless, there are eight primary weaknesses worth considering: the total amount of money spent on campaigns, the time candidates spend raising funds, the advantages of incumbency, the incentives for the wealthy to run, candidates' dependence on "special interests," the role of "soft money," the exemption for "issue advocacy," and the role of independent expenditures. Taken together, these problems paint a campaign system that has two systemic and overreaching defects. First, the system lacks real competition and true accountability to voters. Second, candidates have become too dependent on fund-raising. As the reader will see, I do not share the concern of some that money is an absolute evil in politics. Rather, I am worried about a system that fundamentally favors certain interests over others and that makes candidates dependent on wealthy contributors.

Money Spent

One of the common criticisms of political campaigns is that they cost too much. As the work of Magleby and Nelson (1990) shows, congressional campaign expenditures jumped from $66 million in 1972 to $407 million in 1988. Even controlling for inflation, campaign costs increased 230% over this period. The rise in spending is particularly apparent in competitive races—those contests in which both candidates have viable chances of winning—where the costs of keeping pace with one's opponent are steep.

Those who criticize such spending generally make one of two points. To those disillusioned by politics, the vast sums spent on political campaigning undoubtedly look like a waste of resources that could be better spent on other matters. They are joined by those who claim that the rate of increase in campaign spending has well eclipsed the percentage of the voting-age population who actually vote. For example, in 1986, less than 40% of adults voted in congressional elections, whereas the increase in campaign spending hit 65% over the previous election (Magleby & Nelson, 1990). Opponents say that this is proof that campaign spending is failing to attract voters to the polls. To those more bold, the high cost of campaigns is turning off voters, disillusioning those who see the petty commercials bought with massive contributions.

These criticisms are strong, but they connect two elements that are not necessarily causal. Voter turnout varied between 55% and 35% from 1972 to 1988, whereas the rate of increase in campaign spending continued to go up. If campaign spending is causing low voter turnout, then we would expect to see a consistently negative relationship between the two (i.e., voter turnout would continue to sink as campaign spending rose). For that matter, I am not entirely convinced that campaign spending is itself a problem. Both Clinton and Dole spent less on campaign advertising in 1996 than did Procter & Gamble to advertise its products over the course of the year. If we consider public life to be important, then we should expect candidates to spend money on voter communication. The nation's highest office undoubtedly is more important than a box of Tide detergent, and we should expect campaigns to be costly. Besides, on a purely utilitarian basis, "If the campaign finance system does not provide adequate channels for individual and group participation, then this energy will spill over into less desirable forms" (Citizens' Research Foundation, 1997, p. ii). If candidates cannot adequately promote themselves under the current system of campaign regulation, they will find ways in which to get around it.

Time Spent Raising Money

That I do not oppose money in politics does not mean that I support the status quo. To the contrary, candidates currently spend too much time and effort amassing campaign contributions. Public officials even tell us this. In a study conducted by the Center for Responsive Politics, 52% of U.S. senators said that fund-raising cut significantly into their time for legislative work. Another 12% of senators said that it had some deleterious effect, but as many as 73% of Senate staff members said that fund-raising had a "significant impact" in taking time away from legislative activity (Magleby & Nelson, 1990). The understood rule now on Capitol Hill is that the campaign never stops. As former House Democratic Whip Tony Coelho says, "It's a crazy system. Members [of Congress] don't have time to be good members anymore" (quoted in Cohn, 1993, p. 70).

Incumbency Bias

Although incumbents might complain about the problems of campaign funding, election results usually find them reelected to office. Since World War II, the reelection rate for House incumbents is 91%. Senators have averaged a little lower, but even in 1986 (a year in which Senate control changed parties), 75% of senators won reelection (Magleby & Nelson, 1990). These results alone are not problematic, but they reflect a system in which incumbents receive several benefits that give them than an extra advantage over challengers.

As members of Congress, incumbents enjoy a "franking" privilege, allowing them to disseminate newsletters to the voters at home detailing their accomplishments on behalf of their constituents. They have government-paid staff to direct their press releases and media appearances, and by virtue of their officeholdings, they gain greater media visibility (Magleby & Nelson, 1990). They also are more successful than challengers at raising funds. As will be discussed later, they have better access to PACs and other special interest giving, and with their reelection rates so high, contributors are loathe to "waste" funds by giving them a challenger. These patterns play out in the average campaign expenditures by congresspersons and their challengers. In 1988 alone, incumbents spent more than three times as much as their opponents; where incumbents spent $767 million, challengers had $243 million to spend (Magleby & Nelson, 1990). In this setting, it is difficult to convince challengers to run given the high investment of time and money needed to even hope to be competitive.

Incentives for the Rich

One way for both incumbents and challengers to fund their campaigns is to draw from their own personal wealth. Under the FECA, candidates face no limits at all in contributing to their own campaigns. With this exemption of sorts in place, we are seeing more self-financed millionaire candidates running for office, with a growing number of them winning.

There are those who do not consider these events to be a problem. Free speech is a hallmark of the American political system, they say, and if a candidate wants to spend his or her own funds to communicate with voters, then we should applaud that candidate's initiative. I join part of this chorus in that I welcome more political communication. But the evolution of self-financed millionaire candidates actually serves to decrease electoral competition and with it political dialogue. In 1997, the Los Angeles-based Citizens' Research Foundation (CRF) gathered nine esteemed political scientists and experts on campaign finance. In writing the group's report, each member expressed the following concern:

> The campaign finance systems in this country too often tend to discourage competition by advantaging . . . wealthy individuals willing to make large contributions to their campaign. Specifically, we are troubled when the financial advantage of [a] . . . wealthy individual willing to make large contributions to his or her campaign discourages individuals who might otherwise become credible candidates and when reporters, other observers, and potential contributors discount a candidacy because of the fund-raising advantage that another candidate enjoys by virtue of . . . personal wealth. Such events threaten electoral competition and undermine fairness. (CRF, 1997, p. 11)

This is not the same as calling for an equalization of political contributions and expenditures. To be sure, campaign contributions should reflect the level of financial support that a candidate enjoys. But this is precisely why self-financed millionaire candidates distort the electoral process. They discourage other candidates from entering a race when the challengers must raise funds from others to compete with a candidate who can just dip into his or her own pockets, and they increase public cynicism about the role of money in campaigns. In a sense, they crowd out the political field, taking us further away from the concept of citizen legislatures to an oligarchal system in which the richest Americans dominate government.

Political Action Committees

If one views the problem of campaign reform from newspaper coverage alone, then the greatest scourge of the current system is PACs. In 1996, there were 4,079 PACs registered with the FEC, of which 1,642 were corporate; 332 were labor; and 838 represented trade, health,or membership groups (Sorauf, 1997). The objections to PACs generally fall into three categories. One is that PACs provide a disproportionately large share of campaign contributions for congressional races (and, to some extent, presidential contests).[1] The second is that those contributions distort the electoral process by systematically favoring particular candidates over others. The third category is that PAC giving is designed to win special favors from Congress, for which the PACs often are successful.

PACs contribute a large share of the total contributions collected in congressional races. In the most recent congressional elections, PACs gave $200 million to congressional candidates, which represented 25% of all candidate receipts (Sorauf, 1997). A mere quarter of all campaign contributions might not convince the neutral observer that PAC giving is problematic until he or she examines the pattern of these contributions. PACs systematically favor incumbents in their giving, and they also provide greater contributions to candidates of the party that controls Congress. As Table 37.1 shows, the three largest categories of PACs gave 75% of their funds to incumbents in 1996, with challengers receiving a mere 13% and candidates in open races (where no incumbents exist) getting 12%.

Partisan contribution patterns also turn up in PAC giving. As Table 37.2 shows, labor, membership, and even corporate PACs gave the sizable majority of their contributions to Democratic House candidates in 1992, when Democrats still had control of the House. However, 4 years later after Republicans had taken control of the chamber, contribution patterns evened out. This trend is shown even better if we look only at corporate PAC contributions, those that make up the greatest portion of all PAC contributions; these changed from a 53%-47% Democratic advantage in 1992 to a 70%-30% Republican edge in 1996.

The very change in corporate PAC spending suggests the strongest objection to PACs—that they are using their money to try to buy favorable treatment from Congress. To paraphrase the Center for Responsive Politics, lucrative PACs, particularly those representing commercial interests, are getting special care from Congress that others do not get (Sorauf, 1997). The implication from the center's data is, as one writer has suggested, that "legislators seem accountable to those who finance their campaigns instead of [to] those who elect them to office" (Cohn, 1993, p. 66). This conclusion still is somewhat controversial in political science, as studies disagree over whether campaign contributions influence con-

TABLE 37.1 1996 Campaign Contributions to House Incumbents, Challengers, and Open Seats by Three Largest PAC Categories

Candidate	Corporate PAC Donations (millions of dollars)	Labor PAC Donations (millions of dollars)	Membership PAC Donations (millions of dollars)	Percentage of These Contributions
Incumbents	43.9	21.7	34.1	75
Challengers	1.8	11.5	3.6	13
Open seats	4.8	5.2	5.5	12

NOTE: PAC = political action committee.

TABLE 37.2 Comparison of House Campaign Contributions to Democrats and Republicans by Three Largest PAC Categories

Year	Party Candidates	Corporate PAC Donations (millions of dollars)	Labor PAC Donations (millions of dollars)	Membership PAC Donations (millions of dollars)	Percentage of These Contributions
1992	Democrats	21.8	26.8	21.6	67
	Republicans	18.4	1.3	14.4	33
1996	Democrats	15.1	35.7	15.8	50
	Republicans	35.2	2.5	27.2	50

NOTE: PAC = political action committee.

gressional voting (Lowenstein, 1989; Magleby & Nelson, 1990; Sorauf, 1997). However, those studies that focus on bill sponsorship or committee deliberations—the real behind-the-scenes work of Congress—find a connection between campaign contributions and favorable legislative treatment (Lowenstein, 1989). Former congresspersons admit as much. Vic Weber, a Minnesota Republican, says, "If nobody else cares about it very much, [the contributor] will get its way. If the public understands the issue at any level, then [the contributor is] not able to buy an outcome that the public may not want. But the fact is that the public doesn't focus on most of the work of the Congress." Mel Levin, a California Democrat, adds, "On the tax side, the appropriations side, the subsidy side, and the expenditure side, decisions are clearly weighted and influenced . . . by who has contributed to candidates" (quoted in Sorauf, 1997, p. 157).

That PACs or other special interests would seek special treatment from Congress is not surprising. Indeed, such petitioning and lobbying is not in itself the problem. It is the very nature, let alone right, of Americans to organize with one another and make their voices heard in government. The Constitution guarantees as much in the rights to assembly, association, and petition. Moreover, American political life depends on "the creation of new forms of association to further people's interests and goals. . . . Such activity inevitably comes with a vibrant democracy" (CRF, 1997, p. 21).

Lest the reader think me inconsistent, I am not arguing that PAC activity *as it currently stands* should remain unchecked. What I mean to say is that, *theoretically,*

PACs and the organized political activity they represent should be viewed favorably. However, problems arise where candidates become so dependent on PAC contributions that the outcome of a PAC's legislative initiative rides as much on how much money the PAC contributed as on the merits of the proposal. So long as congressional candidates are dependent on campaign contributions for elections, and so long as certain interests have greater ability to contribute than others, legislative outcomes might be tipped in favor of the wealthiest interests.

Soft Money

In an exemption created entirely by the FEC, political parties may use contributions not subject to the FECA to pay for candidate listings, advertisements, and other "get out the vote" activities on behalf of the party's entire ticket of candidates. Called "soft money," these funds get their name because they are not limited by the "hard" contribution limits of the FECA. National party organizations can solicit "unlimited contributions from individuals or gifts from sources such as corporations and labor unions that have long been banned from giving money in federal elections" (Corrado, 1997, p. 34). Over the past decade, soft money contributions have risen over 10 times, with the Republicans receiving $138.2 million and the Democrats $123.9 million in 1996 (Corrado, 1997).

In a sense, soft money is an administrative loophole. That is, by excepting certain contributions from federal contribution limits, soft money allows political parties to raise unlimited funds from contributors for party-building activities. However, the presence of such immense contributions gives the appearance of impropriety. Although an average citizen cannot afford to provide substantial sums to a party, others can. During the 1980s, the Kroch family (the founders of McDonald's restaurants) gave millions of dollars to the Democratic Party in soft money, and during the 1990s, corporations and wealthy individuals evade federal contribution restrictions by providing the Democratic and Republican parties substantial soft funds.[2] Although each contributor might have a different motive in hand, one cannot avoid the impression that contributors are buying access or even legislative or executive action. Granted, it is difficult for one contributor to get much special attention from a congressperson or the president when he or she gives to the candidate's party and not to the candidate himself or herself. But if a donor supplemented his or her other political contributions with substantial soft money donations, then the donor surely would receive close attention from the politicians of the party to which he or she contributes.

Soft money weakens public confidence in the electoral system. When certain interests can evade the strictures of the FECA and essentially "buy" attention with their large contributions, the system fundamentally favors some over others. But it also is disillusioning to see the lengths to which party leaders will go to raise soft money. In 1996, we watched as Clinton seemed to turn the White House into a bed-and-breakfast operation for large donors. Although not clearly illegal, there is something unseemly about the nation's chief executive officer appearing to sell perks to the highest bidder. The soft money loophole only increases party leaders' dependence on high-dollar contributors while reinforcing the notion that money can buy governmental access or results.

Finally, soft money has created a cottage industry in evading the FECA. Although soft money originally was designed to enhance party organizations by allowing them to engage in voter registration and other grassroots activities, the two major parties have used this small exception to create a giant avenue for campaign spending. As the CRF (1997) explains,

> In 1996 particularly, the state parties used soft money supplied by the national party committees to pay for election year radio and television advertising. . . . This advertising is not the "party building" envisioned by the authorizing legislation. It augments the soft money circumvention, and it undermines accountability. (p. 6)

Issue Advocacy

Like soft money, the FECA exempts another form of canvassing called "issue advocacy," although this latter form of communication can be carried on by many more interests than just political parties.

Issue advocacy is best understood by comparison to its opposite, "express advocacy." Under the FECA, anyone who sponsors advertisements containing express advocacy must pay for the ads with "hard" (i.e., federal) funds. For example, if a PAC wished to run a series of radio advertisements that expressly advocated the election of a federal candidate, then the PAC would be limited to using contributions it received from individuals or other PACs in amounts under $1,000. The PAC also would have to disclose the cost of the advertisements to the FEC.

However, express advocacy has a very limited definition, covering only those communications that " 'expressly advocate' the election or defeat of a clearly identified federal candidate through the use of words such as 'vote for,' 'oppose,' 'support, and the like" (Potter, 1997, p. 227). Political advertising that does not use these words is called issue advocacy and can be paid for from funds that do not meet the FECA.

The sheer possibilities for issue advocacy become readily apparent, allowing corporations, unions, PACs, individuals, and political parties to use unlimited funds to pay for any political advertisement that does not reach express advocacy. For example, if a corporation wanted to praise a candidate's voting record without specifically calling on voters to "elect" the candidate, then the company could draw unlimited funds from its treasury (and not its PAC) to pay for the ad. Or, as we saw in 1996, the AFL-CIO ran a series of ads disparaging several Republican legislators. But because the union did not directly advocate the candidates' "defeat," it was able to pay for the ads directly from its treasury.

We see many more examples of candidates or other organizations using this exemption to run titular campaign ads. In 1997, Senator Alphonse D'Amato placed $2 million in television ads extolling his fight to shut down an incinerator plant (Bernstein, 1997). But because the ads did not expressly advocate his election, he was able to pay for them from whatever sources, and in whatever amounts, he chose.

I am well aware that issue advocacy has a strong backer in the First Amendment, and I have no interest in limiting people or organizations from the free exercise of their ideas and viewpoints. However, when issue advocacy allows individuals or groups to spend unlimited funds on behalf of an election, we face a problem of electoral accountability. One of the very reasons we have campaign finance regulations is to maintain electoral competition, but this value is at risk when anyone with a little creativity and a lot of money can circumvent the express advocacy standard and spend unlimited amounts to influence election outcomes. As the Supreme Court itself has said, there is implicit danger when "corrosive and distorting" aggregations of wealth can dominate the electoral system, even though they have "little or no correlation to the public's support" for political ideas (*Austin v. Michigan Chamber of Commerce,* 1990, p. 659).

Independent Expenditures

To the extent that an individual or a group wishes to expressly advocate the election or defeat of a federal candidate, the FECA permits the person or group to make "independent expenditures" so long as the funds used meet the provisions of the federal election laws. This means that a PAC could take out an ad in favor of a candidate provided that it paid for the advertisement from contributions it received from individuals or other PACs in amounts less than $1,000. So too, a wealthy individual could sponsor an ad opposing a candidate, but the funds would have to be his or her own. Both the wealthy individual and any other individual or group that makes independent expenditures must disclose and report their expenditures to the FEC.

The central problem of independent expenditures, and the one that trips up some sponsors, is that the advertisements or other communications they produce must be independent of the candidate they support or oppose. This standard is fairly simple to meet when an expenditure opposes a candidate, but when an allied group wishes to help a candidate, it can be difficult to remain separate. Supporters naturally want to communicate with a candidate and his or her staff, but to conduct independent expenditures, they cannot coordinate with the campaign or seek its advice in producing or distributing their ads.

This requirement has become even more complicated in the past couple of years, as the Supreme Court recently ruled that political parties can set up independent expenditure committees on behalf of their candidates. So, what we have now are offices in the national parties specifically designed to remain separate from the candidates under whose banners they run. The prospects of one office within the party actively assisting its candidates while a separate independent expenditure committee is kept at arms length is so preposterous as to make a mockery of campaign finance regulations.

Independent expenditures also present the problem of accountability, much as described for issue advocacy. Independent expenditures total several million dollars each election cycle. In 1992 alone, the American Medical Association's PAC spent more than $1 million, or a quarter of its budget, on independent expenditures for specific candidates (Cohn, 1993).

> But neither PACs nor the independent expenditures they sponsor appear on election ballots. Although independent expenditures can shape campaign discourse and popular opinion, they cannot be electorally rewarded or punished for their conduct. Thus, despite their disclosure, independent expenditures lack accountability [to the voters]. (CRF, 1997, p. 16)

Problems With Reform

Congress

As the preceding discussion illuminates, there is no dearth of problems that campaign reform might address. But such efforts are stymied by some fundamental flaws in the system. Even if the FECA were tightened to close the loopholes for soft money, issue advocacy, and the like, the FEC as presently constituted would lack the power to enforce the rules effectively. This is not actually a criticism of the FEC itself, for Congress has intentionally tried to keep the commission weak. Unlike many other independent agencies, Congress denies the FEC the resources necessary to handle its expanding workload. The FEC is denied multi-year budgeting authority, its budget requests are routinely pushed aside, and all the while Congress keeps up a running criticism of the agency. One need only consider the FEC's unfulfilled requests to understand Congress's deliberate indifference to the agency.[3] Among other things, the FEC's only enforcement technique is criminal sanctions. Matters generally reach the commission long after an election has been decided, and without powers to conduct random inspections or to pursue injunctive relief, the FEC must resign itself to criminal prosecutions by the Justice Department as deterrence for future elections.

That Congress would effectively neuter the FEC is not surprising considering that incumbents have few incentives to change the system. By their very election, congresspersons have mastered the campaign finance system, and given that incumbents win reelection at a phenomenally high rate, they have no reason to mess with a scheme that benefits their interests. But it is not just the threat of losing future elections that concerns members of Congress. As former FEC Chairman Trevor Potter says, legislators fear that the FEC "will use any new powers to intervene directly in campaigns, harass candidates and parties, and threaten political freedom" (quoted in Mann, 1997, p. 280). There is some truth to this concern in that a powerful FEC would have powers to intervene soon after a campaign violation occurred. But this is not harassment so much as it is effective policing. Besides, Congress has already shown itself able to control the FEC so that it does not harass or threaten candidates or political parties.

Public Will

Congress also faces little pressure from the general public to complete campaign finance reform. Although there is evidence that the public is increasingly disillusioned with or disconnected from government, few citizens cite campaign reform as an important remedy. In a nationwide survey, only 14% of citizens ranked campaign reform as a top legislative priority. In fact, an even greater percentage, 25%, called such reform a low priority ("Congressional Campaign Reform," 1994). Some of these results might reflect the public's ignorance about government and politics. In the same survey, only 25% of respondents knew that Republicans control both houses of Congress, and a paltry 3% were able to identify what PACs do ("Congressional Campaign Reform," 1994). It also might be the case that "campaign finance reform" sounds vague or confusing to the public, for when the problem is stylized as "money and politics," 69% of respondents are bothered by the amount of money spent on campaigns ("Congressional Campaign Reform," 1994). Nonetheless, when only one in seven people thinks that campaign reform is a top priority, there is little incentive for Congress to act.

Supreme Court

Even if Congress were inclined to take decisive action on campaign finance, its options are limited by the Supreme Court. In the court's seminal case of *Buckley v. Valeo* (1976), the justices equated political expenditures with an individual's right of free speech, saying that any restrictions on campaign spending or independent expenditures would be unconstitutional. The court allowed contribution limits to stand, but under current judicial doctrine, it is unconstitutional to restrict political expenditures. Granted, campaign spending is limited by what a candidate is allowed to raise, but the court's rule allows self-financed candidates to dig deep in their own pockets and well outspend their opponents. Furthermore, any organization with a rich treasury may spend unlimited amounts on issue advocacy. This advantage becomes all the more serious in referenda campaigns, where given the court's decision in *First National Bank of Boston v. Bellotti* (1978), corporations and other wealthy interests may drown out their opponents with a slew of ads. Although high spending does not guarantee a favorable vote, electoral competition is at risk when one side can so dominate the airwaves and drown out the other's message.

Unexpected Effects

Finally, there is the problem of unintended consequences. Even if Congress were to pass campaign finance reform, political pros might find a way in which to get around the restrictions, creating an even greater problem in response. For example, several of the reform proposals before Congress would outlaw PACs. However, candidates still are going to need money to run. If they cannot get large chunks of contributions from PAC donations, then they are going to have to spend even more of their legislative time soliciting contributions. In addition, the special interest organizations that sponsor many PACs would find a way in which to get around the rule. If an organization's PAC could give only $1,000 to a candidate (as opposed to the $5,000 now in effect), then it likely would organize some of its members to donate on their own. This is similar to "bundling," where an organization bundles together its members' contributions to give to a candidate. But in a postreform world, organizations would informally rally their members to contribute directly to specific candidates. Donors would know what they had given, candidates would know who gave, but there would be no public disclosure. According to Coelho, "Many groups do that now. It's not bundling, and it would be perfectly legal, even under the proposed [reforms]" (quoted in Cohn, 1993, p. 69).

Potential Solutions

There are a number of proposals presently before Congress to reform the campaign finance system. The most prominent of them, popularly called McCain-Feingold for its Senate sponsors, would eliminate PACs and restrict soft money and lobbying. Others would limit union or corporate contributions, and still others would completely dismantle contribution limits. However, whether or not these proposals are submitted in good faith, they all suffer from one of two contradictory but fatal weaknesses. Either proponents think it is necessary to remove money from politics, or they believe that candidates or contributors should have free reign to raise and spend money as they see fit.

As I said earlier, money is not an absolute evil in politics. Electoral contests are some of the most fundamental building blocks of a functioning democracy, and candidates need to be able to communicate their ideas and positions to voters. This process takes money. Money buys advertisements, it funds mailings, it purchases buttons and bumper stickers, and it pays for campaign staff. To remove money from politics is to limit the ability of candidates to effectively reach voters. Moreover, candidates likely would find a way in which to get around an absolute prohibition. Political professionals are quite adept at finding loopholes in statutory restrictions. Candidates are going to seek campaign money, and if the law does not provide suitable avenues for raising funds, then politicians will look to sources outside public scrutiny. The answer is not in changing candidates' instincts but rather in altering the incentive structure of campaign funding.

At the same time, I reject the notion that individuals and groups have an absolute right to raise and spend any amount of funds they wish. When money enters the equation, campaigns no longer are soap box debates. Candidates do not rise or fall merely on the basis of their ideas, positions, or attitudes; rather, they win by spending money to reach voters. To accept a system that gives a fundamental advantage to the richest candidates is to say that equal opportunity does not apply to public service. We have long passed the point where a candidate's reserves mainly reflect his popular support in the electorate. In an era where millionaires finance their candidacies, where professional fund-raisers are the most sought-after campaign professionals, and where incumbents use the resources of office to retain their seats, it is simply unreasonable to think that an average citizen still has a fair and competitive chance at office. To be sure, there are exceptions, particularly among one-issue challengers, but an average challenger really cannot compete against the wealthy opponent or the political professional. Indeed, it is hardly surprising that "dozens of rising stars, Democrats and Republicans alike, [have] decided not to run for Congress . . . in what political strategists describe as a growing trend" (Berke, 1998, p. A10).

One of the solutions that has been floated is to reconfigure *Buckley v. Valeo* by amending the U.S. Constitution. Because *Buckley* holds that political expenditures constitute free speech, only a constitutional amendment would permit restrictions on campaign expenditures or independent spending. At first blush, the proposal is enticing. With a cap placed on campaign expenditures, challengers would have an easier time staying competitive. Soft money could be reigned in, and independent expenditures could be kept within reasonable limits. But as attractive as this proposal might be, it attacks the problem from the wrong end. We should encourage political communication, at least that from candidates to the voters. Although I reject the notion that money *is* speech, money does make campaign speech possible. How are we to say when voters have heard enough from the candidates? Indeed, in a hotly contested campaign, we might want both candidates to spend extra time speaking to voters. The central problem is not necessarily too much money chasing voters but rather that the system fundamentally prevents some candidates from getting a fair hearing. The only area in which we should countenance spending restrictions is soft money, and here the solution only requires legislation to close an administrative loophole.[4]

This is not to say that other restrictions are unnecessary. Indeed, the whole subject of issue advocacy reflects a Supreme Court that fails to understand the political process and a Congress unwilling to change it. Television advertisements within 10 days of an election that disparage a candidate's issue positions but do not specifically use the word "defeat" in their script are just as much a campaign advertisement as one run by the candidate's opponent. It is problematic enough that independent groups can swamp a candidate's advertising, effectively steering an election's mandate away from the candidate's positions to those not even on the ballot. But when issue advocacy masquerades as election advertising, it allows groups to use funds that are illegal under the FECA and also permits them to avoid disclosure and reporting. What is needed here is a fine-tuning of the distinction between issue advocacy and express advocacy. As the FEC has correctly advanced for some time now, there ought to be a presumption that any advertising about the candidates within 4 weeks of an election is presumptively express advocacy and not issue advocacy. With judicial deference, Congress could adopt this new rule.[5]

Perhaps the greatest change necessary in the current system is how and where candidates obtain their contributions. Initially, it is time to raise the $1,000 contribution limit set in place nearly 20 years ago. Even with a relatively low inflation rate as of late, this amount has actually dropped in real terms. If candidates cannot raise sufficient sums according to the federal election laws, then they are necessarily going to look for other sources. Indeed, the rise of self-financed candidates might reflect a growing frustration among potential challengers in having to raise hundreds of thousands of dollars in $1,000 increments. By increasing the contribution ceiling to $3,000, the law not only would restore the real value of the FECA's limits[6] but also would provide candidates with a more reasonable chance to raise funds from individuals.

But the real solution is to provide some sort of public financing to otherwise qualified candidates. Undoubtedly, this proposal has its detractors, for few Americans are interested in spending tax dollars on what they consider to be an ineffectual or (at worst) corrupt political system ("Congressional Campaign Reform," 1994). But to the extent that money has corrupted politics, it is because either a relatively few have access to it or because top contributors are acquiring special access or treatment. Done right, public financing could alleviate many of these problems. Public financing need not provide every candidate funding, nor should it be designed to equalize campaign funds among opponents. Rather, once candidates pass threshold criteria (including petition signatures or an amount of funds raised on their own), they would be entitled to benchmark funding. The concept here is to provide candidates a basic floor of funding—a minimal amount to compete plausibly. Payments could be made by check, in vouchers for television time, or even for subsidized postage. Moreover, by offering candidates funding, public financing could require certain responsibilities of them. For example, those accepting public support might have to agree to public debates. Certainly, voters would be better informed if candidates had to face them in a series of unscripted questions from the public itself.

Yet, the greatest advantage of public financing is that it removes candidates from some of the pressures and dangers of raising funds. With a minimum floor provided by federal funds, candidates no longer would have to spend as much time soliciting donors on their own. Incumbents would be forced to face real competitors with sufficient funds to make credible races, and self-financed candidates would not be able to intimidate others from running. To be sure, millionaire candidates still could easily outspend their opponents, but it never has been shown that greater campaign spending *automatically* wins elections. Although campaign funding is correlated with victory, it is instead having a minimum amount to run a credible race that makes the difference. The work of Jennifer Steen, who also appears in this book (Chapter 10), supports this conclusion, although we also see anecdotal evidence on the national level where candidates such as Minnesota Senator Paul Wellstone and California Congresswoman Loretta Sanchez have been able to beat their wealthy opponents with a sufficient floor of funding.

PACs also would have less influence to offer and, therefore, to demand from "their" legislators. With candidates less dependent on contributors to support their races, PACs would become one of many sources of campaign funding, not the motherlode they are currently. Public financing is not a panacea, but anything that reduces candidates' dependence on donors would help to attack many of the weaknesses in the current system.

Finally, by giving every qualified candidate a reasonable chance at basic funding, it is more likely that candidates' positions, and not those of outside groups, would dominate elections. There still would be heated contests, with outside groups pouring in lots of independent ads. But to the extent that more candidates can afford to run, each with sufficient funding, the level of debate likely would rise from the candidates themselves.

Conclusion

That I have proposed these reforms does not mean that I am confident they will be enacted any time soon. It would take an extra chapter or more to discuss the public and legislative apathy that frustrates campaign reform. But this is not a problem we can sweep under the rug, seemingly oblivious to its effects during a period of economic prosperity. The electoral process is getting away from us. More and more qualified and concerned individuals are choosing not to run for office. We are at the point where we have a permanent legislative class, where most potential challengers have no realistic chance at election wholly apart from the strength of their backgrounds or beliefs. Money dominates the current system. Money is not necessarily bad in politics, and there are ways in which to enhance or even expand campaigning. But the present arrangement is systematically disenfranchising certain voters and interests. This is a strong statement, no doubt, but the consequences of inaction are that serious.

Notes

1. Because presidential candidates raise funds only during the primary campaign (the two major party candidates accept federal funding for the general election), the opportunities for PAC contributions are cut in half. Moreover, because presidential candidates necessarily raise funds nationally, individual donations predominate over PAC contributions.

2. The Democrats did establish voluntary limits on soft money for the 1988 elections.

3. Among the requests made by the FEC to Congress that have yet to be enacted are authority to mandate electronic filing, authority to conduct random audits, and explicit authority to refer appropriate matters to the Justice Department for prosecution at any stage of its proceedings (Mann, 1997).

4. The rationale for restricting soft money is not that the expenditures have become too great (although they are significant) but that contributions to fund soft money activities are unregulated. High-dollar donations present a real risk of political corruption, something that is unlikely to occur in federal legislative races where candidates are limited in receiving contributions.

5. That is, Congress needs to pass a law redefining express advocacy, which the courts must uphold if challenged.

6. Compared to existing law, $3,000 in 1998 dollars would better approximate the FECA's original limit of $1,000 as measured in 1974 dollars.

References

Austin v. Michigan Chamber of Commerce, 494 U.S. 652 (1990).

Berke, R. L. (1998, March 15). More and more resist pressure to run for office. *San Francisco Examiner.*

Bernstein, A. (1997, January 12). Roadblocks to campaign reform. *Washington Post.*

Buckley v. Valeo, 424 U.S. 1 (1976).

Citizens' Research Foundation (1997). *New realities, new thinking: Report of the Task Force on Campaign Finance Reform.* Los Angeles: Author.

Cohn, J. S. (1993, Fall). Money talks, reform walks. *The American Prospect,* pp. 66-72.

Congressional campaign reform: Public perceptions. (1994, September 26). *The Polling Report,* pp. 1, 5.

Corrado, A. (1997). Money and politics. In A. Corrado, T. E. Mann, D. R. Ortiz, T. Potter, & F. J. Sorauf (Eds.), *Campaign finance reform: A sourcebook.* Washington, DC: Brookings Institution.

Corrado, A., & Ortiz, D. R. (1997). Recent innovations. In A. Corrado, T. E. Mann, D. R. Ortiz, T. Potter, & F. J. Sorauf (Eds.), *Campaign finance reform: A sourcebook.* Washington, DC: Brookings Institution.

First National Bank of Boston v. Bellotti, 435 U.S. 765 (1978).

Lowenstein, D. H. (1989). On campaign finance reform: The root of all evil is deeply rooted. *Hofstra Law Review, 18.*

Magleby, D. B., & Nelson, C. J. (1990). *The money chase.* Washington, DC: Brookings Institution.

Mann, T. E. (1997). The Federal Election Commission: Implementing and enforcing federal campaign finance law. In A. Corrado, T. E. Mann, D. R. Ortiz, T. Potter, & F. J. Sorauf (Eds.), *Campaign finance reform: A sourcebook.* Washington, DC: Brookings Institution.

Potter, T. (1997). Issue advocacy and express advocacy. In A. Corrado, T. E. Mann, D. R. Ortiz, T. Potter, & F. J. Sorauf (Eds.), *Campaign finance reform: A sourcebook.* Washington, DC: Brookings Institution.

Sandalow, M. (1997, March 17). The campaign finance controversy *San Francisco Chronicle.*

Shaw, G. (1996, October 31). Both parties soiled by scandal that's certain to linger. *Buffalo News.*

Sorauf, F. J. (1997). Political action committees. In A. Corrado, T. E. Mann, D. R. Ortiz, T. Potter, & F. J. Sorauf (Eds.), *Campaign finance reform: A sourcebook.* Washington, DC: Brookings Institution.

38

The Cyberspace Election of the Future

DENNIS W. JOHNSON

Although the 1996 presidential debates were fairly unremarkable, Bob Dole earned a modest footnote in American politics and campaigns. He was the first presidential candidate to mention his campaign's Web site to a nationwide audience. In the closing minutes of the debate on October 6, 1996, Dole said that he wanted to appeal to younger voters: "I ask for your support. I ask for your help. And if you really want to get involved, just tap into my homepage: www.dolekemp96org." As Schwartz (1996) notes, "Even Dole, who once simply called his site 'my whatchamacallit,' can reel off the on-line address" (although Dole misplaced the dot between 96 and org.).[1] Voters apparently were listening, as more than 2 million visited the Dole-Kemp Web site immediately following the debate. Although still a novelty item during the 1996 election, the Internet as a campaign communication tool had arrived.

Some 80 years ago, candidates and campaigns were relatively slow in adapting to the new communication tool of radio and were equally slow in using television when it came on the scene near mid-century. But in recent years, candidates have jumped fairly quickly onto the latest forms of communication. During the late 1980s, fax broadcasting, videocassettes, and cable television advertising became widespread in campaigns. In the 1992 presidential campaign, Jerry Brown announced his 800 telephone number every chance he could, Bill Clinton's campaign used e-mail and satellite downlinks, and candidates for many offices were discovering the reinvigorated, but old-fashioned, format of talk show programs and other forms of free media as effective communication tools.

In 1994, few candidates had Web sites, but as on-line use and technology became more commonplace, campaigns began to use this new tool.[2] Campaigns were participating in the same communications revolution that was transforming the rest of society. As Westen (1996) notes, in 1995, a "great digital phase shift" occurred. In that year, for the first time, "personal computers outsold television sets, the number of e-mail messages surpassed surface mail messages, and data traffic over telephone networks . . . exceeded voice traffic" (p. 59). In 1995, many advocacy group, candidate, and party Web sites were developed including *Town Hall,* the self-described conservative shopping mall. At its unveiling, *Town Hall* President Timothy Butler boldly stated his vision of politics and communications: "TV and radio are the old war. The new war is the battle for minds on the Internet" (quoted in Kurtz, 1995, p. A1).

The first concerted use of Web sites for campaign reporting came during the 1996 presidential election. On Election Night, media Web sites received their first big test, with millions of Internet users checking election returns. CBS estimated that there were 10 million "hits" on its Web site, *PoliticsNow*[3] had five times the usual traffic on Election Night, and CNN estimated 50 million hits on its Web site. Internet users were able to see projected outcomes and early exit poll information. It was possible, for example, to find out on-line and before television viewers that Clinton had received 70% of the Hispanic votes in California and that 46% of voters with incomes below $15,000 in Virginia had voted for Dole (Hilzenrath, 1996).

By 1998, there was an explosion in campaign Web sites; Web pages about politics, issues, and causes; media sites dedicated to politics; and government sites devoted to election information, voter registration, lobbying, and financial disclosure. Even more impetus was given to the Internet by the smell of political scandal. Michael Kinsley, editor of the on-line magazine *Slate,* observes that the Clinton intern scandal was "to the Internet what the Kennedy assassination was to TV news—its coming of age as a media force" (Kinsley, 1998, p. 41). The Monica Lewinsky story spread like cyberfire. On the day it broke, January 18, 1998, there was 1 Web site posting;[4] by the next day, there were 17 postings; and by January 24, there were 633 postings (Greenman, 1998). Web site entrepreneur and gossip Matt Drudge claimed 7 million hits on his *Drudge Report* during the month following the scandal.

There is no doubt that the Internet will be an important political communications tool in campaigns during the next decade. Many observers see the Internet as the dominant new force. Political consultant Phil Noble, whose business includes a newsletter on political uses of the Internet, states that 1998 "will be the last election year of the old media age and the first year of the new media, or digital, age" (Noble, 1998, p. 1). Microsoft Chairman Bill Gates believes that the Internet will become the "primary conduit" for political discourse in future elections (Gates, 1995, pp. 271-272). Others are not so sure. While acknowledging the great growth of political Internet sites and their use in recent elections, Margolis, Resnick, and Tu (1997) argue that the Internet will not be a revolutionary, paradigm-shifting tool but rather will be just one more weapon in the communications arsenal of campaigns, reinforcing—not replacing—the existing dynamics of American politics. Haase (1998) is even less enthusiastic, noting that in 1998, for all the talk about Web sites, the Internet still was a "campaign tool in search of a job."

The Net Citizen

A number of surveys have shown that on-line users were just the type of citizens whom many candidates wanted to attract. Compared to non-Web users, the "digital citizens" or "netizens" were younger, better educated, more affluent, and more likely to be engaged in politics. Men use the Web somewhat more than do women (Bimber, 1998; Georgia Tech Graphics, Visualization, and Usability Center, 1996; Westen, 1998). Katz (1998) takes this description further, describing the digital citizen as optimistic, tolerant, civic-minded, and radically committed to change. Katz sees an emerging "Digital Nation," a "new social class"— young, educated, affluent, richer, and disproportionately White. The closest thing to a political dogma in the digital world, according to Katz, is "ingrained libertarianism."

Coming to adulthood in the next decade is a new generation of on-line users. Don Tapscott, who coined the terms "Net Generation" and "N-Generation," states that there will be about 88 million young people in the United States and Canada in the year 2000. This is the generation growing up comfortable with the Web (Tapscott, 1997). Children with no recollection of the 1980s can easily surf to their favorite Web sites and chat rooms and can create their own homepages. In many circles, if an individual is 13 years old and does not know HTML format, then he or she may be considered "truly retarded."[5]

Will technological facility translate into greater interest in politics once the new generation has reached adulthood? Katz argues that it will. He sees the digital young possessing the three most powerful political forces: technology, education, and communication. With these, the "ascending young citizens of the Digital Nation can, if they wish, construct a more civil society, a new politics based on rationalism, shared information, the pursuit of truth, and new kinds of community" (Katz, 1997).

Yet, we need to step back for a moment. Although a popular image has nearly every American armed with the latest high-tech gizmo, most citizens are not so equipped. For example, a 1997 survey found that only 2% of the American population were "super-connected" to technology; these individuals exchanged e-mail at least 3 days a week and used a laptop computer, a cell phone, a beeper, and a home computer. An additional 7% were "connected"; they used all but one of these technologies. Fully 62% of the population were "semi-connected"; they exchange e-mail at least once a week and use at least one of the other technologies regularly. The remaining 29% of the population were "unconnected"; they used none of the targeted technologies.[6] Another study found that less than 40% of American homes have personal computers and that only 20 million homes have computers with modems (Rose, 1998).

The Internet still is a work in progress, attracting much attention and interest from a dedicated minority but not yet reaching the point of critical mass consumption. Surely, that critical mass has yet to come to politics and elections. The Media Studies Center in late 1996 found that 28% of voters had access to the Internet but that less than 1% relied on the Internet for information on presidential campaigns. Just 6% of all voters had visited a politically oriented Web site during the 1996 election cycle (Media Studies Center, 1996). Less than 2 years later, the Pew Research Center (1998) concluded that Internet use was "skyrocketing," with more than a third (36%) of Americans going on-line from their homes or offices. But those who go on-line are far more interested in information about hobbies, movies, health/science, finances, weather, and entertainment than about politics.

Citizen Access to Campaign and Policy Information

The Electronically Informed Citizen

For the politically engaged and motivated, the Internet is an extraordinary tool. Vast amounts of public information once difficult to obtain or plainly out of reach are now accessible over the Internet. Citizens can easily check voting records of members of Congress through *Project Vote Smart* and votes of state legislators through a growing number of state sites. Through another Web site, *Smart Voter,* and its "My Ballot" page, a citizen can, by simply entering his or her address and zip code, find out about voter registration and access nonpartisan information on candidates and initiatives. *Smart Voter* then produces a ballot, showing all the candidates and issues for that particular jurisdiction.[7] Also, scores of special interest group Web sites provide lists of their legislative demons and heroes including the League of Conservation Voters, the Christian Coalition, the National Rifle Association, and Handgun Control.[8]

The politically curious can go even further. Each of the major news organizations has its own Web site or portions of a Web site dedicated to politics. The ultimate sources for day-to-day information on campaigns and elections are the *National Journal*'s "Hotline" and *Congressional Quarterly*'s "Politics for Pros," both of which supply a stream of election analysis, polls, campaign ad tracking, and summaries of stories from hundreds of newspapers and other newscasts for the information-starved political junkie. Nearly every political columnist has a Web page, and the most prominent are now conveniently linked from one site, the *Drudge Report,* the Internet's cybergossip corner for breaking political stories.

Citizens interested in policy questions are served by a wide array of Web sites. One of the best is the *Policy Network,* which links viewers with a variety of policy organizations. Voters can tap into conservative *Town Hall,* or they can check the Republican and Democratic national party homepages, the senatorial and congressional campaign committees, and virtually all state political parties. Electronic magazines, such as *Salon* and *Slate,* have special emphases on politics and policy. The White House, nearly all 100 U.S. senators, and about 330 House members had established Web sites by the end of 1997.[9]

Third-party fringe groups, and other organizations that would be crowded out of traditional communications space can find equal voice on the Internet. The Greens Party, the Reform Party, Democratic Socialists of America, the U.S. Taxpayers Party, the John Birch Society, the Feminist Majority, and many others all have created Web sites, establishing a true marketplace of ideas.

State Voting and Election Information

In past decades, it was very difficult for citizens to learn about campaign finances, lobbying records, or votes taken in state legislatures. Records were either nonexistent, inaccessible, or available only in the state capitol. Through the Internet, state election boards and other agencies are making many public records truly accessible. In October 1997, California enacted landmark legislation mandating electronic filing of state political disclosure records. California joined 13 other states that passed legislation in 1997 promoting electronic disclosure, and 17 other states have enacted, or are considering, mandatory or voluntary electronic filing and on-line disclosure requirements. The California law probably is the most comprehensive in the nation, requiring electronic filing by 1999–2000 for all statewide and legislative candidates who raise or spend $50,000, along with mandatory electronic filing for all other entities such as political parties, political action committees (PACs), lobbyists, major donors, and slate mailer committees. In addition, the California Voter Foundation publishes a Web site, *Digital Sunlight,* which monitors financial disclosures in California elections and has links to many useful database and disclosure resources.

Through its Web site, the Federal Election Commission (FEC) makes it easier to register to vote. Citizens can download the FEC's National Mail Voter Registration Form, fill it out, and mail it to their respective state election boards. Currently, the National Mail Voter Registration Form is accepted in 23 states, and many state boards of elections also are making their registration forms, election guides, and other information available to the public.

On-Line Debate

Two nonpartisan projects have demonstrated how on-line democracy can give all candidates a chance to be heard. This is especially important for minor or third-party candidates who cannot raise funds for television or direct mail expenditures.

Minnesota E-Democracy

Months before the 1998 Minnesota gubernatorial primaries, candidates were given the chance to participate in an electronic debate, courtesy of Minnesota E-Democracy, a nonprofit, nonpartisan citizens organization.[10] The 12 candidates were given the opportunity to respond to six policy issues posed by a panel of journalists. The 300-word responses were posted on the *E-Democracy* Web site, and visitors could view the responses, receive them by e-mail, and interact through the site's chat room, "MN-Forum."

One great attraction for candidates is that marginal candidates, or candidates with little funding, could post their messages and answers to debate questions just as could the best funded. Jesse Ventura, candidate for the underdog Reform Party, stated that the on-line debate was "truly made for my campaign. It's reaching a huge amount of people at a very low price" (quoted in Raney, 1998a, p. C1). In a remarkable three-way general election, the former professional wrestler won the governorship and credited his Web site as one of the reasons for his upset victory.

Democracy Network

The 1998 California gubernatorial primary was an extraordinary event. It was the most expensive primary in history, dominated by paid television commercials, whereas television stations virtually abandoned coverage of the races. Finally, when there was a televised debate, only 4 of the 17 gubernatorial candidates were allowed to participate.

Through the *Democracy Network,* or *DNet,* all candidates were given the opportunity to post their answers to debate questions over the Internet. *DNet,* a project of the Center for Governmental Studies, made space available on its Web site for all the gubernatorial candidates—regardless of their predicted chances of winning—to debate one another and to answer questions from voters. *DNet* is particularly valuable for local campaigns, where it often is more difficult to find out who is on the ballot and what the candidates stand for. To assist voters, *DNet* has developed an innovative "Issue Grid." Candidates can post policy positions (up to 1,000 words) on a preselected issue or create their own issues. Voters then could click on the race, compare candidate responses, or even e-mail comments to the candidates (Westen, 1998).[11] The *Democracy Network,* working with state chapters of the League of Women Voters and other groups, planned to have *DNet* sites up in nine other states before the 1998 November elections.[12]

Campaigns and the Internet

By 1998, campaign Web sites were standard, almost indispensable, communication tools. Approximately 5 months before the November elections, *Political Resources Directory,* a reference publication for campaigns and the election industry, listed 125 campaign Web sites for the Senate or Congress; 98 for governor, state legislator, or other state office; and 29 for local office.[13] In California's crowded 1998 primary, there were more than 90 statewide candidates, nine ballot initiatives, and dozens of congressional, state senate, and assembly races. Kim

Alexander of the California Voter Foundation noted that more than 80% of the California candidates had Web sites ("Web Sites," 1998).

A closer look at some of the campaign Web sites shows their strengths and shortcomings as communication tools.

Minnesota Governor's Race

In 1998, the Minnesota gubernatorial primary featured a crowded field of 12 candidates including the "three sons": Mike Freeman, Ted Mondale, and Skip Humphrey.[14] Each had a campaign Web site, as did candidates Mark Dayton, Norm Coleman, Joanne Benson, Dick Borrell, John Marty, Allen Quist, Ken Pentel, and Ventura. All sites, except those of Borrell, Pentel, and Quist, had easily remembered Web site addresses. Graphics varied from the bland, unimaginative, poster board-like (Mondale, Borrell, and Benson), and primitive (Pentel) to the more visually appealing (Freeman, Humphrey, Marty, Dayton). Benson's page scrolled the following message at the bottom of the homepage: "the candidate with experience and integrity." Marty's featured RealAudio campaign ads as well as a clever message stating that the candidate would not accept any PAC money, special interest or soft money, or money from large contributors. Most of the Web sites adopted fairly standard subheadings—biography, position papers, press releases, event schedules, candidate accomplishments, how to volunteer, how to contact the campaign, e-mail address, endorsements, and links to other sites. Except for Pentel, none of the candidates' homepages mentioned party affiliation. The Freeman and Humphrey Web sites were the most informative, giving a sense of momentum and excitement. The Web sites also emphasized the positive; only one, Marty's, attacked another candidate, accusing Coleman of cozying up to professional hockey investors. Each of the sites gave useful information to prospective voters, especially the Ventura site, which helped to energize volunteers and supporters during the final days of the general campaign. The next time there is a governor's race in Minnesota, in 2002, the candidate Web sites undoubtedly will be transformed from the rather innocuous Web sites found in 1998 to multimedia, interactive communication platforms.

Warm and Fuzzy

Jonathan Miller, a Democratic candidate for Congress in Kentucky's 6th district in 1998, had a family-friendly Web site featuring the young and handsome candidate, his wife, and his children. His Web site had links to *Yahooligans* (*Yahoo*'s search engine for kids), *Kids Voting USA*, *PBS for Kids*, and *Great Kids* (stories for children); he even had a link to the family dog, Jake.[15] Many campaign Web sites take this soft approach—candidates with kids, hugging, and happy and smiling faces, complete with down-home touches such as recipes for mom's chocolate cream pie. Here is the late 1990s version of Ronald Reagan's 1984 soft glow reelection campaign ads: "Morning in America" comes to the Internet.

Visit With Me and My Opponents

Al Checchi spent a record $40 million of his own money for the California gubernatorial open primary in June 1998. His campaign Web site, like many others, provided viewers with favorable news clippings about himself, but it also featured negative news articles about his opponents. His elaborate, well-constructed site gave a wealth of information and was generous in providing links to the campaign Web sites of Gray Davis, Jane Harman, and fringe Republican candidate Dennis Peron as well as Dan Lungren's official attorney general site.

Local Politics Web Sites

Candidates throughout the country and far down the electoral ladder now have their own campaign Web sites. Typical was Andrew "Bud" Beaty, 1998 candidate for city council in Wichita Falls, Texas, who used the well-worn campaign theme, "It's time for a change," let folks know that he was not part of the north side Wichita Falls "power structure," and implored citizens to "Vote Early . . . Vote Bud." Hundreds of other candidates for local office—school board, small-town mayor, selectperson, sheriff, and many other offices—used on-line communications in 1998 with varying degrees of ingenuity and inventiveness.[16] Most were simple poster board sites with stiff pictures of candidates, occasional American flags, very little visual inventiveness, and few links to other sites. The best were as good as a well-designed print mailer created on a small campaign budget.

Campaigns have used the Internet as a communication device, as a tool for recruitment volunteers and fund-raising, and (inevitably) to attack opponents.

The Interactive Web Site

Jim Gilmore, 1997 Republican gubernatorial candidate in Virginia, effectively drove home one winning theme: Elect me and I'll get rid of your car tax. In Virginia, as in other states, the personal property tax on automobiles was very unpopular, and Gilmore's pledge struck a chord with voters. In all his communications, Gilmore hammered away at this pledge. His Web site, considered by many as the best in the state elections that year, reinforced Gilmore's message. A voter could go to Gilmore's Web site, type in the estimated value of his or her automobile and the name of the county or city in which the voter lived, and immediately would be told how much he or she would save under the Gilmore tax cut over the next 5 years. The voter also would read how Gilmore's opponent's plan just was not going to help the voter. This interactive feature made the Web site all the more attractive—Here is what Gilmore will do for me, and here is how much I will save (I calculated it myself) if I vote for him.

Attack Politics

One of the first uses of the Internet to attack another local opponent was in 1998 in Virginia Beach, Virginia, when city council challenger A. M. "Don"

Weeks used his Web site to chastise incumbent Louisa M. Strayhorn for missing hundreds of votes and spending more than $24,000 on taxpayer-funded trips during the previous 4 years. "Is Councilwoman Louisa Strayhorn doing her share of the work? No. Never has there been a more obvious lack of leadership on city council from the Kempsville District." This fairly tame and unremarkable criticism of one candidate by another received free media attention from the local newspaper; it was newsworthy only because it occurred on-line (Abrams, 1998). So far, there have been few attacks or even criticisms of other candidates over the Internet. As Americans get more used to going on-line for election information, perhaps the attacks will sharpen and become commonplace. But it also is possible that this form of communication, by its very nature, will not become a vehicle for screaming, red-hot attack politics. Much will depend on what is considered acceptable over the Internet. Right now, we simply do not know what Internet use will bear or tolerate. Campaigns are gingerly testing citizen tolerance for another on-line vehicle, political e-mail.

Political "Spam"

In the vocabulary of on-line use, "spam" is the electronic equivalent of junk mail. Many Internet users, and especially e-mail users, receive 20 or 30 spammed commercial messages a day. Soon, they also might receive messages from candidates and issue advocacy organizations. Electronic direct mail has enormous potential as a communication tool; it can reach specific segmented audiences with well-defined messages, with audio and video added, at a fraction of the cost of conventional direct mail.

One early use of unsolicited e-mail messages was from municipal court Judge Caryl Anne Lee of Orange County, California, in her bid for superior court in 1998. Her campaign sent e-mails to 68,000 voters at a cost of $299, compared to $28,500 for traditional direct mail. The e-mail was fairly inoffensive, reminding citizens to vote and linking them with Lee's Web site (Gornstein, 1998). The campaign generated 1,000 "hits" on its Web site (Raney, 1998b).

On a much larger scale, Democratic consultant Robert Barnes backed off of a plan to distribute a half million e-mails to California voters just before the June 1998 primaries. The e-mail would have promoted a slate of Democratic candidates, but one of the candidates decided against launching this spam barrage.[17] Despite the decision not to send out e-mails, Barnes argued that this was a legitimate form of political free speech. "We're not selling a product. We are pushing issues advocacy [and] candidate advocacy" (Raney, 1998c, 1998d, p. C1).

The ultimate question is whether voters consider unsolicited e-mails from candidates an invasion of privacy, another unwanted piece of junk mail, or welcome information from a campaign. In March 1998, a political advocacy group in Seattle, Washington, the Citizens Committee for the Right to Keep and Bear Arms, sent out—without fanfare—2 million pieces of e-mail in conjunction with a membership drive. The response to the e-mail was 10 times better, per dollar, than with conventional direct mail. Furthermore, the group received only two dozen complaints about the e-mail messages (Raney, 1998b).

If the Seattle and California examples are any indication, then we probably will see spammed messages commonplace in future elections.

Reaching Volunteers

One of the first effective uses of the Internet as a tool for recruiting volunteers came during the 1996 presidential primaries. Republican candidate Patrick Buchanan aggressively sought recruits for the "Buchanan Brigade" over the Internet as well as through a more old-fashioned form of communication, conservative talk radio programs. The reelection campaign of Senator John Kerry, a Massachusetts Democrat, also used the Internet as an effective tool for recruiting volunteers (Rash, 1997). It is now commonplace for campaign Internet sites to include a page on how and when to volunteer.

Fund-raising Vehicle

The Internet had limited use in the 1996 cycle as a fund-raising vehicle. The Dole presidential campaign was able to raise less than $100,000 through Internet solicitation, but that still was far more than the Clinton campaign raised on the Web (Friedly, 1998). During the 1998 cycle, there was a marked increase in on-line fund-raising, but it has far to go to reach its full potential. In early 1998, only the National Republican Congressional Committee accepted credit card contributions over a secure Internet connection, but now candidates are beginning to have secure credit card connections as well. Senate candidate Scotty Baesler, a Kentucky Democrat, as well as incumbents Barbara Mikulski, a Maryland Democrat, and Chris Dodd, a Connecticut Democrat, have on-line sites that will accept credit card information. Certainly, by the year 2000, campaigns and political party organizations will have the capacity to receive credit card contributions over secure Web site addresses.

New products are being developed that will enable donors to look up a candidate's or party's Web site, choose to make a donation, and have that donation directly transferred from a financial institution to the candidate's or party's account. Electronic banking, electronic stock purchases, and more commonly electronic purchases of consumer goods have become commonplace. What is familiar and increasingly acceptable in the commercial marketplace will be used by candidates, parties, and causes as they seek donations.

Mail Order Catalog

The reelection Web site of Senator Barbara Boxer, a California Democrat, had an on-line store, a unique fund-raising and marketing device. Fans and supporters could "join the fight for a sound economy, a beautiful environment, human rights, civil rights, and a woman's right to choose" by purchasing "your feisty Boxer T-shirt [$10], your classic Boxer shorts [$15], and [by] display[ing] a Boxer bumper strip on your car [$1]." Boxer's Web page was clever (using a boxing match motif), upbeat, and (as it said) feisty. The Web page also encouraged viewers to send the Boxer message to a friend's e-mail.

Internal to the campaign, the Internet has become an important tool for targeting voters, polling and focus group research, and campaign research.

Targeting Voters

Sophisticated campaigns rely on voter contact and targeting consultants to provide them with the most up-to-date and accurate information on probable voters. Targeting consultants can provide detailed demographic and past voting information on a precinct-level or even block-by-block level. Currently, voter information is prepared and updated through paper reports, diskettes, or CD-ROMs. Soon, all of this will change. Bill Daly, a pioneer in the field of voter contact services, writes, "Before the year 2000, you will be able to get on the Web, 24 hours a day, [7] days a week, call up any set of criteria that is coded into a voter file, and get a specific count back almost immediately" (Daly, 1997–1998, p. 48). Voter files, Daly notes, will not change a lot, but what will change is the speed of getting files downloaded from a vendor's voter file.

Also available for targeting voters will be the personal identification information (the "cookies") provided by Internet users when they log onto commercial Web services. This information, together with other demographic and voter history data, will permit even more accurate targeting and segmentation of voter interests and concerns.

The exchange of targeting data between consultant and campaign is an example of *Intranet* use, which has enormous potential for campaigns. Very soon, a campaign will be able to download polling data and a focus group analysis immediately from its polling consultant or view several different versions of campaign videos. In future campaigns, virtually every aspect of internal campaign communications can be transmitted through a secure Intranet connection.

Cyber-polling

One of the first congressional cyber-polls was conducted in the 26th district of New York in early March 1996 when on-line voters examined the positions of Representative Maurice Hinchey, a Democrat, and two challengers. *Votelink,* an on-line news channel in Boulder, Colorado, was hired to conduct the poll, limiting responses to those living in the zip codes in the 26th district boundaries. By the end of the election 1996 cycle, cyber-polling had become quite common, some of it done internally by campaigns, some done by news organizations. One study found 57 Web site polls operating during the 1996 presidential campaign (Wu & Weaver, 1997). However, there should be no confusion between cyber-polls, or polls conducted over 800 telephone numbers, and sound, methodologically reliable survey research. Cyber-polling is pseudo-polling. On-line surveys lack the essential ingredient of any legitimate, accurate poll—random responses. The population is skewed because Internet users tend to be better educated and more affluent than the rest of society. Furthermore, through Internet polling, it often is possible to stuff the ballot box by voting more than once. Campaign cyber-polls never should be taken seriously by the press or the public, but because of their uniqueness, they will, at least for a while, be newsworthy curiosities. In future elections, cyber-polling undoubtedly will become more of a fixture.

Future campaigns also will use the Internet to conduct focus group sessions, with participants monitoring and evaluating candidate speeches, campaign commercials, and issues. Much of what is done today by traditional focus groups or electronic dial meter groups might be replicated on-line in campaigns of the next decade.

Researching Candidates

A real revolution has occurred in researching the records of candidates and opponents. The Internet now provides extraordinary access to public record documents, newspaper and video archives, government documents, voting records, financial disclosure information, and much more. The information available to the resourceful and creative research team has grown exponentially, making research easier (with more readily available information) but also harder (with a flood of information that has to be synthesized and strategically crafted).

Real Time, Rapid-Response Campaigns

Over the past decade, the pace of campaign communications has accelerated dramatically. Now with the Internet, the tempo has quickened even more. The effective rapid-response campaign has done its research in advance; downloaded on-line data; anticipated media and opponent questions and prepared responses; lined up surrogates; prepared radio and television spots; and used satellite feeds, faxes, and Internet connections to fight back and counter charges.

Voting on the Internet

Oregon voters experimented with mail-in ballots during a special election for Senate in 1996. Many people liked the idea. In 1998, a poll indicated that some 42% of voters in Oregon preferred the convenience of mail-in ballots to the traditional voting at an elementary school or fire department. Mail-in balloting is just a few steps removed from voting over the Internet, and early response to that idea is equally positive as voting through the mail. A nationwide poll in 1996 found that nearly half of the respondents would rather vote by computer than at a polling booth (Westen, 1998, p. 49).

Web voting could offer maximum convenience. During the allotted time to vote (say, 30 days before the election), at my leisure and in the privacy of my own home, I can make my choice. I always have been sure about three candidates and will not even bother to look at their Web sites. But I am not sure about the candidates for the two other offices, and I still do not fully understand one of the ballot issues. Time to download election literature, print it out, and study. I am sitting with a cup of coffee, in my stocking feet, an hour before I go to work. Time to vote. There will be no lines to fight, no pesky poll watchers trying to persuade me at the last minute.

Security and voter fraud issues would not present any greater problem than they present for automatic teller machines or for commercial enterprises selling goods via the Internet. A decade from now, it might be standard to have my left thumbprint taken when I register to vote or to have my voice recorded into a voice recognition software system. The official election Web site might simply ask me to place my left thumbprint in the small box in the corner of the screen and then clearly state into the built-in microphone in the computer my full name, birthday, and election PIN number. I am double-checked for security now, and state board of elections files confirm that I am a registered voter. On the screen, an official ballot pops up, with all the candidates and issues for my political jurisdiction. I am too lazy to click my voting preference on the electronic ballot; instead, I will just do it orally: "My name is Dennis W. Johnson, my birthday is November 22, and my PIN number is 311-43AQ. I vote for Taylor for governor, Ibana for lieutenant governor, and Giles for mayor. I choose not to vote for the offices of Congress and attorney general, and I vote yes on Initiative 10 and no on Initiative 14. This ends my vote." The computer screen confirms my vote, thanks me, and bids me a pleasant day.

Certainly, Web site voting will not be for everyone. Many citizens want the psychological comfort and personal attention of precinct voting, whereas others will feel that we have lost a fiber of our citizenship once we retreat to voting by isolated computer. Some will feel uncomfortable or technologically inept. Much the same feelings must be experienced by those who would rather wait in line to be assisted by a bank clerk than to use the ATM machine. Of course, citizens who have no access to computers or their WebTV equivalent a decade from now must be guaranteed access to traditional precinct voting.

The Cyberspace Election: A Realistic Appraisal

In the first several years of campaign on-line use, we have seen the extraordinary possibilities of the Internet.

The Plugged-In Voter and Activist

The real beneficiaries of Internet campaigns are those who are already decidedly engaged in politics—citizens who attend city council meetings, join the League of Women Voters, watch C-Span and the Newshour with Jim Lehrer, read the editorial page of the newspaper, and volunteer on campaigns. For this small minority of citizens, the Internet gives them the raw material to become even more informed and active. This hardy band of citizens will love *E-Democracy* and the *Democracy Network, Smart Voter,* CNN's "AllPolitics," the "Hotline," and "Politics for Pros."

Registration and Voting Made Easier

Soon, voter registration and actual voting on the Internet will become commonplace. The technologies are familiar, and the security and voter fraud concerns are solvable. We might, a decade from now, look back at the late 20th century and its quaint system of precinct voting. We might lose a bit of America, standing shoulder to shoulder with neighbors we have not spoken to since the last election, waiting to get our names checked off before entering the polling booths. But this also might be a Norman Rockwell nostalgia for an American that never was. Yet, the overriding impulse is toward convenience brought about by technology. Just as we now purchase all sorts of goods via the Internet, do our banking on-line, and send cyber-greeting cards to loved ones and "thank you" notes through e-mail, we probably will think nothing of voting through cyberspace a decade from now.

New Voices Now Heard

Internet sites are ideal forums for voices that were once left out. Instead of the dominant, elite voices, new players can emerge through electronic communications. Many commentators and critics have bewailed the shallowness, predictability, and "horse race" nature of traditional media coverage of campaigns. An exasperated Katz (1998) writes of the 1996 presidential campaign, "By spring '96, it seemed clear to me that this campaign was a metaphor for all that doesn't work in both journalism and politics. I couldn't bear the *New York Times* pundits, CNN's politico-sports talk, the whoring Washington talk shows, the network stand-ups."

A number of politics- or issues-related sites reflect the attitude of the creators of the *Skeleton Closet,* a Web site devoted to digging up dirt on all presidential candidates. On the homepage, the creators of the *Skeleton Closet* say that they are a group of friends "who were fed up with politics—especially media coverage of politics—and decided to do something besides bitch and drink, like everybody else does."

The Web became a vehicle through which every voice can be heard, and every good intention can be aired. Every opinion, however wacky or small-minded, can have its day. As Selnow (1998) describes it, we find over the Internet "a grand collision within the diversity of opinions, conflicts, and prejudices that rock and roll across America" (p. 118).

Anyone could play the Internet game. Drudge, with no background in journalism or the media, became something of a Walter Winchell of the Internet—a source of political gossip and rumor who often scooped traditional media sources and, critics charge, was loose and easy with fact and source checking. He became not only a White House irritant but also the first, and to this point the only, Internet "celebrity."

Lowering the Cost of Elections

One of the most promising aspects of Internet campaigning is that it might drive down the cost of electioneering. In 1996, winning campaigns averaged $673,000 for Congress and $4,700,000 for Senate seats (Makinson, 1997). Many local races, especially those in urban areas with expensive media markets, cost well over $1 million. What drives up the cost are ads purchased on television. If—and this is a very big *if*—candidate commercials on the Internet catch on and effectively communicate to voters with the same force and persuasiveness as those on television, then the far less expensive Internet communications can help to drive down the cost of campaigning. E-mail spammed messages, if they are accepted by the on-line public, promise to significantly cut the cost of communicating with voters. No doubt, traditional direct mail firms will take a great interest in co-opting this technology.

More immediately, Internet campaigns are helpful to marginal and fringe candidates. In traditional communications, such as through television, they barely are covered by free media and cannot afford paid media. The Internet helps, but it performs no miracles. Fringe and marginal candidates still will lose by overwhelming numbers, but at least they have the satisfaction of knowing that their Web pages and messages were available for all who wanted to view them.

Alternative to Television

One disturbing trend noted in the 1998 elections was that television stations were rationing advertising space to candidates. This was evident in California, which witnessed a frenzy of paid television advertisements for candidates. By law, stations must provide access to federal candidates at the lowest unit rate, but state and local candidates are at the mercy of sales and marketing decisions of local television stations. As Democratic media consultant Steve McMahon observes, "Stations would rather run Pizza Hut ads than ads for candidates because stations make more money on Pizza Hut" (quoted in Sobel, 1998, p. 1). The irony here is that the more candidates use television for advertisement, the more pressure there will be to ration or crowd out local candidates. Internet advertising might relieve some of that pressure and give candidates another mechanism for getting their messages to voters.

Although the Internet has enormous potential, the realities of campaigning and elections present a sobering side.

Increase in Citizen Participation Not Likely

The creators and backers of the *Democracy Network* are hoping to increase citizen awareness of candidates and issues and to increase voter participation. It will, however, be an uphill battle. For decades, there had been a steady erosion of citizen trust and confidence in politicians and institutions. During the early 1990s, that distrust was coupled with frustration and anger. Since then, we have moved to a more pernicious stage, with disengagement and disinterest. There are some hopeful signs as grassroots organizations push for greater citizen involvement and local campaign finance reform. But the enemy is deeply rooted apathy, and no amount of Internet connectedness, by itself, can significantly widen the circle of those interested and participating in civic life.

The N-Generation as a New Civic Force?

Undoubtedly, members of the upcoming Net Generation will see extraordinary changes in communications. We have only begun to see the possibilities of the Internet and cannot imagine the impact of the Internet's successor. Will the Net Generation, armed with instant and virtual communications, somehow create a more civil society that is filled with the pursuit of truth and nurtured by rationalism and shared information? I wish it were true. We know that, typically, young adults show the least interest of any age group in voting or participating in politics. It is very difficult to fathom how Internet technology will transform this (or any) generation into eager civic participants, rationally pursuing truth and committed to radical change. More likely, the Net Generation will be seduced by the commercial glitter—not the civic lessons—of the Internet of the near future.

That Internet will come through some version of WebTV, with flat-screened, high-definition, incredibly fast transfer of data, split-screened (for multiple viewing) and interactive. Broadband Internet service is just around the corner, with cable modems or DSL technology providing access 100 times faster than a conventional 28.8-kps modem. Once broadband reaches the mass market, around the year 2005, CD-quality sound, three-dimensional effects, and movie-quality videos will be readily accessible. Deep-pocketed media conglomerates surely will invest heavily, providing the flash, excitement, and brilliance. Today, there are some 320 million Web pages accessible to casual browsers (Lawrence & Giles, 1998). Millions will be added each year. When so much is available, who among the fickle and disinterested consumers, especially the Net Generation, will want to "watch" dull campaign Internet sites?

Not the "Killer App"

Campaign consultants are a very pragmatic bunch. A hardened veteran campaigner would ask this simple question: Can you name one political race, anywhere in the country, that was won or lost because of the Internet? So far, in the infancy of the Internet, it is difficult to name such a race, although perhaps the 1998 Minnesota governor's race was one such contest. Reporter David L. Haase looked at the California primary elections of 1998 and was not impressed with on-line coverage. "At best, plugged-in voters can expect a replay of the 1996 election when having a Web site was novel, hip, and with it but did not contribute much to a single campaign victory" (Haase, 1998).

Television is the dominant medium by far, with direct mail coming in second. Far, far behind is the Internet. Given that less than 1% of voters relied on the Internet for the 1996 presidential elections and that only 6% of voters had visited a political Web site that year, this still is a communications mode in its infancy. Since 1996, far more citizens now use the Internet (Pew Research Center, 1998), yet it still is far from being the dominant vehicle of communication. Any campaign that bets its money solely on the Internet surely will lose.

The Internet is not, in the parlance of the software world, a "killer app" (or killer application). It is not a communications tool that will sweep away all others. It is only one more arrow—and a minor one at that—in the campaign's quiver. If someday the Internet becomes the dominant force with near total market penetration, and Internet campaigning becomes the "killer app," it still will not fulfill the promise of "leveling the playing field." The Internet will become the tool of choice for the best financed, most resourceful campaigns. They will have the fanciest Web sites, with all the three-dimensional, video, and interactive bells and whistles, skillfully merging their Web sites into coordinated communication packages. The Internet will help the needy, but it also will become another weapon in the arsenal of the well endowed.

APPENDIX

Web Sites Cited in Chapter (beginning with http://www.)

Andrew "Bud" Beaty for city council wf.quik.com/budbeaty
Joanne Benson for governor (Minnesota, 1998) benson-for-governor.org
John Birch Society jbs.org
Dick Borrell for governor (Minnesota, 1998) soncom.com/borrell
Barbara Boxer campaign for U.S. senator (California, 1998) boxer98.org
California Voter Foundation Digital Sunlight digitalsunlight.org
Al Checchi for governor (California, 1998) alchecchi.com
Christian Coalition cc.org
Cloakroom (*National Journal*) cloakroom.com
CNN AllPolitics allpolitics.com
Norm Coleman for governor (Minnesota, 1998) coleman98.org
Conservative Political Action Conference cpac.org
Gray Davis for governor (California, 1998) gray-davis.com
Mark Dayton for governor (Minnesota, 1998) daytonformn.org
Democracy Network dnet.org
Democratic Socialists of America dsausa.org
Drudge Report drudgereport.com
Minnesota E-Democracy e-democracy.org
Federal Election Commission National Mail Voter Registration fec.gov/votregis/vr.htm
Feminist Majority feminist.org
Mike Freeman for governor (Minnesota, 1998) freeman98.org
Georgia Tech semiannual Web survey cc.gatech.edu/gvu/user_surveys
Greens Party green.com
Jim Gilmore for governor (Virginia, 1997) gilmorenet.com
Jane Harman for governor (California, 1998) janeharmanforgovernor.com
Hotline (*National Journal*) cloakroom.com
Humphrey for governor (Minnesota, 1998) humphrey98.org
League of Conservation Voters lcv.org

Dan Lungren for governor (California, 1998) `lungrenforgovernor.org`
John Marty for governor (Minnesota, 1998) `johnmarty.org`
Men's Issues Page `vix.com/pub/men`
Jonathan Miller for Congress (Kentucky, 1998) `millerin98.com`
Ted Mondale for governor (Minnesota, 1998) `tedmondale.org`
National Rifle Association `nra.org`
Ken Pentel for governor (Minnesota, 1998) `jimn.org/pentel`
Dennis Peron for governor (California, 1998) `marijuana.org/peron57.htm`
Project Vote Smart `vote-smart.org`
Policy Network `policy.com`
Politics Online `politicsonline.com`
Politics for Pros (*Congressional Quarterly*) `politics.cq.com`
Political Resources Directory `politicalresources.com`
Allen Quist for governor (Minnesota, 1998) `prairie.lakes.com/quist`
Reform Party `reformparty.com`
Town Hall `townhall.com`
Salon Magazine `salonmagazine.com`
Slate Magazine `slate.com`
Skeleton Closet `realchange.com`
Smart Voter `smartvoter.org`
U.S. Taxpayers Party `ustaxpayers.org`
Voter Information Services Inc. `vis.org`
Washington WebWorks `washwebworks.com`
White House `whitehouse.gov`
Wired/Merrill Lynch Forum Digital Citizen Survey `hotwired.com/special/citizen`

Notes

1. A computer prankster beat the Dole-Kemp campaign to the punch by registering `dole96.org` and then offering his own parody of the presidential homepage, claiming 20 million "hits." As Cornfield and Arterton (1997) observe, "[In] today's cyberspace, an anonymous [prankster] could communicate on an equal footing with a good portion of the American political establishment" (pp. 86-87).

2. All Web site addresses cited in this chapter are listed in the Appendix.

3. *PoliticsNow,* one of the first on-line sites devoted to campaigns and elections, was terminated in March 1997.

4. The first posting was `alt.current-events.clinton.whitewater`.

5. This was gleaned from a conversation with my 13-year-old niece, Lauren Johnson. See also McGrath (1998, p. 63).

6. The *Wired/Merrill Lynch Forum* Digital Citizen Survey was conducted by Luntz Research Companies in September 1997.

7. *Smart Voter* is a component of the League of Women Voters Education Fund's "Vision 2000" campaign, with the technology developed by Smart Valley Inc., a nonprofit trade association of high-tech companies in Silicon Valley (Duskin, 1998).

8. Voter Information Services Inc., a nonpartisan, nonprofit voter education organization, publishes congressional voting records for more than 30 advocacy groups.

9. In mid-1995, just 10 senators and 4 representatives had developed Web sites. Some congressional Web sites give useful information, with extensive links to federal agencies and related sites. Some Web sites are mere facades, offering little in the way of information and wrapped more in family photos and homegrown recipes. Warren (1997) grouses, "Congress is doing well in giving the facade of real access" (p. 2936). The White House official Web page is at `http://www.whitehouse.gov`, not to be confused with `http://www.whitehouse.com`, which is a porn site.

10. Minnesota E-Democracy posted an election guide for the 1994 statewide campaigns, claiming to be the world's first organized election-oriented Web site and providing the world's first organized on-line electronic debates. *E-Democracy*'s "MN-Politics" claims to be the world's largest state-level political e-mail forum.

11. By 1999, the *Democracy Network* hopes to have available audio and video responses as well as written responses.

12. The sites will be in Florida, Illinois, Maryland, Massachusetts, New York, Orgeon, Pennsylvania, Texas, and Washington, according to the *DNet* homepage.

13. Many other sites were not listed with the *Political Resources Directory*.

14. Their well-known fathers were former Governor and U.S. Agriculture Secretary Orville Freeman; former U.S. Senator, Vice President, and presidential candidate Walter Mondale; and former U.S. Senator, Vice President, and presidential candidate Hubert H. Humphrey.

15. Miller, a protegé of Vice President Al Gore, came in sixth in a field of seven Democratic candidates.

16. A listing of local campaign Web sites, updated monthly, is found in the *Political Resources Directory* Web site.

17. Slate mailers are popular forms of advertising in California, where there often are long and complicated ballots.

References

Abrams, M. (1998, April 16). Web attacks over Beach councilwoman Strayhorn's travel raises issues of digital debate in election. *The Virginian-Pilot.* Available on Internet: http://www.piloton line.com/news/nw0416web.html.

Bimber, B. (1998, June/July). The gender gap in electronic democracy. *The National Voter,* pp. 8-9.

Cornfield, M., & Arterton, F. C. (1997). "Is this for real?" Democratic politics and the Internet. In *The Internet as paradigm* (pp. 85-102). Washington, DC: Institute for Information Studies.

Daly, B. (1997-1998, December/January). Accessing voter files with the Web. *Campaigns & Elections,* pp. 48-49.

Duskin, M. S. (1998, June/July). Smart voter. *The National Voter,* p. 11.

Friedly, J. (1998, March 18). Fundraisers predict surge in Internet spending. *The Hill,* p. 18.

Gates, B. (1995). *The road ahead.* New York: Viking-Penguin.

Georgia Tech Graphics, Visualization, and Usability Center. (1996, December). World Wide Web survey: Sixth semiannual survey. Available on Internet: http://www.cc.gatech.edu/gvu/user_surveys.

Gornstein, L. (1998, May 30). 68,000 getting judge's campaign e-mail. *Orange County Register* (California). Available on Internet: http://www.ocregister.com/politics/spam030w.shtml.

Greenman, B. (1998, April). Intern-net: The test marketing of the news. *Yahoo! Internet Life,* pp. 86-87.

Haase, D. L. (1998, May 26). Plugged-in politics. *Indianapolis Star/News.* Available on Internet: http://www.starnews.com/news/elections/8/may/0526SN_haase.html.

Hilzenrath, D. (1996, November 10). Mixed returns on the Net. *Washington Post,* p. A1.

Katz, J. (1997, April). Birth of a digital nation. *The Netizen.* Available on Internet: http://www.wired.com/wired/5.04/netizen.html.

Katz, J. (1998). The digital citizen. *The Netizen.* Available on Internet: http://www.hot-wired.com/special/citizen.

Kinsley, M. (1998, February 2). In defense of Matt Drudge. *Time,* p. 41.

Kurtz, H. (1995, June 3). The right: Casting its net. *Washington Post,* p. A1.

Lawrence, S., & Giles, C. L. (1998, April 3). Searching the World Wide Web. *Science, 280,* 98-100.

Makinson, L. (1997, November 25). *The big picture: Money follows power shift on Capitol Hill.* Washington, DC: Center for Responsive Politics.

Margolis, M., Resnick, D., & Tu, C. (1997). Campaigning on the Internet: Parties and candidates on the World Wide Web in the 1996 primary season. *Harvard International Journal of Press/Politics, 2*(3), 59-78.

McGrath, C. (1998, May 17). Being 13. *New York Times Magazine,* p. 63.

Media Studies Center. (1996, December 2). *Survey profiles voters' use of media.* Available on Internet: http://www.mediastudies.org/new.html.

Noble, P. (1998, January 7). The net difference: Conditions right for political Internet in 1998. *netpulse,* p. 1.

Pew Research Center. (1998). *Biennial News Consumption Survey.* Available on Internet: `http://www.people-press.org/med98rpt.htm`.

Raney, R. F. (1998a, March 2). In on-line debate, candidates focus on issues without spin. *New York Times,* p. C1.

Raney, R. F. (1998b, June 7). New issue for political campaigns: The spam question. *New York Times,* p. C1.

Raney, R. F. (1998c, June 2). Political consultant decides not to send bulk e-mail. *New York Times,* p. C1.

Raney, R. F. (1998d, May 27). Spam in California political race may backfire. *New York Times,* p. C1.

Rash, W., Jr. (1997). *Politics on the Nets: Wiring the political process.* New York: Freeman.

Rose, F. (1998, April). The television space race. *Wired.* Available on Internet: `http://www.wired.com/wired/6.04/mtsv.html`.

Schwartz, J. (1996, October 8). Looking for Dole on Web? Dot's the real way home. *Washington Post,* p. A17.

Selnow, G. W. (1998). *Electronic whistle-stops: The impact of the Internet on American politics.* Westport, CT: Praeger.

Sobel, L. (1998, June 10). TV stations ration campaign advertising, citing high demand. *The Hill,* p. 1.

Tapscott, D. (1997). *Growing up digital: The rise of the Net Generation.* New York: McGraw-Hill.

Warren, J. (1997, November 29). Law makers gingerly step into the information age. *Congressional Quarterly Weekly Report,* p. 2936.

Web sites. (1998, February 11). *netpulse.* Available on Internet: `netpulse@politicsonline.com`.

Westen, T. (1996). 2004: A digital scenario. In A. Corrado & C. M. Firestone (Eds.), *Elections in cyberspace: Toward a new era in American politics* (pp. 57-68). Washington, DC: Aspen Institute.

Westen, T. (1998, Spring). Can technology save democracy? *National Civic Review,* pp. 47-56.

Wu, W., & Weaver, D. (1997). On-line democracy or on-line demagoguery? Public opinion "polls" on the Internet. *Harvard International Journal of Press/Politics, 2*(4), 71-86.

39

Political Marketing and Political Propaganda

NICHOLAS O'SHAUGHNESSY

This chapter argues that the phenomenon of political marketing is a misnomer and that marketing is a misleading conceptual framework that fails to adequately describe this field. Political marketing is a conceptual hybrid; much of what is called marketing cannot possibly be so, and what we need is the support of another conceptual framework to properly understand the phenomenon. We must speak a hyphenated language because our meaning is an amalgam of marketing and propaganda. Behind this assertion lies the belief that they really do represent separate though related conceptual domains.

Of course, there are commonalties between propaganda and marketing. But it might be more accurate to depict them as opposite ends of a continuum rather than as generically distinct. There is a gray area, and the two terms are commonly regarded as interchangeable because analogous tools and methods are employed. Moreover, both focus on the presentation of utopian vistas or ideal types to satisfy the aspirations of reference groups. Indeed, it could be argued that the difference between propaganda and marketing is not conceptual but rather merely a difference in intensity. Certainly, aspects of consumer marketing have been categorized by some sociologists as straight propaganda. For example, Schudson (1984) does so in his book, *Advertising: The Uneasy Persuasion,* when he describes advertising as "capitalist realism," explicitly equating it with the idealized typifications of Soviet propaganda from the Zhadanov era onward (or self-described "socialist realism").

But I seek to argue that the term "political marketing" beguiles us by superficial similarities between politics and consumerism into assuming a conceptual uniformity. There are differences created by a radical distinction between the product market and political market situations. In particular, negative political advertising alone may disqualify politics from admission into the consumer marketing category, for negative advertising, with its emphasis on polarities, vilifications of enemies, and value conflicts, coupled with its need to create and sustain social discontent, has recognizably far more in common with war propaganda than with the selling of a product or service. For example, the U.S. presidential election of 1964 is now remembered primarily by one advertisement ("Daisy"), shown only once, in which a little girl counting flower petals was followed by a nuclear countdown and explosion (O'Shaughnessy, 1990). This advertisement helped to create and sustain—particularly with the publicity it aroused—a positioning strategy for Lyndon Johnson as the peace candidate, a positioning that his subsequent actions in leading America further into Vietnam betrayed. Clearly, there is a considerable difference between historically resonant images such as this and any type of consumer advertising, yet we often confuse the two. Those who claim that the attempt to distinguish between marketing and propaganda is merely a fabrication of a difference that is no difference should be answered with these and similar examples.

"Marketing" refers both to a theoretical body of knowledge and to a core of professional practice that has strong public associations with the promotion of food, domestic goods, and the like. The term "political marketing" is an explicit association between politics and consumer situations. I argue that to do this is to neutralize what is really going on by connecting it with the rituals of the everyday, for so-called political marketing, or what we might call "political marketing-propaganda," does influence the type of government that societies get and the value systems they publicly affirm. Ansolabhere and Iyengar (1995) discovered that exposure to a single campaign advertisement in experiments increased support for the sponsoring candidate by nearly 8% and that in the 1988, 1992, and 1998 elections, the victors in one in three U.S. Senate races, one in three governorship contests, and one in nine U.S. House races won by 7% or less. These authors claim that "more intensive advertising by the losers might have reversed these outcomes." If the phenomenon is indeed that important, then we need a language that accurately describes its content rather than one that actively misleads.

Toward a Definition of Propaganda

Before proceeding further, it is necessary to define the elusive term "propaganda." Schumpeter (1965) saw the contemporary use of the term "propaganda" as being merely "any statement emanating from a source that we do not like" (cited in Salmon, 1989). Jowett, less frivolously perhaps, sees propaganda as a "careful and predetermined plan of prefabricated symbol manipulation to communicate to an audience in order to fulfill an objective" (Jowett & O'Donnell, 1992). Propaganda is "the deliberate and systematic attempt to shape perceptions, manipulate cognitions, and direct behavior to achieve a response that furthers the desired intent of the propagandist." Smith, Lasswell, and Casey (1946) sought to distinguish between propaganda and education by arguing that the former is concerned with attitudes on controversial issues, whereas the latter is concerned with attitudes on noncontroversial issues (cited in Salmon, 1989).

Therefore, Jowett sees one distinguishing property of propaganda as being the deliberate intent to influence, but then the same could be said of much human communication; rarely indeed is the communicator entirely neutral about the consequences of his or her message. However, by choosing the word "manipulation," Jowett gives shade and direction to his meaning and coheres with the many other scholars who integrate this word into their definitions. For Pritkanis, "The word propaganda has since evolved to mean mass suggestion or influence through the manipulation of symbols and the psychology of the individual" (Pritkanis & Aronson, 1992). For O'Dwyer, it is "manipulative effort for the source's own benefit rather than the benefit of the receiver" (quoted in Salmon, 1989). Salmon (1989) argues that the word has attracted negative connotations "and now refers to a form of communication in which a communicator "manipulates others."

Another commonly attributed feature of propaganda is that of explicit bias. Propaganda originally was defined as the dissemination of biased ideas and opinions, often through the use of lies and deception. The French authority on propaganda, Jaques Ellul, argues that nearly all biased messages were propagandist, even when the biases were unconscious (Ellul, 1973). Certainly, the best propaganda sometimes is the most unselfconscious; all those schoolbooks and stories that once extolled the glories of the British Empire certainly were not seen by their authors as propaganda. Although all propaganda is necessarily biased, much bias is not propagandist.

Bias, manipulation, and intent to influence certainly are features of propaganda but are unsatisfactory as a comprehensive definition because they do not clearly distinguish it as a category separate from social and political marketing. Attempts to define the term objectively also are distorted by the accumulated meanings of the concept through history. The working definition cannot be separated out from the overlay of colloquial uses, which really relate to particular employments of propaganda rather than being descriptive of some essence. This excessively localized vernacular meaning is carrying an idea of Goebbels' stridency and failing, therefore, to immunize us against other, more sophisticated forms of propaganda.

The preceding definitions of propaganda are true but inadequate. Any definition of propaganda is both subjective and open to criticism, since implicit in the definition we choose is our own particular theory about the nature of propaganda; indeed, this also is the case with the definition of marketing. In the absence of any unchallenged lexical or scholarly authority, I hazard the following subjective assertions about the action of propaganda in modern history and the properties it exhibits. Propaganda is not synonymous with persuasion and is a distinctive branch of high-pressure advocacy. Propaganda simplifies and exaggerates; it often is propelled by a clear, purposive, and coherent ideology. Idealism, even utopianism, may motivate its sponsors and often may characterize its imagery. Propaganda eschews argumentative interchange; seldom is there any element of give-and-take.

Toward a Definition of Marketing

Marketing is a derivative of what people seek insofar as this can be determined. It is not simply the attempt to persuade them to a point of view. The essence of marketing is reciprocity. "Consumers" themselves bring something to bear on the selling; they are not passive objects, and the process is an interactive one.

The marketing concept is distinguished, above all, by the emphasis that is placed on customer focus. Identifying the needs and wants of customers and fashioning products and communications shaped by that understanding is the core of the marketing task. Such understanding is garnered through market intelligence; therefore, value is not defined in any absolute or objective sense but rather is defined subjectively from the market's viewpoint. The marketing approach is sensitive to the fact that any customer base is not some amorphous, undifferentiated mass. Moreover, marketing involves the integration of some total "offer" into an overall strategy. Interpreting the customers is something more than merely mapping out what customers say about themselves and acting accordingly; rather, it is the activity of surfacing their latent wants, the underlying desires that they cannot articulate fully. I intend to show how and in what way much of this is alien to the idea of propaganda.

Hence, this article attempts to sort out a real conceptual confusion between political marketing and political propaganda. Even in sophisticated discourse, the words "propaganda" and "marketing" are used almost interchangeably, for here are related but distinct areas. In establishing their boundaries, we identify the subtleties of each by comparing it to a conceptually distinct other. Such definitions are, of course, not rigid. They shade into each and represent distinct but not discrete categories. For example, the proposition that propaganda is pushed forward by ideology rather than pulled by magnetic consumer focus does not mean that ideologically defined marketing artifacts are rare. The argument is necessarily pitched at a level of generality. If the assertion is that marketing communications may invite several interpretations or are less utopian or less prone to ad hominem arguments, it does not mean that every example of marketing will do this; it merely means that each will exhibit a generic tendency to do so.

Key differences between marketing and propaganda may be summarized as follows. Marketing, at least if its exponents are fully educated in the marketing concept (which is not always the case), is based on some research-defined conception of audience wants. The message can be framed accordingly. By contrast, propaganda is didactic. Consumer marketing may appear more ideologically ambivalent because principle and ideology play a smaller role, and therefore, consumer marketing phenomena often permit a greater latitude of interpretability. Consumer advertising also appeals to values, but the values are less defined because the target market almost inevitably is ideologically heterodox. Thus, consumer product advertising that makes explicit and exclusive appeals to family values might alienate single people in the target market, so the advertising might imply family values without explicitly articulating them.

Negative Advertising

A key argument is that the political addiction to negative advertising disqualifies American politics from being "mere" marketing alone.

A different technique is underpinned by a different, harsher moral ethos. Such negative advertising can, of course, be ideological. An example of this would be Jesse Helms's advertisement against a black candidate, Harvey Gant (O'Shaughnessy, 1990). White hands crumpled a letter of rejection with the following text: "You needed that job. And you were the most qualified. But they had to give it to a minority because of racial quotas. Is that really fair?" Such an advertisement increases social tension because it is racially exclusivist. But it also performs the happy duty of deflecting attention from the candidate and his personality. It illustrates how politics, even more than consumer marketing, is about value affirmation. In this case, the advertisement is really about tribal loyalty.

There is considerable negative campaigning in American politics. Bill Clinton's campaign sponsored 15 months of negative advertising during the 1996 presidential primary, but this was undetected because it occurred in nonmetropolitan regions, "below the radar screen of the national press" (Johnson, 1997). Moreover, negative advertising can be used by pressure groups against their ideological enemies. One example would be the famous anti-abortion video, *The Silent Scream,* a classic piece of propaganda and an investment with a big publicity dividend (Arterton, 1985). Guggenheim was particularly vitriolic on the subject:

> In the last 10 years, Americans have been forced to endure an epidemic of negative political advertising. Visual and aural manipulation abounds. Every tool of the advertising craft has been exercised to prove opponents lazy, dishonest, unpatriotic, dumb, cruel, unfeeling, unfaithful, and even criminal. . . . Ask any seasoned media advertiser, and he will tell you what he can do best in 30 seconds. Create doubt. Build fear. Exploit anxiety. Hit and run. The 30- and 60-second commercials are ready-made for the innuendo and half-truths. Because of their brevity, the audience forgives their failure to qualify, to explain, to defend. (quoted in O'Shaughnessy, 1990)

Just how extreme negative advertising can be is exemplified in several recent cases (Johnson, 1997). When Harold See was a candidate in the 1996 Alabama Supreme Court election, one advertisement showed a skunk fading or "morphing" into the image of See with the words "Some things you can smell a mile away. . . . Harold See doesn't think average Alabamians are smart enough to serve on juries." Stamped on his face were the words "slick Chicago lawyer." A self-styled "Committee for Family Values" produced an advertisement claiming that See had a secret past in which he had abandoned his family, allegations he strongly disputed. In fact, he won the election. Another case, in California, concerned the murder of 12-year-old Polly Klaas. In 1996, one of the Democratic candidates for Congress, Walter Capps, was attacked in commercials as follows: "When the murderer of Polly Klaas got the death penalty he deserved, two people were disappointed . . . Richard Allen Davies, the murderer. And Walter Capps."

Commercials showed images of Davies and Capps with the labels "the murderer" (Davies) and "the liberal" (Capps). And Congressman Vic Fazio found that the face of Davies was morphed through computer graphics into his own, even though he had not voted against the death penalty for several decades.

Thus, the argument is that we are discussing two separate domains at this level and that the negative advertising that punctuates America's political campaigns has a limited amount in common with consumer marketing.

Of course, the most famous negative commercial featured Willie Horton, who raped and killed after having been given weekend parole in Massachusetts (Klein, 1988). Horton was black. Silent prisoners were shown walking through a revolving door. This advertisement hit American liberalism at its most vulnerable point—inability to sound determined on crime, even though this was now a central choice criterion for America's political consumers. These commercials are regarded as the most effective of recent times. Shortly after the Horton ad, George Bush soared past Michael Dukakis in the opinion polls. Then, because Democrats always had been more believable on quality of life issues, film of noxious Boston Harbor was shown repeatedly and helped to challenge Dukakis's assumption of the moral high ground.

Then there is the "Daisy" commercial (discussed earlier) and its consequences. To compare this or the Bush advertisements with straight consumer advertising is to invest them with an insignificance they do not deserve, for the fear aroused in Daisy is not about a headache but rather about the future of the entire human race. Daisy and other important political advertisements belong to a different generic entity. In fact, their negativity is extreme; the implication was actually that Barry Goldwater would take the country into nuclear war, and therefore, Johnson became the peace candidate. There is no ambiguity about the Daisy commerical, the vulnerable image of the small girl with her symbolism of our future, as contrasted with a male voice in nuclear countdown. Johnson's voice appears as an unobtrusive note of externalized authority: "These are the stakes—to make a world in which all of God's children can live or to go into the dark. We must either love each other, or we must die." The nuclear explosion is a harbinger of Armageddon, a signifier of the extinction of the human race. Clearly, one can be accused of the fallacy of selection of instances, but what is important here is not quantification but rather historical significance. Horton and Daisy are significant in American history.

Ansolabhere and Iyengar (1995) provide substantial empirical evidence for the effectiveness of this negative advertising. Thus, although a marketing tool certainly is being used—a brief half minute of images and information—that is where the resemblance with consumer advertising ends. These advertisements fulfill all requirements of classic propaganda, and they bear comparison with the tactics of Goebbels in, for example, his campaign against the deputy Berlin police chief, Isidore Weiss (Herzstein, 1979). Such "advertisements" are (a) ideological, (b) highly emotional, (c) full of value-laden symbols, (d) without ambiguity in their projection of a world of black and white polarities, and (e) vindictive. Thus, the more accurate characterization of modern political communications phenomena is that of a marketing-propaganda hybrid, and although a consumer advertisement might possess some of these characteristics, it would be surprising if it possessed all of them.

An orthodox marketing approach probably would have defined the persuasion objectives differently, with the aim of at least getting opponents to question the vehemence of their resolve and reassuring neutrals. The task of persuading core supporters would not have been achieved at the cost of alienating other constituencies whose support or neutrality could be solicited. The advertisement probably would have been more ambivalent, permitting supporters, the neutral, and even the opposition, a limited degree of latitude in affixing their own meanings. Thus, the purposes of propaganda are not identical to and coterminous with those of marketing. Marketing's objectives are to attract/convert/retain and reinforce, and marketers seldom would be so cavalier with their messages as to antagonize people actively. Instead, partly through the agency of para-language, the messages and storylines of much commercial advertising are more universally acceptable because they are ambivalent (Cook, 1994). For example, Calvin Klein advertisements would seem vulgar if put into explicit words (O'Shaughnessy, 1995).

Manipulation

Political propaganda involves a large element of disguise or even duplicity. For example, some advertisements are deliberately made to resemble television news features; this is one of the techniques pioneered by Joe Napolitan. In fact, voters seem not to distinguish retrospectively between television advertising and television news, and elections can be fought virtually without candidates, especially if they are unpopular. One Walter Mondale advertisement did not feature the candidate himself, with his lugubrious television manner. Instead, it showed a roller-coaster, which acted as a mobile metaphor for Ronald Reagan's handling of the economy. Much of Helms's advertising showed the senator only briefly, and in his opening half-hour advertisement, Helms himself appeared for just a few seconds. A typical advertisement would feature the following words being written on the screen and spoken by an actor: "I voted against the Martin Luther King holiday. Where do you stand, Jim?" When the unpopular Nelson Rockefeller seemed sentenced to defeat, puppets of fish did the talking (reporter fish: "Already 130 new sewage treatment plants are getting underway"; fish puppet: "Yeah, well it was pretty smelly down here") (Perry, 1968). Henry Cabot Lodge's effective 1960 campaign film was composed entirely of stills because the candidate was a cumbersome television performer (Nimmo, 1970). The candidate might not appear, and his or her party affiliation might not even be mentioned. When consultant James Severin was running a Republican for governor of Alabama, no mention was made of his political affiliation, and he became the first Republican to be elected in 115 years (O'Shaughnessy, 1990).

Patricians became plebeian, an American political tradition. In the early 19th century, supporters of the cousin of an English lord, Benjamin Harrison, carried around models of log cabins to indicate an allegedly humble birth. More recently, the patrician Pierre du Pont was transformed into the "descendants of immi-grants." Harvard University lawyer Bruce Babbit became the "scion of a frontier family," and voters were reminded of Dukakis's "Greek immigrant" parents, although not of his father's Harvard medical degree (Diamond & Bates, 1988). Bob Dole became "someone from the people, someone who made it the hard way," for whom "a little bit of Russell goes with him everywhere."

It is a question of degree. Although manipulation most certainly would be part of any colloquial definition of propaganda, for many it also would be the essence of marketing, despite the new existence of ethics courses in business schools. To point up the duplicity of political marketing propaganda would, under this argu-ment, say nothing about its generic classification. Whereas Bush's 1988 Boston Harbor commercial might have successfully falsified Dukakis's excellent environ-mental record, is it not also the case that marketers tamper with images, for example, putting marbles in soup to make it look thicker? What is the difference?

Partly, the difference is a function of consequence because both political marketing and consumer marketing deliberately use vagueness. But consider the following example. In 1968, advertisements showed footage of Vietnam with Richard Nixon's voice saying,

> Never has so much military, economic, and diplomatic power been used as ineffec-tively as in Vietnam. And if, after all of this time and all of this support, there is still no end in sight, then I say the time has come for the American people to turn to new leadership, not tied to the policies and mistakes of the past. I pledge to you: We will have an honorable end to the war in Vietnam. (cited in Nimmo, 1970)

This says nothing; it merely gives impressions that, for example, Americans under Nixon would leave Vietnam fast. Clearly, then, the significance of this rhetoric is much greater than product consumer rhetoric, even if the methods are identical.

Partly too, it is a function of degree. Consumer marketing sometimes is manipulative, but even its critics might be reluctant to claim that it is almost in-variably manipulative. That is not the case with political marketing-propaganda, where deceitful methods might even be the norm rather than the exception.

Yet, the point is still unproven, and we have so far failed to ground it in the distinct category of propaganda. But further consider this evidence: What is called political marketing sometimes goes well beyond the boundaries of distortion to the upper realms of fantastic invention and lying. Johnson (1997) gives the example of Lyndon Johnson during the 1930s doctoring a photograph showing him with the president such that a third politician was airbrushed out of existence. Nixon did the same type of thing during the late 1940s. Earlier, of course, Stalin had notoriously done this to an image of himself and Lenin. One diminutive senator was made to appear bigger by being filmed in a chamber with small 19th-century seats. Another senator was seriously ill, but a creditable shot of his reelection announcement was made by judicious editing of reams of film (Sabato, 1981). He died soon afterward.

The point is that technological resources are being actively used to edit truth. According to Johnson (1997), researchers at the University of Oklahoma analyzed more than 2,000 political commercials from 1952 to 1992 and established that 15% contained "some ethically questionable use of technology." A 1996 study found that 28% of the 188 commercials scrutinized contained questionable use of technology—"news conferences that were never held, debates that never took place, use of audio or video to stereotype or ridicule opponents." In the film *Forrest Gump,* the hero is made, via digital technology, to blend into a 1962 White House ceremony, and John F. Kennedy's face is made to appear as though he is talking to Gump. This method is used in American politics, and one researcher who contrasted original and doctored versions of the same advertisement found that viewers gave higher marks to the deceptive advertisement (Johnson, 1997). Even Virginia Senator John Warner found that his consultant had doctored a photograph in the Senate race. Moreover, as the political dimension of business expands, especially in certain industries, the temptation is to also use the techniques of political propaganda deception. For example, a "Committee to Save Our Children" created advertisements critical of government, but this committee was merely the front organization for major environmental polluters (Johnson, 1997). Also, Californians were deceived by misleading political advertising into signing a petition, but the deceitfulness of big tobacco companies was behind all of this.

Therefore, the claim is that such activities belong to a different realm from those of conventional consumer marketing and should not be allied, and indeed dignified, by a common terminology. It might be merely a question of degree, but when the degrees become sufficiently extensive, it qualifies for the creation of a separate generic category.

Saturation Effects and New Media

Ellul (1973) claims that saturation effects are an important determinant of the effectiveness of propaganda. That is part of propaganda's definition, and the aim of political campaigning is similar, so that media that play a secondary role in consumer marketing play a primary role in political marketing-propaganda. Telephone banks, for example, can reach 1,000 people instantly, including unlisted numbers, and they can target the right people (e.g., they were used effectively by Steve Forbes in the 1996 U.S. presidential election). Fax bank companies also are very active in the political arena, with companies able to send out 500 faxes at once. Because of the political context, such intrusive media may enjoy greater legitimacy in political solicitation than in commercial solicitation.

Direct mail is another medium appropriated by political propagandists. Congresspersons can be bombarded with pressure group letters. For example, pro-lifers can send thousands of letters off to Congress with only 1 day's notice. In just 1 week, Communications Management Inc. sent 2,000 mailgrams to Senator Charles Percy regarding gas price decontrol; the firm had traced sympathetic citizens with the polling census and asked permission to send in their names. Craver Matthews, a political consulting firm, illustrates this point about the volume of transmission well, for the firm can send 1 million pieces of mail in 12 hours (O'Shaughnessy, 1990). Even during the 1930s, Father Charles Coughlin could use his polemical radio broadcasts to pressure Congress with 200,000 telegrams the following day (Warren, 1996).

The internet also is of growing propaganda significance. Internet users are much more likely to be registered to vote, but in particular, the Internet offers the unique quality of interactivity. As a result, propaganda becomes more powerful because it is coproduced, leading to elements of self-persuasion.

Propaganda is, increasingly, the political task. In the words of one member of Congress, "I am not only a news maker but [also] a news man, perhaps the most widely read journalist in my district. I have a radio show, a television program, and a news column with a circulation larger than that of most of the weekly newspapers in my district" (quoted in O'Shaughnessy, 1990).

The aim of much propaganda is to talk to the faithful, so essentially private media are required (e.g., cable). Because the audience is select, the compromises of mainstream media are not needed—exactly the types of compromises that mainstream marketing must make. Audiences can be addressed in their own language—the language of emotion and irrationality—and this is possible because so much information about individuals is now made available. In addition to this distinctive media set, political communication involves a different dynamic from consumer marketing. The fluidity of political situations is now extreme in that parties and politicians can post immediate replies on their Web sites, whereas previously there would have been a 1- or 2-day delay for a measured response.

But not all media with specific marketing propaganda applications are new. One of the phenomena of American politics over the past decade has been the invention of radio as a political medium—*re*invention, in fact, given that Coughlin was the first and most significant exponent some 60 years ago (Warren, 1996). Talk radio hosts, as well as single-issue groups, have become among the most important politicians in America today. What they offer is propaganda, and to employ the word "marketing" in this connection is misconceived. This is a medium of reinforcement, not recruitment, speaking to middle-aged provincial White males (they have the highest voter registration of all groups and comprise 10% of the adult population) in their own language, articulating their anger, and ministering to their self-pity. There are approximately 1,000 talk radio programs, and Rush Limbaugh alone has an audience of some 20 million.

New Actors

In addition to different media and a faster pace, political theater is now crowded with new actors. My claim is that all of these trends contribute to the propagandizing of the American political process. Issue advocacy is becoming more powerful now as outside groups nationalize local campaigns and "flood the airwaves" and television. The year 1996 saw the first real use of issue advocacy, but it was even more salient in 1998, changing the dynamics of campaigns (Johnson, 1997). Moreover, powerful companies and organizations have become increasingly politicized by using the methods of political marketing-propaganda themselves (O'Shaughnessy, 1995). Advertising is increasingly being brought to bear on major legislation such as trade agreements and health care.

Particular users of propaganda have been political action committees and pressure groups, such as the National Rifle Association (NRA) (Anderson, 1996). But unlike the case of consumer marketing, there is no actual need to reach a broad public given that single-issue evangelists are soliciting their own, a task made much easier by new technologies allied with precision marketing techniques such as direct mail. They speak to their own in the strident language of noncompromise, and their own hear them well. The propaganda task is to persuade supporters to give, and then the money can be used in election campaigns to pick off politically dubious candidates. Thus, the NRA is rightly feared. In one case, a senator up for reelection attempted to stop the bill that made illegal bullets capable of piercing police armor. He defied the Senate leadership "with irrelevant and dilatory amendments," yet the ban was enacted after "a bitter [6]-year struggle against the gun lobby" (*New York Times,* December 27, 1976).

Measurements of Effectiveness

A recent study (Kuhn, 1991) illuminates why the appeal of political propaganda might work, for it focuses on just how reluctant people are to engage intellectually with any alternative or oppositional views and, therefore, how vulnerable they might be to propaganda. They merely seek to have their prejudices confirmed by pseudo-evidence:

- The respondents in the study (a wide cross section of people in the United States) commonly viewed pseudo-evidence (just the plausibility of the argument) as powerful in persuading them as genuine evidence when it came to establishing the correctness of ideas or hypotheses.
- Respondents commonly were unable to envision alternatives or counterarguments to their own "theories," simply continuing to stick to positions that they thought others would endorse.
- Even when respondents did entertain alternative explanations, they sought more to rebut them than to seriously consider them as rival explanations. Predisposition to certain beliefs made it difficult to entertain other explanations.
- Respondents whose dispositions were to see positions as either right or wrong, or to see all alternative explanations as equally defensible, saw little value in even engaging in argument.
- The study found that only 9% to 20% of respondents had the necessary understanding needed to generate and evaluate alternatives to reach a reasoned judgment, with the author of the study arguing that without such understanding, "people have little incentive or disposition to develop argumentative skills."

Political scientists have, in the past, sought to claim that television political advertising has a limited impact (Abramson, 1985). On the evidence specifically for the effectiveness of negative advertising, or what I argue is the core of political propaganda, positive-negative versions of the same advertisement in Ansolabhere and Iyengar (1995) experiments led to a 9.5 percentage point versus a 19.0 percentage point lead. For low-interest voters, the negative advertising created a 24 percentage point increase in favor of their party; thus, "weak partisans are easily made into strong partisans." The authors also found that "a negative advertisement from a Democrat[ic] candidate increased the Democrats' vote margin by [9] points among Republican viewers." They conclude that moving independent voters actually requires negative advertising, an astonishing conclusion. They point out that in 1992, 50 states with 62% of the voting-age population suffered full negative campaigns. On the evidence for the effectiveness of political advertising generally, they point out that in the 1992 presidential campaign, more than half of voters could remember information that came from political advertisements. The authors also note the way in which negative advertising freezes out the center from political participation in elections, for negative races reduce turnout by more than 7% and, therefore, must contribute to the 35% drop in public confidence in government registered over the past 40 years.

Political Marketing

The thesis of this chapter, however, is not that all purchased political communication is entirely (or largely) propagandist but that it is a marketing-propaganda hybrid. As such, there also is much that we witness in the practice of political communication that shares a great deal in common with consumer marketing. The techniques, imagery, and codes have an immediate familiarity and resonate with our existing consumer literacy.

It is the locus of policy in voter opinion, which contemporary research and modeling techniques refine and direct, that enables us to make the connection between politics and marketing. The history of the past 20 years in American politics has, indeed, been a story of heightened sensitivity to public opinion, and the traditional mediating institutions such as the political parties themselves have declined in power. Thus, much American political communication can be legitimately diagnosed by the term "political marketing." The ideological turnaround of the Clinton administration in his first term was a good example of this.

> Clinton gave people what they wanted to hear. Through focus groups, mall testing, survey research, and electronic dial groups, Clinton's media advisers knew exactly what the public wanted to hear, with just the right language, words, and phrases that would resonate with the American public. . . . But the real communications failure was in what Clinton and Dole did not say. (Johnson, 1997)

As with consumer marketing, market research does affect the political agenda. Consultant Joe White pointed out how, in 1986, drugs became an issue not because consultants unilaterally decided this but rather because most young parents themselves had known drugs at school and had become seriously alarmed by that stage (quoted in O'Shaughnessy, 1990). Congressional candidates everywhere volunteered for testing and were filmed dutifully carrying their samples of urine. In addition, much political marketing, as well as being rooted in consumer research, contains the same stylistic references as does consumer product advertising. This is especially true of presidential campaigns, for example, Reagan's famous "Morning in America" sequence, which was classic lifestyle advertising depicting happy citizens, sport and leisure activities, and social rituals such as weddings. This was pure imagery without content, and one could interpret it however one wished. The real aim was to create a "feel good" emotion.

The establishment and sitting tenants and presidential candidates can sustain this type of marketing approach. By contrast, the propaganda element often arises by giving the campaign a structuralist duality. The candidate can make bland speeches but use hard-hitting negative advertisements, avoiding the compromise of personal dignity by too direct an association with the propaganda of attack. Thus, there can be two campaigns, with the negative campaign ostensibly run by a separate group of ideological well-wishers who can be conveniently disowned (e.g., Bush's 1988 American presidential campaign and the Horton advertisement).

From the "Eisenhower Answers America" series (Griese, 1975), to Wallace Wilkinson's "new day of new ideas" (*New York Times,* May 31, 1981), to the image of Tip O'Neill driving a stalling car ("The Democrats are running out of gas"), to advice seminars such as "campaigning with dignity, maintaining the judicial image," much American political advertising is not propaganda and has the same essential blandness of consumer advertising. Often, it draws from the same symbolic stock as does consumer advertising. For example, in 1984, the Republican National Committee frequently showed a sequence with a girl riding through the countryside with her boyfriend (O'Shaughnessy, 1990). The couple are wholesome and attractive, so this appeared to be a health advertisement of some kind. But no, the girl begins talking to us about politics. She is intelligent and college educated—no clone—and she explains to us firmly and persuasively why she is a Republican. Reagan himself was a past master of the bland. Chagal (1981) sums up the prototype Reagan oration as follows: "a 20-minute orator's stew consisting of small-town Protestant safe jokes, bursts of passion against harmless targets, and lots of appeals to down-home patriotism."

Conclusion

Interviews with political consultants themselves suggest disagreement as to whether they are in the marketing or propaganda business. Tony Schwartz, the creator of the propagandist Daisy advertisement, regards political promotion as selling voters their preconceived notions, through which voters reaffirm themselves (quoted in O'Shaughnessy, 1990). Schwartz argues that political advertising should resonate with voters and is critical of what he calls the transportation idea of communication, that is, believing that meaning is a coproduction between sender and receiver. He is dismissive of the mediocrity of conventional advertising ("I wouldn't sell soap the way they sell soap"). By contrast, consultant David Garth disputes the term "marketing" and claims that political consultants "chase advertising out of the field." His theory is that political persuasion should be "a high-energy information bombardment and no mood stuff." He claims that politicians do not have to change position because consultants find ways of making that position salable. Schwartz and Garth are among the most eminent political consultants of all time, yet the definitions of political persuasion they articulated to me are underpinned by entirely different paradigms. Schwartz will take it *from* the voter as a classic marketing man, whereas Garth will take it *to* the voter, the hypodermic model of communication.

Moreover, politics is about personality, and in a sense, personality is the product. So too is ideology. A politics entirely constructed around market research would appear insincere to voters, and such an ethos could not sustain a party in office for very long. This, in fact, is the dilemma that faces Britain's Labour Party. One could add to the conventional marketing mix the "two P's" of political marketing: personality and principle. Moreover, the emotional content of politics can be greater because politics is so concerned with the affirmation of values. Thus, a political issue is not merely a product to be merchandised but rather a vibrant value symbol connecting with an individual's sense of who and what he or she is at the deepest level. When Roger Ailes, in an interview (O'Shaughnessy, 1990), caricatured the Democrats' pluralism as being about "lesbian Navahos," he was expressing a doubtless passionately felt but also polarizing value position. In such cases, political views and decisions are part of the social self-construction, the self-articulation or public persona, of the individual, arguably at a more fundamental level than a Hermes scarf or handbag.

For such reasons, "marketing" by itself will not do as a term because it caricatures as a process of commercial expression and exchange what is, in fact, a more subtle process. In addition, even if a political consultant did conceive of politics in purely marketing terms, he or she would have less freedom to maneuver than would the vendors of a product. For example, the consultant's actions are circumscribed by the existing known public personality of the politician, and that personality also is vulnerable in various ways, so the political communicator's task is not to change the personality as a product can be changed or upgraded (he or she might lack that freedom) but rather to get it to be perceived in different ways. Thus, White describes how one of his gubernatorial candidates, a man with a stutter, won his election due to a campaign that turned this disadvantage into an asset, with the candidate explaining what a handicapped childhood was like, with the candidate recalling how he had to work three times as hard at everything, and with the unscripted words of an 85-year-old widow endorsing him (quoted in O'Shaughnessy, 1990).

It might be claimed that to seek to distinguish marketing from propaganda really amounts to fabricating a difference that is no difference. In other words, the process yields no theoretical insight or practical value. Why, then, is the exercise meaningful?

First, it is meaningful because there is value in precision and no merit in vague terminologies. Thus, if "propaganda" is used simply to stigmatize any type of communication with which we disagree, then we have to find new and wordy formulations to describe the important phenomena that the term once signified. But precision never can be absolute. With any concept, there are, in fact, different definitions; to define a concept also is to enunciate a theory about the nature of that concept. Second, words direct our perceptions. If we use them vaguely or interchangeably (as we do here), then we become desensitized to important phenomena in the environment. Terms do duty as sensitizing concepts. There also is a broader context. This chapter has claimed that citizens today live in a propaganda-saturated environment. However, because propaganda in popular discourse is equated only with totalitarian societies, either we do not perceive its contemporary operation or we assume that it is adequately counteracted by a socially pluralist culture with many information systems. But if we do not have a language to describe a phenomenon, then very often either we fail to see it or we describe it with a different language that confuses it with other marginally related social phenomena. An important part of education is to alert people to the types of propaganda-driven activity competing for their attention, allegiance, votes, and money. Yet, if we deny ourselves an accurate language, then this task of education can hardly begin.

References

Abramson, J. (1985). Democratic theory and communications technology. In *Project on new communication technologies, public policy, and democratic values* (chap. 4). Cambridge, MA: Harvard University, John F. Kennedy School of Government.

Anderson, J. (1996). *Inside the NRA*. Beverly Hills, CA: Dove Books.

Ansolabhere, S., & Iyengar, S. (1995). *Going negative: How political advertisements shrink polarize the electorate*. New York: Free Press.

Arterton, C. (1985). Communications technology and governances. In *Project on new communication technologies, public policy, and democratic values*. Cambridge, MA: Harvard University, John F. Kennedy School of Government.

Chagal, D. (1981). *The new kingmakers*. New York: Harcourt, Brace, Jovanovich.

Cook, G. (1994). *The discourse of advertising*. London: Routledge and Kegan Paul.

Diamond, E., & Bates, S. (1988, February 15). Hot spots. *New York*.

Ellul, J. (1973). *Propaganda: The formation of men's attitudes*. New York: Vintage Books.

Griese, N. H. (1975). Rosser Reeves and the 1952 Eisenhower TV spot blitz. *Journal of Advertising, 4*(4), 34-38.

Herzstein, R. E. (1979). *The war that Hitler won*. London: Hamish Hamilton.

Johnson, D. (1997, February). *Political communication in the information age*. Seminar, Wissenchafts-zentrum-Berlin, Berlin.

Jowett, G. S., & O'Donnell, V. (1992). *Propaganda and persuasion*. Newbury Park, CA: Sage.

Klein, J. (1988, October 24). *New York Times*.

Kuhn, D. (1991). *The skills of argument*. Cambridge, UK: Cambridge University Press.

Nimmo, D. (1970). *The political persuaders.* Englewood Cliffs, NJ: Prentice Hall.

O'Shaughnessy, N. J. (1990). *The phenomenon of political marketing.* London: Macmillan.

O'Shaughnessy, N. J. (1995). *Competitive marketing: A strategic approach.* London: Routledge.

Perry, J. M. (1968). *The new politics.* London: Weidenfeld and Nicolson.

Pritkanis, A., & Aronson, E. (1992). *Age of propaganda.* San Francisco: Freeman.

Sabato, L. (1981). *The rise of political consultants: New ways of winning elections.* New York: Basic Books.

Salmon, C. T. (1989). Campaigns for social "improvement": An overview of values, rationales, and impacts. *Sage Annual Reviews of Communication Research, 18.*

Schudson, M. (1984). *Advertising: The uneasy persuasion.* New York: Basic Books.

Schumpeter, J. (1965). *Socialism and democracy.* London: Unwin.

Smith, B. L., Lasswell, H. D., & Casey, R. D. (1946). *Propaganda, communication, and public opinion.* Princeton, NJ: Princeton University Press.

Warren, D. (1996). *Radio priest.* New York: Free Press.

40

Money and Politics

J. HARRY WRAY

This chapter argues that the role of money in the American political system is problematic. Before this argument can be developed, it is important to clarify two very common but ambiguously used terms in our political lexicon: "politics" and "democracy."

Politics and Democracy

When asked to define the term "politics," most Americans describe a tactical form of behavior that they consider at least slightly illicit and often thoroughly corrupt. "Office politics," for example, is conniving behavior in the workplace. "A political decision" suggests an unsavory desertion of principle in the interests of expedience, and a "political person" is one who constantly calibrates decisions according to narrowly perceived self-interest. Politics, in other words, is something that conscientious and right-thinking people avoid, and a politician is one who exists just a little closer to the primal ooze than the rest of us, in the nether region shared with prostitutes, used car dealers, and lawyers of all sorts.

Some astute observers have noted that in a representative democracy, politicians always will have an image problem.[1] Their hold on public trust is unavoidably tenuous. It is not that their self-interested behavior is inherently offensive. Our entire economic order, after all, is based on the premise that people act in self-interested ways. Politicians are distinctive, however, in that they represent themselves as acting in *our* interests, not their own. Often, they do act in our interests, but they are self-interested as well, and this duplicity offends.

Furthermore, as Garry Wills (1975) has noted, politicians always are compromising their principles. They habitually seem to be "selling out." That is not the "American Way," or at least it is not supposed to be. We admire people who stand on their principles and refuse to compromise. Paradoxically, politicians in a representative democracy must compromise to sustain the system. Each of us want our perspectives to prevail in politics. A representative politician seeks to broker these competing claims in ways that will not be so offensive as to prevent reelection. Some compromise inevitably is a part of this process. To most of the rest of us, who do not spend much time thinking about the differences between private and public life, such behavior indicates a flaw in character and increases our cynicism of politicians and politics.

Political scientists tend to think about politics in a less tactical way. Strategies and tactics do interest them, but these rarely are regarded as *defining,* or even distinctive of, the world of politics. Typically, the point of departure for political scientists is the substantive result of strategies and tactics, so politics is seen as integral to distribution. Definitions of politics always are contentious. None is completely satisfying. One that is broadly shared by political scientists, however, is that *politics is the authoritative allocation of values for society.* Normally, this process of allocation is observed in the context of governmental or quasi-governmental institutions. Although this definition is not perfect, it does help to illuminate the concept of politics in a number of ways.

What does it mean to allocate, or to distribute, values? Values are things desired and may be usefully conceived as being of two sorts. There are nonmaterial values that we often seek to distribute or restrict. Does a woman have an inherent right to abort an at least potential child? What are appropriate limits of television violence? Can a local government display a nativity scene during the holiday season? Does the Ku Klux Klan have the right to stage a rally in the middle of a Black neighborhood? Can pornographers use the Internet? Although it might be argued that some of these questions contain a material component (e.g., pornographers can make money marketing their wares on the Internet), they are mostly nonmaterial. They raise the question: What values should we value? Even the most casual observer of the political scene will recognize that the political system is continuously involved with struggles to resolve such issues.

Values also may be material; that is, they may be tangible goodies that we desire. Here, too, the work of the political process is obvious. Who should be taxed, and how much? How much money should be spent on national defense? Where should we build roads? Should the growth of tobacco be subsidized? Who is entitled to receive disability checks? Should there be import quotas on Japanese-built videocassette recorders? Who is entitled to student financial aid? Such familiar questions underscore this core dimension of politics. Politics is not the only way in which material goods are distributed in society. Another very powerful mechanism for doing so is the market, which is commonly considered to be "free," or wholly distinct, from the realm of politics. In our society, people may buy peaches or pineapples, Melissa Ethridge or Ice T, food processors or frozen dinners, according to their wherewithal and personal values. Unlike in some "command economies," the government does not intrude on such decisions.

It is a misconception, however, to regard these decisions as either private or free, for politics inevitably is involved in establishing the structures and boundaries of the market system. Despite the prevalence of free market rhetoric,

Americans recognize the need to control it. Politics is the system that does, as it establishes the rules of the game for our market economy. We do not believe, for example, that people or plutonium should be bought and sold in the marketplace. We want to know that the meat we buy is not tainted and that toys will not harm our children. We want automobiles to be manufactured in such a way as to not ravage our environment. We believe that workers are entitled to safe working conditions. We even rescue major corporations from bad business decisions that they have made. In these, and in many other ways, politics intrudes on the market and, therefore, is involved with the distribution of goods in this sphere.

The allocation of values involves struggle, so there always are winners and losers in politics. A common American bromide holds that people should be free to do anything they wish so long as they do not harm anyone else. The problem with this is that politics is almost exclusively about matters (values) in which people *do* feel that they have something to gain or lose. Some people suffer from defense cuts, whereas others gain. This holds for nonmaterial values as well, where gains and losses are less tangible. Proponents of prayer in schools think that no one is hurt by allowing this practice, but their opponents disagree.

The "*authoritative* allocation of values" means that the allocative decisions are broadly accepted by citizens as legitimate. This does not mean that the decisions are universally liked or that once decisions are made, there can be no more effort to overturn them. Liberals or conservatives might disagree with the enactment of a new welfare law, but they at least tentatively comply with the law, even as they might seek to overturn it. There are exceptions to this general rule. Some who feel passionately about an issue, such as civil rights activists in the 1960s and some abortion opponents today, might break the law and accept the punishment of the state. These acts of conscience, they hope, will goad other citizens and ultimately politicians into changing the law.

Allocating decisions "for society" is perhaps the most troublesome part of our definition of politics. On the one hand, politics often involves decisions that are quite narrow and focused. On the other hand, it can be argued that some very powerful private organizations (e.g., perhaps Microsoft) make allocative decisions for society. Boundary questions, troublesome for any definition, are notorious for this part of our definition of politics. The term "for society" is meant to distinguish politics from what occurs in relatively cohesive groups, where values also are allocated but only for members of that group. When a religious organization asks its members not to eat meat on Fridays, it is allocating values for the members of that group and is not political in our sense. If this organization sought to have a law passed banning the consumption of meat in general, then it would become political.

The second term that needs to be considered is "democracy." Many Americans today would be surprised to learn that democracy is an idea that has come into vogue comparatively recently. The term has been around for centuries, but for most of the history of Western political thought, it has represented an arrangement to be avoided. Americans think of themselves as a great democratic people, yet even during our own constitutional period, the term "democrat" was widely considered to be an epithet. For the Founding Fathers' generation, a democrat was an unscrupulous scoundrel who pandered to the ill-conceived whims of the masses.

Once democratic sentiment began to grow in this country, however, it was irresistible, and now other types of ideas seem arcane. Although some might grouse about how ill prepared people are to participate in political life, no one seriously proposes an alternative in which some segment of the society—the rich, the college educated, certified political scientists (a few of whom are "certifiable")—should govern. The collapse of authoritarian regimes in Eastern Europe and the old Soviet Union has convinced many that we are on the threshold of a worldwide democratic era. As never before, democracy seems to be an idea whose time has arrived.

Ironically, the idea of democracy, to which we seem so deeply committed, is not one that is clearly grasped. "Democracy" is a term frequently used in public discourse, especially around the Fourth of July and during political campaigns, and yet most Americans stumble when asked what the term means. Usually, they will identify some feature of our political system with democracy, as if to suggest that because we talk so much about democracy, democracy must be, in some sense, what we do.

A typical conversation about democracy in America might well begin with some floundering statement to the effect that the term means "the people rule." When asked what it means for the people to rule, a common assertion is that in America people rule because we have elections. If it is noted that many authoritarian political systems hold elections, then the determined American democrat usually will fall back to the position that elections must provide "choices." But not just any choices will do. The choices must be meaningful to citizens, and in any case elections can only be a first step toward democratic governance, not its guarantor.

The true test of democracy is not how leaders are selected but rather how political decisions are made. *A democratic government is one in which people have an approximately equal chance to influence the outcomes and policies of the government.* It is a system in which no one is guaranteed to win, and all are taken seriously. Obviously, there is a utopian strain in this concept. The world is unlikely to have a society that is the perfect expression of this standard, but because the standard has content, it does help sort out those societies that are more or less democratic, and it also helps to answer whether some political change would move us closer to, or pull us further from, a democratic ideal.

Americans seem comfortable with the idea of representative democracy. There are some occasions, such as state and local ballot initiatives, when citizens participate directly in policy formulation. For the most part, however, policy is formulated *indirectly* through elected representatives. Therefore, the democratic standard must be applicable along two dimensions: Citizens must have an approximately equal chance to influence both the selection of representatives and their subsequent political actions.

These two definitions, politics as the authoritative allocation of values for society and democracy as a political system in which citizens have an approximately equal chance to influence the decisions of the government, help to clear away the underbrush for the consideration of the role of money in political life.

If one assumes that democratic governance, in the sense defined here, is and ought to be an overriding goal of our social system, then the way in which we finance our political campaigns is problematic. This is so because of the confluence of three crucial facts. As we shall see, the existence of any one, or any two, of these facts would not necessarily pose a problem, and the existence of all three would pose a problem only if democratic governance were taken seriously.

Fact 1: Political Campaigns in the United States Are Privately Financed

By world standards, we have an unusual way of financing political campaigns. Ours is a helter-skelter, free-for-all system in which candidates for political office are responsible for raising the money necessary for conducting viable political campaigns. Each politician is an entrepreneur who either must invest his or her own money to pay for campaigns or appeal to private individuals and groups for financial support.

The single federal political office that is a partial exception to this rule is the presidency. Candidates for president, if they are seeking either the Republican or Democratic Party nomination, may qualify for some federal support of their campaigns if they first raise enough private money to demonstrate the "seriousness" of their candidacies and if they continue to do well in party primaries. Those who gain the nominations of the major parties are entitled to additional support for the general campaign provided that they agree to accept no further private money. The parties themselves, as opposed to the candidates, can accept private money, and because parties shoulder a significant portion of campaign finance costs, presidential candidates work very hard assisting parties in their fund-raising activities.

Notice who is left out of this system of public finance. It discriminates significantly against minor party presidential candidates. Such candidates are entitled to support only *after* the election, and then only if they have reached a threshold of voter support in that election—a system designed to encourage their continuing obscurity. All other candidates for federal office, and the vast majority of candidates for state and local office, are entirely on their own with respect to campaign fund-raising. Our campaign finance laws are complex. In theory, there are limits to what an individual may contribute, but there are so many loopholes that inventive contributors may give virtually as much as they please.

It is worth noting that this system of campaign finance is unusual. Finance systems vary from nation to nation, but the extensiveness of our commitment to private financing makes the United States distinctive among democratic nations. However, this system is not in itself inherently subversive of democracy. Two other conditions are necessary to make it so.

Fact 2: The Results of Our Distributive System Are Such That There Is Great Economic Inequality in Our Society

To see why this is a necessary condition, consider an alternative distributive result. Imagine a country that used a system of private finance for political campaigns but had a distribution system in which everyone was rewarded equally. Suppose that everyone in this economically egalitarian society made $30,000 a year. In such a society, the private financing of campaigns would pose no problem for democracy. Citizen A might decide to contribute $5,000 to a political campaign, whereas Citizen B chooses to refurbish his home entertainment center. Citizen A presumably would gain political influence as a result of her contribution, but Citizen B would have no basis for complaint. He might have gained an equal amount of influence, but he made another decision, perhaps because he cared less about politics. The democratic condition of having an equal opportunity to influence the political process holds.

Obviously, the real system of distribution in the United States is very different from that described in the preceding paragraph, and most people are glad that it is. Unlike the political sphere, where we believe that people ought to be equally regarded, in the economic sphere, we believe that people ought to be rewarded differently according to their hard work, talents, and so forth. Our belief in this is such that we have generated the most unequal economic distributive system in the modern industrial world.

Recall that politics is the authoritative allocation of values for society. Simply put, we have consented to a distribution that generates enormous economic inequality. And economic inequality is growing. In 1996, census bureau data on income trends showed that the top 5% of households received 21.4% of national income, the greatest proportion since the bureau began reporting such data in 1967. The distribution of wealth, which includes assets as well as income, is even more unequal. In 1950, the top 1% in our society owned 28% of the wealth; by 1996, the proportion had risen to 38%. The richest 20% of Americans are *13* times richer than the poorest 20%. In France the factor is 6, and in Japan it is 4 (Longworth, 1997).

Problems for democracy arise when we allow the inequality generated by our economic system to spill into the political realm, as it does with our system of campaign finance. In the egalitarian economic system described earlier, private financing posed no problem because contributions required equality of sacrifice. In our system, that is not the case. A wealthy person can contribute substantial amounts to political campaigns without any personal sacrifice, whereas even small contributions are beyond the reach of people at the lower levels of our economic spectrum.

Thus, the level playing field required by a democracy is tilted substantially by economic inequality. Ross Perot serves as a prominent illustration of this point. In 1992, Perot decided to run for president. Because he financed his own campaign and received no federal money, he was not bound by any federal finance laws. In 1992, he spent $70 million on his campaign. Aside from his enormous wealth, there was little to separate Perot from millions of other nonpoliticians. His ideas were ordinary, his grasp of economics was tenuous, and his sense of politics was naive. He was a petulant and sometimes paranoid campaigner. Yet, he had a huge impact on the 1992 campaign, not only altering its dialogue but ultimately receiving 19% of the popular vote—more than any third-party candidate since Teddy Roosevelt in 1912. To the vast majority of Americans, $70 million is an unfathomable amount of money. For Perot, however, it is a pittance. In 1992, his net worth was listed at $1.3 billion. If he made no money in 1992, his campaign expenses would have reduced his fortune to $1.23 billion, a level still somewhat above the poverty line.

Fact 3: Political Campaigns in the United States Are Very Expensive

Campaign costs vary substantially from country to country. Some countries provide free television time for candidates. Some have much simpler electoral systems. In England, for example, federal campaigns last about 3 or 4 weeks from start to finish. Even with the existence of Facts 1 and 2, money would pose no substantial threat to democracy if a credible campaign could be mounted without much need for money. Such a reality would render the first two conditions irrelevant.

In our society, however, this is not the case. The design of our electoral system ensures that campaigns will be expensive. Fixed and frequent elections guarantee that our politicians will spend an inordinate amount of time campaigning. The rise of the primary system in this century increased the number of times that candidates need to make expensive mass appeals to the public.

Nonconstitutional factors contribute to the rising costs of political campaigns as well. The evaporation of political parties as grassroots organizations has eliminated the reserve army of volunteers that once was crucial to campaigns. The rise of the electronic media as central elements in campaigns has greatly increased costs, as the creation and display of ads and the reliance on market professionals become more necessary. The increasing costs of campaigns have increased the costs of campaigns, as politicians are forced to spend money to raise it. Finally, campaign costs have increased because there are a large number of willing contributors seeking to get into the political game. The money is there, and it is very hard for politicians to resist. All of these factors, and others as well, contribute to the skyrocketing costs of political campaigns.

In 1860, Abraham Lincoln spent $100,000 getting elected president. Even controlling for the substantial inflation since that time, Lincoln spent only a small fraction of what candidates today must spend. Federal campaign costs have been on an upward spiral since the 1950s, and according to the Center for Responsive Politics, they took a quantum leap in 1996. The center, which is the major public interest analyst of public spending, issued a study noting that $2.2 billion was spent on federal elections in 1996, a 37% increase over the $1.6 billion that was spent just 4 years earlier.[2]

Because democracy implies widespread participation, it is expensive. It takes money to reach voters, but if the result is a better informed electorate, then democracy is enhanced and the costs are perhaps justified. Sadly, this is not the case. There is overwhelming evidence that levels of political information held by citizens are very low and that they have not been moved by the rising tide of political money. The majority cannot identify their representative or their two senators. Policy knowledge, such as President Bill Clinton's proposal to lower the age for Medicare eligibility, is sparser still.[3] Candidates are spending huge sums of money, but they are not doing so in ways that inform citizens of significant policy options.

Consequences

The confluence of the three facts just discussed does not edify democracy; on the contrary, it diminishes democracy. There are several ways in which this can be seen.

Money and Time

Like everyone else, politicians wish to be successful at their work. Some measure that success by reelection, which indicates voter approval. Others see reelection as instrumental to success; holding office allows them to do other things that they consider valuable. In either case, money is increasingly important, and politicians are spending ever greater amounts of time in the money chase. The candidates who spend the most do not always win, although usually they do. In 1994, the winners of elections to the U.S. House of Representatives spent an average of $516,000, whereas the losers spent an average of $239,000. For the Senate, winners and losers spent averages of $4,570,000 and $3,427,000, respectively. In the 1996 U.S. congressional elections, losers were outspent by winners approximately 90% of the time.[4]

Thus, money must be a constant concern of politicians. Representatives stand for election biannually. Any or all of these elections can be quite expensive. Even those representing districts normally considered "safe" will stockpile funds to guard against the possibility of a heavily funded candidate emerging in some future election. Powerful Democratic politicians Dan Rostenkowski and Tom Foley were upset by well-heeled opponents, and Republican Newt Gingrich has survived two similarly close elections. The fact that our election laws allow money raised but not spent for one election to be used in a completely different campaign further entices politicians down the money trail. Gingrich, for example, is entitled to use funds raised for past House campaigns in campaigns for the Senate or the presidency.

The growing concern for money serves to distract politicians from their constitutional duties. Today, federal politicians engage in two campaigns. The first is the traditional public campaign culminating in an election. The second, newer "money campaign" is far less public and is interminable—the campaign to build and maintain a healthy "war chest." Individual solicitations, fund-raising events, preparation of elaborate brochures to court political action committees (PACs), and the like take growing bites out of a politician's day. During Clinton's first term, he actively participated in 185 fund-raising events for himself and others. These do not include individual phone solicitations that congressional investigations showed were substantial. This is *inherently* corrupting. The politician is forced to pay attention to this second campaign to survive, with the result that the quality of his or her public life inevitably is diminished.

There is a second facet of the money-time connection. It is relevant not only to politicians but also to those who elect them. Harvard political scientist Sidney Verba and his associates recently completed a massive study of political participation in America (Verba, Schlozman, & Brady, 1995). This study carefully assessed trends in various forms of political participation. One of the authors' most important findings was that there has been a decline in voluntary political activity such as ringing doorbells, licking envelopes, and phoning potential voters and an increase in monetary contributions. In short, money is replacing time as the major form of citizen activity. The authors muse about the consequence of this shift: "As resources for politics, time and money have obvious differences. Time is more evenly distributed than money. . . . When dollars substitute for hours as the essential unit of political input, participation becomes more unequal" (Verba, Schlozman, & Brady, 1997, p. 79).

Whose Voice?

This leads to a second consequence of the American political money system. All of us might have been created equal, but as the pigs in George Orwell's classic *Animal Farm* first noted, some are more equal than others. Clearly, our system guarantees that the rich will have a disproportionate say in political decision making.

Consider the rational democratic political candidate. (Here, "rational" is used in the conventional economic sense of maximizing self-interest.) The problem faced by that candidate is how to win the votes of at least half of the electorate. Charisma and personality always have been important in the voting decision, but issues have been important as well. Candidates seek to put together a configuration of issue positions that, in combination, will appeal to a majority of the voters, and in this crude way the representative ideal is approached.

Money can easily upset this process. Imagine that our rational candidate, who happens to represent an urban district, is approached by a wheat growers PAC interested in gaining "access" for the purpose of eliciting support for wheat subsidies. Because no wheat growers reside in the district, and because such subsidies would raise the price of wheat-related products, we can imagine that such subsidies are not in the interests of her constituents. What should the candidate do?

Because it goes against the interests of her district, the vote is potentially dangerous. But our rational candidate would be aware of the fact that issue knowledge is minimal in her district. Not many voters would know of her vote. On the other hand, her opponent might well try to advertise her unpopular vote unless he also received similar contributions. Even if the opponent did advertise the vote, our rational candidate would realize that probably only a few voters would get this message and that many of these would dismiss it as "just politics." In many cases, votes can be hidden or obscured in committees, through unrecorded oral votes, or (perhaps) by not voting.

Money is attractive because it is fungible. It does not need to be spent in a manner that connects it to its source. In our example, the candidate would not have to spend the money raised from wheat interests trumpeting the importance of price supports for the product. Instead, she might spend the money to create an ad attacking her opponent, to operate a phone bank, to conduct a poll, or on any other activity she considers efficacious. If the rational candidate concludes that the votes she would gain with the contribution would more than offset the votes she would lose by her "unpopular" vote, then she would take the money.

In the real world, of course, candidates are not purely rational. Political ideologies, moral impulses, party loyalty, and other things may enter into a decision to accept or reject such money. On the other hand, with money's increasing significance, the pressures to make the "rational" decision are constant and substantial. In many cases, the connections between the interests of potential contributors and the interests of the district are not clearly evident. In such cases, the pressure to take the money is significantly increased.

Roger Tamraz offered a rare glimpse into the money campaign in his 1997 testimony before the Senate select committee investigating campaign finance.[5] Tamraz, a wealthy oil magnate, was interested in promoting his vision of a $2.5 billion oil pipeline in the Caspian Sea and wanted "access" to the Clinton administration to solicit support for this project. Although he had already given $95,000 to the Democratic Party, he was excluded from a political breakfast with Vice President Al Gore after the Democratic National Committee received a memo from Gore's office identifying Tamraz as "an American citizen with a shady and untrustworthy reputation." Subsequent conversations with Democratic Party officials led Tamraz to contribute an additional $75,000 to the party. At this point, the sun evidently shined brightly on him. He was admitted to four White House functions including a dinner with Clinton at which he promoted his pipeline dreams.

Tamraz's testimony before the Senate committee was interesting because it was so candid. He had been involved in the money campaign for years, contributing to Republicans as well as Democrats, and he knew that the senators sitting across the table from him had been involved as well. Posturing before the nation's television cameras, the senators professed shock at Tamraz's words. They were nonplussed when his candor extended to them as he frankly told the committee what everyone in the room already knew: This was nothing more than business as usual in modern politics.

There is a more direct way in which to see the disproportionate influence granted to wealthy citizens by the present political money system. In increasing numbers, wealthy citizens occupy political office. Simply on the basis of congressional salaries, members of Congress are among the top 10% of income earners, and most members of Congress are able to supplement their salaries significantly in a number of ways. After the 1996 elections, according to the director of the Center for Responsive Politics, at least 28 U.S. senators were millionaires—a proportion 5,000 times greater than that in the general population (Miller, 1995). Not all millionaires think alike, but there are powerful and understandable pulls on the wealthy toward the status quo. Most people who gain positions of privilege will develop rationales of desert. They will come to believe that they have earned and deserve those positions. From this, it is only a small step to the conviction that our political and social system must be fundamentally sound because it has allowed meritorious people, such as millionaires like themselves, to get or remain ahead—and to dismiss critics as prisoners of envy.

If the wealthy have a disproportionate say in our political system, then the less well-off are underrepresented. One consequence of this is that the less well-off are far less likely to participate in politics, even in the simple act of voting, than are better off citizens. Political withdrawal, in turn, accelerates the downward spiral of exclusion. The present political money system increases the difficulty of the less well-off in finding a champion.

The contrasting images of conservatism and liberalism, as embodied by leading political figures, are useful illustrations. Conservatives seem robust, virile, vigorous, and self-confident. Think of Gingrich, Ronald Reagan, Jack Kemp, Trent Lott, Pat Buchanan, and Phil Gramm. By contrast, liberals—or those who have been identified as liberals—seem tentative, timid, and wimpy. Think of Clinton, Gore, George McGovern, Jimmy Carter, Mario Cuomo, and Michael Dukakis. Perhaps the one exception is Jesse Jackson, the lone champion of robust liberalism. Lingering racism, however, has limited Jackson's ability to appeal to the broader liberal community. It is possible that conservatism is inherently more virile than liberalism, but I think that the main problem lies elsewhere. Conservatives and liberals face very different realities in the political money system.

As troubadours of the status quo, conservatives are invigorated by the money system. The more they blast away, the greater the pleasure of monied interests. As spokespersons for social equity, liberals are chastened by the money system. Not all monied interests are conservative. Labor unions and the entertainment industry, for example, give significant amounts to liberals. One can find the occasional liberal corporate magnate as well. Considered as wholes, however, conservative money overwhelms liberal money, so the money system works very differently for liberals from how it does for conservatives. Liberals must constantly worry about alienating political capital. Any Democratic presidential nominee immediately signals Wall Street, through campaign appointments, policy pronouncements, addresses to economic clubs, and the like, that he or she is "reasonable." In this way, the political voice of liberalism is made tentative. By contrast, Republican nominees feel no need for similar overtures to labor unions.

Structuring Political Discourse

A third consequence of our political money system is that it structures political discourse. Because this is the raison d'être of contributions, this result should not be surprising. People who contribute to political campaigns are not moved by charitable impulse. Donations are given in the hope of some return. Givers seek to influence the allocation of values that is the essence of politics. Considered theoretically, the number of issues that politicians might address is infinite. And there are myriad ways in which to frame those issues that are considered. Thus, although contributions do not determine the content of political discourse, they do substantially shape it. Three examples will serve as illustrations.

For decades, U.S. political leaders have kept a vigilant watch over events in the Middle East. We are particularly interested in sustaining political regimes that are friendly to us, even if these regimes oppress their own citizens. We provide arms to help them sustain their power, and we will not hesitate to intervene militarily if this becomes necessary. This policy enjoys bipartisan support because both parties consider maintaining friendly regimes in that area to be vital to our national interests. Why this is so is obvious. We have an oil-based economy, and the Middle East has bountiful oil supplies. Over the past few decades, we have imported between 25% and 40% of the oil we use from that region. If we are required to prop up oppressive but friendly regimes or to place our young men and women in harm's way to maintain these interests, so be it. The real political world can be messy.

This wisdom is so conventional that it is noncontroversial. The sense that this policy is legitimate is shared by citizens. But there is another way in which to think about this issue, although it is not very evident in Washington, D.C., or in the national media. This alternative perspective is raised by the question: Do we need to be dependent on Middle East oil? Most of us take present levels of oil consumption as a given when considering our interests in the Middle East because that is the way in which the issue is framed. Careful research, however, indicates that we can cut our oil consumption in half *without reducing our standard of living* (Stobaugh & Yergin, 1979).

This could be accomplished by a series of unglamorous steps including requirements for solar-friendly construction, tax breaks for home weatherization, greatly expanded mass transportation systems, higher fuel consumption standards for automobiles, and the encouragement of solar energy projects. Besides reducing oil consumption, this shift would have the additional benefits of linking us to renewable energy supplies as well as creating additional jobs.

One would think that discussion of this option would be high on the agenda of national political life. A reconstructed energy policy would mean that we no longer would have to prop up tawdry and oppressive political regimes or risk the lives of our own citizens. In addition, this policy would significantly decrease the drain on the world's finite energy supplies, improve the quality of the environment, and create jobs. The rationality of the policy seems overwhelming.

Theoretical rationality and political rationality, however, are not the same. Political rationality must be deduced from within the context of the current money system. Consider that of the 20 largest *Fortune* 500 corporations, 8 come from the oil and automobile industries. Not only do all of these companies have well-heeled PACs (their subsidiaries have them as well), they also are larded with wealthy individuals, such as Tamraz, who contribute significantly to the campaign process on an individual basis. To these interests, the present system is rational. An oil-driven, autocentric society makes a great deal of sense to them. Given their need for private campaign contributions, it makes sense to politicians as well.

The effort to establish a national health care system provides a second example of how the money system structures political discourse. At present, more than 40 million Americans have no health care. These are not our poorest citizens, for whom government-sponsored Medicaid provides some assistance. Most of those without medical coverage work, but they work for employers that do not provide health coverage as part of their benefits packages. All other industrialized nations of the world have some system of national health care. Even though they provide universal coverage, many of these systems are less expensive than ours. In Canada, for example, not only is the health care system significantly less expensive than ours, but according to surveys, Canadians are much more satisfied with their system than Americans are with ours. Given that we are the wealthiest nation in the world, it might seem strange to an outsider that we do not have a system that guarantees universal health care. Gallup polls have noted in recent years that a solid majority of Americans support national health care.

For all these reasons, health care became a major issue in the 1992 presidential campaign. When the candidate who was its major proponent was elected along with a majority of his party in both houses of Congress, it seemed that health care was an idea whose time had come. In fact, health care became the major policy initiative of Clinton's first term.

It is at this point that the political money system becomes an important part of the story. In considering the type of system to introduce, the Clinton administration dismissed the Canadian option, despite its many virtues. Even though a single-payer system was simple, straightforward, and efficient, it was not considered to be politically viable. The single-payer system would replace profit-seeking insurance companies with a not-for-profit government-sponsored administration. Because the insurance companies were big players in the political money system, the Clinton administration devised a convoluted and complex national health system that left these companies in the game. Although the single-payer system was proposed as an alternative by Democratic Senator Paul Wellstone, it never went anywhere. Public attention was drawn toward the more complex scheme of the president.

Complexity presents its own political problems, however, as the Clinton health initiative illustrated. In advocating change, policymakers must be able to communicate clearly what the change would mean to the average citizen. If they cannot do so, then the opponents of change will use the complexity to instill doubt in the public. In politics, ambiguity often is the handmaiden of defeat. The opponents of national health care, including insurance companies, waged a massive public relations campaign to instill doubt about the president's proposal. The once solid public support for national health care that helped to elect the president began to erode. This made it much easier for politicians, who during this period were receiving large campaign donations from interests opposing the program, to resist it. The status quo was sustained. In short, the money system trapped national health care policy on the horns of a dilemma. To keep money players in the health care game, a complex scheme was devised. The complexity of this scheme was used by those very players the administration sought to appease to help defeat it.

The third example of how money structures political considerations is political reform. Americans are very cynical about politics these days. In stark contrast to national attitudes of 40 years ago, a substantial majority of our citizens believe that our government does not care very much about what they think. They see politicians as catering to special interests and economic elites and as being primarily concerned about promoting their own careers. Such attitudes have generated a rich harvest of what might be called "antipolitician" politicians, who build political careers by running against the government in Washington. Examples of this breed abound in the presidential selection process of recent decades and include Carter, Reagan, Dukakis, Buchanan, Jerry Brown, Paul Tsongas, and Lamar Alexander. Perhaps the apotheosis of this sentiment was reached in the 1996 campaign, which featured three antigovernment candidates: an incumbent president claiming to be in the process of "reinventing government"; a Republican challenger who, having built a successful career as a very effective political insider, resigned as Senate majority leader to make his newborn antigovernment campaign plausible; and perpetual political crank Perot.

It is not surprising that the sentiment of recent decades has generated much talk about political reform. What is illustrative for our purposes is how that talk has been channeled. There has been tremendous interest in term limits, as a way in which to root out corruption, and comparatively little about campaign finance reform, even though it is more obviously connected to corruption. Term limits were a key part of the Republicans' "Contract With America," a series of proposals on which party candidates for the House campaigned in 1994.

Republicans had long despaired of gaining majority control of the House. Through the 1980s, they had pushed for term limits as a way of forcing well-funded incumbent Democrats out of office. Statistical data clearly showed that they had a much better chance of winning open seats than of upsetting incumbents. This political ploy had a public rationale. It was presented as political "reform"—a way in which to root out corruption. The argument for term limits was that longevity in office promoted cozy relationships between incumbents and special interests and, in consequence, encouraged corruption. Requiring periodic turnovers of members of Congress would sever these unseemly relationships.

There are numerous arguments opposing term limits, but for our purposes, we focus on their efficacy in reducing corruption. In point of fact, they likely would have the opposite effect for two reasons. First, newly elected officials usually are the least knowledgeable about the details of public policy; therefore, they are the most susceptible to the importunings of special interests. Second, as members of Congress approached the forced terminations of their careers, they would be much more likely to curry favor with special interests. Well-paying jobs are not easy to find in middle age. The most simple way of getting one is to ingratiate oneself to those with the wherewithal to bestow employment. Because they would be retiring from public office anyway, incumbents would not have the fear of public sanction to rein them in. This type of career shift is already a common enough practice in Washington. Under term limits, it likely would become rampant.

The Republicans seized on term limits as a way of building political capital in their wars with the Democrats. It is a simple idea, one easily grasped by a public frustrated with politicians. Polls show that term limits are very popular. But term limits offer the veneer of reform without its substance. Ultimately, their effect would be to increase public cynicism further. When the Republicans actually gained control of the House after the 1994 elections, they faced a Hobson's choice: If they did not pass term limit legislation, they would be seen as reneging on their promise to implement the Contract With America; but now term limits was an issue that would work against them as the new majority party. In the end, some party defections caused the narrow defeat of term limits. It was the only part of the contract that was defeated in the House.

The moral of this tale is not the success or failure of this legislation. It is how national interest in reform was channeled by politicians toward a safe harbor. Term limits would not alter existing relations of power and make people feel that the government was responsive to them. The clearest way in which to do this is through campaign finance reform. A national survey conducted during the Senate Governmental Affairs Committee hearings on campaign finance, which ended amid partisan bickering and a failure to accomplish anything in the way of reform, shows that the role of money in our political life is one of the major sources of popular discontent with and cynicism toward politics. The survey reveals that 3 out of 4 citizens believe that congressional representatives are more responsive to monied interests outside their district than to their own constituents, and 7 out of 10 respondents stated that the two political parties are equally likely to engage in questionable fund-raising activities. Fully 70% of the respondents favored campaign finance reform, but most held forth little hope for it happening.[6]

Conclusion

We have shown how the confluence of three conditions—privately financed political campaigns, great economic inequality, and sharply escalating campaign costs—serves to subvert democracy. People in our system have widely varying abilities to influence the outcomes of government. Those in economically advantageous positions have far greater opportunity to influence the "authoritative allocation of values" that is the core of the political process.

The democratic prospect can be improved by altering any of these conditions. Of the three, attempts to enhance democracy by reducing economic inequality are least likely to be effective. The levels of economic equality necessary for political equality are so radically different from our current situation, so counter to our cultural traditions, and so contradictory of conventional economic wisdom that this path is not viable.

Some would argue that addressing the first or third condition is not a viable strategy either. Certainly, changing the current private political money system faces two immediate problems. The first is that reforms would have to be introduced by those who are the major beneficiaries of the current system. Incumbent politicians are advantaged in this system because they are proven winners. Contributors seeking influence recognize this; therefore, they find it more efficient to spend money on those already in power than to spend it on unproven challengers. The second obstacle is that finance reform is not very salient to citizens. When asked about this issue, citizens obviously care, but there is little evidence that it is fundamental to many voters.

These two problems, however, might not be as intractable as they seem. In this age of deep political cynicism, it would astonish most people to know that a great many of this nation's leaders enter politics for noble reasons. Conservative or liberal, they begin in politics with ideas about how to make life better. For such individuals, the constant money chase is demeaning. Many have confessed as much in private interviews. Some, such as Democratic Senator Bill Bradley and Republican Congressman Vin Weber, have resigned from office partly in despair over the money chase. The bipartisan MacCain-Feingold Campaign Reform Bill had majority support in the Senate before it was killed on a technicality by Majority Leader Trent Lott. Although it fell far short of the type of reform needed to democratize our system, it was an indication that the natives are restless, even with a system that favors them.

Continuing public cynicism toward politics also increases pressure for reform. All of us like to be well thought of by others. In politics, this type of emotional return is diminishing. Politicians always have had to face the problem of being reviled by about half the population. Their solace has been that they have been loved by the other half. There can be little pleasure in an occupation that is universally reviled, however, and this is especially so when that occupation requires public ratification. Despite the advantages incumbents have in the current system, their need for dignity might edge them toward reform.

Still, public cynicism needs to be galvanized into action. Cynicism is not the same as anger. So far, public concern about the money chase has not boiled over into the campaign process. People are turned off, but they are not fired up. Public concern is mostly latent. It needs some individual or precipitating event to elevate it in the public consciousness.

Other countries simply impose spending limits on political parties and candidates. In the wake of Watergate, Congress passed legislation having such limits. In *Buckley v. Valeo,* however, the Supreme Court ruled that such limitations violated constitutionally guaranteed free speech. Spending money, the court ruled, is a form of political expression and cannot be restricted by government fiat. This ruling is controversial, but it expressed a strong majority sentiment on the court and is unlikely to be overruled by the more conservative present court.

This does not mean, however, that democratic reform is precluded. A recent initiative enacted by voters in the state of Maine is attracting significant attention.[7] Once candidates for state office in Maine pass a qualification threshold by raising a reasonable amount of money in small donations, they receive a fixed amount of money for their campaigns. Candidates must agree not to raise or spend any additional private money whatsoever to qualify for public funds. In the event that they are being outspent significantly by a candidate using private funds, their allocation is increased. If a private organization, such as a PAC, wages a heavily funded independent campaign against a candidate, then the candidate is entitled to public funds to counteract the campaign. The Maine law does not violate the *Buckley* provisions because it is voluntary. If they wish, candidates may spend private money and avoid the restrictions that come with the public funds.

A federally implemented program similar to the one in Maine obviously would cost money, but the overall costs of campaigns likely would drop dramatically. There would be no reason to spend money because it is there, which has significantly contributed to increasing costs in recent years. Furthermore, political analysts estimate that about one quarter of campaign expenditures goes for raising money, a cost that no longer would be relevant to publicly financed candidates. The costs of political campaigns could be further reduced by a significant amount if there were a requirement for free television time in relevant markets. Because the airwaves are publicly owned, stations enter into contracts with the federal government for their use. Under the Federal Communications Act, the stations agree to operate in the "public interest, convenience, and necessity." This is why stations have some public interest programming. Free campaign time, standard in other countries, could easily be incorporated under these provisions.

Despite these things, ending the political money chase will cost something, and supporters of the current system will play this issue like a Stradivarius. What must be recognized is that the current system is far more expensive. Although the costs are partially hidden, we pay for the current system every time an unworthy contractor receives a government contract, every time a special interest gets a tax favor, and every time a wise government policy is overlooked. And we pay for it with lost dignity that comes with the recognition that many of us do not matter politically. Democracy might be a comparatively new idea and an unfinished dream, but it is a dream worth pursuing.

Notes

1. See, for example, Walzer (1973) and Wills (1975).
2. The report is summarized in "Campaign Costs Soar" (1997).
3. For an excellent review of levels of political knowledge in this country, see Delli Carpini and Keeter (1996).
4. Data are from a poll conducted in April 1997 by Princeton Survey Research Associates for the Center for Responsive Politics (1997). Data on the 1996 election are reported in Starr (1997).
5. Information on Tamraz is from Ottaway and Morgan (1997).
6. This survey was conducted in April 1997 by the Princeton Survey Research Associates for the Center For Responsive Politics (1997).
7. See Miller (1997). The January/February 1998 issue of *The American Prospect* is largely devoted to campaign finance reform and contains several articles of interest.

References

Campaign costs soar to record $2.2 billion. (1997, November 25). *Chicago Tribune,* sec. 1, p. 6.
Center For Responsive Politics. (1997). *The price of admission: 1994 election statistics at a glance.* Available on Internet: http://www.crp.org.
Delli Carpini, M. X., & Keeter, S. (1996). *What Americans know about politics and why it matters.* New Haven, CT: Yale University Press.

Longworth, R. C. (1997, October 5). A bottom line blight on American life. *Chicago Tribune,* sec. 2, p. 1.

Miller, E. S. (1995, November/December). Playing to play. *Sojourners, 24*(5), 3-6.

Miller, E. S. (1997, January/February). Clean elections, how to. *The American Prospect,* pp. 56-59.

Ottaway, D., & Morgan, D. (1997, September 9). For DNC donor, resistance was overcome. *Washington Post,* p. A1.

Starr, P. (1997, January/February). Democracy v. dollar. *The American Prospect,* pp. 6-9.

Stobaugh, R., & Yergin, D. (Eds.). (1979). *Energy future.* New York: Random House.

Verba, S., Schlozman, K. L., & Brady, H. E. (1995). *Voice and equality: Civic volunteerism and American politics.* Cambridge, MA: Harvard University Press.

Verba, S., Schlozman, K. L., & Brady, H. E. (1997, May/June). The big tilt. *The American Prospect,* pp. 27-33.

Walzer, M. (1973). Politics and the problem of dirty hands. *Philosophy and Public Affairs, 2,* 160-180.

Wills, G. (1975, September). Hurrah for politicians. *Harpers,* pp. 45-50.

Index

About the Editor

Bruce I. Newman is nationally and internationally known as one of the leading authorities on the subject of political marketing. He has published numerous articles and five books on the subject of politics and marketing including *The Marketing of the President* (1994) and *The Mass Marketing of Politics: Democracy in an Age of Manufactured Images* (1999). He also is the coauthor of two books on the subject of consumer psychology, *Consumption Values and Market Choices* (1991) and *Customer Behavior* (1998). He served as an adviser to senior presidential aides in the Clinton White House on communication strategy for the 1996 presidential election. He is an associate professor in the marketing department of the Kellstadt Graduate School of Business at DePaul University. Prior to that, he was on the faculties of Baruch College, City University of New York, and the University of Wisconsin–Milwaukee. He also was a visiting professor at Trinity College in Dublin, Ireland, and a visiting scholar at FMD Research Institute in Oslo, Norway. He received his B.S., M.B.A., and Ph.D. (1981) in marketing from the University of Illinois in Champaign-Urbana. He currently sits on the editorial boards of *Psychology and Marketing* and *Werbeforschung & Praxis*. He lectures around the world on the subjects of political marketing and voting behavior and is a frequent contributor to the mass media. He has appeared on nationally syndicated television and radio talk shows in the United States and the United Kingdom. He has been quoted numerous times in national newspapers and has written op-ed articles appearing in the *Christian Science Monitor,* the *Sunday Telegraph,* and the *Chicago Tribune.* In 1993, he received the Ehrenring (Ring of Honor) from the Austrian Advertising Research Association in Vienna for his research in political marketing. He is the first American recipient of this award in the 30 years it has been given out.

About the Contributors

Michaela Adami specialized in advertising and market research during her studies of commercial science at the Vienna University of Economics and Business Administration. Since 1997, she has been a Ph.D. candidate at the university's Institute of Advertising and Market Research, where she focuses on nonverbal image measurement. Since 1998, she has been the marketing director of Premiere PAY TV Austria.

Nigel Allington is Fellow of Gonville and Caius College at Cambridge University and Lecturer in Economics at Cardiff University. He is the author of *Learning and Liberty: The Idea of the University Revisited* (1992, with Nicholas O'Shaughnessy).

Paul R. Baines is Lecturer in Marketing at Middlesex University Business School in London. He currently is conducting research in the area of determining the transferability of U.S. political campaign practice for U.K. political parties. He is a doctoral student at the Manchester School of Management, where he received his M.Phil. for research into marketing planning for political parties. He is the author and coauthor of several articles on the use of marketing techniques in nonconventional environments such as for political parties and candidates and soccer clubs.

Knut Bergmann currently is dividing his time between working as a political consultant for the head office of a bank and writing his doctoral thesis in which he will provide an analysis of the strategies and mechanisms underlying the "Americanization" of Germany's election campaign in 1998. He studied political science, psychology, and law in Bonn, Germany, from 1992 to 1998. During these years, he also worked for a member of Parliament and for several companies in the departments of communications and public relations. In his master's thesis, he gave an extensive analysis of the German general election campaign in 1994. He has published several articles about political communications in Germany.

George Bishop is Professor of Political Science and Director of the Graduate Certificate Program in Public Opinion and Survey Research at the University of Cincinnati. An active member of the American Association for Public Opinion Research and a past president of the Midwest Association for Opinion Research (NAPOR), he received the 1994 MAPOR Fellow Award for distinguished scholarship in public opinion and survey research. He has published numerous articles in journals such as *Public Opinion Quarterly*, as well as various book chapters, on survey question effects in public opinion polls. He has been a guest professor at the Center for Survey Research and Methodology in Mannheim, Germany, and a senior consultant with Burke Marketing in Cincinnati, Ohio. He also has taught as a visiting faculty member in the Summer Institute in Survey Research at the University of Michigan.

Patrick Butler is Lecturer in Business Studies at Trinity College in Dublin, Ireland. Formerly at the University of Ulster, he teaches a variety of undergraduate, postgraduate, and executive development programs. He has a wide range of research interests including political marketing, arts management, and electronic commerce. He has published in the *European Journal of Marketing, International Journal of Bank Marketing,* and *Harvard International Journal of Press/ Politics,* among others, and has presented his research at many international conferences. He is involved in management consulting and development in Ireland and abroad, through European Union and United Nations projects.

Neil Collins is Professor of Public Administration at the National University of Ireland, Cork. He has published in the areas of marketing both political parties and public sector services. He has worked at universities in Ireland, the United Kingdom, and the United States. His major research interests are in Irish and European Union politics.

Wojciech Cwalina is Assistant Professor in the Department of Experimental Psychology at the Catholic University of Lublin in Poland. His research specialties include political marketing psychology, organizational and management psychology, and analysis of media coverage. Among his publications are numerous articles in psychological journals and chapters in books about political marketing and mass communication. He works as a marketing specialist and campaign adviser for the Solidarity Election Action in Lower Silesia Division.

Rob Daves is director of polling and news research at the *Star Tribune* in Minneapolis, Minnesota, where he directs the Minnesota Poll. He worked in newspapers as a reporter, copy editor, and news editor before training in market and public opinion research. He is past president of the Midwest Association for Public Opinion Research and a member of the American Association for Public

Opinion Research and the Research Federation of the Newspaper Association of America. Other book chapters he has written address how polls ascertain likelihood to vote, deliberative polling, and allocating undecided respondents in preelection polls. He received his M.A. in journalism from the University of North Carolina at Chapel Hill and a B.S. in sociology from Western Carolina University.

Dietmar Ecker took over the majority of the communications and lobbying agency, Ecker & Partner, in June 1998. With its 12 employees, the agency ranks among the top 10 agencies in Austria. Ecker & Partner stands for integrative customer care in all aspects of the communication business. Through strategic communication consulting and network construction, the agency provides the requested presence for its clients in their target group. The target is to elaborate tailor-made approaches in small teams. He is the former press officer of Ferdinand Lacina, minister of finance.

Andrzej Falkowski is Professor of Experimental Psychology at the Catholic University of Lublin in Poland, where his research specialty is cognitive psychology including consumer behavior, marketing, and political advertising. He is a Fulbright Scholar (University of Michigan). Mentioned in *Who's Who in the World* and in *Men of Achievement*, his publications include numerous articles in consumer behavior and cognitive psychology journals as well as the following books: *Psychological Judgment and the Process of Perception* (1992) and *A Similarity Relation in Cognitive Processes: An Ecological and Information Processing Approach* (1995).

Hanne Gardner worked in industrial and consumer marketing for major companies such as Rowntree and Nestle before becoming Senior Lecturer in the Department of Retailing and Marketing and Business Studies at Manchester Metropolitan University. She earned both her B.S. and her M.S. at the University of Manchester Institute of Science and Technology. Her research interests include culture and retailing as well as political marketing.

Jon B. Gould is Assistant Professor of Government and Politics and Visiting Assistant Professor of Law at George Mason University. He was formerly a Visiting Scholar at the Institute of Governmental Studies at the University of California, Berkeley. A lawyer and political scientist, he has extensive experience in campaigning and election law. He has served as chair of the American Bar Association's Election Law Committee; been general counsel of College Democrats of America and its project, Vote for a Change; advised the Clinton-Gore 1996 campaign manager, and worked on the legal staff of the Dukakis-Bentsen 1988 campaign. He consults internationally on issues of constitutional and electoral reform.

Phil Harris is Co-director of the Centre for Corporate and Public Affairs at Manchester Metropolitan University. He is a member of the Senate and Fellow of the Chartered Institute of Marketing, Deputy Chairman of the Academy of

Marketing, and author of the forthcoming text, *Political Marketing* (with Dominic Wring). He was a candidate in the 1992 British general election and the 1994 European elections, and he is past vice chairman of the Liberal Party. He has authored more than 100 articles and papers on issues such as joint ventures, lobbying, political marketing, and industrial marketing. He was editor of a special edition of the *European Journal of Marketing* on political marketing and recently organized the "Machiavelli at 500" seminar in Manchester.

Peter D. Hart is Founder and Chief Executive Officer of Peter D. Hart Research Associates, which has conducted more than 5,000 public opinion surveys among more than 3 million individuals since 1971. An established leader in survey research, he (along with Robert Teeter) has been the pollster for NBC News and the *Wall Street Journal* since 1989. His firm has conducted strategic planning projects for corporate clients such as American Airlines, Microsoft, Time Warner, Chrysler, and AT&T. He appears frequently on the major television programs that discuss public policy issues including *Meet the Press, The Today Show,* and C-SPAN. From 1974 to 1990, he was the leading analyst on public opinion for CBS Election Night coverage with Dan Rather, and since 1990, he has been the leading analyst for NBC's Election Night coverage with Tom Brokaw and Tim Russert.

Andreas Herrmann is Professor of Marketing at the University of Mainz. Previously, he was an assistant professor of marketing at the University of Mannheim and a marketing manager at Audi. His favorite areas of research are product development, product and price bundling, and multivariate analysis. He is the author of about 100 articles and five books on subjects such as product management and customer retention in the automotive industry.

Jürgen Hofrichter is a senior researcher in the field of political and electoral research at Infratest dimap in Berlin. Infratest dimap is responsible for electoral research and anaylsis and the presentation of television graphics on the German public television channel, ARD, during German elections. After receiving his sociology degree from the University of Mannheim, he was a researcher and then the managing director at the Centre for European Survey Analyses and Studies from 1987 to 1993. From 1993 to 1996, he was team director for media research and later for social research in the market research institute, MARPLAN, in Offenbach, Germany.

Frank Huber is Assistant Professor of Marketing at the University of Mannheim in Germany. He received his Ph.D. in 1998 and his M.B.A. in 1993 at the same university and in the same subject. He received the Pro-Marketing Award of the University of Mannheim for his master's thesis, *Behavioral Approaches of Market Segmentation in Fashion Marketing: A LISREL Application.* Since 1993, he has published two books and more than 90 articles in international and German journals, books, and conference proceedings. His main research topics are customer satisfaction, loyalty, retention, customer perceptions of brands, and the analysis of data with multivariate techniques.

Dennis W. Johnson is Associate Dean of the Graduate School of Political Management at George Washington University in Washington, D.C. He is author of *No Place for Amateurs: The Professionalization of Modern Campaigns* (Routledge, forthcoming), from which his chapter in this book is adapted. He has worked in senior staff positions in both the U.S. House of Representatives and the U.S. Senate and ran his own political consulting business for 6 years. He has a Ph.D. in political science from Duke University.

Linda Lee Kaid is Professor of Communication and George Lynn Cross Research Professor at the University of Oklahoma, where she also serves as Director of the Political Communications Center and supervises the Political Commercial Archive. She received her Ph.D. from Southern Illinois University in 1974. Her research specialties include political advertising and news coverage of political events. A Fulbright Scholar, she also has done work on political television in several Western European countries. She is the author or editor of 12 books, has written more than 80 journal articles and book chapters, and has presented more than 100 convention papers on various aspects of political communication.

Dennis F. Kinsey is Assistant Professor of Public Relations in the S. I. Newhouse School of Public Communications at Syracuse University. He is a former vice president of Decision Research Corporation, a public opinion research and political consulting firm with headquarters in Cleveland, Ohio. As vice president of that company, he conducted research for clients as diverse as the reelection campaign of Ohio Governor Richard F. Celeste and the California Trial Lawyers Association. He has consulted for numerous elected officials including Congressman Edward Feighan, Judge Carl B. Stokes, and Ohio Treasurer Mary Ellen Withrow. He has published in *Journalism Educator, Journal of Advertising Research, Operant Subjectivity, Political Communication,* and *Political Psychology.*

Neil Kotler is a program specialist at the Smithsonian Institution. He received his B.A. (1962) from Brandeis University, his M.A. (1963) from the University of Wisconsin–Madison, and his Ph.D. in political science (1974) from the University of Chicago. He is a former legislative director in the U.S. House of Representatives; professor at the University of Texas at Austin, Dartmouth College, and DePaul University; and Peace Corps volunteer in Ethiopia. He is the editor of several publications including *The Statue of Liberty Revisited; Making a Universal Symbol; Sharing Innovation: Global Perspectives on Food, Agriculture, and Rural Development;* and *Completing the Food Chain: Strategies for Combating Hunger and Malnutrition.* He also is the coauthor of *Museum Strategy and Marketing.*

Philip Kotler is the S. C. Johnson and Son Distinguished Professor of International Marketing in the Kellogg Graduate School of Management at Northwestern University. He has been honored as one of the world's leading marketing thinkers. He received his M.A. in economics (1953) from the University of Chicago and his Ph.D. in economics (1956) from the Massachusetts Institute of

Technology and has received honorary degrees from DePaul University, the University of Zurich, Stockholm University, and Athens University of Economics and Business. He is the author of more than 100 articles and 17 books including *Marketing Management, Strategic Marketing for Nonprofit Organizations, Social Marketing, Marketing Places, and Museum Strategy and Marketing.* He has been a consultant to IBM, General Electric, AT&T, Bank of America, Merck, Motorola, Ford, and other leading corporations.

Sidney Kraus is Professor of Communication at Cleveland State University. He is a specialist on televised presidential debates and political communication. Two of his books have been cited as among 25 of the most important books on media and politics by the Freedom Forum Media Studies Center at Columbia University. A second edition of his award-winning book, *Televised Presidential Debates and Public Policy,* will be published in 1999. Other books include *The Great Debates: Kennedy vs. Nixon, 1960, The Great Debates: Carter vs. Ford, 1976, The Effects of Mass Communication on Political Behavior, Mass Media and Political Thought: An Information Processing Approach,* and *Mass Communication and Political Information Processing.*

Gregory G. Lebel teaches Campaign Organization in the Graduate School of Political Management at George Washington University in Washington, D.C. He is Interim Executive Director of the Interfaith Alliance, a national grassroots organization of clergy and people of faith promoting the positive role of religion in public life and presenting an alternative religious voice to that of the Christian Coalition and other religious right groups. He has more than 20 years of experience in managing public and nonprofit organizations including past work on the presidential campaigns of Senators Gary Hart and Al Gore as well as numerous state, local, and congressional campaigns.

Barbara Lindsay is a prominent member of the Fawcett Society and a researcher at the Centre for Corporate and Public Affairs at Manchester Metropolitan University. She is a member of the Advisory Board of the public policy "think tank," the Centre for Reform, and is an active member of the Cunliffe Centre for the Study of Constitutionalism at Sussex University. She has published extensively in the fields of political, social, and women's issues during the past 20 years.

Andrew Lock is Pro-Vice Chancellor and Dean of the Faculty of Management and Business at Manchester Metropolitan University. He holds a B.A. from the University of Leeds in England and a master's and Ph.D. from London Business School. He previously taught at Kingston Polytechnic (now Kingston University) and at the University of British Columbia. He currently is chair of the Association of Business Schools under the EQUIS scheme and of MBAs through the Association of MBAs. His current research interests are in political marketing and the development and management of business education.

Hans Lugmayr works for the Austrian minister of agriculture, for different county politicians, and for federations in business and agriculture, among other things. Lugmayr once worked in Tyrol for Austrian Radio and subsequently joined an advertising agency in Germany. After his return to Austria, he founded Marketing Agency C&M.

Michael L. Mezey has been Dean of the College of Liberal Arts and Sciences at DePaul University since 1993. He earned his B.A. at the College of the City of New York and his M.A. and Ph.D. in political science at Syracuse University. He served on the faculties at the University of Virginia and the University of Hawaii before joining the DePaul faculty as chair of the Department of Political Science in 1977. He is the author of numerous scholarly papers, articles, and book chapters in the areas of American politics, legislative politics, and comparative legislative behavior. He has published two books, *Comparative Legislatures* (1979) and *Congress, the President, and Public Policy* (1989).

Dorina Miron is a Ph.D. candidate in mass communication at the University of Alabama and a research assistant with the Institute for Communication Research. She has an M.A. in philology from the University of Bucharest in Romania and an M.A. in journalism from the University of Missouri. Her areas of expertise include mass communication theory and research methods, media effects, and the role of mass media in the electoral process. Her main research interests include transnational advertising, cultural customization of mass communication addressed to foreign publics, election campaigns, voting behavior, and Central and Eastern European politics.

Pama Mitchell is director of polling for the *Atlanta Journal-Constitution* in Georgia and also conducts public opinion research for other media and nonprofit clients through her consulting company, Mitchell Research Design. She has a Ph.D. in mass communication research from the School of Journalism at the University of North Carolina (UNC) at Chapel Hill, where she also received an M.A. in media studies. Her previous positions include manager of surveys for CBS News Election and Survey Unit and writer-producer for public television in North Carolina. She taught broadcast journalism on the faculty of East Carolina University and broadcast advertising copywriting in an adjunct position at UNC at Chapel Hill.

Philip Morgan is Lecturer in Human Resource Management at Cardiff University. He is the author of *Privatisation and the Welfare State* (1995) and the forthcoming *Essays on the Theory and Practice of Privatisation* (with Nigel Allington).

Dan Nimmo is retired from full-time teaching and currently is a Visiting Scholar in Political Science at Baylor University. He is author and editor of numerous books in the areas of politics and the media, political campaigning, and political persuasion as well as a contributor to professional journals in political science, communications, and sociology. His most recent work is *Political Commentators in the United States in the 20th Century* (1997).

Daniel Odescalchi is President of Strategic Advantage International, a political consulting firm based in New York State. After years of assisting candidates at the state and federal levels, in 1992 he began consulting for the new democratic parties in Eastern Europe. He consulted for the prime minister of Hungary and the Hungarian Democratic Forum, the Democratic Convention in Romania, the Party of Coexistence in Slovakia, and the Alternative Council of Ministers in Bosnia Hercegovina. Having become an expert on postcommunism voter trends, he has spoken on the topic extensively. In 1995, he returned to the United States to become deputy national political director for the presidential bid of Republican Steve Forbes.

Nicholas O'Shaughnessy is Lecturer in Marketing at the Judge Institute of Management Studies and Fellow of Hugh's Hall at Cambridge University. He has a forthcoming publication, *Propaganda, Polemic, and Persuasion: The Marketing of Discontent at the End of the Twentieth Century.*

Richard M. Perloff is Professor of Communication at Cleveland State University. He is the author of *Political Communication: Politics, Press, and Public in America.* His book, *The Dynamics of Persuasion,* was named one of the "Outstanding Books of 1993" by the journal *Choice.* Nationally known for his scholarship on the third-person effect and perceptions of media impact, he has written more than 40 journal articles and book chapters. He served as president of the Midwest Association for Public Opinion Research; is on the editorial board of the *Journal of Communication;* and has written human interest features, historical articles, and opinion pieces for a variety of newspapers. He received his Ph.D. from the University of Wisconsin–Madison (1978) and has been a faculty member at Cleveland State since 1979.

Fritz Plasser is Professor of Political Science in the Department of Political Science at the University of Innsbruck in Austria. His research focuses on comparative studies of voting behavior and party system change, role of mass media in political campaigns, political marketing, and the role of U.S. consultants for professionalization of the electoral process in media-centered democracies. His recent publications include *Political Culture in East Central Europe* (1996), *The American Democracy* (1997), *Democratic Consolidation in East-Central Europe* (1998, with others), and *Party Responses to the Erosion of Voter Loyalities in Western Europe* (forthcoming, as coeditor).

Eric W. Rademacher is Research Associate at the Institute for Policy Research at the University of Cincinnati and is completing his doctorate in political science. His dissertation examines the impact of various data adjustment techniques on preelection projection estimates.

Lilia Raycheva is Associate Professor and Vice Dean in the School of Journalism and Mass Communication at St. Kliment Okhridsky Sofia University in Bulgaria. A Fulbright Scholar, she also has done postdoctoral work in film and television at Columbia University and New York University. She has received numerous grants and awards from organizations such as Bulgarian National Television, the Union of Bulgarian Journalists, the Open Society Fund, the American Council of Learned Societies, and the Cox Center in Georgia. She has authored or edited seven books and has produced and directed many programs for Bulgarian television. Her main interests include film and television language, elections, and media system development, and the role of television in politics.

Mike Rice is co-founder and co-owner of Varoga & Rice, a national research and general consulting agency with offices in Texas and California. As research director for the California Democratic Party, he helped design the party's remote-access, on-line research system. A research instructor at Democratic National Committee training academies and an expert on the federal Freedom of Information Act and state public record laws, he has worked in each of the three most recent California gubernatorial elections. His campaign victories have included those of U.S. senators and representatives, big-city mayors, and more than 20 candidates for California's state assembly.

Jennie Roberts works for the successful public relations firm, Buchanan Communications. She was a pupil at Alrincham Grammar School for Girls before studying for a a B.A. in international history and politics at the University of Leeds. After graduating from Leeds in 1996, she completed a master's degree in public relations at Manchester Metropolitan University, during which time she wrote her study of the 1997 general election campaign. In 1997, she embarked on a career in financial public relations.

Jolán Róka is Senior Research Professor at the University of Budapest. She specializes in the study of Hungarian media and has presented papers on the role of voter manipulation in media at many conferences including the 1994 British Film Institute conference in London. She also works with public opinion, imagery in politics, and political advertising. She is head of the Department of Media Studies at the University of Szeged in Hungary.

Judith-Rae E. Ross has a career that combines teaching, journalism, public service, and political consulting. With a Ph.D. in French intellectual history from the University of Illinois at Chicago, she currently teaches history at DePaul University, serves as an elected trustee of Niles Township, and is a political consultant. Her media experience spans both newspaper writing and television. Her newspaper writing experience includes 5 years with Lerner newspapers. She is a frequent op-ed writer for Pioneer Press, and since 1994, she has been a regular panelist on cable television.

Christian Scheucher is an adviser to the Austrian People's Party. He is in charge of research operations, campaign planning, and strategy development. He holds an M.P.A. from the John F. Kennedy School of Government at Harvard University and a master's in political science from the University of Vienna. He has been advising candidates and organizations in several European countries. He has spoken and published in Austria and internationally about campaigning, lobbying, political communications, and research. He teaches a course on campaign management at the University of Vienna. He is a member of the European Association of Political Consultants.

Hans Schmid is the founder of GGK Austria, the leading Austrian advertising agency. He is the founder of more than 20 companies in Austria and Central Europe. He studied at the Wirtschaftsuniversität Wien in Vienna.

Dan Schnur is an adviser to Republican candidates and causes, specializing in message development and media relations. He has several years of experience in state and national politics including 5 years as chief press spokesman for former California Governor Pete Wilson. His experience also includes work for the Reagan-Bush 1984 and Bush-Quayle 1988 presidential campaigns as well as the Republican National Committee and the California Republican Party. He is a Visiting Instructor at the Institute of Governmental Studies at the University of California, Berkeley, and a Visiting Lecturer at the Jesse M. Unruh Institute of Politics at the University of Southern California.

Günter Schweiger is Professor of Marketing Research and Advertising and head of the marketing department at Wirtschaftsuniversität Wien in Austria. He is the author or editor of 28 books and about 100 articles in scholarly journals in the areas of image research, market research, communication strategy, export marketing, advertising research, industrial marketing, and brand management. He is Editor of *Werbeforschung & Praxis,* a periodical of the Austrian and German Advertising Research Association, and is Coeditor of *Der Markt,* a periodical of the Austrian Marketing Research Association.

Christian Senft is head of the Department of Public Affairs and Political Management of the Christian Democratic Union in Berlin. He also works as a political adviser for the mayor of Berlin and as a political consultant for national and federal election campaigns. He studied business administration, marketing, and political science at the University of Technology in Berlin and is a doctoral student at the University of Innsbruck in Austria.

Elaine Sherman is Professor of Marketing and International Business at Hofstra University. She also regularly conducts public and political opinion polls for a major cable television network. Her research interests include direct marketing, the Internet and electronic commerce, the elderly market, quality of life issues, and consumer behavior. She has written more than 50 articles and given many lectures on marketing and public poll topics to audiences throughout the world.

She is a senior project director with the Market Discovery Group, a research agency specializing in strategic assignments for major corporations.

Jennifer A. Steen is a doctoral candidate in the Department of Political Science at the University of California, Berkeley, where she is writing her dissertation on the increasing number of self-financed candidates in congressional elections. Her research on campaign finance and other electoral issues is inspired by her earlier experience as a campaign consultant. Most recently, she served as campaign manager for U.S. Representative Jane Harman's successful 1996 reelection effort. She has served the Democratic Party as a precinct captain, national convention delegate, and presidential elector. During 1998–1999, she holds the Robert W. Hartley Research Fellowship in Governmental Studies at the Brookings Institution.

Wayne P. Steger is Assistant Professor of Political Science at DePaul University. He teaches courses on Congress, the presidency, parties and elections, and research methods. His articles on presidential-congressional relations, presidential foreign policy choice, media coverage of presidential elections, and epistemology have appeared in *American Politics Quarterly, Presidential Studies Quarterly, Congress & the Presidency,* and the *PRG Report.*

Michael Strugl currently is working as a freelance creative director for the advertising agency, Zoffel-Hoff & Partner, in the political communication department. In this position, he has already played a key role in campaigns for the German Christian Democratic Union and the South Tyrolian People's Party as well as in state and local campaigns. His career started in the public relations and communication department for the Upper Austrian People's Party. In 1995, he became deputy managing director for his party and was responsible for marketing, organization, services, and education. In 1997, he worked as campaign manager for the election campaign of the governor of Upper Austria. In the same year, he became a member of the Austrian Bundesrat, the second chamber of Austria's Parliament.

Alfred J. Tuchfarber directs the Ohio Poll, a quarterly survey of Ohio residents conducted by the Institute for Policy Research at the University of Cincinnati. In presidential and gubernatorial election years, Ohio Poll election surveys are used to project statewide election results. He also is Professor of Political Science, Associate Professor of Medicine, Director of the Institute for Policy Research, and Co-director of the Institute for Health Policy and Health Services Research at the university. He has published extensively on survey methodology, public opinion, and political behavior.

Craig Varoga is co-founder and co-owner of Varoga & Rice, a national research and general consulting agency with offices in Texas and California. He was national director of state research for the 1996 Clinton-Gore presidential campaign and has been the Democratic National Committee's lead trainer for congressional managers. He has managed campaigns throughout the United

States including those of Houston Mayor Lee Brown, former Houston Mayor Bob Lanier, and Congressman Ken Bentsen. He writes a monthly column for *Campaigns & Elections* magazine and authored *It's a Fact* (1983), a trivia book.

Nadja Vetter works as a public relations executive with a corporate and financial public relations agency. She graduated from Manchester Metropolitan University in 1998. During her studies, she did extensive research on various aspects of lobbying and wrote her M.A. dissertation on the strategic importance of corporate lobbying. In 1995, she completed her B.A. in international relations at the University of Geneva.

Klaus Weissmann has served as assistant for economic affairs and political marketing for the Austrian People's Party since 1997. He also worked as a political consultant in Scotland during the 1997 campaign and in Eastern Europe, focusing on strategic media planning and international public relations. His political training experience began in 1993 with Communication Skills International. He conducted media training for Austrian and European politicians in several state and local campaigns. Currently, he works in the head office (Corporate Communication) of Europe's leading specialist in applied chemistry and one of the best-known producers of brand-name articles through Central and Eastern Europe.

Wolfram Wickert recently was appointed as spokesman for the European Union and G8 summits that are organized and hosted by the German government. In 1997, he founded a political initiative that successfully supported the new German chancellor, Gerhard Schröder, during his election campaign. He published a historical novel with political reference to the Third Reich and several modern political cartoons. In 1969, he joined the staff of Chancellor Willy Brandt's government as spokesman for 3 years. He also worked at the German embassy in New Delhi, India, and in the office of Chancellor Helmut Schmidt. After the reunification of Germany, he worked for the state government of Brandenburg.

J. Harry Wray is Associate Professor of Political Science at DePaul University, where he served as department chair for 6 years. Prior to coming to DePaul, he taught at Duke University and the University of North Carolina. He received his B.A. from Whittier College, his M.A. from the University of California, Los Angeles, and his Ph.D. from the University of North Carolina at Chapel Hill. In addition to numerous articles in professional journals, he is coauthor of *American Politics and Everyday Life* and author of *American Political Culture* (Prentice Hall, forthcoming).

Dominic Wring is Lecturer in Communication and Media Studies and a member of the Communication Research Centre at Loughborough University. He is co-convenor of the U.K. Political Studies Association Media and Politics Group and deputy chair of the U.K. Academy of Marketing special interest group on political marketing. His work on election campaigning and political communication has appeared in a variety of journals and books. He currently is completing a historical study of the marketing of the Labour Party in Britain.